Microsoft® Office 2007
Advanced Concepts and Techniques

Gary B. Shelly

Thomas J. Cashman

Misty E. Vermaat

Contributing Authors

Mary Z. Last

Philip J. Pratt

Jeffrey J. Quasney

Susan L. Sebok

Jeffrey J. Webb

COURSE TECHNOLOGY
CENGAGE Learning™

Australia • Brazil • Japan • Korea • Mexico • Singapore • Spain • United Kingdom • United States

COURSE TECHNOLOGY
CENGAGE Learning

Microsoft Office 2007
Advanced Concepts and Techniques
Gary B. Shelly, Thomas J. Cashman,
Misty E. Vermaat

Executive Editor: Alexandra Arnold

Senior Product Managers: Reed Curry, Mali Jones

Product Manager: Heather Hawkins

Associate Product Manager: Klenda Martinez

Editorial Assistant: Jon Farnham

Senior Marketing Manager: Joy Stark-Vancs

Marketing Coordinator: Julie Schuster

Print Buyer: Julio Esperas

Director of Production: Patty Stephan

Lead Production Editor: Matthew Hutchinson

Production Editors: Cathie DiMassa, Jill Klaffky,
    Phillipa Lehar

Developmental Editors: Jill Batistick,
    Amanda Brodkin, Laurie Brown, Lyn Markowicz

Proofreaders: John Bosco, Kim Kosmatka

Indexer: Rich Carlson

QA Manuscript Reviewers: John Freitas,
    Serge Palladino, Chris Scriver, Danielle Shaw,
    Marianne Snow, Teresa Storch

Art Director: Bruce Bond

Cover and Text Design: Joel Sadagursky

Cover Photo: Jon Chomitz

Compositor: GEX Publishing Services

Printer: Banta Menasha

For product information and technology assistance, contact us at
Cengage Learning Customer & Sales Support, 1-800-354-9706
For permission to use material from this text or product, submit all requests online at **cengage.com/permissions**
Further permissions questions can be emailed to
permissionrequest@cengage.com

softcover binding:
ISBN-13: 978-1-4188-4332-8
ISBN-10: 1-4188-4332-6

hardcover-spiral binding:
ISBN-13: 978-1-4188-4333-5
ISBN-10: 1-4188-4333-4

Course Technology
25 Thomson Place
Boston, Massachusetts 02210
USA

Cengage Learning is a leading provider of customized learning solutions with office locations around the globe, including Singapore, the United Kingdom, Australia, Mexico, Brazil, and Japan. Locate your local office at:
international.cengage.com/region

Cengage Learning products are represented in Canada by Nelson Education, Ltd.

For your lifelong learning solutions, visit **course.cengage.com**

Purchase any of our products at your local college store or at our preferred online store **www.ichapters.com**

Printed in the United States of America
7 8 9 10

Microsoft® **Office 2007**
Advanced Concepts and Techniques

Contents

Microsoft Office **Word 2007**

CHAPTER FOUR

Creating a Document with a Title Page, Table, Chart, and Watermark

Microsoft Office **Excel® 2007**

CHAPTER FOUR
Financial Functions, Data Tables, and Amortization Schedules

Microsoft Integration 2007

INTEGRATION CASE STUDIES
Microsoft Office 2007 Integration Case Studies

Appendices

APPENDIX A
Project Planning Guidelines

APPENDIX B
Introduction to Microsoft Office 2007

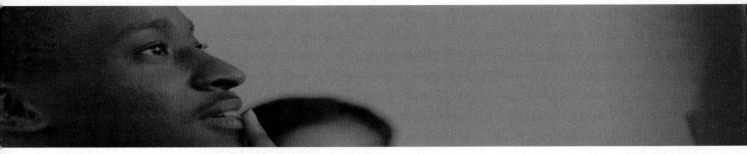

Preface

The Shelly Cashman Series® offers the finest textbooks in computer education. We are proud of the fact that our series of Microsoft Office 4.3, Microsoft Office 95, Microsoft Office 97, Microsoft Office 2000, Microsoft Office XP, and Microsoft Office 2003 textbooks have been the most widely used books in education. With each new edition of our Office books, we have made significant improvements based on the software and comments made by instructors and students.

Microsoft Office 2007 contains more changes in the user interface and feature set than all other previous versions combined. Recognizing that the new features and functionality of Microsoft Office 2007 would impact the way that students are taught skills, the Shelly Cashman Series development team carefully reviewed our pedagogy and analyzed its effectiveness in teaching today's Office student. An extensive customer survey produced results confirming what the series is best known for: its step-by-step, screen-by-screen instructions, its project-oriented approach, and the quality of its content.

We learned, though, that students entering computer courses today are different than students taking these classes just a few years ago. Students today read less, but need to retain more. They need not only to be able to perform skills, but to retain those skills and know how to apply them to different settings. Today's students need to be continually engaged and challenged to retain what they're learning.

As a result, we've renewed our commitment to focusing on the user and how they learn best. This commitment is reflected in every change we've made to our Office 2007 books.

Objectives of This Textbook

Microsoft Office 2007: Advanced Concepts and Techniques is intended for a second course on Office 2007 applications. This book assumes that students are familiar with the fundamentals of Microsoft Windows Vista, Microsoft Office Word 2007, Microsoft Office Excel 2007, Microsoft Office Access 2007, Microsoft Office PowerPoint 2007, and Microsoft Office Outlook 2007. These fundamentals are covered in the companion textbook *Microsoft Office 2007: Introductory Concepts and Techniques, Windows Vista Edition*. The objectives of this book are:

- To go beyond the fundamentals and offer an in-depth presentation to Microsoft Office Word 2007, Microsoft Office Excel 2007, Microsoft Office Access 2007, Microsoft Office PowerPoint 2007, Microsoft Office Outlook 2007, and Microsoft Office 2007 Integration.

- To expose students to practical examples of the computer as a useful tool

- To acquaint students with the proper procedures to create and enhance documents, worksheets, databases, and presentations suitable for coursework, professional purposes, and personal use

- To help students discover the underlying functionality of Office 2007 so they can become more productive

- To develop an exercise-oriented approach that allows learning by doing

INSTRUCTOR'S MANU

include chapter ob
quick quizzes, figu
page. The new for
chapter easily.

LECTURE SUCCESS S

correspond to cert
project in a chapte

SYLLABUS Sample s
syllabi cover polici

FIGURE FILES Illustr
Use this ancillary t
lecture with an ov
ancillary can be an

POWERPOINT PRESE

system that provid
Use this presentati
and knowledge bas
that use multiple l

SOLUTIONS TO EXER

the Chapter Reinf
below, are also inc

RUBRICS AND ANN

framework for assi
that correspond to
with the correct sc

TEST BANK & TEST

types (40 multiple
types (5 modified
Thinking question
the test bank to 1
appropriate, figur
The test bank cor
objective-based te
use. ExamView er
designed specifica
QuickTest Wizar
Technology's que

LAB TESTS/TEST OU

and are supplied
covered in the ch

DATA FILES FOR ST

exercises are incl
to your students
inside back cover

The Shelly Cashman Approach

Features of the Shelly Cashman Series Microsoft Office 2007 books include:

- **Project Orientation** Each chapter in the book presents a project with a practical problem and complete solution in an easy-to-understand approach.

- **Plan Ahead Boxes** The project orientation is enhanced by the inclusion of Plan Ahead boxes. These new features prepare students to create successful projects by encouraging them to think strategically about what they are trying to accomplish before they begin working.

- **Step-by-Step, Screen-by-Screen Instructions** Each of the tasks required to complete a project is clearly identified throughout the chapter. Now, the step-by-step instructions provide a context beyond point-and-click. Each step explains why students are performing a task, or the result of performing a certain action. Found on the screens accompanying each step, call-outs give students the information they need to know when they need to know it. Now, we've used color to distinguish the content in the call-outs. The Explanatory call-outs (in black) summarize what is happening on the screen and the Navigational call-outs (in red) show students where to click.

- **Q&A** Found within many of the step-by-step sequences, Q&As raise the kinds of questions students may ask when working through a step sequence and provide answers about what they are doing, why they are doing it, and how that task might be approached differently.

- **Experimental Steps** These new steps, within our step-by-step instructions, encourage students to explore, experiment, and take advantage of the features of the Office 2007 new user interface. These steps are not necessary to complete the projects, but are designed to increase the confidence with the software and build problem-solving skills.

- **Thoroughly Tested Projects** Unparalleled quality is ensured because every screen in the book is produced by the author only after performing a step, and then each project must pass Course Technology's Quality Assurance program.

- **Other Ways Boxes and Quick Reference Summary** The Other Ways boxes displayed at the end of most of the step-by-step sequences specify the other ways to do the task completed in the steps. Thus, the steps and the Other Ways box make a comprehensive reference unit. A Quick Reference Summary at the end of the book contains all of the tasks presented in the chapters, and all ways identified of accomplishing the tasks.

- **BTW** These marginal annotations provide background information, tips, and answers to common questions that complement the topics covered, adding depth and perspective to the learning process.

- **Integration of the World Wide Web** The World Wide Web is integrated into the Office 2007 learning experience by (1) BTW annotations that send students to Web sites for up-to-date information and alternative approaches to tasks; (2) a Microsoft Business Certification Program Web page so students can prepare for the certification examinations; (3) a Quick Reference Summary Web page that summarizes the ways to complete tasks (mouse, Ribbon, shortcut menu, and keyboard); and (4) the Learn It Online section at the end of each chapter, which has chapter reinforcement exercises, learning games, and other types of student activities.

- **End-of-Chapter Student Activities** Extensive student activities at the end of each chapter provide the student with plenty of opportunities to reinforce the materials learned in the chapter through hands-on assignments. Several new types of activities have been added that challenge the student in new ways to expand their knowledge, and to apply their new skills to a project with personal relevance.

Q&A

What is a maximized window?

A maximized window fills the entire screen. When you maximize a window, the Maximize button changes to a Restore Down button.

Other Ways

1. Click Italic button on Mini toolbar
2. Right-click selected text, click Font on shortcut menu, click Font tab, click Italic in Font style list, click OK button
3. Click Font Dialog Box Launcher, click Font tab, click Italic in Font style list, click OK button
4. Press CTRL+I

BTW

Minimizing the Ribbon
If you want to minimize the Ribbon, right-click the Ribbon and then click Minimize the Ribbon on the shortcut menu, double-click the active tab, or press CTRL+F1. To restore a minimized Ribbon, right-click the Ribbon and then click Minimize the Ribbon on the shortcut menu, double-click any top-level tab, or press CTRL+F1. To use commands on a minimized Ribbon, click the top-level tab.

To the Student . . . Getting the Most Out of Your Book

Welcome to *Microsoft Office 2007: Advanced Concepts and Techniques.* You can save yourself a lot of time and gain a better understanding of the Office 2007 programs if you spend a few minutes reviewing the figures and callouts in this section.

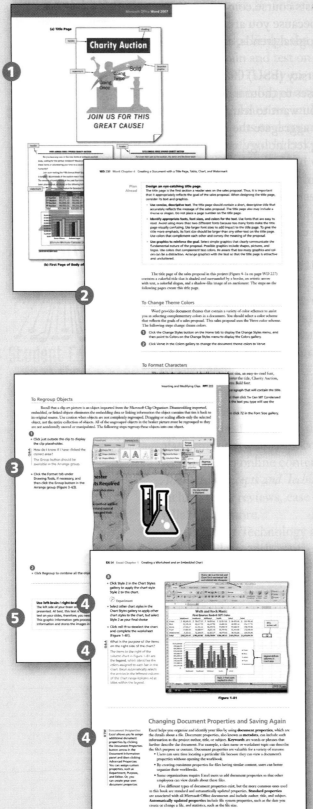

1 PROJECT ORIENTATION
Each chapter's project presents a practical problem and shows the solution in the first figure of the chapter. The project orientation lets you see firsthand how problems are solved from start to finish using application software and computers.

2 PROJECT PLANNING GUIDELINES AND PLAN AHEAD BOXES
Overall planning guidelines at the beginning of a chapter and Plan Ahead boxes throughout encourage you to think critically about how to accomplish the next goal before you actually begin working.

3 CONSISTENT STEP-BY-STEP, SCREEN-BY-SCREEN PRESENTATION
Chapter solutions are built using a step-by-step, screen-by-screen approach. This pedagogy allows you to build the solution on a computer as you read through the chapter. Generally, each step includes an explanation that indicates the result of the step.

4 MORE THAN JUST STEP-BY-STEP
BTW annotations in the margins of the book, Q&As in the steps, and substantive text in the paragraphs provide background information, tips, and answers to common questions that complement the topics covered, adding depth and perspective. When you finish with this book, you will be ready to use the Office programs to solve problems on your own. Experimental steps provide you with opportunities to step out on your own to try features of the programs, and pick up right where you left off in the chapter.

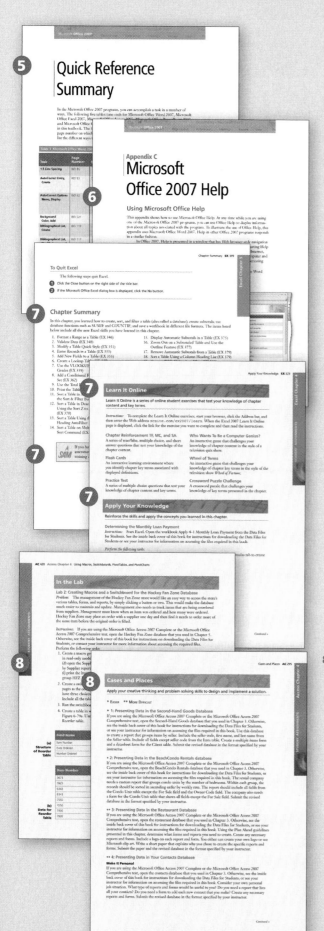

5 OTHER WAYS BOXES AND QUICK REFERENCE SUMMARY
Other Ways boxes that follow many of the step sequences and a Quick Reference Summary at the back of the book explain the other ways to complete the task presented, such as using the mouse, Ribbon, shortcut menu, and keyboard.

6 EMPHASIS ON GETTING HELP WHEN YOU NEED IT
The first project of each application and Appendix C show you how to use all the elements of Office Help. Being able to answer your own questions will increase your productivity and reduce your frustrations by minimizing the time it takes to learn how to complete a task.

7 REVIEW, REINFORCEMENT, AND EXTENSION
After you successfully step through a project in a chapter, a section titled Chapter Summary identifies the tasks with which you should be familiar. Terms you should know for test purposes are bold in the text. The SAM Training feature provides the opportunity for addional reinforcement on important skills covered in each chapter. The Learn It Online section at the end of each chapter offers reinforcement in the form of review questions, learning games, and practice tests. Also included are exercises that require you to extend your learning beyond the book.

8 LABORATORY EXERCISES
If you really want to learn how to use the programs, then you must design and implement solutions to problems on your own. Every chapter concludes with several carefully developed laboratory assignments that increase in complexity.

About Our New Cover Look

Learning styles of students have changed, but the
Shelly Cashman Series' dedication to their success has
remained steadfast for over 30 years. We are committed
to continually updating our approach and content to
reflect the way today's students learn and experience new
technology.

This focus on the user is reflected in our bold new cover
design, which features photographs of real students
using the Shelly Cashman Series in their courses. Each
book features a different user, reflecting the many ages,
experiences, and backgrounds of all of the students
learning with our books. When you use the Shelly
Cashman Series, you can be assured that you are learning
computer skills using the most effective courseware
available.

We would like to thank the administration and faculty
at the participating schools for their help in making
our vision a reality. Most of all, we'd like to thank the
wonderful students from all over the world who learn
from our texts and now appear on our covers.

Microsoft Office 2007

4 Creating a Document with a Title Page, Table, Chart, and Watermark

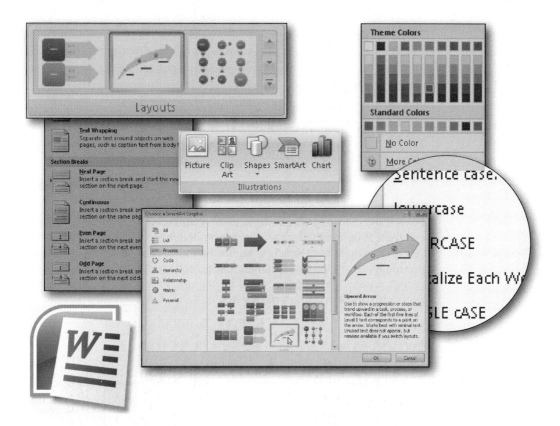

Objectives

You will have mastered the material in this project when you can:

- Border and shade a paragraph
- Insert and format a SmartArt graphic
- Insert a watermark
- Insert a section break
- Insert a Word document in an open document
- Insert headers and footers

- Modify and format a Word table
- Sum columns in a table
- Create a chart from a Word table
- Add picture bullets to a list
- Create and apply a character style
- Draw a table

Creating a Document with a Title Page, Table, Chart, and Watermark

Introduction

During the course of your business and personal life, you may want or need to present a recommendation to a person or group of people for their consideration. You might suggest they purchase a product, such as vehicles or books, or contract a service, such as designing their Web page or remodeling their house. Or, you might try to convince an audience to take an action, such as signing a petition, joining a club, or donating to a cause. You may be asked to request funds for a new program or activity or to promote an idea, such as a benefits package to company employees or a budget plan to upper management. To present your recommendations, you may find yourself writing a proposal.

A proposal generally is one of three types: sales, research, or planning. A **sales proposal** sells an idea, a product, or a service. A **research proposal** usually requests funding for a research project. A **planning proposal** offers solutions to a problem or improvement to a situation.

Project Planning Guidelines

The process of developing a document that communicates specific information requires careful analysis and planning. As a starting point, establish why the document is needed. Once the purpose is determined, analyze the intended readers of the document and their unique needs. Then, gather information about the topic and decide what to include in the document. Finally, determine the document design and style that will be most successful at delivering the message. Details of these guidelines are provided in Appendix A. In addition, each project in this book provides practical applications of these planning considerations.

Project — Sales Proposal

Sales proposals describe the features and value of products and services being offered, with the intent of eliciting a positive response from the reader. Desired outcomes include the reader accepting ideas, purchasing products, volunteering time, or contributing to a cause. A well-written proposal can be the key to obtaining the desired results.

The project in this chapter follows generally accepted guidelines for writing short sales proposals and uses Word to create the sales proposal shown in Figure 4–1. The sales proposal in this chapter is designed to persuade readers to donate items or volunteer their time for a charity auction. The proposal has a colorful title page to attract readers' attention. To add impact, the sales proposal has a watermark of an auctioneer behind the text and graphics on each page. It also uses tables, a chart, and a bulleted list to summarize and highlight important data.

(a) Title Page

(b) First Page of Body of Proposal   **(c) Second Page of Body of Proposal**

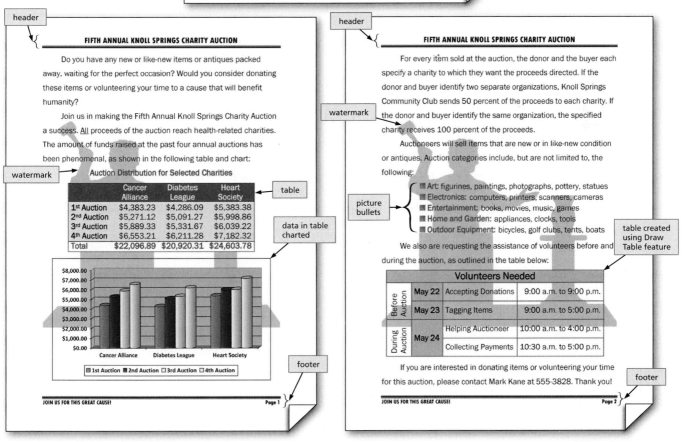

Figure 4–1

Overview

As you read through this chapter, you will learn how to create the sales proposal shown in Figure 4–1 on the previous page by performing these general tasks:

- Create a title page.
- Save the title page.
- Insert a draft of the body of the sales proposal below the title page.
- Edit and enhance the draft of the body of the sales proposal.
- Save the sales proposal.
- Print the sales proposal.

Plan Ahead

General Project Guidelines

When creating a Word document, the actions you perform and decisions you make will affect the appearance and characteristics of the finished document. As you create a sales proposal, such as the project shown in Figure 4–1, you should follow these general guidelines:

1. **Identify the nature of the proposal.** A proposal may be solicited or unsolicited. If someone else requests that you develop the proposal, it is solicited. Be sure to include all requested information in a solicited proposal. When you write a proposal because you recognize a need, the proposal is unsolicited. With an unsolicited proposal, you must gather information you believe will be relevant and of interest to the intended audience.

2. **Design an eye-catching title page.** The title page should convey the overall message of the sales proposal. Use text, graphics, formats, and colors that reflect the goals of the sales proposal. Be sure to include a title.

3. **Compose the text of the sales proposal.** Sales proposals vary in length, style, and formality, but all are designed to elicit acceptance from the reader. The sales proposal should have a neat, organized appearance. A successful sales proposal uses succinct wording and includes lists for textual messages. Write text using active voice, instead of passive voice. Assume readers of unsolicited sales proposals have no previous knowledge about the topic. Be sure the goal of the proposal is clear. Establish a theme and carry it throughout the proposal.

4. **Enhance the sales proposal with appropriate visuals.** Use visuals to add interest, clarify ideas, and illustrate points. Visuals include tables, charts, and graphical images (i.e., pictures, clip art).

5. **Proofread and edit the proposal.** Carefully review the sales proposal to be sure it contains no spelling, grammar, mathematical, or other errors. Check that transitions between sentences and paragraphs are smooth. Ensure that the purpose of the proposal is stated clearly. Ask others to review the proposal and give you suggestions for improvements.

When necessary, more specific details concerning the above guidelines are presented at appropriate points in the chapter. The chapter also will identify the actions performed and decisions made regarding these guidelines during the creation of the sales proposal shown in Figure 4–1.

BTW

Certification
The Microsoft Certified Application Specialist (MCAS) program provides an opportunity for you to obtain a valuable industry credential — proof that you have the Word 2007 skills required by employers. For more information see Appendix G or visit the Word 2007 Certification Web page (scsite.com/wd2007/cert).

To Start Word

If you are using a computer to step through the project in this chapter and you want your screens to match the figures in this book, you should change your computer's resolution to 1024 × 768. For information about how to change a computer's resolution, read Appendix D.

The following steps start Word and verify Word settings.

Note: If you are using Windows XP, see Appendix F for alternate steps.

1 Click the Start button on the Windows Vista taskbar to display the Start menu.

2 Click All Programs at the bottom of the left pane on the Start menu to display the All Programs list and then click Microsoft Office in the All Programs list to display the Microsoft Office list.

3 Click Microsoft Office Word 2007 in the Microsoft Office list to start Word and display a new blank document in the Word window.

4 If the Word window is not maximized, click the Maximize button on its title bar to maximize the window.

5 If the Print Layout button is not selected, click it so that Word is in Print Layout view.

6 If your zoom level is not 100%, click the Zoom Out or Zoom In button as many times as necessary until the Zoom level button displays 100% on its face.

To Display Formatting Marks

It is helpful to display formatting marks that indicate where in the document you pressed the ENTER key, SPACEBAR, and other keys. The following steps display formatting marks.

1 If necessary, click Home on the Ribbon to display the Home tab.

2 If the Show/Hide ¶ button on the Home tab is not selected already, click it to display formatting marks on the screen.

Creating a Title Page

A **title page** is a separate cover page that contains, at a minimum, the title of the document. For a sales proposal, the title page usually is the first page of the document. Solicited proposals often have a specific format for the title page. Guidelines for the title page of a solicited proposal may stipulate the margins, spacing, layout, and required contents such as title, sponsor name, author name, date, etc. With an unsolicited proposal, by contrast, you can design the title page in a way that best presents its message.

<table>
<tr><td>Plan
Ahead</td><td>

Design an eye-catching title page.
The title page is the first section a reader sees on the sales proposal. Thus, it is important that it appropriately reflects the goal of the sales proposal. When designing the title page, consider its text and graphics.

- **Use concise, descriptive text.** The title page should contain a short, descriptive title that accurately reflects the message of the sales proposal. The title page also may include a theme or slogan. Do not place a page number on the title page.

- **Identify appropriate fonts, font sizes, and colors for the text.** Use fonts that are easy to read. Avoid using more than two different fonts because too many fonts make the title page visually confusing. Use larger font sizes to add impact to the title page. To give the title more emphasis, its font size should be larger than any other text on the title page. Use colors that complement each other and convey the meaning of the proposal.

- **Use graphics to reinforce the goal.** Select simple graphics that clearly communicate the fundamental nature of the proposal. Possible graphics include shapes, pictures, and logos. Use colors that complement text colors. Be aware that too many graphics and colors can be a distraction. Arrange graphics with the text so that the title page is attractive and uncluttered.

</td></tr>
</table>

The title page of the sales proposal in this project (Figure 4–1a on page WD 227) contains a colorful title that is shaded and surrounded by a border, an artistic arrow with text, a colorful slogan, and a shadow-like image of an auctioneer. The steps on the following pages create this title page.

To Change Theme Colors

Word provides document themes that contain a variety of color schemes to assist you in selecting complementary colors in a document. You should select a color scheme that reflects the goals of a sales proposal. This sales proposal uses the Verve color scheme. The following steps change theme colors.

1 Click the Change Styles button on the Home tab to display the Change Styles menu, and then point to Colors on the Change Styles menu to display the Colors gallery.

2 Click Verve in the Colors gallery to change the document theme colors to Verve.

To Format Characters

The title in the sales proposal should use a large font size, an easy-to-read font, and be the focal point on the page. The following steps enter the title, Charity Auction, centered and using 72-point Tw Cen MT Condensed Extra Bold font.

1 Click the Center button on the Home tab to center the paragraph that will contain the title.

2 Click the Font box arrow on the Home tab. Scroll to and then click Tw Cen MT Condensed Extra Bold (or a similar font) in the Font gallery, so that the text you type will use the selected font.

3 Click the Font Size box arrow on the Home tab and then click 72 in the Font Size gallery, so that the text you type will use the selected font size.

4 Type `Charity Auction` as the title.

To Border a Paragraph

When you click the Border button on the Home tab, Word applies the most recently defined border, or, if one has not been defined, it applies the default border to the current paragraph.

In this project, the title in the sales proposal has a 6-point gray border around it. You can use the Borders gallery to add borders to any or all edges of a paragraph. To specify a different point size and color, however, you use the Borders and Shading dialog box. The following steps add a 6-point gray outside border around a paragraph.

1

- With the insertion point in the paragraph to border, click the Border button arrow on the Home tab to display the Border gallery (Figure 4–2).

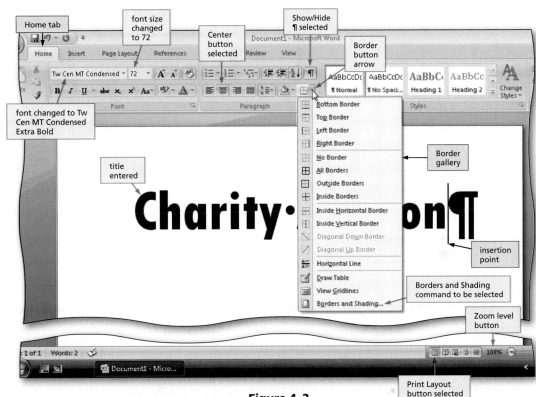

Figure 4–2

2

- Click Borders and Shading in the Border gallery to display the Borders and Shading dialog box.

- Click Box in the Setting area, which will place a border on each edge of the paragraph.

- Click the Width box arrow and then click 6 pt to make the border much thicker.

- Click the Color box arrow and then click Gray-50%, Text 2, which is the fourth color in the first row in the Color gallery (Figure 4–3).

Q&A What is the purpose of the buttons in the Preview area?

They are toggles that display and remove the top, bottom, left, and right borders from the diagram in the preview area.

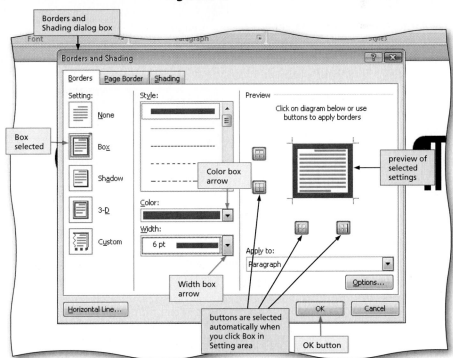

Figure 4–3

3

- Click the OK button to place a 6-point gray outside border around the title (Figure 4–4).

Q&A How would I remove an existing border from a paragraph?

Click the Border button arrow on the Home tab and then click the border in the Border gallery that identifies the border you wish to remove.

Other Ways

1. Click Page Borders on Page Layout tab, click Borders tab in Borders and Shading dialog box, select desired border, click OK button

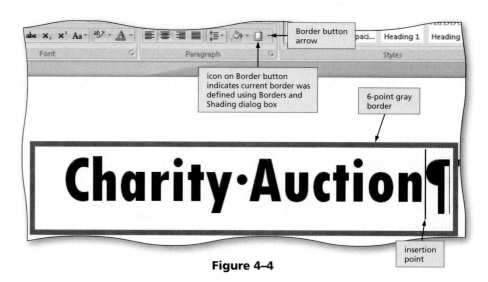

Figure 4–4

To Shade a Paragraph

To make the title of the sales proposal more eye-catching, it is shaded in a dark pink. When you shade a paragraph, Word shades the rectangular area behind any text or graphics in the paragraph from the left margin of the paragraph to the right margin. If the paragraph is surrounded by a border, Word shades inside the border. The following steps shade a paragraph.

1

- Click the Shading button arrow on the Home tab to display the Shading gallery.

- Point to Pink, Accent 2, Darker 25% (sixth color in the fifth row) to display a live preview of this color of shading (Figure 4–5).

Q&A Why did the text color change to white in the shaded paragraph?

When the color is Automatic, it usually is black. If you select a dark shading color, Word automatically changes the text color to white so that it is easier to read.

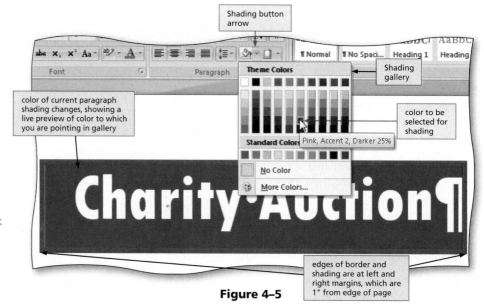

Figure 4–5

Experiment

- Point to various colors in the Shading gallery and watch the paragraph shading color change.

2

- Click Pink, Accent 2, Darker 25% to shade the current paragraph.

Other Ways

1. Click Border button arrow, click Borders and Shading, click Shading tab, click Fill   box arrow, select desired color, click OK button

To Change Left and Right Paragraph Indent

The border and shading currently extend from the left margin to the right margin (shown in Figure 4–5). In the sales proposal, the edges of the border and shading are closer to the text in the title. If you want the border and shading to start and end at a location different from the margin, change the left and right paragraph indent.

The Increase Indent and Decrease Indent buttons on the Home tab change the indent by ½-inch. To set precise indent values, use the Page Layout tab. The following steps change the left and right paragraph indent using the Page Layout tab.

1

- If the rulers are not displayed already, click the View Ruler button on the vertical scroll bar so that you can see the indent markers in relation to the margins.

- Click Page Layout on the Ribbon to display the Page Layout tab.

- With the insertion point in the paragraph to indent, click the Indent Left box up arrow three times to display 0.3" in the Indent Left box and adjust the paragraph left indent by 0.3".

- Click the Indent Right box up arrow three times to display 0.3" in the Indent Right box and adjust the paragraph right indent by 0.3" (Figure 4–6).

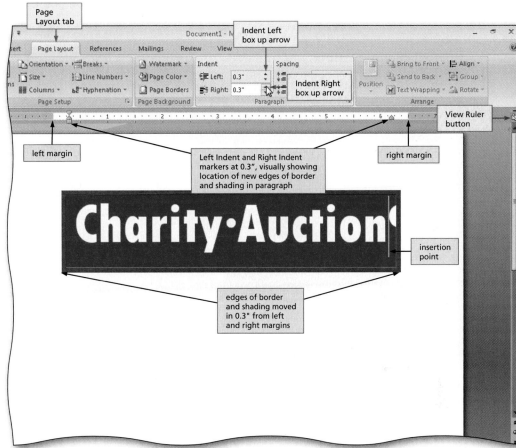

Figure 4–6

 **Experiment**

- Repeatedly click the Indent Right and Indent Left box up and down scroll arrows and watch the left and right edges of the paragraph change in the document window. When you have finished experimenting, set the left and right indent each to 0.3".

2

- Click the View Ruler button on the vertical scroll bar again to hide the ruler because you are finished using it.

Other Ways
1. Drag Left Indent and Right Indent markers on ruler 2. Click Paragraph Dialog Box Launcher on Home tab, click Indents and Spacing tab, set indentation values, click OK button 3. Right-click paragraph, click Paragraph on shortcut menu, click Indents and Spacing tab, set indentation values, click OK button

To Clear Formatting

The title is finished. When you press the ENTER key to advance the insertion point from the end of the first line to the beginning of the second line on the title page, the border and shading are carried forward to line 2, and any text you type will be 72-point Tw Cen MT Condensed Extra Bold font. The paragraphs and characters on line 2 should not have the same paragraph and character formatting as line 1. Instead, they should be formatted using the Normal style. The following steps clear formatting, which applies the Normal style formats to the location of the insertion point.

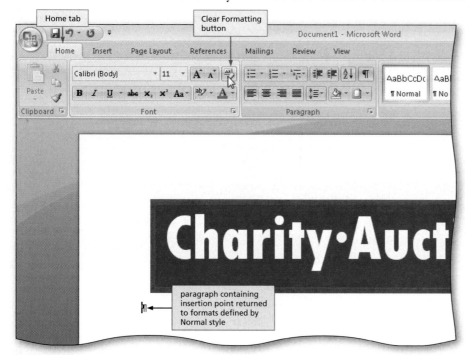

Figure 4–7

1 If necessary, position the insertion point at the end of line 1, as shown in Figure 4–6 on the previous page.

2 Press the ENTER key.

3 Display the Home tab.

4 Click the Clear Formatting button on the Home tab to apply the Normal style to the location of the insertion point (Figure 4–7).

Q&A Could I have clicked Normal in the Styles gallery instead of the Clear Formatting button?

Yes.

SmartArt Graphics

Microsoft Office 2007 includes **SmartArt graphics**, which are visual representations of ideas. Many different types of SmartArt graphics are available, allowing you to choose one that illustrates your message best. Table 4–1 identifies the purpose of some of the more popular SmartArt types. Within each type, Office provides numerous layouts. For example, you can select from more than 20 different layouts of lists.

Table 4–1 SmartArt Graphic Types	
Type	**Purpose**
List	Shows nonsequential or grouped blocks of information
Process	Shows progression, timeline, or sequential steps in a process or workflow
Cycle	Shows continuous sequence of steps or events
Hierarchy	Illustrates organization charts, decision trees, hierarchical relationships
Relationship	Compares or contrasts connections between concepts
Matrix	Shows relationships of parts to a whole
Pyramid	Shows proportional or interconnected relationships with the largest component at the top or bottom

SmartArt graphics contain shapes. You can add text to shapes, add more shapes, or delete shapes. You also can modify the appearance of a SmartArt graphic by applying styles and changing its colors.

To Insert a SmartArt Graphic

Below the title on the title page in this project is an artistic arrow with the text, Going Once, Going Twice, Sold. You use a SmartArt graphic in Word to create this arrow. The following steps insert a SmartArt graphic centered below the title on the title page.

1

- With the insertion point on the blank paragraph below the title (shown in Figure 4–7), click the Center button on the Home tab so that the inserted SmartArt graphic will be centered below the title.

2

- Display the Insert tab.

- Click the Insert SmartArt Graphic button on the Insert tab to display the Choose a SmartArt Graphic dialog box (Figure 4–8).

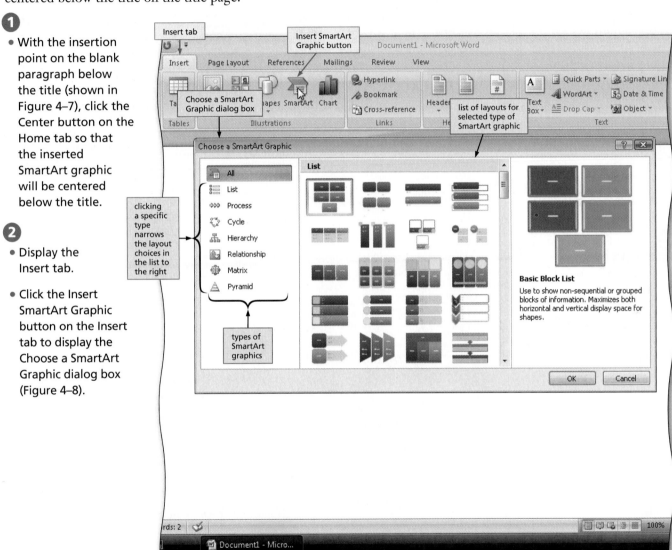

Figure 4–8

Experiment

- Click various SmartArt graphic types on the left of the dialog box and watch the related layout choices appear in the list to the right.

Experiment

- Click various layouts in the list of layouts to the right to see the preview and description of the layout appear on the far right of the dialog box.

4

- Click Process on the left of the dialog box to display the layout choices related to a process SmartArt graphic.

- If necessary, scroll through the list of layouts until Upward Arrow appears. Click Upward Arrow, which displays a preview and description of the Upward Arrow layout (Figure 4–9).

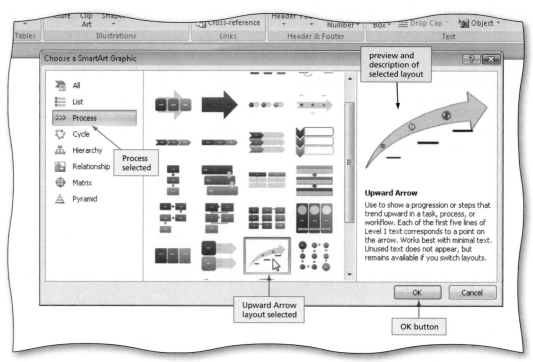

Figure 4–9

5

- Click the OK button to insert the Upward Arrow SmartArt graphic in the document at the location of the insertion point (Figure 4–10).

 Can I change layout of the inserted SmartArt graphic?

Yes. Click the More button in the Layouts gallery in the SmartArt Tools Design tab to display the list of layouts.

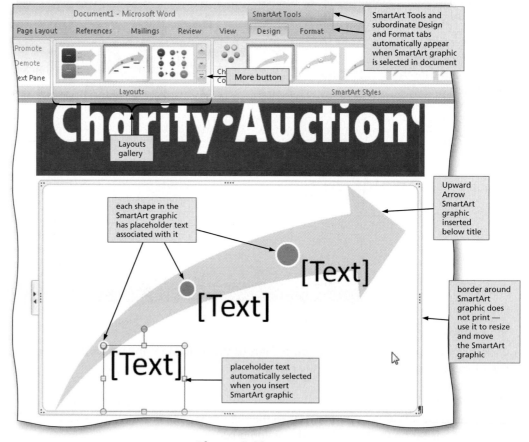

Figure 4–10

To Add Text to a SmartArt Graphic

In this title page, the graphic has the words Going Once, Going Twice, Sold, on the arrow. You can enter text in the placeholder text in the SmartArt graphic or in the Text pane. The Text pane, which is a separate window that can be displayed next to the SmartArt graphic, has placeholder text that duplicates the text in the SmartArt graphic.

The text you enter in a placeholder text wordwraps just as text wordwraps between the margins of a document. The following steps add text to the SmartArt graphic using the placeholder text in the graphic.

1

- Type `Going Once` in the selected lower-left placeholder text.

Q&A What if my placeholder text is no longer selected?

Click it to select it.

Q&A What if the Text pane appears next to the SmartArt graphic?

Close the Text pane by clicking its Close button or clicking the Text Pane button on the Design tab.

2

- Click the middle placeholder text to select it. Type `Going Twice` and then click the upper-right placeholder text to select it.

- Type `Sold` as the final text in the graphic (Figure 4–11).

Q&A How do I edit placeholder text if I make a mistake?

Click the placeholder text to select it and then correct the entry.

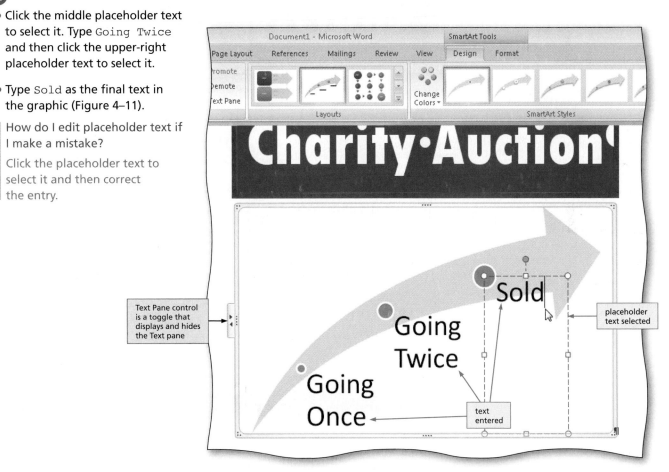

Figure 4–11

Other Ways
1. Click Text Pane control, enter text in Text pane, close Text pane   2. Click Text Pane button on SmartArt Tools Design tab, enter text in Text pane, click Text Pane button again

To Change Colors of a SmartArt Graphic

In this project, the arrow on the title page is blue instead of pink. Word provides a variety of colors for a SmartArt graphic and the shapes in the graphic. The following steps change the colors of the SmartArt graphic.

1

- With the SmartArt graphic selected, click the Change Colors button on the Design tab to display the Change Colors gallery.

Q&A

What if the Design tab in the SmartArt Tools tab no longer is the active tab?

Click the SmartArt graphic to select it and then click Design on the Ribbon.

2

- Scroll to and then point to Colored Outline - Accent 5 in the Change Colors gallery to display a live preview of that color applied to the SmartArt graphic in the document (Figure 4–12).

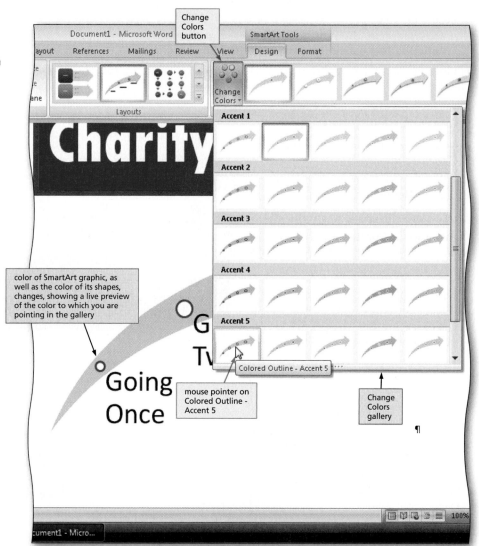

Figure 4–12

Experiment

- Point to various colors in the Change Colors gallery and watch the colors of the graphic change in the document window.

3

- Click Colored Outline - Accent 5 in the Change Colors gallery to apply the selected color to the SmartArt graphic (Figure 4–13).

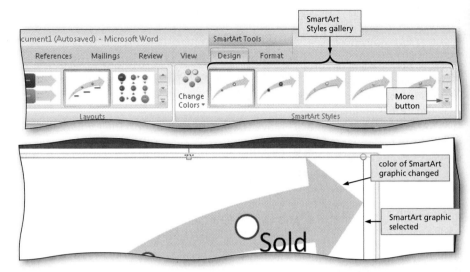

Figure 4–13

To Apply a SmartArt Style

The next step is to apply a SmartArt style to the SmartArt graphic. Word provides a SmartArt Styles gallery, allowing you to change the SmartArt graphic's format to a more visually appealing style. The following steps apply a SmartArt style to the SmartArt graphic.

1

- With the SmartArt graphic still selected, click the More button in the SmartArt Styles gallery (shown in Figure 4–13) to expand the SmartArt Styles gallery.

2

- Point to Polished in the 3-D area of the SmartArt Styles gallery to display a live preview of that style applied to the graphic in the document (Figure 4–14).

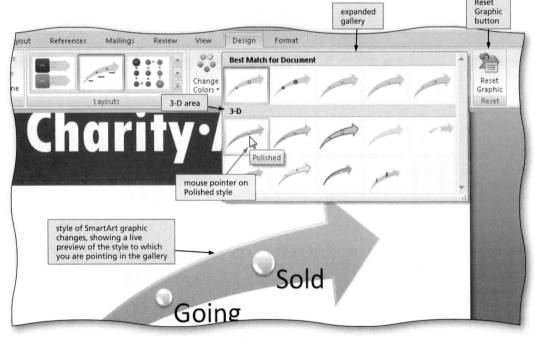

Figure 4–14

 Experiment

- Point to various SmartArt styles in the SmartArt Styles gallery and watch the style of the graphic change in the document window.

3

- Click Polished in the SmartArt Styles gallery to apply the selected style to the SmartArt graphic.

BTW

Resetting Graphics
If you want to remove all formats from a SmartArt graphic and start over, you would click the Reset Graphic button on the SmartArt Tools Design tab (Figure 4-14 on the previous page).

To Format Text Using the Mini Toolbar

The last step in formatting the SmartArt is to make the word, Sold, stand out more. The following steps use the Mini toolbar to increase the font size of the word, Sold, to 44 point, bold it, and change its color to dark pink.

1 Double-click the word, Sold, to select it.

2 Move the mouse pointer into the Mini toolbar, so that it changes to a bright toolbar.

3 Click the Bold button on the Mini toolbar to bold the selected text.

4 Click the Font Size box arrow on the Mini toolbar and then click 44 in the Font Size gallery to change the font size of the selected text.

5 Click the Font Color button arrow and then click Pink, Accent 2, Darker 25% to change the color of the selected text (Figure 4–15).

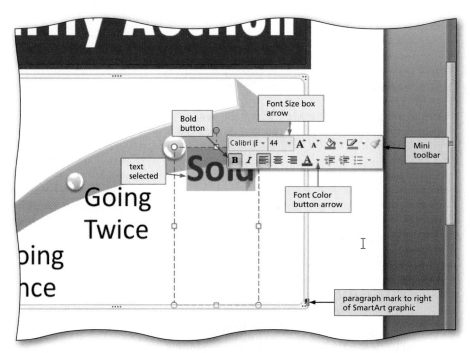

Figure 4–15

To Format Characters and Modify Character Spacing Using the Font Dialog Box

In this project, the next step is to enter and format the text at the bottom of the title page. This text is the theme of the proposal and is formatted so that it is noticeable. Its characters are 48-point bold, italic, and dark pink. Each letter in this text displays a shadow. A **shadow** is a light gray duplicate image that appears on the lower-right edge of a character or object. Also, you want extra space between each character so that the text spans across the width of the page.

You could use buttons on the Home tab to apply some of these formats. The shadow effect and expanded spacing, however, are applied using the Font dialog box. Thus, the next steps apply all above-mentioned formats using the Font dialog box.

1

- Position the insertion point on the paragraph mark to the right of the SmartArt graphic and then press the ENTER key to position the insertion point centered below the SmartArt graphic.

- Type Join us for this great cause!

- Select the sentence you just typed and then click the Font Dialog Box Launcher on the Home tab to display the Font dialog box. If necessary, click the Font tab in the dialog box.

- Click Bold Italic in the Font style list.

- Scroll through the Size list and then click 48.

- Click the Font color box arrow and then click Pink, Accent 2, Darker 25% in the Font color gallery.

- Click Shadow in the Effects area so that each character displays a shadow on its lower-right edge (Figure 4–16).

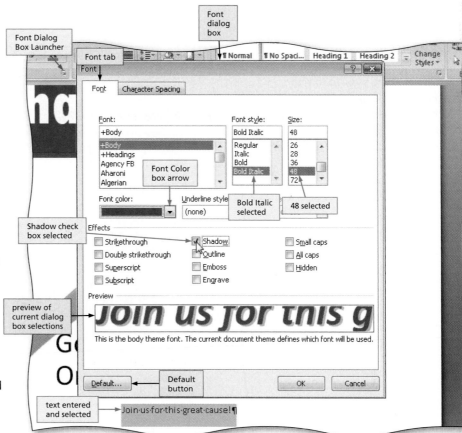

Figure 4–16

2

- Click the Character Spacing tab to display the Character Spacing sheet in the dialog box.

- Click the Spacing box arrow and then click Expanded to increase the amount of space between characters by 1 pt, which is the default.

- Click the Spacing By box up arrow until the box displays 5 pt so that 5 points of blank space are displayed between each character (Figure 4–17).

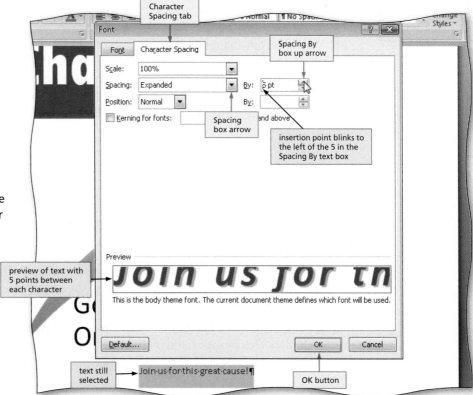

Figure 4–17

3

● Click the OK button to apply font changes to the selected text. If necessary, scroll so that the selected text is displayed completely in the document window (Figure 4–18). (Leave the text selected for the next set of steps.)

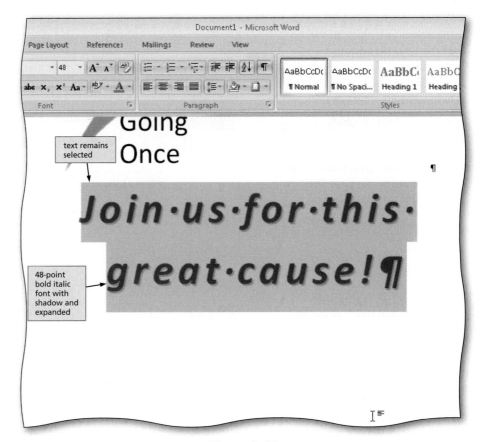

Figure 4–18

Other Ways

1. Right-click selected text, click Font on shortcut menu, select formats, click OK button

TO MODIFY THE DEFAULT FONT SETTINGS

You can change the default font so that the current document and all future documents use the new font settings. That is, if you quit Word, restart the computer, and restart Word, documents you create will use the new default font.

If you wanted to change the default font from 11-point Calibri to another font, font style, font size, font color, and/or font effects, you would perform the following steps.

1. Display the Font dialog box.
2. Make desired changes to the font settings in the Font dialog box.
3. Click the Default button (shown in Figure 4–16 on the previous page).
4. When the Microsoft Word dialog box is displayed, click the Yes button.

TO RESET THE DEFAULT FONT SETTINGS

To change the font settings back to the default, you would follow the above steps, using the default font settings when performing Step 2. If you do not remember the default settings, you would perform the following steps to restore the original Normal style settings.

1. Quit Word.
2. Use Windows Explorer to locate the normal.dotm file (be sure that hidden files and folders are displayed and include system and hidden files in your search).
3. Rename the normal.dotm file to oldnormal.dotm file so that the normal.dotm file no longer exists.
4. Start Word, which will recreate a normal.dotm file using the original default settings.

Character Effects

In addition to a shadow, the Font sheet in the Font dialog box (Figure 4–16 on page WD 241) contains many other character effects you can add to text in a document. Table 4–2 illustrates the result of each of these effects.

Table 4–2 Character Effects Available in the Font Dialog Box		
Type of Effect	**Plain Text**	**Formatted Text**
Strikethrough	Auction	~~Auction~~
Double strikethrough	Auction	~~Auction~~
Superscript	1st	1ST
Subscript	H2O	H$_2$O
Shadow	Auction	**Auction**
Outline	Auction	Auction
Emboss	Auction	Auction
Engrave	Auction	Auction
Small caps	Auction	Auction
All caps	Auction	AUCTION
Hidden	Auction	

The last entry in Table 4–2 shows the hidden format. **Hidden text** does not print but is part of the document. When the Show/Hide ¶ button on the Home tab is not selected, hidden text does not appear on the screen. When the Show/Hide ¶ button is selected, Word displays hidden text on the screen.

To Change Case of Text

To make the title text at the bottom of the sales proposal more pronounced, it is formatted in all capital letters. The following steps capitalize all letters in selected text.

1
- With the text still selected, click the Change Case button on the Home tab to display the Change Case gallery (Figure 4–19).

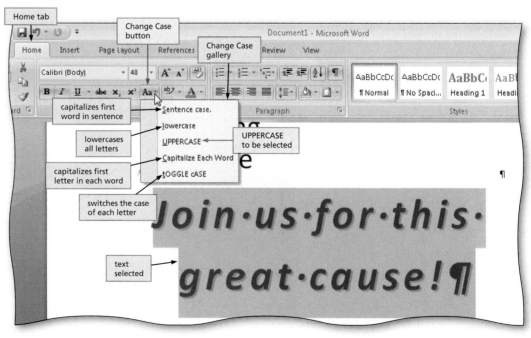

Figure 4–19

2

- Click UPPERCASE to change the characters in the selected text to all capital letters.

- Press the END key to deselect the text and position the insertion point at the end of the document (Figure 4–20).

Q&A

Could I have used the All caps check box in the Effects area of the Font dialog box to format this text in all capital letters?

Yes, but because the dialog box was closed already, the Change Case button was used.

text formatted in all capital letters

insertion point

Figure 4–20

Other Ways

1. Right-click selected text, click Font on shortcut menu, click Font tab, click All caps check box, click OK button

2. Press SHIFT+F3 repeatedly until text displays all caps

To Zoom One Page

The next step in creating the title page is to place the auctioneer graphic on it. You want to see the entire page while inserting this graphic. Thus, you zoom so that the entire page is displayed in the document window. Instead of using the Zoom slider to set the zoom, you can use the One Page button to quickly display the entire page in the document window. The following step zooms one page.

1

- Click View on the Ribbon to display the View tab.

- Click the One Page button on the View tab to display the entire page centered in the document window (Figure 4–21).

View tab

One Page button

entire one-page document is displayed centered in document window

Other Ways

1. Click Zoom level button on status bar, click Whole page in the Zoom dialog box, click OK button

Figure 4–21

To Create a Watermark

A **watermark** is text or a graphic that is displayed on top of or behind the text in a document. For example, a catalog may print the words, Sold Out, on top of sold-out items. The first draft of a five-year-plan may have the word, Draft, printed behind the text of the document. Some companies use their logos or other graphics as watermarks on documents to add visual appeal to the document.

In this project, a picture of an auctioneer is displayed behind all text and graphics as a watermark. The auctioneer picture is located on the Data Files for Students. See the inside back cover of this book for instructions on downloading the Data Files for Students, or contact your instructor for information about accessing the required files. The following steps create a picture watermark.

1

- Display the Page Layout tab.

- Click the Watermark button on the Page Layout tab to display the Watermark gallery (Figure 4–22).

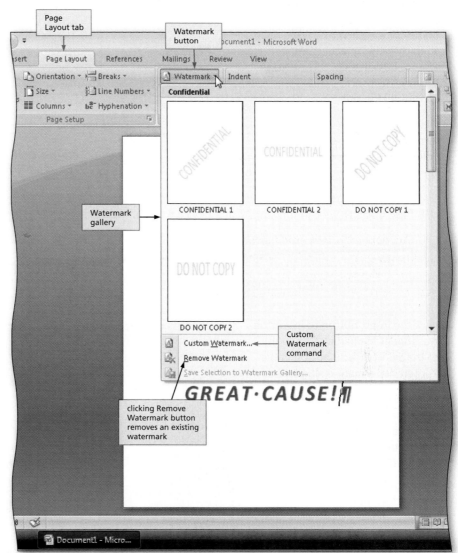

Figure 4–22

2

- Click Custom Watermark to display the Printed Watermark dialog box.

- With your USB flash drive connected to one of the computer's USB ports, click Picture watermark and then click the Select Picture button to display the Insert Picture dialog box.

- If the Folders list is displayed below the Folders button, click the Folders button to remove the Folders list.

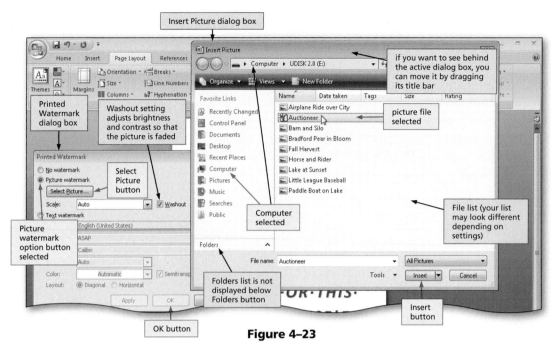

Figure 4–23

- Click Computer in the Favorite Links section and then double-click UDISK 2.0 (E:) to select the USB flash drive, Drive E in this case, as the device that contains the picture.

- Click Auctioneer to select the file name (Figure 4–23).

Q&A What if the picture is not on a USB flash drive?

Use the same process, but select the device containing the picture in the Favorite Links section.

3

- Click the Insert button to insert the Auctioneer file name to the right of the Select Picture button in the Printed Watermark dialog box.

- Click the OK button in the Printed Watermark dialog box to insert the watermark in the document, faded behind the text and SmartArt graphic (Figure 4–24).

Q&A How would I remove a watermark from a document?

Click the Watermark button on the Page Layout tab and then click Remove Watermark, or click No watermark in the Printed Watermark dialog box (Figure 4–23).

Q&A How would I create a text watermark?

Click Text watermark in the Printed Watermark dialog box (Figure 4–23), select the text for the watermark or enter your own text, select formats for the text, and then click the OK button.

Figure 4–24

To Change Spacing Above a Paragraph and Set Zoom Level

To make the text, JOIN US FOR THIS GREAT CAUSE!, stand out more, this project positions it below the bottom of the auctioneer watermark. Currently, the Spacing Before this paragraph is 0 pt (shown in Figure 4–24). The following steps change the Spacing Before to 150 points and then change the zoom level back to 100% because you are finished with the title page.

1 With the insertion point in the paragraph to adjust, click the Spacing Before box up arrow on the Page Layout tab as many times as necessary until 150 pt is displayed in the Spacing Before box (Figure 4–25).

2 Change the zoom level to 100%.

Figure 4–25

To Reveal Formatting

Sometimes, you want to know what formats were applied to certain text items in a document. For example, you may wonder what font, font size, font color, and other effects were applied to the last paragraph of the title page. To display formatting applied to text, use the Reveal Formatting task pane. The next step illustrates how to reveal formatting.

1

- With the insertion point in the text for which you want to reveal formatting, press SHIFT+F1 to show formatting applied to the location of the insertion point in the Reveal Formatting task pane (Figure 4–26).

Experiment

- Click the Font collapse button to hide the Font formats. Click the Font expand button to redisplay the Font formats.

Q&A Why do some of the formats in the Reveal Formatting task pane appear as links?

Clicking a link in the Reveal Formatting task pane displays an associated dialog box, allowing you to change the format of the current text. For example, clicking the Font link in the Reveal Formatting task pane displays the Font dialog box. If you make changes in the Font dialog box and then click the OK button, Word changes the format of the current text.

2

- Close the Reveal Formatting task pane by clicking its Close button.

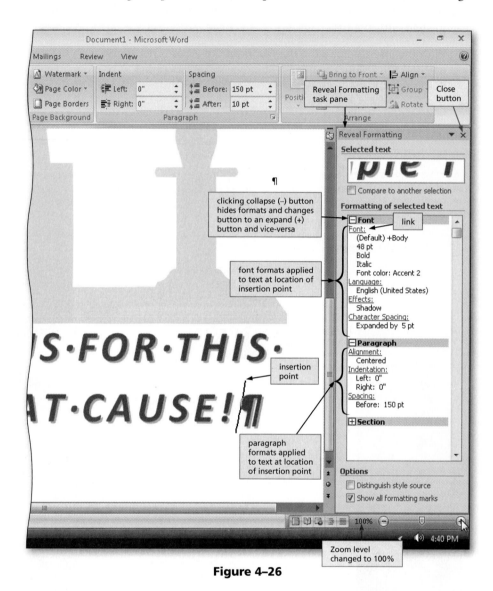

Figure 4–26

To Save a Document

The title page for the sales proposal is complete. Thus, the next step is to save it.

1 With a USB flash drive connected to one of the computer's USB ports, click the Save button on the Quick Access Toolbar to display the Save As dialog box.

2 Type `Charity Auction Title Page` in the File name text box to change the file name.

3 If Computer is not displayed in the Favorite Links section, drag the top or bottom edge of the Save As dialog box until Computer is displayed.

④ Click Computer in the Favorite Links section, and then double-click your USB flash drive in the list of available drives.

⑤ Click the Save button in the Save As dialog box to save the document on the USB flash drive with the file name, Charity Auction Title Page.

Inserting an Existing Document in an Open Document

Assume you already have prepared a draft of the body of the proposal and saved it with the file name, Charity Auction Draft. You would like the draft to display on a separate page following the title page. Once the two documents are displayed on the screen together as one document, you save this active document with a new name so that each of the original documents remains intact.

Plan Ahead

> **Compose the sales proposal.**
> Be sure to include basic elements in your sales proposal:
>
> • **Include an introduction, body, and conclusion.** The introduction could contain the subject, purpose, statement of problem, need, background, or scope. The body may include costs, benefits, supporting documentation, available or required facilities, feasibility, methods, timetable, materials, or equipment. The conclusion summarizes key points or requests an action.
>
> • **Use headers and footers.** Headers and footers help to identify every page. A page number should be in either the header or footer. If the sales proposal is disassembled, the reader can use the headers and footers to determine the order and pieces of your proposal.

In the following pages, you will insert the draft of the proposal below the title page and then edit the draft as follows: customize its font set, delete a page break, and cut some text.

Sections

All Word documents have at least one section. A Word document can be divided into any number of sections. During the course of creating a document, you will create a new **section** if you need to change the top margin, bottom margin, page alignment, paper size, page orientation, page number position, or contents or position of headers, footers, or footnotes in just a portion of the document.

The next two pages of the sales proposal require page formatting different from that of the title page. The title page will not have a header or footer and the next two pages will have a header and footer.

When you want to change page formatting for a portion of a document, you create a new section in the document. Each section then may be formatted differently from the others. Thus, the title page formatted with no header or footer will be in one section, and the next two pages of the proposal that will have a header and footer will be in another section.

To Insert a Next Page Section Break

The next two pages of the sales proposal have a header, but the title page does not. One way to specify different headers in a document is to divide it into sections. When you insert a section break, you specify whether the new section should begin on a new page.

In this project, the title page is separate from the next two pages. Thus, the section break should contain a page break. The following steps insert a next page section break, which instructs Word to begin the new section on a new page in the document.

1

- With the insertion point at the end of the title page, click the Breaks button on the Page Layout tab to display the Breaks gallery (Figure 4–27).

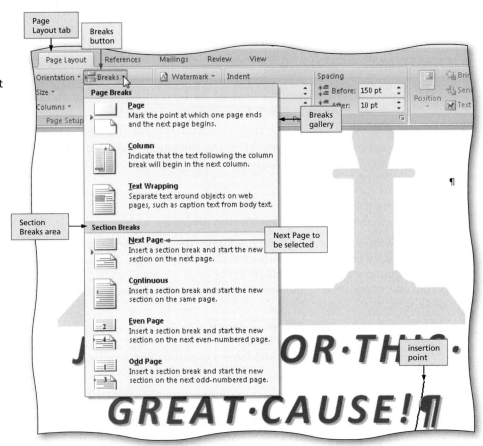

Figure 4–27

2

- Click Next Page in the Section Breaks area of the Breaks gallery to insert a next page section break in the document at the location of the insertion point. If necessary, scroll so that your screen matches Figure 4–28.

 Q&A Why is the watermark in the new page?

A watermark is a page format that automatically is carried forward to subsequent pages.

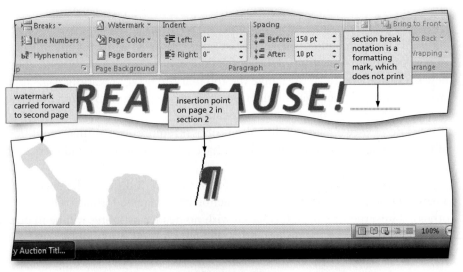

Figure 4–28

To Delete a Section Break

Word stores all section formatting in the section break. If you wanted to delete a section break and all associated section formatting, you would perform the following tasks.

1. Select the section break notation by dragging through it.

2. Right-click the selection and then click Cut on the shortcut menu.

or

1. Position the insertion point immediately to the left or right of the section break notation.

2. Press the DELETE key to delete a section break to the right of the insertion point or press the BACKSPACE key to delete a section break to the left of the insertion point.

To Clear Formatting

When you create a section break, Word carries forward any formatting at the location of the insertion point to the next section. Thus, the current paragraph has 150 points of spacing before the paragraph and the text is formatted the same as the last line of the title page. In this project, the paragraphs and characters on the second page should return to the Normal style. Thus, the following steps clear formatting.

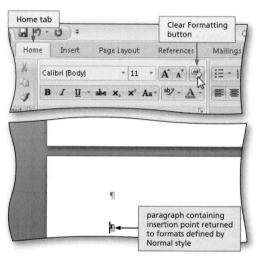

1 Display the Home tab.

2 With the insertion point positioned on the paragraph mark on the second page (shown in Figure 4–28), click the Clear Formatting button on the Home tab to apply the Normal style to the location of the insertion point (Figure 4–29).

Figure 4–29

To Insert a Word Document in an Open Document

The next step is to insert the draft of the sales proposal at the top of the second page of the document. The draft is located on the Data Files for Students. See the inside back cover of this book for instructions on downloading the Data Files for Students, or contact your instructor for information about accessing the required files. The following steps insert the draft of the proposal in the open document.

- Be sure the insertion point is positioned on the paragraph mark at the top of page 2.

- Display the Insert tab.

- With your USB flash drive connected to one of the computer's USB ports, click the Object button arrow to display the Object menu (Figure 4–30).

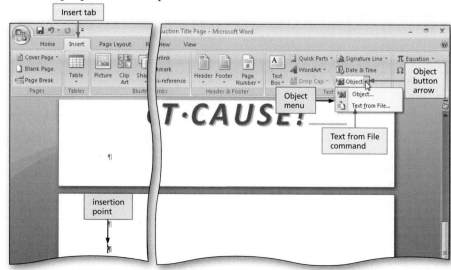

Figure 4–30

2

- On the Object menu, click Text from File to display the Insert File dialog box.

- If the Folders list is displayed below the Folders button, click the Folders button to remove the Folders list.

- If necessary, click Computer in the Favorite Links section and select the USB flash drive, Drive E in this case, in the list of files.

- Click Charity Auction Draft to select the file name (Figure 4–31).

 Q&A How do I open the file if I am not using a USB flash drive?

Use the same process, but be certain to select your device in the Computer list.

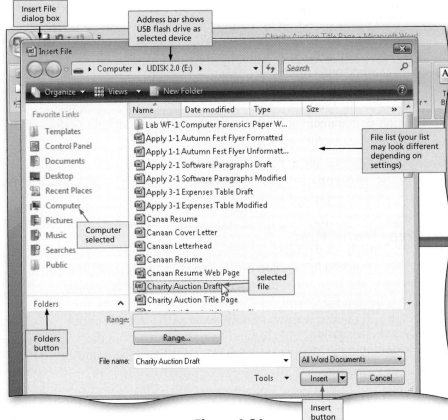

Figure 4–31

3

- Click the Insert button in the dialog box to insert the file, Charity Auction Draft, in the open document at the location of the insertion point.

Q&A Where is the insertion point?

When you insert a file in an open document, Word positions the insertion point at the end of the inserted document.

- Press SHIFT+F5 to position the insertion point on line 1 of page 2, which was its location prior to inserting the new Word document (Figure 4–32).

Q&A What is the purpose of SHIFT+F5?

The shortcut key, SHIFT+F5, positions the insertion point at your last editing location. Word remembers your last three editing locations, which means you can press this shortcut key repeatedly to return to one of your three most recent editing locations.

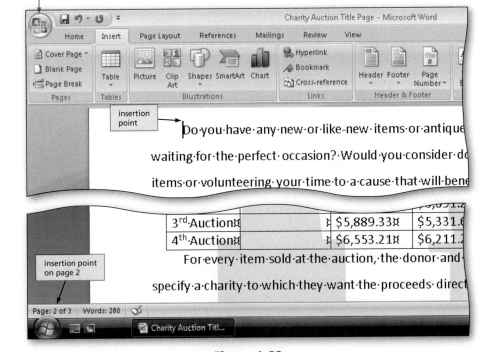

Figure 4–32

To Save an Active Document with a New File Name

The current file name on the title bar is Charity Auction Title Page, yet the active document contains both the title page and the draft of the sales proposal. To keep the title page as a separate document called Charity Auction Title Page, you should save the active document with a new file name. If you save the active document by clicking the Save button on the Quick Access Toolbar, Word will assign it the current file name. You want the active document to have a new file name. The following steps save the active document with a new file name.

1 With the USB flash drive containing the Charity Auction Title Page connected to one of the computer's USB ports, click the Office Button and then click Save As on the Office Button menu to display the Save As dialog box.

2 Type `Charity Auction Proposal` in the File name text box to change the file name.

3 If Computer is not displayed in the Favorite Links section, drag the top or bottom edge of the Save As dialog box until Computer is displayed.

4 If necessary, click Computer in the Favorite Links section, and then double-click your USB flash drive in the list of available drives.

5 Click the Save button in the Save As dialog box to save the document on the USB flash drive with the file name, Charity Auction Proposal.

BTW

Inserting Documents
When you insert a Word document in another Word document, the entire inserted document is placed at the location of the insertion point. If the insertion point, therefore, is positioned in the middle of the open document when you insert another Word document, the open document continues after the last character of the inserted document.

To Print Specific Pages in a Document

The title page is the first page of the proposal. The body of the proposal spans the second and third pages. The next steps print a hard copy of only the body of the proposal.

1

• Ready the printer.

• Click the Office Button to display the Office Button menu.

• Point to Print on the Office Button menu and then click Print on the submenu to display the Print dialog box.

• Click Pages in the Page range area of the dialog box and then type 2–3 in the Pages text box (Figure 4–33).

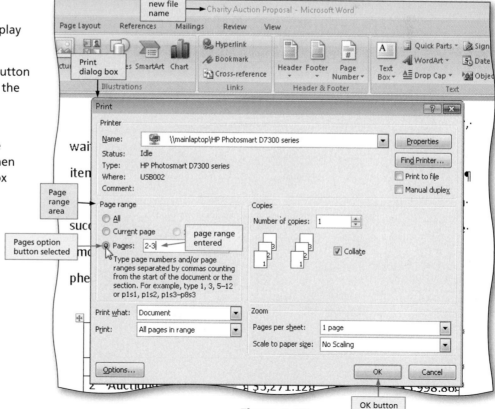

Figure 4–33

2

- Click the OK button to print the inserted draft of the sales proposal (Figure 4–34).

Q&A What if I wanted to print pages from a certain point to the end of a document?

You would enter the page number followed by a dash in the Pages text box. For example, 5- will print from page 5 to the end of the document. To print up to a certain page, put the dash first (e.g., -5 will print pages 1 through 5).

Q&A Why does my document wrap on different words than Figure 4–34?

Differences in wordwrap are related to the printer used by your computer.

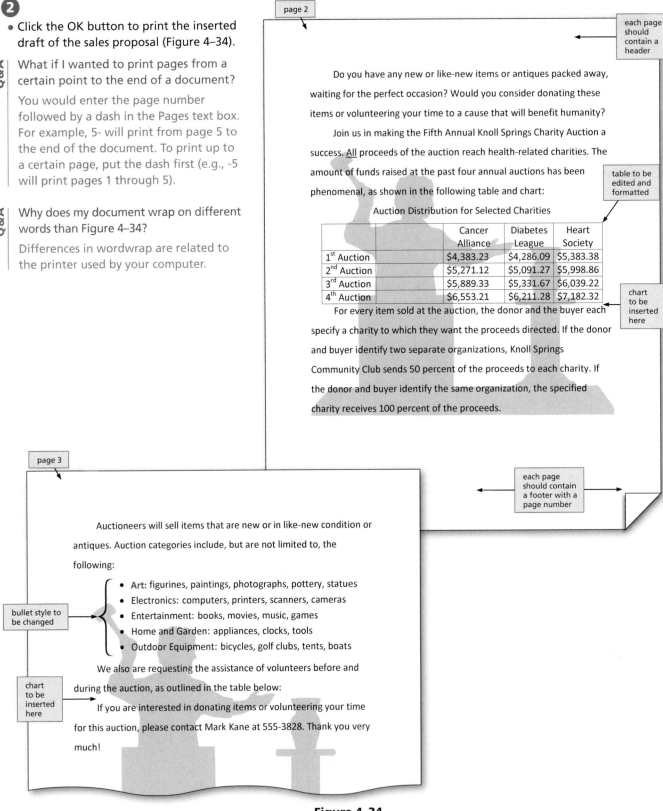

page 2

each page should contain a header

Do you have any new or like-new items or antiques packed away, waiting for the perfect occasion? Would you consider donating these items or volunteering your time to a cause that will benefit humanity?

Join us in making the Fifth Annual Knoll Springs Charity Auction a success. All proceeds of the auction reach health-related charities. The amount of funds raised at the past four annual auctions has been phenomenal, as shown in the following table and chart:

table to be edited and formatted

Auction Distribution for Selected Charities

	Cancer Alliance	Diabetes League	Heart Society
1st Auction	$4,383.23	$4,286.09	$5,383.38
2nd Auction	$5,271.12	$5,091.27	$5,998.86
3rd Auction	$5,889.33	$5,331.67	$6,039.22
4th Auction	$6,553.21	$6,211.28	$7,182.32

chart to be inserted here

For every item sold at the auction, the donor and the buyer each specify a charity to which they want the proceeds directed. If the donor and buyer identify two separate organizations, Knoll Springs Community Club sends 50 percent of the proceeds to each charity. If the donor and buyer identify the same organization, the specified charity receives 100 percent of the proceeds.

each page should contain a footer with a page number

page 3

Auctioneers will sell items that are new or in like-new condition or antiques. Auction categories include, but are not limited to, the following:

bullet style to be changed

- **Art:** figurines, paintings, photographs, pottery, statues
- Electronics: computers, printers, scanners, cameras
- Entertainment: books, movies, music, games
- Home and Garden: appliances, clocks, tools
- Outdoor Equipment: bicycles, golf clubs, tents, boats

We also are requesting the assistance of volunteers before and during the auction, as outlined in the table below:

chart to be inserted here

If you are interested in donating items or volunteering your time for this auction, please contact Mark Kane at 555-3828. Thank you very much!

Figure 4–34

Other Ways

1. Press CTRL+P

To Customize Theme Fonts

After reviewing the draft in Figure 4–34, you notice its text is based on the Office font set, which uses Cambria for headings and Calibri for body text. You prefer different fonts for the sales proposal, specifically Tw Cen MT Condensed Extra Bold for headings and Franklin Gothic Book for body text. These two fonts are not defined in a font set. Thus, the following steps create a customized theme font set for this document.

- Display the Home tab. Click the Change Styles button on the Home tab to display the Change Styles menu.

- Point to Fonts on the Change Styles menu to display the Fonts gallery.

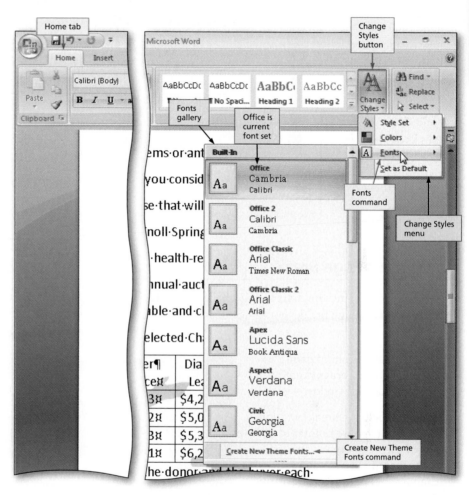

Figure 4–35

2
- Click Create New Theme Fonts in the Fonts gallery to display the Create New Theme Fonts dialog box.

- Click the Heading font box arrow; scroll to and then click Tw Cent MT Condensed Extra Bold (or a similar font).

- Click the Body font box arrow; scroll to and then click Franklin Gothic Book (or a similar font).

- Enter Charity Auction Proposal as the name for the new theme font (Figure 4–36).

Figure 4–36

3

- Click the Save button in the dialog box to create the customized theme font with the name, Charity Auction Proposal, and apply the new heading and body fonts in the current document (Figure 4–37).

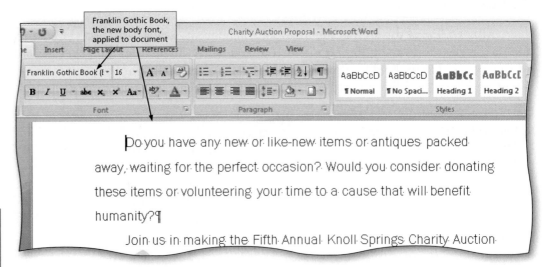

Franklin Gothic Book, the new body font, applied to document

Figure 4–37

To Delete a Page Break

After reviewing the draft in Figure 4–34 on page WD 254, you notice it contains a page break below the third paragraph. This page break should not be in the document. The following steps delete a page break.

1

- Scroll to the bottom of page 2 to display the page break notation in the document window.

- To select the page break notation, position the mouse pointer to the left of the page break and then click when the mouse pointer changes to a right-pointing arrow (Figure 4–38).

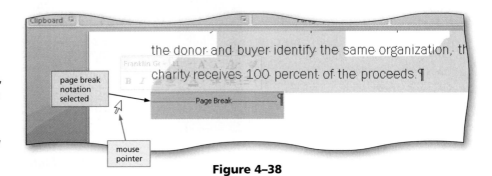

page break notation selected

mouse pointer

Figure 4–38

2

- Press the DELETE key to remove the page break from the document (Figure 4–39).

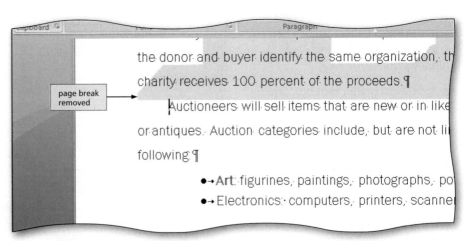

page break removed

Figure 4–39

To Cut Text

The last line of the draft document contains the phrase, Thank you very much! You decide to shorten it simply to say, Thank you! The following steps cut text from a document.

- Scroll to the end of the document and select the words, very much (Figure 4–40).

text to be deleted is selected

Figure 4–40

- Click the Cut button on the Home tab to remove the selected text from the document (Figure 4–41).

Q&A

When you cut items, are they placed on the Clipboard?

Yes. You then can paste items from the Clipboard in the document by clicking the Paste button on the Home tab or by using the Clipboard task pane.

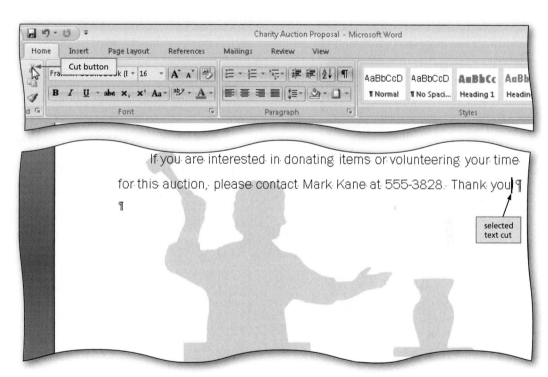

selected text cut

Figure 4–41

Other Ways

1. Right-click selected text, click Cut on shortcut menu
2. Press CTRL+X

Creating Headers and Footers

A **header** is text that prints at the top of each page in the document. A **footer** is text that prints at the bottom of each page. In this proposal, you want the header and footer to display on each page after the title page; that is, you do not want the header and footer on the title page. Recall that the title page is in a separate section from the rest of the sales proposal. Thus, the header and footer should not be in section 1, but they should be in section 2. The steps on the following pages explain how to create a header and footer in section 2 only.

To Go To a Section

Because the header and footer should be only on the pages in section 2 of the document, you should be sure the insertion point is in section 2 when you create the header and footer. The following steps position the insertion point in section 2, specifically, the beginning of section 2.

1
- Click the 'Page number in document' button on the status bar to display the Find and Replace dialog box.

Experiment
- Scroll through the 'Go to what' list in the dialog box to see the many areas you can go to in a document.

2
- Click Section in the 'Go to what' area to select it.

- Type 2 in the 'Enter section number' text box (Figure 4–42).

3
- Click the Go To button in the dialog box to position the insertion point at the beginning of section 2 in the document.

- Click the Close button in the dialog box.

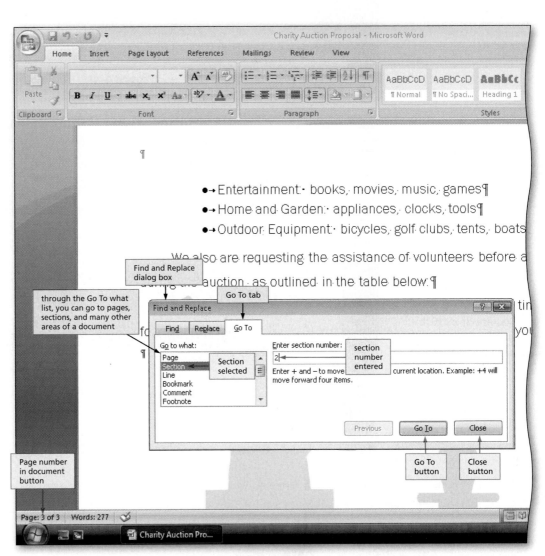

Figure 4–42

Other Ways

1. Click Select Browse Object button on vertical scroll bar, click Browse by Section
2. Click Find button arrow on Home tab, click Go To
3. Press CTRL+G

To Create a Header Different from the Previous Section Header

The next step is to instruct Word that the header and footer to be added should be in only the current (second) section of the document so that the header and footer do not appear on the title page.

1

- Display the Insert tab.

- Click the Header button on the Insert tab and then click Edit Header in the Header gallery to switch to the header for section 2 (Figure 4–43).

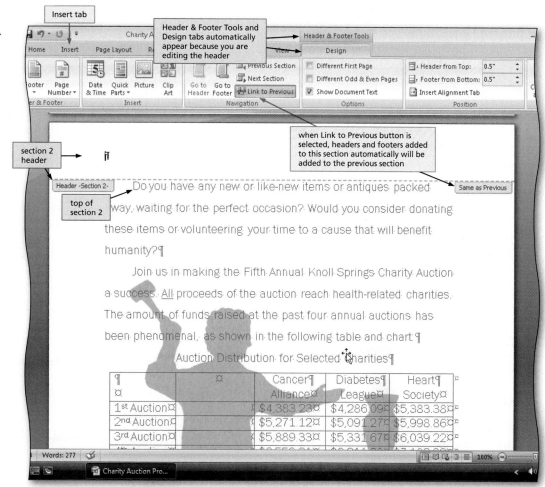

Figure 4–43

2

- If the header displays the tab, Same as Previous, in its lower-right corner, click the Link to Previous button on the Design tab to remove the Same as Previous tab, which means that the headers and footers entered in section 2 will not be copied to section 1.

Q&A What if I wanted a header and footer to appear in all sections?

You would leave the Link to Previous button selected on the Design tab.

BTW

Sections
To see formatting associated with a section, double-click the section break notation to display the Page Setup dialog box. You can change margin settings and page orientation for a section in the Margins tab. To change paper sizes for a section, click the Paper tab. The Layout tab allows you to change header and footer specifications and vertical alignment for the section. To add a border to a section, click the Borders button in the Layout sheet.

To Insert a Formatted Header

Word provides several built-in preformatted header designs for you to insert in documents. The following steps insert a formatted header in section 2 of the sales proposal.

1

- Click the Header button on the Design tab to display the Header gallery (Figure 4–44).

 **Experiment**

- Scroll through the list of built-in headers to see the variety of available formatted header designs.

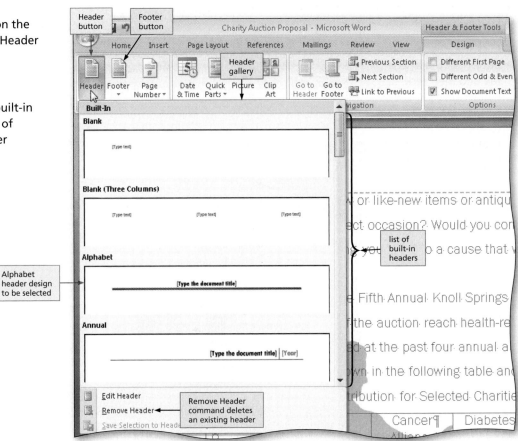

Figure 4–44

2

- Scroll to and then click the Alphabet header design to insert it in the header of section 2.

- Click the content control, Type the document title, and then type FIFTH ANNUAL KNOLL SPRINGS CHARITY AUCTION as the header text (Figure 4–45).

 What if I wanted to delete a header?

You would click Remove Header in the Header gallery (Figure 4–44).

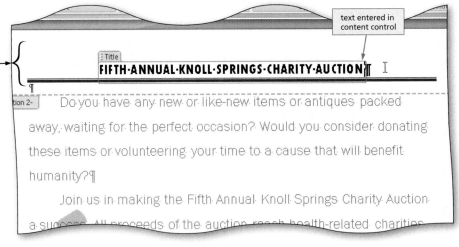

Figure 4–45

Other Ways

1. Click Header button on Insert tab, select desired header in list

Edit

The sa...
that wa...
and fiv...
show t...
remain...

> **Enh**
> Stud...
> tabl...
> reac...
> doc...

charti...

1
2
3
4

To Fc

identif...

1 If...

2 Se...

3 Bc...

To Dc

delete...

1

• Posit...
top c...
and...
chan...
arrov...
colur...
(Figu...

To Insert a Formatted Footer

The next step is to insert the footer. Word provides the same built-in preformatted footer designs as header designs. The footer design that corresponds to the header just inserted contains text at the left margin and a page number at the right margin. The following steps insert a formatted footer in section 2 of the sales proposal that corresponds to the header just inserted.

1 Click the Go to Footer button on the Design tab to display the footer in the document window.

2 Click the Footer button on the Design tab to display the Footer gallery.

3 Click the Alphabet footer design to insert it in the footer of section 2.

4 Click the content control, Type text, and then type JOIN US FOR THIS GREAT CAUSE! as the text (Figure 4–46).

Q&A Why is the page number a 2?

The page number is 2 because, by default, Word begins numbering pages from the beginning of the document.

BTW **Headers and Footers**
If a portion of a header or footer does not print, it may be in a nonprintable area. Check the printer manual to see how close the printer can print to the edge of the paper. Then, click the Page Setup Dialog Box Launcher on the Page Layout tab, click the Layout tab in the dialog box, adjust the From edge text box to a value that is larger than the printer's minimum margin setting, click the OK button, and then print the document again.

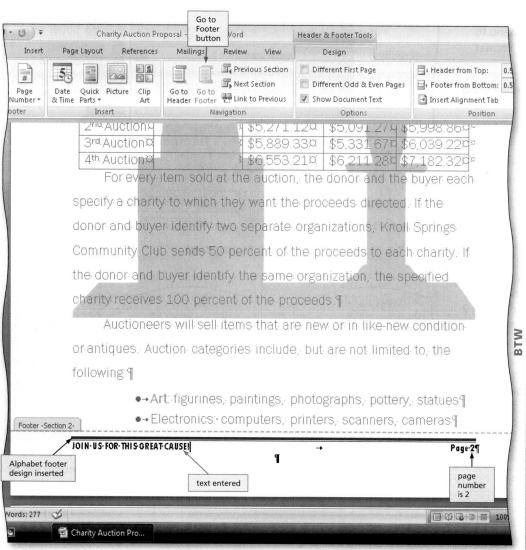

BTW **Page Numbers**
If Word displays {PAGE} instead of the actual page number, press ALT+F9 to turn off field codes. If Word prints {PAGE} instead of the page number, click the Office Button, click the Word Options button, click Advanced in the left pane, scroll to the Print area, remove the check mark from the 'Print field codes instead of their values' check box, and then click the OK button.

Figure 4–46

To Apply a Table Style

The table in the document looks dull. The following steps apply a table style to the table.

1 Display the Design tab.

2 With the insertion point in the table, be sure just these check boxes contain check marks in the Design tab: Header Row, Total Row, and First Column.

3 Click the More button in the Table Styles gallery to expand the Table Styles gallery.

4 Scroll to and then click Colorful List in the Table Styles gallery to apply the Colorful List style to the table (Figure 4–55).

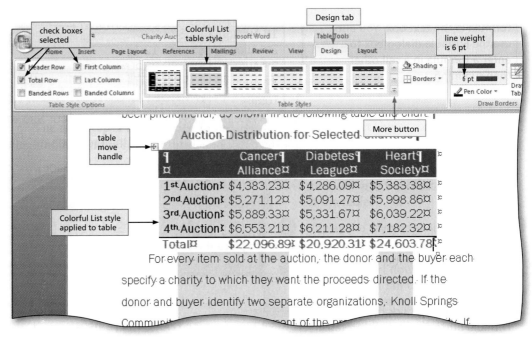

Figure 4–55

To Center a Table

The next step is to center the table horizontally between the page margins.

1 Position the mouse pointer in the table so that the table move handle appears (shown in Figure 4–55).

Q&A What if the table move handle does not appear?

You can select the table by clicking the Select Table button on the Layout tab and then clicking Select Table in the menu.

2 Click the table move handle to select the table.

3 Move the mouse pointer into the Mini toolbar and then click the Center button on the Mini toolbar, or click the Center button on the Home tab, to center the selected table between the left and right margins. (Leave the table selected for the next set of steps.)

To Border a Table

The table in this project has a 1-point, gray border. Earlier in this chapter when you created the title page, the border line weight was changed to 6 point and the border color changed to gray. Because the table border should be 1 point, you will change the line weight before adding the border to the table. The following steps add a border to a table.

- With the table still selected, click the Line Weight box arrow on the Design tab and then click 1 pt in the Line Weight gallery.

- Click the Borders button arrow on the Design tab to display the Borders gallery (Figure 4–56).

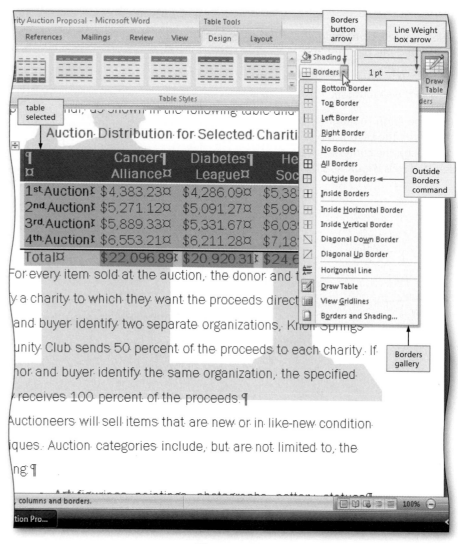

Figure 4–56

- Click Outside Borders to add a 1-point, gray border to the selected table.

- Click in the table to remove the selection.

Tables
If you wanted to move a table to a new location, you would point to the upper-left corner of the table until the table move handle appears (shown in Figure 4-55), point to the table move handle, and then drag it to move the entire table to a new location.

To Align Data in Cells

The next step is to change the alignment of the data in cells that contain the dollar amounts. In addition to aligning text horizontally in a cell (left, center, or right), you can align it vertically within a cell (top, center, bottom). When the height of the cell is close to the same height as the text, however, differences in vertical alignment are not readily apparent, which is the case for this table. Later in this chapter, you will align cell contents in a table that clearly will show variations in the vertical alignment. The following step right-aligns data in cells.

1

- Select the cells containing dollar amounts by dragging through them.

- Display the Layout tab.

- Click the Align Top Right button on the Layout tab to right-align the contents of the selected cells (Figure 4–57).

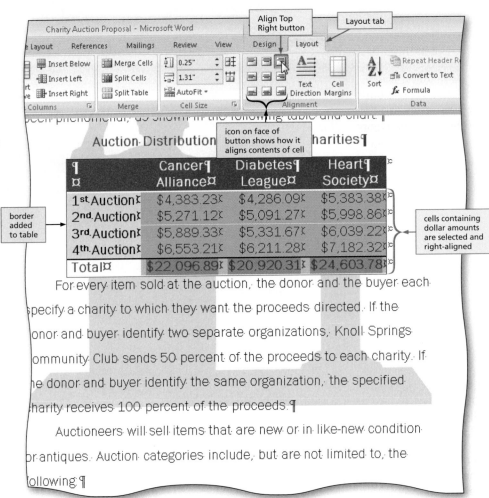

Figure 4–57

Charts
If Microsoft Excel is installed on your computer and you wanted to create a chart from an Excel worksheet, you would click the Insert Chart button on the Insert tab. If Microsoft Excel is not installed on your computer, clicking the Insert Chart button starts the Microsoft Graph program.

Charting a Word Table

When you create a Word table, you easily can chart its data using an embedded charting program called **Microsoft Graph**. Graph has its own menus and commands because it is a program embedded in Word. Using Graph commands, you can modify the appearance of the chart once you create it.

To create a chart from a Word table, the first row and left column of the selected cells in the table must contain text labels, and the other cells in the selected cells must contain numbers. The table in the Charity Auction Proposal meets these criteria. In the following pages, you will chart a table, move the legend to a different location, resize the chart, and change the chart type.

To Chart a Table

To chart a Word table, first select the rows and columns in the table to be charted. In this project, you do not want to chart the last row in the table that contains the totals. Thus, you will select the first five rows in the table and then chart the selected cells. The following steps chart a table.

- Point to the left of, or outside, the first row in the table (the column headings) until the mouse pointer changes to a right-pointing arrow and then drag downward until the first five rows in the table are selected. (Do not select the Total row.)

- Display the Insert tab.

- Click the Object button arrow to display the Object menu (Figure 4–58).

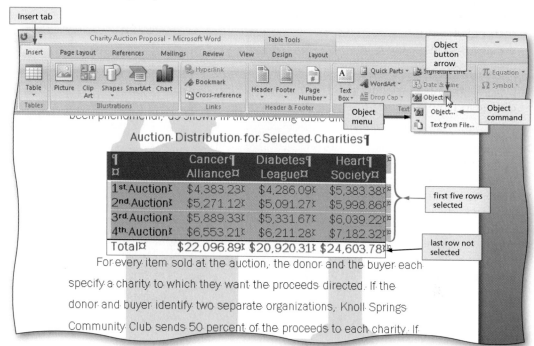

Figure 4–58

- Click Object on the Object menu to display the Object dialog box.

- If necessary, click the Create New tab. Select Microsoft Graph Chart in the Object type list (Figure 4–59).

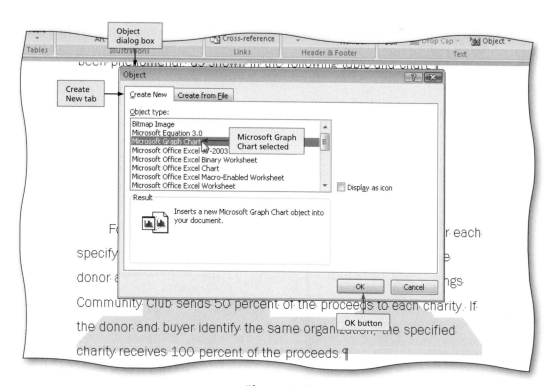

Figure 4–59

3

- Click the OK button to start the Microsoft Graph program, which creates a chart of the selected rows in the table (Figure 4–60).

- Close the Datasheet window by clicking its Close button.

Q&A

What is the Datasheet window?

Graph places the contents of the table in a **Datasheet window**, also called a **datasheet**. Graph then charts the contents of the datasheet. Although you can modify the contents of the datasheet, it is not necessary in this project. Thus, the datasheet is closed.

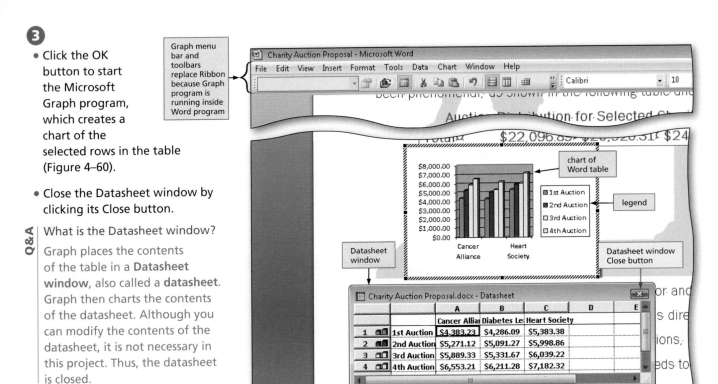

			A	B	C	D	E
			Cancer Allian	Diabetes Le	Heart Society		
1		1st Auction	$4,383.23	$4,286.09	$5,383.38		
2		2nd Auction	$5,271.12	$5,091.27	$5,998.86		
3		3rd Auction	$5,889.33	$5,331.67	$6,039.22		
4		4th Auction	$6,553.21	$6,211.28	$7,182.32		

Figure 4–60

To Move Legend Placement in a Chart

The first step in changing the chart is to move the legend so that it displays below the chart instead of to the right of the chart. The **legend** is a box that identifies the colors assigned to categories in the chart. The following steps move the legend in the chart.

1

- If necessary, scroll to display the chart in the document window.

- Right-click the legend in the chart to display a shortcut menu related to legends (Figure 4–61).

Q&A

What if Microsoft Graph is no longer active; that is, what if the Word Ribbon is displayed instead of the Graph menus and toolbars?

While working in Graph, you may inadvertently click somewhere outside the chart, which exits Graph and returns to Word. If this occurs, simply double-click the chart to return to Graph.

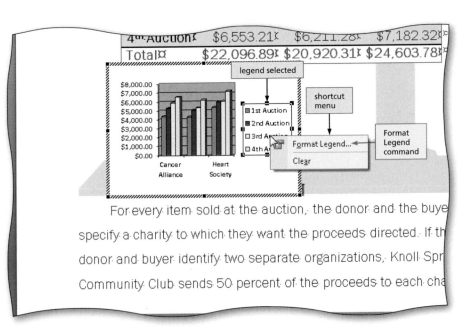

Figure 4–61

- Click Format Legend on the shortcut menu to display the Format Legend dialog box.

- Click the Placement tab, if necessary.

- Click Bottom in the Placement area (Figure 4–62).

- Click the OK button to place the legend below the chart.

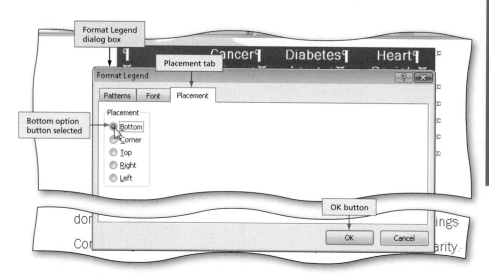

Figure 4–62

To Resize a Chart

The next step is to resize the chart so that it is bigger. You resize a chart the same way you resize any other graphical object. That is, you drag the chart's sizing handles. The following steps resize the chart.

- Point to the bottom-right sizing handle on the chart and drag downward and to the right as shown in Figure 4–63.

2

- Release the mouse button to resize the chart (shown in Figure 4–64 on the next page).

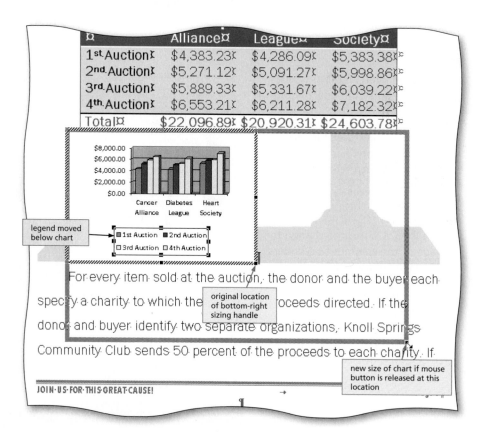

Figure 4–63

To Change the Chart Type

The next task is to change the chart type so that the columns have a cylindrical shape instead of a rectangular shape. The following steps change the chart type.

- Right-click an area of white space in the chart to display a shortcut menu (Figure 4–64).

Q&A What if my shortcut menu differs from the one shown in the figure?

Right-click a different area of white space in the chart.

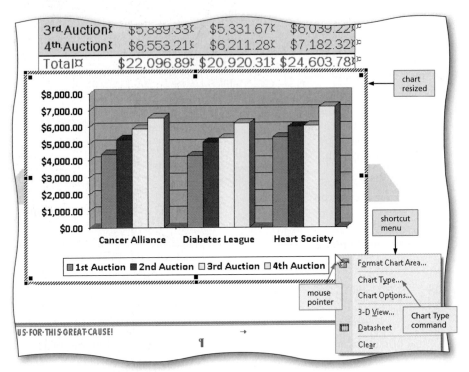

Figure 4–64

- Click Chart Type on the shortcut menu to display the Chart Type dialog box.

- If necessary, click the Standard Types tab. In the Chart type list, scroll to and then select Cylinder (Figure 4–65).

3

- Click the OK button to change the shape of the columns to cylinders (shown in Figure 4–66).

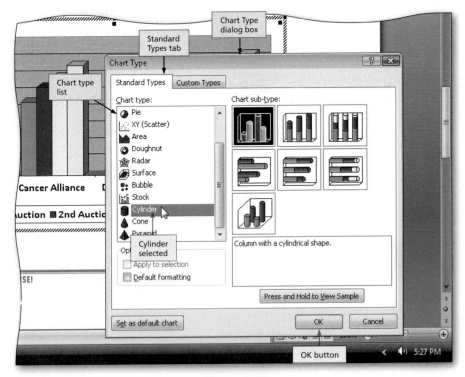

Figure 4–65

To Exit Graph and Return to Word

The modified chart is finished. The next step is to exit Graph and return to Word. In Word, you place an outside border on the chart to give it a finished look and add a blank line above the chart to separate it from the table.

- Click somewhere outside the chart to close the Graph program and return to Word.

- If necessary, scroll to display the chart in the document window.

Q&A

What if I want to modify an existing chart after I close Graph?

You would double-click the chart to reopen the Graph program. When you are finished making changes to the chart, click anywhere outside the chart to return to Word.

2

- Display the Home tab.

- Click the chart to select it. Click the Border button arrow on the Home tab and then click Outside Borders in the Border gallery to place the same border around the chart that is around the table.

- Click the Line spacing button on the Home tab and then click Add Space Before Paragraph to place a blank line above the chart.

- Click to the right of the chart to deselect it (Figure 4–66).

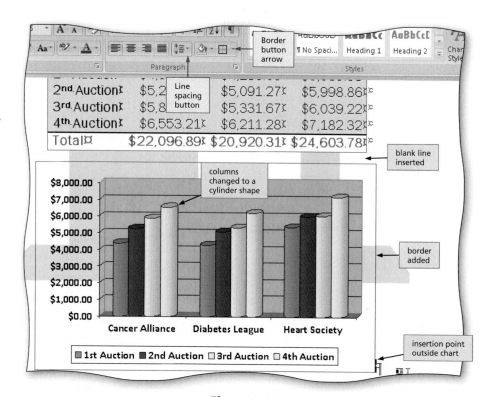

Figure 4–66

Working with Formats, Styles, and Bulleted Lists

On the last page of the sales proposal, the auction categories at the beginning of each bulleted item are emphasized. The draft of the sales proposal formatted the first auction category, Art, in bold and dark pink. All the remaining auction categories should use this format. Also, the bullet character at the beginning of each category is a picture bullet, instead of the standard dot. The following pages illustrate steps used to format the text and bullets in the auction categories:

1. Find the bold, dark pink format.
2. Create a character style for the format.
3. Select the auction categories to be formatted.
4. Apply the style.
5. Customize bullets in a list.

To Find a Format

The last page of the proposal has a bulleted list. The text at the beginning of each bulleted paragraph identifies a specific auction category. The first bullet, identified with the text, Art, has been formatted as bold and dark red. To find this text in the document, you could scroll through the document until it is displayed on the screen. A more efficient way is to find the bold, dark red format using the Find and Replace dialog box. The following steps find a format.

1

- Click the Find button on the Home tab to display the Find and Replace dialog box.

- If Word displays a More button in the Find and Replace dialog box, click it so that it changes to a Less button and expands the dialog box.

- Click the Format button to display the Format menu (Figure 4–67).

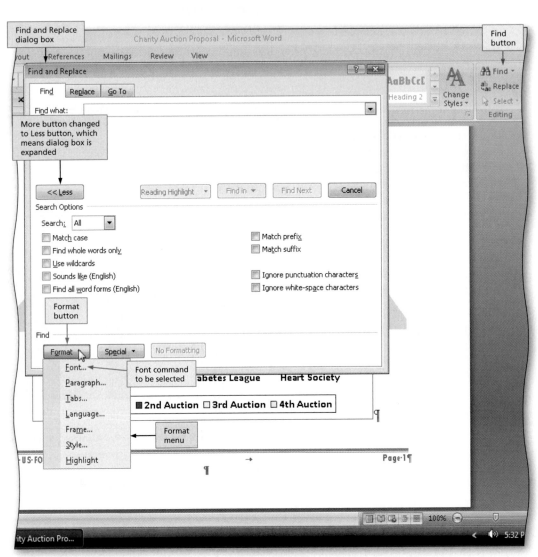

Figure 4–67

2

• Click Font on the Format menu to display the Find Font dialog box. If necessary, click the Font tab.

• In the dialog box, click Bold in the Font style list.

• In the dialog box, click the Font color box arrow and then click Pink, Accent 2, Darker 25% (Figure 4–68).

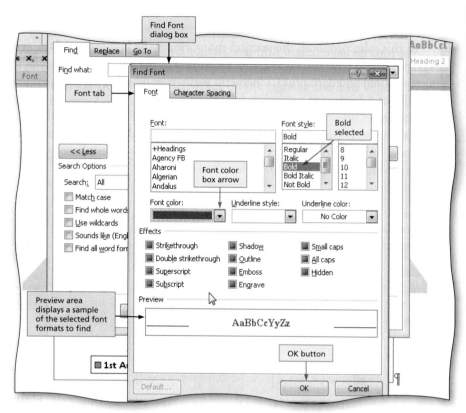

Figure 4–68

3

• Click the OK button to close the Find Font dialog box.

• When the Find and Replace dialog box is active again, click its Find Next button to locate and highlight in the document the first occurrence of the specified format (Figure 4–69).

Q&A How do I remove a find format?

You would click the No Formatting button in the Find and Replace dialog box.

4

• Click the Cancel button in the Find and Replace dialog box because the located occurrence is the one you wanted to find.

Q&A Can I search for (find) special characters such as page breaks?

Yes. To find special characters, you would click the Special button in the Find and Replace dialog box.

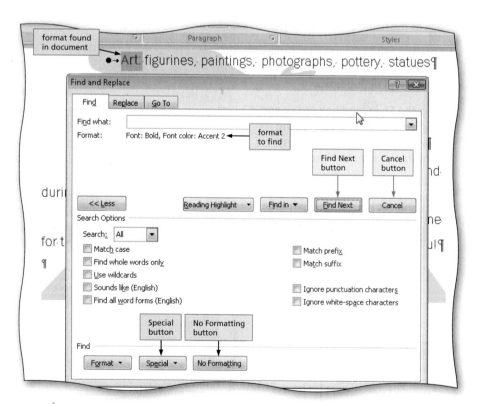

Figure 4–69

Other Ways

1. Click Select Browse Object button on vertical scroll bar, click Find icon

2. Press CTRL+F

To Customize Bullets in a List

The bulleted list in the sales proposal draft uses default bullet characters. You want to use a more visually appealing picture bullet. The following steps change the bullets in the list from the default to picture bullets.

- Select all the paragraphs in the bulleted list.

- Click the Bullets button arrow on the Home tab to display the Bullets gallery (Figure 4–73).

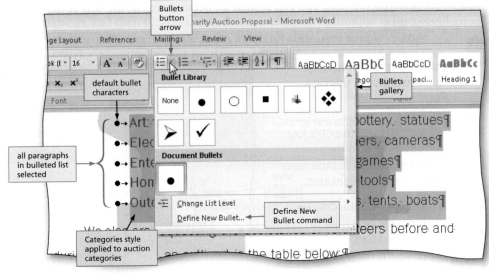

Figure 4–73

- Click Define New Bullet in the Bullets gallery to display the Define New Bullet dialog box.

- Click the Picture button in the Define New Bullet dialog box to display the Picture Bullet dialog box.

- Scroll through the list of picture bullets and then select the picture bullet shown in Figure 4–74 (or a similar picture bullet).

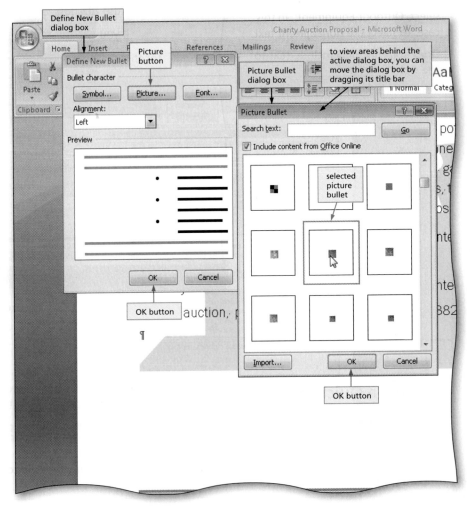

Figure 4–74

- Click the OK button in the Picture Bullet dialog box.

- Click the OK button in the Define New Bullet dialog box to change the bullets in the selected list to picture bullets.

- When the Word window is visible again, click in the selected list to remove the selection (Figure 4–75).

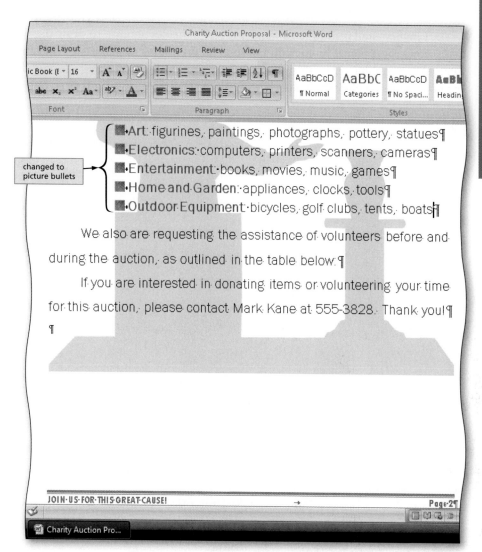

Figure 4–75

Drawing a Table

The next step is to insert a table above the last paragraph of the proposal (shown in Figure 4–1 on page WD 227). As previously discussed, a Word table is a collection of rows and columns; the intersection of a row and a column is called a cell. Cells are filled with data.

When you want to create a simple table, one with the same number of rows and columns, select the dimension of the table in the Table gallery. To create a more complex table, use Word's **Draw Table feature**. The table to be created at this point in the project is a complex table because it contains a varying number of columns per row. The following pages discuss how to use Word's Draw Table feature.

BTW

Page Breaks and Tables
If you do not want a page break to occur in the middle of a table, position the insertion point in the table, click the Table Properties button on the Table Tools Layout tab, click the Row tab in the dialog box, remove the check mark from the 'Allow row to break across pages' check box, and then click the OK button.

To Draw an Empty Table

The first step is to draw an empty table in the document. To draw the boundary, rows, and columns of the table, you drag a pencil pointer on the screen. Do not try to make the rows and columns evenly spaced as you draw them. After you draw the table, you will instruct Word to space them evenly. If you make a mistake while drawing the table, you can click the Undo button on the Quick Access Toolbar to undo your most recent action(s). The following steps draw an empty table.

- Display the Insert tab.

- Click the Table button on the Insert tab to display the Table gallery (Figure 4–76).

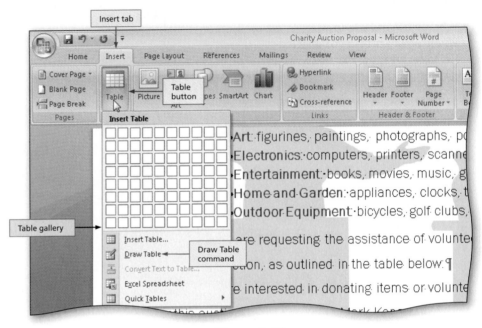

Figure 4–76

- Click Draw Table in the Table gallery.

- Position the mouse pointer, which has a pencil shape, where you want the upper-left corner of the table, as shown in Figure 4–77.

- Verify the insertion point is positioned exactly as shown in Figure 4–77.

Figure 4–77

- Drag the pencil pointer downward and to the right until the dotted rectangle, which indicates the proposed table's size, is positioned similarly to the one shown in Figure 4–78.

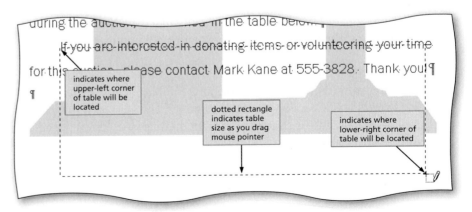

Figure 4–78

4

- Release the mouse button to draw the table border.

Q&A What if Word wraps the text around the table?

Right-click the table, click Table Properties on the shortcut menu, click the Table tab, click None in the Text wrapping area, and then click the OK button.

Q&A What if the table is not positioned as shown in Figure 4–79?

Click the Undo button on the Quick Access Toolbar and then repeat Steps 1 through 4.

- Position the pencil pointer in the table as shown in Figure 4–79.

Q&A What if I do not have a pencil pointer?

Click the Draw Table button on the Design tab.

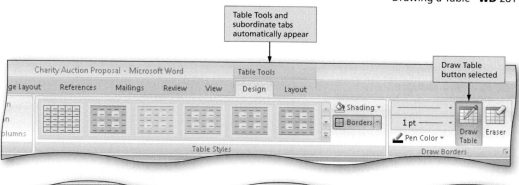

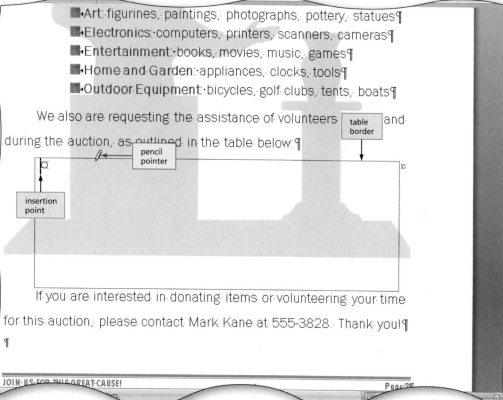

Figure 4–79

5

- Drag the pencil pointer down to the bottom of the table border to draw a vertical line.

- Drag the pencil pointer from top to bottom of the table border two more times to draw two more vertical lines, as shown in Figure 4–80.

- Position the pencil pointer in the table as shown in Figure 4–80.

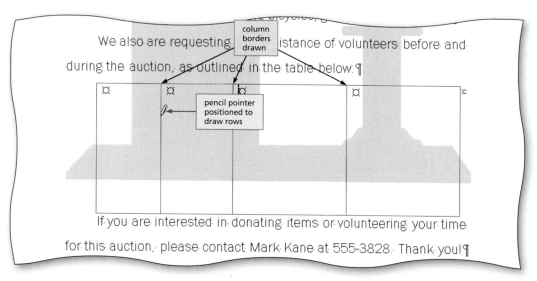

Figure 4–80

- Draw three horizontal lines to form the row borders, similarly to those shown in Figure 4–81.

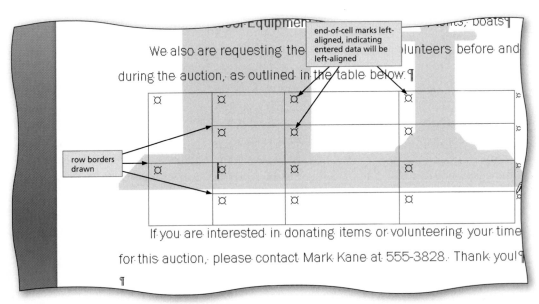

Figure 4–81

To Erase Lines in a Table

After drawing rows and columns in the table, you may want to remove a line. In this table, one line needs to be removed (shown in Figure 4–82). The following step erases a line in a table.

- Click the Eraser button on the Design tab, which causes the mouse pointer to change to an eraser shape.

- Click the line you wish to erase (Figure 4–82).

- Click the Eraser button on the Design tab to turn off the eraser.

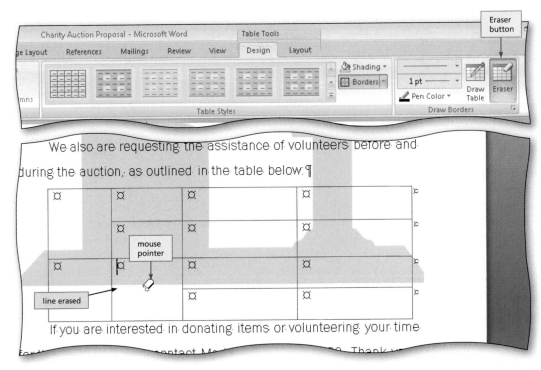

Figure 4–82

To Distribute Rows

Because you drew the table borders with the mouse, some of the rows may be varying heights. The following step spaces the row heights evenly.

1

- Display the Layout tab.

- Click the Select Table button on the Layout tab and then click Select Table on the menu to select the table.

- Click the Distribute Rows button on the Layout tab to make the height of the rows uniform (Figure 4–83).

Q&A Can I make the columns even too?

Yes. You would click the Distribute Columns button on the Layout tab.

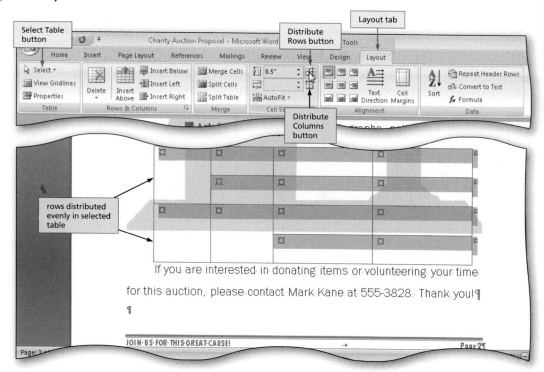

Figure 4–83

To Single-Space Table Contents

You want the data you type within the cells to be single-spaced, instead of 1.15 spacing. That is, you want any data that wraps within a cell to be single-spaced. The following steps single-space the table cells.

1 With the table still selected, press CTRL+1.

To Enter Data in a Table

The next step is to enter the data in the table. To advance from one column to the next, press the TAB key. When the insertion point is in the rightmost column, also press the TAB key to advance to the next row; do not press the ENTER key. The following steps enter the data in this table.

1 Click in the first cell of the table. Type Before Auction and then press the TAB key.

2 Type May 22 and then press the TAB key. Type Accepting Donations and then press the TAB key. Type 9:00 a.m. to 9:00 p.m. and then press the TAB key.

3 Press the TAB key. Type May 23 and then press the TAB key. Type Tagging Items and then press the TAB key. Type 9:00 a.m. to 5:00 p.m. and then press the TAB key.

BTW

Deleting Table Contents
If you wanted to delete the contents of a table and leave an empty table in the document, select the table contents and then press the DELETE key.

④ Type `During Auction` and then press the TAB key. Type `May 24` and then press the TAB key. Type `Helping Auctioneer` and then press the TAB key. Type `10:00 a.m. to 4:00 p.m.` and then press the TAB key.

⑤ Press the TAB key two times. Type `Collecting Payments` and then press the TAB key. Type `10:30 a.m. to 5:00 p.m.` to complete the table entries (Figure 4–84).

BTW

Table Wrapping
If you wanted text to wrap around a table, instead of displaying above and below the table, do the following: right-click the table, click Table Properties on the shortcut menu, click the Table tab, click Around in the Text wrapping area, and then click the OK button.

Before Auction¤	May 22¤	Accepting Donations¤	9:00 a.m. to 9:00 p.m.¤
	May 23¤	Tagging Items¤	9:00 a.m. to 5:00 p.m.¤
During Auction¤	May 24¤	Helping Auctioneer¤	10:00 a.m. to 4:00 p.m.¤
		Collecting Payments¤	10:30 a.m. to 5:00 p.m.¤

table data entered

If you are interested in donating items or volunteering your time for this auction, please contact Mark Kane at 555-3828. Thank you!¶

Figure 4–84

To Display Text in a Cell Vertically

The data you enter in cells displays horizontally. You can rotate the text so that it displays vertically. Changing the direction of text adds variety to your tables. The following step displays text in table cells vertically.

①
• Select the cells containing the words, Before Auction and During Auction.

• Click the Text Direction button on the Layout tab twice so that the text reads from bottom to top in each cell (Figure 4-85).

Q&A

Why do you click the Text Direction button twice?

The first time you click the Text Direction button, the text in the cell reads from top to bottom. The second time you click it, the text displays so it reads from bottom to top (Figure 4–85). If you would click the button a third time, the text would display horizontally again.

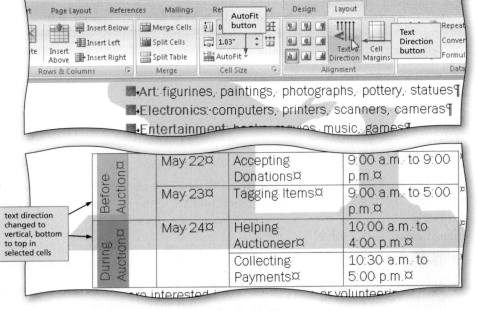

Figure 4–85

To Resize Table Columns to Fit Table Contents

Each table cell should be as wide as the longest entry in the table. The following step instructs Word to fit the width of the columns to the contents of the table.

1 With the insertion point in the table, click the AutoFit button on the Layout tab and then click AutoFit Contents on the AutoFit menu, so that Word automatically adjusts columns based on the text in the table.

To Change Column Width

The AutoFit Contents command did not fit the vertical text correctly. Notice in Figure 4–86 that the column containing the Before Auction and After Auction text is not wide enough to fit the contents. Thus, you will manually make this table column wider. When the insertion point is in a table, the ruler displays column markers that indicate the beginning and ending of columns. The following steps use the ruler to change column width.

1

- Click the View Ruler button on the vertical scroll bar to display the rulers on the screen.

- Position the mouse pointer on the first Move Table Column marker on the ruler (Figure 4–86).

2

- Drag the Move Table Column marker rightward until the word, Auction, appears in the table cells (shown in Figure 4–87 on the next page).

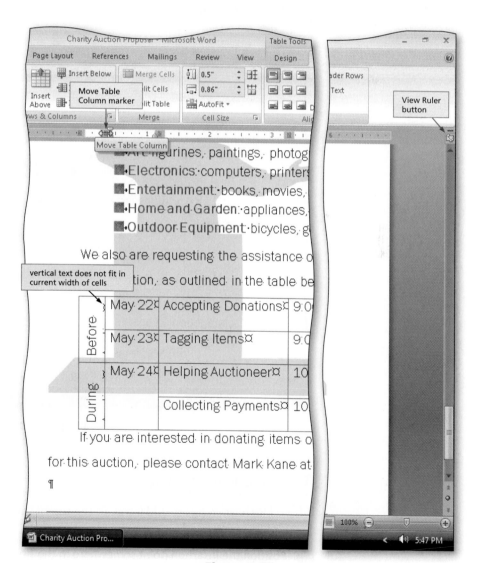

Figure 4–86

Other Ways

1. Drag column boundary (vertical gridline to right of column in table)
2. Click Properties button on Layout tab, click Column tab, enter width, click OK button

Table Columns
If you hold down the ALT key while dragging a column marker on the ruler or a column boundary in the table, the width measurements of all columns appear on the ruler as you drag the column marker or boundary.

To Align Data in Cells

The next step is to change the alignment of the data in cells. All text that displays horizontally should be centered vertically. The dates and tasks should be left-aligned, and the times should be right-aligned. The following steps align data in cells.

1 Select the cells containing the dates and the tasks.

2 Click the Align Center Left button on the Layout tab to center the selected text vertically at the left edge of the cells (Figure 4–87).

3 Select the cells containing the times (the rightmost column).

4 Click the Align Center Right button on the Layout tab to center the selected text vertically at the right edge of the cells.

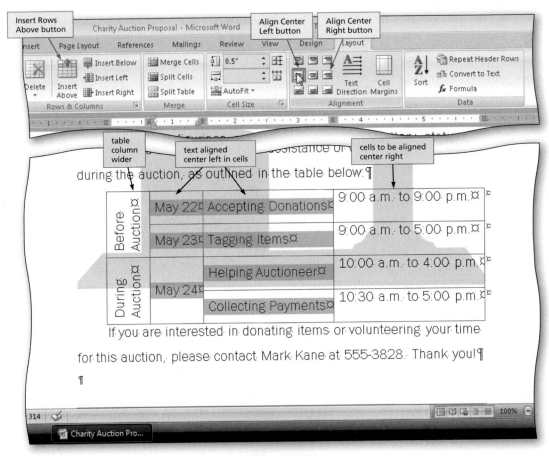

Figure 4–87

To Add a Row to a Table

The next step is to add a row to the top of the table for the table title. The following steps add a row to a table.

1 Position the insertion point somewhere in the first row of the table.

2 Click the Insert Rows Above button on the Layout tab to add a row above the current row.

To Merge Cells

The top row of the table is to contain the table title, which should be centered above the columns of the table. The row just added has one cell for each column, in this case, four cells. The title of the table, however, should be in a single cell that spans across all rows. Thus, the following steps merge the four columns into a single column.

1

- Verify the cells to merge are selected, in this case, the entire first row (Figure 4–88).

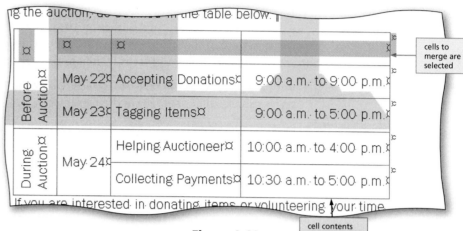

Figure 4–88

2

- Click the Merge Cells button on the Layout tab to merge the four cells into one cell (Figure 4–89).

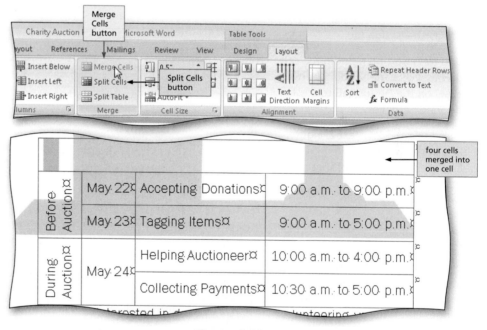

Figure 4–89

Other Ways
1. Right-click selected cells, click Merge Cells on shortcut menu

To Split Table Cells

Instead of merging multiple cells into a single cell, sometimes you want to split a single cell into multiple cells. If you wanted to split cells, you would perform the steps below and at the top of the next page.

1. Position the insertion point in the cell to split.

2. Click the Split Cells button on the Layout tab, or right-click the cell and then click Split Cells on the shortcut menu.

3. When Word displays the Split Cells dialog box, enter the number of columns and rows into which you want the cell split.

4. Click the OK button.

To Enter and Format Text in a Table Cell

The next task is to format and enter the title in the merged cell. The cell uses the formats that were in the leftmost cell, which means its contents are aligned vertically bottom to top. The following steps format and enter text in the merged cell.

1 With the first row of the table still selected, click the Text Direction button so that the text will be displayed horizontally in the merged cell.

2 Click the Align Center button so that the text will be centered in the cell.

3 Type Volunteers Needed as the table title.

To Shade a Table Cell

The next step is to shade the cell containing the title, Volunteers Needed, in gray. The following steps shade a cell.

1

- Display the Design tab.

- With the insertion point in the cell to shade, click the Shading button arrow on the Design tab to display the Shading gallery.

- Point to Gray-50%, Text 2, Lighter 60% in the Shading gallery to display a live preview of that shading color applied to the current cell in the table (Figure 4–90).

Experiment

- Point to various colors in the Shading gallery and watch the shading color of the current cell change.

2

- Click Gray-50%, Text 2, Lighter 60% in the Shading gallery to apply the selected style to the current cell.

Q&A How would I remove shading from a cell?

Click the Shading button arrow and then click No Color in the Shading gallery.

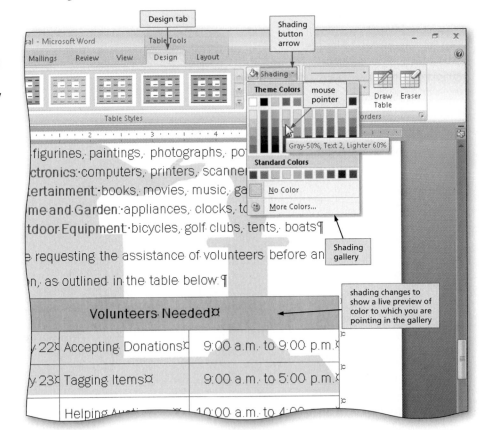

Figure 4–90

To Format and Shade More Cells and Change Table Border Color

With the title shaded gray, the text is a little difficult to read. Thus, you will increase the font size and bold the text. Also, the date cells should be bold and shaded the same color as the title cell.

1 Select the table title, Volunteers Needed, and then bold it. Change its font size to 20 point.

2 Select the dates (May 22, May 23, May 24) and bold them.

3 Shade the date cells Gray-50%, Text 2, Lighter 60%.

4 Select the entire table. Click the Border button arrow on the Design tab and then click Borders and Shading in the Border gallery to display the Borders and Shading dialog box.

5 If necessary, click All in the Setting area so that all borders in the table are formatted.

6 Click the Color box arrow and then click Pink, Accent 2, Darker 25% in the Color gallery to change the border colors in the preview area (Figure 4–91).

7 Click the OK button to change border colors in the selected table.

8 Click outside the table to remove the selection.

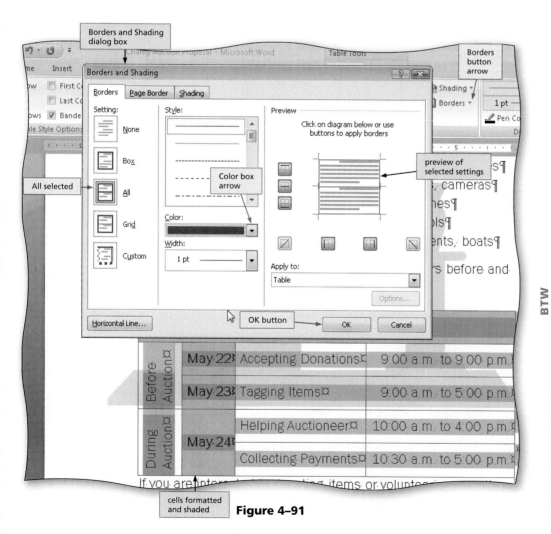

Figure 4–91

BTW

Conserving Ink and Toner
You can instruct Word to print draft quality documents to conserve ink or toner by clicking the Office Button, clicking the Word Options button, clicking Advanced in the left pane of the Word Options dialog box, scrolling to the Print area, placing a check mark in the 'Use draft quality' check box, and then clicking the OK button. Click the Office Button, point to Print, and then click Quick Print.

To Change Row Height

The next step is to narrow the height of the row containing the table title. The steps below change a row's height.

- Point to the bottom border of the first row. When the mouse pointer changes to a double-headed arrow, drag up until the proposed row border looks like Figure 4–92.

- Release the mouse button to resize the row at the location of the dotted line.

Other Ways

1. Click Table Properties button on Layout tab, click Row tab, enter row height in Specify height box, click OK button

2. Right-click row, click Table Properties on shortcut menu, click Row tab, enter row height in Specify height box, click OK button

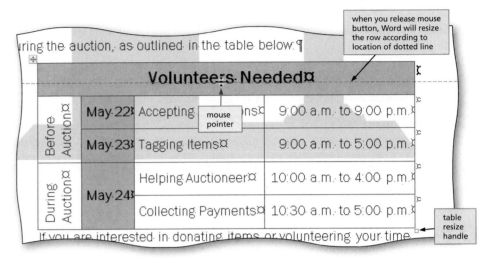

Figure 4–92

To Add a Blank Line Above a Paragraph

The table is complete. The next step is to add a blank line above the last paragraph to put a space between the table and the paragraph.

1 Position the insertion point in the last paragraph of the proposal and then press CTRL+0 (the numeral zero) to add a blank line above the paragraph (Figure 4–93).

Q&A What if the last paragraph spills onto the next page?

You can make the table smaller so the paragraph fits at the bottom of the page. To do this, drag the table resize handle (shown in Figure 4–92) that appears in the lower-right corner of the table inward.

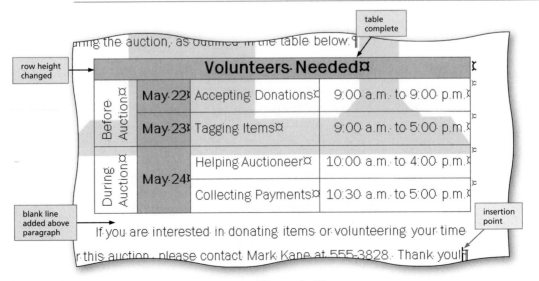

Figure 4–93

To Check Spelling, Save, Print, and Quit Word

The following steps check the spelling of the document, save the document, and then print the document.

1 Click the Spelling & Grammar button on the Review tab. Correct any misspelled words.

2 Save the sales proposal again with the same file name.

3 Print the sales proposal (shown in Figure 4–1 on page WD 227).

4 Quit Word.

BTW | **Quick Reference** For a table that lists how to complete the tasks covered in this book using the mouse, Ribbon, shortcut menu, and keyboard, see the Quick Reference Summary at the back of this book, or visit the Word 2007 Quick Reference Web page (scsite.com/wd2007/qr).

Chapter Summary

In this chapter, you learned how to add a border and shading to a paragraph, insert and format a SmartArt graphic, insert a watermark, insert a Word document in an open document, insert formatted headers and footers, modify and format an existing Word table, chart a Word table using Microsoft Graph, and use the Draw Table feature. The items listed below include all the new Word skills you have learned in this chapter.

1. Border a Paragraph (WD 231)
2. Shade a Paragraph (WD 232)
3. Change Left and Right Paragraph Indent (WD 233)
4. Insert a SmartArt Graphic (WD 235)
5. Add Text to a SmartArt Graphic (WD 237)
6. Change Colors of a SmartArt Graphic (WD 238)
7. Apply a SmartArt Style (WD 239)
8. Format Characters and Modify Character Spacing Using the Font Dialog Box (WD 240)
9. Modify the Default Font Settings (WD 242)
10. Reset the Default Font Settings (WD 242)
11. Change Case of Text (WD 243)
12. Zoom One Page (WD 244)
13. Create a Watermark (WD 245)
14. Reveal Formatting (WD 248)
15. Insert a Next Page Section Break (WD 250)
16. Delete a Section Break (WD 251)
17. Insert a Word Document in an Open Document (WD 251)
18. Print Specific Pages in a Document (WD 253)
19. Customize Theme Fonts (WD 255)
20. Delete a Page Break (WD 256)
21. Cut Text (WD 257)
22. Go To a Section (WD 258)
23. Create a Header Different from the Previous Section Header (WD 259)
24. Insert a Formatted Header (WD 260)
25. Insert a Formatted Footer (WD 261)
26. Format Page Numbers to Start at a Different Number (WD 262)
27. Delete a Column (WD 263)
28. Add Columns (WD 264)
29. Sum Columns in a Table (WD 265)
30. Border a Table (WD 267)
31. Align Data in Cells (WD 268)
32. Chart a Table (WD 269)
33. Move Legend Placement in a Chart (WD 270)
34. Resize a Chart (WD 271)
35. Change the Chart Type (WD 272)
36. Exit Graph and Return to Word (WD 273)
37. Find a Format (WD 274)
38. Create a Character Style (WD 276)
39. Select Nonadjacent Text (WD 277)
40. Customize Bullets in a List (WD 278)
41. Draw an Empty Table (WD 280)
42. Erase Lines in a Table (WD 282)
43. Distribute Rows (WD 283)
44. Display Text in a Cell Vertically (WD 284)
45. Change Column Width (WD 285)
46. Merge Cells (WD 287)
47. Split Table Cells (WD 287)
48. Shade a Table Cell (WD 288)
49. Change Row Height (WD 290)

 If you have a SAM user profile, you may have access to hands-on instruction, practice, and assessment. Log in to your SAM account (http://sam2007.course.com) to launch any assigned training activities or exams that relate to the skills covered in this chapter.

Learn It Online

Test your knowledge of chapter content and key terms.

Instructions: To complete the Learn It Online exercises, start your browser, click the Address bar, and then enter the Web address scsite.com/wd2007/learn. When the Word 2007 Learn It Online page is displayed, click the link for the exercise you want to complete and then read the instructions.

Chapter Reinforcement TF, MC, and SA
A series of true/false, multiple choice, and short answer questions that test your knowledge of the chapter content.

Flash Cards
An interactive learning environment where you identify chapter key terms associated with displayed definitions.

Practice Test
A series of multiple choice questions that test your knowledge of chapter content and key terms.

Who Wants To Be a Computer Genius?
An interactive game that challenges your knowledge of chapter content in the style of a television quiz show.

Wheel of Terms
An interactive game that challenges your knowledge of chapter key terms in the style of the television show *Wheel of Fortune*.

Crossword Puzzle Challenge
A crossword puzzle that challenges your knowledge of key terms presented in the chapter.

Apply Your Knowledge

Reinforce the skills and apply the concepts you learned in this chapter.

Working with a Complex Table
Instructions: Start Word. Open the document, Apply 4-1 Awesome Antiques Draft, from the Data Files for Students. See the inside back cover of this book for instructions on downloading the Data Files for Students, or contact your instructor for information about accessing the required files.

The document contains a Word table that you are to modify. The modified table is shown in Figure 4–94.

AWESOME ANTIQUES					
SECOND QUARTER SALES REPORT					
		APRIL	MAY	JUNE	TOTAL
ZONE 1	BOSTON	98,764	102,987	110,864	312,615
	CHICAGO	76,432	69,075	87,952	233,459
	DETROIT	68,064	71,536	70,443	210,043
ZONE 2	DENVER	100,987	98,221	103,416	302,624
	HOUSTON	64,842	69,844	70,009	204,695
	SEATTLE	88,513	87,990	92,752	269,255
TOTAL SALES		497,602	499,653	535,436	1,532,691

Figure 4–94

Perform the following tasks:

1. Use the Split Cells command or the Split Cells button on the Table Tools Layout tab to split the first row into two rows (one column). In the new cell below the company name, type `Second Quarter Sales Report` as the subtitle.

2. Add a row to the bottom of the table. In the newly added bottom row, use the Merge Cells command or the Merge Cells button on the Layout tab to merge the first two cells into a single cell. Type `Total Sales` in the merged cell.

3. Use the Formula button on the Layout tab to place totals in the bottom row for the April, May, and June columns.

4. Use the Formula button to place totals in the right column. Start in the bottom-right cell and work your way up the table. *Hint:* The formula should be =SUM(LEFT).

5. Select the cells containing the row headings, Zone 1 and Zone 2. Use the Text Direction button on the Layout tab to position the text vertically from bottom to top. Change the alignment of these two cells to Align Center. Click in the table to remove the selection.

6. Change the width of the column containing the Zone 1 and Zone 2 text so that it is narrower.

7. Create a customized theme font set that uses the Copperplate Gothic Bold font for both headings and body fonts. Save the theme font with the name Awesome Antiques.

8. Apply the Light List – Accent 3 table style to the table.

9. Use the Distribute Rows button to make all the rows the same size.

10. Select all the cells in the columns containing the April, May, and June sales and then use the Distribute Columns button to make these columns evenly spaced.

11. Align top center the first two rows of the table.

12. Align center the cells containing the column headings, April, May, June, and Total.

13. Align center right the cells containing numbers.

14. Align center left the cells containing these labels: Boston, Chicago, Detroit, Denver, Houston, Seattle, and Total Sales.

15. Center the entire table across the width of the page.

16. Shade the bottom row and the rightmost column Olive Green, Accent 3, Lighter 80%.

17. Shade the bottom-right cell Olive Green, Accent 3.

18. Change the font size of the first row title to 18 point.

19. Shade the first row Red, Accent 2, Darker 50%.

20. Change the document properties as specified by your instructor.

21. Save the modified file with the file name, Apply 4-1 Awesome Antiques Modified.

22. Print the revised table.

23. Position the insertion point in the first row of the table. Display the Reveal Formatting task pane. On your printout, write down all the formatting assigned to this row.

Extend Your Knowledge

Extend the skills you learned in this chapter and experiment with new skills. You may need to use Help to complete the assignment.

Embedding an Excel Chart in a Word Document

Instructions: Start Word. Open the document, Extend 4-1 Housing Table, from the Data Files for Students. See the inside back cover of this book for instructions on downloading the Data Files for Students, or contact your instructor for information about accessing the required files.

You will use Excel to create a chart of a Word table. If you do not have Excel on your computer, do not follow the steps below; instead, use Microsoft Graph to create a chart of the table and format the chart.

Perform the following tasks:

1. Use Help to learn about adding an Excel chart to a Word document. (*Hint:* Press the F1 key while pointing to the Insert Chart button on the Insert tab.)

2. Copy the first five rows of the Word table to the Clipboard (all rows except for the total row).

3. Position the insertion point below the Word table because Excel positions the chart at the location of the insertion point. Click the Insert Chart button on the Insert tab. Select the 3-D Column chart in the Insert Chart dialog box.

4. In Excel, use Help to learn about working in Excel and pasting.

5. Paste the Word table data from the Office Clipboard with cell A1 of Excel worksheet being the upper-left corner for the pasted table. Drag the lower-right corner of the range so that it does not include column D. Close the Excel window.

6. Move the legend to the bottom of the chart (Figure 4–95).

7. Right-click the chart and change the chart type to a type other than 3-D Column.

8. Use the Chart Styles gallery on the Chart Tools Design tab on the Ribbon to change the style of the chart so that it is not Style 2.

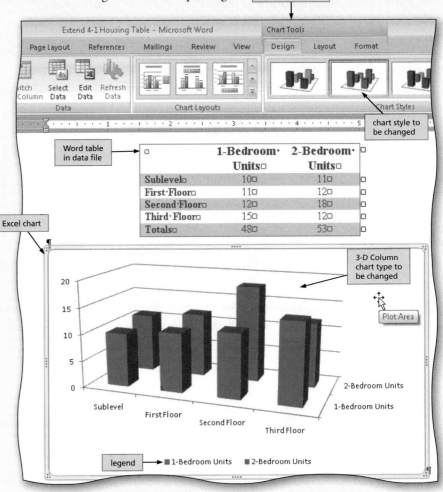

Figure 4–95

9. Use the buttons on the Chart Tools Layout tab on the Ribbon to add a title to the chart, the x-axis, and the y-axis.

10. Change the document properties, as specified by your instructor. Save the revised document using a new file name and then submit it in the format specified by your instructor.

Make It Right

Analyze a document and correct all errors and/or improve the design.

Formatting a Title Page

Instructions: Start Word. Open the document, Make It Right 4-1 Title Page Draft, from the Data Files for Students. See the inside back cover of this book for instructions on downloading the Data Files for Students, or contact your instructor for information about accessing the required files.

The document is a title page that is missing elements and that is not formatted ideally (Figure 4–96). You are to remove the header and edit the border, shading, SmartArt, watermark, and text.

Figure 4–96

Perform the following tasks:

1. Remove the header from the title page.

2. Modify the border so that it surrounds all edges of the title.

3. Modify the paragraph shading in the title so that both lines of the title are shaded.

Continued >

Make It Right *continued*

4. Increase the size of the SmartArt graphic on the title page. The text in the middle shape in the SmartArt is not correct. Change the word, Success, to Dedication in the middle shape. Change the colors of the SmartArt graphic and then change the SmartArt style.

5. Change the zoom to one page. Increase the size of the watermark so that it fills the page.

6. Change the character spacing of the last line on the title page from condensed to expanded.

7. Add or remove space above or below paragraphs so that all contents of the title page fit on a single page. Change the zoom back to 100%.

8. Increase fonts so they are easy to read. Use the Change Font Case button to change capitalization.

9. Change the document properties, as specified by your instructor. Save the revised document with a new file name and then submit it in the format specified by your instructor.

In the Lab

Design and/or create a document using the guidelines, concepts, and skills presented in this chapter. Labs are listed in order of increasing difficulty.

Lab 1: Creating a Proposal that has a SmartArt Graphic and Uses the Draw Table Feature

Problem: The owner of the Clean Fleet Auto has hired you to prepare a sales proposal describing their services, which will be mailed to local businesses.

Perform the following tasks:

1. Change the theme colors to the Metro color scheme.

2. Create the title page as shown in Figure 4–97a. Be sure to do the following:

   (a) Insert the SmartArt graphic, add text to it, and change its colors and style as specified in the figure.

   (b) Change the fonts, font sizes, font colors, and font effects. Add the borders and paragraph shading. Indent the left and right edges of the title paragraph by 0.4 inches. Expand the characters in the text, ON-SITE CLEANING, by 5 points. In the company name at the bottom of the title page, add a shadow to the characters.

6-point outside border; color: Gold, Accent 3, Darker 25%

72-point Broadway font

shading color: Turquoise, Accent 4, Darker 50%

48-point bold, italic, font; color: Turquoise, Accent 4, Darker 50%

picture watermark

SmartArt graphic – Type: Relationship Layout: Linear Venn Colors: Colored Fill - Accent 1 Style: Polished

48-point bold font; color: Gold, Accent 3, Darker 25%

Figure 4–97 (a)

(c) Create the picture watermark. The picture is called Car Wash and is available on the Data Files for Students. See the inside back cover of this book for instructions on downloading the Data Files for Students, or contact your instructor for information about accessing the required files.

3. At the bottom of the title page, insert a next page section break. Clear formatting.

4. Create a customized theme font set that uses the Broadway font for headings and Verdana font for body text. Save the theme font with the name Clean Fleet. Increase the font size of the body text on the second page to 14 point.

5. Create the second page of the proposal as shown in Figure 4–97b.

(a) Insert the formatted header using the Pinstripes design. The header should appear only on the second page (section) of the proposal. Format the header text as shown in the figure.

(b) Change the bullets in the bulleted list to gold picture bullets.

(c) Draw the table with the Draw Table feature. The border should have a 1-point line weight with a color of Gold, Accent 3, Darker 25%. Distribute rows in the table so that they are all the same height. Center the table. Single-space the contents of the table and change spacing after paragraphs to 0 point. Change the direction of the row title, Cars; make the column width of this column narrower; and align center the text. Change the alignment of the title and column headings to align center; the second column to align center left; and the cells with numbers to align center right. Distribute the columns with numbers so that they are the same width. Shade the table cells as specified in the figure.

(d) Create a character style for the first word in the products list of bold with the color Gold, Accent 3, Darker 25%. Apply the character style to the first word in each paragraph in the bulleted list.

6. Check the spelling. Change the document properties, as specified by your instructor. Save the document with Lab 4-1 Clean Fleet Auto Proposal as the file name.

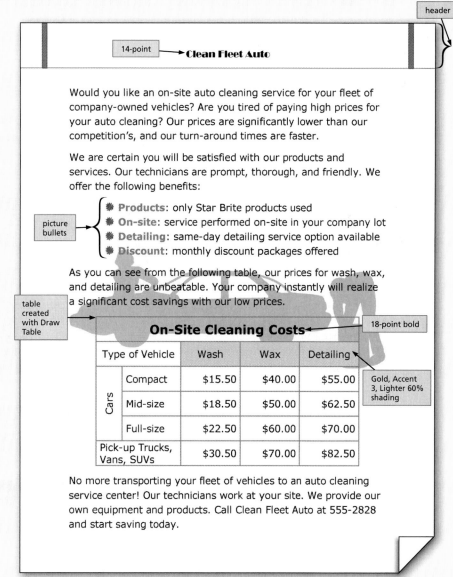

Figure 4–97 (b)

In the Lab

Lab 2: Creating a Proposal that Includes a SmartArt Graphic, a Table and a Chart

Problem: The owner of the Deli Express has hired you to prepare a sales proposal describing their foods and services, which will be mailed to all community residents.

Perform the following tasks:

1. Change the theme colors to the Opulent color scheme.
2. Create the title page as shown in Figure 4–98a. Be sure to do the following:

   (a) Insert the SmartArt graphic, add text to it, insert the pictures, and change its colors and style as specified in the figure. The three picture files are called Sub Sandwich, Salad, and Soup and are available on the Data Files for Students. See the inside back cover of this book for instructions on downloading the Data Files for Students, or contact your instructor for information about accessing the required files. (*Hint:* To insert a picture, double-click the picture placeholder to display the Insert Picture dialog box, locate the picture file, and then click the Insert button.)

   (b) Change the fonts, font sizes, font colors, and font effects. Include the border and paragraph shading around the company name. Add a shadow to and expand the characters in the text, Let us feed your crowd!, by 5 points.

   (c) Create a horizontal text watermark that says, Great Food.

3. At the bottom of the title page, insert a next page section break. Clear formatting.

4. Create a customized theme font set that uses the Cooper Black font for headings and Berlin Sans FB Demi font for body text. Save the theme font with the name Deli Express. Increase the font size of the body text on the second page to 14 point.

72-point Cooper Black font with color of White, Background 1

shading color: Orange, Accent 3

3-point double line outside border; color: Pink, Text 2, Darker 25%

SmartArt graphic – Type: List Layout: Horizontal Picture List Colors: Colorful Range – Accent Colors 2 to 3 Style: Powder

105-point Berlin Sans FB Demi font for text watermark; color: White, Background 1, Darker 50%

72-point Berlin Sans FB Demi font; color: Pink, Text 2, Darker 25%

Figure 4–98 (a)

5. Create the second page of the proposal as shown in Figure 4–98b.

   (a) Insert the formatted header using the Alphabet design. The header should appear only on the second page of the proposal. Format the header text as shown in the figure.

   (b) Insert the formatted footer using the Alphabet design. The footer should appear only on the second page of the proposal. Replace the page number with the telephone number.

   (c) The bulleted list has pink picture bullets.

   (d) Create a 4 × 4 table. Apply the table style indicated in the figure. Align top center the column headings and the numbers. Center the table between the page margins.

   (e) Chart the table. Resize the chart so that it is wider. Change the chart type to cylinder. Move the legend. Add a ½-point outline with a color of Black, Text 1, Lighter 50% around the chart. Insert a blank line above the chart.

   (f) Create a character style for the first word in the menu items list of underlined with the color Lavender, Background 2, Darker 50%. Apply the character style to the first word in each paragraph in the bulleted list.

6. Check the spelling. Change the document properties, as specified by your instructor. Save the document with Lab 4-2 Deli Express Proposal as the file name.

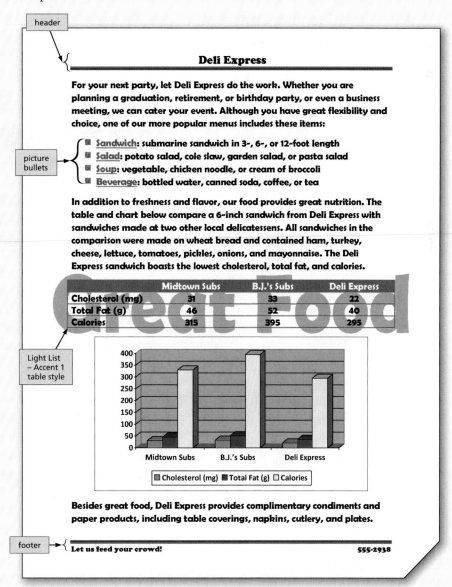

Figure 4–98 (b)

In the Lab

Lab 3: Enhancing a Draft of a Proposal

Problem: You work in the district office of Ashton Community School District. Your boss has prepared a draft of a proposal requesting voters pass the upcoming referendum. You decide to enhance the proposal by adding picture bullets, another table, and a chart. You also prepare a title page that includes a SmartArt graphic.

Perform the following tasks:

1. Change the theme colors to the Solstice color scheme.

2. Create a title page similar to the one shown in Figure 4–99a. The picture for the watermark is called School and is available on the Data Files for Students. See the inside back cover of this book for instructions on downloading the Data Files for Students, or contact your instructor for information about accessing the required files. The SmartArt graphic has been resized so that it is wider and also each individual chevron in the graphic was selected and flipped vertically. Use Help to learn how to flip a graphic.

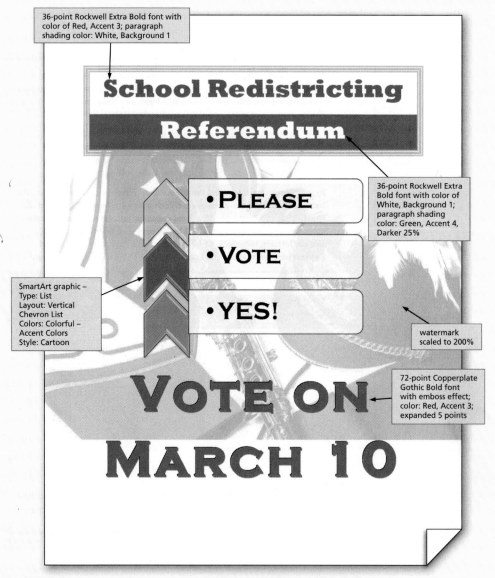

Figure 4–99 (a)

3. Insert a next page section break. Clear formatting. Insert the draft of the body of the proposal below the title page. The draft is called Lab 4-3 School Proposal Draft on the Data Files for Students (shown in Figure 4–99b).

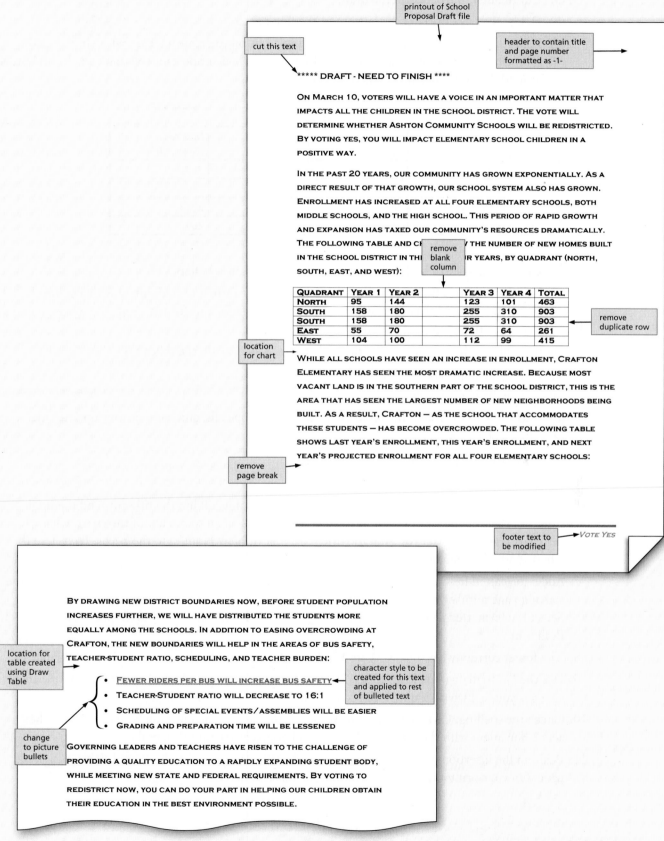

Figure 4–99 (b)

Continued >

In the Lab *continued*

4. On the first page of the body of the draft, do the following:

   (a) Cut the first line of text in the draft.

   (b) Delete the page break at the bottom of the first page.

   (c) Below the third paragraph, use the Draw Table button to create a table that is similar to the following. Select appropriate fonts and font colors, shade important cells, add a colorful border around the table, and align data in the cells as shown.

	Enrollment Figures per School		
	School	Last Year	This Year	Next Year (Projected)
	Crafton	342	418	475
VOTE YES	Grover Cleveland	200	212	220
	Cummings	240	252	267
	Idlewild	210	233	260

   (d) Change the style of bullet characters in the list to picture bullets.

   (e) Use the Find and Replace dialog box to find the font format of underlined with a color of Gold, Accent 2, Darker 50%. Create a character style for this format. Apply the character style to each of the remaining bulleted paragraphs of text.

5. On the table on the second page of the body of the proposal, do the following:

   (a) Delete the duplicate row for South.

   (b) Delete the blank column.

   (c) Add a row to the top of the table for a title, merge the cells, and enter an appropriate title.

   (d) Align right all numbers.

   (e) Apply a table style to the table.

   (f) Center the table.

6. Chart the first four columns of the last five rows of the table (all but the title row and the total column). Enlarge the chart so that it is wider. Move the legend to the left of the chart. Change the chart type to cylinder bar. Add the title, Number of New Homes, to the z-axis. *Hint*: Use the Chart Options command.

7. Add a formatted header using the Stacks design. Enter an appropriate document title. Change the starting page number to 1. Format the page number so that it has dashes on each side (e.g., -1-). Select the formatted page number and change it to the Body font: 11-point Copperplate Gothic Bold font.

8. The footer currently has the text, Vote Yes. Edit the footer so that its text reads: Vote on March 10!

9. Use the Go to dialog box to go to section 1 and then to section 2. Make any additional formatting changes you feel would improve the document.

10. Check the spelling. Change the document properties, as specified by your instructor. Save the active document with the file name, Lab 4-3 School Redistricting Proposal.

11. Position the insertion point in the first line of the title page. Display the Reveal Formatting task pane. On your printout, write down all formatting assigned to this paragraph.

Cases and Places

Apply your creative thinking and problem solving skills to design and implement a solution.

• Easier ••More Difficult

• 1: Create a Sales Proposal for a Veterinarian's Office

You are participating in an internship this summer at a local veterinarian's office. Because it is a fairly new practice, business is not as brisk as the veterinarian would like. She has asked you to design a sales proposal that will be sent to area residents; data for the table is shown below. The title page is to contain the name, PetCare Animal Hospital, formatted with a border and shading. Include an appropriate SmartArt graphic and a watermark. Include the slogan, Full-Service Care for Pets. The second page of the proposal should contain the following: first paragraph — We know you love your pets. When they need medical attention, you can be confident when you turn to us. Pet Care Animal Hospital offers full-service care, 24 hours a day, 365 days a year for the following types of animals:; list with picture bullets — Cats, Dogs, Birds, Small pocket pets; next paragraph — Accredited by the American Veterinary Group, PetCare Animal Hospital meets strict guidelines in patient care, surgery, and sanitation. Our staff is dedicated to providing your pet with the highest quality of care and state-of-the-art medical treatment. The table below lists some of our general practice services and surgeries:; paragraph below table — You are invited to tour our new facilities and to meet with our staff at any time. Stop by our office at 22 West Barrington in Stillwater anytime, or call us at 555-9092 for an appointment. We look forward to serving you and your faithful friend.

General Practice	Wellness checkups
	Immunizations
	Dental care
	Parasite control
Treatments and Surgery	Emergency surgery
	Spaying and neutering
	Oral surgery
	Chemotherapy

•• 2: Create a Planning Proposal for a Property Management Group

Your boss at Stefanson Property Management has asked you to create a planning proposal for a potential new client, Crescent Apartments. The apartment complex consists of 12 buildings, with between 20 to 30 units per building, a pool area, a clubhouse, and extensive grounds and parking. Typically, outside contractors are hired to perform maintenance duties at a cost of more than $130,000 per year. Signing a yearly contract with Stefanson Property Management can save Crescent Apartments nearly half their yearly maintenance costs. Included in Stefanson's yearly cost are groundskeeping ($23,000), snow removal ($12,300), electrical ($10,500), HVAC (heating, ventilation, and air conditioning) ($18,500), and plumbing ($8,000). General maintenance and repairs are charged at a per job basis. For additional charges, Stefanson can complete other tasks, such as painting, replacing flooring, installing cabinets, and removing wallpaper. Create a proposal for your boss to present to the owner of Crescent Apartments that outlines the services provided, the cost, and other key information. Place the company name, appropriate SmartArt graphic, and the company slogan ("Efficient property management") on the title page. Be sure the body of the proposal includes the following items: a list with picture bullets, a table, a chart, a watermark, a header, and a footer.

Continued >

Cases and Places continued

•• 3: Create a Proposal for an Alumni Club

To satisfy part of the community service requirements for your scholarship, you have volunteered in the Alumni Club office on your campus. Part of your new duties involves informing members of the many benefits to which they are entitled as alumni. Create a proposal that alerts alumni to the benefits of membership. Some of the benefits include staying in touch with other alumni; receiving a free monthly magazine; access to the campus Career and Opportunity Center; automobile, health, and life insurance plans; credit card with no annual fee; various discounts on airfare, car rental, and hotel rooms; club-sponsored outings; and discount event tickets. The Alumni Club has a Web site where members can look up other members, visit the campus store, register for outings, or obtain information about promotions and discounts for alumni. Several events have been scheduled, including a spring dance, a 20-year reunion dinner, a seminar about using the Web effectively in job searches, and a dinner and silent auction for charity. Use the techniques you learned in this chapter to create a sales proposal, selling the idea of membership to recent alumni. Place the club name, appropriate SmartArt graphic, and the slogan "Join the Circle!" on the title page. Be sure the proposal includes the following items: a list with picture bullets, a table with totals, a chart, a watermark, a header with a page number, and a footer.

•• 4: Create a Proposal for a Club or Event at your School

Make It Personal

As a college student, you are aware of the many clubs, activities, and events on your campus. Some students join clubs that let them interact with like-minded students; others engage in activities that will help them in their area of study. While most students like the college they attend, improvements always can be made. For example, you might be a nursing student who sees a need for a forum for other student nursing majors to get together and discuss their clinical experiences. You could be a business major who thinks a club on campus would provide a good outlet for business majors. Maybe you subscribe to a cause or idea that is not represented on your campus. If you are a music buff, you might want to organize and schedule musical gatherings. Keeping your major or area of interest in mind, create a proposal for a new club or event for your campus that solicits members or attendees. Provide information about the club or event, including its name, meeting/event location and time, and purpose. Include a title page with appropriate SmartArt graphic, the club or event name, and a suitable slogan. Be sure the proposal contains the following items: a list with picture bullets, a table, a chart, a header with a page number, a footer, and a watermark.

•• 5: Create a Research Proposal for New Computers

Working Together

Wayfield Industries is a food service provider with a main office and a staff of five salespeople. The sales staff covers a 300-mile area around River Oaks, selling primarily to restaurants, schools, and hotels. Increasingly, it has become apparent that the salespeople need constant computer access in order to service their accounts efficiently. Your boss at Wayfield Industries has asked you to create a research proposal that outlines the cost of providing each of the five salespeople with a notebook computer. He wants at least three different brands of computers to compare, and each must meet the following minimum requirements: 2 GB RAM, 17-inch display, 120 GB hard disk, and an Intel Core Duo processor. It is vital that the notebook computers have a built-in wireless connection for accessing the Internet, at least three USB 2.0 ports, and a CD/DVD drive. In addition, he has asked that you list any features the different brands might include that are desirable, such as built-in fingerprint scanners, additional USB ports, second battery, preinstalled software, or free upgrades. Assign each team member a computer brand to research. Gather information about the required features and capabilities listed above. As a team, compile the information about each type of computer researched and prepare a proposal. Create an appropriate title page that includes a formatted title and appropriate SmartArt graphic. Be sure the proposal contains a watermark, a list with picture bullets, a table, a chart, a header, a footer, and page numbers.

5 Generating Form Letters, Mailing Labels, and Directories

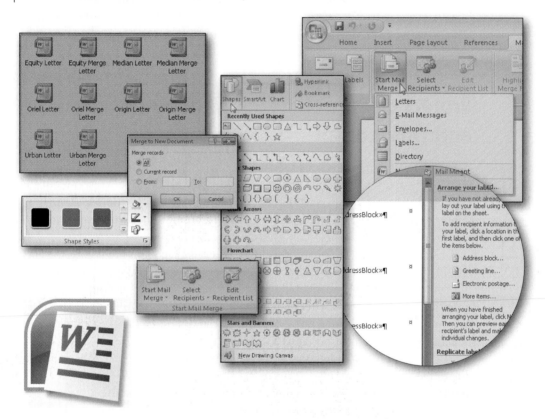

Objectives

You will have mastered the material in this chapter when you can:

- Explain the merge process
- Use the Mail Merge task pane and the Mailings tab on the Ribbon
- Use a letter template as the main document for a mail merge
- Insert and format a shape on a drawing canvas
- Create and edit a data source
- Insert merge fields in a main document
- Create a multilevel list
- Use an IF field in a main document
- Merge and print form letters
- Sort data records
- Address and print mailing labels and envelopes
- Merge all data records to a directory
- Change page orientation
- Modify table properties

5 | Generating Form Letters, Mailing Labels, and Directories

Introduction

People are more likely to open and read a personalized letter than a letter addressed as Dear Sir, Dear Madam, or To Whom It May Concern. Typing individual personalized letters, though, can be a time-consuming task. Thus, Word provides the capability of creating a form letter, which is an easy way to generate mass mailings of personalized letters. The basic content of a group of form letters is similar. Items such as name and address, however, vary from one letter to the next. With Word, you also easily can address and print mailing labels or envelopes for the form letters.

Project — Form Letters, Mailing Labels, and Directories

Both businesses and individuals regularly use form letters to communicate via the postal service or e-mail with groups of people. Types of form letter correspondence include announcements of sales to customers, notices of benefits to employees, invitations to the public to participate in a sweepstakes giveaway, and letters of job application to potential employers.

The project in this chapter follows generally accepted guidelines for writing form letters and uses Word to create the form letters shown in Figure 5–1. The form letters inform health club members of club improvements and notifies members of a monthly rate increase. Each form letter states the club member's membership type and his or her new monthly amount due. The new rate for the Standard Plan is $75 per month, and the new rate for the Premium Plan is $105 per month.

To generate form letters, such as the ones shown in Figure 5–1, you create a main document for the form letter (Figure 5–1a), create or specify a data source (Figure 5–1b), and then merge, or *blend*, the main document with the data source to generate a series of individual letters (Figure 5–1c). In Figure 5–1a, the main document represents the portion of the form letter that repeats from one merged letter to the next. In Figure 5–1b, the data source contains the name, address, and membership type for different club members. To personalize each letter, you merge the member data in the data source with the main document for the form letter, which generates or prints and an individual letter for each club member listed in the data source.

Word provides two methods of merging documents: the Mail Merge task pane and the Mailings tab on the Ribbon. The Mail Merge task pane displays a wizard, which is a step-by-step progression that guides you through the merging process. The Mailings tab provides buttons and boxes you use to merge documents. This chapter illustrates both techniques.

(a) Main Document for the Form Letter

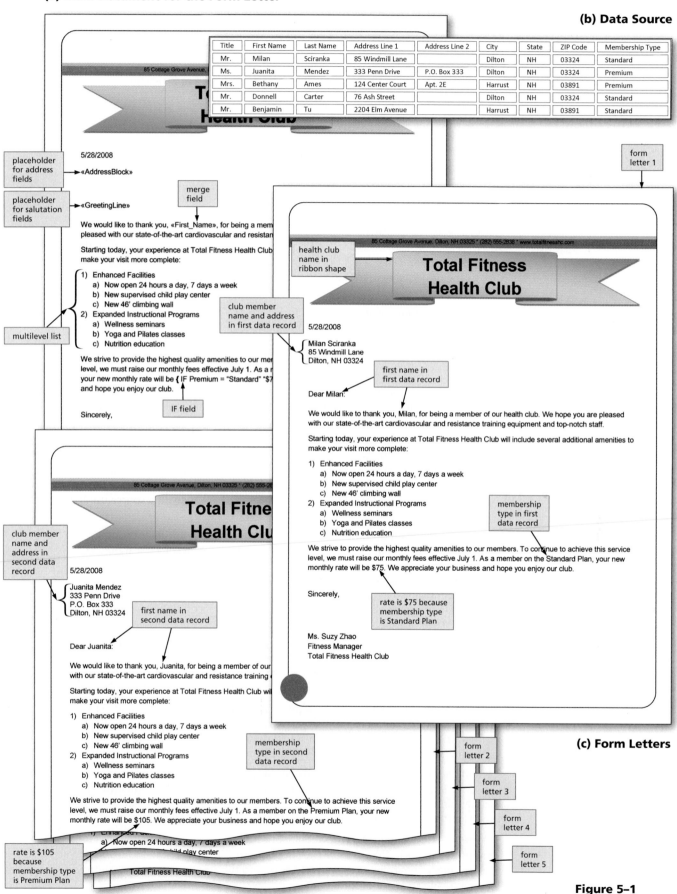

Figure 5–1

Overview

As you read through this chapter, you will learn how to create and generate the form letters shown in Figure 5–1 on the previous page, along with mailing labels, envelopes, and a directory, by performing these general tasks:

- Identify a template as the main document for the form letter.
- Create a letterhead for the main document.
- Type the contents of the data source.
- Compose the remainder of the main document, below the letterhead.
- Address and print mailing labels and envelopes using the data source.
- Create a directory, which displays the contents of the data source.

Plan Ahead

General Project Guidelines

When creating a Word document, the actions you perform and decisions you make will affect the appearance and characteristics of the finished document. As you create form letters, such as the project shown in Figure 5–1, and related documents, you should follow these general guidelines:

1. **Identify the main document for the form letter.** When creating form letters, you either can type the letter from scratch in a blank document window or use a letter template. A letter template saves time because the word processing program prepares a letter with text and/or formatting common to all letters. Then, you customize the resulting letter by selecting and replacing prewritten text.

2. **Design a creative letterhead.** Use text, graphics, formats, and colors that reflect you or your business. Include a name, postal mailing address, and telephone number. If you have an e-mail address and Web address, include those as well.

3. **Create or specify the data source.** The **data source** contains the variable, or changing, values for each letter. A data source can be an Access database table, an Outlook contacts list, or an Excel worksheet. If the necessary and properly organized data already exists in one of these Office programs, you can instruct Word to use the existing file as the data source for the mail merge. Otherwise, you can create a new data source using one of these programs.

4. **Compose the main document for the form letter.** A **main document** contains the constant, or unchanging, text, punctuation, spaces, and graphics. It should reference the data in the data source properly. The finished main document letter should look like a symmetrically framed picture with evenly spaced margins, all balanced below an attractive letterhead. The content of the main document for the form letter should contain proper grammar, correct spelling, logically constructed sentences, flowing paragraphs, and sound ideas. Be sure to proofread it carefully.

5. **Merge the main document with the data source to create the form letters.** **Merging** is the process of combining the contents of a data source with a main document. You can print the merged letters on the printer or place them in a new document, which you later can edit. You also have the option of merging all data in a data source, or just merging a portion of it.

6. **Generate mailing labels and envelopes.** To generate mailing labels and envelopes for the form letters, follow the same process as for the form letters. That is, determine the appropriate data source, create the label or envelope main document, and then merge the main document with the data source to generate the mailing labels and envelopes.

7. **Create a directory of the data source.** A **directory** is a listing of the contents of the data source. To create a directory, follow the same process as for the form letters. That is, determine the appropriate data source, create the directory main document, and then merge the main document with the data source to create the directory.

When necessary, more specific details concerning the above guidelines are presented at appropriate points in the chapter. The chapter also will identify the actions performed and decisions made regarding these guidelines during the creation of the form letters shown in Figure 5–1, and related documents.

To Start Word

If you are using a computer to step through the project in this chapter and you want your screens to match the figures in this book, you should change your computer's resolution to 1024 × 768. For information about how to change a computer's resolution, read Appendix D.

The following steps start Word and verify Word settings.

1 Start Word.

2 If the Word window is not maximized, click its Maximize button.

3 If the Print Layout button is not selected, click it so that Word is in Print Layout view.

4 If your zoom level is not 100%, click the Zoom Out or Zoom In button as many times as necessary until the Zoom level button displays 100% on its face.

5 If the Show/Hide ¶ button on the Home tab is not selected already, click it to display formatting marks on the screen.

Identifying the Main Document for Form Letters

The first step in the mail merge process is to identify the type of document you are creating for the main document. Typical installations of Word support five types of main documents: letters, e-mail messages, envelopes, labels, and a directory. In this section of the chapter, you create letters as the main document. Later in this chapter, you will specify labels, envelopes, and a directory as the main document.

Identify the main document for the form letter. Be sure the main document for the form letter includes all essential business letter elements. All business letters should contain a date line, inside address, message, and signature block. Many business letters contain additional items such as a special mailing notation(s), an attention line, a salutation, a subject line, a complimentary close, reference initials, and an enclosure notation.

Plan Ahead

To Identify the Main Document for the Form Letter Using the Task Pane

This project uses a letter template as the main document for the form letter. Word provides five styles of merge letter templates: Equity, Median, Oriel, Origin, and Urban. The following steps use the Mail Merge task pane to identify the Equity Merge Letter template as the main document for a form letter.

1
- Click Mailings on the Ribbon to display the Mailings tab.

- Click the Start Mail Merge button on the Mailings tab to display the Start Mail Merge menu (Figure 5–2).

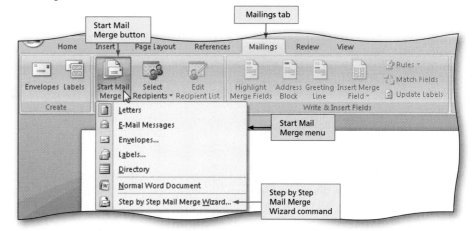

Figure 5–2

2

- Click Step by Step Mail Merge Wizard on the Start Mail Merge menu to display the Mail Merge wizard in the Mail Merge task pane (Figure 5–3).

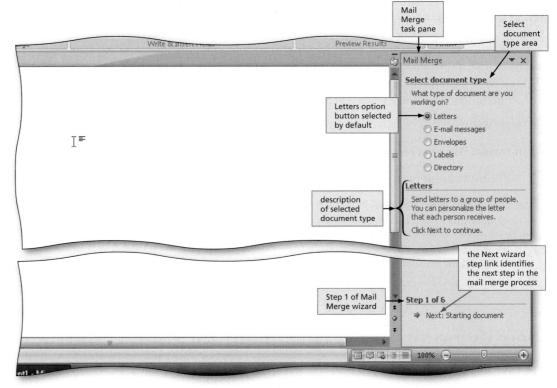

Figure 5–3

3

- Click the 'Next wizard step' link at the bottom of the Mail Merge task pane to display Step 2 of the Mail Merge wizard.

- Click 'Start from a template' in the 'Select starting document' area and then click the 'Select mail merge template' link to display the Select Template dialog box.

- Click the Letters tab in the dialog box and then click Equity Merge Letter, which shows a preview of the selected template in the Preview area (Figure 5–4).

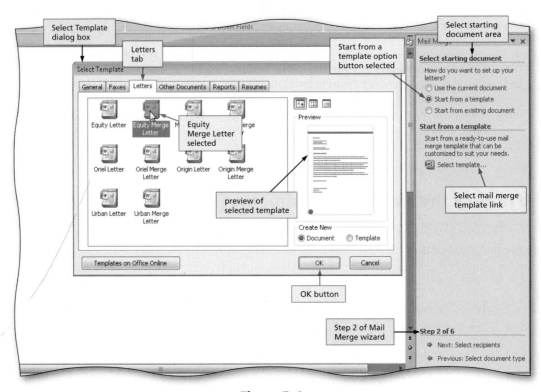

Figure 5–4

 Experiment

- Click various Merge Letter templates in the Letters tab and watch the preview display at the right edge of the dialog box. When finished experimenting, click the Equity Merge Letter template.

4

- Click the OK button to display a letter in the document window that is based on the Equity Merge Letter template (Figure 5–5).

5

- Click the Close button in the upper-right corner of the Mail Merge task pane title bar to close the Mail Merge wizard.

Q&A Why am I closing the Mail Merge task pane?

You temporarily are stopping the merge process while you create the letterhead for the form letter. When you are ready to continue with the merge process, you will redisplay the Mail Merge task pane.

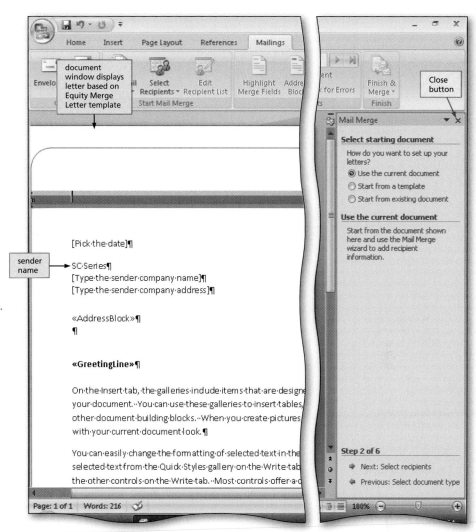

Figure 5–5

Other Ways

1. Click Office Button, click New, click Installed Templates, click Equity Merge Letter, click Create button. Click Start Mail Merge button on Mailings tab, click Letters

To Print the Document

The next step is to print the letter that Word generated, which is based on the Equity Merge Letter template.

1 Ready the printer. Display the Office Button menu, point to Print, and then click Quick Print to print the document that is based on the Equity Merge Letter template (Figure 5–6 on the next page).

Q&A What are the content controls in the document?

A content control contains instructions for filling in areas of the document. To select a content control, click it. Later in this chapter, you will personalize the content controls.

Q&A Why does SC Series display as the sender name?

Word places the user name associated with your copy of Microsoft Word as the sender name. SC Series, which stands for Shelly Cashman Series, is the user name associated with this copy of Word.

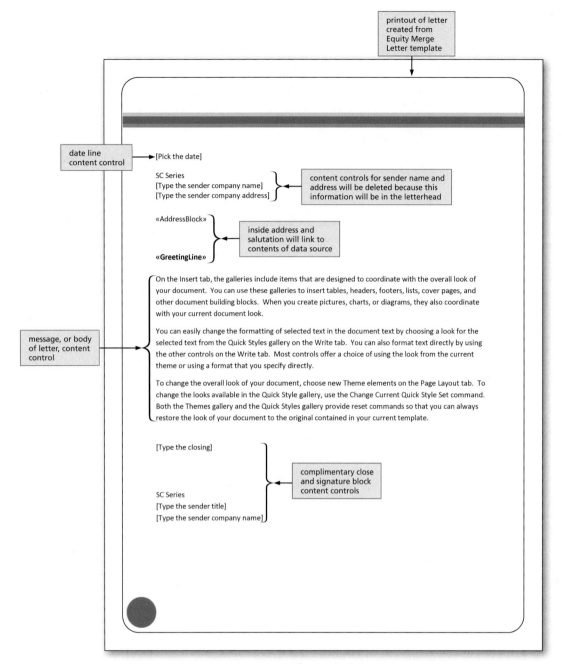

Figure 5–6

TO CHANGE THE USER NAME AND INITIALS

If you wanted to change the user name and initials associated with your copy of Microsoft Word, you would perform the following steps.

1. Display the Office Button menu and then click the Word Options button to display the Word Options dialog box.

2. Click Popular in the left pane.

3. Enter your name in the User name text box.

4. Enter your initials in the Initials text box.

5. Click the OK button.

To Change Theme Colors and Fonts

BTW

Changing Margins
If you want to see the current margin settings, display the ruler and then hold down the ALT key while pointing to the margin boundary (where the blue meets the white on the ruler). To see the numeric margin settings while changing the margins, hold down the ALT key while dragging the margin boundary on the ruler.

The form letter in this project uses the Equity color scheme and Office Classic 2 font set. The following steps change theme colors and the font set.

1 Display the Home tab. Click the Change Styles button on the Home tab, point to Colors on the Change Styles menu, and then click Equity in the Colors gallery to change the document theme colors to Equity.

2 Click the Change Styles button on the Home tab; point to Fonts on the Change Styles menu; if necessary, scroll to Office Classic 2 in the Fonts gallery; and then click Office Classic 2 to change the document theme fonts to Office Classic 2.

To Change the Margin Settings

Word is preset to use standard 8.5-by-11-inch paper, with 1-inch top, bottom, left, and right margins. If you change the default margin settings, the new margin settings affect every page in the document. If you wanted the margins to affect just a portion of the document, you would divide the document into sections as discussed in Chapter 4, which would enable you to specify different margin settings for each section.

The form letter in this chapter has .75-inch left and right margins and 1-inch top and bottom margins, so that more text can fit from left to right on the page. The following steps change margin settings.

1
- Display the Page Layout tab.
- Click Margins button on the Page Layout tab to display the Margins gallery (Figure 5–7).

2
- Click Moderate in the Margins gallery to change the left and right margins to .75-inches.

Q&A What if the margin settings I want are not in the Margins gallery?

You can click the Custom Margins command in the Margins gallery and then enter your desired margin values in the top, bottom, left, and right text boxes in the dialog box.

Q&A Why does my document wrap on different words?

Differences in wordwrap relate to the printer used by your computer. Thus, it is possible that the same document could wordwrap differently if associated with a different printer.

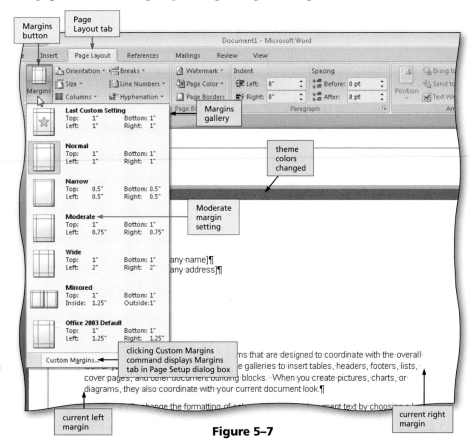

Figure 5–7

Other Ways	
1. Position mouse pointer on margin boundary on ruler; when mouse pointer	changes to two-headed arrow, drag margin boundary on ruler

Working with Shapes and the Drawing Canvas

The letterhead for the form letter consists of the company address, telephone number, and Web site information in a line above the company name, which is surrounded by a ribbon-like shape (Figure 5–1 on page WD 307). Word has a variety of predefined shapes, which are a type of drawing object, that you can insert in documents. A **drawing object** is a graphic that you create using Word. The following pages create the letterhead for the form letter.

To Enter Text in a Table Row

The orange bar at the top of the form letter is actually a three-row table, with each row containing a different shading color. The following steps enter the company address, telephone number, and Web site information in the second row of the table.

1 Click the dark orange bar to position the insertion point in the second row of the table.

2 Center the insertion point in the cell.

3 Type 85 Cottage Grove Avenue, Dilton, NH 03324 * (282) 555-2838 * www.totalfitnesshc.com in the table cell (Figure 5–8).

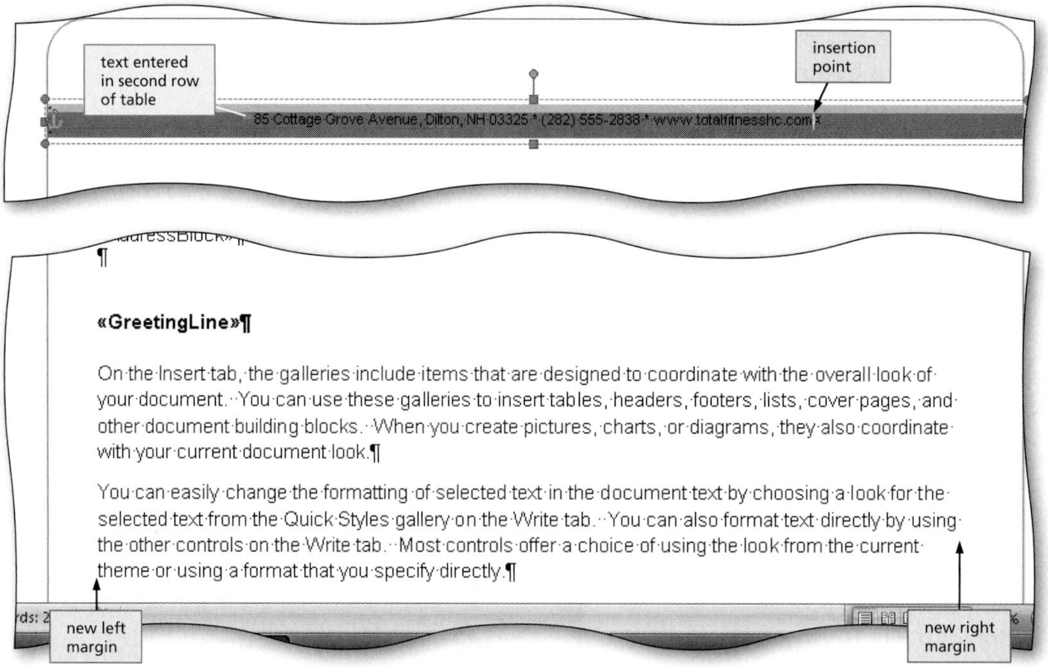

BTW

Drawing Canvas
If you want the drawing canvas to be displayed automatically when you insert a shape, click the Office Button; click the Word Options button on the Office Button menu; click Advanced in the left pane; if necessary, scroll to the Editing options area; place a check mark in the Automatically create drawing canvas when inserting AutoShapes check box; and then click the OK button. With this check box selected, you would skip the steps on page WD 315.

text entered in second row of table

insertion point

85 Cottage Grove Avenue, Dilton, NH 03325 * (282) 555-2838 * www.totalfitnesshc.com

«AddressBlock»¶
¶

«GreetingLine»¶

On the Insert tab, the galleries include items that are designed to coordinate with the overall look of your document. You can use these galleries to insert tables, headers, footers, lists, cover pages, and other document building blocks. When you create pictures, charts, or diagrams, they also coordinate with your current document look.¶

You can easily change the formatting of selected text in the document text by choosing a look for the selected text from the Quick Styles gallery on the Write tab. You can also format text directly by using the other controls on the Write tab. Most controls offer a choice of using the look from the current theme or using a format that you specify directly.¶

new left margin

new right margin

Figure 5–8

To Insert a Drawing Canvas

The next step is to insert the ribbon-like shape that will contain the company name. When you insert shapes, it is recommended you insert them in a drawing canvas. A **drawing canvas** is a rectangular boundary between your shape and the rest of the document; it also is a container that helps you to resize and arrange shapes on the page. The next steps insert a drawing canvas in a document.

①

- With the insertion point in the second row of the table, display the Insert tab.

- Click the Shapes button on the Insert tab to display the Shapes gallery (Figure 5–9).

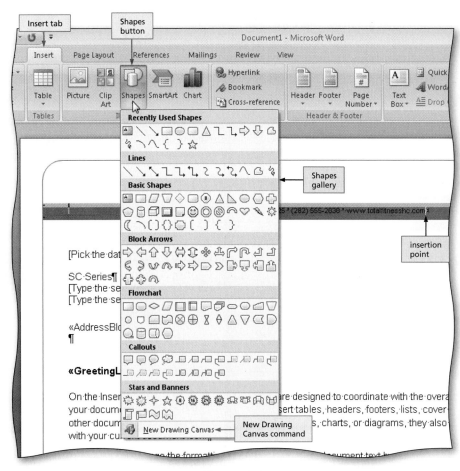

Figure 5–9

②

- Click New Drawing Canvas in the Shapes gallery to insert a drawing canvas at the location of the insertion point (Figure 5–10).

Q&A What is the patterned rectangle around the drawing canvas?

It indicates the drawing canvas is selected. You also can use it to resize or move the drawing canvas and its contents.

Q&A Can I change the colors of the drawing canvas?

Yes. You can use the Drawing Tools Format tab to change colors and other formats of the drawing canvas.

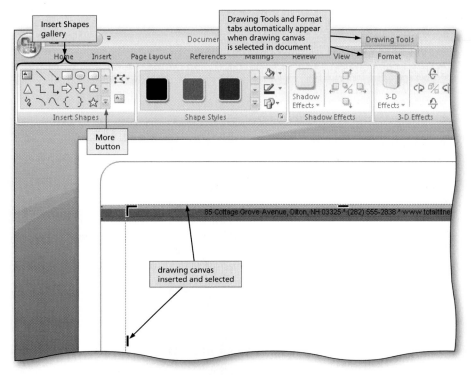

Figure 5–10

To Insert a Shape

The next step is to draw a ribbon shape in the drawing canvas. Examples of predefined shapes in Word include rectangles, circles, triangles, arrows, flowcharting symbols, stars, banners, and callouts. The following steps insert a ribbon shape in the drawing canvas.

1

- Click the More button in the Insert Shapes gallery on the Format tab (shown in Figure 5–10 on the previous page), which shows more gallery options (Figure 5–11).

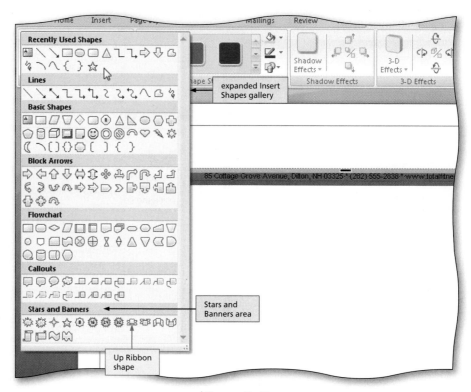

Figure 5–11

2

- Click the Up Ribbon shape in the Stars and Banners area of the Insert Shapes gallery, which removes the gallery and changes the mouse pointer to the shape of a crosshair.

- Position the mouse pointer (a crosshair) on the left of the drawing canvas below the shaded table, as shown in Figure 5–12.

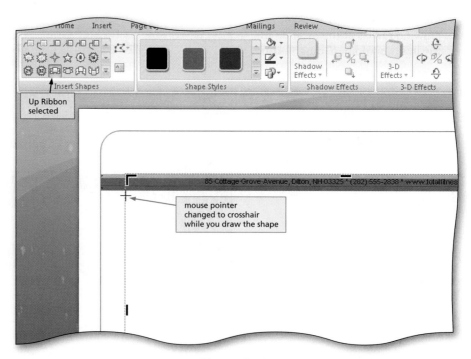

Figure 5–12

- Drag the mouse, as shown in Figure 5–13, to the right and downward to form the ribbon shape.

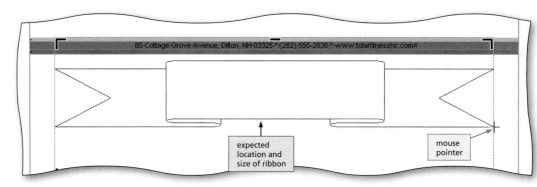

Figure 5–13

- Release the mouse button so that Word draws the shape in the drawing canvas. If your shape is not the same approximate height and width as shown in Figure 5–14, drag the shape's sizing handles to resize it, or enter the appropriate values in the Shape Height and Shape Width text boxes on the Format tab.

Q&A

What is the purpose of the rotate and adjustment handles?

When you drag an object's **rotate handle**, which is the green circle, Word rotates the object in the direction you drag the mouse. When you drag an object's **adjustment handle**, which is the yellow diamond, Word changes the object's shape.

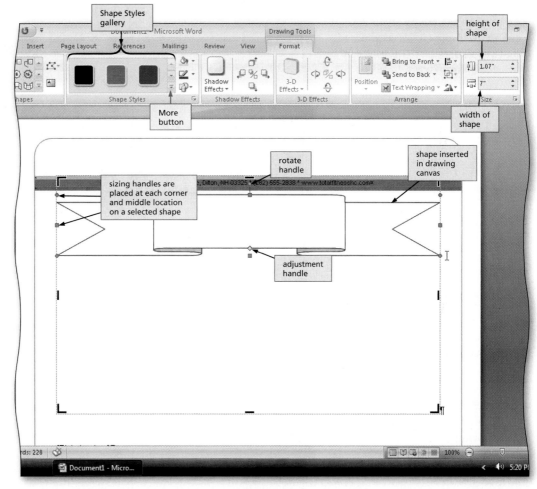

Figure 5–14

Q&A

What if I wanted to delete a shape and start over?

With the shape selected, press the DELETE key.

Other Ways

1. Click Shapes button on Insert tab, select desired shape

To Apply a Shape Style

The next step is to apply a style to the shape, so that it is more colorful. Word provides a Shape Styles gallery, allowing you to change the look of the shape to a more visually appealing style. The following steps apply a style to the shape.

1

- With the shape still selected, click the More button in the Shape Styles gallery (shown in Figure 5–14 on the previous page) to expand the Shape Styles gallery.

2

- Point to Diagonal Gradient - Accent 2 in the Shape Styles gallery to display a live preview of that style applied to the shape in the document (Figure 5–15).

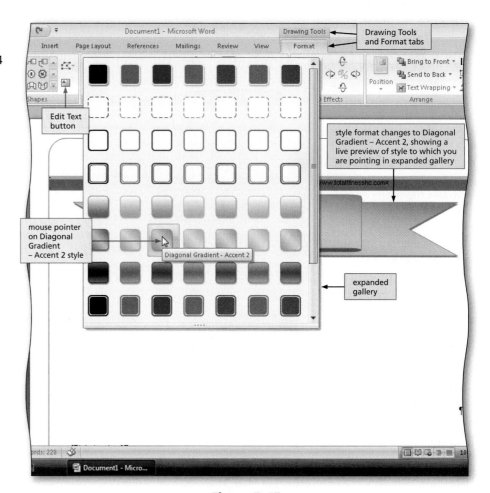

Figure 5–15

Experiment

- Point to various styles in the Shape Styles gallery and watch the style of the shape change in the drawing canvas.

3

- Click Diagonal Gradient - Accent 2 in the Shape Styles gallery to apply the selected style to the shape.

Other Ways

1. Click Advanced Tools Dialog Box Launcher in Shape Styles group, select desired colors, click OK button

2. Right-click shape, click Format AutoShape on shortcut menu, select desired colors, click OK button

To Add Formatted Text to a Shape

The next step is to add the company name to the shape, centered with a 26-point bold font. The following steps add text to a shape.

1

- Click the Edit Text button on the Drawing Tools Format tab (shown in Figure 5–15) to place an insertion point in the shape and display the Text Box Tools and its subordinate Format tab on the Ribbon (Figure 5–16).

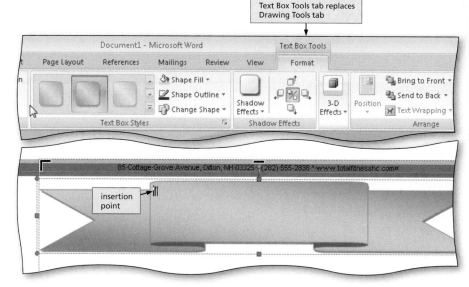

Figure 5–16

2

- Display the Home tab.

- Click the Center button on the Home tab.

- Click the Bold button on the Home tab.

- Change the font size to 26 point.

- Type Total Fitness and then press SHIFT+ENTER to insert a line break character.

- Type Health Club on the second line of the shape (Figure 5–17). (If all the letters in the company name do not fit in the shape, drag the sizing handles on the shape until all text is displayed in the shape.)

 Why insert a line break instead of pressing the ENTER key?

The default space after a paragraph is 8 points. To suppress paragraph spacing between lines, insert a line break.

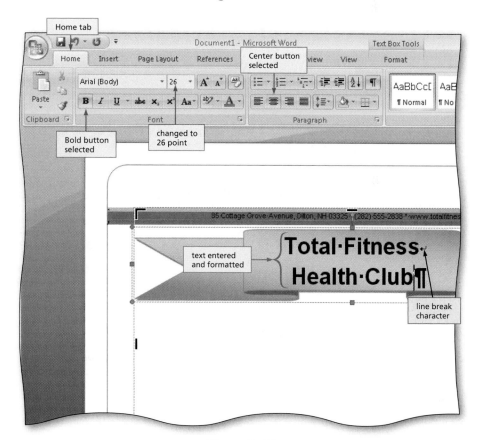

Figure 5–17

Other Ways
1. Right-click shape, click Add Text on shortcut menu

To Resize a Drawing Canvas

Recall that you drew the ribbon shape in a drawing canvas. The height of the drawing canvas is almost four inches, which is too tall for this letter. You want the drawing canvas to touch the bottom of the shape, to leave plenty of room for the letter. The following steps resize a drawing canvas.

- Click in the drawing canvas in an area outside the shape to select the drawing canvas.

- Position the mouse pointer on the bottom-middle sizing handle until the mouse pointer shape changes to a T.

- Drag the bottom-middle sizing handle upward, as shown in Figure 5–18, until the dotted line touches the bottom of the shape.

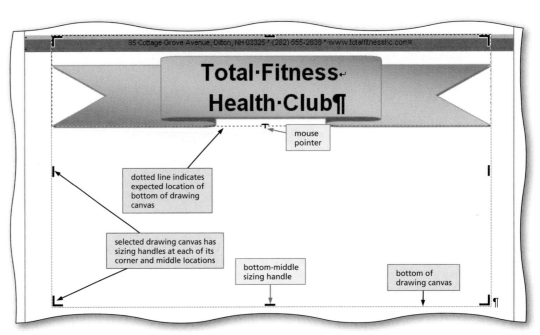

Figure 5–18

- Release the mouse button to resize the drawing canvas (Figure 5–19).

Q&A

Can I move the shape around in the drawing canvas?

Yes. You can drag the shape to any location in the drawing canvas.

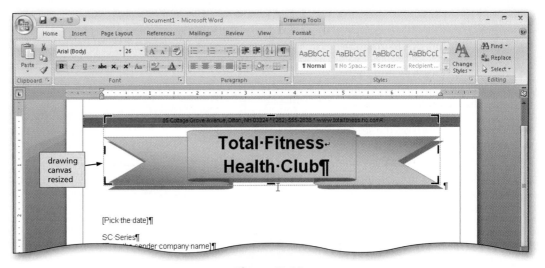

Figure 5–19

Other Ways

1. Enter new values in Shape Width and Shape Height text boxes on Format tab

2. Right-click drawing canvas, click Format Drawing Canvas on shortcut menu, click Size tab, enter height and width values in text boxes, click OK button

To Create a Folder while Saving

You have performed several tasks while creating this project and should save it. You want to save this and all other documents created in this chapter in a folder called Total Fitness. This folder does not exist, so you must create it. Rather than creating the folder in Windows, you can create folders in Word, which saves time. The following steps create a folder during the process of saving a document.

1

- With a USB flash drive connected to one of the computer's USB ports, click the Save button on the Quick Access Toolbar to display the Save As dialog box.

- Type Health Club Form Letter in the File name text box to change the file name.

- If Computer is not displayed in the Favorite Links section, drag the top or bottom edge of the Save As dialog box until Computer is displayed.

- Click Computer in the Favorite Links section, and then double-click your USB flash drive in the list of available drives.

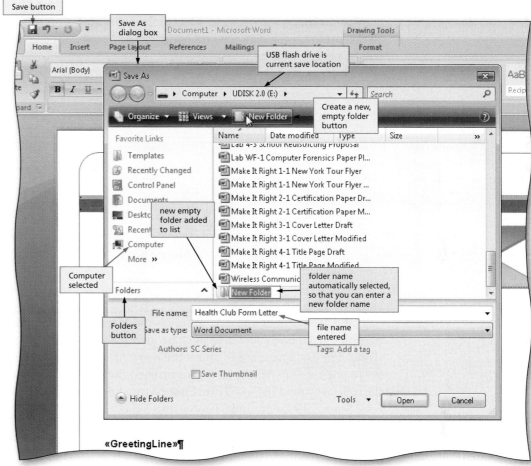

- Click the 'Create a new, empty folder' button in the Save As dialog box to display a folder with the name New Folder selected in the dialog box (Figure 5–20).

Figure 5–20

2

- Type Total Fitness as the new folder name and then press the ENTER key to create the new folder on the USB flash drive.

- Click the Save button in the Save As dialog box to save the Health Club Form Letter in the Total Fitness folder on the USB flash drive.

Q&A

Can I create a folder in any other dialog box?

Yes. Any dialog box that displays a File list, such as the Open and Insert File dialog boxes, also has the 'Create a new, empty folder' button, allowing you to create a new folder in Word instead of using Windows Vista for this task.

Other Ways
1. Press F12

Creating a Data Source

A data source is a file that contains the data that changes from one merged document to the next. As shown in Figure 5–21, a data source often is shown as a table that consists of a series of rows and columns. Each row is called a **record**. The first row of a data source is called the **header record** because it identifies the name of each column. Each row below the header row is called a **data record**. Data records contain the text that varies in each copy of the merged document. The data source for this project contains five data records. In this project, each data record identifies a different club member. Thus, five form letters will be generated from this data source.

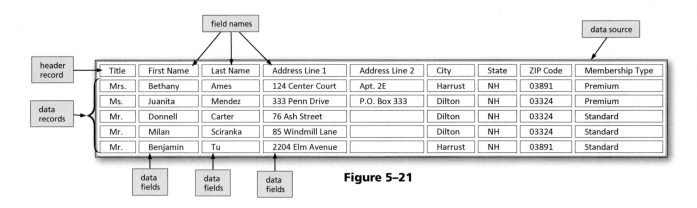

field names									data source
Title	First Name	Last Name	Address Line 1	Address Line 2	City	State	ZIP Code	Membership Type	
Mrs.	Bethany	Ames	124 Center Court	Apt. 2E	Harrust	NH	03891	Premium	
Ms.	Juanita	Mendez	333 Penn Drive	P.O. Box 333	Dilton	NH	03324	Premium	
Mr.	Donnell	Carter	76 Ash Street		Dilton	NH	03324	Standard	
Mr.	Milan	Sciranka	85 Windmill Lane		Dilton	NH	03324	Standard	
Mr.	Benjamin	Tu	2204 Elm Avenue		Harrust	NH	03891	Standard	

header record → Title row

data records → rows below

data fields (columns)

Figure 5–21

Each column in the data source is called a **data field**. A data field represents a group of similar data. Each data field must be identified uniquely with a name, called a **field name**. For example, First Name is the name of the data field (column) that contains the first names of club members. In this project, the data source contains nine data fields with the following field names: Title, First Name, Last Name, Address Line 1, Address Line 2, City, State, ZIP Code, and Membership Type.

Plan Ahead

Create the data source.
When you create a data source, you will need to determine the fields it should contain. That is, you will need to identify the data that will vary from one merged document to the next. Following are a few important points about fields:

- For each field, you may be required to create a field name. Because data sources often contain the same fields, some programs create a list of commonly used field names that you may use.

- Field names must be unique; that is, no two field names may be the same.

- Fields may be listed in any order in the data source. That is, the order of fields has no effect on the order in which they will print in the main document.

- Organize fields so that they are flexible. For example, break the name into separate fields: title, first name, and last name. This arrangement allows you to print a person's title, first name, and last name (e.g., Mr. Roger Bannerman) in the inside address but only the title and last name in the salutation (Dear Mr. Bannerman).

BTW

Fields and Records
Field and record are terms that originate from the computer programming field. Do not be intimidated by these terms. A field is simply a column in a table, and a record is a row. Instead of as a field, some programmers identify a column of data as a variable or an attribute. All three terms (field, variable, and attribute) have the same meaning.

To Create a New Data Source

Word provides a list of 13 commonly used field names. This project uses 8 of the 13 field names supplied by Word: Title, First Name, Last Name, Address Line 1, Address Line 2, City, State, and ZIP Code. This project does not use the other five field names supplied by Word: Company Name, Country or Region, Home Phone, Work Phone, and E-mail Address. Thus, you will delete these five field names. Then, you will add one new field name (Membership Type) to the data source. The following steps create a new data source for a mail merge.

1

• Display the Mailings tab.

• Click the Start Mail Merge button on the Mailings tab and then click Step by Step Mail Merge Wizard to redisplay the Mail Merge task pane.

• Click 'Type a new list' in the Select recipients area, which displays the 'Type a new list' area.

• Click the 'Create new recipient list' link to display the New Address List dialog box (Figure 5–22).

Q&A

When would I use the other two option buttons in the Select recipients area?

If you had a data source already created, you would use the first option: Use an existing list. If you wanted to use your Outlooks contacts list as the data source, you would choose the second option.

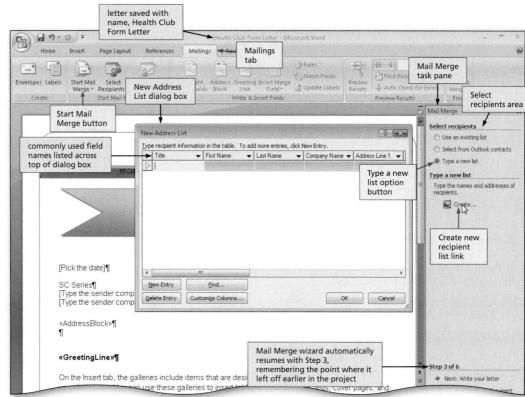

Figure 5–22

2

• Click the Customize Columns button to display the Customize Address List dialog box (Figure 5–23).

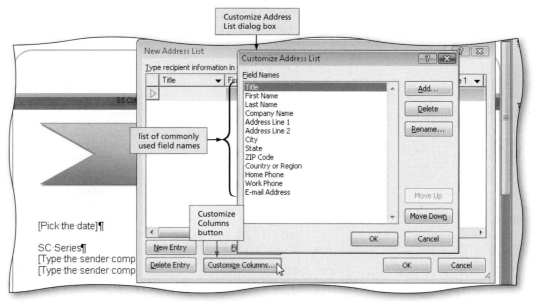

Figure 5–23

● Click Company Name in the Field Names list and then click the Delete button to display a dialog box asking if you are sure you want to delete the selected field (Figure 5–24).

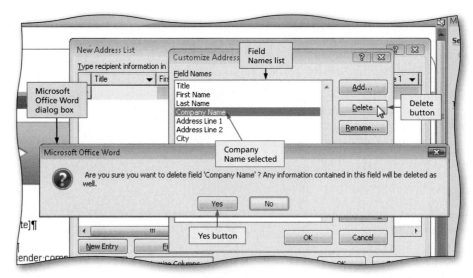

Figure 5–24

● Click the Yes button in the Microsoft Office Word dialog box.

● Click Country or Region in the Field Names list. Click the Delete button. Click the Yes button to remove the field.

● Click Home Phone in the Field Names list. Click the Delete button. Click the Yes button to remove the field.

● Use this same procedure to delete the Work Phone and E-mail Address fields (Figure 5–25).

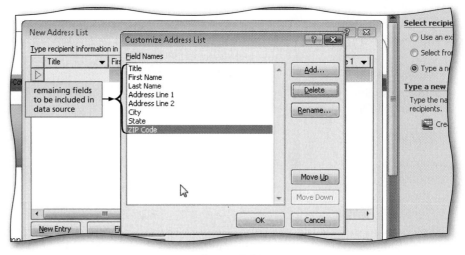

Figure 5–25

● Click the Add button to display the Add Field dialog box.

● Type Membership Type in the 'Type a name for your field' text box (Figure 5–26).

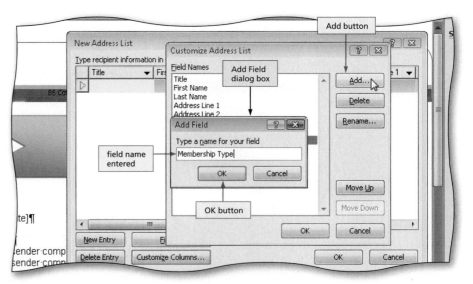

Figure 5–26

6

- Click the OK button to close the Add Field dialog box and add the Membership Type field name to the bottom of the Field Names list (Figure 5–27).

Can I change the name of a field?

Yes. Select the field, click the Rename button, type the new name, and then click the OK button.

Could I add more field names to the list?

Yes. You would click the Add button for each field name you want to add.

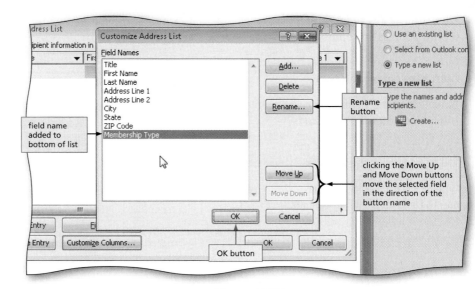

Figure 5–27

7

- Click the OK button to close the Customize Address List dialog box, which positions the insertion point in the Title text box for the first record (row) in the New Address List dialog box (Figure 5–28).

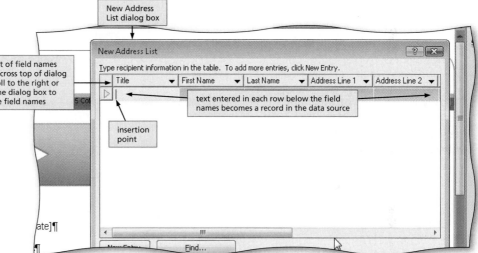

Figure 5–28

8

- Type Mr. and then press the TAB key to enter the title for the first data record.

- Type Milan and then press the TAB key to enter the first name.

- Type Sciranka and then press the TAB key to enter the last name.

- Type 85 Windmill Lane and then press the TAB key to enter the first address line (Figure 5–29).

What if I notice an error in an entry?

Click the entry and then correct the error as you would in the document window.

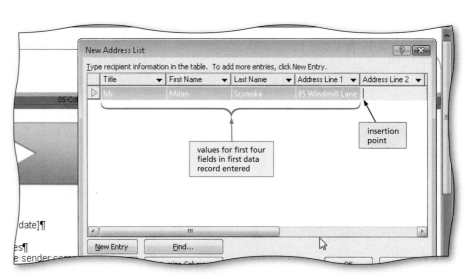

Figure 5–29

9

- Press the TAB key to leave the second address line empty.

- Type `Dilton` and then press the TAB key to enter the city.

- Type `NH` and then press the TAB key to enter the state code.

- Type `03324` and then press the TAB key to enter the ZIP code.

- Type `Standard` to enter the membership type (Figure 5–30).

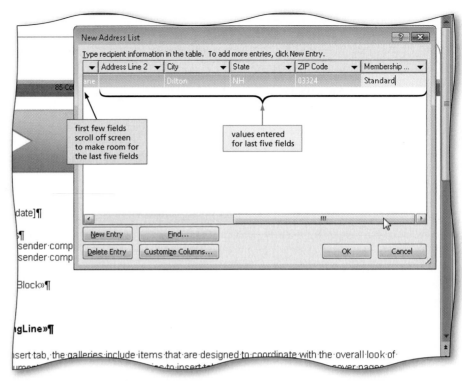

Figure 5–30

10

- Click the New Entry button to add a new blank record and position the insertion point in the Title field of the new record (Figure 5–31).

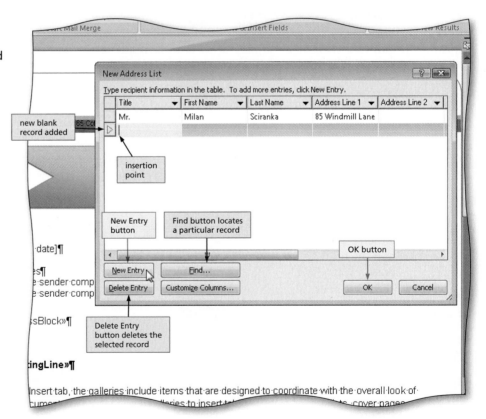

Figure 5–31

To Enter More Records

The following steps enter the remaining four records in the New Address List dialog box.

1 Type Ms. and then press the TAB key. Type Juanita and then press the TAB key. Type Mendez and then press the TAB key.

2 Type 333 Penn Drive and then press the TAB key. Type P.O. Box 333 and then press the TAB key.

3 Type Dilton and then press the TAB key. Type NH and then press the TAB key. Type 03324 and then press the TAB key.

4 Type Premium and then click the New Entry button.

Q&A Instead of clicking the New Entry button, can I press the TAB key at the end of one row to add a new blank record?

Yes. Pressing the TAB key at the end of a row has the same function as clicking the New Entry button.

5 Type Mrs. and then press the TAB key. Type Bethany and then press the TAB key. Type Ames and then press the TAB key.

6 Type 124 Center Court and then press the TAB key. Type Apt. 2E and then press the TAB key.

7 Type Harrust and then press the TAB key. Type NH and then press the TAB key. Type 03891 and then press the TAB key.

8 Type Premium and then click the New Entry button.

9 Type Mr. and then press the TAB key. Type Donnell and then press the TAB key. Type Carter and then press the TAB key.

10 Type 76 Ash Street and then press the TAB key twice.

11 Type Dilton and then press the TAB key. Type NH and then press the TAB key. Type 03324 and then press the TAB key.

12 Type Standard and then click the New Entry button.

13 Type Mr. and then press the TAB key. Type Benjamin and then press the TAB key. Type Tu and then press the TAB key.

14 Type 2204 Elm Avenue and then press the TAB key twice.

15 Type Harrust and then press the TAB key. Type NH and then press the TAB key. Type 03891 and then press the TAB key.

16 Type Standard and then click the OK button (shown in Figure 5–31), which displays the Save Address List dialog box (shown in Figure 5–32 on the next page).

BTW

Certification
The Microsoft Certified Application Specialist (MCAS) program provides an opportunity for you to obtain a valuable industry credential — proof that you have the Word 2007 skills required by employers. For more information see Appendix G or visit the Word 2007 Certification Web page (scsite.com/wd2007/cert).

To Save the Data Source when Prompted by Word

When you click the OK button in the New Address List dialog box, Word displays the Save Address List dialog box so that you can save the data source. The following steps save the data source in the Total Fitness folder created earlier in this project.

1

- Type Health Club Members in the File name text box.

- If necessary, locate and select the USB flash drive and then double-click the Total Fitness folder to open the folder (Figure 5–32).

Q&A

What is a Microsoft Office Address Lists file type?

It is a Microsoft Access database file. If you are familiar with Microsoft Access, you can open the Health Club Members file in Access. You do not have to be familiar with Access or have Access installed on your computer, however, to continue with this mail merge process. Word simply stores a data source as an Access table because it is an efficient method of storing a data source.

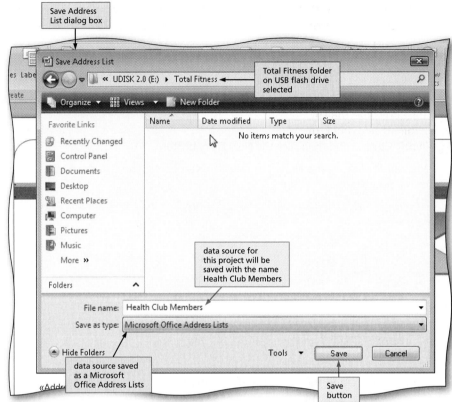

Figure 5–32

2

- Click the Save button in the Save Address List dialog box to save the data source in the Total Fitness folder on the USB flash drive using the file name, Health Club Members, and then display the Mail Merge Recipients dialog box (Figure 5–33).

3

- Click the OK button to close the Mail Merge Recipients dialog box.

- Click the Close button on the Mail Merge task pane title bar because you are finished with the wizard.

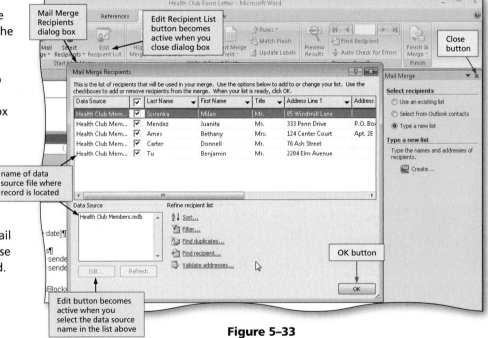

Figure 5–33

Editing Records in the Data Source

All of the data records have been entered in the data source and saved with the file name, Health Club Members. To add or edit data records in the data source, you would click the Edit Recipient List button on the Mailings tab to display the Mail Merge Recipients dialog box (shown in Figure 5–33). Click the data source name in the Data Source list and then click the Edit button in the Mail Merge Recipients dialog box to display the data records in a dialog box similar to the one shown in Figure 5–31 on page WD 326. Then, add or edit records as described in the previous steps. If you want to edit a particular record and the list of data records is long, you can click the Find button to locate an item, such as the first name, quickly in the list.

To delete a record, select it using the same procedure described in the previous paragraph. Then, click the Delete Entry button in the dialog box (Figure 5–31 on page WD 326).

Composing the Main Document for the Form Letters

The next step is to enter and format the text and fields in the main document for the form letters (shown in Figure 5–1a on page WD 307). With the letterhead for the form letters complete, you will follow these steps to compose the remainder of the main document for the form letter.

1. Format the date line and enter the date
2. Delete the company content controls
3. Edit the greeting line (salutation)
4. Enter text and insert merge fields
5. Create a multilevel list
6. Insert an IF field
7. Merge the letters

To Change Spacing Before Paragraphs

The default amount of space above (before) the date line paragraph is 36 points. In this project, it is reduced to 24 points to be sure the entire letter fits on a single page. The following steps change the spacing before to 24 point.

1 Click the date content control to select it.

2 Display the Page Layout tab.

3 Click the Spacing Before box down arrow on the Page Layout tab as many times as necessary until 24 pt is displayed in the Spacing Before text box.

BTW

Saving Data Sources
Word, by default, saves a data source in the My Data Sources folder on your hard disk. Likewise, when you open a data source, Word initially looks in the My Data Sources folder for the file. The default file type for a new data source created in Word is called Microsoft Office Address Lists. If you are familiar with Microsoft Access, you can open and view these file types in Access using the Microsoft Office Access file type.

To Enter the Date

The next step is to enter the date. You can click the date content control and type the correct date, or you can click the box arrow and select the date from a calendar. The following steps use the calendar to enter the date.

- With the date content control selected, click its box arrow to display a calendar.

- Scroll through the calendar months until May, 2008 is displayed (Figure 5–34).

- Click 28 in the calendar to display 5/28/2008 in the date line of the form letter (shown in Figure 5-35).

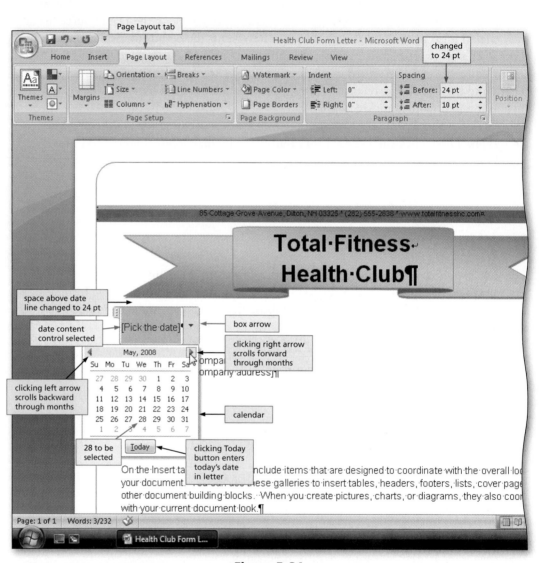

Figure 5–34

To Delete Content Controls

Earlier in this chapter, you created the letterhead for the main document for the form letter. Thus, the letter does not require the company content controls below the date. The following steps delete these content controls.

1 Select the three lines of company content controls by dragging through them (Figure 5–35).

2 Press the DELETE key to delete the selected content controls.

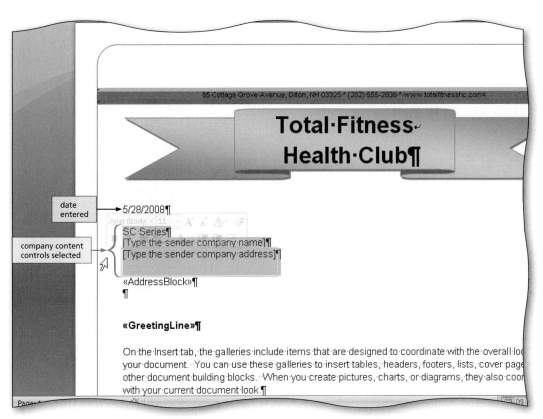

Figure 5–35

Merge Fields

In this form letter, the inside address appears below the date line, and the salutation is below the inside address. The contents of the inside address and salutation are located in the data source. To link the data source to the main document, you insert the field names from the data source in the main document.

In the main document, field names linked to the data source are called **merge fields** because they merge, or combine, the main document with the contents of the data source. When a merge field is inserted in the main document, Word surrounds the field name with merge field characters (shown in Figure 5–36 on the next page). The **merge field characters**, which are chevrons, mark the beginning and ending of a merge field. Merge field characters are not on the keyboard; therefore, you cannot type them directly in the document. Word automatically displays them when a merge field is inserted in the main document.

Most letters contain an address and salutation. For this reason, Word provides an AddressBlock merge field and a GreetingLine merge field. The **AddressBlock merge field** contains several fields related to an address: title, first name, middle name, last name, suffix, company, street address 1, street address 2, city, state, and ZIP code. When Word uses the AddressBlock merge field, it automatically looks for any fields in the associated data source that are related to an address and then formats the address block properly when you merge the data source with the main document. For example, if your inside address does not use a middle name, suffix, or company, Word omits these items from the inside address and adjusts the spacing so that the address prints correctly.

The Mail Merge template automatically inserted the AddressBlock and GreetingLine merge fields in the form letter. If you wanted to insert these merge fields in a document, you would click the Address Block button or the Greeting Line button on the Mailings tab.

BTW

Fields
When you insert fields in a document, the displayed fields may be surrounded by braces instead of chevrons and extra instructions may appear between the braces. If this occurs, then field codes have been turned on. To turn off field codes so that they do not display, press ALT+F9.

To Edit the GreetingLine Merge Field

The **GreetingLine merge field** contains text and fields related to a salutation. The default greeting for the salutation is in the format, Dear Joshua, followed by a comma. In this letter, you want a more formal ending to the salutation — a colon. Also, the GreetingLine merge field is formatted in bold. You do not want the salutation to print in bold. The following steps edit the GreetingLine merge field.

1

- Select the GreetingLine merge field by clicking to its left.

Q&A Why does the GreetingLine merge field turn gray?

Word, by default, shades a field in gray when the insertion point is in the field. The shading displays on the screen to help you identify fields; the shading does not print on a hard copy. To select an entire field, double-click it.

- Display the Home tab. Click the Bold button on the Home tab to remove the bold format from the GreetingLine merge field.

- Right-click the GreetingLine merge field (Figure 5–36).

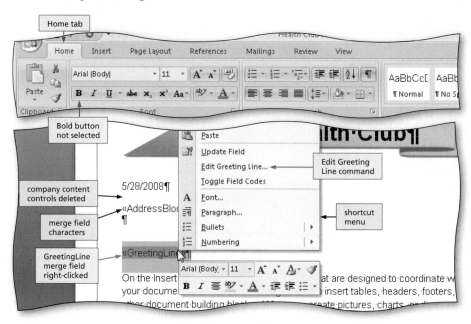

Figure 5–36

2

- Click Edit Greeting Line on the shortcut menu to display the Modify Greeting Line dialog box.

- Click the rightmost 'Greeting line format' box arrow and then click the colon (:) in the list (Figure 5–37).

3

- Click the OK button to modify the greeting line format.

Q&A Will I notice a change in the GreetingLine merge field?

No. The new format will be displayed later in this chapter when you merge the form letter to the data source.

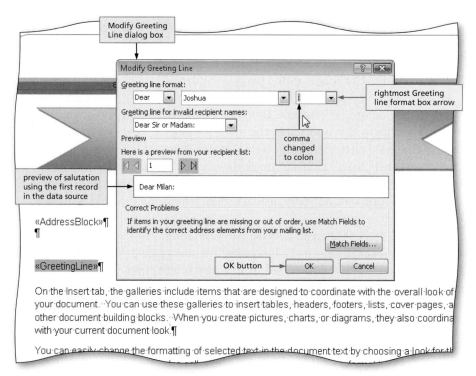

Figure 5–37

To Begin Typing the Body of the Form Letter

The next step is to begin typing the message, or body of the letter, which is to be located where Word has the content control, Type the body of the letter. The following steps begin typing the letter in the location of the content control.

1 Click the body of the letter to select the content control (Figure 5–38).

2 With the content control selected, type `We would like to thank you,` and then press the SPACEBAR.

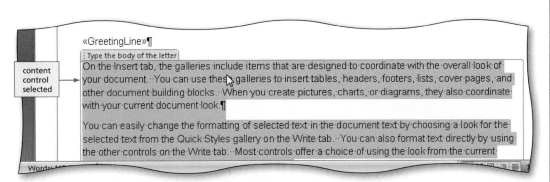

Figure 5–38

BTW

Insert Merge Field Button
If you click the Insert Merge Field button instead of the Insert Merge Field button arrow (Figure 5–39), Word displays the Insert Merge Field dialog box instead of the Insert Merge Field menu. To insert fields from the dialog box, click the field name and then click the Insert button. The dialog box remains open so that you can insert multiple fields, if necessary. When finished inserting fields, click the Close button in the dialog box.

To Insert a Merge Field in the Main Document

The first sentence in the first paragraph of the letter states the first name of the member. To instruct Word to use data fields from the data source, you insert merge fields in the main document for the form letter. The following steps insert a merge field at the location of the insertion point.

1

• Display the Mailings tab.

• Click the Insert Merge Field button arrow on the Mailings tab to display the Insert Merge Field menu (Figure 5–39).

Q&A

Why is the underscore character in some of the field names?

Word places an underscore character in place of the space in merge fields.

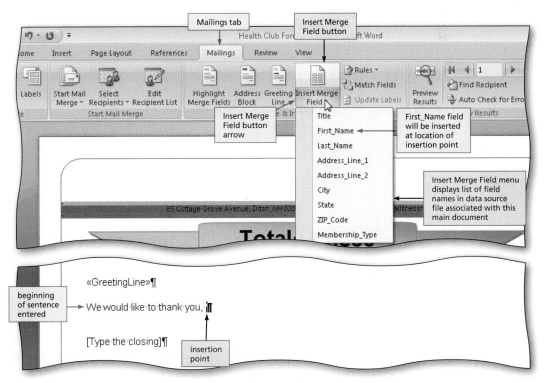

Figure 5–39

②

- Click First_Name to insert the selected merge field in the document at the location of the insertion point (Figure 5–40).

Q&A

Will First_Name print when I merge the form letters?

No. When you merge the data source with the main document, the first name (e.g., Milan) will print at the location of the merge field, First_Name.

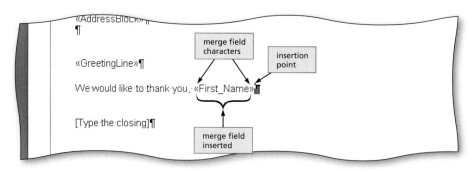

Figure 5–40

Other Ways

1. Click Insert Merge Field button on Mailings tab, click desired field, click Insert button, click Close button

To Enter More Text

The next step is to enter the remainder of the first paragraph and the beginning of the second paragraph.

① With the insertion point at the location shown in Figure 5–40, type a comma, press the SPACEBAR, and then type for being a member of our health club. We hope you are pleased with our state-of-the-art cardiovascular and resistance training equipment and top-notch staff.

② Press the ENTER key. Type Starting today, your experience at Total Fitness Health Club will include several additional amenities to make your visit more complete: and then press the ENTER key (Figure 5–41).

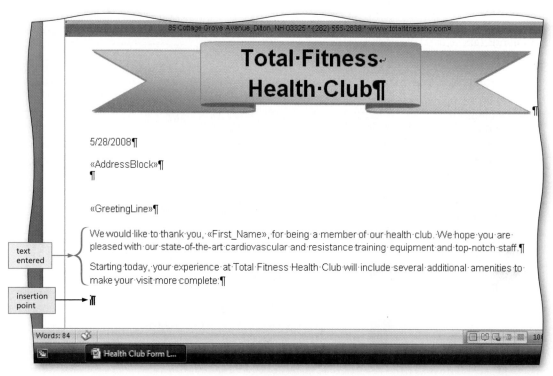

Figure 5–41

To Create a Multilevel List

The next step is to enter a multilevel list in the form letter (shown in Figure 5–1a on page WD 307). A **multilevel list** is a list that contains several levels of items, with each level displaying a different numeric, alphabetic, or bullet symbol.

To ensure that no existing formatting will affect the multilevel list, the first step in creating the list is to clear formatting. The following steps create a multilevel list.

1
- Scroll to display the insertion point higher in the document window.

- Display the Home tab and then click the Clear Formatting button to remove any existing formatting.

- Click the Multilevel List button on the Home tab to display the Multilevel List gallery.

- Position the mouse pointer in the second style in the first row in the List Library area to see a preview of the style (Figure 5–42).

 Experiment
- Point to various list styles in the gallery to see the list style previews.

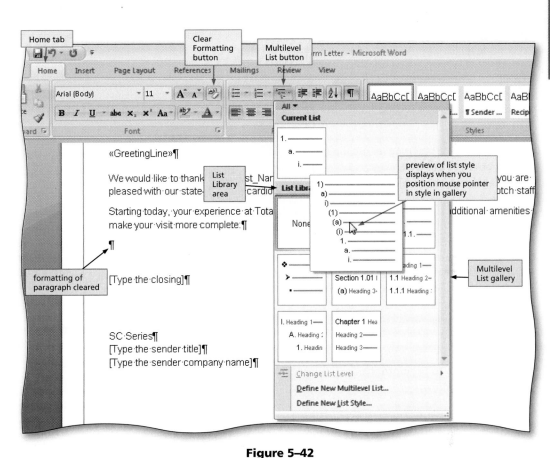

Figure 5–42

2
- Click the desired list style (second style in the first row in List Library area) to apply the selected multilevel list style to the current paragraph.

- Type `Enhanced Facilities` and then press the ENTER key to enter this first-level list item (Figure 5–43).

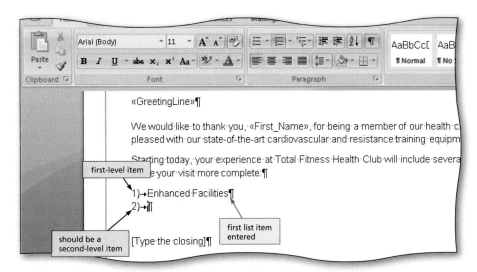

Figure 5–43

3

- Press the TAB key to demote the current list item to a second-level list item that is indented below the first list item.

- Type Now open 24 hours a day, 7 days a week and then press the ENTER key to enter a second-level list item.

- Type New supervised child play center and then press the ENTER key to enter a second-level list item.

- Type New 46' climbing wall and then press the ENTER key to enter a second-level list item (Figure 5–44).

Q&A

Can I adjust the level of a list item after it is typed?

Yes. With the insertion point in the item to adjust, click the Increase Indent or Decrease Indent button on the Home tab, press TAB or SHIFT+TAB, or right-click the list item and then click the desired command on the shortcut menu.

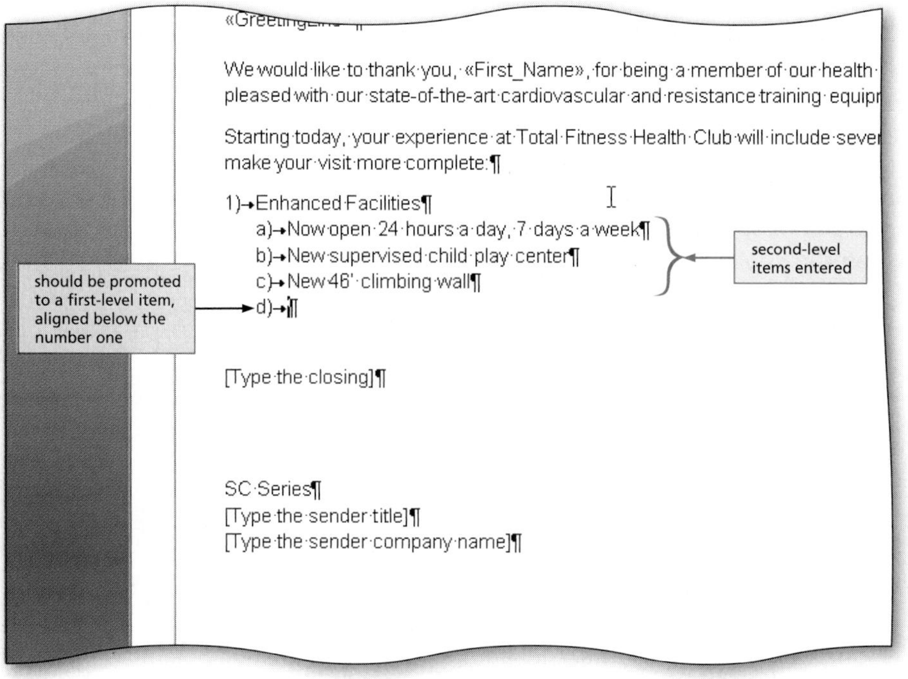

Figure 5–44

4

- Press SHIFT+TAB to promote the current list item.

- Type Expanded Instructional Programs and then press the ENTER key.

- Press the TAB key to demote the current list item, which will be Wellness seminars.

- Type Wellness seminars and then press the ENTER key.

- Type Yoga and Pilates classes and then press the ENTER key.

- Type Nutrition education and then press the ENTER key three times to end the numbered list (Figure 5–45).

Q&A

Why did the automatic numbering stop?

Word turns off automatic numbering when you press the ENTER key without entering text next to a numbered or bulleted list item. Another way to stop automatic numbering is to click the Numbering button on the Home tab.

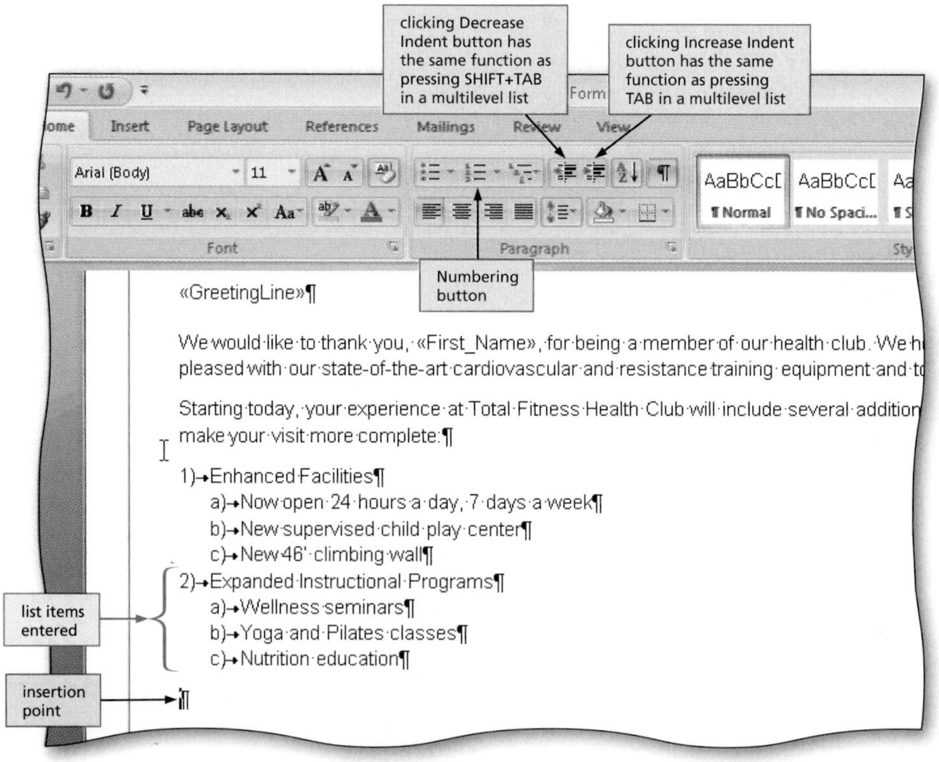

Figure 5–45

To Enter More Text and a Merge Field

The next paragraph states the member's membership type, which is a merge field. The following step enters the beginning of the next paragraph with the merge field.

1 Type We strive to provide the highest quality amenities to our members. To continue to achieve this service level, we must raise our monthly fees effective July 1. As a member on the **and then press the** SPACEBAR.

2 Display the Mailings tab. Click the Insert Merge Field button arrow on the Mailings tab and then click Membership_Type on the Insert Merge Field menu.

3 Press the SPACEBAR and then type Plan, your new monthly rate will be **and then press the** SPACEBAR.

IF Fields

In addition to merge fields, you can insert Word fields that are designed specifically for a mail merge. An **IF field** is an example of a Word field. One form of the IF field is called an **If...Then:** If a condition is true, then perform an action. For example, If Mary owns a house, then send her information about homeowner's insurance. Another form of the IF field is called an **If...Then...Else:** If a condition is true, then perform an action; else perform a different action. For example, If John has an e-mail address, then send him an e-mail message; else send him the message via the postal service.

In this project, the form letter checks the club member's membership type. If the membership type is Standard, then the new monthly rate is $75; else if the membership type is Premium, then the new monthly rate is $105. Thus, you will use an If...Then... Else: If the membership type is equal to Standard, then print $75 on the form letter, else print $105.

The phrase that appears after the word If is called a rule or a condition. A **condition** consists of an expression, followed by a comparison operator, followed by a final expression.

Expression The expression in a condition can be a merge field, a number, a series of characters, or a mathematical formula. Word surrounds a series of characters with quotation marks ("). To indicate an empty, or null, expression, Word places two quotation marks together ("").

Comparison Operator The comparison operator in a condition must be one of six characters: = (equal to or matches the text), <> (not equal to or does not match text), < (less than), <= (less than or equal to), > (greater than), >= (greater than or equal to).

If the result of a condition is true, then Word evaluates the **true text**. If the result of the condition is false, Word evaluates the **false text** if it exists. In this project, the first expression in the condition is a merge field (Membership_Type); the comparison operator is equal to (=); and the second expression is the text "Standard". The true text is "$75". The false text is "$105". The complete IF field is as follows:

IF Membership_Type = "Standard"   "$75"   "$105"

condition   true text   false text

To Insert an IF Field in the Main Document

The following steps insert this IF field in the form letter: If the membership type is Standard, then the new monthly rate is $75; else if the membership type is Premium, then the new monthly rate is $105.

1

- With the insertion point positioned as shown in Figure 5–46, click the Rules button on the Mailings tab to display the Rules menu (Figure 5–46).

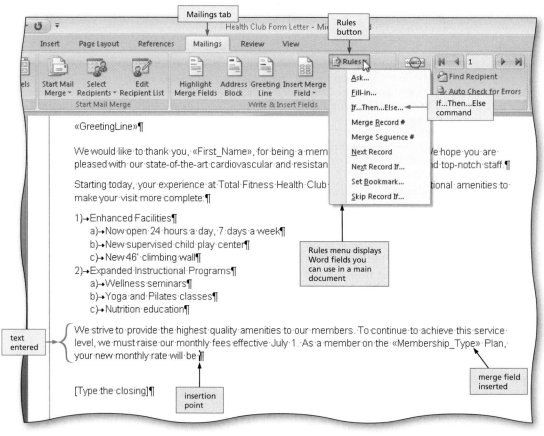

Figure 5–46

2

- Click If...Then...Else on the Rules menu to display the Insert Word Field: IF dialog box (Figure 5–47).

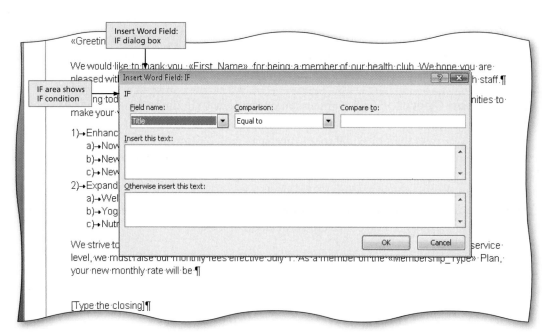

Figure 5–47

- Click the Field name box arrow to display the list of fields in the data source.

- Scroll through the list of fields in the Field name list and then click Membership_Type.

- Position the insertion point in the Compare to text box and then type `Standard` as the comparison text.

- Press the TAB key and then type `$75` as the true text.

- Press the TAB key and then type `$105` as the false text (Figure 5–48).

Q&A Does the capitalization matter in the comparison text?

Yes. The text, Standard, is different from the text, standard, in a comparison. Be sure to enter the text exactly as you entered it in the data source.

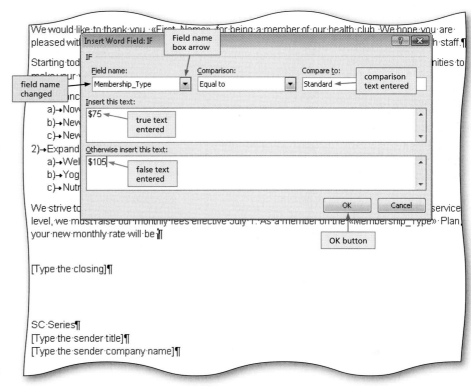

Figure 5–48

- Click the OK button to insert the IF field at the location of the insertion point (Figure 5–49).

Q&A Why does the main document display $75 instead of the IF field instructions?

The $75 is displayed because the first record in the data source has a membership type of Standard. Word, by default, evaluates the IF field using the current record and displays the results, called the **field results**, in the main document instead of displaying the IF field instructions. Later in the chapter, you will view the IF field instructions.

b)→New super...
c)→New 46' climbing wall¶
2)→Expanded Instructional Programs¶
    a)→Wellness seminars¶
    b)→Yoga and Pilates classes¶
    c)→Nutrition education¶

We strive to provide the highest quality amenities to our members. To continue to achieve this service level, we must raise our monthly fees effective July 1. As a member on the «Membership_Type» Plan, your new monthly rate will be $75¶

[Type the closing]¶

insertion point

field results are displayed for entered IF field, instead of IF field instructions

SC Series¶
[Type the sender title]¶
[Type the sender company name]¶

ords: 165   100%

Figure 5–49

BTW

Word Fields

In addition to the IF field, Word provides other fields that may be used in form letters. For example, the ASK and FILLIN fields prompt the user to enter data for each record in the data source. The SKIP RECORD IF field instructs the mail merge not to generate a form letter for a data record if a specific condition is met.

To Enter More Text in Content Controls

The following steps enter the text in the remainder of the form letter.

1. Type a PERIOD and then press the SPACEBAR. Type We appreciate your business and hope you enjoy our club.

2. If necessary, scroll to display the closing and signature block in the document window.

3. Select the closing content control and then type Sincerely, as the closing.

4. Select the sender name content control. (If your sender name content control already displays a name, drag through the name to select it also.) Type Ms. Suzy Zhao as the sender name.

5. Select the sender title content control and then type Fitness Manager as the sender title.

6. Select the sender company name content control and then type Total Fitness Health Club as the sender company name (Figure 5–50).

BTW

Opening Main Document Files

When you open a main document, Word attempts to open the associated data source file too. If the data source is not in the same location (i.e., drive and folder) as it was when it originally was saved, Word may display a dialog box indicating that it could not find the data source. When this occurs, click the Find Data Source button in the dialog box to display the Open Data Source dialog box, which is where you can locate the data source file. If Word does not display a dialog box with the Find Data Source button, then the data source is not associated with the main document. To associate the data source with the main document, click the Select Recipients button on the Mailings tab, click Use Existing List, and then locate the data source file. When you save the main document, Word will associate the data source with the main document.

we would like... ...for being a me... ...hope you are pleased with our state-of-the-art cardiovascular and resistance training equipment and top-notch staff.¶

Starting today, your experience at Total Fitness Health Club will include several additional amenities to make your visit more complete:¶

1)→Enhanced Facilities¶
  a)→Now open 24 hours a day, 7 days a week¶
  b)→New supervised child play center¶
  c)→New 46' climbing wall¶
2)→Expanded Instructional Programs¶
  a)→Wellness seminars¶
  b)→Yoga and Pilates classes¶
  c)→Nutrition education¶

We strive to provide the highest quality amenities to our members. To continue to achieve this service level, we must raise our monthly fees effective July 1. As a member on the «Membership_Type» Plan, your new monthly rate will be $75. We appreciate your business and hope you enjoy our club.¶

closing entered → Sincerely,¶

sender name entered

sender title entered → Ms. Suzy Zhao¶
  Fitness Manager¶

company name entered → Total Fitness Health Club¶

main document for form letter complete

company name content control still selected

Words: 171

Health Club Form L...

Figure 5–50

To Save a Document Again

The main document for the form letter now is complete. Thus, you should save it again.

1. Save the main document for the form letter again with the same file name, Health Club Form Letter.

To Display a Field Code

The instructions in the IF field are not displayed in the document; instead, the field results are displayed for the current record (Figure 5–51). The instructions of an IF field are called as **field codes**, and the default for Word is for field codes not to be displayed. Thus, field codes do not print or show on the screen unless you turn them on. You use one procedure to show field codes on the screen and a different procedure to print them on a hard copy.

You might want to turn on a field code to verify its accuracy or to modify it. Field codes tend to clutter the screen. Thus, most Word users turn them off after viewing them. The following steps show a field code on the screen.

1

- Right-click the dollar amount, $75, to display a shortcut menu (Figure 5–51).

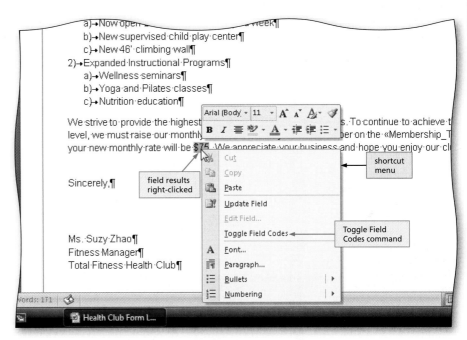

Figure 5–51

2

- Click Toggle Field Codes on the shortcut menu to display the field code instead of the field results for the IF field (Figure 5–52).

Q&A Will displaying field codes affect the merged documents?

No. Displaying field codes has no effect on the merge process.

Q&A What if I wanted to display all field codes in a document?

You would press ALT+F9. Then, to hide all the field codes, press ALT+F9 again.

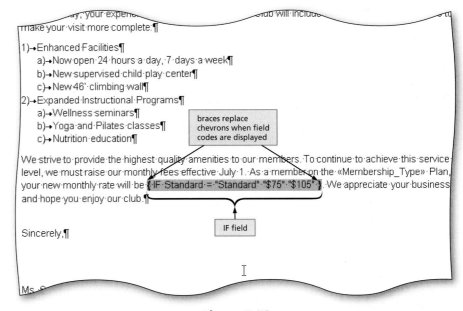

Figure 5–52

Other Ways

1. With insertion point in field, press SHIFT+F9

To Print Field Codes in the Main Document

When you merge or print a document, Word automatically converts field codes that show on the screen to field results. You may want to print the field codes version of the form letter, however, so that you have a hard copy of the field codes for future reference. When you print field codes, you must remember to turn off the field codes option so that merged documents print field results instead of field codes. The following steps print the field codes in the main document and then turn off the print field codes option.

1

- Display the Office Button menu and then click the Word Options button to display the Word Options dialog box.

- Click Advanced in the left pane to display advanced options in the right pane. Scroll to the Print area in the right pane of the dialog box.

- Place a check mark in the 'Print field codes instead of their values' check box (Figure 5–53).

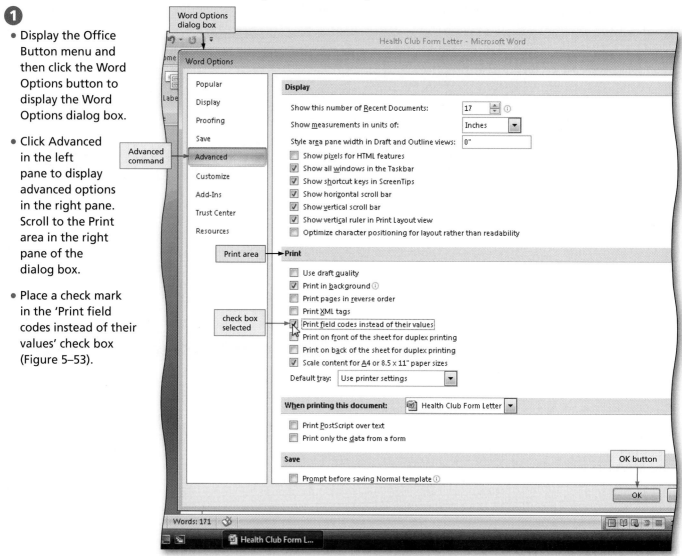

Figure 5–53

2

- Click the OK button to instruct Word to show field codes when the document prints.

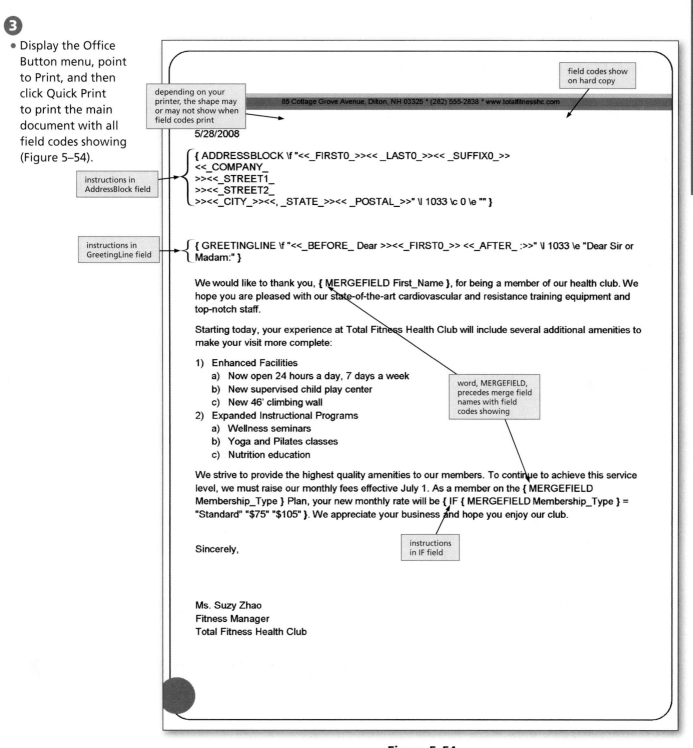

3

- Display the Office Button menu, point to Print, and then click Quick Print to print the main document with all field codes showing (Figure 5–54).

field codes show on hard copy

depending on your printer, the shape may or may not show when field codes print

85 Cottage Grove Avenue, Dilton, NH 03325 * (282) 555-2838 * www.totalfitnesshc.com

5/28/2008

instructions in AddressBlock field

{ ADDRESSBLOCK \f "<<_FIRST0_>><< _LAST0_>><< _SUFFIX0_>>
<<_COMPANY_
>><<_STREET1_
>><<_STREET2_
>><<_CITY_>><<, _STATE_>><< _POSTAL_>>" \l 1033 \c 0 \e "" }

instructions in GreetingLine field

{ GREETINGLINE \f "<<_BEFORE_ Dear >><<_FIRST0_>> <<_AFTER_ :>>" \l 1033 \e "Dear Sir or Madam:" }

We would like to thank you, { MERGEFIELD First_Name }, for being a member of our health club. We hope you are pleased with our state-of-the-art cardiovascular and resistance training equipment and top-notch staff.

Starting today, your experience at Total Fitness Health Club will include several additional amenities to make your visit more complete:

1) Enhanced Facilities
   a) Now open 24 hours a day, 7 days a week
   b) New supervised child play center
   c) New 46' climbing wall
2) Expanded Instructional Programs
   a) Wellness seminars
   b) Yoga and Pilates classes
   c) Nutrition education

word, MERGEFIELD, precedes merge field names with field codes showing

We strive to provide the highest quality amenities to our members. To continue to achieve this service level, we must raise our monthly fees effective July 1. As a member on the { MERGEFIELD Membership_Type } Plan, your new monthly rate will be { IF { MERGEFIELD Membership_Type } = "Standard" "$75" "$105" }. We appreciate your business and hope you enjoy our club.

instructions in IF field

Sincerely,

Ms. Suzy Zhao
Fitness Manager
Total Fitness Health Club

Figure 5–54

4

- Display the Office Button menu and then click the Word Options button to display the Word Options dialog box.

- Click Advanced in the left pane to display advanced options in the right pane. Scroll to the Print area in the right pane of the dialog box.

- Remove the check mark in the 'Print field codes instead of their values' check box.

- Click the OK button to instruct Word to print field results the next time you print.

To Merge the Form Letters to the Printer

The data source and main document for the form letter are complete. The next step is to merge them to generate the individual form letters. The following steps merge the form letters, sending the merged letters to the printer.

- Click the Finish & Merge button on the Mailings tab to display the Finish & Merge menu (Figure 5–55).

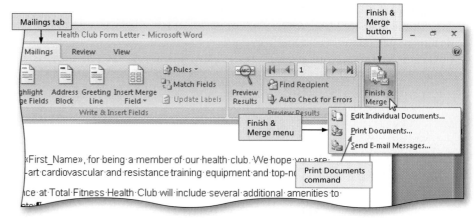

Figure 5–55

- Click Print Documents to display the Merge to Printer dialog box.

- If necessary, click All to select it (Figure 5–56).

Q&A

Do I have to merge all records?

No. Through this dialog box you can merge the current record or a range of record numbers.

❸

- Click the OK button to display the Print dialog box.

- Click the OK button in the Print dialog box to print five separate letters, one for each club member in the data source, as shown in Figure 5–1c on page WD 307. (If Word displays a message about locked fields, click its OK button.)

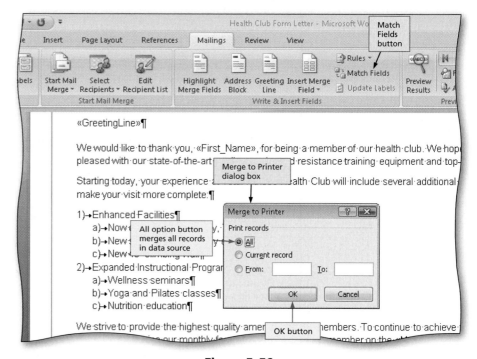

Figure 5–56

Correcting Errors in Merged Documents

If you notice errors in the printed form letters, edit the main document the same way you edit any other document. Then, save the changes and merge again. If the wrong field results print, Word may be mapping the fields incorrectly. To view fields, click the Match Fields button on the Mailings tab (Figure 5–56). Then, review the list of fields in the list. For example, the Last Name should map to the Last Name field in the data source. If it does not, click the box arrow to change the name of the data source field.

To Merge to a New Document Window

Instead of immediately printing the merged form letters, you could send them to a new document window, where you can view the merged form letters on the screen to verify their accuracy before printing them. When you are finished viewing the merged form letters, you can print them as you print any other Word document.

In addition, you can edit the contents of individual merged letters. You also can save the merged form letters in a file or close the document window without saving them.

If you wanted to merge to a new document window, you would perform the following steps.

1. Click the Finish & Merge button on the Mailings tab and then click Edit Individual Documents to display the Merge to New Document dialog box.

2. Click All.

3. Click the OK button to merge the form letters to a new document window.

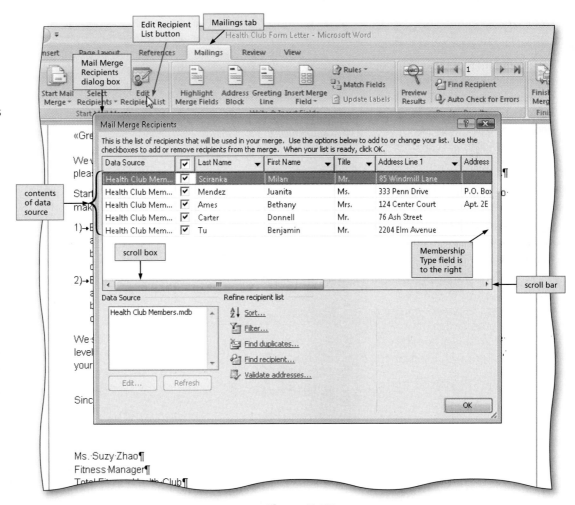

BTW

Locking Fields
If you wanted to lock a field so that its field results cannot be changed, click the field and then press CTRL+F11. To subsequently unlock a field so that it may be updated, click the field and then press CTRL+SHIFT+F11.

To Select Records to Merge

Instead of merging and printing all of the records in the data source, you can choose which records will merge, based on a condition you specify. The dialog box in Figure 5–56 allows you to specify by record number which records to merge. Often you merge based on the contents of a specific field. For example, you may want to merge and print only those club members whose membership type is Premium. The following steps select records for a merge.

1

• Click the Edit Recipient List button on the Mailings tab to display the Mail Merge Recipients dialog box (Figure 5–57).

Figure 5–57

2

- Drag the scroll box to the right edge of the scroll bar in the Mail Merge Recipients dialog box so that the Membership Type field appears in the dialog box.

- Click the box arrow to the right of the field name, Membership Type, to display sort and filter criteria for the Membership Type field (Figure 5–58).

Q&A

What are the filter criteria in the parenthesis?

The (All) option clears any previously set filter criteria. The (Blanks) option selects records that contain blanks in that field, and the (Nonblanks) option selects records that do not contain blanks in that field. The (Advanced) option displays the Filter and Sort dialog box, which allows you to perform more advanced record selection operations.

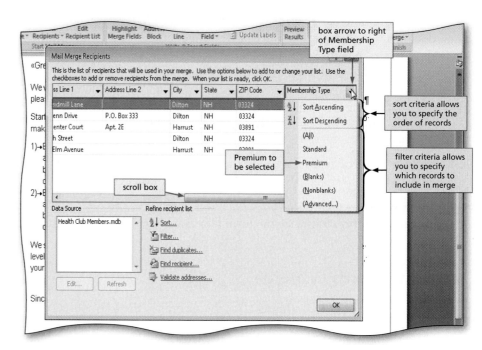

Figure 5–58

3

- Click Premium to reduce the number of data records displayed in the Mail Merge Recipients dialog box to two, because two club members have a membership type of Premium (Figure 5–59).

- Click the OK button to close the Mail Merge Recipients dialog box.

Q&A

What happened to the other three records that did not meet the criteria?

They still are part of the data source, just not appearing in the Mail Merge Recipients dialog box. When you clear the filter, all records will reappear.

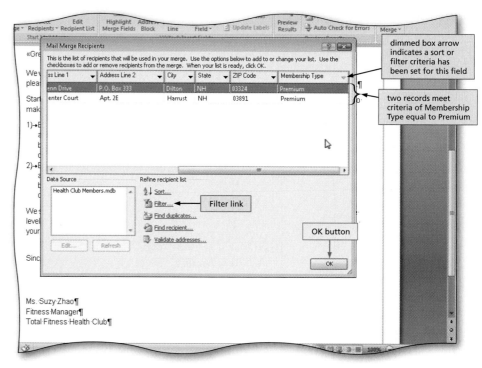

Figure 5–59

Other Ways

1. Click Filter link in Mail Merge Recipients dialog box, click Filter Records tab, enter filter criteria, click OK button

To Merge the Form Letters to the Printer

The next step is to merge the selected records. To do this, you follow the same steps described earlier. The difference is that Word will merge only those records that meet the criteria specified, that is, just those with a membership type of Premium.

1 Click the Finish & Merge button on the Mailings tab to display the Finish & Merge menu.

2 Click Print Documents to display the Merge to Printer dialog box. If necessary, click All in the dialog box.

3 Click the OK button to display the Print dialog box.

4 Click the OK button in the Print dialog box to print two separate letters, one for each club member whose membership type is Premium (Figure 5–60). (If Word displays a message about locked fields, click its OK button.)

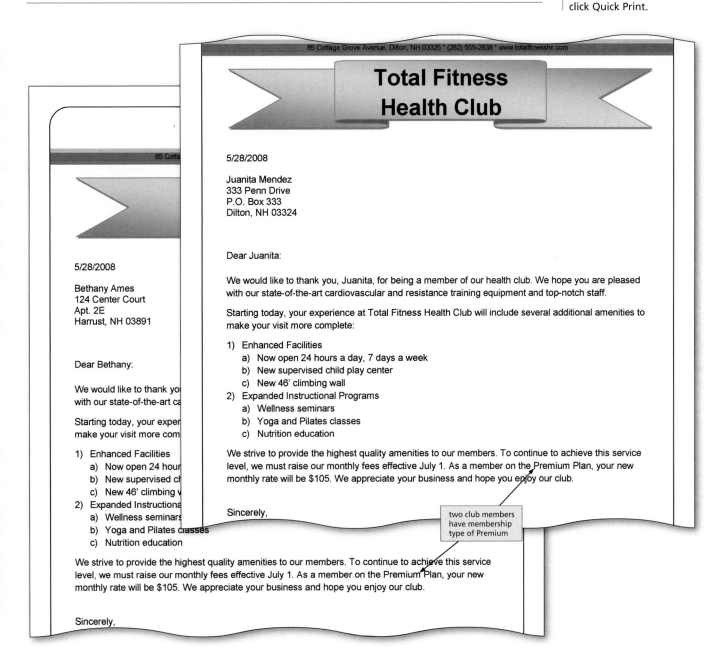

Figure 5–60

To Remove a Merge Condition

You should remove the merge condition so that future merges will not be restricted to club members with a membership type of Premium.

1 Click the Edit Recipient List button on the Mailings tab to display the Mail Merge Recipients dialog box.

2 Click the Filter link in the dialog box (shown in Figure 5–59 on page WD 346) to display the Filter and Sort dialog box.

3 If necessary, click the Filter Records tab.

4 Click the Clear All button in the dialog box. Click the OK button in each of the two open dialog boxes.

To Sort the Data Records in a Data Source

If you mail the form letters using the U.S. Postal Service's bulk rate mailing service, the post office requires that you sort and group the form letters by ZIP code. Thus, the following steps sort the data records by ZIP code.

1

- Click the Edit Recipient List button on the Mailings tab to display the Mail Merge Recipients dialog box.

- Scroll to the right until the ZIP Code field shows in the dialog box.

- Position the mouse pointer on the ZIP Code field name (Figure 5–61).

BTW

Validating Addresses
If you have installed address validation software, you can click the Validate addresses link in the Mail Merge Recipients dialog box to validate your recipients' addresses. If you would like information about installing address validation software and have not yet installed the software, click the Validate addresses link in the Mail Merge Recipients dialog box and then click the Yes button in the Microsoft Office Word dialog box to display a related Microsoft Office Web page.

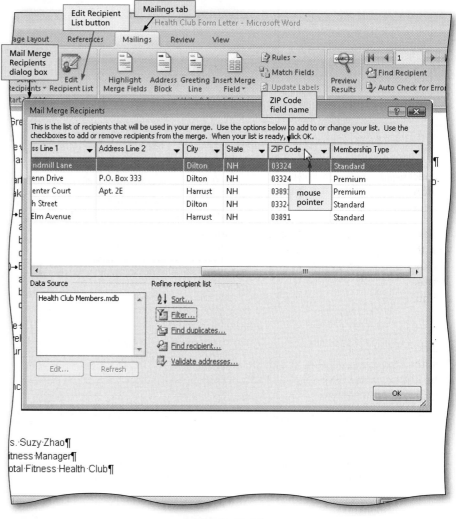

Figure 5–61

2

- Click the ZIP Code field name to sort the data source records in ascending (smallest to largest) order by ZIP Code (Figure 5–62).

- Click the OK button to close the Mail Merge Recipients dialog box.

In what order would the form letters print if I merged them again now?

Word would print them in ZIP code order; that is, the records with ZIP Code 03324 would print first, and the records with ZIP Code 03891 would print last.

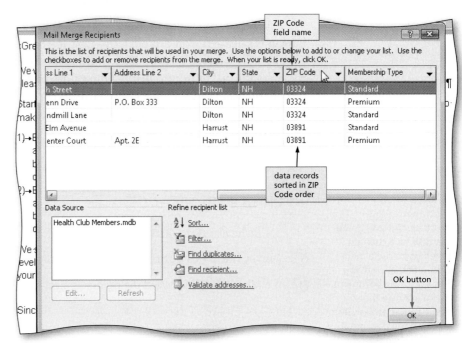

Figure 5–62

To View Merged Data in the Main Document

You can verify the order of the data records without printing them by viewing field results instead of merge fields. The following steps view merged data.

1

- If necessary, scroll up to display the AddressBlock merge field in the document window.

- Click the View Merged Data button on the Mailings tab to display the values in the first data record, instead of the merge fields (Figure 5–63).

2

- Click the View Merged Data button on the Mailings tab again to display the merge fields in the main document, instead of the field values.

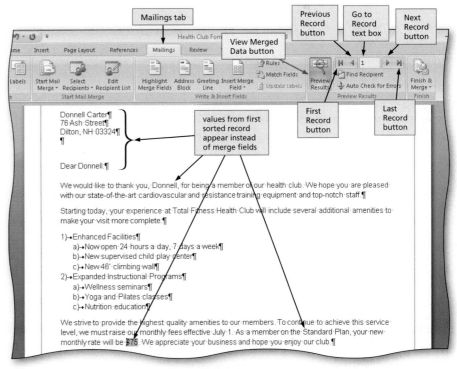

Figure 5–63

Displaying Data Source Records in the Main Document

When you are viewing merged data in the main document (the View Merged Data button is selected), you can click the Last Record button (Figure 5–63 on the previous page) on the Mailings tab to display the values from the last record in the data source, the First Record button to display the values in record one, the Next Record button to display the values in the next consecutive record number, or the Previous Record button to display the values from the previous record number. You also can display a specific record by clicking the Go to Record text box, typing the record number you would like to be displayed in the main document, and then pressing the ENTER key.

To Close a Document

The health club form letter is complete. Thus, the next step is to close the document.

1 Display the Office Button menu and then click Close.

2 If a Microsoft Office Word dialog box is displayed, click the Yes button to save the changes.

Addressing and Printing Mailing Labels and Envelopes

Now that you have merged and printed the form letters, the next step is to print addresses on mailing labels to be affixed to envelopes for the form letters. The mailing labels will use the same data source as the form letter, Health Club Members. The format and content of the mailing labels will be exactly the same as the inside address in the main document for the form letter. That is, the first line will contain the club member's title and first name followed by the last name. The second line will contain his or her street address, and so on. Thus, you will use the AddressBlock merge field in the mailing labels.

Plan Ahead

> **Generate mailing labels and envelopes.**
> An envelope should contain the sender's full name and address in the upper-left corner of the envelope. It also should contain the addressee's full name and address, positioned approximately in the vertical and horizontal center of the envelope. The address can be typed directly on the envelope or on a mailing label that is affixed to the envelope.

You follow the same basic steps to create the main document for the mailing labels as you did to create the main document for the form letters. The major difference is that the data source already exists because you created it earlier in this project.

To Address and Print Mailing Labels Using an Existing Data Source

To address mailing labels, you specify the type of labels you intend to use. Word will request the label information, including the label vendor and product number. You can obtain this information from the box of labels. For illustration purposes in addressing these labels, the label vendor is Avery and the product number is J8158. The next steps address and print mailing labels using an existing data source.

1

- Display the Office Button menu. Click New on the Office Button menu to display the New Document dialog box. With Blank document selected, click the Create button to open a new blank document window.

- Display the Mailings tab.

- Click the Start Mail Merge button on the Mailings tab and then click Step by Step Mail Merge Wizard to display Step 1 of the Mail Merge wizard in the Mail Merge task pane.

- Specify labels as the main document type by clicking Labels in the 'Select document type' area (Figure 5–64).

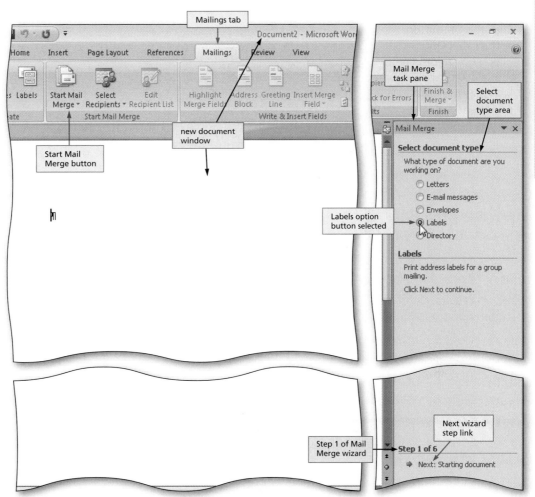

Figure 5–64

2

- Click the 'Next wizard step' link at the bottom of the Mail Merge task pane to display Step 2 of the Mail Merge wizard.

- In the Mail Merge task pane, click the 'Select label size' link to display the Label Options dialog box.

- Select the label vendor and product number (in this case, Avery A4/A5 and J8158), as shown in Figure 5–65.

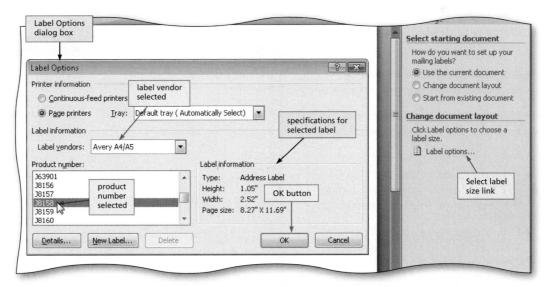

Figure 5–65

3

- Click the OK button in the Label Options dialog box to display the selected label layout as the main document (Figure 5–66).

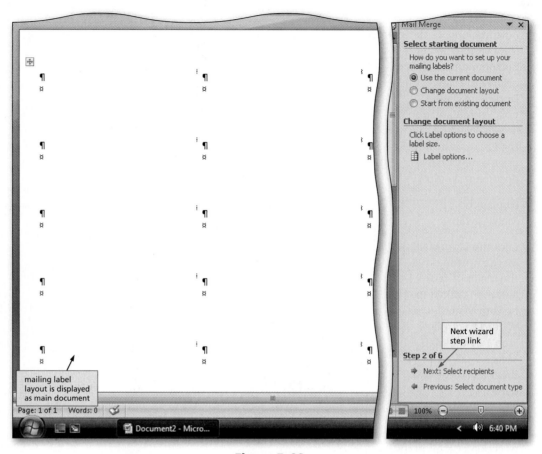

Figure 5–66

4

- Click the 'Next wizard step' link at the bottom of the Mail Merge task pane to display Step 3 of the Mail Merge wizard, which allows you to select the data source.

- If necessary, click 'Use an existing list' in the Select recipients area.

- Click the 'Select recipient list file' link to display the Select Data Source dialog box.

- If necessary, locate and select the USB flash drive and then double-click the Total Fitness folder to select it.

- Click the file name, Health Club Members, to select the data source you created earlier in the chapter (Figure 5–67).

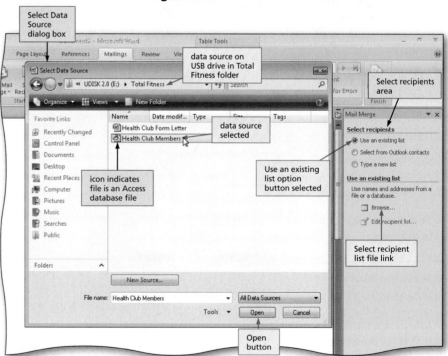

Figure 5–67

Q&A

Why did Word initially open the All Data Sources folder in the Select Data Source dialog box?

The All Data Sources folder is the default folder for storing data source files. Word looks in that folder first for an existing data source.

5

- Click the Open button to display the Mail Merge Recipients dialog box (Figure 5–68).

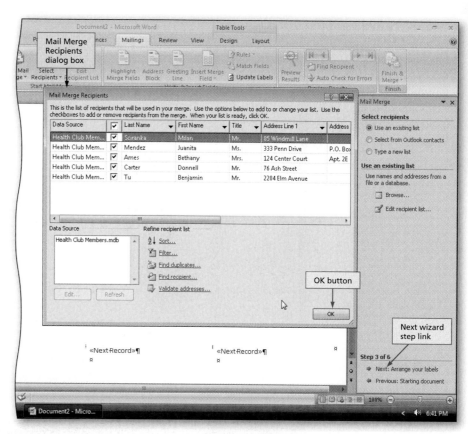

Figure 5–68

6

- Click the OK button to close the dialog box.

- At the bottom of the Mail Merge task pane, click the 'Next wizard step' link to display Step 4 of the Mail Merge wizard in the Mail Merge task pane.

- In the Mail Merge task pane, click the 'Insert formatted address' link to display the Insert Address Block dialog box (Figure 5–69).

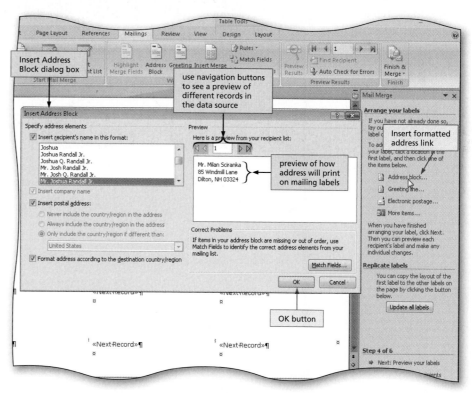

Figure 5–69

• Click the OK button to close the dialog box and insert the AddressBlock mail merge field in the first label of the main document (Figure 5–70).

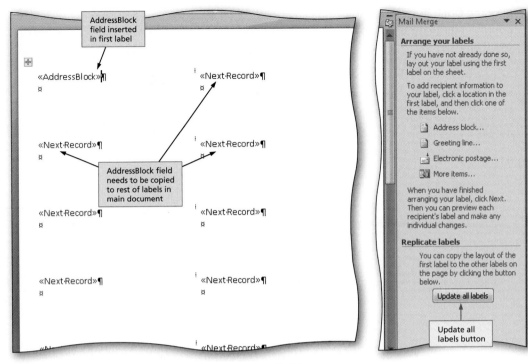

Figure 5–70

• Click the 'Update all labels' button to copy the layout of the first label to the remaining label layouts in the main document (Figure 5–71).

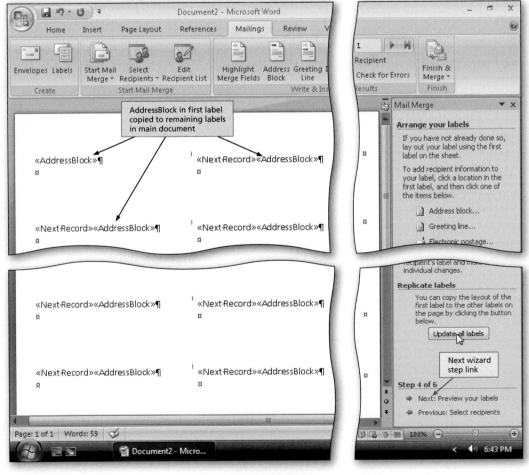

Figure 5–71

9

- Click the 'Next wizard step' link at the bottom of the Mail Merge task pane to display Step 5 of the Mail Merge wizard, which shows a preview of the mailing labels in the document window (Figure 5–72).

What if I do not want a blank space between each line in the printed mailing addresses?

You would select all the mailing labels by pressing CTRL+A and then change the Spacing Before to 0 pt on the Page Layout tab.

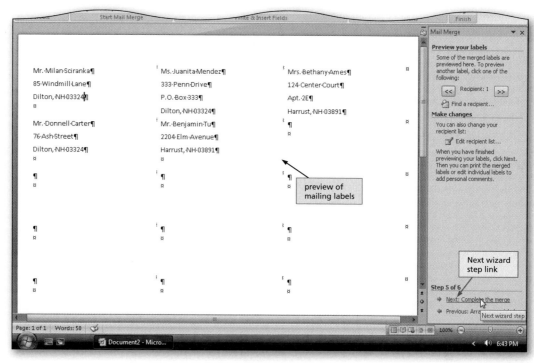

Figure 5–72

10

- Click the 'Next wizard step' link at the bottom of the Mail Merge task pane to display Step 6 of the Mail Merge wizard.

- In the Mail Merge task pane, click the 'Merge to printer' link to display the Merge to Printer dialog box (Figure 5–73).

- If necessary, click All in the dialog box so that all records in the data source will be included in the merge.

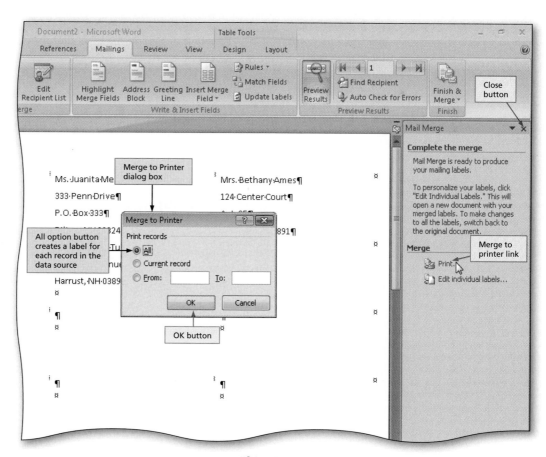

Figure 5–73

- If necessary, insert a sheet of blank mailing labels in the printer.

- Click the OK button to display the Print dialog box.

- Click the OK button in the Print dialog box to print the mailing labels (Figure 5–74).

- Click the Close button at the right edge of the Mail Merge task pane.

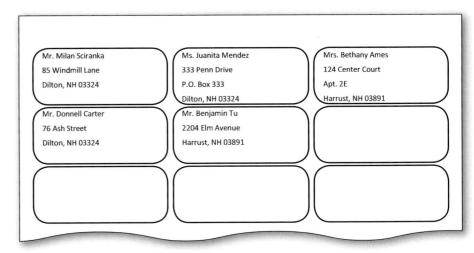

Figure 5–74

To Save the Mailing Labels

The following steps save the mailing labels.

1. With a USB flash drive connected to one of the computer's USB ports, click the Save button on the Quick Access Toolbar to display the Save As dialog box.

2. Type `Health Club Mailing Labels` in the File name text box to change the file name.

3. If necessary, locate and select your USB flash drive in the list of available drives and then double-click the Total Fitness folder to open the folder.

4. Click the Save button in the Save As dialog box to save the document in the Total Fitness folder on the USB flash drive with the file name, Health Club Mailing Labels.

To Address and Print Envelopes Using an Existing Data Source

Instead of addressing mailing labels to affix to envelopes, your printer may have the capability of printing directly on envelopes. To print the address information directly on envelopes, follow the same basic steps as you did to address the mailing labels. The following steps address envelopes using an existing data source.

Note: If your printer does not have the capability of printing envelopes, skip these steps and proceed to the next section titled, Merging All Data Records to a Directory. If you are in a laboratory environment, ask your instructor if you should perform these steps or skip them.

1. Display the Office Button menu. Click New on the Office Button menu to display the New Document dialog box. With Blank document selected, click the Create button to open a new blank document window.

2 Click the Start Mail Merge button on the Mailings tab and then click Step by Step Mail Merge Wizard to display Step 1 of the Mail Merge wizard in the Mail Merge task pane. Specify envelopes as the main document type by clicking Envelopes in the 'Select document type' area.

3 Click the 'Next wizard step' link at the bottom of the Mail Merge task pane to display Step 2 of the Mail Merge wizard. In the Mail Merge task pane, click the Set Envelope Options link to display the Envelope Options dialog box.

4 Select the envelope size and then click the OK button in the Envelope Options dialog box, which displays the selected envelope layout as the main document.

5 If your envelope does not have a pre-printed return address, position the insertion point in the upper-left corner of the envelope layout and then type a return address.

6 Click the 'Next wizard step' link at the bottom of the Mail Merge task pane to display Step 3 of the Mail Merge wizard, which allows you to select the data source. If necessary, click 'Use an existing list' in the Select recipients area. Click the 'Select recipient list file' link to display the Select Data Source dialog box. If necessary, locate and select the USB flash drive and then double-click the Total Fitness folder to select it. Click the file name, Health Club Members, to select the data source you created earlier in the chapter. Click the Open button, which displays the Mail Merge Recipients dialog box, and then click the OK button to close the dialog box. At the bottom of the Mail Merge task pane, click the 'Next wizard step' link to display Step 4 of the Mail Merge wizard in the Mail Merge task pane.

7 Position the insertion point in the middle of the envelope. In the Mail Merge task pane, click the 'Insert formatted address' link to display the Insert Address Block dialog box. Click the OK button to close the dialog box and insert the AddressBlock mail merge field in the envelope layout of the main document (Figure 5–75).

8 Click the 'Next wizard step' link at the bottom of the Mail Merge task pane to display Step 5 of the Mail Merge wizard, which shows a preview of an envelope in the document window.

9 Click the 'Next wizard step' link at the bottom of the Mail Merge task pane to display Step 6 of the Mail Merge wizard. In the Mail Merge task pane, click the 'Merge to printer' link to display the Merge to Printer dialog box. If necessary, click All in the dialog box so that all records in the data source will be included in the merge.

10 If necessary, insert blank envelopes in the printer. Click the OK button to display the Print dialog box. Click the OK button in the Print dialog box to print the address on the envelopes. Click the Close button at the right edge of the Mail Merge task pane.

BTW

AddressBlock Merge Field
Another way to insert the AddressBlock merge field in a document is to click the Address Block button on the Mailings tab.

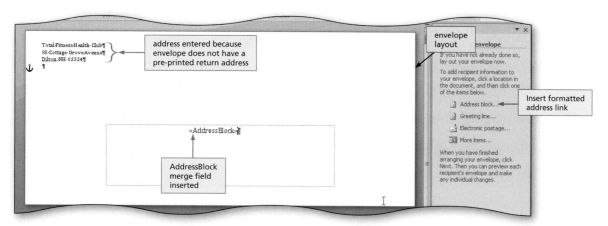

Figure 5–75

To Save the Envelopes

The following steps save the envelopes.

1 With a USB flash drive connected to one of the computer's USB ports, click the Save button on the Quick Access Toolbar to display the Save As dialog box.

2 Type `Health Club Envelopes` in the File name text box to change the file name.

3 If necessary, locate and select your USB flash drive in the list of available drives and then double-click the Total Fitness folder to open the folder.

4 Click the Save button in the Save As dialog box to save the document in the Total Fitness folder on the USB flash drive with the file name, Health Club Envelopes.

Merging All Data Records to a Directory

You may want to print the data records in the data source. Recall that the data source is saved as a Microsoft Access database table. Thus, you cannot open the data source in Word. To view the data source, you click the Edit Recipient List button on the Mailings tab, which displays the Mail Merge Recipients dialog box. This dialog box, however, does not have a Print button.

When you merge to a directory, the default organization of a directory places each record one after next, similar to the look of entries in a telephone book. The directory in this chapter is more organized with the rows and columns divided and field names placed above each column (shown in Figure 5–1b on page WD 307). To accomplish this look, the following steps are required:

1. Create a directory, placing a separating character between each merge field.
2. Convert the directory to a table, using the separator character as the identifier for each new column.
3. Change the page orientation from portrait to landscape, so that all records fit across one row.
4. Merge the directory to a new document, which creates a table of all records in the data source.
5. Format the table containing the directory.
6. Sort the table by last name, so that it is easy to locate a particular record.

To Merge to a Directory

One way to print the contents of the data source is to merge all data records in the data source into a single document, called a **directory**. That is, a directory does not merge each data record to a separate document; instead, a directory lists all records together in a single document. The next steps merge the data records in the data source to a directory. For illustration purposes, these steps use the buttons on the Mailings tab rather than using the Mail Merge task pane.

- Display the Office Button menu and then click New to display the New Document dialog box. With Blank document selected, click the Create button to open a new blank document window.

- Display the Mailings tab.

- Click the Start Mail Merge button on the Mailings tab to display the Start Mail Merge menu (Figure 5–76).

2

- Click Directory as the main document type.

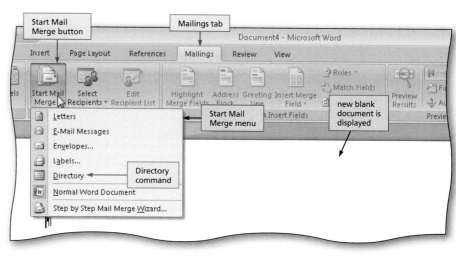

Figure 5–76

3

- Click the Select Recipients button on the Mailings tab to display the Select Recipients menu (Figure 5–77).

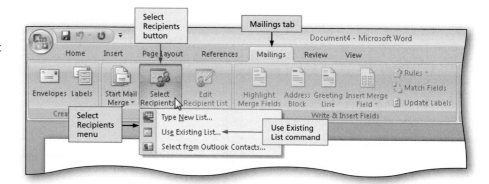

Figure 5–77

4

- Click Use Existing List on the Select Recipients menu to display the Select Data Source dialog box.

- If necessary, locate and select the USB flash drive and then double-click the Total Fitness folder to select it.

- Click the file name, Health Club Members, to select the data source you created earlier in the chapter (Figure 5–78).

5

- Click the Open button to associate the selected data source with the current main document.

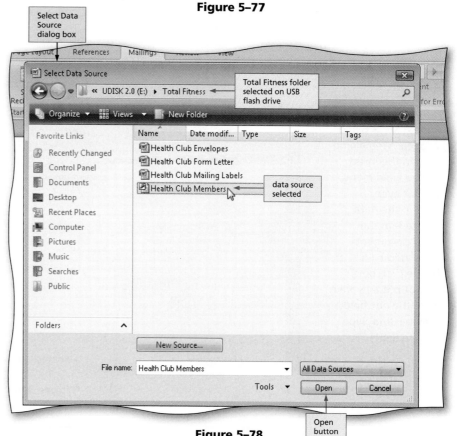

Figure 5–78

- Click the Insert Merge Field button arrow on the Mail Merge toolbar to display the Insert Merge Field menu (Figure 5–79).

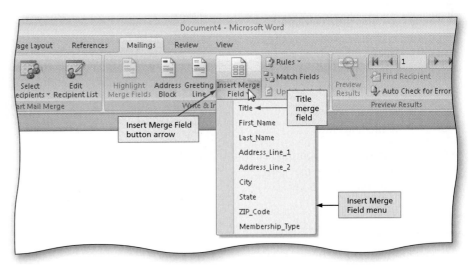

Figure 5–79

- Click Title on the Insert Merge Field menu to insert the merge field in the document.

- Press the HYPHEN (-) key to place the hyphen character after the inserted merge field (Figure 5–80).

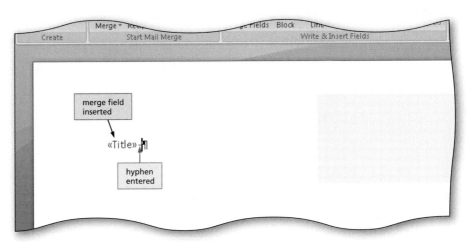

Figure 5–80

- Repeat Steps 6 and 7 for each remaining field in the Insert Merge Field menu, so that every field in the data source is in the main document separated by a hyphen, except do not put a hyphen after the last field: Membership_Type (Figure 5–81).

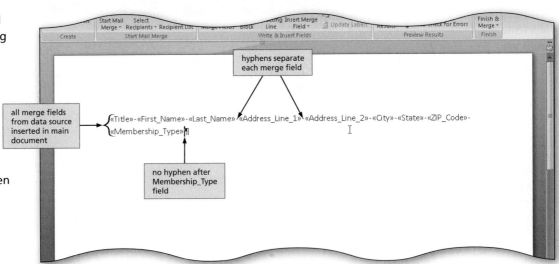

Figure 5–81

To Convert Text to a Table

If you merge the records now, they will print in one long list, one record below the next. Instead of a long list, you want each data record to be in a single row and each merge field to be in a column. That is, you want the directory to be in a table form. The following steps convert the text containing the merge fields to a table.

1

- Press CTRL+A to select the entire document, because you want all document contents to be converted to a table.

- Display the Insert tab.

- Click the Table button on the Insert tab to display the Table gallery (Figure 5–82).

Can I convert a section of a document to table?

Yes, simply select the characters, lines, or paragraphs to be converted before displaying the Convert Text to Table dialog box.

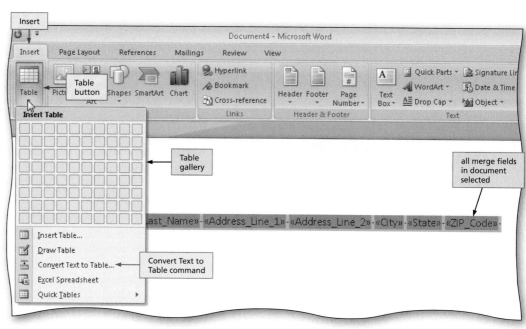

Figure 5–82

2

- Click Convert Text to Table to display the Convert Text to Table dialog box.

- If necessary, type 9 in the Number of columns box because the resulting table should have 9 columns.

- If necessary, click Other in the 'Separate text at' area and then type a hyphen (-) in the text box (Figure 5–83).

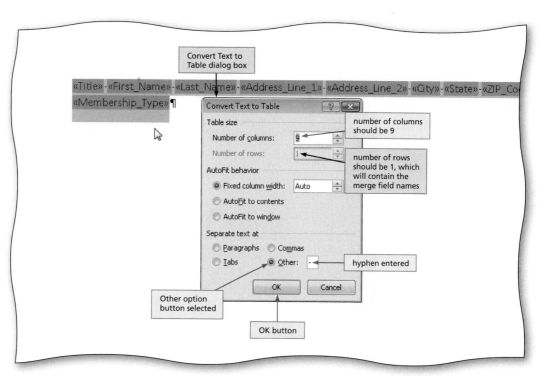

Figure 5–83

3

- Click the OK button to convert the selected text (the merge fields) to a table (Figure 5–84).

Q&A

Can I format the table?

Yes. You can use any of the commands on the Table Tools subordinate tabs to change the look of the table.

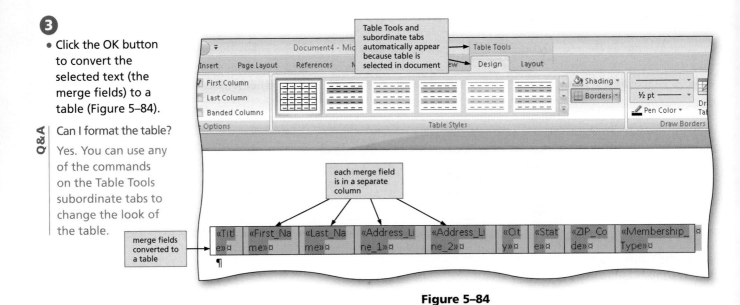

Figure 5–84

To Change Page Orientation

Notice in Figure 5–84 that none of the merge field names fit across the width of their columns. That is, they wrap to a second line. This is because the contents of the cells are too wide to fit on a piece of paper in portrait orientation. When a document is in **portrait orientation**, the short edge of the paper is the top of the document. You can instruct Word to layout a document in **landscape orientation**, so that the long edge of the paper is the top of the document. The following steps change the orientation of the document from portrait to landscape.

1

- Display the Page Layout tab.

- Click the Page Orientation button on the Page Layout tab to display the Page Orientation gallery (Figure 5–85).

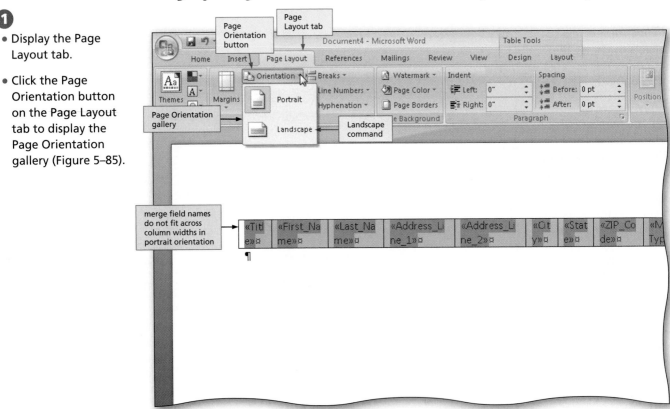

Figure 5–85

2

- Click Landscape in the Page Orientation gallery to change the page orientation to landscape (Figure 5–86).

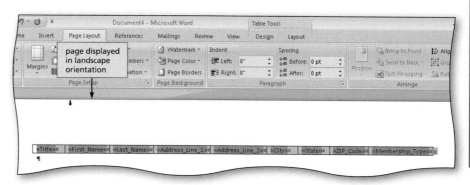

Figure 5–86

To Merge to a New Document Window

The next step is to merge the data source and the directory main document to a new document window, so that you can edit the resulting document. The following steps merge to a new document window.

1

- Display the Mailings tab.

- Click the Finish & Merge button on the Mailings tab to display the Finish & Merge menu (Figure 5–87).

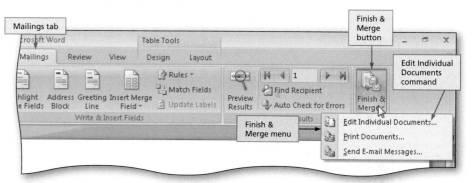

Figure 5–87

2

- Click Edit Individual Documents on the Finish & Merge menu to display the Merge to New Document dialog box.

- If necessary, click All in the dialog box.

- Click the OK button to merge the data records to a directory in a new document window (Figure 5–88).

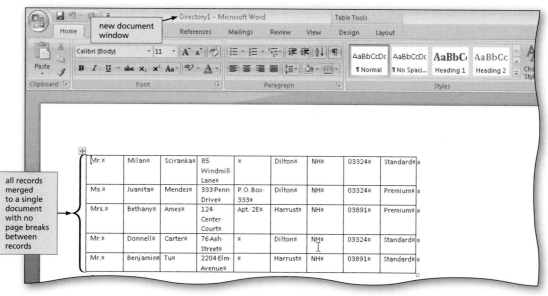

Figure 5–88

To Modify and Format a Table

The table would be more descriptive if the field names were displayed in a row above the actual data. The following steps add a row to the top of a table and format the data in the new row.

1 Add a row to the top of the table by positioning the insertion point in the first row of the table and then clicking the Insert Rows Above button on the Layout tab.

2 Click in the first (leftmost) cell of the new row. Type `Title` and then press the TAB key. Type `First Name` and then press the TAB key. Type `Last Name` and then press the TAB key. Type `Address Line 1` and then press the TAB key. Type `Address Line 2` and then press the TAB key. Type `City` and then press the TAB key. Type `State` and then press the TAB key. Type `ZIP Code` and then press the TAB key. Type `Membership Type` as the last entry in the row.

3 Make all columns as wide as their contents using the AutoFit Contents command.

To Modify Table Properties

The next step is to increase the left and right margin in each cell of the table and place a .05-inch space between each cell, so that the table is easier to read. To make these changes, you use the Table Properties dialog box. You also can center the table between the left and right margins in this dialog box. The following steps use the Table Properties dialog box.

- Click the Table Properties button on the Layout tab to display the Table Properties dialog box.

- Click the Options button to display the Table Options dialog box.

- Click the Left box up arrow until 0.15" is displayed in the Left text box.

- Click the Right box up arrow until 0.15" is displayed in the Right text box.

- Place a check mark in the 'Allow spacing between cells' check box and then click the up arrow until 0.05" is displayed in this text box (Figure 5–89).

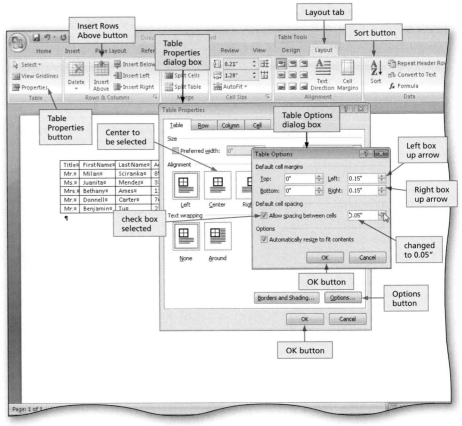

Figure 5–89

2

- Click the OK button to close the Table Options dialog box.
- Click Center in the Alignment area.
- Click the OK button to apply the modified properties to the table (Figure 5–90).

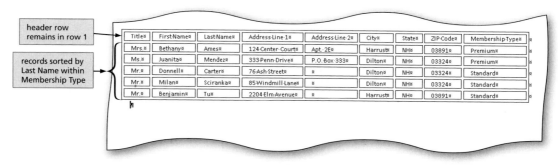

Figure 5–90

Other Ways

1. Right-click table, click Table Properties on shortcut menu

To Sort a Table

The next step is to sort the table. In this project, the table records are displayed in membership type order. Within each membership type, the records should be sorted by club member last name. The following steps sort a table.

1

- Click the Sort button on the Layout tab (shown in Figure 5–89) to display the Sort dialog box.
- Click Header row so that the first row is left in its current location when the table is sorted.
- Click the Sort by box arrow; scroll to and then click Membership Type.
- Click the first Then by box arrow and then click Last Name (Figure 5–91).

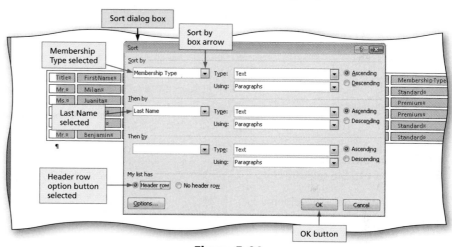

Figure 5–91

2

- Click the OK button to sort the records in the table in ascending Last Name order within ascending Membership Type order (Figure 5–92).

Q&A

What does ascending mean?

With the Last Name and Membership Type data, ascending means alphabetical. With the dates, ascending means the earliest date is at the top of the list, and for numbers, ascending order puts the smallest numbers first.

Figure 5–92

To Format Text as Hidden

You want to add a note to the top of this table, but do not want the note to print. To do this, you format the text as hidden. The following steps enter text and then format it as hidden.

- Click in the top-left corner of the table and then press the ENTER key to position the insertion point on a blank line above the table.

- **Type** Table last updated on May 28.

- Select the text just entered above the table.

- Click Font Dialog Box Launcher to display the Font dialog box. If necessary, click the Font tab.

- In the Effects area, click Hidden (Figure 5–93).

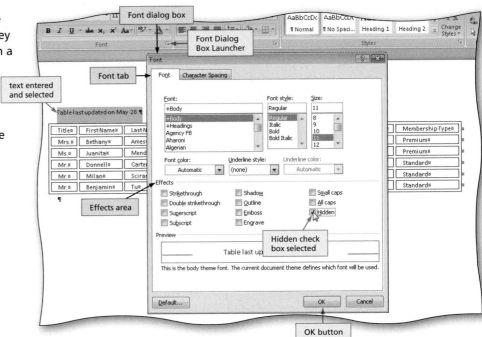

Figure 5–93

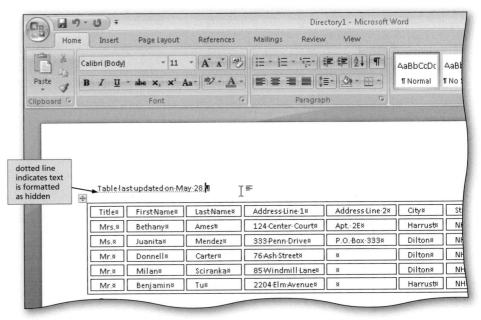

- Click the OK button to apply the hidden effect to the selected text.

- Click anywhere in the document to remove the highlight (Figure 5–94).

Figure 5–94

Other Ways

1. Right-click selected text, click Font on shortcut menu, click Font tab, click Hidden, click OK button

To Hide Hidden Text

Hidden text appears on the screen only when the Show/Hide ¶ button on the Home tab is selected. The following step hides text formatted as hidden.

1

- If the Show/Hide ¶ button on the Home tab is selected, click it to deselect it (Figure 5–95).

Q&A How do I show the hidden text again?

Click the Show/Hide ¶ button on the Home tab again.

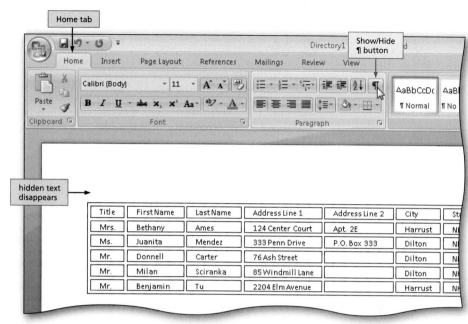

Figure 5–95

Other Ways

1. Press CTRL+SHIFT+*

To Print a Document

The following step prints the directory in landscape orientation.

1 Display the Office Button menu, point to Print, and then click the Quick Print button on the Home tab to print the directory in landscape orientation (Figure 5–96).

Q&A If Microsoft Access is installed on my computer, can I use that to print the data source?

As an alternative to merging to a directory and printing the results, if you are familiar with Microsoft Access and it is installed on your computer, you can open and print the data source in Access.

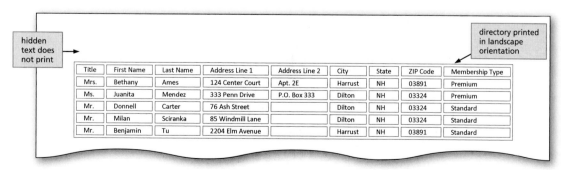

Figure 5–96

To Save the Directory

The following steps save the directory.

1 With a USB flash drive connected to one of the computer's USB ports, click the Save button on the Quick Access Toolbar to display the Save As dialog box.

2 Type `Health Club Member Directory` in the File name text box to change the file name.

3 If necessary, locate and select your USB flash drive in the list of available drives and then double-click the Total Fitness folder to open the folder.

4 Click the Save button in the Save As dialog box to save the document in the Total Fitness folder on the USB flash drive with the file name, Health Club Member Directory.

To Quit Word

The following steps close all open documents and quit Word.

1 Display the Office Button menu and then click the Exit Word button to close all open documents and quit Word.

2 When Word asks if you want to save the document used to create the directory, click the No button. For all other documents, click the Yes button to save the changes.

Opening a Main Document

You open a main document as you open any other Word document (i.e., clicking Open on the Office Button menu). If Word displays a dialog box indicating it will run an SQL command, click the Yes button (Figure 5–97).

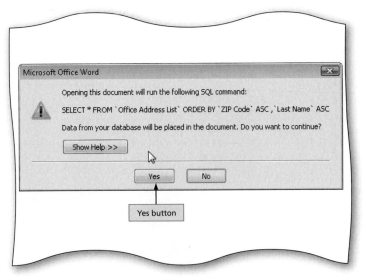

Figure 5–97

BTW

Converting Main Document Files
If you wanted to convert a mail merge main document to a regular Word document, you would open the main document, click the Start Mail Merge button on the Mailings tab, and then click Normal Word Document on the Start Mail Merge menu.

When you open a main document, Word attempts to open the associated data source file, too. If the data source is not in exactly the same location (i.e., drive and folder) as when it originally was saved, Word displays a dialog box indicating that it could not find the data source (Figure 5–98). When this occurs, click the Find Data Source button to display the Open Data Source dialog box, which allows you to locate the data source file.

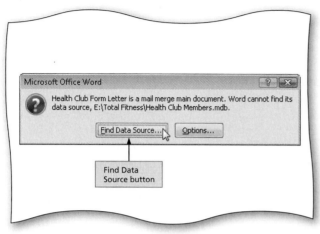

Figure 5–98

Chapter Summary

In this chapter, you have learned how to create and print form letters, create a data source, insert and format shapes, create a multilevel list, address mailing labels and envelopes from a data source, and merge to a directory. The items listed below include all the new Word skills you have learned in this chapter.

1. Identify the Main Document for the Form Letter Using the Task Pane (WD 308)
2. Change the User Name and Initials (WD 312)
3. Change the Margin Settings (WD 313)
4. Insert a Drawing Canvas (WD 314)
5. Insert a Shape (WD 316)
6. Apply a Shape Style (WD 318)
7. Add Formatted Text to a Shape (WD 319)
8. Resize a Drawing Canvas (WD 320)
9. Create a Folder while Saving (WD 321)
10. Create a New Data Source (WD 323)
11. Save the Data Source when Prompted by Word (WD 328)
12. Enter the Date (WD 330)
13. Edit the GreetingLine Merge Field (WD 332)
14. Insert a Merge Field in the Main Document (WD 333)
15. Create a Multilevel List (WD 335)
16. Insert an IF Field in the Main Document (WD 338)
17. Display a Field Code (WD 341)
18. Print Field Codes in the Main Document (WD 342)
19. Merge the Form Letters to the Printer (WD 344)
20. Merge to a New Document Window (WD 345, WD 363)
21. Select Records to Merge (WD 345)
22. Remove a Merge Condition (WD 348)
23. Sort the Data Records in a Data Source (WD 348)
24. View Merged Data in the Main Document (WD 349)
25. Address and Print Mailing Labels Using an Existing Data Source (WD 350)
26. Address and Print Envelopes Using an Existing Data Source (WD 356)
27. Merge to a Directory (WD 358)
28. Convert Text to a Table (WD 361)
29. Change Page Orientation (WD 362)
30. Modify Table Properties (WD 364)
31. Sort a Table (WD 365)
32. Format Text as Hidden (WD 366)
33. Hide Hidden Text (WD 367)

If you have a SAM user profile, you may have access to hands-on instruction, practice, and assessment. Log in to your SAM account (http://sam2007.course.com) to launch any assigned training activities or exams that relate to the skills covered in this chapter.

Learn It Online

Test your knowledge of chapter content and key terms.

Instructions: To complete the Learn It Online exercises, start your browser, click the Address bar, and then enter the Web address scsite.com/wd2007/learn. When the Word 2007 Learn It Online page is displayed, click the link for the exercise you want to complete and then read the instructions.

Chapter Reinforcement TF, MC, and SA
A series of true/false, multiple choice, and short answer questions that test your knowledge of the chapter content.

Flash Cards
An interactive learning environment where you identify chapter key terms associated with displayed definitions.

Practice Test
A series of multiple choice questions that test your knowledge of chapter content and key terms.

Who Wants To Be a Computer Genius?
An interactive game that challenges your knowledge of chapter content in the style of a television quiz show.

Wheel of Terms
An interactive game that challenges your knowledge of chapter key terms in the style of the television show *Wheel of Fortune*.

Crossword Puzzle Challenge
A crossword puzzle that challenges your knowledge of key terms presented in the chapter.

Apply Your Knowledge

Reinforce the skills and apply the concepts you learned in this chapter.

Working with a Form Letter
Instructions: Start Word. Open the document, Apply 5-1 Green Grove Form Letter, from the Data Files for Students. See the inside back cover of this book for instructions on downloading the Data Files for Students, or contact your instructor for information about accessing the required files. When you open the main document, if Word displays a dialog box about an SQL command, click the Yes button. If Word prompts for the name of the data source, select Apply 5-1 Green Grove Customers on the Data Files for Students.

The document is a main document for a Green Grove form letter. You are to edit the greeting line field, print the form letter with field codes displaying, add a record to the data source, and then merge the form letters to a file.

Perform the following tasks:
1. Edit the date content control so that it contains the date 1/15/2008.
2. Edit the GreetingLine merge field so that the salutation ends with a colon (:).
3. Save the modified main document for the form letter with the name Apply 5-1 Green Grove Format Letter Modified.
4. View merged data in the document. Use the navigation buttons in the Preview Results group to display merged data from various records in the data source. What is the last name of the first record? The third record? The fifth record?
5. Print the form letter by clicking the Office Button, pointing to Print, and then clicking Quick Print (Figure 5–99).

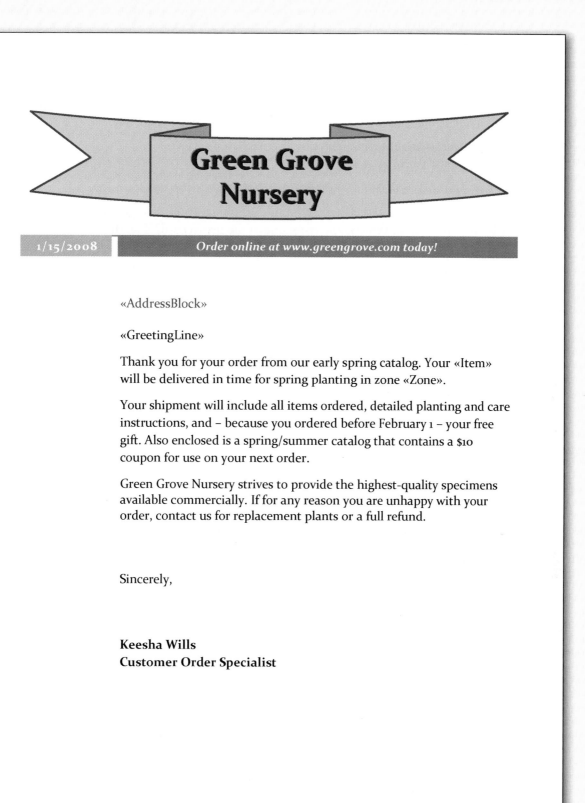

Green Grove Nursery

1/15/2008 — *Order online at www.greengrove.com today!*

«AddressBlock»

«GreetingLine»

Thank you for your order from our early spring catalog. Your «Item» will be delivered in time for spring planting in zone «Zone».

Your shipment will include all items ordered, detailed planting and care instructions, and – because you ordered before February 1 – your free gift. Also enclosed is a spring/summer catalog that contains a $10 coupon for use on your next order.

Green Grove Nursery strives to provide the highest-quality specimens available commercially. If for any reason you are unhappy with your order, contact us for replacement plants or a full refund.

Sincerely,

Keesha Wills
Customer Order Specialist

Figure 5–99

6. Print the form letter with field codes, that is, with the 'Print field codes instead of their values' check box selected. Be sure to deselect this check box after printing the field codes version of the letter. How does this printout differ from the one in Instruction #5?

Continued >

Apply Your Knowledge *continued*

7. Add a record to the data source that contains your personal information. Type hostas in the Item field and 2 in the Zone field. *Hint*: Click the Edit Recipient List button; click the data source name, Apply 5-1 Green Grove Customers in the Data Source area of the Mail Merge Recipients dialog box; and then click the Edit button in the Mail Merge Recipients dialog box.

8. In the data source, change Regina Herrera's last name to Gonzales.

9. Sort the data source by the Last Name field.

10. Save the main document for the form letter again.

11. Use the navigation buttons in the Preview Results group to display merged data from various records in the data source. What is the last name of the first record? The third record? The fifth record?

12. Merge the form letters to a new document. Save the new document with the name Apply 5-1 Green Grove Merged Form Letters. Print the document containing the merged form letters.

13. Merge the form letters directly to the printer.

Extend Your Knowledge

Extend the skills you learned in this chapter and experiment with new skills. You may need to use Help to complete the assignment.

Working with Word Fields and Multilevel Lists

Instructions: Start Word. Open the document, Extend 5-1 Far Horizons Form Letter, from the Data Files for Students. See the inside back cover of this book for instructions on downloading the Data Files for Students, or contact your instructor for information about accessing the required files. When you open the main document, if Word displays a dialog box about an SQL command, click the Yes button. If Word prompts for the name of the data source, select Extend 5-1 Far Horizons Customers on the Data Files for Students.

The document is a main document for a Far Horizons form letter (Figure 5–100). You will change the margins, change the shape, change the numbering format in the multilevel list, add a field to the data source, modify an IF field, and add a Fill-in field.

Perform the following tasks:

1. Use Help to learn about margins, shapes, multilevel lists, mail merge, IF fields, and Fill-in fields.

2. Change the top margin to 0.5" (one-half inch).

3. Change the shape at the top of the letter. *Hint*: Click the Change Shape button on the Text Box Tools Format tab.

4. Change the color of the shape. Add a shadow effect to the shape. Change the color of the shadow.

5. Change the numbering format of the multilevel list.

6. Add a field to the data source called Cruise Type. Enter field values for each record, i.e., Alaskan, Caribbean, etc.

7. In the first sentence and also in the last sentence of the main document, insert the new field called Cruise Type, just before the word, cruise.

8. Edit the IF field so that two-berth cabins cost $700. *Hint*: Display the IF field code in the document window and edit the IF field directly in the document.

9. At the bottom of the document, just above the horizontal line, insert a Fill-in field, so that you can type a different personalized note to each customer. When you merge the letters, type an appropriate note to each customer. The notes should be meaningful to the recipient, such as related to their local sports team, weather, a recent telephone call, etc.

10. Print the form letter by clicking the Office Button, pointing to Print, and then clicking Quick Print.

11. Print the form letter with field codes, that is, with the 'Print field codes instead of their values' check box selected. Be sure to deselect this check box after printing the field codes version of the letter. How does this printout differ from the one in Instruction #10?

12. Change the document properties, as specified by your instructor. Save the revised document using a new file name.

13. Merge the form letters to a new document and then submit it in the format specified by your instructor.

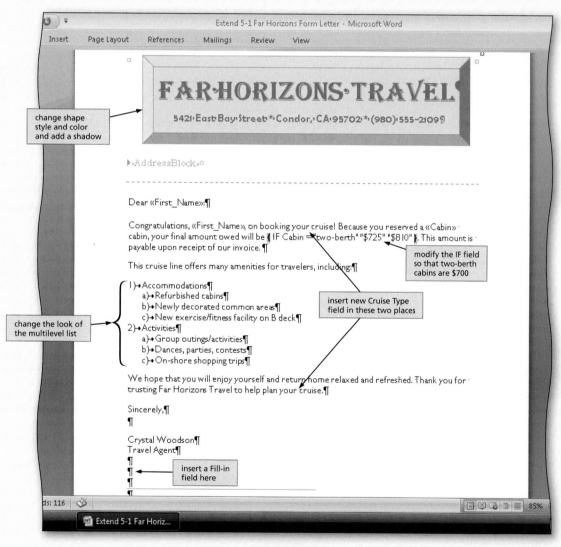

Figure 5–100

Make It Right

Analyze a document and correct all errors and/or improve the design.

Working with a Form Letter and Multilevel List

Instructions: Start Word. Open the document, Make It Right 5-1 Arrow Appliance Form Letter, from the Data Files for Students. See the inside back cover of this book for instructions on downloading the Data Files for Students, or contact your instructor for information about accessing the required files. When you open the main document, if Word displays a dialog box about an SQL command, click the Yes button. If Word prompts for the name of the data source, select Make It Right 5-1 Arrow Appliance Customers on the Data Files for Students.

The document is a form letter that is missing fields and is not formatted appropriately (Figure 5–101). You are to resize the shape, insert an AddressBlock field and a GreetingLine field, insert merge fields, switch merge fields, and promote and demote multilevel list items.

Perform the following tasks:

1. Resize the shape so that the entire company name, Arrow Appliance, is visible.
2. Insert the AddressBlock field above the date.
3. Insert the GreetingLine field below the date. Use an appropriate salutation and punctuation.
4. The end of the first sentence is missing the merge field, Appliance.
5. In the second sentence, remove the ZIP Code field.
6. In the third sentence of the first paragraph, the two merge fields for Term and Appliance should be reversed.
7. Format the multilevel list so that it is more organized. It should have two levels. You will need to demote some levels and promote others. Sort the list within each level.
8. In the data source, find the record whose last name is Franc. Fix the State and ZIP Code entries in this record.
9. In the data source, find the misspelling dryr and correct its spelling to dryer.
10. Change the document properties, as specified by your instructor. Save the revised document using a new file name.
11. Specify that only customers who purchased a refrigerator should be included in a merge. Merge these form letters to the printer. Clear the filter.
12. Identify another type of filter for this data source and merge those form letters to a new document. On the printout, write down the filter you used.
13. Merge all the records to a new document in last name order.

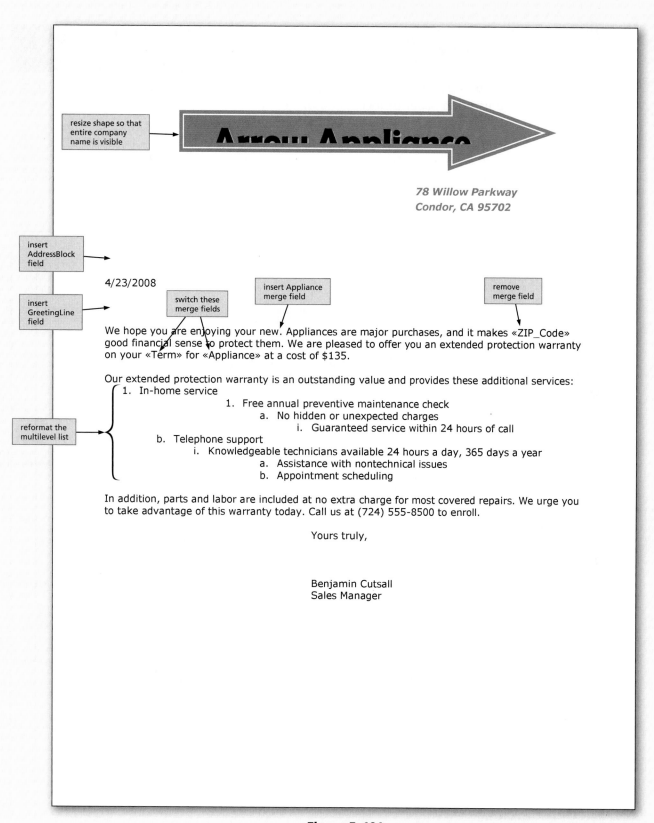

Figure 5–101

STUDENT ASSIGNMENTS

In the Lab

Design and/or create a document using the guidelines, concepts, and skills presented in this chapter. Labs are listed in order of increasing difficulty.

Lab 1: Creating a Form Letter Using a Template, a Data Source, Mailing Labels, and a Directory

Problem: The owner of Diamond Eye Care has asked you to send a letter to patients that are due for an eye exam. You decide to create the form letter shown in Figure 5–102a.

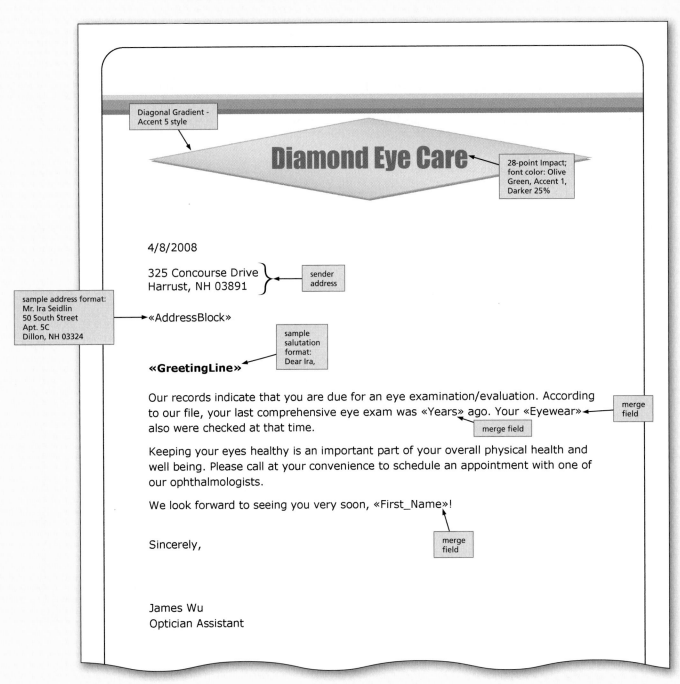

Figure 5–102 (a)

Perform the following tasks:

1. Use the Equity Merge Letter template to create a form letter.

2. Insert a drawing canvas and then a diamond shape inside the drawing canvas. Add text to and format the shape as shown in Figure 5-102a.

3. Type a new data source using the data shown in Figure 5–102b. Delete field names not used, and add two field names: Years and Eyewear. Save the data source with the file name, Lab 5-1 Diamond Eye Care Patients, in a folder called Lab 5-1 Diamond Eye Care. *Hint*: You will need to create the folder while saving.

Title	First Name	Last Name	Address Line 1	Address Line 2	City	State	ZIP Code	Years	Eyewear
Mr.	Ira	Seidlin	50 South Street	Apt. 5C	Dillon	NH	03324	two years	contacts
Mr.	Roberto	Abela	909 Pillston Ct.		Dillon	NH	03324	three years	glasses
Ms.	Leslie	Gerhard	2328 N. 128 Blvd.	Apt. 410	Harrust	NH	03891	two years	glasses
Ms.	Matilda	Jung	876 O'Toole Drive		Harrust	NH	03891	four years	contacts
Ms.	Emily	Stefanson	62 Harbor Ct.		Dillon	NH	03324	three years	contacts

Figure 5–102 (b)

4. Save the main document for the form letter with the file name, Lab 5-1 Diamond Eye Care Form Letter, in the folder called Lab 5-1 Diamond Eye Care. Compose the form letter for the main document as shown in Figure 5–102a. Insert the merge fields as shown in Figure 5–102a. Change the theme colors to Paper. Change the theme fonts to the Aspect font set.

5. Save the main document for the form letter again. Print the main document.

6. Merge the form letters to the printer.

7. In a new document window, address mailing labels using the same data source you used for the form letters. Save the mailing labels with the name, Lab 5-1 Diamond Eye Care Labels, in the Lab 5-1 Diamond Eye Care folder.

8. In a new document window, specify the main document type as a directory. Insert all merge fields in the document. Convert the list of fields to a Word table (the table will have 10 columns). Change the page layout to landscape orientation. Merge the directory layout to a new document window. Add a row to the top of the table and insert field names in the empty cells. Bold the text in the first row. Resize the columns so that the table columns look like Figure 5–102b. Add 0.05" between each table cell and center the table using the Table Properties dialog box.

9. Insert your name as text above the table. Format your name as hidden text. Hide the text on the screen. Then, reveal the text on the screen.

10. Save the directory with the name, Lab 5-1 Diamond Eye Care Directory, in the folder named Lab 5-1 Diamond Eye Care. Print the directory (your name should not print because it is hidden).

11. Sort the table in the directory by the Last Name field. Print the sorted directory.

In the Lab

Lab 2: Creating a Form Letter with an IF Field and a Multilevel List

Problem: As the president of the Athletic Booster Club, you send a letter to new members, thanking them for their support. You create the form letter shown in Figure 5–103a. The membership type will vary, depending on the donation amount.

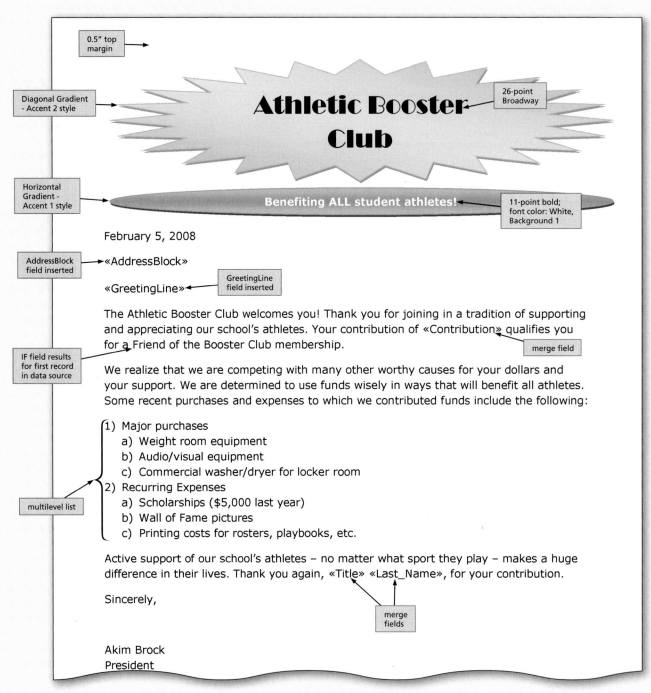

Figure 5–103 (a)

Perform the following tasks:

1. Do not use a template to create this form letter. Select 'Use the current document', which should be a blank document in the document window.

2. Insert a drawing canvas and then a 24-point star shape inside the drawing canvas. Also insert an oval shape in the drawing canvas below the star shape. Add text to and format the shapes as shown in Figure 5-103a.

3. Change the margins to Moderate (1-inch top and bottom; .75-inch left and right). Then, use the Custom Margins command to change the top margin to .5-inch.

4. Type a new data source using the data shown in Figure 5–103b. Delete field names not used, and add one field name: Contribution. Save the data source with the file name, Lab 5-2 Booster Club Members, in a folder called Lab 5-2 Booster Club. *Hint*: You will need to create the folder while saving.

Title	First Name	Last Name	Address Line 1	Address Line 2	City	State	ZIP Code	Contribution
Mr.	Adam	Willis	2445 Saren Lane	Apt. 402	Blackburg	TX	77490	$50.00
Ms.	Maxine	Tremain	8950 Treeway Ct.		Blackburg	TX	77490	$50.00
Ms.	Kim	Chung	5056 E. Fourth St.	Apt. 1A	Blackburg	TX	77490	$200.00
Mr.	David	Goldberg	17 South Street		Delman	TX	79006	$100.00
Mr.	Apurv	Patel	32 Fountain Square		Delman	TX	79006	$50.00

Figure 5–103 (b)

5. Save the main document for the form letter with the file name, Lab 5-2 Booster Club Form Letter, in the folder named Lab 5-2 Booster Club. Compose the form letter for the main document as shown in Figure 5–103a. Edit the GreetingLine field so that it shows a colon at the end of the salutation (e.g., Dear Mr. Willis:). Insert the merge fields as shown in the figure. Create the multilevel list as shown in the figure. Change the theme colors to Oriel. Change the theme fonts to the Aspect font set. The IF field tests if Contribution is less than or equal to 50; if it is, then print the text, Friend of the Booster Club; otherwise print the text, Super Booster.

6. Save the main document for the form letter again. Print the main document twice: once with field codes displaying and once without field codes.

7. Merge the form letters to the printer.

8. In a new document window, address mailing labels using the same data source you used for the form letters. Save the mailing labels with the name, Lab 5-2 Booster Club Labels, in the Lab 5-2 Booster Club folder. Merge and print the mailing labels.

9. If your printer allows and your instructor requests it, in a new document window, address envelopes using the same data source you used for the form letters. Save the envelopes with the file name, Lab 5-2 Booster Club Envelopes, in the folder named Lab 5-2 Booster Club. Merge and print the envelopes.

Continued >

10. In a new document window, specify the main document type as a directory. Insert all merge fields in the document. Convert the list of fields to a Word table (the table will have nine columns). Change the page layout to landscape orientation. Merge the directory layout to a new document window. Add a row to the top of the table and insert field names in the empty cells. Bold the text in the first row. Change the top, bottom, left, and right page margins to Narrow (one-half inch). Resize the columns so the table looks like Figure 5–103b on the previous page. Add 0.1" above and below each table cell and between each cell using the Table Properties dialog box. Center the table between the margins.

11. Insert your name as text above the table. Format your name as hidden text.

12. Save the directory with the name, Lab 5-2 Booster Club Directory, in the folder named Lab 5-2 Booster Club. Print the directory (your name should not print because it is hidden).

13. Sort the table in the directory by the Last Name field within the ZIP Code field. Print the sorted directory.

14. Save the directory again.

In the Lab

Lab 3: Designing a Data Source, Form Letter, and Mailing Labels from Sample Letters

Problem: The circulation manager at Squireman Publications would like to send a thank-you letter to magazine subscribers. Sample drafted letters are shown in Figure 5–104a and Figure 5-104b on page WD 382.

Perform the following tasks:

1. Decide which fields should be in the data source. Write the field names down on a piece of paper.

2. In Word, identify a main document for the letters.

3. Create a data source containing five records, which consists of data from the two letters shown in Figure 5–104 and then add three more records with your own data. Save the data source with the file name, Lab 5-3 Squireman Publications Address List, in a folder named Lab 5-3 Squireman Publications.

4. Save the main document for the form letter with the file name, Lab 5-3 Squireman Publications Form Letter. Enter the shape in the document and enter text and fields of the main document for the form letter shown in Figure 5–104.

5. Print the main document twice, once with field codes displaying and once without field codes.

6. Merge and print the form letters.

7. Merge the data source to a directory. Convert it to a Word table. Add an attractive border to the table and apply any other formatting you feel necessary. Print the table. Save the file using the name Lab 5-3 Squireman Publications Directory.

Squireman Publications

202 West Squire Boulevard * Micheltown, DE 19722 * squireman@link.net

Matthew Mason
7676 Independence Parkway
Rocktown, AR 71672

2/19/2008

Dear Mr. Mason:

Thank you for your recent subscription. Your first issue of *Off-Roading Journal* will be delivered to you next month. As a premium for your one-year subscription, we have enclosed a calendar and memo pad as your free gift.

We appreciate your business and hope that you will enjoy every issue of *Off-Roading Journal*. Should you have any questions, please feel free to contact us at the address or e-mail address above. Thank you again, Matthew!

Yours truly,

Dashuan Titus
Circulation Manager

Figure 5–104 (a)

Continued >

STUDENT ASSIGNMENTS

In the Lab *continued*

Squireman Publications

202 West Squire Boulevard * Micheltown, DE 19722 * squireman@link.net

Lee Sun
42 W. 18th Street
Apt. 9C
Ponrolet, MI 49155

2/19/2008

Dear Mr. Sun:

Thank you for your recent subscription. Your first issue of *Aspiring Gourmet* will be delivered to you next month. As a premium for your two-year subscription, we have enclosed a slimline calculator as your free gift.

We appreciate your business and hope that you will enjoy every issue of *Aspiring Gourmet*. Should you have any questions, please feel free to contact us at the address or e-mail address above. Thank you again, Lee!

Yours truly,

Dashuan Titus
Circulation Manager

Figure 5–104 (b)

Cases and Places

Apply your creative thinking and problem solving skills to design and implement a solution.

● Easier   ●● More Difficult

● 1: Create a Form Letter for a Charitable Organization

Charitable Outreach is a local organization that contributes volunteers, money, and other donations to area charities. As a volunteer, you have been asked by the director to send letters to past donors thanking them for their donation and alerting them to the organization's current needs. Create a form letter using the following information: Insert a shape of your choice in a drawing canvas, and insert the text Charitable Outreach within the shape. Format the shape and the text using the Styles button on the Ribbon. The organization's address is 75 Welton Plaza, Twister, OK 74519 and their telephone is (217) 555-6542. Create the data source shown in Figure 5–105. After the salutation, the first paragraph should read: Thank you for your recent contribution of «amount». As you know, Charitable Outreach is a nonprofit organization dedicated to improving the quality of life for all residents in a three-county region. Donors like you, «first name», have made possible the following fundraisers:. Create a multilevel list for the following items: 1) Spring events - Dinner dance, Golf outing, Garden tour; 2) Fall events - Harvest Ball, Bonfire, Football weekend trip. Last paragraph: Our tradition of community outreach would not be possible without donors like you. We thank you for your support and look forward to seeing you at our next event. Use your name in the signature block. Address and print accompanying labels or envelopes for the form letters.

Title	First Name	Last Name	Address Line 1	Address Line 2	City	State	Zip Code	Amount
Ms.	Lucy	Song	4483 W. 119th Street	Apt. 12L	Twister	OK	74519	$100.00
Mr.	Arnold	Green	15 N. Commerce Street		Twister	OK	74519	$75.00
Mr.	Miguel	Arroyo	P. O. Box 244	125 Main Street	Sandfly	OK	74877	$25.00
Ms.	Joseph	Ipolito	709 Placid Way		Twister	OK	74519	$100.00
Ms.	LaToya	Carrothers	323 Eaton Parkway		Sandfly	OK	74877	$200.00

Figure 5–105

●● 2: Create a Memo Form Letter for Company Training

You work part-time at HomeCare, a home health care service. Your boss has just announced that all company computers are being upgraded to run Windows Vista and Office 2007. He needs to schedule training sessions for employees in the two departments he oversees, accounting and communications. He has asked you to create a memo that can be sent to both departments and gives the pertinent information. If your instructor approves, change the user name and initials associated with your copy of Word to your name and initials. Then, use a suitable memo template and include the following information: The memo should be sent to both departments. The accounting department should be informed that they are going to receive training on Microsoft Excel 2007, and the communications department will receive training on Microsoft Word 2007 (use an IF field in the To: portion of the memo template to accomplish this). The training session for Accounting will be held on March 26 from 1:00 - 4:00 p.m.; the training session for Communications will be held on the same day from 8:00 - 11:00 a.m. Both sessions will meet in Conference Room G. Merge and print the memos, then merge the data source to a directory. Convert the directory to a Word table and apply formatting to make the table more attractive and readable.

Continued >

Cases and Places *continued*

• • 3: Create a Form Letter for a Mail-Order Company

Nature Pride Naturals, where you work part-time, is a mail-order company specializing in vitamins, herbal remedies, and organic foods and beverages. Your boss has asked you to design a form letter that can be sent to customers thanking them for their orders and listing the new specials. This month, organic teas and multivitamins are featured items. The teas are 100 percent organic, handpicked, and are caffeine- and pesticide-free. The multivitamins are available in 50-, 100-, and 200-caplet bottles (use a multilevel list for this). You also must inform the customers that you have enclosed a coupon for their next order. If they spent less than $50.00, they received a 10 percent off coupon; if they spent more than $50.00, they received a 15 percent off coupon (use an IF field for this). Obtain the names and addresses of at least five classmates, friends, or family members and use them as records in the data source. Create a directory of the data source records. Address accompanying labels or envelopes for the form letters.

• • 4: Create a Form Letter as the Cover Letter for your Resume

Make It Personal

Whether it is now or after graduation, at some point in your life you will need to search for a job. Suppose you already have your resume prepared and want to send it to a group of potential employers. Design an accompanying cover letter for your resume using the skills and techniques you learned in this chapter. Obtain a recent newspaper and cut out at least three classified advertisements for jobs in which you are interested or are in your current field of study. Also, find two job listings on the Web. Create a cover letter for your resume that can be sent as a form letter. Make sure it contains your name, address, telephone number, and e-mail address (if you have one). Use the information in the advertisements you found to create the data source. The data source should contain the five employers' names, addresses, and the job title for which you are applying. Address accompanying labels or envelopes for the cover letters. Also, create a directory of the data source records and format it as a Word table. Use the concepts and skills you learned in this chapter to format the form letter and directory. Submit the want ads with your printouts.

• • 5: Create Form Letters Using Different Types of Data Sources

Working Together

This chapter illustrated using one type of data source for merging form letters. Other types of data sources, however, can be used for a merge operation. As a starting point for this assignment, select either the form letter created in this chapter, the Apply Your Knowledge letter, or any of the other assignments completed and the data source. Divide into teams, then create and merge form letters as follows:

1. One or more team members should merge the contents of the data source to e-mail addresses. It may be necessary to use Help in Word to accomplish this.

2. One or more team members should use Microsoft Office Access 2007 to view, format, and print the contents of a data source created in Word. It may be necessary to use Help in Access.

3. One or more team members should use Microsoft Office Excel 2007 to create a table and then use that table as the data source in the merge document. It may be necessary to use Help in both Word and in Excel for instructions on creating and saving a worksheet in the proper format for a mail merge.

4. One or more team members should use Microsoft Office Outlook recipients as a data source in a mail merge document. It may be necessary to use Help in both Word and in Outlook.

Then, as a team, develop a PowerPoint slide show that outlines the steps required to complete the four tasks listed above. Present the slide show to your classmates.

6 | Creating a Professional Newsletter

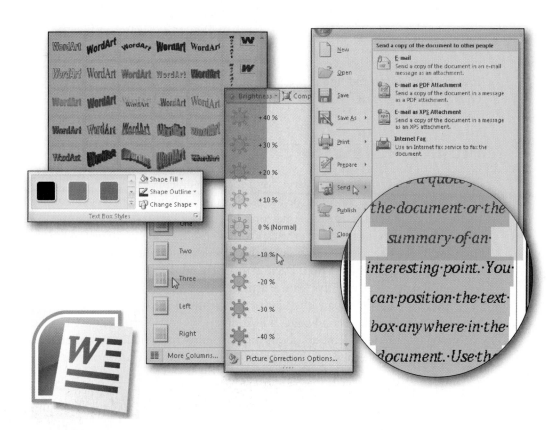

Objectives

You will have mastered the material in this chapter when you can:

- Create and format WordArt
- Insert a symbol in a document
- Insert and format a floating graphic
- Format a document in multiple columns
- Format a character as a drop cap
- Insert a column break
- Modify a style

- Place a vertical rule between columns
- Insert and format a text box
- Copy and paste using a split window
- Balance columns
- Modify and format a SmartArt graphic
- Add a page border

6 | Creating a Professional Newsletter

Introduction

Professional looking documents, such as newsletters and brochures, often are created using desktop publishing software. With desktop publishing software, you can divide a document in multiple columns, wrap text around diagrams and other graphical images, change fonts and font sizes, add color and lines, and so on, to create an attention-grabbing document. Desktop publishing software, such as Adobe PageMaker or QuarkXpress, enables you to open an existing word processing document and enhance it through formatting not provided in your word processing software. Word, however, provides many of the formatting features that you would find in a desktop publishing program. Thus, you can use Word to create eye-catching newsletters and brochures.

Project — Newsletter

A newsletter is a publication geared for a specific audience that is created on a recurring basis, such as weekly, monthly, or quarterly. The audience may be subscribers, club members, employees, customers, patrons, etc.

The project in this chapter uses Word to produce the two-page newsletter shown in Figure 6–1. The newsletter is a monthly publication, called Health Bits, which is for members of Health Bits Group. Each issue of Health Bits contains a feature article and announcements. This month's feature article discusses health concerns related to computer use. The feature article spans the first two columns of the first page of the newsletter and then continues on the second page. The announcements, located in the third column of the first page, remind members about the upcoming meeting, inform them about member discounts, and advise them of the topic of the next month's feature article.

Overview

As you read through this chapter, you will learn how to create the newsletter shown in Figure 6–1 by performing these general tasks:

- Create the nameplate on the first page of the newsletter.
- Format the first page of the body of the newsletter.
- Create a pull-quote on the first page of the newsletter.
- Create the nameplate on the second page of the newsletter.
- Format the second page of the body of the newsletter.
- Print the newsletter.

The project in this chapter involves several steps requiring you to drag the mouse. If you drag to the wrong location, you may want to cancel an action. Remember that you always can click the Undo button on the Quick Access Toolbar to cancel your most recent action.

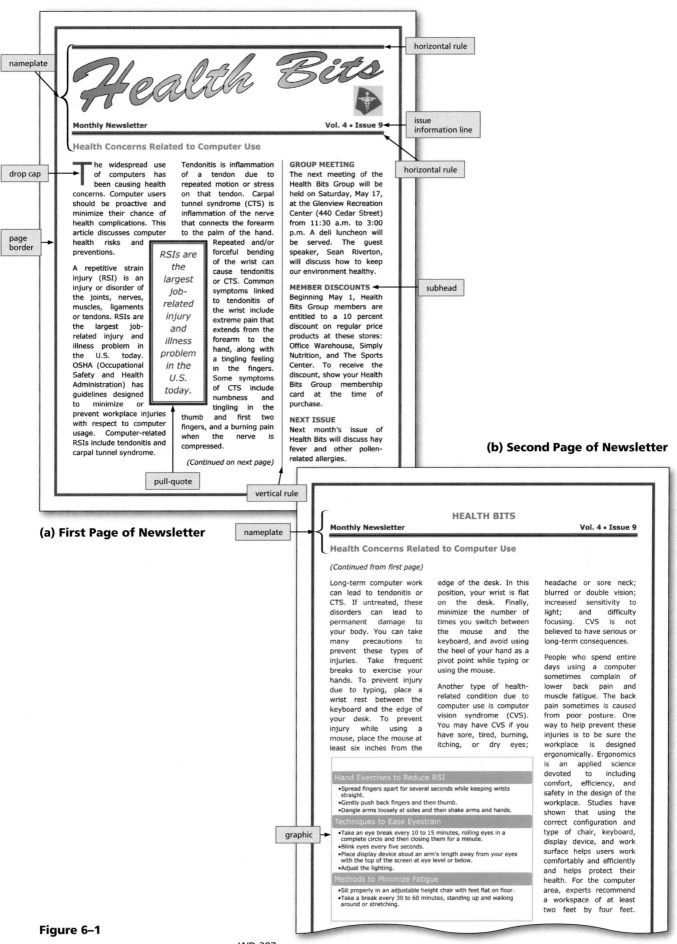

Figure 6–1

(a) **First Page of Newsletter**

(b) **Second Page of Newsletter**

The Health Bits newsletter incorporates the desktop publishing features of Word. The body of each page of the newsletter is divided in three columns. A variety of fonts, font sizes, and colors add visual appeal to the document. The first page has text wrapped around a pull-quote, and the second page has text wrapped around a graphic. Horizontal and vertical lines separate distinct areas of the newsletter, including a page border around the perimeter of each page.

Desktop Publishing Terminology

As you create professional looking newsletters and brochures, you should be familiar with several desktop publishing terms. Figure 6–1 on the previous page identifies these terms:

- A **nameplate**, or **banner**, is the portion of a newsletter that contains the title of the newsletter and usually an issue information line.
- The **issue information line** identifies the specific publication.
- A **ruling line**, usually identified by its direction as a **horizontal rule** or **vertical rule**, is a line that separates areas of the newsletter.
- A **subhead** is a heading within the body of the newsletter.
- A **pull-quote** is text that is *pulled*, or copied, from the text of the document and given graphical emphasis.

Plan Ahead

General Project Guidelines

When creating a Word document, the actions you perform and decisions you make will affect the appearance and characteristics of the finished document. As you create a newsletter, such as the project shown in Figure 6–1, you should follow these general guidelines:

1. **Create the nameplate.** The nameplate visually identifies the newsletter. Usually, the nameplate is positioned horizontally across the top of the newsletter, although some nameplates are vertical. The nameplate typically consists of text, graphics, and ruling lines.

2. **Determine content for the body of the newsletter.** Newsletters typically have one or more articles that begin on the first page. Include articles that are interesting to the audience. Incorporate color, appropriate fonts and font sizes, and alignment to provide visual interest. Use pull-quotes, graphics, and ruling lines to draw the reader's attention to important points. Avoid overusing visual elements — too many visuals can give the newsletter a cluttered look.

3. **Bind and distribute the newsletter.** Many newsletters are printed and mailed to recipients. Some are placed in public locations, free for interested parties. Others are e-mailed or posted on the Web for users to download. Printed newsletters typically are stapled at the top, along the side, or on a fold. For online newsletters, be sure the newsletter is in a format that most computer users will be able to open.

When necessary, more specific details concerning the above guidelines are presented at appropriate points in the chapter. The chapter also will identify the actions performed and decisions made regarding these guidelines during the creation of the newsletter shown in Figure 6–1.

To Start Word

If you are using a computer to step through the project in this chapter and you want your screens to match the figures in this book, you should change your computer's resolution to 1024 × 768. For information about how to change a computer's resolution, read Appendix D.

The following steps start Word and verify Word settings.

1 Start Word.

2 If the Word window is not maximized, click its Maximize button.

3 If the Print Layout button on the status bar is not selected, click it so that Word is in Print Layout view.

4 If your zoom level is not 100%, click the Zoom Out or Zoom In button as many times as necessary until the Zoom level button displays 100% on its face.

5 If the Show/Hide ¶ button on the Home tab is not selected already, click it to display formatting marks on the screen.

6 If the rulers are not displayed already, click the View Ruler button on the vertical scroll bar because you will use the rulers to perform tasks in this project.

To Set Custom Margins

Recall that Word is preset to use standard 8.5-by-11-inch paper, with 1-inch top, bottom, left, and right margins. In Chapter 5, you changed the margins by selecting predefined settings in the Margins gallery. For the newsletter in this chapter, all margins (left, right, top, and bottom) are .75 inches, which is not a predefined setting in the Margins gallery. Thus, the following steps set custom margins.

1

• Display the Page Layout tab.

• Click the Margins button on the Page Layout tab to display the Margins gallery (Figure 6–2).

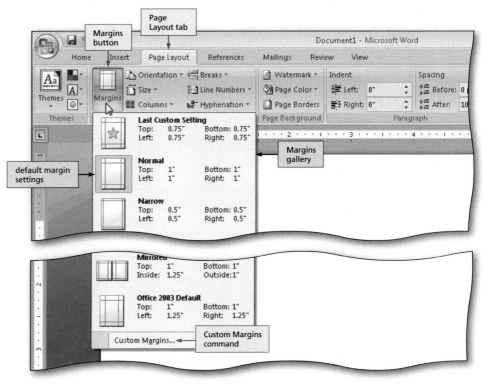

Figure 6–2

2

- Click Custom Margins in the Margins gallery to display the Page Setup dialog box. If necessary, click the Margins tab in the dialog box.

- Type .75 in the Top text box to change the top margin setting and then press the TAB key to position the insertion point in the Bottom text box.

- Type .75 in the Bottom text box to change the bottom margin setting and then press the TAB key.

- Type .75 in the Left text box to change the left margin setting and then press the TAB key.

- Type .75 in the Right box to change the right margin setting (Figure 6–3).

3

- Click the OK button to set the custom margins for this document.

Other Ways
1. Position mouse pointer on margin boundary on ruler; when mouse pointer changes to two-headed arrow, drag margin boundaries on ruler

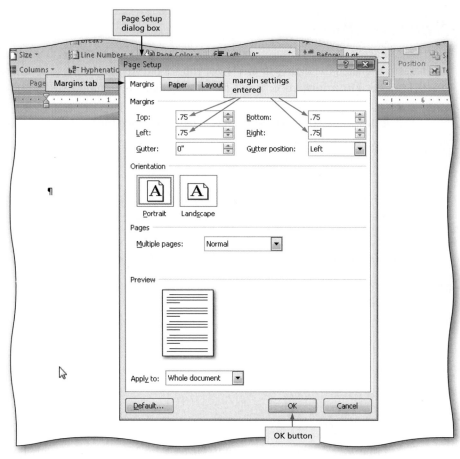

Figure 6–3

{}
BTW

Saving Modified Themes
If you want to save a modified theme so that you can use it again in another document, modify the theme colors or fonts (as described in the steps to the right), click the Themes button on the Page Layout tab, click Save Current Theme in the Themes gallery, enter a theme name in the File name text box, and then click the Save button.

To Change Theme Colors and Fonts

The newsletter in this chapter uses the Metro color scheme and Aspect font set. The following steps change the theme colors to the Metro color scheme and the theme fonts to the Aspect font set.

1 Display the Home tab. Click the Change Styles button on the Home tab, point to Colors on the Change Styles menu, and then click Metro in the Colors gallery to change the document theme colors to Metro.

2 Click the Change Styles button on the Home tab, point to Fonts on the Change Styles menu, and then click Aspect in the Fonts gallery to change the document theme fonts to Aspect.

Creating the Nameplate

The nameplate on the first page of this newsletter consists of the information above the multiple columns (Figure 6–1a on page WD 387). In this project, the nameplate includes the newsletter title, Health Bits, the issue information line, and the title of the feature article. The steps on the following pages create the nameplate for the first page of the newsletter in this project.

Create the nameplate.
The nameplate should catch the attention of readers, enticing them to read the newsletter. The nameplate typically consists of the title of the newsletter and the issue information line. Some also include a subtitle, a slogan, and a graphical image or logo. Guidelines for the newsletter title and other elements in the nameplate are as follows:

- Compose a title that is short, yet conveys the contents of the newsletter. In the newsletter title, eliminate unnecessary words such as these: the, newsletter. Use a decorative font in as large a font size as possible so that the title stands out on the page.

- Other elements on the nameplate should not compete in size with the title. Use colors that complement the title. Select easy-to-read fonts.

- Arrange the elements of the nameplate so that it does not have a cluttered appearance. If necessary, use ruling lines to visually separate areas of the nameplate.

Plan Ahead

The following pages use the steps outlined below to create the nameplate for the newsletter in this chapter.

1. Enter and format the newsletter title using WordArt.
2. Add a horizontal rule above the newsletter title.
3. Enter the issue information line.
4. Add a horizontal rule below the issue information line.
5. Insert and format an appropriate clip art image.
6. Enter the feature article title.

BTW

WordArt
WordArt is not treated as Word text. If you misspell text in WordArt and then spell check the document, Word will not flag the misspelled text in the WordArt.

To Insert WordArt

In Chapter 5, you added a shape drawing object to a document. Recall that a drawing object is a graphic you create using Word. Another type of drawing object, called **WordArt**, enables you to create special effects such as shadowed, rotated, stretched, skewed, and wavy text.

This project uses WordArt for the newsletter title, Health Bits, to draw the reader's attention to the nameplate. The following steps insert WordArt.

- Display the Insert tab.

- Click the WordArt button on the Insert tab to display the WordArt gallery (Figure 6–4).

Q&A

Why will I choose WordArt style 1?

You want to add your own special text effects to the WordArt, and WordArt style 1 is the most basic style.

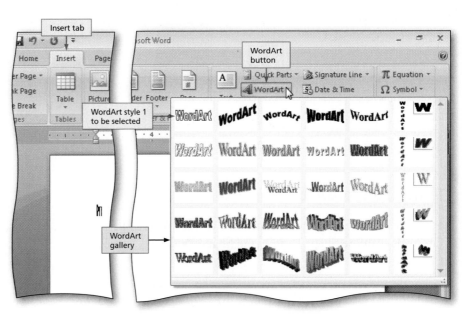

Figure 6–4

2

- Click WordArt style 1, the style in the upper-left corner of the WordArt gallery, to display the Edit WordArt Text dialog box.

3

- Type `Health Bits` in the Text text box, as the WordArt text.

- Click the Font box arrow in the dialog box; scroll to and then click Brush Script MT, or a similar font, to change the font of the WordArt text.

- Click the Size box arrow in the dialog box; scroll to and then click 72 to change the font size of the WordArt text (Figure 6–5).

Figure 6–5

4

- Click the OK button to display the WordArt text in the document window (Figure 6–6).

Q&A

How do I correct a mistake in the WordArt text?

Click the Edit Text button on the WordArt Tools Format tab, or right-click the WordArt and then click Edit Text on the shortcut menu, to redisplay the Edit WordArt Text dialog box.

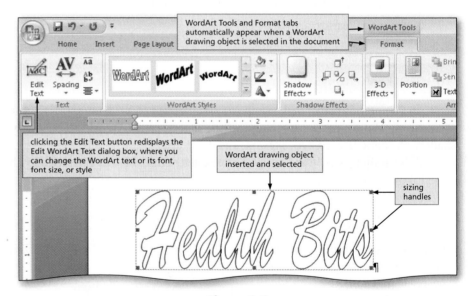

Figure 6–6

To Resize WordArt

You resize WordArt the same way you resize any other graphic. That is, you can drag its sizing handles or enter values in the Shape Height and Shape Width text boxes. The next steps resize the WordArt.

1 Drag the bottom-right sizing handle to the right and slightly downward until the WordArt size is similar to Figure 6–7.

2 If the values in the Shape Height and Shape Width text boxes are not approximately equal to 1.4" and 7", respectively, change their values so that the WordArt is similar in size to Figure 6–7.

Figure 6–7

To Change the WordArt Fill Color

The next step is to change the color of the WordArt so that it displays a green to yellow to green gradient color effect. **Gradient** means the colors blend into one another. In this newsletter, the yellow color is in the middle of the WordArt text, which blends into the green color to the edges of the WordArt text. The following steps change the fill color of the WordArt.

1

• With the WordArt selected, click the Shape Fill button arrow on the WordArt Tools Format tab to display the Shape Fill gallery.

Q&A The Shape Fill gallery did not display. Why not?

Be sure you click the Shape Fill button arrow, which is to the right of the Shape Fill button. If you mistakenly click the Shape Fill button, Word places a default fill in the selected WordArt instead of displaying the Shape Fill gallery.

• Point to Gradient in the Shape Fill gallery to display the Gradient gallery (Figure 6–8).

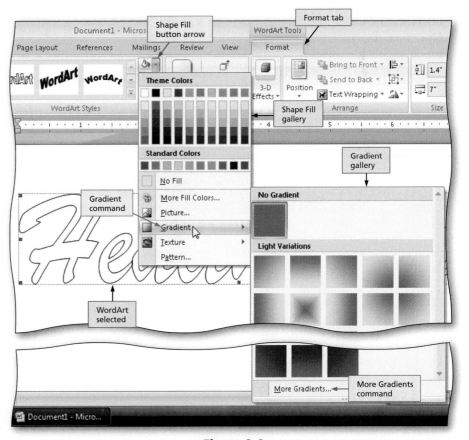

Figure 6–8

2

- Click More Gradients in the Gradient gallery to display the Fill Effects dialog box. If necessary, click the Gradient tab in the dialog box.

- In the Colors area, click Two colors, which causes two separate color text boxes to appear in the dialog box (Figure 6–9).

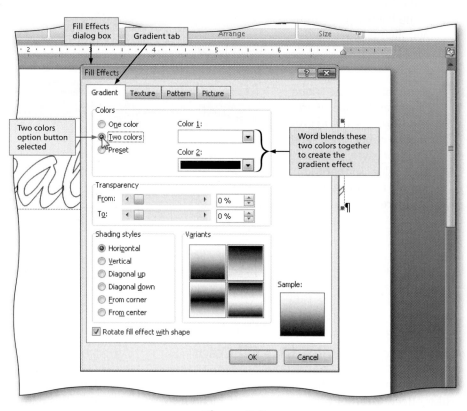

Figure 6–9

3

- Click the Color 1 box arrow and then click Gold, Accent 3, Lighter 60% (third row, seventh column) in the color gallery.

- Click the Color 2 box arrow and then click Green, Accent 1, Darker 25% (fifth row, fifth column) in the color gallery.

- Click From center in the Shading styles area and then, if necessary, click the left variant in the Variants area (Figure 6–10).

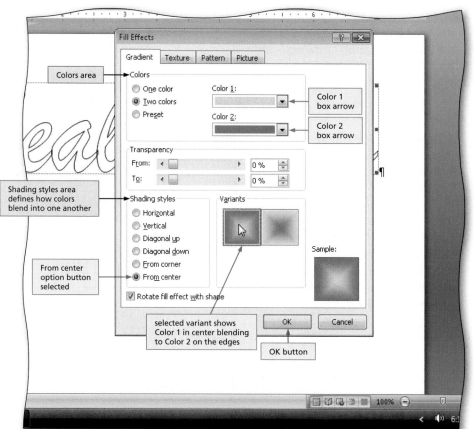

Figure 6–10

4

- Click the OK button to change the colors of the WordArt (Figure 6–11).

colors changed to gradient blend of green and yellow

Figure 6–11

Other Ways

1. Right-click WordArt, click Format WordArt on shortcut menu, click Fill Effects button, select desired options, click OK button in each dialog box

To Change the WordArt Shape

Word provides a variety of shapes to make your WordArt more interesting. For the newsletter in this chapter, the WordArt slants at an upward angle to make room for a graphic on the right edge of the nameplate. The following steps change the WordArt to a cascade up shape.

1

- Click the Change WordArt Shape button on the Format tab to display the WordArt Shape gallery (Figure 6–12).

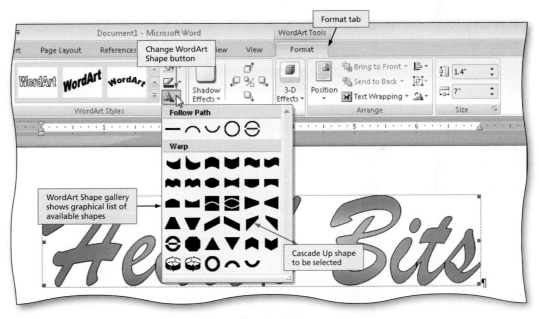

Format tab

Change WordArt Shape button

WordArt Shape gallery shows graphical list of available shapes

Cascade Up shape to be selected

Figure 6–12

2

- Click the Cascade Up shape in the WordArt Shape gallery to instruct Word to form itself into the Cascade Up shape (Figure 6–13).

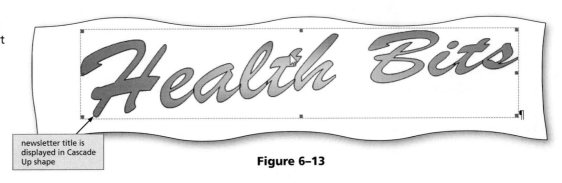

newsletter title is displayed in Cascade Up shape

Figure 6–13

BTW

Deleting WordArt Graphics
If you want to delete a WordArt graphic, you would right-click it and then click Cut on the shortcut menu, or click it and then press the DELETE key.

To Center the Newsletter Title

The next step is to center the paragraph containing the WordArt.

1 Click the paragraph mark to the right of the WordArt text to deselect the WordArt and position the insertion point in the paragraph containing the WordArt.

2 If necessary, display the Home tab, and then click the Center button on the Home tab to center the paragraph containing the WordArt.

Q&A Will I notice a change after centering the WordArt?

Because the WordArt object extends from the left to the right margins, you may not notice a difference in its position after clicking the Center button.

To Border One Edge of a Paragraph

In Word, you use borders to create ruling lines. As discussed in previous projects, Word can place borders on any edge of a paragraph; that is, Word can place a border on the top, bottom, left, and right edges of a paragraph.

In this project, the title of the newsletter has a 3-point, decorative, dark-pink border above it. The following steps place a border above a paragraph.

- Click the Border button arrow on the Home tab and then click Borders and Shading in the Border gallery to display the Borders and Shading dialog box.

- Click Custom in the Setting area because you are setting just a top border.

- Scroll through the style list and click the style shown in Figure 6–14, which has a thick middle line between two thin lines.

- Click the Color button arrow and then click Pink, Accent 2, Darker 50% (sixth column in the last row of Theme Colors) in the Color gallery.

- Click the Top Border button in the Preview area of the dialog box to show a preview of the selected border style (Figure 6–14).

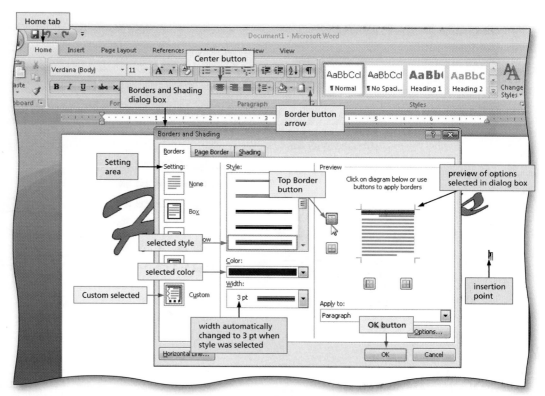

Figure 6–14

Q&A What is the purpose of the buttons in the Preview area?

They are toggles that display and remove the top, bottom, left, and right borders from the diagram in the Preview area.

3

• Click the OK button to place the defined border above the newsletter title (Figure 6–15).

How would I change an existing border?

First, you remove the border by clicking the Border button arrow on the Home tab, and then click the border in the Border gallery that identifies the border you wish to remove. Then, add a new border as described in these steps.

Figure 6–15

Other Ways

1. Click Page Borders on Page Layout tab, click Borders tab in Borders and Shading dialog box, select desired border, click OK button

To Clear Formatting

When you press the ENTER key at the end of the newsletter title to advance the insertion point to the next line, Word carries forward formatting. You do not want the paragraphs and characters on line 2 to have the same formatting as line 1. Instead, you clear formatting so that the characters on line 2 use the Normal style. The following steps clear formatting after pressing the ENTER key.

1 With the insertion point positioned at the end of line 1 (shown in Figure 6–15), press the ENTER key.

2 Click the Clear Formatting button on the Home tab to remove any existing formatting.

To Set a Right-Aligned Tab Stop

The issue information line in this newsletter contains the text, Monthly Newsletter, at the left margin and the volume and issue number at the right margin (shown in Figure 6–1a on page WD 387). A paragraph cannot be formatted as both left-aligned and right-aligned. To place text at the right margin of a left-aligned paragraph, you must set a tab stop at the right margin. The steps on the next page set a right-aligned tab stop at the right margin.

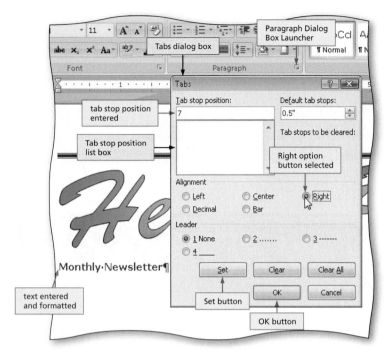

Figure 6–16

1. Click the Bold button on the Home tab. Click the Font Color button arrow on the Home tab and change the font color to Pink, Accent 2, Darker 50%. Type Monthly Newsletter on line 2 of the newsletter.

2. Click the Paragraph Dialog Box Launcher to display the Paragraph dialog box and then click the Tabs button in the Paragraph dialog box to display the Tabs dialog box.

3. Type 7 in the Tab stop position text box, which is the location of the right margin.

4. Click Right in the Alignment area to specify alignment for text at the tab stop (Figure 6–16).

5. Click the Set button in the Tabs dialog box to set a right-aligned custom tab stop, which places the entered tab stop position, the number 7 in this case, in the Tab stop position list box.

6. Click the OK button to place a right tab marker at the 7" mark on the ruler.

To Insert a Symbol

In the newsletter in this chapter, a large round dot is between the volume number and issue number. This special symbol (the large round dot) is not on the keyboard. You insert dots and other symbols, such as letters in the Greek alphabet and mathematical characters, using the Symbol dialog box.

The following steps insert a dot symbol between the volume and issue numbers in the issue information line of the newsletter.

1
- Press the TAB key. Type Vol. 4 and then press the SPACEBAR.

- Display the Insert tab.

- Click the Symbol button on the Insert tab (Figure 6–17).

Q&A What if the symbol I want to insert already appears in the Symbol gallery?

You can click any symbol shown in the Symbol gallery to insert it in the document.

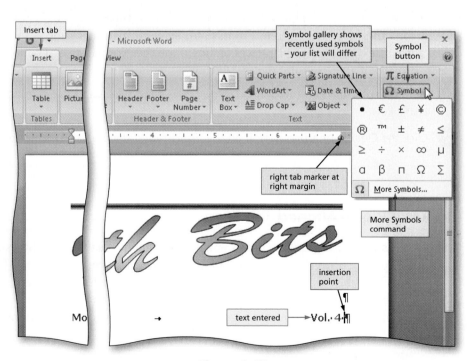

Figure 6–17

2

- Click More Symbols in the Symbol gallery to display the Symbol dialog box.

- If Symbol is not the font displayed in the Font box, click the Font box arrow in the dialog box and then scroll to Symbol and click it.

- In the list of symbols, if necessary, scroll to and then click the dot symbol shown in Figure 6–18.

- Click the Insert button to place the dot symbol in the document to the left of the insertion point (Figure 6–18).

Q&A Why is the Symbol dialog box still open?

The Symbol dialog box remains open, allowing you to insert additional symbols.

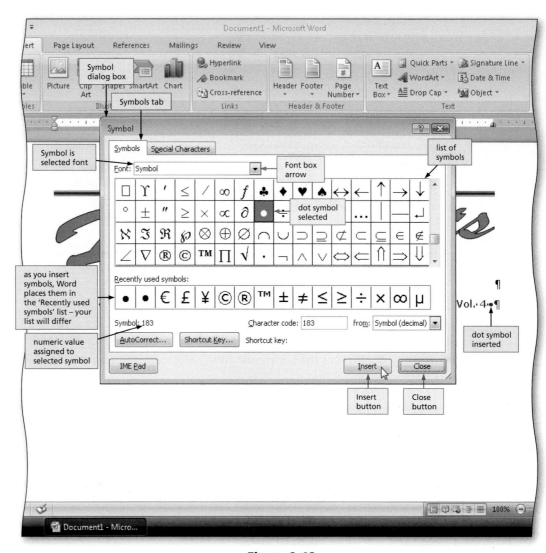

Figure 6–18

3

- Click the Close button in the Symbol dialog box.

Other Ways

1. While holding ALT key, with the NUM LOCK key on, use numeric keypad to type ANSI character code for symbol

To Enter Text and Add a Border

The next step is to finish entering text in the issue information line and then place a border immediately below the issue information line. The border has the same format as the one above the newsletter title. The steps on the next page enter text and add the border.

BTW

Inserting Special Characters
In addition to symbols, you can insert a variety of special characters including dashes, hyphens, spaces, apostrophes, and quotation marks. Click the Special Characters tab in the Symbols dialog box, click the desired character in the Character list, click the Insert button, and then click the Close button.

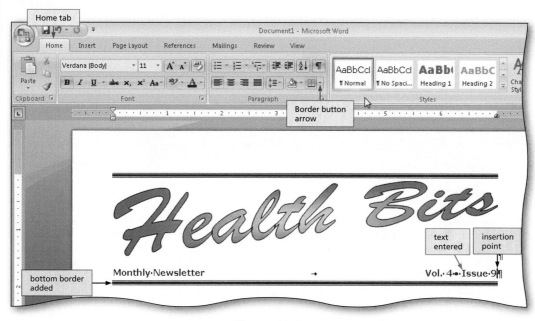

Figure 6–19

Press the SPACEBAR. Type Issue 9 at the end of the issue information line.

Display the Home tab. Click the Border button arrow on the Home tab and then click Bottom Border in the Border gallery to place a bottom border on the current paragraph using the same formats as the previously defined border (Figure 6–19).

Q&A What if my border is not the same as the one above the title?

Remove the border just added and then define a new bottom border using the Borders and Shading dialog box.

To Save a Document

The next step is to save the newsletter because you have performed many steps thus far.

1. With a USB flash drive connected to one of the computer's USB ports, click the Save button on the Quick Access Toolbar to display the Save As dialog box.

2. Save the document on a USB flash drive with the file name, Health Bits Newsletter.

To Insert Clip Art from the Web

The next step is to insert an image of a caduceus (a symbol often associated with health care) from the Web in the nameplate.

1. Display the Insert tab. Click the Clip Art button on the Insert tab to display the Clip Art task pane.

2. In the Clip Art task pane, type caduceus in the Search for text box.

3. Click the Go button to display a list of clips that match the description, caduceus.

4. Scroll to and then click the clip art of the caduceus that matches the one in Figure 6–20. (If the clip art image does not appear in the task pane, click the Close button on the Clip Art task pane and then proceed to the shaded steps on the next page.)

5. Click the Close button on the Clip Art task pane title bar to close the task pane.

Q&A What if my clip art image is not in the same location as in Figure 6–20?

The clip art image may be in a different location, depending on the position of the insertion point when you inserted the image. In a later section, you will move the image to a different location.

Note: The following steps assume your computer is connected to the Internet. If it is not, go directly to the shaded steps on the next page that are titled To Insert a Graphic File from the Data Files for Students.

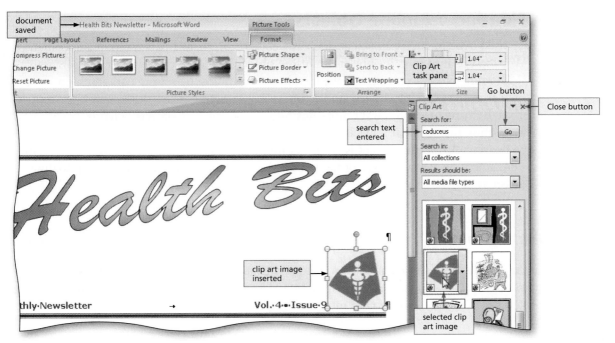

Figure 6–20

To Insert a Graphic File from the Data Files for Students

If you do not have access to the Internet, you can insert the clip art file in the Word document from the Data Files for Students. See the inside back cover of this book for instructions on downloading the Data Files for Students, or contact your instructor for information about accessing the required files. Only perform these steps if you were not able to insert the caduceus clip art from the Web in the steps at the bottom of the previous page.

1 Display the Insert tab. Click the Insert Picture from File button on the Insert tab to display the Insert Picture dialog box.

2 With your USB flash drive connected to one of the computer's USB ports, locate and then click the file called Caduceus on the USB flash drive to select the file.

3 Click the Insert button in the dialog box to insert the picture at the location of the insertion point in the document (shown in Figure 6–20).

To Resize the Clip Art Image

The clip art image is too big. It should be about one-quarter of its current size. The following steps resize the clip art image.

1 Drag the top-right sizing handle inward until the size of the clip art image is similar to Figure 6–21.

2 If necessary, double-click the clip art image to display the Picture Tools Format tab. If the values in the Shape Height and Shape Width text boxes are not approximately equal to .67 each, change their values so that the clip art image size is similar to Figure 6–21.

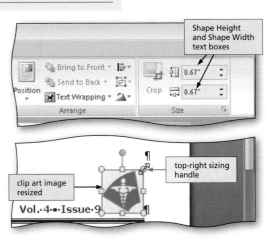

Figure 6–21

Floating vs. Inline Objects

When you insert an object, such as a clip art image, in a paragraph in a document, Word inserts it as an inline object. An **inline object** is an object that is part of a paragraph. With inline objects, you change the location of the object by setting paragraph options, such as centered, right-aligned, and so on.

In many cases, you want more flexibility in positioning objects. That is, you want to position the object at a specific location in a document. To do this, the object must be floating. A **floating object** is an object that can be positioned at a specific location in a document or in a layer over or behind text in a document. You can position a floating object anywhere on the page.

To Format a Graphic as Floating

In the nameplate of the newsletter in this chapter, the caduceus image is positioned at the right edge of the nameplate between the newsletter title and the issue information line. The following steps change the image from an inline object to a floating object, which will enable you to move the graphic to any location on the page.

1

- If necessary, double-click the clip art image to display the Picture Tools Format tab.

- Click the Text Wrapping button on the Format tab to display the Text Wrapping menu (Figure 6–22).

Q&A

Does Word have different types of floating formats?

Yes. Square wraps text in a box around an object; Tight wraps text around the shape of the object; Behind Text places the object behind the text without wrapping; In Front of Text places the object in front of the text without wrapping; Top and Bottom places text above and below the object; and Through runs text through the object.

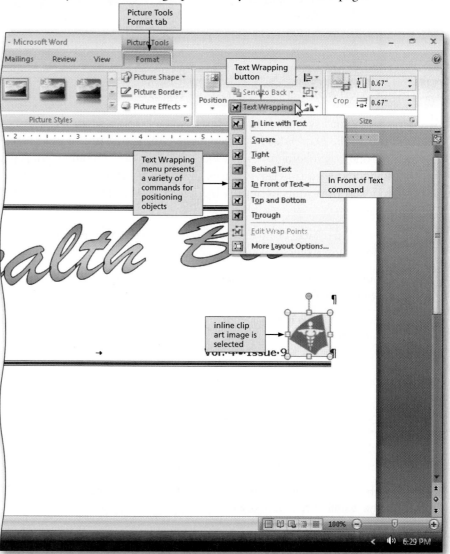

Figure 6–22

2

- In the Text Wrapping menu, click In Front of Text so that the image changes to a floating object that can be positioned in front of text on the page (Figure 6–23).

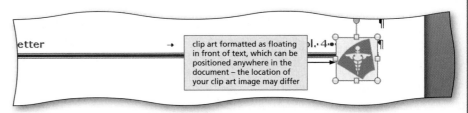

Figure 6–23

To Move a Graphic

The next step is to move the clip art image up so that it is positioned between the newsletter title and the issue information line.

1 Point to the middle of the graphic, and when the mouse pointer has a four-headed arrow attached to it, drag the graphic to the location shown in Figure 6–24.

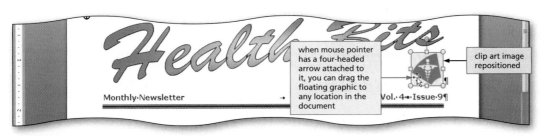

Figure 6–24

To Flip a Graphic

The next step is to flip the clip art image so that the arc is facing the opposite direction. The following steps flip a graphic horizontally.

1

- With the graphic still selected, click the Rotate button on the Format tab to display the Rotate gallery (Figure 6–25).

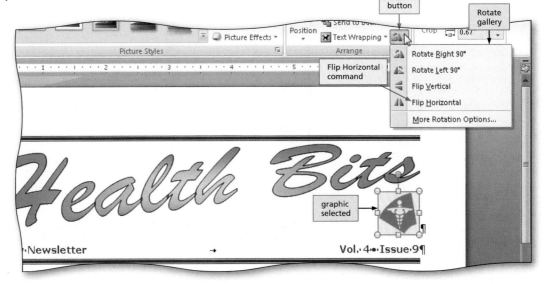

Figure 6–25

- Click Flip Horizontal on the Rotate gallery, so that Word flips the graphic to display its mirror image (Figure 6–26).

Q&A Can I flip a graphic vertically?

Yes, you would click the Flip Vertical command in the Rotate gallery.

with clip art image flipped horizontally, arc now displays in opposite direction

Vol.·4·••·Issue·9¶

Figure 6–26

To Adjust the Brightness of a Graphic

In this newsletter, the clip art image is a bit darker so that its colors blend more with the colors in the newsletter title. In Word, you can increase or decrease the brightness of a graphic. The following steps adjust a graphic's brightness.

- Click the Brightness button on the Format tab to display the Brightness gallery.

- Point to -10 % in the Brightness gallery to display a live preview of that decrease in brightness applied to the selected clip art image (Figure 6–27).

Experiment

- Point to various percentages in the Brightness gallery and watch the clip art image colors lighten and darken.

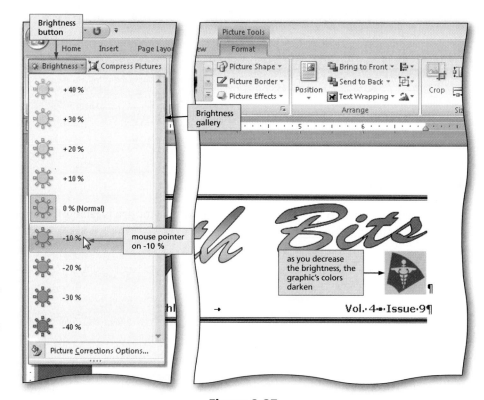

as you decrease the brightness, the graphic's colors darken

Vol.·4·••·Issue·9¶

Figure 6–27

- Click -10 % in the Brightness gallery to darken the clip art image.

Q&A Can I remove all formatting applied to a graphic and start over?

Yes, you would click the Reset Picture button on the Format tab to return a graphic to its original settings.

Other Ways

1. Right-click image, click Format Picture on shortcut menu, click Picture in left pane, drag Brightness slider, click Close button

To Clear Formatting

The next step is to enter the title of the feature article below the horizontal rule. To do this, you position the insertion point at the end of the issue information line (after the 9 in Issue 9) and then press the ENTER key. Recall that the issue information line has a bottom border. When you press the ENTER key in a bordered paragraph, Word carries forward any borders to the next paragraph. Thus, after you press the ENTER key, you should clear formatting to format the new paragraph to the Normal style. The following steps clear formatting.

1 Click at the end of line 2 (the issue information line) so that the insertion point is immediately after the 9 in Issue 9. Press the ENTER key.

2 Display the Home tab. Click the Clear Formatting button on the Home tab to apply the Normal style to the location of the insertion point.

To Enter Text as a Heading Style

Below the bottom border in the nameplate is the title of the feature article, Health Concerns Related to Computer Use, which is formatted in a Heading 2 style. The following steps enter text using the Heading 2 style.

1 Click Heading 2 on the Home tab.

2 Type Health Concerns Related to Computer Use to enter the feature title in the Heading 2 style.

To Modify a Style Using the Modify Style Dialog Box

The Heading 2 style uses a bright green color. In this newsletter, you would like the Heading 2 style to be one shade darker. The following steps modify a style.

1
- Right-click Heading 2 on the Home tab to display a shortcut menu (Figure 6–28).

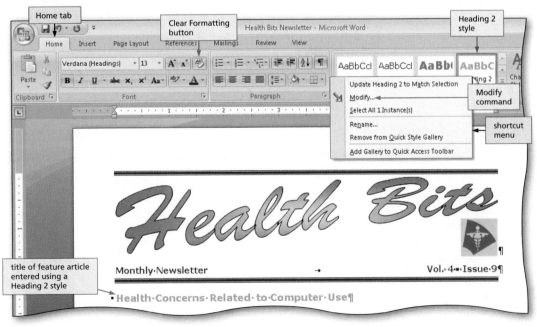

Figure 6–28

2

- Click Modify on the shortcut menu to display the Modify Style dialog box.

- Click the Color box arrow and then click Green, Accent 1, Darker 25% to change the color to a darker shade of green.

- Place a check mark in the Automatically update check box so that any additional changes you make to the Heading 2 style will automatically modify the style (Figure 6–29).

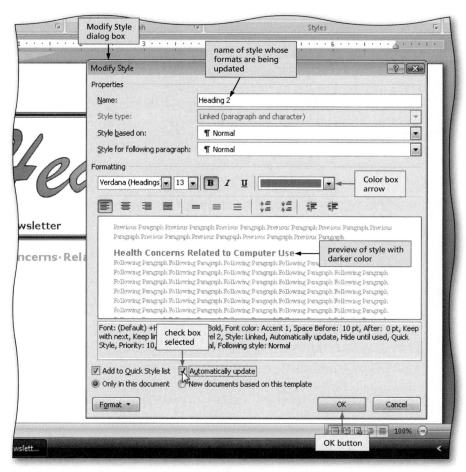

Figure 6–29

3

- Click the OK button to update the Heading 2 style (Figure 6–30).

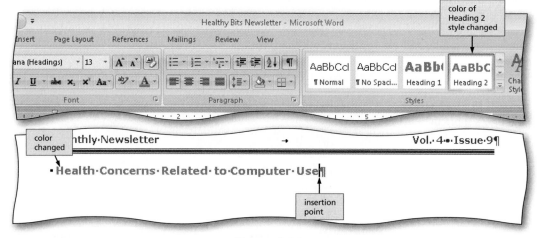

Figure 6–30

Other Ways

1. Click Styles Dialog Box Launcher, point to style name in list, click box arrow next to style name, click Modify in menu, change settings, click OK button

2. Click Styles Dialog Box Launcher, click Manage Styles button, select style name in list, click Modify button, change settings, click OK button in each dialog box

To Save a Document Again

The nameplate for the newsletter is complete. You should save the newsletter again.

 1 Save the newsletter again with the same file name, Health Bits Newsletter.

Formatting the First Page of the Body of the Newsletter

The next step is to format the first page of the body of the newsletter. The body of the newsletter in this chapter is divided in three columns (Figure 6–1a on page WD 387). The first two columns contain the feature article and the third column contains announcements. The characters in the paragraphs are aligned on both the right and left edges — similar to newspaper columns. The first letter in the first paragraph is much larger than the rest of the characters in the paragraph. A vertical rule separates the second and third columns. The steps on the following pages format the first page of the body of the newsletter using these desktop publishing features.

Plan Ahead

Determine the content for the body of the newsletter.
While content and subject matter of newsletters may vary, the procedures used to create newsletters are similar:

- **Write the body copy.** Newsletters should contain articles of interest and relevance to readers. Some share information, while others promote a product or service. Use active voice in body copy, which is more engaging than passive voice. Proofread the body copy to be sure it is error free. Check all facts for accuracy.

- **Organize body copy in columns.** Most newsletters divide body copy in columns. The body copy in columns, often called **snaking columns** or newspaper-style columns, flows from the bottom of one column to the top of the next column.

- **Format the body copy.** Begin the feature article on the first page of the newsletter. If the article spans multiple pages, use a continuation line, called jump or jump line, to guide the reader to the remainder of the article. The message at the end of the article on the first page of the newsletter is called a **jump-to line**, and a **jump-from line** marks the beginning of the continuation, which is usually on a subsequent page.

- **Maintain consistency.** Be consistent with placement of body copy elements in newsletter editions. If the newsletter contains announcements, for example, position them in the same location in each edition so that readers easily can find them.

- **Maximize white space.** Allow plenty of space between lines, paragraphs, and columns. Tightly packed text is difficult to read. Separate the text adequately from graphics, borders, and headings.

- **Incorporate color.** Use colors that complement those in the nameplate. Be careful not to overuse color. Restrict color below the nameplate to drop caps, subheads, graphics, and ruling lines. If you do not have a color printer, still change the colors because the colors will print in shades of black and gray. These shades add variety to the newsletter.

(continued)

Plan
Ahead

(continued)

- **Select and format subheads.** Develop subheads with as few words as possible. Readers should be able to identify content of the next topic by glancing at a subhead. Subheads should be emphasized in the newsletter but should not compete with text in the nameplate. Use a larger, bold, or otherwise contrasting font for subheads so that they stand apart from the body copy. Use this same format for all subheads for consistency. Leave a space above subheads to visually separate their content from the previous topic. Be consistent with spacing above and below subheads throughout the newsletter.

- **Divide sections with vertical rules.** Use vertical rules to guide the reader through the newsletter.

- **Enhance the document with visuals.** Add energy to the newsletter and emphasis to important points with graphics, pull-quotes, and other visuals such as drop caps to mark beginning of an article. Use these elements sparingly, however, so that the newsletter does not look crowded. Fewer, large visuals are more effective several smaller ones. If you use a graphic that you did not create, be sure to obtain permission to use it in the newsletter and give necessary credit to the creator of the graphic.

Columns

When you begin a document in Word, it has one column. You can divide a portion of a document or the entire document in multiple columns. Within each column, you can type, modify, or format text.

To divide a portion of a document in multiple columns, you use section breaks. Word requires that a new section be created each time you alter the number of columns in a document. Thus, if a document has a nameplate (one column) followed by an article of three columns followed by an article of two columns, the document would be divided in three separate sections.

Plan
Ahead

Organize body copy in columns.
Be consistent from page to page with number of columns. Narrow columns generally are easier to read than wide ones. Columns, however, can be too narrow. A two- or three-column layout generally is appealing and offers a flexible design. Try to have between five and fifteen words per line. To do this, you may need to adjust the column width, the font size, or the leading (line spacing). Font size of text in columns should be no larger than 12 point but not so small that readers must strain to read the text.

BTW

Certification
The Microsoft Certified Application Specialist (MCAS) program provides an opportunity for you to obtain a valuable industry credential — proof that you have the Word 2007 skills required by employers. For more information see Appendix G or visit the Word 2007 Certification Web page (scsite.com/ wd2007/cert).

To Insert a Continuous Section Break

In this chapter, the nameplate is one column and the body of the newsletter is three columns. Thus, you must insert a continuous section break below the nameplate. The term, continuous, means the new section should be on the same page as the previous section, which, in this case, means that the three columns of body copy will be positioned directly below the nameplate on the first page of the newsletter. The following steps insert a continuous section break.

1

- With the insertion point at the end of the feature article title (shown in Figure 6–30 on page WD 406), press the ENTER key to position the insertion point below the article title.

- Display the Page Layout tab.

- Click the Insert Page and Section Breaks button on the Page Layout tab to display the Insert Page and Section Breaks gallery (Figure 6–31).

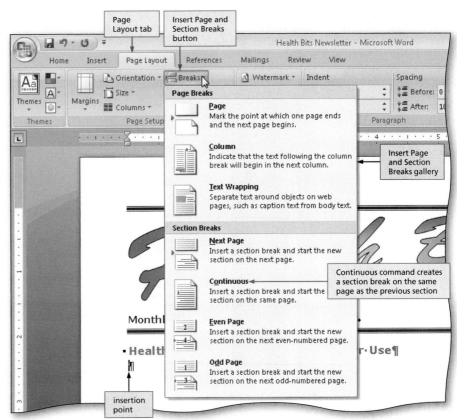

Figure 6–31

2

- Click Continuous in the Insert Page and Section Breaks gallery to insert a continuous section break above the insertion point (Figure 6–32).

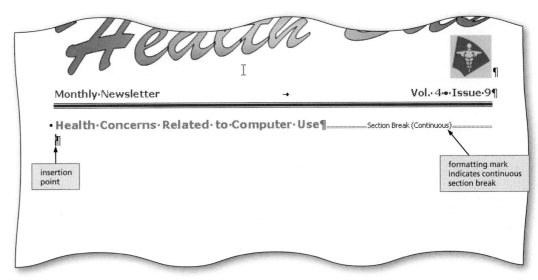

Figure 6–32

To Change the Number of Columns

The document now has two sections. The nameplate is in the first section, and the insertion point is in the second section. The second section should be formatted to three columns. Thus, the following steps format the second section in the document to three columns.

1

• Click the Columns button on the Page Layout tab to display the Columns gallery (Figure 6–33).

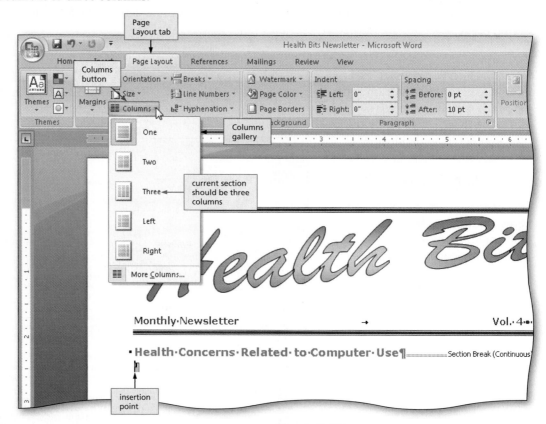

Figure 6–33

2

• Click Three in the Columns gallery to divide the section containing the insertion point in three evenly sized and spaced columns (Figure 6–34).

Q&A

What if I want columns of different widths?

You would click the More Columns command in the Columns gallery, which displays the Columns dialog box. In this dialog box, you can specify varying column widths and spacing.

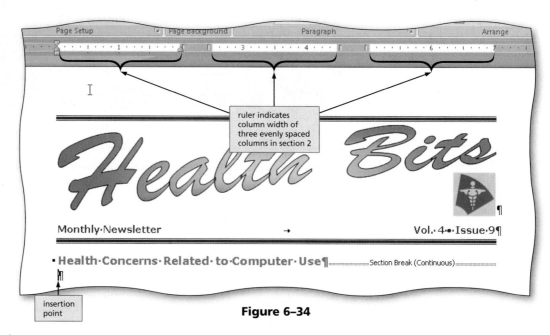

Figure 6–34

To Justify a Paragraph

The text in the paragraphs of the body of the newsletter is **justified**, which means that the left and right margins are aligned, like the edges of newspaper columns. The following step enters the first paragraph of the feature article using justified alignment.

1

- Display the Home tab.

- Click the Justify button on the Home tab so that Word aligns both the left and right margins of typed text.

- Type the first paragraph of the feature article (Figure 6–35): The widespread use of computers has been causing health concerns. Computer users should be proactive and minimize their chance of health complications. This article discusses computer health risks and preventions.

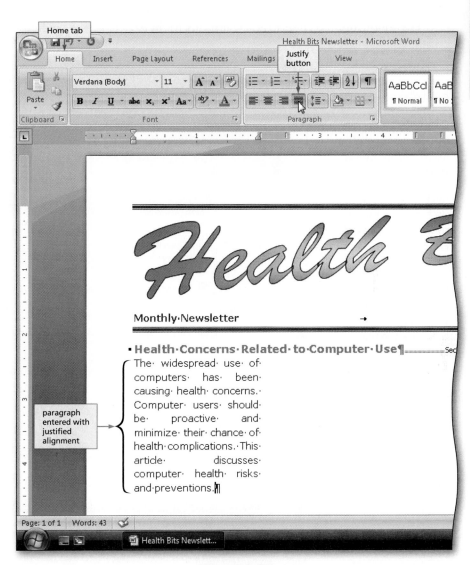

Figure 6–35

Q&A

Why do some words have extra space between them?

When a paragraph is formatted to justified alignment, Word places extra space between words so that the left and right edges of the paragraph are aligned. To remedy big gaps, sometimes called rivers, you can add or rearrange words, change the column width, change the font size, and so on.

Other Ways

1. Right-click paragraph, click Paragraph on shortcut menu, click Indents and Spacing tab, click Alignment box arrow, click Justified, click OK button

2. Click Paragraph Dialog Box Launcher, click Indents and Spacing tab, click Alignment box arrow, click Justified, click OK button

3. Press CTRL+J

To Insert a File in a Column of the Newsletter

Instead of typing the rest of the feature article in the newsletter in this chapter, the next step is to insert a file named Health Bits Main Article in the newsletter. This file, which contains the remainder of the feature article, is located on the Data Files for Students. See the inside back cover of this book for instructions on downloading the Data Files for Students, or contact your instructor for information about accessing the required files.

The following steps insert the Health Bits Main Article file in a column of the newsletter.

1

- Press the ENTER key.

- Display the Insert tab.

- Click the Insert Object button arrow on the Insert tab to display the Object menu.

- Click Text from File on the Object menu to display the Insert File dialog box.

- With your USB flash drive connected to one of the computer's USB ports, locate and then click the file called Health Bits Main Article on the USB flash drive to select the file (Figure 6–36).

Figure 6–36

2

- Click the Insert button to insert the file, Health Bits Main Article, in the file Health Bits Newsletter at the location of the insertion point.

- Scroll so that the bottom of the first page appears in the document window so that you can see how the article fills the three columns on the first and second pages (Figure 6–37).

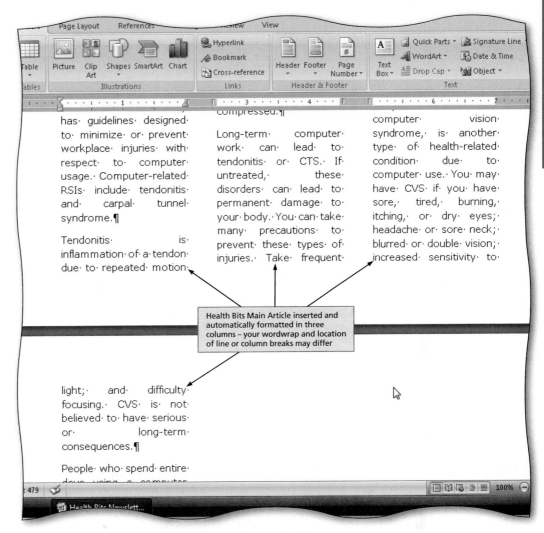

> Health Bits Main Article inserted and automatically formatted in three columns – your wordwrap and location of line or column breaks may differ

Figure 6–37

To Change Spacing below a Paragraph

The space between the feature article title and the text in the feature article is tight. To improve readability, this newsletter has additional white space below the feature article title. The following steps increase the spacing below the paragraph containing the feature article title.

1 Scroll to the top of the document and then position the insertion point in the paragraph to be adjusted, in this case, the paragraph containing the article title.

2 Display the Page Layout tab.

3 Click the Spacing After box up arrow on the Page Layout tab as many times as necessary until 12 pt is displayed in the Spacing After text box (Figure 6–38 on the next page).

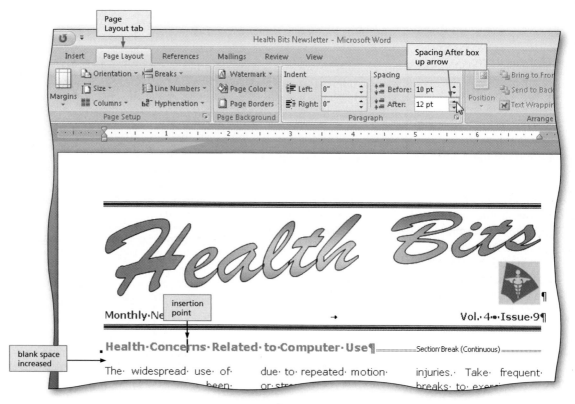

Figure 6–38

To Increase Column Width

The columns in the newsletter currently contain many rivers due to the justified alignment in the narrow column width. To eliminate some of the rivers, you increase the size of the columns slightly in this newsletter. The following steps increase column widths.

- Position the insertion point somewhere in the feature article text.

- Click the Columns button on the Page Layout tab to display the Columns gallery (Figure 6–39).

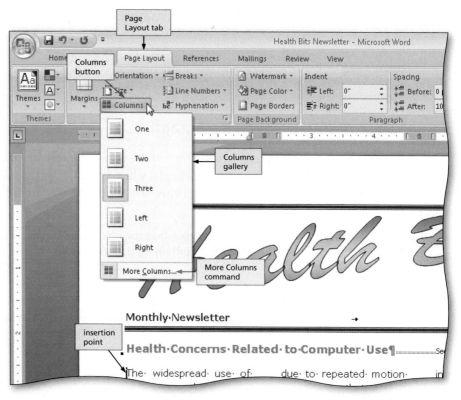

Figure 6–39

2

- Click More Columns in the Columns gallery to display the Columns dialog box.

- In the 'Width and spacing' area, click the Width box up arrow as many times as necessary until the Width box reads 2.1" (Figure 6–40).

Q&A

How would I make the columns different widths?

You would remove the check mark from the 'Equal column width' check box and then set the individual column widths in the dialog box.

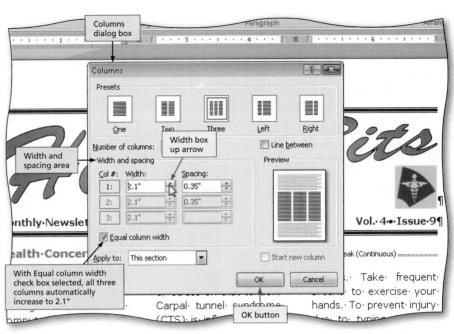

Figure 6–40

3

- Click the OK button to make the columns slightly wider (Figure 6–41).

Figure 6–41

Other Ways

1. Double-click space between columns on ruler, enter column width in dialog box, click OK button

2. Drag column boundaries on ruler

To Format a Letter as a Drop Cap

The first letter in the feature article in this newsletter is formatted as a drop cap. A **drop cap** is a capital letter whose font size is larger than the rest of the characters in the paragraph. In Word, the drop cap can sink into the first few lines of text, or it can extend into the left margin, which often is called a stick-up cap. In this newsletter, the paragraph text wraps around the drop cap.

The following steps create a drop cap in the first paragraph of the feature article in the newsletter.

- Position the insertion point somewhere in the first paragraph of the feature article.

- Display the Insert tab.

- Click the Drop Cap button on the Insert tab to display the Drop Cap gallery (Figure 6–42).

Experiment

- Point to various commands in the Drop Cap gallery to see a live pre-view of the drop cap formats in the document.

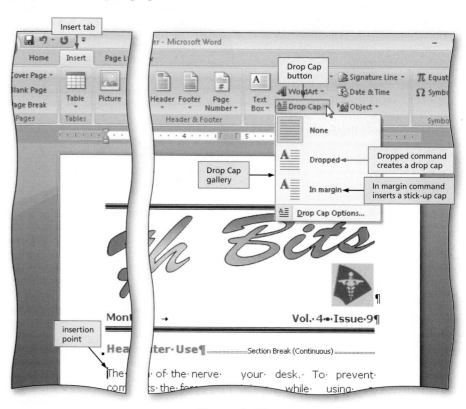

Figure 6–42

- Click Dropped in the Drop Cap gallery to format the T in the word, The, as a drop cap and wrap subsequent text in the paragraph around the drop cap (Figure 6–43).

Q&A

What is the outline around the drop cap in the document?

When you format a letter as a drop cap, Word places a frame around it. A **frame** is a container for text that allows you to position the text anywhere on the page. Word formats a frame for the drop cap so that text wraps around it. The frame also contains a paragraph mark nonprinting character to the right of the drop cap, which may or may not be visible on your screen.

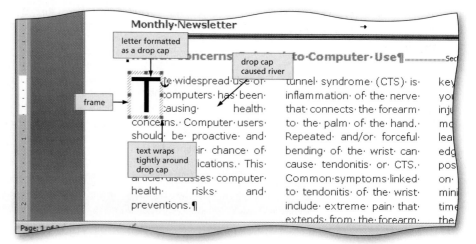

Figure 6–43

To Format the Drop Cap

The drop cap caused a river in the third line of the paragraph, and the drop cap also is too close to the text in the first line of the paragraph. You will resize the frame around the drop cap to remedy these two problems. Also, the drop cap is to be a gold color. The following steps apply these formats to the drop cap.

- Drag the right-middle sizing handle on the frame slightly rightward until the text in the first three lines of the paragraph looks like Figure 6–44.

Q&A What if my frame no longer is displayed?

Click the drop cap to select it. Then, click the blue selection rectangle to display the frame.

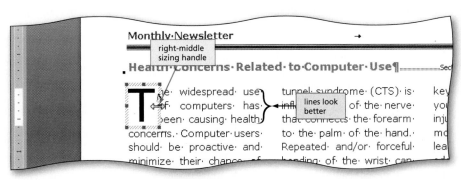

Figure 6–44

Q&A What if the drop cap moves on the page?

Position the mouse pointer on an edge of the drop cap frame and when the mouse pointer has a four-headed arrow attached to it, drag the drop cap to the correct location.

- Triple-click inside the frame to select the drop cap.

- Right-click the selected drop cap to display the Mini toolbar. Click the Font Color button arrow on the Mini toolbar to display the Font Color gallery (Figure 6–45).

- Click Gold, Accent 3, Darker 50% (seventh color in the last row of Theme Colors) to change the color of the drop cap.

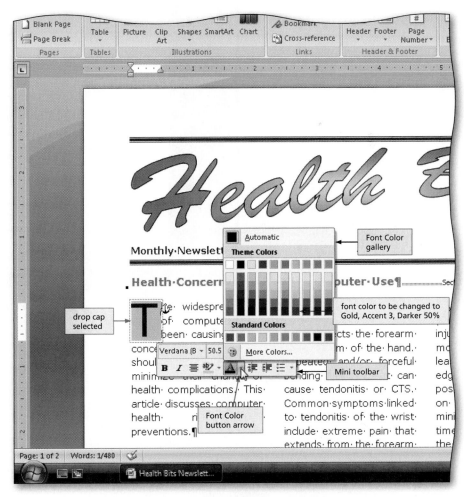

Figure 6–45

To Insert a Next Page Section Break

The third column on the first page of the newsletter is not a continuation of the feature article. The third column, instead, contains several member announcements. The feature article continues on the second page of the newsletter (shown in Figure 6–1b on page WD 387). Thus, you must insert a next page section break at the bottom of the second column so that the remainder of the feature article moves to the second page. The following steps insert a next page section break at the bottom of the second column.

1

- Scroll to display the bottom of the second column of the first page of the newsletter in the document window. Position the insertion point to the left of the L in the paragraph beginning with the word, Long-term.

- Display the Page Layout tab.

- Click the Insert Page and Section Breaks button on the Page Layout tab to display the Insert Page and Section Breaks gallery (Figure 6–46).

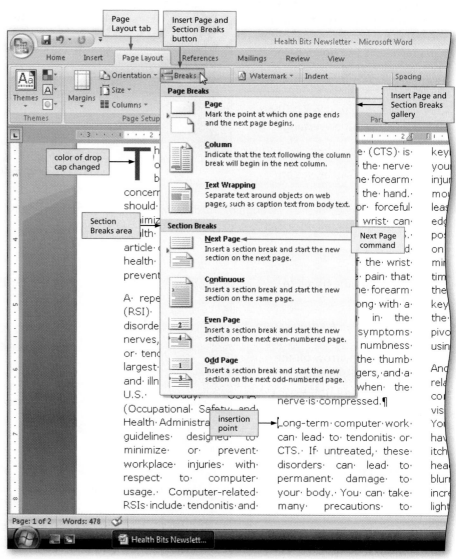

Figure 6–46

2

- In the Section Breaks area in the gallery, click Next Page to insert a section break and position the insertion point on the next page (Figure 6–47).

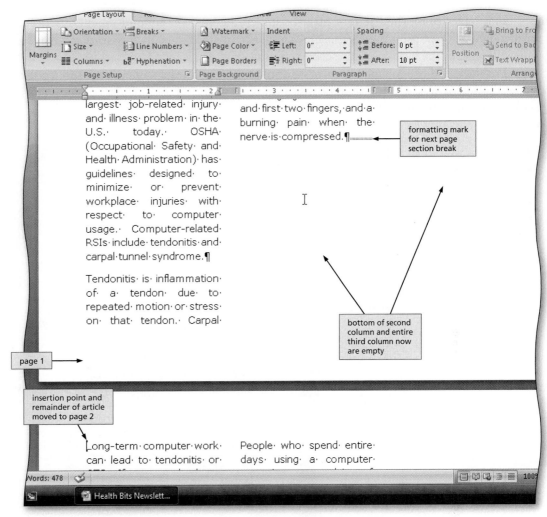

Figure 6–47

To Enter Text

The next step is to insert a jump-to line at the end of the second column, informing the reader where to look for the rest of the feature article. The following steps insert text at the bottom of the second column.

1 Scroll to display the bottom of the second column of the first page of the newsletter in the document window and then position the insertion point between the paragraph mark and the section break notation.

2 Press the ENTER key twice to insert a blank line for the jump-to text above the section break notation.

3 Press the UP ARROW key to position the insertion point on the blank line.

4 Press CTRL+R to right align the paragraph mark. Press CTRL+I to turn on the italic format. Type (Continued on next page) as the jump-to text and then press CTRL+I again to turn off the italic format.

BTW

Quick Reference
For a table that lists how to complete the tasks covered in this book using the mouse, Ribbon, shortcut menu, and keyboard, see the Quick Reference Summary at the back of this book, or visit the Word 2007 Quick Reference Web page (scsite.com/wd2007/qr).

To Insert a Column Break

In the Health Bits newsletters, for consistency, the member announcements always begin at the top of the third column. If you insert the Health Bits Announcements at the current location of the insertion point, however, they will begin at the bottom of the second column.

For the member announcements to be displayed in the third column, you insert a **column break** at the bottom of the second column, which places the insertion point at the top of the next column. Thus, the next step is to insert a column break at the bottom of the second column.

- Position the insertion point to the left of the paragraph mark of the line containing the next page section break, which is the location where the column break should be inserted.

- Click the Insert Page and Section Breaks button on the Page Layout tab to display the Insert Page and Section Breaks gallery (Figure 6–48).

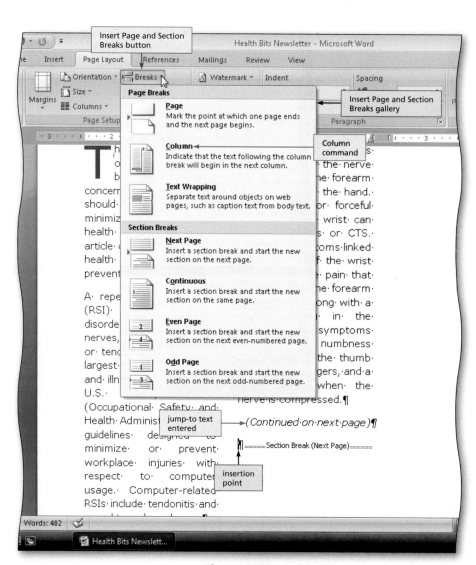

Figure 6–48

2

- Click Column in the Insert Page and Section Breaks gallery to insert a column break at the bottom of the second column on page 1 and move the insertion point to the top of the third column (Figure 6–49).

What if I wanted to remove a column break?

You would double-click it to select it and then click the Cut button on the Home tab or press the DELETE key.

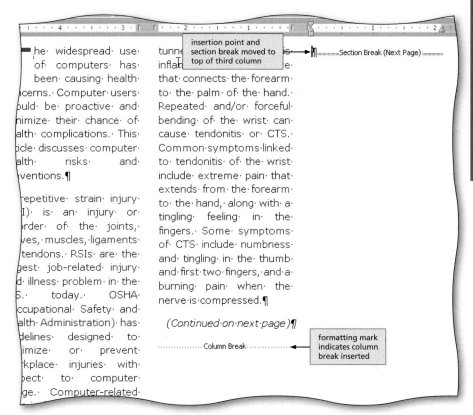

Figure 6–49

Other Ways
1. Press CTRL+SHIFT+ENTER

To Save a Document Again

You have performed several steps since the last save. Thus, you should save the newsletter again.

1 Save the newsletter again with the same file name, Health Bits Newsletter.

To Insert a File in a Column of the Newsletter

So that you do not have to enter the entire third column of announcements in the newsletter, the next step in the project is to insert the file named Health Bits Announcements in the third column of the newsletter. This file contains the three announcements: the first about a group meeting, the second about member discounts, and the third about the topic of the next newsletter issue.

The Health Bits Announcements file is located on the Data Files for Students. See the inside back cover of this book for instructions on downloading the Data Files for Students, or contact your instructor for information about accessing the required files. The steps below and at the top of the next page insert a file in a column of the newsletter.

1 With the insertion point at the top of the third column, display the Insert tab.

2 Click the Insert Object button arrow on the Insert tab to display the Object menu and then click Text from File on the Object menu to display the Insert File dialog box.

3 With your USB flash drive connected to one of the computer's USB ports, locate and then click the file called Health Bits Announcements on the USB flash drive to select the file.

4 Click the Insert button to insert the file, Health Bits Announcements, in the file Health Bits Newsletter in the third column of the newsletter.

Q&A What if text from the announcements column spills onto the second page of the newsletter?

You will format text in the announcements column so that all of its text fits in the third column of the first page.

5 Press SHIFT+F5 to return the insertion point to the last editing location, that is, the top of the third column on the first page of the newsletter.

To Format Text as a Heading Style

The announcements in the third column contain three subheads that need to be formatted so that they better identify their respective messages. The following steps apply the Heading 3 style to the first subhead in the announcements column.

1 Position the insertion point somewhere in the subhead, GROUP MEETING.

2 Display the Home tab.

3 Click the More button in the Styles gallery to expand the gallery. Click Heading 3 in the expanded Styles gallery to apply the Heading 3 style to the paragraph containing the insertion point (Figure 6–50).

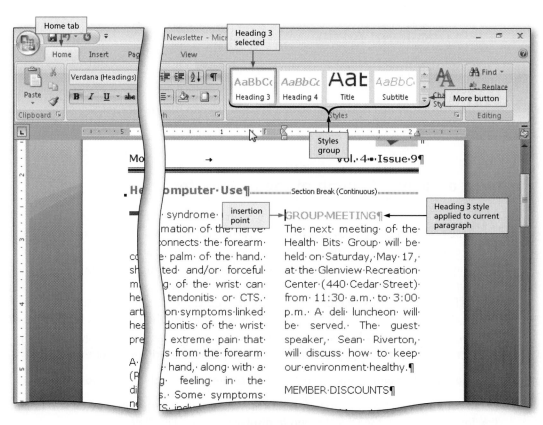

Figure 6–50

To Format More Text as a Heading Style

The following steps apply the Heading 3 style to the second and third subheads in the announcements column.

1 Position the insertion point somewhere in the subhead, MEMBER DISCOUNTS.

2 Click Heading 3 in the Styles gallery to apply the Heading 3 style to the second subhead in the announcements column.

3 Position the insertion point somewhere in the subhead, NEXT ISSUE, and then apply the Heading 3 style to this third subhead in the announcements column.

4 If an extra blank paragraph mark along with the next page section break is on the second page of the newsletter instead of the first page, position the insertion point on the paragraph mark at the end of the paragraph below the NEXT ISSUE subhead and then press the DELETE key so that the second page of the newsletter contains the remainder of the feature article (Figure 6–51).

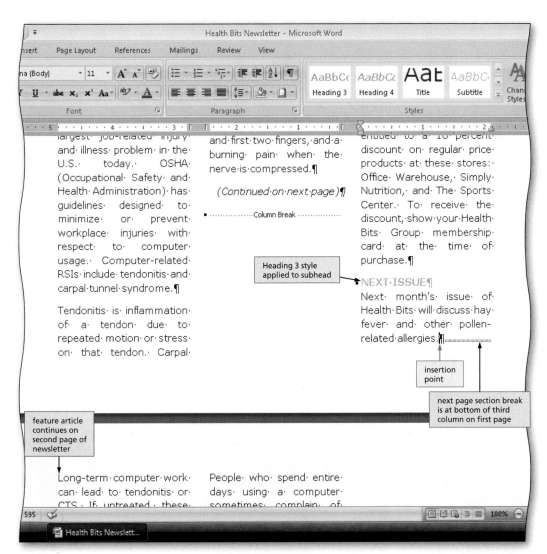

Figure 6–51

To Update a Style to Match a Selection

Instead of bright green, the subheads in this newsletter are the same gold color as the drop cap. The following steps change the color of the characters in the first subhead and then update the Heading 3 style so that all other subheads match this modified text.

1

- Scroll to and then select the line containing the subhead, GROUP MEETING.

- Right-click the selected subhead text to display the Mini toolbar and shortcut menu.

- Click the Font Color button on the Mini toolbar to change the color of the selected subhead to Gold, Accent 3, Darker 50%.

Q&A What if my Font Color button does not display the correct color?

Click the Font Color button arrow and select the correct color in the Font Color gallery.

2

- Right-click the selected subhead text again and then point to Styles on the shortcut menu to display the Styles menu (Figure 6–52).

3

- On the Styles menu, click Update Heading 3 to Match Selection, which modifies the Heading 3 style to match the formats of the selected text and changes all other Heading 3 text in the document to the updated style.

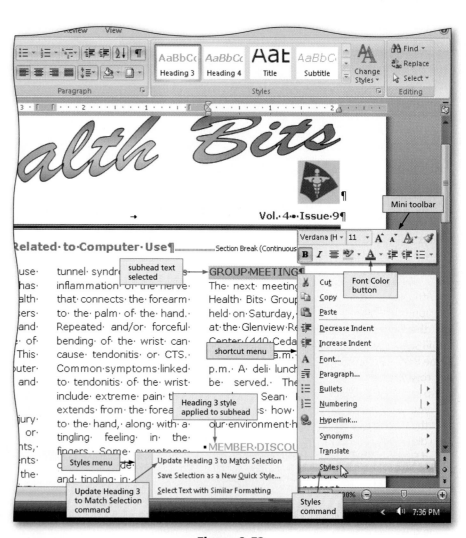

Figure 6–52

Other Ways

1. Right-click style name in Styles gallery on Home tab, click Update [style name] to Match Selection on shortcut menu

Vertical Rules

In newsletters, you often see a vertical rule separating columns. The newsletter in this chapter has a vertical rule between the second and third columns, that is, between the feature article and the announcements.

Divide sections with vertical rules.
If a multi-column newsletter contains a single article, place a vertical rule between every column. If different columns present different articles, place a vertical rule between each article.

Plan Ahead

To Place a Vertical Rule between Columns

In Word, a vertical rule is created with a left or right border that is spaced several points from the text. A point is approximately 1/72 of an inch. The following steps place a vertical rule between the second and third columns of the newsletter.

- Change the zoom level to 70% and then scroll through the document so that the entire third column is displayed in the document window.

- Drag through all of the text in the third column of the newsletter to select it.

- With the third column of page 1 in the newsletter still selected, click the Borders button arrow on the Home tab and then click Borders and Shading in the Borders gallery to display the Borders and Shading dialog box.

- If necessary, click the Borders tab in the dialog box.

- Click the Left Border button in the Preview area (Figure 6–53).

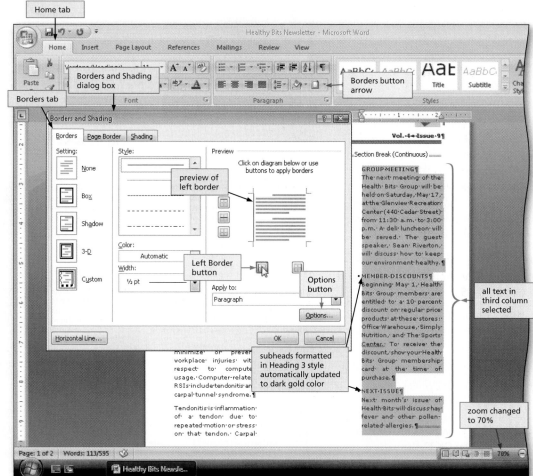

Figure 6–53

2

- Click the Options button to display the Border and Shading Options dialog box.

- In the dialog box, change the Left text box to 10 pt, which instructs Word to move the left border 10 points from the edge of the paragraph (Figure 6–54).

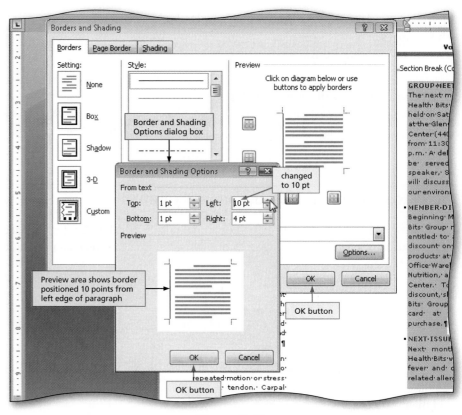

Figure 6–54

3

- Click the OK button in each open dialog box to draw a left border that is positioned 10 points from the edge of the text.

- Click in the document to remove the selection from the third column (Figure 6–55).

 Q&A

How would I place a vertical rule between every column in a newsletter?

You would click the Columns button on the Page Layout tab, click the More Columns command in the Columns gallery, place a check mark in the Line between check box, and then click the OK button.

- Change the zoom level to 100% so that the newsletter text is easier to read.

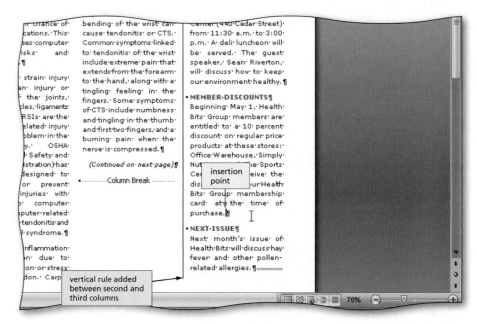

Figure 6–55

Other Ways

1. Click Page Borders button on Page Layout tab, click Borders tab in Borders and Shading dialog box, select desired border, click Options button, adjust border from text, click OK button in each dialog box

Creating a Pull-Quote

A pull-quote is text pulled, or copied, from the text of the document and given graphical emphasis so that it stands apart and commands the reader's attention. The newsletter in this project has a pull-quote on the first page between the first and second columns (Figure 6–1a on page WD 387).

Enhance the document with pull-quotes.
Because of their bold emphasis, pull-quotes should be used sparingly in a newsletter. Pull-quotes are useful for breaking the monotony of long columns of text. Typically, quotation marks are used only if you are quoting someone directly. If you use quotation marks, use curly (or smart) quotation marks instead of straight quotation marks.

Plan Ahead

To create the pull-quote in this newsletter, follow this general procedure:

1. Create a **text box**, which is a container for text that allows you to position the text anywhere on the page.

2. Copy the text from the existing document to the Clipboard and then paste the text from the Clipboard to the text box.

3. Resize the text box.

4. Move the text box to the desired location.

To Insert a Text Box

The first step in creating the pull-quote is to insert a text box. A text box is like a frame; the difference is that a text box has more graphical formatting options than does a frame. Word provides a variety of built-in text boxes, saving you the time of formatting the text box. The following steps insert a built-in text box.

1

- Scroll to display the top portion of the newsletter in the document window and position the insertion point at an approximate location for the pull-quote (you will position the pull-quote at the exact location in a later step).

- Display the Insert tab.

- Click the Text Box button on the Insert tab to display the Text Box gallery (Figure 6–56).

Experiment

- Scroll through the Text Box gallery to see the variety of text box styles available.

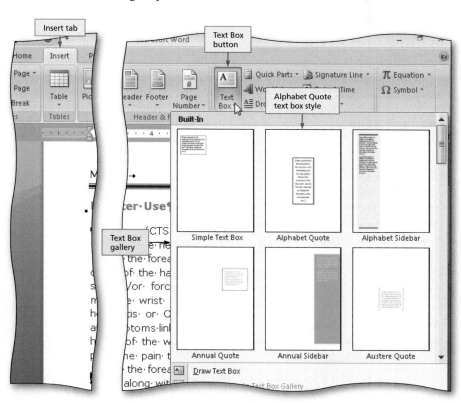

Figure 6–56

- Click Alphabet Quote in the Text Box gallery to insert that text box style in the document (Figure 6–57).

Q&A Does my text box need to be in the same location as Figure 6–57?

No. You will move the text box later.

Q&A The layout of the first page is all messed up because of the text box. What do I do?

You will enter text in the text box and then position it in the correct spot. At that time, the layout of the first page will be fixed.

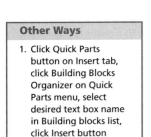

Other Ways

1. Click Quick Parts button on Insert tab, click Building Blocks Organizer on Quick Parts menu, select desired text box name in Building blocks list, click Insert button

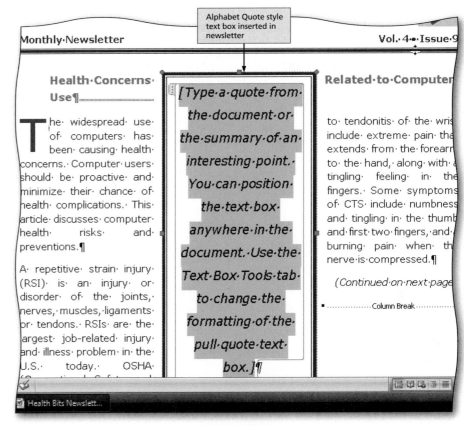

Figure 6–57

To Copy and Paste

The next step in creating the pull-quote is to copy text from the newsletter to the Clipboard and then paste the text into the text box. The item being copied is called the **source object**. The object to which you are pasting is called the **destination object**. Thus, the source object is a sentence in the body copy of the newsletter, and the destination object is the text box. The following steps copy and then paste the sentence.

- If necessary, scroll to display the second paragraph in the newsletter and then select its second sentence, which is the text for the pull-quote: RSIs are the largest job-related injury and illness problem in the U.S. today.

- If necessary, display the Home tab.

- With the sentence to be copied selected, click the Copy button on the Home tab (Figure 6–58).

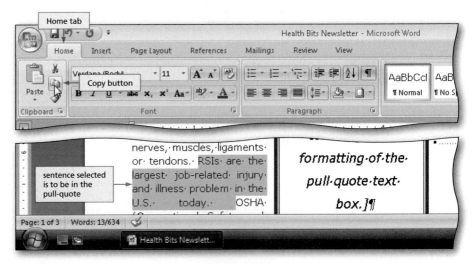

Figure 6–58

2

- If necessary, scroll to display the text box in the document window. Click the text in the text box to select it.

- Click the Paste button on the Home tab to paste the contents of the Clipboard in the text box, which replaces the selected text.

Q&A Why did the Paste menu appear below the Paste button?

You clicked the Paste button arrow instead of the Paste button.

3

- Because you want the pasted text to use the formats that were in the text box (the destination) instead of the formats of the copied text (the source), click the Paste Options button to display the Paste Options menu (Figure 6–59).

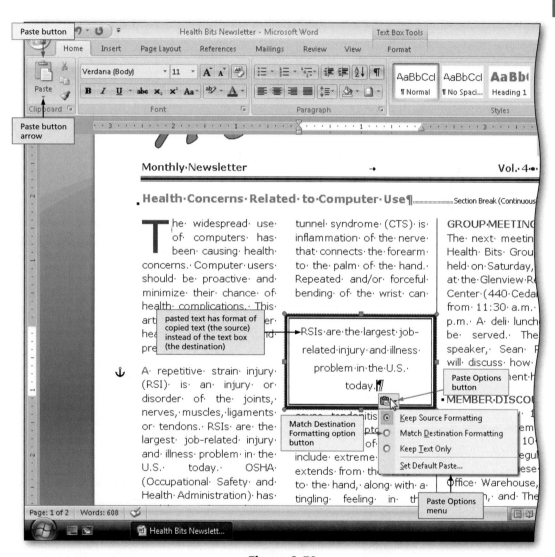

Figure 6–59

Q&A What if the Paste Options button does not appear?

Format the text in the text box to italic with a font size of 14 point and then skip Step 4 on the next page.

Q&A What if my pasted text already is formatted like the destination (i.e., looks like Figure 6–60 on the next page)?

Skip steps 3 and 4.

4

- Click Match Destination Formatting on the Paste Options menu to format the pasted text the same as the destination, which in this case, is the text box contents (Figure 6–60).

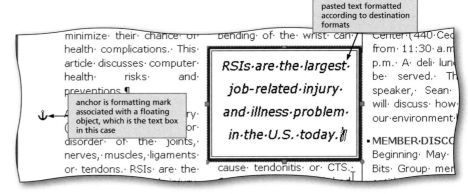

Figure 6–60

To Format Text

The next steps format the text in the pull-quote to color the text and change line spacing to 1.15.

1 Triple-click the pull-quote text to select it.

2 Use the Font Color button arrow to change the pull-quote's font color to Pink, Accent 2, Darker 50%.

3 Click in the pull-quote text to remove the selection.

4 Click the Line spacing button and then click 1.15 in the Line spacing gallery to change the line spacing of the pull-quote (Figure 6–61).

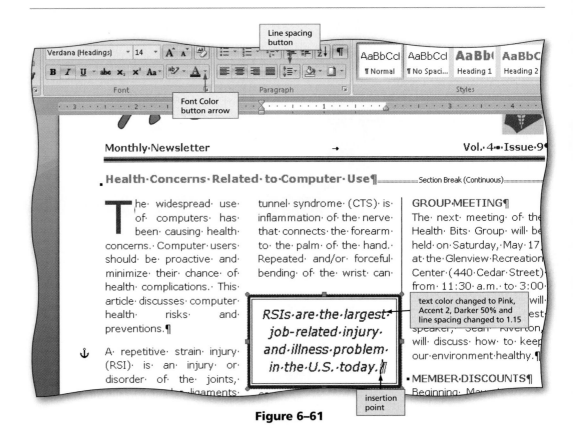

Figure 6–61

To Resize a Text Box

The next step in formatting the pull-quote is to resize the text box. You resize a text box the same way as any other object. That is, you drag its sizing handles. The following steps resize the text box.

1 If necessary, click the edge of the text box to select it.

2 Drag the right-middle sizing handle inward about one inch to make the pull-quote narrower so that the pull-quote text looks like Figure 6–62.

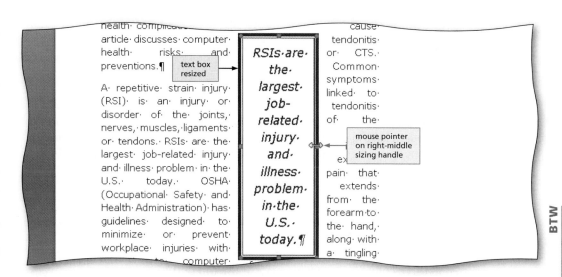

Figure 6–62

BTW

Moving Text Boxes
To move a text box using the keyboard, select the text box and then press the arrow keys on the keyboard. For example, each time you press the DOWN ARROW key, the selected text box moves down one line.

To Position a Text Box

The final step is to position the pull-quote text box between the first and second columns of the newsletter. The following step moves the text box to the desired location.

1

• With the text box still selected, drag the text box to its new location (Figure 6–63). You may need to drag and/or resize the text box a couple of times so that it looks similar to this figure.

• Click outside the text box to remove the selection.

Q&A Why does my text wrap differently around the text box?

Differences in wordwrap relate to the printer used by your computer. Thus, your document may wordwrap around the text box differently.

Figure 6–63

To Save a Document Again

You have performed several steps since the last save. You should save the newsletter again.

 Save the newsletter again with the same file name, Health Bits Newsletter.

Formatting the Second Page of the Newsletter

The second page of the newsletter (Figure 6–1b on page WD 387) continues the feature article that began in the first two columns on the first page. The nameplate on the second page is simpler than the one on the first page of the newsletter. In addition to the text in the feature article, page two contains a graphic. The following pages format the second page of the newsletter in this project.

Plan Ahead	**Create the nameplate.** The top of the inner pages of a newsletter may or may not have a nameplate. If you choose to create one for your inner pages, it should not be the same as, or compete with, the one on the first page. Inner page nameplates usually contain only a portion of the nameplate from the first page of a newsletter.

To Change Column Formatting

The document currently is formatted in three columns. The nameplate at the top of the second page, however, should be in a single column. The next step, then, is to change the number of columns at the top of the second page from three to one.

As discussed earlier in this project, Word requires a new section each time you change the number of columns in a document. Thus, you first must insert a continuous section break and then format the section to one column so that the nameplate can be entered on the second page of the newsletter. The following steps insert a continuous section break and then change the column format.

- Scroll through the document and then position the mouse pointer at the upper-left corner of the second page of the newsletter (to the left of L in Long-term).

- Display the Page Layout tab.

- Click the Insert Page and Section Breaks button on the Page Layout tab to display the Insert Page and Section Breaks gallery (Figure 6–64).

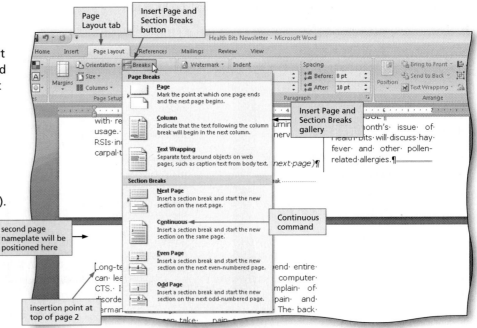

Figure 6–64

2

- Click Continuous in the Insert Page and Section Breaks gallery to insert a continuous section break above the insertion point.

- Press the UP ARROW key to position the insertion point to the left of the continuous section break just inserted.

- Click the Columns button on the Page Layout tab to display the Columns gallery (Figure 6–65).

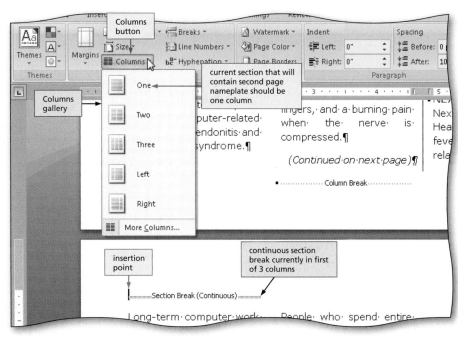

Figure 6–65

3

- Click the One in the Columns gallery to format the current section to one column, which now is ready for the second page nameplate (Figure 6–66).

Q&A

Can I change the column format of existing text?

Yes. If you already have typed text and would like it to be formatted in a different number of columns, select the text, click the Columns button on the Page Layout tab, and then click the number of columns desired in the Columns gallery. Word automatically creates a new section for the newly formatted columns.

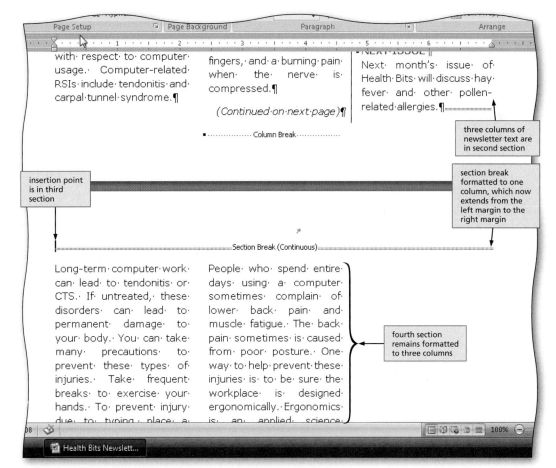

Figure 6–66

To Format and Enter Text

The following steps describe how to enter the newsletter title at the top of the second page in the third section.

1 With the insertion point to the left of the section break notation in the third section, press the ENTER key twice. Press the UP ARROW key to position the insertion point on the blank line above the continuous section break.

2 Display the Home tab. Click Heading 1 in the Styles gallery on the Home tab. Click the Center button on the Home tab to center the paragraph mark and insertion point.

3 Type HEALTH BITS as the newsletter title and then press the ENTER key.

To Split the Window

The rest of the nameplate on the second page is identical to the nameplate on the first page. That is, the issue information line is below the newsletter title, followed by a horizontal rule, which is followed by the title of the feature article. The next step is to copy these lines from the nameplate on the first page and then paste them on the second page.

To simplify this process, you would like to view the nameplate on the first page and the nameplate on the second page on the screen at the same time. Word allows you to split the window in two separate panes, each containing the current document and having its own scroll bar. This enables you to scroll to and view two different portions of the same document at the same time. The following steps split the Word window.

- Position the mouse pointer on the split box at the top of the vertical scroll bar, which changes the mouse pointer to a resize pointer (Figure 6–67).

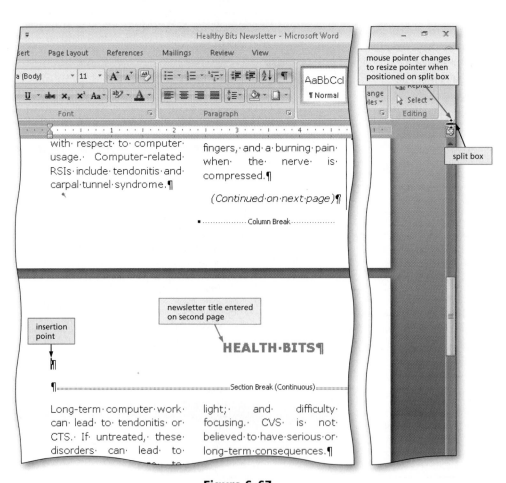

Figure 6–67

2

- Double-click the resize pointer to divide the document window in two separate panes - both the upper and lower panes display the current document (Figure 6–68).

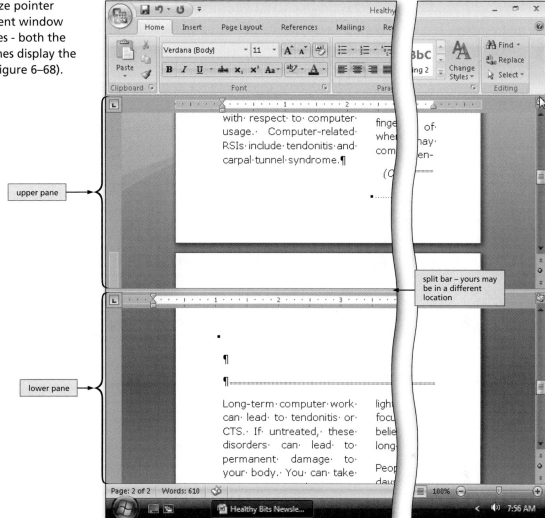

Figure 6–68

To Arrange All Open Word Documents on the Screen

If you have multiple Word documents open and want to view all of them at the same time on the screen, you can instruct Word to arrange all the open documents on the screen from top to bottom. If you wanted to arrange all open Word documents on the same screen, you would perform the following steps.

1. Click Arrange All on the View tab to display each open Word document on the screen.

2. To make one of the arranged documents fill the entire screen again, maximize the window by clicking its Maximize button or double-clicking its title bar.

To Copy and Paste Using Split Windows

The next step is to copy the bottom of the nameplate from the first page to the second page nameplate using the split window. The following steps copy and then paste using the split window.

1

- In the upper pane, scroll to display the nameplate on page 1.

- In the lower pane, scroll to display the nameplate on page 2.

- Select the issue information line and the feature article title on page 1.

- Click the Copy button on the Home tab to copy the selected text to the Clipboard (Figure 6–69).

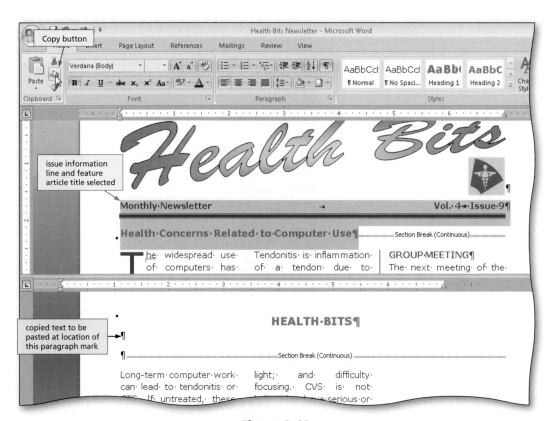

Figure 6–69

2

- Position the insertion point in the lower pane on the paragraph mark below the newsletter title.

- Click the Paste button on the Home tab to paste the issue information line and feature article title on the second page of the newsletter.

- If an extra paragraph mark appears below the feature article title, remove it (Figure 6–70).

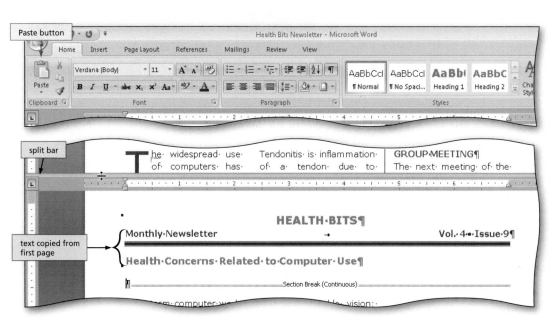

Figure 6–70

To Remove a Split Window

The next step is to remove the split window so that you can continue formatting the second page of the newsletter. The following step removes a split window.

1 Double-click the split bar, or click the Remove Split button on the View tab, or press ALT+SHIFT+C, to remove the split window and return to a single Word window on the screen.

To Enter Text

The second page of the feature article on the second page of this newsletter begins with a jump-from line (the continued message) immediately below the nameplate. The following steps enter the jump-from line.

1 With the insertion point on the line immediately below the pasted text, press CTRL+I to turn on the italic format. Type `(Continued from first page)` and then press CTRL+I to turn off the italic format.

2 If the continuous section break is on the line below the jump-from line, press the DELETE key to move it up to the same line as the jump-from line (Figure 6–71).

BTW

Using a Split Window to Copy Text
To move or copy text between parts of a long document, split the window into two panes. Display the text or graphics you want to move or copy in one pane and the destination for the text or graphics in the other pane, and then select and drag the text or graphics across the split bar.

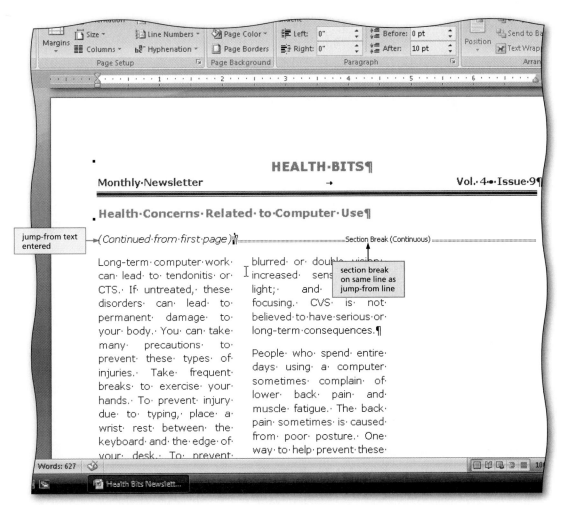

Figure 6–71

To Balance Columns

Currently, the text on the second page of the newsletter completely fills up the first column and almost fills the second column. The third column is empty. The text in the three columns should consume the same amount of vertical space. That is, the three columns should be balanced. To balance columns, you insert a continuous section break at the end of the text. The following steps balance columns.

 1

- Scroll to the bottom of the text in the second column on the second page of the newsletter and then position the insertion point at the end of the text.

- If an extra paragraph mark is below the last line of text, press the DELETE key to remove the extra paragraph mark.

- Display the Page Layout tab.

- Click the Insert Page and Section Breaks button on the Page Layout tab to display the Insert Page and Section Breaks gallery (Figure 6–72).

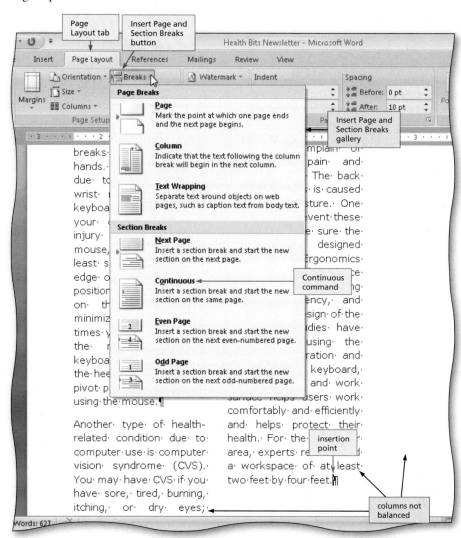

Figure 6–72

 2

- Click Continuous in the Insert Page and Section Breaks gallery to insert a continuous section break, which balances the columns on the second page of the newsletter (Figure 6–73).

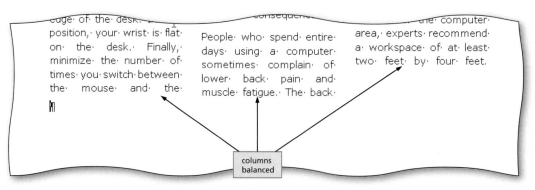

Figure 6–73

To Save a Document Again

You have performed several steps since the last save. Thus, you should save the newsletter again.

1 Save the newsletter again with the same file name, Health Bits Newsletter.

Modifying and Formatting a SmartArt Graphic

Recall from Chapter 4 that Microsoft Office 2007 includes **SmartArt graphics**, which are visual representations of ideas. Many different types of SmartArt graphics are available, allowing you to choose one that illustrates your message best.

In this newsletter, a SmartArt graphic is positioned in the lower-left corner of the second page, just below the first and second columns. Because the columns are small in the newsletter, it is best to work with a SmartArt graphic in a separate document window so that you easily can see all of its components. When finished editing the graphic, you can copy and paste it in the newsletter. You will follow these steps for the SmartArt graphic in this newsletter:

1. Open the document that contains the SmartArt graphic for the newsletter.

2. Modify the layout of the graphic. Add a shape and text to the graphic.

3. Copy and paste the graphic in the newsletter.

4. Resize the graphic and add a border to it.

To Open a Document from Word

The first draft of the SmartArt graphic is in a file called Hand and Eye Chart on the Data Files for Students. See the inside back cover of this book for instructions on downloading the Data Files for Students, or contact your instructor for information about accessing the required files. The following steps open the Hand and Eye Chart file from the USB flash drive.

1 With your USB flash drive connected to one of the computer's USB ports, click the Office Button and then click Open on the Office Button menu to display the Open dialog box.

2 Locate and select the Hand and Eye Chart file on the USB flash drive. Click the Open button to open the selected file and display its contents in the Word window.

3 Click the graphic to select it and display the SmartArt Tools tab and its subordinate tabs on the Ribbon (Figure 6–74).

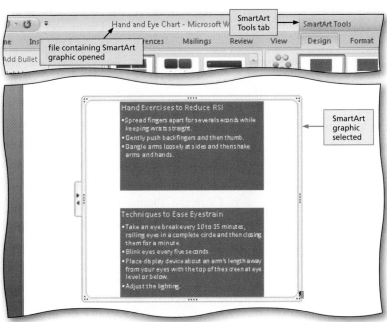

Figure 6–74

To Change the Layout of a SmartArt Graphic

The SmartArt graphic currently uses the Basic Block List layout. This newsletter uses the Vertical Bullet List layout. The following step changes the layout of an existing SmartArt graphic.

- If necessary, display the SmartArt Tools Design tab.

- With the SmartArt graphic selected, locate and click the Vertical Bullet List layout in the Layouts gallery to change the layout of the SmartArt graphic (Figure 6–75).

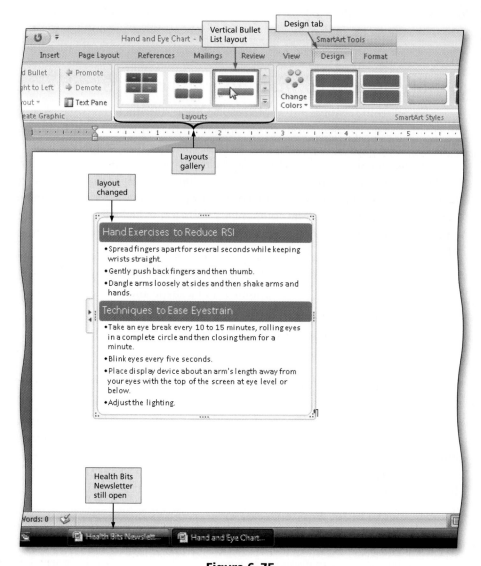

Figure 6–75

To Modify Theme Effects

If you wanted to change the theme effects, which would change the look of graphics such as SmartArt graphics, you would perform the following steps.

1. Click the Theme Effects button on the Page Layout tab.
2. Click the desired effect in the Theme Effects gallery.

To Add a Shape to a SmartArt Graphic

The current SmartArt graphic has two shapes — one for hand exercises and one for easing eyestrain. This newsletter has a third shape that outlines methods to minimize fatigue. The following step adds a shape to a SmartArt graphic.

1

- With the diagram selected, click the Add Shape button on the Design tab to add a shape to the SmartArt graphic (Figure 6–76).

Q&A Why did my screen display a menu instead of adding a shape?

You clicked the Add Shape button arrow instead of the Add Shape button. Clicking the Add Shape button adds the shape automatically; clicking the Add Shape button arrow displays a menu allowing you to specify the location of the shape.

Q&A How do I delete a shape?

Select the shape by clicking it and then press the DELETE key, or right-click the shape and then click Cut on the shortcut menu.

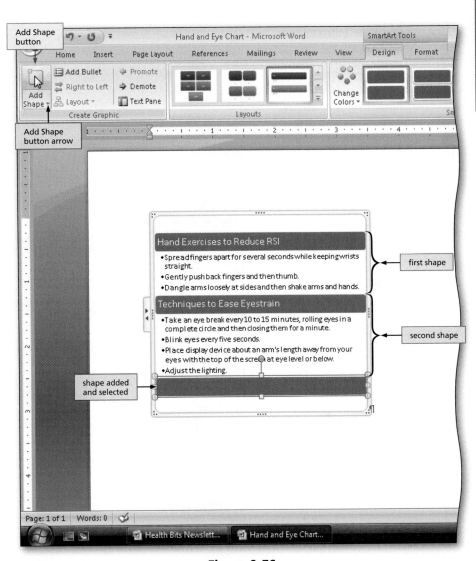

Figure 6–76

To Save Customized Themes

When you modify the theme effects, theme colors, or theme fonts, you can save the modified theme for future use. If you wanted to save a customized theme, you would perform the following steps.

1. Click the Themes button on the Page Layout tab to display the Themes gallery.
2. Click Save Current Theme in the Themes gallery.
3. Enter a theme name in the File name text box.
4. Click the Save button to add the saved theme to the Themes gallery.

To Add Text to a SmartArt Graphic through the Text Pane

In Chapter 4, you added text directly to the shapes in the SmartArt graphic. In this project, you enter the text through the Text pane. The following step uses the Text pane to add text to a shape.

1

- Click the Text Pane button on the Design tab to display the Text pane to the left of the SmartArt graphic.

- Scroll to the bottom of the Text pane and then, if necessary, position the insertion point to the right of the bullet that has no text to its right.

- Type Methods to Minimize Fatigue as the text for the shape (Figure 6–77).

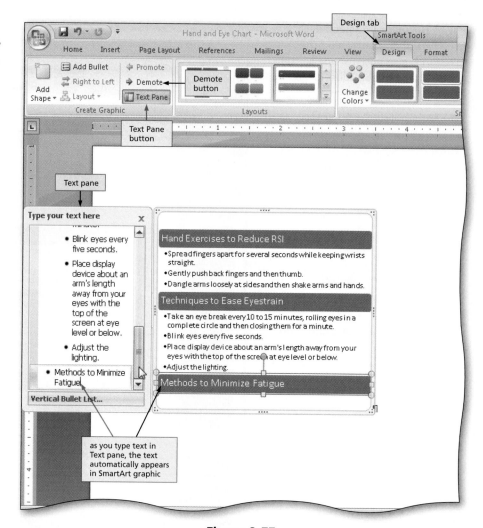

Figure 6–77

BTW

Demoting Text Pane Text

Instead of pressing the TAB key in the Text pane, you could click the Demote button on the Design tab to increase the indent for a bullet. You also can click the Promote button to decrease the indent for a bullet.

To Enter More Text to a SmartArt Graphic

The following steps enter the remaining text in the SmartArt graphic.

1 Press the ENTER key to add a new bullet and then press the TAB key to indent the bullet.

2 Type Sit properly in an adjustable height chair with feet flat on floor.

3 Press the ENTER key to add a new bullet.

4 Type Take a break every 30 to 60 minutes, standing up and walking around or stretching. (Figure 6–78).

5 Click the Close button on the Text Pane title bar to close the Text pane.

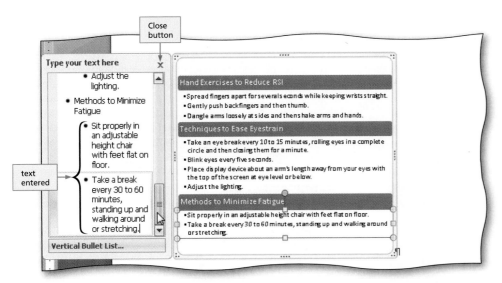

Figure 6–78

To Save an Active Document with a New File Name

To preserve the contents of the original Hand and Eye Chart file, you should save the active document with a new file name. The following steps save the active document with a new file name.

1 With the USB flash drive containing the Hand and Eye Chart file connected to one of the computer's USB ports, click the Office Button and then click Save As on the Office Button menu to display the Save As dialog box.

2 Save the document on the USB flash drive with the file name, Hand and Eye Chart Modified.

To Copy and Paste a SmartArt Graphic

The next step is to copy the SmartArt graphic from this document window and then paste it in the newsletter. The following steps use the Clipboard task pane to copy the graphic and then paste it in the second page of the newsletter.

1

- Display the Home tab.

- Click the Clipboard Dialog Box Launcher on the Home tab to display the Clipboard task pane.

- If the Office Clipboard in the Clipboard task pane is not empty, click the Clear All button in the Clipboard task pane.

- If necessary, click the SmartArt graphic to select it.

- Click the Copy button on the Home tab to copy the selected SmartArt graphic to the Office Clipboard (Figure 6–79).

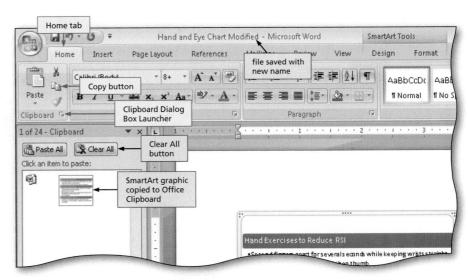

Figure 6–79

- Click Health Bits Newsletter - Microsoft Word program button on the Windows Vista taskbar to display the newsletter document.

- Position the insertion point at the bottom of the second page of the newsletter and then click the Paste button on the Home tab to paste the SmartArt graphic in the newsletter (Figure 6–80).

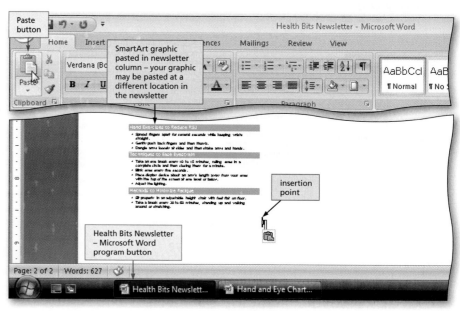

Figure 6–80

To Format a Graphic as Floating

The text in the newsletter should wrap around the graphic in a square shape. Thus, the next step is to change the graphic from inline to floating with a wrapping style of square. Perform the following steps to format the graphic as floating with square wrapping.

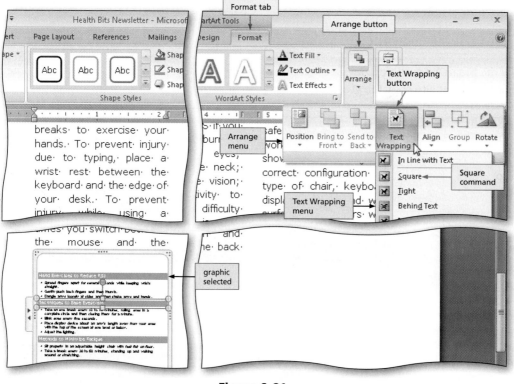

Figure 6–81

1 If necessary, double-click the SmartArt graphic to select it.

2 Display the SmartArt Tools Format tab on the Ribbon.

3 With the SmartArt graphic selected, click the Arrange button on the Format tab and then click the Text Wrapping button on the Arrange menu to display the Text Wrapping menu (Figure 6–81).

4 Click Square on the Text Wrapping menu to change the graphic from inline to floating with square wrapping.

To Resize and Position the SmartArt Graphic

The next task is to increase the size of the SmartArt graphic so that it is as wide as the first two columns in the newsletter and then position it in the bottom-left corner of the second page. The following steps resize and then position the graphic.

1 Drag the upper-right corner sizing handle outward until the graphic is approximately the same size as shown in Figure 6–82.

2 Point to the frame on the graphic and when the mouse has a four-headed arrow attached to it, drag the graphic to the location shown in Figure 6–82. You may have to drag the graphic a couple of times to position it similarly to the figure.

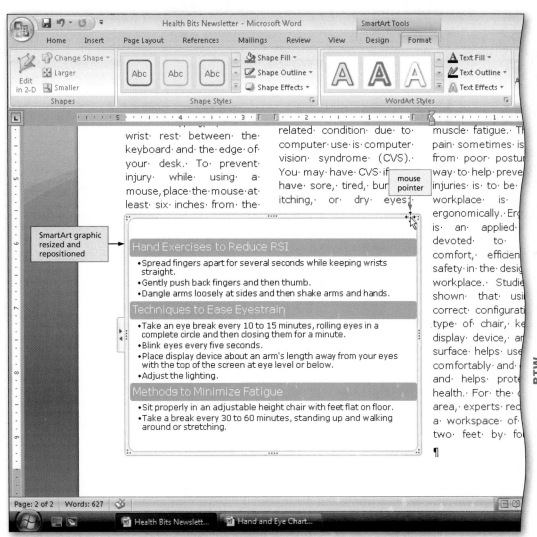

Figure 6–82

BTW

Space Around Graphics
The space between a graphic and the text, which sometimes is called the **run-around**, should be at least 1/8" and should be the same for all graphics in a document. Adjust the run-around of a selected floating graphic by doing the following: click the Arrange button on the SmartArt Tools Format tab, click the Position button on the Arrange menu, click the More Layout Options on the Position menu, adjust the values in the 'Distance from text' text boxes, and then click the OK button.

To Add an Outline to a SmartArt Graphic

The SmartArt graphic in this newsletter has a green outline around it. The following steps add an outline to a SmartArt graphic.

- Click the Shape Outline button arrow on the Format tab to display the Shape Outline gallery.

- Point to Green, Accent 1 in the Shape Outline gallery to display a live preview of that color outline applied to the SmartArt graphic in the document (Figure 6–83).

 Experiment

- Point to various colors in the Shape Outline gallery and watch the outline color around the SmartArt graphic change.

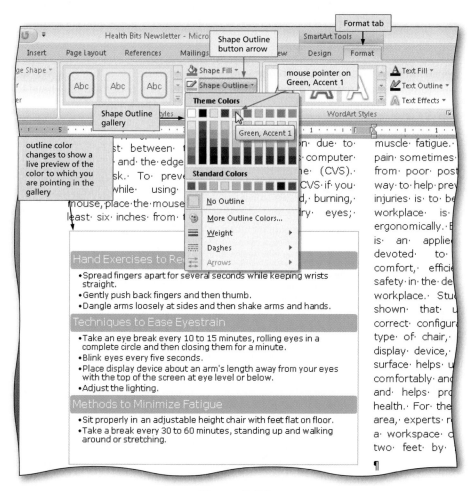

Figure 6–83

2

- Click Green, Accent 1 in the Shape Outline gallery to apply the selected outline color to the SmartArt graphic.

Q&A

Can I change other aspects of a graphic?

Yes. Through the Design and Format tabs, you can change the size of a shape, fill and outline colors, text styles and colors, and more.

- Click outside the graphic so that it is no longer selected.

Other Ways

1. Right-click selected graphic, click Format Object on shortcut menu, click Line Color in left pane, click Solid line, select color, click Close button

Finishing and Distributing the Newsletter

With the text and graphics in the newsletter entered and formatted, the next step is to look at the newsletter as a whole and determine if it looks finished in its current state. To give the newsletter a finished look, you will add a border to its edges.

Then, you will distribute the newsletter via e-mail. When you e-mail the newsletter, however, you cannot be certain that it will print correctly for the recipients because printers wordwrap text differently. To ensure that the newsletter will look the same on the recipients as on your computer, you will save the newsletter in a special format that allows others to view the document as you see it.

The following pages finish the document and then distribute it via e-mail.

To Zoom Two Pages

The last step in formatting the newsletter is to place a border around its edges. You can place both pages in the document window at once so that you can see all the page borders applied. The following steps zoom two pages.

1 Display the View tab.

2 Click the Two Pages button on the View tab to display both entire pages of the newsletter in the document window (Figure 6–84).

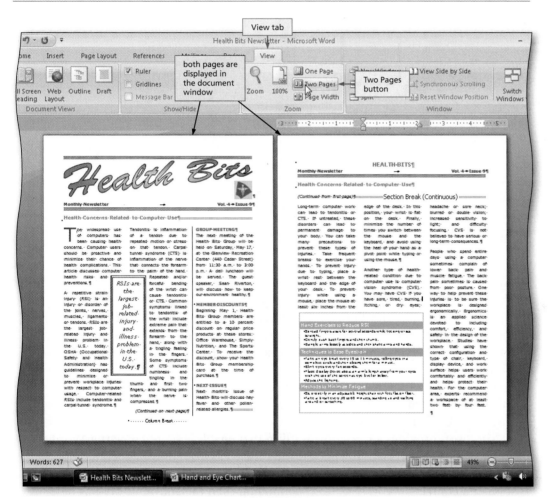

Figure 6–84

To Add a Page Border

This newsletter has a 4½ point gold border around the perimeter of each page. The steps below and on the next page add a page border around the pages of the newsletter.

1 Display the Page Layout tab.

2 Click the Page Borders button on the Page Layout tab to display the Borders and Shading dialog box. If necessary, click the Page Border tab.

Q&A | What if I cannot select the Page Borders button because it is dimmed?

Click somewhere in the newsletter to make the newsletter the active document and then redo Step 2.

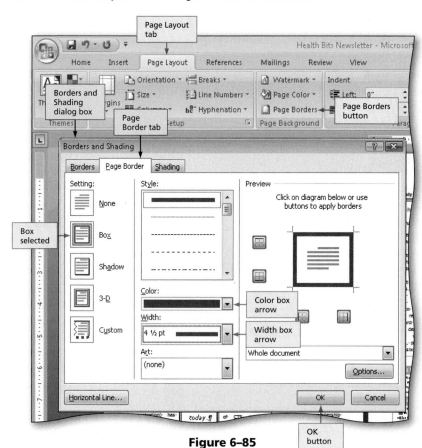

Figure 6–85

③ Click Box in the Setting area to specify a border on all four sides.

④ Click the Color box arrow and then click Gold, Accent 3, Darker 50% in the Color gallery.

⑤ Click the Width box arrow and then click 4 ½ pt (Figure 6–85).

⑥ Click the OK button to place the defined border on each page of the newsletter.

BTW

Printing Borders
In Word, page borders are positioned 24 points from the edge of the page. Many printers cannot print text and graphics that close to the edge of the page. To alleviate this problem, you may need to change the Measure from setting in the Borders and Shading Options dialog box so that the border is positioned from the edge of the text, instead of the edge of the page.

PDF

PDF, which stands for Portable Document Format, is a file format created by Adobe Systems that shows all elements of a printed document as an electronic image. Users can view a PDF document without the software that created the original document. Thus, the PDF format enables users easily to share documents with others. To view, navigate, and print a PDF file, you use a program called **Acrobat Reader**, which can be downloaded free from Adobe's Web site. Figure 6–86 shows the newsletter in this chapter opened in an Acrobat Reader window.

Microsoft provides a free add-in utility that enables you to convert a Word document to a PDF format. To check if the utility has been downloaded to your computer, click the Office Button menu and then point to Save As. If your Save As submenu contains the PDF or XPS command, then the add-in utility has been installed. If your Save As submenu contains the 'Find add-ins for other file formats' command, then the add-in utility has not been installed. To download the add-in utility, click 'Find add-ins for other file formats' on the Save As submenu to display the 'Enable support for other file formats, such as PDF and XPS' Help window. Scroll through the Help window and then click the Microsoft Save as PDF or XPS Add-in for 2007 Microsoft Office Programs command, which displays a Web page on Microsoft's site. Follow the instructions at that Web page to download and install the add-in utility.

With the PDF add-in utility installed on your computer, you can save your documents as PDF files or e-mail the document to others as a PDF file.

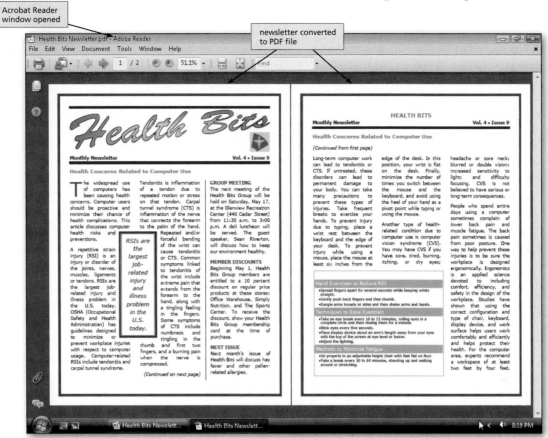

Figure 6–86

To E-Mail a Document as a PDF

If the PDF add-in utility is installed on your computer, you can e-mail the document displayed in the Word window as a PDF file. The original Word document remains intact — Word creates a copy of the file in a PDF format and attaches the PDF file to the e-mail message using your default e-mail program. The following steps e-mail a PDF of the current document, assuming you use Outlook as your default e-mail program.

1
• Click the Office Button and then point to Send on the Office Button menu (Figure 6–87).

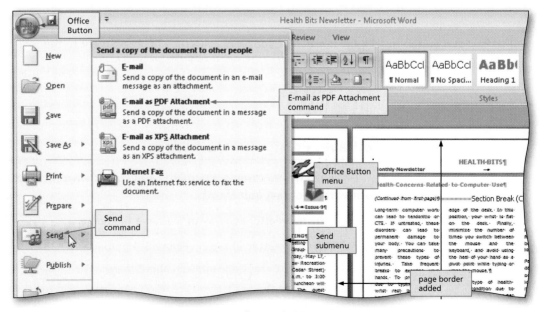

Figure 6–87

2

- Click E-mail as PDF Attachment on the Send submenu, which converts the current document to a PDF file, starts your default e-mail program, and attaches the PDF file to the e-mail message.

Q&A

What if the E-mail as PDF Attachment command is not on my Send submenu?

The PDF add-in utility has not been installed on your computer. See the discussion in the previous section for information about installing the PDF add-in utility.

- If necessary, maximize the e-mail window.

- Fill in the To text box with the recipient's e-mail address.

- Fill in the message (Figure 6–88).

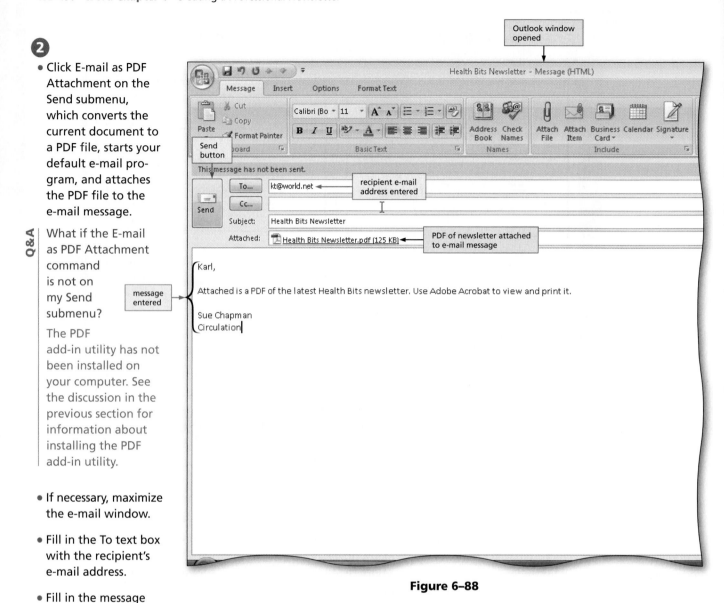

Figure 6–88

3

- Click the Send button to send the e-mail message along with the PDF attachment to the recipient named in the To text box.

To Save, Print, and Quit Word

The newsletter now is complete. You should save the document, print the document, and then quit Word.

1 Save the newsletter again with the same file name.

2 Print the newsletter (shown in Figure 6–1 on page WD 387).

Q&A What if an error message appears about margins?

Depending on the printer you are using, you may need to set the margins differently for this project.

What if one or more of the borders do not print?

Click the Page Borders button on the Page Layout tab, click the Options button in the dialog box, click the Measure from box arrow and click Text, change the four text boxes to 15 pt, and then click the OK button in each dialog box. Try printing the document again. If the borders still do not print, adjust the text boxes in the dialog box to a number smaller than 15 point.

3 Quit Word, closing all open documents.

Conserving Ink and Toner

You can instruct Word to print draft quality documents to conserve ink or toner by clicking the Office Button, clicking the Word Options button, clicking Advanced in the left pane of the Word Options dialog box, scrolling to the Print area, placing a check mark in the 'Use draft quality' check box, and then clicking the OK button. Click the Office Button, point to Print, and then click Quick Print.

Chapter Summary

In this chapter, you have learned how to create a professional looking newsletter using Word's desktop publishing features such as WordArt, columns, horizontal and vertical rules, and pull-quotes. The items listed below include all the new Word skills you have learned in this chapter.

1. Set Custom Margins (WD 389)
2. Insert WordArt (WD 391)
3. Change the WordArt Fill Color (WD 393)
4. Change the WordArt Shape (WD 395)
5. Border One Edge of a Paragraph (WD 396)
6. Insert a Symbol (WD 398)
7. Format a Graphic as Floating (WD 402)
8. Move a Graphic (WD 403)
9. Flip a Graphic (WD 403)
10. Adjust the Brightness of a Graphic (WD 404)
11. Modify a Style Using the Modify Style Dialog Box (WD 405)
12. Insert a Continuous Section Break (WD 409)
13. Change the Number of Columns (WD 410)
14. Justify a Paragraph (WD 411)
15. Insert a File in a Column of the Newsletter (WD 412)
16. Increase Column Width (WD 414)
17. Format a Letter as a Drop Cap (WD 416)
18. Format the Drop Cap (WD 417)
19. Insert a Next Page Section Break (WD 418)
20. Insert a Column Break (WD 420)
21. Update a Style to Match a Selection (WD 424)
22. Place a Vertical Rule between Columns (WD 425)
23. Insert a Text Box (WD 427)
24. Copy and Paste (WD 428)
25. Position a Text Box (WD 431)
26. Change Column Formatting (WD 432)
27. Split the Window (WD 434)
28. Arrange All Open Word Documents on the Screen (WD 435)
29. Copy and Paste Using Split Windows (WD 436)
30. Remove a Split Window (WD 437)
31. Balance Columns (WD 438)
32. Change the Layout of a SmartArt Graphic (WD 440)
33. Modify Theme Effects (WD 440)
34. Add a Shape to a SmartArt Graphic (WD 441)
35. Save Customized Themes (WD 441)
36. Add Text to a SmartArt Graphic through the Text Pane (WD 442)
37. Copy and Paste a SmartArt Graphic (WD 443)
38. Add an Outline to a SmartArt Graphic (WD 446)
39. E-Mail a Document as a PDF (WD 449)

If you have a SAM user profile, you may have access to hands-on instruction, practice, and assessment. Log in to your SAM account (http://sam2007.course.com) to launch any assigned training activities or exams that relate to the skills covered in this chapter.

Learn It Online

Test your knowledge of chapter content and key terms.

Instructions: To complete the Learn It Online exercises, start your browser, click the Address bar, and then enter the Web address scsite.com/wd2007/learn. When the Word 2007 Learn It Online page is displayed, click the link for the exercise you want to complete and then read the instructions.

Chapter Reinforcement TF, MC, and SA
A series of true/false, multiple choice, and short answer questions that test your knowledge of the chapter content.

Flash Cards
An interactive learning environment where you identify chapter key terms associated with displayed definitions.

Practice Test
A series of multiple choice questions that test your knowledge of chapter content and key terms.

Who Wants To Be a Computer Genius?
An interactive game that challenges your knowledge of chapter content in the style of a television quiz show.

Wheel of Terms
An interactive game that challenges your knowledge of chapter key terms in the style of the television show *Wheel of Fortune*.

Crossword Puzzle Challenge
A crossword puzzle that challenges your knowledge of key terms presented in the chapter.

Apply Your Knowledge

Reinforce the skills and apply the concepts you learned in this chapter.

Working with Desktop Publishing Elements of a Newsletter
Instructions: Start Word. Open the document, Apply 6-1 Totally Toned Newsletter Draft, from the Data Files for Students. See the inside back cover of this book for instructions on downloading the Data Files for Students, or contact your instructor for information about accessing the required files.

The document contains a newsletter that you are to modify. The modified newsletter is shown in Figure 6–89.

Perform the following tasks:
1. Change the column width of the columns in the body of the newsletter to 2.1".
2. Change the WordArt shape to Chevron Up.
3. Move the graphic of the weight lifter to the location shown in Figure 6–89.
4. Adjust the brightness of the graphic of the weight lifter to +20 %.
5. In the issue information line, insert a dot symbol between the volume and issue.
6. Change the alignment of the paragraph containing the drop cap from left-aligned to justified.
7. Change the color of the subhead, Weight Room Makeover, to Red, Accent 3, Darker 25%. Select the subhead and then update all Heading 3 styles to match the selection.
8. Add a shape to the bottom of the SmartArt graphic and then insert the text, Nutrition, in the bottom shape. Be sure the inserted text is formatted the same as the text in the other two shapes.
9. If necessary, move the SmartArt graphic so that it is positioned similarly to the one in Figure 6–89.
10. If necessary, move the pull-quote so that it is positioned similarly to the one shown in Figure 6–89.
11. Change the document properties as specified by your instructor.

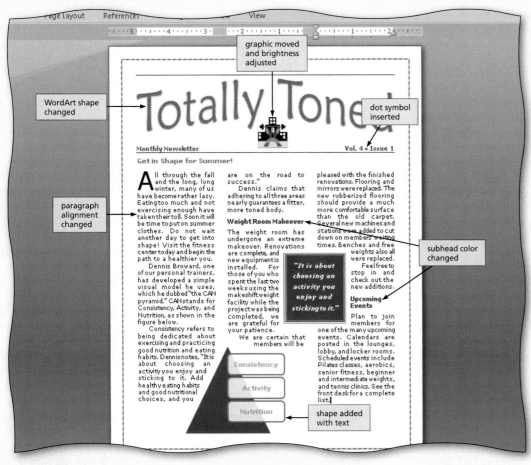

Figure 6–89

12. Save the modified file with the file name, Apply 6-1 Totally Toned Newsletter Modified.

13. Submit the revised newsletter in the format specified by your instructor.

Extend Your Knowledge

Extend the skills you learned in this chapter and experiment with new skills. You may need to use Help to complete the assignment.

Adding a Table to a Newsletter and Enhancing a Nameplate

Instructions: Start Word. Open the document, Extend 6-1 Park Department Newsletter Draft, from the Data Files for Students. See the inside back cover of this book for instructions on downloading the Data Files for Students, or contact your instructor for information about accessing the required files.

You will add a table to the bottom of the newsletter, change the format of the WordArt, change the look of the horizontal rules, change the symbol in the issue information line, add a drop cap, and place vertical rules between each column in the newsletter.

Perform the following tasks:

1. Use Help to review how to create and format a table, if necessary, and to learn about WordArt options, borders, symbols, drop caps, lines between columns, and tabs.

Continued >

Extend Your Knowledge *continued*

2. Insert a continuous section break at the end of the third column of the newsletter to balance the columns. Change the number of columns in the new section from three to one. Change the style of the paragraph in the new section to No Spacing. Use the Table command on the Insert menu to insert a table that has eight rows and three columns. Enter the data in the table as shown in Figure 6–90. Format the table using a table style of your preference.

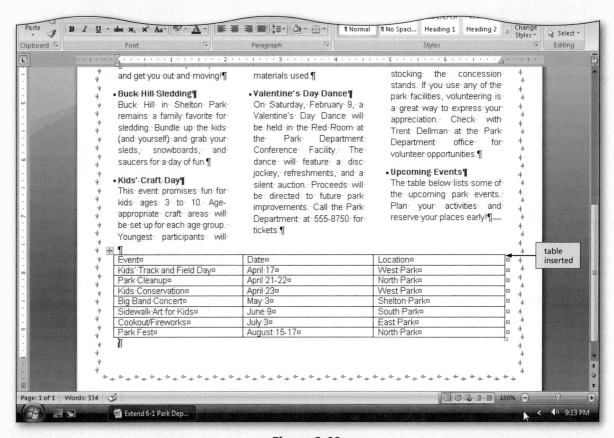

Figure 6–90

3. Change the WordArt to a style other than WordArt style 1. Add a fill texture to the WordArt. Add a Shadow Effect to the WordArt.

4. Remove the horizontal rules (top and bottom borders). Add decorative, colored ruling lines in the same position that are different from the default.

5. Change the symbol between the volume and issue in the information line to a symbol other than the dot.

6. Add a drop cap to the first paragraph in the body of the newsletter. Change the number of lines to drop from three to two lines.

7. Place a vertical line between the three columns in the body of the newsletter.

8. If the newsletter flows to two pages, reduce the size of elements such as WordArt or clip art or the table, or adjust spacing above or below paragraphs so that the newsletter fits on a single page. Make any other necessary adjustments to the newsletter.

9. Clear all tabs in the issue information line in the nameplate. Insert a right-aligned tab stop at the 7" mark. Fill the tab space with a leader character of your choice.

10. Change the document properties as specified by your instructor.

11. Save the revised document with a new file name and then submit it in the format specified by your instructor.

Make It Right

Analyze a document and correct all errors and/or improve the design.

Formatting a Newsletter

Instructions: Start Word. Open the document, Make It Right 6-1 Spring Projects Newsletter Draft, from the Data Files for Students. See the inside back cover of this book for instructions on downloading the Data Files for Students, or contact your instructor for information about accessing the required files.

The document is a newsletter whose elements are not formatted properly (Figure 6–91). You are to edit and format the WordArt, format the clip art image and columns, add a drop cap, format the SmartArt graphic, and add a border.

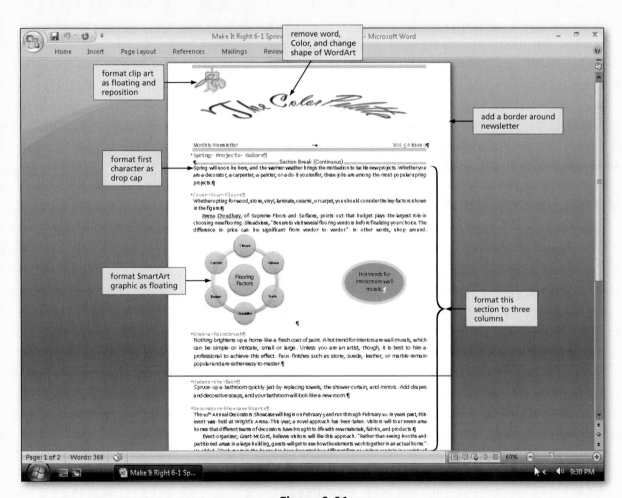

Figure 6–91

Perform the following tasks:

1. Change the theme colors to a color scheme other than Verve.

2. Remove the word, Color, from the WordArt, so that the newsletter title is The Palette. Change the shape of the WordArt so that the text is more readable.

3. Format the clip art image of the color palette to floating (In Front of Text) and then position the image in an open space on the nameplate. If necessary, adjust the size of the WordArt and the clip art image so that they have a pleasing appearance in the nameplate.

Continued >

Make It Right *continued*

4. Change the number of columns in the body of the newsletter from one to three.

5. Format the first letter in the first paragraph of text as a drop cap. Color the drop cap.

6. If necessary, insert a column break so that the subhead, Decorators Showcase Starts, begins at the top of the third column.

7. Format the SmartArt graphic as floating with a Tight wrapping style. Move the SmartArt graphic to the bottom-left corner of the newsletter. Change the theme effects to one other than Office. Save the modified theme.

8. Position the pull-quote near the Grab a Paintbrush section of the newsletter.

9. Add an attractive border around the edge of the newsletter. Do not use the default single line, black border.

10. If the newsletter flows to two pages, reduce the size of elements such as WordArt or clip art or the pull-quote, or adjust spacing above or below paragraphs so that the newsletter fits on a single page. Make any other necessary adjustments to the newsletter.

11. Change the document properties, as specified by your instructor. Save the revised document with a new file name and then submit it in the format specified by your instructor.

In the Lab

Design and/or create a document using the guidelines, concepts, and skills presented in this chapter. Labs are listed in order of increasing difficulty.

Lab 1: Creating a Newsletter with a Pull-Quote and an Article on File

Problem: You are an editor of the newsletter, Memory Lane. The next edition is due out in one week. This issue's article will discuss the new exhibit (Figure 6–92). The text for the feature articles in the newsletter is in a file on the Data Files for Students. See the inside back cover of this book for instructions on downloading the Data Files for Students, or contact your instructor for information about accessing the required files. You need to create the nameplate and the pull-quote.

Perform the following tasks:

1. Change all margins to .75 inches. Depending on your printer, you may need different margin settings.

2. Create the nameplate using the formats identified in Figure 6–92. Create the title using WordArt. Insert the dot symbol between the volume and issue on the issue information line. Use the Clip Art task pane to locate the image shown, or use a similar graphic (or you can insert the picture called Clock, which is on the Data Files for Students). Resize the image to the size shown in the figure. Format the image as floating and then position it as shown.

3. Create a continuous section break below the nameplate.

4. Format section 2 to three columns.

5. Insert the Lab 6-1 Memory Lane Articles, which is located on the Data Files for Students, in section 2 below the nameplate.

6. Format the newsletter according to Figure 6–92. Columns should have a width of 2" with spacing of 0.5". Resize the drop cap so that it is not so close to the text. Position the border between the second and third column 15 points from the left edge of the text.

7. Insert a continuous section break at the end of the document to balance the columns.

8. Format the subheads, New Artifacts and Next Month's Issue, using the Heading 2 style. Be sure the New Artifacts subhead starts at the top of the third column. If necessary, insert a column break.

9. Insert a Pinstripes Quote text box for the pull-quote. The text for the pull-quote is in the second column of the article. Copy the text and then paste it in the text box. Change the style of the text box to Diagonal Gradient - Accent 5. Resize the text box so that it is similar in size to Figure 6–92. Position the text box as shown in Figure 6–92.

10. Add the page border as shown in the figure. (*Hint:* Use the Art box arrow in the Page Border tab of the Borders and Shading dialog box.)

11. View the document in print preview. If it does not fit on a single page, click the Shrink to Fit button on the Print Preview tab or reduce the size of the WordArt or adjust spacing above and below paragraphs.

12. Save the document with Lab 6-1 History Museum Newsletter as the file name and then submit it in the format specified by your instructor.

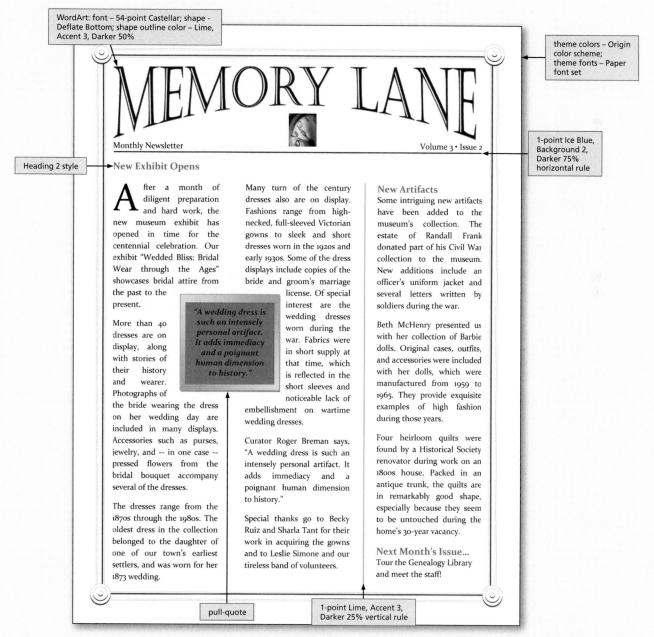

Figure 6–92

In the Lab

Lab 2: Creating a Newsletter with a SmartArt Graphic and an Article on File

Problem: You are responsible for the monthly preparation of The Free Press, a newsletter for community members. The next edition discusses upcoming community activities (Figure 6–93). This article already has been prepared and is on the Data Files for Students. See the inside back cover of this book for instructions on downloading the Data Files for Students, or contact your instructor for information about accessing the required files. You need to create the nameplate and the SmartArt graphic.

Perform the following tasks:

1. Change all margins to .75 inches. Depending on your printer, you may need different margin settings.

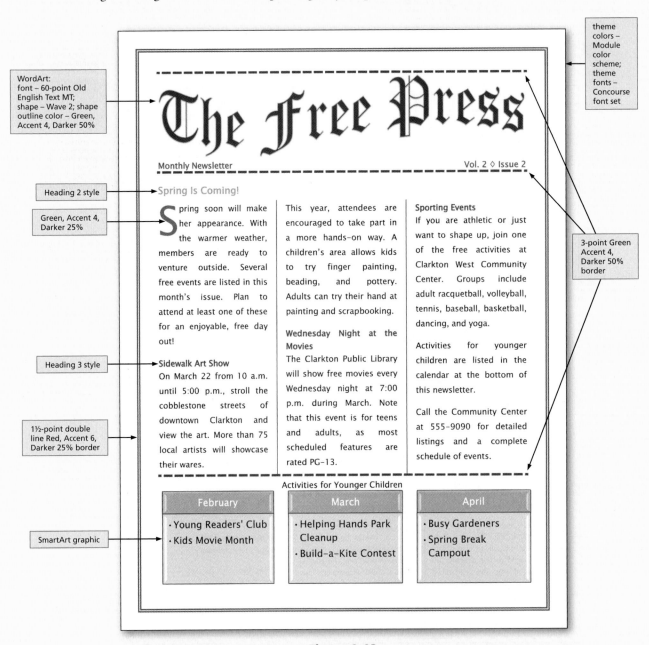

Figure 6–93

2. Create the nameplate using the formats identified in Figure 6–93. Create the title using WordArt. Insert the diamond symbol between the volume and issue on the issue information line.

3. Create a continuous section break below the nameplate.

4. Format section 2 to three columns.

5. Insert the Lab 6-2 Free Press Articles, which is located on the Data Files for Students, in section 2 below the nameplate.

6. Format the newsletter according to Figure 6–93. Columns should have a width of 2.1" with spacing of 0.35". Format the subheads using the Heading 3 style. Change the Heading 3 style to Red, Accent 6, Darker 25%. Save this new format as part of the Heading 3 style.

7. Insert a continuous section break at the end of the document to balance the columns.

8. Add the page border as shown in the figure.

9. Open a new document window and create the SmartArt graphic shown in Figure 6–93. Use the Horizontal Bullet List layout. Add text shown in the figure. Apply the Cartoon SmartArt style. Save the graphic with the file name, Lab 6-2 Activities for Children Graphic. Use the Office Clipboard to copy and paste the SmartArt graphic to the bottom section of the newsletter. Change its color to Colored Fill - Accent 1. Add the title and border above the SmartArt graphic.

10. Arrange both documents (the graphic and the newsletter) on the screen. Scroll through both open windows. Maximize the newsletter window.

11. View the document in print preview. If it does not fit on a single page, click the Shrink to Fit button on the Print Preview tab or reduce the size of the WordArt or adjust spacing above and below paragraphs.

12. Save the newsletter using Lab 6-2 Free Press Newsletter as the file name and submit it in the format specified by your instructor.

In the Lab

Lab 3: Creating a Newsletter from Scratch

Problem: You work part-time for Bowl-a-Rama Lanes, which publishes a monthly newsletter. Figure 6–94 on the next page shows the contents of the next issue.

Perform the following tasks:

1. Change all margins to .75 inches. Depending on your printer, you may need different margin settings.

2. Create the nameplate using the formats identified in Figure 6–94. Create the title using WordArt. Insert the diamond symbol between the volume and issue on the issue information line. Use the Clip Art task pane to locate the images shown or similar images (or you can insert the pictures called Bowling Ball and Bowling Pins, which are on the Data Files for Students). Resize the images and position them as shown in the figure. Flip the image of the bowling ball.

3. Create a continuous section break below the nameplate. Format section 2 to two columns. Enter the text in section 2 using justified paragraph formatting. Place a vertical rule between the columns in section 2.

4. Insert a Braces Quote 2 text box for the pull-quote. Copy the text for the pull-quote from the newsletter and then paste it in the text box. Change the fill of the text box to Tan, Background 2, Darker 50% and the outline to Orange, Accent 1, Darker 25%. Resize and position the text box so that it is similar in size and location to Figure 6–94.

5. Insert a continuous section break at the end of the second column in section 2. Format section 3 to one column. Create the table as shown at the bottom of the newsletter in section 3.

Continued >

STUDENT ASSIGNMENTS

In the Lab continued

6. Make any additional formatting required in the newsletter so that it looks like the figure. The entire newsletter should fit on a single page.

7. Save the document with Lab 6-3 Eleventh Frame Newsletter as the file name and then submit it in the format specified by your instructor.

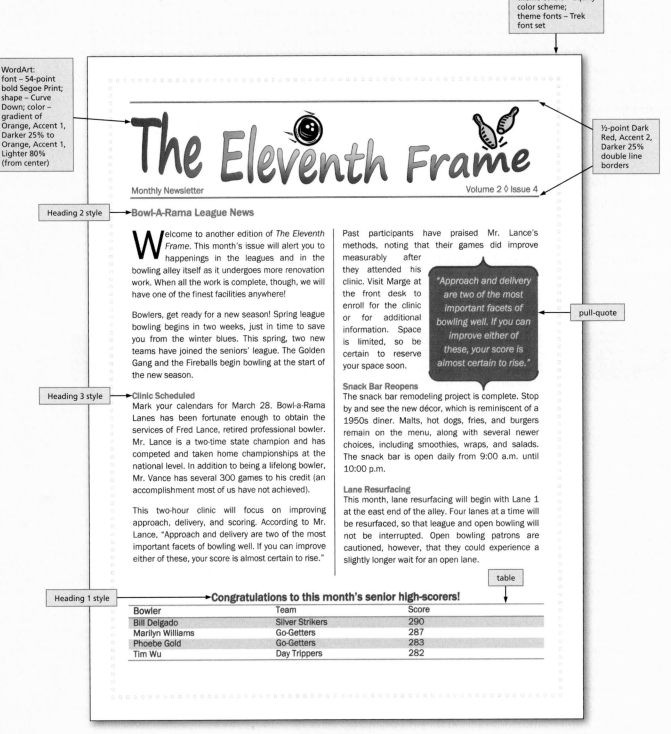

Figure 6–94

Cases and Places

Apply your creative thinking and problem solving skills to design and implement a solution.

● Easier   ●● More Difficult

● 1: Create a Page in this Textbook

For the final project in your computer concepts class, you have been assigned the task of creating page WD 452 in this textbook. The page contains many desktop publishing elements: nameplate, horizontal rules, columns of text, balanced columns, and a variety of font sizes, font colors, and shading. Use WordArt for the text in the nameplate. Split the Word window and copy the Learn It Online nameplate to the location for the Apply Your Knowledge nameplate in the middle of the page. Then, edit the WordArt text in the pasted nameplate to Apply Your Knowledge. Use the concepts and techniques presented in this chapter to format your Word document so that it looks as much like page WD 452 as possible.

●● 2: Create a Newsletter for Residents of an Active Adult Community

As a part-time office assistant at an active adult community, you have been asked to produce a monthly newsletter to help residents get better acquainted with each other and with the many activities and events available at the social center. The community has individual patio homes, several common areas, a park, and a social center. The social center has one large and three smaller rooms available at no cost to residents for events such as showers, parties, reunions, lunches, lectures, and so on. Several events have been scheduled for the next month. For example, on July 3, residents are invited to a cookout and fireworks in the park area. On August 21 and 22, a community garage sale will be set up in the east commons area. The social center events include a free blood pressure screening in Room B, a senior Pilates class in Room A, and a Civil War lecture in Room A. The newsletter should welcome the three new residents that recently moved into the community. Use your library, the Internet, personal experiences, or other resources to obtain more information about active adult communities so that you can elaborate on the information presented here. Organize the information and create a newsletter. The newsletter should contain at least two of these graphic elements: clip art image, picture, SmartArt graphic, pull-quote. Enhance the newsletter with a drop cap, WordArt, color, ruling lines, and a page border.

●● 3: Create a Newsletter about Library Happenings

As a part-time library assistant, you have been asked by the director to create a monthly newsletter. The director wants the first issue to publicize the new technology center and to alert patrons to the many events scheduled at the library this month. Especially important, he believes, are the children's reading program, the used book sale, and upcoming author lectures. He also wants you to list the new releases in both fiction and nonfiction. Use your library, the Internet, personal experiences, or other resources to assist you with elaborating on information presented here. Organize the information and create a newsletter. The newsletter should contain at least two of these graphic elements: clip art image, picture, SmartArt graphic, pull-quote. Enhance the newsletter with a drop cap, WordArt, color, ruling lines, and a page border. Use leader characters to fill the tab space in the issue information line.

Continued >

STUDENT ASSIGNMENTS

Cases and Places *continued*

•• 4: Create a Newsletter about a Topic that Interests You

Make It Personal

What are your interests and hobbies? How do you pass the time? Do you belong to any clubs or organizations? In this assignment, you are to create a newsletter that discusses or highlights an activity or interest of yours. If you are an avid traveler, you could create a newsletter highlighting recent or upcoming trips. If you belong to a club or organization, create a newsletter that covers club activities and members. Perhaps you have a hobby that you can translate into a newsletter, such as photography, quilting, scuba diving, gardening, or sports. Students with jobs could write a newsletter about company happenings and fellow employees, and music or movie buffs could write reviews and news as articles in the newsletter. Organize the information and create a newsletter. The newsletter should contain at least two of these graphic elements: clip art image, picture, SmartArt graphic, pull-quote. Enhance the newsletter with a drop cap, WordArt, color, ruling lines, and a page border.

•• 5: Create a Newsletter that Highlights an Aspect of Your School or Community

Working Together

Find a group, club, event, or facility at your school or organization that you believe could be better publicized or utilized. For example, you could compile a newsletter about the career center, the library, or recreation facility at your school. If your school has a drama or choir department, you could create a newsletter about past and upcoming performances, student actors/singers, and so on. If your school does not have these facilities, find an organization in your community. One team member should gather information for a feature article that highlights the facility or group's purpose or history. Another member should interview its president, director, resource person, or other willing party. Another team member should compile a list of features or upcoming events and activities. Copy all team members' text to the Office Clipboard and then use the Paste All command to compile all the gathered information into a single newsletter. The newsletter should contain at least one clip art image, a picture, a SmartArt graphic, and a pull-quote. Enhance the newsletter with a drop cap, WordArt, color, ruling lines, and a page border.

Integration Feature

Linking an Excel Worksheet and Chart to a Word Document

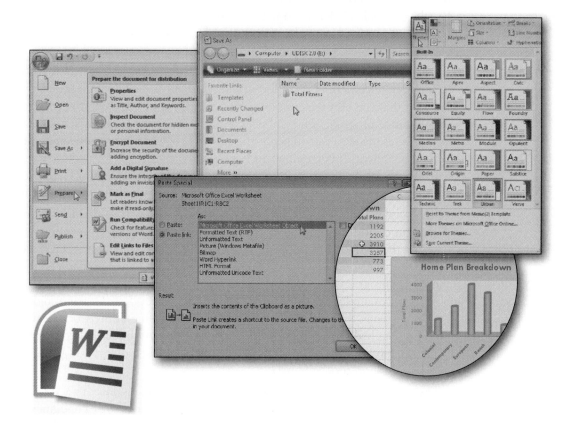

Objectives

You will have mastered the material in this feature when you can:

- Apply a theme to a document
- Update the body text style
- Link an Excel worksheet to a Word document
- Link an Excel chart to a Word document

- Break links
- Save a document so that it is compatible with a previous version of Word
- E-mail a document

Integration Feature Introduction

With Microsoft Office, you can copy part or all of a project created in one Office program to a project created in another Office program. The item being copied is called the **object**. For example, you could copy an Excel worksheet (the object) that is located in an Excel workbook (the source document) to a Word document (the destination document). That is, an object can be copied from a source document to a destination document.

Project — Document Containing Linked Objects

You can use one of three techniques to copy objects from one program to another: copy and paste, embed, or link.

- **Copy and paste**. When you copy an object and then paste it, the object becomes part of the destination document. You edit a pasted object using editing features of the destination program. For example, when you select an Excel worksheet in an Excel workbook, click the Copy button on Excel's Home tab, and then click the Paste button on Word's Home tab, each row in the Excel worksheet becomes a separate paragraph in the Word document and each column is separated by a tab character.

- **Embed**. When you embed an object, like a pasted object, it becomes part of the destination document. The difference between an embedded object and a pasted object is that you edit the contents of an embedded object using the editing features of the source program. The embedded object, however, contains static data; that is, any changes made to the object in the source program are not reflected in the destination document. If you embed an Excel worksheet in a Word document, the Excel worksheet remains as an Excel worksheet in the Word document. When you edit the Excel worksheet from within the Word document, you will use Excel editing features.

- **Link**. A linked object, by contrast, does not become a part of the destination document even though it appears to be a part of it. Rather, a connection is established between the source and destination documents so that when you open the destination document, the linked object appears as part of it. When you edit a linked object, the source program starts and opens the source document that contains the linked object. For example, when you edit a linked worksheet, Excel starts and displays the Excel workbook that contains the worksheet; you then edit the worksheet in Excel. Unlike an embedded object, if you open the Excel workbook that contains the Excel worksheet and then edit the Excel worksheet, the linked object will be updated in the Word document, too.

The project in this feature links an Excel worksheet and chart to a Word document (a memo). Because the worksheet and chart are inserted in the Word document as a link, any time you open the memo in Word, the latest version of the Excel worksheet data is displayed in the memo. Figure 1a shows the memo draft (without any links to Excel); Figure 1b shows the Excel worksheet and chart; and Figure 1c shows the final copy of the memo linked to the Excel worksheet and chart.

BTW

Linked Objects
When you open a document that contains linked objects, Word displays a dialog box asking if you want to update the Word document with data from the linked file. Click the Yes button only if you are certain the linked file is from a trusted source; that is, you should be confident that the source file does not contain a virus or other potentially harmful program before you instruct Word to link the source file to the destination document.

(a) Draft of Word Document (containing no links)

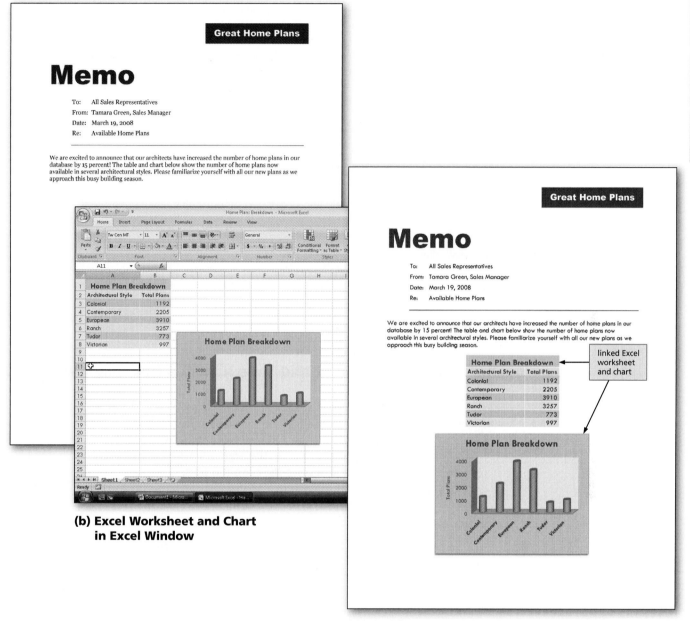

**(b) Excel Worksheet and Chart
in Excel Window**

**(c) Modified Word Document Linked to Excel
Worksheet and Chart**

Figure 1

Overview

As you read through this feature, you will learn how to create the document with the links shown in Figure 1c and then e-mail a copy of the document without links by performing these general tasks:

- Open and re-format the memo.
- Link the Excel worksheet and chart to the memo.
- Edit the Excel worksheet and update the Word document.
- Prepare the memo to be e-mailed to users who may have earlier versions of Word.

Plan Ahead

General Project Guidelines

When creating a Word document that contains an object created in another Office program, the actions you perform and decisions you make will affect the appearance and characteristics of the finished document. When you create a document that is to contain another Office program's object, such as the project shown in Figure 1 on the previous page, you should follow these general guidelines:

1. **Determine how to copy the object.** You can copy and paste, embed, or link an object created in another Office program to the Word document.

   - If you simply want to use the object's data and have no desire to use the object in the source program, then copy and paste the object.

   - If you want to use the object in the source program but you want the object's data to remain static if it changes in the source document, then embed the object.

   - If you want to ensure that the most current version of the object appears in the destination document, then link the object. If the source file is large, such as a video clip or a sound clip, link the object to keep the size of the destination document smaller.

2. **Be certain files from others are virus free.** When using objects created by others, do not use the source document until you are certain it does not contain a virus or other malicious program. Use an antivirus program to verify that any files you use are free of viruses and other potentially harmful programs.

To Open a Word Document and Save It with a New File Name

The first step in this integration feature is to open the draft of the memo that is to contain links to the Excel worksheet and chart objects. The memo file, named Home Plans Memo Draft, is located on the Data Files for Students. See the inside back cover of this book for instructions on downloading the Data Files for Students, or contact your instructor for information about accessing the required files.

To preserve the contents of the original Home Plans Memo Draft file, you will save it with a new file name. The following steps open the memo in Word and save it with a new file name.

1. Start Word and then open the file named Home Plans Memo Draft from the Data Files for Students.

2. Click the Office Button and then click Save As on the Office Button menu to display the Save As dialog box.

3. Type Home Plans Memo Modified in the File name text box to change the file name.

4. Locate and select your USB flash drive in the list of available drives.

5. Click the Save button in the Save As dialog box to save the document on the USB flash drive with the new file name, Home Plans Memo Modified.

6. If the zoom level is not 100%, change it to 100%.

BTW

Certification
The Microsoft Certified Application Specialist (MCAS) program provides an opportunity for you to obtain a valuable industry credential — proof that you have the Word 2007 skills required by employers. For more information see Appendix G or visit the Word 2007 Certification Web page (scsite.com/wd2007/cert).

To Change the Document Theme

The projects in previous chapters have used a color scheme from one document theme and a font set from another document theme. In this feature, the modified memo uses the Median color scheme and Median font set. Instead of changing the color scheme and font set individually, Word provides a means of changing the entire document theme (color scheme, font set, and effects) at once. The following steps change the document theme.

- Display the Page Layout tab.

- Click the Themes button on the Page Layout tab to display the Themes gallery (Figure 2).

Experiment

- Point to various themes in the Themes gallery and watch the color scheme and font set change in the document window.

- Click Median in the Themes gallery to change the document theme to Median.

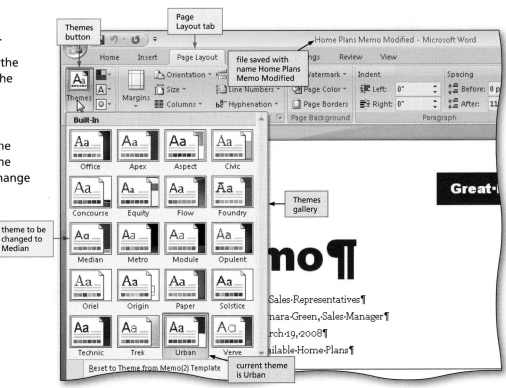

Figure 2

To Update the Body Text Style

The font size of the body text in the memo document is a little small, making it difficult for some people to read. The following steps increase the font size by one point and then update the Body Text style to reflect this change.

1 Triple-click the paragraph of text in the memo to select it. Right-click the selected text to display the Mini toolbar and shortcut menu.

2 Click the Grow Font button on the Mini toolbar to increase the font size of the selected text to 12 point.

3 Right-click the selected text again and then point to Styles on the shortcut menu to display the Styles menu (Figure 3 on the next page).

4 On the Styles menu, click Update Body Text to Match Selection, which modifies the Body Text style to match the formats of the selected text and then changes all other text formatted using the Body Text style in the document to the updated style.

Update Body Text to Match Selection command

shortcut menu

Styles command

Synonyms

Translate

me·Plans¶

Styles

Update Body Text to Match Selection

Save Selection as a New Quick Style...

Select Text with Similar Formatting

e·number·of·home·plans·in·our

paragraph selected and font size changed

We·are·excited·to·annou
database·by·15·percent!
available·in·several·archit
approach·this·busy·building·season.¶

Tw Cen MT 12

B *I*

Styles menu

Font Size changed to 12

Grow Font button

Figure 3

Linking an Excel Worksheet and Chart

The next step in this integration feature is to link the Excel worksheet and chart (the objects), which are located in the Excel workbook called Home Plans Breakdown (the source document), to the Home Plans Memo Modified file (the destination document). To link the worksheet to the memo in this feature, you will follow these general steps:

1. Start Excel and open the Excel workbook that contains the objects (worksheet and chart) to be linked.

2. Select the object (worksheet or chart) in Excel and then copy the selected object to the Clipboard.

3. Switch to Word and link the copied object using the Paste Special command.

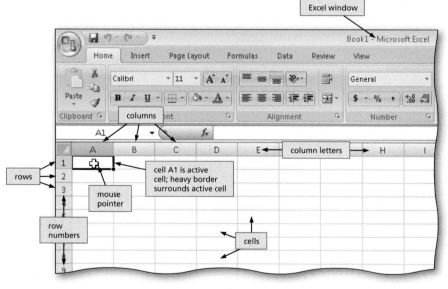

Excel window

rows

columns

A1

mouse pointer

cell A1 is active cell; heavy border surrounds active cell

row numbers

column letters

cells

Figure 4

Excel Basics

The Excel window contains a rectangular grid that consists of columns and rows. A column letter above the grid identifies each column. A row number on the left side of the grid identifies each row. The intersection of each column and row is a cell. A cell is referred to by its unique address, which is the coordinates of the intersection of a column and a row. To identify a cell, specify the column letter first, followed by the row number. For example, cell reference A1 refers to the cell located at the intersection of column A and row 1 (Figure 4).

To Start Excel and Open an Excel Workbook

The Excel worksheet to be linked to the memo is in an Excel workbook called Home Plans Breakdown, which is located on the Data Files for Students. See the inside back cover of this book for instructions on downloading the Data Files for Students, or contact your instructor for information about accessing the required files.

The next steps start Excel and open the workbook called Home Plans Breakdown. (Do not quit Word or close the open Word document before starting these steps.)

1 Click the Start button on the Windows Vista taskbar to display the Start menu.

2 Point to All Programs on the Start menu, click Microsoft Office in the All Programs list, and then click Microsoft Office Excel 2007 in the Microsoft Office list to start Excel and display a new blank workbook in the Excel window.

3 If the Excel window is not maximized, click the Maximize button on its title bar to maximize the window.

4 With your USB flash drive connected to one of the computer's USB ports, click the Office Button in the Excel window to display the Office Button menu and then click Open on the Office Button menu to display the Open dialog box.

5 Locate and select your USB flash drive in the list of available drives.

6 Click Home Plans Breakdown to select the file name and then click the Open button to open the selected file and display the Home Plans Breakdown workbook in the Excel window.

BTW

Opening Word Documents
When you open a document that contains a linked object, Word attempts to locate the source file associated with the link. If Word cannot find the source file, click the Office Button, point to Prepare, and then click Edit Links to Files to display the Links dialog box. Next, select the appropriate source file in the list, click the Change Source button, locate the source file, and then click the OK button.

To Link an Excel Worksheet to a Word Document

The next step is to copy the Excel worksheet to the Clipboard and then use the Paste Link command in Word to link the Excel worksheet from the Clipboard to the Word document. The following steps link the Excel worksheet to the Word document.

1

- In the Excel window, drag through cells in the range A1 through B8 to select them.

- In the Excel window, click the Copy button on the Home tab to copy the selected cells to the Clipboard (Figure 5).

Q&A What is the dotted line around the selected cells?

Excel surrounds copied cells with a moving marquee to help you visually identify the copied cells.

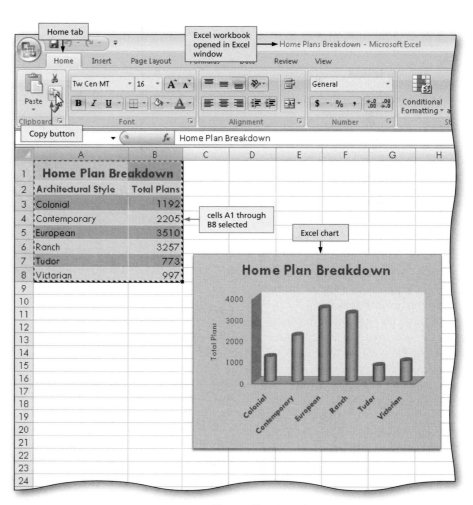

Figure 5

- Click the Home Plans Memo Modified - Microsoft Word program button on the taskbar to switch to the Word window.

- Position the insertion point at the end of the paragraph of text and then press the ENTER key. Center the paragraph mark below the paragraph of text so that the linked worksheet will be centered on the page.

- Scroll so that the paragraph in the memo is near the top of the document window.

- In Word, click the Paste button arrow on the Home tab to display the Paste menu (Figure 6).

Q&A The Paste menu did not display on my screen. Why not?

You clicked the Paste button instead of the Paste button arrow. Click the Undo button on the Quick Access Toolbar and then click the Paste button arrow.

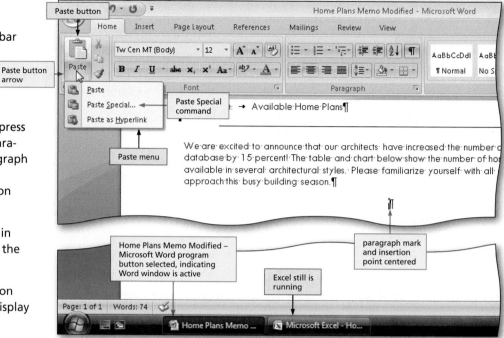

Figure 6

- Click the Paste Special command on the Paste menu to display the Paste Special dialog box.

- Click Paste link to select the option button.

- Select Microsoft Office Excel Worksheet Object in the As list (Figure 7).

Q&A What if the Paste link option button is dimmed?

Click the Microsoft Excel – Home Plans Breakdown program button on the taskbar, select cells A1 through B8 again, click the Copy button in Excel again, click the Home Plans Memo Modified - Microsoft Word program button again, click the Paste button arrow, and then repeat Step 3.

Q&A What if I wanted to embed an object instead of link it?

You would select the Paste option button in the dialog box instead of the Paste link option button.

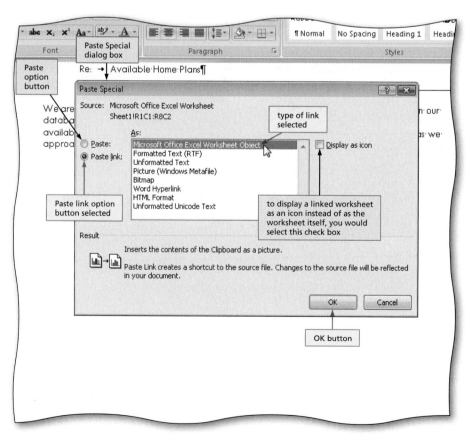

Figure 7

4

• Click the OK button to insert the Excel worksheet as a linked object at the location of the insertion point (Figure 8).

What if I wanted to delete the linked worksheet?

You would select the linked worksheet and then press the DELETE key.

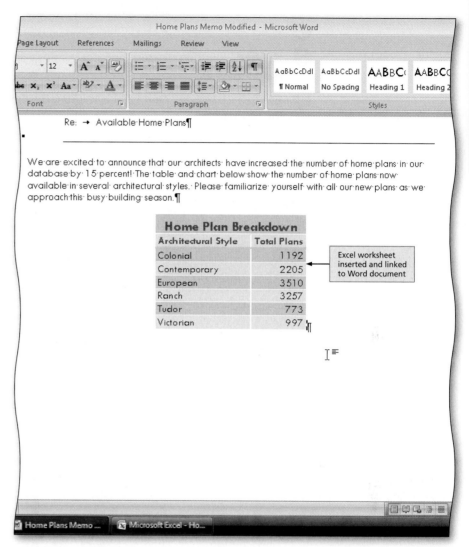

Figure 8

Other Ways

1. To link an entire source file, click the Object button on the Insert tab, click Create from File tab, locate file, click 'Link to file' check box, click OK button

To Link an Excel Chart to a Word Document

The next step is to copy the Excel chart to the Clipboard and then use the Paste Special command in Word to link the Excel chart from the Clipboard to the Word document. The following steps link the Excel chart to the Word document.

1 Click the Microsoft Excel - Home Plans Breakdown program button on the taskbar to switch to the Excel window.

2 In the Excel window, click an edge of the chart to select the chart. Click the Copy button on the Home tab to copy the selected Excel chart to the Clipboard.

3 Click the Home Plans Memo Modified - Microsoft Word program button on the taskbar to switch to the Word window. With the insertion point to the right of the linked worksheet, press the ENTER key.

4 In Word, click the Paste button arrow on the Home tab to display the Paste menu and then click the Paste Special command on the Paste menu to display the Paste Special dialog box.

⑤ Click Paste link to select the option button.

⑥ Select Microsoft Office Excel Chart Object in the As list.

⑦ Click the OK button to insert the Excel chart as a linked object at the location of the insertion point (Figure 9).

⑧ Switch back to Excel. Quit Excel by clicking the Close button on the upper-right corner of the title bar.

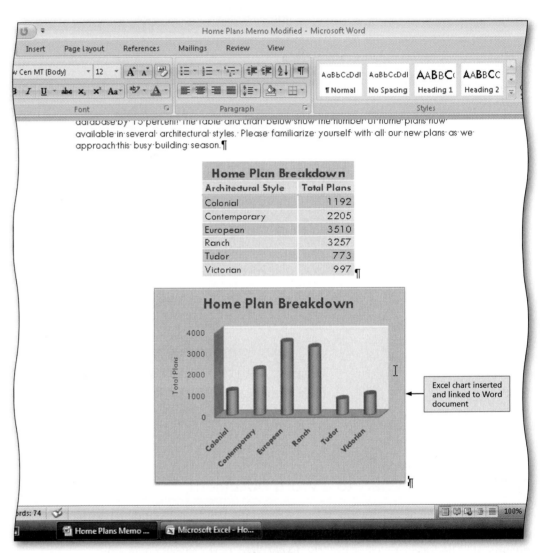

Figure 9

To Copy and Paste Excel Data

If you wanted to copy and paste the chart data, instead of link it, you would perform the following steps.

1. Start Excel.

2. In Excel, select the worksheet cells and then click the Copy button on the Home tab to copy the selected cells to the Clipboard.

3. Switch to Word. Click the Paste button on the Home tab in Word to paste the contents of the Clipboard in the Word document at the location of the insertion point.

To Save a Document Again

You have performed several modifications to this memo file. Thus, you should save it again.

1 Click the Save button on the Quick Access Toolbar to save the document **again** with the same file name, Home Plans Memo Modified.

Editing a Linked Worksheet

At a later time, you may find it necessary to change the data in the Excel worksheet. Any changes you make to the Excel worksheet while in Excel will be reflected in the Excel worksheet and chart in the Word document because the objects are linked to the Word document.

To Edit a Linked Object

The following steps change the number of European home plans from 3510 to 3910 in the Excel worksheet.

1

- In the Word document, double-click the Excel worksheet to start the Excel program and open the source document that contains the linked worksheet.

- If necessary, maximize the Excel window.

- With the Excel worksheet displaying on the screen, click cell B5 to select it.

- Type 3910 and then press the ENTER key to change the value in cell B5, which also automatically updates the associated bar in the chart (Figure 10).

Figure 10

2

- Click the Save button on the Quick Access Toolbar to save the changes.
- Quit Excel.

3

- With the Word window redisplaying on the screen, if necessary, scroll to display the worksheet and chart in the document window.
- To update the worksheet with the edited Excel data, click the worksheet in the Word document and then press the F9 key (Figure 11).

4

- To update the chart with the edited Excel data, click the chart in the Word document and then press the F9 key.

Q&A

Do I always need to press the F9 key to update linked objects?

No. When you open a Word document containing links, Word asks if you want to update the document with the linked files. If you click the Yes button, Word automatically updates links in the opened document.

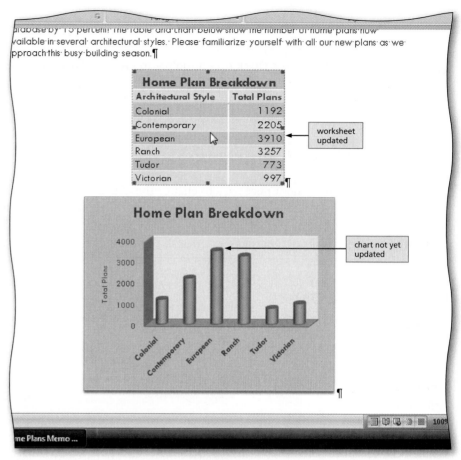

Figure 11

To Save a Document Again and Print It

You are finished with the memo. Thus, you should save it again and then print it.

1 Save the document again with the same file name, Home Plans Memo Modified.

2 Print the memo (Figure 1c on page WD 465).

Preparing the Memo To Be E-Mailed to Users with Earlier Versions of Word

When e-mailing a Word document to others, you want to ensure they will be able to open it and use it. Before e-mailing this memo, take these two steps:

1. **Convert any linked or embedded objects to Word objects.** If you send a Word document that contains a linked Excel object, users will be asked by Word if they want to update the links when they open the Word document. If users are unfamiliar with links, they will not know how to answer the question. Further, if

they do not have the source program, such as Excel, they may not be able to open the Word document.

2. **Save the Word 2007 document in an earlier version of Word.** If you send a document created in Word 2007 to users that have an earlier version of Word, such as Word 2003, they will not be able to open the Word 2007 document. This is because Word 2007 saves documents in a format that is not backward compatible. Word 2007 documents have a file type of .docx, and previous versions of Word have a .doc file type.

The following pages explain these procedures and then e-mail the document.

To Break Links

To convert a linked or embedded object to a Word object, you break the link. That is, you break the connection between the source document and the destination document. When you break a linked Excel worksheet or chart (each of which is an object), the linked worksheet or chart becomes a Word object, a graphic in this case. The following steps break the links to the Excel worksheet and chart.

1

• Click the Office Button and then point to Prepare on the Office Button menu (Figure 12).

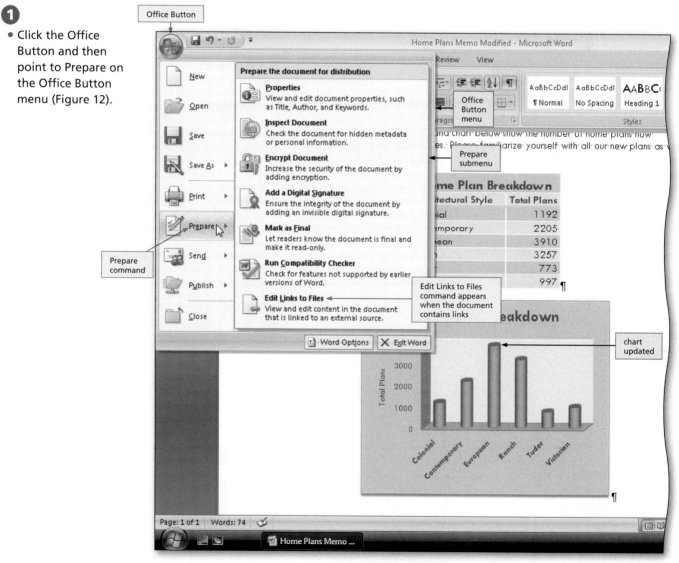

Figure 12

2

- Click Edit Links to Files on the Prepare submenu to display the Links dialog box.

- If necessary, click the first source file listed in the dialog box to select it.

- Click the Break Link button, which displays a dialog box asking if you are sure you want to break the selected links (Figure 13).

3

- Click the Yes button in the dialog box to remove the source file from the list (break the link).

4

- Click the remaining source file listed in the dialog box, if necessary. Click the Break Link button and then click the Yes button in the Microsoft Office Word dialog box to break the remaining link.

5

- Use the Save As command on the Office Button menu to save the file with the name, Home Plans Memo Modified Without Links.

- Double-click the worksheet object in the Word document to be sure that the link has been broken (Figure 14).

Q&A

Why did the Picture Tools tab appear on the Ribbon?

The worksheet now is a Word graphic. When you double-click a graphic, Word displays the Picture Tools tab so that you can edit the picture.

Other Ways

1. Right-click link, point to Linked Worksheet Object, click Links on shortcut menu, select link, click Break Link button, click Yes button, click OK button

2. Select link, press CTRL+SHIFT+F9

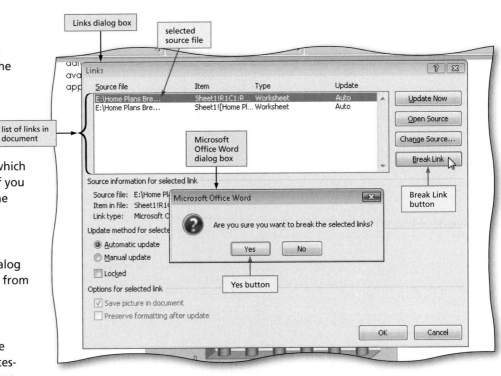

Figure 13

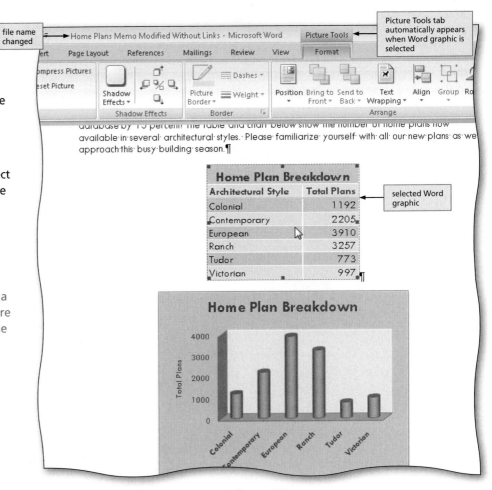

Figure 14

To Save a Word 2007 Document in a Previous Word Format

Documents saved in the Word 2007 format cannot be opened in previous versions of Word. To ensure that all Word users can open your Word 2007 document, you should save the Word 2007 document in a previous version format. The following steps save a Word 2007 document in the Word 97-2003 format.

 1

- Click the Office Button and then point to Save As on the Office Button menu (Figure 15).

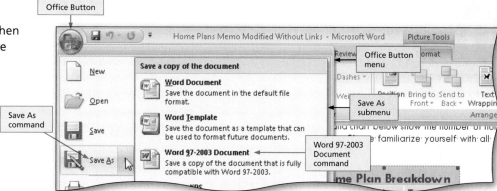

Figure 15

 2

- Click Word 97-2003 Document on the Save As submenu to display the Save As dialog box with Word 97-2003 Document already filled in the 'Save as type' box.

- If necessary, locate and select the USB flash drive in the list of available drives (Figure 16).

 3

- Click the Save button in the dialog box to save the file in a Word 97-2003 format.

Q&A

How can I tell a Word 2007 file from a Word 97-2003 file?

For files saved in the Word 97-2003 format, the Word title bar displays the text, [Compatibility Mode], next to the file name. The file properties also show the file type. You can view the file properties when you open or save a document. Or, click the Document Properties button in the Document Information Panel, click Advanced Properties, and then click the General tab.

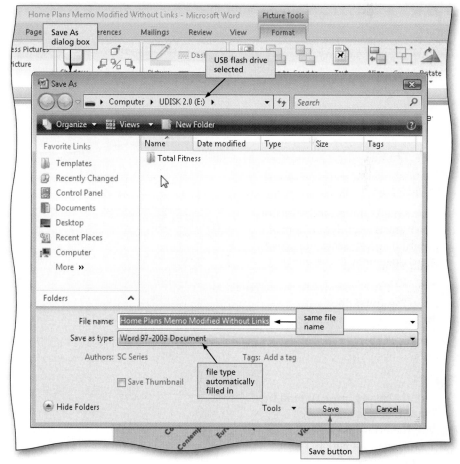

Figure 16

Other Ways

1. Click Office Button, click Save As, change file type to Word 97-2003 Document, click Save button in dialog box

2. Press F12, change file type to Word 97-2003 Document, click Save button in dialog box

To E-Mail a Document as an Attachment

The final step in this feature is to e-mail the Home Plans Memo Modified Without Links document saved in the Word 97-2003 format. The following steps e-mail a document as an attachment, assuming you use Outlook as your default e-mail program.

1

- Click the Office Button and then point to Send on the Office Button menu (Figure 17).

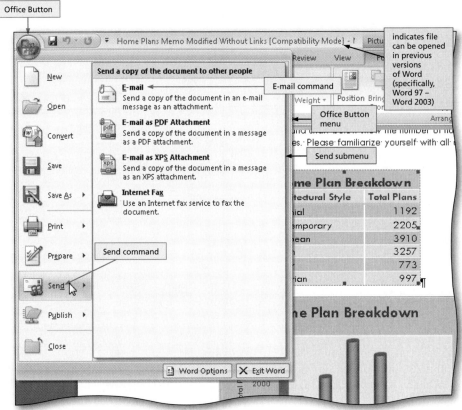

Figure 17

2

- Click E-mail on the Send submenu, which starts your default e-mail program and attaches the active Word document to the e-mail message.

- Fill in the To text box with the recipient's e-mail address.

- Fill in the message (Figure 18).

3

- Click the Send button to send the e-mail message along with the attachment to the recipient named in the To text box.

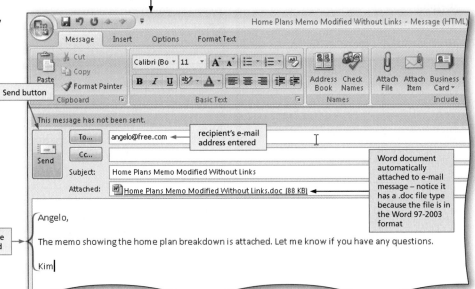

Figure 18

To Quit Word

You are finished with the project in this feature and should quit Word.

1 Quit Word.

Feature Summary

In this feature, you have learned how to apply a theme, update body text, link an Excel worksheet and chart to a Word document, break links, save a document in a previous Word format, and e-mail a document. The items listed below include all the new Word skills you have learned in this feature.

1. Change the Document Theme (WD 467)
2. Update the Body Text Style (WD 467)
3. Link an Excel Worksheet to a Word Document (WD 469)
4. Link an Excel Chart to a Word Document (WD 471)
5. Copy and Paste Excel Data (WD 472)
6. Edit a Linked Object (WD 473)
7. Break Links (WD 475)
8. Save a Word 2007 Document in a Previous Word Format (WD 477)
9. E-Mail a Document as an Attachment (WD 478)

 If you have a SAM user profile, you may have access to hands-on instruction, practice, and assessment. Log in to your SAM account (http://sam2007.course.com) to launch any assigned training activities or exams that relate to the skills covered in this feature.

In the Lab

Design and/or create a document using the guidelines, concepts, and skills presented in this chapter. Labs are listed in order of increasing difficulty. Note: These labs use files from the Data Files for Students. See the inside back cover of this book for instructions on downloading the Data Files for Students, or contact your instructor for information about accessing the required files.

Lab 1: Linking an Excel Worksheet to a Word Document

Problem: Charlotte Keyes, director at County Library, has created an Excel worksheet that lists the circulation figures for the library branches. She would like you to modify a draft memo so that it includes the Excel worksheet.

Instructions:
1. Open the memo called Lab IF-1 County Library Memo Draft from the Data Files for Students.
2. Use the Save As command to save the memo with the name, Lab IF-1 County Library Memo Modified.
3. Change the document theme to Trek.
4. Change the paragraph of body text to 12 point. Update the Body Text style.
5. Use the Copy and Paste Special commands to link the worksheet in the Lab IF-1 Circulation Figures Excel workbook, which is on the Data Files for Students, to the Word memo file.
6. Save the Word memo file again. Submit the memo in the format specified by your instructor.

In the Lab

Lab 2: Linking Data from an Excel Worksheet and an Excel Chart to a Word Document

Problem: Mario Joseph, manager at Party Palace, has created an Excel worksheet that lists the company's recent sales figures. He also has charted the data in Excel. He would like you to prepare a memo that includes the Excel table and chart.

Instructions:

1. Open the memo called Lab IF-2 Party Palace Memo Draft from the Data Files for Students.

2. Use the Save As command to save the memo with the name, Lab IF-2 Party Palace Memo Modified.

3. Change the document theme to Module.

4. Change the paragraph of body text to 12 point. Update the Body Text style.

5. Use the Copy and Paste Special commands to link the worksheet in the Lab IF-2 Party Supply Sales Excel workbook, which is on the Data Files for Students, to the Word memo file.

6. Use the Copy and Paste Special commands to link the chart in the Lab IF-2 Party Supply Sales Excel workbook, which is on the Data Files for Students, to the memo file. If necessary, resize the chart so all memo contents fit on a single page.

7. Save the Word memo file again. Submit the memo in the format specified by your instructor.

8. Break the links in the Word memo file. Save the modified file with the name, Lab IF-2 Party Palace Memo Modified Without Links. Submit the memo in the format specified by your instructor.

9. Save the memo file in the Word 97-2003 format. Submit the memo in the format specified by your instructor.

10. If your instructor approves, e-mail the file created in Step 9 to him or her.

In the Lab

Lab 3: Creating an Excel Worksheet and Linking It to a Word Document

Problem: As a part-time computer assistant at Secondhand Stories, your boss has asked you to create an Excel worksheet that lists the units sold by inventory category and then prepare a memo that links the Excel worksheet to a memo.

Instructions:

1. Create an Excel worksheet that has two columns (Item and Units Sold) and five rows (Books, 17252; Music CDs, 10256; Computer Games, 1632; Movies, 3598; Stationery, 5450). Format the worksheet. Save the Excel workbook with the name, Lab IF-3 Secondhand Stories Sales.

2. Create a memo to All Staff. Save the memo using the file name, Lab IF-3 Secondhand Stories Memo. Use this paragraph of text in the memo: Inventory finally is complete – thank you all for your hard work! The table below shows the number of items sold from inventory by category.

3. Use the Copy and Paste Special commands to link the Excel worksheet data to the Word memo file.

4. Save the Word memo file again. Submit the memo in the format specified by your instructor.

5. Quit Excel. Edit the linked worksheet. Change the number of Computer Games to 7632. Save the worksheet again.

6. Update the linked Excel worksheet in the Word memo. Save the memo again. Submit the memo in the format specified by your instructor.

4 Financial Functions, Data Tables, and Amortization Schedules

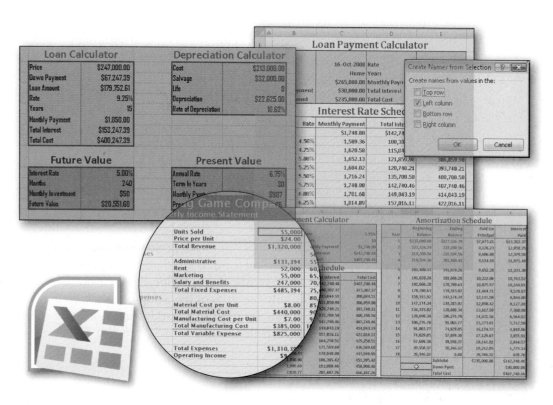

Objectives

You will have mastered the material in this chapter when you can:

- Control the color and thickness of outlines and borders

- Assign a name to a cell and refer to the cell in a formula using the assigned name

- Determine the monthly payment of a loan using the financial function PMT

- Use the financial functions PV (present value) and FV (future value)

- Create a data table to analyze data in a worksheet

- Add a pointer to a data table

- Create an amortization schedule

- Analyze worksheet data by changing values

- Use names and the Set Print Area command to print sections of a worksheet

- Set print options

- Protect and unprotect cells in a worksheet

- Use the formula checking features of Excel

- Hide and unhide cell gridlines, rows, columns, sheets, and workbooks

4 | Financial Functions, Data Tables, and Amortization Schedules

Introduction

Two of the more powerful aspects of Excel are its wide array of functions and its capability of organizing answers to what-if questions. In this chapter, you will learn about financial functions such as the PMT function, which allows you to determine a monthly payment for a loan, and the PV function, which allows you to determine the present value of an investment.

In earlier chapters, you learned how to analyze data by using Excel's recalculation feature and goal seeking. This chapter introduces an additional what-if analysis tool, called data tables. You use a data table to automate data analyses and organize the answers returned by Excel. Another important loan analysis tool is the Amortization Schedule section. An amortization schedule shows the beginning and ending balances and the amount of payment that applies to the principal and interest over a period.

In previous chapters, you learned how to print in a variety of ways. This chapter continues with a discussion about additional methods of printing using names and the Set Print Area command.

Finally, this chapter introduces you to cell protection; hiding and unhiding rows, columns, sheets, and workbooks; and formula checking. **Cell protection** ensures that users do not change values inadvertently that are critical to the worksheet. **Hiding** portions of a workbook lets you show only the parts of the workbook that the user needs to see. The **formula checker** checks the formulas in a workbook in a manner similar to the way the spell checker checks for misspelled words.

Project — Loan Payment Calculator with Data Table and Amortization Schedule

The project in the chapter follows proper design guidelines and uses Excel to create the worksheet shown in Figure 4–1. Braden Mortgage operates as a small home loan institution. The company's Chief Financial Officer has asked for a workbook that calculates loan payment information, displays an amortization schedule, and displays a table that shows loan payments for varying interest rates. To ensure that the loan officers do not delete the formulas in the worksheet, she has asked that cells in the worksheet be protected so they cannot be changed accidently.

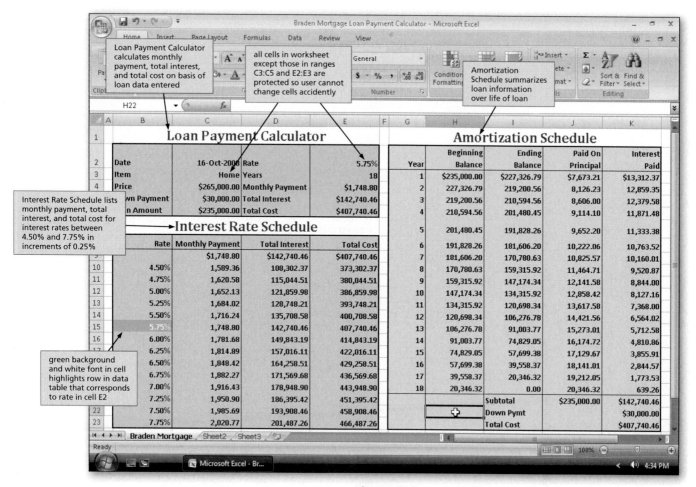

Figure 4–1

The requirements document for the Braden Mortgage Loan Payment Calculator worksheet is shown in Figure 4–2 on the next page. It includes the needs, source of data, summary of calculations, special requirements, and other facts about its development.

Overview

As you read this chapter, you will learn how to create the worksheet shown in Figure 4–1 by performing these general tasks:

- Create and format the Loan Payment Calculator section and use the payment function
- Create and format a data table that includes the interest rate schedule
- Create and format the amortization schedule and use the present value and future value functions
- Create and test print areas in the worksheet
- Protect cells in the worksheet
- Check the formulas in the worksheet

REQUEST FOR NEW WORKBOOK

Date Submitted:	May 5, 2008
Submitted By:	Elana Hughes
Worksheet Title:	Loan Payment Calculator
Needs:	An easy-to-read worksheet (Figure 4-3) that: 1. determines the monthly payment, total interest, and total cost for a loan; 2. shows a data table that answers what-if questions based on changing interest rates; 3. highlights the rate in the data table that matches the actual interest rate; and 4. shows an amortization schedule that lists annual summaries.
Source of Data:	The data (item, price of the item, down payment, interest rate, and term of the loan in years) is determined by the loan officer and customer when they initially meet to review the loan. The Excel Data Table command creates the data table.

Calculations:	1. The following calculations must be made for each loan:
	   a. Loan Amount = Price – Down Payment
	   b. Monthly Payment = PMT function
	   c. Total Interest = 12 × Years × Monthly Payment – Loan Amount
	   d. Total Cost = 12 × Years x Monthly Payment + Down Payment
	 2. The amortization schedule involves the following calculations:
	   a. Beginning Balance = Loan Amount
	   b. Ending Balance = PV function or 0
	   c. Paid on Principal = Beginning Balance – Ending Balance
	   d. Interest Paid = 12 × Monthly Payment – Paid on Principal or 0
	   e. Paid on Principal Subtotal = SUM function
	   f. Interest Paid Subtotal = SUM function

Special Requirements	1. Assign names to the ranges of the three major sections of the worksheet and the worksheet itself, so that the names can be used to print each section separately. 2. Protect the worksheet in such a way that the loan officers cannot enter data into wrong cells mistakenly.

Approvals

Approval Status:	X	Approved
		Rejected
Approved By:	Jorge Martin, Chief Information Officer	
Date:	May 12, 2008	
Assigned To:	J. Quasney, Spreadsheet Specialist	

Figure 4–2

General Project Decisions

While creating an Excel worksheet, you need to make several decisions that will determine the appearance and characteristics of the finished worksheet. As you create the worksheet required to meet the requirements shown in Figure 4–2, you should follow these general guidelines:

Plan
Ahead

1. Create and format the Loan Payment Calculator section of the worksheet. The Loan Payment Calculator section requires a compact and understandable interface where both loan officers and customers can view the results of possible loan situations quickly. This section requires complex financial calculations such as present value and future value of a loan. Excel's financial functions can be used to solve these problems. As with the other two sections of the worksheet, this section of the worksheet should be formatted to make it distinct from the other two sections of the worksheet.

2. Create and format the Interest Rate Schedule section of the worksheet. The Interest Rate Schedule depends on values in the Loan Payment Calculator section of the worksheet. If those values are placed in the top row of the Interest Rate Schedule, then payment, interest, and cost values for various interest rates can be computed in the columns in this section.

3. Create and format the Amortization Schedule section of the worksheet. The amortization schedule relies on formulas specified in the requirements document (Figure 4–2). This section of the worksheet also should include subtotals and a total to provide additional insight to the users of the worksheet.

4. Specify and name print areas of the worksheet. As specified in the requirements document, users of the worksheet require the option to print the individual sections of the worksheet. Excel allows you to name these sections and then print the sections by name.

5. Determine which cells to protect and unprotect in the worksheet. When creating a workbook that will be used by others, the spreadsheet designer should consider which cells another user should be able to manipulate. For the Loan Payment Calculator, the user needs to modify only the item, price, down payment, rate, and number of years of the loan. All other cells in the worksheet should be protected from input by the user of the worksheet.

   In addition, using a sketch of the worksheet can help you visualize its design. The sketch of the worksheet (Figure 4–3) consists of titles, column and cell headings, location of data values, and a general idea of the desired formatting.

   As shown in the worksheet sketch shown in Figure 4–3, the three basic sections of the worksheet are (1) the Loan Payment Calculator on the upper–left side, (2) the Interest Rate Schedule data table on the lower–left side, and (3) the Amortization Schedule on the right side. The worksheet will be created in this order.

(continued)

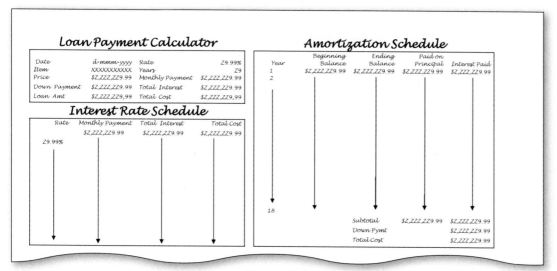

Figure 4–3

Plan Ahead

(continued)

When necessary, more specific details concerning the above guidelines are presented at appropriate points in the chapter. The chapter also will identify the actions you perform and decisions made regarding these guidelines during the creation of the worksheet shown in Figure 4–1 on page EX 267.

Figure 4–1 on page EX 267.

With a good understanding of the requirements document, an understanding of the necessary decisions, and a sketch of the worksheet, the next step is to use Excel to create the worksheet.

To Start Excel

If you are using a computer to step through the project in this chapter and you want your screen to match the figures in this book, you should change your computer's resolution to 1024×768. For information about how to change a computer's resolution, see page APP 21 in Appendix E.

The following steps, which assume Windows is running, start Excel based on a typical installation of Microsoft Office on your computer. You may need to ask your instructor how to start Excel for your computer.

1 Click the Start button on the Windows Vista taskbar to display the Start menu.

2 Click All Programs at the bottom of the left pane on the Start menu to display the All Programs list.

3 Click Microsoft Office in the All Programs list to display the Microsoft Office list.

4 Click Microsoft Office Excel 2007 to start Excel and display a blank worksheet in the Excel window.

5 If the Excel window is not maximized, click the Maximize button next to the Close button on its title bar to maximize the window.

6 If the worksheet window in Excel is not maximized, click the Maximize button next to the Close button on its title bar to maximize the worksheet window within Excel.

To Bold the Entire Worksheet

The following steps assign a bold format to the entire worksheet so that all entries will be emphasized.

1 Click the Select All button immediately above row heading 1 and to the left of column heading A.

2 Click the Bold button on the Home tab on the Ribbon.

BTW

Good Worksheet Design
Do not create worksheets as if you are going to use them only once. Carefully design worksheets as if they will be on display and evaluated by your fellow workers. Smart worksheet design starts with visualizing the results you need. A well-designed worksheet often is used for many years.

BTW

Multiple Worksheets
You can have more than one instance of Excel running. Besides opening multiple workbooks in Excel, you can run multiple instances of Excel. Each instance of Excel will show as a button on the Windows Vista taskbar. When you first install Excel, Excel shows all open workbooks in the taskbar. To change this behavior, click the Excel Options button on the Office Button menu, click Advanced, remove the checkmark from the 'Show all windows in the Taskbar' check box, and then click the OK button.

To Enter the Section Title, Row Titles, System Date, Document Properties, and Save the Workbook

The next step is to enter the Loan Payment Calculator section title, row titles, system date, document properties, and then save the workbook. To make the worksheet easier to read, the width of column A will be decreased to 1.57 characters and used as a separator between the Loan Payment Calculator section and the row headings on the left. Using a column as a separator between sections on a worksheet is a common technique employed by spreadsheet specialists. The width of columns B through E will be increased so the intended values fit. The height of row 1, which contains the title, will be increased so it stands out. The worksheet title also will be changed to the Title cell style.

The following steps enter the section title, row titles, system date, document properties, and then save the workbook.

1 Select cell B1. Enter `Loan Payment Calculator` as the section title. Select the range B1:E1. Click the Merge & Center button on the Ribbon.

2 With cell B1 active, click the Cell Styles button on the Ribbon and then select the Title cell style in the Cell Styles gallery.

3 Position the mouse pointer on the bottom boundary of row heading 1. Drag down until the ScreenTip indicates Height: 23.25 (31 pixels). Position the mouse pointer on the bottom boundary of row heading 2. Drag down until the ScreenTip indicates Height: 30.00 (40 pixels).

4 Select cell B2 and then enter `Date` as the row title and then press the TAB key.

5 With cell C2 selected, enter `=now()` to display the system date.

6 Right–click cell C2 and then click Format Cells on the shortcut menu. When Excel displays the Format Cells dialog box, click the Number tab, click Date in the Category list, scroll down in the Type list, and then click 14–Mar–2001. Click the OK button.

7 Enter the following row titles:

Cell	Entry	Cell	Entry
B3	Item	D2	Rate
B4	Price	D3	Years
B5	Down Payment	D4	Monthly Payment
B6	Loan Amount	D5	Total Interest
		D6	Total Cost

8 Position the mouse pointer on the right boundary of column heading A and then drag to the left until the ScreenTip indicates Width: 1.57 (16 pixels).

9 Position the mouse pointer on the right boundary of column heading B and then drag to the right until the ScreenTip indicates Width: 13.86 (102 pixels).

10 Click column heading C to select it and then drag through column headings D and E. Position the mouse pointer on the right boundary of column heading C and then drag until the ScreenTip indicates Width: 16.29 (119 pixels).

11 Double–click the Sheet1 tab and then enter `Braden Mortgage` as the sheet name. Right–click the tab and then click Tab Color. Click Light Green (column 5, row 1) in the Standard Colors area and then select cell D6 (Figure 4–4 on the next page).

BTW

Global Formatting
To assign formats to all the cells in all the worksheets in a workbook, click the Select All button, right-click a tab, and click Select All Sheets on the shortcut menu. Next, assign the formats. To deselect the sheets, hold down the SHIFT key and click the Sheet1 tab. You also can select a cell or a range of cells and then select all sheets to assign formats to that cell or a range of cells on all sheets in a workbook.

BTW

Concatenation
You can concatenate text, numbers, or text and numbers from two or more cells into a single cell. The ampersand (&) is the concatenation operator. For example, if cell A1 = AB, cell A2 = CD, cell A3 = 25, and you assign cell A4 the formula =A1&A2&A3, then ABCD25 displays in cell A4.

12. Update the document properties with your name and any other relevant information.

13. With a USB flash drive connected to one of the computer's USB ports, click the Save button on the Quick Access Toolbar. Save the workbook using the file name `Braden Mortgage Loan Payment Calculator` on the USB flash drive.

Shortcut Menus
Excel requires that you point to the object (cell, range, toolbar) on the screen when you right-click to display the corresponding shortcut menu. For example, if you select the range G6:J14 and right-click with the mouse pointer on cell A1, then the shortcut menu pertains to cell A1 and not the selected range G6:J14.

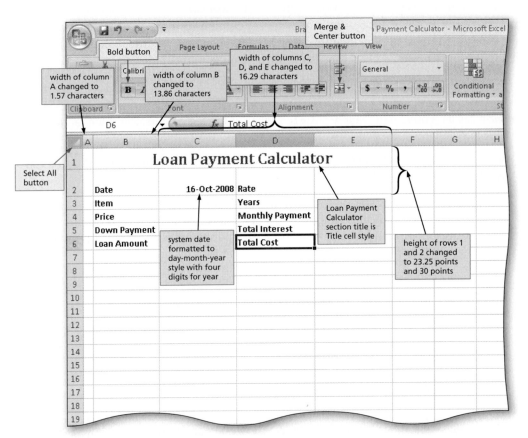

Figure 4–4

Adding Custom Borders and a Background Color to a Range

In previous projects, you were introduced to outlining a range using the Borders button on the Home tab on the Ribbon. The Borders button, however, offers only a limited selection of border thicknesses. To control the color and thickness, Excel requires that you use the Border sheet in the Format Cells dialog box.

To Add Custom Borders and a Background Color to a Range

The following steps add a thick black border and a light blue background color to the Loan Payment Calculator section. Rather than using the Fill Color button to color the background of a range as was done in previous projects, the steps use the Fill sheet in the Format Cells dialog box. To subdivide the row titles and numbers further, light borders also are added within the section as shown in Figure 4–1 on page EX 267.

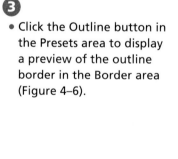

- Select the range B2:E6 and then right–click to display the shortcut menu (Figure 4–5).

2

- Click Format Cells on the shortcut menu.

- When Excel displays the Format Cells dialog box, click the Border tab.

- Click the medium line style in the Style area (column 2, row 5).

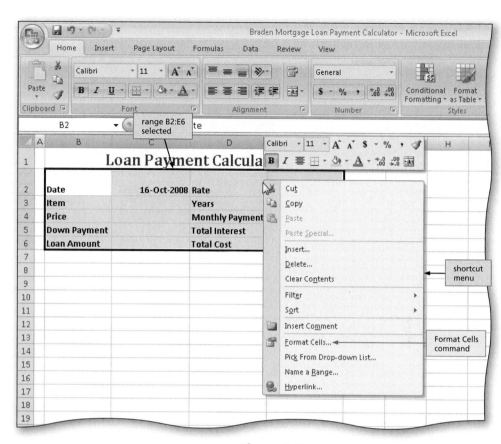

Figure 4–5

3

- Click the Outline button in the Presets area to display a preview of the outline border in the Border area (Figure 4–6).

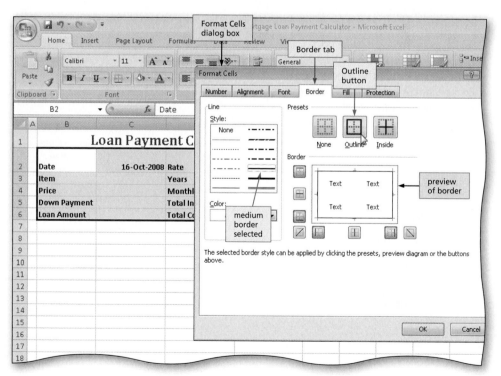

Figure 4–6

4

- Click the light border in the Style area (column 1, row 7) and then click the Vertical Line button in the Border area to preview the black vertical border in the Border area (Figure 4–7).

Q&A

How should I create my desired border?

As shown in Figure 4–7, you can add a variety of borders with different colors to a cell or range of cells to improve its appearance. It is important that you select border characteristics in the order specified in the steps; that is, (1) choose the border color; (2) choose the border line style; and (3) choose the border type. If you attempt to do these steps in any other order, you may not end up with the desired borders.

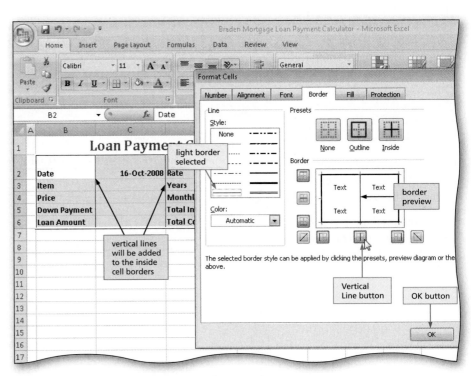

Figure 4–7

5

- Click the Fill tab and then click light blue (column 9, row 3) in the Background Color area.

- Click the OK button and then select cell B8 to deselect the range B2:E6, add a black outline with vertical borders to the right side of each column in the range B2: E6, and add a light blue fill color to the range (Figure 4–8).

Other Ways

1. Select range, click Fill Color button arrow on Home tab on Ribbon, click color, click Borders button arrow on Ribbon, click border

2. Click Format Cells: Font Dialog Box Launcher on Ribbon, click Fill tab, click color, click Borders tab, click border

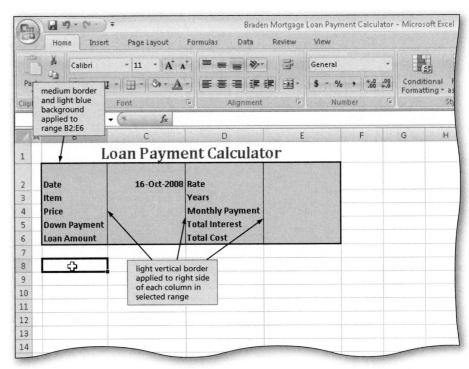

Figure 4–8

To Format Cells before Entering Values

While usually you format cells after you enter values in cells, Excel also allows you to format cells before you enter the values. For example, at the beginning of this project, bold was applied to all the cells in the blank worksheet. The steps on the next page assign the Currency style format with a floating dollar sign to the ranges C4:C6 and E4:E6 before the values are entered.

1 Select the range C4:C6. While holding down the CTRL key, select the nonadjacent range E4:E6.

2 Right–click one of the selected ranges and then click Format Cells on the shortcut menu.

3 When Excel displays the Format Cells dialog box, click the Number tab. Click Currency in the Category list and then click the second format, $1,234.10, in the Negative numbers list. Click the OK button to assign the Currency style format with a floating dollar sign to the ranges C4:C6 and E4:E6.

Q&A

What will happen when I enter values in those cells?

As you enter numbers into these cells, Excel will display the numbers using the Currency style format. You also could have selected the range B4:E6 rather than the nonadjacent ranges and assigned the Currency style format to this range, which includes text. The Currency style format has no impact on text in a cell.

BTW

When to Format
Excel lets you format (1) before you enter data; (2) when you enter data, through the use of format symbols; (3) incrementally after entering sections of data; and (4) after you enter all the data. Spreadsheet specialists usually format a worksheet in increments as they build the worksheet, but occasions do exist where it makes sense to format cells before you enter any data.

To Enter the Loan Data

As shown in the Source of Data section of the Request for New Workbook document in Figure 4–2 on page EX 268, five items make up the loan data in the worksheet: the item to be purchased, the price of the item, the down payment, the interest rate, and the number of years until the loan is paid back (also called the term of the loan). These items are entered into cells C3 through C5 and cells E2 and E3. The steps below describe how to enter the following loan data: Item — Home; Price — $265,000.00; Down Payment — $30,000.00; Interest Rate — 5.75%; and Years — 18.

1 Select cell C3. Type Home and then click the Enter box in the formula bar. With cell C3 still active, click the Align Text Right button on the Ribbon. Select cell C4 and then enter 265000 for the price of the house. Select cell C5 and then enter 30000 for the down payment.

2 Select cell E2. Enter 5.75% for the interest rate. Select cell E3 and then enter 18 for the number of years to complete the entry of loan data in the worksheet (Figure 4–9 on the next page).

Q&A

Why are the entered values already formatted?

The values in cells C4 and C5 in Figure 4–9 are formatted using the Currency style with two decimal places, because this format was assigned to the cells prior to entering the values. Excel also automatically formats the interest rate in cell E2 to the Percent style with two decimal places, because the percent sign (%) was appended to 5.75 when it was entered.

BTW

Entering Percents
When you format a cell to display percentages, Excel assumes that whatever you enter into that cell in the future will be a percentage. Thus, if you enter the number .5, Excel translates the value as 50%. A potential problem arises, however, when you start to enter numbers greater than or equal to one. For instance, if you enter the number 25, do you mean 25% or 2500%? If you want Excel to treat the number 25 as 25% instead of 2500% and Excel interprets the number 25 as 2500%, click the Excel Options button on the Office Button menu. When the Excel Options dialog box is displayed, click the Advanced button and make sure the 'Enable automatic percent entry' check box is selected.

BTW

Managing Range Names

When you insert a column into a worksheet range that includes a named range, Excel automatically updates the named range to include the inserted column. To delete a named range, click the Name Manager button on the Formulas tab, select the name in the Name Manager dialog box, and then click the Delete button (Figure 4-12 on page EX 278).

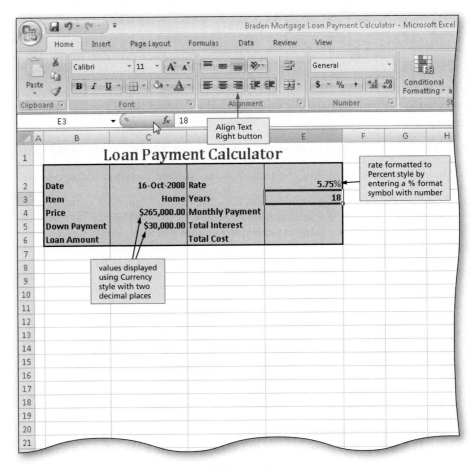

Figure 4–9

BTW

Cell References in Formulas

Are you tired of writing formulas that make no sense when you read them because of cell references? The Name Manager can help add clarity to your formulas by allowing you to assign names to cells. You then can use the names, such as Amount, rather than the cell reference, such as H10, in the formulas you create. To access the Name Manager, click the Formulas tab on the Ribbon and then click the Name Manager button.

Creating Cell Names Based on Row Titles

Worksheets often have column titles at the top of each column and row titles to the left of each row that describe the data within the worksheet. You can use these titles within formulas when you want to refer to the related data by name. A cell **name** is created from column and row titles through the use of the Name command on the Insert menu. You also can use the same command to define descriptive names that are not column titles or row titles to represent cells, ranges of cells, formulas, or constants.

Naming a cell that you plan to reference in a formula helps make the formula easier to read and remember. For example, the loan amount in cell C6 is equal to the price in cell C4 minus the down payment in cell C5. Therefore, according to what you learned in earlier projects, you can enter the loan amount formula in cell C6 as =C4 – C5. By naming cells C4 and C5 using the corresponding row titles in cells B4 and B5, however, you can enter the loan amount formula as =Price – Down Payment, which is clearer and easier to understand than =C4 – C5.

To Create Names Based on Row Titles

The following steps assign the row titles in the range B4:B6 to their adjacent cell in column C and assigns the row titles in the range D2:D6 to their adjacent cell in column E.

1

- Select the range B4:C6.
- Click the Formulas tab on the Ribbon (Figure 4–10).

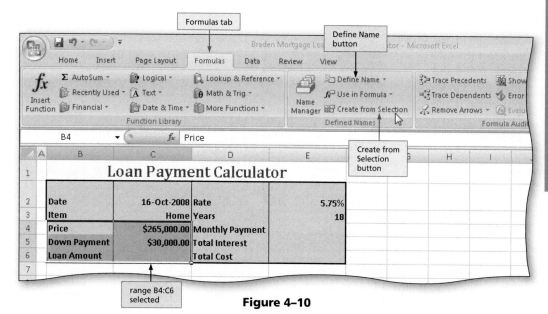

Figure 4–10

2

- Click the Create from Selection button on the Ribbon to display the Create Names from Selection dialog box (Figure 4–11).

Q&A How does Excel determine which option to automatically select in the the Create Names from Selection dialog box?

Excel automatically selects the Left column check box in the 'Create names from values in the' area because the left column of the cells selected in Step 1 contains text.

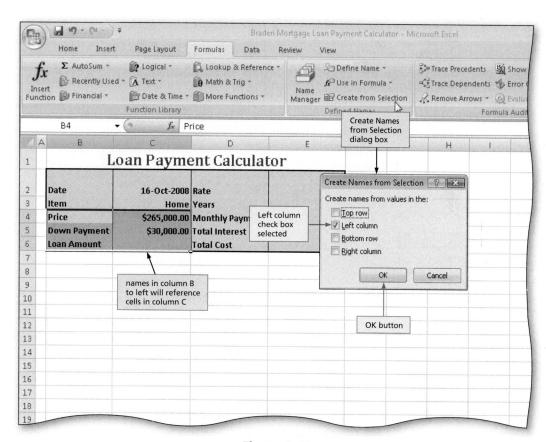

Figure 4–11

3

- Click the OK button.

- Select the range D2:E6 and then click the Create from Selection button on the Ribbon.

- Click the OK button on the Create Names from Selection dialog box to assign names to the range E2:E6.

4

- Select cell B8 to deselect the range D2:E6 and then click the Name box arrow in the formula bar to view the names created (Figure 4–12a).

Q&A

How can the cell names be used?

You now can use the assigned names in formulas to reference cells in the ranges C4:C6 or E2:E6. Excel is not case–sensitive with respect to names of cells. Hence, you can enter the names of cells in formulas in uppercase or lowercase letters. To use a name that is made up of two or more words in a formula, you should replace any space with the underscore character (_). For example, the name, Down Payment, is written as down_payment or Down_Payment when you want to reference the adjacent cell C5. Figure 4–12b shows the Name Manager dialog box that displays when you click the Name Manager button.

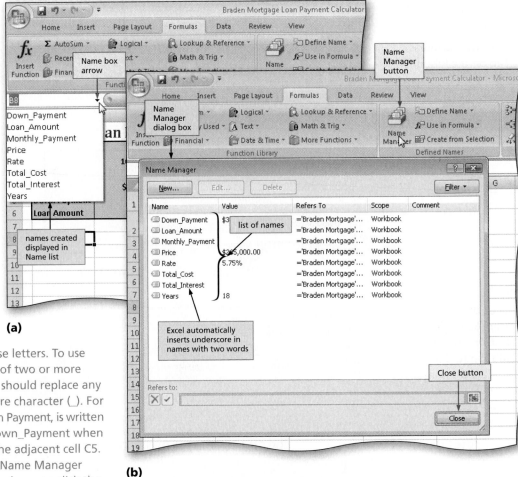

Figure 4–12

Other Ways

1. Select cell or range, type name in Name box, press ENTER key
2. Select cell or range, on Formulas tab on Ribbon click Define Name button, [type name], click OK button
3. Select cell or range, on Formulas tab on Ribbon click Name Manager button, click New, [type name], click OK button, click Close button

More About Cell Names

If you enter a formula using Point mode and click a cell that has an assigned name, then Excel will insert the name of the cell rather than the cell reference. Consider these additional points regarding the assignment of names to cells:

1. A name can be a minimum of 1 character to a maximum of 255 characters.
2. If you want to assign a name that is not a text item in an adjacent cell, use the Define Name button on the Formulas tab on the Ribbon (Figure 4–10 on the previous page) or select the cell or range and then type the name in the Name box in the formula bar.
3. Names are absolute cell references. This is important to remember if you plan to copy formulas that contain names, rather than cell references.
4. Excel displays the names in alphabetical order in the Name list when you click the Name box arrow and in the Name Manager dialog box when you click the Name Manager button on the Formulas tab on the Ribbon (Figures 4–12a and 4–12b).

5. Names are **global** to the workbook. That is, a name assigned to a cell or cell range on one worksheet in a workbook can be used on other sheets in the same workbook to reference the named cell or range.

Spreadsheet specialists often assign names to a cell or range of cells so they can select them quickly. If you want to select a cell or range of cells using the assigned name, you can click the Name box arrow (Figure 4–12a) and then click the name of the cell you want to select. This method is similar to using the F5 key to select a cell, but it is much quicker. When you select a name that references a range in the Name list, Excel highlights the range on the worksheet.

BTW

Entering Interest Rates
An alternative to requiring the user to enter an interest rate in percent form, such as 7.75%, is to allow the user to enter the interest rate as a number without an appended percent sign (7.75) and then divide the interest rate by 1200, rather than 12.

To Enter the Loan Amount Formula Using Names

To determine the loan amount in cell C6, subtract the down payment in cell C5 from the price in cell C4. As indicated earlier, this can be done by entering the formula =C4 – C5 or by entering the formula =price – down_payment in cell C6. You also can use Point mode to enter the formula, as shown in the following steps.

1
- Select cell C6.

- Type = (equal sign), click cell C4, type – (minus sign), and then click cell C5 to display the formula in cell C6 and in the formula bar using the names of the cells rather then the cell references (Figure 4–13).

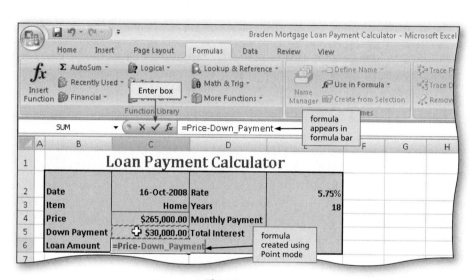

Figure 4–13

2
- Click the Enter box to assign the formula =Price – Down_Payment to cell C6 (Figure 4–14).

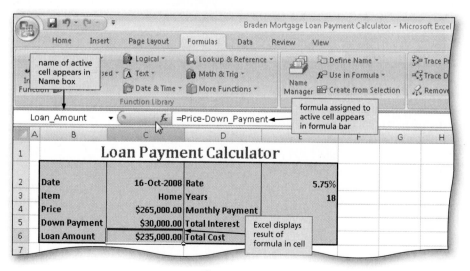

Figure 4–14

To Enter the PMT Function

The next step is to determine the monthly payment for the loan in cell E4. You can use Excel's PMT function to determine the monthly payment. The **PMT function** has three arguments — rate, payment, and loan amount. Its general form is:

=PMT(rate, periods, loan amount)

where rate is the interest rate per payment period, periods is the number of payments, and loan amount is the amount of the loan.

In the worksheet shown in Figure 4–14 on the previous page, Excel displays the annual interest rate in cell E2. Financial institutions, however, calculate interest on a monthly basis. Therefore, the rate value in the PMT function is rate / 12 (cell E2 divided by 12), rather than just rate (cell E2). The periods (or number of payments) in the PMT function is 12 * years (12 times cell E3) because there are 12 months, or 12 payments, per year.

Excel considers the value returned by the PMT function to be a debit and, therefore, returns a negative number as the monthly payment. To display the monthly payment as a positive number, begin the function with a negative sign instead of an equal sign. The PMT function for cell E4 is:

$$-\text{PMT}(\underbrace{\text{rate / 12}}_{\text{monthly interest rate}}, \underbrace{\text{12 * years}}_{\text{number of payments}}, \underbrace{\text{loan\_amount}}_{\text{loan amount}})$$

The following steps use the keyboard, rather than Point mode, to enter the PMT function to determine the monthly payment in cell E4.

1

- Select cell E4. Type `-pmt(rate / 12, 12*years, loan_amount` as the function to display the PMT function in cell E4 and in the formula bar (Figure 4–15).

Q&A

What happens as I enter the function?

The ScreenTip shows the general form of the PMT function. The arguments in brackets in the ScreenTip are optional and not required for the computation described here. The Formula AutoComplete list shows functions and cell names that match the letters that you type on the keyboard. You can type the complete cell name, such as Loan_Amount, or select the cell name from the list. Excel will add the closing parenthesis to the function automatically. Excel also may scroll the worksheet to the right in order to accommodate the display of the ScreenTip.

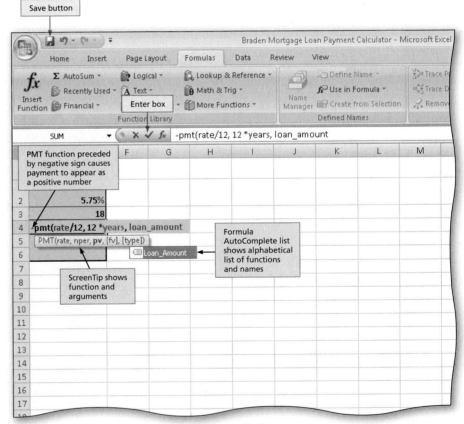

Figure 4–15

2

- If necessary, scroll the worksheet to the left using the horizontal scrollbar.

- Click the Enter box in the formula bar to complete the function (Figure 4–16).

Q&A

What does Excel display after I click the Enter box?

Excel displays the monthly payment $1,748.80 in cell E4, based on a loan amount of $235,000.00 (cell C6) with an annual interest rate of 5.75% (cell E2) for a term of 18 years (cell E3), as shown in Figure 4–16.

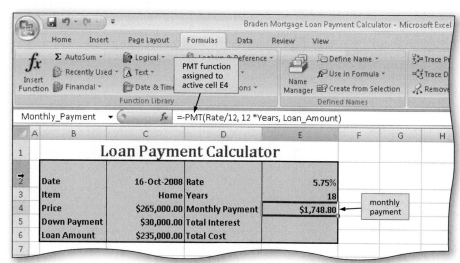

Figure 4–16

Other Ways

1. Click Formulas tab on Ribbon, click Financial button on Ribbon, select PMT function, enter arguments, click OK button

2. Click Insert Function button in formula bar, select Financial category, select PMT function, click OK button, enter arguments, click OK button

Other Financial Functions

In addition to the PMT function, Excel provides more than 50 additional financial functions to help you solve the most complex finance problems. These functions save you from entering long, complicated formulas to obtain needed results. Table 4–1 summarizes three of the more frequently used financial functions.

Table 4–1 Financial Functions

Function	Description
FV (rate, periods, payment)	Returns the future value of an investment based on periodic, constant payments, and a constant interest rate.
PMT (rate, periods, loan amount)	Calculates the payment for a loan based on the loan amount, constant payments, and a constant interest rate.
PV (rate, periods, payment)	Returns the present value of an investment. The present value is the total amount that a series of future payments is worth now.

To Determine the Total Interest and Total Cost

The next step is to determine the total interest the borrower will pay on the loan (the lending institution's gross profit on the loan) and the total cost the borrower will pay for the item being purchased. The total interest (cell E5) is equal to the number of payments times the monthly payment, less the loan amount:

=12 * years * monthly_payment – loan_amount

The total cost of the item to be purchased (cell E6) is equal to the price plus the total interest:

=price + total_interest

The steps on the next page enter formulas to determine the total interest and total cost using names.

BTW

Range Finder
Remember to check all formulas carefully. You can double-click a cell with a formula and Excel will use Range Finder to highlight the cells that provide data to the formula. While Range Finder is active, you can drag the outlines from one cell to another to change the cells referenced in the formula, provided the cells have not been named.

1 Select cell E5. Use Point mode and the keyboard to enter the formula `=12 * years * monthly_payment - loan_amount` to determine the total interest.

2 Select cell E6. Use Point mode and the keyboard to enter the formula `=price + total_ interest` to determine the total cost.

3 Select cell B8 to deselect cell E6 (Figure 4–17).

4 Click the Save button on the Quick Access Toolbar to save the workbook using the file name Braden Mortgage Loan Payment Calculator.

Q&A

What are the new values displayed by Excel?

Excel displays a total interest (the lending institution's gross profit) of $142,740.46 in cell E5 and a total cost of $407,740.46 in cell E6, which is the total cost of the home to the borrower (Figure 4–17).

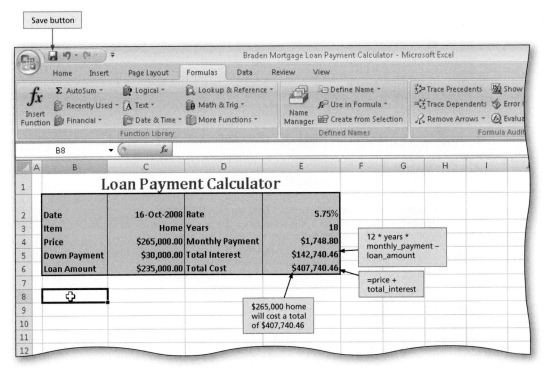

Figure 4–17

To Enter New Loan Data

Assume you want to purchase a Prius for $25,500.00. You have $5,280.00 for a down payment and you want the loan for a term of five years. Braden Mortgage currently is charging 10.25% interest for a five–year auto loan. The following steps show how to enter the new loan data.

1 Select cell C3. Type `Prius` and then press the DOWN ARROW key.

2 In cell C4, type `25500` and then press the DOWN ARROW key.

3 In cell C5, type `5280` and then select cell E2.

4 In cell E2, type `10.25%` and then press the DOWN ARROW key.

5 In cell E3, type 5 and then select cell B8 to recalculate the loan information in cells C6, E4, E5, and E6 (Figure 4–18).

Q&A What do the results of the new calculation mean?

As you can see from Figure 4–18, the monthly payment for the Prius is $432.11. By paying for the car over a five–year period at an interest rate of 10.25%, you will pay total interest of $5,706.40 on the loan and pay a total cost of $31,206.40 for a $25,500.00 Prius.

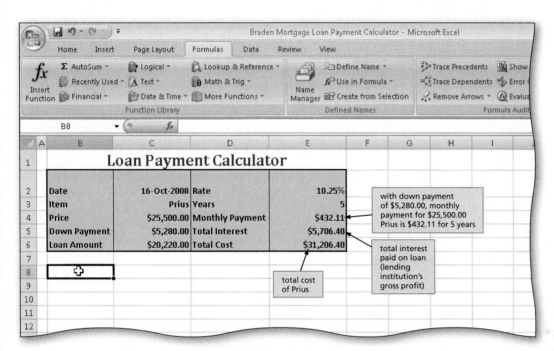

Figure 4–18

To Enter the Original Loan Data

The following steps re–enter the original loan data.

1 Select cell C3. Type Home and then press the DOWN ARROW key.

2 In cell C4, type 265000 and then press the DOWN ARROW key.

3 In cell C5, type 30000 and then select cell E2.

4 In cell E2, type 5.75 and then press the DOWN ARROW key.

5 In cell E3, type 18 and then select cell B8.

Q&A What is happening on the worksheet as I enter the original data?

Excel instantaneously recalculates all formulas in the worksheet each time you enter a value. Excel displays the original loan information as shown in Figure 4–17.

Q&A Can the Undo button on the Quick Access Toolbar be used to change back to the original data?

Yes, but the Undo button must be clicked five times, once for each data item.

Using a Data Table to Analyze Worksheet Data

Data Tables
Data tables have one purpose: to organize the answers to what-if questions. You can create two kinds of data tables. The first type involves changing one input value to see the resulting effect on one or more formulas. The second type involves changing two input values to see the resulting effect on one formula.

You already have seen that if you change a value in a cell, Excel immediately recalculates and displays the new results of any formulas that reference the cell directly or indirectly. But what if you want to compare the results of the formula for several different values? Writing down or trying to remember all the answers to the what–if questions would be unwieldy. If you use a data table, however, Excel will organize the answers in the worksheet for you automatically.

A **data table** is a range of cells that shows the answers generated by formulas in which different values have been substituted. Data tables are built in an unused area of the worksheet (in this case, the range B7:E23). Figure 4–19 illustrates the makeup of a one–input data table. With a **one–input data table**, you vary the value in one cell (in this worksheet, cell E2, the interest rate). Excel then calculates the results of one or more formulas and fills the data table with the results.

An alternative to a one–input table is a two–input data table. A **two–input data table** allows you to vary the values in two cells, but you can apply it to only one formula. A two–input data table example is illustrated in the Extend Your Knowledge exercise on page EX 325.

The interest rates that will be used to analyze the loan formulas in this project range from 4.50% to 7.75%, increasing in increments of 0.25%. The one–input data table shown in Figure 4–20 illustrates the impact of varying the interest rate on three formulas: the monthly payment (cell E4), total interest paid (cell E5), and the total cost of the item to be purchased (cell E6). The series of interest rates in column B are called **input values**.

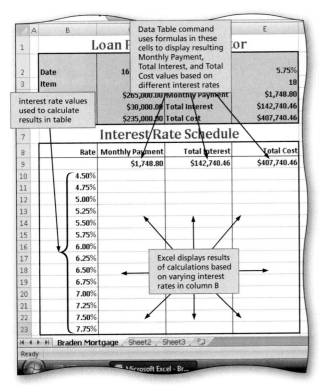

Figure 4–19

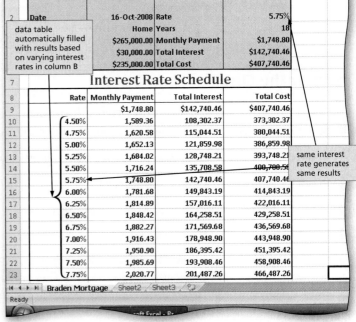

Figure 4–20

To Enter the Data Table Title and Column Titles

The first step in constructing the data table shown in Figure 4–20 is to enter the data table section title and column titles in the range B7:E8 and adjust the heights of rows 7 and 8.

1 Click the Home tab on the Ribbon. Select cell B7. Enter `Interest Rate Schedule` as the data table section title.

2 Select cell B1. Click the Format Painter button on the Ribbon. Select cell B7 to copy the format of cell B1.

3 Enter the column titles in the range B8:E8 as shown in Figure 4–21. Select the range B8:E8 and then click the Align Text Right button on the Ribbon to right–align the column titles.

4 Position the mouse pointer on the bottom boundary of row heading 7. Drag down until the ScreenTip indicates Height: 23.25 (31 pixels). Position the mouse pointer on the bottom boundary of row heading 8. Drag down until the ScreenTip indicates Height: 18.00 (24 pixels). Click cell B10 to deselect the range B8:E8 (Figure 4–21).

BTW

Selecting Cells
If you double-click the top of the heavy black border surrounding an active cell, Excel will make the first nonblank cell in the column active. If you double-click the left side of the heavy black border surrounding the active cell, Excel will make the first nonblank cell in the row the active cell. This procedure works in the same fashion for the right border and the bottom border of the active cell.

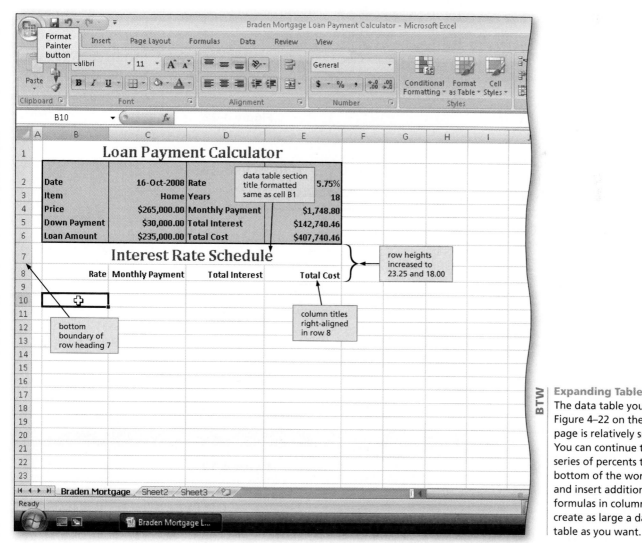

BTW

Expanding Tables
The data table you see in Figure 4–22 on the next page is relatively small. You can continue the series of percents to the bottom of the worksheet and insert additional formulas in columns to create as large a data table as you want.

Figure 4–21

To Create a Percent Series Using the Fill Handle

The next step is to create the percent series in column B using the fill handle. These percent figures will serve as the input data for the data table.

- With cell B10 selected, enter 4.50% as the first number in the series.

- Select cell B11 and then enter 4.75% as the second number in the series.

- Select the range B10:B11.

- Drag the fill handle through cell B23 to create the border of the fill area as indicated by the shaded border (Figure 4–22). Do not release the mouse button.

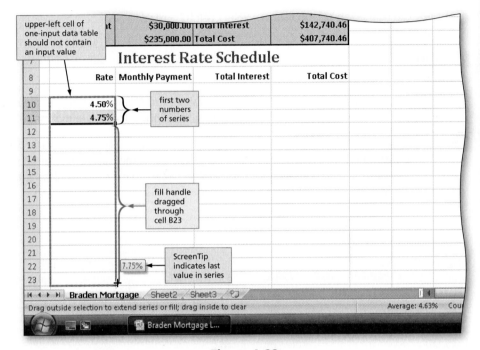

Figure 4–22

- Release the mouse button to generate the percent series from 4.50 to 7.75% and display the Auto Fill Options button. Click cell C9 to deselect the range B10:B23 (Figure 4–23).

Q&A

What is the purpose of the percent figures in column B?

Excel will use the percent figures in column B to calculate the formulas to be evaluated and entered at the top of the data table in row 9. This series begins in cell B10, not cell B9, because the cell immediately to the left of the formulas in a one–input data table should not include an input value.

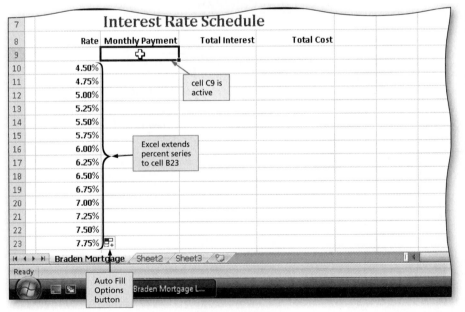

Figure 4–23

Other Ways

1. Right–drag fill handle in direction to fill, click Fill Series on shortcut menu

2. Select range, click Fill button on Home tab on Ribbon, click Down

To Enter the Formulas in the Data Table

The next step in creating the data table is to enter the three formulas at the top of the table in cells C9, D9, and E9. The three formulas are the same as the monthly payment formula in cell E4, the total interest formula in cell E5, and the total cost formula in cell E6. The number of formulas you place at the top of a one–input data table depends on the application. Some one–input data tables will have only one formula, while others might have several. In this case, three formulas are affected when the interest rate changes.

Excel provides four ways to enter these formulas in the data table: (1) retype the formulas in cells C9, D9, and E9; (2) copy cells E4, E5, and E6 to cells C9, D9, and E9, respectively; (3) enter the formulas =monthly_payment in cell C9, =total_interest in cell D9, and =total_cost in cell E9; or (4) enter the formulas =e4 in cell C9, =e5 in cell D9, and =e6 in cell E9.

The best alternative to define the formulas in the data table is the fourth one, which involves using the cell references preceded by an equal sign. This is the best method because: (1) it is easier to enter the cell references; (2) if you change any of the formulas in the range E4:E6, the formulas at the top of the data table are updated automatically; and (3) Excel automatically assigns the format of the cell reference (Currency style format) to the cell. Using the names of the cells in formulas is nearly as good an alternative, but if you use cell names, Excel will not assign the format to the cells. The following steps enter the formulas of the data table in row 9.

1 With cell C9 active, type =e4 and then press the RIGHT ARROW key.

2 Type =e5 in cell D9 and then press the RIGHT ARROW key.

3 Type =e6 in cell E9 and then click the Enter box to complete the assignment of the formulas and Currency style format in the range C9:E9 (Figure 4–24).

Q&A

Why are these cells assigned the values of cells in the Loan Payment Calculator area of the worksheet?

It is important to understand that the entries in the top row of the data table (row 9) refer to the formulas that the loan department wants to evaluate using the series of percentages in column B. Furthermore, recall that when you assign a formula to a cell, Excel applies the format of the first cell reference in the formula to the cell. Thus, Excel applies the Currency style format to cells C9, D9, and E9 because that is the format of cells E4, E5, and E6.

BTW

Formulas in Data Tables

Any experienced Excel user will tell you that to enter the formulas at the top of the data table, you should enter the cell reference or name of the cell preceded by an equal sign (Figure 4–24). This ensures that if you change the original formula in the worksheet, Excel automatically will change the corresponding formula in the data table. If you use a cell reference, Excel also copies the format to the cell. If you use a name, Excel does not copy the format to the cell.

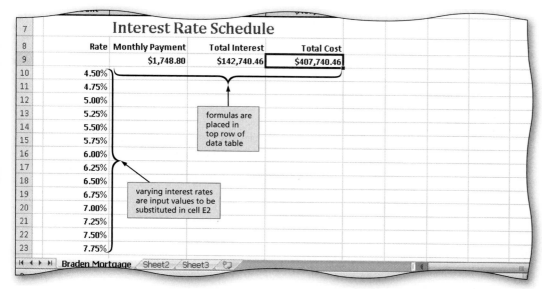

Figure 4–24

To Define a Range as a Data Table

After creating the interest rate series in column B and entering the formulas in row 9, the next step is to define the range B9:E23 as a data table. The Data Table command on the What–If Analysis button on the Data tab on the Ribbon is used to define the range B9:E23 as a data table. Cell E2 is the input cell, which means it is the cell in which values from column B in the data table are substituted in the formulas in row 9.

- Select the range B9:E23.

- Click the Data tab on the Ribbon and then click the What–If Analysis button on the Ribbon to display the What–If Analysis menu (Figure 4–25).

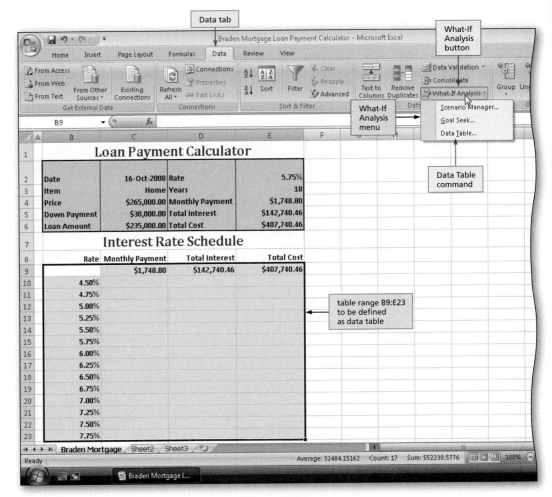

Figure 4–25

2

- Click Data Table on the What–If Analysis menu.

- When Excel displays the Data Table dialog box, click the 'Column input cell' box, and then click cell E2 in the Loan Payment Calculator section (Figure 4–26).

Q&A

What is the purpose of clicking cell E2?

The purpose of clicking cell E2 is to select it for the Column input cell. A marquee surrounds the selected cell E2, indicating it will be the input cell in which values from column B in the data table are substituted in the formulas in row 9. $E$2 now appears in the Column input cell box in the Data Table dialog box.

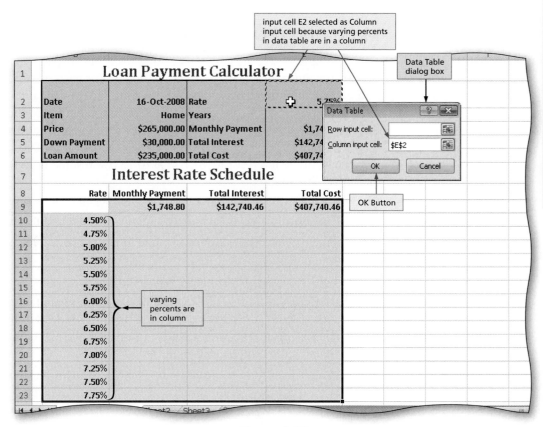

Figure 4–26

3

- Click the OK button to create the data table (Figure 4–27).

Q&A

How does Excel create the data table?

Excel calculates the results of the three formulas in row 9 for each interest rate in column B and immediately fills columns C, D, and E of the data table. The resulting values for each interest rate are displayed in the corresponding rows.

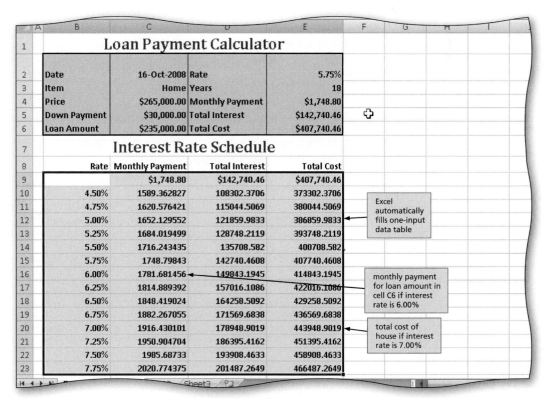

Figure 4–27

More About Data Tables

In Figure 4–27, the data table shows the monthly payment, total interest, and total cost for the interest rates in the range B10:B23. For example, if the interest rate is 5.75% (cell E2), the monthly payment is $1,748.80 (cell E4). If the interest rate is 7.75% (cell B23), however, the monthly payment is $2,020.77 rounded to the nearest cent (cell C23). If the interest rate is 7.00% (cell B20), then the total cost of the house is $443,948.90 rounded to the nearest cent (cell E20), rather than $407,740.46 (cell E6). Thus, a 1.25% increase from the interest rate of 5.75% to 7.00% results in a $36,208.44 increase in the total cost of the house.

The following list details important points you should know about data tables:

1. The formula(s) you are analyzing must include a cell reference to the input cell.

2. You can have as many active data tables in a worksheet as you want.

3. While only one value can vary in a one–input data table, the data table can analyze as many formulas as you want.

4. To include additional formulas in a one–input data table, enter them in adjacent cells in the same row as the current formulas (row 9 in Figure 4–27 on the previous page) and then define the entire new range as a data table by using the Table command on the Data menu.

5. You delete a data table as you would delete any other item on a worksheet. That is, select the data table and then press the DELETE key.

To Format the Data Table

The following steps format the data table to improve its readability.

1 Select the range B8:E23. Right–click the selected range and then click Format Cells on the shortcut menu. When Excel displays the Format Cells dialog box, click the Border tab, and then click the medium line style in the Style area (column 2, row 5). Click the Outline button in the Presets area. Click the light border in the Style area (column 1, row 7) and then click the Vertical Line button in the Border area to preview the black vertical border in the Border area.

2 Click the Fill tab and then click the light red color box (column 6, row 2). Click the OK button.

3 Select the range B8:E8. Click the Home tab on the Ribbon and then click the Borders button to assign a light bottom border.

4 Select the range C10:E23 and right–click. Click Format Cells on the shortcut menu. When Excel displays the Format Cells dialog box, click the Number tab. Click Currency in the Category list, click the Symbol box arrow, click None, and then click the second format, 1,234.10, in the Negative numbers list. Click the OK button to display the worksheet as shown in Figure 4–28.

5 Click the Save button on the Quick Access Toolbar to save the workbook using the file name Braden Mortgage Loan Payment Calculator.

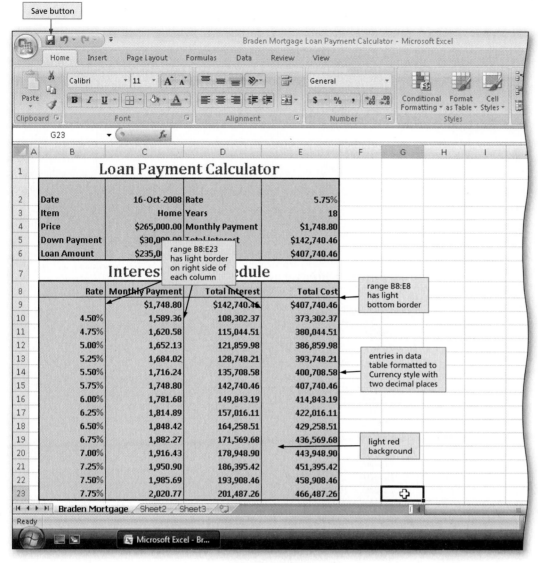

Figure 4–28

Adding a Pointer to the Data Table Using Conditional Formatting

If the interest rate in cell E2 is between 4.50% and 7.75% and its decimal portion is a multiple of 0.25 (such as 6.25%), then one of the rows in the data table agrees exactly with the monthly payment, interest paid, and total cost in the range E4:E6. For example, in Figure 4–28, row 15 (5.75%) in the data table agrees with the results in the range E4: E6, because the interest rate in cell B15 is the same as the interest rate in cell E2. Analysts often look for the row in the data table that agrees with the input cell results.

BTW

Conditional Formatting
You can add as many conditional formats to a range as you like. After adding the first condition, click the Conditional Formatting button on the Home tab on the Ribbon and then click New Rule to add more conditions. If more than one condition is true for a cell, then Excel applies the formats of each condition, beginning with the first.

To Add a Pointer to the Data Table

To make the row stand out, you can add formatting that serves as a pointer to a row. To add a pointer, you can use conditional formatting to make the cell in column B that agrees with the input cell (cell E2) stand out, as shown in the following steps.

- Select the range B10:B23.

- Click the Conditional Formatting button on the Home tab on the Ribbon to display the Conditional Formatting menu (Figure 4–29).

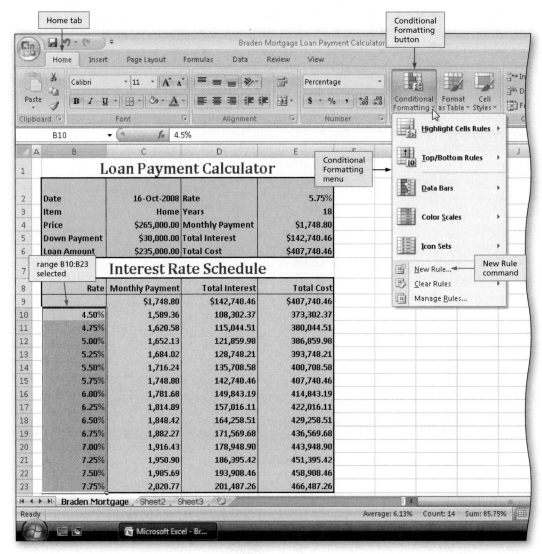

Figure 4–29

2

- Click New Rule on the Conditional Formatting menu.

- When Excel displays the New Formatting Rule dialog box, click 'Format only cells that contain' in the Select a Rule Type box. Select Cell Value in the left list in the 'Format only cells with' area and then select equal to in the middle list.

- Type =$E$2 in the right box.

- Click the Format button, click the Fill tab, and then click Green (column 5, row 7) on the Background color palette.

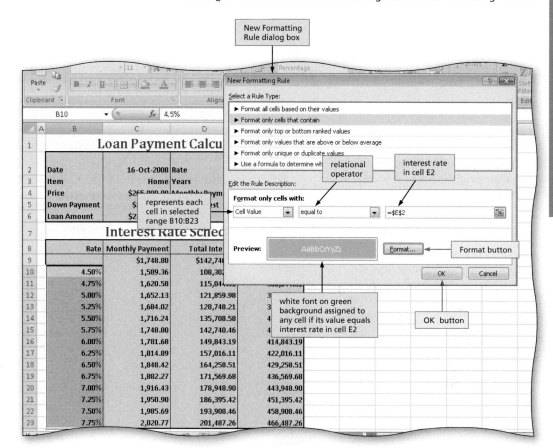

Figure 4–30

- Click the Font tab, click the Color box arrow, and then click White (column 1, row 1) on the Color palette in the Theme area.

- Click the OK button in the Format Cells dialog box to display the New Formatting Rule dialog box as shown in Figure 4–30.

3

- Click the OK button in the New Formatting Rule dialog box. Click cell G23 to deselect the range B10:B23 (Figure 4–31).

Q&A

How does Excel apply the conditional formatting?

Cell B15 in the data table, which contains the value, 5.75%, appears with white font on a green background, because the value 5.75% is the same as the interest rate value in cell E2.

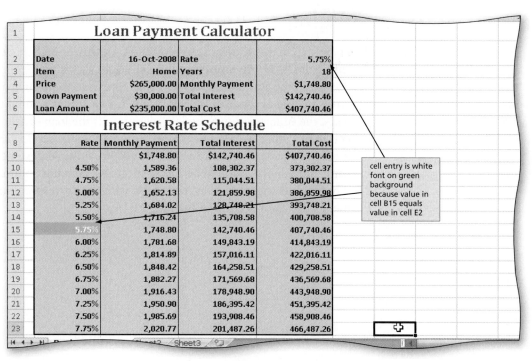

Figure 4–31

4

- Select cell E2 and then enter `7.25` as the interest rate (Figure 4–32).

5

- Enter `5.75` in cell E2 to return the Loan Payment Calculator section and Interest Rate Schedule section to their original states as shown in Figure 4–31.

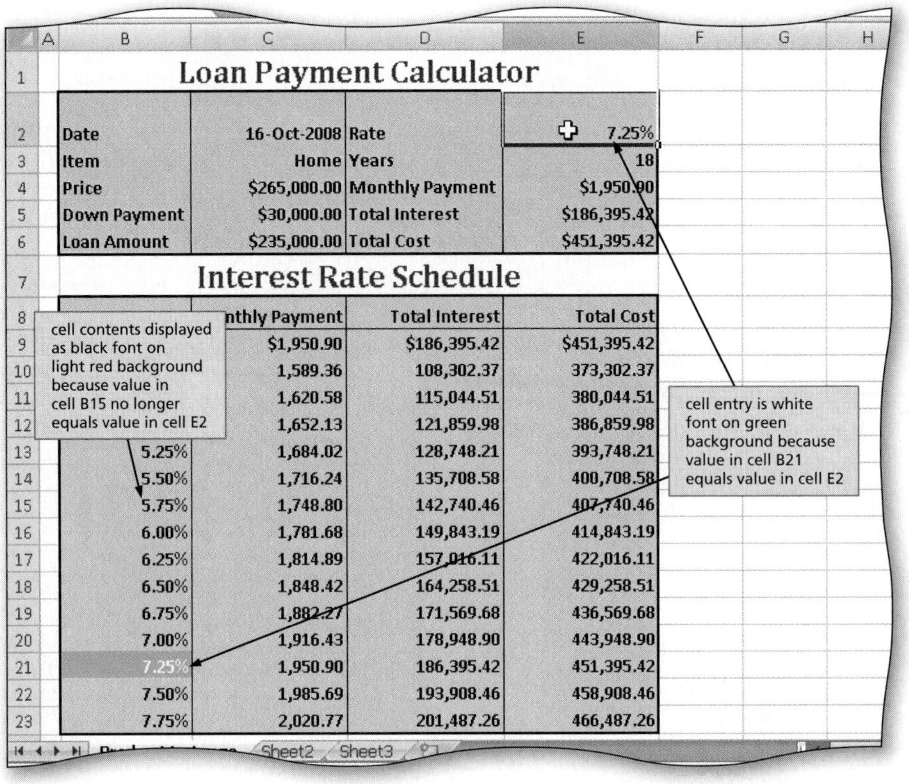

Figure 4–32

Q&A

What happens when the interest rate is changed from 5.75?

Excel immediately displays the cell containing the new rate with a white font on a green background and displays cell B15 with black bold font on a light red background (Figure 4–32). Thus, the white font on a green background serves as a pointer in the data table to indicate the row that agrees with the input cell (cell E2). When the loan officer using this worksheet enters a different percent in cell E2, the pointer will move or disappear. It will disappear whenever the interest rate in cell E2 is outside the range of the data table or its decimal portion is not a multiple of 0.25, such as when the interest rate is 8.25% or 5.80%.

Other Ways

1. Press ALT+O, D

Creating an Amortization Schedule

BTW

Amortization Schedules
Hundreds of Web sites offer amortization schedules. To find these Web sites, use a search engine, such as Google at google.com, and search using the keywords, amortization schedule.

The next step in this project is to create the Amortization Schedule section on the right side of Figure 4–33. An **amortization schedule** shows the beginning and ending balances of a loan, and the amount of payment that applies to the principal and interest for each year over the life of the loan. For example, if a customer wanted to pay off the loan after six years, the Amortization Schedule section tells the loan officer what the payoff would be (cell I8 in Figure 4–33). The Amortization Schedule section shown in Figure 4–33 will work only for loans of up to 18 years. You could, however, extend the table to any number of years. The Amortization Schedule section also contains summaries in rows 21, 22, and 23. These summaries should agree exactly with the corresponding amounts in the Loan Payment Calculator section in the range B1:E6.

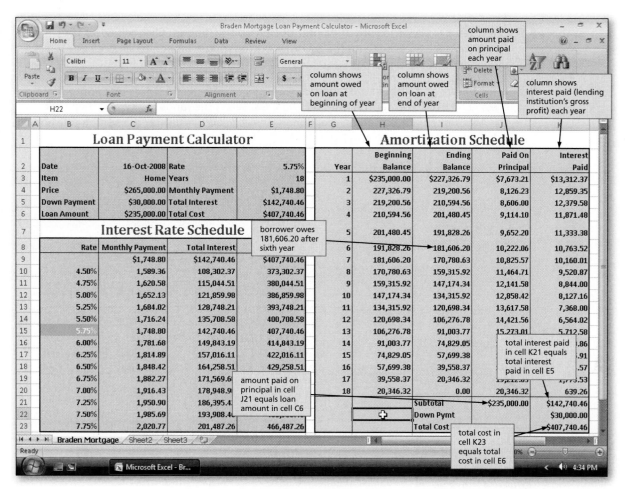

Figure 4–33

To Change Column Widths and Enter Titles

The first step in creating the Amortization Schedule section is to adjust the column widths and enter the Amortization Schedule section title and column titles, as shown in the following steps.

1. Position the mouse pointer on the right boundary of column heading F and then drag to the left until the ScreenTip shows Width: 1.57 (16 pixels).

2. Position the mouse pointer on the right boundary of column heading G and then drag to the left until the ScreenTip shows Width: 8.43 (64 pixels).

3. Drag through column headings H through K to select them. Position the mouse pointer on the right boundary of column heading K and then drag to the right until the ScreenTip shows Width: 14.00 (103 pixels).

4. Select cell G1. Type `Amortization Schedule` as the section title. Press the ENTER key.

BTW

Column Borders
In this chapter, columns A and F are used as column borders to divide sections of the worksheet from one another, as well as from the row headings. A column border is an unused column with a significantly reduced width. You also can use row borders to separate sections of a worksheet.

5 Select cell B1. Click the Format Painter button on the Ribbon. Click cell G1 to copy the format of cell B1. Click the Merge & Center button on the Ribbon to split cell G1. Select the range G1:K1 and then click the Merge & Center button on the Ribbon.

6 Enter the column titles in the range G2:K2 as shown in Figure 4–34. Where appropriate, press ALT+ENTER to enter the titles on two lines. Select the range G2:K2 and then click the Align Text Right button on the Ribbon. Select cell G3 to display the section title and column headings as shown in Figure 4–34.

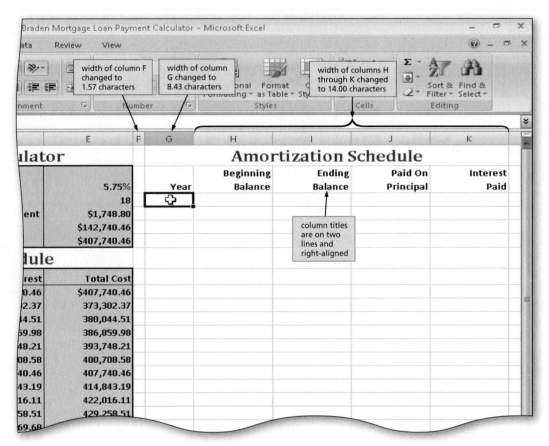

Figure 4–34

To Create a Series of Integers Using the Fill Handle

The next step is to create a series of numbers, using the fill handle, that represent the years during the life of the loan. The series begins with 1 (year 1) and ends with 18 (year 18).

1 With cell G3 active, enter 1 as the initial year. Select cell G4 and then enter 2 to represent the next year.

2 Select the range G3:G4 and then point to the fill handle. Drag the fill handle through cell G20 to create the series of integers 1 through 18 in the range G3:G20 (Figure 4–35).

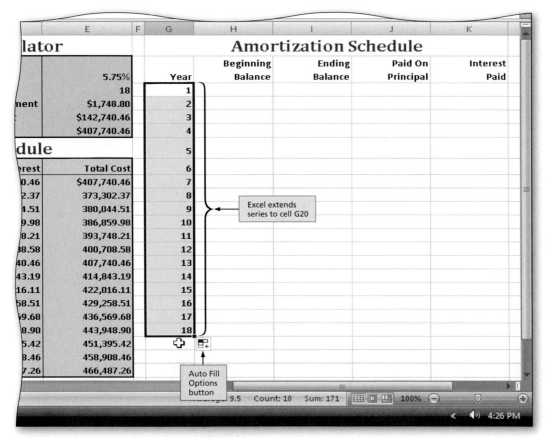

Figure 4–35

To Enter the Formulas in the Amortization Schedule

The next step is to enter the four formulas that form the basis of the amortization schedule in row 3. Later, these formulas will be copied through row 20. The formulas are summarized in Table 4–2.

Tab Stop	Tab Marker	Result of Pressing Tab Key	Example
Table 4–2 Formulas for the Amortization Schedule			
H3	Beginning Balance	=C6	The beginning balance (the balance at the end of a year) is the initial loan amount in cell C6.
I3	Ending Balance	=IF(G3 <= $E$3, PV($E$2 /12, 12 * ($E$3 – G3), –$E$4), 0)	The ending balance (the balance at the end of a year) is equal to the present value of the payments paid over the remaining life of the loan.
J3	Paid On Principal	=H3 – I3	The amount paid on the principal at the end of the year is equal to the beginning balance (cell H3) less the ending balance (cell I3).
K3	Interest Paid	=IF(H3 > 0, 12 * $E$4 – J3, 0)	The interest paid during the year is equal to 12 times the monthly payment (cell E4) less the amount paid on the principal (cell J3).

Of the four formulas in Table 4–2, the most difficult to understand is the PV function that will be assigned to cell I3. The **PV function** returns the present value of an annuity. An **annuity** is a series of fixed payments (such as the monthly payment in cell E4) made at the end of each of a fixed number of periods (months) at a fixed interest rate. You can use the PV function to determine how much the borrower of the loan still owes at the end of each year.

The PV function can determine the ending balance after the first year (cell I3) by using a term equal to the number of months for which the borrower still must make payments. For example, if the loan is for 18 years (216 months), then the borrower still owes 204 payments after the first year (216 months – 12 months). The number of payments outstanding can be determined from the formula 12 * (E3 – G3) or 12 * (18 – 1), which equals 204. Recall that column G contains integers that represent the years of the loan. After the second year, the number of payments remaining is 192, and so on.

If you assign the PV function as shown in Table 4–2 to cell I3 and then copy it to the range I4:I20, the ending balances for each year will display properly. If the loan is for less than 18 years, however, then the ending balances displayed for the years beyond the time the loan is due are invalid. For example, if a loan is taken out for 5 years, then the rows representing years 6 through 18 in the amortization schedule should be 0. The PV function, however, will display negative numbers even though the loan already has been paid off.

To avoid this, the worksheet should include a formula that assigns the PV function to the range I3:I20 as long as the corresponding year in column G is less than or equal to the number of years in cell E3. If the corresponding year in column G is greater than the number of years in cell E3, then the ending balance for that year and the remaining years should be 0. The following IF function causes the value of the PV function or 0 to display in cell I3 depending on whether the corresponding value in column G is less than or equal to the number of years in cell E3. Recall that the dollar signs within the cell references indicate the cell reference is absolute and, therefore, will not change as you copy the function downward.

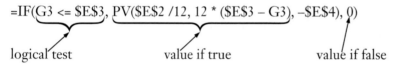

=IF(G3 <= $E$3, PV($E$2 /12, 12 * ($E$3 – G3), –$E$4), 0)

logical test   value if true   value if false

In the above formula, the logical test determines if the year in column G is less than or equal to the term of the loan in cell E3. If the logical test is true, then the IF function assigns the PV function to the cell. If the logical test is false, then the IF function assigns zero (0) to the cell.

The PV function in the IF function includes absolute cell references (cell references with dollar signs) to ensure that the references to cells in column E do not change when the IF function later is copied down the column.

The following steps enter the four formulas shown in Table 4–2 into row 3. Row 3 represents year 1 of the loan.

1

- Select cell H3 and then enter =c6 as the beginning balance of the loan.

- Select cell I3 and then type =if(g3 <= e3, pv(e2 / 12, 12 * (e3 – g3), –e4), 0) as the entry (Figure 4-36).

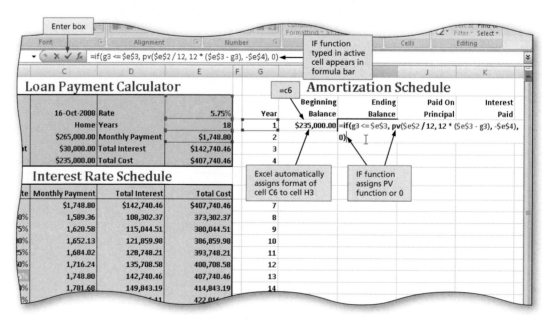

Figure 4–36

2

- Click the Enter box in the formula bar to insert the formula (Figure 4–37).

Q&A

What happens when the Enter box is clicked?

Excel evaluates the IF function in cell I3 and displays the result of the PV function (227326.7922) because the value in cell G3 (1) is less than or equal to the term of the loan in cell E3 (18). With cell I3 active, Excel also displays the formula in the formula bar. If the borrower wanted to pay off the loan after one year, the cost would be $227,326.79.

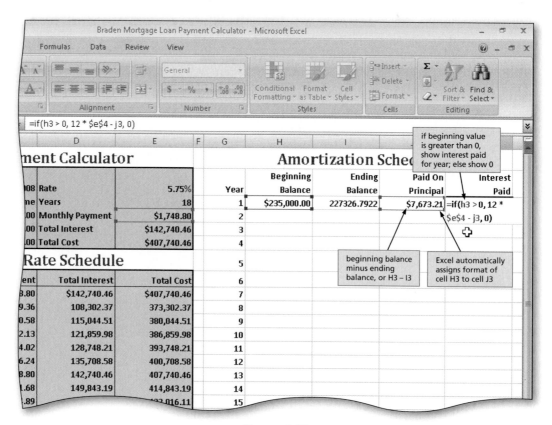

Figure 4–37

3

- Select cell J3. Type =h3 – i3 and then press the RIGHT ARROW key.

- Type =if(h3 > 0, 12 * e4 – j3, 0) in cell K3 to display the amount paid on the principal after 1 year ($7,673.21) in cell J3, using the same format as in cell H3 (Figure 4–38).

Figure 4–38

4

- Click the Enter box in the formula bar to complete the entry (Figure 4–39).

Q&A

What happens when the Enter box is clicked?

Excel displays the interest paid after 1 year (13312.37332) in cell K3. Thus, the lending institution's gross profit for the first year of the loan is $13,312.37.

Q&A

Why are some of the cells in the range H3:K3 formatted?

When you enter a formula in a cell, Excel assigns the cell the same format as the first cell reference in the formula. For example, when you enter =c6 in cell H3, Excel assigns the format in cell C6 to cell H3. The same applies to cell J3. Although this method of formatting also works for most functions, it does not work for the IF function. Thus, the results of the IF functions in cells I3 and K3 are displayed using the General style format, which is the format of all cells when you open a new workbook.

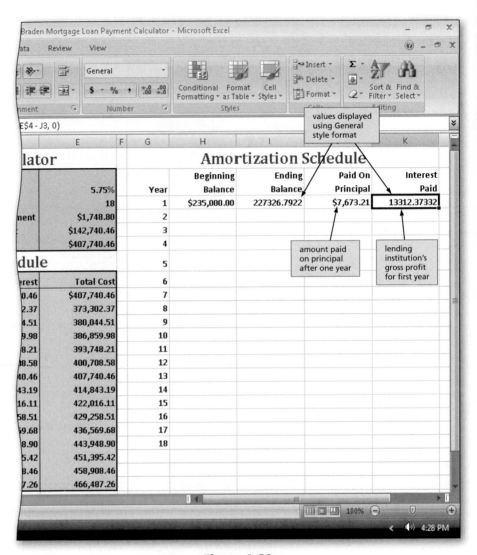

Figure 4–39

To Copy the Formulas to Fill the Amortization Schedule

With the formulas entered into the first row, the next step is to copy them to the remaining rows in the amortization schedule. The required copying is straightforward, except for the beginning balance column. To obtain the next year's beginning balance (cell H4), last year's ending balance (cell I3) must be used. After cell I3 is copied to cell H4, then H4 can be copied to the range H5:H20.

1

- Select the range I3:K3 and then drag the fill handle down through row 20 to copy the formulas in cells I3, J3, and K3 to the range I4:K20 (Figure 4–40).

Q&A

Why do some of the numbers seem incorrect?

Many of the numbers displayed are incorrect because most of the cells in column H do not contain beginning balances.

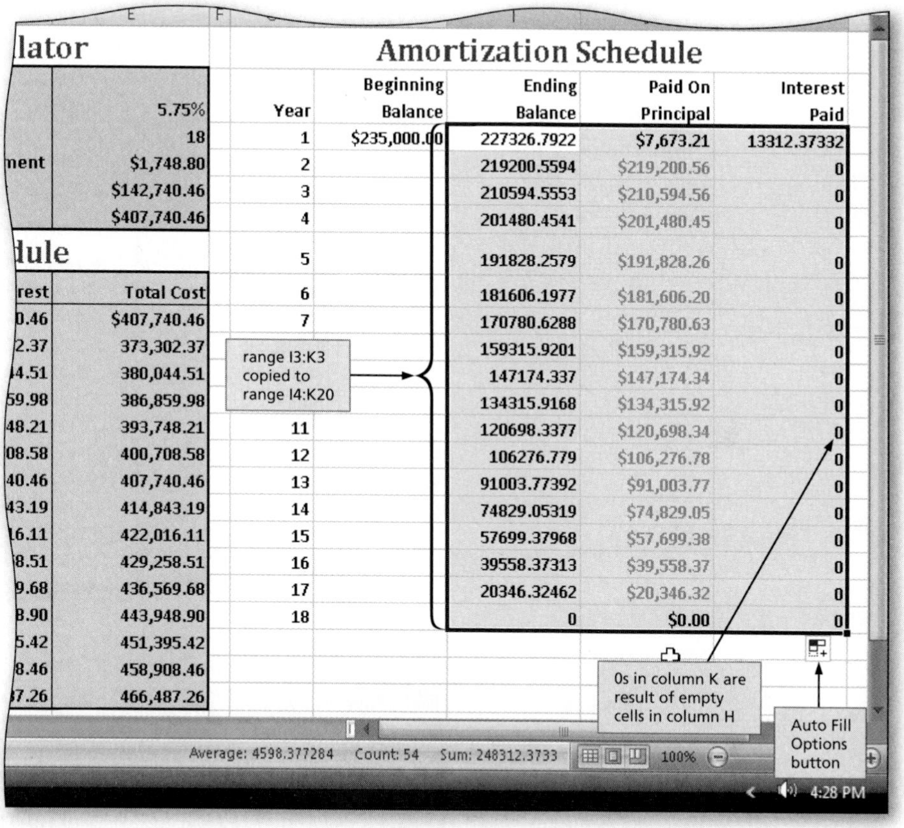

Figure 4–40

2

- Select cell H4, type =i3 as the cell entry, and then click the Enter box in the formula bar to display the ending balance (227326.7922) for year 1 as the beginning balance for year 2 (Figure 4–41).

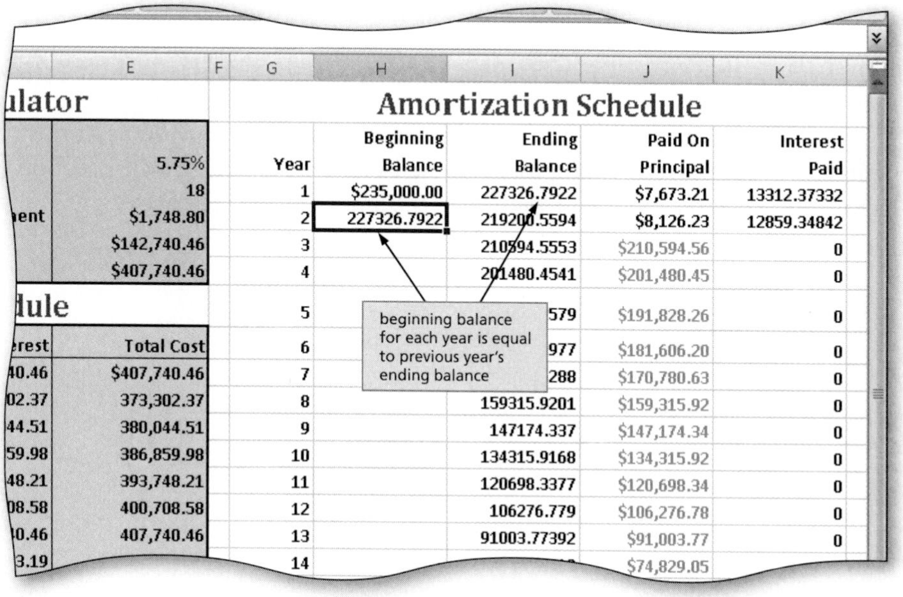

Figure 4–41

3

- With cell H4 active, drag the fill handle down through row 20 to copy the formula in cell H4 (=I3) to the range H5:H20 (Figure 4–42).

Q&A

What happens after the fill operation is complete?

Because the cell reference I3 is relative, Excel adjusts the row portion of the cell reference as it is copied downward. Thus, each new beginning balance in column H is equal to the ending balance of the previous year.

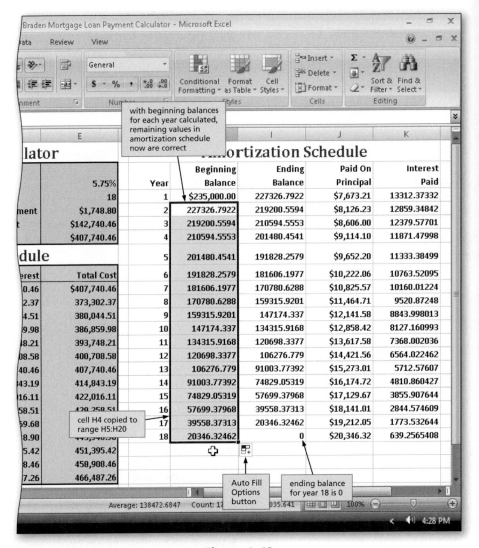

Figure 4–42

To Enter the Total Formulas in the Amortization Schedule

The next step is to determine the amortization schedule totals in rows 21 through 23. These totals should agree with the corresponding totals in the Loan Payment Calculator section (range B1:E6). The following steps show how to enter the total formulas in the amortization schedule.

1 Select cell I21. Enter `Subtotal` as the row title. Select the range J21:K21. Click the Sum button on the Ribbon.

2 Select cell I22. Type `Down Pymt` as the row title. Select cell K22 and then enter `=c5` as the down payment.

3 Select cell I23. Type `Total Cost` as the row title. Select cell K23, type `=j21 + k21 + k22` as the total cost, and then click the Enter box in the formula bar to complete the amortization schedule totals (Figure 4–43).

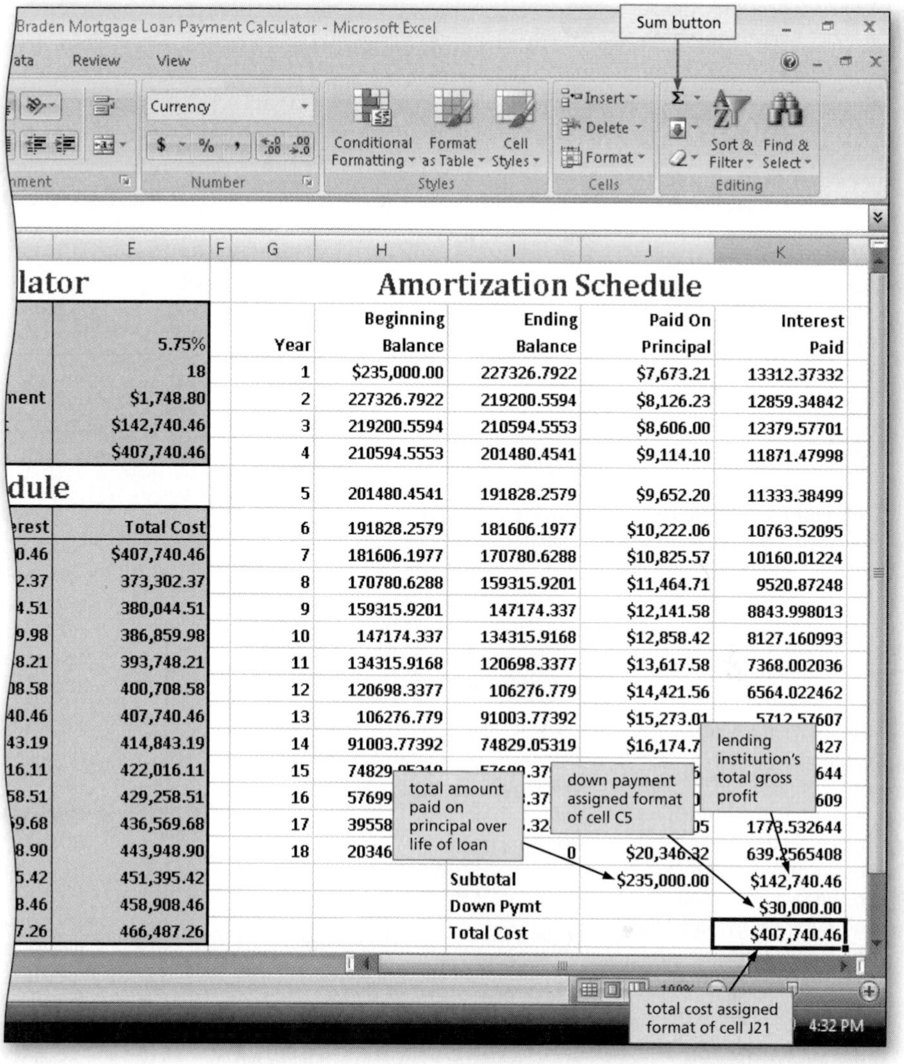

Q&A What was accomplished in the previous steps?

The formula assigned to cell K23 (=j21 + k21 + k22) sums the total amount paid on the principal (cell J21), the total interest paid (cell K21), and the down payment (cell K22). Excel assigns cell J21 the same format as cell J3, because cell J3 is the first cell reference in =SUM(J3:J20). Furthermore, because cell J21 was selected first when the range J21:K21 was selected to determine the sum, Excel assigned cell K21 the same format it assigned to cell J21. Finally, cell K22 was assigned the Currency style format, because cell K22 was assigned the formula =c5, and cell C5 has a Currency style format. For the same reason, the value in cell K23 appears in Currency style format.

Figure 4–43

To Format the Numbers in the Amortization Schedule

The final step in creating the amortization schedule is to format it so it is easier to read. The formatting is divided into two parts: (1) formatting the numbers and (2) adding borders and background.

When the beginning balance formula (=c6) was entered earlier into cell H3, Excel automatically copied the Currency style format along with the value from cell C6 to cell H3. The steps on the next page use the Format Painter button to copy the Currency style format from cell H3 to the range I3:K3. Then the Comma style will be assigned to the range H4:K20.

① Select cell H3. Click the Format Painter button on the Home tab on the Ribbon. Drag through the range I3:K3 to assign the Currency style format to the cells.

② Select the range H4:K20 and then right–click. Click Format Cells on the shortcut menu. When Excel displays the Format Cells dialog box, click the Number tab. Click Currency in the Category list, click the Symbol box arrow, click None, and then click the second format, 1,234.10, in the Negative numbers list. Click the OK button.

③ Select cell H21 to deselect the range H4:K20 to display the numbers in the amortization schedule as shown in Figure 4–44.

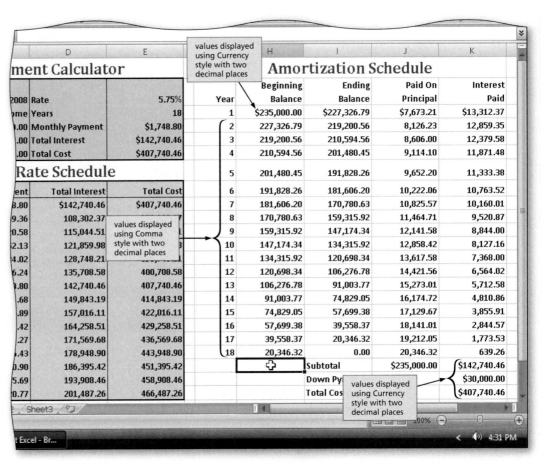

Figure 4–44

To Add Borders and a Background to the Amortization Schedule

The following steps add the borders and a background to the amortization schedule.

① Select the range G2:K23. Right–click the selected range and then click Format Cells on the shortcut menu. When Excel displays the Format Cells dialog box, click the Border tab.

② Click the medium line style in the Style area (column 2, row 5). Click the Outline button in the Presets area.

③ Click the light line style in the Style area (column 1, row 7). Click the vertical line button in the Border area.

④ Click the Fill tab and then click light blue (column 5, row 2). Click the OK button.

5 Select the range G2:K2. Click the Borders button on the Home tab on the Ribbon to assign the range a light bottom border.

6 Select the range G20:K20 and then click the Borders button on the Home tab on the Ribbon to assign the range a light bottom border. Select cell H22 to display the worksheet as shown in Figure 4–45.

7 Click the Save button on the Quick Access Toolbar to save the workbook using the file name, Braden Mortgage Loan Payment Calculator.

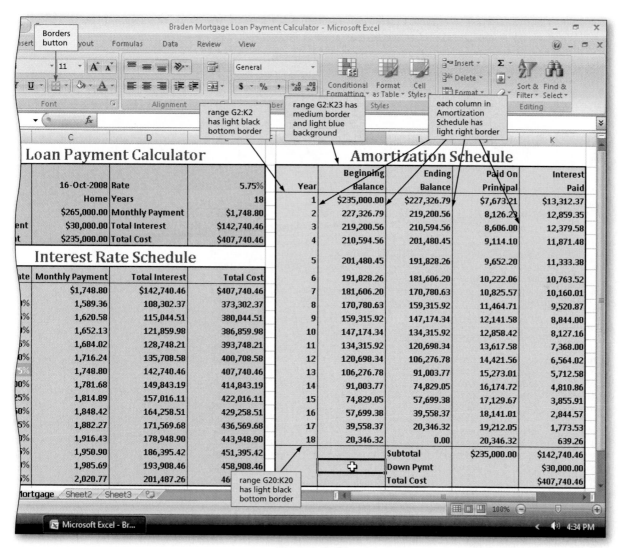

Figure 4–45

To Enter New Loan Data

With the Loan Payment Calculator, Interest Rate Schedule, and Amortization Schedule sections of the worksheet complete, you can use them to generate new loan information. For example, assume you want to purchase a pontoon boat for $41,550.00. You have $6,000.00 for a down payment and want the loan for 5 years. Braden Mortgage currently is charging 7.25% interest for a 5–year loan. The steps on the next page enter the new loan data.

1 Select cell C3. Type `Pontoon Boat` and then press the DOWN ARROW key.

2 In cell C4, type `41550` and then press the DOWN ARROW key.

3 In cell C5, type `6000` as the down payment.

4 Select cell E2, type `7.25` and then press the DOWN ARROW key.

5 In cell E3, type `5` and then press the DOWN ARROW key. Select cell H22 to display the worksheet as shown in Figure 4–46.

Q&A

What happens on the worksheet when the new data is entered?

As shown in Figure 4–46, the monthly payment for the pontoon boat is $708.13 (cell E4). The total interest is $6,938.00 (cell E5) and the total cost for the boat is $48,488.00 (cell E6). Because the term of the loan is for 5 years, the rows for years 6 through 18 in the Amortization Schedule section display 0.00.

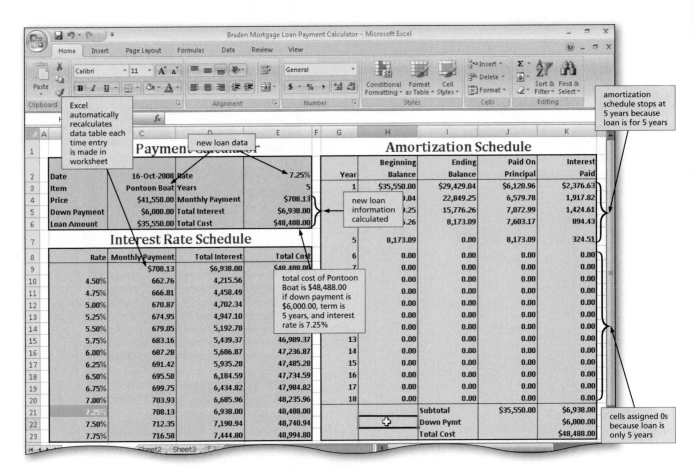

Figure 4–46

To Enter the Original Loan Data

The following steps enter the original loan data.

1 Select cell C3. Type `Home` and then press the DOWN ARROW key.

2 In cell C4, type `265000` and then press the DOWN ARROW key.

3 In cell C5, type `30000` as the down payment.

④ Select cell E2, type 5.75 and then press the DOWN ARROW key.

⑤ In cell E3, type 18 and then click the Enter box in the formula bar or press the ENTER key to complete the entry of the original load data. Select cell H22.

Printing Sections of the Worksheet

In Chapter 2, you learned to print a section of a worksheet by selecting it and using the Selection option in the Print dialog box (see page EX 134). If you find yourself continually selecting the same range in a worksheet to print, you can set a specific range to print each time you print the worksheet by using the Set Print Area command. When you set a range to print using the Set Print Area command, Excel will continue to print only that range until you clear it using the Clear Print Area command.

To Set Up a Worksheet to Print

This section describes print options available in the Sheet sheet in the Page Setup dialog box (Figure 4–47). These print options pertain to the way the worksheet will appear in the printed copy or when previewed. One of the more important print options is the capability of printing in black and white. Printing in black and white not only speeds up the printing process, but also saves ink. This is especially true if you have a color printer and need only a black and white printed copy of the worksheet. The following steps ensure any printed copy fits on one page and prints in black and white.

①

- Click the Page Layout tab on the Ribbon and then click the Page Setup Dialog Box Launcher on the Ribbon.

- When Excel displays the Page Setup dialog box, click the Page tab and then click Fit to in the Scaling area to set the worksheet to print on one page (Figure 4–47).

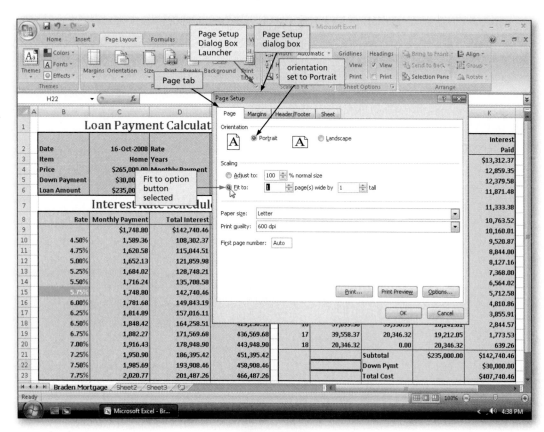

Figure 4–47

2

- Click the Sheet tab and then click 'Black and white' in the Print area to select the check box (Figure 4–48).

3

- Click the OK button.

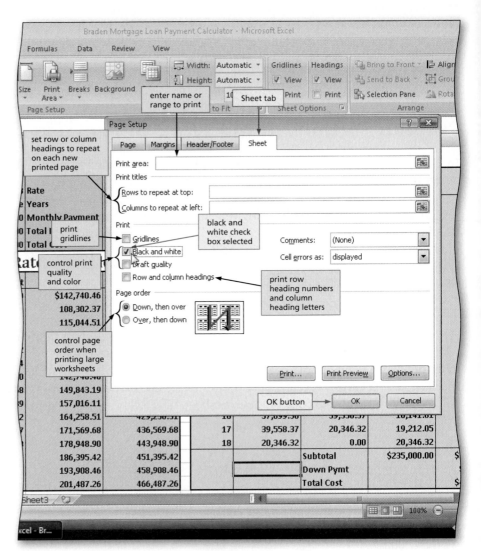

Figure 4–48

More About Print Options

Table 4–3 summarizes the print options available on the Sheet sheet in the Page Setup dialog box.

Table 4–3 Print Options Available Using the Sheet Sheet in the Page Setup Dialog Box	
Print Option	**Description**
Print area box	Excel prints from cell A1 to the last occupied cell in a worksheet unless you instruct it to print a selected area. You can select a range to print with the mouse, or you can enter a range or name of a range in the Print area box. Nonadjacent ranges will print on a separate page.

Table 4–3 Print Options Available Using the Sheet Tab in the Page Setup Dialog Box (*continued*)

Print Option	Description
Print titles area	This area is used to instruct Excel to print row titles and column titles on each printed page of a worksheet. You must specify a range, even if you are designating one column (e.g., 1:4 means the first four rows).
Gridlines check box	A check mark in this check box instructs Excel to print gridlines.
Black and white check box	A check mark in this check box speeds up printing and saves colored ink if you have colors in a worksheet and a color printer.
Draft quality check box	A check mark in this check box speeds up printing by ignoring formatting and not printing most graphics.
Row and column headings check box	A check mark in this check box instructs Excel to include the column heading letters (A, B, C, etc.) and row heading numbers (1, 2, 3, etc.) in the printout.
Comments box	Indicates where comments are to be displayed on the printout.
Cell errors as box	Indicates how errors in cells should be displayed on the printout.
Page order area	Determines the order in which multipage worksheets will print.

To Set the Print Area

The following steps print only the Loan Payment Calculator section by setting the print area to the range B1:E6.

1

- Select the range B1:E6 and then click the Print Area button on the Ribbon to display the Print Area menu (Figure 4–49).

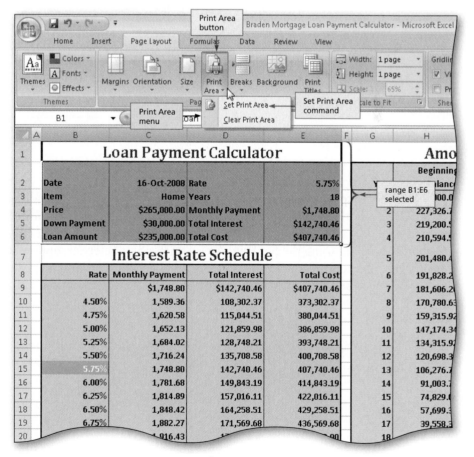

Figure 4–49

● Click Set Print Area on the Print Area menu.

● Click the Office Button and then click Print on the Office Button menu. When Excel displays the Print dialog box, click the OK button to print the selected area (Figure 4–50).

❸

● Click the Print Area button on the Ribbon and then click the Clear Print Area command on the Print Area menu to reset the print area to the entire worksheet.

Q&A

What happens when I set a print area?

Once you set a print area, Excel will continue to print the specified range, rather than the entire worksheet. If you save the workbook with the print area set, then Excel will remember the settings the next time you open the workbook and print only the specified range. To remove the print area so that the entire worksheet prints, click Clear Print Area on the Print Area menu as described in Step 3.

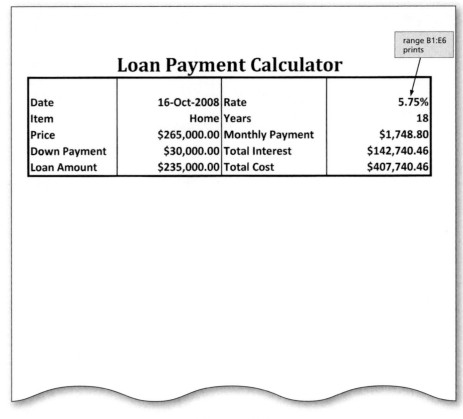

Loan Payment Calculator

range B1:E6 prints

Date	16-Oct-2008	Rate	5.75%
Item	Home	Years	18
Price	$265,000.00	Monthly Payment	$1,748.80
Down Payment	$30,000.00	Total Interest	$142,740.46
Loan Amount	$235,000.00	Total Cost	$407,740.46

Figure 4–50

Other Ways

1. Press ALT+F, T, S

To Name and Print Sections of a Worksheet

With some spreadsheet applications, you will want to print several different areas of a worksheet, depending on the request. Rather than using the Set Print Area command or manually selecting the range each time you want to print, you can name the ranges using the Name box in the formula bar. You then can use one of the names to select an area before using the Set Print Area command or Selection option button. The following steps name the Loan Payment Calculator section, the Interest Rate Schedule section, the Amortization Schedule section, and the entire worksheet, and then print each section using the Selection option button in the Print dialog box.

①

- Click the Page Setup Dialog Box Launcher, click the sheet tab, and, if necessary, click 'Black and white' to deselect the check box.

- Click the OK button to close the Page Setup dialog box.

- If necessary, select the range B1:E6, click the Name box, and then type `Loan_Payment` as the name of the range (Figure 4–51).

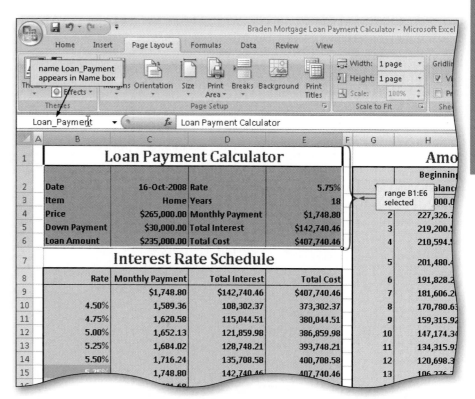

Figure 4–51

②

- Press the ENTER key.

- Select the range B7:E23, click the Name box, type `Interest_Schedule` as the name of the range, and then press the ENTER key.

- Select the range G1:K23, click the Name box, type `Amortization_Schedule` as the name of the range, and then press the ENTER key.

- Select the range B1:K23, click the Name box, type `All_Sections` as the name of the range, and then press the ENTER key.

- Select cell H22 and then click the Name box arrow in the formula bar to display the Name list with the new range names (Figure 4–52).

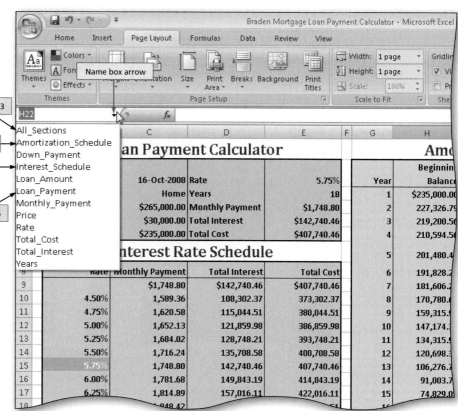
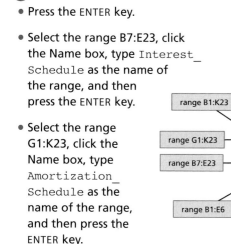

Figure 4–52

3

- Click Loan_Payment in the Name list to select the range B1:E6.

- Click the Office Button and then click Print on the Office Button menu to display the Print dialog box.

- When Excel displays the Print dialog box, click Selection in the Print what area (Figure 4–53).

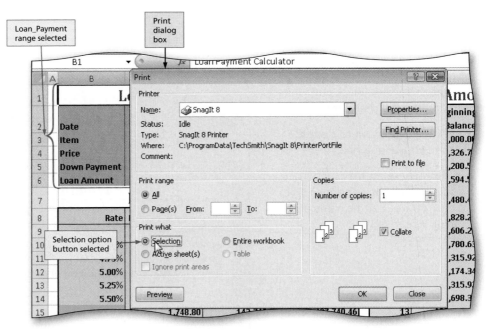

Figure 4–53

4

- Click the OK button to print the Loan_Payment range.

- One at a time, use the Name box to select the names Interest_Schedule, Amortization_Schedule, and All_Sections, and then print them following the instructions in Step 3 (Figure 4–54).

5

- Click the Save button on the Quick Access Toolbar to save the workbook using the file name, Braden Mortgage Loan Payment Calculator.

Q&A
Why does the All_Sections range print on one page?

Recall that the Fit to option was selected earlier (Figure 4–47 on page EX 307). This selection ensures that each of the printouts fits across the page in portrait orientation.

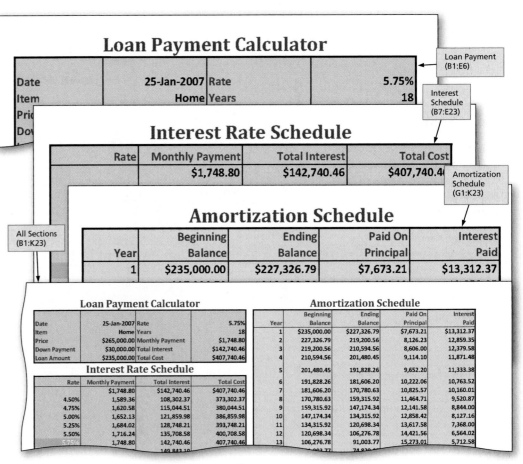

Figure 4–54

Other Ways

1. Select cell or range, on Formulas tab on Ribbon, click Define Name button, [type name], click OK button

2. Select cell or range, on Formulas tab on Ribbon, click Name Manager button, click New, [type name], click OK button, click Close button

Protecting the Worksheet

When building a worksheet for novice users, you should protect the cells in the worksheet that you do not want changed, such as cells that contain text or formulas.

When you create a new worksheet, all the cells are assigned a locked status, but the lock is not engaged, which leaves cells unprotected. **Unprotected cells** are cells whose values you can change at any time. **Protected cells** are cells that you cannot change.

You should protect cells only after the worksheet has been tested fully and the correct results appear. Protecting a worksheet is a two–step process:

1. Select the cells you want to leave unprotected and then change their cell protection settings to an unlocked status.

2. Protect the entire worksheet.

At first glance, these steps may appear to be backwards. Once you protect the entire worksheet, however, you cannot change anything, including the locked status of individual cells.

To Protect a Worksheet

In the Loan Payment Calculator worksheet (Figure 4–55), the user should be able to make changes to only five cells: the item in cell C3; the price in cell C4; the down payment in cell C5; the interest rate in cell E2; and the years in cell E3. These cells must remain unprotected so that users can enter the correct data. The remaining cells in the worksheet should be protected so that the user cannot change them.

The following steps show how to protect the Loan Payment Calculator worksheet.

1

• Select the range C3:C5.

• Hold down the CTRL key and then select the nonadjacent range E2:E3.

• Right–click one of the selected ranges to display the shortcut menu (Figure 4–55).

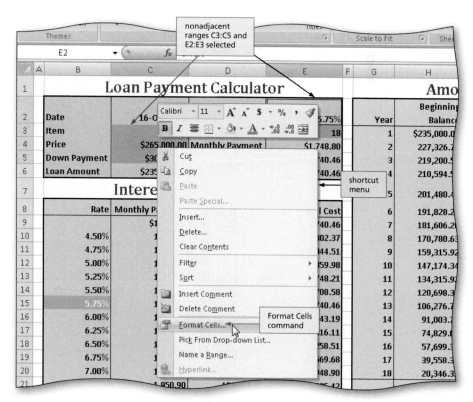

Figure 4–55

2

- Click Format Cells on the shortcut menu.

- When Excel displays the Custom Lists dialog box, click the Protection tab, and then click Locked to remove the check mark (Figure 4–56).

What is the meaning of the Locked check box ?

Excel displays the Protection sheet in the Custom Lists dialog box with the check mark removed from the Locked check box (Figure 4–56). This means the selected cells (C3:C5 and E2:E3) will not be protected when the Protect command is invoked later.

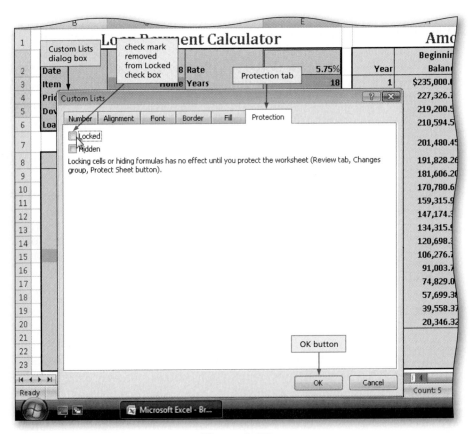

Figure 4–56

3

- Click the OK button and then select cell H22 to deselect the ranges C3:C5 and E2:E3.

- Click the Review tab on the Ribbon (Figure 4–57).

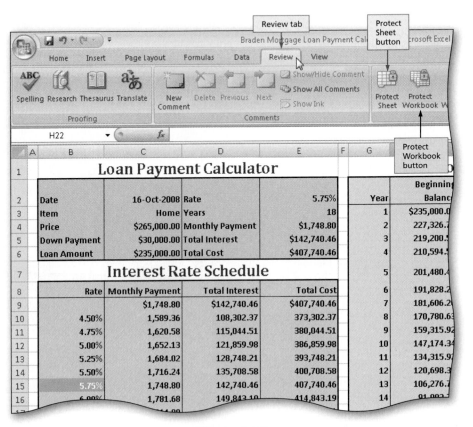

Figure 4–57

4

- Click the Protect Sheet button on the Ribbon to display the Protect Sheet dialog box.

- When Excel displays the Protect Sheet dialog box, make sure the Protect worksheet and contents of locked cells check box at the top of the dialog box and the first two check boxes in the list contain check marks (Figure 4–58).

Q&A

What do the three checked check boxes mean?

With all three check boxes selected, the worksheet is protected from changes to contents (except the cells left unlocked). The two check boxes in the list allow the user to select any cell on the worksheet, but the user can change only unlocked cells.

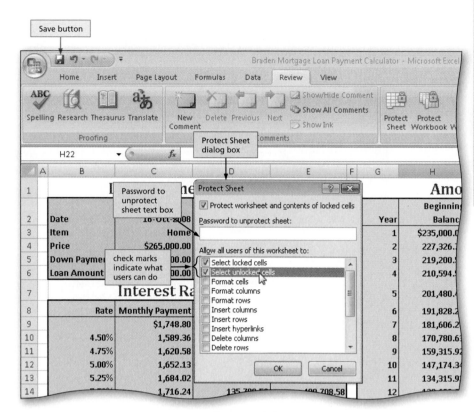

Figure 4–58

5

- Click the OK button in the Protect Sheet dialog box.

- Click the Save button on the Quick Access Toolbar.

Other Ways

1. Click Format Cells Dialog Box Launcher, click Protection tab, remove check mark from Locked check box, click OK button

More About Worksheet Protection

All the cells in the worksheet are protected, except for the ranges C3:C5 and E2:E3. The Protect Sheet dialog box in Figure 4–58 lets you enter a password that can be used to unprotect the sheet. You should create a **password** when you want to keep others from changing the worksheet from protected to unprotected. The check boxes in the list in the Protect Sheet dialog box also give you the option to modify the protection so that the user can make certain changes, such as formatting cells or inserting hyperlinks.

If you want to protect more than one sheet in a workbook, select each sheet before you begin the protection process or click the Protect Workbook button on the Review tab on the Ribbon, instead of clicking the Protect Sheet button (Figure 4–57). If you want to unlock cells for specific users, you can use the Allow Users to Edit Ranges button on the Review tab on the Ribbon.

When this workbook is put into production, users will be able to enter data in only the unprotected cells. If they try to change any protected cell, such as the monthly payment in cell E4, Excel displays a dialog box with an error message as shown in Figure 4–59 on the next page. An alternative to displaying this dialog box is to remove the check mark from the 'Select unlocked cells' check box in the Protect Sheet dialog box (Figure 4–58). With the check mark removed, the user cannot select a locked cell.

To unprotect the worksheet so that you can change all cells in the worksheet, unprotect the document by clicking the Unprotect Sheet button on the Review tab on the Ribbon.

BTW

Using Protected Worksheets
You can move from one unprotected cell to another unprotected cell in a worksheet by using the tab and SHIFT+TAB keys. This is especially useful when the cells are not adjacent to one another.

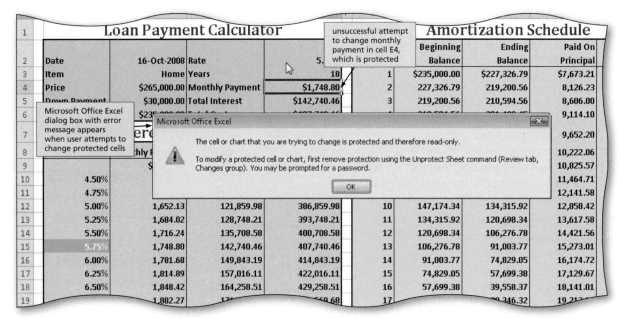

Figure 4–59

To Hide and Unhide a Sheet

You can hide rows, columns, and sheets that contain sensitive data. Sheets are hidden by first selecting one or more of them and then using the Hide command on the sheet tab's shortcut menu (Figure 4–60). Later, you can use the Unhide command on the same shortcut menu to unhide sheets. You also learned earlier in Chapter 2 (page EX 126) that you can use the mouse and keyboard to hide and unhide rows and columns. The following steps show how to hide and then unhide a sheet.

- If the Braden Mortgage sheet is not active, click its sheet tab.

- Right–click the sheet tab to display the shortcut menu (Figure 4–60).

Figure 4–60

2
- Click Hide on the shortcut menu to hide the Braden Mortgage sheet.

3
- Right–click any sheet tab to display the shortcut menu.

4
- Click Unhide on the shortcut menu to open the Unhide dialog box.

5
- When Excel displays the Unhide dialog box, if necessary, click Braden Mortgage in the Unhide sheet list (Figure 4–61).

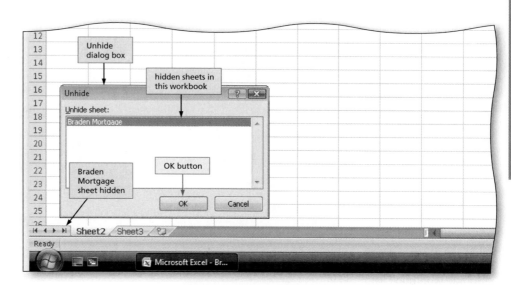

Figure 4–61

When should I hide a sheet?

Hiding sheets in a workbook is not uncommon when working with complex workbooks that have one sheet with the results the user needs to see and one or more sheets with essential data that is unimportant to the user, and thus hidden from view. The fact that a sheet is hidden does not mean the data and formulas on the hidden sheets are unavailable for use on other sheets in the workbook. This same logic applies to hidden rows and columns.

6
- Click the OK button to unhide the Braden Mortgage sheet as it was shown in Figure 4–60.

To Hide and Unhide a Workbook

You hide an entire workbook by using the Hide button on the View tab on the Ribbon. Some users employ this command when they leave a workbook up on an unattended computer and do not want others to be able to see the workbook. The Hide command is also useful when you have several workbooks opened simultaneously and want the user to be able to view only one of them. The following steps show how to hide and unhide a workbook.

1
- Click the View tab on the Ribbon (Figure 4–62).

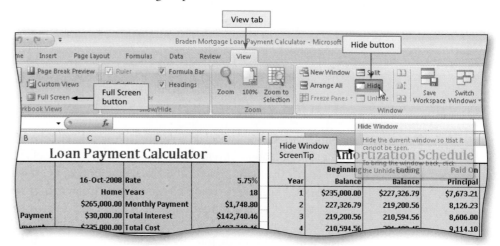

Figure 4–62

● Click the Hide button
on the Ribbon to hide
the Braden Mortgage
workbook.

● Click the Unhide
button on the
Ribbon.

● When Excel displays
the Unhide dialog
box, if necessary, click
Braden Mortgage
Loan Payment
Calculator in the
Unhide workbook list
(Figure 4–63).

Q&A

What else can I hide?

You can hide most
window elements
in order to display
more rows of
worksheet data.
These window
elements include
the Ribbon, formula
bar, and status bar.
The Excel window
elements can be
hidden by using the
Full Screen button
on the View tab on
the Ribbon (Figure 4–62
on the previous page).
These elements remain hidden only as long as the workbook is open. They redisplay when
you close the workbook and open it again.

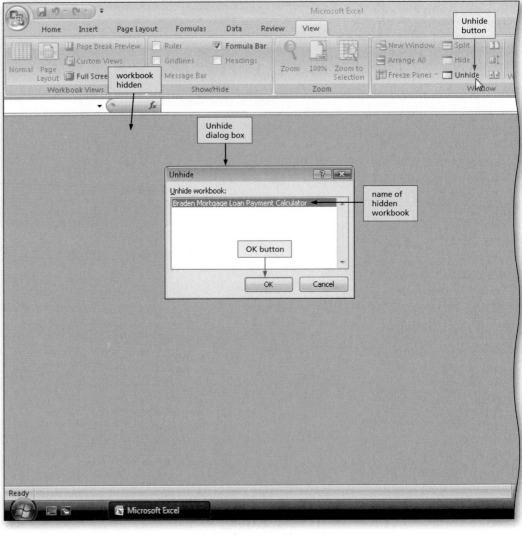

Figure 4–63

④

● Click the OK button to unhide the Braden Mortgage Loan Payment Calculator workbook as
it was shown in Figure 4–62 on the previous page.

Formula Checking

Similar to the spell checker, Excel has a **formula checker** that checks formulas in a worksheet
for rule violations. You invoke the formula checker by clicking the Error Checking command
on the Tools menu. Each time Excel encounters a cell with a formula that violates one of
its rules, it displays a dialog box containing information about the formula and a suggestion
on how to fix the formula. Table 4–4 lists Excel's error checking rules. You can choose
which rules you want Excel to use by enabling and disabling them in the Formulas area in
the Excel Options dialog box shown in Figure 4–64 on page EX 320.

Table 4–4 Error Checking Rules		
Rule	**Name of Rule**	**Description**
1	Cells containing formulas that result in an error	The cell contains a formula that does not use the expected syntax, arguments, or data types.
2	Inconsistent calculated column formula in tables	The cell contains formulas or values that are inconsistent with the column formula or tables.
3	Cells containing years represented as 2 digits	The cell contains a text date with a two–digit year that can be misinterpreted as the wrong century.
4	Numbers formatted as text or preceded by an apostrophe	The cell contains numbers stored as text.
5	Formulas inconsistent with other formulas in the region	The cell contains a formula that does not match the pattern of the formulas around it.
6	Formula that omits cells in a region	The cell contains a formula that does not include a correct cell or range reference.
7	Unlocked cells containing formulas	The cell with a formula is unlocked in a protected worksheet.
8	Formulas referring to empty cell	The cells referred to in a formula are empty.
9	Data entered in a table is invalid	The cell has a data validation error.

To Enable Background Formula Checking

Through the Excel Options dialog box, you can enable background formula checking. **Background formula checking** means that Excel continually will review the workbook for errors in formulas as you create or manipulate it. The following steps enable background formula checking.

1 Click the Office Button on the Ribbon, click the Excel Options button, and then click the Formulas button.

2 If necessary, click 'Enable background error checking' in the Error Checking area to select it.

3 Click any check box in the 'Error checking rules' area that does not contain a check mark (Figure 4–64 on the next page).

4 Click the OK button.

Q&A How can I decide which rules to have the background formula checker check?

You can decide which rules you want the background formula checker to highlight by adding and removing check marks from the check boxes in the 'Error checking rules' area (Figure 4–64). If you add or remove check marks, then you should click the Reset Ignored Errors button to reset error checking.

BTW

Excel Help
The best way to become familiar with Excel Help is to use it. Appendix C includes detailed information about Excel Help and exercises that will help you gain confidence in using it.

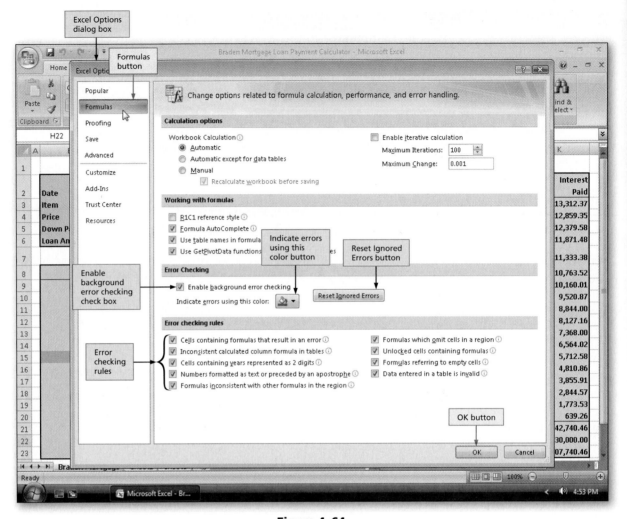

Figure 4–64

More About Background Formula Checking

BTW

Quick Reference
For a table that lists how to complete the tasks covered in this book using the mouse, Ribbon, shortcut menu, and keyboard, see the Quick Reference Summary at the back of this book, or visit the Excel 2007 Quick Reference Web page (scsite.com/ex2007/qr).

When a formula fails to pass one of the rules and background formula checking is enabled, then Excel displays a small green triangle in the upper–left corner of the cell assigned the formula in question.

Assume, for example, that background formula checking is enabled and that cell E4, which contains the PMT function in the Braden Mortgage workbook, is unlocked. Because rule 7 in Table 4–4 stipulates that a cell containing a formula must be locked, Excel displays a green triangle in the upper–left corner of cell E4.

When you select the cell with the green triangle, a Trace Error button appears next to the cell. If you click the Trace Error button, Excel displays the Trace Error menu (Figure 4–65). The first item in the menu identifies the error (Unprotected Formula). The remainder of the menu lists commands from which you can choose. The first command locks the cell. Invoking the Lock Cell command fixes the problem so that the formula no longer violates the rule. The Error Checking Options command instructs Excel to display the Excel Options dialog box with the Formulas area active, as shown in Figure 4–64.

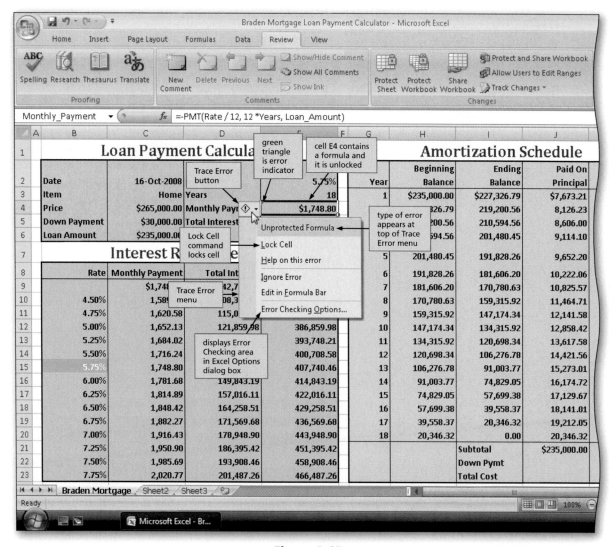

Figure 4–65

The background formula checker can become annoying when you are creating certain types of worksheets that may violate the formula rules until referenced cells contain data. It is not unusual to end up with green triangles in cells throughout your worksheet. If this is the case, then disable background formula checking by removing the check mark from the 'Enable background error checking' check box (Figure 4–64) and use the Error Checking button on the Formulas tab on the Ribbon to check your worksheet once you have finished creating it.

It is strongly recommended that you use background formula checking or the Error Checking button on the Formulas tab on the Ribbon during the testing phase to ensure the formulas in your workbook do not violate the rules listed in Table 4–4.

To Quit Excel

The following steps quit Excel.

1 Click the Close button on the right side of the title bar.

2 If Excel displays a Microsoft Office Excel dialog box, click the No button.

BTW

Certification
The Microsoft Certified Application Specialist (MCAS) program provides an opportunity for you to obtain a valuable industry credential – proof that you have the Excel 2007 skills required by employers. For more information, see Appendix G or visit the Excel 2007 Certification Web page (scsite.com/ex2007/cert).

Chapter Summary

In this chapter, you learned how to use names, rather than cell references, to enter formulas, use financial functions, such as the PMT and PV functions, analyze data by creating a data table and amortization schedule, set print options and print sections of a worksheet using names and the Set Print Area command, protect a worksheet or workbook, and hide and unhide rows, columns, sheets, and workbooks. The items listed below include all the new Excel skills you have learned in this chapter.

1. Add Custom Borders and a Background Color to a Range (EX 272)
2. Create Names Based on Row Titles (EX 276)
3. Enter the Loan Amount Formula Using Names (EX 279)
4. Enter the PMT Function (EX 280)
5. Create a Percent Series Using the Fill Handle (EX 286)
6. Define a Range as a Data Table (EX 288)
7. Add a Pointer to the Data Table (EX 292)
8. Enter the Formulas in the Amortization Schedule (EX 297)
9. Copy the Formulas to Fill the Amortization Schedule (EX 301)
10. Set Up a Worksheet to Print (EX 307)
11. Set the Print Area (EX 309)
12. Name and Print Sections of a Worksheet (EX 310)
13. Protect a Worksheet (EX 313)
14. Hide and Unhide a Sheet (EX 316)
15. Hide and Unhide a Workbook (EX 317)
16. Enable Background Formula Checking (EX 319)

If you have a SAM user profile, you may have access to hands-on instruction, practice, and assessment. Log in to your SAM account (http://sam2007.course.com) to launch any assigned training activities or exams that relate to the skills covered in this chapter.

Learn It Online

Learn It Online is a series of online student exercises that test your knowledge of chapter content and key terms.

Instructions: To complete the Learn It Online exercises, start your browser, click the Address bar, and then enter the Web address scsite.com/ex2007/learn. When the Excel 2007 Learn It Online page is displayed, click the link for the exercise you want to complete and then read the instructions.

Chapter Reinforcement TF, MC, and SA
A series of true/false, multiple choice, and short answer questions that test your knowledge of the chapter content.

Flash Cards
An interactive learning environment where you identify chapter key terms associated with displayed definitions.

Practice Test
A series of multiple choice questions that test your knowledge of chapter content and key terms.

Who Wants To Be a Computer Genius?
An interactive game that challenges your knowledge of chapter content in the style of a television quiz show.

Wheel of Terms
An interactive game that challenges your knowledge of chapter key terms in the style of the television show *Wheel of Fortune*.

Crossword Puzzle Challenge
A crossword puzzle that challenges your knowledge of key terms presented in the chapter.

Apply Your Knowledge

Reinforce the skills and apply the concepts you learned in this chapter.

Determining the Monthly Loan Payment
Instructions: Start Excel. Open the workbook Apply 4–1 Monthly Loan Payment from the Data Files for Students. See the inside back cover of this book for instructions for downloading the Data Files for Students or see your instructor for information on accessing the files required in this book.

Perform the following tasks.
1. Use the Create from Selection button in the Defined Names group on the Formulas tab to create names for cells in the range C4:C9 using the row titles in the range B4:B9.
2. Enter the formulas shown in Table 4–5.

Table 4–5 Data Table Formulas

Cell	Formula
C8	=Price – Down_Payment
C9	=– PMT(Interest_Rate/12, 12 * Years, Loan_Amount)
F4	=C9
G4	=+12 * C7 * C9 + C5
H4	=G4 – C4

Continued >

Apply Your Knowledge *continued*

3. Use the Data Table button in the What–If Analysis gallery on the Data tab to define the range E4:
   H19 as a one–input data table. Use cell C6 (interest rate) as the column input cell. Format the data
   table so that it appears as shown in Figure 4–66.

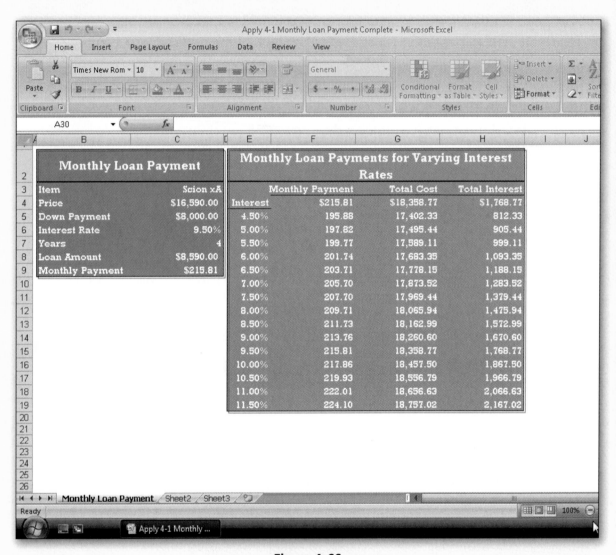

Figure 4–66

4. Use the Page Setup dialog box to select the Fit to and Black and white options. Use the Set Print
   Area command to select the range B2:C9 and then use the Print command on the Office Button
   menu to print. Use the Clear Print Area command to clear the print area. Name the following
   ranges: B2:C9 – Calculator; E2:H19 – Rate_Schedule; and B1:H19 – All_Sections. Print each range
   by selecting the name in the Name box and using the Selection option in the Print dialog box.

5. Unlock the range C3:C7. Protect the worksheet so that the user can select only unlocked cells.

6. Press CTRL+` and print the formulas version in landscape orientation. Press CTRL+` to display the
   values version.

7. Hide and then unhide the Monthly Loan Payment sheet. Hide and then unhide the workbook.
   Unprotect the worksheet and then hide columns E through H. Print the worksheet. Select columns
   D and I and unhide the hidden columns. Hide rows 11 through 19. Print the worksheet. Select
   rows 10 and 20 and unhide rows 11 through 19. Protect the worksheet.

8. Change the document properties as specified by your instructor. Change the worksheet header with your name, course number, and other information as specified by your instructor. Save the workbook using the file name, Apply 4–1 Monthly Loan Payment Complete.
9. Determine the monthly payment and print the worksheet for each data set: (a) Item = Home; Price = $310,000.00; Down Payment = $62,000.00; Interest Rate = 6.75%; Years = 20; (b) Item = Jacuzzi; Price = $19,000.00; Down Payment = $0.00; Interest Rate = 8.80%; Years = 5. You should get the following monthly payment results: (a) $1,885.70; (b) $392.57.
10. Submit the assignment as requested by your instructor.

Extend Your Knowledge

Extend the skills you learned in this chapter and experiment with new skills. You may need to use Help to complete the assignment.

Two–Input Data Table

Instructions: Start Excel. Open the workbook Extend 4–1 401(k) Planning Sheet from the Data Files for Students. See the inside back cover of this book for instructions for downloading the Data Files for Students or see your instructor for information on accessing the files required in this book. You have been asked to include a two–input data table (Figure 4–67) on the existing 401(k) Planning Sheet worksheet that shows the future value that results from varying the expected annual return (cell C8) and employee percent invested (cell C5). Complete the following tasks to create the two–input data table.

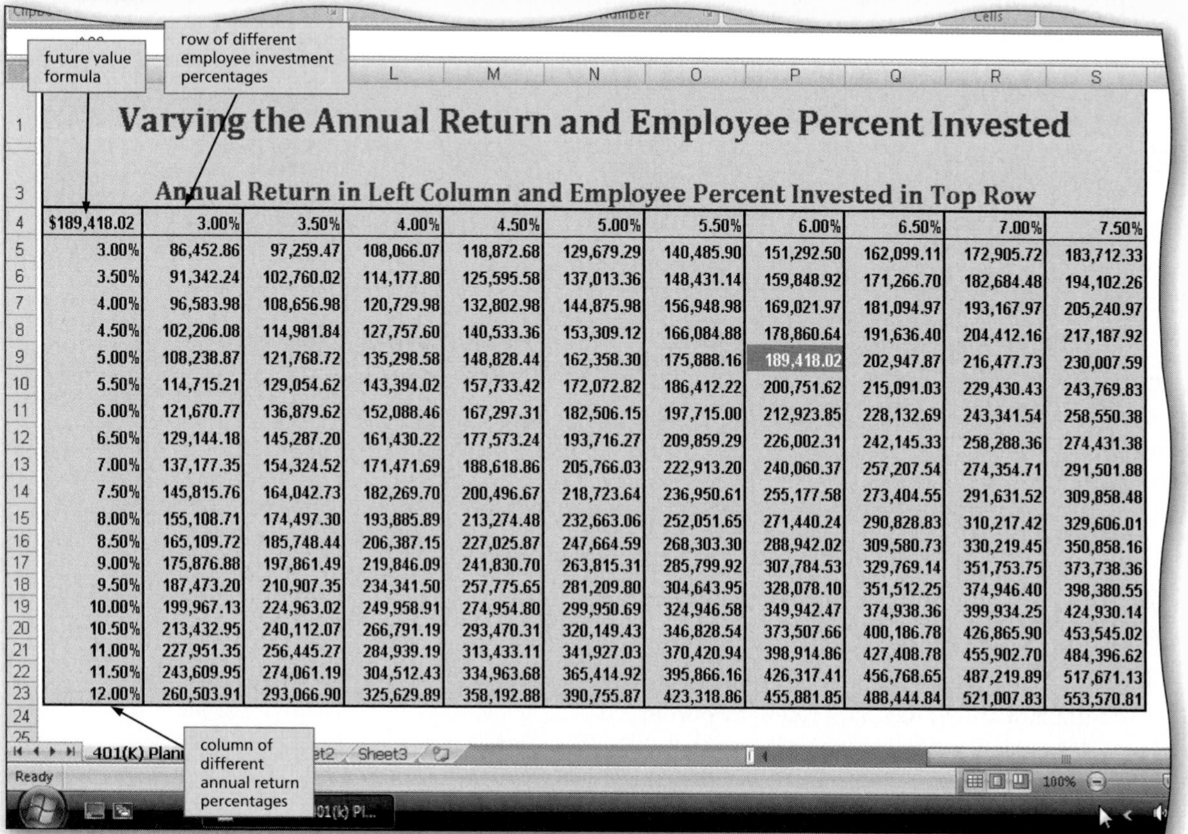

$189,418.02	3.00%	3.50%	4.00%	4.50%	5.00%	5.50%	6.00%	6.50%	7.00%	7.50%
3.00%	86,452.86	97,259.47	108,066.07	118,872.68	129,679.29	140,485.90	151,292.50	162,099.11	172,905.72	183,712.33
3.50%	91,342.24	102,760.02	114,177.80	125,595.58	137,013.36	148,431.14	159,848.92	171,266.70	182,684.48	194,102.26
4.00%	96,583.98	108,656.98	120,729.98	132,802.98	144,875.98	156,948.98	169,021.97	181,094.97	193,167.97	205,240.97
4.50%	102,206.08	114,981.84	127,757.60	140,533.36	153,309.12	166,084.88	178,860.64	191,636.40	204,412.16	217,187.92
5.00%	108,238.87	121,768.72	135,298.58	148,828.44	162,358.30	175,888.16	189,418.02	202,947.87	216,477.73	230,007.59
5.50%	114,715.21	129,054.62	143,394.02	157,733.42	172,072.82	186,412.22	200,751.62	215,091.03	229,430.43	243,769.83
6.00%	121,670.77	136,879.62	152,088.46	167,297.31	182,506.15	197,715.00	212,923.85	228,132.69	243,341.54	258,550.38
6.50%	129,144.18	145,287.20	161,430.22	177,573.24	193,716.27	209,859.29	226,002.31	242,145.33	258,288.36	274,431.38
7.00%	137,177.35	154,324.52	171,471.69	188,618.86	205,766.03	222,913.20	240,060.37	257,207.54	274,354.71	291,501.88
7.50%	145,815.76	164,042.73	182,269.70	200,496.67	218,723.64	236,950.61	255,177.58	273,404.55	291,631.52	309,858.48
8.00%	155,108.71	174,497.30	193,885.89	213,274.48	232,663.06	252,051.65	271,440.24	290,828.83	310,217.42	329,606.01
8.50%	165,109.72	185,748.44	206,387.15	227,025.87	247,664.59	268,303.30	288,942.02	309,580.73	330,219.45	350,858.16
9.00%	175,876.88	197,861.49	219,846.09	241,830.70	263,815.31	285,799.92	307,784.53	329,769.14	351,753.75	373,738.36
9.50%	187,473.20	210,907.35	234,341.50	257,775.65	281,209.80	304,643.95	328,078.10	351,512.25	374,946.40	398,380.55
10.00%	199,967.13	224,963.02	249,958.91	274,954.80	299,950.69	324,946.58	349,942.47	374,938.36	399,934.25	424,930.14
10.50%	213,432.95	240,112.07	266,791.19	293,470.31	320,149.43	346,828.54	373,507.66	400,186.78	426,865.90	453,545.02
11.00%	227,951.35	256,445.27	284,939.19	313,433.11	341,927.03	370,420.94	398,914.86	427,408.78	455,902.70	484,396.62
11.50%	243,609.95	274,061.19	304,512.43	334,963.68	365,414.92	395,866.16	426,317.41	456,768.65	487,219.89	517,671.13
12.00%	260,503.91	293,066.90	325,629.89	358,192.88	390,755.87	423,318.86	455,881.85	488,444.84	521,007.83	553,570.81

Figure 4–67

Continued >

Extend Your Knowledge *continued*

1. Enter the data table title and subtitle as shown in cells I1 and I3 in Figure 4–67. Change the width of column H to 0.50 characters. Merge and center the titles over columns I through S. Format the titles as shown using the Title cell style for both the title and subtitle, a font size of 22 for the title, and a font size of 16 for the subtitle. Change the column widths of columns I through S to 11.00 characters.

2. For a two–input data table, the formula you are analyzing must be assigned to the upper–left cell in the range of the data table. Cell C14 contains the future value formula to be analyzed. Therefore, enter =C14 in cell I4.

3. Use the fill handle to create two lists of percents (a) 3.00% through 12.00%, in increments of 0.50% in the range I5:I23; and (b) 3.00% through 7.50% in increments of 0.50% in the range J4:S4.

4. Select the range I4:S23. Click the Data tab on the Ribbon and then click the What–If Analysis button on the Ribbon. Click the Data Table command on the What–If Analysis gallery. When Excel displays the Table dialog box, enter c5 (employee percent invested) in the Row input cell box and c8 (expected annual return) in the Column input cell box. Click the OK button to populate the table.

5. Format the two–input data table as shown in Figure 4–67.

6. Use conditional formatting to change the format of the cell in the two–input data table that is equal to the future value in cell C14 to white bold font on a red background.

7. Protect the worksheet so that the user can select only unlocked cells (C3:C6 and C8:C9).

8. Change the document properties as specified by your instructor. Change the worksheet header with your name, course number, and other information requested by your instructor. Change the print orientation to landscape. Print the worksheet using the Fit to option. Print the formulas version of the worksheet.

9. Save the workbook using the file name Extend 4–1 401(k) Planning Sheet Complete.

Make It Right

Analyze a workbook and correct all errors and/or improve the design.

Functions, Custom Borders, Cell Names, What–If Analysis, and Protection

Instructions: Start Excel. Open the workbook Make It Right 4–1 Financial Calculator. See the inside back cover of this book for instructions for downloading the Data Files for Students, or see your instructor for information on accessing the files required for this book. Correct the following design and formula problems so that the worksheet appears as shown in Figure 4–68.

1. The worksheet is protected with no unprotected cells. Unprotect the worksheet so that the worksheet can be edited.

2. Correct the Monthly Payment formula in cell C7 and the Total Interest formula in cell C8. The monthly payment should equal $2,078.97 and the total interest should equal $419,214.32.

3. Change the thick box border to a dark red thick box border. Change the thick border separating columns B and C to a dark red light border.

4. Use Goal Seek to change the down payment in cell C3 so that the monthly payment is $1,850.00 as shown in Figure 4–68.

5. Name the range B1:C9, Loan_Calculator.

6. Assign the names in column E to the adjacent cells in column F. Edit the formulas in cells F5 and F6 and change the cell references to their corresponding names.

	A	B	C	D	E	F	G	H	I	J
1		Loan Calculator			Depreciation Calculator					
2		Price	$247,000.00		Cost	$213,000.00				
3		Down Payment	$67,247.39		Salvage	$32,000.00				
4		Loan Amount	$179,752.61		Life	8				
5		Rate	9.25%		Depreciation	$22,625.00				
6		Years	15		Rate of Depreciation	10.62%				
7		Monthly Payment	$1,850.00							
8		Total Interest	$153,247.39							
9		Total Cost	$400,247.39							
10		Future Value			Present Value					
11		Interest Rate	5.00%		Annual Rate	6.75%				
12		Months	240		Term In Years	30				
13		Monthly Investment	$50		Monthly Pymt	$987				
14		Future Value	$20,551.68		Present Value	$152,174.36				
15										
16					Depreciation Analysis					
17		Life		5	6	7	8	9	10	
18		Depreciation	$22,625.00	36,200.00	30,166.67	25,857.14	22,625.00	20,111.11	18,100.00	
19		Rate of Depreciation	10.62%	17.00%	14.16%	12.14%	10.62%	9.44%	8.50%	
20										

Figure 4–68

7. Correct the second and third arguments in the Future Value function in cell C14. Display the future value as a positive number.

8. Change the Present Value function in cell F14 so that the present value displays as a positive number.

9. Complete the one–input data table in the range B17:I19 that determines the depreciation and rate of depreciation for varying years of life (cell F4). Format the numbers in the data table so that they appear as shown in Figure 4–68.

10. Change the document properties as specified by your instructor. Change the worksheet header with your name, course number, and other information requested by your instructor.

11. Unlock the cells containing data (C2:C3, C5:C6, F2:F4, C11:C13, F11:F13). Protect the worksheet so that the user can select only cells with data.

12. Save the workbook using the file name, Make It Right 4–1 Financial Calculator Complete, and submit the revised workbook as requested by your instructor.

In the Lab

Create a workbook using the guidelines, concepts, and skills presented in this chapter. Labs are listed in order of increasing difficulty.

Lab 1: 401(k) Retirement Savings Model

Problem: You have been asked by the human resources department to develop a retirement planning worksheet that will allow each current and prospective employee to see the effect (dollar accumulation) of investing a percent of his or her monthly salary over a period of years (Figure 4–69 on the next page). The plan calls for the company to match an employee's investment, dollar for dollar, up to 3%. Thus, if an employee invests 6% of his or her annual salary, then the company matches the first 3%. If an employee invests only 2% of his or her annual salary, then the company matches the entire 2%. The human resources department wants a one–input data table to show the future value of the investment for different periods.

Continued >

In the Lab *continued*

	A	B	C	D	E	F	G	H	I	J
1		— Retirement Planning Sheet								
2										
3		Employee Name	Paul Morimoto		Years	Future Value	Employee Investment			
4		Annual Salary	$82,000.00			$680,299.52	$147,600.00			
5		Percent Invested	6.00%		5	43,464.49	24,600.00			
6		Company Match	3.00%		10	103,567.94	49,200.00			
7		Annual Return	6.50%		15	186,680.03	73,800.00			
8		Years	30		20	301,608.87	98,400.00			
9		Monthly Contribution			25	460,534.46	123,000.00			
10		Employee	$410.00		30	680,299.52	147,600.00			
11		Employer	$205.00		35	984,194.46	172,200.00			
12		Total	$615.00		40	1,404,425.64	196,800.00			
13		Future Value	$680,299.52		45	1,985,528.59	221,400.00			
14					50	2,789,087.82	246,000.00			
15										

Figure 4–69

Instructions: With a blank worksheet on the screen, perform the following tasks.

1. Change the font of the entire worksheet to bold and apply the Trek theme to the worksheet. Change the column widths to the following: A and D = 0.50; B = 20.00; C, F, and G = 13.00. Change the row heights to the following: 2 = 16.50; and 3 = 32.25. The height of row 1 will be adjusted automatically when a cell style is applied to the worksheet title.

2. In cell B1, enter Retirement Planning Sheet as the worksheet title. Merge and center cell B1 across columns B through G. Apply the Title cell style to cell B1, change the font size to 24 point, and change the font color to Orange, Accent 6 (column 10, row 1 in the Theme colors area on the Font Color palette). Draw a medium black border around cell B1.

3. Enter the row titles in column B, beginning in cell B3 as shown in Figure 4–69. Add the data in Table 4–6 to column C. Use the dollar and percent signs format symbols to format the numbers in the range C4:C7.

Table 4–6 401(k) Planning Sheet Employee Data	
Row Title	**Item**
Employee Name	Paul Morimoto
Annual Salary	$82,000.00
Percent Invested	6.00%
Company Match	3.00%
Annual Return	6.50%
Years	30

4. Use the Create from Selection button on the Formulas tab on the Ribbon to assign the row titles in column B (range B3:B13) to the adjacent cells in column C. Use these names to enter the following formulas in the range C10:C13. Step 4e formats the displayed results of the formulas.

   a. Employee Monthly Contribution (cell C10) = Annual_Salary * Percent_Invested / 12

   b. Employer Monthly Contribution (cell C11) = IF(Percent_Invested < Company_Match, Percent_Invested * Annual_Salary / 12, Company_Match * Annual_Salary / 12)

   c. Total Monthly Contribution (cell C12) = SUM(C10:C11)

   d. Future Value (cell C13) = –FV(Annual_Return/12, 12 * Years, Total)

   e. If necessary, use the Format Painter button on the Home tab on the Ribbon to assign the Currency style format in cell C4 to the range C10:C13.

The Future Value function (FV) in Step 4d returns to the cell the future value of the investment. The future value of an investment is its value at some point in the future based on a series of payments of equal amounts made over a number of periods earning a constant rate of return.

5. Add borders to the range B3:C13 as shown in Figure 4–69.

6. Use the concepts and techniques developed in this project to add the data table in Figure 4–69 to the range E3:G14 as follows.

   a. Enter and format the table column titles in row 3.

   b. Use the fill handle to create the series of years beginning with 5 and ending with 50 in increments of 5 in column E, beginning in cell E5.

   c. In cell F4, enter =C13 as the formula. In cell G4, enter =12 * C10 * C8 as the formula (using cell references in the formulas means Excel will copy the formats).

   d. Use the Data Table command on the What–If Analysis gallery on the Data tab on the Ribbon to define the range E4:G14 as a one–input data table. Use cell C8 as the column input cell.

   e. Format the numbers in the range F5:G14 to the Comma style format. Underline rows 3 and 4 as shown in Figure 4–69. Add borders to the range E3:G14 as shown in Figure 4–69.

7. Use the Conditional Formatting button on the Home tab on the Ribbon to add a red pointer that shows the row that equates the years in cell C8 to the Years column in the data table. Use a white font color for the pointer. Add the background color Light Yellow, Background 2 (column 3, row 1 in the Theme colors area on the Fill Color palette) as shown in Figure 4–69.

8. Change the document properties as specified by your instructor. Change the worksheet header with your name, course number, and other information as specified by your instructor.

9. Spell check and formula check the worksheet. Use Range Finder (double–click cell) to check all formulas.

10. Print the worksheet.

11. Print the formulas version of the worksheet.

12. Unlock the cells in the range C3:C8. Protect the worksheet. Allow users to select only unlocked cells.

13. Save the workbook using the file name Lab 4–1 Retirement Planning Sheet.

14. Hide and then unhide the Retirement Planning Sheet sheet. Hide and then unhide the Workbook. Unprotect the worksheet and then hide columns D through G. Print the worksheet. Select columns C and H and unhide the hidden columns. Hide rows 1 and 2. Print the worksheet. Click the Select All button and unhide rows 1 and 2.

15. Close the workbook without saving changes. Open the workbook Lab 4–1 Retirement Planning Sheet. Determine the future value for the data in Table 4–7. Print the worksheet for each data set. The following Future Value results should display in cell C13: Data Set 1 = $165,108.38; Data Set 2 = $549,735.86; and Data Set 3 = $1,241,885.59. Quit Excel without saving the workbook.

16. Submit the assignment as requested by your instructor.

Table 4–7 Future Value Data			
	Data Set 1	**Data Set 2**	**Data Set 3**
Employee Name	Paula Rios	Sam Vinci	Gupta Ghandi
Annual Salary	$101,000.00	$78,000.00	$41,000.00
Percent Invested	2.00%	4.5%	6%
Company Match	2.00%	3%	3%
Annual Return	6.50%	7.00%	8.5%
Years	20	30	40

In the Lab

Lab 2: Quarterly Income Statement and Break–Even Analysis

Problem: You are a consultant to The Bean Bag Game Company. Your area of expertise is cost–volume–profit or CVP (also called break–even analysis), which investigates the relationship among a product's expenses (cost), its volume (units sold), and the operating income (gross profit). Any money a company earns above the break–even point is called operating income, or gross profit (row 21 in the Break–Even Analysis table in Figure 4–70). You have been asked to prepare a quarterly income statement and a data table that shows revenue, expenses, and income for units sold between 40,000 and 120,000 in increments of 5,000.

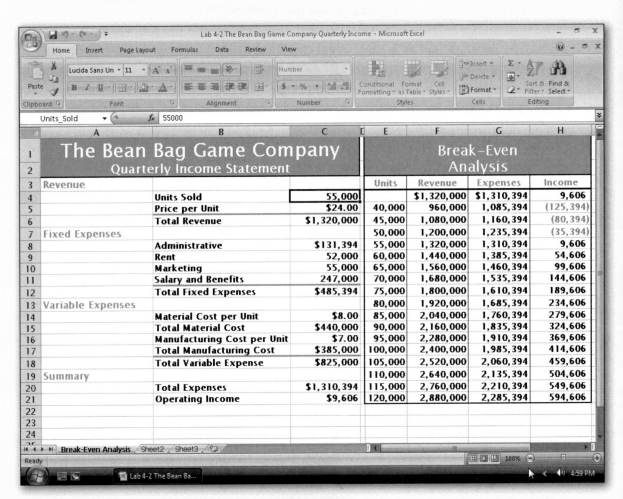

Figure 4–70

Instructions: With a blank worksheet on the screen, perform the following tasks.

1. Apply the Concourse theme to the worksheet. Change the font of the entire worksheet to bold. Change the column widths to the following: A = 21.00; B= 26.00; C = 12.78; D = 0.50; E= 7.44; and F through H = 11.22. Change the heights of rows 1 and 2 to 30.00 and 19.50 respectively. Name the sheet tab Break–Even Analysis and color the tab Orange, Accent 3 (column 7, row 1 on the Tab Color palette).

2. Enter the worksheet titles: The Bean Bag Game Company in cell A1, and Quarterly Income Statement in cell A2. Apply the Title cell style to both cells. Change the font sizes in cells A1 and A2 to 24 and 16 respectively. One at a time, merge and center cells A1 and A2 across columns A through C. Change the background color of cells A1 and A2 to Orange, Accent 3 (column 7, row 1 on the Fill Color palette). Change the font color to White, Background 1 (column 1, row 1 on the Font Color palette). Add a thick border to the range A1:A2.

3. Enter the row titles in columns A and B as shown in Figure 4–70. Change the font size of the row titles in column A to 12–point and change the font color to Orange, Accent 3. Add the data shown in Table 4–8 in column C. Use the dollar sign ($) and comma (,) format symbols to format the numbers in column C as you enter them.

Table 4–8 Annual Income Data

Title	Cell	Item
Units Sold	C4	55,000
Price per Unit	C5	$24.00
Administrative	C8	$131,394
Rent	C9	$52,000
Marketing	C10	$55,000
Salary and Benefits	C11	$247,000
Material Cost per Unit	C14	$8.00
Manufacturing Cost per Unit	C16	$7.00

4. Use the Create from Selection button on the Formulas tab on the Ribbon to assign the row titles in column B in the range B4:B21 to the adjacent cells in column C. Use these names to enter the following formulas in column C:

   a. Total Revenue (cell C6) = Units Sold * Price per Unit (or =C4 * C5)

   b. Total Fixed Expenses (cell C12) = SUM(C8:C11)

   c. Total Material Cost (cell C15) = Units Sold * Material Cost per Unit (or =C4 * C14)

   d. Total Manufacturing Cost (cell C17) = Units Sold * Manufacturing Cost per Unit (or =C4 * C16)

   e. Total Variable Expenses (cell C18) = Total Material Cost + Total Manufacturing Cost (or =C15 + C17)

   f. Total Expenses (cell C20) = Total Fixed Expenses + Total Variable Expense (or =C12 + C18)

   g. Operating Income (cell C21) = Total Revenue – Total Expenses (or =C6 – C20)

5. If necessary, use the Format Painter button on the Home tab on the Ribbon to assign the Currency style format in cell C8 to the unformatted dollar amounts in column C.

6. Add a thick orange bottom border to the ranges B5:C5, B11:C11, and B17:C17 as shown in Figure 4–70.

7. Use the concepts and techniques presented in this project to add the data table to the range E1:H21 as follows:

   a. Add the data table titles and format them as shown in Figure 4–70.

   b. Create the series in column E from 40,000 to 120,000 in increments of 5,000, beginning in cell E5.

   c. Enter the formula =c6 in cell F4. Enter the formula =c20 in cell G4. Enter the formula =c21 in cell H4. If necessary, adjust the column widths.

   d. Use the Data Table command in the What–If Analysis gallery on the Data tab on the Ribbon to define the range E4:H21 as a one–input data table. Use cell C4 (Units Sold) as the column input cell.

   e. Use the Format Cells command on the shortcut menu to format the range F5:H21 to the Comma style format with no decimal places and negative numbers in red with parentheses. Add a medium outline border and light vertical borders to the range E1:H21.

Continued >

8. Change the document properties as specified by your instructor. Change the worksheet header with your name, course number, and other information as specified by your instructor.

9. Spell check and formula check the worksheet. Use Range Finder (double–click cell) to check all formulas.

10. Use the Page Setup Dialog Box Launcher on the Page Layout tab on the Ribbon to select the Fit to and 'Black and white' options.

11. Unlock the following cells: C4, C5, C14, and C16. Protect the workbook so the user can select only unlocked cells.

12. Save the workbook using the file name, Lab 4–2 The Bean Bag Game Company Quarterly Income.

13. Print the worksheet. Print the formulas version of the worksheet.

14. Determine the operating income for the data sets in Table 4–9. Print the worksheet for each data set. You should get the following Operating Income results in cell C21: Data Set 1 = $333,606; Data Set 2 = ($453,894); and Data Set 3 = $50,106.

15. Hide and then unhide the Break–Even Analysis sheet. Hide and then unhide the workbook. Unprotect the worksheet and then hide columns D through H. Print the worksheet. Select columns C and I and unhide the hidden columns. Hide rows 7 through 21. Print the worksheet. Select rows 6 and 22 and unhide rows 7 through 21. Do not save the workbook.

Table 4–9 Operating Income Data				
Title	**Cell**	**Data Set 1**	**Data Set 2**	**Data Set 3**
Units Sold	C4	84,000	42,000	119,000
Price per Unit	C5	$19.00	$15.00	$21.00
Material Cost per Unit	C14	$4.00	$4.75	$10.00
Manufacturing Cost per Unit	C16	$5.25	$9.50	$6.50

16. Submit the assignment as requested by your instructor.

In the Lab

Lab 3: Loan Analysis and Amortization Schedule

Problem: The manager of eLoans Unlimited, Inc., an Internet–based lending institution, has asked you to create the loan analysis worksheet shown in Figure 4–71. She also wants you to demonstrate the goal seeking capabilities of Excel.

Instructions:

1. Apply the Aspect theme to a new worksheet. Bold the entire worksheet and change all the columns to a width of 17.00. Change column A to a width of 0.41.

2. Enter the worksheet title in cell B1, apply the Title cell style, and change its font size to 24-point. Enter the worksheet subtitle in cell B2, apply the Title cell style, and change its font size to 16-point. One at a time, merge and center cells B1 and B2 across columns B through F.

3. Enter the row titles for the ranges B3:B5 and E3:E5 as shown in Figure 4–71. Use the Create from Selection button on the Formulas tab on the Ribbon to assign the row titles in the ranges B3:B5 and E3:E5 to the adjacent cells in ranges C3:C5 and F3:F5, respectively.

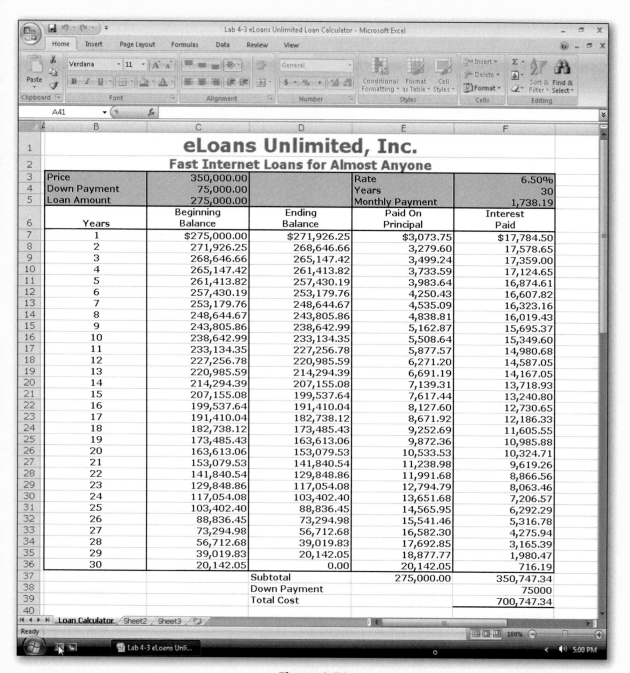

Figure 4–71

4. Enter 350000 (price) in cell C3, 75000 (down payment) in cell C4, 6.50% (interest rate) in cell F3, and 30 (years) in cell F4. Determine the loan amount by entering the formula =Price − Down_Payment in cell C5. Determine the monthly payment by entering the PMT function −PMT(Rate / 12, 12 * Years, Loan_Amount) in cell F5.

5. Create the amortization schedule in the range B6:F36 by assigning the formulas and functions to the cells indicated in Table 4–10 on the next page. Use names when appropriate. The years in column B starting at cell B7 should extend from 1 to 30 years.

6. Enter the total titles in the range D37:D39 as shown in Figure 4–71.

7. Change the sheet tab name and color as shown in Figure 4–71.

8. Change the document properties as specified by your instructor. Change the worksheet header with your name, course number, and other information requested by your instructor.

Continued >

In the Lab *continued*

9. Spell check and formula check the worksheet. Use Range Finder (double–click cell) to check all formulas listed in Table 4–10.

Table 4–10 Cell Assignments

Cell	Formula or Function
C7	=C5
D7	=IF(B7 <= $F$4, PV($F$3 / 12, 12 * ($F$4 − B7), −$F$5),0)
E7	=C7 − D7
F7	=IF(C7 > 0, 12 * $F$5 − E7, 0)
C8	=D7
E37	=SUM(E7:E36)
F37	=SUM(F7:F36)
F38	=C4
F39	=E37 + F37 + F38

10. Use the Page Setup command to select the Fit to and 'Black and white' options.

11. Unlock the cells in the ranges C3:C4 and F3:F4. Protect the worksheet so that users can select any cell in the worksheet, but can change only the unlocked cells.

12. Save the workbook using the file name Lab 4–3 eLoans Unlimited Loan Calculator.

13. Print the worksheet. Print the formulas version of the worksheet.

14. Use Excel's goal seeking capabilities to determine the down payment required for the loan data in Figure 4–71 if the monthly payment is set to $1,000.00. The down payment that results for a monthly payment of $1,000.00 is $191,789.18. Print the worksheet with the new monthly payment of $1,000.00. Close the workbook without saving changes.

15. Hide and then unhide the Loan Payment Calculator sheet. Hide and then unhide the workbook. Unprotect the worksheet and then hide columns D through F. Print the worksheet. Select columns C and G and unhide the hidden columns. Hide rows 6 through 39. Print the worksheet. Select rows 5 and 40 and unhide rows 6 through 39. Do not save the workbook.

Cases and Places

Apply your creative thinking and problem solving skills to design and implement a solution.

● EASIER ●● MORE DIFFICULT

● 1: Break–Even Analysis

You can calculate the number of units you must sell to break even (break–even point) if you know the fixed expenses, the price per unit, and the expense (cost) per unit. You have been hired by Fairview Clothing to create a data table that analyzes the break–even point for prices between $8.00 and $14.25 in increments of $0.25. The following formula determines the break–even point:

Break–Even Point = Fixed Expenses / (Price per Unit – Expense per Unit)

Assume Fixed Expenses = $800,000; Price per Unit = $8.50; and Expense per Unit = $4.10. Enter the data and formula into a worksheet and then create the data table. Use the Price per Unit as the input cell and the break–even value as the result. For a price per unit of $10.50, the data table should show a break–even point of 125,000 units. Protect the worksheet.

● 2: Salvage Value of an Asset

Jack Hollinsworth, owner of Hollinsworth Bakery, recently purchased a new commercial–sized oven for his business. Jack wants a worksheet that uses the financial function SLN to show the oven's straight–line depreciation and a formula to determine the annual rate of depreciation. Straight–line depreciation is based on an asset's initial cost, how long it can be used (called useful life), and the price at which it eventually can be sold (called salvage value). Jack has supplied the following information:

Cost = $124,857; Salvage = $30,000; Life = 8 years; and Annual Rate of Depreciation = SLN / Cost

Jack is not sure what selling price the oven will bring in 8 years. Create a data table that shows straight–line depreciation and annual rate of depreciation for salvage from $25,000 to $35,000 in $500 increments. Use Excel Help to learn more about the SLN function. Protect the worksheet.

● 3: Saving for College

Your friends' dream for their one–year–old son is that one day he will attend their alma mater, Tesla University. For the next 15 years, they plan to make monthly payment deposits to a 529 College Savings plan at a local bank. The account pays 4.5% annual interest, compounded monthly. Create a worksheet for your friends that uses a financial function to show the future value (FV) of their investment and a formula to determine the percentage of the college's tuition saved. They have supplied the following information:

Out of State Annual Tuition = $40,000; Rate (per month) = 4. 5% / 12; Nper (number of monthly payments) = 15 * 12; Pmt (payment per period) = $375; and percentage of Tuition Saved = FV / Tuition for four years

Your friends are not sure how much they will be able to save each month. Create a data table that shows the future value and percentage of tuition saved for monthly payments from $250 to $850, in $50 increments. Protect the worksheet.

Continued >

Cases and Places *continued*

•• 4 Saving for a Dream Home

Make It Personal

Find a home in your area that you would like to someday purchase. Based on the estimated current price of the home, determine how much money you need to save each month so that in seven years, you have enough to make a down payment of 10% of the current estimated value. Assume that you can save the money in an account that is getting a 5.75% return. Create a worksheet that determines how much you have to save each month so that in seven years the value of the account is 10% of the current estimated value. *Hint:* Use the FV function with a monthly savings of $400. Then use the Goal Seek command to determine the monthly savings amount. Protect the worksheet.

•• 5 Paying Off a Car Loan

Working Together

Jackie Waltrip is retiring from her teaching job, but before leaving her job, she wants to settle her account with her union's credit union. Jackie has seven years remaining on a ten–year car loan, with an interest rate of 10.25% and a monthly payment of $450.00. The credit union is willing to accept the present value (PV) of the loan as a payoff. Develop an amortization schedule that shows how much Jackie must pay at the end of each of the ten years. As a team, use Excel Help to learn more about present value. Then, design and create a worksheet that includes the beginning and ending balance, the amount paid on the principal, and the interest paid for years four through ten. Because she has paid for the three years already, determine only the ending balance (present value) for year three. Submit the worksheet as requested by your instructor and include a one–page paper on one of the following topics: (1) error checking; (2) elements you can protect in a workbook; or (3) present value.

5 | Creating, Sorting, and Querying a Table

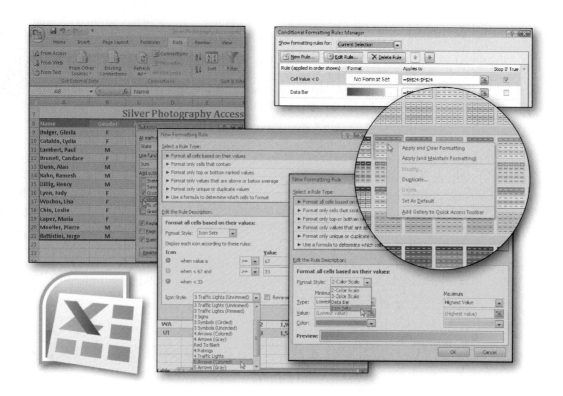

Objectives

You will have mastered the material in this chapter when you can:

- Create and manipulate a table
- Delete sheets in a workbook
- Validate data
- Add calculated columns to a table
- Use icon sets with conditional formatting
- Use the VLOOKUP function to look up a value in a table
- Print a table
- Add and delete records and change field values in a table

- Sort a table on one field or multiple fields
- Display automatic subtotals
- Use Group and Outline features to hide and unhide data
- Query a table
- Apply database functions, the SUMIF function, and the COUNTIF function
- Save a workbook in different file formats

5 | Creating, Sorting, and Querying a Table

Introduction

A **table**, also called a **database**, is an organized collection of data. For example, a list of friends, a list of students registered for a class, a club membership roster, and an instructor's grade book can be arranged as tables in a worksheet. In these cases, the data related to a person is called a **record**, and the data items that make up a record are called **fields**. For example, in a table of sales reps, each sales rep would have a separate record; each record might include several fields, such as name, age, hire date, state, and sales quota. A record in a table also can include fields (columns) that contain formulas and functions. A field, or column, that contains formulas or functions is called a **calculated column**. A calculated column displays results based on other columns in the table.

A worksheet's row-and-column structure can be used to organize and store a table. Each row of a worksheet can store a record, and each column can store a field. Additionally, a row of column headings at the top of the worksheet can store field names that identify each field. Excel's built-in data validation features help ensure data integrity of the data entered in the table.

After you enter a table onto a worksheet, you can use Excel to (1) add and delete records; (2) change the values of fields in records; (3) sort the records so Excel displays them in a different order; (4) determine subtotals for numeric fields; (5) display records that meet comparison criteria; and (6) analyze data using database functions. This chapter illustrates all six of these table capabilities.

Project — Silver Photography Accessories Sales Rep Table

The project in the chapter follows proper design guidelines and uses Excel to create the worksheet shown in Figure 5–1. Silver Photography Accessories sells equipment to photography stores throughout the western United States. The company's sales director has asked for a workbook that summarizes key information about sales reps and their performance. The data in the workbook should be easy to summarize, sort, edit, and query.

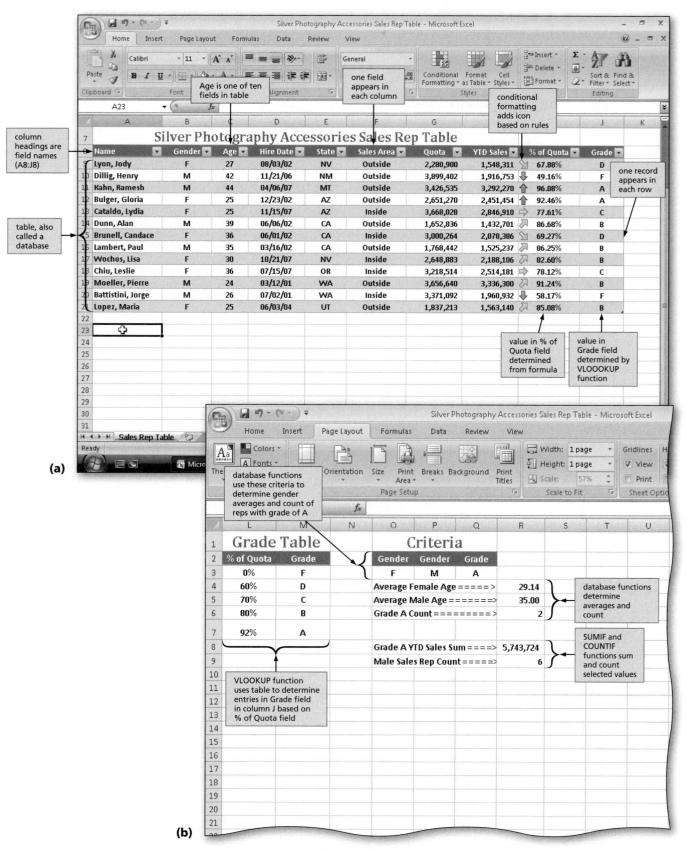

Figure 5–1

The requirements document for the Silver Photography Accessories Sales Rep table is shown in Figure 5–2. It includes the needs, source of data, calculations, special requirements, and other facts about its development.

REQUEST FOR NEW WORKBOOK

Date Submitted:	June 3, 2008
Submitted By:	Rose Veccos
Worksheet Title:	Silver Photography Accessories Sales Rep Table
Needs:	Create a sales representative table (Figure 5-3a) that can be sorted, queried, maintained, and printed to obtain meaningful information. Using the data in the table, compute statistics that include the average female age, average male age, grade A count, sum of YTD Sales for those with grade A, and the count of the male sales reps as shown in Figure 5-3b.
	The table field names, columns, types of data, and column widths are described in Table 5-1. Because Rose will use the table online as she travels among the offices, it is important that it be readable and that the table is visible on the screen. Therefore, some of the column widths listed in Table 5-1 are determined from the field names and not the maximum length of the data. The last two fields (located in columns I and J) use a formula and function to determine values based on data within each sales representative record.
Source of Data:	Rose will supply the sales representative data required for the table.
Calculations:	Include the following calculations:
	1. % of Quota field in table = YTD Sales / Quota
	2. Grade field in table = VLOOKUP function that uses the Grade table in Figure 5-3b
	3. Average Female Age = AVERAGE function that uses the Criteria table in Figure 5-3b
	4. Average Male Age = AVERAGE function that uses the Criteria table in Figure 5-3b
	5. Grade A Count = DCOUNT function that uses the Criteria table in Figure 5-3b
	6. Grade A YTD Sales Sum = SUMIF function
	7. Male Sales Rep Count = COUNTIF function
Special Requirements:	1. Delete unused sheets.
	2. A Criteria area will be created above the table, in rows 1 through 6, to store criteria for use in a query. An Extract area will be created below the table, beginnning in row 25, to receive records that meet a criteria.
	3. Save the table as a CSV (Comma delimited) file.

Approvals

Approval Status:	X	Approved
		Rejected
Approved By:	Rose Veccos	
Date:	June 10, 2008	
Assigned To:	J. Quasney, Spreadsheet Specialist	

Figure 5–2

BTW

Excel as a Database Tool
Even though Excel is not a true database management system, such as Access or Oracle, it does give you many of the same basic capabilities. For example, in Excel you can create a list; add, change, and delete data in the list; use computational fields; sort data in the list; query the list; and create forms and reports.

The VLOOKUP function will be used to determine the grades in column J in Figure 5–1a, based on the grade table in columns L and M in Figure 5–1b. The DAVERAGE function will be used to find the average age of female and male sales reps in the table (range O4:R5 in Figure 5–1b). The DCOUNT function will be used to count the number of sales reps that received a grade of A (range O6:R6 in Figure 5–1b). These two functions require that a **criteria area** (range O1:Q3) be set up to tell Excel what items to average and count. Icon sets will be used to provide a visual means of identifying grades based on a conditional formatting rule. Finally, the SUMIF and COUNTIF functions will be used to sum selectively the sales of sales reps that received a grade of A and count the number of male sales reps in the table (range O8:R9 in Figure 5–1b).

Table 5–1 on the next page describes the field names, columns, types of data, and column widths to use when creating the table.

Overview

As you read this chapter, you will learn how to create the worksheet shown in Figure 5–1 by performing these general tasks:

- Create and format the sales rep table
- Sort the sales rep table
- Display subtotals by grouping the sales reps
- Obtain answers to questions about the sales reps using a variety of methods to query the sales rep table
- Extract records from the table based on given criteria
- Save the worksheet in different file formats

General Project Decisions

Plan
Ahead

While creating an Excel worksheet, you need to make several decisions that will determine the appearance and characteristics of the finished worksheet. As you create the worksheet required to meet the requirements shown in Figure 5–2, you should follow these general guidelines:

1. Create and format the sales rep table. The sales rep table should include the data provided in Table 5–1. The table should be formatted so that the records are easily distinguised. The data in the worksheet should start several rows from the top in order to leave room for the criteria area. Using banded rows to format the table provides greater readability. The last two columns require calculations for the % of Quota and Grade. The Grade can be obtained using Excel's VLOOKUP function. Totals also should be added to the table for the sales reps' average age, the sum of the sales reps' quotas, and the sum of the sales reps' year-to-date sales.

2. Sort the sales rep table. The user of the worksheet should be able to sort the table in a variety of manners and sort using multiple fields at the same time. Excel includes simple and advanced methods for sorting tables.

3. Display subtotals by grouping the sales reps. The user of the worksheet should be able to create subtotals of groups of sales reps after sorting the table. Excel's grouping features provide for subtotaling.

4. Obtain answers to questions (queries) about the sales reps using a variety of methods to query the sales rep table. A query can include filters, the use of which results in the table displaying only those records that meet certain criteria. Or, a query can include a calculation based on data in the table that then is displayed in the worksheet outside of the table.

5. Extract records from the table based on given criteria. A criteria area and extract area can be created on the worksheet. The criteria area can be used to enter rules regarding which records to extract, such as all female representatives with a grade of A. The extract area can be used to store the records that meet the criteria. The column headings from the table should be used as column headings in both the criteria and extract areas of the worksheet.

(continued)

Plan Ahead

(continued)

6. Save the worksheet in different file formats. A variety of circumstances may require a worksheet to be saved in a different file format. For example, the data in a worksheet may need to be used in another program that is not capable of reading the Excel file format. The CSV (comma delimited) file format is a file format that is one of the most commonly used.

In addition, using a sketch of the worksheet can help you visualize its design. The sketch of the table (Figure 5–3a) consists of the title, column headings, location of data values, and an idea of the desired formatting. The sketch does not show the criteria area above the table and the extract area below the table, which are included as requirements in the requirements document (Figure 5–2). The general layout of the grade table, criteria area, and required statistics are shown in Figure 5–3b.

When necessary, more specific details concerning the above guidelines are presented at appropriate points in the chapter. The chapter also will identify the actions you perform and decisions made regarding these guidelines during the creation of the worksheet shown in Figure 5–1 on page EX 339.

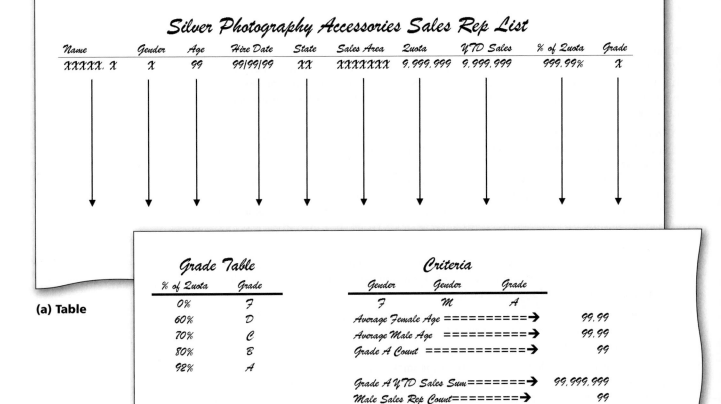

(a) Table

(b) Grade Table, Criteria, and Statistics

Figure 5–3

With a good understanding of the requirements document, an understanding of the necessary decisions, and a sketch of the worksheet, the next step is to use Excel to create the worksheet.

Table 5–1 Column Information for Silver Photography Accessories Sales Rep Table

Column Headings (Field Names)	Column in Worksheet	Type of Data	Column Width	Description as It Pertains to a Sales Rep
Name	A	Text	16.43	Last name and first name
Gender	B	Text	11.57	Male or female
Age	C	Numeric	8.29	Age in years
Hire Date	D	Date	13.14	Date hired
State	E	Text	9.43	Sales territory
Sales Area	F	Text	14.00	Inside or outside sales
Quota	G	Numeric	13.29	Annual sales quota
YTD Sales	H	Numeric	13.29	Year-to-date sales
% of Quota	I	YTD Sales / Quota	14.57	Percent of annual quota met
Grade	J	VLOOKUP function	10.29	Grade indicates how much of quota has been met

To Start Excel

If you are using a computer to step through the project in this chapter and you want your screen to match the figures in this book, you should change your computer's resolution to 1024 × 768. For information about how to change a computer's resolution, see page APP 21 in Appendix E.

The following steps, which assume Windows is running, start Excel based on a typical installation of Microsoft Office on your computer. You may need to ask your instructor how to start Excel for your computer.

Note: If you are using Windows XP, see Appendix F for alternate steps.

1 Click the Start button on the Windows Vista taskbar to display the Start menu.

2 Click All Programs at the bottom of the left pane on the Start menu to display the All Programs list.

3 Click Microsoft Office in the All Programs list to display the Microsoft Office list.

4 Click Microsoft Office Excel 2007 to start Excel and display a blank worksheet in the Excel window.

5 If the Excel window is not maximized, click the Maximize button next to the Close button on its title bar to maximize the window.

6 If the worksheet window in Excel is not maximized, click the Maximize button next to the Close button on its title bar to maximize the worksheet window within Excel.

BTW

Starting Excel
If you plan to open an existing workbook, you can start Excel and open the workbook at the same time by double-clicking the workbook file name in Windows Explorer.

To Enter the Column Headings for a Table

Plan
Ahead

Create and format the sales rep table.
One way to create a table in Excel is to follow these five steps: (1) enter the column headings (field names); (2) define a range as a table using the Format as Table command; (3) format the insert row immediately below the column headings; (4) set up data validation using the Data Validation command; and (5) enter records into the table. The following pages illustrate the process of creating the Silver Photography Accessories Sales Rep table using these five steps.

BTW

Setting Up a List
When creating a list, leave several rows empty above the list on the worksheet to set up a criteria area for querying the list. Some spreadsheet specialists also leave several columns empty to the left of the list, beginning with column A, for additional worksheet activities. A range of blank rows or columns on the side of a list is called a moat of cells.

The following steps change the column widths to those specified in Table 5–1, enter the table title, and enter and format the column headings. These steps also change the name of Sheet1 to Sales Rep Table, delete the unused sheets in the workbook, and save the workbook using the file name, Silver Photography Accessories Rep Table.

Although Excel does not require a table title to be entered, it is a good practice to include one on the worksheet to show where the table begins. With Excel, you usually enter the table several rows below the first row in the worksheet. These blank rows later will be used as a criteria area to store criteria for use in a query.

Note: The majority of tasks involved in entering and formatting the table title and column headings of a list are similar to what you have done in previous chapters. Thus, if you plan to complete this chapter on your computer and want to skip the set of steps below, open the workbook Silver Photography Accessories Sales Rep Table from the Data Files for Students.

1 Use the mouse to change the column widths as follows: A = 16.43, B = 11.57, C = 8.29, D = 13.14, E = 9.43, F = 14.00, G = 13.29, H = 13.29, I = 14.57, and J = 10.29.

2 Enter `Silver Photography Accessories Sales Rep Table` as the table title in cell A7.

BTW

Merging and Centering Across a Selection
You merge and center when you want to treat the range of cells over which you center as a single cell. You center across a selection when you want the selected range of cells to be independent of one another. With most workbooks, it makes little difference whether you center using one technique or the other. Thus, most spreadsheet specialists use the merge and center technique because the procedure is available as a button on the Home tab on the Ribbon.

3 Apply the Title cell style to cell A7. Click the Font Color button on the Home tab on the Ribbon and then click Red, Accent 2 (column 6, row 1) on the Font Color palette.

4 Select the range A7:H7. Right-click the selected range and then click Format Cells on the shortcut menu. When Excel displays the Format Cells dialog box, if necessary, click the Alignment tab, click the Horizontal box arrow in the Text alignment area, click Center Across Selection in the Horizontal list, and then click the OK button.

5 Enter the column headings in row 8 as shown in Figure 5–4. Center the column headings in the range B8:H8.

6 Apply the Heading 3 cell style to the range A8:H8.

7 Double-click the Sheet1 tab at the bottom of the screen. Type `Sales Rep Table` as the sheet name. Press the ENTER key. Right-click the tab, point to Tab Color on the shortcut menu, and then click Red, Accent 2 (column 6, row 1).

8 Click the Sheet2 tab, hold down the CTRL key, and then click the Sheet3 tab. Right-click the selected sheet tabs and then click Delete on the shortcut menu to delete the selected sheets from the workbook.

9 Update the document properties with your name and any other relevant information.

10 With a USB flash drive connected to one of the computer's USB ports, click the Save button on the Quick Access Toolbar. Save the workbook using the file name, Silver Photography Accessories Sales Rep Table on the USB flash drive. (Figure 5–4).

Q&A When should the Center Across Selection alignment be used instead of the Merge & Center button on the Ribbon?

In Step 4, the Center Across Selection horizontal alignment was used to center the table title in row 7 horizontally across the range A7:H7. In earlier chapters, the Merge & Center button on the Home tab on the Ribbon was used to center text across a range. The major difference between the Center Across Selection horizontal alignment and the Merge & Center button is that, unlike the Merge & Center button, the Center Across Selection horizontal alignment does not merge the selected cell range into one cell.

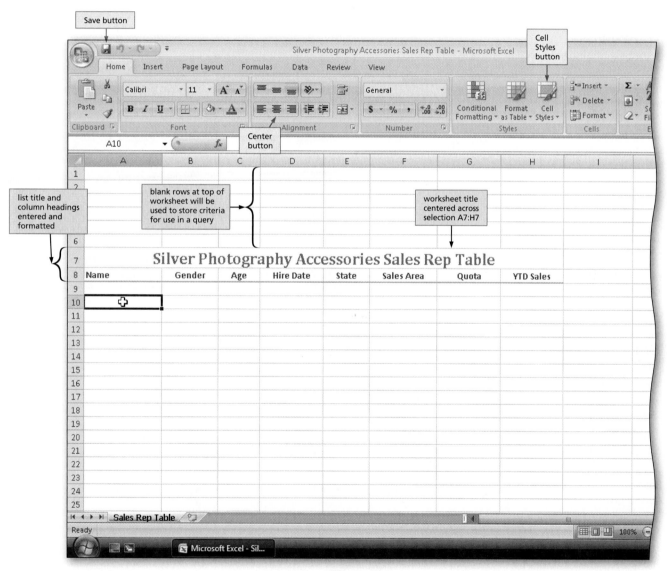

Figure 5–4

To Format a Range as a Table

The following steps define the range A8:H8 as a table by applying a table quick style to the range. Excel allows you to enter data in a range either before defining it as a table or after defining it as a table. This chapter uses the latter procedure because it offers additional tools that help ensure data integrity, such as data validation.

- Select the range A8:H8.

- Click the Format as Table button on the Home tab on the Ribbon to display the Table Style gallery (Figure 5–5).

Experiment

- Point to a number of table quick styles in the Table Style gallery to preview them on the worksheet.

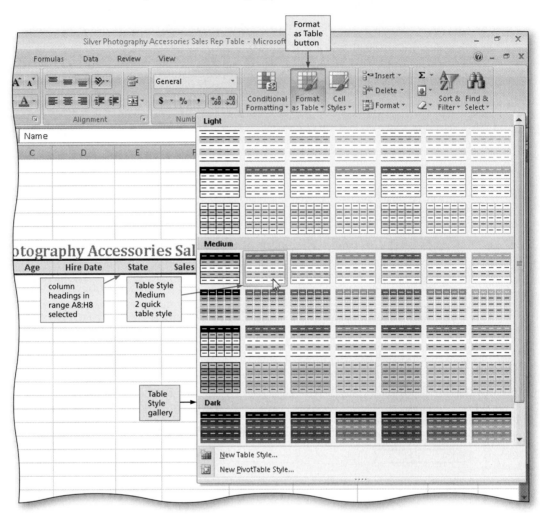

Figure 5–5

- Click the Table Style Medium 2 quick table style in the Table Style gallery.

- When Excel displays the Format As Table dialog box, click the 'My table has headers' check box to select it (Figure 5–6).

Q&A

Why is the range A8:H8 already selected in the Format As Table dialog box?

Because the range A8:H8 was selected before clicking the Format As Table button, Excel automatically selects this range for the 'Where is the data for your table?' box.

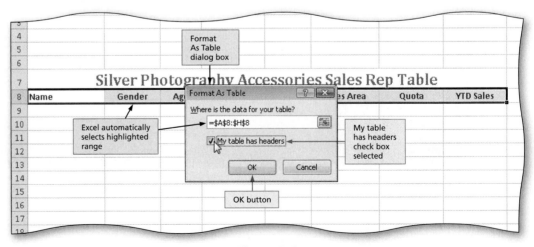

Figure 5–6

3
- Click the OK button to create a table from the selected column headings and corresponding cells in the row below it.

- Scroll down until row 7 is at the top of the worksheet window (Figure 5–7).

Q&A

Why does Excel indicate that the cells in row 9 are in the table?

Excel automatically creates an empty row in the table so that you are ready to enter the first record in the table.

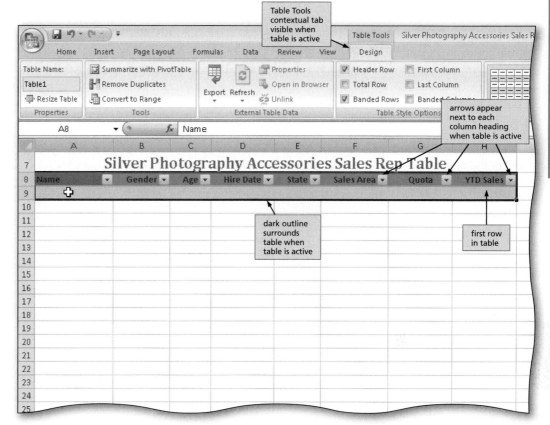

Figure 5–7

Other Ways

1. Select range, on Insert tab on Ribbon click Table, click OK button
2. Select range, press ALT+H+T, select quick style
3. Select range, press ALT+D, I, C

To Format the First Row in an Empty Table

If the table contains no data, as in Figure 5–7, then Excel sets the format of the cells in the first row to the default associated with the table quick style chosen when the table was created. That is, if you assigned any formats to the first row before it became part of a table, then those formats are lost when the table is created. For this reason, if you create an empty table and want the records to be formatted in a different manner associated with the selected quick style, you must format the first row after you create the table, as shown in the following steps.

1 Select the range B9:H9 and then click the Center button on the Home tab on the Ribbon.

2 Right-click cell D9. Click Format Cells on the shortcut menu. When Excel displays the Format Cells dialog box, click the Number tab, click Date in the Category list, click 03/14/01 in the Type list, and then click the OK button.

3 Select the range G9:H9 and then click the Comma Style button on the Ribbon. Click the Decrease Decimal button on the Ribbon twice so columns G and H will display whole numbers.

Q&A

Why are no changes apparent on the worksheet?

No visible changes appear on the worksheet, because the table contains no records. As records are entered into the table, the assigned formats will apply, even as more rows are added to the table.

To Validate Data

Excel has built-in **data validation** features to ensure that the data you enter into a cell or range of cells is within limits. For example, the cells in the Gender column in Figure 5–8 should be either an F for female or an M for male. Any entry other than M or F is invalid and should not be allowed. The following steps show how to use the Data Validation button on the Data tab on the Ribbon to ensure that Excel will accept only an entry of F or M in the Gender column.

- Select cell B9, the cell in the insert row below the Gender column heading in cell B8.

- Click the Data tab on the Ribbon and then point to the Data Validation button on the Ribbon (Figure 5–8).

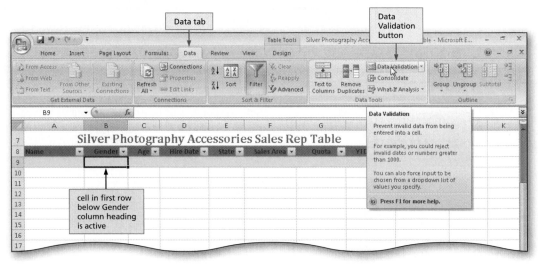

Figure 5–8

- Click the Data Validation button on the Ribbon to display the Data Validation dialog box.

- When Excel displays the Data Validation dialog box, if necessary, click the Settings tab, click the Allow box arrow, and then click List in the Allow list.

- Type F,M in the Source box.

- Click the In-cell dropdown check box to clear it (Figure 5–9).

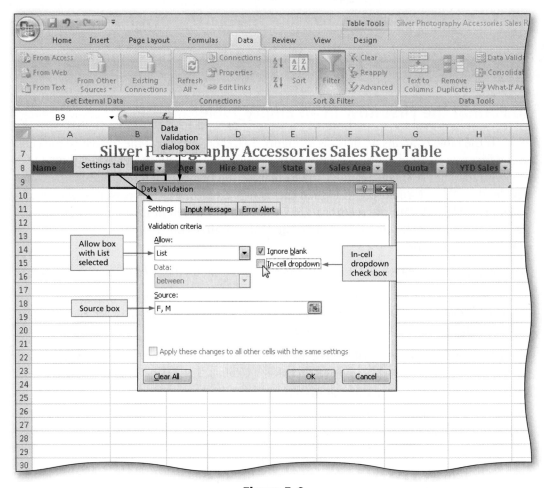

Figure 5–9

3

- Click the Error Alert tab.

- If necessary, click 'Show error alert after invalid data is entered' to select it.

- If necessary, click the Style box arrow and then click Stop in the Style list.

- Type Gender Invalid in the Title text box.

- Type Gender code must be an F or M. in the Error message box (Figure 5–10).

4

- Click the OK button.

Q&A

Why are no changes evident on the worksheet?

No immediate changes appear on the worksheet. If, however, you try to enter any value other than F or M in cell B9, Excel rejects the data and displays the Gender Invalid dialog box created in Step 3.

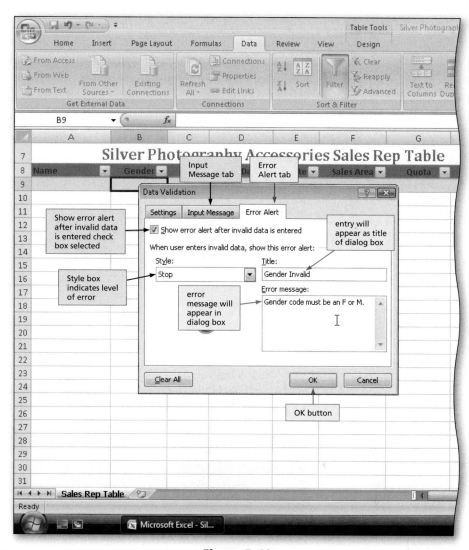

Figure 5–10

Other Ways

1. Press ALT+A, V, V

BTW

Lists
To change an active list back to a normal range of cells, right-click the range, point to Table on the shortcut menu, and then click Convert to Range on the Table submenu.

BTW

Validation
Data validation rules can be mandatory or cautionary. If the rule is mandatory (a Stop), then Excel rejects the cell entry via a dialog box (Figure 5–11) and gives you a chance to correct it. If the rule is cautionary (a Warning), Excel displays a dialog box to warn you of the invalid entry and then gives you a chance to redo the cell entry or leave it as entered.

Data Validation Errors and Criteria

The Style box in the Error Alert sheet shown in Figure 5–10 sets the level of error. Valid entries include Stop, Warning, and Information. Figure 5–11 shows the Gender Invalid dialog box that Excel displays when a user enters a value other than F or M into a cell in the Gender column in the table. The Retry button leaves the invalid value in the cell for you to change. The Cancel button removes the invalid value.

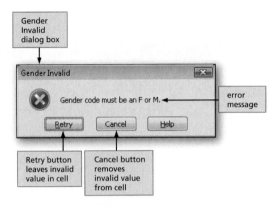

Figure 5–11

BTW

Garbage In Garbage Out (GIGO)
In information processing, the phrase "garbage in, garbage out", or GIGO (pronounced gee-go), is used to describe the output of inaccurate information that results from the input of invalid data.

Excel's built-in data validation features are powerful and easy to use. The different data validation criteria allowed by Excel and summarized in Table 5–2 can be selected in the Allow list in the Settings sheet in the Data Validation dialog box (Figure 5–9 on page EX 348).

Table 5–2 Types of Data Validation Criteria Allowed	
Allows	**Description**
Any value	Allows the user to enter anything in the cell. Any value is the default for all cells in a worksheet.
Whole number	Allows whole numbers in a specific range.
Decimal number	Allows decimal numbers in a specific range.
List	Allows the user to enter only an item from a list. Useful when working with codes, such as M for male and F for female.
Date	Allows a range of dates.
Time	Allows a range of times.
Text length	Allows a certain length of text.
Custom	Allows you to specify a formula that will validate the data entered by the user. For example, the formula <3 would require the cell entry to be less than 3.

BTW

Bypassing Validation
Excel ignores data validation when you paste data from the Office Clipboard or use the mouse to copy by dragging.

Although this chapter validates only the values entered into the Gender column, Table 5–2 shows that you can validate, in one way or another, all of the columns in the Silver Photography Accessories Sales Rep Table. For example, you can validate the data entered in the Age column by establishing limits for a whole number between 18 and 65. Or, you can validate the data entered in the Hire Date column to ensure the user enters a date between 1960 and 2008.

To Modify a Table Quick Style

Before entering records in the table, the quick style that was used to create the table should be modified to make the table more readable. A bold font style with a black font color for the table's entries makes them more readable. The following steps create a new table quick style by copying the Table Style Medium 2 quick style and then modify the new quick style to apply a bold font style and black font color to the entire table.

1

• If necessary, select cell A9 to activate the table.

• Click the Format as Table button on the Home tab on the Ribbon and then right-click the Table Style Medium 2 quick table style to display the shortcut menu (Figure 5–12).

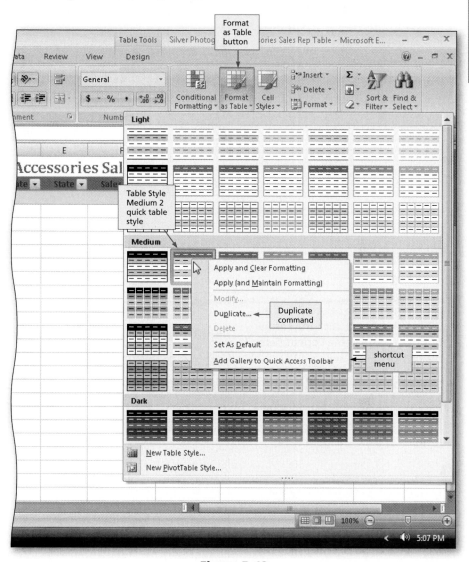

Figure 5–12

● Click Duplicate on the shortcut menu to display the Modify Table Quick Style dialog box.

● When Excel displays the Modify Table Quick Style dialog box, type `TableStyleMedium2 – Custom` in the Name text box (Figure 5–13).

Q&A

What elements of a table can I customize?

The Table Element list in the Modify Table Quick Style dialog box allows you to choose almost any aspect of a table to modify. You can change the formatting for each element listed in the Table Element list by clicking the element and then clicking the Format button to display the Format Cells dialog box with which you are familiar.

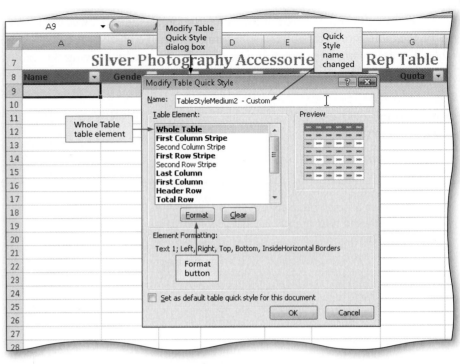

Figure 5–13

● With Whole Table selected in the Table Element list, click the Format button to display the Format Cells dialog box.

● Select Bold in the Font style list.

● Click the Color box arrow and then click the Black, Text 1 color (column 2, row 1) (Figure 5–14).

4

● Click the OK button to close the Format Cells dialog box.

● Click the OK button to close the Modify Table Quick Style dialog box.

● Select the range A8:H8 and then apply the White, Background 1 (column 1, row 1) font color to the range.

Q&A

Why should the color of the header row be changed to white?

The white font color allows the text in the header rows to stand out against the background color of the header row.

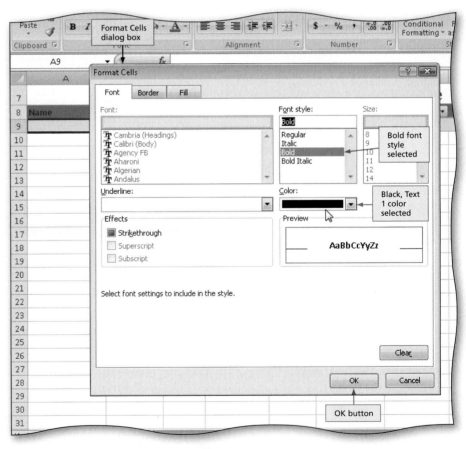

Figure 5–14

To Enter Records into a Table

The next step is to enter the sales reps' records into the table. As indicated earlier, the computational fields in columns I and J will be added after the data is in the table.

1

- If necessary, select cell A9 to activate the table.

- Type sales rep information for row 9 as shown in Figure 5–15. After typing the data for a field, press the RIGHT ARROW key to move to the next field. After you type the YTD sales, press the TAB key to start a new record.

- Type sales rep information for row 10 as shown in Figure 5–15. After typing the data for a field, press the RIGHT ARROW key to move to the next field. After you type the YTD sales, click cell A12 to select it (Figure 5–15).

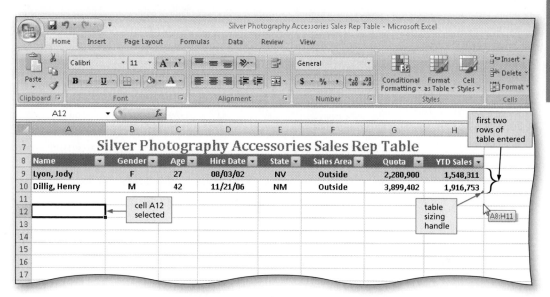

Figure 5–15

Q&A Is row 10 now part of the table?

Yes. Pressing the TAB key adds the next row below the table to the table. Row 10 is now part of the sales rep table.

2

- Drag the table sizing handle to the top of cell H12 to add another row to the table (Figure 5–16).

Q&A Why does row 11 have a different background color than row 10?

The quick style used to create the table includes a type of formatting called row banding. **Row banding** causes adjacent rows to have different formatting so that each record in the table is distinguished from surrounding rows.

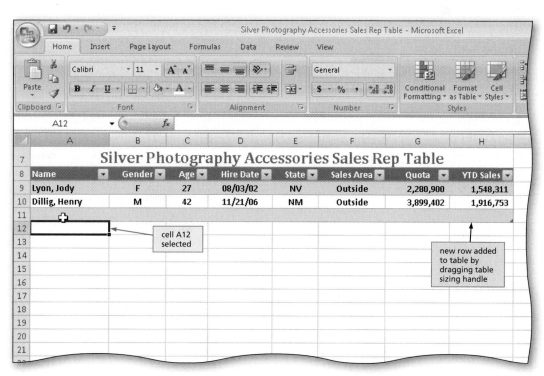

Figure 5–16

3

- Enter the sales rep record for the third sales rep as shown in Figure 5–17.

- Drag the table sizing handle to cell H21 to add 10 new rows to the table (Figure 5–17).

Q&A

Why were all of the rows not added to the table in Step 1?

Steps 1 through 3 demonstrate three different methods of adding rows to a table. The first method can be used when you are adding a number of rows to the table and do not know how many rows you are going to add. The second method can be used when you need to add one additional row to a table that you previously created. The third method can be used when you know exactly how many rows you need in a table.

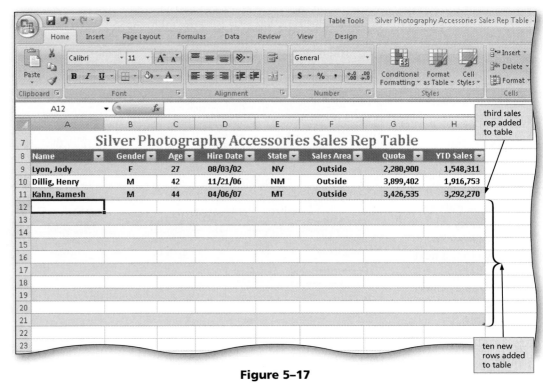

Figure 5–17

4

- Enter the remaining sales reps' records as shown in Figure 5–18.

- Select cell A23 (Figure 5–18).

Q&A

What happens if I enter an invalid Gender code?

If you entered an incorrect Gender code while entering the sales reps' records, then Excel should have displayed the dialog box in Figure 5–11 on page EX 350. After you click the Retry or Cancel button in the error message dialog box, Excel requires you to reenter all values up to and including the value in error.

	Silver Photography Accessories Sales Rep Table						
Name	Gender	Age	Hire Date	State	Sales Area	Quota	YTD Sales
Lyon, Jody	F	27	08/03/02	NV	Outside	2,280,900	1,548,311
Dillig, Henry	M	42	11/21/06	NM	Outside	3,899,402	1,916,753
Kahn, Ramesh	M	44	04/06/07	MT	Outside	3,426,535	3,292,270
Bulger, Gloria	F	25	12/23/02	AZ	Outside	2,651,270	2,451,454
Cataldo, Lydia	F	25	11/15/07	AZ	Inside	3,668,028	2,846,910
Dunn, Alan	M	39	06/06/02	CA	Outside	1,652,836	1,432,701
Brunell, Candace	F	36	06/01/02	CA	Inside	3,000,264	2,078,386
Lambert, Paul	M	35	03/16/02	CA	Outside	1,768,442	1,525,237
Wochos, Lisa	F	30	10/21/07	NV	Inside	2,648,883	2,188,106
Chiu, Leslie	F	36	07/15/07	OR	Inside	3,218,514	2,514,181
Moeller, Pierre	M	24	03/12/01	WA	Outside	3,656,640	3,336,300
Battistini, Jorge	M	26	07/02/01	WA	Inside	3,371,092	1,960,932
Lopez, Maria	F	25	06/03/04	UT	Outside	1,837,213	1,563,140

Figure 5–18

Other Ways

1. Press ALT+J, T

Adding Computational Fields to the Table

The next step is to add the computational fields % of Quota in column I and Grade in column J. The first computational field involves dividing the YTD Sales in column H by the Quota in column G. The second computational field involves a table lookup to determine a grade based upon the % of Quota in column I.

To Add New Fields to a Table

Adding new fields to a table in a worksheet illustrates another of Excel's powerful table capabilities. As shown in the following steps, if you add a new column heading in a column adjacent to the current column headings in the table, then Excel automatically adds the adjacent column to the table's range and copies the format of the table heading to the new column headings. Adding a new row to a table works in a similar manner.

The first step in adding the two new fields is to enter the two column headings, or field names, in cells I8 and J8, enter the first % of Quota formula in cell I9, and then format the two cells immediately below the new column headings. The formula for the % of Quota in cell I9 is YTD Sales / Quota or =H9 / G9. After the formula is entered in cell I9, the formula is automatically copied to the range I10:I21. When you enter a formula in the first row of a field, Excel creates a calculated column. A calculated column is a column in a table in which each row uses a common formula that references other fields in the table.

1

- Select cell I8, type % of Quota, click cell J8, type Grade.

- Select cell I9, enter =h9 / g9 as the formula, and then click the Enter button on the formula bar (Figure 5–19).

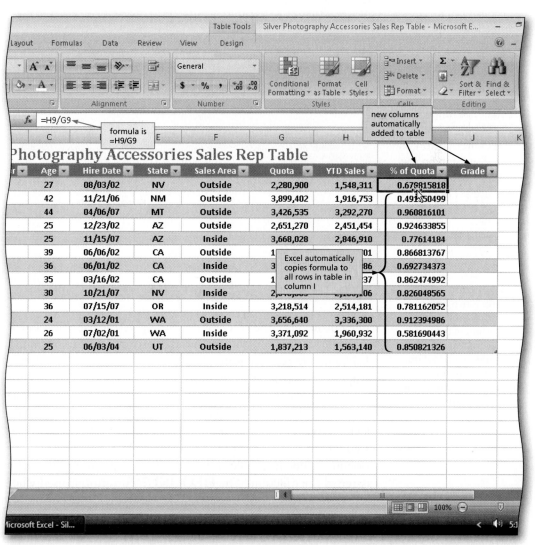

Figure 5–19

2

- Select the range I9:I21 and then click the Percent Style button on the Ribbon. Click the Increase Decimal button on the Ribbon twice.

- Click the Center button on the Ribbon to center the range I9:I21 (Figure 5–20).

- Select the range A7:J7, right-click the selected range, click Format Cells on the shortcut menu, click the Alignment tab, click the Horizontal box arrow, click Center Across Selection, and then click the OK button.

3

- Select the range J9:J21 and then click the Center button on the Home tab on the Ribbon. Select cell J9 to deselect the range J9:J21.

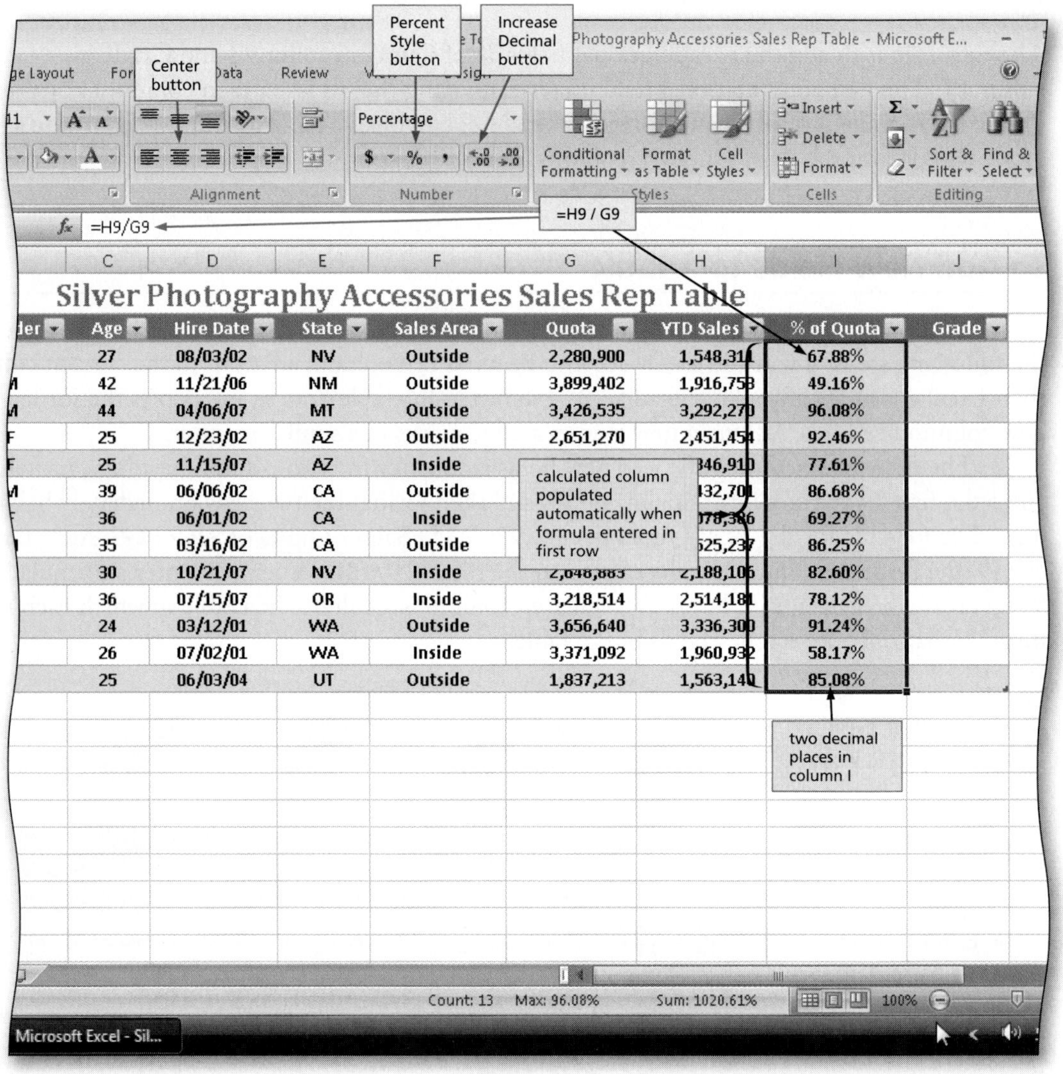

Figure 5–20

Lookup Functions
Lookup functions are powerful, useful, and interesting in the way they work. For additional information on lookup functions, enter **vlookup** in the Search box in the Excel Help window.

Adding a Lookup Table

The entries in the % of Quota column give the user an immediate evaluation of where each sales rep's YTD Sales stand in relation to their annual quota. Many people, however, dislike numbers as an evaluation tool. Most prefer simple letter grades, which, when used properly, can group the sales reps in the same way an instructor groups students by letter grades. Excel contains functions that allow you to assign letter grades based on a table.

Excel has several lookup functions that are useful for looking up values in tables, such as tax tables, discount tables, parts tables, and grade tables. The two most widely used lookup functions are the HLOOKUP and VLOOKUP functions. Both functions look up a value in a table and return a corresponding value from the table to the cell assigned the function. The **HLOOKUP function** is used when the table direction is horizontal, or across the worksheet. The **VLOOKUP function** is used when a table direction is vertical, or down the worksheet. The VLOOKUP function is by far the most often used because most tables are vertical, as is the table in this chapter.

The grading scale in this chapter (Table 5–3) is similar to one that your instructor uses to determine your letter grade. As shown in Table 5–3, any score greater than or equal to 92% equates to a letter grade of A. Scores greater than or equal to 80 and less than 92 are assigned a letter grade of B, and so on.

The VLOOKUP function requires that the table indicate only the lowest score for a letter grade. Furthermore, the table entries must be in sequence from lowest score to highest score. Thus, the entries in Table 5–3 must be resequenced for use with the VLOOKUP function so they appear as shown in Table 5–4.

The general form of the VLOOKUP function is:

=VLOOKUP(lookup_value, table_array, col_index_num)

To Create a Lookup Table

The VLOOKUP function searches the far-left column of the **table array**. The far-left column of the table_array contains what are called the **table arguments**. In this example, the table arguments are made up of percentages (see Table 5–4). The VLOOKUP function uses the % of Quota value (called the lookup_value) in the record of a sales rep to search the far-left column of the table array for a particular value and then returns the corresponding **table value** from the column indicated by the col_index_num value. In this example, the grades are in the second or far-right column.

For the VLOOKUP function to work correctly, the table arguments must be in ascending sequence, because the VLOOKUP function will return a table value based on the lookup_value being less than or equal to the table arguments. Thus, if the % of Quota value is 77.61% (fifth record in table), then the VLOOKUP function returns a grade of C, because 77.61% is greater than or equal to 70% and less than 80%.

The following steps create the grade table in the range L1:M7.

1 Select column headings L and M. Point to the boundary on the right side of the column M heading above row 1 and then drag to the right until the ScreenTip indicates, Width: 11.00 (82 pixels).

2 Select cell L1 and then enter Grade Table as the table title.

3 If necessary, scroll the worksheet to the left and click cell A7 to select it. Scroll the worksheet to the right so that cell L1 is visible. Click the Format Painter button on the Ribbon and then click cell L1. Drag through cell M1 and then click the Merge & Center button on the Home tab on the Ribbon.

4 Select the range I8:J8. While holding down the CTRL key, point to the border of the range I8:J8 and drag to the range L2:M2 to copy the column headings, % of Quota and Grade.

Table 5–3 Typical Grade Table

% of Quota	Grade
92% and higher	A
80% to 91%	B
70% to 79%	C
60% to 69%	D
0 to 59%	F

Table 5–4 Typical Grade Table Modified for VLOOKUP Function

% of Quota	Grade
0	F
60%	D
70%	C
80%	B
92%	A

BTW

The VLOOKUP Function
A score that is outside the range of the table causes the VLOOKUP function to return an error message (#N/A) to the cell. For example, any % of Quota score less than zero in column I of Figure 5–20 would result in the error message #N/A being assigned to the corresponding cell.

5 Enter the table entries in Table 5–4 in the range L3:M7. Select the range L3:M7, click the Bold button on the Ribbon, and then click the Center button on the Ribbon. Select cell J9 to deselect the range L3:M7 (Figure 5–21).

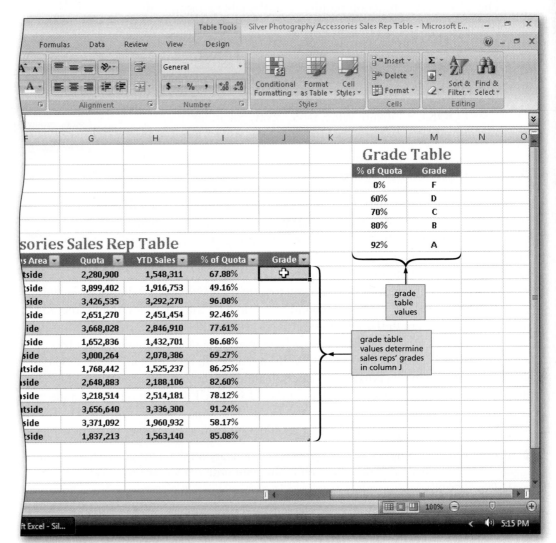

Figure 5–21

BTW

Sensitive Information in a List
If you have a list with one or more columns of sensitive information, such as salary information, you can hide the columns by selecting them and then pressing CTRL+0. Next, password protect the worksheet. To view the hidden columns, unprotect the worksheet, select the two adjacent columns, and then press CTRL+SHIFT+RIGHT PARENTHESIS.

To Use the VLOOKUP Function to Determine Letter Grades

The following steps show how to use the VLOOKUP function and the grade table to determine the letter grade for each sales rep based on the sales rep's % of Quota value. In this case, cell I9 is the lookup_value; $L$3:$M$7 is the table_array; and 2 is the col_index_num in the table_array.

1

- With cell J9 selected, type =vlookup(i9, l3:m7, 2 as the cell entry (Figure 5–22).

Q&A

Why are absolute cell references used in the function?

It is most important that you use absolute cell references ($) for the table_array ($L$3:$M$7) in the VLOOKUP function or Excel will not adjust the cell references when it creates the calculated column in the next step. This will cause unexpected results in column J.

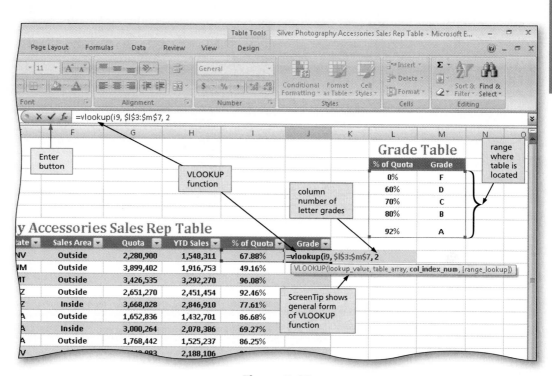

Figure 5–22

2

- Click the Enter button to create a calculated column for the Grade field (Figure 5–23).

Q&A

What happens when the Enter button is clicked?

Because the cell I9 is the first record in a table, Excel creates a calculated column in column I by copying the VLOOKUP function through row 21. As shown in Figure 5–23, any % of Quota value below 60 in column I returns a grade of F in column J. The 13th record (Lopez in row 21) receives a grade of B because its % of Quota value is 85.08%. A % of Quota value of 92% is required to move up to the next letter grade. The second record (Dillig) receives a grade of F because his % of Quota value is 49.16%, which is less than 60%.

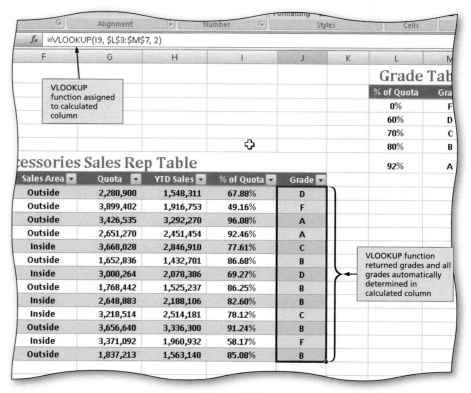

Figure 5–23

- Scroll the worksheet so that row 7 is the top row and then select cell A23 to show the completed sales rep table (Figure 5–24).

Q&A

How is the VLOOKUP function determining the grades?

From column J, you can see that the VLOOKUP function is not searching for a table argument that matches the lookup_ value exactly. The VLOOKUP function begins the search at the top of the table and works down- ward. As soon as it finds the first table argument greater than the lookup_ value, it returns the previous table value. The letter grade of F is returned for any value greater than or equal to 0 (zero) and less than 60. A score less than 0 returns an error message (#N/A) to the cell assigned the VLOOKUP function.

Name	Gender	Age	Hire Date	State	Sales Area	Quota	YTD Sales	% of Quota	Grade
Lyon, Jody	F	27	08/03/02	NV	Outside	2,280,900	1,548,311	67.88%	D
Dillig, Henry	M	42	11/21/06	NM	Outside	3,899,402	1,916,753	49.16%	F
Kahn, Ramesh	M	44	04/06/07	MT	Outside	3,426,535	3,292,270	96.08%	A
Bulger, Gloria	F	25	12/23/02	AZ	Outside	2,651,270	2,451,454	92.46%	A
Cataldo, Lydia	F	25	11/15/07	AZ	Inside	3,668,028	2,846,910	77.61%	C
Dunn, Alan	M	39	06/06/02	CA	Outside	1,652,836	1,432,701	86.68%	B
Brunell, Candace	F	36	06/01/02	CA	Inside	3,000,264	2,078,386	69.27%	D
Lambert, Paul	M	35	03/16/02	CA	Outside	1,768,442	1,525,237	86.25%	B
Wochos, Lisa	F	30	10/21/07	NV	Inside	2,648,883	2,188,106	82.60%	B
Chiu, Leslie	F	36	07/15/07	OR	Inside	3,218,514	2,514,181	78.12%	C
Moeller, Pierre	M	24	03/12/01	WA	Outside	3,656,640	3,336,300	91.24%	B
Battistini, Jorge	M	26	07/02/01	WA	Inside	3,371,092	1,960,932	58.17%	F
Lopez, Maria	F	25	06/03/04	UT	Outside	1,837,213	1,563,140	85.08%	B

table is complete

Figure 5–24

Other Ways

1. Click Insert Function box in formula bar, click 'Or select a category' box arrow, click Lookup & Reference, click VLOOKUP in 'Select a function' list
2. Click Formulas tab on Ribbon, click Lookup & Reference button, click VLOOKUP

BTW

Using HLOOKUP
HLOOKUP uses the same arguments as VLOOKUP, but searches rows of information instead of columns. HLOOKUP also uses the row_index_num argument instead of the col_index_num argu- ment, as shown in Figure 5–22 on page EX 359. When using HLOOKUP, be sure to sort the values in the first row of the table_array in ascending order to find an approximate match. Otherwise, specify FALSE as the range_lookup to find an exact match.

Guidelines for Creating a Table in Excel

When you create a table in Excel, you should follow some basic guidelines, as listed in Table 5–5.

Table 5–5 Guidelines for Creating a Table in Excel

Table Size and Workbook Location

1. Do not enter more than one table per worksheet.

2. Maintain at least one blank row between a table and other worksheet entries.

3. A table can have a maximum of 16,384 fields and 1,048,576 records on a worksheet.

Column Headings (Field Names)

1. Place column headings (field names) in the first row of the table.

2. Do not use blank rows or rows with dashes to separate the column headings (field names) from the data.

3. Apply a different format to the column headings and the data. For example, bold the column headings and format the data below the column headings using a regular style. Most quick table styles follow these guidelines.

4. Column headings (field names) can be up to 32,767 characters in length. The column headings should be meaningful.

Contents of Table

1. Each column should have similar data. For example, Hire Date should be in the same column for all sales reps.

2. Format the data to improve readability, but do not vary the format of the data in a column.

Conditional Formatting

Excel provides a variety of formatting options for visually representing the value in a cell based on its value. Conditional formatting allows you to create rules that change the formatting of a cell or range of cells based on the value of a cell. Excel includes five types of conditional formats: highlight, top and bottom rules, data bars, color scales, and icon sets. You can combine different types of formats on any cell or range. For example, based on a cells value, you can format it to include both an icon and a specific background color. You also can apply multiple conditional formatting rules to a cell or range.

The Conditional Formatting Rules Manager dialog box allows you to view all of the rules for the current selection or for the entire workbook. You open the dialog box by clicking the Conditional Formatting button on the Home tab on the Ribbon and then clicking the Manage Rules command on the Conditional Formatting menu. The dialog box also allows you to view and change the order in which the rules are applied to a cell or range. You also can stop the application of subsequent rules after one rule is found to be true. For example, if the first rule specifies that a negative value in the cell results in a red background color applied to the cell, then you may not want to apply any other conditional formats to the cell. In this case, put a check mark in the Stop If True column for the rule in the Conditional Formatting Rules Manager dialog box.

The project in this chapter uses an icon set as a type of conditional format. The exercises at the end of this chapter include instructions regarding the use of other types of conditional formats.

To Add a Conditional Formatting Rule with an Icon Set

The Grade field was added to the table in order to provide a visual cue to the user of the worksheet regarding each sales rep's performance. One method to achieve a similar result is to display an icon next to the % of Quota percentage for each sales rep. Conditional formatting provides a number of icons, including icons with the appearance of traffic signals, flags, bars, and arrows. Icon sets include sets of three, four, or five icons. You use an icon set depending on how many ways you need to group your data. For example, in the case of grades for the sales reps, there are five different grades and, therefore, an icon set that includes five icons should be used. You define rules for the conditions under which each icon of the five is displayed in a cell. The following steps add a conditional format to the % of Quota field in the Sales Rep table.

- Select the range I9:I21 and then click the Conditional Formatting button on the Home tab on the Ribbon.

- Click New Rule on the Conditional Formatting menu.

- When the New Formatting Rule dialog box is displayed, click the Format Style box arrow and point to Icon Sets in the list (Figure 5–25).

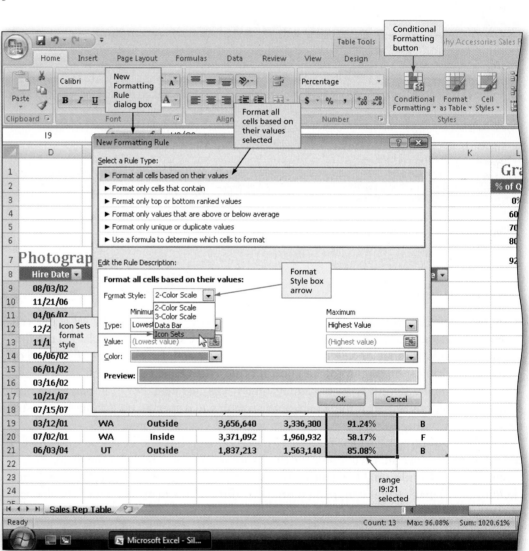

Figure 5–25

- Click Icon Sets in the list to display the Icon area in the Edit the Rule Description area.

- Click the Icon Style box arrow to display the Icon Style list and then scroll and point to 5 Arrows (Colored) in the list (Figure 5–26).

Experiment

- Click a variety of icon styles in the Icon Styles list to view the options in the Edit the Rule Description area for each option.

❸

- Click 5 Arrows (Colored) in the list.

- Click the top Type box arrow and then click Number in the list.

- Change the Type to Number for the remaining Type boxes.

- Type 0.92 in the first Value box, 0.8 in the second Value box, and 0.7 in the third Value box.

- Type 0.6 in the final Value box and then press the TAB key to complete the conditions (Figure 5–27).

Q&A

Why do the numbers next to each icon change as I type?

The area below the word Icon represents the current conditional formatting rule. Excel automatically updates this area as you change the conditions on the right side of the Edit the Rule Description area. Use this area as an easy-to-read status of the conditions that you are creating.

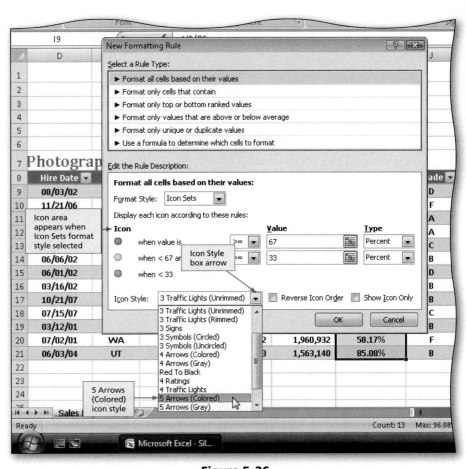

Figure 5–26

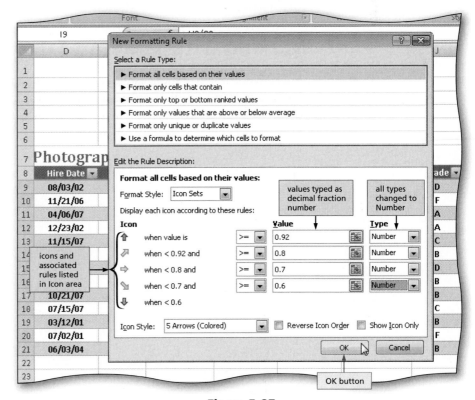

Figure 5–27

4

- Click the OK button to display icons in each row of the table in the % of Quota field.

- Select cell A23 (Figure 5–28).

Q&A

What do the icons represent?

In addition to the Grade field, the conditional formatting icons provide a visual representation of the sales reps' progress on attaining their sales quotas. The green arrow and its direction represents a grade of A, the red arrow and its direction a grade of F, and the three different yellow arrows and their directions represent the B, C, and D levels.

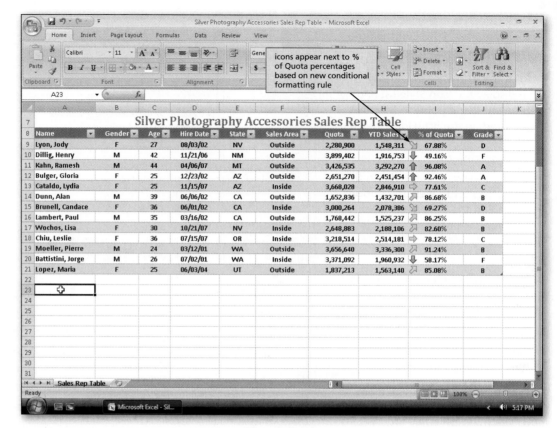

Figure 5–28

Working with Tables in Excel

When a table is active, the Design tab on the Ribbon provides powerful commands that allow you to alter the appearance and contents of a table quickly. This section explores the use of some of these commands, such as toggling total and header rows in a table.

To Use the Total Row Check Box

The Total Row check box on the Design tab allows you to insert a row at the bottom of the table called the **total row**. Within the total row, it sums the values in the far-right column of the table, if the values are numeric. If the values in the far-right column of the table are text, then Excel counts the number of records. For example, in Figure 5–30 on the next page, the 13 in cell J22 on the right side of the total row is a count of the number of sales rep records. Excel provides additional computations for the total row, as shown in the following steps.

1

• Select cell A9 to make the table active and then click the Design tab on the Ribbon (Figure 5–29).

🔎 **Experiment**

• Select a variety of combinations of check boxes in the Table Styles Options group on the Design tab on the Ribbon. When finished, make sure that the check boxes are set as shown in Figure 5–29.

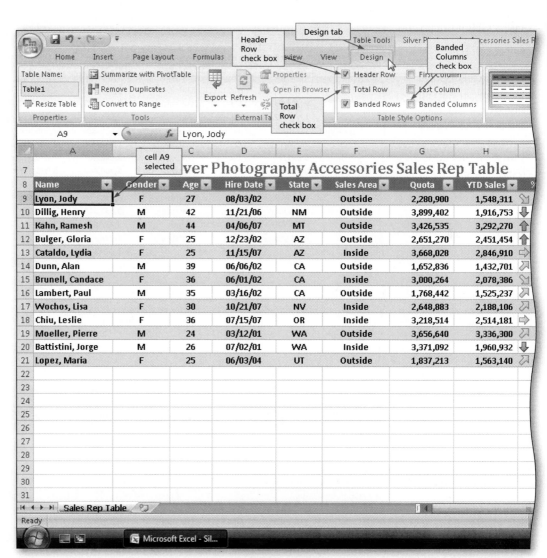

Figure 5–29

2

- Click the Total Row check box on the Ribbon to add the total row and display the record count in the far-right column of the table, column J.

- Select cell H22.

- When Excel displays an arrow on the right side of the cell, click the arrow to display a list of available statistical functions (Figure 5–30).

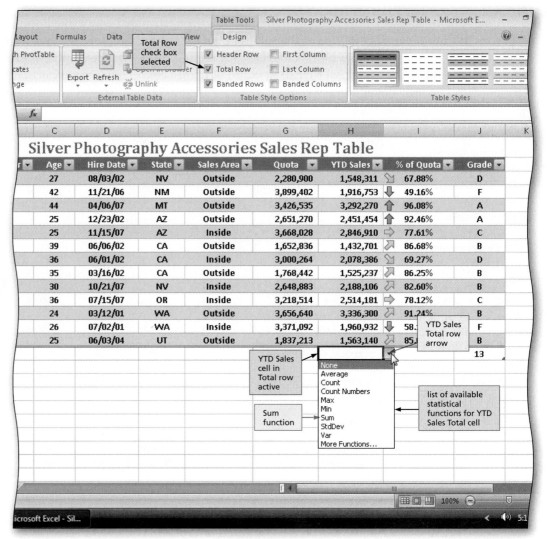

Figure 5–30

3

- Click Sum in the list.

- Select cell G22, click the arrow on the right side of the cell, and then click Sum in the list.

- Select cell C22, click the arrow on the right side of the cell, and then click Average in the list.

- Select cell A9 (Figure 5–31).

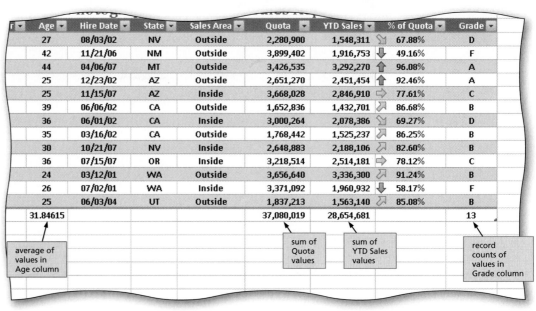

Figure 5–31

4

- Click the Total Row check box on the Ribbon to hide the total row (Figure 5–32).

Experiment

- Click the Header Row, Banded Rows, and Banded Columns check boxes on the Ribbon. When finished viewing the formatting caused by checking these check boxes, uncheck the check boxes.

Q&A

What are banded columns?

As you have learned, banded rows include alternating colors every other row. Similarly, banded columns provide alternating colors every other column. You also can include a different color for the first and/or last column in a table. The quick style that you choose for a table must have these colors defined in the quick style. The quick style used in this chapter does not include special formatting for the first and last columns.

	A	B	C	D	E	F	G	H	
7				Silver Photography Accessories Sales Rep Table					
8	Name	Gender	Age	Hire Date	State	Sales Area	Quota	YTD Sales	
9	Lyon, Jody	F	27	08/03/02	NV	Outside	2,280,900	1,548,311	
10	Dillig, Henry	M	42	11/21/06	NM	Outside	3,899,402	1,916,753	
11	Kahn, Ramesh	M	44	04/06/07	MT	Outside	3,426,535	3,292,270	
12	Bulger, Gloria	F	25	12/23/02	AZ	Outside	2,651,270	2,451,454	
13	Cataldo, Lydia	F	25	11/15/07	AZ	Inside	3,668,028	2,846,910	
14	Dunn, Alan	M	39	06/06/02	CA	Outside	1,652,836	1,432,701	
15	Brunell, Candace	F	36	06/01/02	CA	Inside	3,000,264	2,078,386	
16	Lambert, Paul	M	35	03/16/02	CA	Outside	1,768,442	1,525,237	
17	Wochos, Lisa	F	30	10/21/07	NV	Inside	2,648,883	2,188,106	
18	Chiu, Leslie	F	36	07/15/07	OR	Inside	3,218,514	2,514,181	
19	Moeller, Pierre	M	24	03/12/01	WA	Outside	3,656,640	3,336,300	
20	Battistini, Jorge	M	26	07/02/01	WA	Inside	3,371,092	1,960,932	
21	Lopez, Maria	F	25	06/03/04	UT	Outside	1,837,213	1,563,140	

Total row hidden

Figure 5–32

To Print the Table

When a table is selected and you display the Print dialog box, an option appears that allows you to print just the contents of the active table. The following steps print the table in landscape orientation using the Fit to option.

- Select cell A9 to make the table active and then click the Page Layout tab on the Ribbon.

- Click the Page Setup Dialog Box Launcher to display the Page Setup dialog box.

- When Excel displays the Page Setup dialog box, click Landscape in the Orientation area and then click Fit to in the Scaling area.

- Click the Print button to display the Print dialog box. When Excel displays the Print dialog box, click Table in the Print what area (Figure 5–33).

- Click the OK button to print the table (Figure 5–34).

- Click the Page Setup Dialog Box Launcher to display the Page Setup dialog box. Click Portrait in the Orientation area and then click Adjust to in the Scaling area.

- Click the OK button to close the Page Setup dialog box.

Figure 5–33

Name	Gender	Age	Hire Date	State	Sales Area	Quota	YTD Sales	% of Quota	Grade
Lyon, Jody	F	27	08/03/02	NV	Outside	2,280,900	1,548,311	67.88%	D
Dillig, Henry	M	42	11/21/06	NM	Outside	3,899,402	1,916,753	49.16%	F
Kahn, Ramesh	M	44	04/06/07	MT	Outside	3,426,535	3,292,270	96.08%	A
Bulger, Gloria	F	25	12/23/02	AZ	Outside	2,651,270	2,451,454	92.46%	A
Cataldo, Lydia	F	25	11/15/07	AZ	Inside	3,668,028	2,846,910	77.61%	C
Dunn, Alan	M	39	06/06/02	CA	Outside	1,652,836	1,432,701	86.68%	B
Brunell, Candace	F	36	06/01/02	CA	Inside	3,000,264	2,078,386	69.27%	D
Lambert, Paul	M	35	03/16/02	CA	Outside	1,768,442	1,525,237	86.25%	B
Wochos, Lisa	F	30	10/21/07	NV	Inside	2,648,883	2,188,106	82.60%	B
Chiu, Leslie	F	36	07/15/07	OR	Inside	3,218,514	2,514,181	78.12%	C
Moeller, Pierre	M	24	03/12/01	WA	Outside	3,656,640	3,336,300	91.24%	B
Battistini, Jorge	M	26	07/02/01	WA	Inside	3,371,092	1,960,932	58.17%	F
Lopez, Maria	F	25	06/03/04	UT	Outside	1,837,213	1,563,140	85.08%	B

Figure 5–34

Sorting a Table

The data in a table is easier to work with and more meaningful if the records are arranged sequentially based on one or more fields. Arranging records in a specific sequence is called **sorting**. Data is in **ascending sequence** if it is in order from lowest to highest, earliest to most recent, or alphabetically from A to Z. For example, the records in the Silver Photography Accessories Sales Rep table were entered in no particular order. Data is in **descending sequence** if it is sorted from highest to lowest, most recent to earliest, or alphabetically from Z to A. The field or fields you select to sort the records are called **sort keys**.

You can sort data in a table using one of the following techniques:

1. Select a cell in the field on which to sort, click the Sort & Filter button on the Home tab on the Ribbon, and then click one of the sorting options on the Sort & Filter menu.

2. With the table active, click the column heading arrow in the column on which to sort and then click one of the sorting options in the table.

3. Use the Sort button on the Data tab on the Ribbon.

4. Right-click anywhere in a table and then point to Sort on the shortcut menu to display the Sort submenu.

To Sort a Table in Ascending Sequence by Name Using the Sort & Filter Button

The following example shows how to sort the table in ascending sequence by name using the Sort & Filter button on the Home tab on the Ribbon.

1

- If necessary, click the Home tab on the Ribbon.

- Select cell A9, click the Sort & Filter button on the Ribbon, and then point to the Sort A to Z command on the Sort & Filter menu (Figure 5–35).

Q&A

What if the column I choose includes numeric or date data?

If the column you choose includes numeric data, then the Sort & Filter menu would show the Sort Smallest to Largest and Sort Largest to Smallest commands instead of the Sort A to Z and Sort Z to A commands. If the column you choose includes date data, then the Sort & Filter menu would show the Sort Oldest to Newest and Sort Newest to Oldest commands instead of the Sort A to Z and Sort Z to A commands.

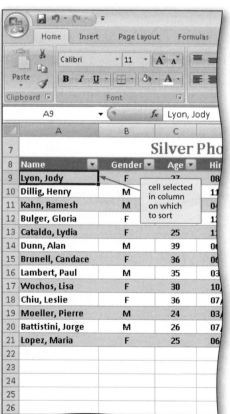
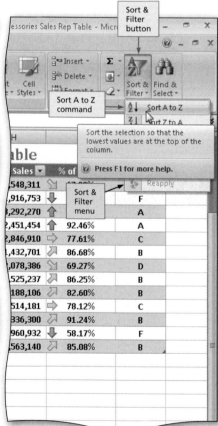

Figure 5–35

2

- Click the Sort A to Z command to sort the sales rep table in ascending sequence by name (Figure 5–36).

Experiment

- Select other fields in the table and use the same procedure to sort on the fields you choose. When you are finished, select cell A9 and repeat the first task in step 2 above.

Other Ways

1. Select field in table, on Data tab on the Ribbon click Sort A to Z button
2. Click column heading arrow of field on which to sort, click Sort A to Z
3. Right-click column to sort, point to Sort on shortcut menu, click Sort A to Z
4. Press ALT+A, A

A9			*fx*	Battistini, Jorge		

	A	B	C	D	E	F	G
7				Silver Photography Accessories Sales Re			
8	Name	Gender	Age	Hire Date	State	Sales Area	Quota
9	Battistini, Jorge	M	26	07/02/01	WA	Inside	3,371,092
10	Brunell, Candace	F	36	06/01/02	CA	Inside	3,000,264
11	Bulger, Gloria	F	25	12/23/02	AZ	Outside	2,651,270
12	Cataldo, Lydia	F	25	11/15/07	AZ	Inside	3,668,028
13	Chiu, Leslie	F	36	07/15/07	OR	Inside	3,218,514
14	Dillig, Henry	M	42	11/21/06	NM	Outside	3,899,402
15	Dunn, Alan	M	39	06/06/02	CA	Outside	1,652,836
16	Kahn, Ramesh	M	44	04/06/07	MT	Outside	3,426,535
17	Lambert, Paul	M	35	03/16/02	CA	Outside	1,768,442
18	Lopez, Maria	F	25	06/03/04	UT	Outside	1,837,213
19	Lyon, Jody	F	27	08/03/02	NV	Outside	2,280,900
20	Moeller, Pierre	M	24	03/12/01	WA	Outside	3,656,640
21	Wochos, Lisa	F	30	10/21/07	NV	Inside	2,648,883
22							

records sorted in ascending sequence by name

Figure 5–36

To Sort a Table in Descending Sequence by Name Using the Sort Z to A button on the Data Tab

The following steps show how to sort the records in descending sequence by name.

1 If necessary, select cell A9.

2 Click the Data tab on the Ribbon.

3 Click the Sort Z to A button on the Ribbon to sort the sales rep table in descending sequence by name (Figure 5–37).

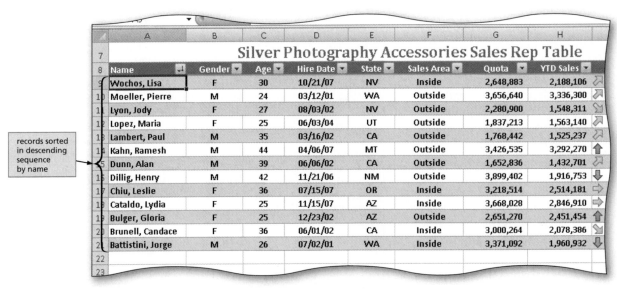

records sorted in descending sequence by name

	A	B	C	D	E	F	G	H
7				Silver Photography Accessories Sales Rep Table				
8	Name	Gender	Age	Hire Date	State	Sales Area	Quota	YTD Sales
9	Wochos, Lisa	F	30	10/21/07	NV	Inside	2,648,883	2,188,106
10	Moeller, Pierre	M	24	03/12/01	WA	Outside	3,656,640	3,336,300
11	Lyon, Jody	F	27	08/03/02	NV	Outside	2,280,900	1,548,311
12	Lopez, Maria	F	25	06/03/04	UT	Outside	1,837,213	1,563,140
13	Lambert, Paul	M	35	03/16/02	CA	Outside	1,768,442	1,525,237
14	Kahn, Ramesh	M	44	04/06/07	MT	Outside	3,426,535	3,292,270
15	Dunn, Alan	M	39	06/06/02	CA	Outside	1,652,836	1,432,701
16	Dillig, Henry	M	42	11/21/06	NM	Outside	3,899,402	1,916,753
17	Chiu, Leslie	F	36	07/15/07	OR	Inside	3,218,514	2,514,181
18	Cataldo, Lydia	F	25	11/15/07	AZ	Inside	3,668,028	2,846,910
19	Bulger, Gloria	F	25	12/23/02	AZ	Outside	2,651,270	2,451,454
20	Brunell, Candace	F	36	06/01/02	CA	Inside	3,000,264	2,078,386
21	Battistini, Jorge	M	26	07/02/01	WA	Inside	3,371,092	1,960,932
22								
23								

Figure 5–37

To Sort a Table Using the Sort Command on a Column Heading AutoFilter Menu

The following step shows how to sort the table by hire date using the Sort Ascending command on a column heading list.

1

- If necessary, click the Home tab on the Ribbon.

- Click the Hire Date arrow to display the Hire Date AutoFilter menu (Figure 5–38).

- Click Sort Oldest to Newest in the Hire Date AutoFilter menu to sort the table in ascending sequence by hire date.

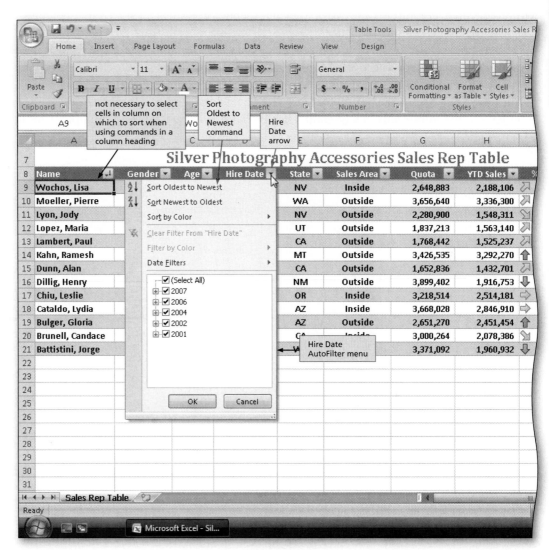

Figure 5–38

Other Ways

1. Select field in table, on Data tab on Ribbon click Sort Oldest to Newest button
2. Right-click column to sort, point to Sort on shortcut menu, click Sort Oldest to Newest
3. Press ALT+A, D

To Sort a Table on Multiple Fields Using the Custom Sort Command

Excel allows you to sort on many fields in a single sort operation. You can sort on a maximum of 256 fields in a single sort operation. For instance, the sort example that follows uses the Custom Sort command on the Sort & Filter menu to sort the Silver Photography Accessories Sales Rep table by quota (column G) within gender (column B) within sales area (column F). The Sales Area and Gender fields will be sorted in ascending sequence; the Quota field will be sorted in descending sequence.

The phrase, sort by quota within gender within sales area, means that the records in the table first are arranged in ascending sequence by sales area (Inside and Outside). Within sales area, the records are arranged in ascending sequence by gender (M or F). Within gender, the records are arranged in descending sequence by the sales rep's quota. In this case, Sales Area is the **major sort key** (Sort by field), Gender is the **intermediate sort key** (first Then by field), and Quota is the **minor sort key** (second Then by field). Sorting a table on multiple fields is illustrated below.

1

- With a cell in the table active, click the Sort & Filter button on the Home tab on the Ribbon to display the Sort & Filter menu (Figure 5–39).

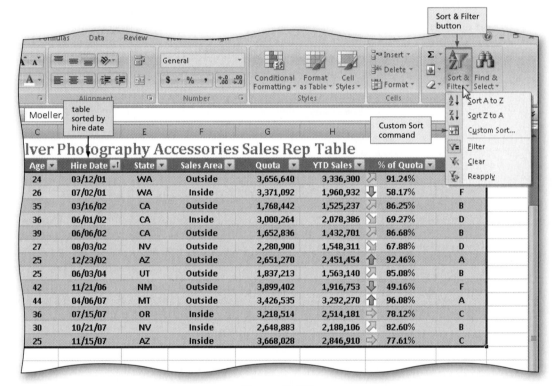

Figure 5–39

2

- Click the Custom Sort command on the Sort & Filter menu to display the Sort dialog box.

- When Excel displays the Sort dialog box, click the Sort by box arrow to display the field names in the table (Figure 5–40).

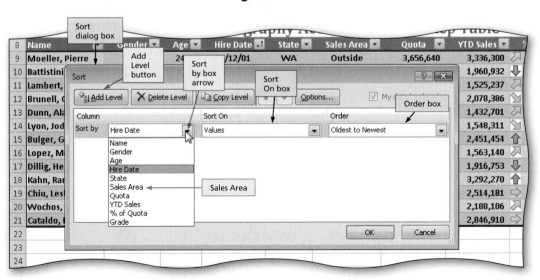

Figure 5–40

3

- Click Sales Area. If necessary, select Values in the Sort On box. If necessary, select A to Z in the Order box.

- Click the Add Level button.

- Click the Then by box arrow and then click Gender in the Then by list. If necessary, select Values in the Sort On box, and if necessary, select A to Z in the Order box.

- Click the Add Level button.

- Click the second Then by box arrow and then click Quota in the Then by list. If necessary, select Values in the Sort On box. Select Largest to Smallest in the Order box (Figure 5–41).

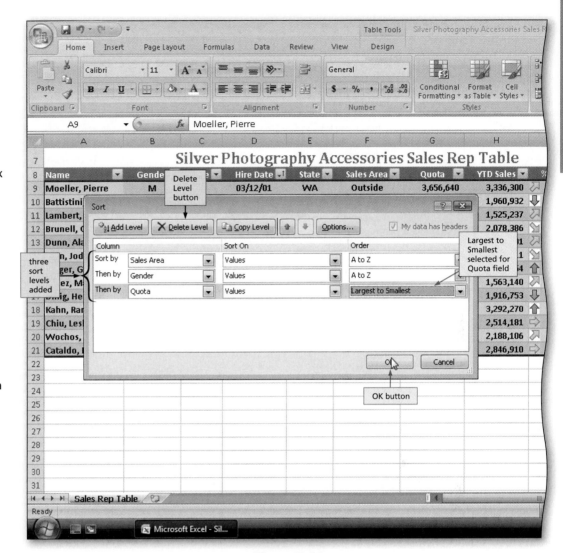

Figure 5–41

4

- Click the OK button to sort the table by quota within gender within sales area (Figure 5–42).

How are the records sorted?

As shown in Figure 5–42, Excel sorts the records in ascending sequence by sales area in column F. Within each sales area, the records are in ascending sequence by gender in column B. Finally, within gender, the records are sorted in descending sequence by the quotas in column G. Remember, if you make a mistake in a sort operation, you can return the records to their original order by clicking the Undo button on the Quick Access Toolbar or by sorting the table by hire date.

within each sales area, records are in ascending sequence by gender

records are in ascending sequence by sales area

within each gender type, records are in descending sequence by quota

Silver Photography Accessories Sales Rep Table

Name	Gender	Age	Hire Date	State	Sales Area	Quota	YTD Sales
Cataldo, Lydia	F	25	11/15/07	AZ	Inside	3,668,028	2,846,910
Chiu, Leslie	F	36	07/15/07	OR	Inside	3,218,514	2,514,181
Brunell, Candace	F	36	06/01/02	CA	Inside	3,000,264	2,078,386
Wochos, Lisa	F	30	10/21/07	NV	Inside	2,648,883	2,188,106
Battistini, Jorge	M	26	07/02/01	WA	Inside	3,371,092	1,960,932
Bulger, Gloria	F	25	12/23/02	AZ	Outside	2,651,270	2,451,454
Lyon, Jody	F	27	08/03/02	NV	Outside	2,280,900	1,548,311
Lopez, Maria	F	25	06/03/04	UT	Outside	1,837,213	1,563,140
Dillig, Henry	M	42	11/21/06	NM	Outside	3,899,402	1,916,753
Moeller, Pierre	M	24	03/12/01	WA	Outside	3,656,640	3,336,300
Kahn, Ramesh	M	44	04/06/07	MT	Outside	3,426,535	3,292,270
Lambert, Paul	M	35	03/16/02	CA	Outside	1,768,442	1,525,237
Dunn, Alan	M	39	06/06/02	CA	Outside	1,652,836	1,432,701

Sales Rep Table

Ready

Microsoft Excel - Sil...

Figure 5–42

5

- After viewing the sorted table, click the Hire Date arrow and then click Sort Oldest to Newest in the Hire Date AutoFilter menu to sort the table into its original sequence.

Other Ways

1. Click minor field column heading arrow, click Sort Z to A button on Data tab on Ribbon, click intermediate field column heading arrow, click Sort A to Z button on Data tab on Ribbon, click major field column heading arrow, click Sort A to Z button on Data tab on Ribbon
2. Press ALT+A, S

Displaying Automatic Subtotals in a Table

Displaying **automatic subtotals** is a powerful tool for summarizing data in a table. To display automatic subtotals, Excel requires that you sort the table on the field on which the subtotals will be based, convert the table to a range, and then use the Subtotal button on the Data tab on the Ribbon. When Excel displays the Subtotal dialog box, you select the subtotal function you want to use.

The field on which you sort prior to clicking the Subtotal button is called the **control field**. When the control field changes, Excel displays a subtotal for the numeric fields selected in the Subtotal dialog box. For example, if you sort on the State field and request subtotals for the Quota and YTD Sales fields, then Excel recalculates the subtotal and grand total each time the State field changes. The most common subtotal used with the Subtotals command is the SUM function, which causes Excel to display a sum each time the control field changes.

To Display Automatic Subtotals in a Table

In addition to displaying subtotals, Excel also creates an outline for the table. The following steps show how to display subtotals for the Quota field and YTD Sales field by state.

1

- Click the State arrow in cell E8 and then click Sort A to Z in the State AutoFilter menu to sort the table in ascending order by State.

- With cell A9 active, right-click anywhere in the table and then point to the Table command on the shortcut menu to display the Table submenu (Figure 5–43).

Q&A

Why does the table need to be converted to a range?

It is most important that you convert the table to a range before attempting to click the Subtotal button. If the table is not converted to a range, then the Subtotal button on the Data tab on the Ribbon is dimmed (not available).

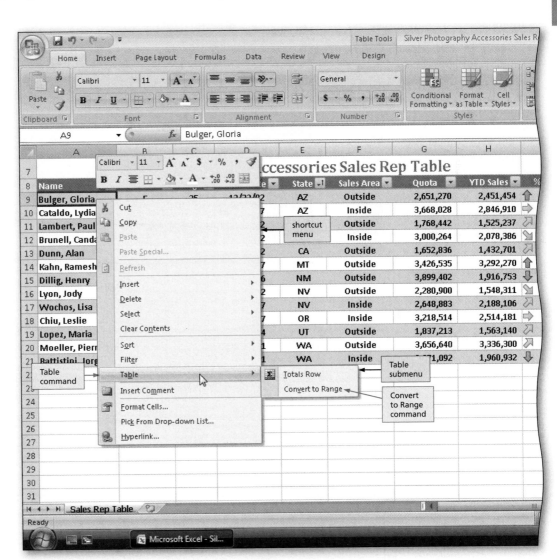

Figure 5–43

2

- Click the Convert to Range command on the Table submenu.

- When Excel displays the Microsoft Excel dialog box, click the Yes button to convert the table to a range.

- Click the Data tab on the Ribbon and then click the Subtotal button on the Ribbon to display the Subtotal dialog box.

- When Excel displays the Subtotal dialog box, click the 'At each change in' box arrow and then click State.

- If necessary, select Sum in the Use function list.

- In the 'Add subtotal to' list, click Grade to clear it and then click Quota and YTD Sales to select them (Figure 5–44).

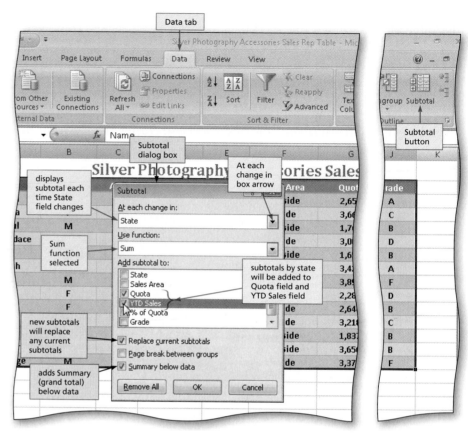

Figure 5–44

3

- Click the OK button to add subtotals to the range (Figure 5–45).

 Q&A

What changes does Excel make to the worksheet?

As shown in Figure 5–45, Excel adds eight subtotal rows and one grand total row to the table, including one subtotal for each different state and one grand total row for the entire table. The names for each subtotal row are derived from the state names and appear in bold. Thus, the text, AZ Total, in cell E11 identifies the subtotal row that contains Quota and YTD Sales totals for Arizona.

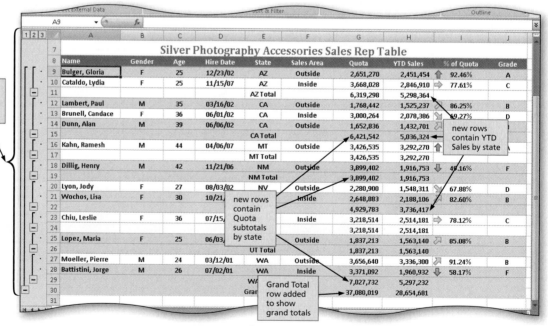

Figure 5–45

Other Ways

1. Press ALT+A, B

To Zoom Out on a Subtotaled Table and Use the Outline Feature

The following steps show how to use the Zoom Out button on the status bar to reduce the magnification of the worksheet so that the table is more readable. The steps also illustrate how to use the outline features of Excel to hide and unhide data and totals.

1
- Click the Zoom Out button on the status bar once to reduce the zoom percent to 90% (Figure 5–46).

2
- Click the row level symbol 2 on the left side of the window to hide all detail rows and display only the subtotal and grand total rows (Figure 5–47).

Q&A

How can I use the outlining features?

By utilizing the **outlining features** of Excel, you quickly can hide and show detail rows. You can click the **row level symbols** to expand or collapse rows in the worksheet. Row level symbol 1, immediately below the Name box, hides all rows except the Grand Total row. Row level symbol 2 hides the detail records so the subtotal rows and Grand Total row appear as shown in Figure 5–47. Row level symbol 3 shows all rows.

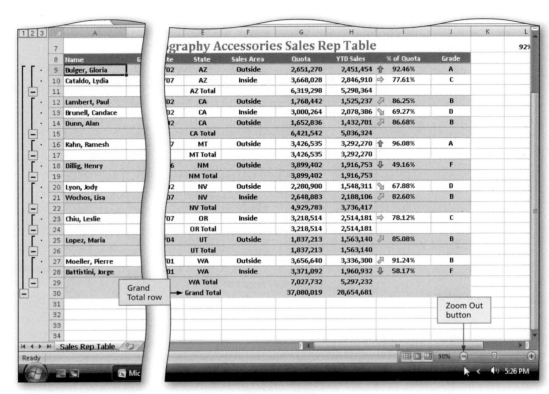

Figure 5–46

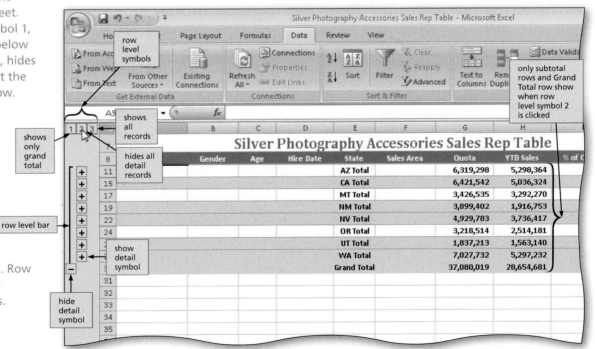

Figure 5–47

- Click each of the lower three show detail symbols (+) on the left side of the window to display detail records for OR, UT, and WA and change the show detail symbols to hide detail symbols (Figure 5–48).

④

- Click the row level symbol 3 on the left side of the window to show all detail rows.

- Click the Zoom In button on the status bar once to change the zoom percent back to 100%.

Q&A

Can I group and outline without subtotals?

Yes. You do not have to use the Subtotals button to outline a worksheet. You can outline a worksheet by using the Group button on the Data tab on the Ribbon. Usually, however, the Group button is useful only when you already have total lines in a worksheet.

Other Ways

1. To group and outline, on Data tab on Ribbon, click Group, click Group

2. To group and outline, press ALT+A, B

3. To zoom, hold CTRL key while scrolling Intellimouse wheel towards you

4. To zoom, press ALT+W, Q, select magnification, press ENTER key

5. To zoom, click Zoom button on View tab on Ribbon, select magnification

Figure 5–48

row level symbol 3

show detail symbols change to hide detail symbols

detail records that correspond to hide detail symbols

show detail symbols unhide corresponding detail records

		Gender	Age	Hire Date	State	Sales Area	Quota	YTD Sales	% of
11					AZ Total		6,319,298	5,298,364	
15					CA Total		6,421,542	5,036,324	
17					MT Total		3,426,535	3,292,270	
19					NM Total		3,899,402	1,916,753	
22					NV Total		4,929,783	3,736,417	
23	Chiu, Leslie	F	36	07/15/07	OR	Inside	3,218,514	2,514,181	78
24					OR Total		3,218,514	2,514,181	
25	Lopez, Maria	F	25	06/03/04	UT	Outside	1,837,213	1,563,140	85
26					UT Total		1,837,213	1,563,140	
27	Moeller, Pierre	M	24	03/12/01	WA	Outside	3,656,640	3,336,300	91.
28	Battistini, Jorge	M	26	07/02/01	WA	Inside	3,371,092	1,960,932	58.
29					WA Total		7,027,732	5,297,232	
30					Grand Total		37,080,019	28,654,681	

BTW

Summarizing Data Using Named Ranges

Another way to summarize data is to use named ranges in formulas. Create a range name for one group of related data, such as WA_Total, and another range name for another group of related data, such as UT_Total. Click a blank cell and then create a formula that adds the sums of each range, using the Use in Formula button to insert range names, such as =SUM(WA_Total)+SUM(UT_Total).

To Remove Automatic Subtotals from a Table

The following steps show how to remove the subtotals and convert the range back to a table.

1

• Click Subtotal on the Ribbon to display the Subtotal dialog box (Figure 5–49).

2

• Click the Remove All button.

3

• Select the range A8:J21 and then click the Home tab on the Ribbon.

• Click the Format as Table button on the Ribbon and then click the Custom quick style in the Format as Table gallery.

• When Excel displays the Format As Table dialog box, click the OK button.

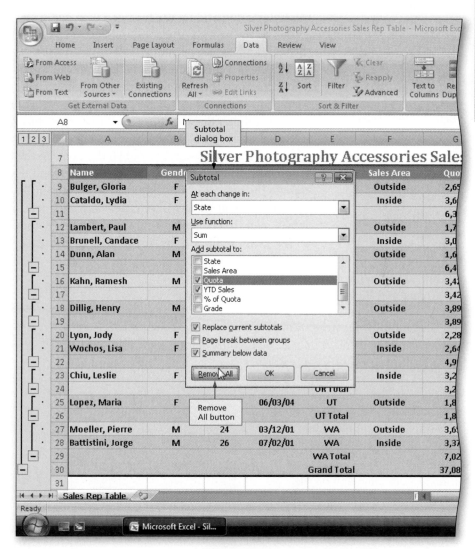

Figure 5–49

Other Ways
1. Press ALT+A, B, ALT+R

To Sort a Table Using a Column Heading List

The following steps sort the Silver Photography Accessories Sales Rep table into its previous sort order, sorted in ascending sequence by hire date.

1 Select cell A9 (or any cell in the table) to make the table active.

2 Click the Hire Date arrow and then click Sort Oldest to Newest in the Hire Date AutoFilter menu to sort the table in ascending sequence by hire date.

Sort Options
You can sort left to right across rows by clicking the Options button in the Sort dialog box (Figure 5–41 on page EX 373) and then clicking Sort left to right in the Orientation area. You also can click Case sensitive to sort lowercase letters before the same capital letters for an ascending sort.

Querying a Table Using AutoFilter

An alternative to using a data form to find records in a table that meet comparison criteria is to use the column heading arrows. The Filter button on the Data tab on the Ribbon or the Filter command on the Sort & Filter menu on the Home tab on the Ribbon places the arrows to the right of the column headings in a table. Thus, the query technique that uses the column heading arrows is called **AutoFilter**.

When you first create a table, Excel automatically enables AutoFilter; the column heading arrows thus appear to the right of the column headings. You can hide the arrows so they do not show by toggling one of the two commands listed above.

AutoFilter displays all records that meet the criteria as a subset of the table by hiding records that do not pass the test. Clicking a column heading arrow causes Excel to display, among other commands, a list of all the items in the field (column) in an AutoFilter menu. If you deselect an item from the AutoFilter menu, Excel immediately hides records that contain the item. The item you deselect from the AutoFilter menu is called the **filter criterion**. If you select a filter criterion from a second column heading while the first is still active, then Excel displays a subset of the first subset. The process of filtering activity based on one or more filter criteria is called a **query**.

To Query a Table Using AutoFilter

The following steps show how to query the Silver Photography Accessories Sales Rep table using AutoFilter, so that the table displays only those records that pass the following test:

Gender = F AND Sales Area = Inside

1

- Click the Gender arrow in cell B8 to display the Gender AutoFilter menu (Figure 5–50).

Q&A

What is displayed below the Text Filters command on the AutoFilter menu?

The list below the Text Filters command is a list of all of the values that occur in the selected column. The top item, (Select All), indicates that all values for this field currently are displayed in the table.

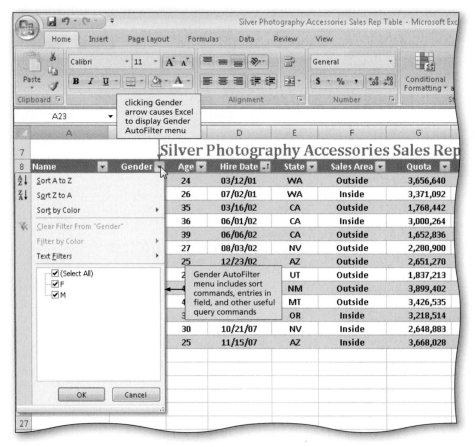

Figure 5–50

2

- Click M in the Gender list to remove the check mark and cause Excel to hide all records representing males, so that only records representing females appear.

- Click the OK button.

- Click the Sales Area arrow in row 8 to display the Sales Area AutoFilter menu (Figure 5–51).

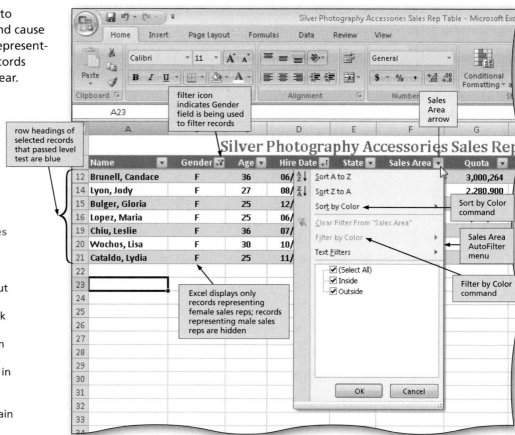

Figure 5–51

3

- Click Outside in the Sales Area list to remove the check mark and hide all records that represent females who are not inside sales reps (Figure 5–52).

- Click the OK button.

Q&A

Why are the row headings of some rows displayed in blue?

Excel displays row headings in blue to indicate that these rows are the result of a filtering process.

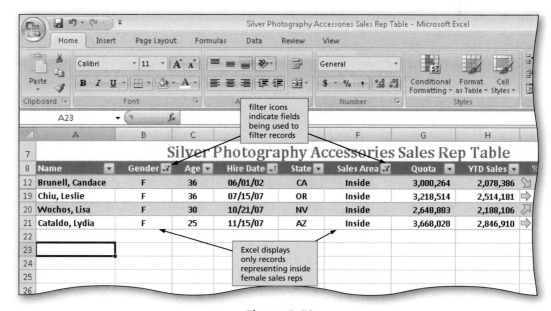

Figure 5–52

Q&A

Are both filters now applied to the table?

Yes. When you select a second filter criterion, Excel adds it to the first. Hence, in the previous steps, each record must pass two tests to appear as part of the final subset of the table.

BTW

Protected Worksheets
The Sort, Subtotal, and
AutoFilter commands
are unavailable if the
worksheet or workbook
is protected, unless you
selected them in the
'Allows users of this
worksheet to' list in the
Protect Sheet dialog box
when you protect the
worksheet or workbook.

BTW

**Creating Formulas for
Filtered Lists**
Excel allows you to create
formulas for filtered lists.
After sorting and filtering
data, click the Subtotal
button on the Data tab.
In the Subtotal dialog
box, click the `At each
change in' box arrow,
select the field to sort,
click the Use function box
arrow, select a function
(such as Sum to total the
values or Count to count
the values), click the
check boxes of the fields
you want to subtotal, and
then click the OK button.

More About AutoFilter

Other important points regarding AutoFilter include the following:

1. When AutoFilter is enabled and records are hidden, Excel displays a filter icon in the table column heading arrows used to establish the filter and the row headings of the selected records in blue.

2. If the column heading arrows do not show, then you must manually enable AutoFilter by clicking the Filter command on the Sort & Filter menu on the Home tab on the Ribbon. The Filter button also is on the Data tab on the Ribbon.

3. To remove a filter criterion for a single field, select the Select All option from the column heading AutoFilter menu for that field.

4. When you create a formula in the total row of a table, the formula automatically recalculates the values even when you filter the list. For example, the results shown in the total row in Figure 5–31 on page EX 366 automatically update if you apply a filter to the table.

5. You can filter and sort a column by color or conditional formatting using the Sort by Color and Filter by Color commands on the AutoFilter menu (Figure 5–51 on the previous page).

To Show All Records in a Table

The following steps illustrate how to show all records in the table following a query.

- With the table active, click the Data tab on the Ribbon and then point to the Filter button on the Ribbon (Figure 5–53).

- Click the Filter button on the Ribbon to display all of the records in the table.

Other Ways

1. Press ALT+A, T
2. Click column heading arrow that includes a filter icon, click (Select All) in AutoFilter menu

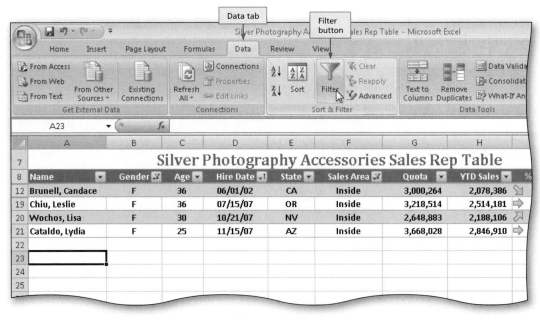

Figure 5–53

To Enter Custom Criteria Using AutoFilter

One of the commands available in all AutoFilter menus is Custom Filter. The Custom Filter command option allows you to enter custom criteria, such as multiple options or ranges of numbers. The following steps show how to enter custom criteria to show records in the table that represent sales reps whose ages are between 30 and 40, inclusive; that is, they are greater than or equal to 30 and less than or equal to 40 (30 ≤ Age ≤ 40).

- Click the Filter button on the Data tab on the Ribbon to display the AutoFilter arrows in the table.

- With the table active, click the Age arrow in cell C8 to display the Age AutoFilter menu.

- When Excel displays the AutoFilter menu, point to the Number Filters command and then point to Custom Filter on the shortcut menu (Figure 5–54).

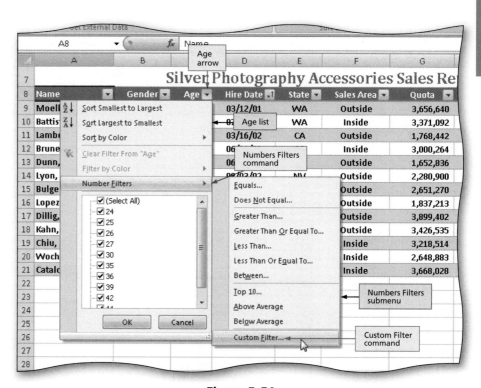

Figure 5–54

- Click Custom Filter.

- When Excel displays the Custom AutoFilter dialog box, click the top-left box arrow, click 'is greater than or equal to' in the list, and then type 30 in the top-right box.

- Click the bottom-left box arrow, click 'is less than or equal to' in the list, and then type 40 in the bottom-right box (Figure 5–55).

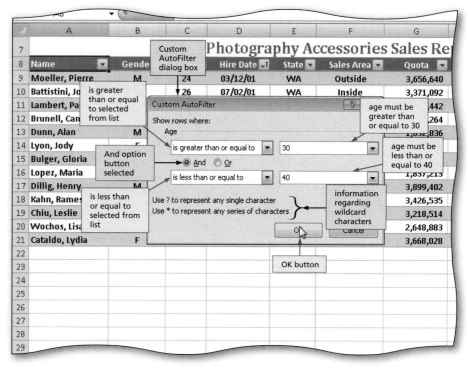

Figure 5–55

3

- Click the OK button in the Custom AutoFilter dialog box to display records in the table that represent sales reps whose ages are between 30 and 40 inclusive (Figure 5–56).

4

- After viewing the records that meet the custom criteria, click the Filter button on the Ribbon.

🔍 **Experiment**

- Create filters on other fields in the table, such as Gender and State. When you are finished, click the Filter button and then repeat the steps above so that the worksheet appears as it does in Figure 5–56.

Filter button

filter icon indicates Age field used to filter records

Silver Photography Accessories Sales Rep Table

Name	Gender	Age	Hire Date	State	Sales Area	Quota	YTD Sales	% of Quota
Lambert, Paul	M	35	03/16/02	CA	Outside	1,768,442	1,525,237	86.25%
Brunell, Candace	F	36	06/01/02	CA	Inside	3,000,264	2,078,386	69.27%
Dunn, Alan	M	39	06/06/02	CA	Outside	1,652,836	1,432,701	86.68%
Chiu, Leslie	F	36	07/15/07	OR	Inside	3,218,514	2,514,181	78.12%
Wochos, Lisa	F	30	10/21/07	NV	Inside	2,648,883	2,188,106	82.60%

records representing sales reps whose ages are greater than or equal to 30 AND less than or equal to 40

Ready   5 of 13 records found

Figure 5–56

Q&A

How are the And and Or option buttons used?

You can click the And option button or the Or option button to select the AND or the OR operator. The AND operator indicates that both parts of the criteria must be true; the OR operator indicates that only one of the two must be true. Use the AND operator when the custom criteria is continuous over a range of values, such as $(30 \le Age \le 40)$. Use the OR operator when the custom criteria is not continuous, such as Age less than or equal to 30 OR greater than or equal to 40 $(30 \le Age \ge 40)$.

Using a Criteria Range on the Worksheet

You can set up a **criteria range** on the worksheet and use it to manipulate records that pass the comparison criteria. Using a criteria range on the worksheet involves two steps:

1. Create the criteria range and name it Criteria.
2. Use the Advanced button on the Data tab on the Ribbon.

To Create a Criteria Range on the Worksheet

To set up a criteria range, first copy the column headings in the table to another area of the worksheet. If possible, copy the field names to rows above the table, in case the table is expanded downward or to the right in the future. Next, enter the comparison criteria in the row immediately below the field names you just copied to the criteria range. Then use the Name box in the formula bar to name the criteria range, Criteria.

The following step shows how to create a criteria range in the range A2:J3 to find records that pass the test:

Gender = F AND Age > 25 AND Grade > C

A grade greater than or equal to C alphabetically means that only sales reps with grades of D and F pass the test.

1

- Click the Home tab on the Ribbon.

- Select the range A7:J8 and then click the Copy button on the Ribbon.

- Click cell A1 and then press the ENTER key to copy the contents on the Office Clipboard to the destination area A1:J2.

- Change the title to Criteria Area in cell A1, enter F in cell B3, enter >25 in cell C3, and then enter >C in cell J3.

- Select the range A2:J3, click the Name box in the formula bar, type Criteria as the range name, press the ENTER key, and then click cell J4 (Figure 5–57).

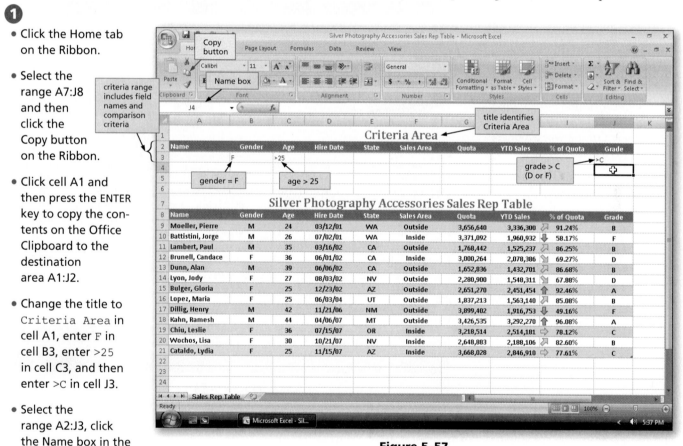

Figure 5–57

Must the text in the column headings in the criteria range match those in the table exactly?

Yes. To ensure the column headings in the criteria range are spelled exactly the same as the column headings in the table, copy and paste the column headings in the table to the criteria range as shown in the previous set of steps.

To Query a Table Using the Advanced Filter Dialog Box

Using the Advanced Filter dialog box is similar to using the AutoFilter query technique, except that it does not filter records based on comparison criteria you select from a table. Instead, this technique uses the comparison criteria set up in a criteria range (A2:J3) on the worksheet.

The following steps show how to use the Advanced Filter dialog box to query a table and show only the records that pass the test established in the criteria range in Figure 5–57 on the previous page (Gender = F AND Age > 25 AND Grade > C).

1

- Select cell A9 to activate the table.

- Click the Data tab on the Ribbon and then click the Advanced button on the Ribbon to display the Advanced Filter dialog box (Figure 5–58).

Q&A

What is displayed already in the Advanced Filter dialog box?

In the Action area, the 'Filter the list, in-place' option button is selected automatically. Excel automatically selects the table (range $A$8:$J$21) in the List range box. Excel also automatically selects the criteria range ($A$2:$J$3) in the Criteria range box, because the name Criteria was assigned to the range A2:J3 earlier.

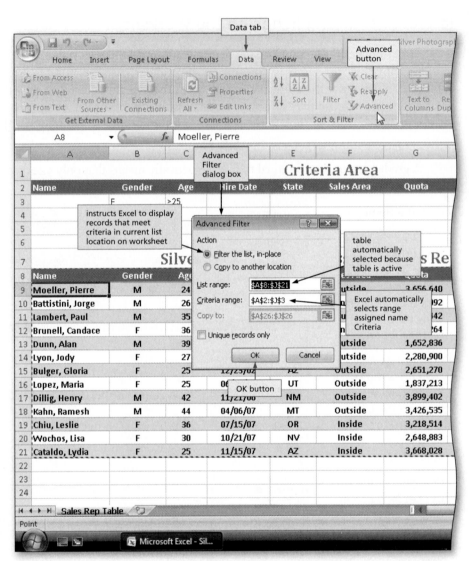

Figure 5–58

2

- Click the OK button in the Advanced Filter dialog box to hide all records that do not meet the comparison criteria (Figure 5–59).

Q&A

What is the main difference between the AutoFilter query technique and using the Advanced Filter dialog box?

Like the AutoFilter query technique, the Advanced Filter command displays a subset of the table. The primary difference between the two is that the Advanced Filter command allows you to create more complex comparison criteria, because the criteria range can be as many rows long as necessary, allowing for many sets of comparison criteria.

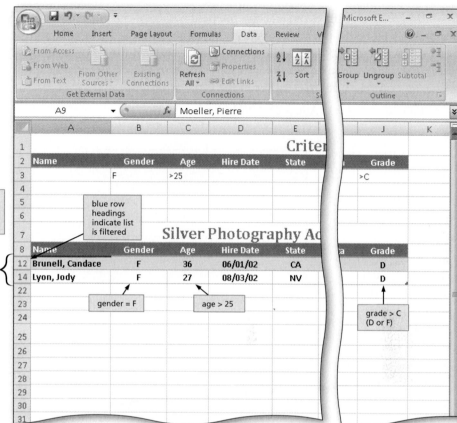

Figure 5–59

To Show All Records in a Table

The following step illustrates how to show all records in the table.

1 Click the Filter button on the Data tab on the Ribbon.

Q&A

Why was AutoFilter turned off?

When the Advanced Filter command is invoked, Excel disables the AutoFilter command, thus hiding the column heading arrows in the active table as shown in Figure 5–59.

Other Ways
1. Press ALT+A, T

Extracting Records

If you select the 'Copy to another location' option button in the Action area of the Advanced Filter dialog box (Figure 5–58), Excel copies the records that meet the comparison criteria in the criteria range to another part of the worksheet, rather than displaying them as a subset of the table. The location where the records are copied is called the **extract range**. Creating an extract range requires steps similar to those used to create a criteria range earlier in the chapter. Once the records that meet the comparison criteria in the criteria range are extracted (copied to the extract range), you can create a new table or manipulate the extracted records.

To Create an Extract Range and Extract Records

To create an extract range, copy the field names of the table and then paste them to an area on the worksheet, preferably well below the table range. Next, name the pasted range Extract by using the Name box in the formula bar. Finally, use the Advanced Filter dialog box to extract the records. The following steps show how to create an extract range below the Silver Photography Accessories Sales Rep table and then extract records that meet the following criteria, as entered earlier in the Criteria range:

Gender = F AND Age > 25 AND Grade > C

- Click the Home tab on the Ribbon.

- Select range A7:J8, click the Copy button on the Ribbon, select cell A25, and then press the ENTER key to copy the contents on the Office Clipboard to the destination area A25:J26.

- Select cell A25 and then type Extract Area as the title.

- Select the range A26:J26, type the name Extract in the Name box in the formula bar, and then press the ENTER key.

- Select cell A9 to activate the table and then click the Data tab on the Ribbon.

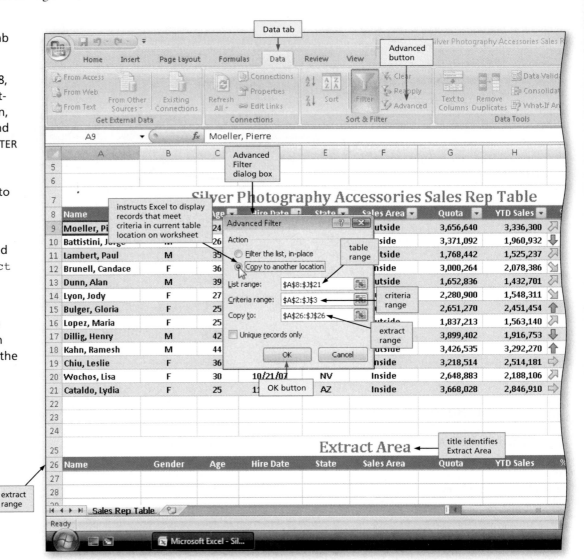

Figure 5–60

- Click the Advanced button on the Ribbon to display the Advanced Filter dialog box.

- When Excel displays the Advanced Filter dialog box, click 'Copy to another location' in the Action area (Figure 5–60).

3

- Click the OK button to copy any records that meet the comparison criteria in the criteria range from the table to the extract range (Figure 5–61).

Q&A

What happens to the rows in the extract range if I perform another advanced filter operation?

Each time the Advanced Filter dialog box is used and the 'Copy to another location' option button is selected, Excel clears cells below the field names in the extract range. Hence, if you change the comparison criteria in the criteria range and then use the Advanced Filter dialog box a second time, Excel clears the previously extracted records before it copies a new set of records that pass the new test.

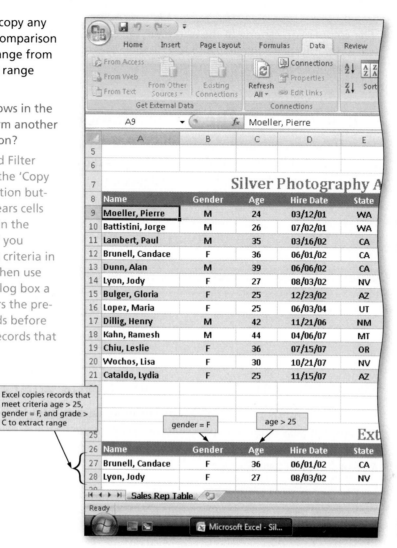

Figure 5–61

Other Ways

1. Press ALT+A, Q

To Enable AutoFilter

As indicated earlier, when the Advanced Filter dialog box is used, Excel disables AutoFilter, thus hiding the column heading arrows in an active table. The following steps show how to enable AutoFilter.

1 Click the Filter button on the Data tab on the Ribbon to display the column heading arrows in the table.

2 Click the Home tab on the Ribbon.

BTW

Setting Up the Extract Range
When setting up the extract range, all of the column headings do not have to be copied in the list to the proposed extract range. Instead, copy only those column headings you want, in any order. You also can type the column headings rather than copy them, although this method is not recommended because it increases the likelihood of misspellings or other typographical errors.

More About the Criteria Range

The comparison criteria in the criteria range determine the records that will pass the test when the Advanced Filter dialog box is used. This section describes examples of different comparison criteria.

A Blank Row in the Criteria Range

If the criteria range contains a blank row, it means that no comparison criteria have been defined. Thus, all records in the table pass the test. For example, the blank row in the criteria range shown in Figure 5–62 means that all records will pass the test.

Figure 5–62

Using Multiple Comparison Criteria with the Same Field

If the criteria range contains two or more entries below the same field name, then records that pass either comparison criterion pass the test. For example, based on the criteria range shown in Figure 5–63, all records that represent sales reps with a State value of MT or NM will pass the test.

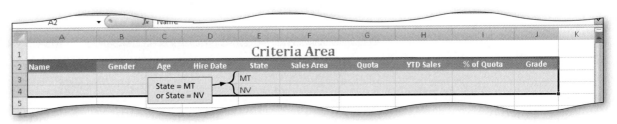

Figure 5–63

The Criteria Area
When you add items in multiple rows to a criteria area, you must redefine the range of the name Criteria before you use it. To redefine the name Criteria, click the Name Manager button on the Formulas tab on the Ribbon. When Excel displays the Name Manager dialog box, select Criteria in the list and then click the Delete button. Next, select the new Criteria area and name it Criteria using the Name box.

If an AND operator applies to the same field name (Age > 50 AND Age < 55), then you must duplicate the field name (Age) in the criteria range. That is, add the field name Age in cell K2 to the right of Grade and then adjust the range assigned to the name Criteria by using the Define Name command on the Formulas tab on the Ribbon.

Comparison Criteria in Different Rows and below Different Fields

When the comparison criteria below different field names are in the same row, then records pass the test only if they pass all the comparison criteria. If the comparison criteria for the field names are in different rows, then the records must pass only one of the tests. For example, in the criteria range shown in Figure 5–64, female sales reps OR outside sales reps pass the test.

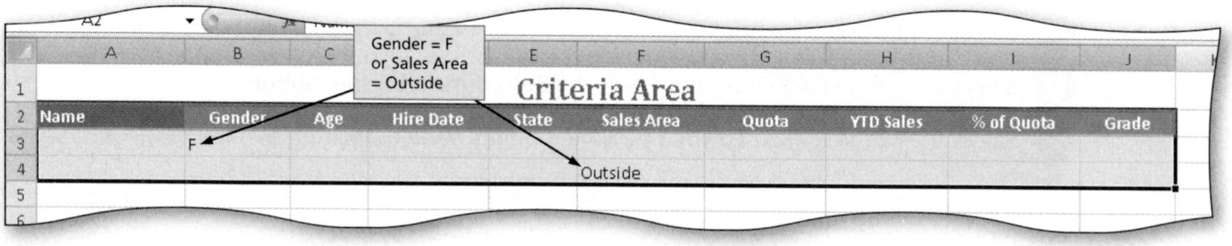

Figure 5–64

Using Database Functions

Excel has 12 **database functions** that can be used to evaluate numeric data in a table. One of the functions is called the DAVERAGE function. As the name implies, the **DAVERAGE function** is used to find the average of numbers in a table field that pass a test. This function serves as an alternative to finding an average using the Subtotal button on the Data tab on the Ribbon. The general form of the DAVERAGE function is:

=DAVERAGE(table range, "field name", criteria range)

where table range is the range of the table, field name is the name of the field in the table, and criteria range is the comparison criteria or test to pass.

Another often used table function is the DCOUNT function. The **DCOUNT function** will count the number of numeric entries in a table field that pass a test. The general form of the DCOUNT function is:

=DCOUNT(table range, "field name", criteria range)

where table range is the range of the table, field name is the name of the field in the table, and criteria range is the comparison criteria or test to pass.

> **BTW**
> **Database Functions**
> Database functions are useful when working with lists of data, such as the one in this chapter. Remembering the function arguments and their order within parentheses is not easy, however. Thus, it is recommended that you use the Insert Function button in the formula bar to assign a database function to your worksheet.

To Use the DAVERAGE and DCOUNT Database Functions

The following steps use the DAVERAGE function to find the average age of female sales reps and the average age of male sales reps in the table. The DCOUNT function is used to count the number of sales reps records that have a grade of A. The first step sets up the criteria areas that are required by these two functions.

1. Select cell O1 and then enter `Criteria` as the criteria area title. Select cell L1, click the Format Painter button on the Ribbon, and then click cell O1. Center the title, Criteria, across the range O1:Q1.

2. Select cell O2 and then enter `Gender` as the field name. Select cell P2 and enter `Gender` as the field name. Select cell Q2 and then enter `Grade` as the field name. Select cell L2. Click the Format Painter button on the Ribbon. Drag through the range O2:Q2.

3. Enter `F` in cell O3 as the Gender code for female sales reps. Enter `M` in cell P3 as the Gender code for male sales reps. Enter `A` in cell Q3 as the Grade value. Select M3, click the Format Painter button on the Ribbon, and then drag through the range O3:Q3.

4. Enter `Average Female Age = = = = = >` in cell O4. Enter `Average Male Age = = = = = = =>` in cell O5. Enter `Grade A Count = = = = = = = = = >` in cell O6.

5. Select cell R4 and then enter `=daverage(a8:j21, "Age", o2:o3)` as the database function.

6. Select cell R5 and then enter `=daverage(a8:j21, "Age", p2:p3)` as the database function.

7 Select cell R6 and then enter =dcount(a8:j21, "Age", q2:q3) as the database function.

8 Select the range O4:R6 and then click the Bold button on the Ribbon.

9 Select the range R4:R5 and then click the Comma Style button on the Ribbon (Figure 5–65).

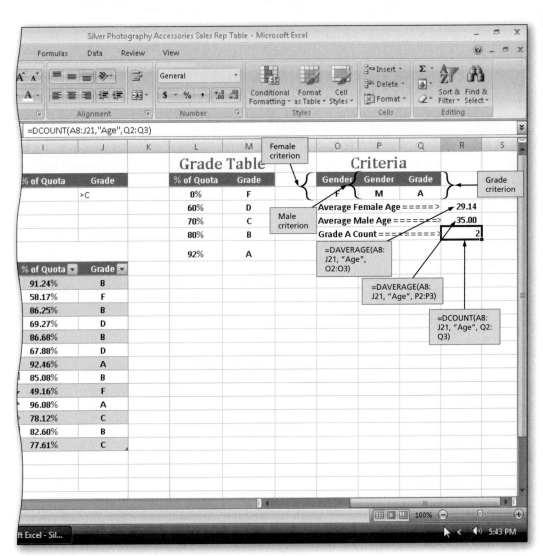

Figure 5–65

More About Using Database Functions

In Figure 5–65, the first value in the DCOUNT function, A8:J21, refers to the table range defined earlier in this chapter (range A8:J21). Instead of using the cell range, you can name the table using the Name box in the formula bar and then use the table name as the first argument in the database functions. Database is the name most often assigned to a table. If the table were named Database, then the DCOUNT function would be entered as:

=DCOUNT(Database, "Age", Q2:Q3)

Excel uses the criteria range Q2:Q3 to select the records in the range Database where the Grade is A; it then counts the numeric Age field in these records to determine the number of records that pass the criteria. Excel requires that you surround the field name Age with quotation marks unless the field has been assigned a name through the Name box in the formula bar.

The third value, Q2:Q3, is the criteria range for the grade count. In the case of the DCOUNT function, it is required that you select a numeric field to count even though the value of the numeric field itself is not used.

Other Database Functions

Other database functions that are similar to the functions described in previous chapters include the DMAX, DMIN, and DSUM functions. For a complete list of the database functions available for use with a table, click the Insert Function box in the formula bar. When Excel displays the Insert Function dialog box, select Database in the 'Or select a category' list. The 'Select a function' box displays the database functions. If you click a database function name, Excel displays a description of the function above the OK button in the Insert Function dialog box.

Using the SUMIF and COUNTIF Functions

The SUMIF and COUNTIF functions are useful when you want to sum values in a range or count values in a range only if they meet criteria. The range need not be a table. For example, assume you want to sum the YTD sales of the sales reps that have a grade of A. Or, assume you want to count the number of male sales reps. The first question can be answered by using the SUMIF function as follows:

=SUMIF(J9:J21,"A",H9:H21)

where the first argument J9:J21 is the range containing the numbers to add, the second argument "A" is the criteria, and the third argument H9:H21 is the range containing the cells with which to compare the criteria.

The second question can be answered by using the COUNTIF function as follows:

=COUNTIF(B9:B21,"M")

where the first argument B9:B21 is the range containing the cells with which to compare the criteria.

To Use the SUMIF and COUNTIF Functions

The following steps enter identifiers and these two functions in the range O8:R9.

1 Enter Grade A YTD Sales Sum = = = => in cell O8.

2 Enter Male Sales Rep Count = = = = = => in cell O9.

3 Select cell R8 and then enter =SUMIF(j9:j21,"A",h9:h21) as the function.

4 Select cell R9 and then enter =COUNTIF(b9:b21,"M") as the function.

5 Select the range O8:R9 and then click the Bold button on the Ribbon.

6 Select cell R8, click the Comma Style button on the Ribbon, and then click the Decrease Decimal button on the Ribbon twice.

7 Double-click the right border of column heading R to change the width of column R to best fit (Figure 5–66).

Q&A

Are there any differences when using these functions on a range?

Yes. The COUNTIF, SUMIF, and database functions will work on any range. The difference between using these functions on a range and table is that if the function references a table, then Excel automatically adjusts the first argument as a table grows or shrinks. The same cannot be said if the function's first argument is a range reference that is not defined as a table.

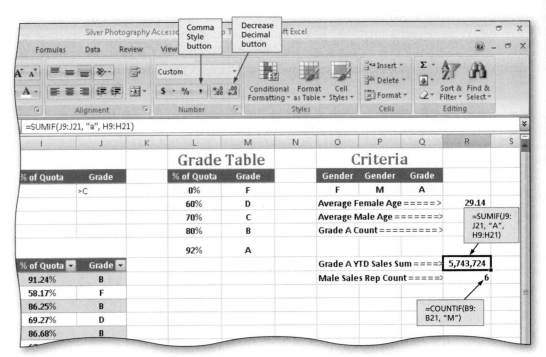

Figure 5–66

To Print the Worksheet and Save the Workbook

The following steps print the worksheet on one page and save the workbook.

1 Select any cell outside the table.

2 Click the Page Layout tab on the Ribbon and then click the Page Setup Dialog Box Launcher to display the Page Setup dialog box.

3 Click Landscape in the Orientation area. Click Fit to in the Scaling area.

4 Click the Print button. When the Print dialog box appears, click the OK button to print the worksheet (Figure 5–67).

5 Click the Save button on the Quick Access Toolbar to save the workbook using the file name, Silver Photography Accessories Sales Rep Table.

6 Click the Page Setup Dialog Box Launcher to display the Page Setup dialog box. Click Portrait in the Orientation area and then click Adjust to in the Scaling area.

7 Click the OK button to close the Page Setup dialog box.

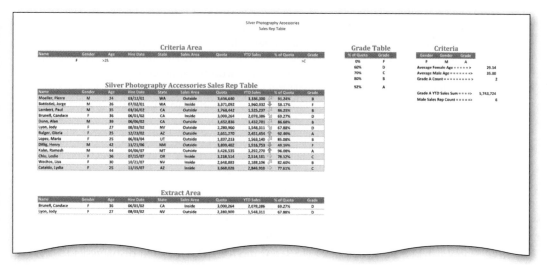

Figure 5–67

Saving a Workbook in Different File Formats

Excel workbooks usually are saved in a file format called **Microsoft Excel Workbook**. A file saved in the Microsoft Excel Workbook file format has a file extension of **xlsx**. A **file extension**, which usually is three or four characters in length, is used by Windows Vista to classify files by application. By default, you do not see the file extensions when you use the Save As or Open dialog boxes, but the file extensions are appended to the file name and separated by a period. Excel allows you to save a workbook in more than 30 different file formats, so that the data can be transferred to other applications easily. Table 5–6 summarizes the more popular file formats available in Excel via the 'Save as type' box in the Save As dialog box.

BTW

Certification
The Microsoft Certified Application Specialist (MCAS) program provides an opportunity for you to obtain a valuable industry credential – proof that you have the Excel 2007 skills required by employers. For more information, see Appendix G or visit the Excel 2007 Certification Web page (scsite.com/ex2007/cert).

Table 5–6 Popular File Formats Available with the Save As Command in Excel	
File Formats	**Extension**
Microsoft Excel Workbook	xlsx
Microsoft Excel 97 – Excel 2003 Workbook	xls
XML Spreadsheet 2003	xml
XML Data	xml
Single File Web Page	mht
Web Page	htm
Template	xltx
Text (Tab delimited)	txt
Unicode Text	txt
CSV (Comma delimited)	csv
Formatted Text (Space delimited)	prn

Plan Ahead	**Save the worksheet in a different file format.**
	Often, the best way to share data in a worksheet with other applications is to save the file as a text file. The CSV file format is most the most common type of text file. When saving data to a text file, Excel will place one row from the worksheet on one line of text. In this case, each sales rep record will be represented on one line of text in the CSV file. The Grade column is not included in the range to save because it is computed using the grade table, which will not be part of the new file.

To Save a Workbook in CSV File Format

The following steps show how to save the table (range A8:I21) in the Silver Photography Accessories Sales Rep Table workbook in a CSV (Comma delimited) file format so that the file can be read by most applications. In this example, the table is copied to a new workbook, saved using the CSV file format, and then displayed and printed in Notepad.

1

- Click the Home tab on the Ribbon.

- Select the table in the range A8:I21.

- Click the Copy button on the Ribbon.

- Click the Office Button and then click New on the Office Button menu.

- When the New Workbook dialog box is displayed, click the Create button.

- With cell A1 selected in the new workbook, click the Paste button on the Ribbon.

- Click the Select All button, point to the right border of the column A heading, and double-click to set all column widths to best fit.

- Select cell A16 (Figure 5–68).

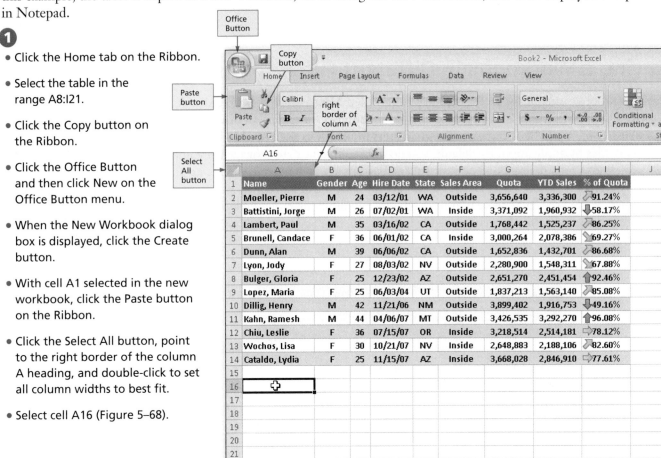

Figure 5–68

2

• With a USB flash drive connected to one of the computer's USB ports, click the Save button on the Quick Access Toolbar. Change the file name to Silver Photography Accessories Sales Rep Table CSV (Figure 5–68).

3

• Click the 'Save as type' box arrow and then scroll down and point to CSV (Comma delimited) in the 'Save as type' list as shown in Figure 5–69.

• Click CSV (Comma delimited) in the Save as type list.

• If necessary, click Computer in the Favorite Links section of the Navigation pane and then double-click UDISK 2.0 (E:) to select the USB flash drive as the new save location. Click the Save button in the Save As dialog box. Click the OK button and the Yes button in the Microsoft Office Excel dialog boxes when they appear.

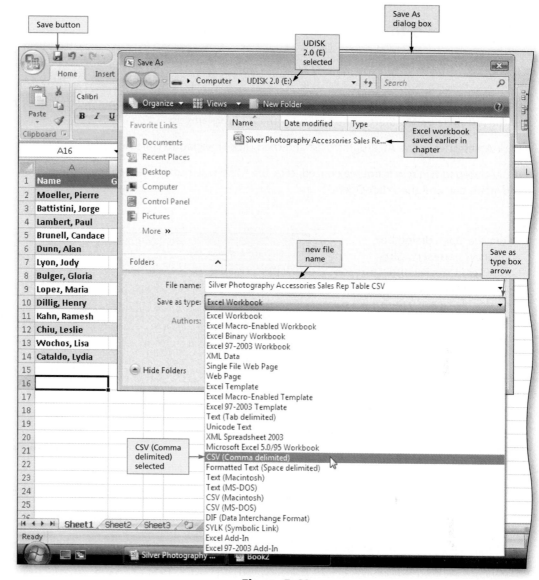

Figure 5–69

• Click the workbook Close button on the right side of the Excel title bar.

Q&A

Can I open the CSV file in Excel?

Yes. If you open the Silver Photography Accessories Sales Rep Table CSV in Excel, it will place the fields from the CSV file in the same cells as shown in Figure 5–68, but without some of the formatting.

Other Ways

1. On Office Button menu click Save As, type file name, select file type, select drive or folder, click Save button in Save As dialog box

2. Press CTRL+S, type file name, select file type, select drive or folder, click Save button in Save As dialog box

To Use Notepad to Open and Print the CSV File

The following steps show how to use Notepad to open and print the CSV file.

1

- Click the Start button on the Windows Vista taskbar to display the Start menu and then click All Programs at the bottom of the left pane on the Start menu to display the All Programs list.

- Click Accessories in the All Programs list and then click Notepad to start Notepad.

- If the Notepad window is not maximized, click the Maximize button next to the Close button on its title bar, click File on the menu bar, and then click Open.

2

- When the Open dialog box appears, if necessary, click Computer in the Favorite Links section of the Navigation pane and then double-click UDISK 2.0 (E:) to select the USB flash drive as the new open location. Select All Files in the 'Files of type' list.

- Double-click Silver Photography Accessories Sales Rep Table CSV to display the file in Notepad (Figure 5–70).

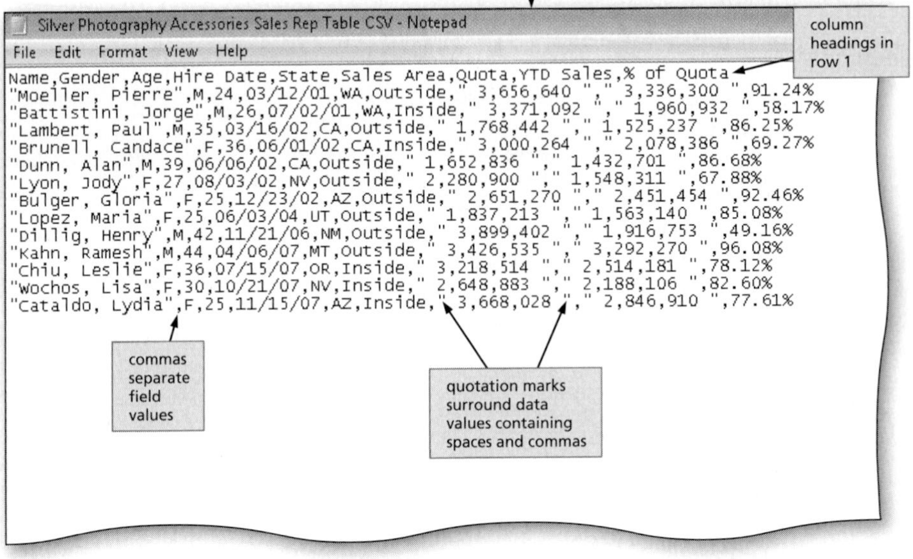

Q&A

What is shown in the CSV file?

Figure 5–70 shows the contents of the Silver Photography Accessories Sales Rep Table CSV file. The column headings are on the first line, separated by commas. Each record is on a separate line. Commas separate the fields in each record; quotation marks surround any fields with data containing spaces or commas. Data saved in this format can be read by most applications, including Excel.

Notepad application active

column headings in row 1

Silver Photography Accessories Sales Rep Table CSV - Notepad

File Edit Format View Help

```
Name,Gender,Age,Hire Date,State,Sales Area,Quota,YTD Sales,% of Quota
"Moeller, Pierre",M,24,03/12/01,WA,Outside," 3,656,640 "," 3,336,300 ",91.24%
"Battistini, Jorge",M,26,07/02/01,WA,Inside," 3,371,092 "," 1,960,932 ",58.17%
"Lambert, Paul",M,35,03/16/02,CA,Outside," 1,768,442 "," 1,525,237 ",86.25%
"Brunell, Candace",F,36,06/01/02,CA,Inside," 3,000,264 "," 2,078,386 ",69.27%
"Dunn, Alan",M,39,06/06/02,CA,Outside," 1,652,836 "," 1,432,701 ",86.68%
"Lyon, Jody",F,27,08/03/02,NV,Outside," 2,280,900 "," 1,548,311 ",67.88%
"Bulger, Gloria",F,25,12/23/02,AZ,Outside," 2,651,270 "," 2,451,454 ",92.46%
"Lopez, Maria",F,25,06/03/04,UT,Outside," 1,837,213 "," 1,563,140 ",85.08%
"Dillig, Henry",M,42,11/21/06,NM,Outside," 3,899,402 "," 1,916,753 ",49.16%
"Kahn, Ramesh",M,44,04/06/07,MT,Outside," 3,426,535 "," 3,292,270 ",96.08%
"Chiu, Leslie",F,36,07/15/07,OR,Inside," 3,218,514 "," 2,514,181 ",78.12%
"Wochos, Lisa",F,30,10/21/07,NV,Inside," 2,648,883 "," 2,188,106 ",82.60%
"Cataldo, Lydia",F,25,11/15/07,AZ,Inside," 3,668,028 "," 2,846,910 ",77.61%
```

commas separate field values

quotation marks surround data values containing spaces and commas

Figure 5–70

3

- Click File on the menu bar and then click Print.

- When the Print dialog box appears, click the Print button to print the CSV version of the Silver Photography Accessories Sales Rep table (Figure 5–71).

- Click the Close button on the right side of the Notepad title bar to quit Notepad.

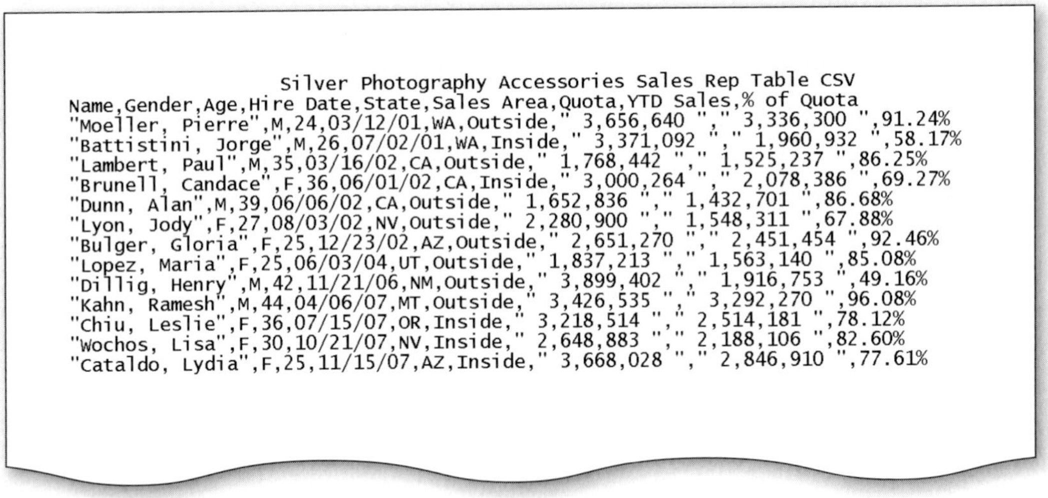

```
                  Silver Photography Accessories Sales Rep Table CSV
     Name,Gender,Age,Hire Date,State,Sales Area,Quota,YTD Sales,% of Quota
     "Moeller, Pierre",M,24,03/12/01,WA,Outside," 3,656,640 "," 3,336,300 ",91.24%
     "Battistini, Jorge",M,26,07/02/01,WA,Inside," 3,371,092 "," 1,960,932 ",58.17%
     "Lambert, Paul",M,35,03/16/02,CA,Outside," 1,768,442 "," 1,525,237 ",86.25%
     "Brunell, Candace",F,36,06/01/02,CA,Inside," 3,000,264 "," 2,078,386 ",69.27%
     "Dunn, Alan",M,39,06/06/02,CA,Outside," 1,652,836 "," 1,432,701 ",86.68%
     "Lyon, Jody",F,27,08/03/02,NV,Outside," 2,280,900 "," 1,548,311 ",67.88%
     "Bulger, Gloria",F,25,12/23/02,AZ,Outside," 2,651,270 "," 2,451,454 ",92.46%
     "Lopez, Maria",F,25,06/03/04,UT,Outside," 1,837,213 "," 1,563,140 ",85.08%
     "Dillig, Henry",M,42,11/21/06,NM,Outside," 3,899,402 "," 1,916,753 ",49.16%
     "Kahn, Ramesh",M,44,04/06/07,MT,Outside," 3,426,535 "," 3,292,270 ",96.08%
     "Chiu, Leslie",F,36,07/15/07,OR,Inside," 3,218,514 "," 2,514,181 ",78.12%
     "Wochos, Lisa",F,30,10/21/07,NV,Inside," 2,648,883 "," 2,188,106 ",82.60%
     "Cataldo, Lydia",F,25,11/15/07,AZ,Inside," 3,668,028 "," 2,846,910 ",77.61%
```

Figure 5–71

To Quit Excel

The following steps quit Excel.

1 Click the Close button on the right side of the title bar.

2 If the Microsoft Office Excel dialog box is displayed, click the No button.

Chapter Summary

In this chapter, you learned how to create, sort, and filter a table (also called a database); create subtotals; use database functions such as SUMIF and COUNTIF; and save a workbook in different file formats. The items listed below include all the new Excel skills you have learned in this chapter.

1. Format a Range as a Table (EX 346)
2. Validate Data (EX 348)
3. Modify a Table Quick Style (EX 351)
4. Enter Records in a Table (EX 353)
5. Add New Fields to a Table (EX 355)
6. Create a Lookup Table (EX 357)
7. Use the VLOOKUP Function to Determine Letter Grades (EX 359)
8. Add a Conditional Formatting Rule with an Icon Set (EX 362)
9. Use the Total Row Check Box (EX 365)
10. Print the Table (EX 368)
11. Sort a Table in Ascending Sequence by Name Using the Sort & Filter Button (EX 369)
12. Sort a Table in Descending Sequence by Name Using the Sort Z to A Button on the Data Tab (EX 370)
13. Sort a Table Using the Sort Command on a Column Heading AutoFilter Menu (EX 371)
14. Sort a Table on Multiple Fields Using the Custom Sort Command (EX 372)

15. Display Automatic Subtotals in a Table (EX 375)
16. Zoom Out on a Subtotaled Table and Use the Outline Feature (EX 377)
17. Remove Automatic Subtotals from a Table (EX 379)
18. Sort a Table Using a Column Heading List (EX 379)
19. Query a Table Using AutoFilter (EX 380)
20. Show All Records in a Table (EX 382)
21. Enter Custom Criteria Using AutoFilter (EX 383)
22. Create a Criteria Range on the Worksheet (EX 385)
23. Query a Table Using the Advanced Filter Dialog Box (EX 386)
24. Create an Extract Range and Extract Records (EX 388)
25. Use the DAVERAGE and DCOUNT Database Functions (EX 391)
26. Use the SUMIF and COUNTIF Functions (EX 393)
27. Save a Workbook in CSV File Format (EX 396)
28. Use Notepad to Open and Print the CSV File (EX 398)

 If you have a SAM user profile, you may have access to hands-on instruction, practice, and assessment. Log in to your SAM account (http://sam2007.course.com) to launch any assigned training activities or exams that relate to the skills covered in this chapter.

Learn It Online

Learn It Online is a series of online student exercises that test your knowledge of chapter content and key terms.

Instructions: To complete the Learn It Online exercises, start your browser, click the Address bar, and then enter the Web address scsite.com/ex2007/learn. When the Excel 2007 Learn It Online page is displayed, click the link for the exercise you want to complete and then read the instructions.

Chapter Reinforcement TF, MC, and SA
A series of true/false, multiple choice, and short answer questions that test your knowledge of the chapter content.

Flash Cards
An interactive learning environment where you identify chapter key terms associated with displayed definitions.

Practice Test
A series of multiple choice questions that test your knowledge of chapter content and key terms.

Who Wants To Be a Computer Genius?
An interactive game that challenges your knowledge of chapter content in the style of a television quiz show.

Wheel of Terms
An interactive game that challenges your knowledge of chapter key terms in the style of the television show *Wheel of Fortune.*

Crossword Puzzle Challenge
A crossword puzzle that challenges your knowledge of key terms presented in the chapter.

Apply Your Knowledge

Reinforce the skills and apply the concepts you learned in this chapter.

Querying a List
Instructions: Assume that the figures that accompany each of the following six problems make up the criteria range for the Fritz's Luxury Kennel Guest List shown in Figure 5–72. Fill in the comparison criteria to select records from the list to solve each of these six problems. So that you understand better what is required for this assignment, the answer is given for the first problem. You can open the workbook Apply 5-1 Fritzs Luxury Kennel Guest List from the Data Files for Students and use the Filter button to verify your answers. See the inside back cover of this book for instructions for downloading the Data Files for Students or see your instructor for information on accessing the files required in this book.

Fritz's Luxury Kennel Guest List

Owner Name	Dog Name	Gender	Age	Breed	Cage Size
Attassi	Max	M	8	Golden Retriever	3
Koblitz	Amber	F	6	Newfoundland	3
Stanley	Goldie	F	9	Beagle	1
Athas	Muffin	M	2	Newfoundland	3
Felski	Claire	F	7	Bulldog	2
Chen	Maynard	M	5	Golden Retriever	3
Richardson	Sparky	F	4	Doberman Pinscher	3
Perez	Rocky	M	3	Bulldog	2
Dunlap	Carmy	F	1	Golden Retriever	2
Seldal	Ziggy	M	11	Beagle	1
Hong	Apollo	M	8	Doberman Pinscher	3

Kennel Guest List Sheet2 Sheet3

Ready

Apply 5-1 Fritz Lux...

Figure 5–72

1. Select records that represent female dogs who are less than 5 years old.

Owner Name	Dog Name	Gender	Age	Breed	Cage Size
		F	<5		

2. Select records that have a breed of Beagle or Bulldog.

Owner Name	Dog Name	Gender	Age	Breed	Cage Size

3. Select records that represent male dogs whose owners' last names begin with the letter A and who are greater than 5 years old.

Owner Name	Dog Name	Gender	Age	Breed	Cage Size

4. Select records that represent female dogs who are at least 4 years old and need a cage size of greater than 1.

Owner Name	Dog Name	Gender	Age	Breed	Cage Size

5. Select records that represent male dogs who are Golden Retrievers or need a cage size of 3.

Owner Name	Dog Name	Gender	Age	Breed	Cage Size

6. Select records that represent dogs who are at least 4 years old and are either the Newfoundland breed or Golden Retriever breed.

Owner Name	Dog Name	Gender	Age	Breed	Cage Size

Extend Your Knowledge

Extend the skills you learned in this chapter and experiment with new skills. You may need to use Help to complete the assignment.

More Conditional Formatting

Instructions: Start Excel. Open the workbook Extend 5-1 Jensen Basketball Poles from the Data Files for Students. See the inside back cover of this book for instructions for downloading the Data Files for Students or see your instructor for information on accessing the files required in this book. You have been asked to add conditional formatting to highlight the lowest and highest total expenses, and to add conditional formatting to show data bars for net income that is greater than zero (Figure 5–73). Complete the following tasks to add and manage conditional formatting rules in the worksheet.

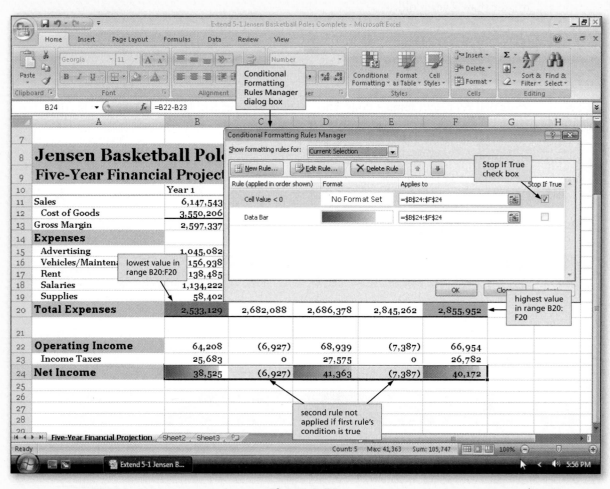

Figure 5–73

1. Save the workbook using the file name, Extend 5-1 Jensen Basketball Poles Complete. Select the range B20:F20. Click the Conditional Formatting button on the Home tab on the Ribbon and then click New Rule. When Excel displays the New Formatting Rule dialog box, select 'Format only top or bottom ranked values' in the Select a Rule Type list. In the 'Format values that rank in the' area, type 1 in the center text box. Click the Format button in the Preview area. When Excel displays the Format Cells dialog box, click the Fill tab, click the green color (column 5, row 7) in the Background Color area, and then click the OK button. Click the OK button in the New Formatting Rule dialog box.

2. With the range B20:F20 selected, add a second rule to the range following the procedure from Step 1. When creating the new rule, select Bottom in the 'Format values that rank in the' list and type 1 in the center text box. Click the Format button and then select the red color (column 2, row 7) in the Background Color area. Click the OK button in the Format Cells dialog box and then click the OK button in the New Formatting Rules dialog box.

3. With the range B20:F20 selected, click the Conditional Formatting button on the Home tab on the Ribbon and then click Manage Rules to view the rules for the range. Click the Close button in the Conditional Formatting Rules Manager dialog box.

4. Select the range B24:F24. Add a new conditional formatting rule to format all cells based on their values. Select the Data Bar format style. Select Red, Accent 1, Darker 25% (column 5, row 5) in the Bar Color palette and then close the New Formatting Rule dialog box.

5. With range B24:F24 selected, add a new conditional formatting rule. Select 'Format only cells that contain' as the rule type. Format only cells with a cell value less than zero. Do not select a format using the Format button. Make sure that the Preview area indicates that no format is set and then click the OK button to add the rule.

6. With the range B24:F24 selected, click the Conditional Formatting button on the Home tab on the Ribbon and then click Manage Rules to view the rules for the range. Click the Stop If True check box for the first rule in the dialog box to ensure that the second rule is not applied to negative values in the range (Figure 5–73). Click the OK button to close the Conditional Formatting Rules Manager dialog box.

7. Change the document properties as specified by your instructor. Change the worksheet header with your name, course number, and other information as specified by your instructor. Change the print orientation to landscape. Print the worksheet using the Fit to option. Save the workbook.

8. Select the range B15:F19. Click the Conditional Formatting button on the Home tab on the Ribbon, point to Color Scales on the Conditional Formatting menu, and then click Green – Yellow – Red Color Scale in the Color Scales gallery. Print the worksheet using the Fit to option. Do not save the workbook. Submit the assignment as requested by your instructor.

Make It Right

Analyze a workbook and correct all errors and/or improve the design.

Tables, Conditional Formatting, and Database Functions

Instructions: Start Excel. Open the workbook Make It Right 5-1 Van Dyl Kitchen Accessories Sales Rep List and then save the file using the file name, Van Dyl Kitchen Accessories Sales Rep List Complete. See the inside back cover of this book for instructions for downloading the Data Files for Students, or see your instructor for information on accessing the files required for this book. Correct the following table, conditional formatting, and database function problems so that the worksheet appears as shown in Figure 5–74.

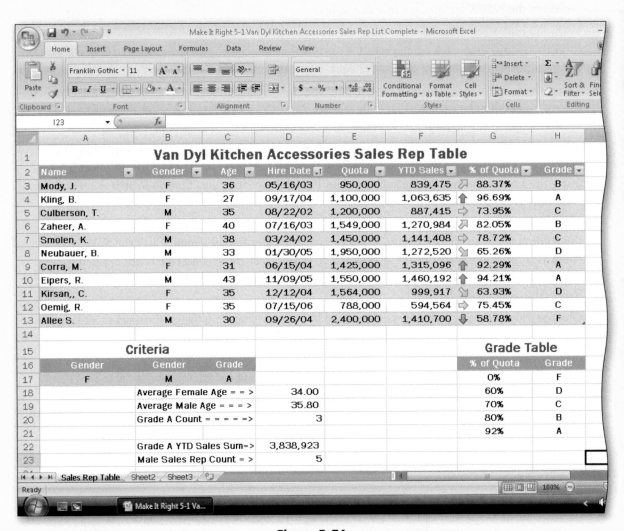

Figure 5–74

1. Use the Table Style Options group on the Design tab on the Ribbon to make certain that the table in the worksheet includes banded rows.

2. The table does not show all of the rows because the Age field is filtered. Ensure that all rows in the table are displayed.

3. The conditional formatting for the % of Quota field uses only four icons in the rule instead of five. Change the icon style of the rule to use 5 Arrows (Colored).

4. The values used by the conditional formatting rule to choose each arrow style are incorrect and should be based on the values listed in the grade table. Edit the conditional formatting rule so that the values in the grade table are reflected in the rules.

5. Correct the third argument in the DAVERAGE function used to calculate the average male age.

6. Correct the second and third arguments in the SUMIF function used to calculate the grade A YTD sales sum.

7. Change the document properties as specified by your instructor. Change the worksheet header with your name, course number, and other information requested by your instructor.

8. Save the workbook and submit the revised workbook as requested by your instructor.

In the Lab

Create a workbook using the guidelines, concepts, and skills presented in this chapter. Labs are listed in order of increasing difficulty.

Lab 1: Creating, Filtering, and Sorting a Table and Determining Subtotals

Problem: You are employed by Whitman Publishing, a company that supplies textbooks to the college market. The national sales force is divided into districts within divisions within regions. The three regions are the Southeast region (1), Midwest region (2), and Western region (3). The director of the Accounting department has asked you to create a sales rep table (Figure 5–75), run queries against the table, generate various sorted reports, and generate subtotal information.

Clipboard	Font			Alignment		Number		Styles	Cells

A23

	A	B	C	D	E	F	G	H	I	J	K	L	M
6	**Whitman Publishing Sales Rep Table**												
7	Region #	Div #	Dist #	Rep #	Lname	Fname	Age	Gender	Quota	Sales			
8	3	C	3	346	Day	Laura	⬇ 32	F	2,000,000	1,167,301			
9	2	D	3	378	Sung	Lee	⬇ 27	M	4,000,000	4,544,023			
10	1	C	3	490	Lawless	Debra	⬆ 56	F	3,500,000	3,823,145			
11	2	C	3	492	Chirac	Fran	⬇ 30	F	4,200,000	3,918,292			
12	2	C	3	501	Lopez	Raul	⇨ 39	M	1,500,000	1,123,444			
13	3	D	2	510	Green	Kim	⬇ 25	F	3,500,000	3,265,942			
14	2	C	1	512	Leuellen	Jim	⬆ 57	M	6,500,000	6,560,345			
15	1	C	3	610	Gandi	Josh	⬇ 28	M	2,500,000	1,269,583			
16	3	C	3	611	Beam	Saul	⬇ 34	M	5,500,000	4,693,219			
17	1	D	1	615	Nickel	Lisa	⬇ 33	F	3,200,000	3,210,459			
18	2	D	2	712	John	Len	⇨ 38	M	11,000,000	9,300,845			
19	1	D	2	715	Lipes	Napoleon	⇨ 47	M	6,000,000	7,121,032			
20	1	D	2	737	Goldberg	Joan	⬆ 62	F	3,000,000	2,034,054			
21	Total						39.077	13	56,400,000	52,031,684			
22													
23	⇳												

Figure 5–75

Continued >

In the Lab *continued*

Instructions Part 1:   Create the table shown in Figure 5–75 on the previous page using the techniques learned in this chapter and following the instructions below.

1. Bold the entire worksheet.
2. Enter the table title in row 6 and apply the Title cell style. Enter and format the field names in row 7.
3. Use the Format as Table button on the Home tab on the Ribbon to create a table using data from the range A7:J7. Use Table Style Medium 3 to format the table. Format the first row below the field names and then enter the rows of data shown in rows 8 through 20 of Figure 5–75. Change the Sheet1 tab name to Whitman Publishing Sales Reps and delete Sheet2 and Sheet3.
4. With a cell in the table active, click the Design tab on the Ribbon and then click the Total Row check box in the Table Style Options group. Show the record count in the Gender column, the average age in the Age column, and sums in the Quota and Sales columns as shown in Figure 5–75.
5. Add the icon set 3 arrows (colored) using conditional formatting to the Age column (G8:G20): Age >=50; 35=<Age<50; Age<35 as shown in Figure 5–75. To add the conditional formatting, select the range G8:G20, click the Conditional Formatting button on the Home tab on the Ribbon, and click the New Rule command. When Excel displays the New Formatting Rule dialog box, click the Icon Style box arrow, scroll up and click 3 Arrows (Colored). Click the Value box and enter the Age limits described earlier. Change the Type boxes to Number.
6. Change the document properties as specified by your instructor. Change the worksheet header with your name, course number, and other information requested by your instructor.
7. Use the Orientation button on the Page Layout tab on the Ribbon to change the orientation to Landscape. Print the table. Save the workbook using the file name, Lab 5-1 Whitman Publishing Sales Rep Table. Submit the assignment as requested by your instructor.

Instructions Part 2:   Open the workbook Lab 5-1 Whitman Publishing Sales Rep Table created in Part 1. Do not save the workbook in this part. Step through each query exercise in Table 5–7 and print (or write down for submission to your instructor) the results for each. To complete a filter exercise, use the AutoFilter technique. If the arrows are not showing to the right of the column headings when the table is active, then click the Filter button on the Data tab on the Ribbon. Select the appropriate arrow(s) to the right of the field names and option(s) on the corresponding menus. Use the Custom Filter option on the Number Filters list for field names that do not contain appropriate selections. Following each query, click the Filter button on the Data tab on the Ribbon twice to clear the query and reactivate the arrows in the field names. You should end up with the following number of records for Filters 1 through 12: 1 = 7; 2 = 6; 3 = 1; 4 = 2; 5 = 4; 6 = 1; 7 = 2; 8 = 3; 9 = 0; 10 = 4; 11 = 9; and 12 = 13. When you are finished querying the table, close the workbook without saving changes. Submit the assignment as requested by your instructor.

Table 5–7 Whitman Publishing Sales Rep Table Filter Criteria

Filter	Region	Div	Dist	Rep	Lname	Fname	Age	Gender	Quota	Sales
1								M		
2		C	3							
3	2	D	2							
4			2						>5,000,000	
5							>30	F		
6							>40 and < 50			
7							>50			>3,500,000
8	1	D								
9	1						<39	F		>4,000,000
10								M	>=5,500,000	
11				>=500						
12	All	All	All	All	All	All	All	All	All	All

Instructions Part 3: Open the workbook Lab 5-1 Whitman Publishing Sales Rep Table created in Part 1. Do not save the workbook in this part. Sort the table according to the following six sort problems. Print the table for each sort problem in landscape orientation using the Fit to option (or write down the last name in the first record for submission to your instructor). Begin problems 2 through 6 by sorting the Rep field in ascending sequence to sort the table back into its original order.

1. Sort the table in descending sequence by region.

2. Sort the table by district within division within region. All three sort keys are to be in ascending sequence.

3. Sort the table by division within region. Both sort keys are to be in descending sequence.

4. Sort the table by representative number within district within division within region. All four sort keys are to be in ascending sequence.

5. Sort the table in descending sequence by sales.

6. Sort the table by district within division within region. All three sort keys are to be in descending sequence.

7. Hide columns I and J by selecting them and pressing CTRL+o (zero). Print the table. Select columns H and K. Press CTRL+SHIFT+RIGHT PARENTHESIS to display the hidden columns. Close the Lab 5-1 Whitman Publishing Sales Rep Table workbook without saving changes. Submit the assignment as requested by your instructor.

Instructions Part 4: Open the Lab 5-1 Whitman Publishing Sales Rep Table workbook created in Part 1 and complete the following tasks. Do not save the workbook in this part.

1. Click a cell in the table to activate the table. Click the Design tab on the Ribbon and then click the Total Row check box to remove the total row. Sort the table by district within division within region. Select ascending sequence for all three sort keys.

2. Select cell A8. Right-click anywhere in the table, point to the Table command on the shortcut menu, and then click the Convert to Range command on the Table submenu. When Excel displays the Microsoft Office Excel dialog box, click the Yes button to convert the table to a range. Click the Data tab on the Ribbon and then click the Subtotal button on the Ribbon. When Excel displays the Subtotal dialog box, click the 'At each change in' box arrow and then click Region #. If necessary, select Sum in the Use function list. In the 'Add subtotal to' list, click Quota and Sales to select them and then click the OK button. Print the table. Click row level symbol 1 and print

Continued >

In the Lab *continued*

the table. Click row level symbol 2 and print the table. Click row level symbol 3. Click the Subtotal button on the Ribbon and then click the Remove All button in the Subtotal dialog box to remove all subtotals. Close the workbook without saving changes. Submit the assignment as requested by your instructor.

Instructions Part 5: Open the Lab 5-1 Whitman Publishing Sales Rep Table workbook created in Part 1. Copy the table (range A7:J20) to a new workbook. Save the new workbook in a CSV (Comma delimited) file format using the file name, Lab 5-1 Whitman Publishing Sales Rep Table CSV. Close the workbook. Start Notepad and open the CSV file. Print the CSV file. Close Notepad. Open the CSV file in Excel. Quit Excel. Submit the assignment as requested by your instructor.

In the Lab

Lab 2: Sorting, Finding, and Advanced Filtering
Problem: Computer Consultants, Inc. specializes in supplying computer consultants to companies in need of programmers. The company uses a table (Figure 5–76) that shows whether a consultant is knowledgeable in a programming language.

The chief financial officer, Cheryl Riiz, has asked you to sort, query, and determine some statistics from the table. Carefully label each required printout by using the part number and step. If a step results in multiple printouts, label them a, b, c, and so on.

Consultant Specialist Table

Name	Gender	Age	Yrs	VBA	VB	C#	C++	Java	COBOL	RPG	HTML	Count
Bhua, Li	M	21	2	N	N	Y	Y	Y	N	N	N	3
Kadafi, Kim	F	22	4	N	Y	Y	N	Y	Y	N	N	4
Kidd, Laura	F	23	1	N	Y	N	N	Y	Y	Y	Y	5
Sea, Tyler	M	24	3	Y	N	N	N	Y	Y	Y	N	4
Jang, Lin	F	25	5	Y	Y	Y	Y	Y	Y	Y	Y	8
White, Danzel	M	25	3	N	Y	Y	N	Y	Y	Y	N	5
Chavez, Juanita	F	26	4	Y	Y	N	Y	N	Y	N	N	4
Naik, Chandana	F	28	9	N	N	N	Y	Y	N	N	Y	3
Biagi, John	M	29	7	N	Y	N	Y	N	Y	N	Y	4
Goldsmith, Ed	M	31	8	Y	Y	Y	N	N	N	N	Y	4
Hatt, Jerimiah	M	32	5	Y	N	N	Y	Y	Y	N	Y	5
Santos, Carlos	M	32	7	Y	N	Y	N	N	N	N	Y	3
Sosa, Flower	F	32	10	N	Y	Y	Y	N	N	Y	Y	5
Dan, Jake	M	34	19	Y	Y	N	N	N	Y	Y	N	4
Harley, Jim	M	38	9	N	N	N	N	N	Y	Y	Y	3
Diaz, Jorge	M	38	15	Y	Y	Y	Y	Y	Y	Y	Y	8
Lock, Nikole	F	42	12	Y	Y	Y	Y	Y	Y	Y	Y	8
Smith, Kylie	F	45	7	Y	Y	Y	Y	N	Y	N	N	5
Brown, Fred	M	50	13	Y	N	N	Y	Y	Y	Y	Y	6
Wongley, Susie	F	65	23	Y	Y	N	N	Y	Y	Y	N	5

Figure 5–76

Instructions Part 1: Start Excel and perform the following tasks.

1. Open the workbook Lab 5-2 Consultant Specialist Table from the Data Files for Students. See the inside back cover of this book for instructions for downloading the Data Files for Students or see your instructor for information on accessing the files required in this book. Do not save the workbook in this part.

2. Complete the following tasks:

   a. Sort the records in the table into descending sequence by name. Susie Wongley should appear first in the table. Li Bhua should appear last. Print the table. Undo the sort.

   b. Sort the records in the table by age within gender. Select ascending sequence for the age and descending sequence for gender. Li Bhua should be the first record. Print the table. Undo the sort.

   c. Sort the table by Java within C++ within C# within VB. Apply sort descending for all four fields. Sort the table first on Java, then C++, then C#, and finally VB. Those who are proficient in all four programming languages will rise to the top of the table. Jorge Diaz should be the first record. Print the table. Close the workbook without saving it. Submit the assignment as requested by your instructor.

Instructions Part 2: Open the workbook Lab 5-2 Consultant Specialist Table (Figure 5–76) from the Data Files for Students. Do not save the workbook in this part. Select a cell within the table. If the column heading arrows do not appear, then click Filter on the Data tab on the Ribbon. Use the column heading arrows to find the records that meet the criteria in items 1 through 4 below. Use the Show All command on the Filter submenu before starting items 2, 3, and 4. Print the table for each problem. You should end up with the following number of records for items 1 through 4: item 1 should have 6; item 2 should have 3; item 3 should have 3; and item 4 should have 7. Close the workbook without saving the changes. Submit the assignment as requested by your instructor.

1. Find all records that represent employees who are male and are proficient in Java.

2. Find all records that represent employees with more than 9 years of experience (Yrs) and who are certified in VB and HTML.

3. Find all records that represent female employees who are at least 30 years old and are proficient in COBOL.

4. Find all records that represent employees who have at least 5 years of experience (Yrs) and who are proficient in VBA and HTML.

Instructions Part 3: Open the workbook Lab 5-2 Consultant Specialist Table from the Data Files for Students and then save the workbook using the file name, Lab 5-2 Consultant Specialist Table Final. Perform the following tasks:.

1. Add a criteria range by copying the table title and field names (range A9:M10) to the range A1:M2 (Figure 5–77). Change cell A1 to Criteria Area and then color the title area as shown in Figure 5–77. Use the Name box in the formula bar to name the criteria range (A2:M3) Criteria.

A	B	C	D	E	F	G	H	I	J	K	L	M	N
					Criteria Area								
Name	Gender	Age	Yrs	VBA	VB	C#	C++	Java	COBOL	RPG	HTML	Count	
	M	>30											

Figure 5–77

Continued >

In the Lab *continued*

2. Add an extract range by copying the table title and field names (range A9:M10) to the range A35:M36 (Figure 5–78). Change cell A35 to Extract Area and then color the title area as shown in Figure 5–78. Use the Name box in the formula bar to name the extract range (range A36:M36) Extract.

	A	B	C	D	E	F	G	H	I	J	K	L	M	N
34														
35	Extract Area													
36	Name	Gender	Age	Yrs	VBA	VB	C#	C++	Java	COBOL	RPG	HTML	Count	
37	Goldsmith, Ed	M	31	8	Y	Y	Y	N	N	N	N	Y	4	
38	Hatt, Jerimiah	M	32	5	Y	N	N	Y	Y	Y	N	Y	5	
39	Santos, Carlos	M	32	7	Y	N	Y	N	N	N	N	Y	3	
40	Dan, Jake	M	34	19	Y	Y	N	N	N	Y	Y	N	4	
41	Harley, Jim	M	38	9	N	N	N	N	N	Y	Y	Y	3	
42	Diaz, Jorge	M	38	15	Y	Y	Y	Y	Y	Y	Y	Y	8	
43	Brown, Fred	M	50	13	Y	N	N	Y	Y	Y	Y	Y	6	
44														

Figure 5–78

3. With the table active, use the Advanced button on the Data tab on the Ribbon to extract records that pass the tests listed below in a through d. Print the entire worksheet using landscape orientation and the Fit to option for each extract.

   a. Extract the records that represent employees who are male and older than 30 (Figure 5–77 on the previous page). You should extract seven records (Figure 5–78).

   b. Extract the records that represent female employees who are proficient in Java, but not in RPG. You should extract two records.

   c. Extract the records that represent male employees who are at least 35 years old and are proficient in at least four programming languages. The field Count in column M uses the COUNTIF function to count the number of Ys in a record. A count of 4 means the record represents a specialist with expertise in four areas. You should extract two records.

   d. Extract the records that represent employees who are proficient in three programming languages or fewer. You should extract 4 records.

4. Change the document properties as specified by your instructor. Change the worksheet header with your name, course number, and other information as specified by your instructor. Save the workbook using the file name, Lab 5-2 Consultant Specialist Table Final. Close the workbook. Submit the assignment as requested by your instructor.

Instructions Part 4:   Open the workbook Lab 5-2 Consultant Specialist Table Final created in Part 3. If you did not complete Part 3, then open Lab 5-2 Consultant Specialist Table from the Data Files for Students. Perform the following tasks:

1. Scroll to the right to display cell G1 in the upper-left corner of the window. Enter the criteria in the range O1:Q3 as shown in Figure 5–79. Enter the row titles in cells O5:O10 as shown in Figure 5–79.

2. Use the database function DAVERAGE and the appropriate criteria in the range O2:Q3 to determine the average age of the males and females in the range. Use the table function DCOUNT and the appropriate criteria in the range O2:Q3 to determine the record count of those who are proficient in HTML. The DCOUNT function requires that you choose a numeric field in the table to count, such as Age.

3. Use the SUMIF function to determine the Java Y Sum Count in cell R9. That is, sum the Count field for all records containing a Y in the Java column. Use the COUNTIF function to determine the HTML N Count in cell R10.

4. Print the worksheet in landscape orientation using the Fit to option. Save the workbook using the file name, Lab 5-2 Consultant Specialist Table Final. Submit the assignment as requested by your instructor.

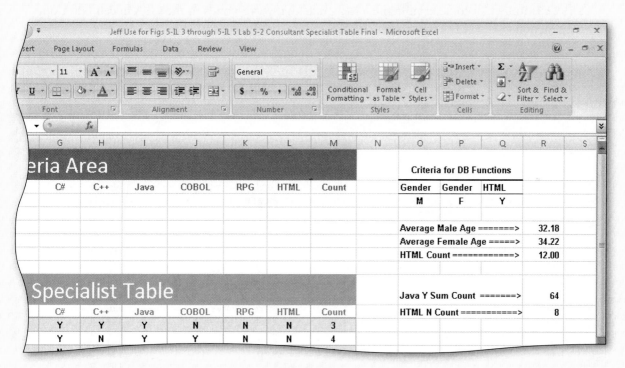

Figure 5–79

In the Lab

Lab 3: Creating a Table with a Lookup Function

Problem: You are a member of the Do-Gooders' Student Club, a club for young adults interested in helping the less fortunate. The president has asked for a volunteer to create a table of the club's members (Figure 5–80). You decide it is a great opportunity to show your Excel skills. Besides including a member's GPA in the table, the president also would like a GPA letter grade assigned to each member based on the GPA value in column G.

Instructions Part 1:   Perform the following tasks to create the table shown in the range A7:H17 in Figure 5–80.

1. Bold the entire worksheet. Create the table shown in Figure 5–80 using the techniques learned in this chapter. Assign appropriate formats to row 8, the row immediately below the field names. Rename the Sheet1 tab and delete Sheet2 and Sheet3.

2. Enter the data shown in the range A8:G17.

3. Enter the Grade table in the range J6:K20. In cell H8, enter the function =vlookup(g8, j8:k20, 2) to determine the letter grade that corresponds to the GPA in cell G8. Copy the function in cell H8 to the range H9:H17.

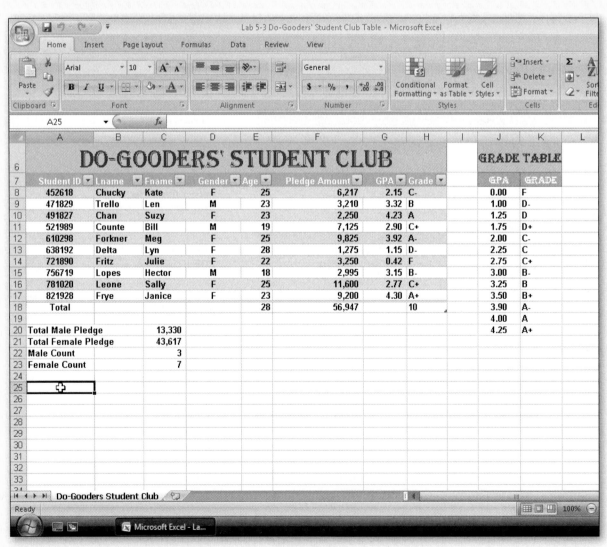

Figure 5–80

4. Select the Total Row option on the Design tab on the Ribbon to determine the maximum age, the pledge amount, and the record count in the Grade column in row 18.

5. Enter the total row headings in the range A20:A23. Use the SUMIF and COUNTIF functions to determine the totals in the range C20:C23.

6. Change the document properties as specified by your instructor. Change the worksheet header with your name, course number, and other information as specified by your instructor.

7. Save the workbook using the file name, Lab 5-3 Do-Gooders' Student Club Table. Print the worksheet in landscape orientation. At the bottom of the printout, explain why the dollar signs ($) are necessary in the VLOOKUP function in Step 3. Submit the assignment as requested by your instructor.

Instructions Part 2: Open the workbook Lab 5-3 Do-Gooders' Student Club Table. Do not save the workbook in this part. Sort the table as follows. Print the table after each sort. After completing the third sort, close the workbook without saving the changes.

1. Sort the table in ascending sequence by the Pledge Amount.

2. Sort the table by GPA within Gender. Use descending sequence for both fields.

3. Sort the table by Age within Gender. Use ascending sequence for both fields.

Instructions Part 3: Open the workbook Lab 5-3 Do-Gooders' Student Club Table and then save the file using the file name, Lab 5-3 Do Gooders' Student Club Table Final. Use the concepts and techniques presented in this chapter to set up a Criteria area above the table, set up an Extract area below the Grade table, and complete the following extractions. Extract the records that meet the following three criteria sets and print the worksheet for each:

1. Gender =F; GPA > 3.50 (Three records pass the test.)

2. Age > 23 (Four records pass the test.)

3. Gender = M; Age < 21 (Two records pass the test.)

Extract the records that meet the following criteria: 21 < Age < 25. It is necessary that you add a second field called Age to the immediate right of the Criteria range, delete the name Criteria, and then define the Criteria range to include the new field. Four records pass the final test. Select a cell outside the table and print the workbook in landscape orientation. Save the workbook with the last criteria range. Submit the assignment as requested by your instructor.

Cases and Places

Apply your creative thinking and problem solving skills to design and implement a solution.

• EASIER   •• MORE DIFFICULT

• 1: Inventory Level Priority

Create an inventory table from the data in Table 5–8. Also include an Amount field and a Priority field. Both are calculated columns. Amount equals Inventory times Price. Create a Priority Code table in the range I1:J6 using the data shown in Table 5–9. Use the VLOOKUP function to determine the priority to assign to each record. Add the total row to the table. Print the worksheet in landscape orientation using the Fit to option. Save the workbook.

Table 5–8 Educational Percussion, Inc. Inventory List			
Item number	**Description**	**Inventory**	**Price**
B60338	Bar Chime	619	14.25
M44910	Maraca	873	9.50
C71610	Castanet	579	17.60
S80787	Shekere	537	22.50
T36275	Tambourine	764	12.45
T74695	Triangle	208	8.30
W59366	Woodblock	268	7.95
C24890	Clave	385	13.80
C87343	Cabasa	387	14.05
W15840	Whistle	699	6.85
C49955	Cowbell	237	18.25

Table 5–9 Priority Codes	
Inventory	**Priority**
0	1
250	2
400	3
600	4
800	5

• 2: Conditional Formatting and Sorting a Table

Open the table created in Cases and Places Exercise 1. Add conditional formatting to the Priority field using the Icon Sets format style and the 5 Ratings icon style. Complete the following three sorts, print each sorted version of the table, and then undo the sorts in preparation for the next sort: (a) sort the table in ascending sequence (smallest to largest) by inventory, (b) sort the table by amount (ascending) within priority code (descending), and (c) sort the table in descending sequence by priority code. With the table sorted by priority, toggle off the total row, convert the table to a range, and then use the Subtotal button on the Data tab on the Ribbon to determine subtotals for each priority code. Print the table with the subtotals. Save the workbook with the subtotals.

• 3: Filtering a Table and Multiple Conditional Formats

Open the table created in Cases and Places Exercise 1. Add a second conditional format to the priority code field using a Data Bar format style and a Bar color of your choice. If necessary remove the subtotals and then convert the range back to a table. Filter (query) the table using the column heading arrows. Make sure you show all records before each query. Print the table for each of the following queries: (1) priority code equal to 2, (2) inventory greater than 250 and less than 600, (3) priority code equals 1 and inventory greater than 30, and (4) price greater than 9.00. The number of records that show in the queries are: (1) 3, (2) 5, (3) 2, and (4) 8.

• • 4: Creating a Table of Companies

Make It Personal

Gather information about companies at which you may want to work in your next job. Obtain information for at least ten companies in five different states. Include company name, state, city, miles from your current residence, and assign a rating for each company between 1 and 4, with 4 being the most preferred. Add a conditional format using the Data Bar format style, edit the formatting rule to show only bars, and change the width of the column to at least 20 characters. Complete the following sorts, print each sorted version of the table, and then undo the sorts in preparation for the next sort: (a) alphabetically (A to Z) by state, and (b) descending (smallest to largest) by miles from home. Filter the list for records with a preference greater than 2. Print the table and then show all of the records. Group the records by state, using the Average function in the Use function list in the Subtotal dialog box. Print the worksheet.

• • 5: Creating a Table of Students

Working Together

Have your group design a table that includes a row for each student. The table should contain the following information: (1) last initial and first initial, (2) gender, (3) age, (4) college start date, (5) resident state, (6) major, (7) credit hours required for degree, (8) credit hours towards degree, (9) percent of degree completed (computational field), (10) anticipated graduation year, and (11) letter grade based on GPA (1 = D, 2 = C, 3 = B, and 4 = A). Use the concepts and techniques introduced in this chapter to design and create a table from the data collected along with a grade field that corresponds to the GPA. Add conditional formatting to the gender, age, percent of degree completed, and anticipated graduation year fields. Also, run sorts, determine subtotals, and use the database, COUNTIF, and SUMIF functions to generate statistics.

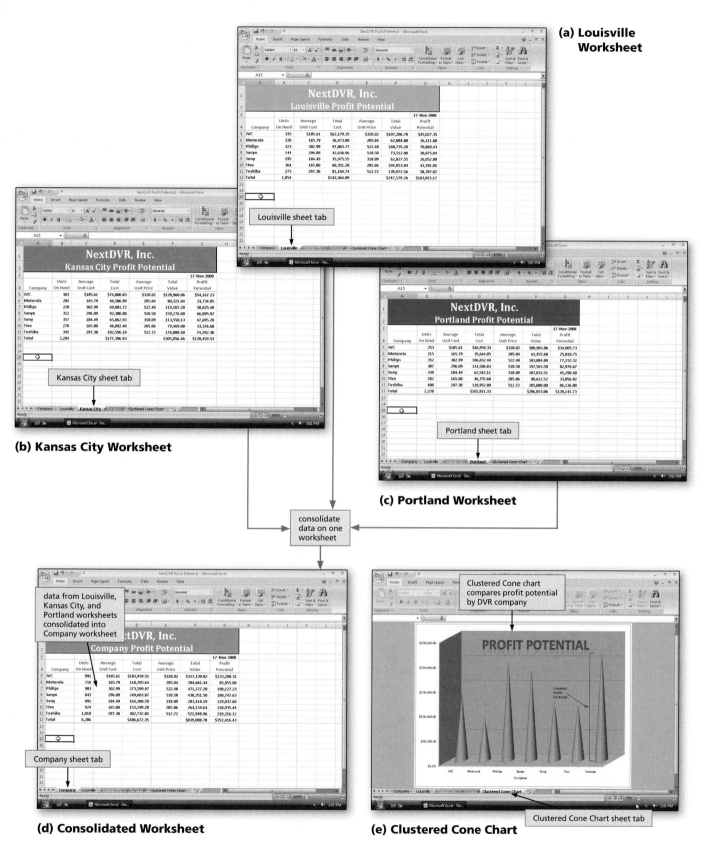

(a) Louisville Worksheet

(b) Kansas City Worksheet

(c) Portland Worksheet

(d) Consolidated Worksheet

(e) Clustered Cone Chart

Figure 6–1

The requirements document for the NextDVR Profit Potential workbook is shown in Figure 6–2. It includes the needs, source of data, summary of calculations, chart requirements, special requirements, and other facts about its development.

REQUEST FOR NEW WORKBOOK

Date Submitted:	October 6, 2008
Submitted By:	Chip Yerkes
Worksheet Title:	NextDVR, Inc. Profit Potential
Needs:	The needs are as follows: 1. A template (Figure 6-3a) that can be used to create similar worksheets. 2. A workbook containing three worksheets for the three regions in which the company operates and one worksheet to consolidate the company data. 3. A chart (Figure 6-3b) that compares the profit potential of the different DVRs in inventory, by company or brand. The chart should be placed on a separate sheet.
Source of Data:	The data will be collected and organized by the chief financial officer, Chip Yerkes.
Calculations:	Include the following formulas in the template for each camera: 1. Total Cost = Units On Hand * Average Unit Cost 2. Average Unit Price = Average Unit Cost / (1 − .42) 3. Total Value = Units On Hand * Average Unit Price 4. Profit Potential = Total Value − Total Cost 5. Use the SUM function to determine totals. 6. After using the template to create the multiple-worksheet workbook, use the SUM function to determine the units on hand totals on the Company sheet (Figure 6-1d). **Note:** Use dummy data in the template to verify the formulas. Round the Average Unit Price to the nearest penny.
Chart Requirements:	Include a chart sheet with a Clustered Cone chart that compares the profit potential for each of the DVR brands listed on the Company sheet. Use a text box to create a callout to highlight the cone representing the DVR brand with the greatest profit potential.
Special Requirements:	Investigate a way NextDVR can consolidate data from multiple workbooks into another workbook.

Approvals

Approval Status:	X	Approved
		Rejected
Approved By:	Jason Ganden	
Date:	October 15, 2008	
Assigned To:	J. Quasney, Spreadsheet Specialist	

Figure 6–2

Overview

As you read this chapter, you will learn how to create the worksheet shown in Figure 6–1 by performing these general tasks:

- Create and format the template
- Add a worksheet to the workbook
- Reference data on other worksheets
- Create a Clustered Cone chart and add WordArt to the chart
- Print the worksheet with proper page breaks
- Create a workspace and consolidate data by linking workbooks

Plan
Ahead

General Project Decisions

While creating an Excel worksheet, you need to make several decisions that will determine the appearance and characteristics of the finished worksheet. As you create the worksheet to meet the requirements shown in Figure 6–2, you should follow these general guidelines:

1. Design the template and plan the formatting. Templates help speed and simplify work because Excel users often work with the same types of problems over and over again. Using a template allows you to begin your work with a preformatted worksheet. In the case of the NextDVR Profit Potential worksheet, the template saves the work of formatting the three region worksheets and the consolidated worksheet. The formatting is done once in the template, and then that formatting automatically is carried over to the new worksheets.

2. Identify additional worksheets needed in the workbook. After the template is created using dummy data and the required formulas (Figure 6–4 on page EX 424) and then saved, it will be copied to a workbook made up of four worksheets. Actual data for the three regions will replace the dummy data on the three region worksheets. The data from the three region worksheets then will be consolidated on the company worksheet.

3. Plan the layout and location of the required chart. The chart requires additional artwork, including a callout, and would therefore be more suited for placement on a new worksheet. A Clustered Cone chart type is a proper choice for this chart because data from a few vendors is compared. The tapering of the cones allows space for additional elements, such as the callout, without any overlapping.

4. Examine the alternatives for printing a number of worksheets, including headers, margins, and page breaks. When working with multiple worksheets, using properly formatted page headers and footers is important. Excel allows you to print page numbers and the sheet name of each sheet. In addition, margins and page breaks also can be adjusted to provide professional looking printed worksheets.

5. Identify workbooks to be consolidated into a workspace and then linked to create a consolidated workbook of the initial workbooks. The special requirement for the project listed in the requirements document (Figure 6–2) asks that methods to combine workbooks together should be investigated. Each of the three regions has sent a similar workbook that represents their own profit potentials. Excel allows you to work with these workbooks in a workspace and then link the workbooks together to provide a consolidated view of the data in the workbooks.

(continued)

Plan Ahead

(continued)

In addition, using a sketch of the worksheet can help you visualize its design. The sketch of the template (Figure 6–3a) consists of titles, column and row headings, location of data values, and a general idea of the desired formatting. The sketch of the Clustered Cone chart (Figure 6–3b) consists of a chart title, which will be added using WordArt, and a callout that emphasizes the cylinder representing the greatest profit potential.

When necessary, more specific details concerning the above guidelines are presented at appropriate points in the chapter. The chapter also will identify the actions you perform and decisions made regarding these guidelines during the creation of the worksheet shown in Figure 6–1 on page EX 419.

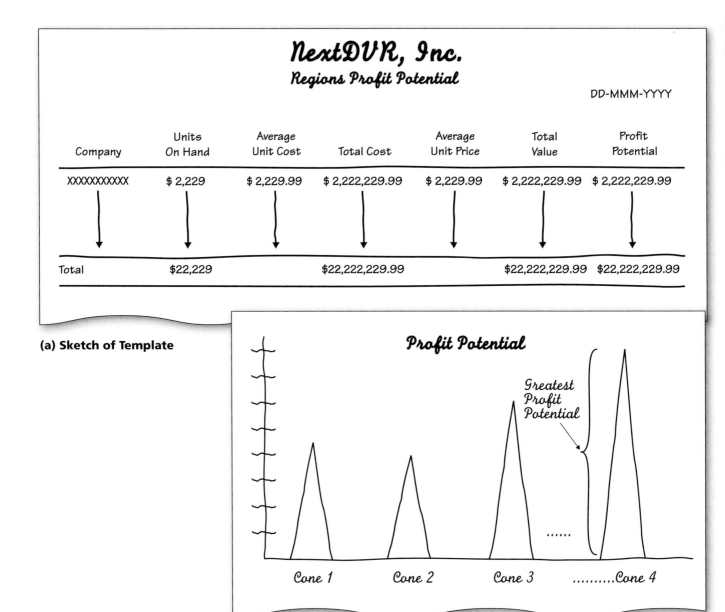

(a) Sketch of Template

(b) Sketch of Clustered Cone Chart

Figure 6–3

With a good understanding of the requirements document, an understanding of the necessary decisions, and a sketch of the template, the next step is to use Excel to create the template.

To Start Excel

If you are using a computer to step through the project in this chapter and you want your screen to match the figures in this book, you should change your computer's resolution to 1024 × 768. For information about how to change a computer's resolution, see page APP 21 in Appendix E.

The following steps, which assume Windows is running, start Excel based on a typical installation of Microsoft Office on your computer. You may need to ask your instructor how to start Excel for your computer.

Note: If you are using Windows XP, see Appendix F for alternate steps.

1 Click the Start button on the Windows Vista taskbar to display the Start menu.

2 Click All Programs at the bottom of the left pane on the Start menu to display the All Programs list.

3 Click Microsoft Office in the All Programs list to display the Microsoft Office list.

4 Click Microsoft Office Excel 2007 to start Excel and display a blank worksheet in the Excel window.

5 If the Excel window is not maximized, click the Maximize button next to the Close button on its title bar to maximize the window.

6 If the worksheet window in Excel is not maximized, click the Maximize button next to the Close button on its title bar to maximize the worksheet window within Excel.

Creating the Template

The first step in building the workbook is to create and save a template that contains the titles, column and row headings, formulas, and formats used on each of the sheets.

Design the template and plan the formatting.	Plan Ahead

Design the template and plan the formatting.
The template will be used to create a number of other worksheets. Thus, it is important to consider the layout, cell formatting, and contents of the page.

- **Set row heights and column widths.** Row heights and column widths should be set to sizes large enough to accommodate future needs.

- **Use placeholders for data when possible.** Placeholders are used in a template to guide users of the template regarding what type of data to enter in cells. For example, the word Region should be used in the subtitle to indicate to a user of the template to place the Region name in the subtitle.

(continued)

Plan Ahead

(continued)

- **Use dummy data to verify formulas.** When a template is created, **dummy data** — that is, sample data used in place of actual data to verify the formulas in the template — should be used in place of actual data to verify the formulas in the template. Selecting simple numbers such as 1, 2, and 3 allows you to check quickly to see if the formulas are generating the proper results. In templates with more complex formulas, you may want to use numbers that test the extreme boundaries of valid data.

- **Format cells in the template.** Formatting should be applied to titles and subtitles that can be changed to provide cues to users of the worksheets. For example, by using a fill color for the title and subtitle, when each regions' worksheets are created, the fill color can be changed. All numeric cell entry placeholders – dummy data – should be properly formatted for unit numbers and currency amounts.

After the template is saved, it can be used every time a similar workbook is developed. Because templates help speed and simplify their work, many Excel users create a template for each application on which they work. Templates can be simple — possibly using a special font or worksheet title; or they can be more complex — perhaps utilizing specific formulas and format styles, such as the template for the NextDVR Profit Potential workbook.

Creating a template, as shown in Figure 6–4, follows the same basic steps used to create a workbook. The only difference between developing a workbook and a template is the file type used to save the template.

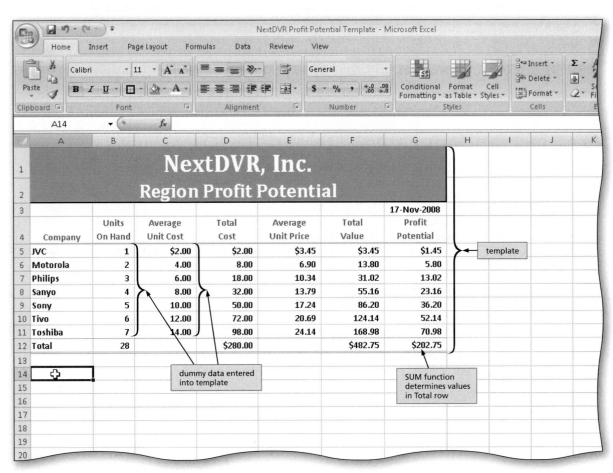

Figure 6–4

To Bold the Font and Adjust the Row Heights and Column Widths of the Template

The first step in creating the template is to change the font style to bold and adjust the height of row 4 to 30.75 points and column widths of columns A and C through G to 13.00 characters.

1 Click the Select All button immediately above row heading 1 and to the left of column heading A and then click the Bold button on the Ribbon. Select cell A1 to deselect the worksheet.

2 Drag the bottom boundary of row heading 4 down until the ScreenTip, Height 30.75 (41 pixels), appears.

3 Drag the right boundary of column heading A to the right until the ScreenTip, Width: 13.00 (96 pixels), appears.

4 Click column heading C, drag through to column heading G, and then drag the right boundary of column heading G right until the ScreenTip, Width: 13.00 (96 pixels), appears. Select cell A1 to deselect columns C through G.

BTW
Selecting a Range of Cells
You can select any range of cells with entries surrounded by blank cells by clicking a cell in the range and pressing CTRL+SHIFT+ASTERISK (*).

To Enter the Title, Subtitle, and Row Titles in the Template

The following steps enter the titles in cells A1 and A2 and the row titles in column A.

1 Type NextDVR, Inc. in cell A1 and then press the DOWN ARROW key.

2 Type Region Profit Potential in cell A2 and then press the DOWN ARROW key twice to make cell A4 active.

3 Type Company and then press the DOWN ARROW key.

4 With cell A5 active, enter the remaining row titles in column A as shown in Figure 6–5 on the next page.

BTW
Displaying Future Dates
You can display a future date, such as tomorrow's date, in a cell by adding a number to the NOW or TODAY function. For example, =NOW()+1 displays tomorrow's date in a cell and =NOW()+14 displays a date two weeks in the future. The function =NOW() – 1 displays yesterday's date.

To Enter Column Titles and the System Date in the Template

The next step is to enter the column titles in row 4 and the system date in cell G3.

1 Select cell B4. Type Units and then press ALT+ENTER. Type On Hand and then press the RIGHT ARROW key.

2 Type Average and then press ALT+ENTER. Type Unit Cost and then press the RIGHT ARROW key.

3 With cell D4 active, enter the remaining column titles in row 4 as shown in Figure 6–5.

4 Select cell G3. Type =now() and then press the ENTER key. Right-click cell G3 and then click Format Cells on the shortcut menu. When Excel displays the Format Cells dialog box, click Date in the Category list and then double-click 3/14/01 13:30 in the Type list. Select cell A14 to deselect cell G3.

Q&A Why was the date not formatted as it appears in Figure 6–4?

The format assigned to the system date in cell G3 is temporary. For now, it ensures that the system date will appear properly, rather than as a series of number signs (#). The system date will be assigned a permanent format later in this chapter.

BTW
Manipulating Dates
You can use the DATE function to change a year, month, and day to a serial number that automatically is formatted to mm/dd/yyyy. For example, if cell A1 equals the year 2008, cell A2 equals the month 2, cell A3 equals day 10, and cell A4 is assigned the function =DATE (A1, A2, A3), then 2/10/2008 appears in cell A4. The DATE function is most useful in formulas where year, month, and day are formulas, not constants.

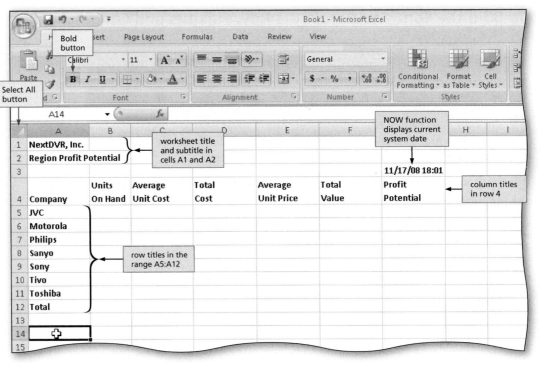

Dummy Numbers

As you develop more sophisticated workbooks, it will become increasingly important that you create good test data to ensure your workbooks are free of errors. The more you test a workbook, the more confident you will be in the results generated. Always take the time to select test data that tests the limits of the formulas.

Figure 6–5

To Enter Dummy Data in the Template Using the Fill Handle

While creating the NextDVR template in this chapter, dummy data is used for the units on hand values in the range B5:B11 and the average unit cost values in the range C5:C11. The dummy data is entered by using the fill handle to create a series of numbers in columns B and C. The series in column B begins with 1 and increments by 1; the series in column C begins with 2 and increments by 2. Recall that you must enter the first two numbers in a series so that Excel can determine the increment amount. If the cell to the right of the start value is empty and you want to increment by 1, however, you can create a series by entering only one number as shown in the following steps.

- Select cell B5.

- Type 1 and then press the ENTER key.

- Select the range B5:C5.

- Drag the fill handle through cells B11 and C11. Do not release the mouse button (Figure 6–6).

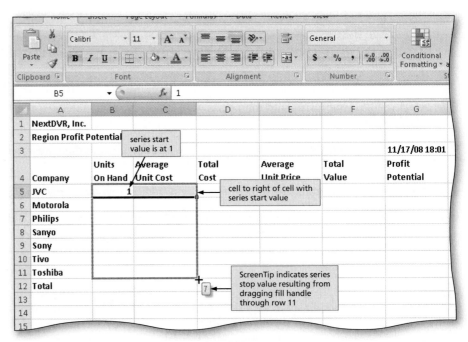

Figure 6–6

2

- Release the mouse button to create the series 1 through 7 in increments of 1 in the range B5:B11 (Figure 6–7).

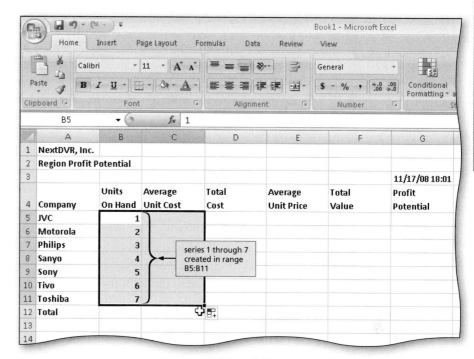

Figure 6–7

3

- Select cell C5. Type 2 and then press the DOWN ARROW key.

- Type 4 and then press the ENTER key.

- Select the range C5:C6. Drag the fill handle through cell C11 to create the series 2 through 14 in increments of 2 in the range C5:C11 (Figure 6–8).

Q&A

What other types of series can I create?

Excel allows you to create many types of series, including a **date series** (Jan, Feb, Mar, etc.), an **auto fill series** (1, 1, 1, etc.), and a **linear series** (1, 2, 3, etc. or 2, 4, 6, etc.), which was created in the previous steps. A fourth type of series is a growth series. A **growth series** multiplies values by a constant factor. You can create a growth

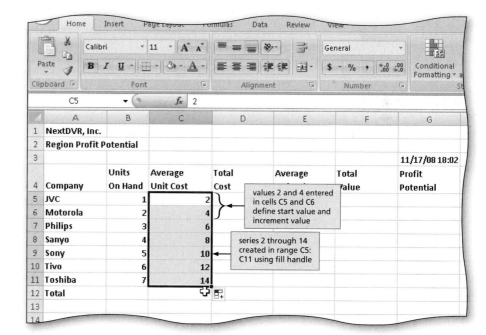

Figure 6–8

series by entering an initial value in the first cell, selecting the range to fill, clicking the Fill button on the Home tab on the Ribbon, clicking Series, clicking Growth in the type area, and then entering a constant factor in the Step value box.

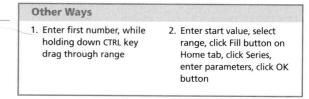

Other Ways

1. Enter first number, while holding down CTRL key drag through range

2. Enter start value, select range, click Fill button on Home tab, click Series, enter parameters, click OK button

BTW

Accuracy
The result of an arithmetic operation, such as multiplication or division, is accurate to the factor with the least number of decimal places.

The ROUND Function and Entering Formulas in the Template

The next step is to enter the four formulas for the first DVR company (JVC) in the range D5:G5. When you multiply or divide decimal numbers that result in an answer with more decimal places than the format allows, you run the risk of the column totals being off by a penny or so. For example, as shown in the worksheet sketch in Figure 6–3a on page EX 422, columns C through G use the Currency and Comma style formats with two decimal places. And yet, the formulas used to calculate values for these columns result in several additional decimal places that Excel maintains for computation purposes. For this reason, it is recommended that you use the **ROUND function** on formulas that potentially can result in more decimal places than the format displays in a given cell. The general form of the ROUND function is

=ROUND (number, number of digits)

where the number argument can be a number, a cell reference that contains a number, or a formula that results in a number; and the number of digits argument can be any positive or negative number used to determine the number of places to which the number will be rounded.

BTW

Fractions
The forward slash (/) has multiple uses. For example, dates often are entered using the slash. In formulas, the slash represents division. What about fractions? To enter a fraction, such as ½, type .5 or 0 ½ (i.e., type zero, followed by a space, followed by the number 1, followed by a slash, followed by the number 2). If you type ½ without the preceding zero, Excel will store the value in the cell as the date January 2.

The following is true about the ROUND function:

1. If the number of digits argument is greater than 0 (zero), then the number is rounded to the specified number of digits to the right of the decimal point.
2. If the number of digits argument is equal to 0 (zero), then the number is rounded to the nearest integer.
3. If the number of digits argument is less than 0 (zero), then the number is rounded to the specified number of digits to the left of the decimal point.

Table 6–1 shows the four formulas to enter in the template in the range D5:G5. The ROUND function is used to round the value resulting from the formula assigned to cell E5 to two decimal places.

Table 6–1 Formulas Used to Determine Profit Potential			
Cell	**Description**	**Formula**	**Entry**
D5	Total Cost	Units On Hand x Average Unit Cost	=B5 * C5
E5	Average Unit Price	ROUND(Average Unit Cost / (1–.42), 2)	=ROUND(C5 / (1–.42), 2)
F5	Total Value	Units On Hand x Average Unit Price	=B5 * E5
G5	Profit Potential	Total Value – Total Cost	=F5 – D5

BTW

Changing Modes
You change from Enter mode or Edit mode to Point mode by typing the EQUAL SIGN (=) followed by clicking a cell or clicking the Insert Function box on the formula bar, selecting a function, and then clicking a cell. You know you are in Point mode when the word Point appears on the left side of the status bar at the bottom of the Excel window.

The most difficult formula to understand in Table 6–1 is the one that determines the average unit price, which also is called the average selling price. To make a net profit, companies must sell their merchandise for more than the unit cost of the merchandise plus the company's operating expenses (taxes, rent, upkeep, and so forth).

To determine what selling price to set for an item, companies often first establish a desired margin and then determine a selling price. Most companies look for a margin of 30% to 75%. NextDVR, Inc., for example, tries to make a margin of 42% on each of its digital cameras. The formula for the average unit price in Table 6–1 helps the company determine the price at which to sell an item so that it ends up with a 42% margin. For example, if an item costs NextDVR $2.00 (the unit cost), then the company must sell it for $3.45 [$2.00 / (1–.42)] to make a 42% margin. Of this $3.45, $2.00 goes to pay the unit cost of the item; the other $1.45 is the gross profit potential (42% x $3.45 = $1.45).

To Enter Formulas Using Point Mode and Determine Totals in the Template

The following steps use Point mode to enter the four formulas in Table 6–1 in the range D5:G5. After the formulas are entered for JVC DVRs in row 5, the formulas will be copied for the remaining six companies. The Sum button then is used to determine the totals in row 12.

1

• Select cell D5, type = to start the formula, click cell B5, type * (asterisk), click cell C5, and then click the Enter box in the formula bar (Figure 6–9).

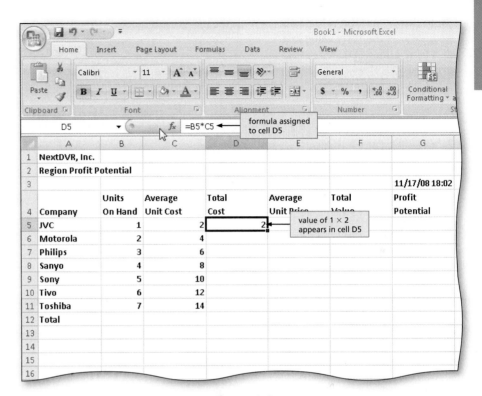

Figure 6–9

2

• Select cell E5, type =round(c5/(1-.42),2), and then click the Enter box in the formula bar to display the formula =ROUND(C5/(1-0.42), 2) in the formula bar and the value 3.45 (3.448276 rounded to two decimal places) as the average unit price in cell E5 (Figure 6–10).

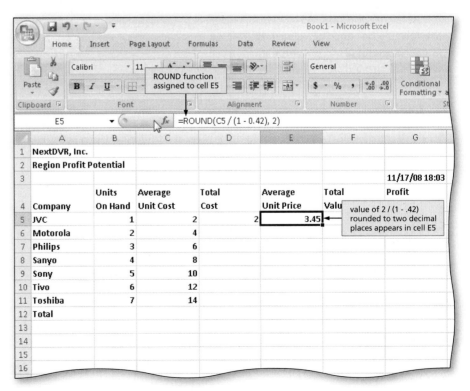

Figure 6–10

3

● Select cell F5, type = to start the formula, click cell B5, type * (asterisk), click cell E5, and then click the Enter box in the formula bar to display the formula =B5*E5 in the formula bar and the value 3.45 (1 x 3.45) as the total value in cell F5 (Figure 6–11).

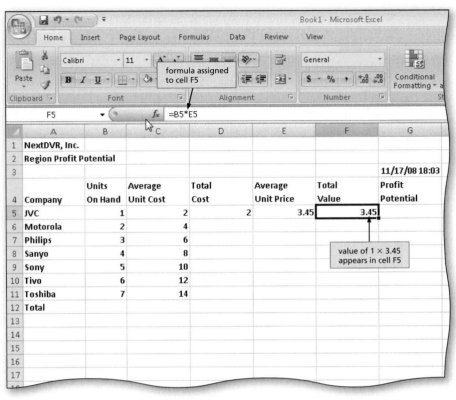

Figure 6–11

4

● Select cell G5, type = to start the formula, click cell F5, type – (minus sign), click cell D5, and then click the Enter box in the formula bar to display the formula =F5 – D5 in the formula bar and the value 1.45 (3.45 – 2) as the profit potential in cell G5 (Figure 6–12).

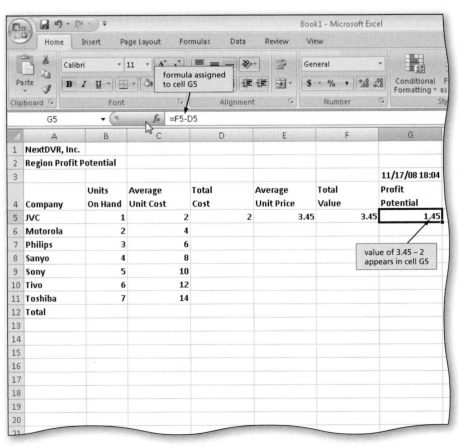

Figure 6–12

5

• Select the range D5:G5 and then point to the fill handle (Figure 6–13).

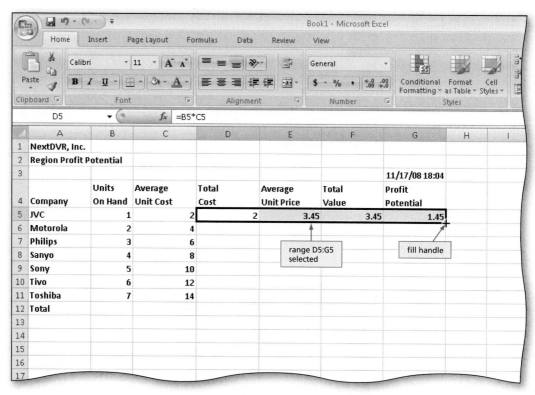

Figure 6–13

6

• Drag down through the range D6:G11 to copy the formulas in the range D5:G5 to the range D6:G11. Excel automatically adjusts the cell references so each formula references the data in the row to which it is copied (Figure 6–14).

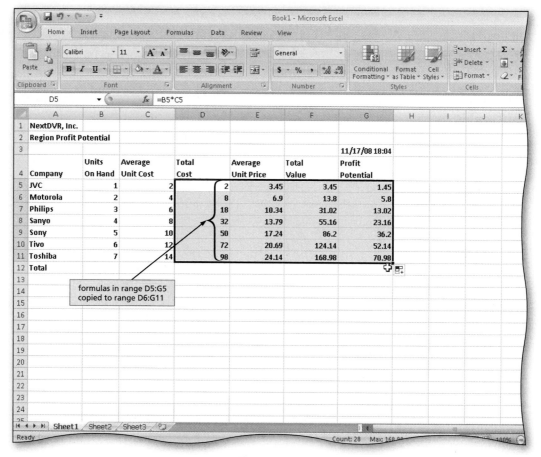

Figure 6–14

7

- Select cell B12, and then click the Sum button on the Ribbon twice.

- Select cell D12 and then click the Sum button twice.

- Select the range F12:G12 and then click the Sum button.

- Select cell A14 to deselect the range F12:G12 and display the values based on the dummy data entered earlier in columns B and C (Figure 6–15).

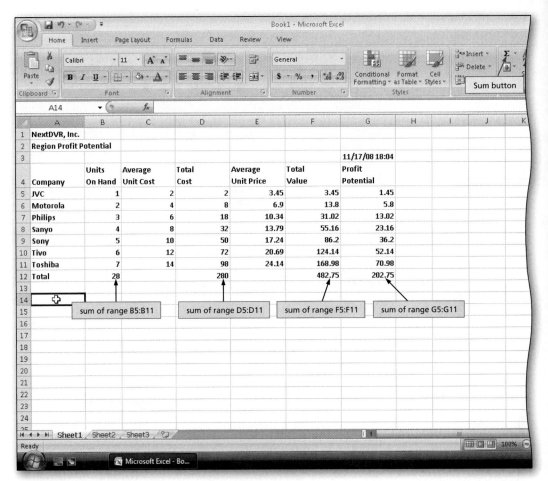

Figure 6–15

To Save the Template

Saving a template is just like saving a workbook, except that the file type Template is selected in the Save as type box in the Save As dialog box. The following steps save the template on a USB drive in drive E using the file name, NextDVR Profit Potential Template.

1

- Update the document properties with your name and any other relevant information.

- With a USB flash drive connected to one of the computer's USB ports, click the Save button on the Quick Access Toolbar to display the Save As dialog box.

- When Excel displays the Save As dialog box, type `NextDVR Profit Potential Template` in the File name box.

- Click the Save as type box arrow and then click Excel Template in the list.

- Select UDISK 2.0 (E:) as the new save location (Figure 6–16).

2

- Click the Save button in the Save As dialog box to save the template on the USB drive and display the file name, NextDVR Profit Potential Template, on the title bar (Figure 6–17 on the next page).

Q&A

Why does Excel change the folder name when the Excel Template file type is chosen?

When the Excel Template file type is chosen in the Save as type box, Excel automatically changes the contents of the Save in box to the Templates folder created when Office 2007 was installed. In a **production environment** — that is, when you are creating a template for a business, school, or personal application — the template typically would be saved in the Templates folder, not on the USB flash drive.

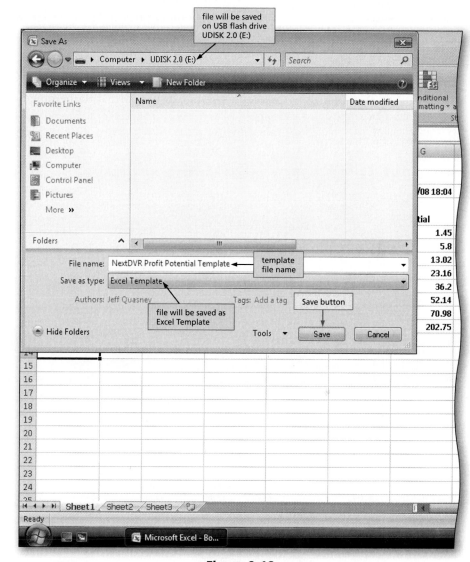

Figure 6–16

Formatting the Template

The next step is to format the template so it appears as shown in Figure 6–17. The following list summarizes the steps required to format the template.

1. Format the titles in cells A1 and A2.
2. Format the column titles and add borders to rows 4 and 12.
3. Assign the Currency style format with a floating dollar sign to the nonadjacent ranges C5:G5 and D12:G12.
4. Assign a Custom style format to the range C6:G11.
5. Assign a Comma style format to the range B5:B12.
6. Create a format style and assign it to the date in cell G3.

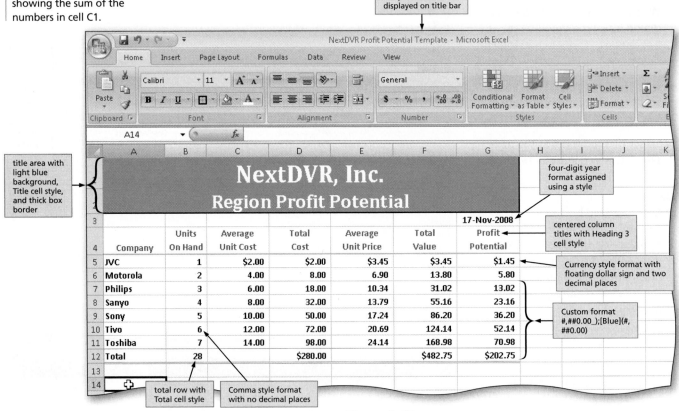

Figure 6–17

To Format the Template Title and Subtitle

The steps used to format the template title and subtitle include changing cell A1 to 28-point with the Title cell style; changing cell A2 to 22-point with the Title cell style; centering both titles across columns A through G; changing the title background color to light blue and the title font to white; and drawing a thick box border around the title area. The color scheme associated with the default Office template also will be changed to a new color scheme. One reason to change the color scheme is to add variety to the look of the worksheet that you create. The following steps format the title and subtitle.

1 Click the Page Layout tab on the Ribbon. Click the Colors button on the Ribbon and then click Apex in the Colors gallery.

2 Select the range A1:A2. Click the Home tab on the Ribbon and apply the Title cell style to the range. Select cell A1. Click the Font Size box arrow on the Ribbon and then click 28 in the Font Size list. Select the range A1:G1. Click the Merge & Center button on the Ribbon.

3 Select cell A2, click the Font Size box arrow on the Ribbon, and then click 22 in the Font Size list. Select the range A2:G2. Click the Merge & Center button on the Ribbon.

4 Select the range A1:A2, click the Fill Color button arrow on the Ribbon, and then click Light Blue (column 7, row 7) on the Fill Color palette.

5 Click the Font Color button arrow on the Ribbon and then click White, Background 1 (column 1, row 1) on the Font Color palette.

6 Click the Borders button arrow on the Ribbon and then click Thick Box Border in the Borders gallery.

7 Select cell A14 to deselect the range A1:A2.

To Format the Column Titles and Total Row

The next steps center and underline the column titles and draw a top and double bottom border on the Total row in row 12.

1 Select the range A4:G4, click the Center button on the Ribbon, and then apply the Heading 3 cell style to the range.

2 Select the range A12:G12, assign the Total cell style to the range, and then select cell A14 (Figure 6–18).

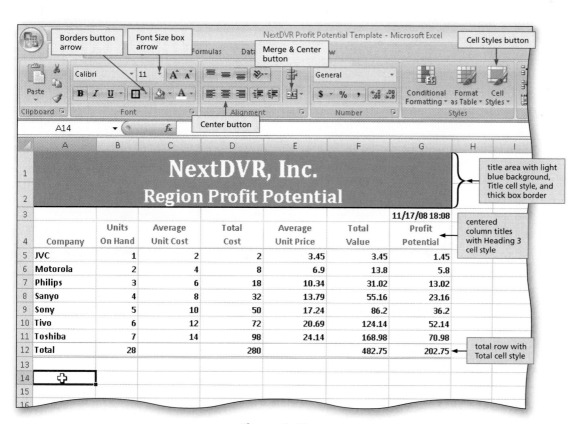

Figure 6–18

To Assign a Currency Style Using the Format Dialog Box

As shown in Figure 6–17 on page EX 434, the template for this chapter follows the **standard accounting format** for a table of numbers; that is, it contains floating dollar signs in the first row of numbers (row 5) and the totals row (row 12). Recall that while a fixed dollar sign always appears in the same position in a cell (regardless of the number of significant digits), a floating dollar sign always appears immediately to the left of the first significant digit in the cell. To assign a fixed dollar sign to rows 5 and 12, select the range and then click the Accounting Number Format button on the Home tab on the Ribbon. Assigning a floating dollar sign, by contrast, requires you to select the desired format in the Format Cells dialog box.

The following steps use the Format Cells dialog box to assign a Currency style with a floating dollar sign and two decimal places to the ranges C5:G5 and D12:G12.

- Select the range C5:G5.

- While holding down the CTRL key, select the nonadjacent range D12:G12 and then right-click the selected ranges to highlight the nonadjacent ranges and display the shortcut menu (Figure 6–19).

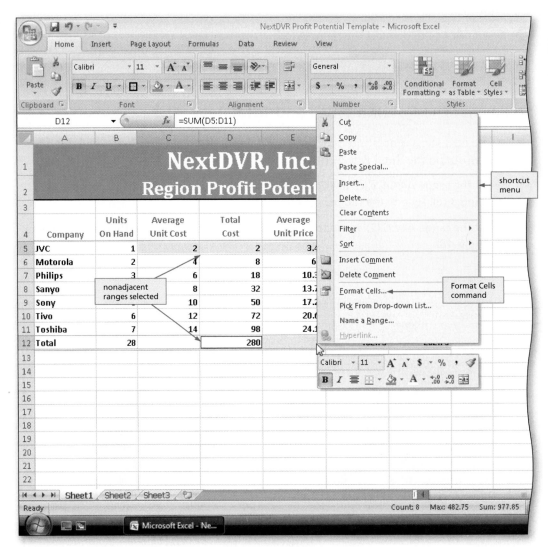

Figure 6–19

2

• Click Format Cells on the shortcut menu.

• When Excel displays the Format Cells dialog box, if necessary click the Number tab, click Currency in the Category list, and then click the red ($1,234.10) in the Negative numbers list (Figure 6–20).

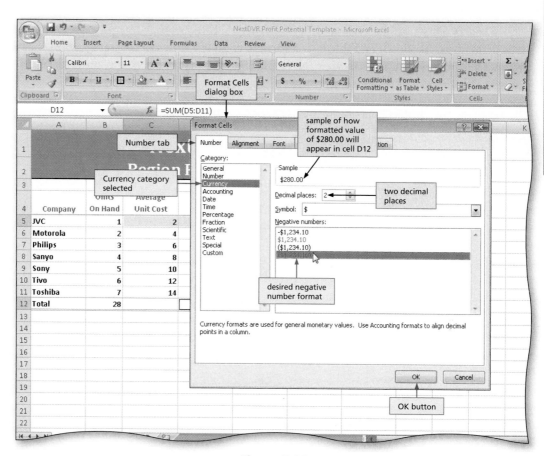

Figure 6–20

3

• Click the OK button to assign the Currency style with a floating dollar sign and two decimal places to the ranges C5:G5 and D12:G12. Select cell A14 to deselect the nonadjacent ranges (Figure 6–21).

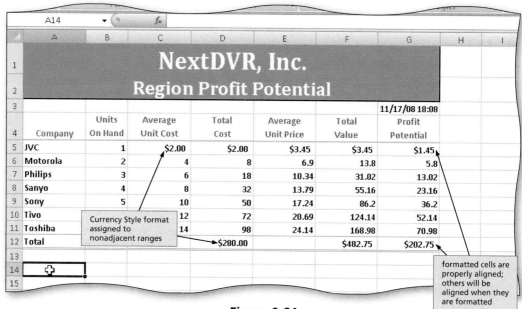

Figure 6–21

Other Ways

1. Press CTRL+1, click Number tab, select format, click OK button

To Create and Assign a Custom Format Code and a Comma Style Format

Excel assigns a format code to every format style listed in the Category list in the Number sheet in the Format Cells dialog box. As shown in Table 6–2, a **format code** is a series of format symbols that defines how a cell entry assigned a format will appear. To view the entire list of format codes that come with Excel, select Custom in the Category list (Figure 6–20 on the previous page).

Table 6–2 Format Symbols in Format Codes		
Format Symbol	**Example of Symbol**	**Description**
# (number sign)	###.##	Serves as a digit placeholder. If the value in a cell has more digits to the right of the decimal point than number signs in the format, Excel rounds the number. Extra digits to the left of the decimal point are displayed.
0 (zero)	0.00	Functions like a number sign (#), except that if the number is less than 1, Excel displays a 0 in the ones place.
. (period)	#0.00	Ensures Excel will display a decimal point in the number. The placement of period symbols determines how many digits appear to the left and right of the decimal point.
% (percent)	0.00%	Displays numbers as percentages of 100. Excel multiplies the value of the cell by 100 and displays a percent sign after the number.
, (comma)	#,##0.00	Displays a comma as a thousands separator.
( )	#0.00;(#0.00)	Displays parentheses around negative numbers.
$ or + or –	$#,##0.00; ($#,##0.00)	Displays a floating sign ($, +, or –).
* (asterisk)	$*##0.00	Displays a fixed sign ($, +, or –) to the left in the cell followed by spaces until the first significant digit.
[color]	#.##;[Red]#.##	Displays the characters in the cell in the designated color. In the example, positive numbers appear in the default color, and negative numbers appear in red.
" " (quotation marks)	$0.00 "Surplus"; $-0.00 "Shortage"	Displays text along with numbers entered in a cell.
_ (underscore)	#,##0.00_)	Skips the width of the character that follows the underscore.

Before creating custom format codes or modifying an existing custom format code, you should understand their makeup. As shown below, a format code can have up to four sections: positive numbers, negative numbers, zeros, and text. Each section is divided by a semicolon.

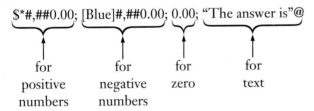

$*#,##0.00; [Blue]#,##0.00; 0.00; "The answer is"@

| for positive numbers | for negative numbers | for zero | for text |

A format code need not have all four sections. For most applications, a format code will have only a positive section and possibly a negative section.

The next step is to create and assign a custom format code to the range C6:G11. To assign a custom format code, you select the Custom category in the Category list in the Format Cells dialog box, select a format code close to the one to be created, and then modify or customize the selected format code. The following steps create and assign a custom format code.

1

- Select the range C6:G11, right-click the selected range, and then click Format Cells on the shortcut menu.

- When Excel displays the Format Cells dialog box, if necessary, click the Number tab, and then click Custom in the Category list.

- If necessary, scroll down and then click #,##0.00_); [Red](#,##0.00) in the Type list.

- In the Type text box, change the word Red to Blue (Figure 6–22).

Q&A

What is displayed in the dialog box?

The Custom format has been modified to show negative numbers in blue. In the Sample area, Excel displays a sample of the custom format assigned to the first number in the selected range.

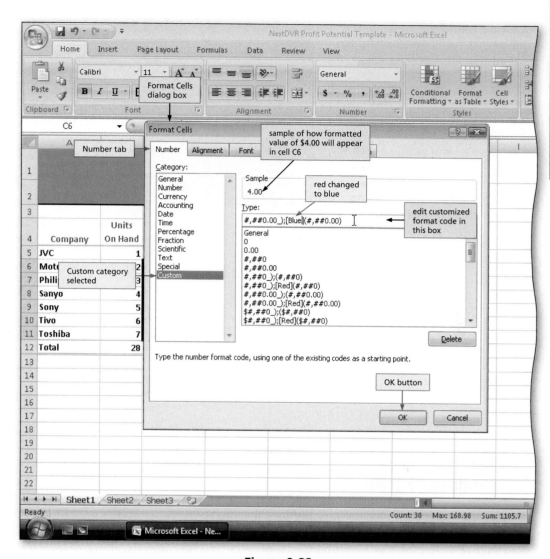

Figure 6–22

2

- Click the OK button to display the numbers in the range C6:G11 using the custom format code created in Step 1.

- Select the range B5:B12, click the Comma Style button on the Ribbon, and then click the Decrease Decimal button on the Ribbon twice to display the numbers in the range B5:B12 using the Comma style format with no decimal places (Figure 6–23).

- Select cell A14.

Q&A

Can I reuse the custom format code?

Yes. When you create a new custom format code, Excel adds it to the bottom of the Type list in the Number sheet in the Format Cells dialog box to make it available for future use.

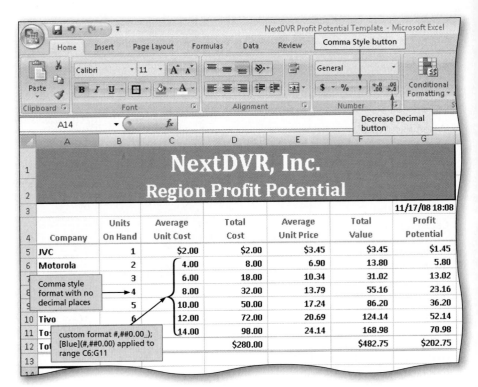

Figure 6–23

To Create a New Style

A **style** is a group of format specifications that are assigned to a style name. Most of the cell styles in the Cell Styles gallery that is displayed when you click the Cell Styles button on the Home tab include formatting only of visual characteristics, such as font, font size, font color, and fill color. Excel makes several general styles available with all workbooks and themes, as described in Table 6–3. You can apply these existing styles to a cell or cells in a worksheet, modify an existing style, or create an entirely new style.

Table 6–3 Styles Available with All Workbooks via the Cell Styles Button on the Home Tab	
Style Name	**Description**
Normal	Number = General; Alignment = General, Bottom Aligned; Font = Arial 10; Border = No Borders; Patterns = No Shading; Protection = Locked
Comma	Number = (*#,##0.00);_(*(#,##0.00);_(*"-"_);_(@_)
Comma(0)	Number = (*#,##0_);_(*(#,##0);_(*"-"_);_(@_)
Currency	Number = ($#,##0.00_);_($*(#,##0.00);_($*"-"??_);_(@_)
Currency(0)	Number = ($#,##0_);_($*(#,##0);_($*"-"_);_(@_)
Percent	Number = 0%

Using the New Cell Style button in the Cell Styles gallery on the Home tab, you can create and then assign a style to a cell, a range of cells, a worksheet, or a workbook in the same way you assign a format using the buttons on the Ribbon. In fact, the Comma Style button, Currency Style button, and Percent Style button assign the Comma, Currency, and Percent styles in Table 6–3, respectively. Excel automatically assigns the Normal style in Table 6–3 to all cells when you open a new workbook.

By right-clicking styles in the Style gallery, you also can delete, modify, and duplicate styles. The Merge Styles button in the Cell Styles gallery allows you to merge styles from other workbooks. You add a new style to a workbook or merge styles when you plan to use a group of format specifications over and over.

The following steps show how to create a new style called Four-Digit Year by modifying the existing Normal style. The new style will include the following formats: Number = 14-Mar-2001 and Alignment = Horizontal Center and Bottom Aligned.

After the Four-Digit Year style is created, it will be assigned to cell G3, which contains the system date.

- Click the Cell Styles button on the Home tab on the Ribbon to display the Cell Styles gallery (Figure 6–24).

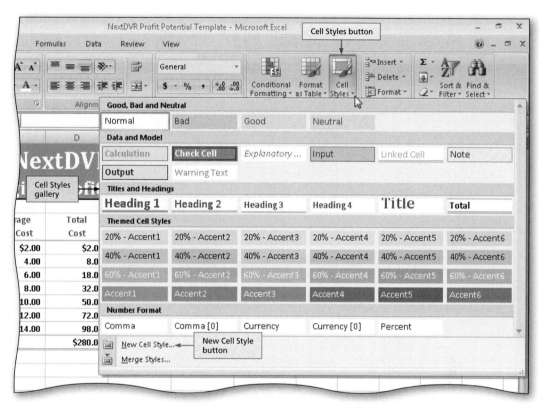

Figure 6–24

2

- Click the New Cell Style button in the Cell Styles gallery.

- When Excel displays the Style dialog box, type `Four-Digit Year` as the new style name (Figure 6–25).

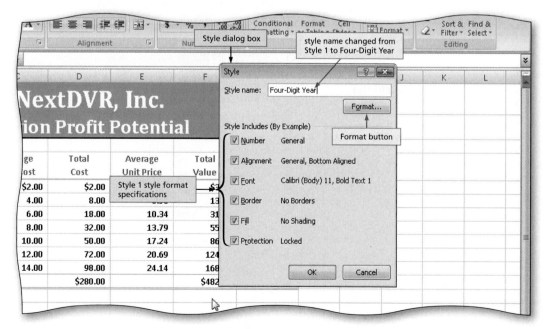

Figure 6–25

- Click the Format button to display the Format Cells dialog box.

- When Excel displays the Format Cells dialog box, if necessary, click the Number tab, click Date in the Category list, and then click 14-Mar-2001 in the Type list (Figure 6–26).

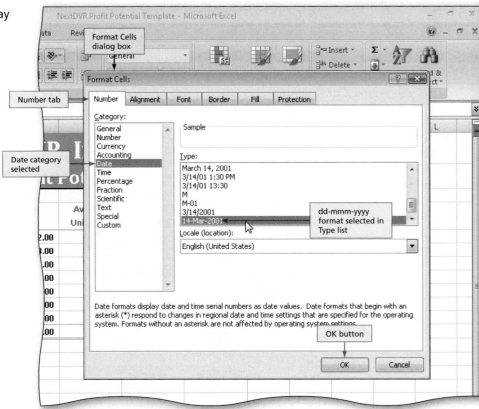

Figure 6–26

- Click the Alignment tab, click the Horizontal box arrow, click Center in the Horizontal list, and then click the OK button.

- When the Style dialog box becomes active, click Font, Border, Fill, and Protection to clear the check boxes (Figure 6–27).

- Click the OK button to add the new Four-Digit Year style to the list of styles available with the NextDVR Profit Potential Template file in the Cell Styles gallery.

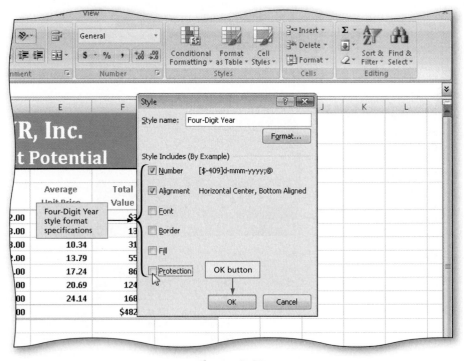

Figure 6–27

Other Ways

1. Press ALT+H, J, N

To Apply a New Style

In earlier steps, cell G3 was assigned the system date using the now() function. The next step is to assign cell G3 the Four-Digit Year style, which centers the contents of the cell and assigns it the date format dd-mmm-yyyy.

1
- Select cell G3 and then click the Cell Styles button on the Ribbon to display the Cell Styles gallery (Figure 6–28).

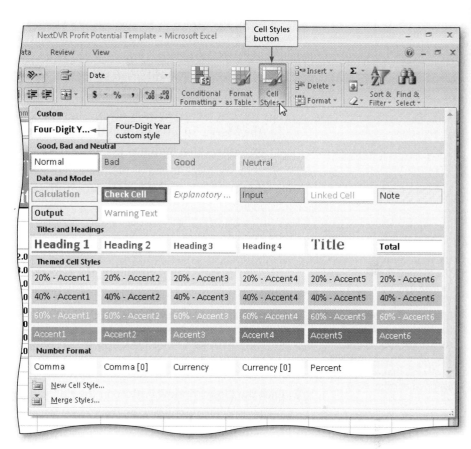

Figure 6–28

2
- Click the Four-Digit Year style to assign the Four-Digit Year style to cell G3 (Figure 6–29).
- Select cell A14.

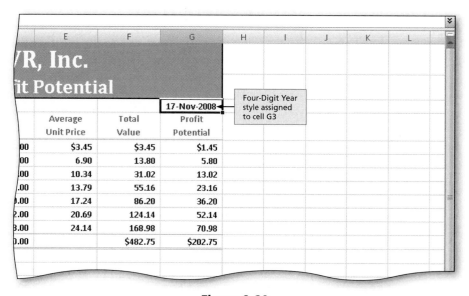

Figure 6–29

Other Ways
1. Press ALT+H, J

More About Using Styles

Keep in mind the following additional points concerning styles:

1. A style affects the format of a cell or range of cells only if the corresponding check box is selected in the 'Style Includes area' in the Style dialog box (Figure 6–27 on page EX 442). For example, if the Font check box is not selected in the Style dialog box, then the cell assigned the style maintains the font format it had before the style was assigned.

2. If you assign two different styles to a range of cells, Excel adds the second style to the first, rather than replacing it.

3. You can merge styles from another workbook into the active workbook by using the Merge Styles button in the Cell Styles gallery. You must, however, open the workbook that contains the desired styles before you use the Merge Styles button.

4. The six check boxes in the Style dialog box are identical to the six tabs in the Format Cells dialog box (Figure 6–26 on page EX 442).

To Spell Check, Save, and Print the Template

With the formatting complete, the next step is to spell check the template, save it, and then print it.

1. Select cell A1. Click the Spelling button on the Review tab. Correct any misspelled words.

2. Click the Save button on the Quick Access Toolbar to save the workbook.

3. Print the workbook.

4. Click the Close Window button on the right side of the worksheet window to close the workbook and leave Excel open.

Using Templates

Before using the template to create the NextDVR Profit Potential workbook, you should be aware of how templates are used and their importance. If you click the New command on the Office Button menu, the New Workbook dialog box is displayed (Figure 6–30). The New Workbook dialog box includes a My templates link in the Templates list, which you can click to view a list of Excel templates that you have saved on your computer in the New dialog box.

Recall that Excel automatically chose Templates as the Save in folder when the template in this chapter initially was saved (Figure 6–16 on page EX 443). Saving templates in the Templates folder, rather than in another folder, is the standard procedure in the business world. If the NextDVR Profit Potential template created in this chapter had been saved in the Templates folder, then the template would appear in the New Workbook dialog box after clicking My templates in the Templates list. The template then could have been selected to start a new workbook.

When you select a template from the New Workbook or New dialog box to create a new workbook, Excel names the new workbook using the template name with an appended digit 1 (for example, Template1). This is similar to what Excel does when you first start Excel and it assigns the name Book1 to the workbook.

Excel provides additional workbook templates, which you can access by clicking the links in the Templates list shown in Figure 6–30. Additional workbook templates also are available on the Web. To access the templates on the Web, click the links in the Microsoft Office Online section of the Templates list.

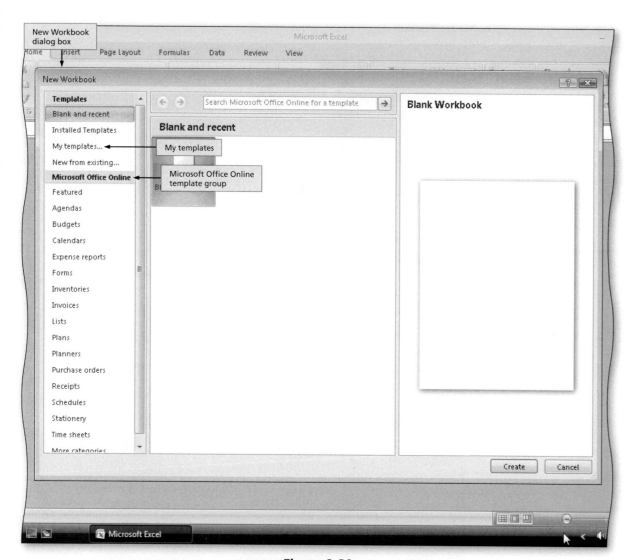

Figure 6–30

Creating a Workbook from a Template

With the template created, the next step is to use it to create the NextDVR Profit Potential workbook shown in Figure 6–1 on page EX 419.

To Open a Template and Save It as a Workbook

The following steps open the NextDVR Profit Potential template and save it as a workbook.

1

• With Excel active, click the Office Button and then click Open on the Office Button menu.

• When Excel displays the Open dialog box, select UDISK 2.0 (E:) in the Address bar.

• Click the file name NextDVR Profit Potential Template to select it (Figure 6–31).

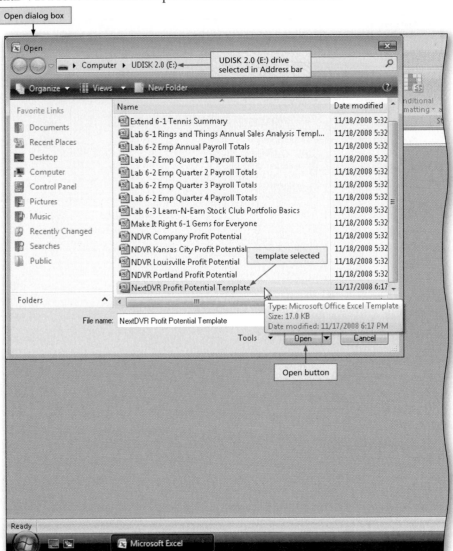

Figure 6–31

2

- Click the Open button in the Open dialog box.

- When Excel displays the NextDVR Profit Potential Template, click the Office Button and then click Save As on the Office Button menu.

- When the Save As dialog box appears, type NextDVR Profit Potential in the File name box.

- Click the Save as type box arrow and then click Excel Workbook (Figure 6–32).

3

- Click the Save button in the Save As dialog box to save the workbook.

Q&A

How does Excel automatically select the file type and file name?

In a production environment in which templates are saved to the Templates folder, Excel automatically selects Excel Workbook as the file type when you attempt to save a template as a workbook. Excel also appends the digit 1 to the template name as described earlier.

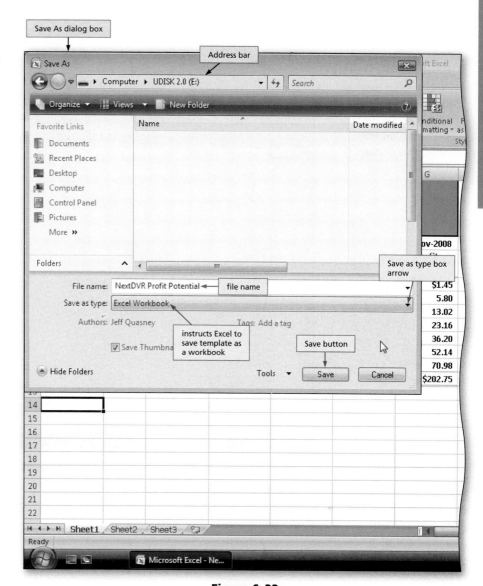

Figure 6–32

To Add a Worksheet to a Workbook

A workbook contains three worksheets by default. The number of worksheets you can have in a workbook is limited only by the amount of memory in your computer.

> **Identify additional worksheets needed in the workbook.**
> The NextDVR Profit Potential workbook requires four worksheets — one for each of the three regions and one for the company totals. Thus, a worksheet must be added to the workbook.

Plan Ahead

When you add a worksheet, Excel places the new sheet tab to the left of the active tab. To keep the worksheet with the dummy data shown in Figure 6–29 on page EX 443 on top — that is, to keep its tab (Sheet1) to the far left — spreadsheet specialists often add a new worksheet between Sheet1 and Sheet2, rather than to the left of Sheet1. The following steps select Sheet2 before adding a worksheet to the workbook.

1

- Click the Sheet2 tab at the bottom of the window and then click the Insert Cells button arrow on the Home tab on the Ribbon to display the Insert menu (Figure 6–33).

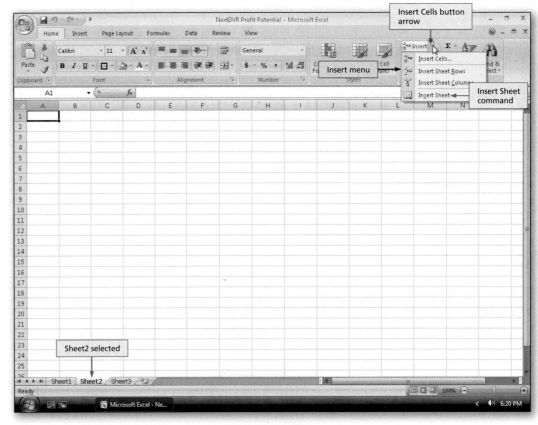

Figure 6–33

2

- Click Insert Sheet to add a fourth worksheet named Sheet 4 between Sheet 1 and Sheet 2 (Figure 6–34).

Q&A

Can I start a new workbook with more sheets?

Yes. An alternative to adding worksheets is to change the default number of worksheets before you open a new workbook. To change the default

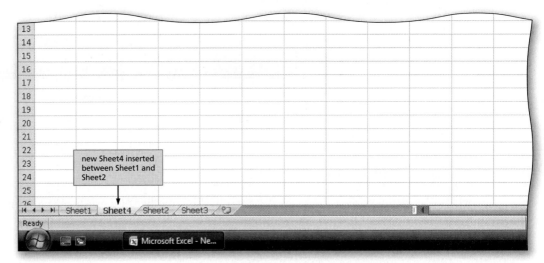

Figure 6–34

number of worksheets in a blank workbook, click the Excel Options button on the Office Button menu, and then change the number in the 'Include this many sheets' box in the 'When creating new workbooks' area of the Excel Options dialog box. Recall from Chapter 4 that you can delete a worksheet by right-clicking the sheet tab of the worksheet you want to delete and then clicking Delete on the shortcut menu.

Other Ways

1. Right-click tab, click Insert on shortcut menu
2. Press ALT+H, I, S

To Copy the Contents of a Worksheet to Other Worksheets in a Workbook

With four worksheets in the workbook, the next step is to copy the contents of Sheet1 to Sheet4, Sheet2, and Sheet3. Sheet1 eventually will be used as the Company worksheet with the consolidated data. Sheet4, Sheet2, and Sheet3 will be used for the three region worksheets.

- Click the Sheet1 tab.

- Click the Select All button and then click the Copy button on the Ribbon (Figure 6–35).

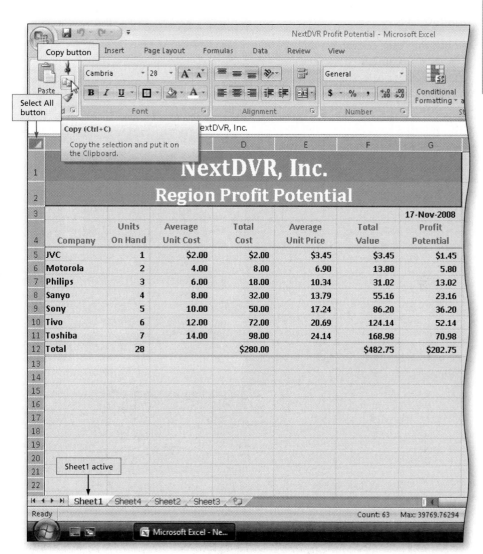

Figure 6–35

2

- Click the Sheet4 tab.

- While holding down the SHIFT key, click the Sheet3 tab so all three blank worksheets in the workbook are selected.

- Click the Paste button on the Ribbon to copy the data on the Office Clipboard to Sheet4, Sheet2, and Sheet3 (Figure 6–36).

Q&A

Why does the word Group appear on the title bar?

Because multiple worksheets are selected, the term [Group] follows the template name on the title bar.

3

- Click the Sheet1 tab and then press the ESC key to remove the marquee surrounding the selection.

- Hold down the SHIFT key and then click the Sheet3 tab. Select cell A14.

- Hold down the SHIFT key and then click the Sheet1 tab to deselect Sheet4, Sheet2, and Sheet3 (Figure 6–37).

- Click the Save button on the Quick Access Toolbar.

Q&A

Can I use the ENTER key to paste the data?

Yes. The ENTER key could have been used to complete the paste operation in Step 2, rather than the Paste button on the Ribbon. Recall that if you complete a paste operation using the ENTER key, then the marquee disappears and the Office Clipboard no longer contains the copied data following the action. Because the Paste button on the Ribbon was used, the ESC key was used in Step 3 to clear the marquee and Office Clipboard of the copied data.

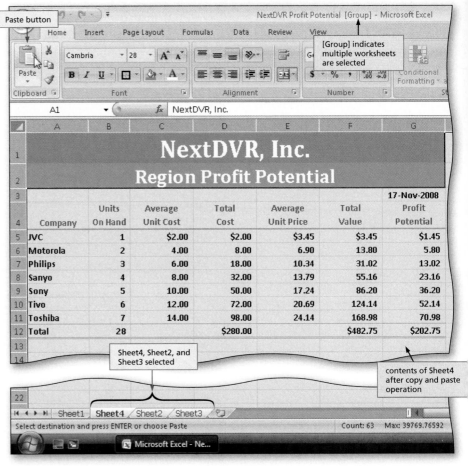

Figure 6–36

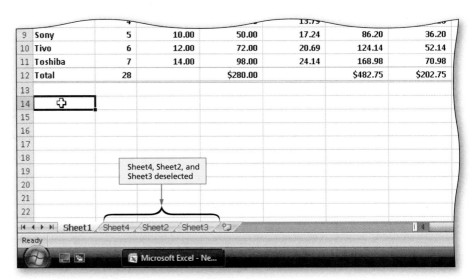

Figure 6–37

Other Ways

1. Select source area, click Copy button on Home tab, select worksheets, click Paste button on Home tab

2. Right-click source area, click Copy on shortcut menu, select worksheets, click Paste on shortcut menu

3. Select source area, press CTRL+C, select worksheets, press CTRL+V

To Drill an Entry through Worksheets

The next step is to replace the dummy numbers in the range C5:C11 with the average unit cost for each type of DVR (Table 6–4). The average unit costs for each category are identical on all four sheets. For example, the average unit cost for the JVC DVR in cell C5 is $185.61 on all four sheets. To speed data entry, Excel allows you to enter a number once and drill it through worksheets so it is entered in the same cell on all the selected worksheets. This technique is referred to as **drilling an entry**. The following steps drill the seven average unit cost entries in Table 6–4 through all four worksheets in the range C5:C11.

Table 6–4 Average Unit Cost Entries	
Company	**Average Unit Cost**
JVC	185.61
Motorola	165.79
Philips	302.99
Sanyo	296.09
Sony	184.49
Tivo	165.80
Toshiba	297.38

1

- With Sheet1 active, hold down the SHIFT key and then click the Sheet3 tab to select all four tabs at the bottom of the window.

- Select cell C5. Type 185.61 and then press the DOWN ARROW key.

- Enter the six remaining average unit costs in Table 6–4 in the range C6:C11 to display the average unit cost entries as shown in Figure 6–38.

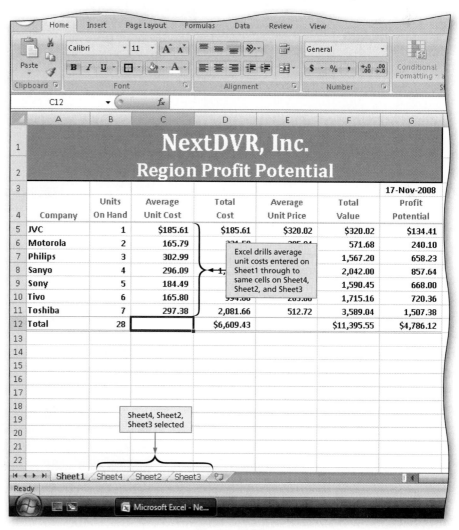

Figure 6–38

2

- Hold down the SHIFT key and then click the Sheet1 tab to deselect Sheet4, Sheet2, and Sheet3.

- One at a time, click the Sheet4 tab, the Sheet2 tab, and the Sheet3 tab to verify that all four sheets are identical (Figure 6–39).

Q&A

What is the benefit of drilling data through worksheets?

In the previous set of steps, seven new numbers were entered on one worksheet. As shown in Figure 6–39, by drilling the entries through the four other worksheets, 28 new numbers now appear, seven on each of the four worksheets. Excel's capability of drilling data through worksheets is an efficient way to enter data that is common among worksheets.

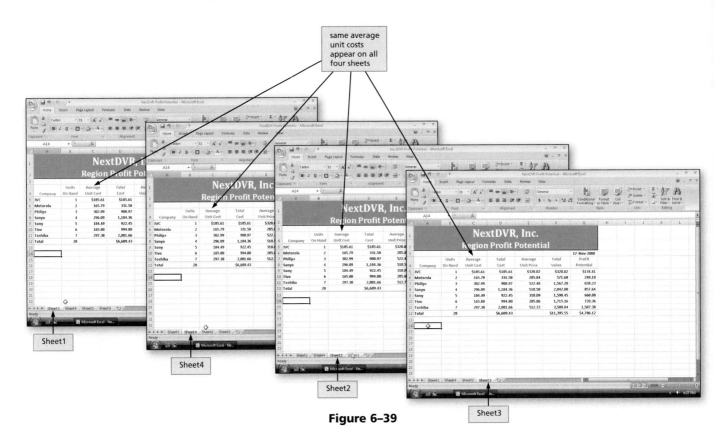

Figure 6–39

To Modify the Louisville Sheet

Drilling an Entry
Besides drilling a number down through a workbook, you can drill a format, a function, or a formula down through a workbook.

With the skeleton of the NextDVR Profit Potential workbook created, the next step is to modify the individual sheets. The following steps modify the Louisville sheet (Sheet 4) by changing the sheet name, tab color, and worksheet subtitle; changing the color of the title area; and entering the units on hand values in column B.

Table 6–5 Louisville Units On Hand	
Cell	**Units on Hand**
B5	335
B6	220
B7	323

Table 6–5 Louisville Units On Hand (continued)	
Cell	**Units on Hand**
B8	144
B9	195
B10	364
B11	273

1 Double-click the Sheet4 tab. Type `Louisville` and then press the ENTER key. Right-click the Louisville tab, point to Tab Color on the shortcut menu, and then click Light Green (column 5, row 1 in the Standard Colors area) on the Color palette.

2 Double-click cell A2, drag through the word, Region, and then type `Louisville` to change the worksheet subtitle.

3 Select the range A1:A2, click the Fill Color button arrow on the Ribbon, and then click Light Green (column 5, row 1 in the Standard Colors area) on the Fill Color palette.

4 Enter the data listed in Table 6–5 in the range B5:B11 (Figure 6–40).

5 Select cell A14 and then click the Save button on the Quick Access Toolbar.

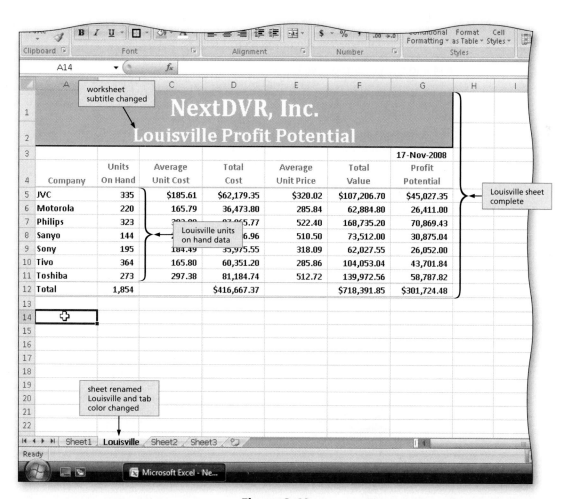

Figure 6–40

BTW

Importing Data
Costs, such as those entered into the range C5:C11, often are maintained in another workbook, a file, or a database. If the costs are maintained elsewhere, ways exist to link to a workbook or import data from a file or database into a workbook. Linking to a workbook is discussed later in this chapter. For information on importing data, see the From Other Sources button on the Data tab on the Ribbon.

To Modify the Kansas City Sheet

The following steps modify the Kansas City sheet (Sheet 2).

Table 6–6 Kansas City Units On Hand	
Cell	**Units on Hand**
B5	403
B6	281
B7	228
B8	312
B9	357
B10	278
B11	345

1 Double-click the Sheet2 tab. Type `Kansas City` and then press the ENTER key. Right-click the Kansas City tab, point to Tab Color on the shortcut menu, and then click Red (column 2, row 1 in the Standard Colors area) on the Color palette.

2 Double-click cell A2, drag through the word, Region, and then type `Kansas City` to change the worksheet subtitle.

3 Select the range A1:A2, click the Fill Color button arrow on the Ribbon, and then click Red (column 2, row 1 in the Standard Colors area) on the Fill Color palette.

4 Enter the data listed in Table 6–6 in the range B5:B11 (Figure 6–41).

5 Select cell A14 and then click the Save button on the Quick Access Toolbar.

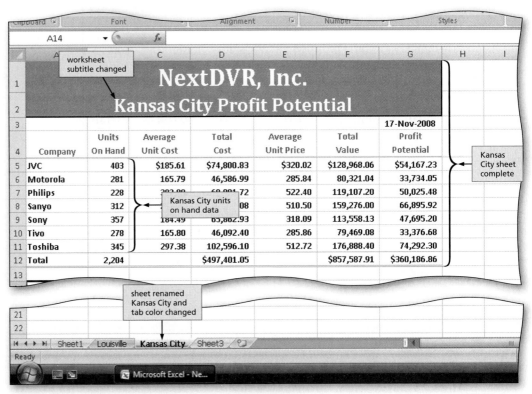

Figure 6–41

To Modify the Portland Sheet

As with the Louisville and Kansas City sheets, the sheet name, tab color, worksheet subtitle, data, and background colors must be changed on the Portland sheet. The following steps modify the Portland sheet.

Table 6–7 Portland Units On Hand	
Cell	**Units on Hand**
B5	253
B6	215
B7	352
B8	387
B9	339
B10	282
B11	400

1 Double-click the Sheet3 tab. Type `Portland` and then press the ENTER key. Right-click the Portland tab, point to Tab Color on the shortcut menu, and then click Purple (column 10, row 1 in the Standard Colors area) on the Color palette.

2 Double-click cell A2, drag through the word, Region, and then type `Portland` to change the worksheet subtitle.

3 Select the range A1:A2, click the Fill Color button arrow on the Ribbon, and then click Purple (column 10, row 1 in the Standard Colors area) on the Fill Color palette.

4 Enter the data listed in Table 6–7 in the range B5:B11 (Figure 6–42).

5 Select cell A14 and then click the Save button on the Quick Access Toolbar.

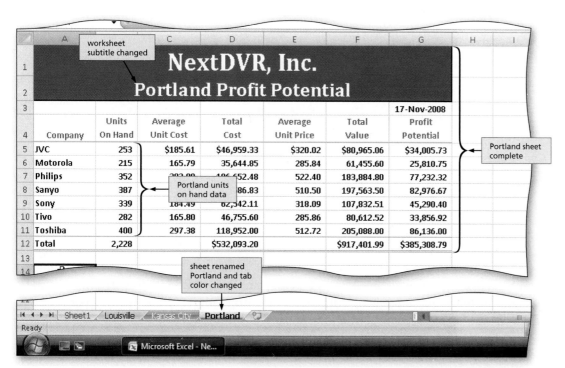

Figure 6–42

Referencing Cells in Other Sheets in a Workbook

With the three region sheets complete, the next step is to modify Sheet1, which will serve as the consolidation worksheet containing totals of the data on the Louisville, Kansas City, and Portland sheets. Because this sheet contains totals of the data, you need to understand how to reference cells in other sheets in a workbook before modifying Sheet1.

To reference cells in other sheets in a workbook, you use the sheet name, which serves as the **sheet reference**, and the cell reference. For example, you refer to cell B5 on the Louisville sheet as shown below.

=Louisville!B5

Using this method, you can sum cell B5 on the three region sheets by selecting cell B5 on the Sheet1 sheet and then entering:

= Louisville!B5 + Kansas City!B5 + Portland!B5

A much quicker way to total the three cells is to use the SUM function as follows:

=SUM(Louisville:Portland!B5)

The SUM argument (Louisville:Portland!B5) instructs Excel to sum cell B5 on each of the three sheets (Louisville, Kansas City, and Portland). The colon (:) between the first sheet name and the last sheet name instructs Excel to include these sheets and all sheets in between, just as it does with a range of cells on a sheet. A range that spans two or more sheets in a workbook such as Louisville:Portland!B5 is called a **3-D range**. The reference to this range is a **3-D reference**.

A sheet reference such as Portland! always is absolute. Thus, the sheet reference remains constant when you copy formulas.

Entering a Sheet Reference

You can enter a sheet reference in a cell by typing the sheet reference or by clicking the appropriate sheet tab while in Point mode. When you click the sheet tab, Excel activates the sheet and automatically adds the sheet name and an exclamation point after the insertion point in the formula bar. Next, select or drag through the cells you want to reference on the sheet.

If the range of cells to be referenced is located on several worksheets (as when selecting a 3-D range), click the first sheet tab and then select the cell or drag through the range of cells. Next, while holding down the SHIFT key, click the sheet tab of the last sheet you want to reference. Excel will include the cell(s) on the first sheet, the last sheet, and any sheets in between.

To Modify the Company Sheet

This section modifies the Company sheet by changing the sheet name, tab color, and subtitle and then entering the SUM function in each cell in the range B5:B11. The SUM functions will determine the total units on hand at the three regions, by company. Cell B5 on the Company sheet, for instance, will contain the sum of the JVC DVR units on hand in cells Louisville!B5, Kansas City!B5, and Portland!B5. Before determining the totals, the following steps change the sheet name from Sheet1 to Company, color the tab, and change the worksheet subtitle to Company Profit Potential.

BTW

Circular References
A circular reference is a formula that depends on its own value. The most common type is a formula that contains a reference to the same cell in which the formula resides.

BTW

3-D References
If you are summing numbers on noncontiguous sheets, hold down the CTRL key rather than the SHIFT key when selecting the sheets.

1 Double-click the Sheet1 sheet tab, type Company and then press the ENTER key. Right-click the Company tab, point to Tab Color on the shortcut menu, and then click Light Blue (column 7, row 1 in the Standard Colors area) on the Color palette.

2 Double-click cell A2, drag through the word, Region, and then type Company as the worksheet subtitle. Press the ENTER key.

To Enter and Copy 3-D References Using the Paste Button Menu

The following steps enter the 3-D references used to determine the total units on hand for each of the seven DVR companies. In these steps, the Formulas command on the Paste button menu on the Ribbon is used to complete the paste operation. When the Formulas command is used, the paste operation pastes only the formulas, leaving the formats of the destination area unchanged.

1
- Select cell B5 and then click the Sum button on the Ribbon to display the SUM function and ScreenTip (Figure 6–43).

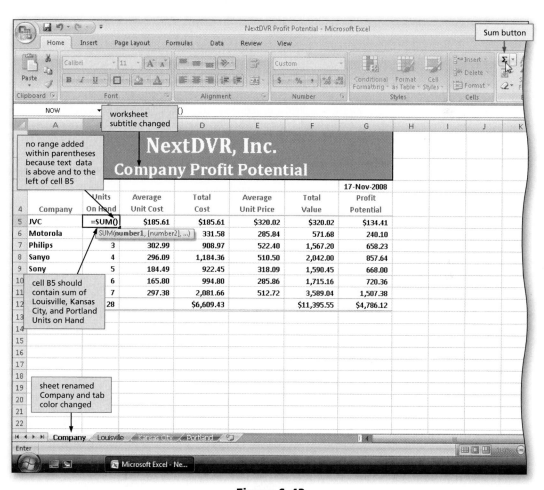

Figure 6–43

● Click the Louisville tab and then click cell B5. While holding down the SHIFT key, click the Portland tab to surround cell Louisville!B5 with a marquee (Figure 6–44).

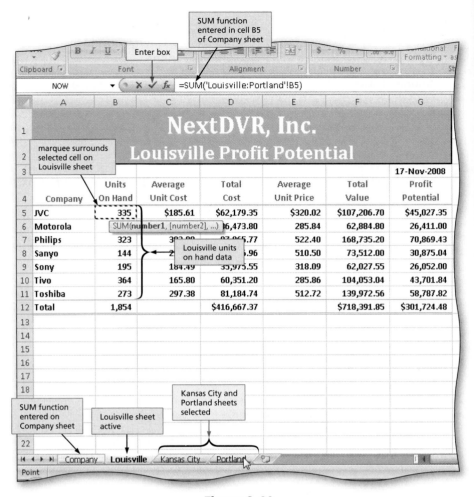

Figure 6–44

● Click the Enter box in the formula bar to enter the SUM function with the 3-D references in cell Company!B5 (Figure 6–45).

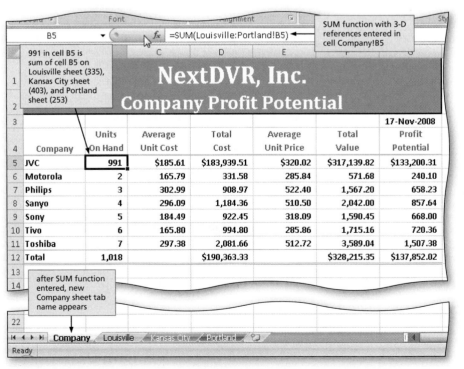

Figure 6–45

4

- With cell B5 active, click the Copy button on the Ribbon to copy the SUM function and the formats assigned to cell B5 to the Office Clipboard (Figure 6–46).

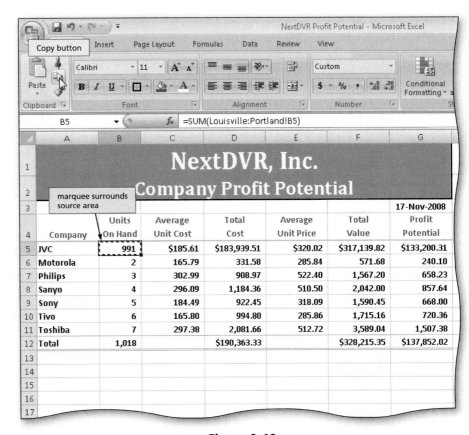

Figure 6–46

5

- Select the range B6:B11 and then click the Paste button arrow on the Ribbon to display the Paste button menu (Figure 6–47).

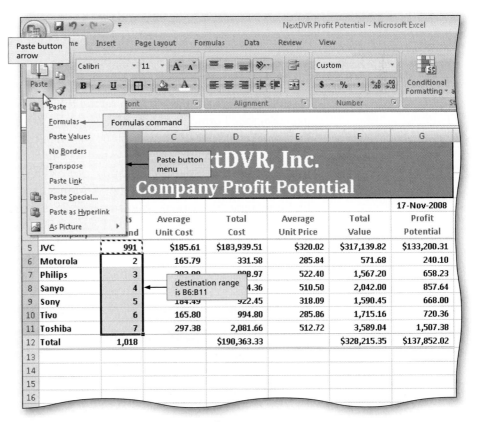

Figure 6–47

6

- Click Formulas on the Paste button menu to copy the SUM function in cell B5 to the range B6:B11 (Figure 6–48) and automatically adjust the cell references in the SUM function to reference the corresponding cells on the three sheets in the workbook.

- Press the ESC key to clear the marquee surrounding cell B5 and then select cell A14 to deselect the range B6:B11.

- Click the Save button on the Quick Access Toolbar to save the NextDVR Profit Potential workbook.

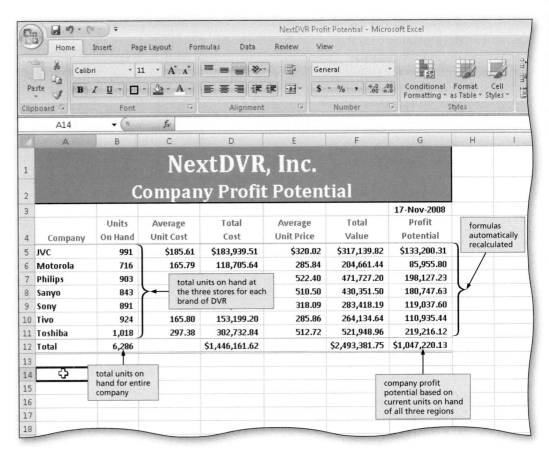

Figure 6–48

More About Pasting

If you click the Paste button on the Ribbon to complete the paste operation, rather than using the Formulas command as shown in Figure 6–47 on the previous page, then any formats assigned to cell B5 also will be copied to the range B6:B11. Completing the paste operation by using the fill handle or by pressing the ENTER key also will copy any formats from the source area to the destination area. When you use the Formulas command on the Paste button menu, Excel copies the SUM function, but not the format, assigned to cell B5. In this example, the format assigned to cell B5 is the same as the format assigned to the range B6:B11, so it does not matter if you use the Paste button or the Formulas command. In many cases, however, the formats of the source area and destination area differ; the Paste button menu, thus, is a useful option to complete the copy and paste operation. Table 6–8 summarizes the commands available on the Paste button menu, as shown in Figure 6–47.

Table 6–8 Paste Button Menu Commands	
Command	**Description**
Paste	Pastes in the same manner as clicking the Paste button.
Formulas	Pastes the formulas from the source area, but not the formats.
Paste Values	Pastes the value of the formula from the source area, but not the formulas or formats.
No Borders	Pastes the formula and all formats from the source area, except for borders.

Table 6–8 Paste Button Menu Commands *(continued)*

Command	Description
Transpose	Pastes the formula and formats from the source area, but transposes the columns and rows. For example, if you are summing numbers in a column in the source area, then Excel will sum numbers in a row in the destination area.
Paste Link	Pastes the cell reference of the source area in the destination area.
Paste Special	Displays the Paste Special dialog box that allows you to choose what you want pasted from the source area to the destination area.
Paste as Hyperlink	Pastes the contents of the Office Clipboard as a hyperlink, which you then can edit.
As Picture	Displays the As Picture submenu, which allows you to convert the contents of the Office Clipboard to an image.

Drawing the Clustered Cone Chart

The requirements document shown in Figure 6–2 on page EX 420 requires a Clustered Cone chart. The **Clustered Cone chart** is similar to a 3-D Bar chart in that it can be used to show trends or illustrate comparisons among items.

BTW

The Move Chart Button
The Move Chart button on the Design contextual tab on the Ribbon can be used to move a chart from a chart sheet to a worksheet. Click the Move Chart button on the Ribbon, select the Object in check box, and then select a destination worksheet for the chart in the Object in list in the Move Chart dialog box.

Plan the layout and location of the required chart.
The Clustered Cone chart in Figure 6–49, for example, compares the total profit potential of the different brands of DVRs in inventory. The chart should be placed on a separate worksheet so that the company and region worksheets maintain a similar look. WordArt is used to draw the reflected chart title, Profit Potential, in an eye-catching and professional format. A text box, arrow, and brace are used to highlight the DVR brand with the greatest profit potential.

Plan Ahead

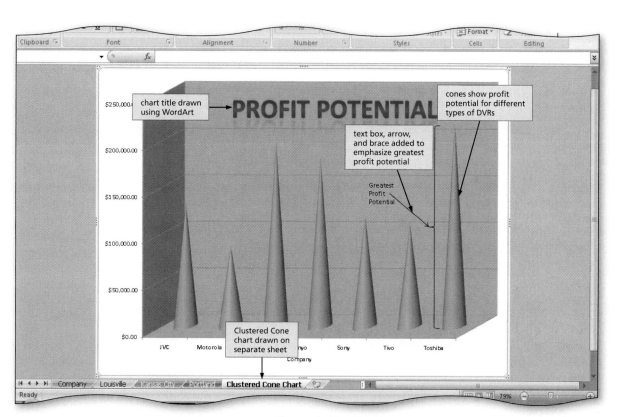

Figure 6–49

To Draw the Clustered Cone Chart

The following steps add a Clustered Cone chart to a new sheet and then change the layout of the chart to rotate it, remove the series label, and add a title to the horizontal axis.

- With the Company sheet active, select the range A5:A11.

- Hold down the CTRL key and then select the range G5:G11.

- Click the Insert tab on the Ribbon.

- Click the Column button on the Ribbon and then click Clustered Cone (column 1, row 4) in the Column gallery to insert a Clustered Cone chart (Figure 6–50).

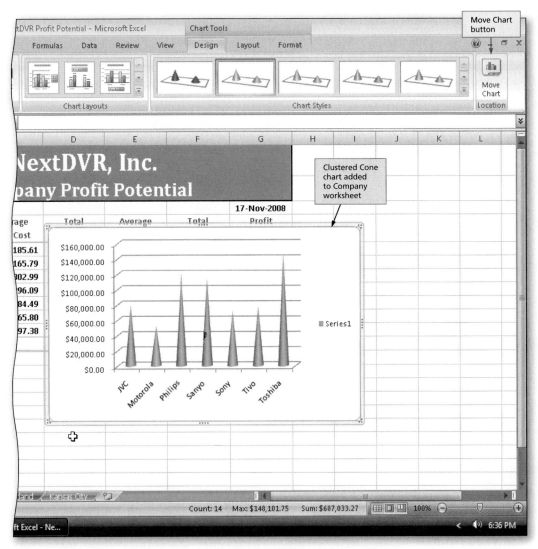

Figure 6–50

BTW

Moving Charts
To move an embedded chart to a new sheet, right-click the chart edge, click the Move Chart command, click the New sheet option button, type a sheet name, and then click the OK button. To move a chart to a chart sheet, click the chart, display the Chart Tools Design tab, and then click the Move Chart button. In the Move Chart dialog box, click the Object in option button, click the Object in box arrow, click a sheet name, and then click the OK button.

2

- Click the Move Chart button on the Ribbon.

- When Excel displays the Move Chart dialog box, click New sheet and then type `Clustered Cone Chart` as the sheet name.

- Click the OK button in the Move Chart dialog box to move the chart to a new sheet (Figure 6–51).

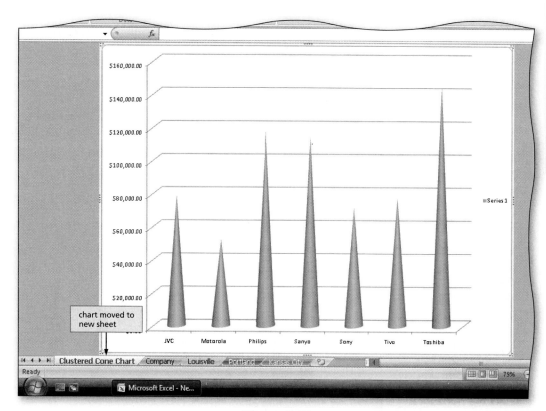

Figure 6–51

3

- Click the Layout tab on the Ribbon and then click the 3-D Rotation button on the Ribbon to display the Format Chart Area dialog box.

- Type 70 in the X text box in the Rotation area to rotate the chart 70% along the X-axis.

- Type 30 in the Y text box in the Rotation area to rotate the chart 30% along the Y-axis.

- Click the Close button in the Format Chart Area dialog box (Figure 6–52).

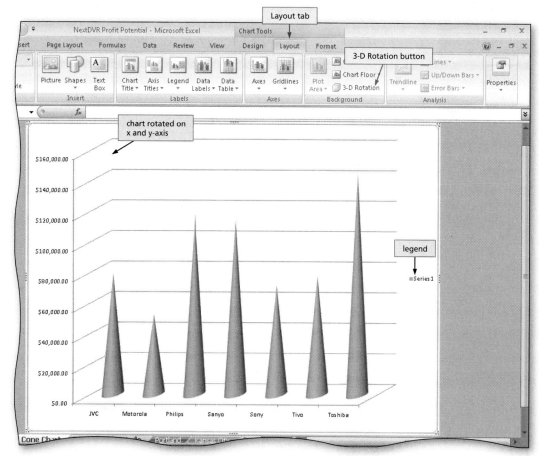

Figure 6–52

4

- Click the Legend button on the Ribbon and then click None to remove the legend from the right side of the chart (Figure 6–53).

5

- Click the Axis Titles button on the Ribbon to display the Axis Titles menu.

- Point to Primary Horizontal Axis Title on the Axis Titles menu and then click Title Below Axis in the Primary Horizontal Axis Title gallery to add a title to the horizontal axis.

- Select the horizontal axis title and type Company as the new title (Figure 6–54).

Q&A

What does the chart show?

The Clustered Cone chart compares the profit potential of the seven different brands of digital cameras. You can see from the chart that, of the DVRs in inventory, the Toshiba brand DVRs have the greatest profit potential and the Motorola brand cameras have the least profit potential.

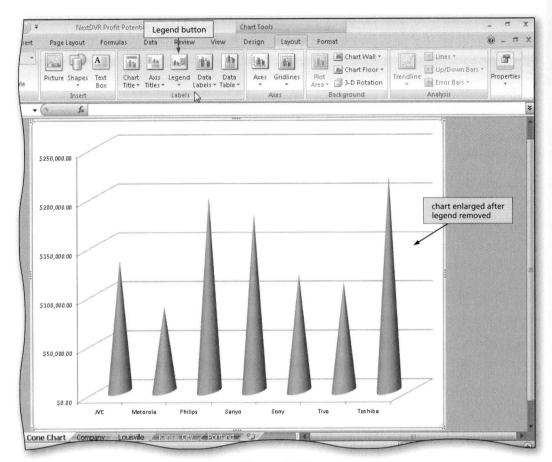

Figure 6–53

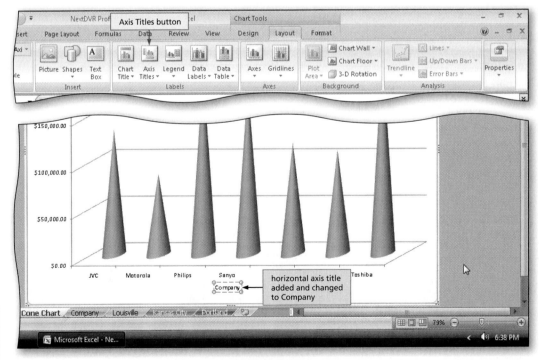

Figure 6–54

Other Ways
1. Select range, click Chart type button in Charts group on Insert tab, click Chart type in gallery
2. Select range, press F11

To Format the Clustered Cone Chart

The following steps color the sheet tab, move the sheet, change the color of the cylinders and the chart walls, and format the y-axis (values axis) and x-axis (category axis).

1 Right-click the Clustered Cone Chart sheet tab, point to Tab Color on the shortcut menu, and then click Aqua, Accent 3 (column 7, row 1) on the Color palette.

2 If necessary, drag the tab split box (Figure 6–55) to the right to ensure all five tabs show. Drag the Clustered Cone Chart sheet tab to the right of the Portland sheet tab.

3 Click the chart wall behind the cones, click the Home tab on the Ribbon, click the Fill Color button arrow on the Ribbon, and then click Lavender, Accent 5, Lighter 40% (column 9, row 4) on the Fill Color palette.

4 Click the floor of the chart below the cones, click the Fill Color button arrow on the Ribbon, and then click White, Background 1, Darker 15% (column 1, row 3) on the Fill Color palette.

5 Click one of the cylinders to select all the cones, click the Fill Color button arrow on the Ribbon, and then click Aqua, Accent 3 (column 7, row 1) on the Fill Color palette.

6 Click the x-axis and then click the Bold button on the Ribbon. Click the y-axis and then click the Bold button on the Ribbon. Click outside the chart area to display the chart as shown in Figure 6–55.

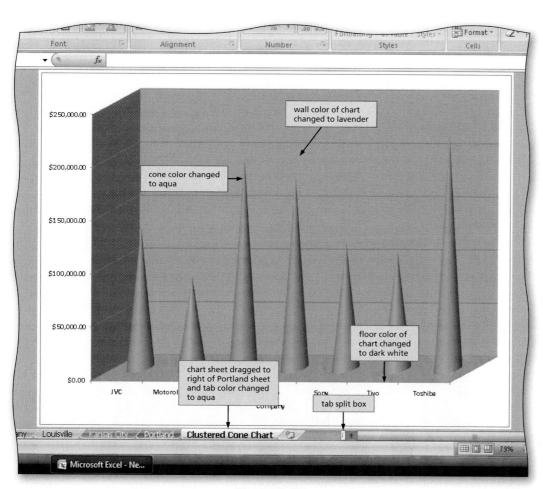

Figure 6–55

To Add a Chart Title Using the WordArt Tool

Earlier, you learned how to add a chart title by using the Chart Title button on the Layout tab on the Chart Tools contextual tab on the Ribbon. You also learned how to format it using the Home tab on the Ribbon. You also can create a chart title using the WordArt tool. The **WordArt tool** allows you to create shadowed, skewed, rotated, and stretched text on a chart sheet or worksheet and apply other special text formatting effects. The WordArt text added to a worksheet is called an **object**. The following steps show how to add a chart title using the WordArt tool.

- With the Clustered Cone Chart sheet active, click anywhere on the chart, and then click the Insert tab on the Ribbon.

- Click the WordArt button on the Ribbon to display the WordArt gallery.

- When Excel displays the WordArt gallery, point to the Gradient Fill – Accent 4, Reflection (column 5, row 4) selection in the WordArt gallery (Figure 6–56).

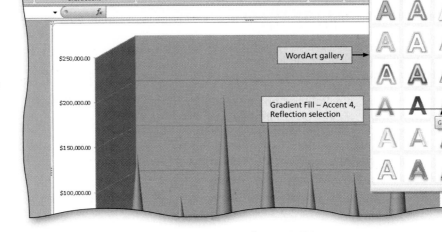

Figure 6–56

- Click the Gradient Fill – Accent 4, Reflection selection in the WordArt gallery to insert a new WordArt object.

- When Excel displays the WordArt object on the chart, type Profit Potential as the title of the Clustered Cone chart (Figure 6–57).

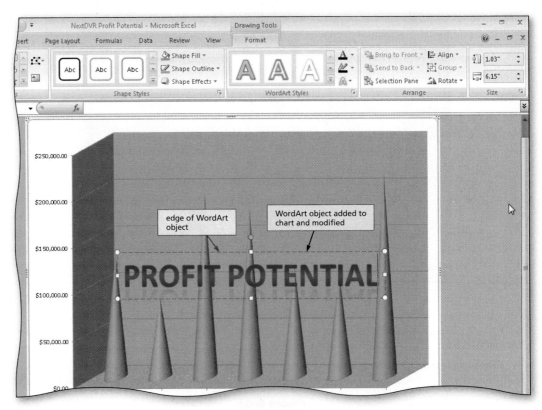

Figure 6–57

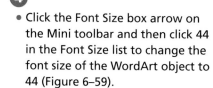

3

- Select the text in the WordArt object to display the Mini toolbar (Figure 6–58).

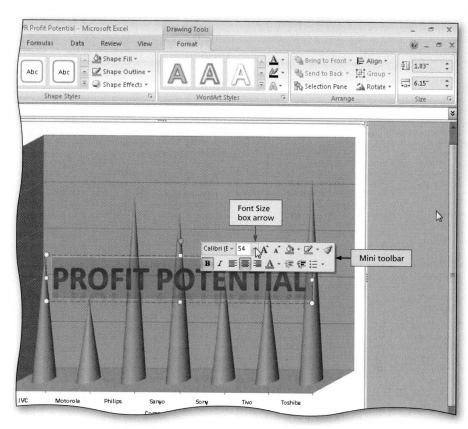

Figure 6–58

4

- Click the Font Size box arrow on the Mini toolbar and then click 44 in the Font Size list to change the font size of the WordArt object to 44 (Figure 6–59).

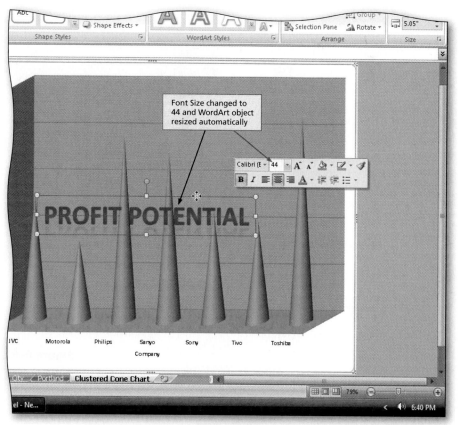

Figure 6–59

● Drag the top edge of the WordArt object so that the object is positioned above the cones in the chart as shown in Figure 6–60.

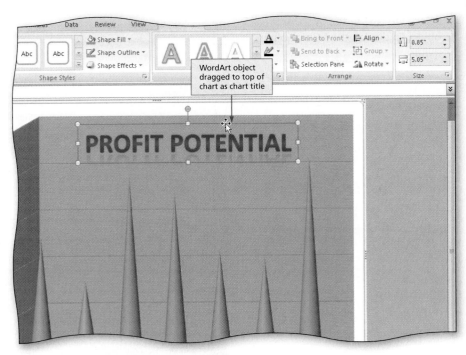

Figure 6–60

● Click outside the chart area to deselect the WordArt object (Figure 6–61).

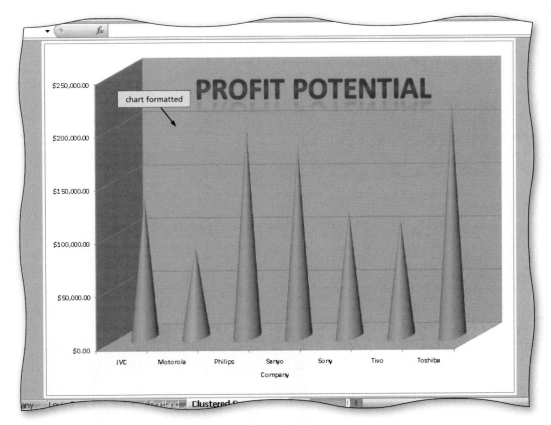

Figure 6–61

Other Ways	
1. Click WordArt button on Insert tab	2. Right-click object, click Format Shape on shortcut menu

To Add a Text Box, Arrow, and Brace to the Chart

A text box, arrow, and a brace can be used to **annotate** (call out or highlight) other objects or elements in a worksheet or chart. For example, in a worksheet, you may want to annotate a particular cell or group of cells by adding a text box, arrow, and brace. In a chart, you may want to emphasize a column or slice of a Pie chart.

A **text box** is a rectangular area of variable size in which you can add text. You use the sizing handles to resize a text box in the same manner you resize an embedded chart or a WordArt object. If the text box has the same color as the background, then the text appears as if it was written freehand, because the box itself does not show. An **arrow** allows you to connect an object, such as a text box, to an item that you want to annotate. A **brace** allows you to point out a large item or a group of items that you want to annotate.

The following steps add the text box, arrow, and brace indicated in the sketch of the chart in Figure 6–3b on page EX 422 and also shown in Figure 6–49 on page EX 461.

1

• Click the Insert tab on the Ribbon.

• Click the Shapes button on the Ribbon to display the Shapes gallery (Figure 6–62).

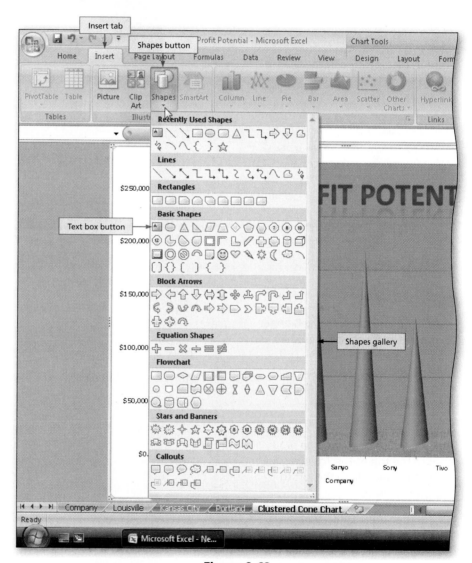

Figure 6–62

2

- Click the Text Box button (column 1, row 1 in the Basic Shapes area) in the Shapes gallery to select it.

- Point to the upper-left corner of the planned text box location, and then drag the crosshair to the lower-right corner.

- With the insertion point active in the text box, type Greatest Profit Potential as the text to display in the text box as shown in Figure 6–63.

 What if the Text Box button is not in that location in the Shapes gallery?

When Excel is first installed on a computer, it places commonly used shapes in the Recently Used Shapes area in the Shapes gallery. If users of your computer have used other shapes, they may have displaced the Text Box button in the Recently Used Shapes area. The Text Box shape also appears as the first shape in the Basic Shapes area in the Shapes gallery.

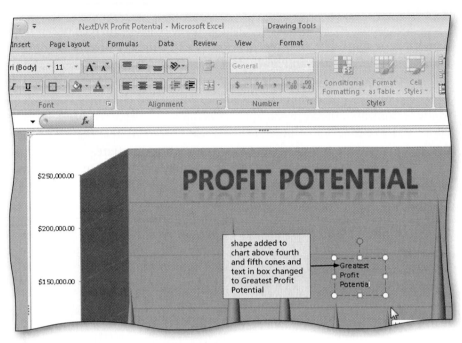

Figure 6–63

3

- Click the Insert tab on the Ribbon, click the Shapes button on the Ribbon, and then click the Left Brace button in the Shapes gallery (column 5, row 4 in the Basic Shapes area).

- Point to the bottom-left corner of the Toshiba cone and then drag up to the top of the Toshiba cone and then slightly to the left to draw the brace.

- Click the Subtle Line - Dark 1 shape style in the Shape Styles group to select it and change the color of the brace (Figure 6–64).

 Why should I add the brace before adding the arrow?

The arrow will connect the text box shape and the brace shape. Placing the start and ending points of the arrow will be easier with the targets already in place.

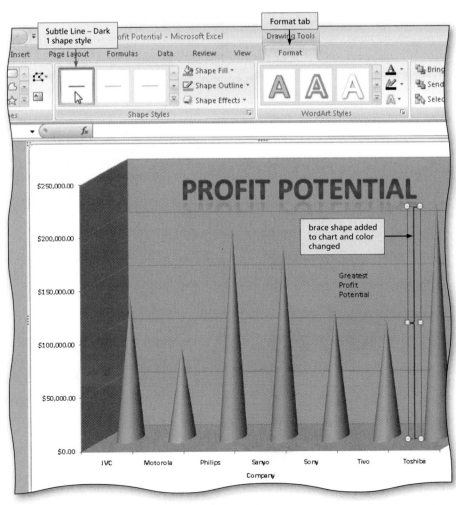

Figure 6–64

4

- Click the Insert tab on the Ribbon, click the Shapes button on the Ribbon, and then click the Arrow button in the Shapes gallery (column 2, row 1 in the Lines area).

- Point immediately to the right of the letter t in Profit in the text box, and then drag the arrow to the center of the brace to draw the arrow.

- Click the Subtle Line - Dark 1 shape style in the Shape Styles group to select it and change the color of the brace.

- Click outside the chart area to deselect the chart (Figure 6–65).

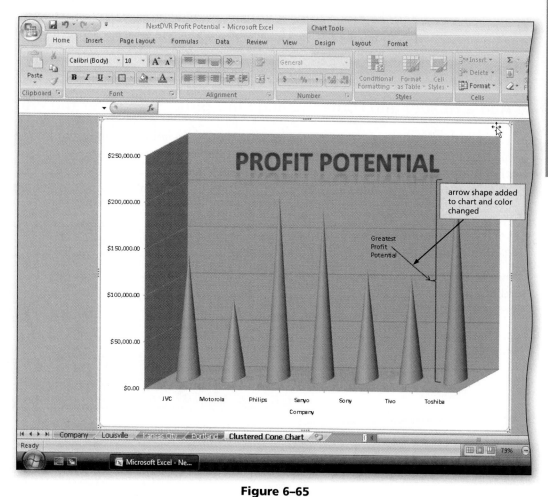

Figure 6–65

5

- Click the Company tab and then select cell A14 to deselect the chart range.

- Click the Save button on the Quick Access Toolbar to save the workbook.

Adding a Header and Footer, Changing the Margins, and Printing the Workbook

A **header** is printed at the top of every page in a printout. A **footer** is printed at the bottom of every page in a printout. By default, both the header and footer are blank. You can change either so that information, such as the workbook author, date, page number, or tab name, prints at the top or bottom of each page.

Sometimes, you will want to change the **margins** to increase or decrease the white space surrounding the printed worksheet or chart. The default margins in Excel for both portrait and landscape orientation are set to the following: Top = .75 inch; Bottom = .75 inch; Left = .7 inch; Right = .7 inch. The header and footer are set at .3 inch from the top and bottom, respectively. You also can center a printout horizontally and vertically.

Changing the header and footer and changing the margins are all part of **page setup**, which defines the appearance and format of a printed worksheet. To change page setup characteristics, select the desired sheet(s) and then click the Page Layout tab on the Ribbon. Remember to select all the sheets you want to modify before you change the headers, footers, or margins, because the page setup characteristics will change only for selected sheets. The headers and footers for chart sheets must be assigned separately from worksheets.

To Add a Header and Footer, Change Margins, and Center the Printout Horizontally

As you modify the page setup, remember that Excel does not copy page setup characteristics when one sheet is copied to another. Thus, even if you assigned page setup characteristics to the template before copying it to the NextDVR Profit Potential workbook, the page setup characteristics would not copy to the new sheet. The following steps use the Page Setup dialog box to change the headers, footers and margins and center the printout horizontally.

1

- With the Company sheet active, scroll to the top of the document.

- While holding down the SHIFT key, click the Portland sheet tab to select the four worksheet tabs.

- Click the Page Layout tab on the Ribbon (Figure 6–66).

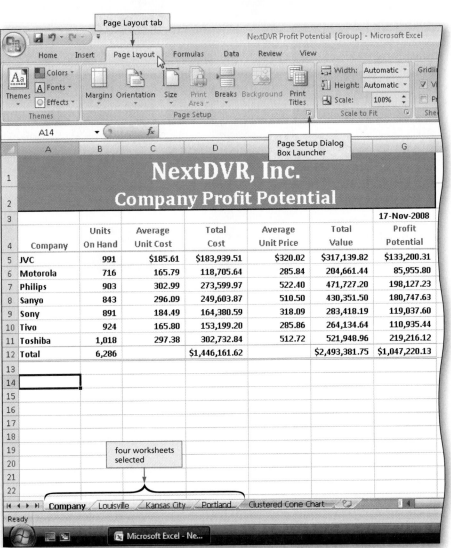

Figure 6–66

2

- Click the Page Setup Dialog Box Launcher to display the Page Setup dialog box.

- When Excel displays the Page Setup dialog box, if necessary, click the Margins tab.

- Double-click the Top box and then type 1.5 to change the top margin to 1.5 inch.

- Enter .5 in both the Left box and Right box to change the left and right margins to .5 inch.

- Click the Horizontally check box in the 'Center on page' area to select it. This will center the worksheet on the page horizontally (Figure 6–67).

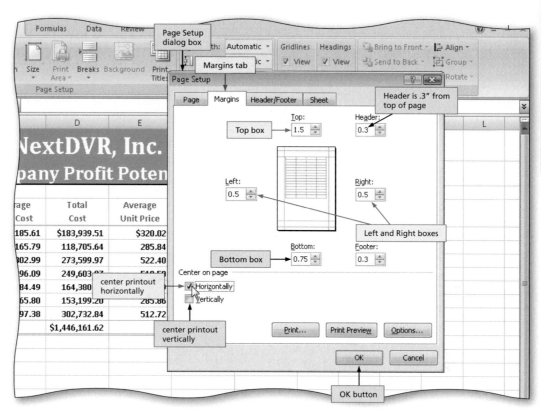

Figure 6–67

3

- Click the OK button in the Page Setup dialog box to close it.

- Click the Page Layout button on the status bar to display the worksheet in Page Layout view (Figure 6–68).

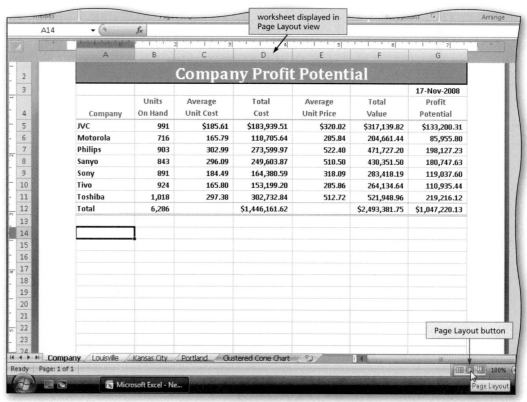

Company	Units On Hand	Average Unit Cost	Total Cost	Average Unit Price	Total Value	Profit Potential
						17-Nov-2008
JVC	991	$185.61	$183,939.51	$320.02	$317,139.82	$133,200.31
Motorola	716	165.79	118,705.64	285.84	204,661.44	85,955.80
Philips	903	302.99	273,599.97	522.40	471,727.20	198,127.23
Sanyo	843	296.09	249,603.87	510.50	430,351.50	180,747.63
Sony	891	184.49	164,380.59	318.09	283,418.19	119,037.60
Tivo	924	165.80	153,199.20	285.86	264,134.64	110,935.44
Toshiba	1,018	297.38	302,732.84	512.72	521,948.96	219,216.12
Total	6,286		$1,446,161.62		$2,493,381.75	$1,047,220.13

Company Profit Potential

Figure 6–68

4

- If necessary, scroll the worksheet up until the Header area is displayed. Click the left Header box, type J. Quasney (or your name if you are stepping through the chapter on a computer), press the ENTER key, and then type Profit Potential to complete the entry.

- Click the center section box and then click the Sheet Name button on the Ribbon to instruct Excel to insert the sheet name that appears on the sheet tab as part of the header.

- Click the right Header box, click the Current Date button on the Ribbon, press the COMMA key, press the SPACEBAR, and then click the Current Time button on the Ribbon to insert the date and time in the Header (Figure 6–69).

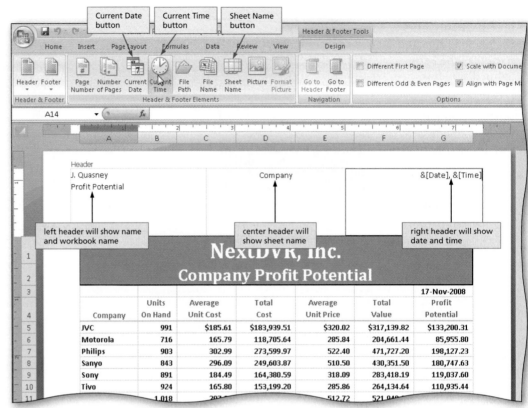

Figure 6–69

5

- Scroll the workbook down to view the Footer area.

- Click the middle section box, type Page, press the SPACEBAR, click the Page Number button on the Ribbon, press the SPACEBAR, type of, press the SPACEBAR, and then click the Number of Pages button on the Ribbon to add the footer (Figure 6–70).

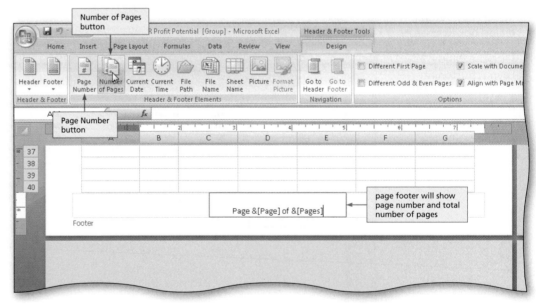

Figure 6–70

Q&A

What does Excel insert when I click a button in the Header & Footer Tools group on the Ribbon?

When you click a button in the Header & Footer Tools group on the Ribbon (Figure 6–70), Excel enters a code (similar to a format code) into the active header or footer section. A code such as &[Page] instructs Excel to insert the page number.

6

- Click anywhere on the worksheet to deselect the page footer.

- Click the Normal view button on the status bar and then select cell A14. Click the Page Layout tab on the Ribbon and then click the Page Setup Dialog Box Launcher on the Ribbon to display the Page Setup dialog box.

- Click the Print Preview button in the Page Setup dialog box to preview the Company sheet (Figure 6–71).

7

- Click the Next Page button and Previous Page button on the Print Preview tab on the Ribbon to preview the other pages.

- After previewing the printout, click the Close Print Preview button on the Ribbon.

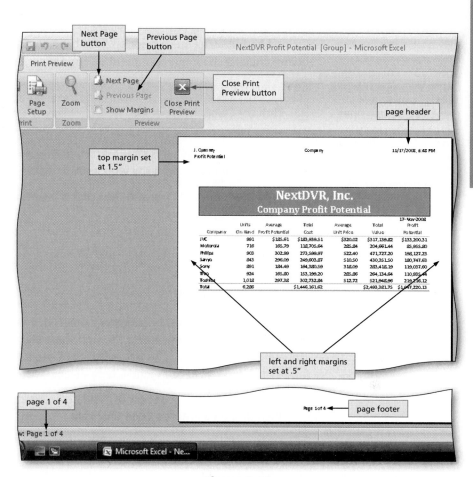

Figure 6–71

To Add a Header to the Clustered Cone Chart Sheet

The following steps add the same header applied to the four worksheets in the previous steps to the Clustered Cone Chart sheet.

1 Click the Clustered Cone Chart tab and then on the Page Layout tab, click the Page Setup Dialog Box Launcher.

2 When Excel displays the Page Setup dialog box, click the Header/Footer tab, click the Custom Header button, and in the left header box type J. Quasney (or your name if you are stepping through the chapter on a computer). Press the ENTER key and then type Profit Potential to complete the entry.

3 In the center header box, type &[Tab] to instruct Excel to print the sheet name in the Center Header section.

4 In the right header box, type &[Date], &[Time] to instruct Excel to print the date and time in the Right Header section.

5 Click the OK button in the Header dialog box and then click the OK button in the Page Setup dialog box.

6 Click the Company tab. Click the Save button on the Quick Access Toolbar to save the workbook.

BTW

Quick Reference
For a table that lists how to complete the tasks covered in this book using the mouse, Ribbon, shortcut menu, and keyboard, see the Quick Reference Summary at the back of this book, or visit the Excel 2007 Quick Reference Web page (scsite.com/ex2007/qr).

To Print All Worksheets in a Workbook

The following steps print all five sheets in the workbook by selecting all the sheets before clicking the Print command on the Office Button menu.

1 Ready the printer.

2 Click the Company sheet tab. While holding down the SHIFT key, click the Clustered Cone Chart tab.

3 Click the Print command on the Office Button menu and then click the OK button in the Print dialog box to print the workbook as shown in Figure 6–72a and 6-72b.

4 Hold down the SHIFT key and then click the Company sheet tab to deselect all sheets but the Company sheet.

To Print Nonadjacent Sheets in a Workbook

In some situations, nonadjacent sheets in a workbook may need to be printed. To select nonadjacent sheets, select the first sheet and then hold down the CTRL key and click the nonadjacent sheets. The following steps show how to print the nonadjacent Company, Louisville, and Clustered Cone Chart sheets.

1 With the Company sheet active, hold down the CTRL key, click the Louisville sheet tab, and then click the Clustered Cone Chart tab.

2 Click the Print command on the Office Button menu and then click the OK button in the Print dialog box.

3 Hold down the SHIFT key and click the Company sheet tab to deselect the Louisville and Clustered Cone Chart sheets.

Selecting and Deselecting Sheets

Beginning Excel users sometimes have difficulty trying to select and deselect sheets. Table 6–9 summarizes how to select and deselect sheets.

Table 6–9 Summary of How to Select and Deselect Sheets	
Task	**How to Carry Out the Task**
Select adjacent sheets	Select the first sheet by clicking its tab and then hold down the SHIFT key and click the sheet tab at the other end of the list of adjacent sheet tabs.
Select nonadjacent sheets	Select the first sheet by clicking its tab and then hold down the CTRL key and click the sheet tabs of the remaining sheets you want to select.
Multiple sheets selected and you want to select a sheet that is selected, but not active (sheet tab name not in bold)	Click the sheet tab you want to select.
Multiple sheets selected and you want to select the active sheet (sheet tab name in bold)	Hold down the SHIFT key and then click the sheet tab of the active sheet.

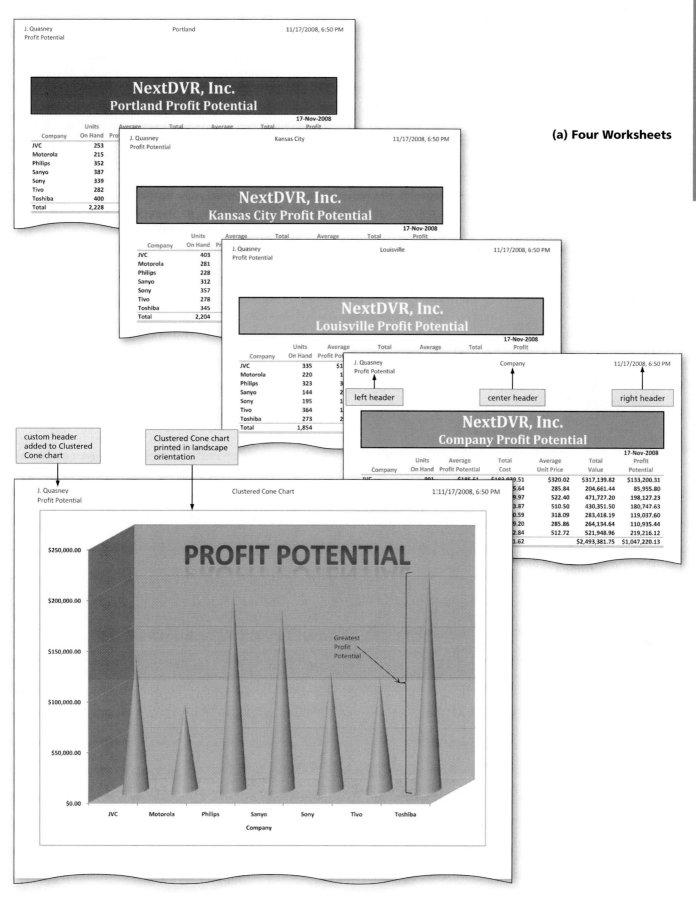

(a) Four Worksheets

custom header added to Clustered Cone chart

Clustered Cone chart printed in landscape orientation

left header

center header

right header

Greatest Profit Potential

(b) 3-D Clustered Cone Chart

Figure 6–72

To Insert and Remove a Page Break

When you print a worksheet or use the Page Setup dialog box, Excel inserts **page breaks** that show the boundaries of what will print on each page. These page breaks are based upon the margins selected in the Margins sheet in the Page Setup dialog box and the type of printer you are using. If the Page breaks option is selected, then Excel displays dotted lines on the worksheet to show the boundaries of each page. For example, the dotted line in Figure 6–73 shows the right boundary of the first page. If the dotted line does not show on your screen, then click Excel Options on the Office Button menu. When Excel displays the Excel Options dialog box, click the Advanced command to display Advanced Excel options. Scroll the window until the 'Display options for this worksheet' area appears. Click the Show page breaks check box (Figure 6–75 on page EX 480).

You can insert both horizontal and vertical page breaks in a worksheet. Manual page breaks are useful if you have a worksheet that is several pages long and you want certain parts of the worksheet to print on separate pages. For example, say you had a worksheet that comprised ten departments in sequence and each department had many rows of information. If you wanted each department to begin on a new page, then inserting page breaks would satisfy the requirement.

To insert a horizontal page break, you select a cell in column A or an entire row that you want to print on the next page and then click the Breaks button on the Page Layout tab. When the Breaks menu is displayed, click the Insert Page Break command. To insert a vertical page break, you select a cell in row 1 or an entire column that you want to print on the next page and then click the Insert Page Break command. Excel displays a dotted line to indicate the beginning of a new page. To remove a page break, you select the cell in the row immediately below or to the right of the dotted line that indicates the page break you want to remove and then click the Remove Page Break command on the Insert Breaks menu. Excel also includes a Page Break view that allows you to change page breaks by dragging them.

The following steps insert both a horizontal and vertical page break.

1
- With the Company sheet active, select cell B12 and then click the Page Layout tab on the Ribbon.

- Click the Breaks button on the Ribbon and then click Insert Page Break on the Breaks menu to insert a page break (Figure 6–73).

Q&A What appears on the worksheet?

Excel inserts a dotted line above row 12 indicating a horizontal page break and inserts a dotted line to the left of column B indicating a vertical page break (Figure 6–73).

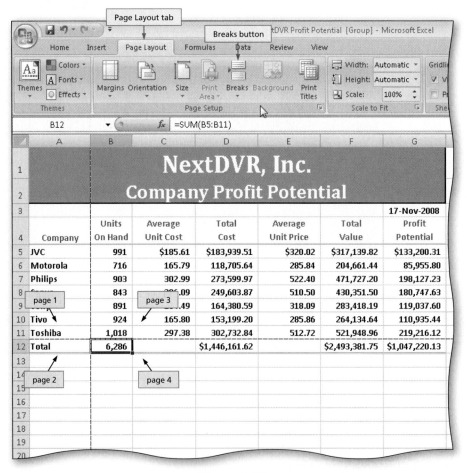

Figure 6–73

2

- With cell B12 active, click the Breaks button on the Ribbon to display the Breaks menu (Figure 6–74).

- Click Remove Page Break to remove the page breaks.

Q&A

Is there a way to move page breaks?

Yes. An alternative to using the Breaks command on the Page Layout tab on the Ribbon to insert page breaks is to click the Page Break Preview button on the status bar. When the Page Break preview appears, you can drag the blue boundaries, which represent page breaks, to new locations.

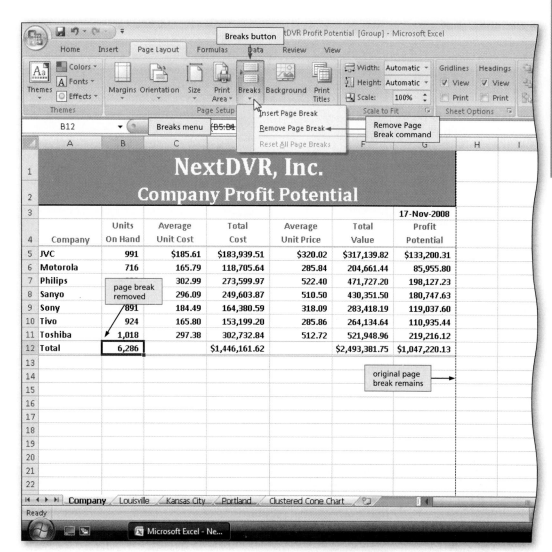

Figure 6–74

Other Ways
1. Click Page Break Preview button on View tab, click OK button, drag page breaks	2. Select cell, press ALT+P, B, I

To Hide Page Breaks

When working with a workbook, page breaks can be an unnecessary distraction, especially to users who have no interest in where pages break. The following steps show how to hide the dotted lines that represent page breaks.

1

- Click the Office Button and then click the Excel Options button on the Office Button menu.

- When Excel displays the Excel Options dialog box, click the Advanced button to display Advanced Excel options.

- Scroll the window until the 'Display options for this worksheet' area appears.

- Click the 'Show page breaks' check box to clear the check box (Figure 6–75).

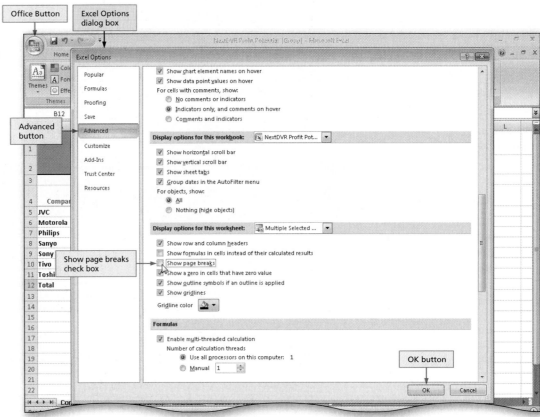

Figure 6–75

2

- Click the OK button to hide the page breaks as shown in Figure 6–76.

Company	Units On Hand	Average Unit Cost	Total Cost	Average Unit Price	Total Value	Profit Potential
						17-Nov-2008
JVC	991	$185.61	$183,939.51	$320.02	$317,139.82	$133,200.31
Motorola	716	165.79	118,705.64	285.84	204,661.44	85,955.80
Philips	903	302.99	273,599.97	522.40		7.23
Sanyo	843	296.09	249,603.87	510.50		7.63
Sony	891	184.49	164,380.59	318.09		7.60
Tivo	924	165.80	153,199.20	285.86	264,134.64	110,935.44
Toshiba	1,018	297.38	302,732.84	512.72	521,948.96	219,216.12
Total	6,286		$1,446,161.62		$2,493,381.75	$1,047,220.13

Company Profit Potential

dotted line representing vertical page break hidden

Figure 6–76

Other Ways

1. Press ALT+P, B, R

Saving a Workbook as a PDF or XPS file

Excel provides additional options for distributing your final workbook project. Often you may want to distribute copies of a workbook to others who do not have access to Excel. The printed pages shown in Figure 6–72 on page EX 477 provide one method for distributing the workbook. Excel also allows you to distribute an electronic version of the printed pages using two different file formats: PDF and XPS. For each of these file formats, the workbook appears in an electronic format to the reader of the workbook, with one worksheet displayed as a separate page. The reader may not make changes to the documents; they, therefore, often are considered electronic printed versions of the workbook.

When you distribute a workbook as a PDF or XPS file, those who want to read the workbook must have a reader program installed. The most common PDF reader is Acrobat Reader from Adobe. Microsoft provides a reader for its newer XPS file format.

To save a workbook in the PDF and XPS file formats, you must install an add-on program from Microsoft's Web site. The add-on program is available as a free download from Microsoft, and a link to the Web site is provided in Excel Help. Once installed, the Save As submenu on the Office Button menu includes a new PDF or XPS command. When you click the command, Excel displays the Publish as PDF or XPS dialog box which allows you to choose a file name for the document, a location to save the document, and other options.

The Find and Replace Commands

A **string** can be a single character, a word, or a phrase in a cell on a worksheet. You display the Find & Select menu by clicking the Find & Select button on the Ribbon. The Find command on the Find & Select menu is used to locate a string. The Replace command on the Find & Select menu is used to locate one string and then replace it with another string. The Find and Replace commands are not available for a chart sheet.

Both the Find and Replace commands cause the Find and Replace dialog box to be displayed. The Find and Replace dialog box has two variations. One version displays minimal options, while the other version displays all of the available options. When you invoke the Find or Replace command, Excel displays the dialog box variation that was used the last time either command was invoked.

BTW

The Find Command
If you want to search only a specified range of a worksheet, then select the range before invoking the Find command. The range can consist of adjacent cells or nonadjacent cells.

To Find a String

The following steps show how to locate the string, Toshiba, in the four worksheets: Company, Louisville, Kansas City, and Portland. The Find and Replace dialog box that displays all the options will be used to customize the search to include the entire workbook and to use the match case and match entire cell contents options. **Match case** means that the search is case sensitive and the cell contents must match the word exactly the way it is typed. **Match entire cell contents** means that the string cannot be part of another word or phrase and must be unique in the cell. Unlike the Spelling command, which starts the spell checker at the active cell and works downward, the Find and Replace commands always begin at cell A1, regardless of the location of the active cell.

- Click the Home tab on the Ribbon.

- With the Company sheet active, click the Find & Select button on the Ribbon (Figure 6–77).

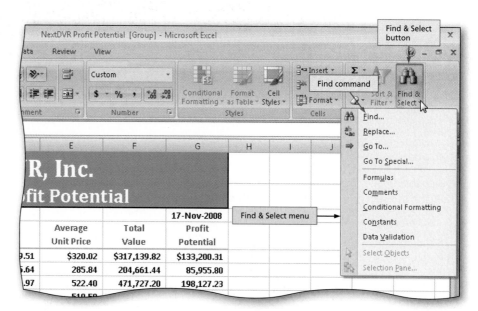

Figure 6–77

2

- Click Find.

- When Excel displays the Find and Replace dialog box, click the Options button so that it appears as shown in Figure 6–78.

- Type Toshiba in the Find what box, click the Within box arrow, select Workbook, and then click the Match case and 'Match entire cell contents' check boxes to select them (Figure 6–78).

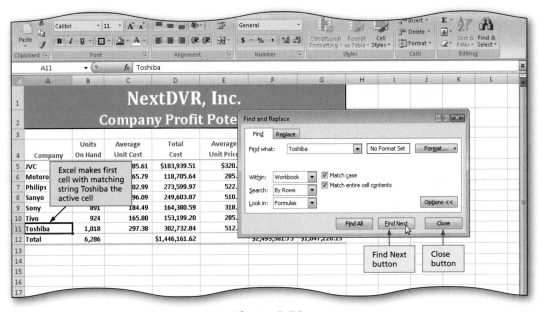

Figure 6–78

Why does the appearance of the Options button change?

The two greater than signs pointing to the left on the Options button indicate that the more comprehensive Find and Replace dialog box is active.

3

- Click the Find Next button to cause Excel to begin the search at cell A1 on the Company sheet and make cell A11 the active cell (Figure 6–79) because it is the first cell to match the search string.

4

- Continue clicking the Find Next button to find the string, Toshiba, on the other sheets in the workbook.

Figure 6–79

- Click the Close button in the Find and Replace dialog box to terminate the process and close the Find and Replace dialog box.

Q&A What if Excel does not find the search string?

If the Find command does not find the string for which you are searching, Excel displays a dialog box indicating it has searched the selected worksheets and cannot find the search string.

Other Ways

1. Press CTRL+F

Working with the Find and Replace Dialog Box

The Format button in the Find and Replace dialog box in Figure 6–78 allows you to fine-tune the search by adding formats, such as bold, font style, and font size, to the string. The Within box options include Sheet and Workbook. The Search box indicates whether the search will be done vertically through rows or horizontally across columns. The Look in box allows you to select Values, Formulas, or Comments. If you select Values, Excel will look for the search string only in cells that do not have formulas. If you select Formulas, Excel will look in all cells. If you select Comments, Excel will look only in comments. If you select the Match case check box, Excel will locate only cells in which the string is in the same case. For example, philips is not the same as Philips. If you select the 'Match entire cell contents' check box, Excel will locate only the cells that contain the string and no other characters. For example, Excel will find a cell entry of Philips, but not Philips DVRs.

To Replace a String with Another String

The Replace command is used to replace the found search string with a new string. You can use the Find Next and Replace buttons to find and replace a string one occurrence at a time, or you can use the Replace All button to replace the string in all locations at once. The following steps show how to use the Replace All button to replace the string, Philips, with the string, Royal Philips, formatted as red italic font.

- With the Company sheet active, click the Find & Select button on the Ribbon and then click Replace.

- When Excel displays the Find and Replace dialog box, type `Philips` in the Find what box and `Royal Philips` in the Replace with box.

- Click the Format button to the right of the Replace with box. When Excel displays the Replace Format dialog box, click the Font tab, click the Color box arrow, click Red (column 2, row 1 in the Standard colors area), click Italic in the Font style list, and then click the OK button.

- If necessary, click the Within box arrow and then click Workbook.

- If necessary, click the Match case and 'Match entire cell contents' check boxes to select them (Figure 6–80).

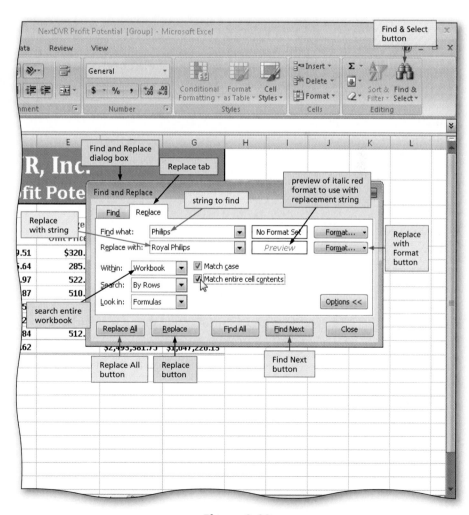

Figure 6–80

2

- Click the Replace All button to replace the string (Figure 6–81).

3

- Click the OK button in the Microsoft Office Excel dialog box.

- Click the Close button in the Find and Replace dialog box.

Q&A

What happens when Excel replaces the string?

Excel replaces the string, Philips, with the replacement string, Royal Philips (cell A7), throughout the four worksheets in the workbook. The replacement string is formatted as red italic font. Excel does not replace the string, Philips, on the Clustered Cone Chart sheet. Excel displays the Microsoft Office Excel dialog box indicating four replacements were made.

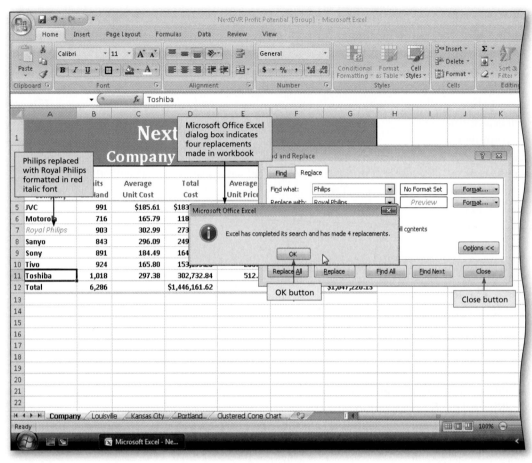

Figure 6–81

Other Ways

1. Press CTRL+H

To Quit Excel

The following steps quit Excel without saving changes to the NextDVR Profit Potential workbook.

1 Click the Close button on the right side of the Excel title bar.

2 When Excel displays the Microsoft Office Excel dialog box, click the No button.

Consolidating Data by Linking Workbooks

Earlier in this chapter, the data from three worksheets were consolidated into another worksheet in the same workbook using 3-D references. An alternative to this method is to consolidate data from worksheets in other workbooks. Consolidating data from other workbooks also is referred to as linking. A **link** is a reference to a cell or range of cells in another workbook. In this case, the 3-D reference also includes a workbook name. For example, the following 3-D reference pertains to cell B5 on the Kansas City sheet in the workbook NDVR Kansas City Profit Potential located on drive E.

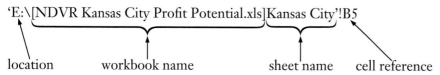

'E:\[NDVR Kansas City Profit Potential.xls]Kansas City'!B5

location   workbook name   sheet name   cell reference

The single quotation marks surrounding the location, workbook name, and sheet name are required if any of the three names contain spaces. If the workbook you are referring to is in the same folder as the active workbook, the location (E:\) is not necessary. The brackets surrounding the workbook name are required.

To illustrate linking cells between workbooks, the Company, Louisville, Kansas City, and Portland worksheets from the workbook created earlier in this chapter are on the Data Files for Students in separate workbooks as described in Table 6–10. In the workbook names in Table 6–10, the NDVR stands for NextDVR. The region workbooks contain the region data, but the NDVR Company workbook does not include any consolidated data. The consolidation of data from the three region workbooks into the NDVR Company Profit Potential workbook will be completed later in this section.

Table 6–10 Workbook Names

Worksheet in NextDVR Profit Potential Workbook	Saved on The Data Files for Students Using the Workbook Name
Company	NDVR Company Profit Potential
Louisville	NDVR Louisville Profit Potential
Kansas City	NDVR Kansas City Profit Potential
Portland	NDVR Portland Profit Potential

The remaining sections of this chapter demonstrate how to search for the four workbooks in Table 6–10 on drive E, how to create a workspace from the four workbooks, and finally how to link the three region workbooks to consolidate the data into the NDVR Company Profit Potential workbook.

BTW

Consolidation
You also can consolidate data across different workbooks using the Consolidate button on the Data tab on the Ribbon, rather than by entering formulas. For more information on the Consolidate button, type consolidate in the Search box in the Excel Help dialog box, and then click the 'Consolidate data in multiple worksheets' link in the Results list.

To Search for and Open Workbooks

Excel has a powerful search tool that you can use to locate workbooks (or any file) stored on disk. You search for files using the Search text box in the Open dialog box. If you view files on the Data Files for Students, then you would see the four workbooks listed in the right column of Table 6–10. The following steps, however, show how to search for workbooks when you cannot remember exactly the name of the file or its location. In this example, the string NDVR (the first four characters in the workbook names) will be used to locate the workbooks. The located workbooks then are opened and **arranged** so that each one appears in its own window.

- Start Excel following the steps on page EX 423 and then click the Office Button.

- Click Open on the Office Button menu and then select UDISK (E:) in the Address bar (Figure 6–82).

- Type NDVR in the Search box.

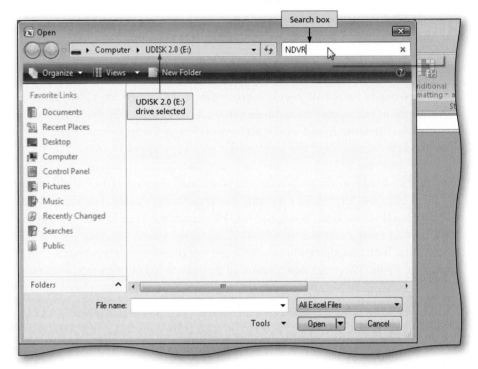

Figure 6–82

2

- Press the ENTER key to display a list of the four workbooks described in Table 6–10 on the previous page in the File list (Figure 6–83).

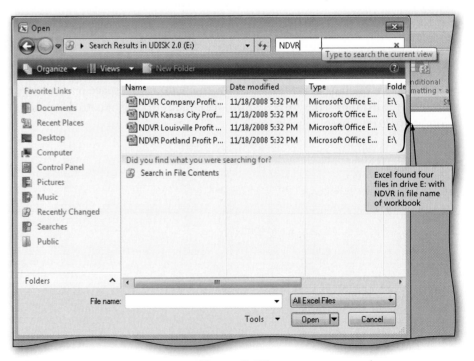

Figure 6–83

3

- In the File list, while holding down the CTRL key, click each of the three region workbook names one at a time and then click the company workbook name.

- Click the Open button to open the four workbooks.

- Click the View tab on the Ribbon and then click the Switch Windows button to display the names of the four workbooks with a check mark to the left of the active workbook (Figure 6–84).

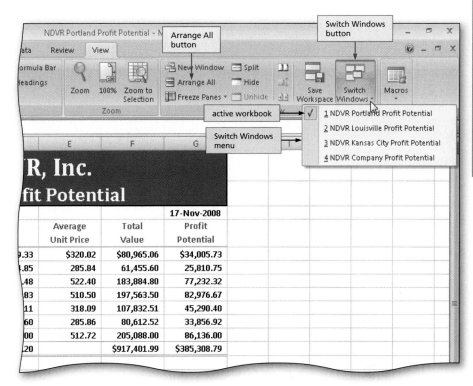

Figure 6–84

4

- Click the Arrange All button on the Ribbon.

- When Excel displays the Arrange Windows dialog box, click Vertical, and then, if necessary, click the 'Windows of active workbook' check box to clear it (Figure 6–85).

 How can I arrange workbooks in the Excel window?

As shown in Figure 6–85, multiple opened workbooks can be arranged in four ways. The option name in the Arrange Windows dialog box identifies the resulting window's configuration. You can modify any of the arranged workbooks by clicking within its window to activate it. To return to showing one workbook, double-click its title bar as described in Step 6 on the next page.

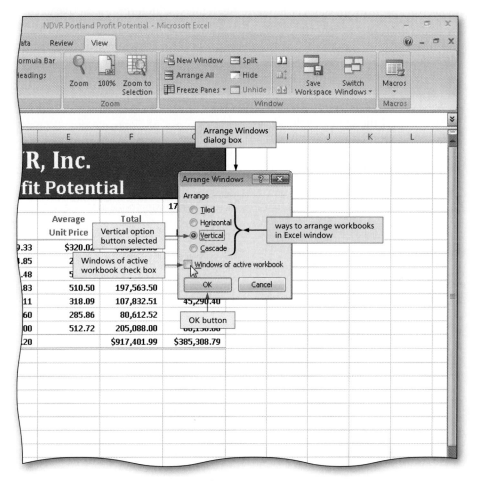

Figure 6–85

- Click the OK button in the Arrange Windows dialog box to display the four opened workbooks as shown in Figure 6–86.

6

- Double-click the NDVR Company Profit Potential title bar to maximize it and hide the other opened workbooks.

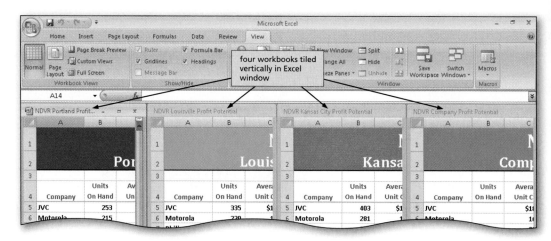

Figure 6–86

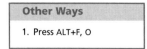

Other Ways
1. Press ALT+F, O

To Create a Workspace File

If you plan to consolidate data from other workbooks, it is recommended that you first bind the workbooks together using a workspace file. A **workspace file** saves information about all the workbooks that are open. The workspace file does not contain the actual workbooks; rather, it stores information required to open the files associated with the workspace file, including file names, which file was active at the time of the save, and other display settings. To create a workspace file, click the Save Workspace button on the View tab on the Ribbon. After you create and save a workspace file, you can open all of the associated files by opening the workspace. The following steps show how to create a workspace file from the files opened in the previous set of steps.

- With the four NDVR workbooks opened and the Company Profit Potential workbook active, if necessary, click the View tab on the Ribbon (Figure 6–87).

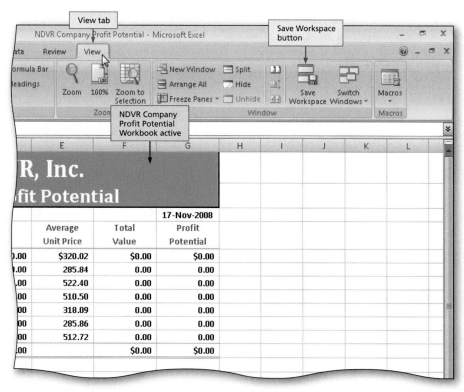

Figure 6–87

2

- Click the Save Workspace button on the Ribbon.

- When Excel displays the Save Workspace dialog box, select UDISK 2.0 (E:) in the Address bar and then type `NextDVR Workspace` in the File name box (Figure 6–88).

Q&A

Can I still open the workbooks separately or must I always open the workspace?

After the workspace is saved to disk, you can open the workbooks one at a time as you did in the past, or you can open all of the associated workbooks by opening the workspace. When you invoke the Open command, workspace file names appear in the Open dialog box, the same as any workbook file name.

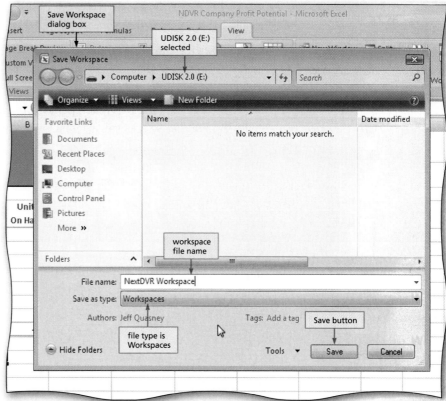

Figure 6–88

3

- Click the Save button in the Save Workspace dialog box to save the file names of the workbooks open, of the workbooks displaying, and other display settings.

- If the Microsoft Office Excel dialog box is displayed for any of the workbooks, click the No button.

- Click the Office Button and then click the Exit Excel button on the Office Button menu to quit Excel.

- If the Microsoft Office Excel dialog box is displayed for any of the workbooks, click the No button.

Other Ways
1. Press ALT+W, K

To Consolidate Data by Linking Workbooks

The following steps show how to open the workspace file NextDVR Workspace and consolidate the data from the three region workbooks into the NDVR Company Profit Potential workbook.

1 Start Excel as described on page EX 423. Click the Office Button and then click Open on the Office Button menu. When Excel displays the Open dialog box, select UDISK 2.0 (E:) in the Address bar. Double-click NextDVR Workspace to open the four workbooks saved in the workspace. Make NDVR Company Profit Potential the active worksheet. If necessary, double-click the NDVR Company Profit Potential window title bar to maximize it.

2 Select cell B5. Click the Sum button on the Home tab on the Ribbon. Click the View tab on the Ribbon and then click the Switch Windows button arrow on the Ribbon. Click NDVR Louisville Profit Potential on the Switch Windows menu. Click cell B5. Delete the dollar signs ($) in the reference to cell B5 in the formula bar. Click immediately after B5 in the formula bar and then press the COMMA key.

Workspace Files
A workspace file saves
display information
about open workbooks,
such as window sizes,
print areas, screen mag-
nification, and display
settings. Workspace files
do not contain the
workbooks themselves.

③ Click the Switch Windows button arrow on the Ribbon and then click NDVR Kansas City
Profit Potential. Select cell B5. Delete the dollar signs ($) in the reference to cell B5 in the
formula bar. Click immediately after B5 in the formula bar and then press the COMMA key.

④ Click the Switch Windows button arrow on the Ribbon and then click NDVR Portland
Profit Potential. Select cell B5. Delete the dollar signs ($) in the reference to cell B5 in the
formula bar. Click the Enter box.

⑤ With cell B5 active in the NDVR Company Profit Potential workbook, drag the cell's fill
handle through cell B11. Select cell B5 (Figure 6–89).

⑥ Click the Save button on the Quick Access Toolbar. If Excel displays a dialog box, select
Overwrite changes. Click the OK button. Click the Office Button, click Print on the Office
Button menu, and then click the OK button in the Print dialog box to print the workbook.

Q&A

Why did the formulas need to be edited for each workbook?

As you link workbooks, remember that the cell reference inserted by Excel each time you
click a cell in a workbook is an absolute cell reference ($B$5). You must edit the formula
and change these to relative cell references because the SUM function later is copied to the
range B6:B11. If the cell references are left as absolute, then the copied function always
would refer to cell B5 in the three workbooks no matter where you copy the SUM function.

Excel Help
The best way to become
familiar with Excel Help
is to use it. Appendix C
includes detailed infor-
mation about Excel Help
and exercises that will
help you gain confidence
in using it.

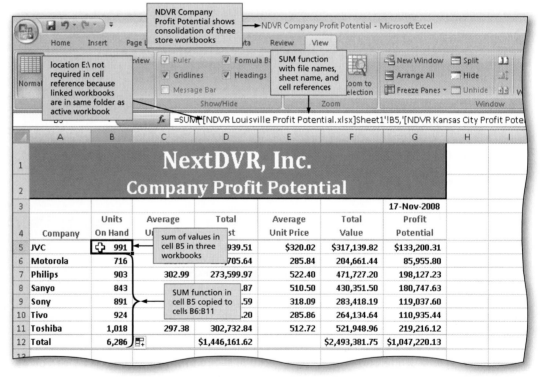

Figure 6–89

Updating Links

Later, if you open the NDVR Company Profit Potential workbook by itself, also
called the **dependent workbook**, Excel will update the links automatically if the linked
workbooks are open. The linked workbooks are called the **source workbooks**. If the linked
workbooks are not open, then Excel displays a security warning in a pane below the Ribbon.
If you click the Options button in the security warning pane, Excel displays the Microsoft

Office Security Options dialog box and asks if you would like to enable automatic update of links. If you click the 'Enable this content' option button and click the OK button in the dialog box, Excel reads the data in the source workbooks and recalculates formulas in the dependent workbook, but it does not open the source workbooks.

If the three source workbooks are open along with the dependent workbook as in the previous set of steps, Excel automatically updates the links (recalculates) in the NDVR Company Profit Potential workbook when a value changes in any one of the source workbooks.

BTW

Certification
The Microsoft Certified Application Specialist (MCAS) program provides an opportunity for you to obtain a valuable industry credential — proof that you have the Excel 2007 skills required by employers. For more information, see Appendix G or visit the Excel 2007 Certification Web page (scsite.com/ex2007/cert).

To Close All Workbooks at One Time and Quit Excel

To close all four workbooks at one time and quit Excel, complete the following steps.

1 Click the Office Button and then click the Exit Excel button on the Office Button menu.

2 If Excel displays the Microsoft Office Excel dialog box, click the No button.

Chapter Summary

In this chapter, you learned how to create and use a template, customize formats, create styles, change chart types, draw and enhance a Clustered Cone chart using WordArt, annotate using text boxes and arrows, use 3-D reference to reference cells in other sheets, add, remove, and change pages breaks, use the Find and Replace commands, and create a workspace file. The items listed below include all the new Excel skills you have learned in this chapter.

1. Save the Template (EX 433)
2. Create and Assign a Custom Format Code and a Comma Style Format (EX 438)
3. Create a New Style (EX 440)
4. Apply a New Style (EX 443)
5. Open a Template and Save It as a Workbook (EX 446)
6. Add a Worksheet to a Workbook (EX 447)
7. Copy the Contents of a Worksheet to Other Worksheets in a Workbook (EX 449)
8. Drill an Entry through Worksheets (EX 451)
9. Enter and Copy 3-D References Using the Paste Button Menu (EX 457)
10. Format the Clustered Cone Chart (EX 465)
11. Add a Chart Title Using the WordArt Tool (EX 466)
12. Add a Text Box, Arrow, and Brace to the Chart (EX 469)
13. Add a Header and Footer, Change Margins, and Center the Printout Horizontally (EX 472)
14. Add a Header to the Clustered Cone Chart Sheet (EX 475)
15. Print All Worksheets in a Workbook (EX 476)
16. Print Nonadjacent Sheets in a Workbook (EX 476)
17. Insert and Remove a Page Break (EX 478)
18. Hide Page Breaks (EX 479)
19. Find a String (EX 481)
20. Replace a String with Another String (EX 483)
21. Search for and Open Workbooks (EX 486)
22. Create a Workspace File (EX 488)
23. Consolidate Data by Linking Workbooks (EX 489)

If you have a SAM user profile, you may have access to hands-on instruction, practice, and assessment. Log in to your SAM account (http://sam2007.course.com) to launch any assigned training activities or exams that relate to the skills covered in this chapter.

Learn It Online

Learn It Online is a series of online student exercises that test your knowledge of chapter content and key terms.

Instructions: To complete the Learn It Online exercises, start your browser, click the Address bar, and then enter the Web address scsite.com/ex2007/learn. When the Excel 2007 Learn It Online page is displayed, click the link for the exercise you want to complete and then read the instructions.

Chapter Reinforcement TF, MC, and SA
A series of true/false, multiple choice, and short answer questions that test your knowledge of the chapter content.

Flash Cards
An interactive learning environment where you identify chapter key terms associated with displayed definitions.

Practice Test
A series of multiple choice questions that test your knowledge of chapter content and key terms.

Who Wants To Be a Computer Genius?
An interactive game that challenges your knowledge of chapter content in the style of a television quiz show.

Wheel of Terms
An interactive game that challenges your knowledge of chapter key terms in the style of the television show *Wheel of Fortune*.

Crossword Puzzle Challenge
A crossword puzzle that challenges your knowledge of key terms presented in the chapter.

Apply Your Knowledge

Reinforce the skills and apply the concepts you learned in this chapter.

Consolidating Data in a Workbook
Instructions: Follow the steps below to consolidate the four quarterly payroll sheets on the Annual Totals sheet in the workbook Apply 6-1 Annual Payroll Totals (Figure 6–90). At the conclusion of the instructions, the Annual Payroll Totals sheet should display as shown in the lower screen in Figure 6–90.

Perform the following tasks.
1. Start Excel. Open the workbook Apply 6-1 Annual Payroll Totals from the Data Files for Students and then save the workbook as Apply 6-1 Annual Payroll Totals Complete. See the inside back cover of this book for instructions for downloading the Data Files for Students or see your instructor for information on accessing the files required in this book. One by one, click the first four tabs and review the quarterly payroll totals. Click the Annual Totals tab.

2. Determine the annual payroll totals on the Annual Totals sheet by using the SUM function and 3-D references to sum the hours worked on the four quarterly sheets in cell B11. Do the same to determine the annual gross pay in cell C11. Copy the range B11:C11 to the range B12:C14 by using the Copy button on the Home tab on the Ribbon and the Formulas command on the Paste button menu on the Home tab on the Ribbon.

3. Change the document properties as specified by your instructor. Select all five worksheets. Add a worksheet header with your name, course number, and other information as specified by your instructor. Add the page number and total number of pages to the footer. Center all worksheets horizontally on the page and print without gridlines. Preview and print the five worksheets. Click the Annual Totals tab to select the sheet.

4. Save the workbook with the new page setup. Close the workbook.

5. Submit the assignment as requested by your instructor.

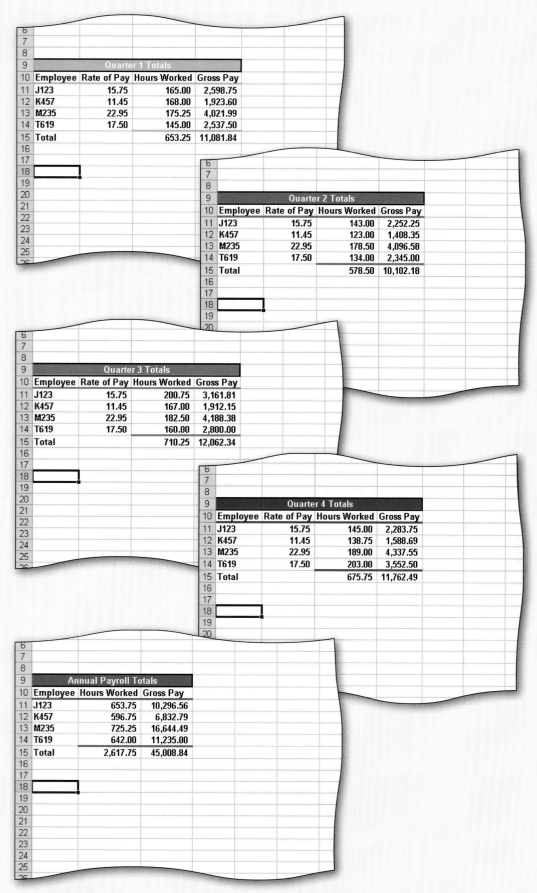

Figure 6–90

Extend Your Knowledge

Extend the skills you learned in this chapter and experiment with new skills. You may need to use Help to complete the assignment.

Making Use of the Chart Tools on the Design Tab

Instructions: Complete the following tasks.

1. Start Excel. Open the workbook Extend 6-1 Tennis Summary from the Data Files for Students and then save the workbook as Extend 6-1 Tennis Summary Complete. See the inside back cover of this book for instructions for downloading the Data Files for Students or see your instructor for information on accessing the files required in this book. Click the Chart tab. Click the chart to select it and display the Design tab on the Ribbon.

2. Click the Change Chart Type button on the Design tab on the Ribbon and then choose a Line chart to change the 3-D Bar chart to a Line chart. One at a time, repeat this step for each of the following chart types: Bar chart, Area chart, Surface chart, and Doughnut chart. Finally, choose the Column chart type 3-D Cone (column 1, row 3).

3. Click the More arrow (lower arrow) in the Chart Layouts group on the Design tab on the Ribbon to display the Chart Layouts gallery. Choose Layout 2 (column 2, row 1) in the Chart Layouts gallery. Repeat this step for the following layouts: Layout 8 and Layout 9. Finally, choose Layout 5 (column 2, row 2).

4. Click the More arrow (lower arrow) in the Chart Styles group on the Design tab on the Ribbon to display the Chart Styles gallery. One at a time, choose three different Chart Styles. Finally, choose Style 38 (column 6, row 5) as shown in Figure 6–91. Remove the axis title from the left side of the chart.

5. Change the document properties as specified by your instructor. Change the Chart sheet header with your name, course number, and other information as specified by your instructor. Change the print orientation to landscape. Print the Chart sheet using the Fit to option. Save the workbook.

6. Submit the assignment as requested by your instructor.

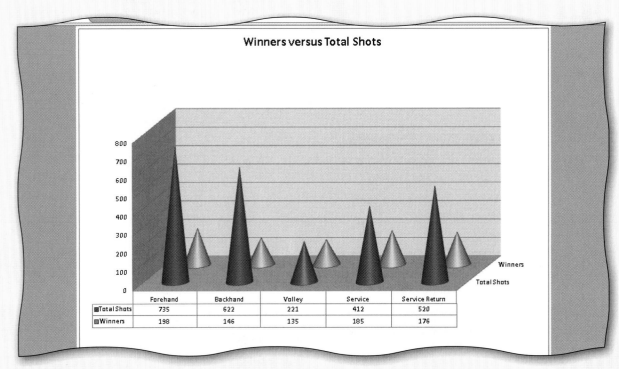

Figure 6–91

Make It Right

Analyze a workbook and correct all errors and/or improve the design.

Chart Manipulation, Using WordArt, and Correcting 3-D Cell References

Instructions: Start Excel. Open the workbook Make It Right 6-1 Gems for Everyone and then save the workbook as Make It Right 6-1 Gems for Everyone Complete. See the inside back cover of this book for instructions for downloading the Data Files for Students or see your instructor for information on accessing the files required in this book. Correct the following design and formula problems so that the Company Totals sheet appears with an embedded chart as shown in Figure 6–92.

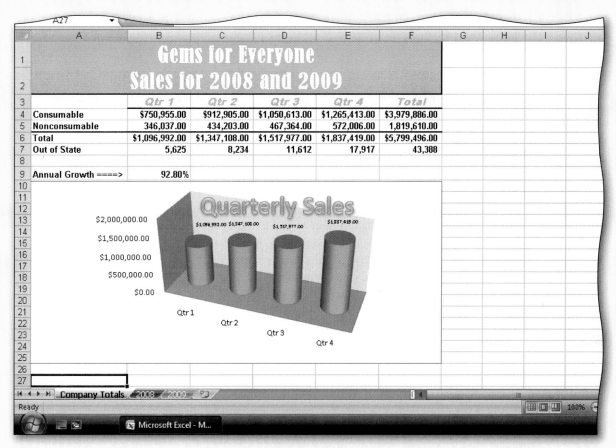

Figure 6–92

Perform the following tasks:

1. Click the Chart sheet tab to display the 3-D Pie chart and then click the chart.

2. Click the Design tab on the Ribbon and then complete the following chart tasks:

   a. Change the 3-D Pie Chart to Clustered Cylinder Chart (column 1, row 2 in the Column area).

   b. Change the chart layout to Layout 4 by clicking the More arrow (lower arrow) in the Chart Layouts group and choosing Layout 4. One at a time, select each of the total numbers at the top of the columns. Change the font size to 6 by typing 6 in the Font Size box on the Home tab on the Ribbon. Drag the total numbers above the cylinders. Delete the Series 1 label below the chart.

   c. Click the More arrow (lower arrow) in the Chart Styles group on the Design tab on the Ribbon to display the Chart Styles gallery. Choose Style 40 (column 8, row 5).

Continued >

Make It Right *continued*

    d. Use the WordArt button on the Insert tab on the Ribbon to add the chart title, Quarterly Sales. Choose the Fill – Accent 6, Warm Matte Bevel (column 2, row 6). Move the chart title above the chart. Change the font size of the chart title to 28.

    e. Click the Design tab on the Ribbon and then click the Move Chart button to move the chart to the Company Totals sheet. Drag the chart to the range A10:F25. Make any necessary adjustments so that the chart appears as shown in Figure 6–92 on the previous page.

3. Select cell B4, the supposed sum of cell B4 on the 2008 and 2009 sheets. Note that the SUM function is not referencing cell B4 on the 2008 sheet. Reenter the SUM function and select the appropriate range to sum. Do the same for cell B5. Copy the range B4:B5 to the range C4:E5.

4. Change the document properties as specified by your instructor. Change the three worksheet headers to include your name, course number, and other information requested by your instructor.

5. Save the workbook, and submit the revised workbook as requested by your instructor.

In the Lab

Create a workbook using the guidelines, concepts, and skills presented in this chapter. Labs are listed in order of increasing difficulty.

Lab 1: Using a Template to Create a Multiple-Sheet Workbook

Problem: Rings and Things is a company that specializes in hand jewelry for women. The company has four stores in Biloxi, Hartford, Peoria, and Seattle and a corporate office in Indianapolis. All of the stores sell their products via direct mail, telesales, and walk-ins. Every year, the corporate officers in Indianapolis use a template to create a year-end sales analysis workbook. The workbook contains four sheets, one for each of the three stores and one sheet to consolidate data and determine the company totals. The Consolidated sheet appears as shown in Figure 6–93.

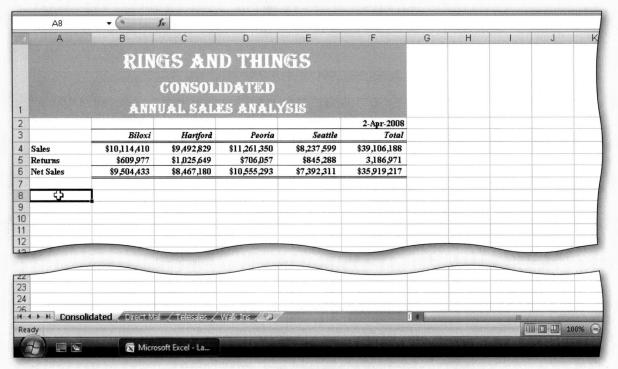

Figure 6–93

The template used to create the annual sales analysis workbook is part of the Data Files for Students. Rebecca Smart, the company's accountant, has asked you to use the template to create the year-end sales analysis workbook.

Instructions Part 1: Perform the following tasks.

1. Open the template Lab 6-1 Rings and Things Annual Sales Analysis Template from the Data Files for Students. See the inside back cover of this book for instructions for downloading the Data Files for Students or see your instructor for information on accessing the files required in this book. Save the template as a workbook using the file name, Lab 6-1 Part 1 Rings and Things Annual Sales Analysis. Make sure Excel Workbook is selected in the 'Save as type' list when you save the workbook.

2. Add a worksheet to the workbook between Sheet1 and Sheet2 and then paste the contents of Sheet1 to the three empty sheets.

3. From left to right, rename the sheet tabs Consolidated, Direct Mail, Telesales, and Walk Ins. Color the tabs as shown in Figure 6–93. On each of the three sales channel sheets, change the subtitle in cell A2 to match the tab name. Use the title, Consolidated, in cell A1 of the Consolidated worksheet. Change the title style for each title area in the range A1:F1 to match its tab color. Enter the data in Table 6–11 into the three sales channel sheets.

Table 6–11 Rings and Things Annual Sales Data by Store and Sales Channel				
		Direct Mail	**Telesales**	**Walk Ins**
Biloxi	Sales	4873275	3291010	1950125
	Returns	275375	289500	45102
Hartford	Sales	5239100	2152675	2101054
	Returns	463201	500250	62198
Peoria	Sales	3925750	4235100	3100500
	Returns	225198	324519	156340
Seattle	Sales	3278109	1975200	2984290
	Returns	352679	125500	367109

4. On the Consolidated worksheet, use the SUM function, 3-D references, and copy and paste capabilities of Excel to total the corresponding cells on the three sales channel sheets. First, compute the sum in cell B4 and then compute the sum in cell B5. Copy the range B4:B5 to the range C4:E5. The Consolidated sheet should resemble Figure 6–93.

5. Change the document properties as specified by your instructor. Select all four sheets. Add a worksheet header with your name, course number, and other information requested by your instructor. Add the page number and total number of pages to the footer. Change the left and right margins to .5.

6. With the four sheets selected, preview and then print the workbook in landscape orientation and use the Black and white option.

7. Save the workbook with the new page setup characteristics. Close the workbook.

8. Submit the assignment as specified by your instructor.

Instructions Part 2: Complete the following tasks.

1. Start Excel. Open the workbook Lab 6-1 Part 1 Rings and Things Annual Sales Analysis and then save the workbook using the file name, Lab 6-1 Part 2 Rings and Things Annual Sales Analysis.

2. Create an embedded Clustered Horizontal Cylinder chart in the range A8:H25 on the Consolidated worksheet by charting the range A3:E5.

Continued >

3. Move the chart to a separate sheet by clicking the Move Chart button on the Design tab on the Ribbon. Name the sheet tab Chart and color the sheet tab red. Drag the Chart sheet tab to the far right.

4. Increase the font size of the labels on both axes to 12-point bold. Increase the font size of the legends on the right side of the chart to 14-point.

5. Apply the chart colors shown in Figure 6–94 to the cylinders and to the walls by right-clicking the items one at a time and selecting the appropriate commands.

6. Use the WordArt button on the Insert tab on the Ribbon to add the chart title Annual Sales and Returns. Select Fill - Accent, 2 Matte Bevel (column 3, row 6) from the WordArt gallery.

7. Add the two text boxes and arrows and change their colors to red as shown in Figure 6–94.

8. Add a header to the Chart sheet with your name, course number, and other information requested by your instructor. Add the page number and total number of pages to the footer. Preview and print all five sheets at one time. Save the workbook and then close the workbook.

9. Submit the assignment as specified by your instructor.

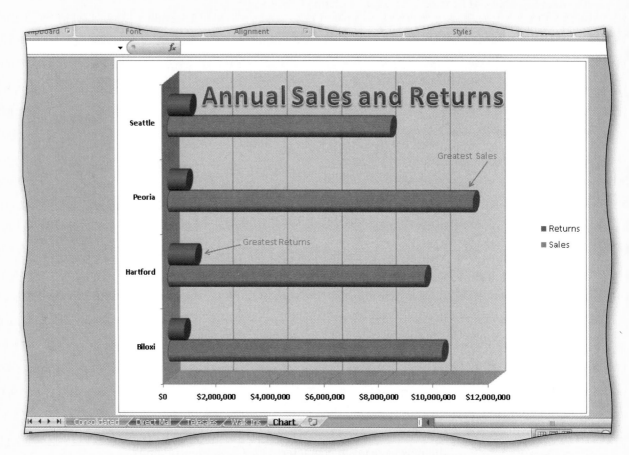

Figure 6–94

Instructions Part 3: Complete the following tasks.

1. Start Excel. Open the workbook Lab 6-1 Part 2 Rings and Things Annual Sales Analysis. Do not save the workbook in this part.

2. Select cell A1 on the Consolidated worksheet. Select all the worksheets except for the Chart sheet.

3. Use the Find & Select button on the Home tab on the Ribbon to list all occurrences of the word, Sales, in the workbook. Use the Find All button in the Find and Replace dialog box. Write down the number of occurrences and the cell locations of the word Sales.

4. Repeat Step 3, but find only cells that match exactly the word Sales. If necessary, click the Options button to display the desired check box. Use the Find & Select button to find all occurrences of the word Sales. Write down the number of occurrences and the cell locations that match exactly with the word Sales.

5. Use the Find & Select button to find all occurrences of the word, sales, in bold white font. For this find operation, clear the check mark from the Match entire cell contents check box.

6. Use the Replace command to replace the word, Sales, with the word, Revenue, on all four sheets. Print the four sheets. Close the workbook without saving changes.

7. Submit the assignment as specified by your instructor.

In the Lab

Lab 2: Consolidating Data by Linking Workbooks

Problem: The Apply Your Knowledge exercise in this chapter calls for consolidating the Hours Worked and Gross Pay from four worksheets on a fifth worksheet in the same workbook (see Figure 6–90 on page EX 493). This exercise takes the same data stored in four separate workbooks and consolidates the Hours Worked and Gross Pay by linking to a fifth workbook.

Instructions Part 1: Perform the following tasks.

1. Start Excel. Open the following five files from the Data Files for Students. See the inside back cover of this book for instructions for downloading the Data Files for Students or see your instructor for information on accessing the files required in this book. You can open them one at a time or you can open them all at one time by selecting the five files and then clicking the Open button.
   - Lab 6-2 Emp Annual Payroll Totals
   - Lab 6-2 Emp Quarter 1 Payroll Totals
   - Lab 6-2 Emp Quarter 2 Payroll Totals
   - Lab 6-2 Emp Quarter 3 Payroll Totals
   - Lab 6-2 Emp Quarter 4 Payroll Totals

2. Click the Switch Windows button on the View tab on the Ribbon and then click Lab 6-2 Emp Annual Payroll Totals.

3. Click the Save Workspace button on the View tab on the Ribbon. When the Save Workspace dialog box is displayed, save the workspace using the file name, Lab 6-2 Emp Payroll Workspace.

4. Close all the open workbooks. Open the workspace Lab 6-2 Emp Payroll Workspace. When the Lab 6-2 Emp Annual Payroll Totals window is displayed, click the Maximize button in the upper-right corner to maximize the window. Save the workbook using the file name, Lab 6-2 Part 1 Emp Annual Payroll Totals.

5. Consolidate the data in the four quarterly payroll workbooks into the range B11:C14 in the workbook Lab 6-2 Part 1 Emp Annual Payroll Totals by doing the following:

   a. Click cell B11. Click the Home tab on the Ribbon and then click Sum button.

   b. Click the Switch Windows button on the View tab on the Ribbon and then click Lab 6-2 Emp Quarter 1 Payroll Totals. When the workbook is displayed, click cell C11, click the Switch Windows button on the View tab on the Ribbon, and then click Lab 6-2 Part 1 Emp Annual

Continued >

In the Lab *continued*

Payroll Totals. Change the absolute cell reference $C$11 in the formula bar to the relative cell reference C11 by deleting the dollar signs. Click immediately after C11 in the formula bar and then press the COMMA key.

c. Click the Switch Windows button on the View tab on the Ribbon and then click Lab 6-2 Emp Quarter 2 Payroll Totals. When the workbook is displayed, click cell C11, click the Switch Windows button on the View tab on the Ribbon, and then click Lab 6-2 Part 1 Emp Annual Payroll Totals. Change the absolute cell reference $C$11 in the formula bar to the relative cell reference C11 by deleting the dollar signs. Click immediately after C11 in the formula bar and then press the COMMA key.

d. Click the Switch Windows button on the View tab on the Ribbon and then click Lab 6-2 Emp Quarter 3 Payroll Totals. When the workbook is displayed, click cell C11, click the Switch Windows button on the View tab on the Ribbon, and then click Lab 6-2 Part 1 Emp Annual Payroll Totals. Change the absolute cell reference $C$11 in the formula bar to the relative cell reference C11 by deleting the dollar signs. Click immediately after C11 in the formula bar and then press the COMMA key.

e. Click the Switch Windows button on the View tab on the Ribbon and then click Lab 6-2 Emp Quarter 4 Payroll Totals. When the workbook is displayed, click cell C11, click the Switch Windows button on the View tab on the Ribbon, and then click Lab 6-2 Part 1 Emp Annual Payroll Totals. Change the absolute cell reference $C$11 in the formula bar to the relative cell reference C11 by deleting the dollar signs. Press the ENTER key to sum the four quarter hours worked. You should end up with an annual total of 653.75 hours worked in cell B11.

f. With the workbook Lab 6-2 Part 1 Emp Annual Payroll Totals window active, select cell B11. Drag the fill handle through cell C11 to display the annual gross pay in cell C11. Select the range B11:C11. Drag the fill handle down to cell C14. When the Auto Fill Options button is displayed next to cell C14, click the Auto Fill Options button and then click the Fill Without Formatting option. The totals in row 15 should be exactly the same as the totals in row 15 in the lower figure of Figure 6–90 on page EX 493.

6. Change the document properties as specified by your instructor. Change the worksheet header with your name, course number, and other information as specified by your instructor. Preview and print the annual payroll totals. Save the workbook using the file name, Lab 6-2 Part 1 Emp Annual Payroll Totals. Close all workbooks. Submit the assignment as requested by your instructor.

Instructions Part 2: Perform the following tasks to update the hours worked for Quarter 2 and Quarter 4.

1. Start Excel. Open Lab 6-2 Emp Quarter 2 Payroll Totals from the Data Files for Students. Change the hours worked for employee K457 in row 12 from 123.00 to 223.25. Save the workbook using the file name, Lab 6-2 Emp Quarter 2 Payroll Totals. Close the workbook.

2. Open Lab 6-2 Emp Quarter 4 Payroll Totals. Change the hours worked for employee M235 in row 13 from 189.00 to 211.00. Save the workbook using the file name, Lab 6-2 Emp Quarter 4 Payroll Totals. Close the workbook.

3. Open Lab 6-2 Part 1 Emp Annual Payroll Totals workbook saved earlier in Part 1 of this exercise. Save the workbook using the file name, Lab 6-2 Part 2 Emp Annual Payroll Totals. Click the Data tab on the Ribbon. Click the Edit Links button in the Connections group on the Data tab. Select each file in the Edit Links dialog box and then click the Update Values button to instruct Excel to apply the current values in the four source workbooks to the consolidated workbook (Figure 6–95).

4. Preview and print the consolidated workbook. Save the workbook. Submit the assignment as requested by your instructor.

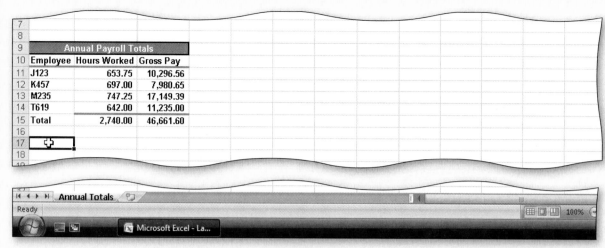

	Annual Payroll Totals	
Employee	Hours Worked	Gross Pay
J123	653.75	10,296.56
K457	697.00	7,980.65
M235	747.25	17,149.39
T619	642.00	11,235.00
Total	2,740.00	46,661.60

Figure 6–95

In the Lab

Lab 3: Returning Real-Time Stock Quotes to the Stock Portfolio Worksheet

Problem: You belong to the Learn-N-Earn Stock Club, which has been investing in the stock market for the past several years. As vice-president of the club, you maintain a summary of the club's stock market investments in an Excel workbook (Figure 6–96a on the next page). Each day you go through the Business section of the newspaper and manually update the current prices in column G to determine the value of the club's equities. You recently heard about the Web query capabilities of Excel and have decided to use them to update the club's stock portfolio automatically.

Instructions: Perform the following steps to have Web queries automatically update the current price in column G and the major indices in the range B12:B15 of Figure 6–96a.

1. Start Excel. Open the workbook Lab 6-3 Learn-N-Earn Stock Club Portfolio Basics from the Data Files for Students and then save the workbook using the file name, Lab 6-3 Learn-N-Earn Stock Club Portfolio. See the inside back cover of this book for instructions for downloading the Data Files for Students or see your instructor for information on accessing the files required in this book. After reviewing the worksheet, you should notice that it lacks current prices in column G and the major indices in the range B12:B15.

2. Click Sheet2 and then select cell A1. Click the Data tab on the Ribbon and then click the Existing Connections button. When Excel displays the Existing Connections dialog box, double-click MSN MoneyCentral Investor Stock Quotes. When Excel displays the Import Data dialog box, click the OK button. When Excel displays the Enter Parameter Value dialog box, click the Learn-N-Earn Portfolio sheet tab at the bottom of the screen and drag through the range B3:B10. Click the 'Use this value/reference for future refreshes' check box to select it. The Enter Parameter Value dialog box should display as shown in Figure 6–96b on the next page. Click the OK button. The Web query should return a worksheet with up-to-date stock quotes similar to the one shown in Figure 6–96c on the next page. Rename the Sheet2 tab Stock Quotes.

3. Click the Learn-N-Earn Portfolio tab. Click cell G3. Type = (equal sign). Click the Stock Quotes tab. Click cell D4. Press the ENTER key. Use the fill handle to copy cell G3 on the Learn-N-Earn Portfolio sheet to the range G4:G10. You now should have current prices for the stock portfolio that are the same as the last prices on the Stock Quotes worksheet in column D.

4. Click Sheet3 and then select cell A1. If necessary, click the Data tab on the Ribbon and then click Existing Connections. When Excel displays the Existing Connections dialog box, double-click MSN Money Central Investor Major Indices. When Excel displays the Import Data dialog box,

Continued >

In the Lab *continued*

click the OK button. Rename the Sheet3 tab Major Indices. The worksheet should be similar to the one shown in Figure 6–96d.

(a) Learn-N-Earn Portfolio Worksheet

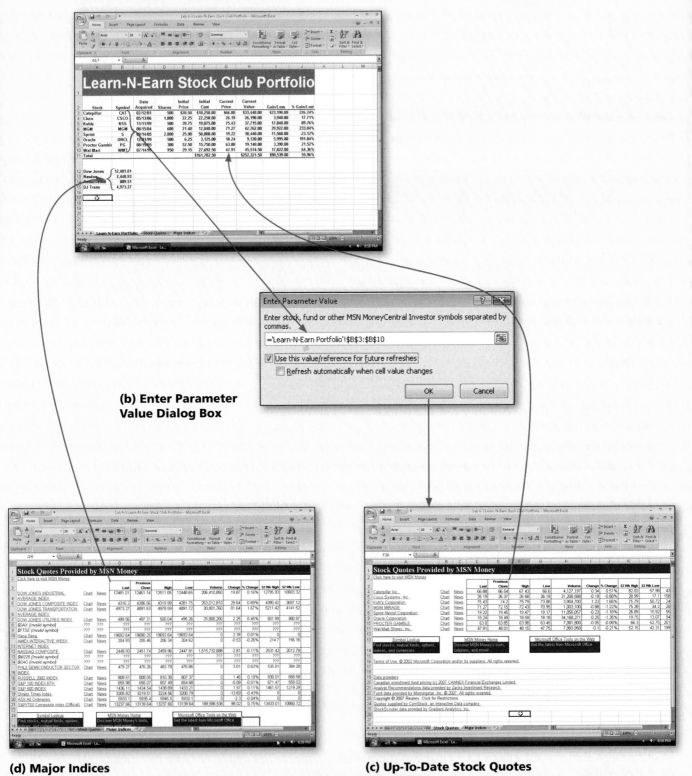

(b) Enter Parameter Value Dialog Box

(d) Major Indices

(c) Up-To-Date Stock Quotes

Figure 6–96

5. Click the Learn-N-Earn Portfolio sheet tab. Select cell B12. Type = (equal sign). Click the Major Indices sheet tab. Select cell D4 (the last Dow Jones Industrial Average Index). Press the ENTER key. Select cell B13. Type = (equal sign). Click the Major Indices tab. Select cell D12 (the last NASDAQ Composite Index). Press the ENTER key. Select cell B14. Type = (equal sign). Click the Major Indices tab. Select cell D16 (the last Russell 2000 Index). Press the ENTER key. Select cell B15. Type = (equal sign). Click the Major Indices tab. Select cell D6 (the last Dow Jones Transportation Average Index). Press the ENTER key. Select cell A16.

6. Change the document properties as specified by your instructor. Select all three worksheets and then change the header with your name, course number, and other information as specified by your instructor. Add a page number as the footer. Change the top margin to 1.5 inches. Select cell A16 and then save the workbook using the file name, Lab 6-3 Learn-N-Earn Stock Club Portfolio.

7. Print the three worksheets using the 'Black and white' option in landscape orientation. Use the Fit to option in the Page sheet in the Page Setup dialog box to print the sheets on one page.

8. Select cell A16 and then save the workbook. Submit the assignment as requested by your instructor.

Cases and Places

Apply your creative thinking and problem solving skills to design and implement a solution.

● EASIER ●● MORE DIFFICULT

● 1: Public Safety Division Budget Proposal

San Pueblo's Public Safety division comprises three departments —Streets and Sanitation, Fire, and Police. The departments have submitted figures comparing this year's budget with next year's budget in four categories (Table 6–12). Develop a template that can be used to prepare each department's budget and the Public Safety division's consolidated total budget within one workbook. Include this year's budget, next year's budget, and the variance [(next year's budget – this year's budget) / this year's budget] for each expenditure. Indicate totals where appropriate. Create an embedded chart on the Public Safety division's worksheet comparing the division's expenditures this year and next.

Table 6–12 San Pueblo's Public Safety Division Expenditures

	Streets and Sanitation		Fire		Police	
	Next Year	This Year	Next Year	This Year	Next Year	This Year
Equipment	212000	198150	62350	78345	225175	220650
Maintenance	68350	62450	22750	17000	98375	102500
Miscellaneous	48125	44520	37600	38200	47500	32800
Salaries and Benefits	116000	112400	198000	211000	150000	162750

● 2: Creating a Consolidated Balance Sheet

Jeans-For-Teens is a New York-based company that sells high-end jeans globally. After launching its Web site five years ago, the company has attracted so many clients from Europe that the own-ers opened a shop in Paris. The New York and Paris shops' assets last year, respectively, were: cash $25,101 and $650,450; accounts receivable $57,190 and $325,860; marketable securities $345,213 and $211,450; inventory $845,258 and $326,120; and equipment $82,250 and $56,200. The liabilities for each store were: notes payable $1,223,010 and $345,000; accounts payable $213,360 and $702,330; and income tax payable $82,100 and $125,350. The stockholders' equity was: common stock $812,300 and $235,000; and retained earnings $324,242 and $162,400.

Use the concepts and techniques presented in this project to design a template as a balance worksheet to reflect the figures above. Include totals for assets, liabilities, and stockholders' equity. Use the template to create a balance worksheet for the New York store, the Paris store, and the consolidated balance worksheet for the corporation.

●● 3: Analyzing Company Profits by Category

Elite Software sells computer software and supplies. Merchandise is divided into six categories based on profit margin: individual application packages (22%), integrated application packages (9%), entertain-ment software (16%), system software (25%), learning aids (18%), and supplies (10%). Last year's sales data has been collected for the State Street and Western Avenue Stores as shown in Table 6–13. Develop a template that can be used to determine marketing strategies for next year. Include sales, profit margins, profits (sales × profit margin), total sales, total profits, and functions to determine the most and least sales, profit margins, and profits. Use the template to create a worksheet for each outlet, a consolidated worksheet for the entire company, and a chart on a separate sheet reflecting the company's profits by category.

STUDENT ASSIGNMENTS

Table 6–13 Last Year's Sales for State Street and Western Avenue Stores

	State Street Store	Western Avenue Store
Individual applications	$148,812	$52,864
Integrated applications	140,135	93,182
Entertainment software	62,912	72,345
System software	22,769	25,278
Learning aids	9,562	21,397
Supplies	44,215	34,921

•• 4: Analyzing Annual College Expenses and Resources

Make It Personal

College expenses are skyrocketing and your resources are limited. To plan for the upcoming year, you have decided to organize your anticipated expenses and resources in a workbook. The data required to prepare the workbook is shown in Table 6–14.

Table 6–14 Next Year's Anticipated College Expenses and Resources

Expenses	Semester 1	Semester 2	Summer
Room and Board	5750	5750	2150
Tuition	8750	8750	2200
Books	1200	1450	230
Clothes	575	350	150
Entertainment	600	500	200
Miscellaneous	400	350	175
Resources			
Savings	2500	2500	500
Parents	5000	7500	1200
Job	1000	1200	400
Financial Aid	6275	3450	2505
Scholarship	2500	2500	500

Create a template with the data for the first semester in Table 6–14 in mind. Use dummy data in the template. Sum both the expenses and resources for the semester in the template. Save the template and then use it to create a workbook with each of the three semesters on a separate worksheet. Use 3-D cell references to consolidate the data on a worksheet in the workbook. Include a 3-D pie chart that compares the annual expenses. Use the concepts and techniques described in this chapter to format the workbook and chart.

•• 5: Creating a Consolidated Budget Proposal Using Linking Techniques

Working Together

Complete the exercise outlined in Cases and Places 1 using separate workbooks for each department, rather than a single workbook. As a team, create an appropriate template. Assign each member of the team one or more of the four required workbooks to build using the template. After the workbooks have been created, use the concepts and techniques presented in this chapter to consolidate the data by creating a workspace and linking the workbooks. Test the linkage to the division workbook by changing values in the department workbooks.

Graphics Feature
SmartArt and Images

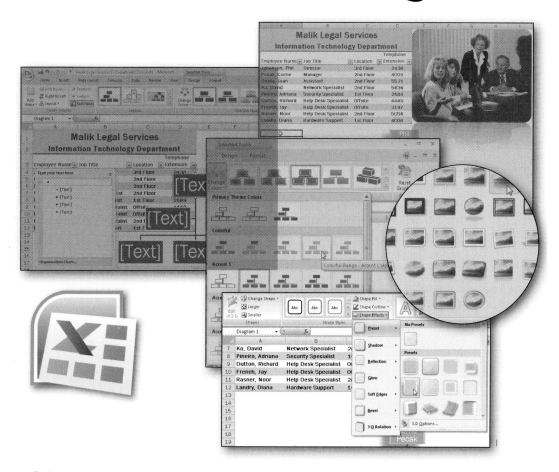

Objectives

You will have mastered the material in this Graphics feature when you can:

- Insert a SmartArt graphic on a worksheet
- Modify a SmartArt graphic
- Add effects to a SmartArt graphic
- Insert an image on a worksheet
- Modify an image on a worksheet

Graphics Feature Introduction

Like a chart, a graphic or image often conveys information or an idea better than words or numbers. You insert and modify graphics and images in order to enhance the visual appeal of an Excel workbook. Many of the skills you learn when working with graphics and images in Excel will be similar when working in Word, PowerPoint, or Outlook.

Project — Adding SmartArt and Images to a Worksheet

The director of the Malik Legal Services Information Technology department would like to enhance the department's directory to be more visually appealing to those inside and outside of the department. The directory currently exists in a table in an Excel worksheet. The director would like a photograph and department organization chart added to the directory.

Figure 1 shows the results of adding and modifying both a SmartArt graphic and an image. The SmartArt graphic is arranged as an organization chart. Other boxes and levels of the organization can be added to the graphic quickly. The SmartArt graphic also can be resized, positioned, and formatted much in the same way in which you have worked with charts in previous chapters. The image on the top right is a photograph that has been inserted into the worksheet, resized, repositioned, and formatted with a rounded corner and reflection.

Overview

As you read through this feature, you will learn how to create and modify SmartArt graphics and insert and modify images by performing the following tasks:

- Insert a SmartArt graphic on a worksheet
- Modify a SmartArt graphic
- Add effects to a SmartArt graphic
- Insert an image on a worksheet
- Modify an image on a worksheet

Plan Ahead

General Project Decisions

1. **Choose the type of graphic to use for the organization chart.** The requirements for the worksheet ask for an organization chart. The SmartArt graphics provided with most Microsoft Office applications include a template for an organization chart. Using the built-in SmartArt graphics organization chart template is, therefore, a good starting point for the chart.

2. **Determine the contents and layout of the organization chart.** The organization chart reflects the hierarchy of the organization that it represents. An organization hierarchy can be inferred from the job titles shown in the table in Figure 1.

3. **Specify the formatting for the organization chart.** Because visual appeal is important, the chart should be formatted with 3-D effects, and colors should be added to make the chart more appealing.

(continued)

(continued)

4. **Obtain the image to be used in the worksheet.** The image to be used is included with the Data Files for Students. Once the image is inserted on the worksheet, the image file no longer is needed because a copy of the image becomes part of the worksheet. When obtaining an image, you must use only those images for which you have permission. Several sources exist that provide royalty-free images, meaning that you do not have to pay for the image to use it.

5. **Determine placement and formatting for the image.** Placing the image to the right of the table is appropriate because the image is not likely to change size over time. The organization chart, however, may change size in the future and should be placed below the table and image. If the organization gets larger, the worksheet provides more space below the table and image for this growth. The image also can be set off from the table by using a rounded border. An artistic reflection of the image provides an additional visual enhancement to the worksheet.

 When necessary, more specific details concerning the above guidelines are presented at appropriate points in the feature. The feature also will identify the actions you perform and decisions made regarding these guidelines during the addition of the organization chart and image to an existing worksheet.

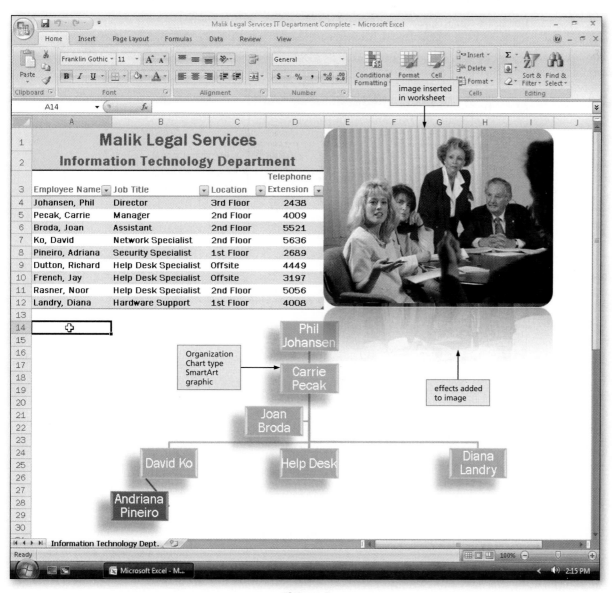

Figure 1

Working with SmartArt Graphics

A SmartArt graphic is a customizable diagram that you use to pictorially present lists, processes, and relationships. For example, the manufacturing process to produce an item can be illustrated with a SmartArt graphic. Excel includes seven types of SmartArt graphics: List, Process, Cycle, Hierarchy, Relationship, Matrix, and Pyramid. Each type of graphic includes several layouts, or templates, from which to choose. After selecting a SmartArt graphic type and layout, you customize the graphic to meet your needs and present your information and ideas in a compelling manner.

To Open a Workbook, Turn Off Gridlines, and Insert an Organization Chart

Many entities maintain an organization chart that represents the hierarchy of the employees in the organization. The following steps open a workbook that contains an employee list, and then add, move, and size a SmartArt organization chart.

- Connect a USB flash drive to one of the computer's USB ports.

- Start Excel and then open the workbook, Malik Legal Services IT Department, from the Data Files for Students.

- Save the workbook using the file name, Malik Legal Services IT Department Complete.

- Click the View tab on the Ribbon and then click the Gridlines check box to turn off gridlines on the worksheet (Figure 2).

Why should I turn off gridlines?

Although useful during the process of creating a worksheet, many spreadsheet specialists remove the gridlines to reduce the clutter on the screen. This is especially true when working with graphics and images on a worksheet.

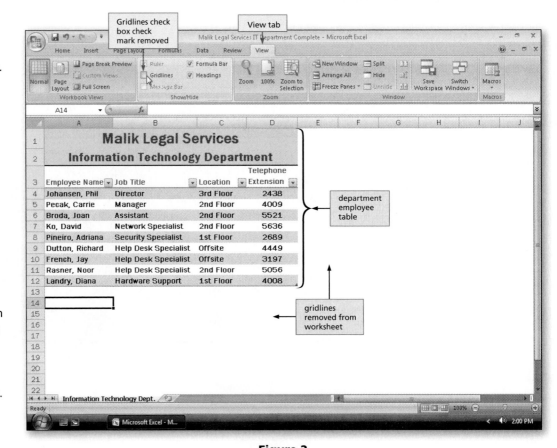

Figure 2

3

- Click the Insert tab on the Ribbon and then click the SmartArt button on the Ribbon to display the Choose a SmartArt Graphic dialog box.

Experiment

- Click a variety of SmartArt graphics types and layouts to view previews of the graphics in the preview area of the Choose a SmartArt Graphic dialog box.

4

- Click Hierarchy in the Type list on the left side of the Choose a SmartArt Graphic dialog box. The middle portion of the dialog box (the layout list) displays a gallery of hierarchy charts, and the right side of the dialog box (the preview area) displays a preview of the selected SmartArt graphic.

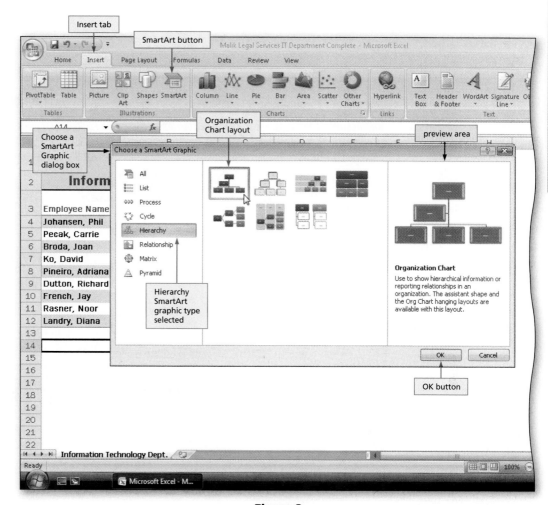

Figure 3

- Click Organization Chart (column 1, row 1) in the layout list to see a preview of the chart in the preview area (Figure 3).

Click the OK button to insert an Organization Chart SmartArt graphic in the worksheet. If necessary, click the Text Pane button on the Ribbon to display the Text pane. (Figure 4).

Q&A What is displayed on the screen?

Two panes are added to the worksheet. The left pane is the Text pane. The Text pane is displayed only when the chart is selected. The Text pane includes one line for each box in the chart and allows you to add text to the chart quickly. The right pane is the SmartArt graphic with the Hierarchy type and the Organization Chart layout. The chart is displayed over the data in the worksheet, but it will be repositioned in the following steps.

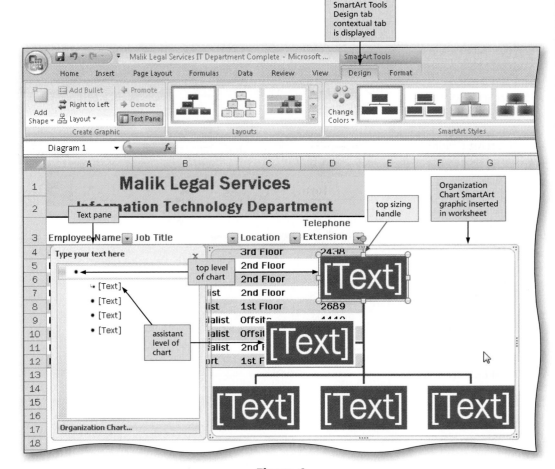

Figure 4

While holding down the ALT key, click and drag the top of the chart to the bottom of row 13.

Click the middle sizing handle on the right edge of the chart and while holding down the ALT

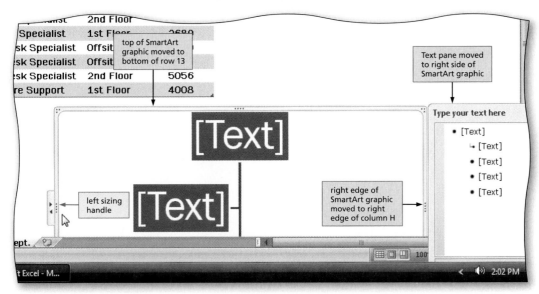

Figure 5

key, drag the sizing handle until the right edge of the chart is aligned with the right edge of column H.

Drag the Text pane to the right side of the chart (Figure 5).

Q&A Why should I drag the Text pane to the right side of the chart?

The chart will be widened further to the left. If the Text pane remains on the left side of the chart, then it will display on top of the resized chart and obscure the view of the chart.

7

- If necessary, scroll the worksheet down until row 30 is displayed.

- Click the middle sizing handle on the left edge of the chart and while holding down the ALT key, drag the sizing handle until the left edge of the chart is aligned with the right edge of column A.

- Click the middle sizing handle on the bottom edge of the chart and while holding down the ALT key, drag the sizing handle until the bottom edge of the chart is aligned with the bottom edge of row 29 (Figure 6).

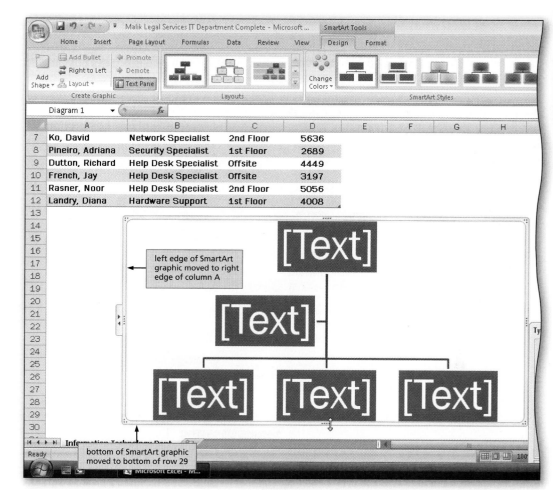

Figure 6

Other Ways	
1. To turn off gridlines, press ALT+W+V+G	2. To insert SmartArt graphic, press ALT+N+M, select layout, click OK button

To Add Shapes and Modify Text in the Organization Chart

The default organization chart layout includes five shapes: a shape for a manager at the top of the chart, a shape for the manager's assistant on the left side in the second row of the chart, and three shapes for subordinates in the third row of the chart. The Malik Legal Services Information Technology department requires two additional shapes in the organization chart: a shape at the top of the chart for the Director level of management, and a shape below the lower-left shape for the Security Specialist job title. The following steps add two new shapes to the organization chart and then modify the text in all of the shapes.

- Right-click the top shape in the organization chart to display the shortcut menu.

- Point to Add Shape on the shortcut menu to display the Add Shape submenu (Figure 7).

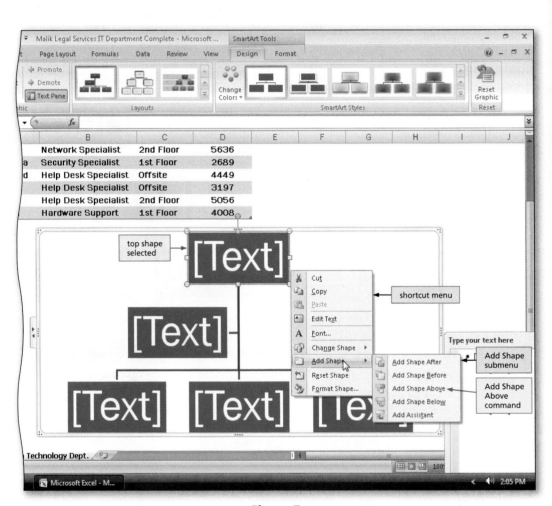

Figure 7

Excel Graphics Feature

2

- Click Add Shape Above to add a new shape to the organization chart (Figure 8).

Why does Excel change the layout of the chart?

When a new shape is added to a SmartArt graphic, Excel rearranges the shapes in the graphic to fit in the same area. In Figure 8, the size of each shape and the font size of the text in each shape is reduced to accommodate the added shape. Excel also arranges the third level of the organization chart in a vertical alignment in order to better fit the added shape.

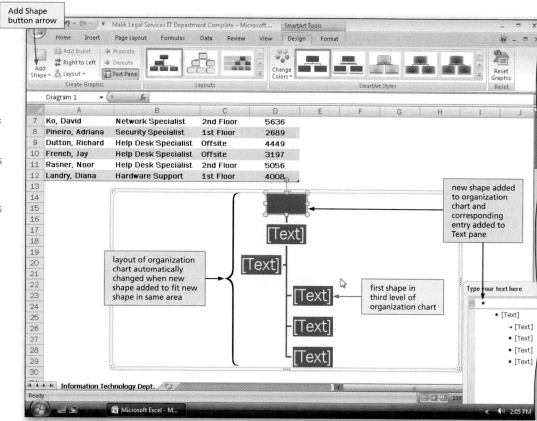

Figure 8

3

- Click the first shape in the third level of the organization chart to select it.

- Click the Add Shape button arrow on the Ribbon to display the Add Shape menu.

- Click Add Shape Below on the Add Shape menu to add a new shape below the first shape in the third level of the organization chart (Figure 9).

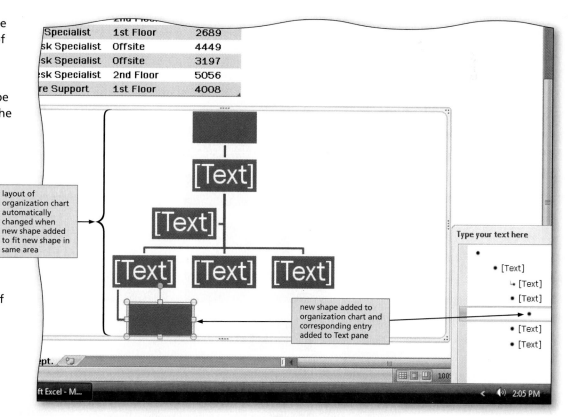

Figure 9

4

- Click the top shape in the organization chart and then type Phil Johansen to add text to the shape (Figure 10).

Q&A

Why does Excel add the same text to the Text pane?

As changes are made to text in the chart, the Text pane reflects those changes as an outline. You can type text in the shapes or type text in the Text pane, as shown in the following step.

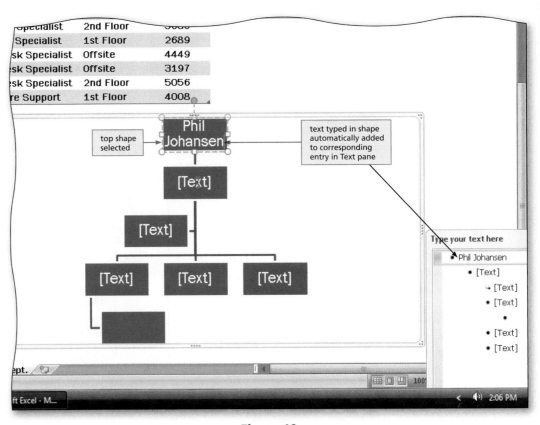

Figure 10

5

- Click the entry under Phil Johansen in the Text pane to select it.

- Type Carrie Pecak in the second line of the Text pane to change the text in the shape in the second level of the organization chart (Figure 11).

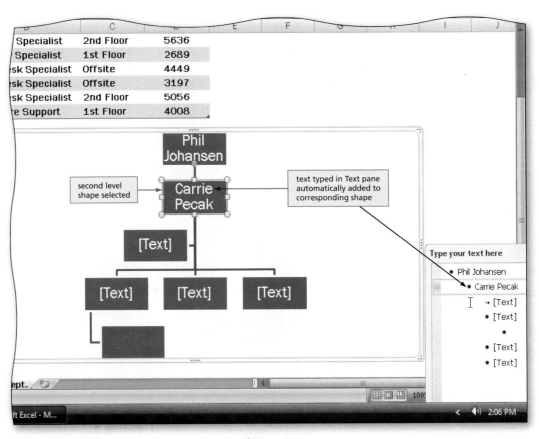

Figure 11

6

- Repeat Step 4 for each of the remaining shapes in the organization chart and enter text in each shape as shown in Figure 12.

- Click the Save button on the Quick Access Toolbar.

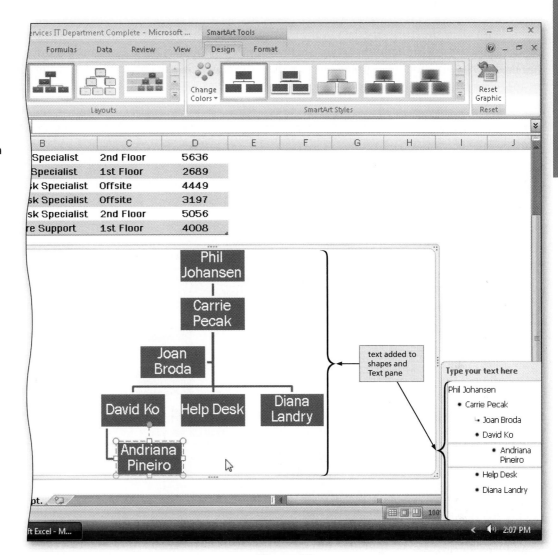

Figure 12

Other Ways

1. Click line in Text pane, press ENTER key

2. Select shape, press CTRL+C, press CTRL+V

To Change the Position of Shapes and Add Effects to the Organization Chart

With all of the necessary data in the chart, the next step is to customize the chart by changing its layout to reflect the structure of the Information Technology department. The shapes in the third and fourth rows of the organization chart should be spread out to reduce the clutter in the chart. The following steps arrange the chart to be more readable and visually appealing.

- Click the lower-right shape in the organization chart (Diana Landry) and then drag the shape to the right until the right edge of the shape is aligned with the right edge of the organization chart as shown in Figure 13.

- Click the shape containing the text, David Ko, and then drag the shape to the left until the right edge of the shape is aligned approximately with the right edge of column B as shown in Figure 13.

- Click the shape containing the text, Andriana Pineiro, and then drag the shape to the left until the lower-left corner of the shape is aligned with the lower-left corner of the organization chart as shown in Figure 13.

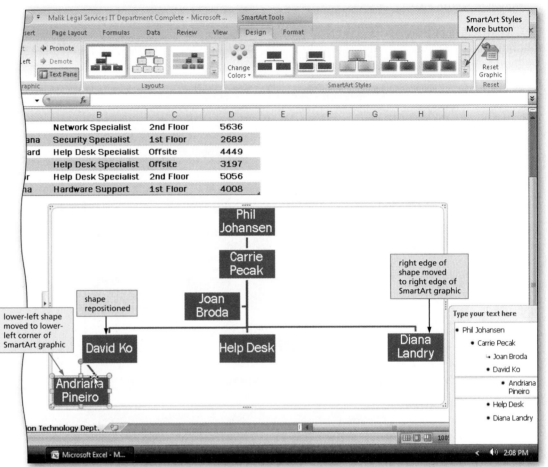

Figure 13

- Click the SmartArt Styles More button to display the SmartArt Styles gallery.

 Experiment

- Point to a variety of SmartArt styles in the SmartArt Styles gallery to preview the styles in the worksheet.

- Point to the Cartoon style in the SmartArt Styles gallery to display a preview of the style in the organization chart (Figure 14).

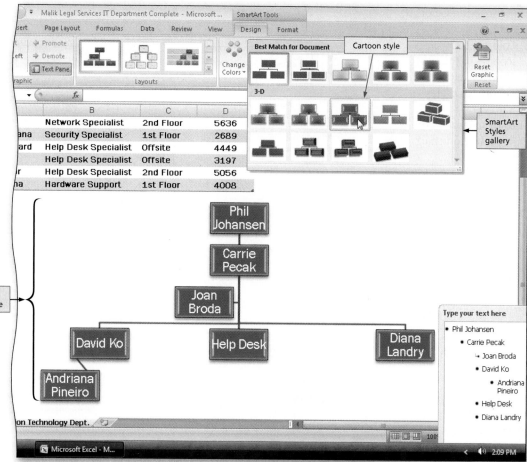

Figure 14

- Click the Cartoon style in the SmartArt Styles gallery to apply the style to the organization chart.

- Click the Change Colors button on the Ribbon to display the Change Colors gallery.

 Experiment

- Point to a variety of color schemes in the Change Colors gallery to preview the color schemes in the worksheet.

- Point to the Colorful Range – Accent Colors 4 to 5 color scheme in the Change Colors gallery to display a preview of the color scheme in the organization chart (Figure 15).

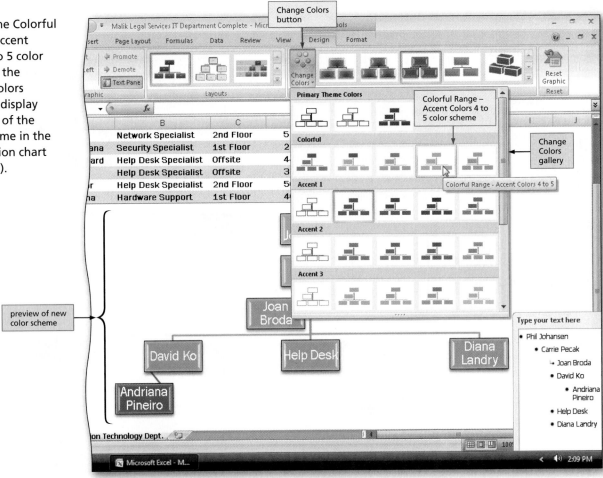

preview of new color scheme

Figure 15

6

- Click the Colorful Range – Accent Colors 4 to 5 color scheme in the Change Colors gallery to apply the color scheme to the organization chart.

- Click the Format tab on the Ribbon. Click the Shape Effects button arrow to display the Shape Effects gallery.

Experiment

- Point to a variety of shape effect types in the Shape Effects gallery and then point to a variety of selections in the galleries to preview the various shape effects in the worksheet.

- Point to the Preset button on the Shape Effects menu to display the Preset gallery.

- Point to the Preset 5 effect in the Preset gallery to display a preview of the effect in the organization chart (Figure 16).

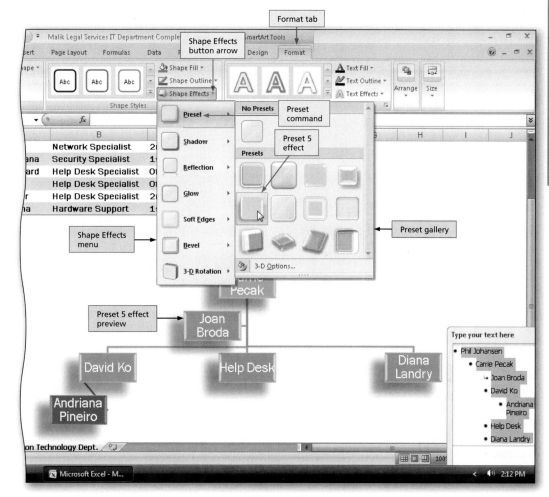

Figure 16

- If necessary, make certain that all of the names are selected in the Text pane.

- Click the Preset 5 effect in the Preset gallery to apply the effect to the organization chart.

- Select cell A14.

- Click the Save button on the Quick Access Toolbar.

Using Images on a Worksheet

Excel allows you to insert images on a worksheet and then modify the image by changing its shape and size, and adding borders and effects. You can enhance a worksheet by including an image such as a corporate logo, photograph, diagram, or map. To use an image, the image must be stored digitally in a file.

Other Ways
1. To change style, select SmartArt graphic, press ALT+J+S+S, click style
2. To change color scheme, select SmartArt graphic, press ALT+J+S+C, click color scheme

To Insert and Modify an Image in the Worksheet

The following steps insert an image of some of the Malik Legal Services Information Technology department members in the worksheet, position and resize the image, and add an effect to the image. The image, which was taken with a digital camera, is available on the Data Files for Students.

- Click the Insert tab on the Ribbon.

- With your USB flash drive connected to one of the computer's USB ports, click the Insert Picture from File button on the Ribbon to display the Insert Picture dialog box.

- If the Folders list is displayed below the Folders button, click the Folders button to remove the Folders list.

- If necessary, click Computer in the Favorite Links section and then scroll until UDISK 2.0 (E:) appears in the list of available drives.

- Double-click UDISK 2.0 (E:) to select the USB flash drive, drive E in this case, as the device that contains the picture. Your USB flash drive may have a different drive letter and name.

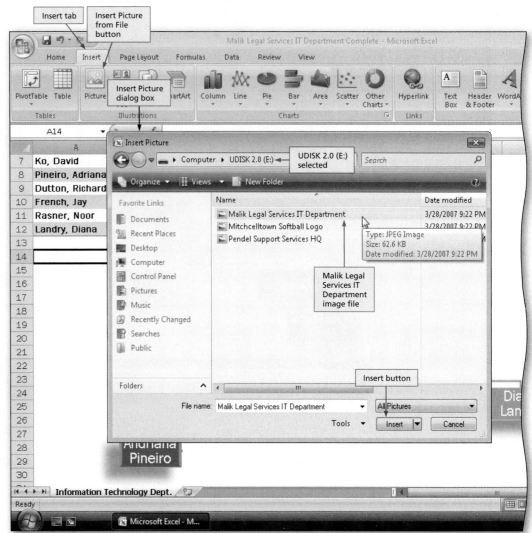

Figure 17

- Click Malik Legal Services IT Department to select the file name (Figure 17).

2

- Click the Insert button to insert the picture in the worksheet (Figure 18).

Q&A

How does Excel determine where to insert the image?

Excel inserts the image so the upper-left corner of the image is located at the upper-left corner of the selected cell, which is cell A14 in Figure 18.

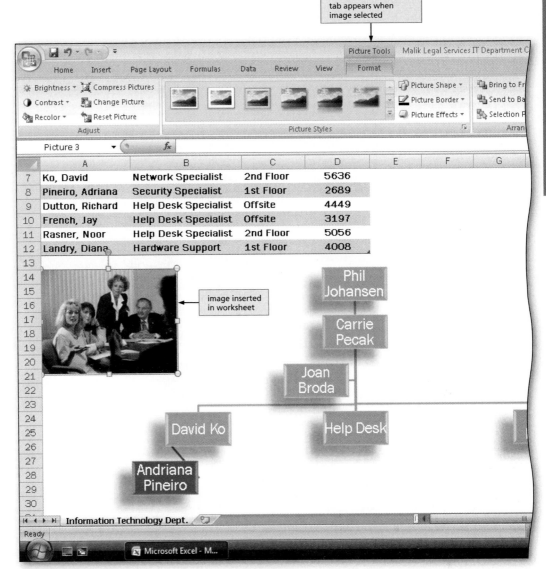

Picture Tools contextual tab appears when image selected

image inserted in worksheet

Figure 18

3

- Scroll the worksheet vertically until row 1 appears.

- Click anywhere in the image and while pressing the ALT key, drag the image so that its upper-left corner is aligned with the upper-left corner of cell E1.

- While pressing the ALT key, drag the lower-right sizing handle of the image to the lower-right corner of cell I12 (Figure 19).

Q&A

Why should I press the ALT key as I drag and resize the image?

When you press the ALT key as you drag or resize an image, Excel snaps, or aligns, the image to the borders of a cell. If you do not hold the ALT key, the corners of the image can be placed anywhere within a cell.

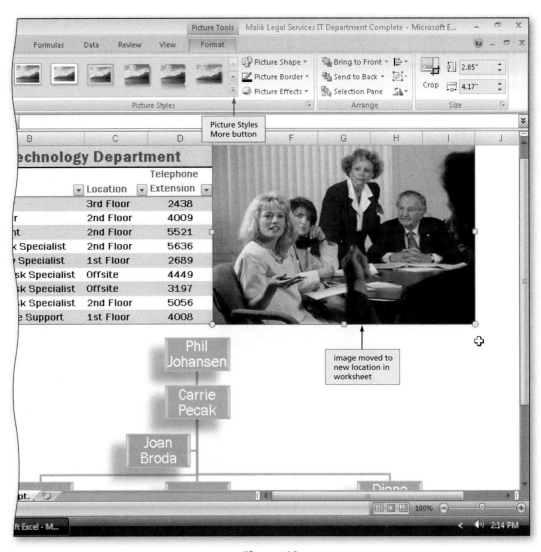

Figure 19

4

- Click the Picture Styles More button on the Ribbon to display the Picture Styles gallery.

Experiment

- Point to a variety of picture styles in the Picture Styles gallery and then point to a variety of styles in the galleries to preview them in the worksheet.

5

- Point to the Reflected Rounded Rectangle picture style (column 5, row 1) to see a preview of the style in the worksheet (Figure 20).

6

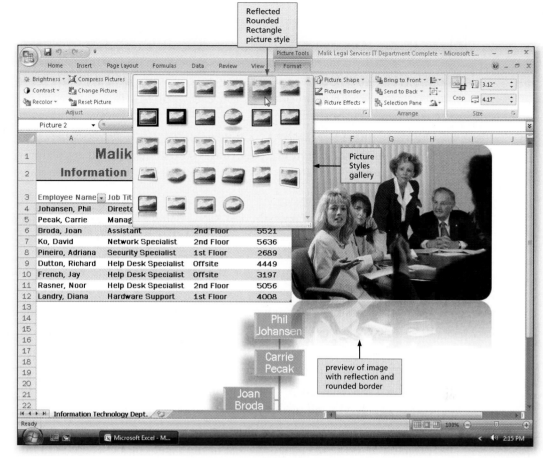

Figure 20

- Click the Reflected Rounded Rectangle picture style to apply the style to the image.
- Click the Save button on the Quick Access Toolbar.

Other Ways
1. Press ALT+N, P

To Quit Excel

The following steps quit Excel.

1 Click the Close button on the right side of the title bar.

2 If Excel displays a Microsoft Office Excel dialog box, click the Yes button to save the workbook.

Feature Summary

This Graphics feature introduced you to inserting and modifying SmartArt graphics and images. The items listed below include all the new Office 2007 skills you have learned in this Web feature.

1. Open a Workbook, Turn Off Gridlines, and Insert an Organization Chart (EX 510)
2. Add Shapes and Modify Text in the Organization Chart (EX 514)
3. Change the Position of Shapes and Add Effects to the Organization Chart (EX 518)
4. Insert and Modify an Image in the Worksheet (EX 522)

In the Lab

Modify a workbook using the guidelines, concepts, and skills presented in this Graphics feature. Labs are listed in order of increasing difficulty.

Lab 1: Inserting a Hierarchy Chart and Image on a Worksheet

Problem: You are the director of your town's softball league and are planning the league's playoff schedule. You want to create a worksheet that illustrates the playoff matchups for the teams in one of the divisions.

Instructions: Start Excel and open the Lab GF-1 Mitchelltown Softball League workbook from the Data Files for Students and then save it as Lab GF-1 Mitchelltown Softball League Complete. Perform the following tasks:

1. Insert a SmartArt graphic using the Hierarchy type and select the Horizontal Hierarchy layout type (column 1, row 2) in the layout area in the Choose a SmartArt Graphic dialog box.

2. Select the hierarchy chart and then click the Right to Left button on the Design tab on the Ribbon to change the layout of the hierarchy chart to read from left to right.

3. Right-click the lower shape in the middle column of the hierarchy chart, point to Add Shape on the shortcut menu, and then click Add Shape Below on the Add Shape submenu.

4. Move and resize the chart so that the upper-left corner of the chart is aligned with the upper-left corner of cell A15 and the lower-right corner of the chart is aligned with the lower-right corner of cell F30.

5. From top to bottom, change the text in the shapes in the left column of the hierarchy chart to read Angels, Sox, Mariners, and Mets. Change the text in both shapes in the middle column of the hierarchy chart to Winner Game 1. Change the text in the shape on the right side of the hierarchy chart to Division Champion.

6. Change the color scheme of the hierarchy chart to Colorful – Accent Colors (column 1, row 2) in the Change Colors gallery.

7. Change the font size of the text in the shapes to 16 using the Font Size box on the Home tab on the Ribbon.

8. Use the Shape Effects gallery to change the effects on the chart to Preset 9 in the Preset gallery.

9. Insert the Mitchelltown Softball League.jpg image file from the Data Files for Students on the worksheet.

10. Move and resize the image so that the upper-left corner of the image is aligned with the upper-left corner of cell A1 and the lower-right corner of the image is aligned with the lower-right corner of cell F6.

11. Select the image. Click the Format tab on the Ribbon and then select the Reflected Perspective Right picture style (column 5, row 4) in the Picture Styles gallery.

12. Change the document properties as specified by your instructor. Change the worksheet header with your name, course number, and other information requested by your instructor. Save the workbook. Submit the assignment as requested by your instructor.

In the Lab

Lab 2: Inserting a Balance Chart and Image on a Worksheet

Problem: Your company is considering moving to a new location. You have been asked to create a high-level overview of the pros and cons regarding the move to the location.

Instructions: Start Excel and open the Lab GF-2 Pendel Support Services workbook from the Data Files for Students and then save it as Lab GF-2 Pendel Support Services Complete. Perform the following tasks:

1. Insert a SmartArt graphic using the Relationship type and select the Balance layout type (column 1, row 1) in the layout area in the Choose a SmartArt Graphic dialog box.

2. Move and resize the chart so that the upper-left corner of the chart is aligned with the upper-left corner of cell A4 and the lower-right corner of the chart is aligned with the middle of the corner of cell H18.

3. Use the Text pane to enter text for the balance chart. Enter the values shown in Table 1, making certain that the pros column shows on the left of the chart. Be sure to delete the unused shape on the right side of the balance chart by right-clicking the shape and then clicking Cut on the shortcut menu. The upper-left shape in the chart should read Pros, and the upper-right shape in the chart should read Cons. Note that the direction of the tilt of the balance chart changes when more pros than cons are entered in the chart.

Table 1 Pros and Cons	
Pros	**Cons**
Central Location	Expensive Lease
Convenient Parking	Congested Area
Closer to Customers	

4. Change the color scheme of the hierarchy chart to Colored Fill – Accent 1 (column 2, row 3) in the Change Colors gallery.

5. Apply the Inset SmartArt style to the balance chart (column 2, row 2) on the SmartArt Styles gallery.

6. Insert the Pendel Support Services Offices.jpg image file from the Data Files for Students on the worksheet.

7. Move and resize the image so that the upper-left corner of the image is aligned with the upper-left corner of cell H4 and the lower-right corner of the image is aligned with the lower-right corner of cell M17.

8. Select the image. Click the Format tab on the Ribbon. Click the Picture Effects button on the Ribbon, point to Shadow in the Picture Effects gallery, and then select Perspective Diagonal Upper Left (column 1, row 8) in the Shadow gallery.

9. Click the Picture Effects button on the Ribbon, point to Bevel in the Picture Effects gallery, and then select Divot (column 1, row 4) in the Bevel gallery.

10. Change the document properties as specified by your instructor. Change the worksheet header with your name, course number, and other information requested by your instructor. Save the workbook. Submit the assignment as requested by your instructor.

4 Creating Reports and Forms

Objectives

You will have mastered the material in this chapter when you can:

- Create reports and forms using wizards
- Group and sort in a report
- Add totals and subtotals to a report
- Resize columns
- Conditionally format controls
- Filter records in reports and forms

- Print reports and forms
- Add a field to a report or form
- Include gridlines
- Add a date
- Change the format of a control
- Move controls

4 | Creating Reports and Forms

Introduction

One of the advantages to maintaining data in a database is the ability to present the data in attractive reports and forms. Reports represent formatted printouts of data in a database. The data can come from one or more tables. Forms, on the other hand, are usually viewed on the screen, although they can be printed. They often are used to view specific data and also may be used to update data. Similar to reports, the data in the form can come from one or more tables. This chapter shows how to create reports and forms by creating two reports and a form. There are several ways to create both reports and forms. The most common is to use the Report or Form Wizard to create an initial report or form. If the layout created by the wizard is satisfactory, you are done. If not, you can use either Layout view or Design view to customize the report or form. In this chapter, you will use Layout view for this purpose. In later chapters, you will learn how to use Design view.

Project — Reports and Forms

JSP Recruiters has realized several benefits from using the database of clients and recruiters. JSP hopes to realize additional benefits using two custom reports that meet their specific needs. The first report is shown in Figure 4–1. The report features grouping. **Grouping** means creating separate collections of records sharing some common characteristic. In the report shown in Figure 4–1, for example, the records have been grouped by city. There are five separate groups: one each for Berls, Berridge, Fort Stewart, Mason, and Tarleton. The appropriate city appears before each group. The rows within the group include the client number, client name, amount paid, and current due. The total of the amount paid and current due amounts for the clients in the group (called a **subtotal**) appears after the group. At the end of the report is a grand total of the amount paid and current due amounts for all groups.

The second report, shown in Figure 4–2, includes subtotals of the amount paid and current due amounts after each group, and displays grand totals at the end. Like the report in Figure 4–1, the data is grouped, although this time it is grouped by recruiter number. This report, however, encompasses data from both the Recruiter table and the Client table. Not only does the recruiter number appear before each group, but the first name and last name of the recruiter appear as well. In addition, the column headings have been split over two lines.

Clients by City

City	Client Number	Client Name	Amount Paid	Current Due
Berls				
	BH72	Berls Hospital	$29,200.00	$0.00
	RM32	Roz Medical	$0.00	$0.00
	WL56	West Labs	$14,000.00	$0.00
			$43,200.00	$0.00
Berridge				
	AC34	Alys Clinic	$0.00	$17,500.00
	FD89	Ferb Dentistry	$21,000.00	$12,500.00
			$21,000.00	$30,000.00
Fort Stewart				
	PR11	Peel Radiology	$31,750.00	$0.00
			$31,750.00	$0.00
Mason				
	MH56	Munn Hospital	$0.00	$43,025.00
			$0.00	$43,025.00
Tarleton				
	FH22	Family Health	$0.00	$0.00
	TC37	Tarleton Clinic	$18,750.00	$31,500.00
			$18,750.00	$31,500.00
			$114,700.00	$104,525.00

Figure 4–1

Clients by Recruiter

Recruiter Number	First Name	Last Name	Client Name	Client Number	Specialties Needed	Amount Paid	Current Due
21	Alyssa	Kerry					
			Alys Clinic	AC34	CNA, PA, Phy, RN	$0.00	$17,500.00
			Ferb Dentistry	FD89	DH, Dnt	$21,000.00	$12,500.00
			Peel Radiology	PR11	RT	$31,750.00	$0.00
						$52,750.00	$30,000.00
24	Camden	Reeves					
			Berls Hospital	BH72	CLS, OT, PA, Phy, PT, RN	$29,200.00	$0.00
			Family Health	FH22	NP, Phy, RN	$0.00	$0.00
			Munn Hospital	MH56	CRNA, OT, Phy, PT, RN	$0.00	$43,025.00
			West Labs	WL56	CLS	$14,000.00	$0.00
						$43,200.00	$43,025.00
27	Jaime	Fernandez					
			Roz Medical	RM32	CNA, NP, PA, Phy, RN	$0.00	$0.00
			Tarleton Clinic	TC37	NP, PA, Phy, RN	$18,750.00	$31,500.00
						$18,750.00	$31,500.00
						$114,700.00	$104,525.00

Thursday, April 24, 2008

Figure 4–2

JSP also wants to improve the data entry process by using a custom form as shown in Figure 4–3. The form has a title and a date. It does not contain all the fields in the Client table, and the fields are in a different order. For this form, JSP likes the appearance of including the fields in a grid.

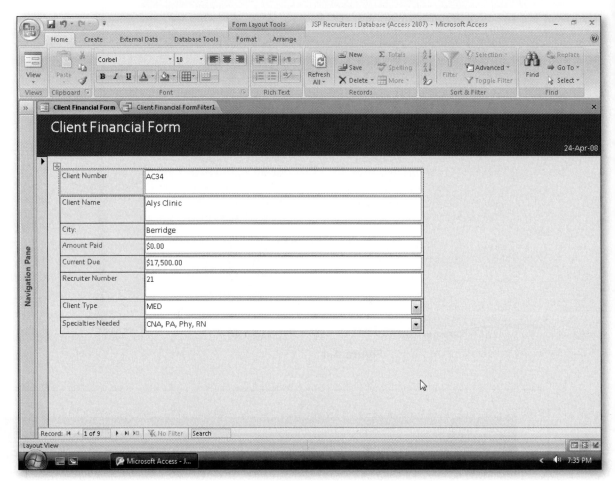

Figure 4–3

Overview

As you read through this chapter, you will learn how to create reports and forms by performing these general tasks:

- Use the Report Wizard to create a report on the Client table.
- Group and sort the report in Layout view.
- Add totals and subtotals to the report.
- Conditionally format a control.
- Filter records in the report.
- Use the Report Wizard to create a report on the Recruiter and Client tables.
- Add a field to the report and include totals.
- Use the Form Wizard to create a form on the Client table.
- Include gridlines and a date in the form.
- Add a field to the form.
- Filter and sort records in the form.

Report and Form Design Guidelines

Plan
Ahead

1. **Determine whether the data should be presented in a report or a form.** Is it necessary to print the data, in which case a report would be the appropriate choice? Is it necessary to view the data on the screen, in which case a form would be the appropriate choice? Is the user going to update data? If so, a form is the appropriate choice.

2. **Determine the intended audience for the report or form.** Who will use the report or form? How will they use it? What data do they need? What level of detail do they need?

3. **Determine the tables that contain the data needed for the report or form.** Is all the data found in a single table or does it come from multiple related tables?

4. **Determine the fields that should appear on the report or form.** What data items are needed by the user of the report or form?

5. **Determine the organization of the report or form.** In what order should the fields appear? How should they be arranged? Should the records in a report be grouped in some way?

6. **Determine the format and style of the report or form.** What should be in the report or form heading? Do you want a title and date, for example? Do you want a logo? What should be in the body of the report and form? What should the style be? In other words, what visual characteristics should the various portions of the report or form have?

7. **Review the report or form after it has been in operation to determine whether any changes are warranted.** Is the order of the fields still appropriate? Are any additional fields required?

When necessary, more specific details concerning the above decisions and/or actions are presented at appropriate points in the chapter. The chapter also will identify the actions performed and decisions made regarding these guidelines in the design of the reports and forms such as those shown in Figures 4–1, 4–2, and 4–3.

Starting Access

If you are using a computer to step through the project in this chapter and you want your screen to match the figures in this book, you should change your screen's resolution to 1024 × 768. For information about how to change a computer's resolution, read Appendix E.

To Start Access

The following steps, which assume Windows Vista is running, start Access.

Note: If you are using Windows XP, see Appendix F for alternate steps.

1 Click the Start button on the Windows Vista taskbar to display the Start menu.

2 Click All Programs at the bottom of the left pane on the Start menu to display the All Programs list and then click Microsoft Office on the All Programs list to display the Microsoft Office list.

3 Click Microsoft Office Access 2007 on the Microsoft Office list to start Access and display the Getting Started with Microsoft Office Access window.

4 If the Access window is not maximized, click the Maximize button on its title bar to maximize the window.

To Open a Database

> **Note:** If you are using Windows XP, see Appendix F for alternate steps.

In Chapter 1, you created your database on a USB flash drive using the file name, JSP Recruiters. There are two ways to open the file containing your database. If the file you created appears in the Recent Documents list, you could click it to open the file. If not, you can use the More button to open the file. The following steps use the More button to open the JSP Recruiters database from the USB flash drive.

1 With your USB flash drive connected to one of the computer's USB ports, click the More button to display the Open dialog box.

2 If the Folders list is displayed below the Folders button, click the Folders button to remove the Folders list.

3 If necessary, click Computer in the Favorites Links section and then double-click UDISK 2.0 (E:) to select the USB flash drive, Drive E in this case, as the new open location.

4 Click JSP Recruiters to select the file name.

5 Click the Open button to open the database.

6 If a Security Warning appears, click the Options button to display the Microsoft Office Security Options dialog box.

7 With the option button to enable the content selected, click the OK button to enable the content.

Report Creation

Unless you want a report that simply lists all the fields and all the records in a table, the simplest way to create a report design is to use the Report Wizard. In some cases, the Report Wizard can produce exactly the desired report. Other times, however, you first must use the Report Wizard to produce a report that is as close as possible to the desired report. Then, use Layout view to modify the report and transform it into the correct report. In either case, once the report is created and saved, you can print it at any time. Access will use the current data in the database for the report, formatting and arranging it in exactly the way you specified when you created the report.

Plan Ahead

> **Determine the tables and fields that contain the data needed for the report.**
>
> 1. **Examine the requirements for the report in general to determine the tables.** Do the requirements only relate to data in a single table, or does the data come from multiple tables? How are the tables related?
>
> 2. **Examine the specific requirements for the report to determine the fields necessary.** Look for all the data items that are specified for the report. Each should correspond to a field in a table or be able to be computed from a field in a table. This information gives you the list of fields.
>
> 3. **Determine the order of the fields.** Examine the requirements to determine the order in which the fields should appear. Be logical and consistent in your ordering. For example, in an address, the city should come before the state and the state should come before the postal code unless there is some compelling reason for another order.

To Create a Simple Report

A report that lists all the fields and all the records in a table without any special features is called a simple report. If you wanted to create a simple report, you would use the following steps.

1. Select the table for the report in the Navigation Pane.
2. Click the Create tab.
3. Click the Report button in the Reports group.

BTW

Creating Simple Reports
You also can base a simple report on a query. To modify a simple report, open the report in Layout view.

To Create a Report Using the Report Wizard

The following steps use the Report Wizard to create an initial version of the Clients by City report. After analyzing requirements, this version is to contain the City, Client Number, Client Name, Amount Paid, and Current Due fields. The fields all come from the Client table, so it is the only table required.

1

- Show the Navigation Pane if it is currently hidden.

- If necessary, click the Client table in the Navigation Pane to select it.

- Click Create on the Ribbon to display the Create tab.

- Click the Report Wizard button on the Create tab to start the Report Wizard (Figure 4–4).

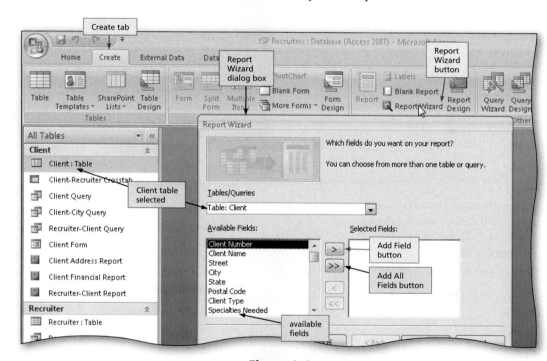

Figure 4–4

2

- Click the City field and then click the Add Field button to add the City field to the list of selected fields (Figure 4–5).

Q&A

Why are there two Specialties Needed fields in the list?

They serve different purposes. If you were to select Specialties Needed, you would get all the specialties for a given client on one line. If you were to select Specialties Needed.Value, each specialty would be on a separate line. You are not selecting either one at this point.

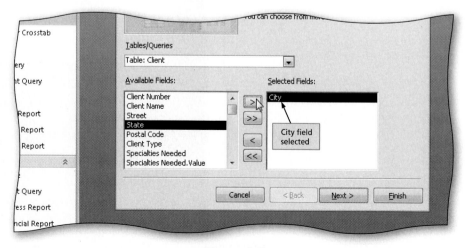

Figure 4–5

● Using the same technique, add the Client Number, Client Name, Amount Paid, and Current Due fields (Figure 4–6).

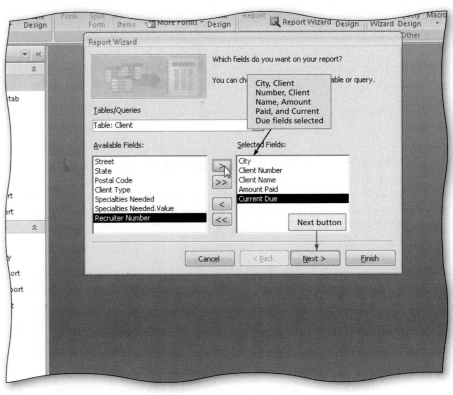

Figure 4–6

④

● Click the Next button to display the next Report Wizard screen (Figure 4–7), which asks for grouping levels.

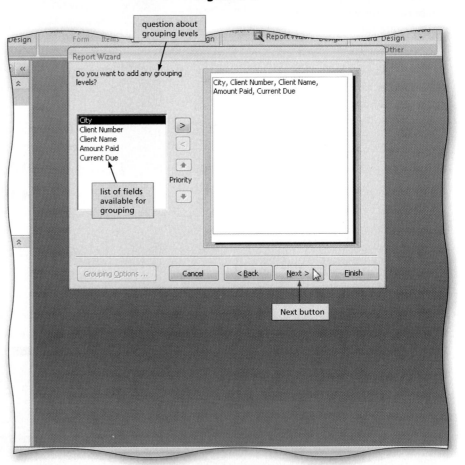

Figure 4–7

5

- Because you do not need to specify grouping levels, click the Next button to display the next Report Wizard screen, which asks for sort order (Figure 4–8).

I thought the report involved grouping. Why do I not specify grouping at this point?

You could. You will specify it later, however, in a way that gives you more control over the grouping that is taking place.

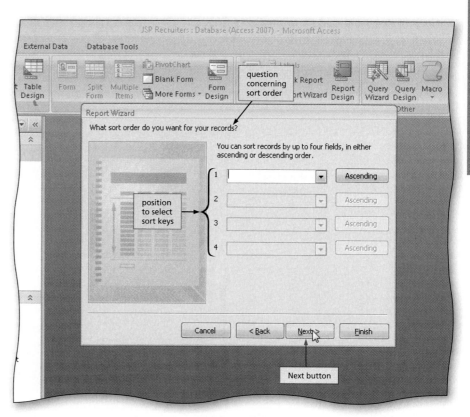

Figure 4–8

6

- Because you do not need to specify a sort order, click the Next button to display the next Report Wizard screen, which asks for your report layout preference (Figure 4–9).

Could I sort here?

You could. Again, in this report you will specify sorting later.

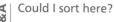 **Experiment**

- Try different layouts to see the effect on the sample layout on the left. When finished, select the Tabular layout.

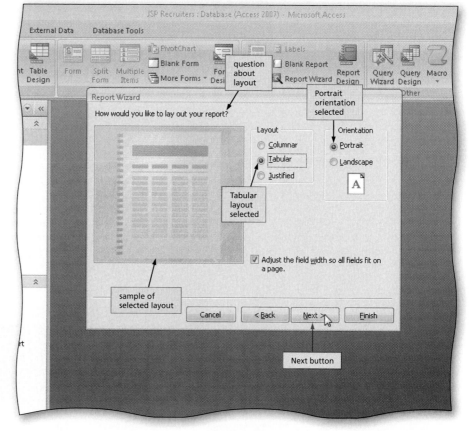

Figure 4–9

● With Tabular layout and Portrait orientation selected, click the Next button to display the next Report Wizard screen, which asks for a style.

● If necessary, click the Module style to select it (Figure 4–10).

 Experiment

● Try different styles to see the effect on the sample on the left. When finished, select the Module style.

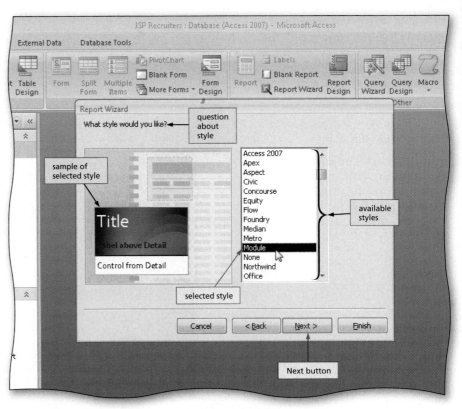

Figure 4–10

⑧

● Click the Next button and then type Clients by City as the report title (Figure 4–11).

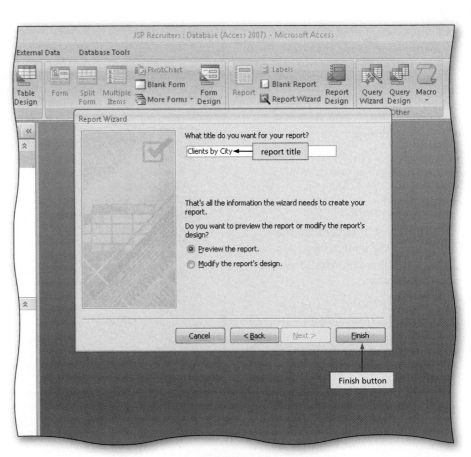

Figure 4–11

9
• Click the Finish
button to produce
the report
(Figure 4–12).

10
• Click the Close
'Clients by City'
button to close
the report.

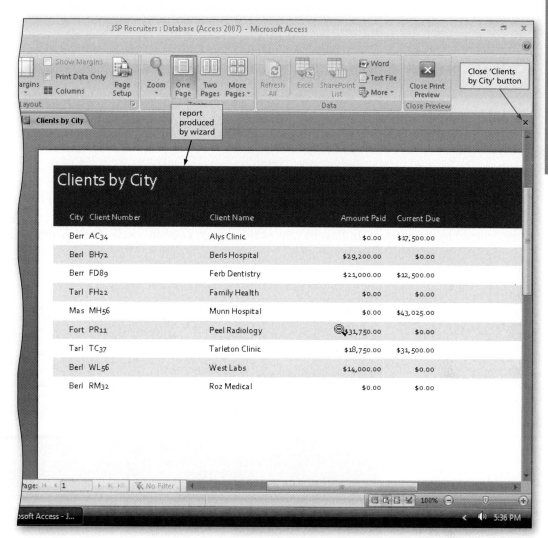

Figure 4–12

Using Layout View in a Report

When working with a report in Access, there are four different ways to view the
report. They are Report view, Print Preview, Layout view, and Design view. Report view
shows the report on the screen. Print Preview shows the report as it will appear when
printed. Layout view is similar to Report view in that it shows the report on the screen,
but it also allows you to make changes to the report. It is usually the easiest way to make
such changes. Design view also allows you to make changes, but it does not show you the
actual report. It is most useful when the changes you need to make are especially complex.
In this chapter, you will use Layout view to modify the report.

<table>
<tr><td>Plan
Ahead</td><td>**Determine the organization of the report or form.**

1. **Determine sort order.** Is there a special order in which the records should appear?

2. **Determine grouping.** Should the records be grouped in some fashion? If so, what should appear before the records in a group? If, for example, clients are grouped by city, the name of the city should probably appear before the group. What should appear after the group? For example, are there some fields for which subtotals should be calculated? If so, the subtotals would come after the group.</td></tr>
</table>

To Group and Sort in a Report

JSP has determined that the records in the report should be grouped by City. That is, all the clients of a given city should appear together immediately after the name of the city. Within the clients in a given city, the clients are to be ordered by client name. In Layout view of the report, you can specify both grouping and sorting by using the Group and Sort button on the Format tab. The following steps open the report in Layout view and then specify both grouping and sorting in the report.

1

- Right-click the Clients by City report in the Navigation Pane to produce a shortcut menu.

- Click Layout View on the shortcut menu to open the report in Layout view.

- Hide the Navigation Pane.

- If a field list appears, close the Field List by clicking its Close button.

- If necessary, click the Group & Sort button on the Format tab to produce the 'Add a group' and 'Add a sort' buttons (Figure 4–13).

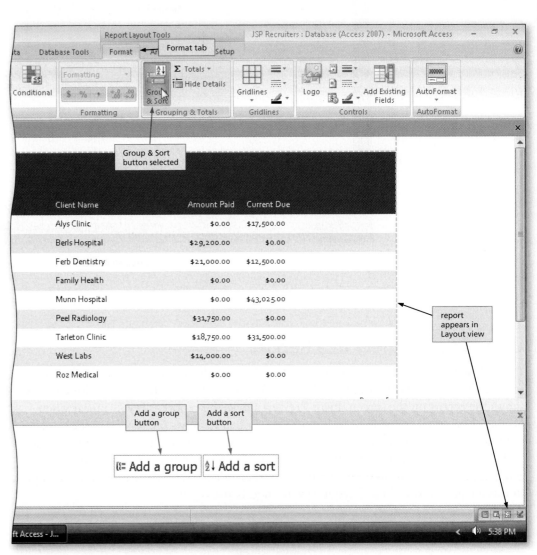

Figure 4–13

Access Chapter 4

2

• Click the 'Add a group' button to
add a group (Figure 4–14).

Figure 4–14

3

• Click the City field in the field
list to group records by city
(Figure 4–15).

Q&A Does the field on which I group
have to be the first field?

No. If you select a field other than
the first field, Access will move
the field you select into the first
position.

Q&A I selected the wrong field for
grouping. What should I do?

Click the arrow next to the control
and select the correct field. If you
decide you do not want to group
after all, click the Delete button
on the right-hand edge of the line
containing the grouping field.

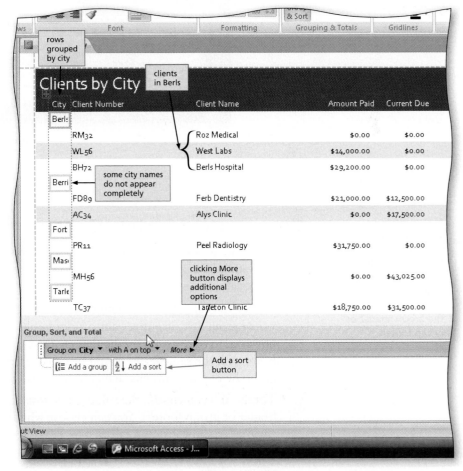

Figure 4–15

4

• Click the 'Add a sort' button to add a sort (Figure 4–16).

5

• Click the Client Name field in the field list to alphabetically sort by client name.

Q&A

I thought the report would be sorted by City, because I chose to group by City. What is the effect of choosing to sort by Client Name?

This sort takes place within groups. You are specifying that within the list of clients of the same city, the clients will be ordered by name.

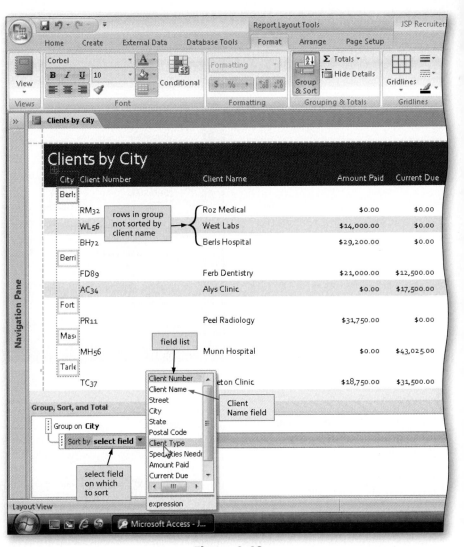

Figure 4–16

BTW

Grouping
You should allow sufficient white space between groups. If you feel the amount is insufficient, you can add more space by enlarging the group header or group footer.

Grouping and Sorting Options

For both grouping and sorting, there is a More button that you can click if you need to specify additional options (see Figure 4–15 on the previous page). The options you then could select are:

• **Value.** You can choose the length of the value on which to group. Typically you would group by the entire value, for example, the entire city name. You could choose, however, to only group on the first character, in which case all clients in cities that begin with the same letter would be considered a group. You also could choose to group by the first two characters or by a custom number of characters.

• **Totals.** You can choose the values to be totaled and where they are to appear (group header or group footer). You can choose whether there is to be a grand total, and also whether to show group totals as a percentage of the grand total.

• **Title.** You can customize the group title.

• **Header section.** You can choose to include or omit a header section for the group.

- **Footer section**. You can choose to include or omit a footer section for the group.
- **Keep together**. You can indicate whether Access is to attempt to keep portions of a group together on a page. The default is that it will not. You can specify that Access is to attempt to keep a whole group together on one page. If the group will not fit on the remainder of the page, Access will move the group header and the records in a group to the next page. Finally, you can choose to have Access keep the header and the first record together on one page. If the header would fit at the bottom of a page, but there would not be room for the first record, Access will move the header to the next page.

Understanding Report Sections

A report is divided into various sections to help clarify the presentation of data. In Design view, which you will use in later chapters, the sections are labeled on the screen. Even though they are not labeled in Layout view, it still is useful to understand the purpose of the various sections. A typical report consists of a Report Header section, Page Header section, Detail section, Page Footer section, and Report Footer section.

The contents of the **Report Header section** print once at the beginning of the report. In the Clients by City report, the title, Clients by City, is in the Report Header section. The contents of the **Report Footer section** print once at the end of the report. In the Clients by City report, the Report Footer section contains the grand totals of Amount Paid and Current Due. The contents of the **Page Header section** print once at the top of each page and typically contain the column headings. The contents of the **Page Footer section** print once at the bottom of each page and often contain a date and a page number. The contents of the **Detail section** print once for each record in the table, for example once for Roz Medical, once for West Labs, and so on. In this report, they contain the client number, client name, amount paid, and current due.

When the data in a report is grouped, there are two additional sections. The contents of the **Group Header section** are printed before the records in a particular group, and the contents of the **Group Footer section** are printed after the group. In the Clients by City report, the Group Header section contains the city name and the Group Footer section contains subtotals of Amount Paid and Current Due.

Understanding Controls

The various objects on a report are called **controls**. All the information on the report is contained in the controls. There is a control containing the title, Clients by City. There is a control containing each column heading (City, Client Number, Client Name, Amount Paid, and Current Due). There is a control in the Group Header section that displays the city and two controls in the Group Footer section. One displays the subtotal of Amount Paid and the other displays the subtotal of Current Due. In the Detail section, there are four controls, one containing the client number, one containing the client name, one containing the amount paid, and one containing the current due amount.

There are three types of controls: bound controls, unbound controls, and calculated controls. **Bound controls** are used to display data that comes from the database, such as the client number and name. **Unbound controls** are not associated with data from the database and are used to display such things as the report's title. Finally, **calculated controls** are used to display data that is calculated from other data, such as a total.

When working in Layout view, Access handles details concerning these controls for you automatically. When working in Design view, you will see and manipulate the controls.

BTW

Report Design Considerations
The purpose of any report is to present specific information. Review your report to see if it conveys the information effectively. Make sure that the meaning of the row and column headings is clear. You can use different fonts and sizes by changing the appropriate properties but do not overuse them. Using too many fonts and sizes makes a report look cluttered and unprofessional. Finally, be consistent when creating reports. Once you decide on a general report style, stick with it throughout your database.

BTW

Controls in Reports and Forms
Controls are objects that display data and perform actions. Controls also allow you to work with labels and images to improve the user interface.

To Add Totals and Subtotals

Along with determining to group data in this report, it also was determined that subtotals of Amount Paid and Current Due should be included. To add totals or other statistics, use the Totals button on the Format tab. You then select from a menu of aggregate functions, functions that perform some mathematical function against a group of records. The available aggregate functions are: Sum (total), Average, Count Records, Count Values, Max (largest value), Min (smallest value), Standard Deviation, and Variance. The following steps add totals of the Amount Paid and Current Due fields. Because the report is grouped, each group will have a subtotal, that is, a total for just the records in the group. At the end of the report, there will be a grand total, that is, a total for all records.

❶

- Click the Amount Paid field on the first record to select the field.

Q&A Does it have to be the first record?

No. You could click the Amount Paid field on any record.

- Click the Totals button on the Format tab to display the list of available calculations (Figure 4–17).

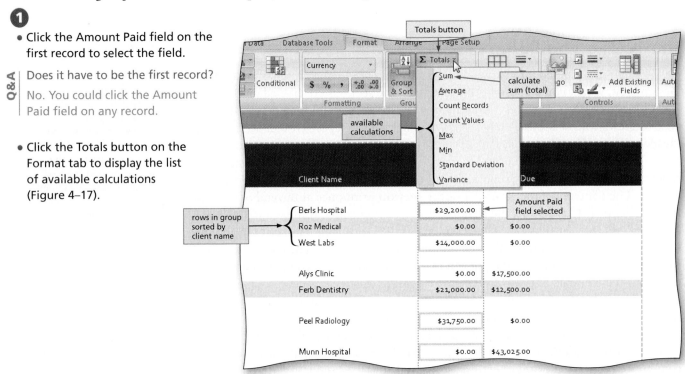

Figure 4–17

❷

- Click Sum to calculate the sum of amount paid values (Figure 4–18).

Q&A Is Sum the same as Total?

Yes.

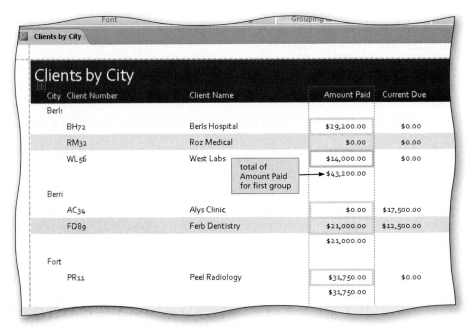

Figure 4–18

3

- Using the same technique as in Steps 1 and 2, add totals for the Current Due field (Figure 4–19).

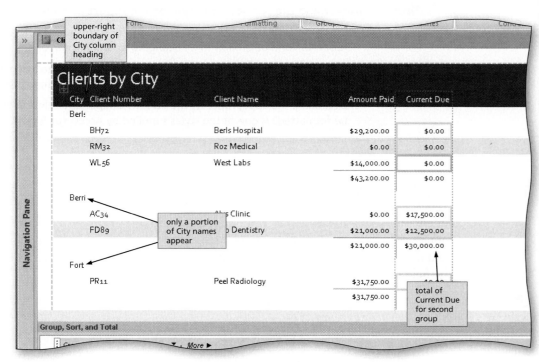

Figure 4–19

To Resize Columns

In some cases, not all the data in the column appears because the column currently is too narrow. To resize a column, point to the boundary of the column so that the mouse pointer becomes a double-headed arrow. You can then drag the boundary of the column to resize the column. The following steps resize the columns.

- If necessary, close the Group, Sort, and Total pane by clicking the Group & Sort button on the Design tab.

- Click the City column heading.

- Point to the right boundary of the City column heading so that the pointer turns into a double-headed arrow.

- Drag the right boundary to the right so that the entire contents of the City column appear (Figure 4–20).

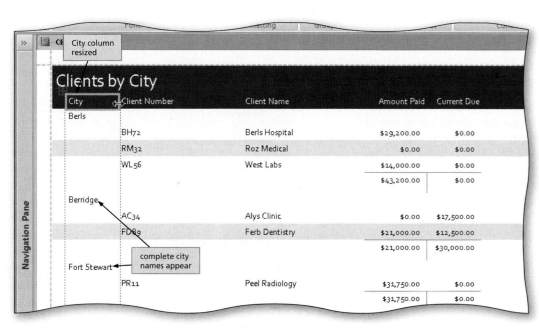

Figure 4–20

<table>
<tr><td>Plan
Ahead</td><td>**Determine the format and style of the report or form.**

1. **Determine whether any special fonts and/or colors are warranted.** Would the look of the report or form be enhanced by changing a font, a color, or any other special effects?

2. **Determine whether conditional formatting is appropriate.** Are there any fields in which you would like to emphasize certain values by giving them a different appearance?

3. **Determine the appearance of the various components.** How should the various portions be formatted? Is one of the styles supplied by Access sufficient?</td></tr>
</table>

To Conditionally Format Controls

You can emphasize values in a column that satisfy some criterion by formatting them differently from other values. This emphasis is called **conditional formatting**. JSP management would like to emphasize values in the Current Due field that are greater than $0.00. The following steps conditionally format the Current Due field so that values in the field that are greater than $0.00 are in red.

- Click the Current Due field on the first record to select the field (Figure 4–21).

Q&A Does it have to be the first record?

No. You could click the field on any record.

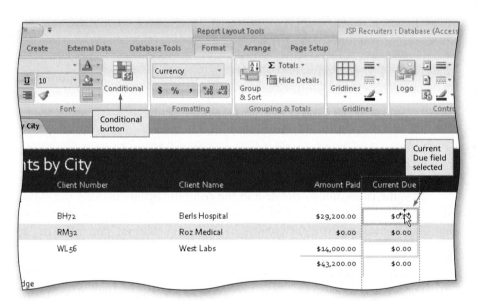

Figure 4–21

- Click the Conditional button on the Format tab to display the Conditional Formatting dialog box.

- Click the box arrow to display the list of available comparison phrases (Figure 4–22).

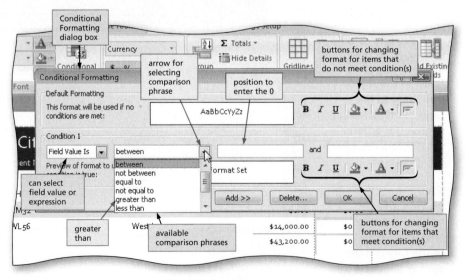

Figure 4–22

- Click greater than to select the greater than operator.

- Type 0 as the greater than value.

- Click the Font/Fore Color button arrow for the format to be used when condition is true to display a color palette (Figure 4–23).

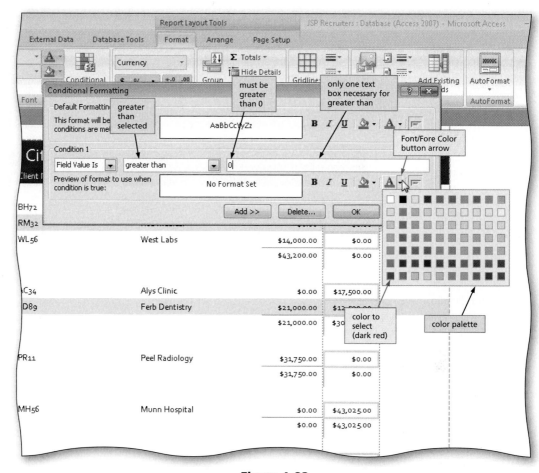

Figure 4–23

4

- Click the dark red color in the lower corner of the color palette to select the color (Figure 4–24).

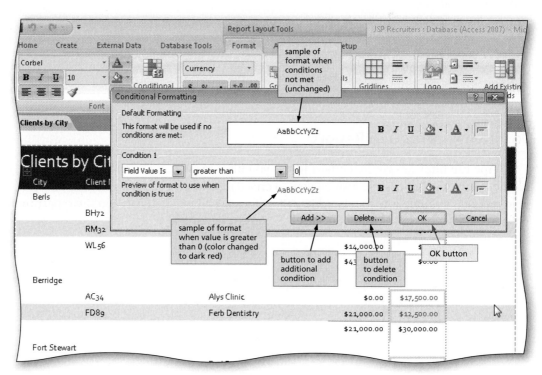

Figure 4–24

5

- Click the OK button in the Conditional Formatting dialog box to change the formatting (Figure 4–25).

Q&A

What if I have more than one condition?

Click the Add button to add additional conditions. You can include up to three conditions. For each condition, you specify the condition and the format to be used when the condition is true.

Q&A

Can I change this conditional formatting at a later time?

Yes. Select the field for which you had applied conditional formatting on any record, click the Conditional button on the Format tab, make the necessary changes, and then click the OK button.

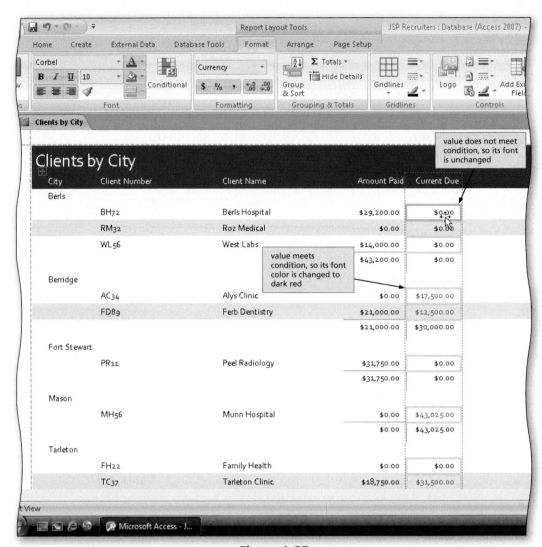

Figure 4–25

To Filter Records in a Report

You can filter records in a report just as you filter records in a datasheet. You can use the filter buttons on the Home tab in exactly the same fashion you do on a datasheet. If the filter involves only one field, right-clicking the field provides a simple way to filter. The following steps filter the records in the report to include only those records on which the amount paid is not $0.00.

①

- Right-click the Amount Paid field on the second record to display the shortcut menu (Figure 4–26).

Q&A

Did I have to pick second record?

No. You could pick any record on which the Amount Paid is $0.00.

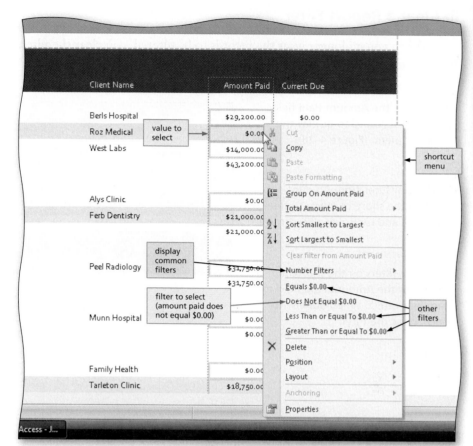

Figure 4–26

②

- Click Does Not Equal $0.00 on the shortcut menu to restrict the records to those on which the Amount Paid is not $0.00 (Figure 4–27).

Q&A

When would you use Number Filters?

You would use Number Filters if you need filters that are not on the main shortcut menu or if you need the ability to enter specific values other than the ones shown on the shortcut menu. If those filters are insufficient for your needs, you can use Advanced Filter/Sort, which is accessible through the Advanced button on the Home tab.

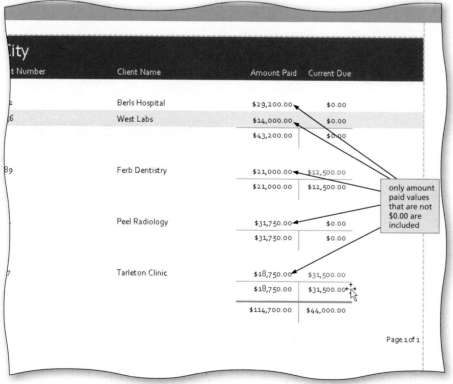

Figure 4–27

To Clear a Report Filter

When you no longer want the records to be filtered, you clear the filter. The following steps clear the filter on the Amount Paid field.

1

- Right-click the Amount Paid field on the first record to display the shortcut menu (Figure 4–28).

2

- Click Clear filter from Amount Paid on the shortcut menu to clear the filter and redisplay all records.

Experiment

- Try other filters on the shortcut menu for the Amount Paid field to see their effect. When done with each, clear the filter.

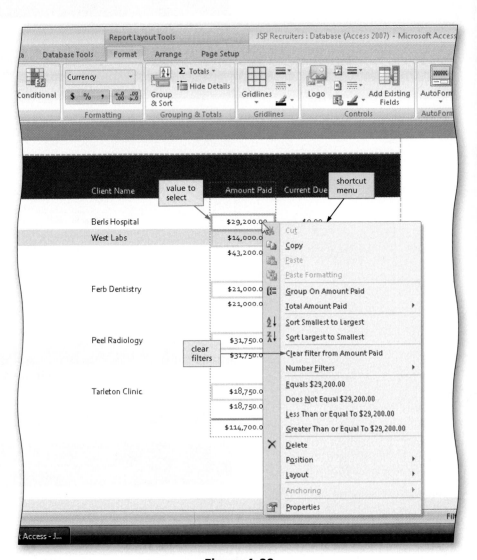

Figure 4–28

To Save and Close a Report

Now that you have completed your work on your report, you should save the report and close it. The following steps first save your work on the report and then close the report.

1 Click the Save button on the Quick Access Toolbar to save your work.

2 Close the Clients by City report.

The Arrange and Page Setup Tabs

When working on a report in Layout view, you can make additional layout changes by using the Arrange and/or Page Setup tabs. The Arrange tab is shown in Figure 4–29. Table 4–1 shows the buttons on the Arrange tab along with the Enhanced ScreenTips that describe their function.

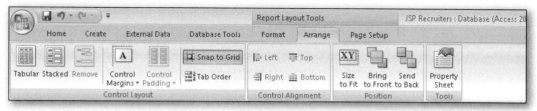

Figure 4–29

Table 4–1 Arrange Tab	
Button	**Enhanced ScreenTip**
Tabular	Create a layout similar to a spreadsheet with labels across the top and data in columns below the labels.
Stacked	Create a layout similar to a paper form, with labels to the left of each field.
Remove	Remove the layout applied to the controls.
Control Margins	Specify the location of information displayed within the control.
Control Padding	Set the amount of spacing between controls and the gridlines of a layout.
Snap to Grid	Snap to grid.
Tab Order	Change the tab order of controls on the page.
Left	Align left.
Right	Align right.
Top	Align top.
Bottom	Align bottom.
Size to Fit	Size to fit.
Bring to Front	Bring the selected object in front of all other objects so that no part of it is hidden behind another object.
Send to Back	Send the selected object behind all other objects.
Property Sheet	Open this object's property sheet to set its properties.

The Page Setup tab is shown in Figure 4–30. Table 4–2 on the next page shows the buttons on the Page Setup tab along with the Enhanced ScreenTips that describe their function.

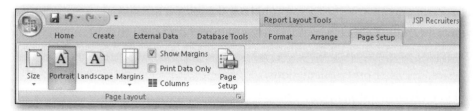

Figure 4–30

Table 4–2 Page Setup Tab	
Button	**Enhanced ScreenTip**
Size	Choose a paper size for the current section.
Portrait	Change to portrait orientation.
Landscape	Change to landscape orientation.
Margins	Select the margin sizes for the entire document or the current section.
Show Margins	Show margins.
Print Data Only	Print data only.
Columns	Columns.
Page Setup	Show the Page Setup dialog box.

To Print a Report

Once you have created a report, you can print it at any time. The printed layout will reflect the layout you created. The data in the report will always reflect current data. The following steps print the Clients by City report.

1 Show the Navigation Pane, ensure the Clients by City report is selected, and then click the Office Button to display the Microsoft Office menu.

2 Point to Print on the Office Button menu and then click Quick Print on the Print submenu to print the report.

Q&A How can I print a range of pages rather than printing the whole report?

Click the Office Button, point to Print on the Office Button menu, click Print on the Print submenu, click the Pages option button in the Print Range box, enter the desired page range, and then click the OK button.

Q&A What should I do if the report is too wide for the printed page?

You can adjust the margins or change the page orientation. You make both types of changes by opening the report in Layout view and then clicking the Page Setup tab. You can click the desired orientation button to change the orientation or click the Margins button to change to some preset margins. For custom margins, click the dialog box launcher in the lower-right corner of the Page Layout group.

TO CREATE A SUMMARY REPORT

You may determine that a report should be organized so that it only shows the overall group calculations, but not all the records. A report that includes the group calculations such as subtotals, but does not include the individual detail lines is called a **summary report**. If you wanted to create a summary report, you could use the following steps.

1. Create report including field on which you will group and fields you wish to summarize.
2. Group the report on the desired field.
3. Add the desired totals or other calculations.
4. Click the Hide Details button on the Format tab.

Multi-Table Reports

You may determine that the data required for a report comes from more than one table. You can use the Report Wizard to create a report on multiple tables just as you can use it to create reports on single tables.

To Create a Report that Involves Multiple Tables

The following steps use the Report Wizard to create a report that involves both the Recruiter and Client tables.

1

- Show the Navigation Pane if it is currently hidden.

- Click the Recruiter table in the Navigation Pane to select it.

- Click Create on the Ribbon to display the Create tab.

- Click the Report Wizard button on the Create tab to start the Report Wizard (Figure 4–31).

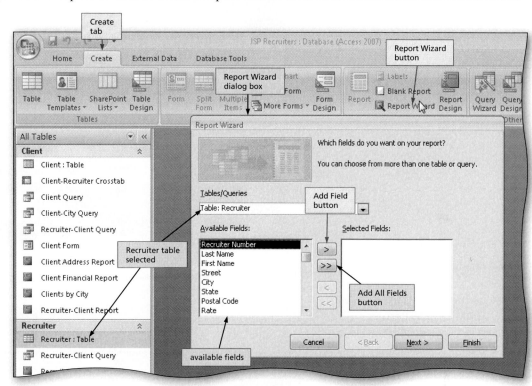

Figure 4–31

2

- Click the Add Field button to add the Recruiter Number field.

- Add the First Name field by clicking it and then clicking the Add Field button.

- Add the Last Name field in the same manner.

- Click the Tables/Queries arrow, and then click Table: Client in the Tables/Queries list box (Figure 4–32).

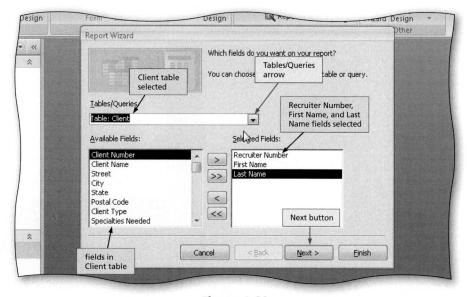

Figure 4–32

3

- Add the Client Number, Client Name, Amount Paid, and Current Due fields by clicking the field and then clicking the Add Field button.

- Click the Next button (Figure 4–33).

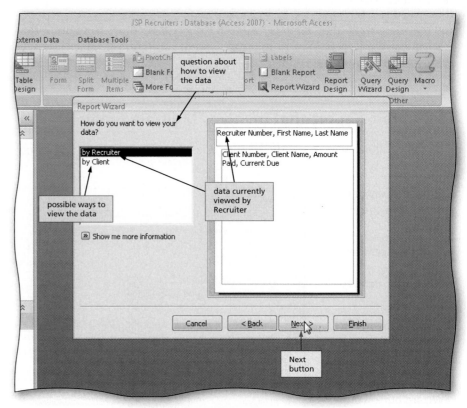

Figure 4–33

4

- Because the report is to be viewed by Recruiter and by Recruiter already is selected, click the Next button (Figure 4–34).

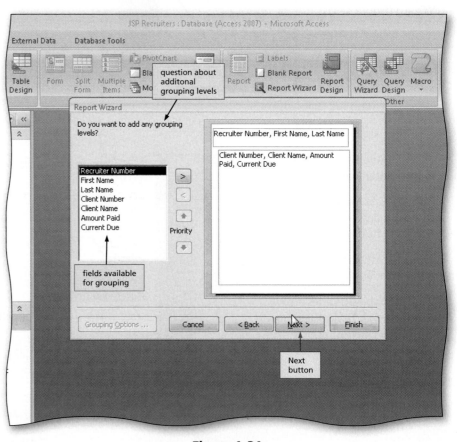

Figure 4–34

5

- Because no additional grouping levels are required, click the Next button.

- Click the box arrow in the text box labeled 1 and then click the Client Name field in the list to select Client Name for the sort order (Figure 4–35).

Q&A When would I use the Summary Options button?

You would use the Summary Options button if you want to specify subtotals or other calculations within the wizard. You can also use it to produce a summary report by selecting Summary Only, which will omit all detail records from the report.

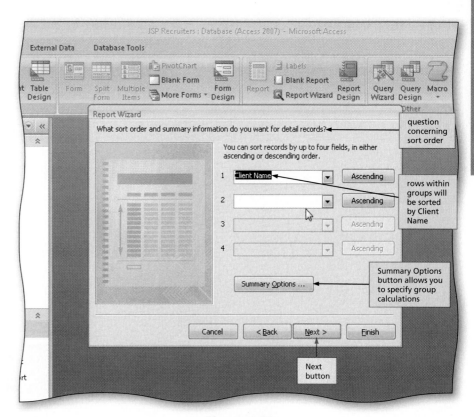

Figure 4–35

6

- Click the Next button, be sure the Stepped layout is selected, and then click the Landscape option button to select Landscape orientation (Figure 4–36).

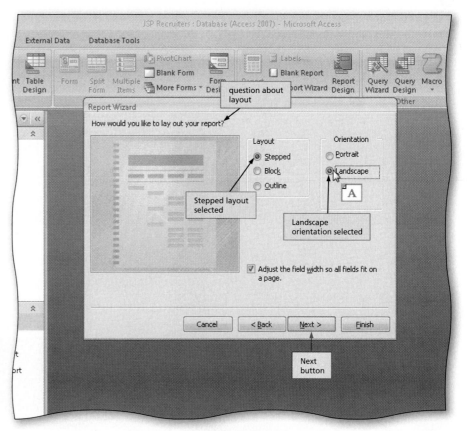

Figure 4–36

● Click the Next button to display the next Report Wizard screen, which asks for a style (Figure 4–37).

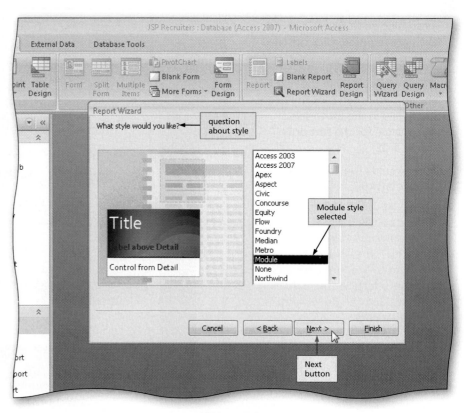

Figure 4–37

● With the Module style selected, click the Next button and then type Clients by Recruiter as the report title (Figure 4–38).

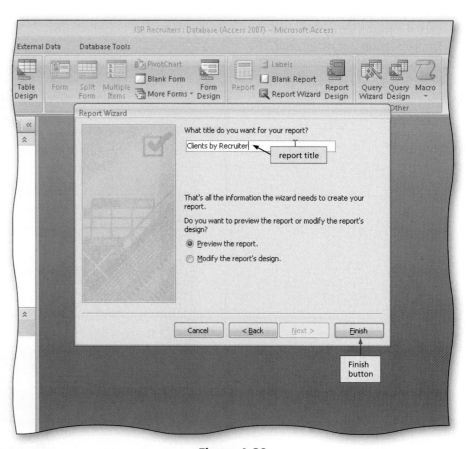

Figure 4–38

9

- Click the Finish button to produce the report (Figure 4–39).

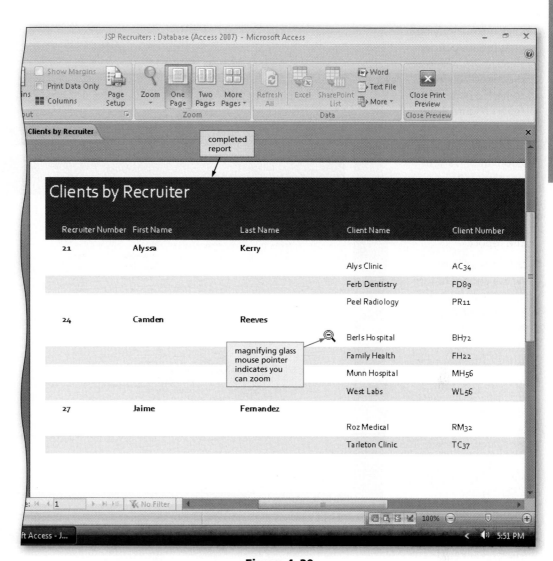

Figure 4–39

● Click the magnifying glass mouse pointer somewhere within the report to view a complete page of the report (Figure 4–40).

 Experiment

● Zoom in on various positions within the report. When finished, view a complete page of the report.

Q&A
Why does Client Name appear before Client Number when we selected Client Number first in the Report Wizard?

When you specify sorting in the Report Wizard, Access places the field on which sorting is to occur first. This reversed the order of the Client Number and Client Name fields.

Q&A
Why are there pound signs (#) in the Current Due column?

The column is too small to hold the entire number. You can resize the column to display the entire number.

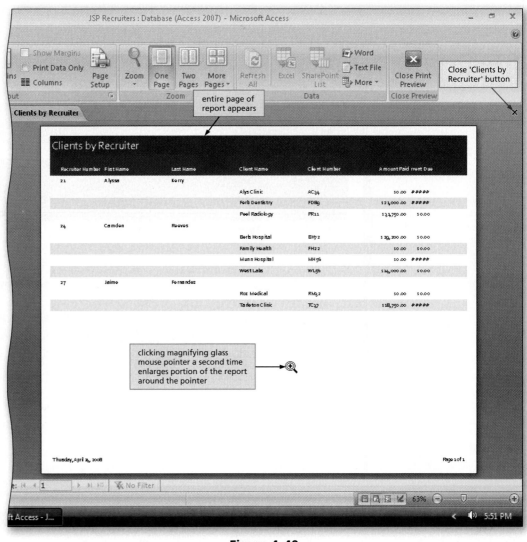

Figure 4–40

● Click the Close 'Clients by Recruiter' button to close the report and remove it from the screen.

To Resize Columns and Column Headings

The following steps resize the columns and the column headings in the Clients by Recruiter report.

- Open the Clients by Recruiter report in Layout view and then hide the Navigation Pane.

- Click the Recruiter Number column heading to select the column.

- Point to the lower boundary of the Recruiter Number column heading so that the mouse pointer changes to a double-headed arrow (Figure 4–41).

Q&A

Could I point to the lower boundary of any other column as well?

Yes. It doesn't matter which one you point to. You will resize all of them at once.

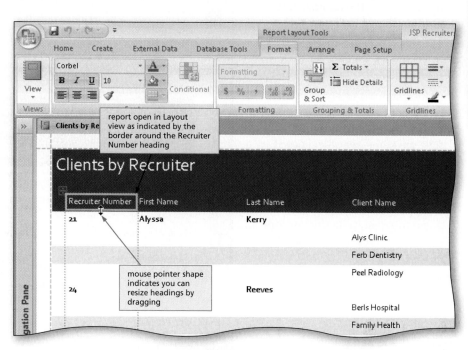

Figure 4–41

- Increase the height of the column headings by dragging the lower portion of the column headings down to the approximate position shown in Figure 4–42 and then point to the right boundary of the Recruiter Number heading so that the mouse pointer changes to a double-headed arrow.

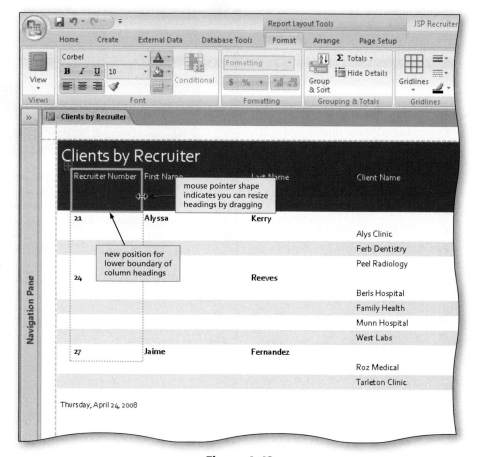

Figure 4–42

3

- Change the width of the Recruiter Number heading by dragging the pointer to the approximate position shown in Figure 4–43.

 Q&A Did I have to do anything special to extend the column heading over two lines?

If the column is too narrow for a two-word name to appear completely, Access will automatically split the name over two lines. If there is sufficient space for the two-word name, Access will not split the name. If you wish to split it you can do so by clicking the name to select it, clicking in front of the second word to produce an insertion point, holding the SHIFT key down and pressing the ENTER key.

Figure 4–43

4

- Using the same technique, change the width of the remaining columns to those shown in Figure 4–44.

Q&A Do I have to be exact?

No. As long as your report looks close to the one in the figure it is fine.

Q&A I'm not very good with dragging the mouse to make fine adjustments. Is there another way?

Yes. If you want to make a slight adjustment to the size of a control, you may find it easier to select the control, hold down the SHIFT key, and then use the appropriate arrow key to resize the control.

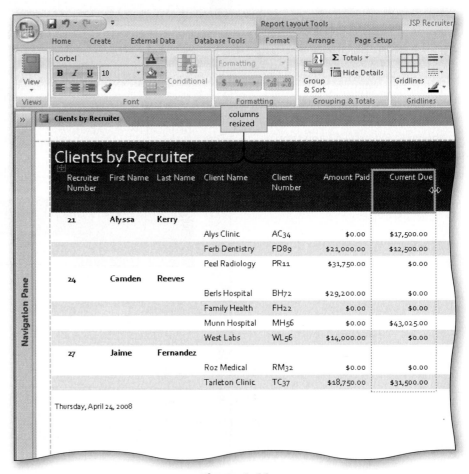

Figure 4–44

> **Review the report after it has been in operation to determine whether any changes are warranted.**
>
> 1. **Determine whether the order of the fields is still the best order.** After a user has worked with a report or form for a period, he or she may feel that another order of the fields would work better than the original order.
>
> 2. **Determine whether any additional fields now are required.** Are there fields missing from the report that would be helpful?

To Add a Field

After reviewing the report, you may decide that the report should contain some additional field. You can use a field list to add the necessary field. The following steps use a field list to add the Specialties Needed field to the Clients by Recruiter report.

- If necessary, click the Add Existing Fields button on the Format tab to display a field list (Figure 4–45).

Q&A

My field list does not look like the one in the figure. It does not have the two tables, and the link at the bottom has Show all tables. Yours has Show only fields in the current record source. What should I do?

Click the 'Show all tables' link. Your field list should then match the one in the figure.

Q&A

What is the purpose of the Edit Table links in the field list?

If you click an Edit Table link, the table will appear in Datasheet view and you can make changes to it.

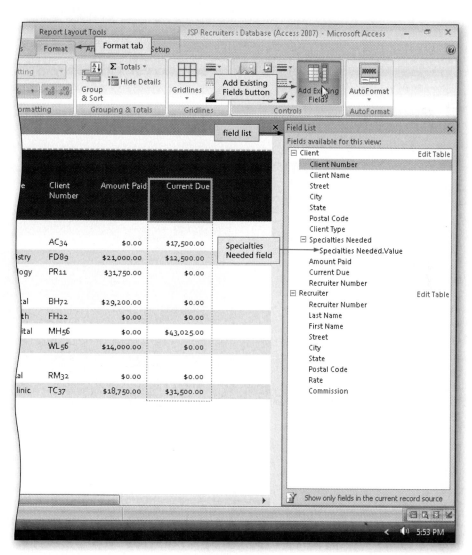

Figure 4–45

2

- Point to the Specialties Needed field, press and hold the left mouse button, and then drag the mouse pointer until the line to the left of the mouse pointer is between the Client Number and Amount Paid fields (Figure 4–46).

Q&A What if I make a mistake?

You can delete the field by clicking the field and then pressing the DELETE key. You can move the field by dragging it to the correct position.

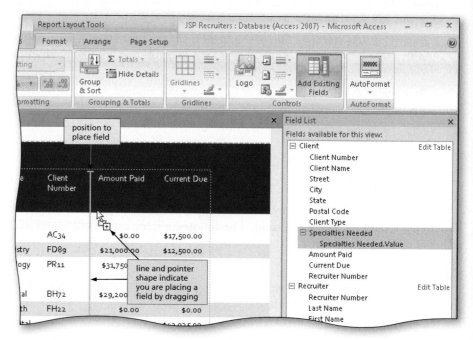

Figure 4–46

3

- Release the left mouse button to place the field (Figure 4–47).

Q&A Could I create a report in Layout view without using the Report Wizard just by dragging the fields into the positions I want?

Yes. You would click the Create tab, and then click Blank Report in the Reports group. You could then drag the fields from the field list.

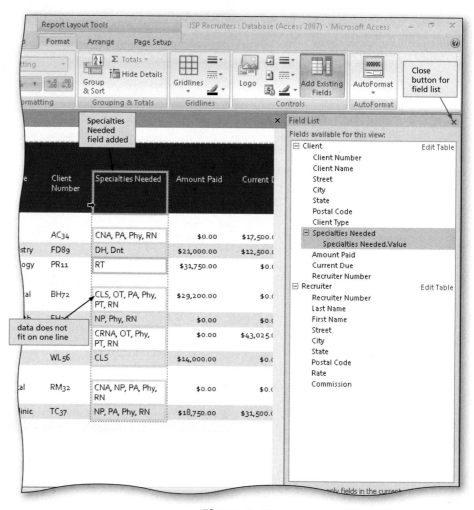

Figure 4–47

4

- Close the field list by clicking its Close button.

Q&A

Could I also close the field list by clicking the Add Existing Field button a second time?

Yes. Use whichever method you find most convenient.

- Drag the right boundary of the Specialties Needed field to the approximate position shown in Figure 4–48.

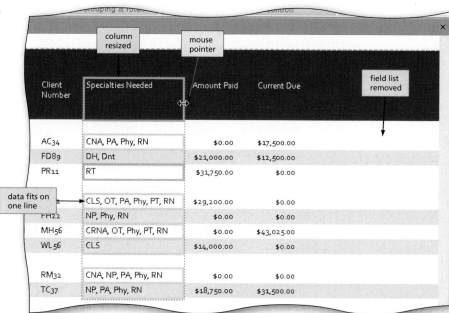

Figure 4–48

Using the Value Property of a Multivalued Field

Rather than adding the Specialties Needed field, you could add the Value property of the Specialties Needed field. To do so, you would drag Specialties Needed.Value rather than Specialties Needed to the report. If you did so, each specialty would be on a separate line, as shown in Figure 4–49. If you compare the report in Figure 4–49 with the one shown in Figure 4–48, you will see that the four specialties needed by Alys Clinic, which appeared on one line in Figure 4–48, occupy four lines in the report shown in Figure 4–49.

BTW

Creating Reports in Layout View
You can create a report in Layout view without using the wizard. To do so, click Create on the Ribbon and then click the Blank Report button on the Create tab.

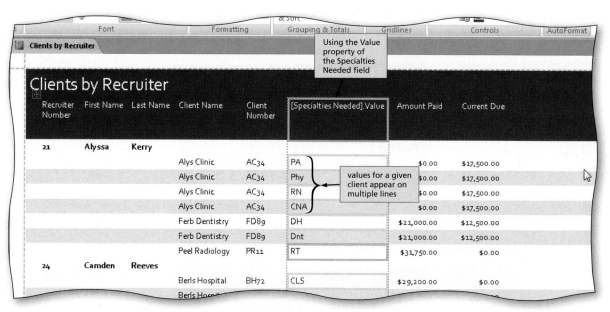

Figure 4–49

To Include Totals

The following steps add totals and subtotals for the Amount Paid and Current Due fields.

- Click the Amount Paid field on the first record to select the field.

- Click the Totals button on the Format tab to display the Totals menu (Figure 4–50).

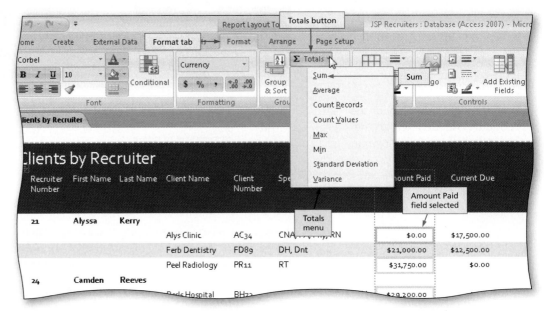

Figure 4–50

2

- Click Sum in the Totals menu to calculate the sum of the amounts paid for the clients of each recruiter as well as the grand total.

- Click the Current Due field on the first record to select the field.

- Click the Totals button on the Format tab to display the Totals menu.

- Click Sum in the Totals menu to calculate the sum of the current due amounts for the clients of each recruiter as well as the grand total (Figure 4–51).

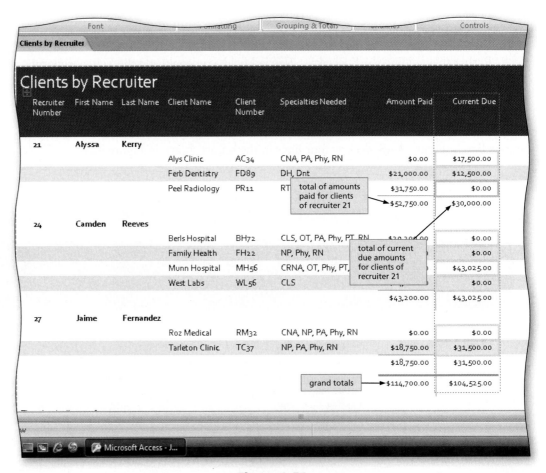

Figure 4–51

To Save and Close a Report

Now that you have completed your work on your report, you should save the report and close it. The following steps first save your work on the report and then close the report.

1 Click the Save button on the Quick Access Toolbar to save your work.

2 Close the Clients by Recruiter report.

To Print a Report

The following steps print the Clients by Recruiter report.

1 With the Clients by Recruiter report selected in the Navigation Pane, click the Office Button to display the Microsoft Office menu.

2 Point to the arrow next to print on the Office Button menu and then click Quick Print on the Print submenu to print the report.

Form Creation

As with reports, it is usually simplest to begin creating a form by using the wizard. Once you have used the Form Wizard to create a form, you can modify that form in either Layout view or Design view.

To Use the Form Wizard to Create a Form

The following steps use the Form Wizard to create an initial version of the Client Financial Form. This version contains the Client Number, Client Name, Client Type, Specialties Needed, Amount Paid, Current Due, and Recruiter Number fields.

1

- Be sure the Navigation Pane appears and the Client table is selected.

- Click Create on the Ribbon to display the Create tab.

- Click the More Forms button on the Create tab to display the More Forms menu (Figure 4–52).

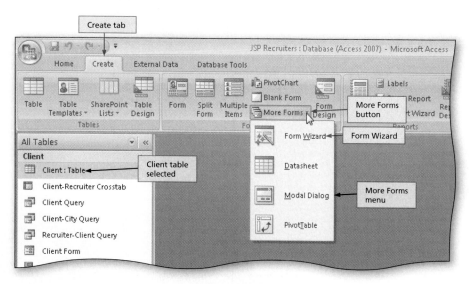

Figure 4–52

- Click Form Wizard on the More Forms menu to start the Form Wizard.

- Add the Client Number, Client Name, Client Type, Specialties Needed, Amount Paid, Current Due, and Recruiter Number fields to the form (Figure 4–53).

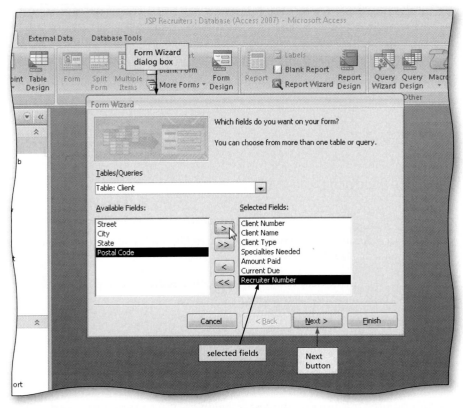

Figure 4–53

- Click the Next button to display the next Form Wizard screen (Figure 4–54).

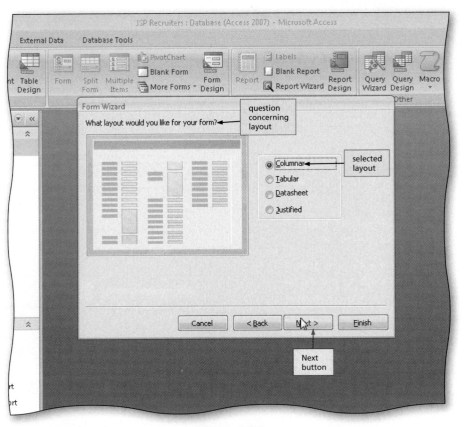

Figure 4–54

• Be sure the Columnar layout is selected, and then click the Next button to display the next Form Wizard screen (Figure 4–55).

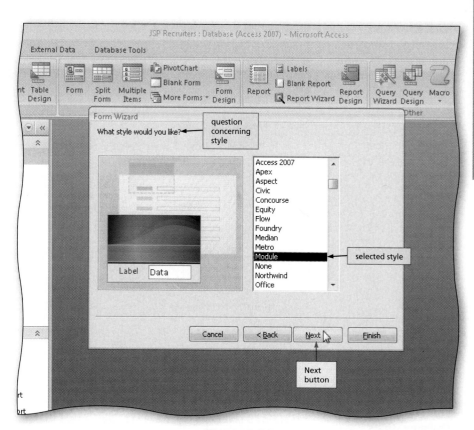

Figure 4–55

5

• Be sure Module is selected, click the Next button, and then type `Client Financial Form` as the title for the form (Figure 4–56).

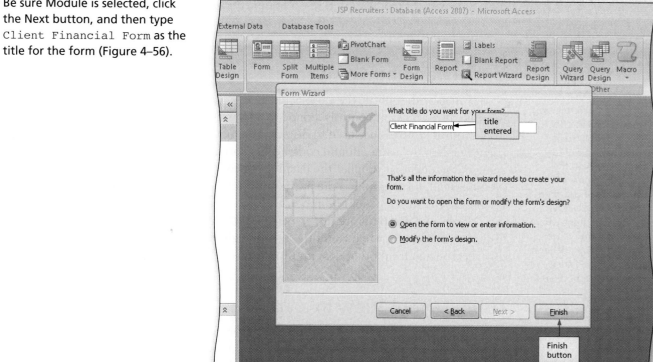

Figure 4–56

6

- Click the Finish button to complete and display the form (Figure 4–57).

7

- Click the Close 'Client Financial Form' button to close the form.

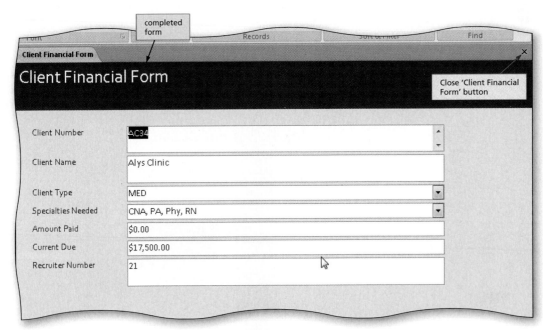

Figure 4–57

BTW

Form Design Considerations
Forms should be appealing visually and present data logically and clearly. Review your form to see if it presents the information effectively. Properly designed forms improve both the speed and accuracy of data entry. Forms that are cluttered or contain too many different effects (colors, fonts, frame styles, and so on) can be very hard on the eyes. Also, some colors are more difficult than others for individuals to see. Be consistent when creating forms. Once you decide on a general style for forms, stick with it throughout your database.

Understanding Form Sections

A form typically has only three sections. The **Form Header section** appears at the top of the form and usually contains the form title. It also may contain a logo and/or a date. The body of the form is in the **Detail section**. The **Form Footer section** appears at the bottom of the form and often is empty.

Understanding Controls

Just as with reports, the various items on a form are called controls. Forms include the same three types of controls: bound controls, unbound controls, and calculated controls. **Bound controls** are used to display data that comes from the database, such as the client number and name. Bound controls have attached labels that typically display the name of the field that supplies the data for the control. The **attached label** for the Client Number field, for example, is the portion of the screen immediately to the left of the field. It contains the words, Client Number.

Unbound controls are not associated with data from the database and are used to display such things as the form's title. Finally, **calculated controls** are used to display data that is calculated from other data in the database.

Using Layout View in a Form

When working with a form in Access, there are three different ways to view the report. They are Form view, Layout view, and Design view. Form view shows the form on the screen and allows you to use the form to update data. Layout view is similar to Form view in that it shows the form on the screen. In Layout view, you cannot update the data, but you can make changes to the layout of the form, which is usually the easiest way to make such changes. Design view also allows you to make changes, but it does not show you the actual form. It is most useful when the changes you need to make are especially complex. In this chapter, you will use Layout view to modify the form.

To Include Gridlines

You can make a variety of changes to the appearance of a form. One change is the inclusion of gridlines. The following steps modify the Client Financial Form to include horizontal and vertical gridlines.

1

- Open the Client Financial Form in Layout view and hide the Navigation Pane.

- If necessary, click Format on the Ribbon to display the Format tab.

- Ensure a field in the form is selected, then click the Gridlines button on the Format tab to display the Gridlines menu (Figure 4–58).

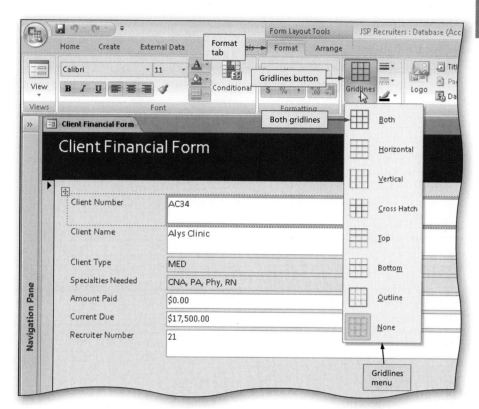

Figure 4–58

2

- Click Both on the Gridlines menu to specify both horizontal and vertical gridlines (Figure 4–59).

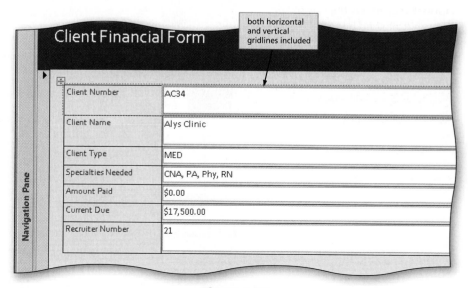

Figure 4–59

To Add a Date

You can add special items to reports and forms, such as a logo or title. You also can add the date and/or the time. In the case of reports, you can add a page number as well. To add any of these items, you use the appropriate button in the Controls group of the Format tab. The following steps use the Date and Time button to add a date to the Client Financial Form.

1

- Click in the Form header, outside the title (Client Financial Form) to select the Form header.
- Click the Date and Time button on the Format tab to display the Date and Time dialog box (Figure 4–60).

Q&A What is the relationship between the various check boxes and option buttons?

If the Include Date check box is checked, you must pick a date format from the three option buttons underneath the check box. If it is not checked, the option buttons will be dimmed. If the Include Time check box is checked, you must pick a time format from the three option buttons underneath the check box. If it is not checked, the option buttons will be dimmed.

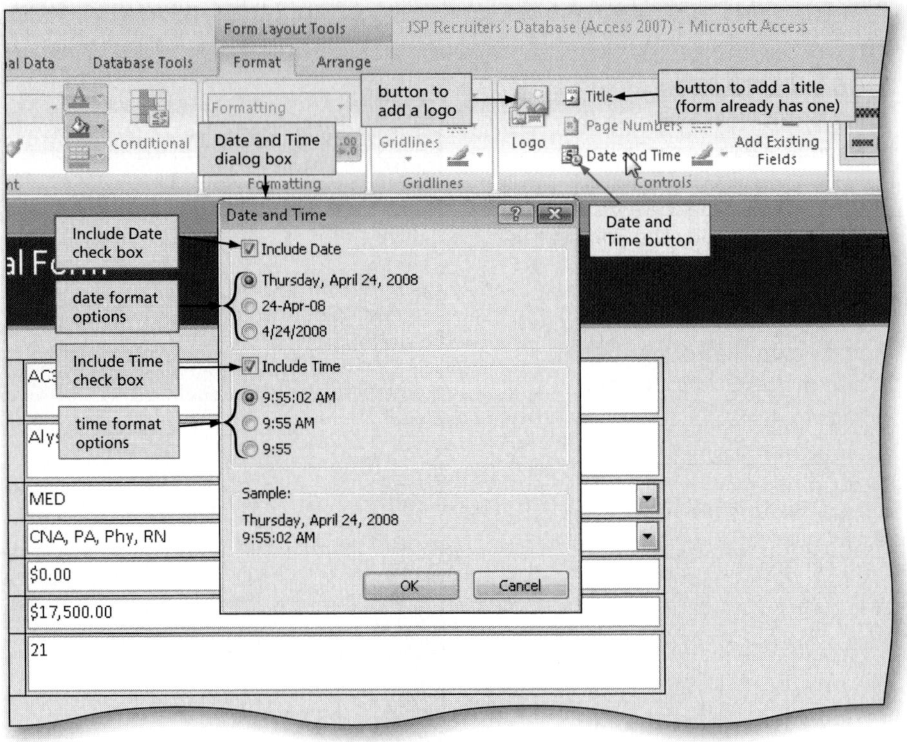

Figure 4–60

2

- Click the option button for the second date format to select the format that shows the day of the month, followed by the abbreviation for the month, followed by the year.
- Click the Include Time check box to remove the check mark (Figure 4–61).

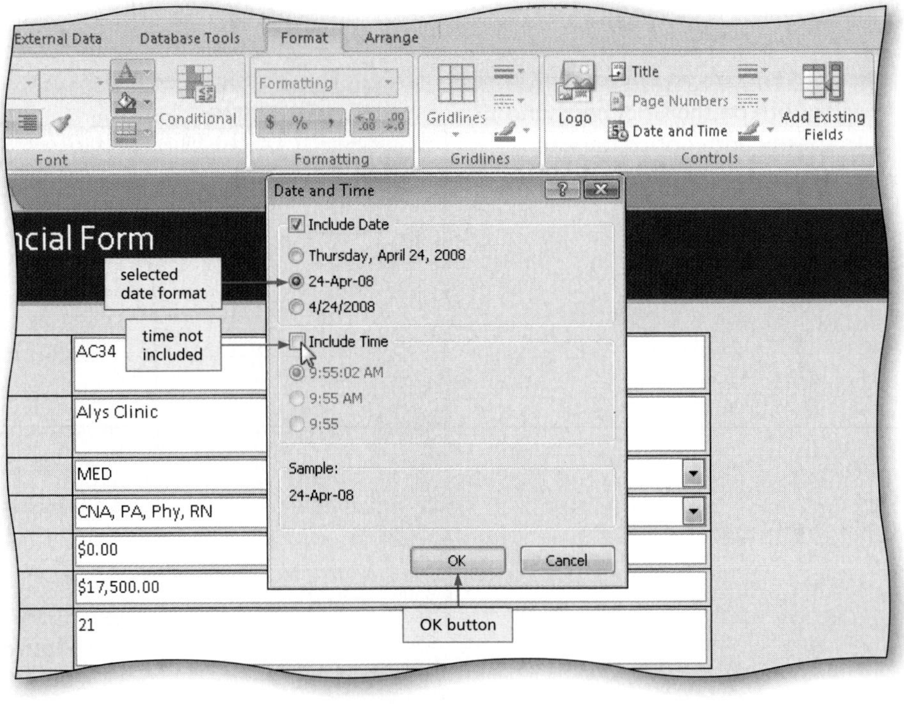

Figure 4–61

❸

- Click the OK button in the Date and Time dialog box to add the date to the form (Figure 4–62).

Q&A Why is the date so dark? I can hardly read it.

The letters are black, which does not work well with this color of the form heading. You need to change the color of the date to make it more visible.

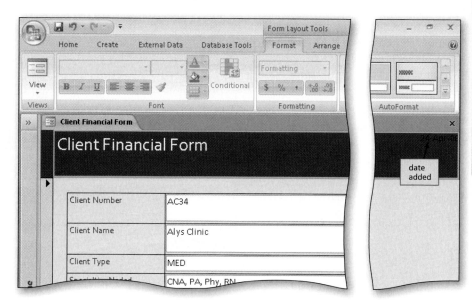

Figure 4–62

To Change the Format of a Control

You can use the buttons in the Font group of the Format tab to change the format of a control. The following steps use the Font Color arrow in the Font group to change the color of the font in the control containing the date to white, so that it will be more visible.

❶

- Click the Date control to select it.

- Be sure the Format tab appears.

- Click the Font Color arrow on the Format tab to display a color palette (Figure 4–63).

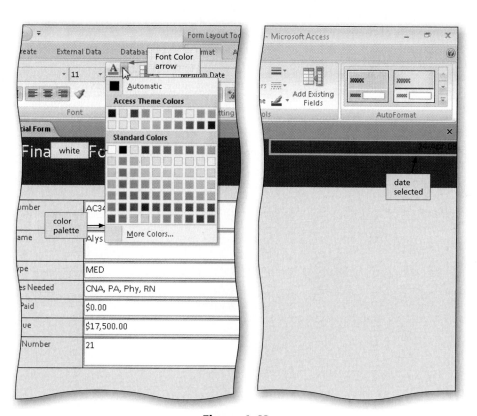

Figure 4–63

● Click the white color in the upper-left corner of the Standard Colors section to change the font color for the date to white (Figure 4–64).

Q&A

Can I change the color of other controls the same way?

Yes. Select the control and then use the same steps to change the font color. You also can use other buttons on the Format tab to bold, italicize, underline, change the font, and so on.

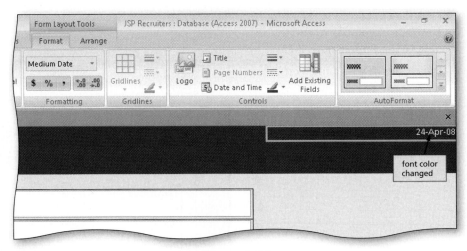

Figure 4–64

To Move a Control

You can move a control by dragging the control. The following steps move the Date control to the lower edge of the form header.

● Point to the Date control so that the mouse pointer changes to a four-headed arrow and then drag the Date control to the lower boundary of the form heading (Figure 4–65).

Q&A

I moved my pointer a little bit and it became a double-headed arrow. Can I still drag the pointer?

If you drag when the pointer is a double-headed arrow, you will resize the control. To move the control, it must be a four-headed arrow.

Q&A

Could I drag other objects as well? For example, could I drag the title to the center of the form header?

Yes. Just be sure you are pointing at the object and the pointer is a four-headed arrow. You then can drag the object to the desired location.

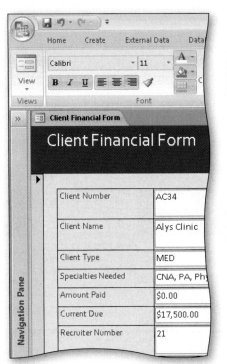
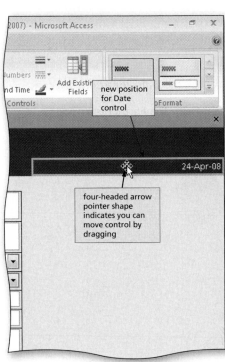

Figure 4–65

**Plan
Ahead**

> **Review the form after it has been in operation to determine whether any changes are warranted.**
>
> 1. **Determine whether the order of the fields is still the best order.** After a user has worked with a form for a period, he or she may feel that another order of the fields would work better than the original order.
>
> 2. **Determine whether any additional fields now are required.** Are there fields missing from the form that would be helpful?

To Move Controls in a Control Layout

The controls for the fields are arranged in control layouts. A **control layout** is a guide that aligns the controls to give the form a uniform appearance. There are two types of control layouts. A **stacked layout** arranges the controls vertically with labels to the left of the control. A **tabular layout** arranges the controls horizontally with the labels across the top, typically in the Form header section. This form contains a stacked layout.

You can move a control within a control layout by dragging the control to the location you want. As you move it, a line will indicate the position where the control will be placed when you release the left mouse button. You can move more than one control in the same operation by selecting both controls prior to moving them.

The following steps move the Client Type and Specialties Needed fields so that they follow the Recruiter Number field.

- Click the control for the Client Type field to select it.

- Hold the SHIFT key down and click the control for the Specialties Needed field to select both fields (Figure 4–66).

Q&A

Why did I have to hold the SHIFT key down when I clicked the control for the Specialties Needed field?

If you did not hold the SHIFT key down, you would select only the Specialties Needed field. The Client Type field no longer would be selected.

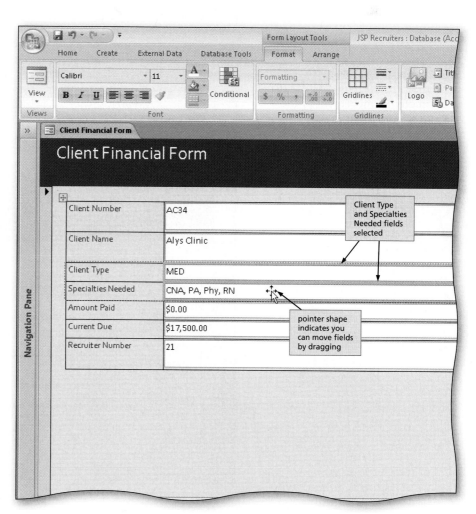

Figure 4–66

2

- Press the left mouse button and then drag the fields to the position shown in Figure 4–67.

Q&A

What is the purpose of the line by the mouse pointer?

It shows you where the fields will be positioned.

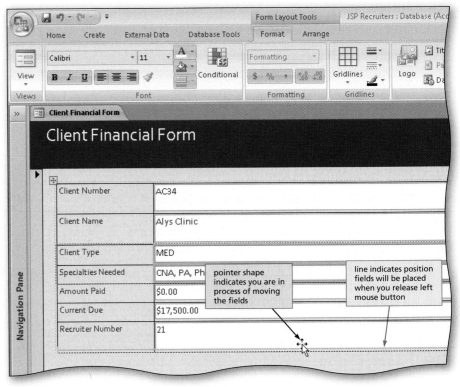

Figure 4–67

3

- Release the left mouse button to complete the movement of the fields (Figure 4–68).

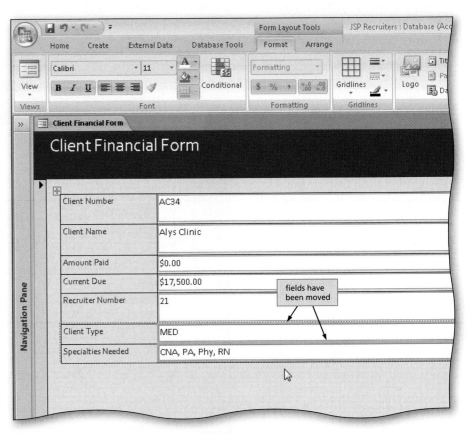

Figure 4–68

To Add a Field

Just as with a report, once you have created an initial form, you may decide that the form should contain an additional field. The following steps use a field list to add the City field to the Client Financial Form.

1

- Be sure the Format tab appears.

- Click the Add Existing Fields button to display a Field List (Figure 4–69).

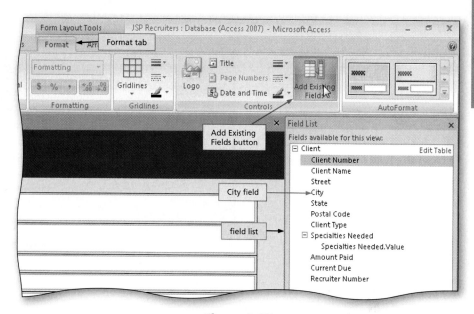

Figure 4–69

2

- Point to the City field in the field list, press the left mouse button, and then drag the pointer to the position shown in Figure 4–70.

Q&A

Does it have to be exact?

The exact pointer position is not critical as long as the line is in the position shown in the figure.

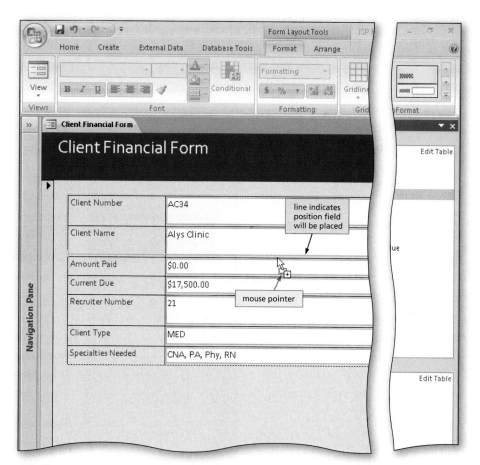

Figure 4–70

3

• Release the left mouse button to place the field (Figure 4–71).

Q&A

What if I make a mistake?

Just as when you are modifying a report, you can delete the field by clicking the field and then pressing the DELETE key. You can move the field by dragging it to the correct position.

4

• Close the field list.

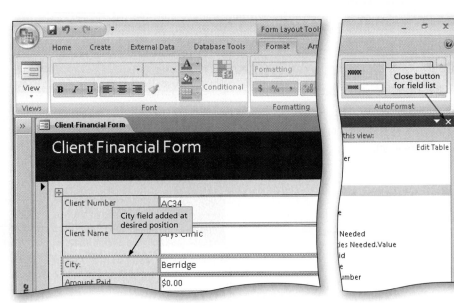

Figure 4–71

To Filter and Sort Using a Form

Just as in a datasheet, you can filter and sort using Advanced Filter/Sort, which is a command on the Advanced menu. The following steps use Advanced Filter/Sort to filter the records to those records whose city begins with the letters, Be. They also sort the records by client name.

1

• Click Home on the Ribbon to display the Home tab.

• Click the Advanced button on the Home tab to display the Advanced menu (Figure 4–72).

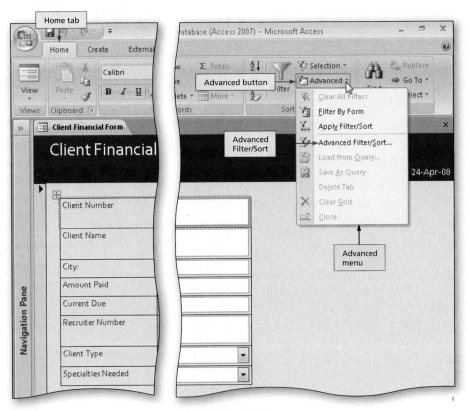

Figure 4–72

2

- Click Advanced Filter/Sort on the Advanced menu.

- Add the Client Name field and select Ascending sort order.

- Add the City field and type like Be* as the criterion for the city field (Figure 4–73).

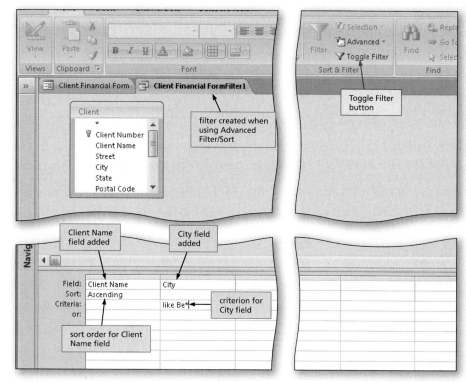

Figure 4–73

3

- Click the Toggle Filter button on the Home tab to filter the records (Figure 4–74).

Q&A

I can see only one record at a time in the form. How can I see which records are included?

You would have to scroll through the records. For example, you could repeatedly press the Next Record button.

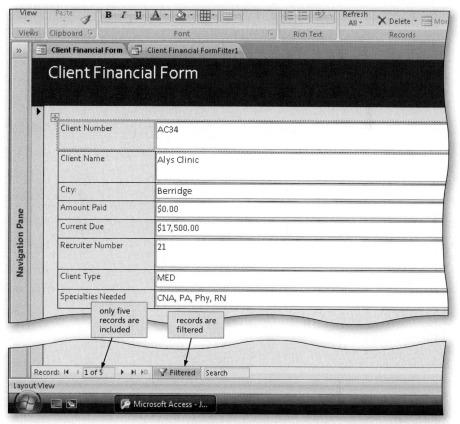

Figure 4–74

BTW

Creating and Removing Layouts
You can create and remove control layouts. To create a tabular layout, select the controls, click Arrange on the Ribbon and then click the Tabular button on the Arrange tab. To create a stacked layout, select the controls, click Arrange on the Ribbon and then click the Stacked button on the Arrange tab. To remove a tabular or stacked layout, select the fields with the layout you want to remove, click Arrange on the Ribbon and then click the Remove button on the Arrange tab.

To Clear a Form Filter

When you no longer want the records to be filtered, you clear the filter. The following steps clear the current filter for the Client Financial Form.

1 Click the Advanced button on the Home tab to display the Advanced menu.

2 Click Clear All Filters on the Advanced menu to clear the filter.

To Save and Close a Form

Now that you have completed your work on your form, you should save the form and close it. The following steps first save your work on the form and then close the form.

1 Click the Save button on the Quick Access Toolbar to save your work.

2 Close the Client Financial Form.

BTW

Creating Forms in Layout View
You can create a form in Layout view without using the wizard. To do so, click Create on the Ribbon and then click the Blank Form button on the Create tab.

To Print a Form

You can print all the records, a range of pages, or a selected record of a form by selecting the appropriate print range. In order to print the selected record, the form must be open. To print all records or a range of pages, the form simply can be highlighted in the Navigation Pane. The following steps open the Client Financial Form and then print the first record in the form, which is the selected record.

1 Open the Client Financial Form and then click the Office Button to display the Office Button menu.

2 Point to Print on the Office Button menu and then click Print on the Print submenu to display the Print dialog box.

3 Click the Selected Record(s) option button in the Page Range box, and then click the OK button.

BTW

Certification
The Microsoft Certified Application Specialist (MCAS) program provides an opportunity for you to obtain a valuable industry credential — proof that you have the Access 2007 skills required by employers. For more information, see Appendix G or visit the Access 2007 Certification Web page (scsite.com/ac2007/cert).

Changing an AutoFormat

An AutoFormat is a predefined style that can be applied to a report or form. You can apply or change an AutoFormat by using the AutoFormat group on the Format tab (see Figure 4–75). In viewing a form in Layout view, two AutoFormat selections appear on the screen. You can use the scroll arrows to see the previous two selections or the next two selections.

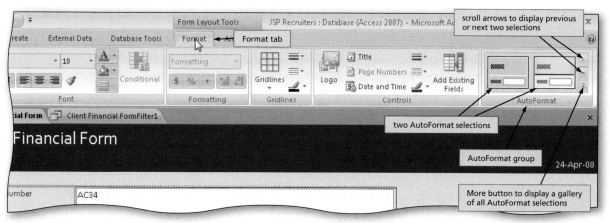

Figure 4–75

As an alternative, you can click the More button to display a gallery of all AutoFormat selections (Figure 4–76). In either case, once you select the desired AutoFormat, the characteristics of the AutoFormat will be applied to the form or report.

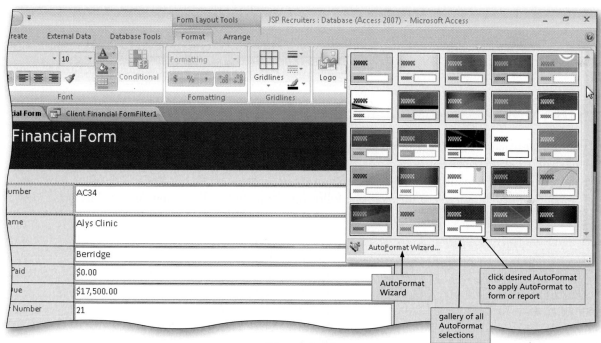

Figure 4–76

You also can use the AutoFormat Wizard to select an AutoFormat. Using the wizard, you can select whether the attributes in the form apply to the font, the color, and or the border. You also can create a new AutoFormat with the characteristics of the current form or report, update the selected AutoFormat with characteristics of the current form or report, or delete the selected AutoFormat.

BTW

Multiple Items Forms and Datasheet Forms
Access includes many different types of forms. A Multiple Items form is a form that shows multiple records in a datasheet with one record per row. To create a Multiple Items form, click the Multiple Items button on the Create tab. A Datasheet form displays a table in a datasheet. To create a Datasheet form, click the More Forms button arrow on the Create tab, and then click Datasheet.

To Apply an AutoFormat

If you wish to apply or change an AutoFormat, you would use the following steps.

1. Click the More button in the AutoFormat group on the Format tab.
2. Click the desired AutoFormat.

BTW

Quick Reference
For a table that lists how
to complete the tasks
covered in this book
using the mouse, Ribbon,
shortcut menu, and
keyboard, see the Quick
Reference Summary at
the back of this book, or
visit the Access 2007 Quick
Reference Web page
(scsite.com/ac2007/qr).

The Arrange Tab

Forms, like reports, have an Arrange tab that you can use to modify the form's layout. However, the Page Setup tab is not available for forms. The buttons on the Arrange tab and the functions of those buttons are just like the ones described in Table 4-1 on page AC 255, with one exception. When working with a form, there is an extra button, the Anchoring button. The function of this button is to tie a control to a section or another control so that it moves or resizes in conjunction with the movement or resizing of its parent.

To Quit Access

You saved all your changes and are ready to quit Access. The following step quits Access.

 Click the Close button on the right side of the Access title bar to quit Access.

Chapter Summary

In this chapter you have learned to use wizards to create reports and forms; modify the layout of reports and forms using Layout view; group and sort in a report, add totals to a report; conditionally format controls; filter records in reports and forms; resize and move controls; add fields to reports and forms; include gridlines; add a date; move controls in a control layout; and change an AutoFormat. The following list includes all the new Access skills you have learned in this chapter.

1. Create a Simple Report (AC 239)
2. Create a Report Using the Report Wizard (AC 239)
3. Group and Sort in a Report (AC 244)
4. Add Totals and Subtotals (AC 248)
5. Resize Columns (AC 249)
6. Conditionally Format Controls (AC 250)
7. Filter Records in a Report (AC 252)
8. Clear a Report Filter (AC 254)
9. Save and Close a Report (AC 254)
10. Print a Report (AC 256)
11. Create a Summary Report (AC 256)
12. Create a Report that Involves Multiple Tables (AC 257)
13. Resize Columns and Column Headings (AC 263)
14. Add a Field (AC 265)
15. Include Totals (AC 268)
16. Use the Form Wizard to Create a Form (AC 269)
17. Include Gridlines (AC 273)
18. Add a Date (AC 274)
19. Change the Format of a Control (AC 275)
20. Move a Control (AC 276)
21. Move Controls in a Control Layout (AC 277)
22. Add a Field (AC 279)
23. Filter and Sort Using a Form (AC 280)
24. Clear a Form Filter (AC 282)
25. Save and Close a Form (AC 282)
26. Print a Form (AC 282)
27. Apply an AutoFormat (AC 284)

 If you have a SAM user profile, you may have access to hands-on instruction, practice, and assessment. Log in to your SAM account (http://sam2007.course.com) to launch any assigned training activities or exams that relate to the skills covered in this chapter.

Learn It Online

Test your knowledge of chapter content and key terms.

Instructions: To complete the Learn It Online exercises, start your browser, click the Address bar, and then enter the Web address scsite.com/ac2007/learn. When the Access 2007 Learn It Online page is displayed, click the link for the exercise you want to complete and then read the instructions.

Chapter Reinforcement TF, MC, and SA
A series of true/false, multiple choice, and short answer questions that test your knowledge of the chapter content.

Flash Cards
An interactive learning environment where you identify chapter key terms associated with displayed definitions.

Practice Test
A series of multiple choice questions that test your knowledge of chapter content and key terms.

Who Wants To Be a Computer Genius?
An interactive game that challenges your knowledge of chapter content in the style of a television quiz show.

Wheel of Terms
An interactive game that challenges your knowledge of chapter key terms in the style of the television show *Wheel of Fortune.*

Crossword Puzzle Challenge
A crossword puzzle that challenges your knowledge of key terms presented in the chapter.

Apply Your Knowledge

Reinforce the skills and apply the concepts you learned in this chapter.

Creating a Report and a Form
Instructions: Start Access. If you are using the Microsoft Office Access 2007 Complete or the Microsoft Office Access 2007 Comprehensive text, open The Bike Delivers database that you used in Chapter 3. Otherwise, see the inside back cover of this book for instructions for downloading the Data Files for Students, or see your instructor for information on accessing the files required in this book.

Continued >

Apply Your Knowledge *continued*

Perform the following tasks:

1. Create the Customers by Courier report shown in Figure 4–77.

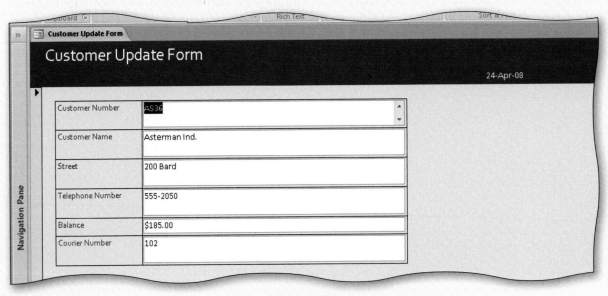

Courier Number	First Name	Last Name	Customer Name	Customer Number	Balance
102	Chou	Dang			
			Asterman Ind.	AS36	$185.00
			CJ Gallery	CJ16	$195.00
			Mentor Group Limited	ME71	$138.00
					$518.00
109	Michelle	Hyde			
			Author Books	AU54	$50.00
			Blossom Shop	BL92	$40.00
			Jordan Place	JO62	$114.00
			Royal Mfg Co.	RO32	$93.00
					$297.00
113	Javier	Lopez			
			Klingon Toys	KL55	$105.00
			Moore Foods	MO13	$0.00
					$105.00
					$920.00

Customers by Courier

Figure 4–77

2. Create the Customer Update Form shown in Figure 4–78 for the Customer table. The form includes the current date and is similar in style to that shown in Figure 4–3 on page AC 236.

Figure 4–78

3. Submit the revised database in the format specified by your instructor.

Extend Your Knowledge

Extend the skills you learned in this chapter and experiment with new skills. You may need to use Help to complete the assignment.

Creating a Summary Report and a Justified Form

Instructions: See the inside back cover of this book for instructions for downloading the Data Files for Students, or see your instructor for information on accessing the files required in this book.

The Plant database contains data for a company that designs and maintains indoor landscapes. You will create the summary report shown in Figure 4–79. You also will create the form shown in Figure 4–80.

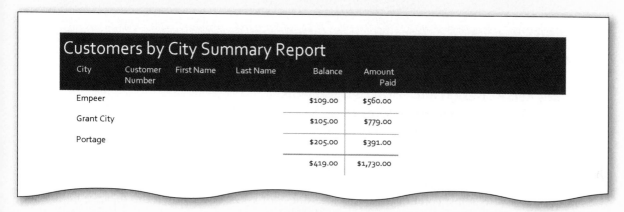

Figure 4–79

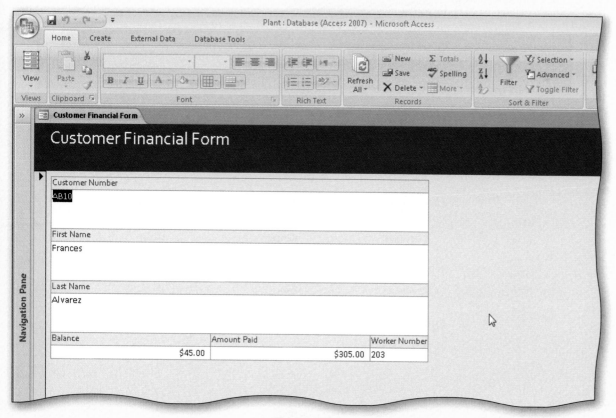

Figure 4–80

Continued >

Extend Your Knowledge *continued*

Perform the following tasks:

1. Create the summary report shown in Figure 4–79 on the previous page. Name the report Customers by City. The title of the report should be Customers by City Summary Report.

2. Create the Customer Financial Form shown in Figure 4–80 on the previous page. Please note that the form uses the Justified layout. Choose your own autoformat and apply it to the form. Save the form as Customer Financial Form AutoFormat.

3. Change the database properties, as specified by your instructor. Submit the revised database in the format specified by your instructor.

Make It Right

Analyze a database and correct all errors and/or improve the design.

Correcting Report Design and Form Design Errors

Instructions: Start Access. Open the Pet database. See the inside back cover of this book for instructions for downloading the Data Files for Students, or see your instructor for information on accessing the files required in this book.

The Pet database contains data for a company that provides a variety of services to pet owners. The owner of the company has created the report shown in Figure 4–81 using the Report Wizard but does not know how to adjust column sizes. She also does not know how to total the Balance field. She would like some way to differentiate customers with a zero balance.

Customers by City

City	Customer Number	First Name	Last Name	Balance
Em				
	BR16	Alex	Breaton	$80.00
	HJ07	Bill	Heijer	$29.00
	MA34	Lisa	Manston	$0.00
	SA23	Maria	Santoro	$0.00
Gra				
	AB10	Frances	Alvarez	$45.00
	FE45	Jean	Ferdon	$0.00
	KL12	Cynthia	Klinger	$60.00
Port				
	GM52	Frank	Gammort	$70.00
	PR80	Martin	Prestz	$95.00
	TR35	Gerry	Trent	$40.00

Figure 4–81

She also created the form shown in Figure 4–82 for the Customer table, but she forgot to add the Pets field. The field should appear before the Balance field.

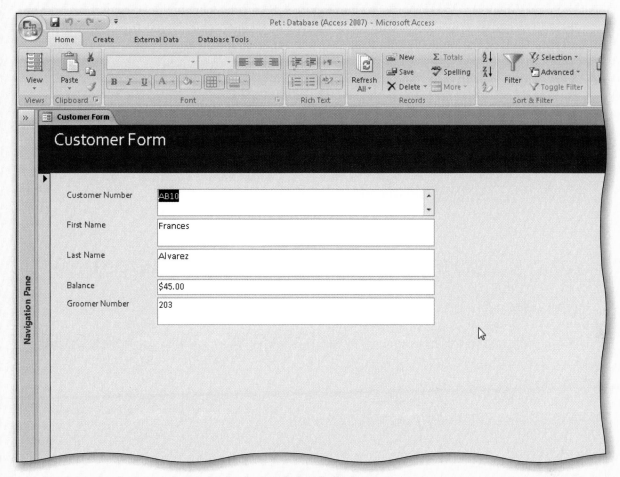

Figure 4–82

Submit the revised database in the format specified by your instructor.

In the Lab

Design, create, modify, and/or use a database following the guidelines, concepts, and skills presented in this chapter. Labs are listed in order of increasing difficulty.

Lab 1: Presenting Data in the JMS TechWizards Database

Problem: The management of JMS TechWizards already has realized the benefits from the database of clients and technicians that you created. The management now would like to prepare reports and forms for the database.

Instructions: If you are using the Microsoft Office Access 2007 Complete or the Microsoft Office Access 2007 Comprehensive text, open JMS TechWizards database that you used in Chapter 3. Otherwise, see the inside back cover of this book for instructions for downloading the Data Files for Students, or see your instructor for information on accessing the files required in this book.

Continued >

In the Lab *continued*

Perform the following tasks:

1. Create the Clients by Type report shown in Figure 4–83 for the Client table. Group the report by Client Type and sort the records within Client Type by Client Name. Include totals for the Billed and Paid fields. If the amount in the Paid field is $0.00, it should appear in red.

Clients by Type

Client Type	Client Number	Client Name	Billed	Paid
MAN				
	AM53	Ashton-Mills	$315.50	$255.00
	SA56	Sawyer Industries	$372.25	$350.00
			$687.75	$605.00
RET				
	BE29	Bert's Supply	$229.50	$0.00
	CR21	Cray Meat Market	$0.00	$0.00
	DE76	D & E Grocery	$485.70	$400.00
	GU21	Grand Union	$228.00	$0.00
	ST21	Steed's Department Store	$0.00	$0.00
	AR76	The Artshop	$535.00	$565.00
			$1,478.20	$965.00
SER				
	GR56	Grant Cleaners	$215.00	$225.00
	ME17	Merry Café	$312.50	$323.50
			$527.50	$548.50
			$2,693.45	$2,118.50

Figure 4–83

2. Create the Clients by Technicians report shown in Figure 4–84. Be sure to adjust the column headings and include totals for the Billed and Paid fields.

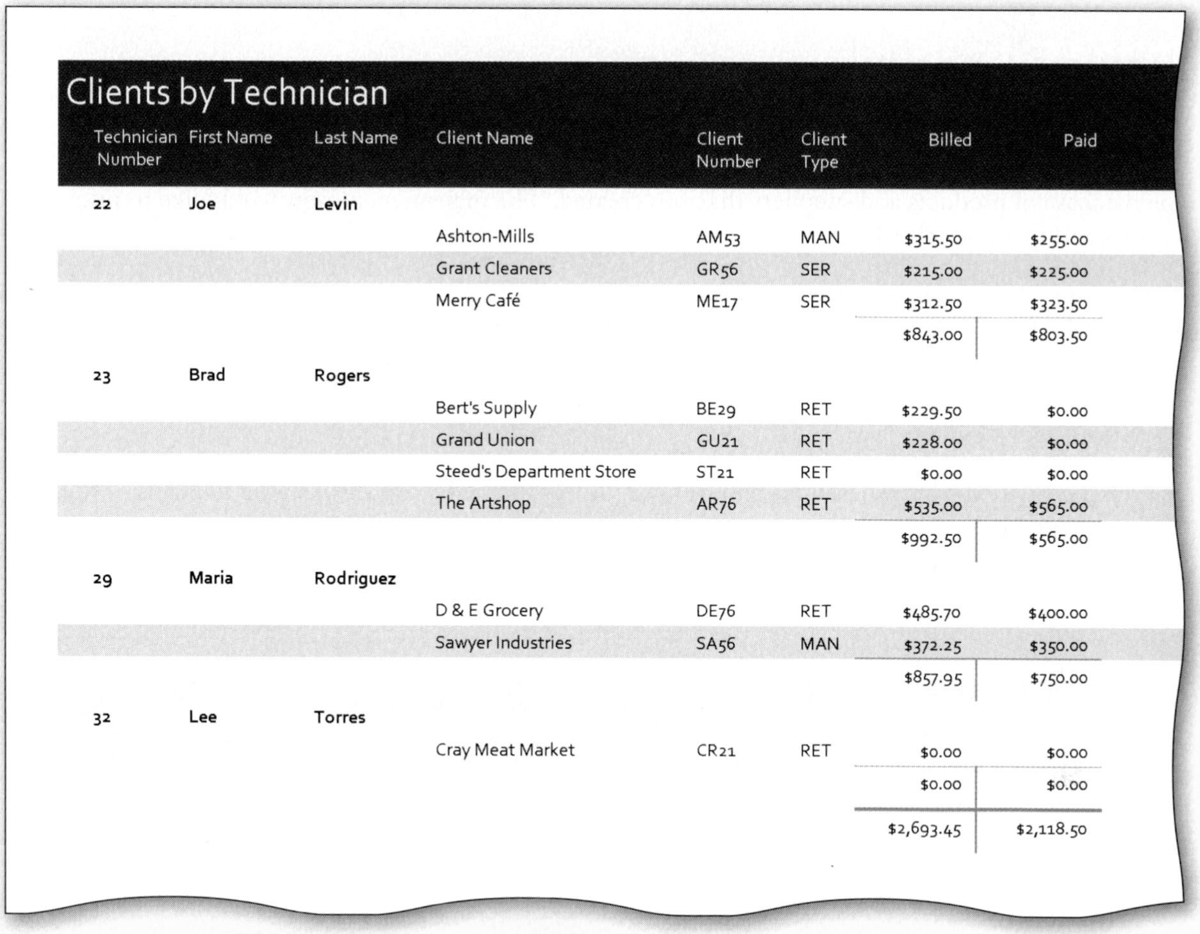

Clients by Technician

Technician Number	First Name	Last Name	Client Name	Client Number	Client Type	Billed	Paid
22	Joe	Levin					
			Ashton-Mills	AM53	MAN	$315.50	$255.00
			Grant Cleaners	GR56	SER	$215.00	$225.00
			Merry Café	ME17	SER	$312.50	$323.50
						$843.00	$803.50
23	Brad	Rogers					
			Bert's Supply	BE29	RET	$229.50	$0.00
			Grand Union	GU21	RET	$228.00	$0.00
			Steed's Department Store	ST21	RET	$0.00	$0.00
			The Artshop	AR76	RET	$535.00	$565.00
						$992.50	$565.00
29	Maria	Rodriguez					
			D & E Grocery	DE76	RET	$485.70	$400.00
			Sawyer Industries	SA56	MAN	$372.25	$350.00
						$857.95	$750.00
32	Lee	Torres					
			Cray Meat Market	CR21	RET	$0.00	$0.00
						$0.00	$0.00
						$2,693.45	$2,118.50

Figure 4–84

3. Create the Client Financial Form shown in Figure 4–85.

Figure 4–85

4. Submit the revised database in the format specified by your instructor.

In the Lab

Lab 2: Presenting Data in the Hockey Fan Zone Database

Problem: The management of the Hockey Fan Zone store already has realized the benefits from the database of products and suppliers that you created. The management now would like to prepare reports and forms for the database.

Instructions: If you are using the Microsoft Office Access 2007 Complete or the Microsoft Office Access 2007 Comprehensive text, open the Hockey Fan Zone database that you used in Chapter 3. Otherwise, see the inside back cover of this book for instructions for downloading the Data Files for Students, or see your instructor for information on accessing the files required in this book.

Perform the following tasks:

1. Create the Items by Type report shown in Figure 4–86 for the Item table. The report is grouped by item type and sorted by description. Calculate the average cost and the average selling price for each item type and for all items.

Items by Type

Item Type	Item Number	Description	Cost	Selling Price
CAP				
	3663	Ball Cap	$11.15	$18.95
	7930	Visor	$11.95	$17.00
			$11.55	$17.98
CLO				
	5923	Jersey	$21.45	$24.75
	7550	Sweatshirt	$19.90	$22.95
	7810	Tee Shirt	$9.50	$14.95
			$16.95	$20.88
NOV				
	3673	Blanket	$29.90	$34.00
	3683	Bumper Sticker	$0.95	$1.50
	4563	Earrings	$4.50	$7.00
	6078	Key Chain	$3.00	$5.00
	6189	Koozies	$2.00	$4.00
	6343	Note Cube	$5.75	$8.00
			$7.68	$9.92
			$10.91	$14.37

Figure 4–86

2. Create the Items by Supplier report shown in Figure 4–87. If there are fewer than 10 items on hand, the value should appear in a red bold font.

Items by Supplier

Supplier Code	Supplier Name	Description	Item Number	On Hand	Cost
AC	Ace Clothes				
		Blanket	3673	5	$29.90
		Jersey	5923	12	$21.45
		Tee Shirt	7810	32	$9.50
LG	Logo Goods				
		Ball Cap	3663	30	$11.15
		Earrings	4563	10	$4.50
		Sweatshirt	7550	8	$19.90
		Visor	7930	9	$11.95
MN	Mary's Novelties				
		Bumper Sticker	3683	50	$0.95
		Key Chain	6078	20	$3.00
		Koozies	6189	35	$2.00
		Note Cube	6343	7	$5.75

Figure 4–87

3. Create the Item Update form shown in Figure 4–88. If there are fewer than 10 items on hand, the value should appear in a red bold font. Notice that the controls have been resized to a smaller width and that the figure shows the form with data for record 2 in the Item table.

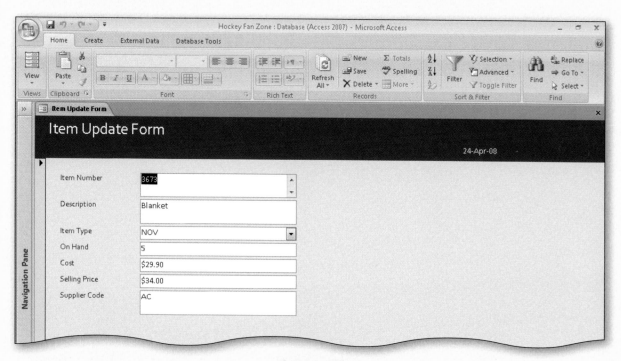

Figure 4–88

4. Submit the revised database in the format specified by your instructor.

In the Lab

Lab 3: Maintaining the Ada Beauty Supply Database

Problem: The management of Ada Beauty Supply already has realized the benefits from the database you created. The management now would like to prepare reports and forms for the database.

Instructions: If you are using the Microsoft Office Access 2007 Complete or the Microsoft Office Access 2007 Comprehensive text, open the Ada Beauty Supply database that you used in Chapter 3. Otherwise, see the inside back cover of this book for instructions for downloading the Data Files for Students, or see your instructor for information on accessing the files required in this book. Submit the revised database in the format specified by your instructor.

Instructions Part 1: Create a report for Ada Beauty Supply. The report should be similar to the Clients by Recruiter report shown in Figure 4–2 on page AC 235 with the records grouped by Sales Rep Number. Include the Sales Rep Number, First Name, and Last Name from the Sales Rep table. Include the Customer Number, Customer Name, Services Offered, Balance, and Amount Paid fields from the Customer table. Provide subtotals and a grand total for the Balance and Amount Paid fields.

Instructions Part 2: Create a Customer Financial Form for Ada Beauty Supply that is similar to the Client Financial form shown in Figure 4–3 on page AC 236. The form should include Customer Number, Customer Name, Amount Paid, Balance, Sales Rep Number, and Services Offered.

Cases and Places

Apply your creative thinking and problem solving skills to design and implement a solution.

• EASIER   •• MORE DIFFICULT

• 1: Presenting Data in the Second-Hand Goods Database

If you are using the Microsoft Office Access 2007 Complete or the Microsoft Office Access 2007 Comprehensive text, open the Second-Hand Goods database that you used in Chapter 3. Otherwise, see the inside back cover of this book for instructions for downloading the Data Files for Students, or see your instructor for information on accessing the files required in this book. Use this database to create a report that groups items by seller. Include the seller code, first name, and last name from the Seller table. Include all fields except seller code from the Item table. Create a multiple items form and a datasheet form for the Item table. Submit the revised database in the format specified by your instructor.

• 2: Presenting Data in the BeachCondo Rentals database

If you are using the Microsoft Office Access 2007 Complete or the Microsoft Office Access 2007 Comprehensive text, open the BeachCondo Rentals database that you used in Chapter 3. Otherwise, see the inside back cover of this book for instructions for downloading the Data Files for Students, or see your instructor for information on accessing the files required in this book. The rental company needs a custom report that groups condo units by the number of bedrooms. Within each group, the records should be sorted in ascending order by weekly rate. The report should include all fields from the Condo Unit table except the For Sale field and the Owner Code field. The company also needs a form for the Condo Unit table that shows all fields except the For Sale field. Submit the revised database in the format specified by your instructor.

•• 3: Presenting Data in the Restaurant Database

If you are using the Microsoft Office Access 2007 Complete or the Microsoft Office Access 2007 Comprehensive text, open the restaurant database that you used in Chapter 3. Otherwise, see the inside back cover of this book for instructions for downloading the Data Files for Students, or see your instructor for information on accessing the files required in this book. Using the Plan Ahead guidelines presented in this chapter, determine what forms and reports you need to create. Create any necessary reports and forms. Include a logo on each report and form. You either can create your own logo or use Microsoft clip art. Write a short paper that explains why you chose to create the specific reports and forms. Submit the paper and the revised database in the format specified by your instructor.

•• 4: Presenting Data in Your Contacts Database

Make It Personal

If you are using the Microsoft Office Access 2007 Complete or the Microsoft Office Access 2007 Comprehensive text, open the contacts database that you used in Chapter 3. Otherwise, see the inside back cover of this book for instructions for downloading the Data Files for Students, or see your instructor for information on accessing the files required in this book. Consider your own personal job situation. What type of reports and forms would be useful to you? Do you need a report that lists all your contacts? Do you need a form to add each new contact that you make? Create any necessary reports and forms. Submit the revised database in the format specified by your instructor.

Continued >

Cases and Places *continued*

•• 5: Understanding Report and Form Formats and Styles

Working Together

The Report and Form Wizards offer several different styles and formats. Each member of the team should pick a different style and create the report shown in Figure 4–2 on page AC 235 and the form shown in Figure 4–3 on page AC 236 using the chosen styles. Compare the styles and as a team vote on which one you prefer. The project included general guidelines for designing reports and forms. Use the Internet to find more information about form design guidelines; for example, there are certain fonts that you should not use for a title and certain colors that are harder for individuals to see. Then, as a group, create a form that illustrates poor design features. Include a short write-up that explains what design principles were violated. Be sure to cite your references. Turn in each of the reports and forms that your team created using different styles. Also, turn in the poorly designed form and the write-up in the format specified by your instructor.

5 | Multi-Table Forms

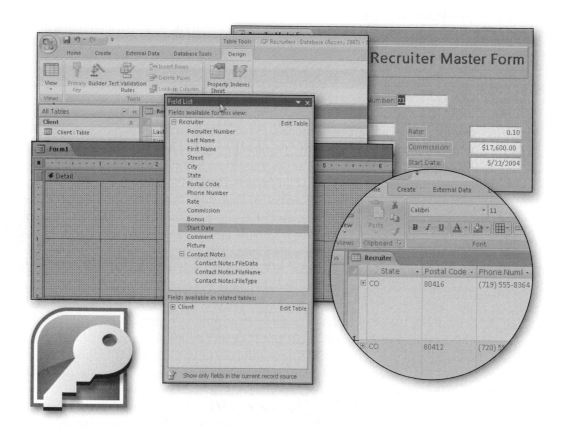

Objectives

You will have mastered the material in this project when you can:

- Use Yes/No, Date, Memo, OLE Object, Attachment, and Hyperlink fields

- Use the Input Mask Wizard

- Update fields and enter data

- Change row and column size

- Create a form with a subform in Design view

- Modify a subform and form design

- Enhance the form title

- Change tab stops and tab order

- Use the form to view data and attachments

- Use Date, Memo, and Yes/No fields in a query

- View object dependencies

5 | Multi-Table Forms

Introduction

This chapter adds several additional fields to the JSP Recruiters database that require special data types. It then creates a form incorporating data from two tables. The two tables, Recruiter and Client, are related in a one-to-many relationship. That is, one recruiter is related to *many* clients, but each client is related to only *one* recruiter. The Recruiter table is called the "one" table in the relationship and the Client table is called the "many" table. The form will show one recruiter at a time, but also will include the many clients of that recruiter. This chapter also creates queries that use the added fields.

Project — Multi-Table Forms

JSP Recruiters uses its database to keep records about clients and recruiters. After several months, however, the administration has found that it needs to maintain additional data on its recruiters. JSP has a bonus program and it needs to add a field that indicates the recruiter's eligibility for the bonus program. JSP needs to store the start date of each recruiter in the database. JSP wants the database to contain a comment about each recruiter as well as the recruiter's picture. Additionally, recruiters now maintain files about potential contacts. Some of these files are maintained in Word and others in Excel. JSP would like a way to attach these files to the corresponding recruiter's record in the database. Finally, JSP wants to add the Phone Number field to the Recruiter table. Users should type only the digits in the telephone number and then have Access format the number appropriately. If the user enters 7195558364, for example, Access will format the number as (719) 555-8364.

After the proposed fields have been added to the database, JSP wants a form created that incorporates both the Client and Recruiter tables. The form includes some of the newly added fields along with some of the existing fields. The form also should include the client number, name, amount paid, and current due amount for the clients of each recruiter. JSP would like to see multiple clients on the screen at the same time (Figure 5–1). The database should provide the capability of scrolling through all the clients of a recruiter and of accessing any of the attachments concerning the recruiter's contact notes. Finally, JSP requires queries that use the Bonus, Start Date, and Comment fields.

Overview

As you read through this chapter, you will learn how to create reports and forms by performing these general tasks:

- Add the Bonus, Start Date, Comment, Picture, and Attachment fields to the Recruiter table and assign each field the appropriate data type.
- Add the Phone Number field to the Recruiter table and create an appropriate input mask.
- Create the Recruiter Master Form and add the fields from the Recruiter table at the appropriate positions.

Figure 5–1

- Add a subform containing the Client Number, Client Name, Amount Paid, and Current Due fields from the Client table.
- Enhance the form by assigning colors and various special effects.
- Create and run queries that involve the Bonus, Start Date, and Comment fields.

Report and Form Design Guidelines

Plan Ahead

1. **When new fields are needed, determine the purpose of those fields to see if they need special data types.** Does the field contain dates? Are the only values for the field Yes or No? Does the field contain an extended description of something? Does the field contain a picture? Is the purpose of the field to contain attachments of files created in other applications?

2. **When a form is required, determine whether the form requires data from more than one table.** Is all the data found in a single table or does it come from multiple related tables?

3. **If the form requires data from more than one table, determine the relationship between the tables.** Identify one-to-many relationships. For each relationship, identify the "one" table and the "many" table.

(continued)

Plan Ahead

(continued)

4. **If the form requires data from more than one table, determine on which of the tables the form is to be based.** Which table contains data that is the main focus of the form? Is it a form about recruiters, for example, that happens to require some client data in order to be effective? Is it a form about clients that also includes some recruiter data as additional information?

5. **Determine the fields from each table that need to be on the form.** How exactly will the form be used? What fields are necessary to support this use? Are there any additional fields that, while not strictly necessary, would make the form more functional? For example, if a user is entering a recruiter number on a form based on clients, it may be helpful also to see the name of the recruiter with that number.

When necessary, more specific details concerning the above decisions and/or actions are presented at appropriate points within the chapter. The chapter also will identify the use of these guidelines in the design of forms such as the one shown in Figure 5–1 on the previous page.

Starting Access

If you are using a computer to step through the project in this chapter and you want your screen to match the figures in this book, you should change your screen's resolution to 1024 × 768. For information about how to change a computer's resolution, read Appendix E.

To Start Access

The following steps, which assume Windows Vista is running, start Access.

Note: If you are using Windows XP, see Appendix F for alternate steps.

1 Click the Start button on the Windows Vista taskbar to display the Start menu.

2 Click All Programs at the bottom of the left pane on the Start menu to display the All Programs list and then click Microsoft Office in the All Programs list to display the Microsoft Office list.

3 Click Microsoft Office Access 2007 on the Microsoft Office list to start Access and display the Getting Started with Microsoft Office Access window.

4 If the Access window is not maximized, click the Maximize button on its title bar to maximize the window.

To Open a Database

In Chapter 1, you created your database on a USB flash drive using the file name, JSP Recruiters. There are two ways to open the file containing your database. If the file you created appears in the Recent Documents list, you could click it to open the file. If not, you can use the More button to open the file. The following steps use the More button to open the JSP Recruiters database from the USB flash drive.

Note: If you are using Windows XP, see Appendix F for alternate steps.

1 With your USB flash drive connected to one of the computer's USB ports, click the More button to display the Open dialog box.

2 If the Folders list is displayed below the Folders button, click the Folders button to remove the Folders list.

3 If necessary, click Computer in the Favorite Links section and then double-click UDISK 2.0 (E:) to select the USB flash drive, Drive E in this case, as the new open location. (Your drive letter might be different.)

4 Click JSP Recruiters to select the file name.

5 Click the Open button to open the database.

6 If a Security Warning appears, click the Options button to display the Microsoft Office Security Options dialog box.

7 With the option button to enable the content selected, click the OK button to enable the content.

Determine the purpose of new fields to see if they need special data types.

Plan
Ahead

1. **Determine whether an input mask is appropriate.** Should the data in the field be displayed in a special way; for example, with parentheses and a hyphen like a phone number or separated into three groups of digits like a Social Security number? Should Access assist the user in entering the data in the right format? For example, should Access automatically insert the parentheses and a hyphen when a user enters a phone number?

2. **Determine whether the Yes/No data type is appropriate.** Are the only possible field values Yes or No? Are the only possible values True or False? Are the only possible values On or Off? If any of these applies, the field is a good candidate for the Yes/No data type.

3. **Determine whether the Date data type is appropriate.** Does the field contain a date? If so, assigning it the Date data type accomplishes several things. First, Access will ensure that the only values entered in the field are legitimate dates. Second, you can perform date arithmetic. For example, you can subtract one date from another to find the number of days between the two dates. Finally, you can sort the field and the dates will sort correctly.

4. **Determine whether the Memo data type is appropriate.** Does the field contain text that is variable in length and that can potentially be very lengthy? If so, the Memo data type is appropriate. If you wish to use special text effects, such as bold and italics, you can assign the field the Memo data type and change the value of the field's Text Format property from Plain Text to Rich Text. You also can collect history on the changes to a memo field by changing the value of the field's Append Only property from No to Yes. If you do so, when you right-click the field and click Show Column History on the shortcut menu, you will see a record of all changes made to the field.

5. **Determine whether the OLE Object data type is appropriate.** Does the field contain objects created by other applications that support **OLE (Object Linking and Embedding)** as a server? Object Linking and Embedding is a feature of Microsoft Windows that creates a special relationship between Microsoft Access and the application that created the object. When you edit the object, Microsoft Access returns automatically to the application that created the object.

6. **Determine whether the Attachment data type is appropriate.** Will the field contain one or more attachments that were created in other application programs? If so, the Attachment data type is appropriate. It allows you to store multiple attachments on each record. You can view and manipulate these attachments in their original application.

7. **Determine whether the Hyperlink data type is appropriate.** Will the field contain links to other Office documents or to Web pages? If so, Hyperlink is appropriate.

BTW

Input Mask Characters
When you create an input mask, Access adds several characters. These characters control the literal values that appear when you enter data. For example, the first backslash in the input mask in Figure 5-8 on page AC 305 displays the opening parenthesis. The double quotes force Access to display the closing parenthesis and a space. The second backslash forces Access to display the hyphen that separates the first and second part of the phone number.

Adding Special Fields

Having analyzed the requirements for the new fields, JSP has determined some new fields to include in the Recruiter table. They need a Phone Number field and they want to assist the users in entering the correct format for a phone number, so it will use an input mask. An **input mask** specifies how data is to be entered and how it will appear. The Bonus field will be a Yes/No field, that is, its Data type will be Yes/No. The Start Date will be a Date field and the Comment field will be a Memo field. Because no special effects are required in the Comment field, the value of the Text Format property will remain Plain Text rather than Rich Text. Because JSP does not require a history of changes to the field, the value of the Append Only property will remain No. The Contact Notes field, which must be able to contain multiple attachments for each recruiter, will be an Attachment field. The only question is the Picture field. It could be either OLE Object or Attachment.

Certainly OLE Object is an appropriate data type for a picture. On the other hand, if an Attachment field contains a picture, the field will display the picture. For other types of attachments, such as Word documents and Excel spreadsheets, however, the Attachment field displays an icon representing the attachment. JSP Recruiters has decided to use OLE Object as the data type for two reasons. First, the form contains another field that must be an Attachment field, the Contact Notes field. In Datasheet view, an Attachment field appears as a paper clip rather than the field name. Thus, if the Picture field also were an Attachment field, the form would display two paper clips, leading to potential confusion. A second potential problem with using an Attachment field for pictures occurs when you have multiple attachments to a record. Only the first attachment routinely appears in the field on either a datasheet or form. Thus, if the picture were not the first attachment, it would not appear.

To Add Fields to a Table

You add the new fields to the Recruiter table by modifying the design of the table and inserting the fields at the appropriate position in the table structure. The following steps add the Bonus, Start Date, Comment, Picture, and Contact Notes fields to the Recruiter table.

1
- If necessary, show the Navigation Pane.

- Right-click the Recruiter table to display a shortcut menu (Figure 5–2).

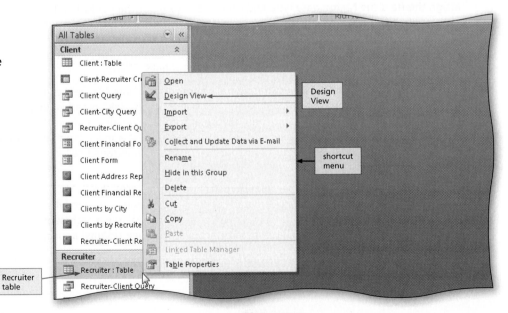

Figure 5–2

2

- Click Design View on the shortcut menu to open the Recruiter table in Design view (Figure 5–3).

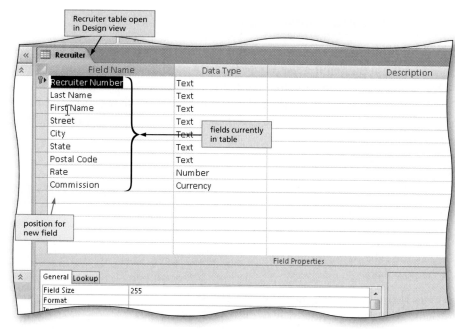

Figure 5–3

3

- Click the first open field to select the position for the first additional field.

- Type Bonus as the field name, press the TAB key, select Yes/No as the data type, and then press the TAB key twice to move to the next field.

- In a similar fashion, add a field with Start Date as the field name and Date/Time as the data type, a field with Comment as the field name and Memo as the data type, a field with Picture as the field name and OLE Object as the data type, and a field with Contact Notes as the field name and Attachment as the data type (Figure 5–4).

 Why use Date as a data type for date fields rather than Text?

If you use Date, the computer will ensure that only legitimate dates are entered in the field. In addition, you can perform appropriate arithmetic with dates. You also can sort by date.

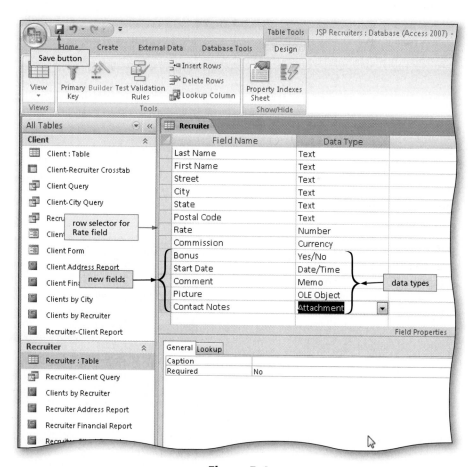

Figure 5–4

4

- Click the Save button on the Quick Access Toolbar to save your changes.

To Use the Input Mask Wizard

An **input mask** specifies how data is to be entered and how it will appear. You can enter an input mask directly or you can use the Input Mask Wizard. The wizard assists you in the creation of the input mask by allowing you to select from a list of the most frequently used input masks.

To use the Input Mask Wizard, select the Input Mask property and then select the Build button. The following steps add the Phone Number field and then specify how the telephone number is to appear by using the Input Mask Wizard.

- Click the row selector for the Rate field (shown in Figure 5–4 on the previous page), and then press the INSERT key to insert a blank row.

- Click the Field Name column for the new field.

- Type Phone Number as the field name and then press the TAB key.

- Click the Input Mask property box (Figure 5–5).

Q&A Do I need to change the data type?

No. Text is the appropriate data type for the Phone Number field.

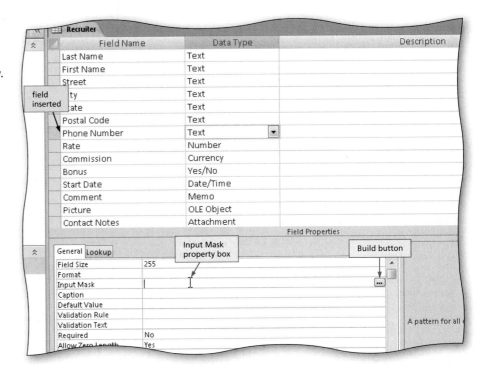

Figure 5–5

- Click the Build button.

- If a dialog box appears asking you to save the table, click the Yes button. (If a dialog box displays a message that the Input Mask Wizard is not installed, check with your instructor before proceeding with the following steps.)

- Ensure that Phone Number is selected (Figure 5–6).

🔎 **Experiment**

- Click different input masks and enter data in the Try It text box to see the effect of the input mask. When done, click the Phone Number input mask.

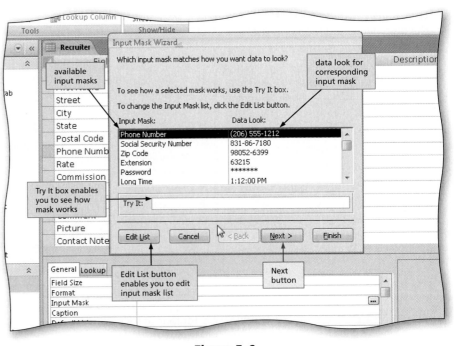

Figure 5–6

- Click the Next button to move to the next screen, where you then are given the opportunity to change the input mask.

- Because you do not need to change the mask, click the Next button a second time (Figure 5–7).

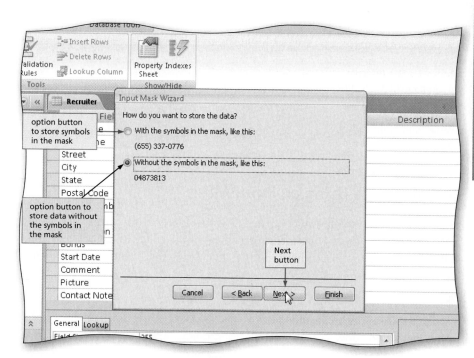

Figure 5–7

- Click the 'With the symbols in the mask, like this' option button, click the Next button, and then click the Finish button (Figure 5–8).

Q&A Why doesn't the data type change to Input Mask?

The data type of the Phone Number field is still Text. The only thing that changed is one of the field properties, the Input Mask property.

Q&A Could I have typed the value in the Input Mask property myself, rather than using the wizard?

Yes. Input masks can be complex, however, so it is usually easier and safer to use the wizard.

5

- Click the Save button on the Quick Access Toolbar to save your changes.

- Close the Recruiter table.

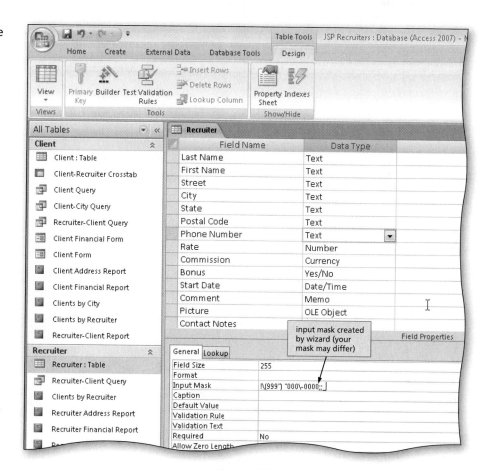

Figure 5–8

Updating the New Fields

After adding the new fields to the table, the next task is to enter data into the fields. The data type determines the manner in which this is accomplished. The following sections cover the methods for updating fields with an input mask, Yes/No fields, date fields, memo fields, OLE fields, and Attachment fields. They also show how you would enter data in Hyperlink fields.

To Enter Data Using an Input Mask

When you are entering data in a field that has an input mask, Access will insert the appropriate special characters in the proper positions. This means Access automatically will insert the parentheses around the area code, the space following the second parenthesis, and the hyphen in the Phone Number field. The following steps use the input mask to add the telephone numbers.

1
- Open the Recruiter table and hide the Navigation Pane.
- Click at the beginning of the Phone Number field on the first record to display an insertion point in the field (Figure 5–9).

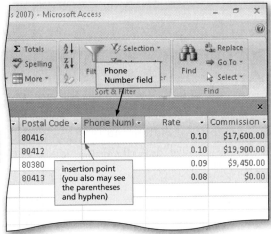

Figure 5–9

2
- Type 7195558364 as the telephone number (Figure 5–10).

Q&A Don't I need to type the parentheses, the space, and the hyphen?

No. Access will insert these automatically.

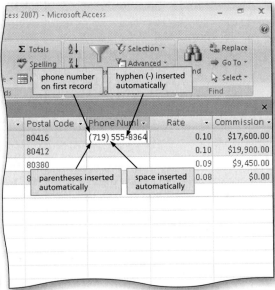

Figure 5–10

3

- Use the same technique to enter the remaining telephone numbers as shown in Figure 5–11.

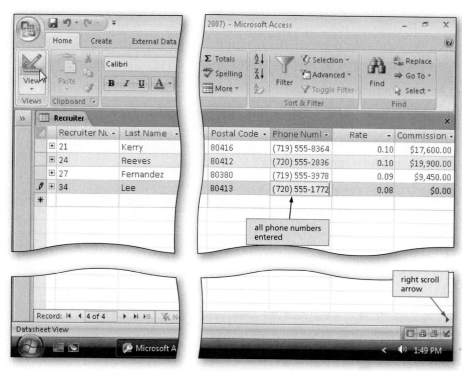

Figure 5–11

To Enter Data in Yes/No Fields

Fields that are Yes/No fields contain check boxes. To set the value to Yes, place a check mark in the check box. To set a value to No, leave the check box blank. The following steps set the value of the Bonus field, a Yes/No field, to Yes for the first two records.

1

- Repeatedly click the right scroll arrow, shown in Figure 5–11, until the new fields appear.

- Click the check box in the Bonus field on the first record to place a check mark in the box (Figure 5–12).

Q&A

What is the meaning of the check mark?

A check mark indicates the value in the Bonus field is Yes. If there is no check mark, the value is No.

2

- Click the check box in the Bonus field on the second record to place a check mark in the box.

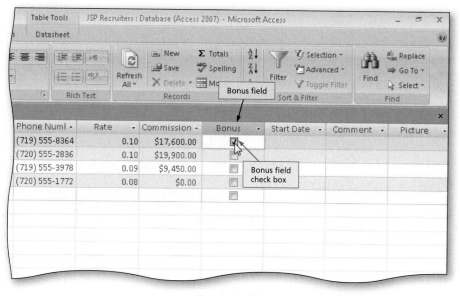

Figure 5–12

To Enter Data in Date Fields

To enter data in date fields, you simply can type the dates and include slashes (/). As an alternative, you can click the field, click the Calendar button that will appear next to the field, and then use the calendar to select the date. The following step adds the Start Dates for the recruiters without using the Calendar button.

- Click the Start Date field on the first record, type 5/22/2004 as the date on the first record, and then press the DOWN ARROW key.

- Type 6/3/2004 as the start date on the second record, and then press the DOWN ARROW key.

- Type 10/3/2006 as the start date on the third record, and then press the DOWN ARROW key.

- Type 12/3/2007 as the start date on the fourth record (Figure 5–13).

Q&A | How do I use the Calendar button?

Click the button to display a calendar. Scroll to the month and year you want and then click the desired day of the month.

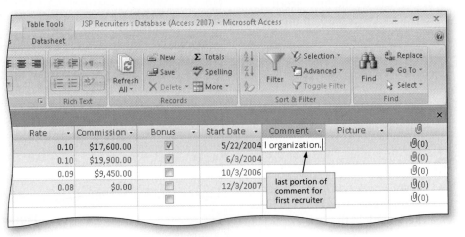

Figure 5–13

 Experiment

- Click the Calendar button and use it to assign a date. When finished, change the date to 12/3/2007.

To Enter Data in Memo Fields

To update a memo field, simply type the data in the field. With the current row and column spacing on the datasheet, only a small portion of the memo will appear. To correct this problem, you will change the spacing later to allow more room for the memo. The following steps enter each recruiter's comment.

- If necessary, click the right scroll arrow so the Comment field appears.

- Click the Comment field on the first record, and then type Master's Degree in Healthcare Management; Treasurer of a national healthcare professional organization. as the entry (Figure 5–14).

Q&A | Why don't I see the whole entry?

Currently, there is not room. You will address this problem shortly.

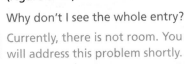

Figure 5–14

2

- Click the Comment field on the second record, and then type `Former hospital administrator; extensive human resources experience; frequent presenter at professional conferences.` as the entry.

- Click the Comment field on the third record, and then type `Former director of human resources at small hospital in Wyoming; Working on a Master's in Healthcare Management.` as the entry.

- Click the Comment field on the fourth record, and then type `Recently retired as a district school nurse; Hired to help expand recruiting services to K-12 school districts.` as the entry (Figure 5-15).

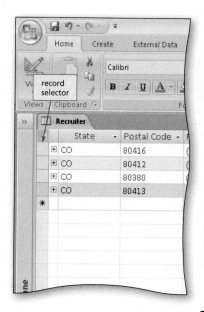

Figure 5–15

To Change the Row and Column Size

Only a small portion of the comments appears in the datasheet. To allow more of the information to appear, you can expand the size of the rows and the columns. You can change the size of a column by using the field selector. The **field selector** is the bar containing the field name. To change the size of a row, you use a record's **record selector**, which is the small box at the beginning of each record.

The following step resizes the column containing the Comment field and the rows of the table so a larger portion of the Comment field text will appear.

1

- Drag the line between the column headings for the Comment and Picture columns to the right to resize the Comment column to the approximate size shown in Figure 5–16.

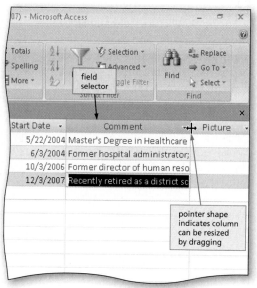

Figure 5–16

• Drag the lower edge of the record selector to approximately the position shown in Figure 5–17.

Q&A

Can rows be different sizes?

No. All rows must be the same size.

Q&A

Why does the value on the last record look different from the others?

It is the one that is currently selected.

Other Ways

1. Right-click record selector, click Row Height to change row spacing

2. Right-click field selector, click Column Width to change column size

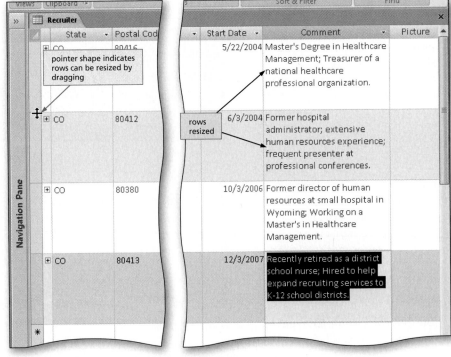

Figure 5–17

To Enter Data in OLE Fields

To insert data into an OLE field, you use the Insert Object command on the OLE field's shortcut menu. The Insert Object command presents a list of the various types of objects that can be inserted. Access then opens the corresponding application to create the object, for example, Microsoft Drawing. If the object already is created and stored in a file, as is the case in this project, you simply insert it directly from the file.

The following steps insert pictures into the Picture field. The steps assume that the pictures are located in a folder called AccessData on your USB drive. If your pictures are located elsewhere, you will need to make the appropriate changes.

1

• Ensure the Picture field appears on your screen, and then right-click the Picture field on the first record to produce a shortcut menu (Figure 5–18).

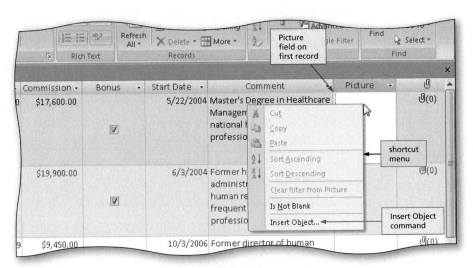

Figure 5–18

- Click Insert Object on the shortcut menu to display the Microsoft Office Access dialog box (Figure 5–19).

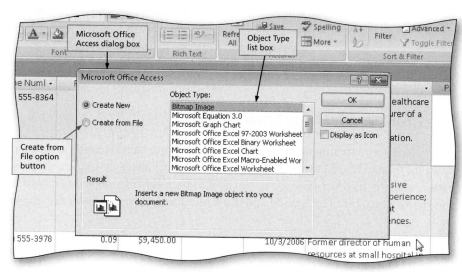

Figure 5–19

- Click the 'Create from File' option button, and then click the Browse button.

- Navigate to the AccessData folder on your USB drive in the Look in box. (If your pictures are located elsewhere, navigate to the folder where they are located instead of the AccessData folder.)

- Click Pict1 and then click the OK button to select the appropriate picture (Figure 5–20).

4

- Click the OK button.

- Insert the pictures into the second, third, and fourth records using the techniques illustrated in Steps 1 through 4. For the second record, select

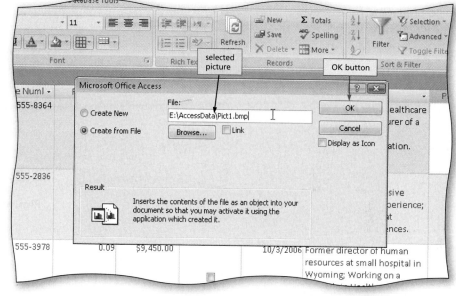

Figure 5–20

the picture named Pict2. For the third record, select the picture named Pict3. For the fourth record, select Pict4.

Bitmap Image

The entries in the Picture field all should be Bitmap images (BMP). They initially may be Pbrush, but, if so, they should change to Bitmap image after you close and reopen the table. If you see the word Package instead of Bitmap image or Pbrush, there is a problem either with the graphics filters that are installed or with the file associations for BMP files. In that case, you can use a slightly different technique to add the pictures. After right-clicking the Picture field, and clicking Insert Object, *do not* click the Create from File button. Instead, select the Paintbrush Picture object type from the list, select the Paste From command on the Edit menu of the Paintbrush window, select the desired BMP file, and then select the Exit command from the File menu to return to the datasheet. The entry in the Picture field then will be Bitmap image, as it should.

To Enter Data in Attachment Fields

To insert data into an Attachment field, you use the Manage Attachments command on the Attachment field's shortcut menu. The Manage Attachments command displays the Attachments dialog box which you can use to attach as many files as necessary to the field. The following steps attach two files to the first recruiter and one file to the fourth recruiter. The second and third recruiters currently have no attachments.

1
- Ensure the Contact Notes field, which has a paper clip in the field selector, appears on your screen, and then right-click the Contact Notes field on the first record to produce a shortcut menu (Figure 5–21).

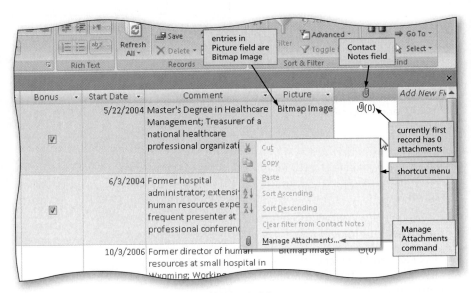

Figure 5–21

2
- Click Manage Attachments on the shortcut menu to display the Attachments dialog box (Figure 5–22).

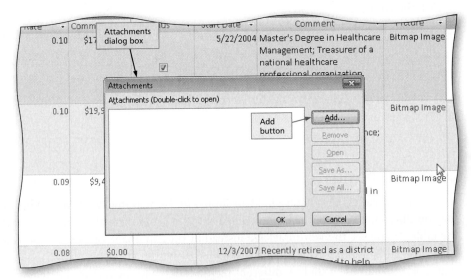

Figure 5–22

3

- Click the Add button in the Attachments dialog box to add an attachment.

- Navigate to the AccessData folder on your USB drive in the Look in box. (If your files are located elsewhere, navigate to the folder where they are located instead of the AccessData folder.)

- Click Alyssa Kerry Clients, a Word file, and then click the Open button to attach the file.

- Click the Add button.

- Click the Alyssa Kerry Potential Clients, an Excel file, and then click the Open button to attach the file (Figure 5–23).

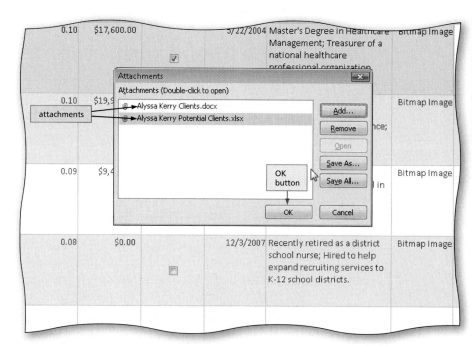

Figure 5–23

4

- Click the OK button in the Attachments dialog box to close the Attachments dialog box.

- Using the same technique, attach the Jan Lee Potential Clients file to the fourth record (Figure 5–24). (The second and third records have no attachments.)

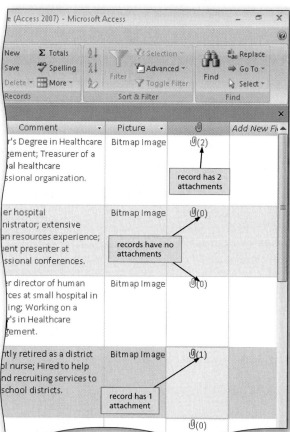

Figure 5–24

To Enter Data in Hyperlink Fields

If you had a Hyperlink field, you would insert data by using the following steps.

1. Right-click the Hyperlink field in which you wish to enter data to display a shortcut menu.
2. Click Hyperlink on the shortcut menu to display the Hyperlink submenu.
3. Click Edit Hyperlink on the Hyperlink submenu to display the Insert Hyperlink dialog box.
4. Type the desired Web address in the Address text box.
5. Click the OK button.

To Save the Properties and Close the Table

The row and column spacing are table properties. When changing any table properties, the changes apply only as long as the table is active *unless they are saved*. Once you have saved them, they will apply every time you open the table.

To undo changes to the row height, right-click the row selector, click Row Height on the shortcut menu, and then click the Standard Height check box in the Row Height dialog box. To undo changes to the column width, right-click the field selector, click Column Width on the shortcut menu, and then click the Standard Width check box in the Column Width dialog box.

The following steps first save the properties and then close the table.

1 Click the Save button on the Quick Access Toolbar to save the changes to the table properties.

2 Close the table.

Viewing Pictures and Attachments in Datasheet View

Although the pictures do not appear on the screen, you can view them within the table. To view the picture of a particular recruiter, right-click the Picture field for the recruiter. Click Bitmap Image Object on the shortcut menu, and then click Open. The picture will appear. Once you have finished viewing the picture, close the window containing the picture by clicking its Close button.

You can view the attachments in the Contact Notes field by right-clicking the field and then clicking Manage Attachments on the shortcut menu. The attachments then appear in the Attachments dialog box. To view an attachment, click the attachment and then click the Open button in the dialog box. The attachment will appear in its original application. After you have finished viewing the attachment, close the original application and close the dialog box.

Multi-Table Form Techniques

With the additional fields in place, JSP Recruiters management is ready to incorporate data from both the Recruiter and Client tables in a single form. The form will display data concerning one recruiter. It also will display data concerning the many clients to which the recruiter is assigned. Formally, the relationship between recruiters and clients is called a **one-to-many relationship** (*one* recruiter services *many* clients). The Recruiter table is the "one" table in this relationship and the Client table is the "many" table.

To include the data for the many clients of a recruiter on the form, the client data will appear in a **subform**, which is a form that is contained within another form. The form in which the subform is contained is called the main form. Thus, the **main form** will contain recruiter data, and the subform will contain client data.

Determine on which of the tables the form is to be based.

1. **Determine the main table the form is intended to view and/or update.** What is the purpose of the form? Which table is it really intended to show? That would be the main table. Is there a table that could be omitted and still have the form make sense? That would NOT be the main table.

2. **Determine how the additional table should fit into the form.** If the additional table is the "many" part of the relationship, the data should probably be in a subform or datasheet. If the additional table is the "one" part of the relationship, the data probably should appear simply as fields on the form.

Plan Ahead

Determine the fields from each table to be included in the form.

1. **Determine the fields from the main table that should be included on the form.** What fields do users want on the form? Is there a particular order for the fields that would be most useful?

2. **Determine the fields from the additional table that should be included on the form.** What fields from the additional table would be helpful in updating or viewing the fields from the main table? Should users be able to change these fields via this form? (Often the answer will be no.)

Plan Ahead

To Create a Form in Design View

You can create a form in Design view, which gives you the most flexibility in laying out the form. You will be presented with a blank design on which you place objects. The following steps create a form in Design view.

1

- Show the Navigation Pane and be sure the Recruiter table is selected.

- Click Create on the Ribbon to display the Create tab (Figure 5–25).

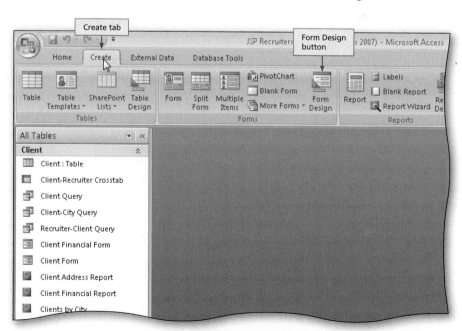

Figure 5–25

- Click Form Design on the Create tab to create a new form in Design view.

- Hide the Navigation Pane.

- If a field list does not appear, click the Add Existing Fields button on the Design tab to display a field list (Figure 5–26). (Your list may show all fields in the Client table.)

- If the fields in the Recruiter table do not appear, click the expand indicator (+) in front of the Recruiter table to display the fields.

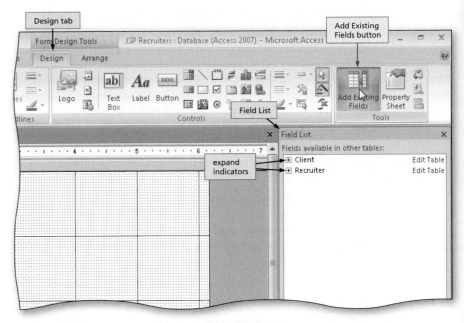

Figure 5–26

To Add a Control for a Field to the Form Design

To place a control for a field on a form, drag the field from the field list to the desired position. When you drag the field, you also drag the attached label for the field. The following steps place the Recruiter Number field on the form.

- Point to the Recruiter Number field in the field list for the Recruiter table, press the left mouse button, and then drag the field to the approximate position shown in Figure 5–27.

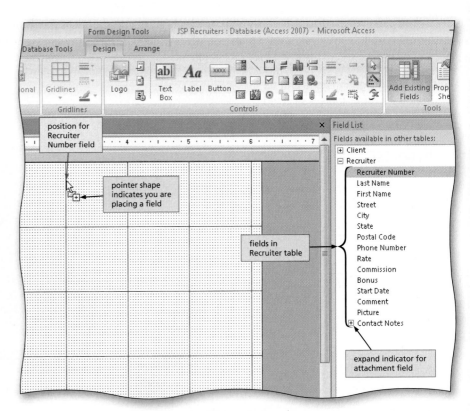

Figure 5–27

2

● Release the left mouse button to place a control for the field (Figure 5–28).

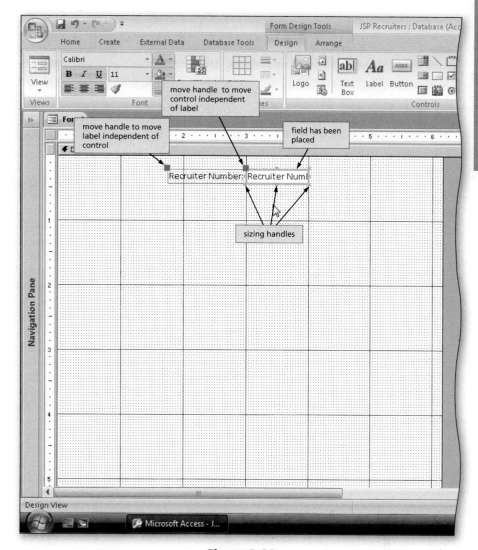

Figure 5–28

To Save the Form

Before continuing with the form creation, it is a good idea to save the form. The following steps save the form and assign it the name Recruiter Master Form.

1 Click the Save button on the Quick Access Toolbar.

2 Type Recruiter Master Form as the name of the form.

3 Click the OK button to save the form.

To Add Controls for Additional Fields

The following step places controls for the First Name, Last Name, Phone Number, Rate, Commission, Start Date, and Bonus fields on the form by dragging the fields from the field list.

1

- Drag the First Name, Last Name, Phone Number, Rate, Commission, Start Date, and Bonus fields to the approximate positions shown in Figure 5–29.

Q&A Do I have to align them precisely?

You can, but you do not need to. In the next steps, you will instruct Access to align the fields properly.

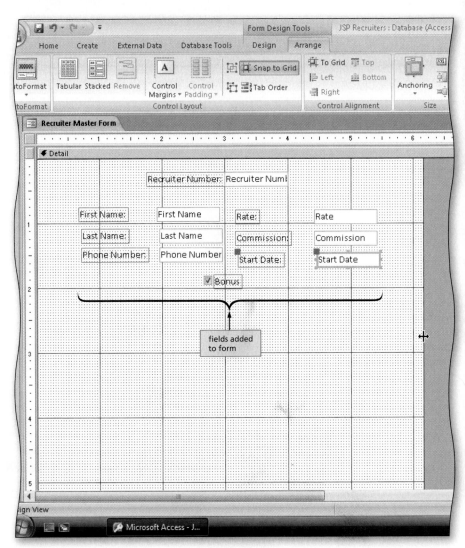

Figure 5–29

To Align Controls

Often, you will want form controls to be aligned in some fashion. For example, the controls may be aligned so their right edges are even with each other. In another case, controls may be aligned so their top edges are even. While you can use the grid that appears in Design view to align controls, it is often easier to use alignment buttons. To ensure that a collection of controls is aligned properly with each other, select all of the affected controls, and then use the appropriate alignment button on the Arrange tab.

There are two ways to select multiple controls. One way is to use a ruler. If you click a position on the horizontal ruler, you will select all the controls for which a portion of the control is under that position on the ruler. Similarly, if you click a position on the vertical ruler, you will select all the controls for which a portion of the control is to the right of that position on the ruler.

The second way to select multiple controls is to select the first control by clicking it. Then, select all the other controls by holding down the SHIFT key while clicking the control.

The following steps select the First Name, Last Name, and Phone Number controls and then align them left.

1

- Click the First Name control (the white space, not the label) to select the control.

- Hold the SHIFT key down and click the Last Name control to select the Last Name control as well.

- Hold the SHIFT key down and click the Phone Number control to select the Phone Number control as well (Figure 5–30).

Q&A

I selected the wrong collection of fields. How can I start over?

Click anywhere outside the controls to deselect the controls, then begin the process again, making sure you do not hold the SHIFT key down when you select the first field.

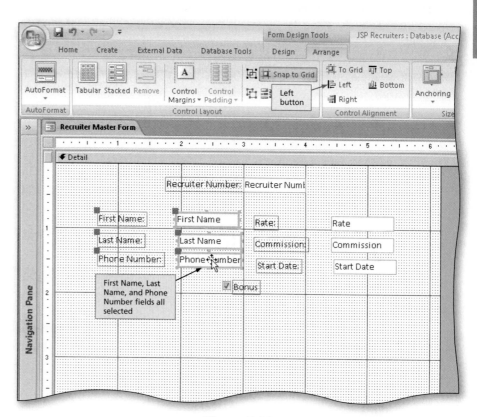

Figure 5–30

2

- Click Arrange on the Ribbon to display the Arrange tab.

- Click the Left button on the Arrange tab to align the controls on the left.

- Release the SHIFT key.

- Using the same technique, align the Rate, Commission, and Start Date fields on the left.

- Click outside any of the selected controls to deselect the controls.

- Fine-tune your layout to match the one in Figure 5–31 by clicking and dragging controls individually.

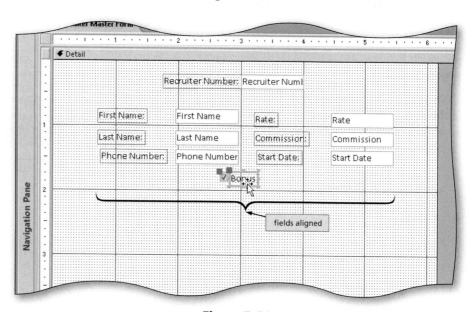

Figure 5–31

To Move the Field List

Dragging from the field list onto the form is a problem if the field list covers the portion of the form where you wish to place the field. If that is the case, you can move the field list to a different location. The following step moves the field list in preparation for placing controls in the area it currently occupies.

- Move the field list to the approximate position shown in Figure 5–32 by dragging its title bar.

Q&A

My field list changed size when I moved it. How can I return it to its original size?

Point to the border of the field list so that the mouse pointer changes to a double-headed arrow. You then can drag to adjust the size.

Q&A

Can I make the field list smaller so I can see more of the screen?

Yes, you can adjust the size to whatever is most comfortable for you.

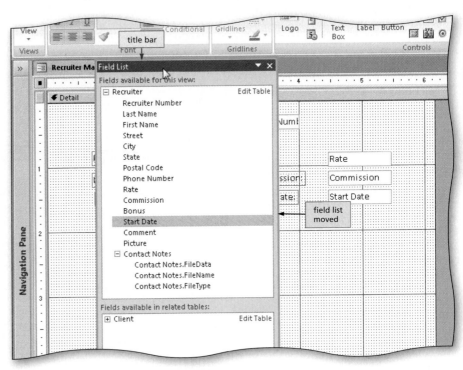

Figure 5–32

To Add Controls for the Remaining Fields

The following steps place controls for the Comment, Picture, and Contact Notes fields and also move their attached labels to the desired position.

- Drag the control for the Comment field from the field list to the approximate position shown in Figure 5–33.

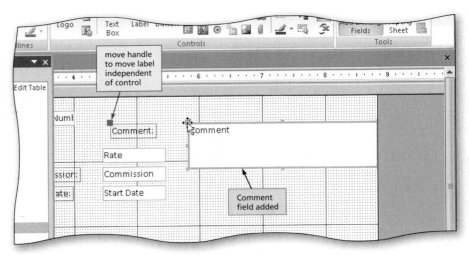

Figure 5–33

2

• Move the label for the Comment field to the position shown in Figure 5–34 by dragging its move handle.

Q&A

I started to move the label and the control moved along with it. What did I do wrong?

You were not pointing at the handle to move the label independent of the control. Make sure you are pointing to the little box in the upper-left corner of the label.

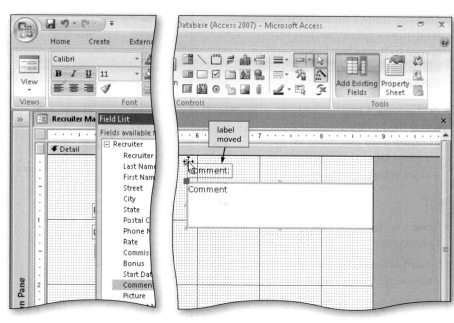

Figure 5–34

3

• Using the same technique, move the control for the Picture field to the approximate position shown in Figure 5–35 and move its label to the position shown in the figure.

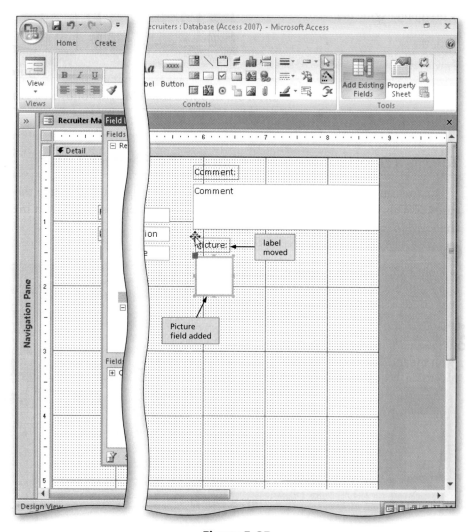

Figure 5–35

5

- Click the Next button.

- Type Clients of Recruiter as the name of the subform (Figure 5–44).

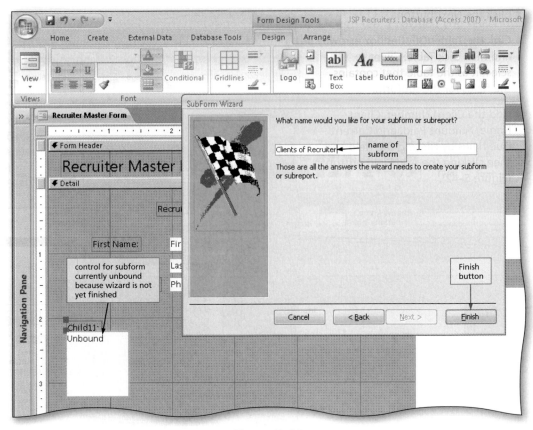

Figure 5–44

6

- Click the Finish button to place the subform (Figure 5–45).

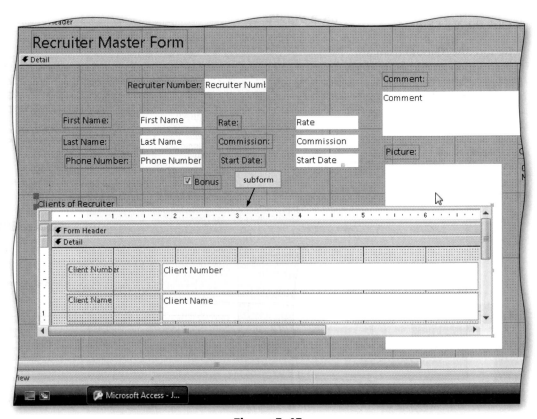

Figure 5–45

7
- Click the subform to select it.
- Move the subform to the approximate position shown in Figure 5–46 by dragging the subform and then resize it to the approximate size shown in the figure by dragging the appropriate sizing handles.

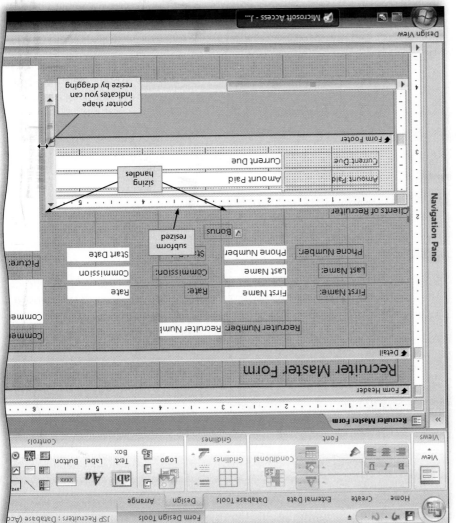

Recruiter Master Form

Figure 5–46

To Close and Save a Form

The following steps first save and then close the Recruiter Master Form.

1 Click the Save button on the Quick Access Toolbar to save the form.

2 Close the form by clicking the Close 'Recruiter Master Form' button.

To Modify a Subform

The next task is to resize the columns in the subform, which appears on the form in Datasheet view. The subform is a separate object in the database. The following steps open the subform and then resize the columns.

1
- Show the Navigation Pane.
- Right-click the Clients of Recruiter form to produce a shortcut menu.
- Click Open on the shortcut menu to open the form.
- Resize the columns to best fit the data by double-clicking the right boundaries of the field selectors (Figure 5–47).

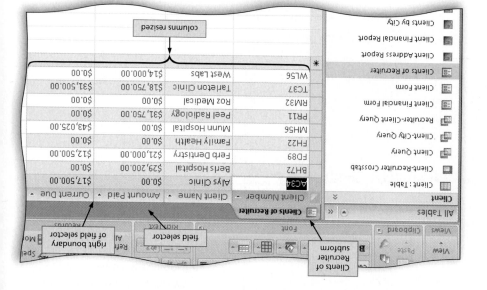

Figure 5–47

2
- Save your changes and then close the subform.
- Open the Recruiter Master Form in Design view and then hide the Navigation Pane.
- Adjust the approximate size and position of the subform to the one shown in Figure 5–48.

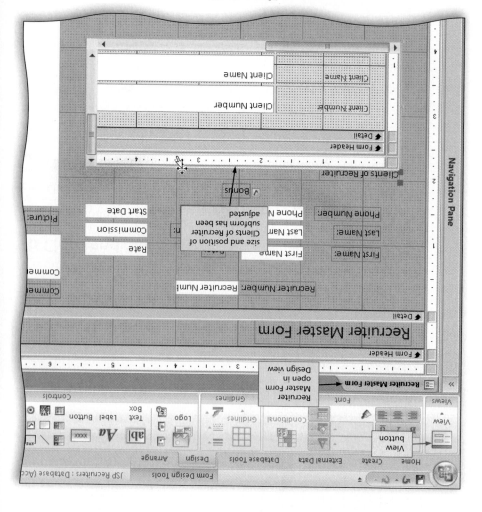

Figure 5–48

3

- Click the View button to view the form in Form view (Figure 5–49).

Q&A

Could I have clicked the View button arrow and then clicked Form View?

Yes. You always can use the arrow. If the icon for the view you want appears on the face of the View button, however, you also can just click the button.

Q&A

Could I have clicked the Form View button in the lower-right corner of the screen to move to Form view?

Yes. Those buttons are always an option. Use whichever approach you find most convenient.

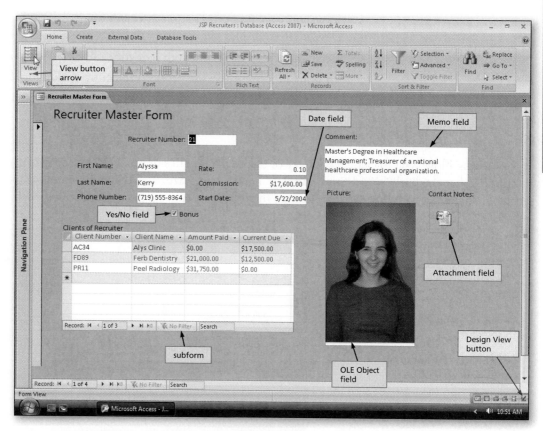

Figure 5–49

Size Mode

The portion of a picture that appears as well as the way it appears is determined by the **size mode**. The possible size modes are as follows:

1. **Clip** — Displays only the portion of the picture that will fit in the space allocated to it.
2. **Stretch** — Expands or shrinks the picture to fit the precise space allocated on the screen. For photographs, usually this is not a good choice, because fitting a photograph to the allocated space can distort the image, giving it a stretched appearance.
3. **Zoom** — Does the best job of fitting the picture to the allocated space without changing the look of the picture. The entire picture will appear and be proportioned correctly. Some white space may be visible around the picture, however.

Currently, the size mode should be Zoom, which is appropriate. If it were not and you wanted to change it, you would use the steps on the next page.

To Change the Size Mode

1. Click the control containing the picture, and then click the Property Sheet button on the Design tab to display the control's property sheet.
2. Click the Size Mode property, and then click the Size Mode property box arrow.
3. Click Zoom and then close the property sheet by clicking its Close button.

To Change Special Effects and Colors

Access allows you to change a variety of the characteristics of the labels in the form. You can change the border style and color, the background color, the font, and the font size. You also can give the label special effects, such as raised or sunken. The following steps change the font color and special effects of the labels.

- Click the View button arrow and then click Design View on the View button menu to return to Design view.

- Click the Recruiter Number label to select it.

- Select each of the remaining labels by holding down the SHIFT key while clicking the label. Be sure to include the label for the subform.

- Release the SHIFT key (Figure 5–50).

Q&A

Does the order in which I select the labels make a difference?

No. The only thing that is important is that they are all selected when you are done.

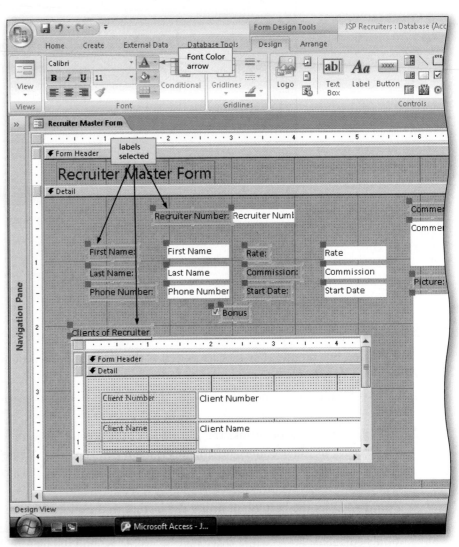

Figure 5–50

2

- Click the Font Color arrow on the Design tab to display a color palette (Figure 5–51).

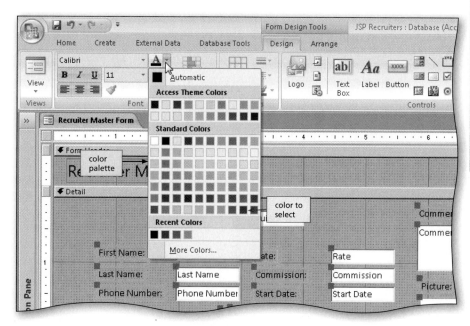

Figure 5–51

3

- Click the blue color in the second position from the right in the bottom row of Standard Colors to change the font color for the labels.

- Click the Property Sheet button on the Design tab to produce the property sheet for the selected labels.

- Change the Border Style to Solid and the Border Width to 3.

- Click the Special Effect property box to display the Special Effect property box arrow (Figure 5–52).

Q&A The property sheet is too small to display the property box arrow. Can I change the size of the property sheet?

Yes. Point to the border of the property sheet so that the mouse pointer changes to a double-headed arrow. You then can drag to adjust the size.

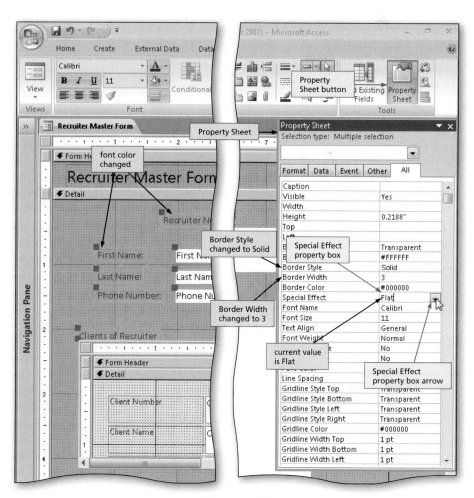

Figure 5–52

• Click the Special Effect property box arrow and then select Etched as the special effect.

Experiment

• Try all the other special effects. In each case, view the form to see the special effect you selected and then return to Design view. When done, select Etched (Figure 5–53).

• Close the property sheet.

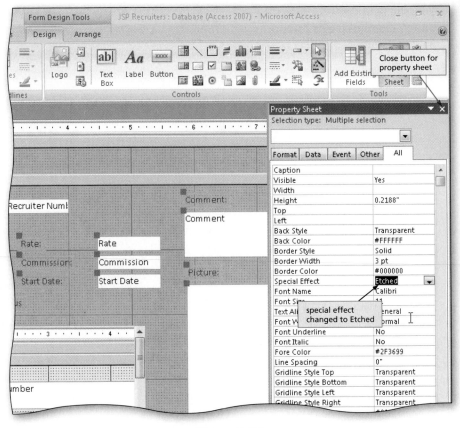

Figure 5–53

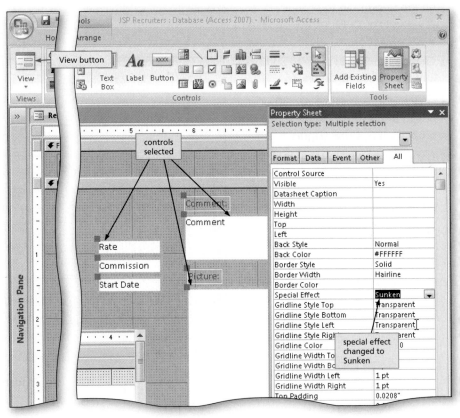

5

• Click the Recruiter Number control (the white space, not the label) to select it.

• Select each of the remaining controls by holding down the SHIFT key while clicking the control. Do not include the subform.

• Click the Property Sheet button on the Design tab to produce the property sheet for the selected controls.

• Select Sunken for the special effect (Figure 5–54).

Figure 5–54

6

- Close the property sheet by clicking its Close button.

- Click the View button to view the form in Form view (Figure 5–55).

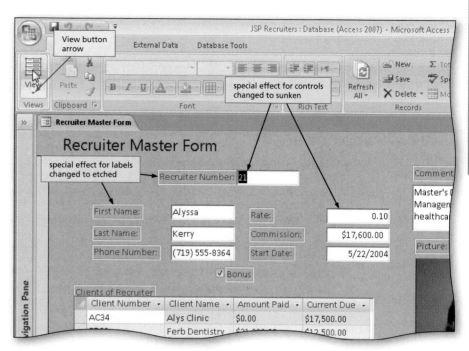

Figure 5–55

To Enhance a Form Title

You can enhance the title in a variety of ways. These include moving it, resizing it, changing the font size, changing the alignment, and assigning it a special effect. The following steps enhance the form title.

1

- Click the View button arrow and then click Design View on the View button menu to return to Design view.

- Resize the Form Header section by dragging down the lower boundary of the section to the approximate position shown in Figure 5–56.

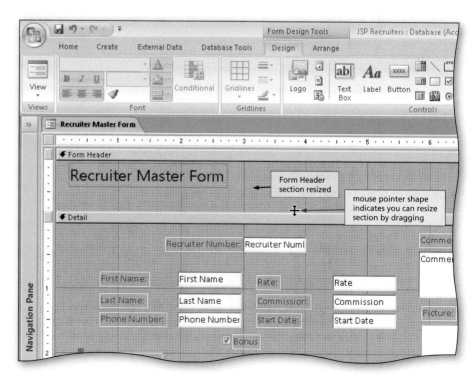

Figure 5–56

- Click the control containing the form title to select the control.

- Drag the control to the approximate position shown in Figure 5–57.

- Drag the lower-right sizing handle to resize the control to the approximate size shown in the figure.

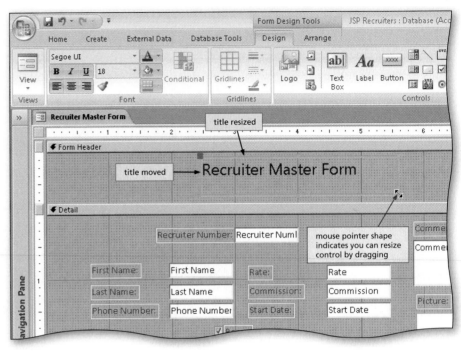

Figure 5–57

- Click the Property Sheet button on the Design tab to display the control's property sheet.

- Click the Special Effect property box, click the Special Effect property box arrow, and then click Raised to change the Special Effect property value to Raised.

- In a similar fashion, change the Font Size property value to 20, the Text Align property value to Distribute, and the Font Weight property value to Semi-bold (Figure 5–58).

- Close the property sheet by clicking its Close button.

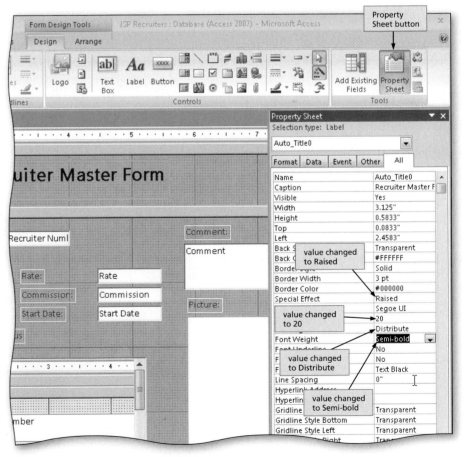

Figure 5–58

To Change a Tab Stop

If users repeatedly press the TAB key to move through the controls on the form, they should bypass the Bonus control, the Picture control, the Contact Notes control, and the subform. In order to force this to happen, the following steps change the value of the Tab Stop property for the control from Yes to No.

- Click the Bonus control to select it.

- Select the Picture control, the Contact Notes control, and the subform by holding down the SHIFT key while clicking each control (Figure 5–59).

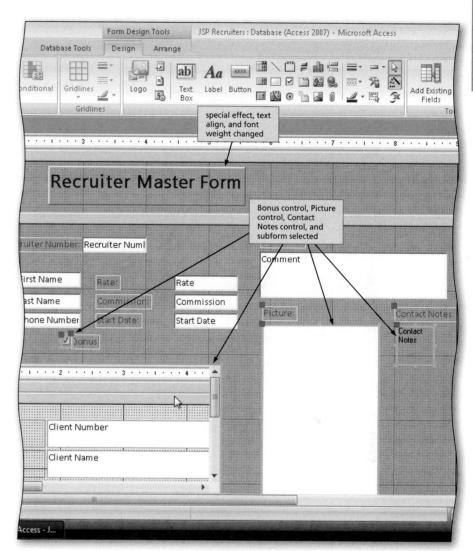

Figure 5–59

- Click the Property Sheet button on the Design tab to display the property sheet. Make sure the All tab is selected, click the down scroll arrow until the Tab Stop property appears, click the Tab Stop property, click the Tab Stop property box arrow and then click No.

- Close the property sheet.

Q&A What is the effect of this change?

When anyone tabs through the controls, they will bypass the Bonus control, the Picture control, the Contact Notes control, and the subform.

Q&A I don't see the Tab Stop property. What did I do wrong?

You clicked the labels for the controls, not the controls.

- Click the Save button on the Quick Access Toolbar to save your changes.

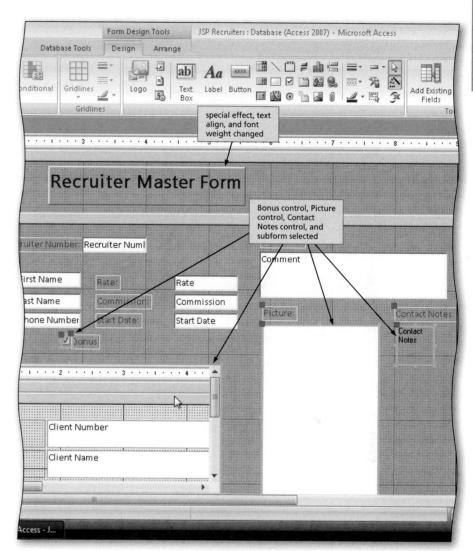

- Click the View button to view the form in Form view. It looks like the one in Figure 5–1 on page AC 299.

- Close the form.

Changing the Tab Order

Users repeatedly can press the TAB key to move through the fields on a form. Access determines the order in which the fields are encountered in this process. If you prefer a different order, you can change the order by clicking the Tab Order button on the Arrange tab. You then can use the Tab Order dialog box (Figure 5–60) to change the order by dragging rows to their desired position as indicated in the dialog box.

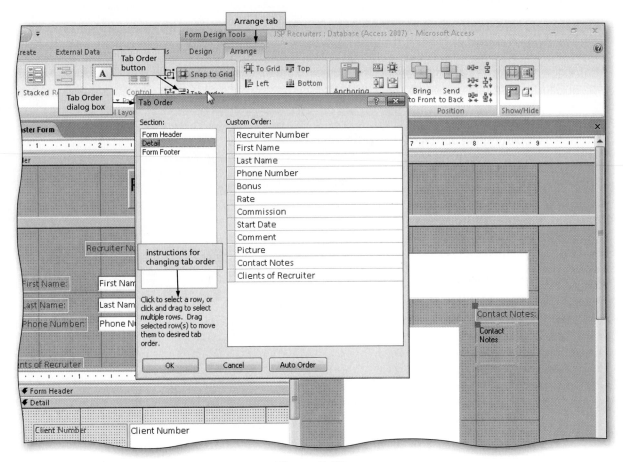

Figure 5–60

TO ANCHOR CONTROLS

The Anchoring button on the Arrange tab allows you to tie (anchor) a control to a section or to another control so that it maintains the same distance between the control and the anchor position. To see the effect of anchoring, objects must appear in overlapping windows. To anchor controls you would use the following steps.

1. Select the control or controls that you want to anchor to the form.

2. Use the Anchor button arrow to display the different anchoring positions and select the desired position.

3. Change to overlapping windows. (Click the Office button, click the Access Options button, click Current Database in the left pane, click the Overlapping Windows option button, and then click the OK button. You will need to close and reopen the database for the change to take effect.)

4. To see the effect of anchoring, open your form and then resize the form by dragging the border of the form. The anchored objects should move appropriately.

5. Change back to tabbed documents. (Follow the instructions in Step 3, replacing the Overlapping Windows with Tabbed Documents.)

To Use the Form

To use a form to view data, right-click the form in the Navigation Pane, and then click Open on the shortcut menu that appears. You then can use the navigation buttons at the bottom of the screen to move among recruiters. You can use the navigation buttons in the subform to move among the clients of the recruiter currently shown on the screen. The following steps use the form to display desired data.

- Show the Navigation Pane if it is currently hidden.

- Right-click Recruiter Master Form and then click Open on the shortcut menu.

- Hide the Navigation Pane.

- Right-click the Contact Notes field to display a shortcut menu (Figure 5–61).

2

- Click the Manage Attachments command on the shortcut menu to display the Attachments dialog box (Figure 5–62).

Q&A

How do I use this dialog box?

Select an attachment and click the Open button to view the attachment. Click the Add button to add a new attachment or the Remove button to remove the selected attachment. You can save the selected attachment as a file in whatever location you specify by clicking the Save button. You can save all attachments at once by clicking the Save All button.

Experiment

- Open each attachment to see how it looks in its original application. When finished, close the original application.

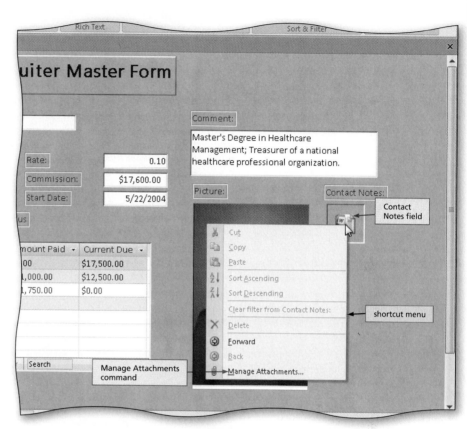

Figure 5–61

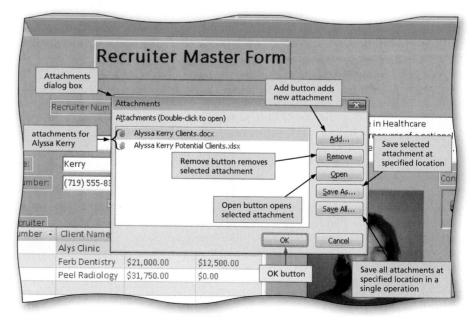

Figure 5–62

3

- Click the OK button to close the Attachments dialog box.

- Click the form's Next record button to display the data for recruiter 24 (Figure 5–63).

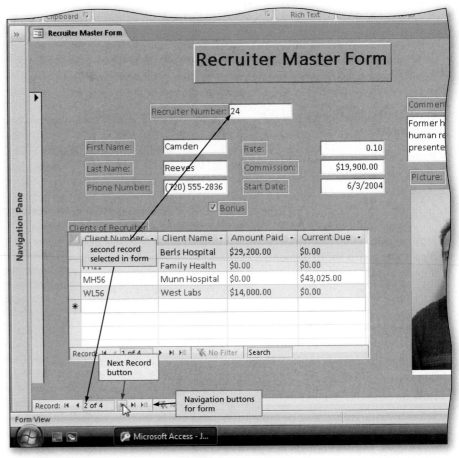

Figure 5–63

4

- Click the subform's Next record button twice to highlight the third client of recruiter 24 (Figure 5–64).

5

- Close the form.

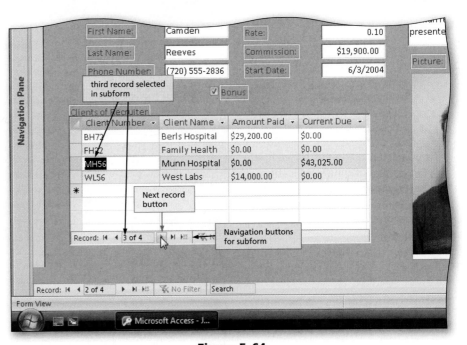

Figure 5–64

Navigation in the Form

The previous steps illustrated the way you work with a main form and subform. Clicking the navigation buttons for the main form moves to a different recruiter. Clicking the navigation buttons for the subform moves to a different client of the recruiter who appears in the main form. The following are other actions you can take within the form.

1. To move from the last field in the main form to the first field in the subform, press the TAB key. To move back to the last field in the main form, press CTRL+SHIFT+TAB.

2. To move from the last field in the subform to the first field in the next record's main form, press CTRL+TAB.

3. To switch from the main form to the subform using the mouse, click anywhere in the subform. To switch back to the main form, click any control in the main form. Clicking the background of the main form will not cause the switch to occur.

To View Object Dependencies

In Access, you can view information on dependencies between database objects. Viewing a list of objects that use a specific object helps in the maintenance of a database and avoids errors when changes are made to the objects involved in the dependency. For example, many items depend on the Recruiter table. By clicking the Object Dependencies button, you can see what items depend on the object. You also can see the items on which the object depends. The following steps view the objects that depend on the Recruiter table.

- Display the Navigation Pane and click the Recruiter table.

- Click Database Tools on the Ribbon to display the Database Tools tab.

- Click the Object Dependencies button on the Database Tools tab to display the Object Dependencies Pane.

- Click the 'Objects that depend on me' option button to select it (Figure 5–65).

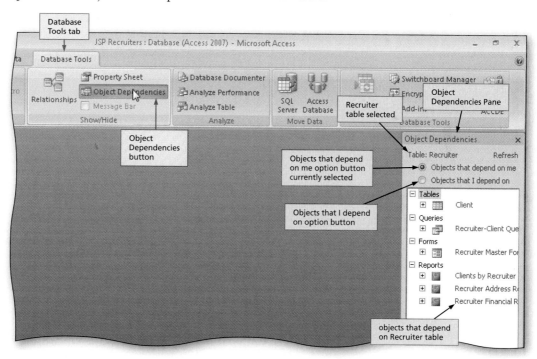

Figure 5–65

Experiment

- Click the 'Objects that I depend on' option button to see the objects on which the Recruiter table depends. Then try both options for other objects in the database. Try clicking the plus sign and the minus sign that appear in front of various objects.

- Close the Object Dependencies Pane by clicking its Close button.

BTW

Searching Memo Fields
When you search memo fields consider alternative spellings. For example, healthcare also can be written as health care.

BTW

Date Fields in Queries
To test for the current date in a query, type Date() in the Criteria row of the appropriate column. Typing <Date() in the Criteria row for Start Date, for example, finds those recruiters who started anytime before the date on which you run the query.

Date, Memo, and Yes/No Fields in Queries

By specifying recruiter start dates using date fields, JSP Recruiters can run queries to find recruiters hired before or after a certain date. Other uses of the date field might include calculating an employee's length of service by subtracting the start date from the current date. Similarly, management can search for recruiters with specific qualifications by adding memos and Yes/No fields.

To use date fields in queries, you simply type the dates including the slashes. To search for records with a specific date, you must type the date. You also can use comparison operators. To find all the recruiters whose start date is prior to January 1, 2005, for example, you type <1/1/2005 as the criterion.

You also can use memo fields in queries. Typically, you will want to find all the records on which the memo field contains a specific word or phrase. To do so, you use wildcards. For example, to find all the recruiters who have the words, Healthcare Management, somewhere in the Comment field, you type *Healthcare Management* as the criterion.

To use Yes/No fields in queries, type the word Yes or the word No as the criterion. You can, if you wish, type True rather than Yes or False rather than No. The following steps create and run queries that use Date, Memo, and Yes/No fields.

To Use Date, Memo, and Yes/No Fields in a Query

The following steps use Date, Memo, and Yes/No fields in queries.

1

- Create a query for the Recruiter table and include the Recruiter Number, Last Name, First Name, Start Date, Comment, and Bonus fields in the query (Figure 5–66).

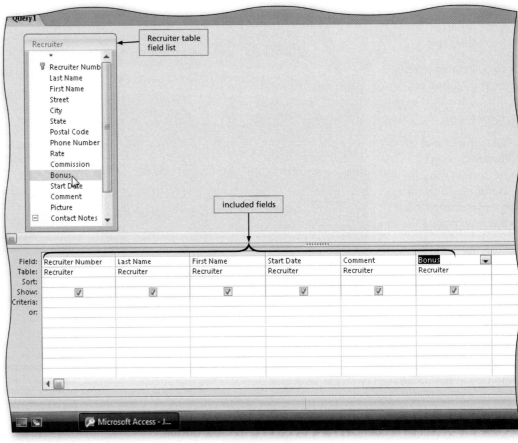

Figure 5–66

2

- Click the Criteria row under the Comment field and then type *Healthcare Management* as the criterion.

- Click the Criteria row under the Start Date field, and then type <1/1/2005 as the criterion (Figure 5–67).

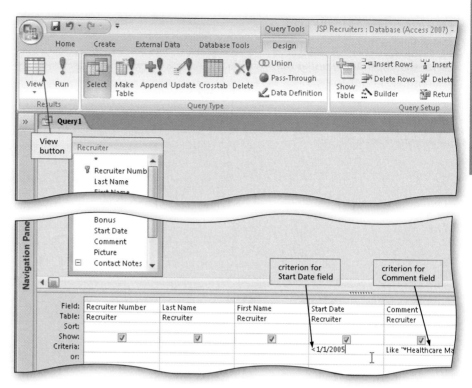

Figure 5–67

3

- Click the View button to view the results (Figure 5–68).

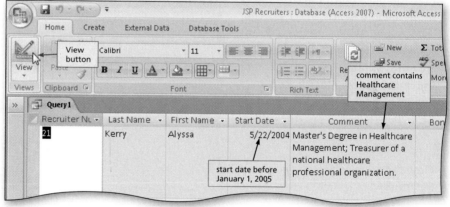

Figure 5–68

4

- Click the View button to return to Design view (Figure 5–69).

Why does the date have number signs (#) around it?

This is the date format in Access. You usually do not have to enter the number signs, because Access will insert them automatically.

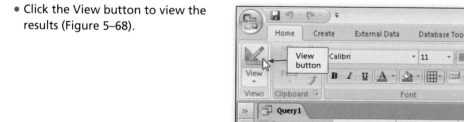

Figure 5–69

5

● Erase the criterion in the Start Date field.

● Click the Criteria row under the Bonus field and then type `Yes` as the criterion (Figure 5–70).

Q&A

Do I have to type Yes?

You also could type True.

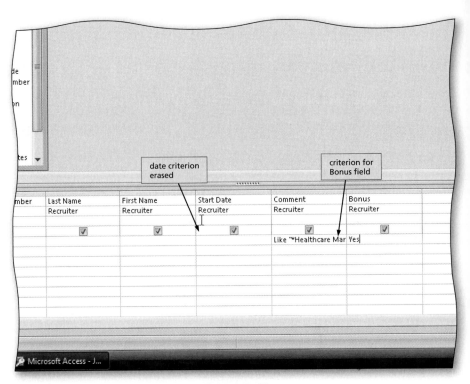

Figure 5–70

6

● Click the View button to view the results (Figure 5–71).

 **Experiment**

● Try other combinations of values in the Start Date field, the Comment field, and/or the Bonus field. In each case, view the results.

7

● Close the query without saving the results.

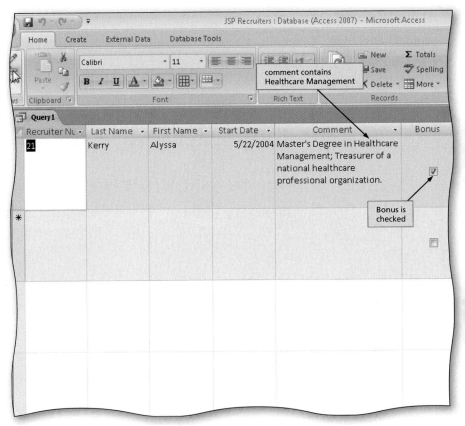

Figure 5–71

Datasheets in Forms

In forms created in Layout view, subforms are not available, but you can achieve similar functionality to subforms by including datasheets. Like subforms, the datasheets contain data for the "many" table in the relationship.

Creating a Simple Form with a Datasheet

If you create a form with the Form button for a table that is the "one" table in a one-to-many relationship, Access automatically includes the "many" table in a datasheet. If you create a form for the Recruiter table, for example, Access will include the Client table in a datasheet, as in Figure 5–72. The clients in the datasheet will be the clients of the recruiter currently on the screen, in this case Alyssa Kerry.

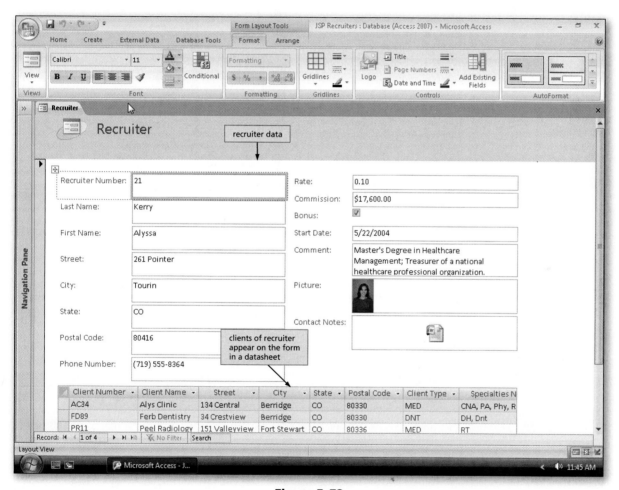

Figure 5–72

To Create a Simple Form with a Datasheet

To create a simple form with a datasheet, you would use the following steps.

1. Select the table that is the "one" part of a one-to-many relationship in the Navigation Pane.

2. Click Create on the Ribbon to display the Create tab.

3. Click the Form button on the Create tab to create the form.

Creating a Form with a Datasheet in Layout View

You can create a form with a datasheet in Layout view. To do so, you would first use the field list to add any fields from the "one" table as shown in Figure 5–73, in which fields from the Recruiter table have been added to the form.

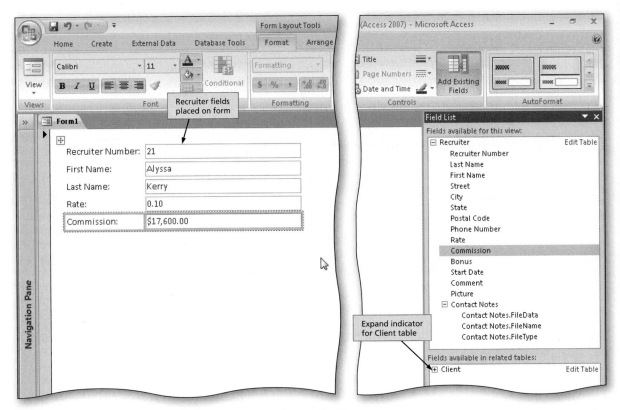

Figure 5–73

Next you would use the field list to add a single field from the "many" table as shown in Figure 5–74, in which the Client Number field has been added. Access automatically will create a datasheet containing this field.

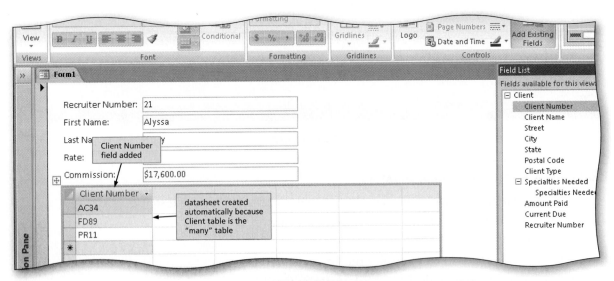

Figure 5–74

Finally, you would click the datasheet to select it and then use the field list to add the other fields from the "many" table that you wish to be included in the form, as shown in Figure 5–75.

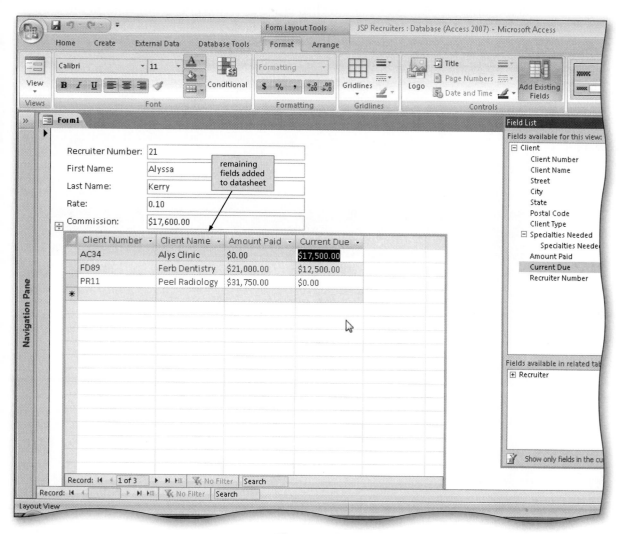

Figure 5–75

TO CREATE A FORM WITH A DATASHEET IN LAYOUT VIEW

Specifically, to create a form with a datasheet in Layout view, you would use the following steps.

1. Click Create on the Ribbon to display the Create tab.

2. Click the Blank Form button on the Create tab to create a form in Layout view.

3. If a field list does not appear, click the Add Existing Fields button on the Format tab to display a field list.

4. Click Show All Tables to display the available tables.

5. Click the Expand indicator (the plus sign) for the "one" table to display the fields in the table and then drag the fields to the desired positions.

6. Click the Expand indicator for the "many" table and drag the first field for the datasheet onto the form to create the datasheet.

7. Click the datasheet to select it and then drag the remaining fields for the datasheet from the field list to the desired locations in the datasheet.

Creating a Multi-Table Form Based on the "Many" Table

All the forms discussed so far in this chapter were based on the "one" table, in this case, the Recruiter table. The records from the "one" table were included in a subform. You also can create a multi-table form based on the "many" table, in this case, the Client table. Such a form is shown in Figure 5–76.

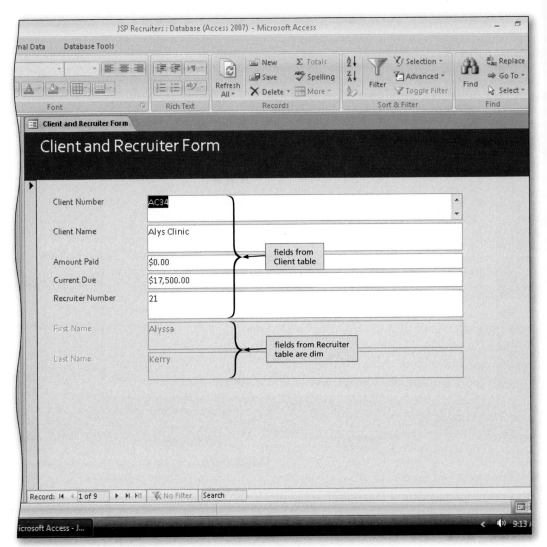

Figure 5–76

In this form, the Client Number, Client Name, Amount Paid, Current Due, and Recruiter Number fields are in the Client table. The First Name and Last Name fields are found in the Recruiter table and help to identify the recruiter whose number appears in the Recruiter Number field. To prevent the user from inadvertently changing the name of a recruiter, those fields have been disabled and appear dimmed. Disabling the fields from the "one" table in a form based on the "many" table is common practice.

TO CREATE A MULTI-TABLE FORM BASED ON THE "MANY" TABLE

To create a multi-table form based on the "many" table, you would use the following steps.

1. Use the Form Wizard to create a form in which you first select fields from the "many" table and then select fields from the "one" table. Be sure the form is organized by the "many" table. Alternatively, you can create the form in Layout view by first placing the fields from the "many" table and then the fields from the "one" table.

2. In Layout view, select each of the fields from the "one" table, click the Property Sheet button on the Design tab to display the property sheet, and then change the value for the Enabled property from Yes to No. This will prevent users from inadvertently updating fields in the "one" table.

BTW | **Quick Reference**
For a table that lists how to complete the tasks covered in this book using the mouse, Ribbon, shortcut menu, and keyboard, see the Quick Reference Summary at the back of this book, or visit the Access 2007 Quick Reference Web page (scsite.com/ac2007/qr).

To Quit Access

You saved all your changes and are ready to quit Access. The following step quits Access.

1 Click the Close button on the right side of the Access title bar to quit Access.

Chapter Summary

In this chapter you have learned to use Yes/No, Date, Memo, OLE Object, and Attachment data types; create and use an input mask; create a form and add a subform; enhance the look of the controls on a form; use a form with a subform; create queries involving Yes/No, Date, and Memo fields; view object dependencies; and create forms containing datasheets in Layout view. The following list includes all the new Access skills you have learned in this chapter.

1. Add Fields to a Table (AC 302)
2. Use the Input Mask Wizard (AC 304)
3. Enter Data Using an Input Mask (AC 306)
4. Enter Data in Yes/No Fields (AC 307)
5. Enter Data in Date Fields (AC 308)
6. Enter Data in Memo Fields (AC 308)
7. Change the Row and Column Size (AC 309)
8. Enter Data in OLE Fields (AC 310)
9. Enter Data in Attachment Fields (AC 312)
10. Enter Data in Hyperlink Fields (AC 314)
11. Save the Properties and Close the Table (AC 314)
12. Create a Form in Design View (AC 315)
13. Add a Control for a Field to the Form Design (AC 316)
14. Add Controls for Additional Fields (AC 318)
15. Align Controls (AC 318)
16. Move the Field List (AC 320)
17. Add Control for the Remaining Fields (AC 320)
18. Use a Shortcut Menu to Change the Fill/Back Color (AC 322)
19. Add a Title (AC 323)
20. Place a Subform (AC 324)
21. Modify a Subform (AC 328)
22. Change the Size Mode (AC 330)
23. Change Special Effects and Colors (AC 330)
24. Enhance a Form Title (AC 333)
25. Change a Tab Stop (AC 335)
26. Use the Form (AC 337)
27. View Object Dependencies (AC 339)
28. Use Date, Memo, and Yes/No Fields in a Query (AC 340)
29. Create a Simple Form with a Datasheet (AC 343)
30. Create a Form with a Datasheet in Layout View (AC 345)
31. Create a Multi-Table Form Based on the "Many" Table (AC 347)

 If you have a SAM user profile, you may have access to hands-on instruction, practice, and assessment. Log in to your SAM account (http://sam2007.course.com) to launch any assigned training activities or exams that relate to the skills covered in this chapter.

Learn It Online

Test your knowledge of chapter content and key terms.

Instructions: To complete the Learn It Online exercises, start your browser, click the Address bar, and then enter the Web address scsite.com/ac2007/learn. When the Access 2007 Learn It Online page is displayed, click the link for the exercise you want to complete and then read the instructions.

Chapter Reinforcement TF, MC, and SA
A series of true/false, multiple choice, and short answer questions that test your knowledge of the chapter content.

Flash Cards
An interactive learning environment where you identify chapter key terms associated with displayed definitions.

Practice Test
A series of multiple choice questions that test your knowledge of chapter content and key terms.

Who Wants To Be a Computer Genius?
An interactive game that challenges your knowledge of chapter content in the style of a television quiz show.

Wheel of Terms
An interactive game that challenges your knowledge of chapter key terms in the style of the television show *Wheel of Fortune*.

Crossword Puzzle Challenge
A crossword puzzle that challenges your knowledge of key terms presented in the chapter.

Apply Your Knowledge

Reinforce the skills and apply the concepts you learned in this chapter.

Adding Date and OLE Fields, Using an Input Mask Wizard, and Querying Date Fields
Instructions: Start Access. If you are using the Microsoft Office Access 2007 Complete or the Microsoft Office Access 2007 Comprehensive text, open The Bike Delivers database that you used in Chapter 4. Otherwise, see your instructor for information on accessing the files required in this book.

Perform the following tasks:

1. Add the Start Date and Picture fields to the Courier table structure, as shown in Figure 5–77. Create an input mask for the Start Date field. Use the Short Date input mask type.

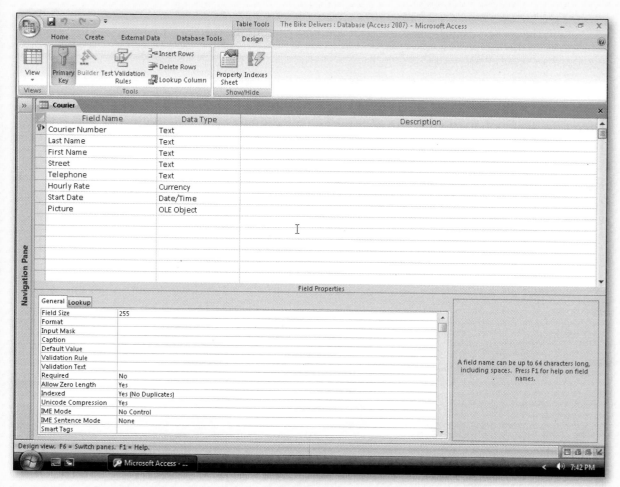

Figure 5–77

2. Add the data shown in Figure 5–78 to the Courier table.

Data for Courier Table		
Courier Number	**Start Date**	**Picture**
102	03/01/2007	Pict2.bmp
109	01/15/2007	Pict4.bmp
113	10/12/2007	Pict3.bmp
117	01/11/2008	Pict1.bmp

Figure 5–78

Continued >

Apply Your Knowledge *continued*

3. Query the Courier table to find all couriers who started after January 1, 2008. Include the Courier Number, First Name, Last Name, and Hourly Rate in the query results. Save the query as Start Date Query.

4. Submit the revised database in the format specified by your instructor.

Extend Your Knowledge

Extend the skills you learned in this chapter and experiment with new skills. You may need to use Help to complete the assignment.

Adding Hyperlink Fields and Creating Multi-Table Forms

Instructions: Start Access. Open the Alyssa Ashton College database. See the inside back cover of this book for instructions on downloading the Data Files for Students, or contact your instructor for more information about accessing the required files.

The human resources director at Alyssa Ashton College maintains a database of faculty candidates. She would like a hyperlink field added to this database. You will add this field. You also will create the form shown in Figure 5–79.

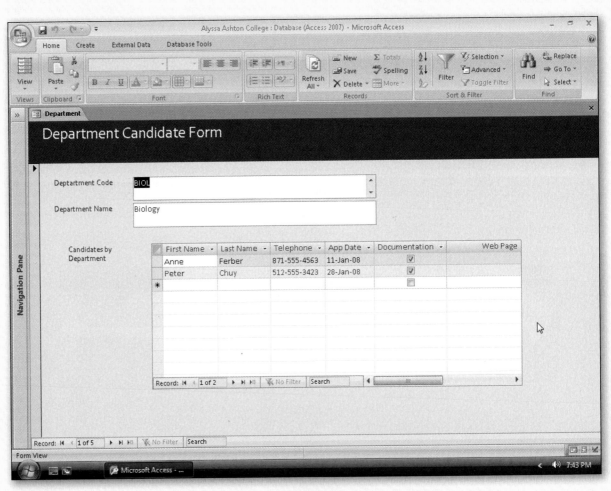

Figure 5–79

Perform the following tasks:

1. Open the Candidate table in Design view and add a hyperlink field. Insert the field after the Documentation field. Use Web Page as the name of the field.

2. Open the Candidate table and add data for the hyperlink field to the first record. If the teachers at your school have individual Web pages, link to one of those pages. Otherwise, use your school home page as the URL.

3. Use the Form Wizard to create the multi-table form shown in Figure 5–79. The Candidate table appears as a subform in the form. The form uses the Module style. Change the title of the form to Department Candidate Form and increase the size of the subform.

4. Change the database properties, as specified by your instructor. Submit the revised database in the format specified by your instructor.

Make It Right

Analyze a database and correct all errors and/or improve the design.

Correcting Form Design Errors

Instructions: Start Access. Open the Landscape Exteriors database. See the inside back cover of this book for instructions on downloading the Data Files for Students, or contact your instructor for more information about accessing the required files.

The Landscape Exteriors database contains data for a company that provides landscaping services. The owner of the company has created the form shown in Figure 5–80 but she has encountered some problems with modifying the form.

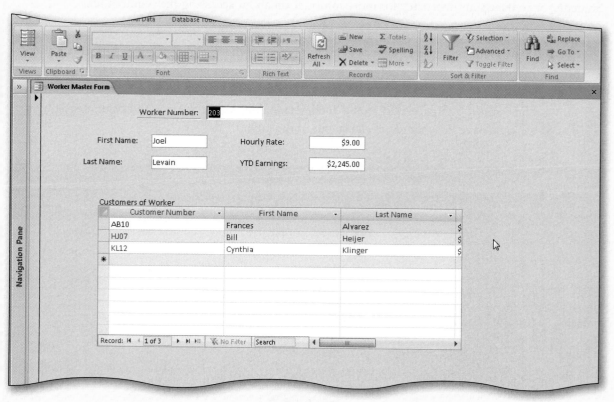

Figure 5–80

Continued >

Make It Right *continued*

The form currently has the chiseled special effect for the Worker Number label. All labels should have a chiseled special effect. The Worker Number control has a sunken special effect. All other controls except the subform also should have the sunken special effect property. The subform is too big and needs to be resized. The First Name and Last Name labels should be aligned to the left. Finally, the form needs a title. The owner would like the title, Worker Master Form. The title should appear above the Worker Number control and should have a raised appearance with a font size of 20 and a font weight of bold.

Submit the revised database in the format specified by your instructor.

In the Lab

Design, create, modify, and/or use a database following the guidelines, concepts, and skills presented in this chapter. Labs are listed in order of increasing difficulty.

Lab 1: Creating Multi-Table Forms for the JMS TechWizards Database

Problem: JMS TechWizards needs to maintain additional data on each technician. The company needs to maintain the date each technician started as well as notes concerning the technician and a picture of the technician. The company wants a form that displays technician information and the clients for which they are responsible.

Instructions: If you are using the Microsoft Office Access 2007 Complete or the Microsoft Office Access 2007 Comprehensive text, open the JMS TechWizards database that you used in Chapter 4. Otherwise, see the inside back cover of this book for instructions on downloading the Data Files for Students, or contact your instructor for more information about accessing the required files.

Perform the following tasks:

1. Add the Start Date, Notes, and Picture fields to the end of the Technician table. The Text Format property for the Notes field should be rich text and users should be able to append data to the Notes field. Save the changes to the structure of the table.

2. Add the data shown in Figure 5–81 to the Technician table. Adjust the row and column spacing to best fit the data. Save the changes to the layout of the table.

Data for Technician Table			
Technician Number	**Start Date**	**Notes**	**Picture**
22	04/02/2007	Has MOS certification in Word, Excel, and Access.	Pict2.bmp
23	05/14/2007	Extensive network experience. Has a good rapport with clients.	Pict3.bmp
29	10/01/2007	Excellent diagnostic skills. Prefers to handle hardware problems.	Pict1.bmp
32	01/14/2008	Has MOS certification in Access.	Pict4.bmp

Figure 5–81

3. Create the form shown in Figure 5–82. Use Technician Master Form as the name of the form and Clients of Technician as the name of the subform. Change the tab order so users tab to the Notes field before the Start Date field. Users should not be able to tab through the Picture control. The title control has the following properties: raised special effect, a font size of 20, a font weight of semi-bold, and a text align of distribute. The remaining labels on the form have a chiseled special effect.

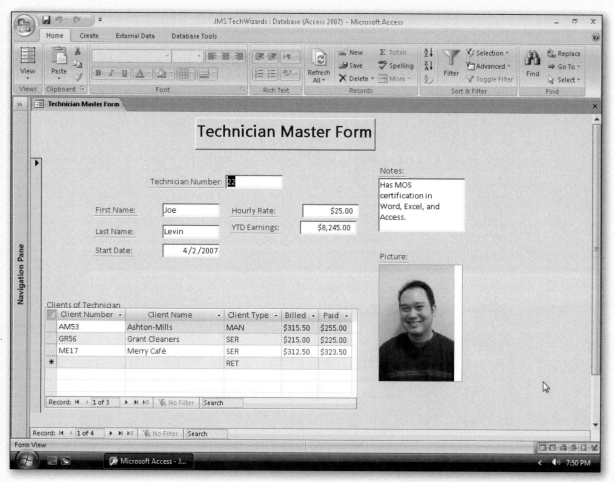

Figure 5–82

4. Query the Technician table to find all technicians who have MOS certification and started before January 1, 2008. Include the Technician Number, First Name, Last Name, and Notes fields in the query results. Save the query as MOS Query.

5. Submit the revised database in the format specified by your instructor.

In the Lab

Lab 2: Adding Fields and Creating Multi-Table Forms in the Hockey Fan Zone Database

Problem: The management of the Hockey Fan Zone store has found that they need to maintain additional data on suppliers. Management needs to know the last date an order was placed and whether the supplier accepts returns. Management also would like to attach Excel files to each supplier's record that contain historical cost data. The Hockey Fan Zone requires a form that displays information about the supplier as well as the items that are purchased from suppliers.

Instructions: If you are using the Microsoft Office Access 2007 Complete or the Microsoft Office Access 2007 Comprehensive text, open the Hockey Fan Zone database that you used in Chapter 4. Otherwise, see the inside back cover of this book for instructions on downloading the Data Files for Students, or contact your instructor for more information about accessing the required files.

Perform the following tasks:
1. Add the fields, Last Order Date, Returns, and Cost History to the end of the Supplier table structure. Last Order Date is a date field, Returns is a Yes/No field, and Cost History is an Attachments field. Create an input mask for the Last Order Date that uses the Short Date mask.
2. Add the data shown in Figure 5–83 to the Supplier table.

Data for Supplier Table			
Supplier Code	**Last Order Date**	**Returns**	**Cost History**
AC	02/25/2008	Yes	AC_History.xlsx
LG	03/21/2008	No	LG_History.xlsx
LG	03/04/2008	Yes	MN_History.xlsx

Figure 5–83

3. Create the form shown in Figure 5–84. Use Supplier Master Form as the name of the form and Items of Supplier as the name of the subform. The title control has the following properties: raised special effect, a font size of 20, a font weight of semi-bold, and a text align of distribute. The remaining labels on the form have a chiseled special effect.

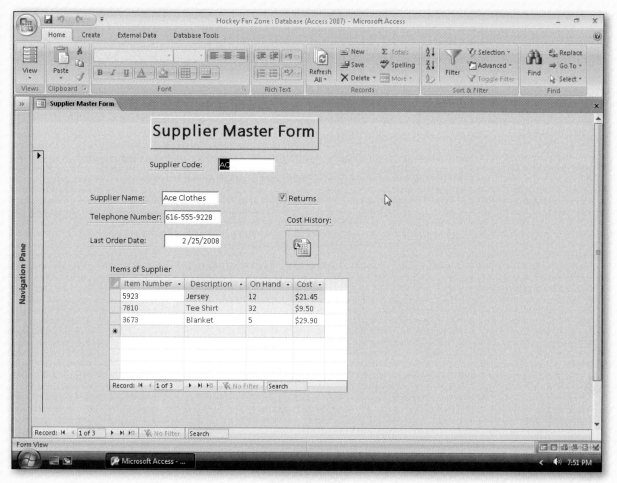

Figure 5–84

4. Query the Supplier table to find all suppliers that accept returns. Include the Supplier Code and Name in the query results. Save the query as Returns Query.

5. Submit the revised database in the format specified by your instructor.

In the Lab

Lab 3: Maintaining the Ada Beauty Supply Database

Problem: The management of Ada Beauty Supply needs to maintain additional data on sales reps. Management needs to store the date the sales rep started, comments about each sales rep, and a picture of the sales rep. Management wants a form that displays sales rep information and the customers they represent.

Instructions: If you are using the Microsoft Office Access 2007 Complete or the Microsoft Office Access 2007 Comprehensive text, open the Ada Beauty Supply database that you used in Chapter 4. Otherwise, see the inside back cover of this book for instructions on downloading the Data Files for Students, or contact your instructor for more information about accessing the required files. Submit the revised database in the format specified by your instructor.

Continued >

In the Lab *continued*

Instructions Part 1:   Add the Start Date, Notes, and Picture fields to the Sales Rep table and then add the data shown in Figure 5–85 to the Sales Rep table. Be sure the datasheet displays the entire comment.

Data for Sales Rep Table			
Sales Rep Number	**Start Date**	**Notes**	**Picture**
44	05/07/2007	Has an AA degree. Working on a BBA in Management.	Pict1.bmp
49	12/12/2006	Mentors new sales reps. Working on BBA in Marketing.	Pict2.bmp
51	02/15/2008	Former beautician. Cannot stand for long periods of time.	Pict3.bmp
55	03/06/2007	Excellent computer skills. Helps to train new employees.	Pict4.bmp

Figure 5–85

Instructions Part 2:   Create the Sales Rep Master Form shown in Figure 5–86. The title control has a raised special effect with a font size of 20, a font weight of semi-bold, and a text align of distribute. The remaining labels on the form have no special effect. Users should not be able to tab to the Picture field.

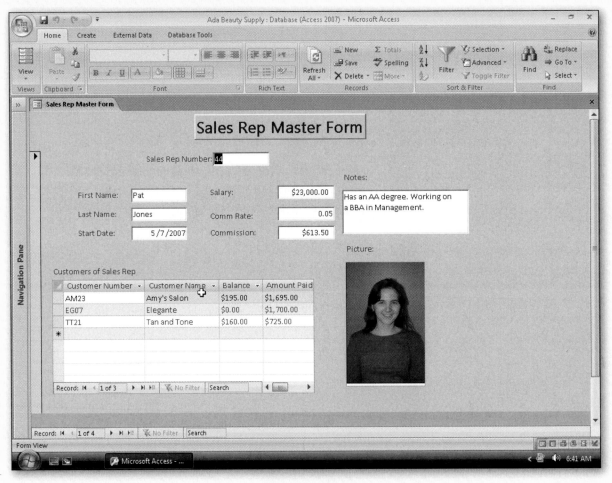

Figure 5–86

Instructions Part 3:   Find all sales reps that are former beauticians. Include the Sales Rep Number, First Name, and Last Name in the query result. Save the query as Beautician Query. Find all sales reps that started after February 1, 2008. Include the Sales Rep Number, First Name, Last Name, and Comm Rate in the query result. Save the query as Start Date Query.

Cases and Places

Apply your creative thinking and problem solving skills to design and implement a solution.

● Easier   ●● More Difficult

● 1: Creating Multi-Table Forms for the Second-Hand Goods Database

If you are using the Microsoft Office Access 2007 Complete or the Microsoft Office Access 2007 Comprehensive text, open the Second-Hand Goods database that you used in Chapter 4. Otherwise, see the inside back cover of this book for instructions on downloading the Data Files for Students, or contact your instructor for more information about accessing the required files. Create a form for the Seller table that is similar in design to the form shown in Figure 5–87. Customize the form by adding your own special effects and changing the background color of the form. Include all fields. Create a form for the Item table that also includes the seller first name and the seller last name. Change the Enabled property for the seller first and last name so users cannot change the seller name data. Name the form Item Update Form. Submit the revised database in the format specified by your instructor.

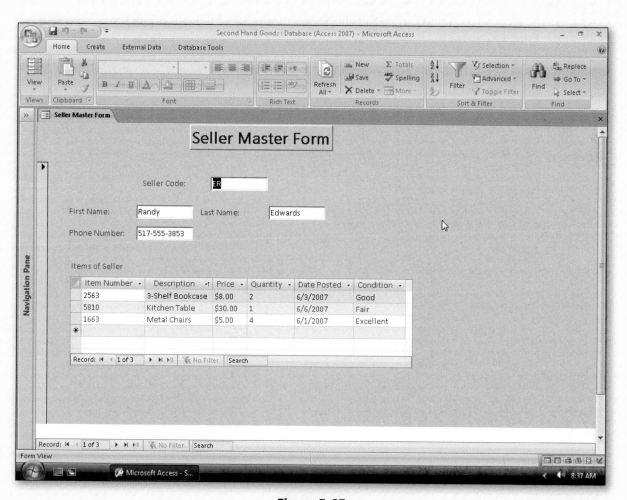

Figure 5–87

Continued >

Cases and Places *continued*

• 2: Adding Fields and Creating Multi-Table Forms for the BeachCondo Rentals Database

If you are using the Microsoft Office Access 2007 Complete or the Microsoft Office Access 2007 Comprehensive text, open the BeachCondo Rentals database that you used in Chapter 4. Otherwise, see the inside back cover of this book for instructions on downloading the Data Files for Students, or contact your instructor for more information about accessing the required files. The rental company needs to store some notes concerning the owner's rental policies. Add a Notes field with a memo data type to the Owner table. Update the table with the data shown in Figure 5–88.

Data for Owner Table	
Owner Number	**Notes**
AB12	Will not rent to families with children under 18.
BE20	Will rent to families with children.
GR50	Allows dogs in unit.
HJ05	Will not rent during the month of April.
HJ05	Allows dogs in unit.

Figure 5–88

Create a form for the Owner table that is similar in design to the form shown in Figure 5–89. Customize the form by changing the special effects, the font color of the labels, and the background color of the form. Query the database to find all owners that allow dogs. Include the owner code, first name, last name, unit number, and weekly rate in the query results. Save the query as Pet Policy Query. Submit the revised database in the format specified by your instructor.

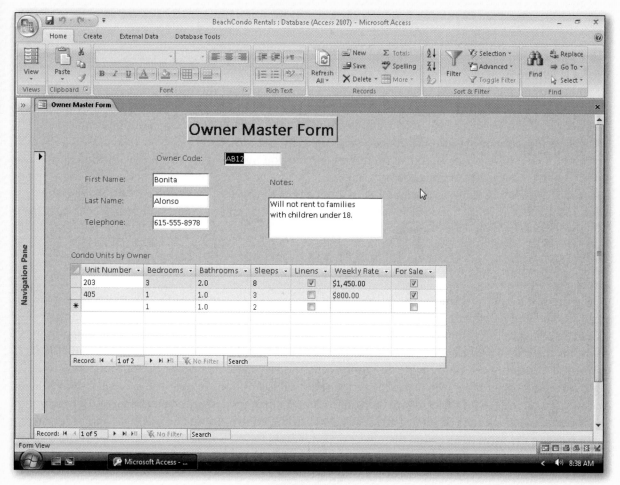

Figure 5–89

•• 3: Adding Fields to the Restaurant Database

If you are using the Microsoft Office Access 2007 Complete or the Microsoft Office Access 2007 Comprehensive text, open the restaurant database that you used in Chapter 4. Otherwise, see the inside back cover of this book for instructions on downloading the Data Files for Students, or contact your instructor for more information about accessing the required files. Using the Plan Ahead guidelines presented in this chapter, determine what additional fields you need to add to your database. For example, many restaurants maintain their own Web sites. You may want to include a hyperlink field for this data. You can use a memo field to store comments or notes about each restaurant. Add these fields to your database and update the fields with appropriate data. Review the different types of forms described in this chapter. Create at least two forms for your database that use these new fields. Use Layout view to create at least one form and then modify the form as necessary. Submit the revised database in the format specified by your instructor.

Continued >

Cases and Places *continued*

•• 4: Adding Fields to Your Contacts Database

Make It Personal

If you are using the Microsoft Office Access 2007 Complete or the Microsoft Office Access 2007 Comprehensive text, open the contacts database that you used in Chapter 4. Otherwise, see the inside back cover of this book for instructions on downloading the Data Files for Students, or contact your instructor for more information about accessing the required files. Consider your own personal job situation. What other fields would be useful to you? Do you need a hyperlink field with the URL of each of the companies in your contact database? Do you need an Attachment field in which to store correspondence that you have sent each company? Do you need to create new forms with the additional fields? Modify the database and create any necessary forms. Submit the revised database in the format specified by your instructor.

•• 5: Understanding Fields, Multi-Table Forms, and Object Dependencies

Working Together

Copy the JSP Recruiters database and rename the database to your team name. For example, if your team is the Fab Five, then name the database Fab Five. As a team, decide if there are any fields that could be added to the Client table. For example, it might be useful to have a hyperlink field that contains the URL for the client. Also, a field that contained additional notes about each client may be appropriate. Modify the Client table design to accommodate these new fields. Then, add data to the fields. You can use existing web pages for various medical institutions in your area. Create a multi-table form based on the Client table and include the recruiter's first and last name on the form. Users should not be able to update the recruiter name fields. Anchor the controls in the Client table and experiment with resizing the form. Determine the object dependencies for each table in the database. Write a short report that explains the importance of understanding object dependencies. Submit the report and the revised database in the format specified by your instructor.

6 | Using Macros, Switchboards, PivotTables, and PivotCharts

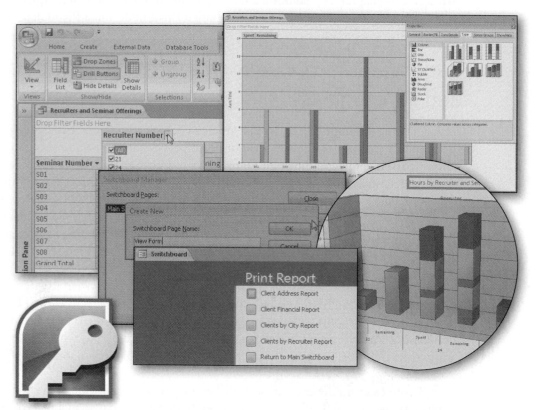

Objectives

You will have mastered the material in this project when you can:

- Create and modify macros and macro groups
- Run macros
- Create a switchboard and switchboard pages
- Modify switchboard pages
- Use a switchboard
- Import data and create a query
- Create a PivotTable

- Change properties in a PivotTable
- Use a PivotTable
- Create a PivotChart and add a legend
- Change the chart type and organization of a PivotChart
- Remove drop zones in a PivotChart
- Assign axis titles and a chart title in a PivotChart
- Use a PivotChart

6 | Macros, Switchboards, PivotTables, and PivotCharts

Introduction

This chapter shows how to create and test macros and how to use these macros in the switchboard system that JSP Recruiters requires. With the switchboard system, users can access any form, table, or report simply by clicking the appropriate buttons on the switchboard. In this chapter, two additional tables are added to the database. A query incorporating these new tables then is used to create both a PivotTable and a PivotChart.

Project — Macros, Switchboards, PivotTables, and PivotCharts

Managers at JSP Recruiters have heard about switchboard systems that enable users to click a button or two to open any form or table, preview any report, or print any report. A **switchboard** like the one shown in Figure 6–1a is a form that includes buttons to perform a variety of actions. In this system, rather than having to use the Navigation Pane, the user simply clicks a button — View Form, View Table, View Report, Print Report, or Exit Application — to indicate the action to be taken. Other than Exit Application, clicking a button leads to another switchboard. For example, when a user clicks the View Form button, Access displays the View Form switchboard, as shown in Figure 6–1b. On this next-level form, the user clicks the button that identifies the form he or she wants to view. Similarly, when the user clicks the View Table button, Access displays a switchboard on which the user clicks a button to indicate the table he or she wants to view. Thus, viewing any form, table, or report, or printing any report requires clicking only two buttons. The administration at JSP would like such a switchboard system because they believe it will improve the user-friendliness of the system, thereby improving employee satisfaction and efficiency.

Before creating the switchboard, JSP will create **macros**, which are collections of actions designed to carry out specific tasks. To perform the actions in a macro, you run the macro. When a macro is run, Access will execute the various steps, called **actions**, in the macro. The switchboard system uses macros. Clicking certain buttons in the switchboard system will cause the appropriate macros to run.

Chapter 2 showed how to create a crosstab query, which is a query that calculates a statistic (for example, sum, average, or count) for data that is grouped by two different types of information. A PivotTable is similar. The PivotTable in Figure 6–1c, for example, displays the sum of hours spent and hours remaining grouped by seminar number and recruiter number. Unlike a crosstab, however, a PivotTable is dynamic, a feature that appeals to JSP. By clicking the plus or minus signs, JSP can expand and contract the level of detail that appears in the chart. Users can dynamically filter the data so that only certain seminars or recruiters are included. They even can use additional fields to filter the data. For example, they could specify that the data is only to reflect seminars offered to certain clients. Finally, they can change the organization. They might prefer to reverse

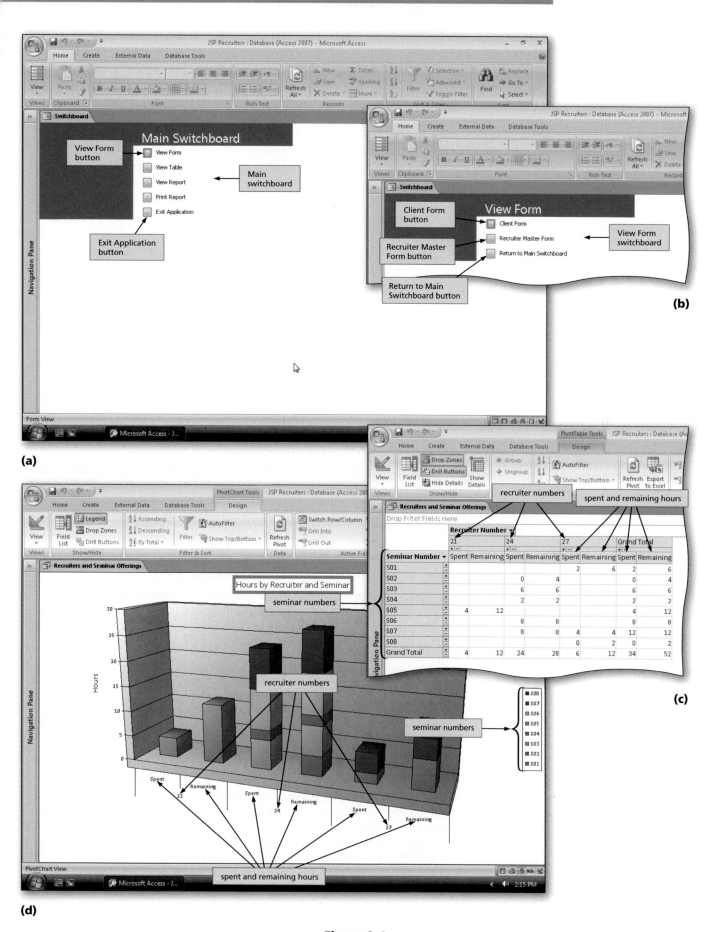

Figure 6–1

the roles of the rows and columns, having the rows represent recruiters and the columns represent seminars. Accomplishing this is a simple matter of dragging the fields to the desired positions.

JSP managers can represent the same data graphically by using a PivotChart like the one in Figure 6–1d on the previous page. In this particular chart, the colors of the sections of the bars represent the different seminars as indicated on the right of the chart. Across the bottom of the chart are the recruiters. The bars represent the hours spent or hours remaining for the recruiter. The total bar, ignoring colors, thus would represent the total hours spent or remaining by the recruiter. Unlike a regular chart, the PivotChart has the same dynamic capabilities as a PivotTable. You can change to a different chart type, you can reverse the roles of the rows and columns, and you can filter data with the same ease you can in a PivotChart.

PivotTables and PivotCharts are normally associated with Microsoft Excel. You always could export data from an Access database to Excel and then use Excel to create a PivotTable or PivotChart. Having PivotTable and PivotChart capabilities within Access, however, means that you do not have to go through that process.

Overview

As you read through this chapter, you will learn how to create macros, switchboards, PivotTables, and PivotCharts by performing these general tasks:

- Create a macro group contain ing the macros that will be used in the switchboard.
- Create a switchboard and add the switchboard pages.
- Add the items and actions to the switchboard pages.
- Create the tables, relationships, and query that will be used in creating a PivotTable and a PivotChart.
- Create and use a PivotTable.
- Create and use a PivotChart.

Plan Ahead

Macro, Switchboard, PivotTable, and PivotChart Design Guidelines

1. **Determine when it would be beneficial to automate tasks in a macro.** Are there tasks involving multiple steps that would be more conveniently accomplished by running a macro than by carrying out all the individual steps? For example, to open a table in read-only mode and then display a message could be accomplished conveniently through a macro. Are there tasks that are to be performed when the user clicks buttons in a switchboard? These tasks can be placed in a macro, which can be run when the button is clicked.

2. **Determine whether it is appropriate to create a switchboard.** If you want to make it easy and convenient for users to perform a variety of tasks just by clicking buttons, consider creating a switchboard. You can associate the performance of the various tasks with the buttons in the switchboard.

3. **Determine the organization of the switchboard.** Determine the various tasks that need to be performed by clicking buttons. Decide the logical grouping of those buttons.

4. **Determine whether it is appropriate to present data as a PivotTable.** Do you need to calculate a statistic for data that is grouped by two different types of information? If so, you can consider either a crosstab query or a PivotTable. If you want the presentation to be interactive, that is, if you want to be able to easily change the organization of the data as well as to filter the data, then a PivotTable is appropriate.

5. **Determine the organization of the PivotTable.** Determine the fields for the rows, columns, data, and filters.

(continued)

(continued)   ◦ **Plan Ahead**

6. **Determine whether it is appropriate to present data as a PivotChart.** Do you want to summarize the same type of data as in a PivotTable, but graphically? Do you need the same ability to be able to change the organization of the presentation as well as to filter the data? If so, a PivotChart is appropriate.

7. **Determine the organization of the PivotChart.** Determine the fields for the x axis and the y axis. Decide which chart type would best display the data.

When necessary, more specific details concerning the above decisions and/or actions are presented at appropriate points in the chapter. The chapter also will identify the use of these guidelines in the design of switchboards, such as the one shown in Figures 6–1a and 6–1b on page AC 363, as well as PivotTables and PivotCharts, such as the ones shown in Figures 6–1c and 6–1d on page AC 363.

Starting Access

If you are using a computer to step through the project in this chapter and you want your screen to match the figures in this book, you should change your screen's resolution to 1024 × 768. For information about how to change a computer's resolution, read Appendix E.

To Start Access

The following steps, which assume Windows Vista is running, start Access.

Note: If you are using Windows XP, see Appendix F for alternate steps.

1 Click the Start button on the Windows Vista taskbar to display the Start menu.

2 Click All Programs at the bottom of the left pane on the Start menu to display the All Programs list and then click Microsoft Office in the All Programs list to display the Microsoft Office list.

3 Click Microsoft Office Access 2007 in the Microsoft Office list to start Access and display the Getting Started with Microsoft Office Access window.

4 If the Access window is not maximized, click the Maximize button on its title bar to maximize the window.

To Open a Database

In Chapter 1, you created your database on a USB flash drive using the file name, JSP Recruiters. There are two ways to open the file containing your database. If the file you created appears in the Recent Documents list, you could click it to open the file. If not, you can use the More button to open the file. The following steps use the More button to open the JSP Recruiters database from the USB flash drive.

Note: If you are using Windows XP, see Appendix F for alternate steps.

1 With your USB flash drive connected to one of the computer's USB ports, click the More button to display the Open dialog box.

2 If the Folders list is displayed below the Folders button, click the Folders button to remove the Folders list.

3 If necessary, click Computers in the Favorite Links section and then double-click UDISK 2.0 (E:) to select the USB flash drive, Drive E in this case, as the new open location. (Your drive letter might be different.)

4 Click JSP Recruiters to select the file name.

5 Click the Open button to open the database.

6 If a Security Warning appears, click the Options button to display the Microsoft Office Security Options dialog box.

7 With the option button to enable the content selected, click the OK button to enable the content.

Creating and Using Macros

Like other applications, Access allows you to create and use macros. Once you have created a macro, you can simply run the macro and Access will perform the various actions you specified. For example, the macro might open a table in Read-Only mode, a mode where changes to the table are prohibited, and then display a message indicating this fact.

A macro consists of a series of actions that Access performs when the macro is run; therefore, you will need to specify the actions when you create the macro. The actions are entered in a special window called a Macro Builder window. Once a macro is created, you can run it from the Navigation Pane by right-clicking the macro and then clicking Run on the shortcut menu. Macros also can be associated with items on switchboards. When you click the corresponding button on the switchboard, Access will run the macro. Whether a macro is run from the Navigation Pane or from a switchboard, the effect is the same: Access will execute the actions in the macro in the order in which they are entered.

In this chapter, you will learn how to create macros to open tables in read-only mode, open forms, preview reports, and print reports. As you enter actions, you will select them from a list box. The names of the actions are self-explanatory. The action to open a form, for example, is OpenForm. Thus, it is not necessary to memorize the specific actions that are available.

To Begin Creating a Macro

The following steps begin creating a macro, the purpose of which is to open the Client table in Read Only mode and then display a message to this effect. You will later add the appropriate actions to the macro.

- If necessary, hide the Navigation Pane.

- Click Create on the Ribbon to display the Create tab.

- Click the Macro button arrow to display the Macro button menu (Figure 6–2).

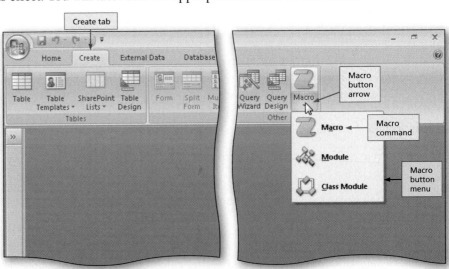

Figure 6–2

2

- Click Macro on the Macro menu to create a new macro (Figure 6–3).

Q&A

Could I just click the Macro button instead of clicking the arrow?

In this case you could. Because the icon on the face of the button is the one for macro, clicking the button would produce the same results as clicking the arrow and then clicking Macro.

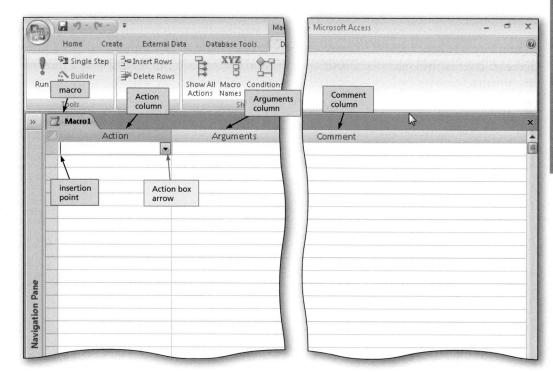

Figure 6–3

The Macro Builder Window

The first column in the Macro Builder window, also called the Macro window, is the Action column (see Figure 6–3). You enter the actions you want the macro to perform in this column. To enter an action, click the arrow in the Action column and then select the action from the list that appears. Many actions require additional information, called the **arguments** of the action. If you select such an action, the arguments will appear in the lower portion of the Macro Builder window and you can make any necessary changes to them. The second column contains the values you have assigned to these arguments. You can use the third column to enter a comment concerning the action if you wish.

The actions, the arguments, and the values for the arguments are shown in Table 6–1.

Table 6–1 Specifications for First Macro

Action	Argument to Change	New Value for Argument
OpenTable	Table Name	Client
	View	Datasheet
	Data Mode	Read Only
MsgBox	Message	Table is open as read-only
	Beep	Yes
	Type	Information
	Title	JSP Recruiters

The macro begins by opening the Client table in read-only mode. That is, users can view the data, but cannot change it. The macro then displays a message indicating that the table is open in this mode. When the users click the OK button, the message will disappear.

To Add Actions to a Macro

To continue creating this macro, enter the actions. For each action, enter the action and comment in the appropriate text boxes, and then make the necessary changes to any arguments. The following steps add the actions to the macro that will open the Client table in Read Only mode and then display a message to this effect. They then save the macro.

1

- Click the box arrow in the first row of the Action column to display a menu of available actions (Figure 6–4).

Q&A How can I tell the purpose of the various actions?

Select an action. A brief description of the action will appear in the lower-right corner of the screen. If you want detailed information on the selected action, press F1.

Experiment

- Select an action and then press F1 to view a detailed description. Close the Access Help window, press the box arrow and repeat the process for other actions. When finished, press the box arrow a final time.

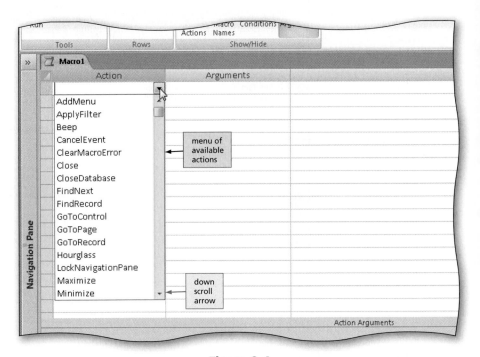

Figure 6–4

2

- Scroll down until OpenTable appears and then click OpenTable to select it as the action (Figure 6–5).

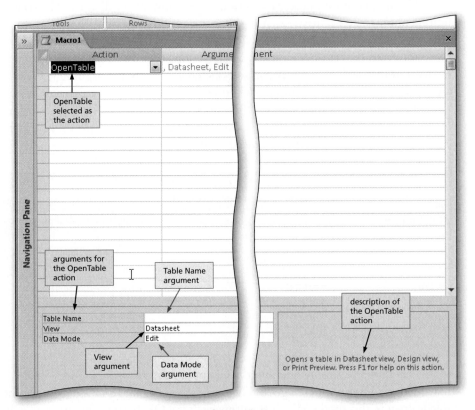

Figure 6–5

3

- Click the Table Name argument to display an arrow.

- Click the arrow to display a list of available tables and then click Client to select the Client table.

- Click the Data Mode argument to display an arrow.

- Click the arrow to display a list of available choices for the Data Mode argument (Figure 6–6).

- Click Read Only to select Read Only as the value for the Data Mode argument.

 How can I tell the meaning of the various options?

A description appears in the lower-right corner of the screen. If that is not sufficient, press F1 for detailed information.

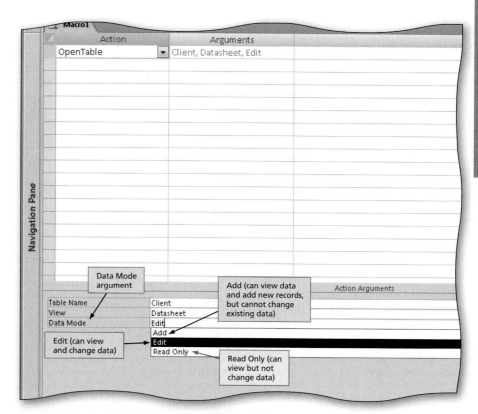

Figure 6–6

4

- Click the second row in the Action column and then click the arrow that appears to display a menu of available actions.

- Scroll down until MsgBox appears and then click MsgBox to select it as the action (Figure 6–7).

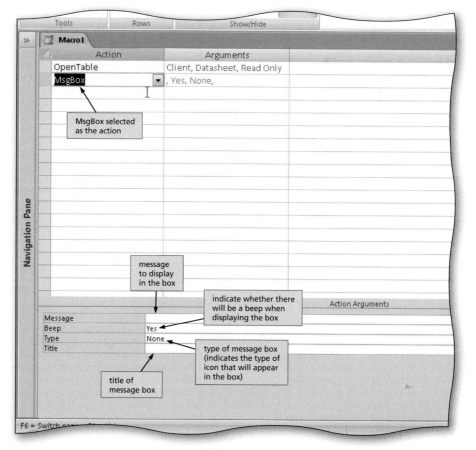

Figure 6–7

- Click the Message argument and type `Table is open as read-only` as the message.

- Click the Type argument, click the arrow that appears, and then select Information as the value for the Type argument.

Q&A How can I tell the meaning of the various possibilities?

When you click the argument, Access displays a general description to the right of the argument. If you want further information at that point, press F1.

- Click the Title argument and type `JSP Recruiters` as the title (Figure 6–8).

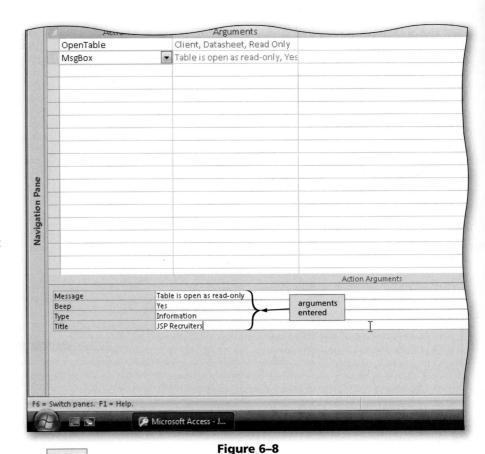

Figure 6–8

- Click the Save button on the Quick Access Toolbar and type `Open Client Table Read Only` as the name of the macro (Figure 6–9).

⑦

- Click the OK button to save the macro.

- Close the macro.

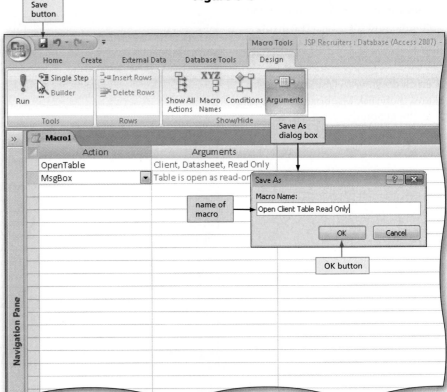

Figure 6–9

Single-Stepping a Macro

You may have problems with a macro. The macro may abort. It may open the wrong table or produce a wrong message. If you have problems with a macro, you can **single-step the macro**, that is, proceed through a macro a step at a time in Design view. To do so, you would open the macro in Design view and then click the Single Step button on the Design tab (Figure 6–10).

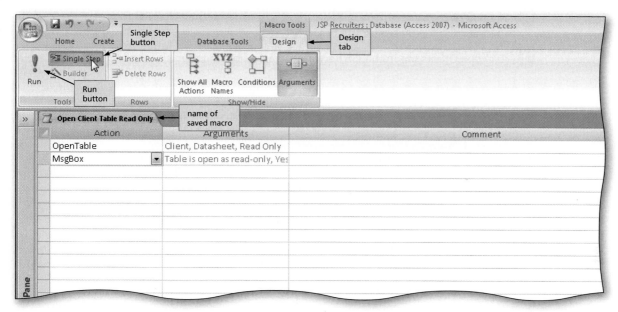

Figure 6–10

You next would click the Run button on the Design tab. Access would display the Macro Single Step dialog box (Figure 6–11). The dialog box shows the action to be executed and the values of the various arguments. You can click the Step button to proceed to the next step. If you want to terminate the process, you can click the Stop All Macros button.

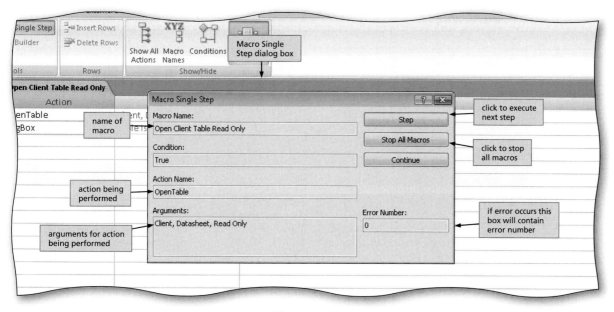

Figure 6–11

To Run a Macro

When you instruct Access to run a macro, Access will execute the steps in the macro. The following steps run the macro that was just created.

1 Show the Navigation Pane and scroll down, if necessary, so that the Open Client Table Read Only macro appears. It should be in a section of the Navigation Pane called Unrelated Objects, because it is not directly related to any of the tables in the database.

2 Right-click the Open Client Table Read Only macro and then click Run on the shortcut menu to run the macro (Figure 6–12).

3 Click the OK button in the JSP Recruiters dialog box and then close the Client table.

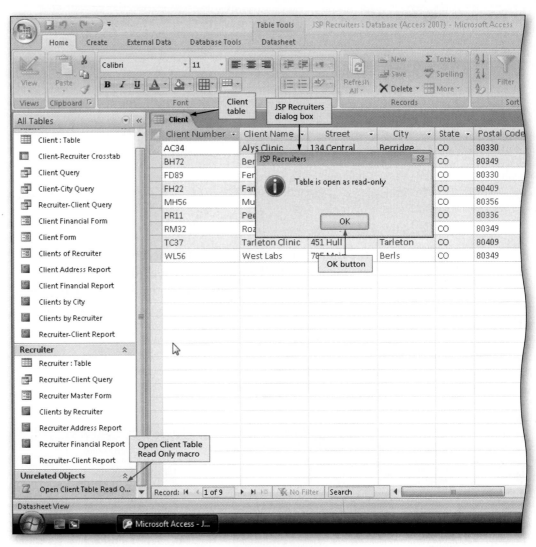

Figure 6–12

To Modify a Macro

You can modify a macro in the same way you first created it. You can change actions and/or arguments. You can insert a new action between two existing actions by clicking the position for the action and pressing the INSERT key to insert a new blank row. The following steps modify the macro you just created, adding a new step to customize the Navigation Pane so that only the tables in the database appear.

1

- Right-click the Open Client Table Read Only macro to display a shortcut menu.

- Click Design View on the shortcut menu to open the macro in Design view.

- Click the row selector on the row containing the MsgBox action to select the row, and then press the INSERT key to insert a new row.

- Click the new row.

- Click the Action column arrow on the new row, scroll down, and select NavigateTo as the action (Figure 6–13).

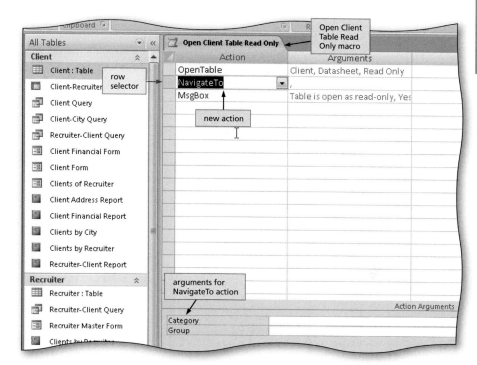

Figure 6–13

2

- Click the Category argument, click the arrow, and then click Object Type as the value for the Category argument.

- Click the Group argument, click the arrow, and then click Tables as the value for the Group argument (Figure 6–14).

- Save and then close the macro.

Q&A

Is it necessary to save and close the macro before running it?

No. You can run it in Design view by clicking the Run button on the Design tab.

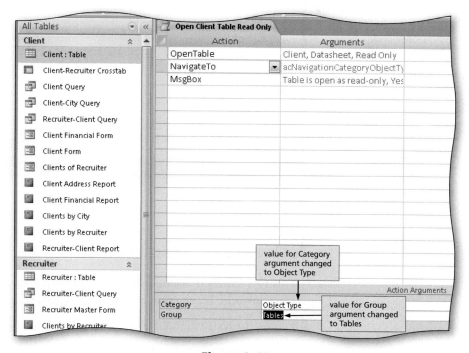

Figure 6–14

To Run the Modified Macro

The following steps run the macro that you just modified.

1 Right-click the Open Client Table Read Only macro and then click Run on the shortcut menu to run the macro (Figure 6–15).

2 Click the OK button in the JSP Recruiters dialog box and then close the Client table.

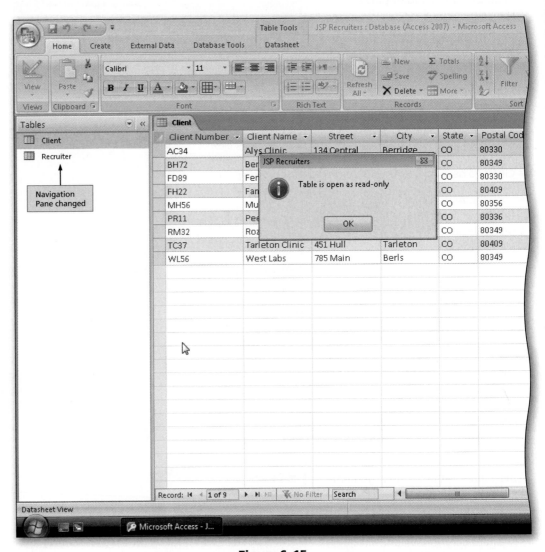

Figure 6–15

To Reverse the Macro Action

The modified macro changed what is displayed in the Navigation Pane. The following steps return the Navigation Pane to its original state.

1 Click the Navigation Pane arrow to produce the Navigation Pane menu.

2 Click Tables and Related Views to once again organize the Navigation Pane by table (Figure 6–16).

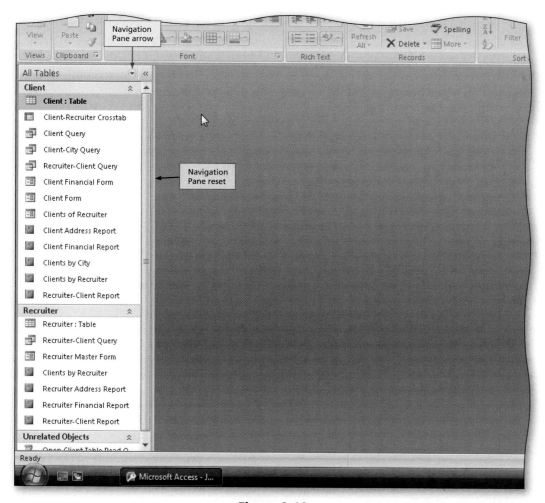

Figure 6–16

Errors in Macros

Macros can contain errors. For example, if you type the name of the table in the Table Name argument of the OpenTable action instead of selecting it from the list, you may type it incorrectly. Access then will not be able to execute the desired action. In that case, a Microsoft Office Access dialog box will appear, indicating the error and solution, as shown in Figure 6–17.

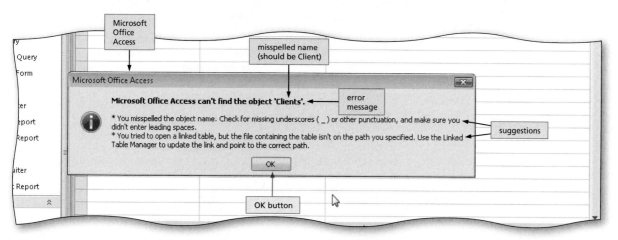

Figure 6–17

If such a dialog box appears, click the OK button. The Action Failed dialog box then appears (Figure 6–18). The dialog box indicates the macro that was being run, the action that Access was attempting to execute, and the arguments for the action. This information tells you which action needs to be corrected. To make the correction, click the Stop All Macros button, and then modify the design of the macro.

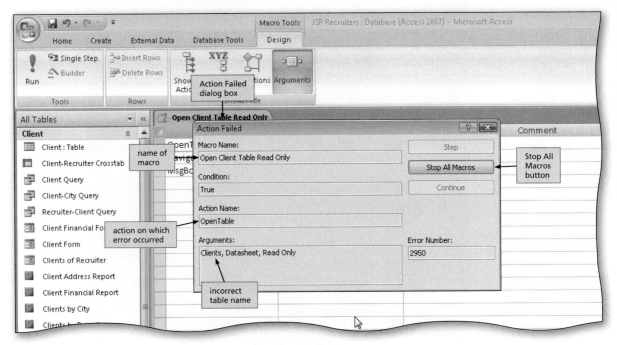

Figure 6–18

Additional Macros

The additional macros to be created are shown in Table 6–2. You will create these macros in the steps starting on page AC 377. The first column gives the name of the macro, and the second column indicates the actions for the macro. The third column contains the values of those arguments that may need to be changed. (Values for any arguments not listed can be left as they are.)

Table 6–2 Specifications for Additional Macros

Macro Name	Action	Argument(s) and Value(s)
Open Client Table	OpenTable	Table Name: Client Data Mode: Read Only
	MsgBox	Message: Table is open as read-only Type: Information Title: JSP Recruiters
Open Recruiter Table	OpenTable	Table Name: Recruiter Data Mode: Read Only
	MsgBox	Message: Table is open as read-only Type: Information Title: JSP Recruiters
Open Client Form	OpenForm	Form Name: Client Form View: Form
Open Recruiter Master Form	OpenForm	Form Name: Recruiter Master Form View: Form

Table 6–2 Specifications for Additional Macros (*continued*)		
Macro Name	**Action**	**Argument(s) and Value(s)**
Preview Client Address Report	OpenReport	Report Name: Client Address Report View: Report
Preview Client Financial Report	OpenReport	Report Name: Client Financial Report View: Report
Preview Clients by City Report	OpenReport	Report Name: Clients by City View: Report
Preview Clients by Recruiter Report	OpenReport	Report Name: Clients by Recruiter View: Report
Print Client Address Report	OpenReport	Report Name: Client Address Report View: Print
Print Client Financial Report	OpenReport	Report Name: Client Financial Report View: Print
Print Clients by City Report	OpenReport	Report Name: Clients by City View: Print
Print Clients by Recruiter Report	OpenReport	Report Name: Clients by Recruiter View: Print

To Create a Macro Group

If you have several macros, you can create a separate file for each one. Alternatively, you can create a single file, called a **macro group**, and place the macros in the single macro group.

To place multiple macros in a macro group, you add the macro names column to the macro and then assign a name to each macro. The following steps create the additional macros shown in Table 6–2 in a macro group called SB Macros, for Switchboard Macros.

❶

- Click Create on the Ribbon to display the Create tab.

- Click the Macro button arrow to display the Macro menu.

- Click Macro on the Macro menu to create a new macro.

- Hide the Navigation Pane.

- Click the Macro Names button on the Design tab to display the Macro Name column (Figure 6–19).

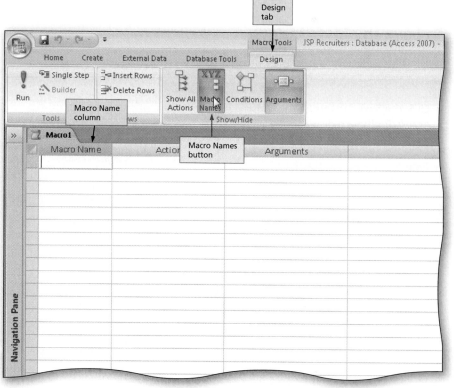

Figure 6–19

- Type the name of the first macro in Table 6–2 on page AC 376 in the Macro Name column on the first row.

- In the Action column on the first row, select the first action in the first macro in Table 6–2 and then make the indicated changes to the arguments in the Actions Arguments pane at the bottom of the screen.

- In the Action column on the second row, select the second action in the first macro in Table 6–2 and then make the indicated changes to the arguments (Figure 6–20).

Q&A

This macro is very similar to the Open Client Table Read Only macro. Is there any way I can modify that macro and create the macro group?

You could, but it probably takes longer to modify the macro than to create a new one. You would need to open the Open Client Table Read Only macro in Design view, add the Action Name column, delete the Navigate To action and then use the Save As command on the Office menu rather than the Save button.

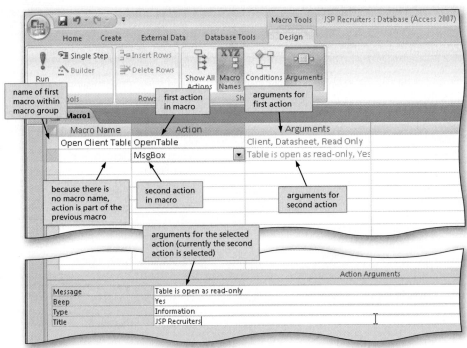

Figure 6–20

To Save the Macro Group

The following steps save the macro group.

- Click the Save button on the Quick Access Toolbar to display the Save As dialog box.

- Type SB Macros as the macro name (Figure 6–21).

- Click the OK button to save the macro group.

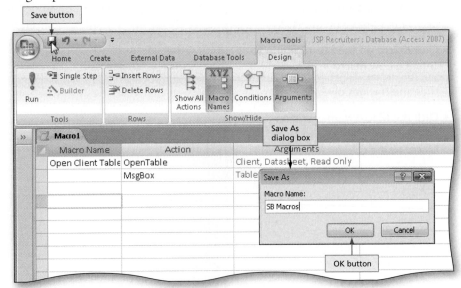

Figure 6–21

To Add the Remaining Macros to the Macro Group

You add the remaining macros to the macro group just as you added the first macro. The following steps add the remaining macros.

• Enter the remaining macro names, actions, and arguments shown in Table 6–2 on pages AC 372 and AC 373 (Figure 6–22).

Q&A

What is the meaning of the symbols that appear in front of the Print macros?

The symbol indicates that the indicated action will not be allowed if the database is not trusted. Because running certain macros can cause potential security risks, Access is alerting you to the threat.

• Click the Save button on the Quick Access Toolbar to save the macro group with the additional macros.

• Close the macro group.

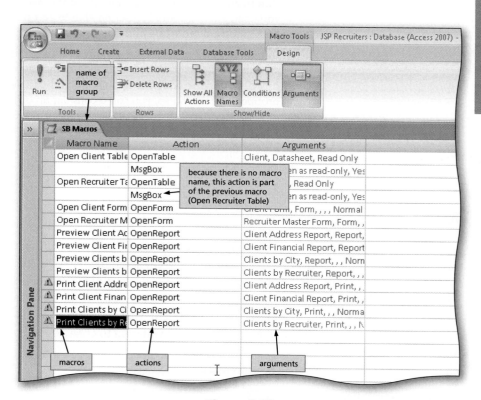

Figure 6–22

Opening Databases Containing Macros

When a database contains macros, there is a chance a computer virus can attach to a macro. By default, Access disables macros when it opens a database and displays a Security Warning. If the database comes from a trusted source and you are sure that it does not contain any macro viruses, click the Options button and then enable the content in the Microsoft Office Security Options dialog box. You can make adjustments to Access security settings by clicking the Access Options button on the Office Button menu and then clicking Trust Center.

Creating and Using a Switchboard

A switchboard (see Figures 6–1a and 6–1b on page AC 363) is a special type of form. It contains buttons you can click to perform a variety of actions. Buttons on the main switchboard can lead to other more specialized switchboards. Clicking the View Form button, for example, causes Access to display the View Form switchboard. Switchboard buttons also can be used to open forms or tables. Clicking the Client Form button on the View Form switchboard opens the Client Form. Still other buttons cause reports to appear in a preview window or print reports.

<table>
<tr>
<td>Plan
Ahead</td>
<td>

Determine the organization of the switchboard.

1. **Determine all the tasks to be accomplished by clicking buttons in the switchboard.** Which tables need to be opened? Which forms? Which queries? Which reports?

2. **Determine any special requirements for the way the tasks are to be performed.** When you open a table, should a user be able to edit data or should the table be open read-only? Should a report be printed or simply viewed on the screen?

3. **Determine how to group the various tasks.** Should the tasks be grouped by function? If so, you could consider an organization such as View Table, View Form, and so on. Within the View Table category, you could list all the tables to be opened. Should the tasks be grouped by table? If so, you could consider an organization in which you are initially presented with a list of tables. When you select a specific table, you would have all the actions that could affect that table, for example, all queries, forms, and reports that are based on that table.

</td>
</tr>
</table>

To Create a Switchboard

JSP Recruiters has determined that they want buttons on the switchboard to view the Client and Recruiter tables in a fashion that does not allow the data to be changed; to view the Client Form and the Recruiter Master Form; to view several reports; and to print the same collection of reports. The overall organization will be by task. Thus, the initial switchboard will contain buttons such as View Form, View Table, View Report, and Print Report.

To create a switchboard, you use the Switchboard Manager button on the Database Tools tab. If you have not previously created a switchboard, you will be asked if you wish to create one. The following steps create a switchboard for the JSP Recruiters database.

- Hide the Navigation Pane if it is not already hidden.

Do I have to hide the Navigation Pane in order to create a switchboard?

No. Hiding it just makes the screen less cluttered. Hiding it is a matter of personal preference.

- Click Database Tools on the Ribbon to display the Database Tools tab.

- Click the Switchboard Manager button on the Database Tools tab (Figure 6–23).

Is the message an error?

No. The message is simply an indication that you have not yet created a switchboard. If you click the Yes button, Access will create one for you.

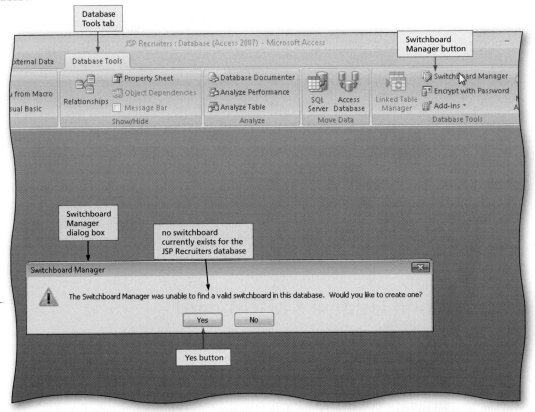

Figure 6–23

2

● Click the Yes
  button to create a
  new switchboard
  (Figure 6–24).

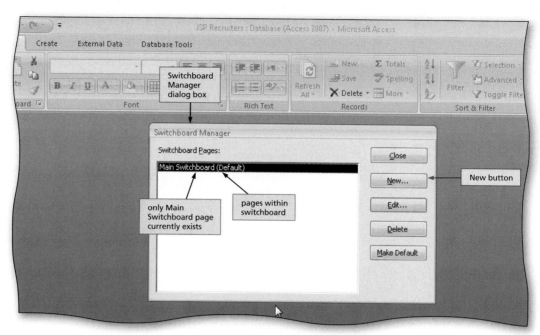

Figure 6–24

Creating Switchboard Pages

The next step in creating the switchboard system is to create the individual switchboards within the system. These individual switchboards are called the **switchboard pages**. The switchboard pages to be created are listed in the first column of Table 6–3. You do not have to create the Main Switchboard page because Access has created it automatically (Figure 6–24). To create each of the other pages, use the New button in the Switchboard Manager dialog box, and then enter the name of the page.

Table 6–3 Specifications for Switchboard Pages and Items

Switchboard Page	Switchboard Item	Command	Additional Information
Main Switchboard	View Form	Go to Switchboard	Switchboard: View Form
	View Table	Go to Switchboard	Switchboard: View Table
	View Report	Go to Switchboard	Switchboard: View Report
	Print Report	Go to Switchboard	Switchboard: Print Report
	Exit Application	Exit Application	None
View Form	Client Form	Run Macro	Macro: Open Client Form
	Recruiter Master Form	Run Macro	Macro: Open Recruiter Master Form
	Return to Main Switchboard	Go to Switchboard	Switchboard: Main Switchboard
View Table	Client Table	Run Macro	Macro: Open Client Table
	Recruiter Table	Run Macro	Macro: Open Recruiter Table
	Return to Main Switchboard	Go to Switchboard	Switchboard: Main Switchboard

Table 6–3 Specifications for Switchboard Pages and Items (*continued*)

Switchboard Page	Switchboard Item	Command	Additional Information
View Report	Client Address Report	Run Macro	Macro: Preview Client Address Report
	Client Financial Report	Run Macro	Macro: Preview Client Financial Report
	Clients by City Report	Run Macro	Macro: Preview Clients by City Report
	Clients by Recruiter Report	Run Macro	Macro: Preview Clients by Recruiter Report
	Return to Main Switchboard	Go to Switchboard	Switchboard: Main Switchboard
Print Report	Client Address Report	Run Macro	Macro: Print Client Address Report
	Client Financial Report	Run Macro	Macro: Print Client Financial Report
	Clients by City Report	Run Macro	Macro: Print Clients by City Report
	Clients by Recruiter Report	Run Macro	Macro: Print Clients by Recruiter Report
	Return to Main Switchboard	Go to Switchboard	Switchboard: Main Switchboard

To Create Switchboard Pages

The following steps create the switchboard pages.

1

- Click the New button in the Switchboard Manager dialog box.

- Type `View Form` as the name of the new switchboard page (Figure 6–25).

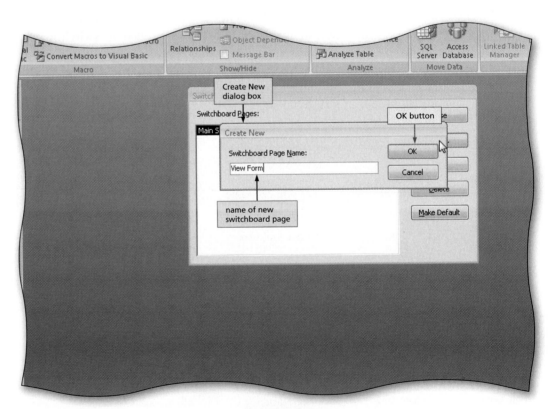

Figure 6–25

2

- Click the OK button to create the View Form switchboard page.

- Use the same technique to create the View Table, View Report, and Print Report switchboard pages (Figure 6–26).

Q&A

Why does Print Report appear at the top of the list?

In the Switchboard Manager dialog box, the pages are listed alphabetically. The switchboard will display the pages in the order in which you entered them. You can change the order of a page when you edit it.

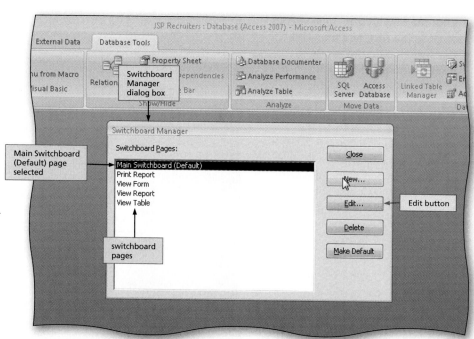

Figure 6–26

To Modify the Main Switchboard Page

The switchboard pages now exist. Currently, there are no actions associated with the pages. You can modify a switchboard page by using the following procedure. Select the page in the Switchboard Manager dialog box, click the Edit button, and then add new items to the page, move existing items to a different position in the list of items, or delete items. For each item, you can indicate the command to be executed when the item is selected.

The following steps modify the Main Switchboard page.

1

- With the Main Switchboard (Default) page selected, click the Edit button to edit the Main switchboard (Figure 6–27).

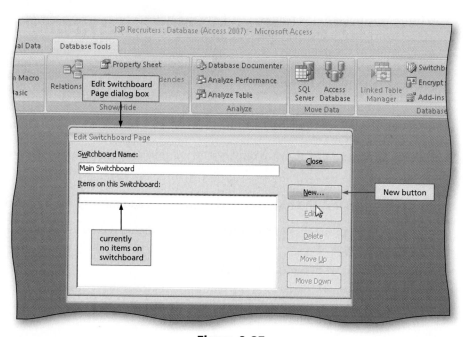

Figure 6–27

2

- Click the New button, type View Form as the text, and then click the Switchboard box arrow to display a menu of available switchboards (Figure 6–28).

Q&A What am I accomplishing here?

There will be a button on the main switchboard labeled View Form. When you click the View Form button on the main switchboard, Access will take the action you indicate, namely it will go to a switchboard page. Whichever page you select for the Switchboard argument is the one to which it will go.

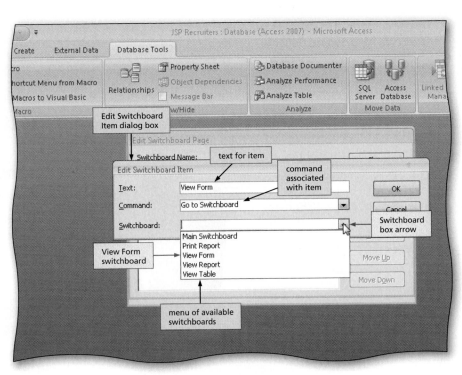

Figure 6–28

3

- Click View Form and then click the OK button to add the item to the switchboard.

- Using the technique illustrated in Steps 2 and 3, add the View Table, View Report, and Print Report items to the Main Switchboard page. In each case, the command is Go to Switchboard. The names of the switchboards are the same as the name of the items. For example, the switchboard for the View Table item is called View Table.

- Click the New button, type Exit Application as the text, and
click the Command box arrow to display a menu of available commands (Figure 6–29).

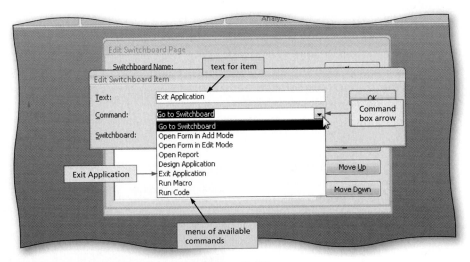

Figure 6–29

4

- Click Exit Application and then click the OK button to add the item to the switchboard.

- Click the Close button in the Edit Switchboard Page dialog box to indicate you have finished editing the Main Switchboard page.

Q&A What is the purpose of the Exit Application button?

The Exit Application button closes the switchboard, closes the database, and returns you to the Getting Starting with Microsoft Office Access screen.

To Modify the Other Switchboard Pages

You modify the other switchboard pages from Table 6–3 on page AC 381 in exactly the same manner you modified the Main Switchboard page. The following steps modify the other switchboard pages.

1
- Click the View Form switchboard page (Figure 6–30).

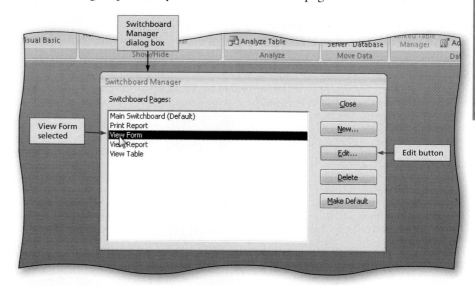

Figure 6–30

2
- Click the Edit button, click the New button to add a new item, type `Client Form` as the text, click the Command box arrow, and then click Run Macro.

- Click the Macro box arrow to display a menu of available macros (Figure 6–31).

Q&A

Why do most of the macro names begin with SB Macros and then a period?

This is the notation used when macros are contained in a macro group. The name of the macro group and a period precede the name of the macro.

Q&A

Why don't I click the New button? How do I add items to the View Form switchboard page?

You are actually editing the page, so you first click the Edit button. You then will be able to add items to the page.

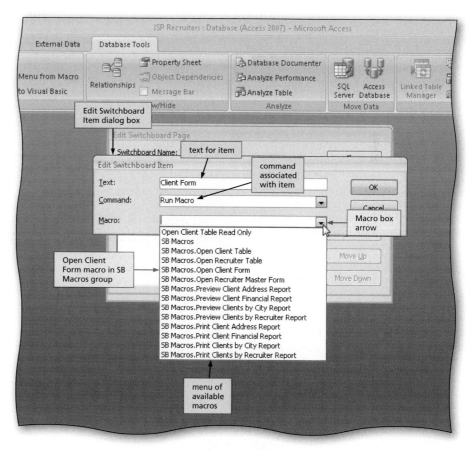

Figure 6–31

- Click Open Client Form, and then click the OK button.

- Click the New button, type `Recruiter Master Form` as the text, click the Command box arrow, and then click Run Macro.

- Click the Macro box arrow, click Open Recruiter Master Form, and then click the OK button.

- Click the New button, type `Return to Main Switchboard` as the text, and click the Switchboard box arrow (Figure 6–32).

Q&A

What is the purpose of the Return to Main Switchboard button?

The Return to Main Switchboard button returns you to the main switchboard page. Because the switchboard is really a series of menus, you always should include a button to return to the main menu, that is, the main switchboard.

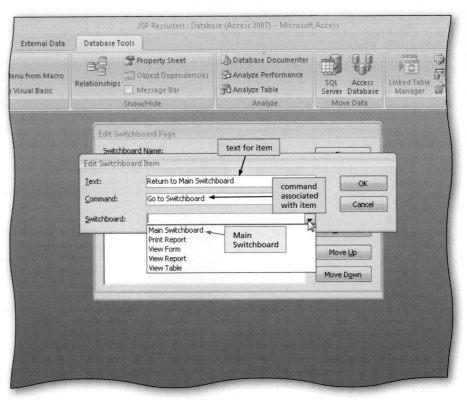

Figure 6–32

- Click Main Switchboard in the list of available switchboards, and then click the OK button.

- Click the Close button in the Edit Switchboard Page dialog box to indicate you have finished editing the View Form switchboard.

- Use the techniques illustrated in Steps 1 through 3 to add the items indicated in Table 6–3 on page AC 381 to the other switchboards (Figure 6–33).

5

- Click the Close button in the Switchboard Manager dialog box.

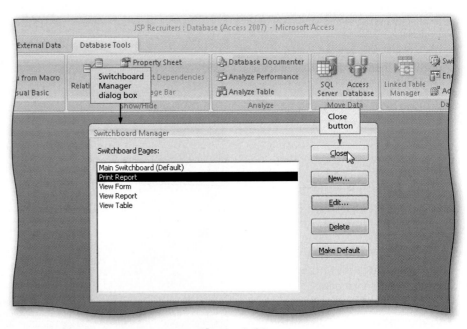

Figure 6–33

To Open a Switchboard

The switchboard is complete and ready for use. Access has created a form called Switchboard that you will run to use the switchboard. It also has created a table called Switchboard Items. Do not modify this table. Switchboard Manager uses this table to keep track of the various switchboard pages and items.

To use the switchboard, select the switchboard in the Navigation Pane, and then click Open on the shortcut menu. The Main Switchboard then will appear. To take any action, click the appropriate buttons. When you have finished, click the Exit Application button. The switchboard will be removed from the screen, and the database will be closed. The following steps open a switchboard system for use.

1

- Show the Navigation Pane, scroll down so that the Switchboard form appears, and then right-click Switchboard (Figure 6–34).

What is the difference between Switchboard and Switchboard Items?

Switchboard is the form. Switchboard Items is a table containing information about the way the switchboard functions. You should not change the Switchboard Items table in any way; otherwise, your switchboard may not function.

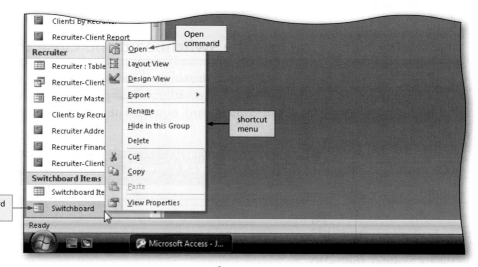

Figure 6–34

2

- Click Open on the shortcut menu to open the switch-board (Figure 6–35).

 **Experiment**

- Try the various buttons on the switchboard to see their effect.

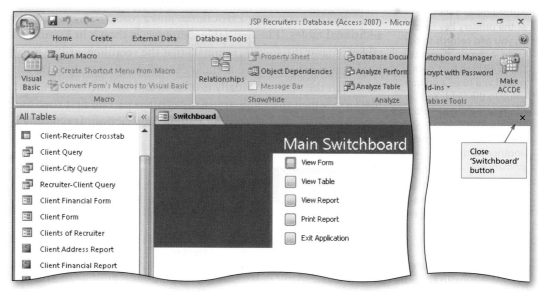

Figure 6–35

BTW

Copy the Structure of a Table
If you want to create a table that has a structure similar to an existing table, you can copy the structure of the table only. To do so, select the existing table in the Navigation Pane and click Copy on the Home tab, then click Paste on the Home tab. When the Paste Table As dialog box appears, type the new table name and click the Structure Only option button. Then, click the OK button. To modify the new table, open it in Design view.

To Open the Database

Because clicking the Exit Application button closed the JSP Recruiters database, you need to open it again. The following steps use the More button to open the JSP Recruiters database from the USB flash drive.

1 With your USB flash drive connected to one of the computer's USB ports, click the More button to display the Open dialog box.

2 If the Folders list is displayed below the Folders button, click the Folders button to remove the Folders list.

3 If necessary, click Computers in the Favorite Links section and then double-click UDISK 2.0 (E:) to select the USB flash drive, Drive E in this case, as the new open location. (Your drive letter might be different.)

4 Click JSP Recruiters to select the file name.

5 Click the Open button to open the database.

6 If a Security Warning appears, click the Options button to display the Microsoft Office Security Options dialog box.

7 With the option button to enable the content selected, click the OK button to enable the content.

To Create the New Tables

You can create new tables in either Datasheet view or Design view. In Design view, you define the structure of the tables. The steps to create the new tables are similar to the steps you used previously to add fields to an existing table and to define primary keys. The only difference is the way you specify a primary key consisting of more than one field. First, you select both fields that make up the primary key by clicking the row selector for the first field, and then hold down the SHIFT key while clicking the row selector for the second field. Once the fields are selected, you can use the Primary Key button to indicate that the primary key consists of both fields.

The following steps create the tables in Design view.

1

• Hide the Navigation Pane.

• Click Create on the Ribbon to display the Create tab (Figure 6–38).

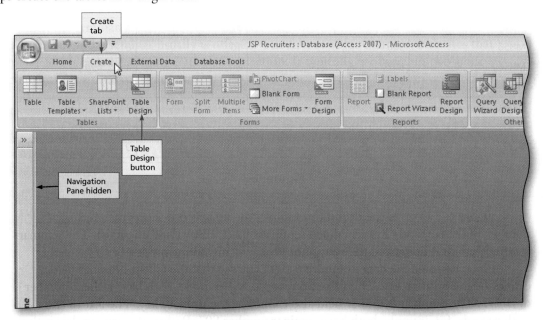

Figure 6–38

2

- Click the Table Design button to create a table in Design view.

- Enter the information for the fields in the Seminar table as indicated in Figure 6–36a on page AC 388, selecting Seminar Number as the primary key.

- Save the table using the name Seminar and close the table.

- Click the Table Design button on the Create tab to create a table in Design view.

- Enter the information for the fields in the Seminar Offerings table as indicated in Figure 6–37a on page AC 389.

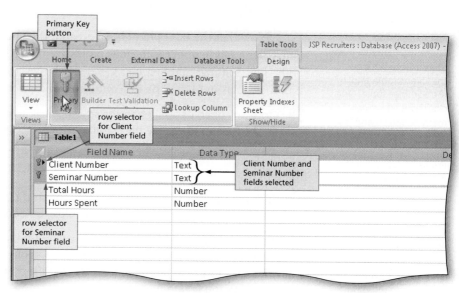

Figure 6–39

- Click the row selector for the Client Number field.

- Hold down the SHIFT key and then click the row selector for the Seminar Number field so both fields are selected.

- Click the Primary Key button on the Design tab to select the combination of the two fields as the primary key (Figure 6–39).

3

- Save the table using the name Seminar Offerings and close the table.

To Import the Data

Now that the tables have been created, you need to add data to them. You either could enter the data, or if the data is already in electronic form, you could import the data. The data for the Seminar and Seminar Offerings tables are on your Data Disk as text files. The following steps import the data.

1 With the JSP Recruiters database open, click the External Data tab on the Ribbon and then click the Text File button in the Import group on the External Data tab to display the Get External Data - Text File dialog box.

2 Click the Browse button and select the location of the files to be imported (for example, the folder called AccessData on drive E:). Select the Seminar text file and click the Open button.

3 Select the 'Append a copy of records to the table' option button and the Seminar table and then click the OK button. Be sure the Delimited option button is selected and click the Next button. Click First Row Contains Field Names check box, click the Next button, and then click the Finish button.

4 Click the Close button to close the Get External Data – Text Box dialog box without saving the import steps.

5 Use the technique shown in Steps 1 through 4 to import the Seminar Offerings text file into the Seminar Offerings table.

BTW

Modify Composite Primary Keys
If you find that you have selected an incorrect field as part of a composite primary key, open the table in Design view, click any field that participates in the primary key, and click the Primary Key button on the Ribbon to remove the primary key. If the fields are adjacent to each other, click the row selector for the first field, hold down the SHIFT key and click the row selector for the second field. Then click the Primary Key button. If the fields are not adjacent to each other, use the CTRL key to select both fields.

To Relate Several Tables

BTW

Many-to-Many Relationships

There is a many-to-many relationship between the Client table and the Seminar table. One client can schedule many seminars and one seminar can be scheduled by many clients. To implement a many-to-many relationship in a relational database management system such as Access, you create a third table, often called a junction or intersection table, that has as its primary key the combination of the primary keys of each of the tables involved in the many-to-many relationship. The primary key of the Seminar Offerings table is the combination of the Client Number and the Seminar Number.

Now that the tables have been created they need to be related to the existing tables. The Client and Seminar Offerings tables are related through the Client Number fields in both. The Seminar and Seminar Offerings tables are related through the Seminar Number fields in both. The following steps illustrate the process of relating the tables.

1 Close any open datasheet on the screen by clicking its Close button. Click Database Tools on the Ribbon to display the Database Tools tab and then click the Relationships button on the Database Tools tab.

2 Click the Show Table button.

3 Click the Seminar Offerings table, click the Add button, click the Seminar table, click the Add button again, and then click the Close button.

4 Point to the Client Number field in the Client table, press the left mouse button, drag to the Client Number in the Seminar Offerings table, and then release the left mouse button. Click the Enforce Referential Integrity check box in the Edit Relationships dialog box and then click the Create button.

5 Drag the Seminar Number field from the Seminar table to the Seminar Offerings table. Click Enforce Referential Integrity check box and then click the Create button to create the relationship (Figure 6–40).

6 Click the Close button in the Relationships group and then click the Yes button to save the changes.

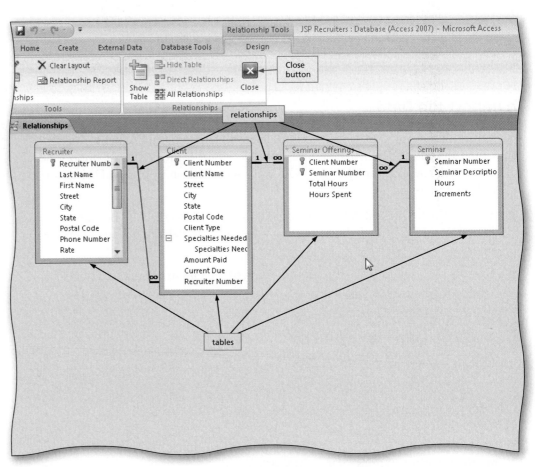

Figure 6–40

PivotTables and PivotCharts

There are two alternatives to viewing data in Datasheet view or Form view. **PivotTable view** presents data as a **PivotTable**, that is, an interactive table that summarizes or analyzes data. PivotChart view presents data as a **PivotChart**, that is, a graphical representation of the data. PivotTables and PivotCharts allow you to view data in multiple dimensions, thus making it valuable for management decision-making. For example, PivotTables and PivotCharts can be used to analyze past data and predict future patterns and trends, a technique known as data mining.

In a PivotTable, you can show different levels of detail easily as well as change the organization or layout of the table by dragging items. You also can filter data by checking or unchecking values in drop-down lists. In a PivotChart, just as in a PivotTable, you can show different levels of detail or change the layout by dragging items. You also can filter data by checking or unchecking values in drop-down lists. You can change the type of chart that appears as well as customize the chart by adding axis titles, a chart title, and a legend. In this section, you will create a PivotTable and a PivotChart. Both the PivotTable and the PivotChart can be based on a table or a query. Both the PivotTable and PivotChart that you create in the following sections are based on a query.

BTW

PivotTable Form
You also can create a PivotTable form. To create a PivotTable form, select the table or query for the PivotTable form in the Navigation Pane, click Create on the Ribbon, click the More Forms button on the Create tab, and then click PivotTable. Click the Field List button on the Design tab to display the PivotTable field list. You then can use the steps shown in Figures 6–47 through 6–50 to create the PivotTable. When finished, save the form. When you open the form, you can use the PivotTable just as in Figures 6–51 through 6–57 on pages AC 400 through AC 402.

To Create the Query

Because the PivotTable and PivotChart you will create will be based on a query, you first must create the query. The following steps create the necessary query.

1

- Click Create on the Ribbon and then click the Query Design button on the Create tab to create a query.

- Click the Recruiter table and then click the Add button to add the Recruiter table to the query.

- Click the Client table and then click the Add button to add the Client table to the query.

- Click the Seminar Offerings table and then click the Add button to add the Seminar Offerings table to the query.

- Click the Close button for the Show Table dialog box.

- Resize the Recruiter and Client field lists so as many fields as possible appear (Figure 6–41).

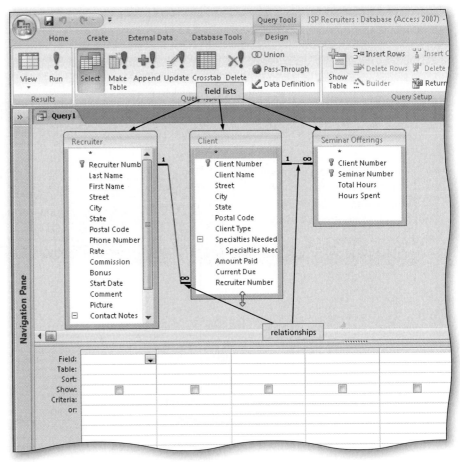

Figure 6–41

- Double-click the Recruiter Number field from the Recruiter table and the Client Number field from the Client table.

- Double-click the Seminar Number and Hours Spent fields from the Seminar Offerings table.

- Right-click the Field row in the first open column to produce a shortcut menu (Figure 6–42).

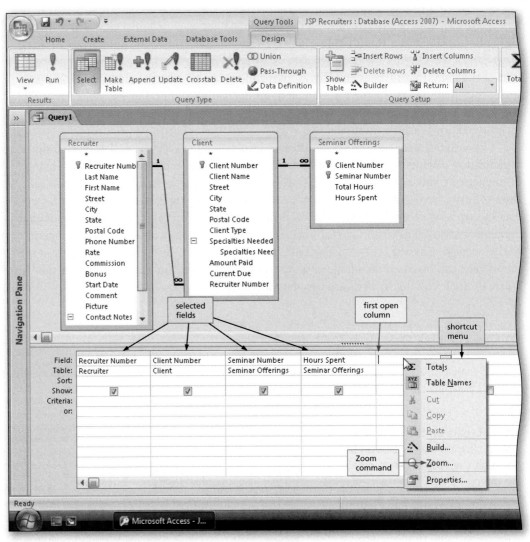

Figure 6–42

3

- Click Zoom on the shortcut menu to display the Zoom dialog box, type Hours Remaining:[Total Hours]-[Hours Spent] in the Zoom dialog box to enter the expression for the field (Figure 6–43).

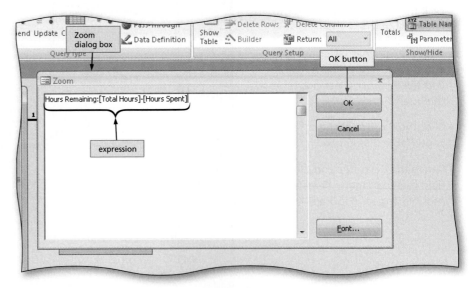

Figure 6–43

4
- Click the OK button and then click the View button on the Design tab to ensure your results are correct.
- Click the Save button on the Quick Access Toolbar and type `Recruiters and Seminar Offerings` as the name of the query (Figure 6–44).

5
- Click the OK button to save the query.
- Close the query.

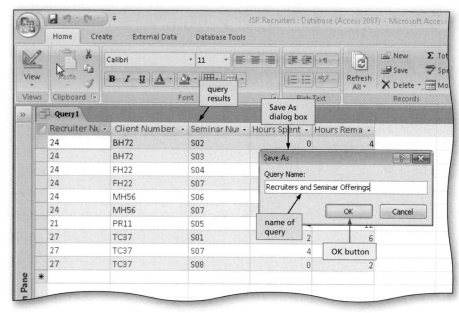

Figure 6–44

PivotTables

Figure 6–45 shows a sample PivotTable. The rows in the table represent the seminars. The columns represent the recruiter numbers. Each column is subdivided into the total of the hours spent and the total of the hours remaining for seminars for those clients assigned to the recruiter. The last column shows the grand total for the items in each row. The last row shows the grand total for items in each column.

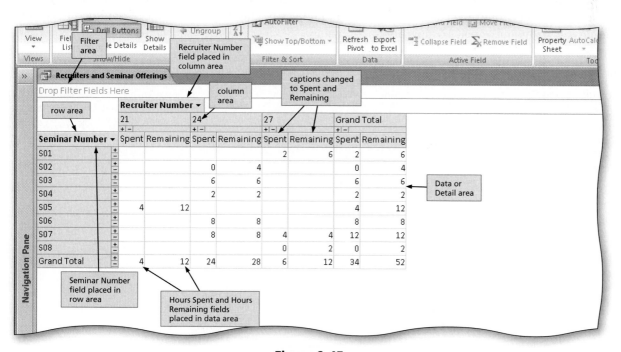

Figure 6–45

BTW

Certification
The Microsoft Certified Application Specialist (MCAS) program provides an opportunity for you to obtain a valuable industry credential—proof that you have the Access 2007 skills required by employers. For more information, see Appendix G or visit the Access 2007 Certification Web page (scsite.com/ac2007/cert).

To create the PivotTable, you place fields in predefined areas of the table called **drop zones**. In the PivotTable in Figure 6–45 on the previous page, the Seminar Number field has been placed in the row zone (also called row area), for example. The drop zones are listed and described in Table 6–4.

Table 6–4 PivotTable Drop Zones	
Zone	**Purpose**
Row	Data from fields in this area will appear as rows in the table.
Column	Data from fields in this area will appear as columns in the table.
Filter	Data from fields in this area will not appear in the table but can be used to restrict the data that appears.
Detail	Data from fields in this area will appear in the detail portion (the body) of the table.
Data	Summary data (for example, a sum) from fields in this area will appear in the detail portion (the body) of the table. Individual values will not appear.

Plan Ahead

Determine the organization of the PivotTable.

1. **Determine the field or fields that will be used for the rows and columns.** What do you want the rows in the grid to represent? What do you want the columns to represent? You can easily reverse the roles later if you wish.

2. **Determine the field or fields that will be summarized in the grid.** Precisely what calculations is the PivotTable intended to present?

3. **Determine the field or fields that will be used to filter the data.** Are there any fields in addition to the ones already identified that will be used to filter the data?

To Create a PivotTable

Applying the steps in the Plan Ahead, JSP Recruiters has determined that the rows will represent the Seminar Number field, the columns will represent the Recruiter Number field, the Hours Spent and Hours Remaining fields will be summarized in the grid. They also have determined that they may occasionally wish to filter the data using the Client Number field. The following steps create the PivotTable using the PivotTable view of the Recruiters and Seminar Offerings query and place fields in appropriate drop zones.

- Show the Navigation Pane, right-click the Recruiters and Seminar Offerings query, click Open on the shortcut menu, and then hide the Navigation Pane.

- Click the View button arrow to display the View button menu (Figure 6–46).

Q&A

Can I just click the View button?

No. Clicking the View button would move to Design view of the query. You want PivotTable view.

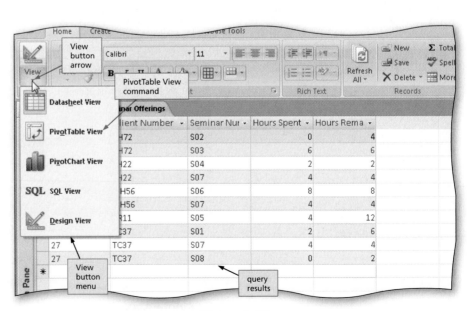

Figure 6–46

2

- Click PivotTable View to switch to PivotTable view of the query.

- If the PivotTable Field List does not appear, click the Field List button on the PivotTable tab to display the field list.

- Click Seminar Number in the field list, and then ensure Row Area appears next to the Add to button (Figure 6–47).

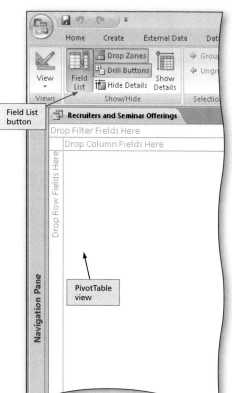
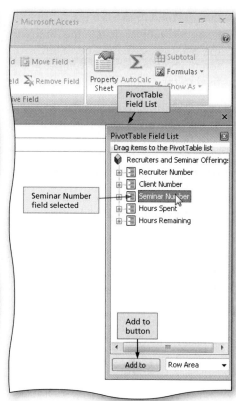

Figure 6–47

3

- Click the Add to button to add the Seminar Number field to the Row area.

- Click the Add to box arrow to display the list of available areas (Figure 6–48).

Q&A Are the areas the same as drop zones?

Yes.

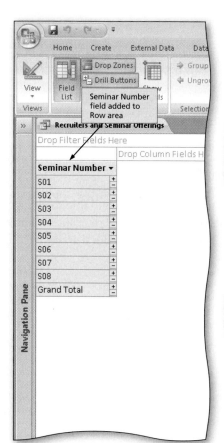
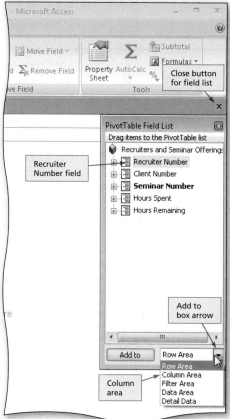

Figure 6–48

- Click Column Area, click the Recruiter Number field in the field list, and then click the Add to button to add the Recruiter Number field to the Column area.

- Click the arrow to display the list of available areas, click Data Area, click Hours Spent, and then click the Add to button to add the Hours Spent field to the Data area.

- Use the same technique to add the Hours Remaining field to the Data area.

- Close the PivotTable Field List by clicking its Close button (Figure 6–49).

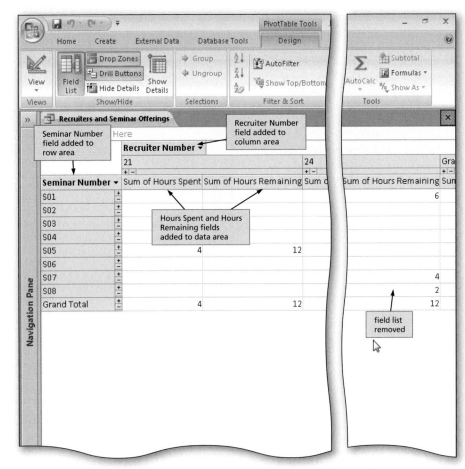

Figure 6–49

Other Ways

1. Click PivotTable View on status bar

To Change Properties in a PivotTable

You can use the property sheet for the objects in a PivotTable to change characteristics of the objects. The following steps use the appropriate property sheet to change the caption for Sum of Hours Spent to Spent and for Sum of Hours Remaining to Remaining in order to reduce the size of the columns in the PivotTable.

1

- Click the Sum of Hours Spent box to select it, and then click the Property Sheet button on the Design tab to display a property sheet.

- Click the Captions tab in the property sheet (Figure 6–50).

2

- Delete the current entry in the Caption property box, type Spent as the new value for the Caption property, and then close the property sheet.

- Use the same technique to change the caption for the Sum of Hours Remaining box to Remaining.

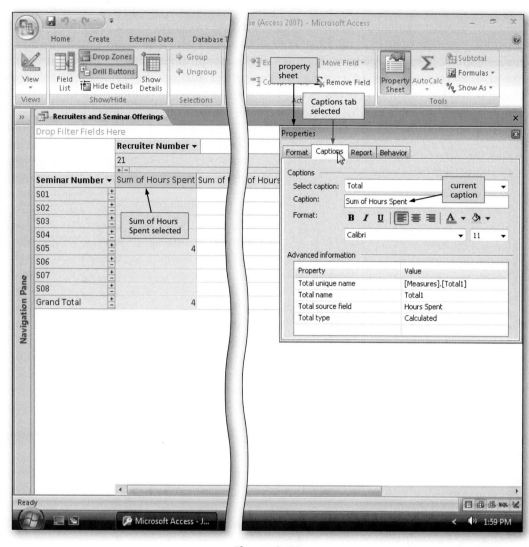

Figure 6–50

To Save the PivotTable Changes

The following step saves the PivotTable changes.

1 Click the Save button on the Quick Access Toolbar.

BTW

Quick Reference

For a table that lists how to complete the tasks covered in this book using the mouse, Ribbon, shortcut menu, and keyboard, see the Quick Reference Summary at the back of this book, or visit the Access 2007 Quick Reference Web page (scsite.com/ac2007/qr).

To Use a PivotTable

To view data using a PivotTable as well as to take advantage of the formatting and filtering that a PivotTable provides, you must open it. If the PivotTable is associated with a query, this would involve opening the query and then switching to PivotTable view. You then can click appropriate plus (+) or minus (–) signs to hide or show data. You also can click appropriate arrows and then check or uncheck the various items that appear to restrict the data that appears. You can drag items from one location to another to change the layout of the PivotTable. The following steps use the PivotTable view of the Recruiters and Seminar Offerings query.

1

- Click the View button arrow, and then click PivotTable View.

Q&A

What if I had closed the query? How would I get back in?

Right-click the query in the Navigation Pane and click Open on the shortcut menu.

- Click the plus sign (+) under recruiter number 21 to remove the details for recruiter number 21 (Figure 6–51).

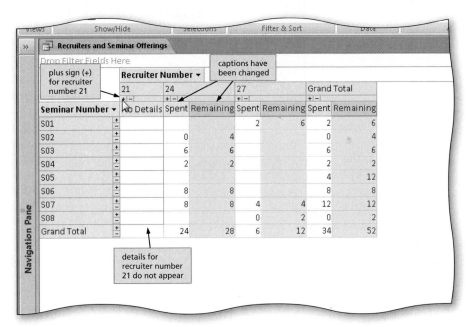

Figure 6–51

2

- Click the minus sign (–) under recruiter number 21 to again display data for recruiter number 21.

- Click the Recruiter Number arrow to display a list of available recruiter numbers (Figure 6–52).

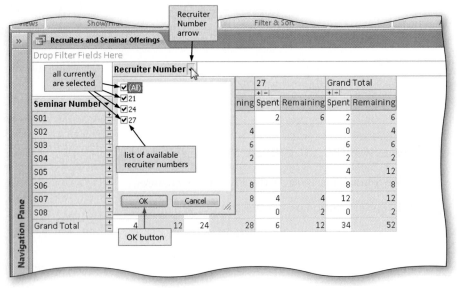

Figure 6–52

3

- Click the Check box for recruiter number 21 to remove the check mark, and then click the OK button to remove the data for recruiter number 21 (Figure 6–53).

Experiment

- Click the Recruiter Number arrow and then try different combinations of check marks to see the effect of your choice.

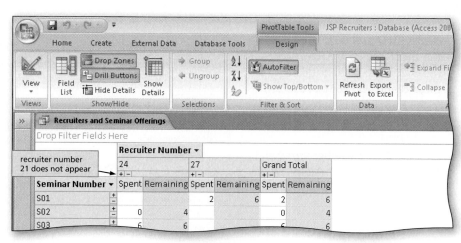

Figure 6–53

4

- Click the Recruiter Number arrow, click the All check box to display all recruiter numbers, and then click the OK button (Figure 6–54).

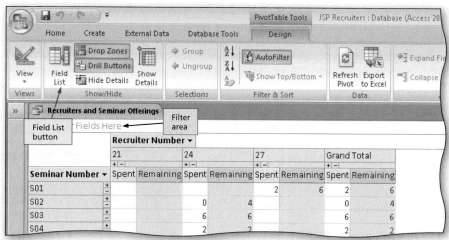

Figure 6–54

5

- Click the Field List button to display the PivotTable Field List. Click Client Number, click the arrow to display a list of available areas, click Filter Area, and then click the Add to button to add the Client Number field to the Filter area.

- Click the Client Number arrow (Figure 6–55).

Q&A

Why do I only see these clients and not the others?

These are the only clients who currently have seminars.

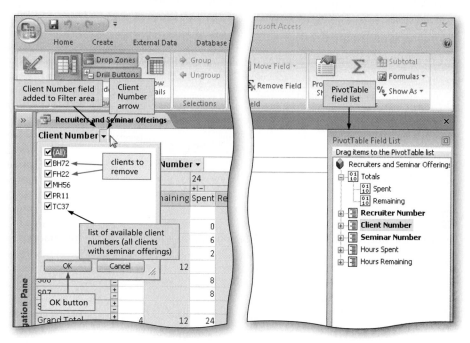

Figure 6–55

6

- Click the check boxes in front of clients BH72 and FH22 to remove the check marks, and then click the OK button so that the data for these clients will not be reflected in the PivotTable (Figure 6–56).

 Experiment

- Click the Client Number arrow and then try different combinations of check marks to see the effect of your choice.

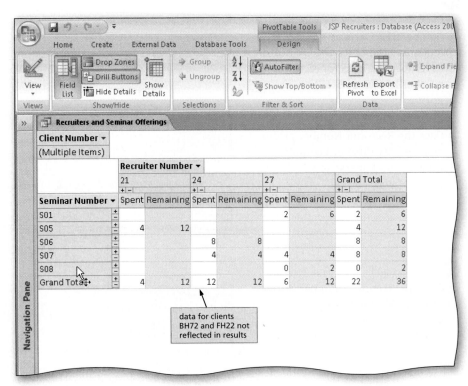

Figure 6–56

7

- Click the Client Number arrow, click the All check box, and then click the OK button to display data for all clients.

- Drag the Recruiter Number field from the Column area to the Row area, and then drag Seminar Number field from the Row area to the Column area to reverse the organization (Figure 6–57).

Q&A I think I dragged to the wrong area. How can I fix it?

You should be able to drag to the correct area. If you would rather start over, close the query without saving it, open the query, and then move to PivotTable view. You then can try again.

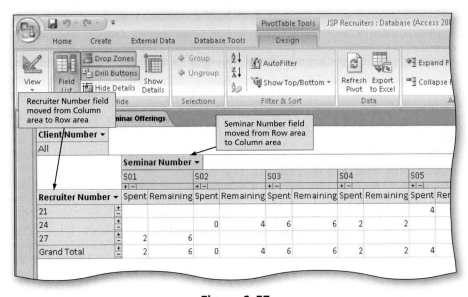

Figure 6–57

8

- Close the Recruiters and Seminar Offerings query without saving your changes.

 Q&A What if I save my changes?

The next time you open the query and move to PivotTable view, you will see the new organization. The roles of the rows and columns would be interchanged.

PivotCharts

If you have not already created a PivotTable for a query or table, you can create a PivotChart for the query or table from scratch by placing fields in appropriate drop zones just as you did when you created a PivotTable. The drop zones are shown in Figure 6–58. Their purpose is described in Table 6–5.

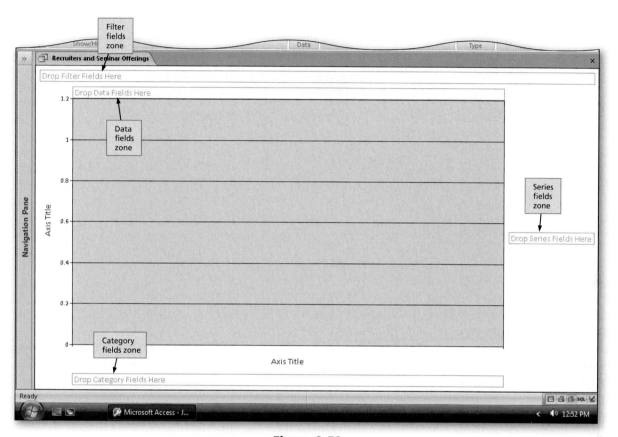

Figure 6–58

Table 6–5 PivotChart Drop Zones

Zone	Purpose	Example
Series	Data from fields in this area will appear as data series, which are represented by colored data markers such as bars. Related markers constitute a series and are assigned a specific color. The names and colors appear in the chart legend.	In the JSP Recruiters PivotChart, the Series area contains the Seminar Number field. The seminar numbers and related colors appear in a legend.
Category	Data from fields in this area will appear as categories, that is, related groups of data. Category labels appear across the x-axis (horizontal) of the chart provided the graph type selected has such an axis.	In the JSP Recruiters PivotChart, the Category area contains the Recruiter Number fields. The recruiter numbers are listed across the x-axis.
Filter	Data from fields in this area will not appear in the chart but can be used to restrict the data that appears.	JSP currently does not use this feature in this PivotChart. If they decide they only want seminars offered to certain clients, they would place the Client Number field in this area.
Data	Data from fields in this area will be summarized within the chart.	In the JSP Recruiters PivotChart, the Data area contains the Hours Spent and Hours Remaining fields. The sum of the values in these fields is represented by the bars in the chart.

Plan
Ahead

Determine the organization of the PivotChart.

1. **Determine the field or fields that will be used for the series.** What field or fields will be represented as data series, that is, as colored data markers like bars? Do you want these represented with a legend?

2. **Determine the field or fields that will be used for the categories.** What field or fields will be represented as categories, that is, as related groups of data? Labels for these fields will appear across the x-axis in those chart types that have an x-axis.

3. **Determine the field or fields that will be used for the data.** Which fields contain the data to be summarized in the chart?

4. **Determine the field or fields that will be used to filter the data.** Are there any fields in addition to the ones already identified that will be used to filter the data?

5. **Determine the type of chart.** What type of chart best represents the data? The most common types of charts are pie charts, line charts and bar charts. A pie chart shows percentages as slices of pies. A line chart uses lines to connect dots that show ordered observations. A bar chart uses bars to show frequencies or values for different categories.

To Create a PivotChart and Add a Legend

If you are using the PivotChart view of a table or query and already have modified the PivotTable view, much of this work already is done. The same information is used wherever possible. You can, of course, modify any aspect of this information. You can remove fields from drop zones by clicking the field name and then pressing the DELETE key. You can add fields to drop zones just as you did with the PivotTable. You also can make other changes, including adding a legend, changing the chart type, changing captions, and adding titles.

JSP Recruiters has applied the steps in the Plan Ahead and determined that seminar numbers will be used for the series, the recruiters will be used for the categories, the Spent and Remaining fields will furnish the data, and the chart type will be 3D Stacked Column.

The following steps create the PivotChart using PivotChart view of the Recruiters and Seminar Offerings query and then add a legend.

- Show the Navigation Pane if it is currently hidden.

- Open the Recruiters and Seminar Offerings query.

- Hide the Navigation Pane.

- Click the View button arrow, and then click PivotChart View.

- If the Chart Field List appears, close the field list by clicking its Close button (Figure 6–59).

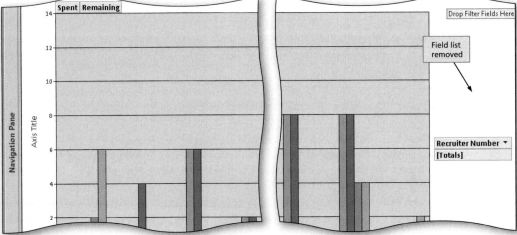

Figure 6–59

Q&A

Where did the data come from?

Because you already have created a PivotTable, Access has represented the data in your PivotTable in the PivotChart. You now can make a variety of changes to this PivotChart.

2

- Click the Legend button on the Design tab to display a legend (Figure 6–60).

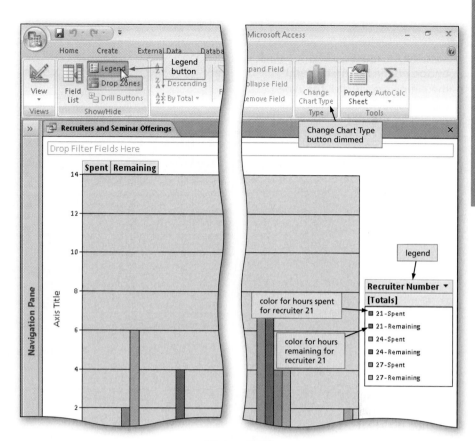

Figure 6–60

Other Ways

1. Click PivotChart View on status bar

To Change the Chart Type

Several types of charts are available. You might find a pie chart more useful than a bar chart, for example. To change the chart type, use the Chart Type button, and then select the desired chart type. The following steps change the chart type to 3D Stacked Column.

1

- If the Change Chart Type button is dimmed, click the Chartspace (that is, the white space in the chart) (Figure 6–61).

Q&A

Does it matter where in the white space I click?

No.

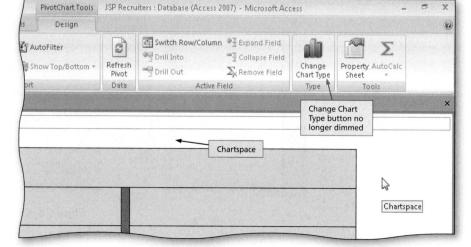

Figure 6–61

②

- Click the Change Chart Type button on the Design tab, and then, if necessary, click the Type tab to display the available chart types (Figure 6–62).

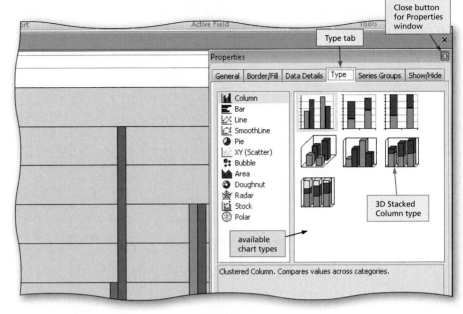

Figure 6–62

③

- Click the 3D Stacked Column type to change the chart type, and then close the Properties window by clicking its Close button (Figure 6–63).

🔍 **Experiment**

- Click the Change Chart Type button and try other chart types to see how they present the data in the PivotChart. When done, select the 3D Stacked Column chart type.

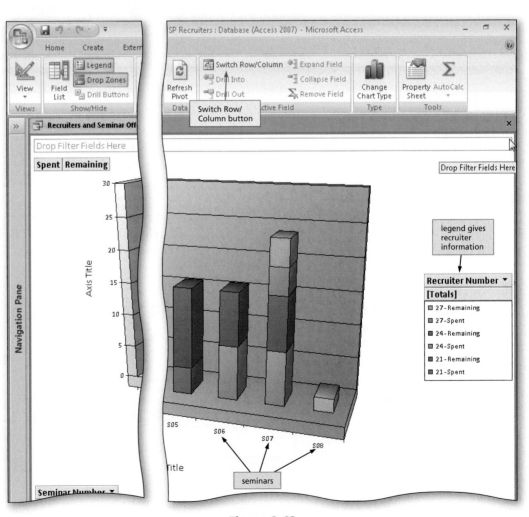

Figure 6–63

To Change PivotChart Orientation

The chart in Figure 6–63 has the seminar numbers along the horizontal axis and recruiter numbers in the legend. The heights of the bars represent the total number of hours for each seminar. Within a bar, the colors represent the recruiter and whether the amount represents hours remaining or hours spent (see legend). To change the chart orientation, you can click the By Row/By Column button. The following step changes the orientation so the recruiter numbers appear along the horizontal axis and the seminars appear in the legend.

1

● Click the Switch Row/Column button on the Design tab to change the organization (Figure 6–64).

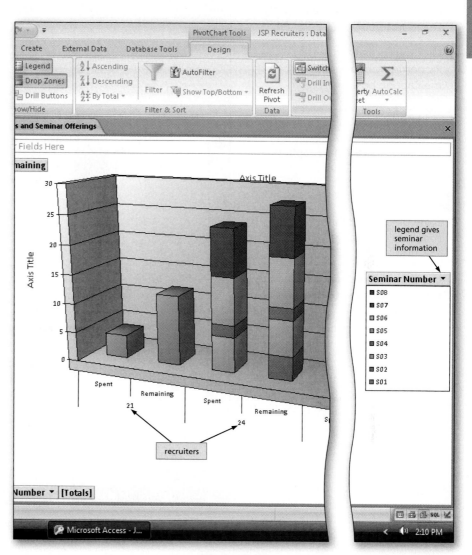

Figure 6–64

To Assign Axis Titles

You can assign titles to an axis by clicking the Axis Title box for the axis you want to change, clicking the Property Sheet button on the Design tab, and then changing the Caption property to the title you want to assign. The following steps change the two axis titles to Hours and Recruiter.

- Click the axis title to the left of the chart, and then click the Property Sheet button on the Design tab.

- Click the Format tab in the Properties window, and then click the Caption box.

- Use the BACKSPACE or DELETE key to delete the old caption.

- Type Hours as the new caption (Figure 6–65).

- Close the property sheet to complete the change of the axis title.

- Use the same technique to change the other axis title to Recruiter.

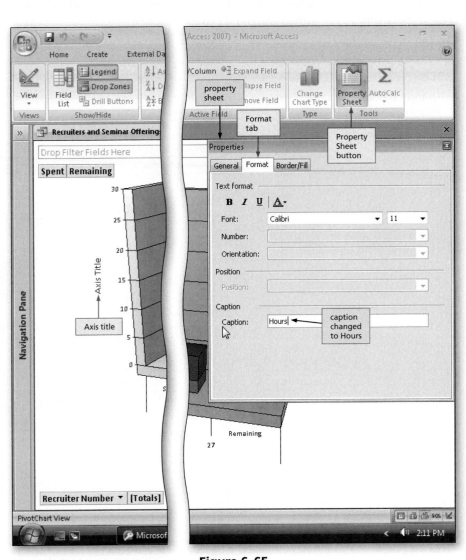

Figure 6–65

To Remove Drop Zones

You can remove the drop zones from the PivotChart to give the chart a cleaner look. To do so, use the Drop Zones button on the Design tab. If you later need to use the drop zones to perform some task, you can return them to the screen by using the Drop Zones button on the Design tab a second time. The following step removes the drop zones.

1

- Click the Drop Zones button on the Design tab to remove the drop zones (Figure 6–66).

Q&A Why remove the drop zones? What if I want to use them later?

The PivotChart has a cleaner look without the drop zones. You can always bring them back whenever you need them by clicking the Drop Zones button again.

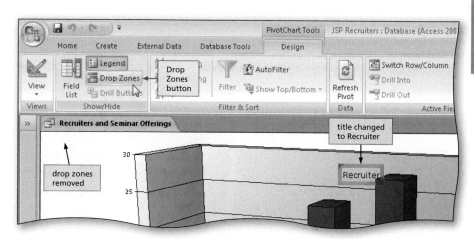

Figure 6–66

To Add a Chart Title

You can add a title to a PivotChart by clicking the Add Title button in the property sheet for the chart. You then can change the Caption property for the newly added title to assign the title of your choice. The following steps add a title to the PivotChart and then change the title's Caption property to Hours by Recruiter and Seminar.

1

- Click anywhere in the Chartspace (the white space) of the PivotChart, click Property Sheet button on the Design tab, and then, if necessary, click the General tab.

- Click the Add Title button (Figure 6–67).

Q&A The title that was added is simply Chart Workspace Title. What if I want a more descriptive title?

In the next step, you will change the title to the one you want.

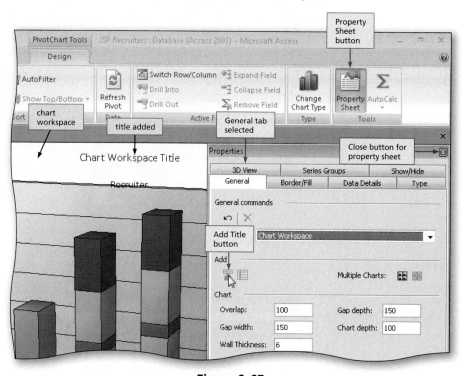

Figure 6–67

2

- Close the property sheet, click the newly added title, and then click the Property Sheet button on the Design tab.

Why did I have to change to a different property sheet?

The property sheet in Step 1 was the property sheet for the chart workspace. To change the title, you need to work with the property sheet for the title.

- Click the Format tab.

- Click the Caption box, and then use the BACKSPACE or DELETE key to erase the old caption.

- Type Hours by Recruiter and Seminar as the new caption and press the ENTER key to change the caption (Figure 6–68).

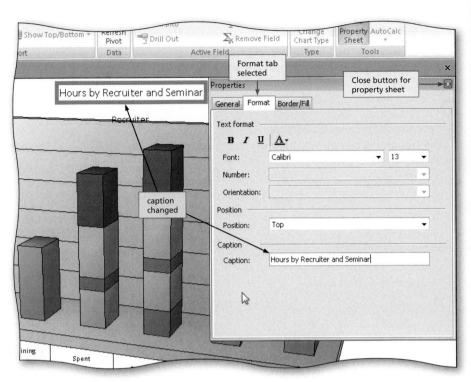

Figure 6–68

3

- Close the property sheet by clicking its Close button (Figure 6–69).

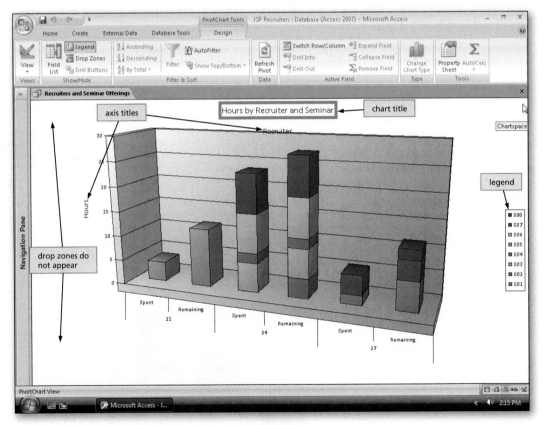

Figure 6–69

To Save the PivotChart Changes

The following step saves the PivotChart changes.

1 Click the Save button on the Quick Access Toolbar.

To Use a PivotChart

To use a PivotChart, you first must open the table or query with which it is associated and then switch to PivotChart view. You then can check or uncheck the various items that appear to restrict the data that appears. In order to do so, the drop zones must appear. If they do not, use the Drop Zones button on the Design tab to display them. You then can click the arrows. You also can drag fields to the drop zones.

You can make the same types of changes you made when you first created the PivotChart. You can change the chart type. You can change the orientation by clicking the By Row/By Column button. You can add or remove a legend. You can change titles. The following steps use the PivotChart view of the Recruiters and Seminar Offerings query.

1

• Be sure the Recruiters and Seminar Offerings query is open in PivotChart view.

• Click the Drop Zones button on the Design tab to display the drop zones (Figure 6–70).

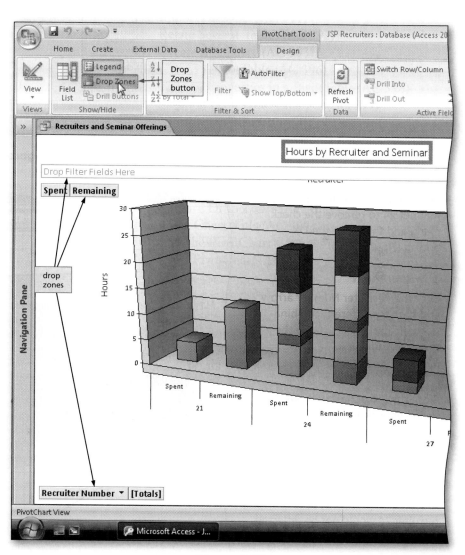

Figure 6–70

Learn It Online

Test your knowledge of chapter content and key terms.

Instructions: To complete the Learn It Online exercises, start your browser, click the Address bar, and then enter the Web address scsite.com/ac2007/learn. When the Access 2007 Learn It Online page is displayed, click the link for the exercise you want to complete and then read the instructions.

Chapter Reinforcement TF, MC, and SA
A series of true/false, multiple choice, and short answer questions that test your knowledge of the chapter content.

Flash Cards
An interactive learning environment where you identify chapter key terms associated with displayed definitions.

Practice Test
A series of multiple choice questions that test your knowledge of chapter content and key terms.

Who Wants To Be a Computer Genius?
An interactive game that challenges your knowledge of chapter content in the style of a television quiz show.

Wheel of Terms
An interactive game that challenges your knowledge of chapter key terms in the style of the television show *Wheel of Fortune*.

Crossword Puzzle Challenge
A crossword puzzle that challenges your knowledge of key terms presented in the chapter.

Apply Your Knowledge

Reinforce the skills and apply the concepts you learned in this chapter.

Adding Tables and Creating PivotTables and PivotCharts
Instructions: Start Access. If you are using the Microsoft Office Access 2007 Complete or the Microsoft Office Access 2007 Comprehensive text, open The Bike Delivers database that you used in Chapter 5. Otherwise, see your instructor for information on accessing the files required in this book. Perform the following tasks:

1. Create two tables in which to store data about the courier services performed for clients. The Services Offered table has the structure shown in Figure 6–73a and the Weekly Services table has the structure shown in Figure 6–73b. The Bike Delivers charges a set fee based on the type of service the client requests. At the end of each week, the company bills the clients.

(a) Structure of Services Offered Table

Field Name	Data Type	Primary Key?
Service Code	Text	Yes
Service Description	Text	
Fee	Currency	

Figure 6–73

Field Name	Data Type	Primary Key?	
Customer Number	Text	Yes	**(b)**
Service Date	Date/Time (change Format Property to Short Date)	Yes	**Structure of Weekly**
Service Time	Date/Time (change Format Property to Medium Time)	Yes	**Services**
Service Code	Text		**Table**

Figure 6–73 (continued)

2. Import the Services Offered.txt file to the Services Offered table and the Weekly Services.txt file to the Weekly Services table.

3. Create a query that includes the Courier, Customer, Services Offered, and Weekly Services tables. Add the Courier Number from the Courier table, the Customer Number and Service Code from the Weekly Services table, and the Service Fee from the Services Offered table to the design grid. Save the query as Couriers and Services.

4. Create the PivotTable shown in Figure 6–74a and the PivotChart shown in Figure 6–74b.

(a) PivotTable

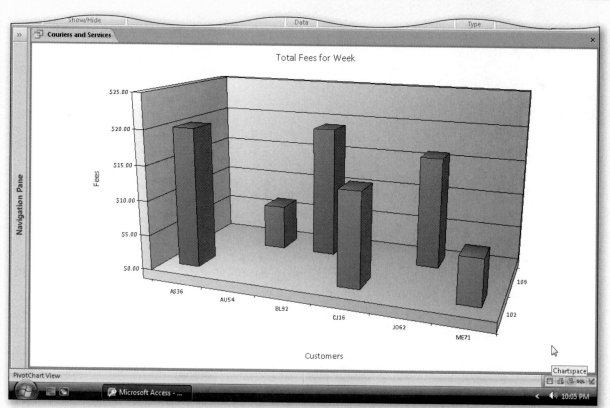

(b) PivotChart

Figure 6–74

5. Submit the revised database in the format specified by your instructor.

Extend Your Knowledge

Extend the skills you learned in this chapter and experiment with new skills. You may need to use Help to complete the assignment.

Modifying Macros and Switchboards

Instructions: Start Access. Open the Regional Books database. See the inside back cover of this book for instructions on downloading the Data Files for Students, or contact your instructor for more information about accessing the required files.

Regional Books, a local bookstore, has created macros and a switchboard. Because the company uses a dark red and gray color scheme on all their publicity materials, they would like the switchboard to reflect those colors. They also would like the name of the store to show on the main switchboard page. You will modify the switchboard page as shown in Figure 6–75. You also will modify a macro.

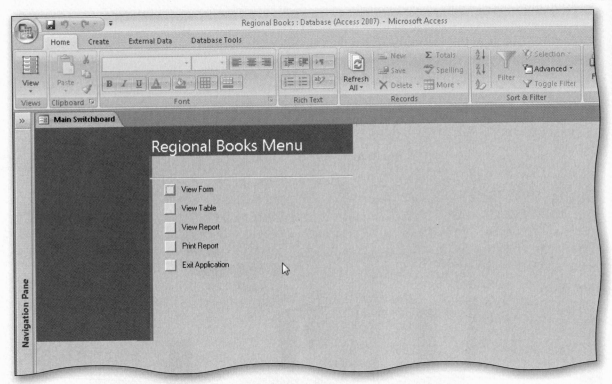

Figure 6–75

Perform the following tasks:

1. Open the switchboard in Design view and change the background color of the form to correspond to the colors shown in Figure 6–75. Change the title to Regional Books Menu.

2. Open the Open Publisher Table macro in Design view and change the Data Mode for the table so that it is read-only. A message box with an appropriate message should appear when the table is opened.

3. Change the database properties, as specified by your instructor. Submit the revised database in the format specified by your instructor.

Make It Right

Analyze a database and correct all errors and/or improve the design.

Correcting Form Design Errors

Instructions: Start Access. Open the College Dog Walkers database. See the inside back cover of this book for instructions on downloading the Data Files for Students, or contact your instructor for more information about accessing the required files.

   The College Dog Walkers database contains data for an organization that provides dog walking services. The owner of the company has created the switchboard shown in Figure 6–76a but he forgot to add the Exit Application button to the main switchboard page. He also forgot to include a button on the View Form page shown in Figure 6–76b to let the user return to the main switchboard page.

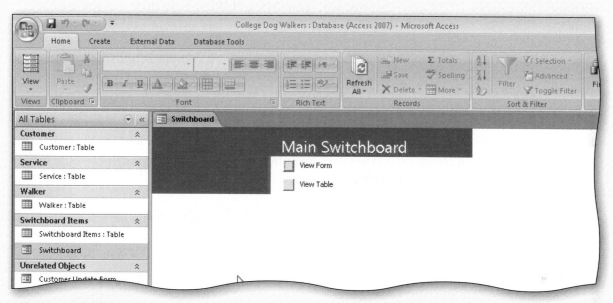

(a) Main Switchboard

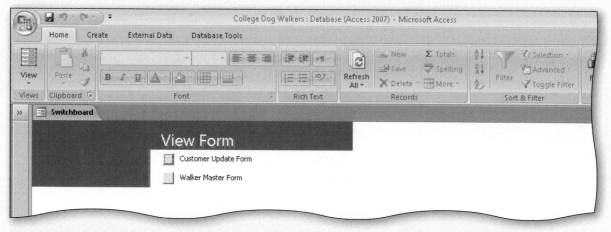

(b) View Form Switchboard Page

Figure 6–76

   Correct these errors, and change the database properties as specified by your instructor. Submit the revised database in the format specified by your instructor.

In the Lab

Design, create, modify, and/or use a database following the guidelines, concepts, and skills presented in this chapter. Labs are listed in order of increasing difficulty.

Lab 1: Creating Macros, a Switchboard, and a PivotTable for the JMS TechWizards Database

Problem: JMS TechWizards would like an easy way to access the various tables, forms, and reports by simply clicking a button or two. This would make the database much easier to maintain and update. The company also needs to keep track of open service requests, that is, uncompleted requests for service.

Instructions: For this assignment you will use the JMS TechWizards database and the data files, Workorders.txt and Category.txt. If you are using the Microsoft Office Access 2007 Complete or the Microsoft Office Access 2007 Comprehensive text, open JMS TechWizards database that you used in Chapter 5. Otherwise, see the inside back cover of this book for instructions on downloading the Data Files for Students, or contact your instructor for more information about accessing the required files. The Workorders.txt and Category.txt files are text files that are included with the Data Files for Students.

Perform the following tasks:

1. Create a macro group that will include macros that will perform the following tasks: (a) open the Client table in read-only mode, (b) open the Technician table in read-only mode (c) open the Client form, (d) open the Technician Master Form, (e) preview the Billing Summary Report, (f) preview the Clients by Technician report, (g) preview the Clients by Type report, (h) print the Billing Summary Report, (i) print the Clients by Technician report, and (j) print the Clients by Type report. Name the macro group JMS Macros.

2. Create a switchboard for the JMS TechWizards database. Use the same design for your switchboard pages as the one illustrated in this chapter. For example, the View Table switchboard page should have three choices: Client Table, Technician Table, and Return to Main Switchboard. Include all the tables, forms, and reports for which you created macros in step 1.

3. Run the switchboard and correct any errors.

4. Create two tables in which to store the open request information. Use Category and Work Orders as the table names. The structure of the Category table is shown in Figure 6–77a and the structure of the Work Orders table is shown in Figure 6–77b. Because the structure of the Work Orders table is similar to the Seminar Offerings table in the JSP Recruiters database, copy the Seminar Offerings table and paste only the structure to the JMS TechWizards database. Import the Category.txt file to the Category table and the Workorders.txt file to the Work Orders table.

(a) Structure of Category Table

Field Name	Data Type	Primary Key?
Category Code	Text	Yes
Category Description	Text	

(b) Structure of Work Orders Table

Field Name	Data Type	Primary Key?
Client Number	Text	Yes
Category Code	Text	Yes
Total Hours (est)	Number	
Hours Spent	Number	

Figure 6–77

5. Add the Category and the Work Orders tables to the Relationships window. Establish a one-to-many relationship between the Category table and the Work Orders table. Establish a one-to-many relationship between the Client table and the Work Orders table.

6. Create a query that joins the Technician table, Client table, and Work Orders table. Include the technician number from the Technician table, the Client Number from the Client table, the category number from the Work Orders table, and hours spent from the Work Orders table in the design grid. Add a calculated field that calculates the hours remaining (Total Hours(est) - Hours Spent). Use Hours Remaining as the name of the calculated field. Run the query and save the query as Technicians and Work Orders.

7. Open the Technicians and Work Orders query and switch to PivotTable view. Create the PivotTable shown in Figure 6–78. Change the captions for the Hours Spent and Hour Remaining fields to Spent and Remaining, respectively.

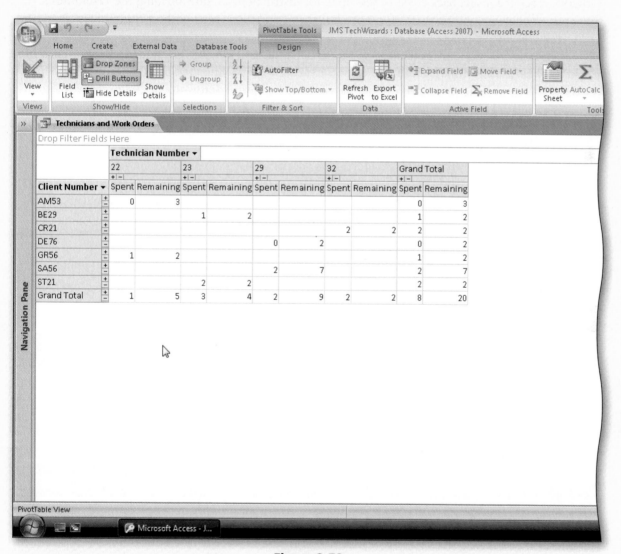

Client Number	Technician Number 22 Spent	22 Remaining	23 Spent	23 Remaining	29 Spent	29 Remaining	32 Spent	32 Remaining	Grand Total Spent	Grand Total Remaining
AM53	0	3							0	3
BE29			1	2					1	2
CR21							2	2	2	2
DE76					0	2			0	2
GR56	1	2							1	2
SA56					2	7			2	7
ST21			2	2					2	2
Grand Total	1	5	3	4	2	9	2	2	8	20

Figure 6–78

8. Submit the revised database in the format specified by your instructor.

In the Lab

Lab 2: Creating Macros and a Switchboard for the Hockey Fan Zone Database

Problem: The management of the Hockey Fan Zone store would like an easy way to access the store's various tables, forms, and reports, by simply clicking a button or two. This would make the database much easier to maintain and update. Management also needs to track items that are being reordered from suppliers. Management must know when an item was ordered and how many were ordered. Hockey Fan Zone may place an order with a supplier one day and then find it needs to order more of the same item before the original order is filled.

Instructions: If you are using the Microsoft Office Access 2007 Complete or the Microsoft Office Access 2007 Comprehensive text, open the Hockey Fan Zone database that you used in Chapter 5. Otherwise, see the inside back cover of this book for instructions on downloading the Data Files for Students, or contact your instructor for more information about accessing the required files. Perform the following tasks:

1. Create a macro group that includes macros to perform the following tasks: (a) open the Item table in read-only mode, (b) open the Supplier table in read-only mode, (c) open the Item Update Form, (d) open the Supplier Master Form, (e) preview the Inventory Status Report, (f) preview the Items by Supplier report, (g) preview the Items by Type report, (h) print the Inventory Status Report, (i) print the Items by Supplier report, and (j) print the Items by Type report. Name the macro group HFZ Macros.

2. Create a switchboard for the Hockey Fan Zone database. Use the same design for your switchboard pages as the one illustrated in this chapter. For example, the View Form switchboard page should have three choices: Item Update Form, Supplier Master Form, and Return to Main Switchboard. Include all the tables, forms, and reports for which you created macros in step 1.

3. Run the switchboard and correct any errors.

4. Create a table in which to store the item reorder information using the structure shown in Figure 6–79a. Use Reorder as the name of the table. Add the data shown in Figure 6–79b to the Reorder table.

Field Name	Data Type	Primary Key?
Item Number	Text	Yes
Date Ordered	Date/Time (Create an Input Mask and use Short Date)	Yes
Number Ordered	Number	

(a) Structure of Reorder Table

Item Number	Date Ordered	Number Ordered
3673	4/15/2008	2
5923	4/21/2008	1
6343	4/1/2008	5
6343	4/4/2008	6
7550	4/3/2008	2
7550	4/5/2008	2
7930	4/11/2008	3
7930	4/14/2008	3

(b) Data for Reorder Table

Figure 6–79

5. Add the Reorder table to the Relationships window and establish a one-to-many relationship between the Item table and the Reorder table.

6. Create a query that joins the Reorder table, Item table, and Supplier table. Include the item number from the Reorder table, the supplier code and number on hand from the Item table, and the number ordered from the Reorder table in the design grid. Run the query and save the query as Supplier and Number of Items.

7. Submit the revised database in the format specified by your instructor.

In the Lab

Lab 3: Creating Macros, a Switchboard, a PivotTable, and a PivotChart for the Ada Beauty Supply Database

Problem: Ada Beauty Supply wants an easy way to access the various tables, forms, and reports by simply clicking a button or two. The company also needs to track active accounts for the current week and wants the ability to easily change the way data is summarized and presented.

Instructions: If you are using the Microsoft Office Access 2007 Complete or the Microsoft Office Access 2007 Comprehensive text, open the Ada Beauty Supply database that you used in Chapter 5. Otherwise, see the inside back cover of this book for instructions on downloading the Data Files for Students, or contact your instructor for more information about accessing the required files. Submit the revised database in the format specified by your instructor.

Instructions Part 1: Create a macro group that includes macros to open the Customer and Sales Rep tables, to open the Customer Financial Form and the Sales Rep Master, and to view and print the Customer Status Report and the Customers by Sales Rep report. Create a switchboard that uses these macros.

Instructions Part 2: The management of Ada Beauty Supply want to maintain data on a weekly basis on the open orders for its customers. These are orders that have not yet been delivered. To track this information requires a new table, an Open Orders table. Create this table using the structure shown in Figure 6–80. Import the Open Orders.txt file into the Open Orders table. Then, update the relationship between the Customer table and the Open Orders table.

Field Name	Data Type	Primary Key?
Order Number	Text	Yes
Amount	Currency	
Customer Number	Text	

Figure 6–80

Continued >

In the Lab *continued*

Instructions Part 3: The management wants to actively track the expected commissions on open orders by sales rep and customer. Create a query that includes the Sales Rep, Open Orders, and Customer tables. Include the sales rep number, customer number, and commission in the design grid. Add a calculated field that calculates the expected commission on the open orders amount, and then create the PivotTable shown in Figure 6–81.

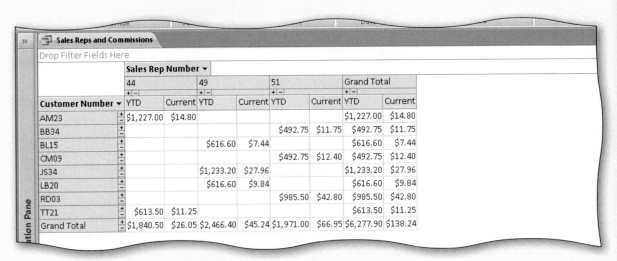

Sales Reps and Commissions								
Drop Filter Fields Here								
		Sales Rep Number ▾						
		44		49		51		Grand Total	
		+–		+–		+–		+–	
Customer Number ▾		YTD	Current	YTD	Current	YTD	Current	YTD	Current
AM23	±	$1,227.00	$14.80					$1,227.00	$14.80
BB34	±					$492.75	$11.75	$492.75	$11.75
BL15	±			$616.60	$7.44			$616.60	$7.44
CM09	±					$492.75	$12.40	$492.75	$12.40
JS34	±			$1,233.20	$27.96			$1,233.20	$27.96
LB20	±			$616.60	$9.84			$616.60	$9.84
RD03	±					$985.50	$42.80	$985.50	$42.80
TT21	±	$613.50	$11.25					$613.50	$11.25
Grand Total	±	$1,840.50	$26.05	$2,466.40	$45.24	$1,971.00	$66.95	$6,277.90	$138.24

Figure 6–81

Cases and Places

Apply your creative thinking and problem solving skills to design and implement a solution.

● EASIER   ●● MORE DIFFICULT

● 1: Creating Macros and a Switchboard for the Second Hand Goods Database

If you are using the Microsoft Office Access 2007 Complete or the Microsoft Office Access 2007 Comprehensive text, open the Second Hand Goods database that you used in Chapter 5. Otherwise, see the inside back cover of this book for instructions on downloading the Data Files for Students, or contact your instructor for more information about accessing the required files. Create a macro group named SHG Macros. The macro group should include macros to open the two tables (Item and Seller), open the two forms (Item Update Form and Seller Master Form), and preview and print the Items by Seller report. For the two open-table macros, select Edit as the Data Mode and do not display a message box. Create the switchboard shown in Figure 6–82a that uses the macros in the macro group. The Forms and Tables switchboard pages are similar in design to the View Form and View Table pages in the chapter. The Reports page is shown in Figure 6–82b. Submit the revised database in the format specified by your instructor.

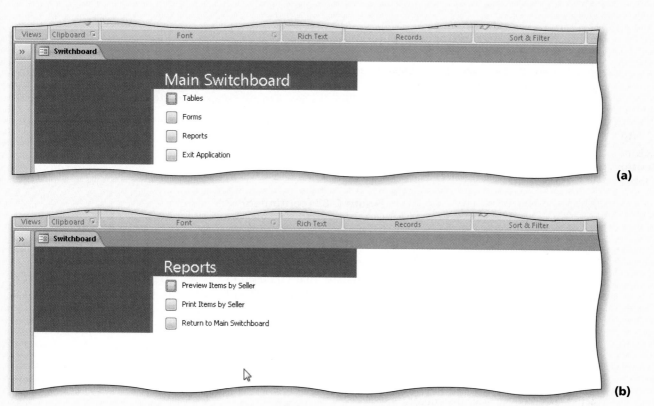

(a)

(b)

Figure 6–82

• 2: Adding Tables, Creating Macros, and a Switchboard for the BeachCondo Rentals Database

If you are using the Microsoft Office Access 2007 Complete or the Microsoft Office Access 2007 Comprehensive text, open the BeachCondo Rentals database that you used in Chapter 5. Otherwise, see the inside back cover of this book for instructions on downloading the Data Files for Students, or contact your instructor for more information about accessing the required files. Create a macro group named BCR Macro Group. The macro group should include macros to open the two tables (Condo Unit and Owner), open the two forms (Condo Unit Form and Owner Master Form) and preview and print the two reports (Available Rentals Report and Condos by Bedroom). Create a switchboard that uses the macros in the macro group. The switchboard should be similar in design to the one created in this chapter. The rental company must keep track of the units that are rented and the individuals who rent the units. Units are rented a week at a time and rentals start on Saturday. The structure of the tables that should contain this data, the Current Rentals and Renter tables, is shown in Figure 6–83a and Figure 6-83b. The data for the two tables is in separate worksheets in the data file, Rentals.xlsx. Create the Current Rentals table in Table Design view. Create the Renter table in Datasheet view. The data type for Renter Number is Text and it is the primary key for the Renter table. Then, import the data from the workbook. Finally, create the necessary relationships. There is a one-to-many relationship between the Renter and the Current Rentals table and a one-to-many relationship between the Condo Unit table and the Current Rentals table. Submit the revised database in the format specified by your instructor.

Field Name	Data Type	Primary Key?
Unit Number	Text	Yes
Start Date	Date/Time	Yes
Length	Number	
Renter Number	Text	

(a) **Structure of Current Rentals Table**

Figure 6–83

Continued >

Cases and Places *continued*

Field Name	Data Type	Primary Key?
Renter Number	Text	Yes
First Name	Text	
Last Name	Text	
Telephone Number	Text	

**(b)
Structure
of Renter
Table**

Figure 6–83 (continued)

••3: Creating Macros and a Switchboard for the Restaurant Database

If you are using the Microsoft Office Access 2007 Complete or the Microsoft Office Access 2007 Comprehensive text, open the restaurant database that you used in Chapter 5. Otherwise, see the inside back cover of this book for instructions on downloading the Data Files for Students, or contact your instructor for more information about accessing the required files. Using the Plan Ahead guidelines presented in this chapter, determine what macros you need to add to your database and if you need a switchboard. Because your database will be used by others who may not be familiar with Access, a switchboard probably would be beneficial. Determine what pages and what actions your switchboard should perform. Create the necessary macros and the switchboard. Submit the revised database in the format specified by your instructor.

••4: Enhancing Your Contacts Database

Make It Personal

If you are using the Microsoft Office Access 2007 Complete or the Microsoft Office Access 2007 Comprehensive text, open the contacts database that you used in Chapter 5. Otherwise, see the inside back cover of this book for instructions on downloading the Data Files for Students, or contact your instructor for more information about accessing the required files. Review the way in which you have used the Contacts database. Are there certain forms, reports, or queries that you open regularly? If so, consider creating a macro to automate these tasks. Review the companies in your database. Have you contacted different individuals at the same company? Are you interested in more than one position at the same company? If the answer is yes, consider creating additional tables similar to the Seminar Offerings table in this chapter. Modify the database and create any necessary forms. Submit the revised database in the format specified by your instructor.

••5: Understanding PivotTables and PivotCharts

Working Together

As a team, research the differences between a crosstab query and a PivotTable. Copy the JMS TechWizards database and rename the database to your team name. For example, if your team is TeamTogether, then name the database TeamTogether TechWizards. Modify the City-Technician crosstab query. What type of modifications are possible to a crosstab query? How difficult is it to make the changes? Create a PivotTable and a PivotChart from the same data. Create a PivotTable form. Discuss when a crosstab is appropriate and when a PivotTable is appropriate and use Microsoft Word to write a short paper that explains the differences. Why would you use a PivotTable form? Submit the Word document and the revised database in the format specified by your instructor.

SQL Feature

Using SQL

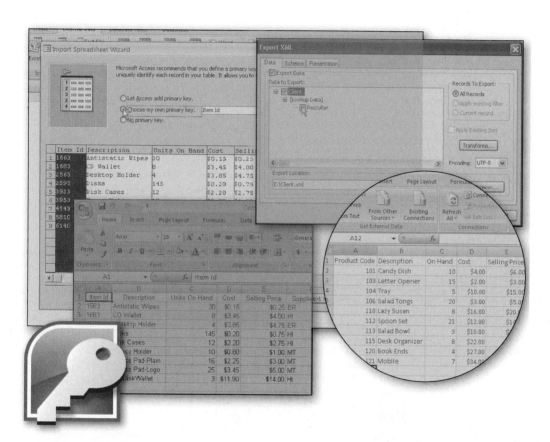

Objectives

You will have mastered the material in this project when you can:

- Change the font or font size for SQL queries
- Include fields and criteria in SQL queries
- Use computed fields and built-in functions in SQL queries
- Sort the results in SQL queries
- Use multiple functions in the same command

- Group the results in SQL queries
- Join tables in SQL queries
- Use subqueries
- Compare SQL queries with Access-generated SQL
- Use INSERT, UPDATE, and DELETE queries to update a database

Context-Sensitive Help in SQL

When you are working in SQL view, you can obtain context-sensitive help on any of the keywords in your query. To do so, click anywhere in the word about which you wish to obtain help, and then press F1.

SQL Feature Introduction

The language called **SQL (Structured Query Language)** is a very important language for querying and updating databases. It is the closest thing to a universal database language, because the vast majority of database management systems, including Access, use it in some fashion. Although some users will be able to do all their queries through the query features of Access instead of SQL, those in charge of administering and maintaining the database system certainly should be familiar with this important language. Access also can be used as an interface to other database management systems, such as SQL Server. To use or interface with SQL Server requires knowledge of SQL.

Project — Using SQL

JSP Recruiters administration realizes that there is a database language for queries that seems to be universal. The language, which is called SQL and is supported by virtually every DBMS, is an extremely powerful tool for querying a database. The administration wants staff at JSP to learn to use this language to broaden their capabilities in accessing JSP Recruiters data. In the process, they would like to create a wide variety of SQL queries. Similar to creating queries in Design view, SQL provides users a way of querying relational databases. In SQL, however, instead of making entries in the design grid, the user must type commands to obtain the desired results, as shown in Figure 1a. You then can click the View button to view the results just as when you are creating queries in Design view. The results for the query in Figure 1a are shown in Figure 1b.

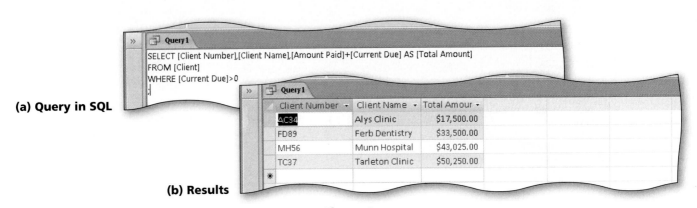

(a) Query in SQL

(b) Results

Figure 1

Overview

As you read through this feature, you will learn how to create SQL queries by performing these general tasks:

- Create queries involving criteria.
- Sort the results of a query.
- Group records in a query and perform group calculations.
- Join tables in queries.
- Create a query that involves a subquery.
- Update data using the INSERT, UPDATE, and DELETE commands.

SQL Query Guidelines

1. **Select the fields for the query.** Examine the requirements for the query you are constructing to determine which fields are to be included.

2. **Determine which table or tables contain these fields.** For each field, determine the table in which it is located.

3. **Determine criteria.** Determine any criteria data you must satisfy to be included in the results. If there are more than two tables in the query, determine the criteria to be used to ensure the data matches correctly.

4. **Determine sort order.** Is the data to be sorted in some way? If so, by what field or fields is it to be sorted?

5. **Determine grouping.** Is the data to be grouped in some way? If so, by what field is it to be grouped? Are there any calculations to be made for the group?

6. **Determine any update operations to be performed.** Determine if rows need to be inserted, changed, or deleted. Determine the tables involved.

When necessary, more specific details concerning the above decisions and/or actions are presented at appropriate points in the feature. The feature also will identify the use of these guidelines in creating SQL queries such as the one shown in Figure 1.

Plan Ahead

Starting Access

If you are using a computer to step through the project in this feature and you want your screen to match the figures in this book, you should change your screen's resolution to 1024×768. For information about how to change a computer's resolution, read Appendix E.

To Start Access

The following steps, which assume Windows Vista is running, start Access.

Note: If you are using Windows XP, see Appendix F for alternate steps.

1 Click the Start button on the Windows Vista taskbar to display the Start menu.

2 Click All Programs at the bottom of the left pane on the Start menu to display the All Programs list and then click Microsoft Office in the All Programs list to display the Microsoft Office list.

3 Click Microsoft Office Access 2007 in the Microsoft Office list to start Access and display the Getting Started with Microsoft Office Access window.

4 If the Access window is not maximized, click the Maximize button on its title bar to maximize the window.

To Open a Database

In Chapter 1, you created your database on a USB flash drive using the file name, JSP Recruiters. There are two ways to open the file containing your database. If the file you created appears in the Recent Documents list, you could click it to open the file. If not, you can use the More button to open the file. The following steps use the More button to open the JSP Recruiters database from the USB flash drive.

Note: If you are using Windows XP, see Appendix F for alternate steps.

1 With your USB flash drive connected to one of the computer's USB ports, click the More button to display the Open dialog box.

2 If the Folders list is displayed below the Folders button, click the Folders button to remove the Folders list.

3 If necessary, click Computer in the Favorite Links section and then double-click UDISK 2.0 (E:) to select the USB flash drive, Drive E in this case, as the new open location. (Your drive letter might be different.)

4 Click JSP Recruiters to select the file name.

5 Click the Open button to open the database.

6 If a Security Warning appears, click the Options button to display the Microsoft Office Security Options dialog box.

7 With the option button to enable the content selected, click the OK button to enable the content.

SQL Background

BTW

Datasheet Font Size
You also can use the Access Options button to change the default font and font size for datasheets. To do so, click Datasheet in the Access Options dialog box and make the desired changes in the default font area.

SQL was developed under the name SEQUEL at the IBM San Jose research facilities as the data manipulation language for IBM's prototype relational model DBMS, System R, in the mid-1970s. In 1980, it was renamed SQL to avoid confusion with an unrelated hardware product called SEQUEL. It is used as the data manipulation language for IBM's current production offerings in the relational DBMS arena — SQL/DS and DB2. Most relational DBMSs, including Microsoft Access and Microsoft SQL Server, use a version of SQL as a data manipulation language.

Some people pronounce SQL by pronouncing the three letters, that is, "ess-que-ell." It is very common, however to pronounce it as the name under which it was developed originally, that is, "sequel." This text assumes you are pronouncing it as the word, sequel. That is why you will see the article, a, used before SQL. If it were pronounced ess-que-ell, you would use the article, an, before SQL. For example, this text will refer to "a SQL query" rather than "an SQL query."

To Change the Font Size

You can change the font and/or the font size for SQL queries using the Access Options button on the Office menu and then Object Designers in the list of options. There usually is not a compelling reason to change the font, unless there is a strong preference for some other font. It often is worthwhile to change the font size, however. With the default size of 8, the queries can be hard to read. Increasing the font size to 10 can make a big difference. The following steps change the font size for SQL queries to 10.

1

- Click the Office
Button to display the
Office Button menu,
and then
click Access
Options to
display the
Access Options
dialog box.

- Click Object
Designers to display
the Object Designers
options.

- In the Query design
area, Click the Size
box arrow, and
then click 10 in the
list that appears to
change the size to
10 (Figure 2).

2

- Click the OK button
to close the Access
Options dialog box.

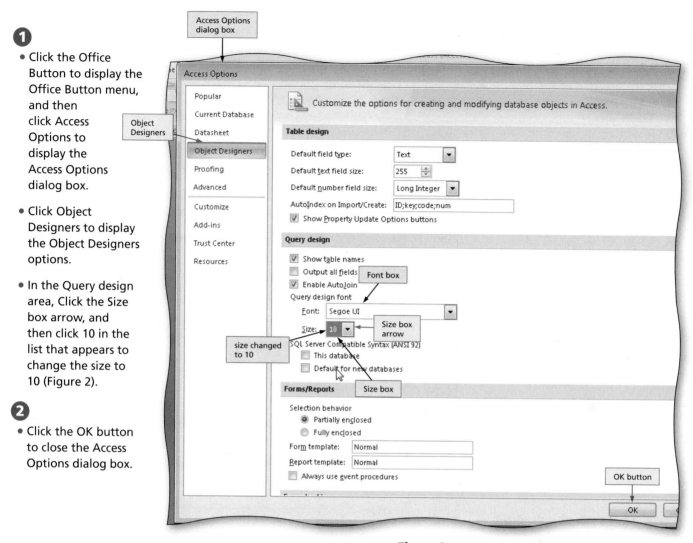

Figure 2

SQL Queries

When you query a database using SQL, you type commands in a blank window rather
than filling in the design grid. When the command is complete, you can view your results
just as you do with queries you create using the design grid.

To Create a New SQL Query

You begin the creation of a new **SQL query**, which is a query expressed using the SQL language, just as you begin the creation of any other query in Access. The only difference is that you will use SQL view instead of Design view. The following steps create a new SQL query.

- Hide the Navigation Pane.

- Click Create on the Ribbon to display the Create tab.

- Click the Query Design button on the Create tab to create a query.

- Close the Show Table dialog box without adding any tables.

- Click the View button arrow to display the View menu (Figure 3).

Q&A Why did the icon on the View button change to SQL and why are there only two items on the menu instead of the usual five?

Without any tables selected, you cannot view any results, nor can you view a PivotTable or PivotChart. You only can use the normal Design view or SQL view.

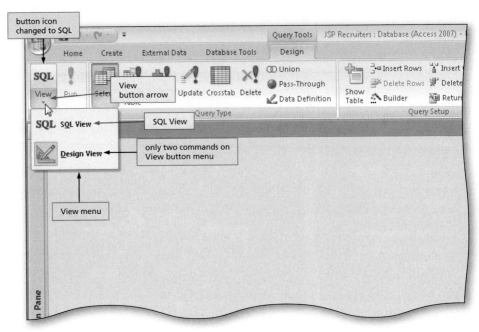

Figure 3

- Click SQL View to view the query in SQL view (Figure 4).

Q&A What happened to the design grid?

In SQL view, you specify the query by typing a SQL command rather than making entries in the design grid.

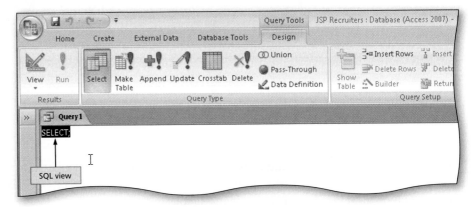

Figure 4

SQL Commands

The basic form of SQL expressions is quite simple: SELECT-FROM-WHERE. The command begins with a **SELECT clause**, which consists of the word, SELECT, followed by a list of those fields you want to include. The fields will appear in the results in the order in which they are listed in the expression. Next there is a **FROM clause**, which consists of the word, FROM, followed by a list of the table or tables involved in the query. Finally, there is an optional **WHERE clause**, which consists of the word, WHERE, followed by any criteria that the data you want to retrieve must satisfy. The command ends with a semicolon (;), which in this text will appear on a separate line.

SQL has no special format rules for placement of terms, capitalization, and so on. In this text, you place the word FROM on a new line, then place the word WHERE, when it is used, on the next line. This makes the commands easier to read. This text also shows words that are part of the SQL language in uppercase and others in a combination of uppercase and lowercase. Because it is a common convention, and necessary in some versions of SQL, place a semicolon (;) at the end of each command.

Unlike some other versions of SQL, Microsoft Access allows spaces within field names and table names. There is a restriction, however, to the way such names are used in SQL queries. When a name containing a space appears in SQL, it must be enclosed in square brackets. For example, Client Number must appear as [Client Number] because the name includes a space. On the other hand, City does not need to be enclosed in square brackets because its name does not include a space. For consistency, all names in this text are enclosed in square brackets. Thus, the City field would appear as [City] even though the brackets technically are not required by SQL.

To Include Only Certain Fields

To include only certain fields, list them after the word SELECT. If you want to list all rows in the table, you do not need to include the word WHERE. The following steps list the number, name, amount paid, and current due amount of all clients.

1

- Type SELECT [Client Number],[Client Name],[Amount Paid],[Current Due] as the first line of the command, and then press the ENTER key.

- Type FROM [Client] as the second line, press the ENTER key and then type a semicolon (;) on the third line.

- Click the View button to view the results (Figure 5).

Q&A

My screen displays a dialog box that asks me to enter a parameter value. What did I do wrong?

You typed a field name incorrectly. Click Cancel to close the dialog box and then correct your SQL statement.

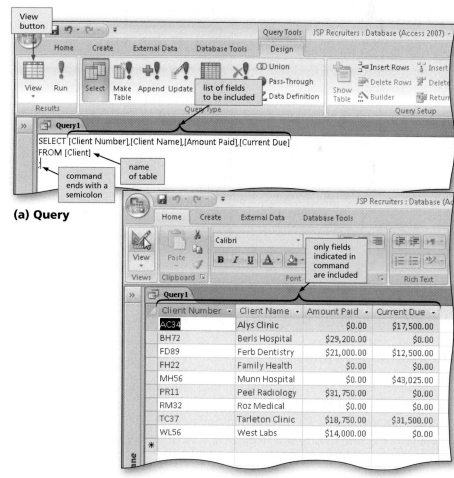

(a) Query

(b) Results

Figure 5

To Prepare to Enter a New SQL Query

To enter a new SQL query, you could close the window, click the No button when asked if you want to save your changes, and then begin the process from scratch. A quicker alternative is to use the View menu and then select SQL View. You then will be returned to SQL view with the current command appearing. At that point, you could erase the current command and then enter a new one. (If the next command is similar to the previous one, it may be simpler to modify the current command instead of erasing it and starting over.) The following steps show how to prepare to enter a new SQL query.

❶

- Click the View button arrow to display the View button menu (Figure 6).

❷

- Click SQL View to return to SQL view.

Q&A Could I just click the View button or do I have to click the arrow?

Because the icon on the button is not the icon for SQL view, you must click the arrow.

Q&A Can I save the query if I want to use it again?

You certainly can. Click the Save button on the Quick Access Toolbar and assign a name in the Save As dialog box.

Figure 6

To Include All Fields

To include all fields, you could use the same approach as in the previous steps, that is, list each field in the Client table after the word SELECT. There is a shortcut, however. Instead of listing all the field names after SELECT, you can use the asterisk (*) symbol. This indicates that you want all fields listed in the order in which you described them to the system during data definition. The following steps list all fields and all records in the Client table.

1

- Delete the current command, type SELECT * as the first line of the command, and then press the ENTER key.

- Type FROM [Client] as the second line, press the ENTER key, and type a semicolon on the third line.

- Click the View button to view the results (Figure 7).

Can I use copy and paste commands when I enter SQL commands?

Yes, you can use copy and paste as well as other editing techniques, such as replacing text.

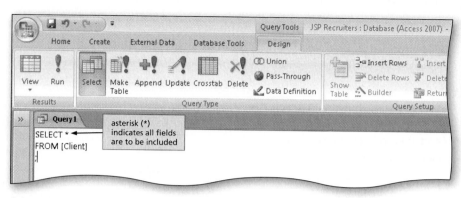

(a) Query

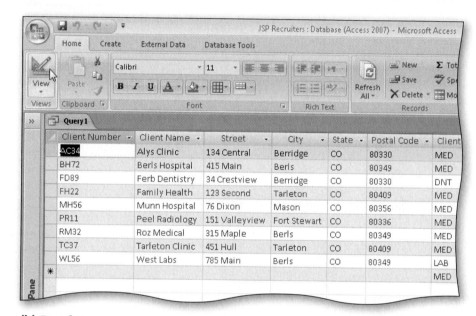

(b) Results

Figure 7

Determine criteria.

Plan Ahead

1. **Determine the fields involved in the criteria.** For any criterion, determine the fields that are included in the criterion. Determine the data types for these fields. If the criterion uses a value that corresponds to a Text field, be sure to enclose the value in single quotation marks.

2. **Determine comparison operators.** When fields are being compared to other fields or to specific values, determine the appropriate comparison operator (equals, less than, greater than, and so on). If a wildcard is involved, then the query will use the LIKE operator.

3. **Determine join criteria.** If tables are being joined, determine the fields that must match.

4. **Determine compound criteria.** If more than one criterion is involved, determine whether all individual criteria are to be true, in which case you will use the AND operator, or whether only one individual criterion needs to be true, in which case you will use the OR operator.

To Use a Criterion Involving a Numeric Field

To restrict the records to be displayed, include the word WHERE followed by a criterion as part of the command. If the field involved is a numeric field, you simply type the value. The following steps list the client number and name of all clients whose current due amount is 0.

- Click the View button arrow, click SQL View to return to SQL view, and then delete the current command.

- Type SELECT [Client Number],[Client Name] as the first line of the command.

- Type FROM [Client] as the second line.

- Type WHERE [Current Due]=0 as the third line and then type a semicolon on the fourth line.

- Click the View button to view the results (Figure 8).

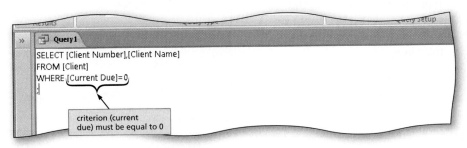

(a) Query

Experiment

- Try the other comparison operators. In each case, view the results to see the effect of your choice.

Q&A On my screen, the clients are listed in a different order. Did I do something wrong?

No. The order in which records appear in a query result is random unless you specifically order the records. You will see how to order records later in this feature.

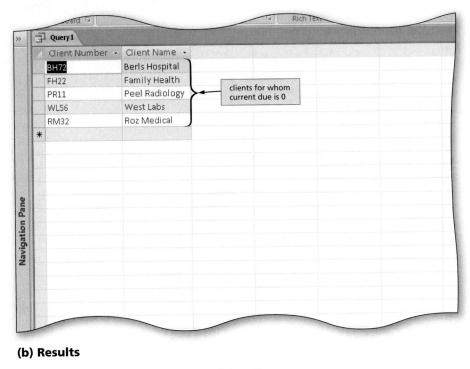

(b) Results

Figure 8

Simple Criteria

The criterion following the word WHERE in the preceding query is called a simple criterion. A **simple criterion** has the form: field name, comparison operator, then either another field name or a value. The possible comparison operators are shown in Table 1. Note that there are two different versions for "not equal to" (<> and !=). You must use the one that is right for your particular implementation of SQL. If you use the wrong one, your system will let you know instantly. Simply use the other.

Table 1 Comparison Operators

Comparison Operator	Meaning
=	Equal to
<	Less than
>	Greater than
<=	Less than or equal to
>=	Greater than or equal to
<> or !=	Not equal to

To Use a Criterion Involving a Text Field

If the criterion involves a text field, the value must be enclosed in single quotation marks. The following example lists all clients located in Berls, that is, all clients for whom the value in the City field is Berls.

- Return to SQL view, delete the previous query, and type SELECT [Client Number],[Client Name] as the first line of the command.

- Type FROM [Client] as the second line.

- Type WHERE [City]='Berls' as the third line and type a semicolon on the fourth line.

- Click the View button to view the results (Figure 9).

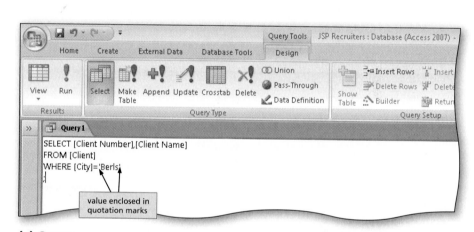

(a) Query

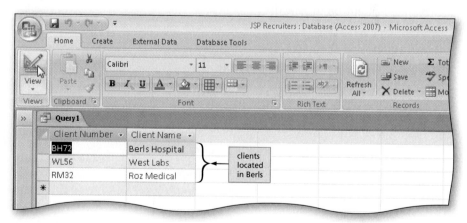

(b) Results

Figure 9

BTW

BETWEEN Operator
The BETWEEN operator allows you to search for a range of values in one field. For example, to find all clients whose amount paid amount is between $20,000 and $30,000, the WHERE clause would be WHERE Amount Paid BETWEEN 20000 AND 30000.

Compound Criteria

The criteria you have seen so far are called simple criteria. The next examples require compound criteria. **Compound criteria** are formed by connecting two or more simple criteria using AND, OR, and NOT. When simple criteria are connected by the word AND, all the simple criteria must be true in order for the compound criterion to be true. When simple criteria are connected by the word OR, the compound criterion will be true whenever any of the simple criteria are true. Preceding a criterion by NOT reverses the truth or falsity of the original criterion. That is, if the original criterion is true, the new criterion will be false; if the original criterion is false, the new one will be true.

To Use a Compound Criterion

The following steps use a compound criterion to display the names of those clients located in Tarleton and for whom the current due amount is 0.

1

- Return to SQL view, delete the previous query, and type SELECT [Client Number],[Client Name] as the first line of the command.

- Type FROM [Client] as the second line.

- Type WHERE [City]='Tarleton' as the third line.

- Type AND [Current Due]=0 as the fourth line and type a semicolon on the fifth line.

- Click the View button to view the results (Figure 10).

Q&A

How do I form compound criteria that involve OR?

You use the same method to form compound criteria involving OR. Simply use the word OR instead of the word AND. In that case, the results would contain those records that satisfied either criterion or both.

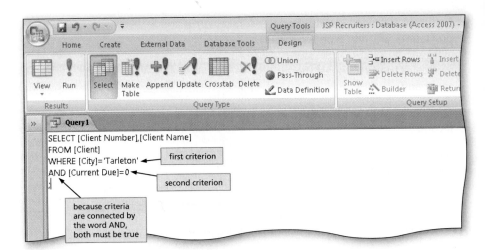

(a) Query

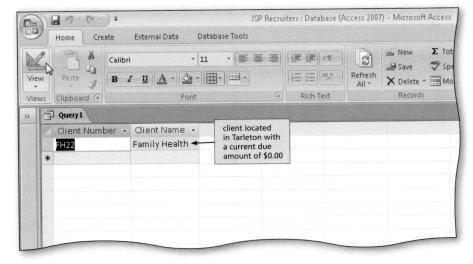

(b) Results

Figure 10

To Use NOT in a Criterion

To use the word NOT in a criterion, precede the criterion with the word NOT. The following steps list the numbers and names of the clients not located in Tarleton.

- Return to SQL view and delete the previous query.

- Type SELECT [Client Number],[Client Name] as the first line of the command.

- Type FROM [Client] as the second line.

- Type WHERE NOT [City]= 'Tarleton' as the third line and type a semicolon on the fourth line.

- View the results (Figure 11).

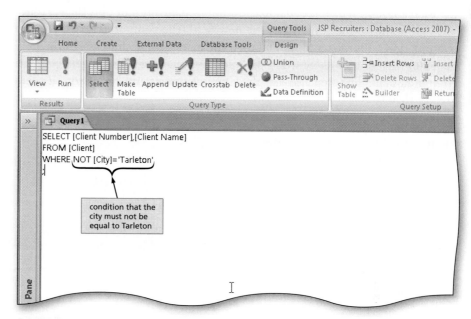

(a) Query

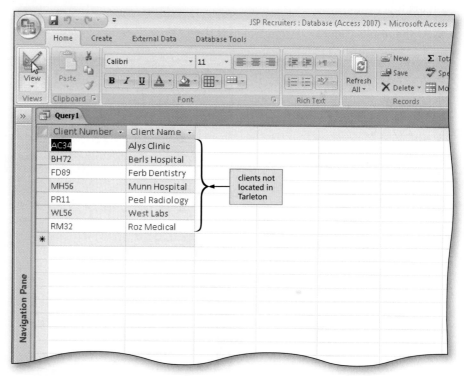

(b) Results

Figure 11

To Use a Computed Field

Just as with queries created in Design view, you can include fields in queries that are not in the database, but that can be computed from fields that are. Such a field is called a **computed** or **calculated field**. Such computations can involve addition (+), subtraction (−), multiplication (*), or division (/). The query in the following step computes the total amount, which is equal to the amount paid amount plus the current due amount.

To indicate the contents of the new field (the computed field), you must name the field by following the computation with the word AS and then the name you wish to assign the field. The name, also called an alias, becomes the column name when the query is run. The following step assigns the name Total Amount to the computed field. The step also lists the Client Number and Name for all clients for which the current due amount is greater than 0.

- Return to SQL view and delete the previous query.

- Type `SELECT [Client Number], [Client Name],[Amount Paid] +[Current Due] AS [Total Amount]` as the first line of the command.

- Type `FROM [Client]` as the second line.

- Type `WHERE [Current Due]>0` as the third line and type a semicolon on the fourth line.

- View the results (Figure 12).

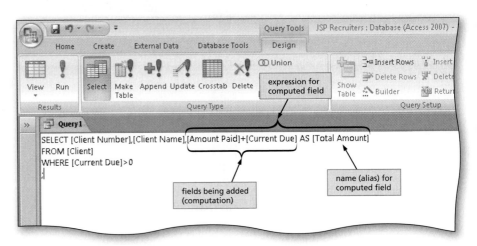

(a) Query

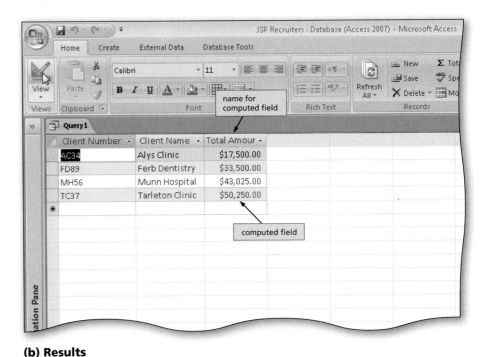

(b) Results

Figure 12

Sorting

The field on which data is to be sorted is called a **sort key**, or simply a **key**. If the data is to be sorted on two fields, the more important key is called the **major sort key** (also referred to as the **primary sort key**) and the less important key is called the **minor sort key** (also referred to as the **secondary sort key**). By following a sort key with the word DESC with no comma in between, you can specify descending sort order. If you do not specify DESC, the data will be sorted in ascending order.

To sort the output, you include an **ORDER BY clause**, which consists of the words ORDER BY followed by the sort key. If there are two sort keys, the major sort key is listed first. In queries that you construct in Design view, the more major sort key must be to the left of the minor sort key in the list of fields to be included. In SQL, there is no such restriction. The fields to be included in the query are in the SELECT clause and the fields to be used for sorting are in the ORDER BY clause. The two clauses are totally independent.

BTW

Union, Pass-Through, and Data Definition Queries
There are three queries that cannot be created in Design view. When you click the button for any of these three queries in Design view, the SQL view window opens. The Union query combines fields from more than one table into one query result set. The Pass-through query enables you to send SQL commands directly to ODBC (Open Database Connectivity) databases using the ODBC database's SQL syntax. The Data Definition query allows you to create or alter database tables or create indexes in Access directly.

Plan Ahead

Determine sort order.

1. **Determine whether data is to be sorted.** Examine the requirements for the query looking for words like "sorted by," "ordered by," "arranged by," and so on.

2. **Determine sort keys.** Look for the fields that follow "sorted by," "ordered by," or any other words that signify sorting. If the requirements for the query included "ordered by client name," then Client Name is a sort key.

3. **If there is more than one sort key, determine which one will be the major sort key and which will be the minor sort key.** Look for words that indicate which field is more important. For example, if the requirements indicate that the results are to be "ordered by amount paid within recruiter number," then Recruiter Number is the more important sort key.

To Sort the Results

The following step lists the client number, name, amount paid amount, current due amount, and recruiter number for all clients. The data is to be sorted by amount paid within recruiter number. That is, within the clients having the same recruiter number, the data is to be sorted further by amount paid amount. This means that the Recruiter Number field is the major (primary) sort key and the Amount Paid field is the minor (secondary) sort key.

1

- Return to SQL view and delete the previous query.

- Type SELECT [Client Number], [Client Name], [Amount Paid], [Current Due], [Recruiter Number] as the first line of the command.

- Type FROM [Client] as the second line.

- Type ORDER BY [Recruiter Number], [Amount Paid] as the third line and type a semicolon on the fourth line.

- View the results (Figure 13).

Experiment

- Try reversing the order of the sort keys to see the effect. Also try to specify descending order for one or both of the sort keys. In each case, view the results to see the effect of your choice.

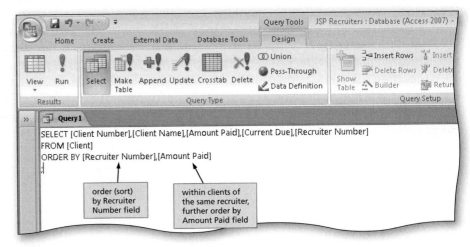

(a) Query

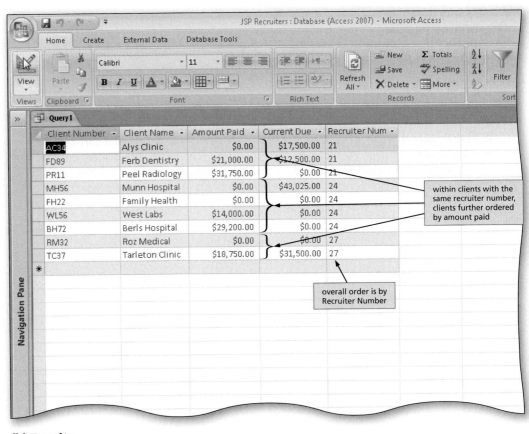

(b) Results

Figure 13

To Use a Built-In Function

SQL has **built-in** functions (also called **aggregate** functions) to calculate the number of entries, the sum or average of all the entries in a given column, and the largest or smallest of the entries in a given column. In SQL, these functions are called COUNT, SUM, AVG, MAX, and MIN, respectively.

The following step counts the number of clients assigned to recruiter number 21 by using the COUNT function with an asterisk (*).

1

- Return to SQL view and delete the previous query.

- Type SELECT COUNT(*) as the first line of the command.

- Type FROM [Client] as the second line.

- Type WHERE [Recruiter Number]='21' as the third line and type a semicolon on the fourth line.

- View the results (Figure 14).

Q&A

Why does Expr1000 appear in the column heading of the results?

Because the column is a computed column, it does not have a name. Access assigns a generic expression name. You can add a name for the column by including the AS clause in the query; it is good practice to do so.

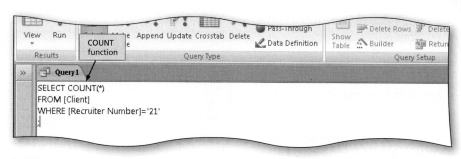

(a) Query

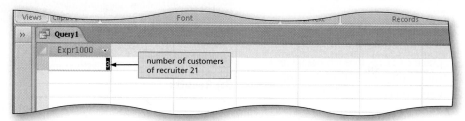

(b) Results

Figure 14

To Use Multiple Functions in the Same Command

The only differences between COUNT and SUM, other than the obvious fact that they are computing different statistics, are that first, in the case of SUM, you must specify the field for which you want a total, instead of an asterisk (*) and second, the field must be numeric. You could not calculate a sum of names or addresses, for example. The following step uses both the COUNT and SUM functions to count the number of clients and calculate the SUM (total) of their Amount Paid amounts.

- Return to SQL view and delete the previous query.

- Type `SELECT COUNT(*), SUM([Amount Paid])` as the first line of the command.

- Type `FROM [Client]` as the second line and type a semicolon on the third line.

- View the results (Figure 15).

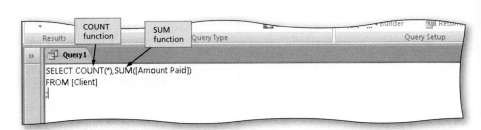

(a) Query

Experiment

- Try using the other functions in place of SUM. In each case, view the results to see the effect of your choice.

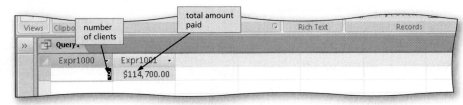

(b) Results

Figure 15

The use of AVG, MAX, and MIN is similar to SUM. The only difference is that a different statistic is calculated.

Grouping

Grouping means creating groups of records that share some common characteristic. In grouping clients by recruiter number, for example, the clients of recruiter 21 would form one group, the clients of recruiter 24 would be a second, and the clients of recruiter 27 would form a third.

Plan Ahead

Determine grouping.

1. **Determine whether data is to be grouped in some fashion.** Examine the requirements for the query to see if they contain individual rows or information about groups of rows.

2. **Determine the field or fields on which grouping is to take place.** By which field is the data to be grouped? Look to see if the requirements indicate a field along with several group calculations.

3. **Determine which fields or calculations are appropriate to display.** When rows are grouped, one line of output is produced for each group. The only things that may appear are statistics calculated for the group or fields whose values are the same for all rows in a group. For example, it would make sense to display the recruiter number, because all the clients in the group have the same recruiter number. It would not make sense to display the client number, because the client number will vary from one row in a group to another. (SQL could not determine which client number to display for the group.)

To Use Grouping

The following step calculates the totals of the Amount Paid fields, called Total Paid, and the Current Due fields, called Total Due, for the clients of each recruiter. To calculate the totals, the command will include the SUM([Amount Paid]) and SUM([Current Due]). To get totals for the clients of each recruiter the command also will include a **GROUP BY clause**, which consists of the words, GROUP BY, followed by the field used for grouping, in this case, Recruiter Number.

Including GROUP BY Recruiter Number will cause the clients for each recruiter to be grouped together; that is, all clients with the same recruiter number will form a group. Any statistics, such as totals, appearing after the word SELECT will be calculated for each of these groups. It is important to note that using GROUP BY does not imply that the information will be sorted.

The step also renames the total amount paid as Total Paid and the total current due as Total Due by including appropriate AS clauses.

1

- Return to SQL view and delete the previous query.

- Type `SELECT [Recruiter Number],SUM([Amount Paid]) AS [Total Paid],SUM([Current Due]) AS [Total Due]` as the first line of the command.

- Type `FROM [Client]` as the second line.

- Type `GROUP BY [Recruiter Number]` as the third line.

- Type `ORDER BY [Recruiter Number]` as the fourth line and type a semicolon on the fifth line.

- View the results (Figure 16).

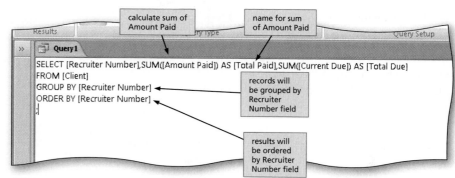

(a) Query

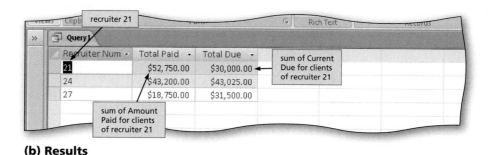

(b) Results

Figure 16

Grouping Requirements

When rows are grouped, one line of output is produced for each group. The only things that may appear are statistics calculated for the group or fields whose values are the same for all rows in a group. For example, it would make sense to display the recruiter number, because all the clients in the group have the same recruiter number. It would not make sense to display the client number, because the client number will vary from one row in a group to another. (SQL could not determine which client number to display for the group.)

To Restrict the Groups that Appear

In some cases you only want to display certain groups. For example, you may want to display only those recruiters for whom the sum of the Current Due amounts are greater than $3,000. This restriction does not apply to individual rows, but instead to groups. Because WHERE applies only to rows, it is not appropriate to accomplish the kind of restriction you have here. Fortunately, there is a clause that is to groups what WHERE is to rows. The clause is the **HAVING clause**, which consists of the word, HAVING, followed by a criterion. It is used in the following step, which restricts the groups to be included to those on which the sum of the current due is greater than $40,000.00.

- Return to SQL view and delete the previous query.

- Click the beginning of the fourth line (ORDER BY [Recruiter Number]) and press the ENTER key to insert a new blank line.

- Click the beginning of the new blank line, and then type HAVING SUM([Current Due])>40000 as the new fourth line.

- View the results (Figure 17).

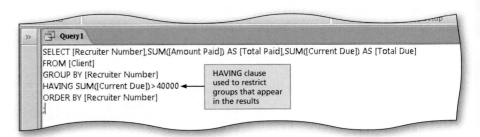

(a) Query

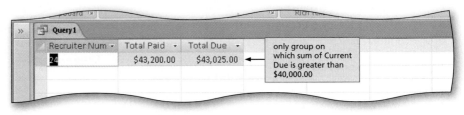

(b) Results

Figure 17

Inner Join
A join that compares the tables in the FROM clause and lists only those rows that satisfy the condition in the WHERE clause is called an inner join. SQL has an INNER JOIN clause. You could replace the FROM and WHERE clauses in the query shown in Figure 18a with FROM Client INNER JOIN Recruiter ON [Client].[Recruiter Number]=[Recruiter]. [Recruiter Number] to get the same results as shown in Figure 18b.

Joining Tables

Many queries require data from more than one table. Just as with creating queries in Design view, it is necessary to be able to **join** tables, that is, to find rows in two tables that have identical values in matching fields. In SQL, this is accomplished through appropriate criteria following the word WHERE.

If you wish to list the client number, name, recruiter number, first name of the recruiter, and last name of the recruiter for all clients, you need data from both the Client and Recruiter tables. The Recruiter Number field is in both tables, the Client Number field is only in the Client table, and the First Name and Last Name fields are only in the Recruiter table. You need to access both tables in your SQL query, as follows:

1. In the SELECT clause, you indicate all fields you wish to appear.

2. In the FROM clause, you list all tables involved in the query.

3. In the WHERE clause, you give the criterion that will restrict the data to be retrieved to only those rows included in both of the two tables, that is, to the rows that have common values in matching fields.

Qualifying Fields

There is a problem in indicating the matching fields. The matching fields are both called Recruiter Number. There is a field in the Client table called Recruiter Number, as well as a field in the Recruiter table called Recruiter Number. In this case, if you only enter Recruiter Number, it will not be clear which table you mean. It is necessary to **qualify** Recruiter Number, that is, to specify to which field in which table you are referring. You do this by preceding the name of the field with the name of the table, followed by a period. The Recruiter Number field in the Client table, for example is [Client].[Recruiter Number].

Whenever there is potential ambiguity, you must qualify the fields involved. It is permissible to qualify other fields as well, even if there is no confusion. For example, instead of [Client Name], you could have typed [Client].[Client Name] to indicate the Client Name field in the Client table. Some people prefer to qualify all fields, and this is not a bad approach. In this text, you only will qualify fields when it is necessary to do so.

To Join Tables

The following step lists the client number, name, recruiter number, first name of the recruiter, and last name of the recruiter for all clients.

①

- Return to SQL view and delete the previous query.

- Type `SELECT [Client Number], [Client Name], [Client]. [Recruiter Number], [First Name], [Last Name]` as the first line of the command.

- Type `FROM [Client], [Recruiter]` as the second line.

- Type `WHERE [Client].[Recruiter Number] = [Recruiter]. [Recruiter Number]` as the third line and type a semicolon on the fourth line.

Q&A

What is the purpose of the WHERE clause?

The WHERE clause specifies that only rows on which the recruiter numbers match are to be included. Specifically, the recruiter number in the Client table ([Client].[Recruiter Number]) must be equal to the recruiter number in the Recruiter table ([Recruiter].[Recruiter Number]). ⌐

- View the results (Figure 18).

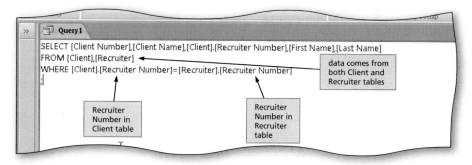

(a) Query

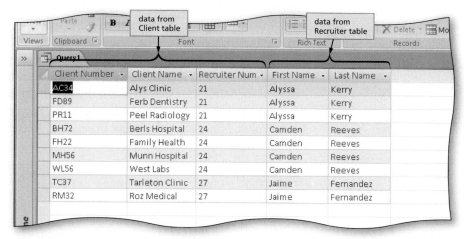

(b) Results

Figure 18

To Restrict the Records in a Join

You can restrict the records to be included in a join by creating a compound criterion. The criterion will include the criterion necessary to join the tables along with a criterion to restrict the records. The criteria will be connected with AND.

The following step lists the client number, client name, recruiter number, first name of the recruiter, and last name of the recruiter for all clients for which the current due amount is greater than 0.

1

- Return to SQL view and delete the previous query.

- Click immediately prior to the semicolon on the last line.

- Type AND [Current Due] > 0 and press the ENTER key.

- View the results (Figure 19).

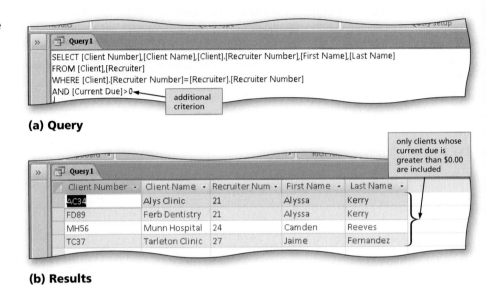

(a) Query

(b) Results

Figure 19

Aliases

When tables appear in the FROM clause, you can give each table an **alias**, or an alternative name, that you can use in the rest of the statement. You create an alias by typing the name of the table, pressing the Spacebar, and then typing the name of the alias. No commas or periods are necessary to separate the two names.

You can use an alias for two basic reasons. The first reason is for simplicity. Figure 20 shows the same query as in Figure 18 on the previous page, but with the Client table assigned the letter, C, as an alias and the Recruiter table assigned the letter, R. When-ever you need to qualify a field name, you can use the alias. Thus, you only need to type R.[Recruiter Number] rather than [Recruiter].[Recruiter Number].

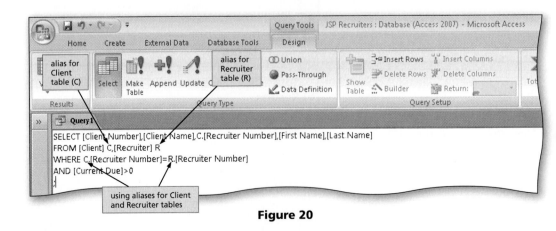

Figure 20

To Join a Table to Itself

The other use of aliases is in joining a table to itself. Joining a table to itself can be useful when you want to compare values in a column to other values in the same column. If you wanted to find the client numbers and names for all clients who are located in the same city and if you had two Client tables in your database, you would simply join the tables looking for rows where the cities were the same. Even though there is only one Client table, however, you actually can treat the Client table as two tables in the query by creating an alias. You would change the FROM clause to:

```
FROM CLIENT F, CLIENT S
```

SQL treats this clause as a query of two tables: one that has the alias F, and another that has the alias S. The fact that both tables are really the single Client table is not a problem. The following step assigns two aliases (F and S) to the Client table and lists the client number and client name of both clients as well as the city in which both are located.

1

- Return to SQL view and delete the previous query.

- Type SELECT F.[Client Number],F.[Client Name], S.[Client Number],S.[Client Name],F.[City] as the first line of the command.

- Type FROM [Client] F, [Client] S as the second line.

- Type WHERE F.[City]=S.[City] as the third line.

- Type AND F.[Client Number]<S. [Client Number] as the fourth line and type a semicolon on the fifth line.

- View the results (Figure 21).

Q&A

Why is the criterion F.[Client Number] < S.[Client Number] included in the query?

If you did not include this criterion, the query would contain four times as many results. On the first row in the results, for example, the first client number is AC34 and the second is FD89. Without this criterion there would be a row on which both the first and second client numbers are AC34, a row on which both are FD89, and a row on which the first is FD89 and the second is AC34. This criteria only selects the one row on which the first client number (AC34) is less than the second (FD89).

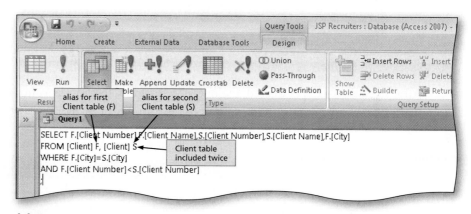

(a) Query

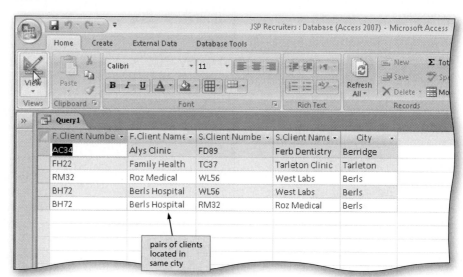

(b) Results

Figure 21

Subqueries

It is possible to place one query inside another. The inner query is called a **subquery** and it is evaluated first. Then the outer query can use the results of the subquery to find its results.

To Use a Subquery

The following step uses the query shown in Figure 22 as a subquery. This query selects recruiter numbers from those records in the Client table on which the city is Berls. In other words, it selects recruiter numbers for those recruiters who have at least one client located in Berls.

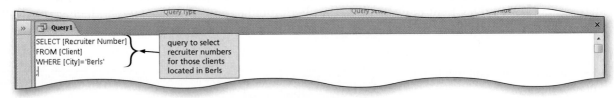

Figure 22

After the subquery is evaluated, the outer query will select the recruiter number, first name, and last name for those recruiters whose recruiter number is in the list produced by the subquery.

- Return to SQL view and delete the previous query.

- Type `SELECT [Recruiter Number],[First Name],[Last Name]` as the first line of the command.

- Type `FROM [Recruiter]` as the second line.

- Type `WHERE [Recruiter Number] IN` as the third line.

- Type `(SELECT [Recruiter Number]` as the fourth line.

- Type `FROM [Client]` as the fifth line.

- Type `WHERE [City]='Berls')` as the sixth line and type a semicolon on the seventh line.

- View the results (Figure 23).

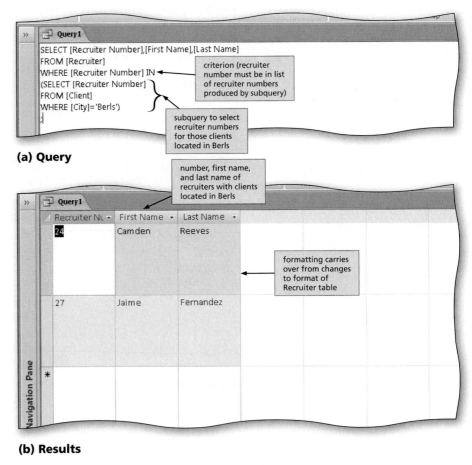

Figure 23

Using an IN Clause

The query in Figure 23 uses an IN clause with a subquery. You also can use an IN clause with a list as an alternative to an OR criterion when the OR criterion involves a single field. For example, to find clients whose city is Berls, Mason, or Tarleton, the criterion using IN would be City IN ('Berls','Mason','Tarleton'). The corresponding OR criterion would be City='Berls' OR City='Mason' OR City='Tarleton'. The choice of which one to use is a matter of personal preference.

You also can use this type of IN clause when creating queries in Design view. To use the criterion in the previous paragraph for example, include the City field in the design grid and enter the criterion in the Criteria row.

Comparison with Access-Generated SQL

When you create a query in Design view, Access automatically creates a corresponding SQL query that is similar to the queries you have created in this feature. The Access query shown in Figure 24, for example, was created in Design view and includes the Client Number and Client Name. The City field has a criterion (Berls), but the City field will not appear in the results.

BTW

Outer Joins
Sometimes you need to list all the rows from one of the tables in a join, regardless of whether they match any rows in the other table. For example, you can perform a join of the Client and Seminar Offerings table but display all clients — even the ones without seminar offerings. This type of join is called an outer join. In a left outer join, all rows from the table on the left (the table listed first in the query) will be included regardless of whether they match rows from the tables on the right (the table listed second in the query). Rows from the right will be included only if they match. In a right outer join, all rows from the table on the right will be included regardless of whether they match rows from the table on the left. The SQL clause for a left outer join is LEFT JOIN and the SQL clause for a right outer join is RIGHT JOIN.

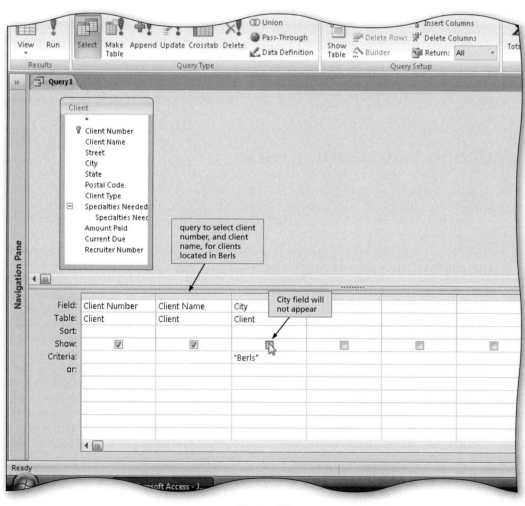

Figure 24

The SQL query that Access generates in correspondence to the Design view query is shown in Figure 25. The query is very similar to the queries you have entered, but there are three slight differences. First, the fields are qualified (Client.[Client Number] and Client.[Client Name]), even though they do not need to be. (Only one table is involved in the query, so no qualification is necessary.) Second, the City field is not enclosed in square brackets. The field legitimately is not enclosed in square brackets because there are no spaces or other special characters in the field name. Finally, there are extra parentheses in the criteria.

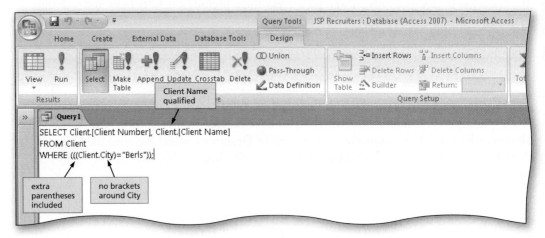

Figure 25

Both the style used by Access and the style you have been using are legitimate. The choice of style is a personal preference.

Updating Data through SQL

Although SQL is often regarded as a language for querying databases, it also contains commands to update databases. You can add new records, update existing records, and delete records.

Plan Ahead

Determine any update operations to be performed.

1. **Determine INSERT operations.** Determine whether new records need to be added. Determine to which table they should be added.

2. **Determine UPDATE operations.** Determine changes that need to be made to existing records. Which fields need to be changed? Which tables contain these fields? What criteria identify the rows that need to be changed?

3. **Determine DELETE operations.** Determine which tables contain records that are to be deleted. What criteria identify the rows that need to be deleted?

To Use an INSERT Command

You can add records to a table by using the SQL INSERT command. The command consists of INSERT INTO followed by the name of the table into which the record is to be inserted. Next is the word VALUE followed by the values for the fields in the record. Values for Text fields must be enclosed within quotes. The following steps add a record that JSP Recruiters wants to add to the Seminar Offerings table. The record is for client PR11 and seminar S01 and indicates that the course will be offered for a total of 8 hours, of which 0 hours already have been spent.

- If necessary, return to SQL view and delete the existing query.

- Type INSERT INTO [Seminar Offerings] as the first line of the command.

- Type VALUES as the second line.

- Type ('PR11','S01',8,0) as the third line and type a semicolon on the fourth line (Figure 26).

- Run the query by clicking the Run button.

- When Access displays a message indicating the number of records to be inserted, click the Yes button to insert the records.

Q&A I clicked the View button and didn't get the message. Do I need to click the Run button?

Yes. You are making a change to the database so you must click the Run button or the change will not be made.

Q&A How can I see if the record was actually inserted?

Use a SELECT query to view the records in the Seminar Offerings table.

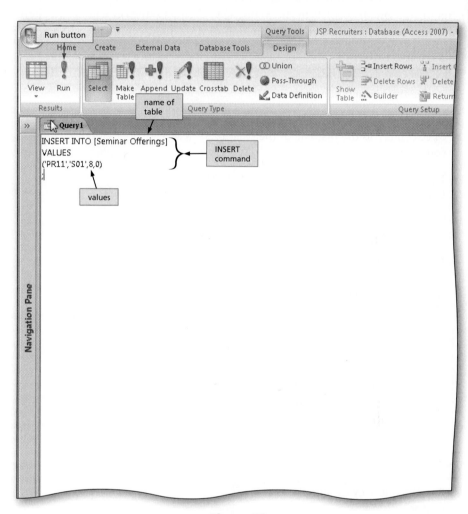

Figure 26

To Use an UPDATE Command

You can update records in SQL by using the UPDATE command. The command consists of UPDATE followed by the name of the table in which records are to be updated. Next, the command contains one or more SET clauses, which consist of the word SET followed by a field to be updated, an equal sign, and the new value. The SET clause indicates the change to be made. Finally, the query includes a WHERE clause. When you execute the command all records in the indicated table that satisfy the criterion will be updated. The following steps use the SQL UPDATE command to perform an update requested by JSP Recruiters. Specifically, they change the Hours Spent to 2 on all records in the Seminar Offerings table on which the client number is PR11 and the seminar number is S01. Because the combination of the Client Number and Seminar Number fields is the primary key, only one record will be updated.

- Delete the existing query.

- Type UPDATE [Seminar Offerings] as the first line of the command.

- Type SET [Hours Spent]=2 as the second line.

- Type WHERE [Client Number]= 'PR11' as the third line.

- Type AND [Seminar Number]= 'S01' as the fourth line and type a semicolon on the fifth line (Figure 27).

Q&A Do I need to change a field to a specific value like 2?

You could use an expression. For example, to add $100 to the Current Due amount, the SET clause would be SET [Current Due]=[Current Due]+100.

- Run the query by clicking the Run button.

- When Access displays a message indicating the number of records to be updated, click the Yes button to update the records.

Q&A How can I see if the update actually occurred?

Use a SELECT query to view the records in the Seminar Offerings table.

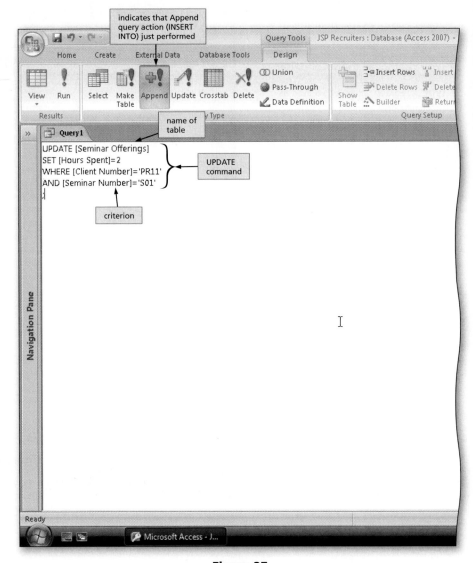

Figure 27

To Use a DELETE Command

You can delete records in SQL by using the DELETE command. The command consists of DELETE FROM followed by the name of the table from which records are to be deleted. Finally, there is a WHERE clause. When you execute the command, all records in the indicated table that satisfy the criterion will be deleted. The following steps use the SQL DELETE command to delete all records in the Seminar Offerings table on which the client number is PR11 and the seminar number is S01, as JSP Recruiters has requested. Because the combination of the Client Number and Seminar Number fields is the primary key, only one record will be deleted.

1

- Delete the existing query.

- Type DELETE FROM [Seminar Offerings] as the first line of the command.

- Type WHERE [Client Number]= 'PR11' as the second line.

- Type AND [Seminar Number]= 'S01' as the third line and type a semicolon on the fourth line (Figure 28).

2

- Run the query by clicking the Run button.

- When Access displays a message indicating the number of records to be deleted, click the Yes button to delete the records.

Q&A

How can I see if the deletion actually occurred?

Use a SELECT query to view the records in the Seminar Offerings table.

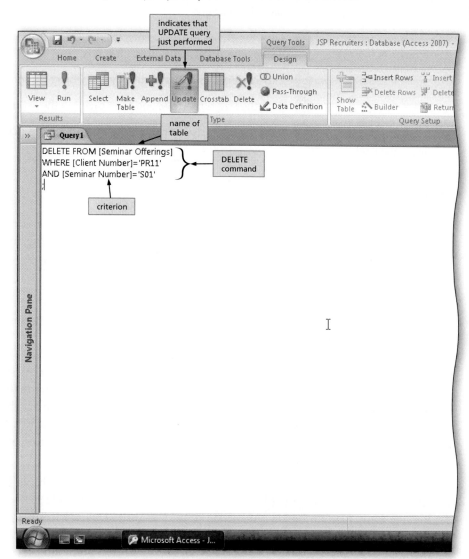

Figure 28

BTW

Certification
The Microsoft Certified Application Specialist (MCAS) program provides an opportunity for you to obtain a valuable industry credential — proof that you have the Access 2007 skills required by employers. For more information, see Appendix G or visit the Access 2007 Certification Web page (scsite.com/ac2007/cert).

Closing the Query and Restoring the Font Size

The following steps close the query and restore the font size to its default setting.

To Close a Query and Restore the Font Size

1 Click the Close 'Query1' button and then click the No button when asked if you want to save the changes.

2 Click the Office Button to display the Office Button menu, and then click Access Options to display the Access Options dialog box.

3 Click Object Designers to display the Object Designers options.

4 Click the Size box arrow, and then click 8 in the list that appears to change the size back to 8.

5 Click the OK button or the Close button for the Access Options dialog box.

BTW

Quick Reference
For a table that lists how to complete the tasks covered in this book using the mouse, Ribbon, shortcut menu, and keyboard, see the Quick Reference Summary at the back of this book, or visit the Access 2007 Quick Reference Web page (scsite.com/ac2007/qr).

To Quit Access

You are ready to quit Access. The following step quits Access.

1 Click the Close button on the right side of the Access title bar to quit Access.

Feature Summary

In this feature you have learned to create SQL queries; include fields in a query; use criteria involving both numeric and text fields as well as use compound criteria; use computed fields, rename the computation; sort the results of a query; use the built-in functions; group records in a query and also restrict the groups that appear in the results; join tables; restrict the records in a join; use subqueries; and use the INSERT, UPDATE, and DELETE commands to update data. Finally, you looked at the SQL query that is generated automatically by Access. The following list includes all the new Access skills you have learned in this feature.

1. Change the Font Size (AC 428)
2. Create a New SQL Query (AC 430)
3. Include Only Certain Fields (AC 431)
4. Prepare to Enter a New SQL Query (AC 432)
5. Include All Fields (AC 432)
6. Use a Criterion Involving a Numeric Field (AC 434)
7. Use a Criterion Involving a Text Field (AC 435)
8. Use a Compound Criterion (AC 436)
9. Use NOT in a Criterion (AC 437)
10. Use a Computed Field (AC 438)
11. Sort the Results (AC 440)
12. Use a Built-In Function (AC 441)
13. Use Multiple Functions in the Same Command (AC 442)
14. Use Grouping (AC 443)
15. Restrict the Groups that Appear (AC 444)
16. Join Tables (AC 445)
17. Restrict the Records in a Join (AC 446)
18. Join a Table to Itself (AC 447)
19. Use a Subquery (AC 448)
20. Use an INSERT Command (AC 451)
21. Use an UPDATE Command (AC 452)
22. Use a DELETE Command (AC 453)
23. Close a Query and Restore the Font Size (AC 454)

In the Lab

Design, create, modify, and/or use a database following the guidelines, concepts, and skills presented in this feature.

Lab 1: Querying the JMS TechWizards Database Using SQL

Problem: The management of JMS TechWizards would like to learn more about SQL and has determined a number of questions it wants SQL to answer. You must obtain the answers to the questions posed by management. Rather than save each query separately, you will copy the SQL query statement to Microsoft Office Word.

Instructions: Start Access. If you are using the Microsoft Office Access 2007 Complete or the Microsoft Office Access 2007 Comprehensive text, open the JMS TechWizards database that you used in Chapter 6. Otherwise, see the inside back cover of this book for instructions on downloading the Data Files for Students, or contact your instructor for more information about accessing the required files.

Perform the following tasks:

1. Open Microsoft Office Word, create a new document, and then type your name at the top. With both Access and Word open on the desktop, create the queries in SQL in Steps 2 through 11 below. For each query, run the query, print the query results (if instructed to do so by your instructor), and copy the SQL command to the Word document. To copy the SQL command, highlight the command and right-click. Click Copy on the shortcut menu. Switch to Word, click the location in the document where the command should appear, right-click, and click Paste on the shortcut menu. Save the document using the file name specified by your instructor.

2. Find all records in the Client table where the billed amount is less than $300.00. Display the client number, name, and technician number in the result.

3. Find all records in the Client table where the billed amount is greater than $350.00 and the city is Anderson. Display all fields in the query result.

4. Find all records in the Client table where the postal code is not 78077. Display the client number, name, and city in the query result.

5. Display the client number, name, technician number, first name, and last name for all clients. Sort the results in ascending order by technician number and client number.

6. Display and print the average billed amount grouped by technician number. Name the average balance as Average Billed.

7. Find the client numbers and names for every pair of clients who are located in the same city.

8. Use a subquery to find all technicians whose clients are located in Kingston. Display the recruiter number, first name, and last name.

9. Add the following record to the Work Orders table.

GR56	4	4	0

10. Update the Hours Spent field to 2 for those records where the Client Number is GR56 and the Category Number is 4.

11. Delete all records where the Client Number is GR56 and the Category Number is 4.

12. Change the document properties for the Word document and save the document using the file name specified by your instructor.

13. Submit in the format specified by your instructor.

In the Lab

Lab 2: Querying the Hockey Fan Zone Database Using SQL

Problem: The management of Hockey Fan Zone would like to learn more about SQL and has determined a number of questions it wants SQL to answer. You must obtain the answers to the questions posed by management.

Instructions: Start Access. If you are using the Microsoft Office Access 2007 Complete or the Microsoft Office Access 2007 Comprehensive text, open the JMS TechWizards database that you used in Chapter 6. Otherwise, see the inside back cover of this book for instructions on downloading the Data Files for Students, or contact your instructor for more information about accessing the required files.

Perform the following tasks:

1. Open Microsoft Office Word, create a new document, and then type your name at the top. With both Access and Word open on the desktop, create the queries in SQL in Steps 2 through 9 below. For each query, run the query, print the query results (if instructed to do so by your instructor), and copy the SQL command to the Word document. To copy the SQL command, highlight the command and right-click. Click Copy on the shortcut menu. Switch to Word, click the location in the document where the command should appear, right-click, and click Paste on the shortcut menu. Save the document using the file name specified by your instructor.

2. Find all records in the Item table where the difference between the cost of the item and the selling price of the item is greater than $4.00. Display the item number, description, cost, and selling price in the query result.

3. Display the item number, description, and total cost (cost * on hand) for all items. Name the computed field Total Cost.

4. Find all items where the description begins with the letter B. Include the item number and description in the query result.

5. Display the supplier name, item number, description, and cost for all items where the number on hand is less than 10. Sort the results in ascending order by supplier name and description.

6. Find the average cost by supplier.

7. Restrict records retrieved in step 6 to only those suppliers where the average cost is less than $20.00.

8. Find the total number of reordered items for each item in the Reorder table. Name the computed field Total Ordered.

9. Use the IN operator to find all items that are clothing or cap type. Display the item number, description, cost, and supplier code in the result. Sort the results by supplier code and item number.

10. Change the document properties for the Word document and save the document using the file name specified by your instructor.

11. Submit in the format specified by your instructor.

3 | Creating a Presentation with Custom Backgrounds and SmartArt Diagrams

Objectives

You will have mastered the material in this chapter when you can:

- Create a presentation from a Microsoft Office Word 2007 outline
- Add a picture to create a custom background
- Add background graphics to slide masters
- Add slide numbers and the date to slide masters
- Apply a WordArt style

- Format WordArt
- Apply effects to pictures
- Insert and modify text boxes
- Apply effects to shapes
- Create a SmartArt graphic
- Use the Text pane to enter placeholder text
- Apply a SmartArt style to a graphic

3 | Creating a Presentation with Custom Backgrounds and SmartArt Diagrams

Introduction

Today's audiences quickly become bored with basic graphics and single-level bulleted lists that are the starting point for most presentations. They often find slide shows visually unappealing and yearn for presentations filled with meaningful content. Currently, PowerPoint commands 95 percent of the presentations graphic software market, and with PowerPoint 2007, it is easy to develop impressive presentations by modifying slide backgrounds, creating diagrams, inserting and modifying tables, and developing new graphics.

Project — Presentation with Custom Backgrounds and SmartArt Diagrams

BTW

Copying SmartArt Graphics
The SmartArt feature is part of Microsoft Office Excel, Word, Outlook, and PowerPoint. You can create graphics in one of these programs and then copy and paste them into another Microsoft Office 2007 program.

The project in this chapter follows visual content guidelines and uses PowerPoint to create the presentation shown in Figure 3–1. This slide show, which discusses electives available in the science curriculum, has a variety of visual elements. This project introduces several techniques to make your presentations more exciting, including WordArt and SmartArt diagrams. A picture is inserted and then given a particular shape, border, and glow effect. The slide backgrounds consist of a picture on the title slide and a custom background on the remaining slides. The slide number and current date are added to the slide master.

Overview

As you read through this chapter, you will learn how to create the presentation shown in Figure 3–1 by performing these general tasks:

- Create a new presentation from an outline created in Microsoft Office Word 2007.
- Format slide master backgrounds.
- Format pictures by applying styles and effects.
- Insert and format SmartArt graphics.
- Change clip art elements.

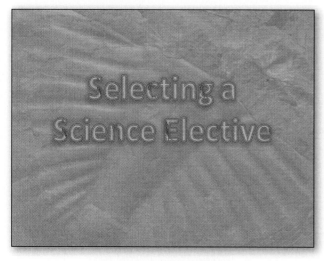

(a) Slide 1 (Title Slide)

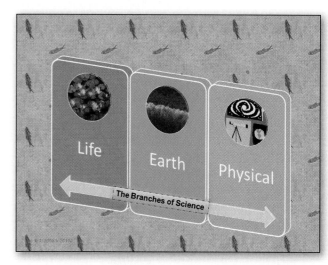

(b) Slide 2 (SmartArt Graphic and Text Box)

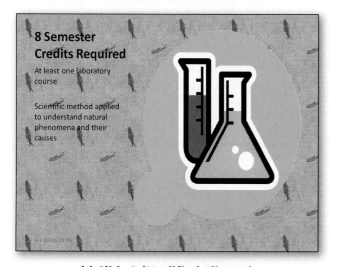

(c) Slide 3 (Modified Clip Art)

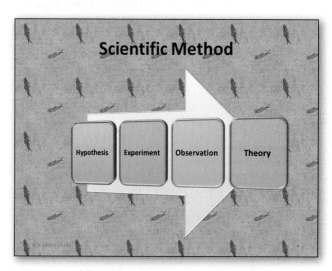

(d) Slide 4 (SmartArt Graphic)

Figure 3–1

General Project Guidelines

When creating a PowerPoint presentation, the actions you perform and decisions you make will affect the appearance and characteristics of the finished document. As you create a presentation with WordArt and SmartArt, such as the project shown in Figure 3–1, you should follow these general guidelines:

1. **Use WordArt in moderation.** Used correctly, the graphical nature of WordArt can add interest and set a tone. Format text with a WordArt style only when needed for special emphasis.

2. **Choose an Appropriate SmartArt Layout.** SmartArt illustrations represent ideas and concepts graphically. Audiences can grasp these visual concepts and recall them more quickly and accurately than viewing text alone. Many SmartArt layouts are available, so select the one that best represents the concept you are attempting to present.

   • List

   • Process

   • Cycle

(continued)

**Plan
Ahead**

**Plan
Ahead**

(continued)

- Hierarchy
- Relationship
- Matrix
- Pyramid

3. **Consider the Verbal Message to Accompany Your Slides.** Slide shows generally accompany a speaker's presentation. They should assist the speaker by providing information presented more effectively visually rather than verbally. As you develop your slides, plan a script for the speaker.

4. **Be Certain You Have Permission to Modify Clips.** Some graphics are protected by trademarks and service marks, so they cannot be modified without permission.

5. **Use Left-Brain / Right-Brain Content Concepts.** Your brain's left hemisphere processes analytical information, such as a mathematical equation or chemical formula. Your brain's right hemisphere, in contrast, responds to sensory information, such as images and music. Construct your PowerPoint slides so the message appeals to the appropriate side of the brain.

When necessary, more specific details concerning the above guidelines are presented at appropriate points in the chapter. The chapter also will identify the actions you perform and decisions you made regarding these guidelines during the creation of the presentation shown in Figure 3–1.

Defining Outline Levels
Imported outlines can contain up to nine outline levels, whereas PowerPoint outlines are limited to six levels (one for the title text and five for body paragraph text). When you import an outline, all text in outline levels six through nine is treated as a fifth-level paragraph.

Creating a Presentation from a Microsoft Office Word 2007 Outline

Many writers begin composing reports and documents by creating an outline. Others review their papers for consistency by saving the document with a new file name, removing all text except the topic headings, and then saving the file again. An outline created in Microsoft Word or another word-processing program works well as a shell for a PowerPoint presentation. Instead of typing text in PowerPoint, as you did in Projects 1 and 2, you can import this outline; add visual elements such as clip art, photos, and graphical bullets, and ultimately create an impressive slide show.

To Start PowerPoint

Note: If you are using Windows XP, see Appendix F for alternate steps.

If you are using a computer to step through the project in this chapter and you want your screens to match the figures in this book, you should change your computer's resolution to 1024×768. For information about how to change a computer's resolution, read Appendix E.

The following steps, which assume Windows Vista is running, start PowerPoint based on a typical installation. You may need to ask your instructor how to start PowerPoint for your computer.

1 Click the Start button on the Windows Vista taskbar, click All Programs at the bottom of the left pane on the Start menu, click Microsoft Office in the All Programs list, and then click Microsoft Office PowerPoint 2007.

2 If the PowerPoint window is not maximized, click the Maximize button next to the Close button on its title bar to maximize the window.

Converting Documents for Use in PowerPoint

PowerPoint can produce slides based on an outline created in Microsoft Word, a word-processing program, or a Web page if the text was saved in a format that PowerPoint can recognize. Microsoft Word 2007 files use the file extension **.docx** in their file names. Text originating in other word-processing programs for later use with PowerPoint should be saved in Rich Text Format (.rtf) or plain text format (.txt). Web page documents that use an HTML extension (.htm) can also be imported.

PowerPoint automatically opens Microsoft Office files, and many other types of files, in the PowerPoint format. The **rich text format** file type is used to transfer formatted documents between applications, even if the programs are running on different platforms, such as PC compatible and Macintosh. When a Word or Rich Text Format document is inserted into a presentation, PowerPoint creates an outline structure based on heading styles in the document. A Heading 1 in a source document becomes a slide title in PowerPoint, a Heading 2 becomes the first level of body text on the slide, a Heading 3 the second level of text on the slide, and so on.

If the original document contains no heading styles, PowerPoint creates an outline based on paragraphs. For example, in a .doc or .rtf file, for several lines of text styled as Normal and broken by paragraphs, PowerPoint turns each paragraph into a slide title.

To Open a Microsoft Word Outline as a Presentation

The text for the Science presentation is contained in a Microsoft Word 2007 file. The following steps open this Microsoft Word outline as a presentation from the Data Files for Students. See the inside back cover of this book for instructions on downloading the Data Files for Students, or contact your instructor for more information about accessing the required files.

1

- Click the Delete button in the Slides group on the Home tab to delete Slide 1 (Figure 3–2).

Must I delete Slide 1 now?

No. PowerPoint will create new slides from the Science Outline, so this current Slide 1 will be blank. You could delete it after you insert the Word outline.

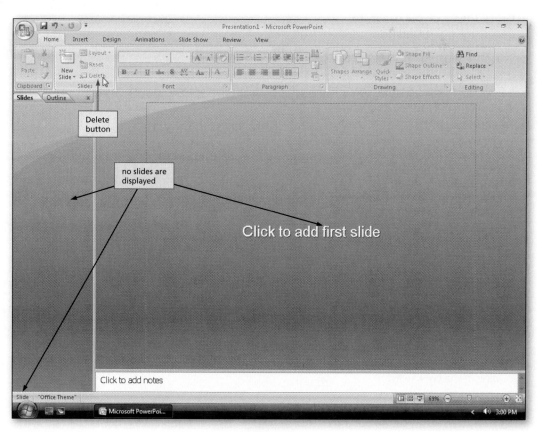

Figure 3–2

- Connect a USB flash drive with the Data Files for Students to one of the computer's USB ports.

- Click the New Slide button arrow to display the Office Theme Layout gallery (Figure 3–3).

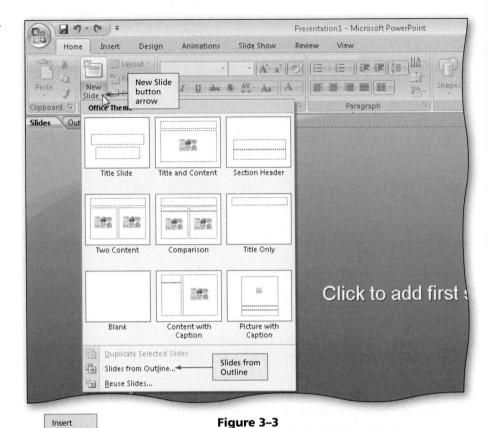

Figure 3–3

3

- Click Slides from Outline in the Office Theme Layout gallery to display the Insert Outline dialog box.

- If the Folders list is displayed below the Folders button, click the Folders button to remove the Folders list.

- If necessary, click Computer in the Favorite Links section to display a list of available drives and then double-click UDISK 2.0 (E:) to select the USB flash drive. (Your USB flash drive may have a different name and letter.)

- Click Science Outline in the File list (Figure 3–4).

Q&A

What if the outline file is not on a USB flash drive?

Use the same process, but be certain to select the device containing the outline in the Look in list.

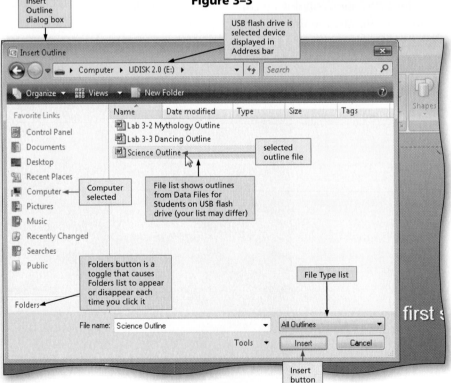

Figure 3–4

4

- Click the Insert button to open the Science Outline and create three slides in your presentation.

- Click the Outline tab in the Tabs pane to view the outline (Figure 3–5).

Q&A

Do I need to see the text as an outline in the Outline tab now?

No, but sometimes it is helpful to view the content of your presentation in this view before looking at individual slides.

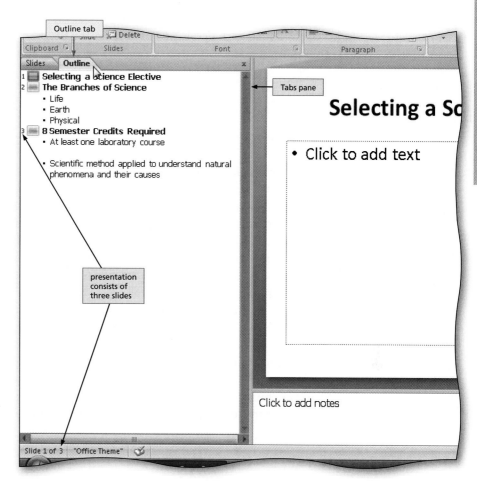

Figure 3–5

Other Ways

1. On Office Button menu click Open, click All Outlines in file type list, click Science Outline, click Open

To Change the Slide 1 Layout to Title Slide

When you started the new presentation, PowerPoint applied the Title and Text slide layout to all slides. You want to apply the Title Slide slide layout to Slide 1 to introduce the presentation. The following steps change the Slide 1 slide layout.

1 Click the Layout button in the Slides group.

2 Click Title Slide to apply that layout to Slide 1.

To Save the Presentation

With all the text for your slides created, you should save the presentation. For a detailed example of the procedure summarized below, refer to pages PPT 28 through PPT 31 in Chapter 1.

Note: If you are using Windows XP, see Appendix F for alternate steps.

1 Connect a USB flash drive to one of the computer's USB ports and then click the Save button on the Quick Access Toolbar.

2 Type Science in the File name text box. Do not press the ENTER key after typing the file name.

③ Click Computer in the Favorite Links section to display a list of available drives and then double-click UDISK 2.0 (E:) to select the USB flash drive.

④ Click the Save button in the Save As dialog box.

Formatting Slide Backgrounds

Resetting Backgrounds
If you have made many changes to the background and want to start the process over, click the Reset Background button in the Format Background dialog box.

A slide's background is an integral part of a presentation because it can generate audience interest. Every slide can have the same background, or different backgrounds can be used in a presentation. This background is considered **fill**, which is the interior of a shape, line, or character. Three fills are available: solid, gradient, and picture or texture. **Solid fill** is one color used throughout the entire slide. **Gradient fill** is one color shade gradually progressing to another shade of the same color or one color progressing to another color. **Picture or texture fill** uses a specific file or an image that simulates a material, such as cork, granite, marble, or canvas.

Once you add a fill, you can adjust its appearance. For example, you can adjust its **transparency**, which allows you to see through the background, so that any text on the slide is visible. You also can select a color that is part of the theme or a custom color. You can use **offsets**, another background feature, to move the background from the slide borders in varying percentage distances. **Tiling options** repeat the background image many times vertically and horizontally on the slide; the smaller the tiling percentage, the greater the number of times the image is repeated.

To Insert a Texture Fill

A wide variety of texture fills are available to give your presentation a unique look. The 24 pictures in the Textures gallery give the appearance of a physical object, such as water drops, sand, tissue paper, and a paper bag. You also can use your own texture pictures for custom backgrounds. When you insert a fill, PowerPoint assumes you want this custom background on only the current slide displayed. To make this background appear on all slides in the presentation, click the Apply to All button in the Format Background dialog box. The following steps insert the Fish fossil fill on all four slides in the presentation.

①
- Click the Slides tab in the Tabs pane to view the slide thumbnails.

- Right-click anywhere on Slide 1 except the title or subtitle text placeholders to display the shortcut menu (Figure 3–6).

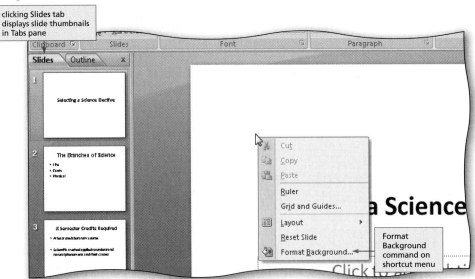

Figure 3–6

- Click Format Background on the shortcut menu to display the Format Background dialog box.

- With the Fill pane displaying, click 'Picture or texture fill' to expand the fill options (Figure 3–7).

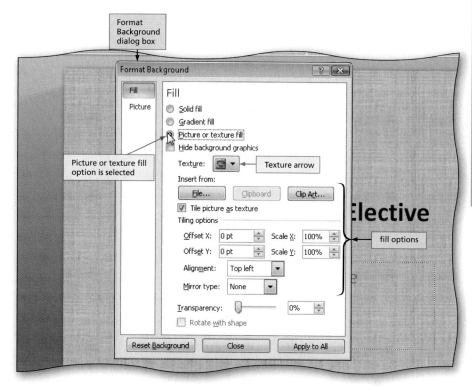

Figure 3–7

3

- Click the Texture arrow to display the Texture gallery (Figure 3–8).

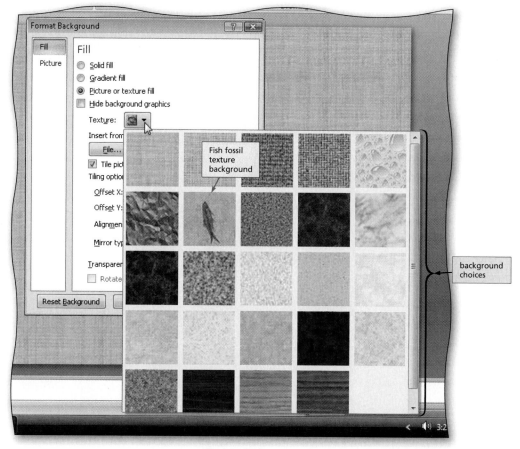

Figure 3–8

4

- Click the Fish fossil background to insert this background on Slide 1 (Figure 3–9).

Q&A

The Format Background dialog box is covering part of the slide. Can I move this box?

Yes. Click the dialog box title and drag it to a different location so that you can view the slide.

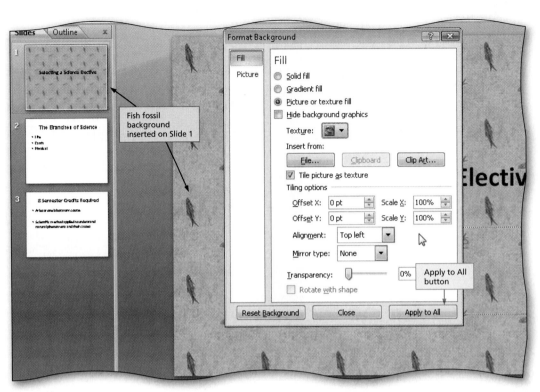

Figure 3–9

5

- Click the Apply to All button to insert the Fish fossil background on all slides (Figure 3–10).

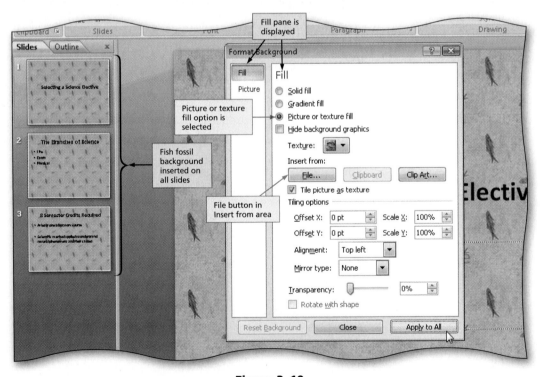

Figure 3–10

Other Ways

1. Click Design tab, click Background Styles in Background group, click Format Background

To Insert a Picture to Create a Background

For variety and interest, you want to use a fossil photograph as the Slide 1 background. This picture is stored on the Data Files for Students. PowerPoint will stretch the height and width of this picture to fill the slide area. The following steps insert the file, Fossil, on only Slide 1.

- If it is not already selected, click the Slide 1 thumbnail in the Tabs pane to select it.

- With the Fill pane displaying and the Picture or texture fill option selected in the Format Background dialog box, click the File button in the Insert from area to display the Insert Picture dialog box.

- If necessary, click Computer in the Favorite Links section and then double-click UDISK 2.0 (E:) to select the USB flash drive.

- Click Fossil to select the file name (Figure 3–11).

Q&A What if the photograph file is not in the file name list?

Use the same process, but be certain to select the location containing the file in the Previous Locations list.

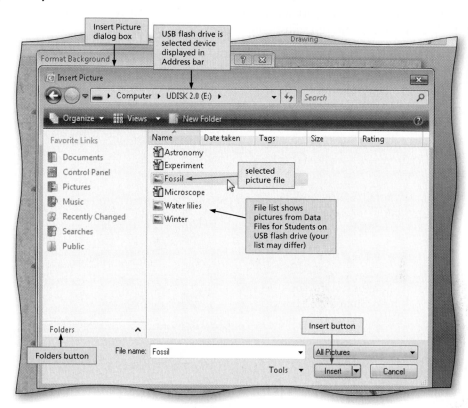

Figure 3–11

- Click the Insert button to insert the Fossil picture as the Slide 1 background (Figure 3–12).

Q&A What if I do not want to use this picture?

Click the Undo button on the Quick Access Toolbar.

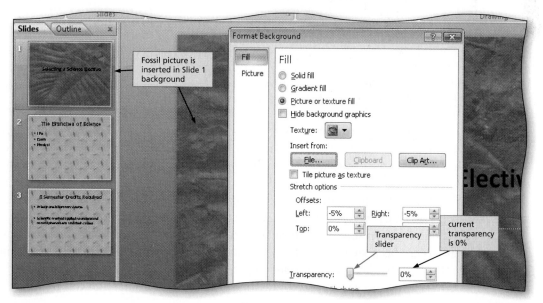

Figure 3–12

To Format the Background Picture Fill Transparency

The Fossil picture on Slide 1 has a rich color and may conflict with text you will add to the title slide. One method of reducing this brightness is to change the transparency. The **Transparency slider** indicates the amount of opaqueness. The default setting is 0, which is fully opaque. The opposite extreme is 100%, which is fully transparent. To change the transparency, you can move the Transparency slider or enter a number in the text box next to the slider. The following step adjusts the transparency to 40%.

- Click the Transparency slider and drag it to the right until 40% is displayed in the Transparency text box (Figure 3–13).

Q&A

Why do the Left and Right offsets in the Stretch options area show a −5 value?

PowerPoint automatically expanded the photograph slightly so that it fills the entire slide.

- Click the Close button to close the Format Background dialog box.

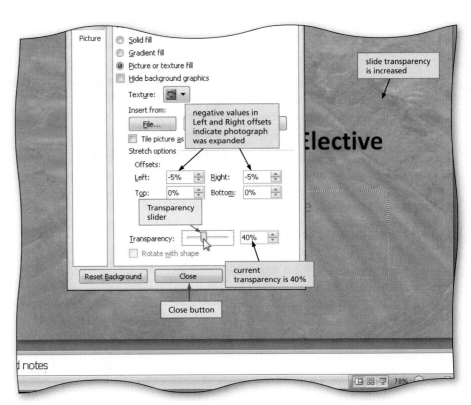

Figure 3–13

To Add Slide Numbers, Date, and Time

Slides can contain information at the top or bottom. The area at the top of a slide is called a header, and the area at the bottom is called a footer. As a default, no information is displayed in the header or footer. You can choose to apply only a header, only a footer, or both a header and footer. In addition, you can elect to have the header or footer display on single slides, all slides, or all slides except the title slide.

Slide numbers help a presenter organize a talk. While few audience members are cognizant of this aspect of a slide, the presenter can glance at the number and know which slide contains particular information. If an audience member asks a question pertaining to information contained on a slide that had been displayed previously or is on a slide that has not been viewed yet, the presenter can jump to that slide in an effort to answer the question. In addition, the slide number helps pace the slide show. For example, a speaker could have the presentation timed so that Slide 4 is displaying three minutes into the talk. The following steps add this number to a slide and also add the current date and time.

- Click Insert on the Ribbon to display the Insert tab.

- Click the Slide Number button in the Text group to display the Header and Footer dialog box.

- If necessary, click the Slide tab to display the Slide sheet (Figure 3–14).

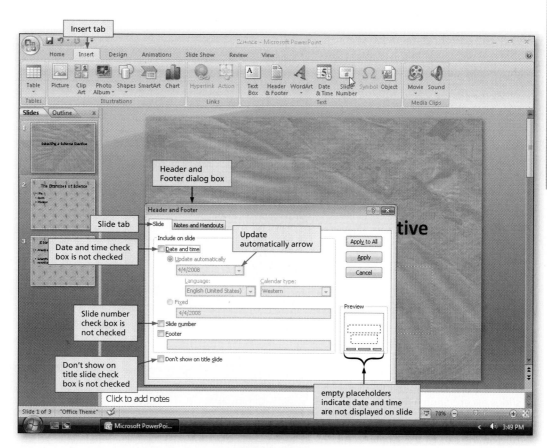

Figure 3–14

②

- Click 'Date and time' to select this check box.

- Click Slide number to select this check box.

- Click 'Don't show on title slide' to select this check box.

- Click the Update automatically arrow in the Date and time area to display the Date and time list (Figure 3–15).

Q&A

What are the black boxes in the Preview area?

The black box in the left footer placeholder indicates the current date and time will appear on the slide; the black box in the right footer placeholder indicates the page number will appear.

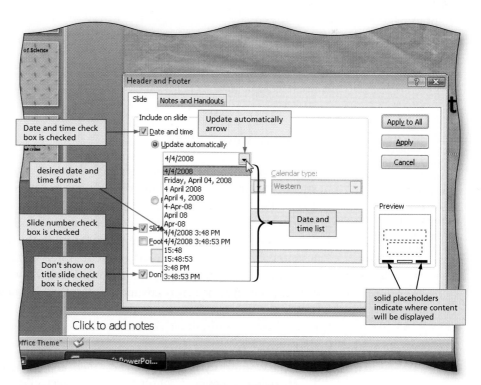

Figure 3–15

3

- Click the current date and time that are displayed in the format shown in Figure 3–16.

What if I want a specific date and time to appear?

Click Fixed in the Date and time area and type the actual information you want your audience to see.

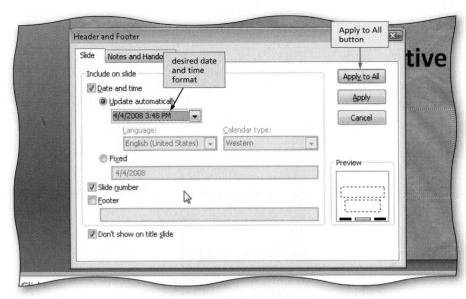

Figure 3–16

4

- Click the Apply to All button to display the slide number on all slides except Slide 1 (Figure 3–17).

When would I click the Apply button instead of the Apply to All button?

Click the Apply button when you want the slide number to appear only on the slide currently selected.

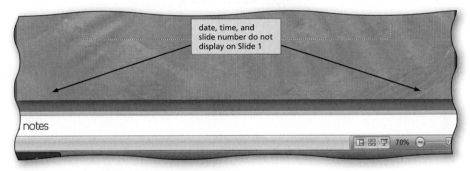

Figure 3–17

Creating Logos
Many companies without graphic arts departments create their logos using WordArt. The bevels, glows, and shadows allow corporate designers to develop unique images with 3-D effects that give depth to their companies' emblems.

Using WordArt

One method of adding appealing visual elements to a presentation is by using **WordArt** styles. This feature is found in other Microsoft Office applications, including Word and Excel. This gallery of decorative effects allows you to type new text or convert existing text to WordArt. You then can add elements such as fills, outlines, and effects.

As with slide backgrounds, WordArt fill in the interior of a letter can consist of a solid color, texture, picture, or gradient. The WordArt **outline** is the exterior border surrounding each letter or symbol. PowerPoint allows you to change the outline color, weight, and style. You also can add an **effect**, which helps add emphasis or depth to the characters. Some effects are shadows, reflections, glows, bevels, and 3–D rotations.

Plan Ahead

Use WordArt in moderation.
Some WordArt styles are bold and detailed, and they can detract from the message you are trying to present if not used carefully. Select a WordArt style when needed for special emphasis, such as a title slide that audience members will see when they enter the room. WordArt can have a powerful effect, so do not overuse it.

To Apply a WordArt Style

The Slide 1 title text imported from the Microsoft Word outline has the default Calibri font with a font size of 44. You quickly can add visual elements to these letters by selecting a text style in the WordArt Quick Style gallery. The following steps apply a WordArt style to the Slide 1 title text.

1

- With Slide 1 displaying, select the title text, Selecting a Science Elective.

- Click Format on the Ribbon under Drawing Tools to display the Format tab.

- Click the More button in the WordArt Styles gallery on the Format tab to display the WordArt Styles gallery (Figure 3–18).

Q&A Why did the Format tab appear automatically on the Ribbon?

It appears when you select text to which you could add a WordArt style or other effect.

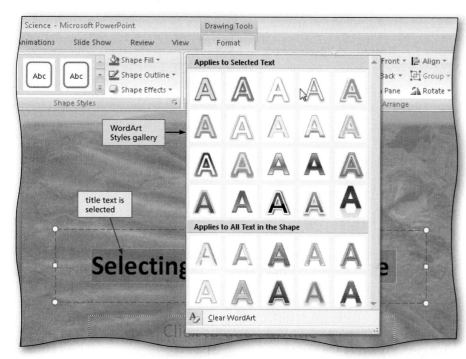

Figure 3–18

2

- Point to Fill – Accent 2, Double Outline – Accent 2 in the Applies to Selected Text area (row 3, column 5) to display a live preview of this style in the title text (Figure 3–19).

 Experiment

- Point to various styles in the WordArt Styles gallery and watch the format of the text and borders change.

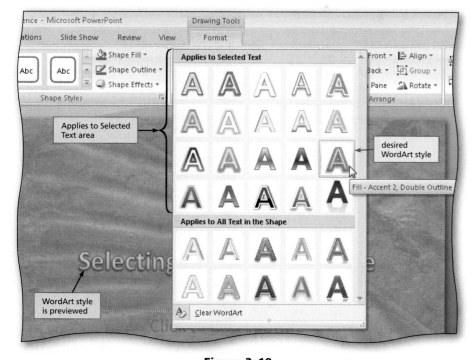

Figure 3–19

- Click Fill – Accent 2, Double Outline – Accent 2 to apply this style to the title text (Figure 3–20).

Q&A

What is a matte bevel style that is part of some of the styles in the gallery?

A matte finish gives a dull and rough effect. A bevel edge is angled or sloped and gives the effect of a three-dimension object.

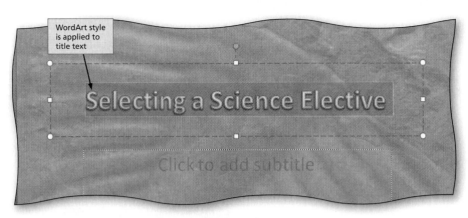

Figure 3–20

To Format the WordArt Text Fill

The Fish fossil image is integral in this presentation on the slide backgrounds, so adding it to the title text WordArt would help reinforce this graphic. The following steps add the Fish fossil as a fill for the WordArt characters on Slide 1.

- With the Slide 1 title text still selected, right-click the text to display the Mini toolbar.

- Click the Increase Font size button on the Mini toolbar repeatedly until the font size increases to 80 point.

- With the Format tab displaying, click the Text Fill arrow in the WordArt Styles group to display the Fill menu (Figure 3–21).

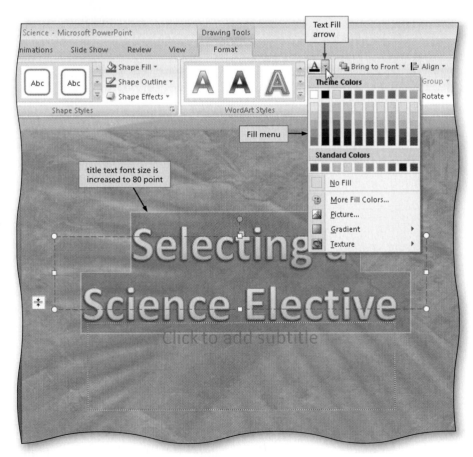

Figure 3–21

2

- Point to Texture on the Fill menu to display the Texture Fill gallery.

- Point to the Fish fossil texture to display a live preview of this texture as the fill for the title text (Figure 3–22).

Experiment

- Point to various styles in the WordArt Styles gallery and watch the format of the text and borders change.

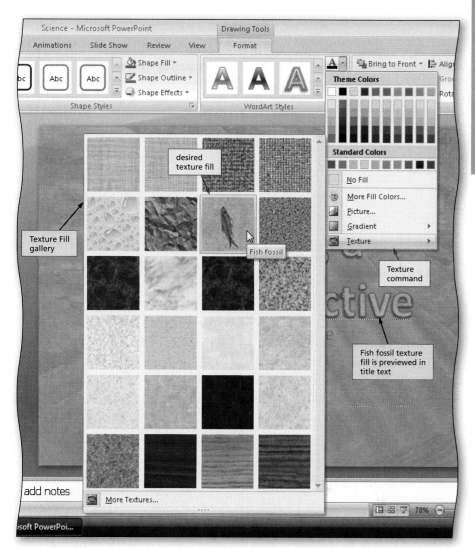

Figure 3–22

3

- Click the Fish fossil texture to apply this texture as the fill for the title text (Figure 3–23).

Q&A

Can I apply this texture simultaneously to text that appears in more than one place on my slide?

Yes. Select one area of text, press and then hold the CTRL key while you select the other text, and then apply the texture.

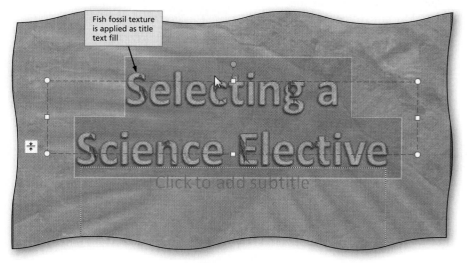

Figure 3–23

To Change the Weight of the WordArt Outline

The WordArt style just applied to this text has a double outline. To emphasize this characteristic, you can increase the width of the lines. As with font size, lines also are measured in point size, and PowerPoint gives you the option to change the line **weight**, or thickness, starting with ¼ point (pt) and increasing in one-fourth-point increments. Other outline options include changing the color and the line style, such as dots or dashes or a combination of dots and dashes. The following steps change the title text outline weight to 4½ pt.

- With the Slide 1 title text still selected and the Format tab displaying, click the Text Outline arrow in the WordArt Styles group to display the Text Outline menu.

- Point to Weight on the Text Outline menu to display the Weight list.

- Point to 4½ pt to display a live preview of this line weight on the title text outline (Figure 3–24).

 **Experiment**

- Point to various line weights in the Weight list and watch the line thickness change.

Q&A Can I make the line width more than 6 pt?

Yes. Click More Lines and increase the amount in the Width box.

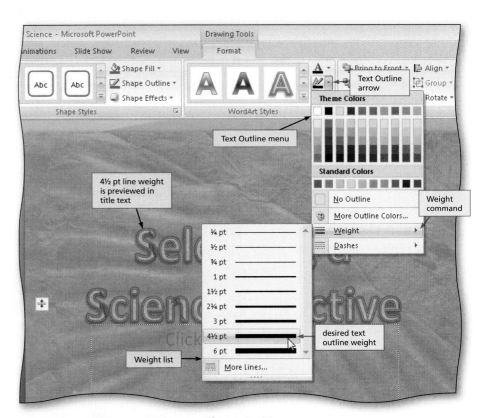

Figure 3–24

- Click 4½ pt to apply this line weight to the title text outline (Figure 3–25).

Q&A Must my text have an outline?

No. To delete the outline, click No Outline in the Text Outline menu.

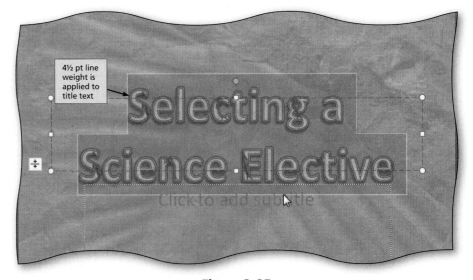

Figure 3–25

To Add a WordArt Text Effect

The Fish fossil fill and thick outline call attention to the Slide 1 title text. For further emphasis, you can add one or more effects. For example, you can add a reflection, which reverses the letters below the text, or a glow, which adds a color around each letter. Once an effect is applied, you often can modify it. For example, you can enhance a shadow effect by changing such elements as its color, size, and angle. The following steps add a glow effect to the WordArt characters on Slide 1.

1

- With the Slide 1 title text still selected and the Format tab displaying, click the Text Effects button in the WordArt Styles group to display the Text Effects list.

- Point to Glow on the Text Effects list to display the Glow gallery (Figure 3–26).

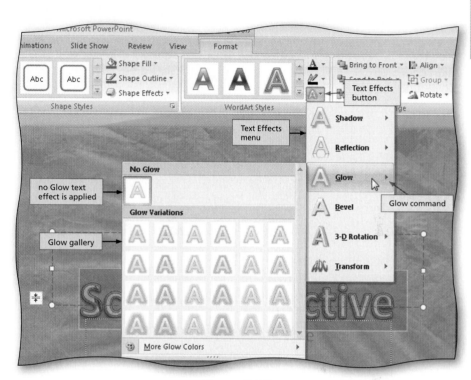

Figure 3–26

2

- Point to Accent color 6, 11 pt glow (row 3, column 6) in the Glow Variations area of the Glow gallery to display a live preview of this effect on the title text (Figure 3–27).

 Experiment

- Point to various Glow Variations in the Glow gallery and watch the colors and sizes change.

Q&A Can I select a color other than the six colors shown in the gallery?

Yes. Click More Glow Colors and then choose a standard or theme color. You also can select a custom color.

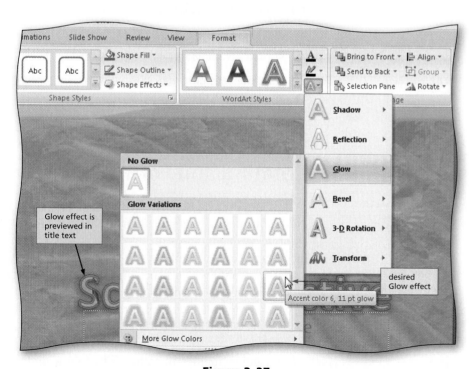

Figure 3–27

• Click Accent color 6, 11 pt glow to apply this effect to the title text (Figure 3–28).

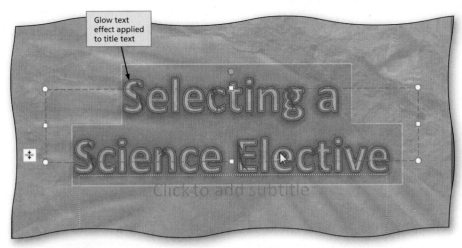

Figure 3–28

To Delete the Subtitle Placeholder

The Slide 1 subtitle placeholder will not be used in this presentation. The following steps delete this placeholder.

1. Click the subtitle text placeholder border two times to change the border to a solid line.

2. Press the DELETE key to delete the placeholder.

To Save an Existing Presentation with the Same File Name

You have made several changes to your presentation since you last saved it. Thus, you should save it again. The following step saves the presentation again.

1. Click the Save button on the Quick Access Toolbar to overwrite the previous Science file on the USB flash drive.

Creating and Formatting a SmartArt Graphic

An illustration often can help convey relationships between key points in your presentation. Numerous studies have shown that audience members recall information more readily and accurately when it is presented graphically rather than textually. Microsoft Office 2007 includes **SmartArt graphics**, which are visual representations of your ideas. The SmartArt layouts have a variety of shapes, arrows, and lines to correspond to the major points you want your audience to remember.

You can create a SmartArt graphic in two ways: select a type and then add text, or convert text already present on a slide to a graphic. Once the SmartArt graphic is present, you can customize its look by changing colors, adding and deleting shapes, adding fill and effects, and including animation. The following table lists some of the popular SmartArt types and their uses:

Type	Purpose
Table 3–1 SmartArt Graphic Layout Types and Purposes	
List	Show nonsequential information
Process	Show steps in a process or timeline
Cycle	Show a continual process
Hierarchy	Create an organizational chart
Relationship	Illustrate connections
Matrix	Show how parts relate to a whole
Pyramid	Show proportional relationships with the largest component at the top or bottom

Plan Ahead

Choose an appropriate SmartArt layout.
If a slide contains key points that show a process or relationship, consider using a SmartArt graphic to add visual appeal and enhance audience comprehension. As you select a layout, determine the number of ideas you need to present and then select a graphic that contains the same number of shapes. For example, the Counterbalance Arrows layout resembles a teeter-totter; it represents the notion that one concept conversely affects another concept, such as the economic principle that supply has an inverse relationship to demand.

To Convert Text to a SmartArt Graphic

You quickly can convert small amounts of slide text into a SmartArt graphic. Once you determine the type of graphic, such as process or cycle, you then have a wide variety of styles from which to choose in the SmartArt Graphic gallery. As with other galleries, you can point to the samples and view a live preview if you desire. The following steps convert the Slide 2 text to the Continuous Picture List graphic, which is part of the List, Process, and Relationship categories.

- Click the Next Slide button to display Slide 2.

- Select the three bulleted list items and then right-click the text to display the shortcut menu.

- Point to Convert to SmartArt in the shortcut menu to display the SmartArt Graphics gallery (Figure 3–29).

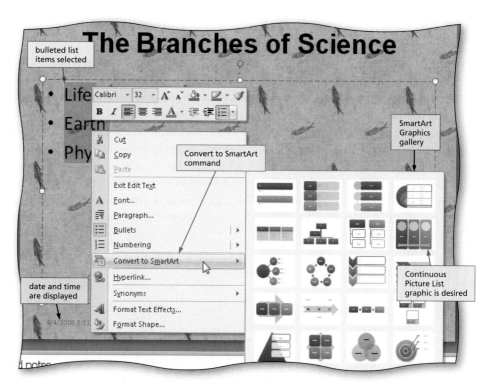

Figure 3–29

2

- Click the Continuous Picture List graphic (row 2, column 4) to apply this shape and convert the text (Figure 3–30).

Q&A

How can I edit the text that displays in the three shapes?

The text also appears in the Text pane displayed to the left of the graphic. Click the text you want to change and make your desired edits.

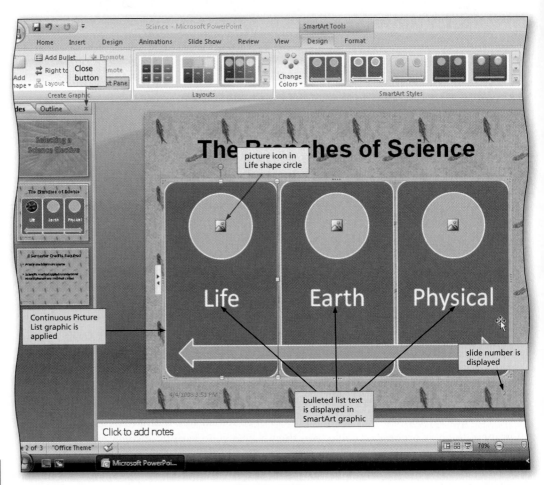

Figure 3–30

Other Ways

1. Click SmartArt button in Illustrations group on Insert tab

To Insert Images from a File into the SmartArt Graphic

The **Text pane** consists of two areas: the top portion has the text that will appear in the SmartArt graphic; the bottom portion gives the name of the graphic and suggestions of what type of information is best suited for this type of visual. The information at the bottom of the Continuous Picture List Text pane indicates that the three circular shapes in the Continuous Picture List graphic are designed to hold images. You can select files from the Clip Organizer or from images you have obtained from other sources, such as a photograph taken with your digital camera. In this presentation, you will add files from the Data Files for Students. See the inside back cover of this book for instructions on downloading the Data Files for Students, or contact your instructor for more information about accessing the required files. The following steps insert three images into the SmartArt graphic.

1

- Double-click the circle picture icon in the Life shape to display the Insert Picture dialog box.

- With your USB flash drive connected to one of the computer's USB ports, double-click UDISK 2.0 (E:) to select the USB flash drive, Drive E in this case, as the device that contains the picture.

- Click Water lilies to select the file name (Figure 3–31).

What if the photograph is not on a USB flash drive?

Use the same process, but be certain to select the location containing the photograph in the File list.

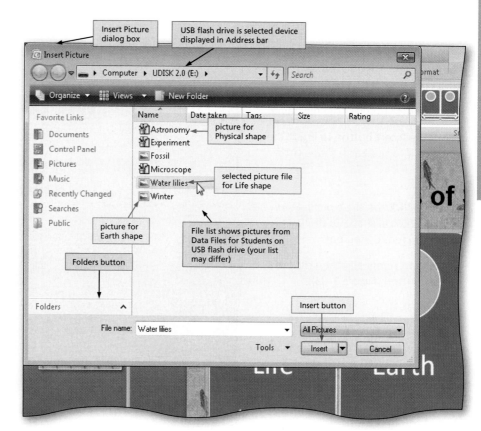

Figure 3–31

2

- Click the Insert button in the dialog box to insert the Water lilies picture into the Life shape circle (Figure 3–32).

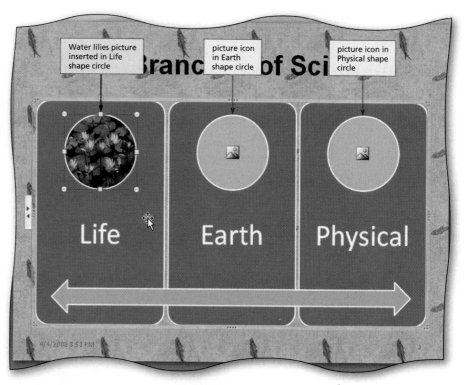

Figure 3–32

3

- Double-click the circle picture icon in the Earth shape to display the Insert Picture dialog box.

- Click Winter to select the file name.

- Click the Insert button to insert the picture into the Earth shape circle.

4

- Double-click the circle picture icon in the Physical shape to display the Insert Picture dialog box.

- Click Astronomy and then click the Insert button (Figure 3–33).

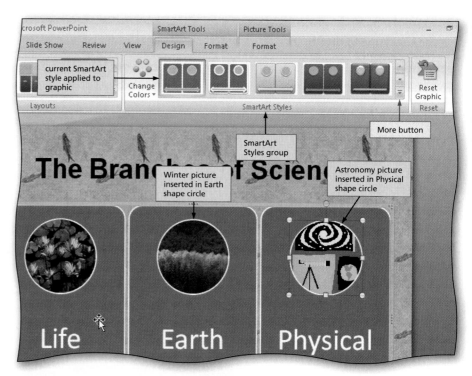

Figure 3–33

To Add a SmartArt Style to the Graphic

You can change the look of your SmartArt graphic easily by applying a **SmartArt Style**. These professionally designed effects have a variety of shape fills, edges, shadows, line styles, gradients, and three-dimensional graphics that allow you to customize the appearance of your presentation. The following steps add the Brick Scene style to the Slide 2 SmartArt graphic.

1

- With the SmartArt graphic still selected and the Design tab active, click the More button in the SmartArt Styles group to expand the SmartArt Styles gallery (Figure 3–34).

How do I select the graphic if it is no longer selected?

Click the graphic anywhere except the images you just added.

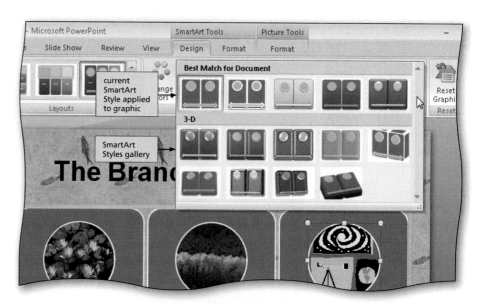

Figure 3–34

- Point to the Brick Scene style (row 2, column 5) in the 3-D category in the SmartArt gallery to display a live preview of this style (Figure 3–35).

Experiment

- Point to various styles in the SmartArt gallery and watch the Continuous Picture List graphic change styles.

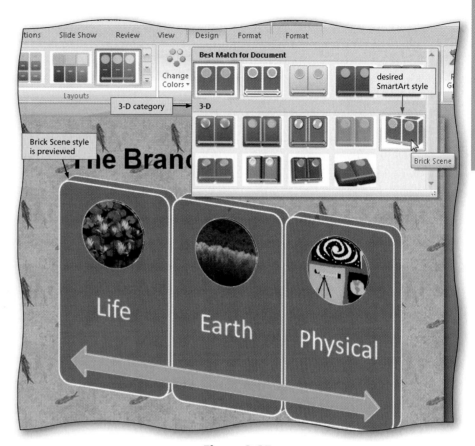

Figure 3–35

- Click Brick Scene to apply this style to the graphic (Figure 3–36).

Figure 3–36

To Change the SmartArt Color

Another modification you can make to your SmartArt graphic is to change its color. As with the WordArt Style gallery, PowerPoint provides a gallery of color options you can preview and evaluate. The following steps change the SmartArt graphic color to a Colorful range.

1

- With the SmartArt graphic still selected and the Design tab active, click the Change Colors button in the SmartArt Styles group to display the Change Colors gallery (Figure 3–37).

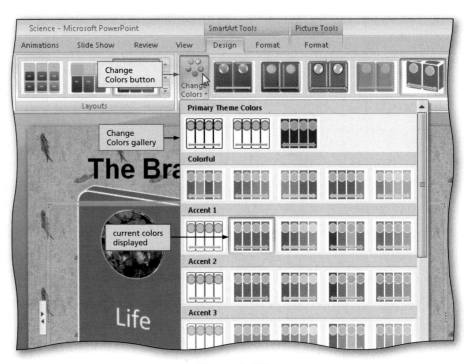

Figure 3–37

2

- Point to Colorful Range – Accent Colors 5 to 6 (row 2, column 5) in the Colorful category to display a live preview of these colors (Figure 3–38).

 **Experiment**

- Point to various colors in the Change Colors gallery and watch the shapes change colors.

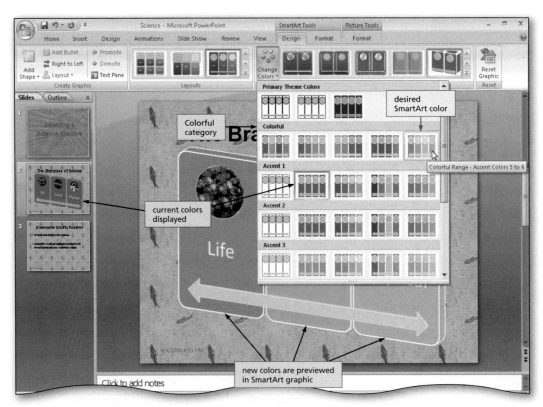

Figure 3–38

3

- Click Colorful Range – Accent Colors 5 to 6 to apply this color variation to the graphic (Figure 3–39).

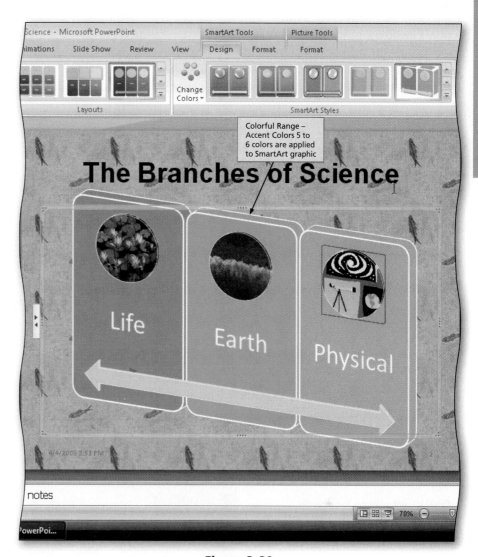

Figure 3–39

Plan Ahead

Consider the verbal message to accompany your slides.

As you design each screen, think about the spoken words that the presenter will use. Audience members want to hear a motivated, passionate speaker who does more than read the text on a screen. Each slide should generate interest, and the speaker should give additional information in an enthusiastic manner. Some speech coaches abide by the principle that a speaker should not say any word that appears on a screen. You should, consequently, make notes as you assemble the slides so that they and the presenter make a unified packaged presentation.

To Insert a Text Box

The arrow in the SmartArt graphic spans across the three shapes. You can add meaningful text to this shape by inserting a **text box**, which is a movable, resizable container. Once you insert this text box, you can add text and graphics and then format these characters and shapes. The following steps cut the text from the slide title, insert a text box on the SmartArt graphic, and then paste the title text in the text box.

1

- Select the Slide 2 title text, The Branches of Science.

- Right-click the selected text to display the shortcut menu (Figure 3–40).

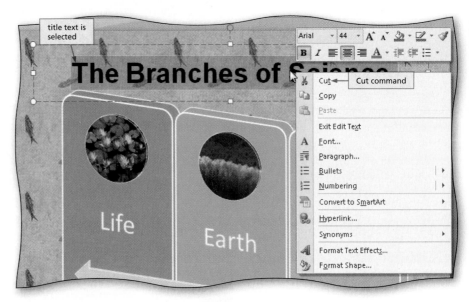

Figure 3–40

2

- Click Cut on the shortcut menu to delete the title text.

- Click Insert on the Ribbon to display the Insert tab.

- Click the Text Box button on the Insert tab.

- Position the mouse pointer on the arrow at the bottom of the three shapes (Figure 3–41).

Q&A

Why did my mouse pointer change shape?

The different shape indicates that PowerPoint is ready to create the text box where you click.

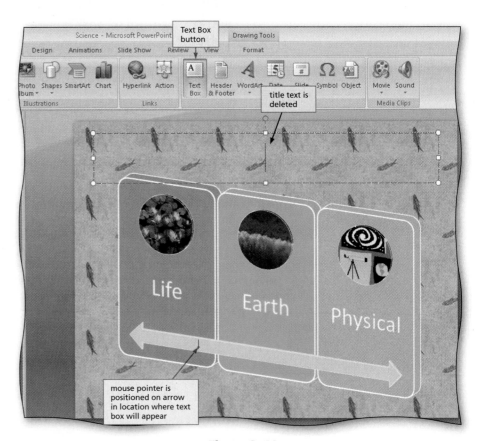

Figure 3–41

3

- Click the arrow to insert a text box.

- Click the Paste button in the Clipboard group on the Home tab to insert the title text in the text box (Figure 3–42).

Q&A

Why does a clipboard icon display near the inserted text box?

The clipboard is the Paste Options button, which presents a variety of methods for inserting the text.

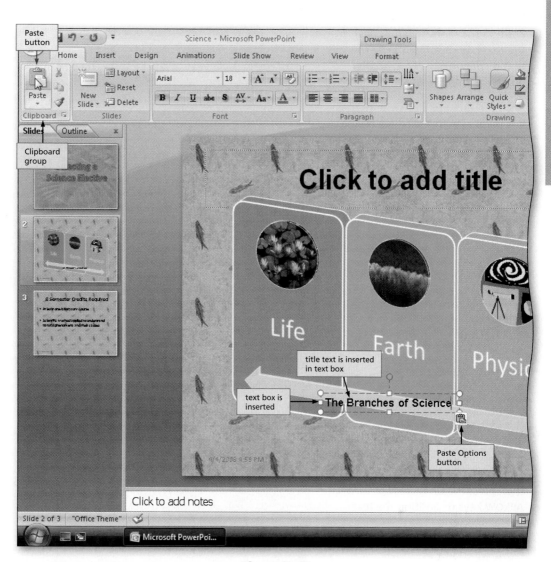

Figure 3–42

To Rotate a Text Box

Once the text box is inserted, you can move it to various locations on the slide. If you need to move it a large distance, select it and drag it to the desired place. In contrast, if you need to move it only a slight increment, use the UP ARROW and DOWN ARROW keys. The text box's orientation on the slide also can change by rotating to the left or right or by flipping horizontally or vertically. Dragging the green **rotation handle** above a selected object allows you to rotate an object in any direction. The steps on the following page rotate the text box.

1

- Position the mouse pointer over the text box rotation handle so that it changes to a Free Rotate pointer (Figure 3–43).

- Drag the text box clockwise so that it is parallel with the arrow on the SmartArt graphic.

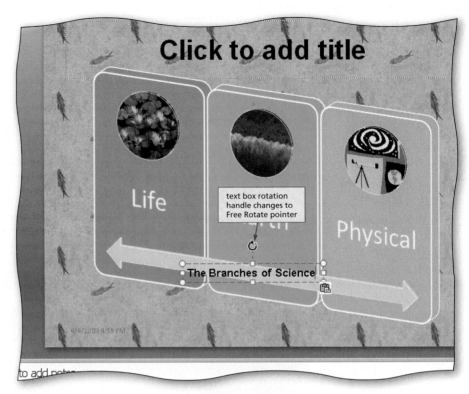

Figure 3–43

2

- If necessary, click an edge of the text box to select the box and then press the UP ARROW or DOWN ARROW keys to position the text box as shown in Figure 3–44.

Q&A

How do I move the text box in small, predefined increments?

To move or nudge the text box shape in very small increments, hold down the CTRL key while pressing the UP ARROW, DOWN ARROW, RIGHT ARROW, or LEFT ARROW keys.

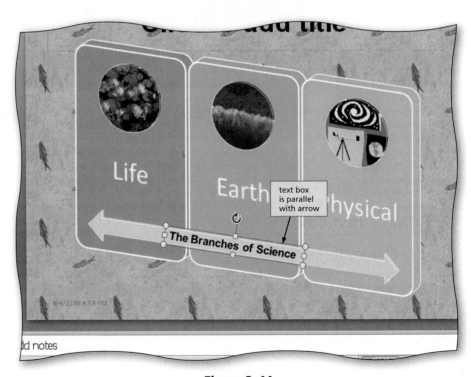

Figure 3–44

Other Ways

1. Click Rotate button in Arrange group on Format tab of Drawing Tools contextual tab

To Format the Text Box

The text box can be formatted in the same manner that shapes are formatted. You can change the fill and outline and also add effects. The following steps add a gradient fill, an outline with dashes and dots, and a glow effect.

1

- With the text box selected, click Format on the Ribbon to display the Format tab under Drawing Tools.

- Click the Shape Fill button in the Shape Styles group on the Format tab to display the Shape Fill menu (Figure 3–45).

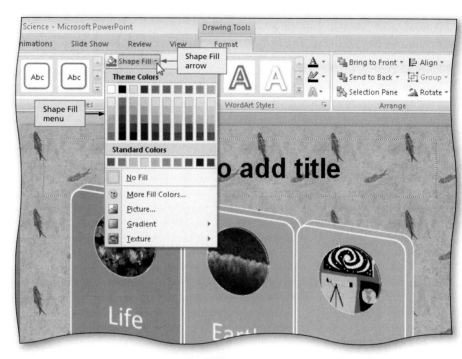

Figure 3–45

2

- Point to Gradient on the Shape Fill menu to display the Gradient gallery.

- Point to Linear Up in the Light Variations area (row 3, column 2) to display a live preview of this gradient in the text box (Figure 3–46).

 Experiment

- Point to various Light and Dark variations in the Gradient gallery and watch the text box fill change.

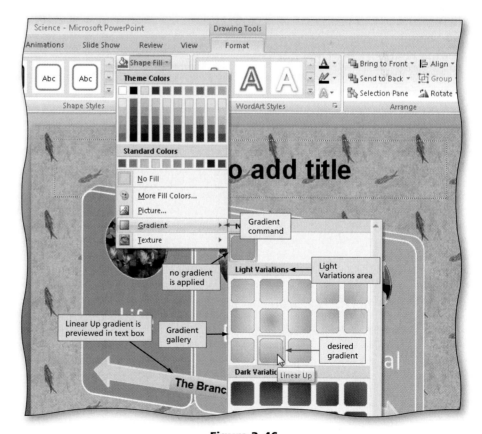

Figure 3–46

- Click Linear Up to apply this gradient to the text box.

- Click the Shape Outline button in the Shape Styles group on the Format tab to display the Shape Outline menu.

- Point to Dashes on the Shape Outline menu to display the Dashes list (Figure 3–47).

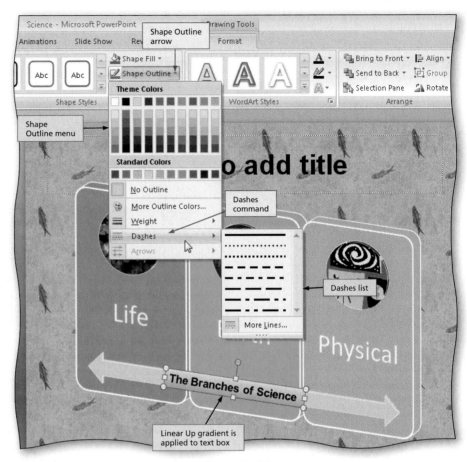

Figure 3–47

- Point to the Long Dash Dot Dot dash to display a live preview of this dash outline in the text box (Figure 3–48).

 **Experiment**

- Point to various dashes and watch the text box outline change.

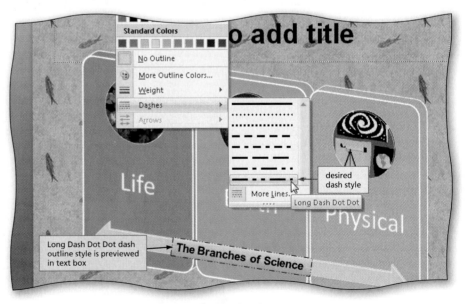

Figure 3–48

5

- Click the Long Dash Dot Dot dash to apply this dash to the text box.

- Click the Shape Effects button in the Shape Styles group on the Format tab to display the Shape Effects list.

- Point to Glow on the Shape Effects list to display the Glow gallery.

- Point to the green Accent color 3, 11 pt glow variation (row 3, column 3) to display a live preview of this glow shape effect in the text box (Figure 3–49).

Experiment

- Point to various glow variations and watch the text box effects change.

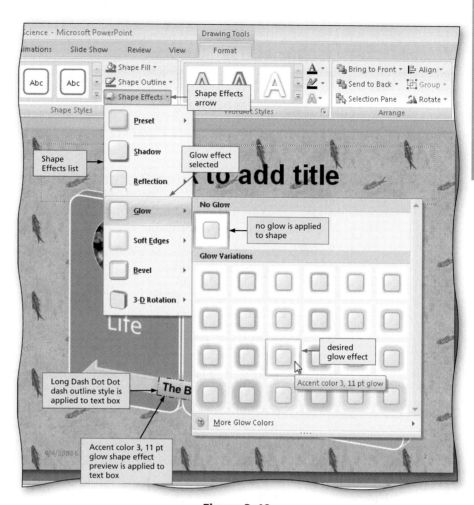

Figure 3–49

6

- Click the Accent color 3, 11 pt glow variation to apply this glow shape effect to the text box (Figure 3–50).

Figure 3–50

To Delete the Title Placeholder

The Slide 2 title placeholder will not be used in this presentation. The following steps delete this placeholder.

1 Double-click the title text placeholder border to change the border to a solid line.

2 Press the DELETE key to delete the placeholder.

To Save an Existing Presentation with the Same File Name

Now that Slide 2 is complete, you should save the presentation. The following step saves the presentation again.

1 Click the Save button on the Quick Access Toolbar to overwrite the previous Science file on the USB flash drive.

Graphic Formats: Vector and Bitmap

A clip art picture is composed of many objects grouped together to form one object. PowerPoint allows you to modify and enhance the clip by disassembling it into the objects. **Disassembling** a clip art picture, also called **ungrouping**, separates one object into multiple objects. Once ungrouped, you can manipulate the individual objects as needed to form a new object. When you ungroup a clip art picture in PowerPoint, it becomes a **drawing object** and loses its link to the Microsoft Clip Organizer. In addition to clips, other drawing objects are curves, lines, arrows, and stars.

Vector Graphics

Objects usually are saved in one of two **graphic formats**: vector or bitmap. A **vector graphic** is a piece of art that has been created by a drawing program such as CorelDRAW or Adobe Illustrator. The clip art pictures used in this project are vector graphic objects and are created as a collection of lines. Vector graphic files store data either as picture descriptions or as calculations. These files describe a picture mathematically as a set of instructions for creating the objects in the picture. These mathematical descriptions determine the position, length, and direction in which the lines are drawn. These calculations allow the drawing program to re-create the picture on the screen as necessary. Because vector graphic objects are described mathematically, they also can be layered, rotated, and magnified with relative ease. Vector graphics also are known as **object-oriented pictures**. Clip art pictures in the Microsoft Clip Organizer that have the file extension of **.wmf** are examples of vector files. Vector files can be ungrouped and manipulated by their component objects. You will ungroup the clip used on Slide 3 in this project.

Bitmap Graphics

A **bitmap graphic** is the other major format used to store objects. These art pieces are composed of a series of small dots, called pixels, which form shapes and lines. A **pixel**, short for **picture element**, is one dot in a grid. A picture that is produced on the computer screen or on paper by a printer is composed of thousands of these dots. Just as a bit is the smallest unit of information a computer can process, a pixel is the smallest element that can display or that printing hardware and software can manipulate in creating letters, numbers, or graphics.

Bitmap graphics are created by digital cameras or in paint programs such as Microsoft Paint. Bitmap graphics also can be produced from **digitizing** art, pictures, or photographs by passing the artwork through a scanner. A **scanner** is a hardware device that converts lines and shading into combinations of the binary digits 0 and 1 by sensing different intensities of light and dark. The scanner shines a beam of light on the picture being scanned. The beam passes back and forth across the picture, sending a digitized signal to the computer's memory. A **digitized signal** is the conversion of input, such as the lines in a drawing, into a series of discrete units represented by the binary digits 0 and 1. **Scanned pictures** are bitmap pictures and have jagged edges. The jagged edges are caused by the individual pixels that create the picture. Bitmap graphics also are known as **raster images**. Pictures in the Microsoft Clip Organizer that have the file extensions of **.jpg** (Joint Photographic Experts Group), **.bmp** (Windows Bitmap), **.gif** (Graphics Interchange Format), and **.png** (Portable Network Graphics) are examples of bitmap graphic files. Bitmap files cannot be ungrouped and converted to smaller PowerPoint object groups. They can be manipulated, however, in an imaging program such as Microsoft Photo Editor. This program allows you to rotate or flip the pictures and then insert them in your slides.

Be certain you have permission to modify clips.
If you change a clip, be certain you have the legal right to do so. For example, corporate logos are designed using specific colors and shapes and often cannot be altered. In addition, you cannot use photographs and illustrations to damage people's reputations by representing them falsely. For instance, you cannot insert a photograph of your former boyfriend or girlfriend, who has made the Dean's List every semester, in a slide that gives information about students who have been placed on academic probation.

Plan
Ahead

Inserting and Modifying Clips

Slide 3 (shown in Figure 3–1c on PPT 163) contains a modified version of a beaker. This clip is from the Microsoft Clip Organizer. You may want to modify a clip art picture for various reasons. Many times you cannot find a clip art picture that precisely illustrates your topic. For example, you want a picture of a man and woman shaking hands, but the only available clip art picture has two men and a woman shaking hands.

Occasionally you may want to remove or change a portion of a clip art picture or you might want to combine two or more clip art pictures. For example, you can use one clip art picture for the background and another picture as the foreground. Still other times, you may want to combine a clip art picture with another type of object. The types of objects you can combine with a clip art picture depend on the software installed on your computer. The **Object type list** in the Insert Object dialog box identifies the types of objects you can combine with a clip art picture. In this presentation, the picture with a beaker contains a green background that is not required to display on the slide, so you will ungroup the clip art picture and remove the background.

BTW

Locating Clip Art
Microsoft Office 2007 includes more then 1,600 clip art images, bullets, lines, and sound files. They were placed in the Office Collections group when the software was installed. Each clip has a variety of keywords that help identify the file; you cannot edit these keywords.

BTW

Cropping Pictures
Use the Crop command to cut unwanted areas from any picture except an animated GIF picture. Select the picture, click the Crop button on the Picture toolbar, position the cropping tool over a center cropping handle, and then drag the handle inward. Click the Crop button again to turn off the cropping command.

Modifying the clip on Slide 3 requires several steps. First, you display Slide 3 and change the slide layout. Then, you insert the beaker picture into the slide. In the next step, you scale the picture to increase its size. Finally, you ungroup the clip, change the color of the liquid in the beaker, and then regroup the component objects. The following steps explain in detail how to insert, scale, ungroup, modify, and regroup a clip art image.

To Change the Slide Layout

For aesthetic reasons, you want the clip art to display prominently on the right side of the slide. The following steps change the slide layout to Content with Caption.

1. Click the Next Slide button to display Slide 3.

2. Click the Layout button in the Slides group on the Ribbon.

3. Click Content with Caption to apply that layout to Slide 3 (Figure 3–51).

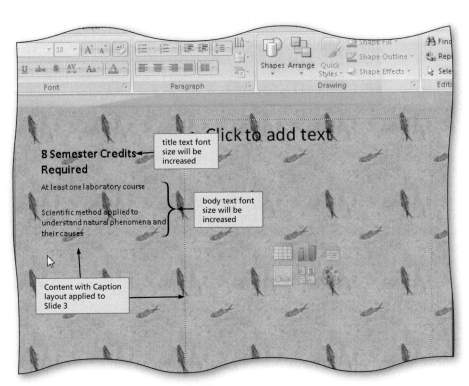

Figure 3–51

To Increase the Font Size

The imported Microsoft Word text can be enlarged to enhance readability. The following steps enlarge the title and body text for Slide 3.

1. Drag through the title text, 8 Semester Credits Required, to select the text and display the Mini toolbar.

2. Move the mouse pointer into the transparent Mini toolbar so that it changes to a bright toolbar and then click the Increase Font Size button on the Mini toolbar three times to change the font size to 32 point.

3 Drag through the two body text paragraphs.

4 Click the Increase Font Size button on the Mini toolbar three times to change the font size to 20 point (Figure 3–52).

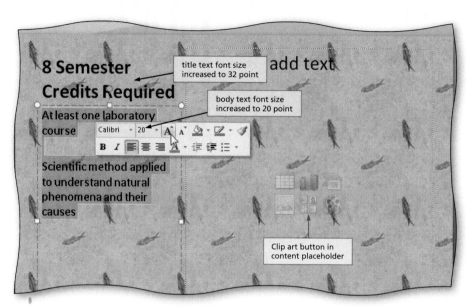

Figure 3–52

To Insert a Clip into a Content Placeholder

The first step in modifying a clip is to insert the picture into a slide. In later steps, you modify the clip. The following steps insert the beaker clip from the Microsoft Clip Organizer. See your instructor if this clip is not available on your system.

1 Click the Clip Art button in the content placeholder (row 2, column 2).

2 Type beaker in the Search for text box and then click the Go button.

3 If necessary, scroll down the list to display the desired clip shown in Figure 3–53 and then click the clip to insert it into the Slide 3 content placeholder.

4 Click the Close button in the Clip Art task pane.

5 If a bullet and the Click to add text paragraph displays behind the clip, click the paragraph and then press the DELETE key to delete the paragraph.

6 If necessary, increase the beaker clip art size by dragging one of the corner sizing handles outward until the clip is the size shown in Figure 3–53. Drag the clip to the location shown in this figure.

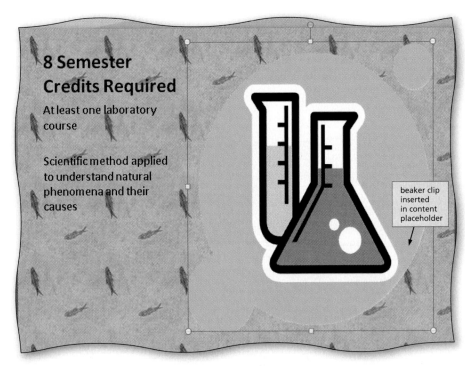

Figure 3–53

To Ungroup a Clip

The next step is to ungroup the beaker clip on Slide 3. When you **ungroup** a clip art picture, PowerPoint breaks it into its component objects. A clip may be composed of a few individual objects or several complex groups of objects. These groups can be ungrouped repeatedly until they decompose into individual objects. Because a clip art picture is a collection of complex groups of objects, you may need to ungroup a complex object into less complex objects before being able to modify a specific object. When you ungroup a clip and click the Yes button in the Microsoft Office PowerPoint dialog box, PowerPoint converts the clip to a PowerPoint object. Recall that a PowerPoint object is an object not associated with a supplementary application. The following steps ungroup a clip.

1

- With the beaker clip selected, click the Format tab under Picture Tools on the Ribbon.

- Click the Group button in the Arrange group on the Format tab (Figure 3–54).

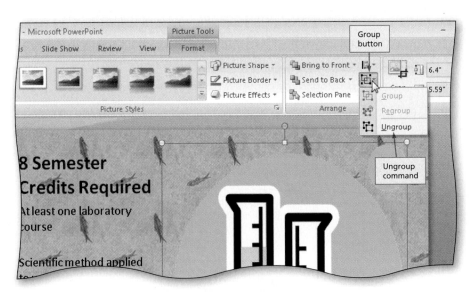

Figure 3–54

2

- Click Ungroup to display the Microsoft Office PowerPoint dialog box.

- Click the Yes button in the Microsoft Office PowerPoint dialog box to convert the clip to a Microsoft Office drawing.

- On the Format tab, click the Group button in the Arrange group and then click Ungroup again to display the objects that comprise the beaker clip (Figure 3–55).

Q&A What if I click the No button?

The clip art picture is displayed on the slide as a clip art picture.

Q&A Why does the Format tab show different options this time?

The clip has become a drawing object, so tools related to drawing now display.

Other Ways

1. Right-click clip, point to Group on shortcut menu, click Ungroup

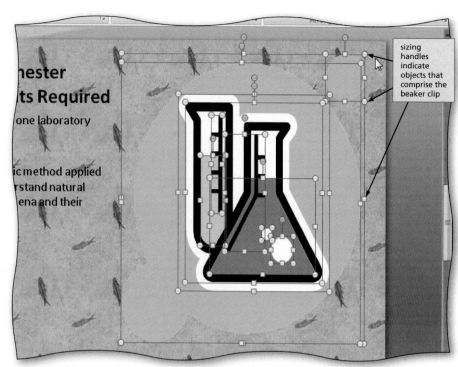

Figure 3–55

To Change the Color of PowerPoint Objects

Now that the beaker picture is ungrouped, you can change the color of the objects. The clip is composed of hundreds of objects, so you must exercise care when selecting the correct object to modify. The following steps change the color of the beaker and test tube liquids.

1

- Click outside the clip area to display clip without the sizing handles around the objects.

- Click the medium blue beaker liquid to display sizing handles around the colored area (Figure 3–56).

Q&A What if I selected a different area?

Click outside the clip and retry.

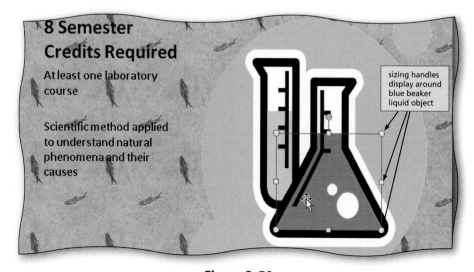

Figure 3–56

2

- Click the Shape Fill arrow in the Shape Styles group to display the Shape Fill menu.

- Point to the color Orange in the Standard Colors area (third color) to display a live preview of the color of the selected liquid in the graphic (Figure 3–57).

Experiment

- Point to various colors and watch the beaker liquid color change.

 Why do those specific colors display in the Standard Colors area?

They are the default colors associated with the Office Theme.

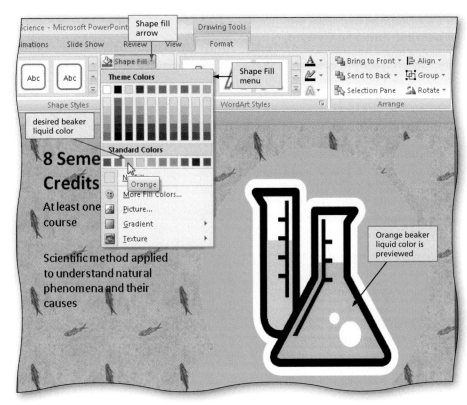

Figure 3–57

3

- Click the color Orange to change the beaker liquid color.

- Click the test tube liquid to display the sizing handles around the colored area (Figure 3–58).

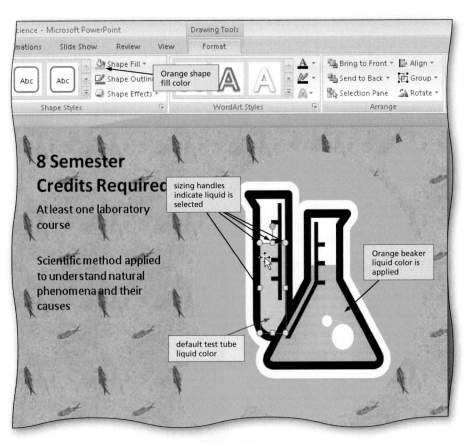

Figure 3–58

4

- Click the Shape Fill button in the Shape Styles group and then point to the Blue color in the Standard Colors area (eighth color) to display a live preview of the color of the selected liquid in the graphic (Figure 3–59).

 Experiment

- Point to various colors and watch the test tube color change.

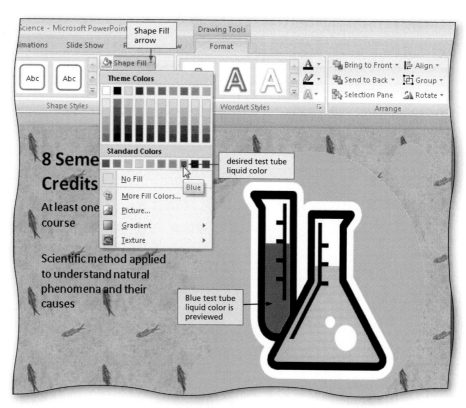

Figure 3–59

5

- Click the Blue color to change the test tube liquid (Figure 3–60).

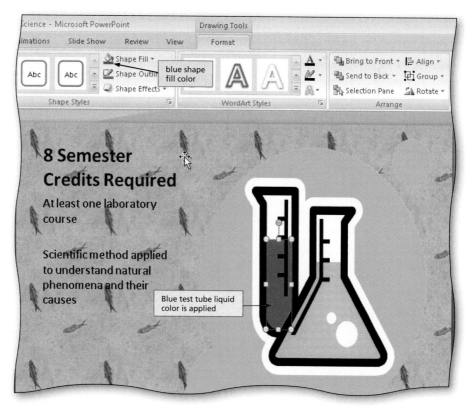

Figure 3–60

Other Ways

1. Right-click object, click Format Shape on shortcut menu, click Color button

To Delete a PowerPoint Object

With the beaker and test tube liquid color changes, you want to delete the green circle in the upper-right corner of the clip. The following steps delete this object.

1

- Click the green circle in the upper-right corner to select it (Figure 3–61).

Figure 3–61

2

- Press the DELETE key to delete this object (Figure 3–62).

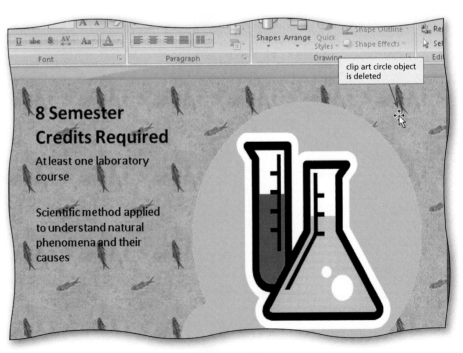

Figure 3–62

To Regroup Objects

Recall that a clip art picture is an object imported from the Microsoft Clip Organizer. Disassembling imported, embedded, or linked objects eliminates the embedding data or linking information the object contains that ties it back to its original source. Use caution when objects are not completely regrouped. Dragging or scaling affects only the selected object, not the entire collection of objects. All of the ungrouped objects in the beaker picture must be regrouped so they are not accidentally moved or manipulated. The following steps regroup these objects into one object.

1

- Click just outside the clip to display the clip placeholder.

Q&A How do I know if I have clicked the correct area?

The Group button should be available in the Arrange group.

- Click the Format tab under Drawing Tools, if necessary, and then click the Group button in the Arrange group (Figure 3–63).

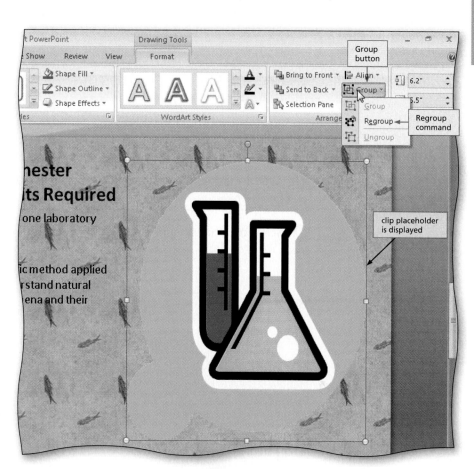

Figure 3–63

2

- Click Regroup to combine all the objects.

Use left-brain / right-brain content concepts.
The left side of your brain screens material analytically and filters out most of the information presented. At best, this text is transferred to your short-term memory. If you have critical text on your slides, therefore, you need to make it stand out by making it visually appealing. This graphic information gets processed by your right brain, which responds to sensory information and stores the images in long-term memory.

Plan
Ahead

Creating and Modifying a SmartArt Diagram

Combining SmartArt Diagrams
Most SmartArt graphics use only a few text fields. If you exceed the number of allocated text panes, PowerPoint will display a red X instead of a bullet. To add more text, insert another SmartArt diagram, drag it to a location where it blends with the first diagram, and then enter the additional text.

The wide variety of SmartArt layouts and styles adds visual interest to your slides. The Microsoft Word outline you imported had bulleted text on Slide 2 that you converted into a SmartArt graphic. You also can create a graphic by selecting a graphic type and then adding text. The second text paragraph on Slide 3 mentions the scientific method, so Slide 4 will explain the steps used in this methodology. The Continuous Block Process SmartArt graphic is an appropriate type to help visualize the scientific method. This graphic type is found in the Process category.

To Insert a Slide and Add Title Text

The final slide in this presentation will use a SmartArt layout. The following steps add a new slide (Slide 4) and then create the title text.

1 Click Home on the Ribbon and then click the New Slide button in the Slides group.

2 Click the Layout button in the Slides group and then click the Title Only layout.

3 Type `Scientific Method` in the title text placeholder.

4 Select the title text and then click the Bold button on the Mini toolbar (Figure 3–64).

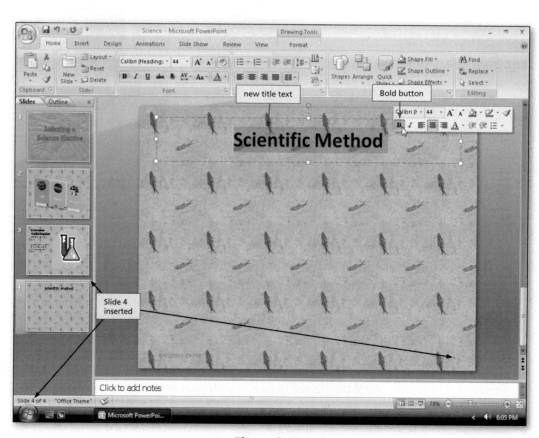

Figure 3–64

To Insert a SmartArt Graphic

The following steps insert the Continuous Block Process SmartArt graphic on Slide 4.

 1

- Click Insert on the Ribbon to display the Insert tab.

- Click the SmartArt button in the Illustrations group to display the Choose a SmartArt Graphic dialog box.

- Click Process in the left pane to display the Process gallery.

- Click the Continuous Block Process graphic (row 2, column 1) to display a preview of this graphic in the right pane (Figure 3–65).

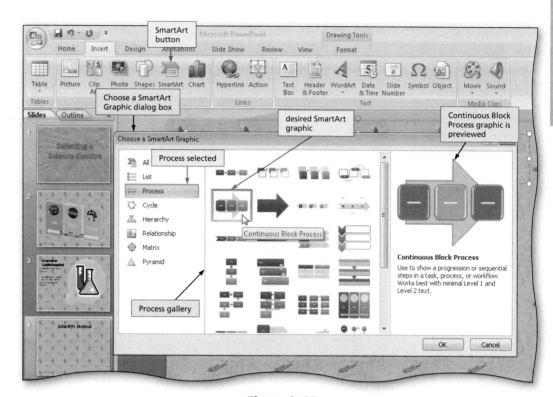

Figure 3–65

2

- Click the OK button to insert this SmartArt graphic on Slide 4 (Figure 3–66). If necessary, click Text Pane in the Create Graphic group to open the text pane if it does not display automatically.

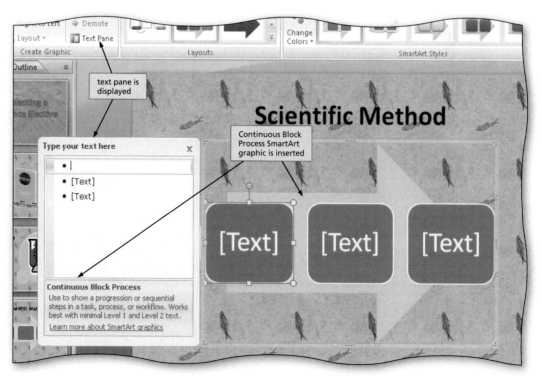

Figure 3–66

Text Pane

The Text pane assists you in creating a graphic because you can direct your attention to developing and editing the message without being concerned with the actual graphic. Each SmartArt graphic has an associated Text pane with bullets that function as an outline and map directly to the image. You can create new lines of bulleted text and then indent and demote these lines. You also can check spelling. The following table shows the character shortcuts you can use to enter Text pane characters.

Table 3–2 Text Pane Keyboard Shortcuts	
Activity	**Shortcut**
Indent text	TAB or ALT+SHIFT+RIGHT ARROW
Demote text	SHIFT+TAB or ALT+SHIFT+LEFT ARROW
Add a tab character	CTRL+TAB
Create a new line of text	ENTER
Check spelling	F7
Merge two lines of text	DELETE at the end of the first text line
Display the shortcut menu	SHIFT+F10
Switch between the Text pane top and the Learn more about SmartArt graphics link at the bottom	CTRL+SHIFT+F
Switch between the SmartArt graphic and the Text pane	CTRL+SHIFT+F2
Close the Text pane	ALT+F4
Switch the focus from the Text pane to the SmartArt graphic border	ESC

To Enter Text in the SmartArt Graphic

The following steps insert four lines of text in the Text pane and in the corresponding SmartArt shapes on Slide 4.

1
- Type Hypothesis in the first bullet line and then press the RIGHT ARROW key to move the insertion point to the second bullet line (Figure 3–67).

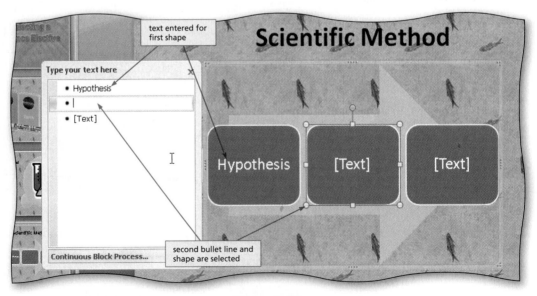

Figure 3–67

2

- Type `Experiment` in the second bullet line and then press the RIGHT ARROW key.

- Type `Observation` in the third bullet line and then press the ENTER key to create a fourth bullet line and shape.

- Type `Theory` in the fourth bullet line. Do not press the ENTER or RIGHT ARROW keys (Figure 3–68).

I mistakenly pressed the ENTER key. How can I delete the bullet line I just added?

Press the BACKSPACE key to delete the line.

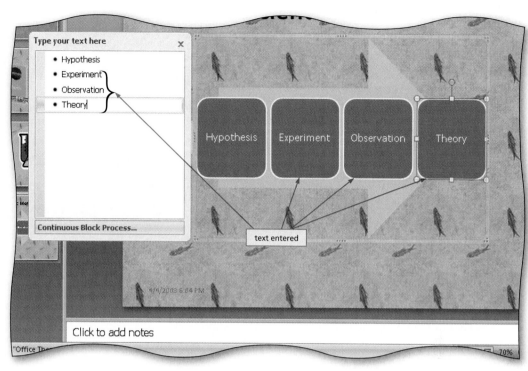

Figure 3–68

To Format the Text Pane Characters

Once the desired characters are entered in the Text pane, you can change the font size, and apply formatting features, such as bold, italic, and underlined text. The following steps format the text by changing the shape text font color and bolding the letters.

1

- With the Text pane open, drag through all four bulleted lines to select the text and display the Mini toolbar (Figure 3–69).

If my Text pane no longer is displayed, how can I get it to appear?

Click the control, which is the tab with two arrows pointing to the right and left, on the left side of the SmartArt graphic.

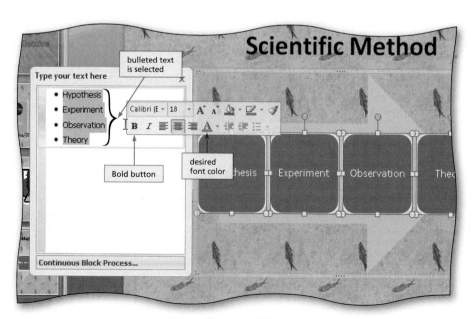

Figure 3–69

2

- Click the Font Color button to change the color of the shape text to the red displayed on the button.

- Click the Bold button on the Mini toolbar to bold the text (Figure 3–70).

Q&A These two formatting changes did not appear in the Text pane. Why?

Not all the formatting changes are evident in the Text pane, but they will appear in the corresponding shape.

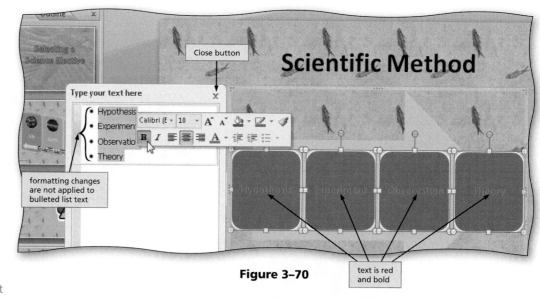

Figure 3–70

To Add a SmartArt Style to the Graphic

With the text entered in the Text pane, you can close it and then add a style to the four SmartArt shapes. The following steps add the Metallic Scene style to the Slide 4 SmartArt graphic.

1 Click the Close button in the SmartArt Text pane so that it no longer is displayed.

2 With the SmartArt graphic still selected, click the More button in the SmartArt Styles group to expand the SmartArt Styles gallery.

3 Click the Metallic Scene style (row 2, column 2) in the 3-D category in the SmartArt gallery to apply this style to the graphic (Figure 3–71).

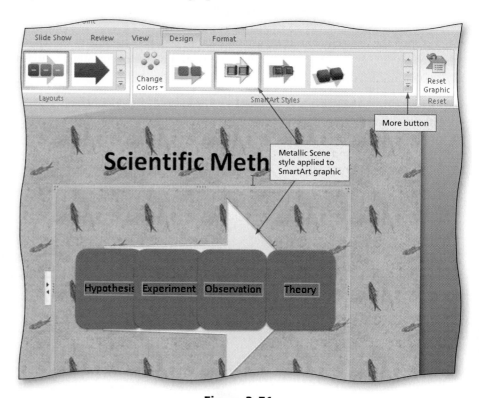

Figure 3–71

To Change the SmartArt Color

A final modification you can make is to change the graphic's color. The following steps change the SmartArt graphic color to the same Colorful range used in the SmartArt graphic in Slide 2.

1 With the SmartArt graphic still selected, click the Change Colors button in the SmartArt Styles group to display the Change Colors gallery.

2 Click the Colorful Range – Accent Colors 5 to 6 (row 2, column 5) in the Colorful category to apply this color variation to the graphic (Figure 3–72).

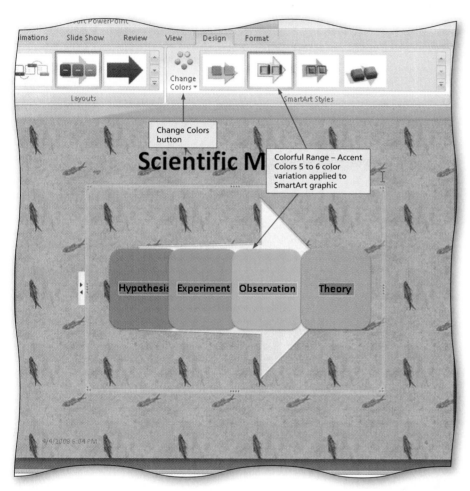

Figure 3–72

To Adjust the SmartArt Graphic Size

When you view the completed graphic, you may decide that individual shapes or the entire art needs to be enlarged or reduced. If you change the size of one shape, the other shapes also may change size to maintain proportions. Likewise, the font size may change in all the shapes if you increase or decrease the font size of one shape. On Slide 4, the SmartArt graphic size can be increased to fill the space and add readability. All the shapes will enlarge proportionally when you adjust the graphic's height and width. The following steps increase the SmartArt graphic size.

- With the SmartArt graphic still selected, press and hold the left mouse button and then drag the bottom-right corner sizing handle diagonally to the location shown in Figure 3–73.

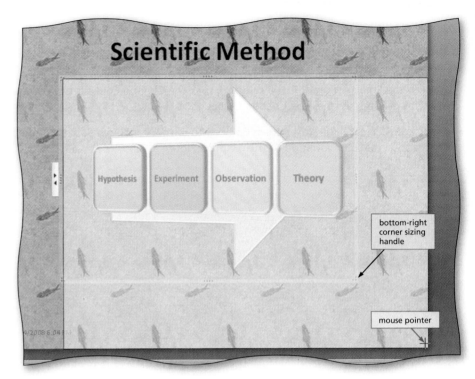

Figure 3–73

- Release the mouse button

- Press the UP and LEFT ARROW keys to position the graphic in the center of the slide below the title text (Figure 3–74).

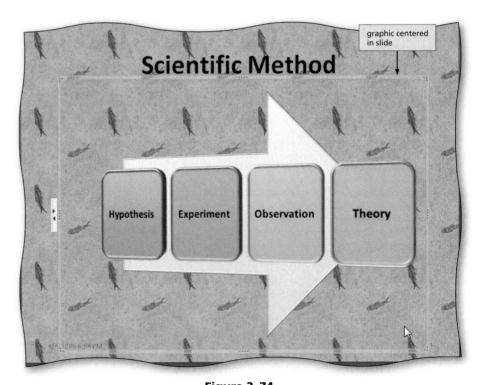

Figure 3–74

To Save an Existing Presentation with the Same File Name

Now that Slide 4 is complete, you should save the presentation. The following step saves the presentation again.

1 Click the Save button on the Quick Access Toolbar to overwrite the previous Science file on the USB flash drive.

To Add a Transition between Slides

A final enhancement you will make in this presentation is to apply the Shape Diamond transition in the Wipes category to all slides and change the transition speed to Slow. The following steps apply this transition to the presentation.

1 Click Animations on the Ribbon to display the Animations tab and then click the More button in the Transition to This Slide group to expand the Transitions gallery.

2 Click the Shape Diamond transition (row 5, column 6) in the Wipes category in the Transitions gallery to apply this transition to Slide 4.

3 Click the Transition Speed arrow in the Transition to This Slide group and then click Slow to change the transition speed for Slide 4.

4 Click the Apply To All button in the Transition to This Slide group to apply this transition and speed to all four slides in the presentation (Figure 3–75).

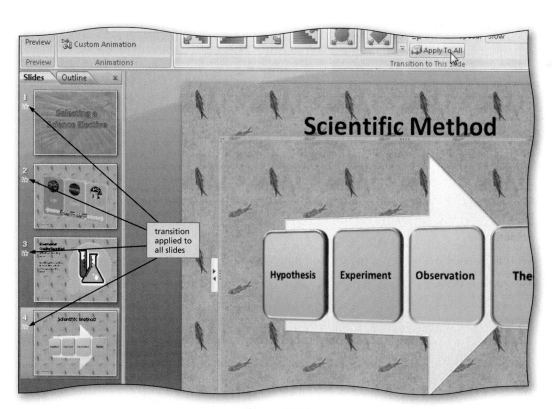

Figure 3–75

To Change Document Properties and Save the Presentation

Before saving the presentation again, you want to add your name, class name, and some keywords as document properties. The following steps use the Document Information Panel to change document properties and then save the project.

1 Click the Office Button to display the Office Button menu, point to Prepare on the Office Button menu, and then click Properties on the Prepare submenu to display the Document Information Panel.

2 Click the Author text box, if necessary, and then type your name as the Author property. If a name already is displayed in the Author text box, delete it before typing your name.

3 Click the Subject text box, if necessary delete any existing text, and then type your course and section as the Subject property.

4 Click the Keywords text box, if necessary delete any existing text, and then type `science electives, required credits, scientific method` as the Keywords property.

5 Click the Close the Document Information Panel button so that the Document Information Panel no longer is displayed.

6 Click the Save button on the Quick Access Toolbar to overwrite the previous Science file on the USB flash drive.

BTW

Quick Reference
For a table that lists how to complete the tasks covered in this book using the mouse, Ribbon, shortcut menu, and keyboard, see the Quick Reference Summary at the back of this book, or visit the PowerPoint 2007 Quick Reference Web page (scsite.com/ppt2007/qr).

To Run an Animated Slide Show

All changes are complete, and the presentation is saved. You now can view the Science presentation. The following step starts Slide Show view.

1 Click Slide 1 in the Slides pane to display the title slide and then click the Slide Show button to display the title slide.

2 Click each slide and view the transition effect and slides.

To Preview and Print Handouts

All changes are complete, and the presentation is saved. You now can create handouts to accompany the slide show. The following steps preview and then print the presentation.

1 Click the Office Button, point to Print, and then click Print Preview on the Print submenu.

2 Click the Print What arrow in the Page Setup group and then click Handouts (4 Slides Per Page) in the Print What list.

3 Click the Print button in the Print group.

4 Click the OK button in the Print dialog box to print the handout (Figure 3–76).

5 Click the Close Print Preview button in the Preview group on the Print Preview tab to return to Normal view.

4/24/2008

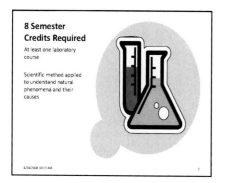

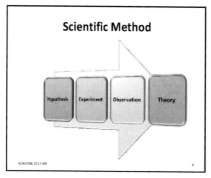

1

Figure 3–76

To Quit PowerPoint

This project is complete. The following steps quit PowerPoint.

1 Click the Close button on the right side of the title bar to quit PowerPoint.

2 If necessary, click the No button in the Microsoft Office PowerPoint dialog box so that any changes you have made are not saved.

Chapter Summary

In this chapter you have learned how to open a Microsoft Word document as a PowerPoint presentation, format a slide background, convert text to a WordArt and to a SmartArt graphic, modify clip art, and insert a SmartArt graphic and then add text. The items listed below include all the new PowerPoint skills you have learned in this chapter.

1. Open a Microsoft Word Outline as a Presentation (PPT 165)
2. Insert a Texture Fill (PPT 168)
3. Insert a Picture to Create a Background (PPT 171)
4. Format the Background Picture Fill Transparency (PPT 172)
5. Add Slide Numbers, Date, and Time (PPT 172)
6. Apply a WordArt Style (PPT 175)
7. Format the WordArt Text Fill (PPT 176)
8. Change the Weight of the WordArt Outline (PPT 178)
9. Add a WordArt Text Effect (PPT 179)
10. Delete the Subtitle Placeholder (PPT 180)
11. Convert Text to a SmartArt Graphic (PPT 181)
12. Insert Images from a File into a SmartArt Graphic (PPT 182)
13. Add a SmartArt Style to the Graphic (PPT 184)
14. Change the SmartArt Color (PPT 186)
15. Insert a Text Box (PPT 188)
16. Rotate a Text Box (PPT 189)
17. Format the Text Box (PPT 191)
18. Insert a Clip into a Content Placeholder (PPT 197)
19. Ungroup a Clip (PPT 198)
20. Change the Color of PowerPoint Objects (PPT 199)
21. Delete a PowerPoint Object (PPT 202)
22. Regroup Objects (PPT 203)
23. Insert a SmartArt Graphic (PPT 205)
24. Enter Text in the SmartArt Graphic (PPT 206)
25. Format the Text Pane Characters (PPT 207)
26. Add a SmartArt Style to the Graphic (PPT 208)
27. Change the SmartArt Color (PPT 209)
28. Adjust the SmartArt Graphic Size (PPT 209)
29. Save an Existing Presentation with the Same File Name (PPT 211)
30. Add a Transition between Slides (PPT 211)

 If you have a SAM user profile, you may have access to hands-on instruction, practice, and assessment. Log in to your SAM account (http://sam2007.course.com) to launch any assigned training activities or exams that relate to the skills covered in this chapter.

Learn It Online

Test your knowledge of chapter content and key terms.

Instructions: To complete the Learn It Online exercises, start your browser, click the Address bar, and then enter the Web address `scsite.com/ppt2007/learn`. When the Office 2007 Learn It Online page is displayed, click the link for the exercise you want to complete and then read the instructions.

Chapter Reinforcement TF, MC, and SA
A series of true/false, multiple choice, and short answer questions that test your knowledge of the chapter content.

Flash Cards
An interactive learning environment where you identify chapter key terms associated with displayed definitions.

Practice Test
A series of multiple choice questions that test your knowledge of chapter content and key terms.

Who Wants To Be a Computer Genius?
An interactive game that challenges your knowledge of chapter content in the style of a television quiz show.

Wheel of Terms
An interactive game that challenges your knowledge of chapter key terms in the style of the television show *Wheel of Fortune*.

Crossword Puzzle Challenge
A crossword puzzle that challenges your knowledge of key terms presented in the chapter.

Apply Your Knowledge

Reinforce the skills and apply the concepts you learned in this chapter.

Changing the Backgrounds, Modifying a Clip, and Applying WordArt
Instructions: Start PowerPoint. Open the presentation, Apply 3–1 Tidal Wave, from the Data Files for Students. See the inside back cover of this book for instructions for downloading the Data Files for Students, or contact your instructor for more information about accessing required files.

The two slides in the presentation present general information about tidal waves. The document you open is an unformatted presentation. You are to insert a texture fill, insert a picture to create a background, modify clip art, and add a WordArt text effect so the slides look like Figure 3–77.

Perform the following tasks:

1. Insert the Water droplets texture fill on the Slide 1 background (row 1, column 5) and change the transparency to 20%. Use your name in place of Student Name and bold and underline your name.

2. On Slide 2, insert the Wave picture from the Microsoft Clip Organizer to create the background and change the transparency to 5%.

3. On Slide 1, apply the WordArt style Fill – Accent 1, Metal Bevel, Reflection (row 6, column 5) to the title text and increase the font size to 80.

4. On Slide 2, apply the WordArt style Fill – Accent 1, Inner Shadow – Accent 1 (row 2, column 4) shown in Figure 3–77b to the text paragraphs. Apply the Glow Variation Accent color 3, 5 pt glow (row 1, column 3).

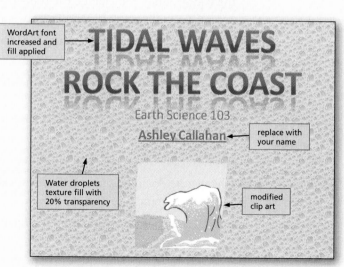

Figure 3–77 (a)

Continued >

Apply Your Knowledge *continued*

5. On Slide 1, ungroup the wave clip and then delete the red and black borders. Regroup the clip.

6. Apply the Wedge wipe transition (row 1, column 5) to all slides.

7. Check the spelling, and then display the revised presentation in Slide Sorter view to check for consistency.

8. Change the document properties, as specified by your instructor. Save the presentation using the file name, Apply 3–1 Sea. Submit the revised document in the format specified by your instructor.

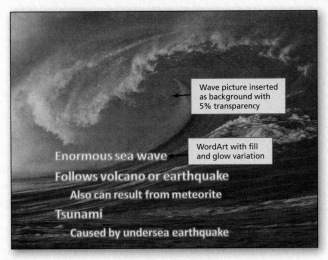

Figure 3–77 (b)

Extend Your Knowledge

Extend the skills you learned in this chapter and experiment with new skills. You may need to use Help to complete the assignment.

Formatting Slide Backgrounds and Converting Text to SmartArt

Instructions: Start PowerPoint. Open the presentation, Extend 3-1 Food Pyramid, from the Data Files for Students. See the inside back cover of this book for instructions for downloading the Data Files for Students, or contact your instructor for more information about accessing required files. The images for the slides were obtained with permission from the MyPyramid.gov Web site, which is sponsored by the United States Department of Agriculture.

You will format slide backgrounds and add your name and slide number to the slide footers. You then will convert bulleted text to a SmartArt graphic.

Perform the following tasks:

1. On Slide 1, insert a texture fill on the background. On Slides 2 through 6, insert a different fill on the backgrounds and change the transparency.

2. On all slides, add slide numbers and your name (Figure 3–78a). To insert your name, click the Footer box on the Slide tab in the Header and Footer dialog box and then type your name in the Footer text box.

3. Convert the bulleted lists on Slides 2 through 6 to the Vertical Block List layout (row 4, column 3 in the List category) SmartArt graphic. Change the color.

4. Apply a fill to the title text on Slides 2 through 6. Change the text outline color to an appropriate color and bold the text.

5. Apply a transition to all slides.

6. Change the document properties, as specified by your instructor. Save the presentation using the file name, Extend 3-1 Revised Pyramid.

7. Submit the revised document in the format specified by your instructor.

Cases and Places *continued*

● 2: Design and Create a Solar System Presentation

In your Astronomy 101 class, you are studying the solar system, concentrating on the planets Mercury and Venus. For extra credit, you create a presentation with a slide featuring each planet. Begin the presentation with a title slide showing one aspect of the solar system as the slide background. Slide 2 should use the Basic Target SmartArt graphic in the Relationships category with the innermost circle representing the Sun, the middle circle representing Mercury, and the outer circle representing Venus. Use the files in the Inner Solar System folder on the Data Files for Students as backgrounds for each slide. Place the information in Table 3–3 in SmartArt diagrams. Apply slide transitions and a footer with page numbers and your name on all slides. Be sure to check spelling.

Table 3–3 Inner Solar System		
Planet	**Features**	**Distance from Sun**
Mercury	Temperature: 950°F sunlit side; −346°F dark side	36 million miles
Venus	Temperature: 55°F to 396°F Atmosphere: Carbon dioxide, nitrogen, and sulfuric acid	67 million miles

●● 3: Design and Create an Exercise Variety Presentation

In January of every year, people make resolutions to exercise on a regular basis. They faithfully begin working out for a few weeks, but then many quit because they become bored with the routine. In an effort to retain members, the fitness center in your community wants to persuade members to participate in a variety of activities to remain motivated. The director has asked you to prepare a presentation showcasing at least four activities and the number of calories burned per hour. You begin by writing an outline of your presentation in Microsoft Word and then show this document to her for approval. Import this document into a PowerPoint presentation and create a slide show. Convert text into a SmartArt graphic. Insert a text box and WordArt on the title slide, and use at least one modified clip from the Microsoft Clip Organizer. Apply a slide transition to all slides.

●● 4 Design and Create a Career Presentation

Make It Personal

Choosing a college major often is difficult. Most students change their major at least twice during their college careers, and many students return to campus to train for a new career after having worked for many years or raised a family. To gain information about a possible career, obtain a copy of the *Occupational Outlook Handbook* in your library, or view the publication online at www.bls.gov/oco/home.htm, and read about your intended field of study. Use the concepts and techniques from this chapter to develop and format a slide show with a title slide and a slide about training requirements, occupational duties, compensation, and employment prospects. Add at least one clip, a texture fill for the background, and a SmartArt graphic. Be sure to check spelling. Print a handout with two slides on each page.

●● 5: Design and Create a Large Deciduous Trees Presentation

Working Together

Homeowners often desire trees as part of their landscaping plans. Many deciduous trees, which drop their leaves in the fall, grow taller than 40 feet. If a tree is going to survive transplanting and grow properly, it must be planted in the proper location. Have each member of your team visit a local nursery or arboretum, or conduct online research and each select one large deciduous tree that is well suited for your environment. Gather information about each tree's botanical and common name, height, and spread. After coordinating the data, create a presentation with a least one slide showcasing each tree, including a photograph and SmartArt. As a group, critique each slide. Submit your assignment in the format specified by your instructor.

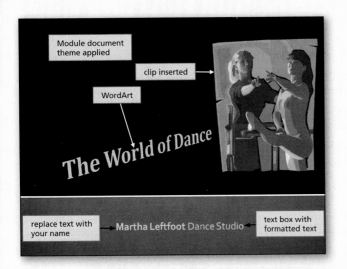

(a)

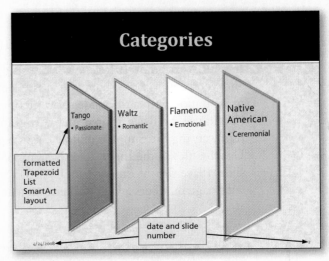

(b)

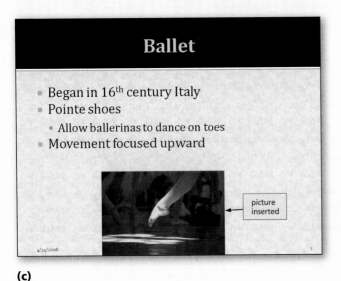

(c)

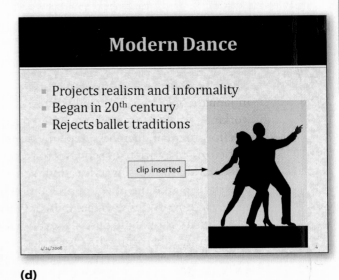

(d)

Figure 3–82

Cases and Places

Apply your creative thinking and problem solving skills to design and implement a solution.

● Easier ●● More Difficult

Note: Remember to use the 7 × 7 rule as you design the presentations: a maximum of seven words on a line and a maximum of seven lines on one slide.

● **1: Design and Create a National Parks Presentation**

The United States Park Service establishes and preserves America's natural resources. Approximately 400 protected areas are part of the system, including the Grand Canyon, the Statue of Liberty, and Gettysburg. The National Park Service, part of the U.S. Department of the Interior, also works with local communities to help them preserve and manage their own local heritage and recreational areas. You and your friends have visited several National Park Service sites and have photos of the landscapes and animals you have seen. These digital photos are in the National Parks Photos folder on the Data Files for Students. Create a presentation using these photos. Apply at least three objectives found at the beginning of this chapter to develop the presentation. Add a title slide with SmartArt. Be sure to check spelling.

Continued >

4 | Working with Information Graphics

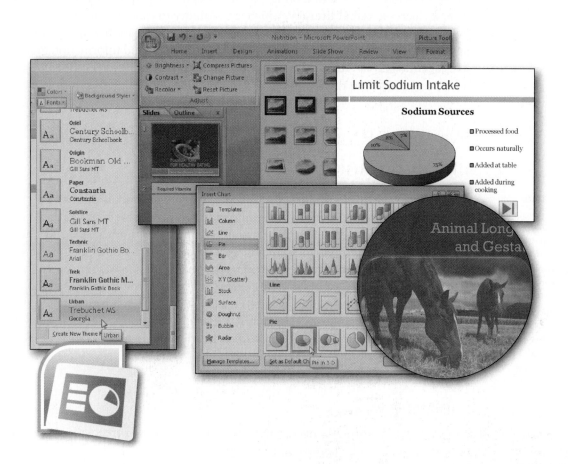

Objectives

You will have mastered the material in this chapter when you can:

- Modify an entire presentation by changing the theme colors and fonts
- Insert pictures and clips into slides without content placeholders
- Format pictures and clips by applying styles and adding borders
- Apply effects to pictures and clips
- Add hyperlinks to a slide
- Create and format a table

- Create a chart
- Find synonyms using the thesaurus
- Add action buttons and action settings
- Display guides to position slide elements
- Hide slides
- Run a slide show with hyperlinks

4 Working with Information Graphics

Introduction

Audiences generally focus first on the visual elements displayed on a slide. Graphical elements increase **visual literacy**, which is the ability to examine and assess these images. They can be divided into two categories: images and information graphics. Images are the clips and photographs you have used in Chapters 2 and 3, and information graphics are tables, charts, graphs, and diagrams. Both sets of visuals help audience members interpret and retain material, so they should be designed and presented with care.

Project — Presentation with a Chart, Table, and Hyperlinks

The project in this chapter follows visual content guidelines and uses PowerPoint to create the presentation shown in Figure 4–1. The slide show uses several visual elements to help audience members understand which vitamins are important in their diet and where sodium is added to food. The three-column table lists six essential vitamins, their sources, and how the body uses them. The three-dimensional pie chart shows four sources of sodium and emphasizes that the largest amount enters the body through processed food. The title slide picture is inserted and then given a particular effect. The document theme's color scheme is changed for visual interest. Action buttons on Slides 2, 3, and 4 help a presenter navigate from one slide to another. In addition, hyperlinks display specific Web sites when clicked during a presentation.

BTW **Enhancing Speaker Confidence**
Using information graphics can help increase your confidence as a speaker. When you rehearse your speech with your PowerPoint charts and tables, you should become confident knowing that these visuals support your verbal message. While you will burn nervous energy as you move toward the screen and point to specific information on these graphics, you should be relieved to know that your audience will be studying your charts and graphs and not focusing on you.

Overview

As you read through this chapter, you will learn how to create the presentation shown in Figure 4–1 by performing these general tasks:

- Format a picture by applying an effect.
- Create a table and chart.
- Change the document theme color scheme.
- Find and replace words.
- Run a slide show with action buttons and hyperlinks.

(a) Slide 1 (Title Slide)

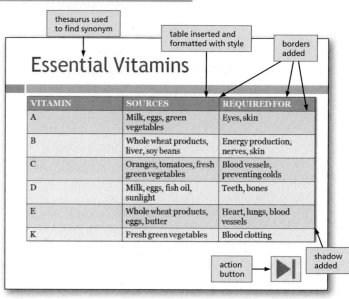

(b) Slide 2

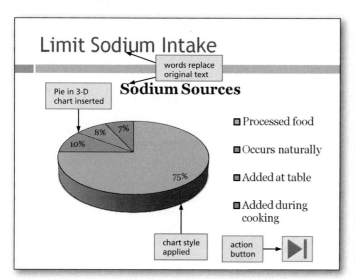

(c) Slide 3

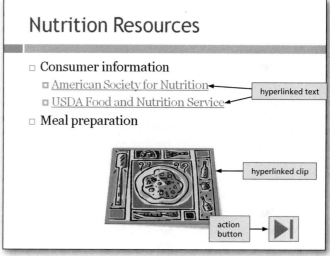

(d) Slide 4

Figure 4–1

General Project Guidelines

When creating a PowerPoint presentation, the actions you perform and decisions you make will affect the appearance and characteristics of the finished document. As you create a presentation with information graphics, such as the project shown in Figure 4–1, you should follow these general guidelines:

1. **Select an appropriate font.** All letters in a particular font are constructed from lines, which are called strokes. The weight, or thickness, of these strokes and their slant, or direction, determine the structure of the font. Some fonts are suited best for titles, and others are most appropriate for the body of the slide.

2. **Choose outstanding hyperlink text or images.** Make the hypertext letters or graphics large so a speaker is prompted to click them during a speaking engagement.

3. **Consider the graphic's function.** Decide precisely what message you want the chart, table, or illustration to convey to the audience. Determine its purpose.

(continued)

Plan Ahead

(continued)

4. **Choose the appropriate chart style.** Most audience members like charts to help them understand the relationships between groups of data. Charts express numbers visually, but you must decide which chart type best conveys the points you are attempting to make in your presentation. PowerPoint presents a variet y of chart layouts, and you must decide which one is effective in presenting the relationships between numbers and to indicate important trends.

5. **Obtain information for the graphic from credible sources.** The text or numbers in the graphics should be current and correct. Verify the sources of the information and be certain you have typed the data correctly. On the slide or during your presentation, acknowledge the source of the information. Give credit to the person or organization that supplied the information for your graphics, if necessary.

6. **Test your visual elements.** Show your slides to several friends or colleagues and ask them to interpret what they see. Time the duration they studied each slide. Have them verbally summarize the information they perceived.

When necessary, more specific details concerning the above guidelines are presented at appropriate points in the chapter. The chapter also will identify the actions you perform and decisions you made regarding these guidelines during the creation of the presentation shown in Figure 4–1.

To Start PowerPoint and Apply a Document Theme

Note: If you are using Windows XP, see Appendix F for alternate steps.

If you are using a computer to step through the project in this chapter and you want your screens to match the figures in this book, you should change your computer's resolution to 1024 × 768. For information about how to change a computer's resolution, read Appendix E.

The following steps start PowerPoint and apply a document theme.

1 Start PowerPoint.

2 If the PowerPoint window is not maximized, click its Maximize button.

3 Apply the Median document theme.

BTW

Increasing Audience Retention
Researchers unanimously conclude that well-constructed information graphics help audience members retain the information you are presenting. Although the exact amount of measured retention varies, one study found that an audience recalled five times more material when it was presented both verbally and visually. These audience members needed to use both senses of sight and hearing to engaged in the presentation and tune out distractions. Their retention ultimately is enhanced.

Developing the Core Presentation Slides

The four slides in your presentation give details about healthy eating. The title slide introduces the topic, Slides 2 and 3 give information about vitamins and sodium, and the final slide contains information about Internet sources for nutritional information. You will enhance all four slides with visual elements, including a photograph, table, chart, and clip.

To Create a Title Slide

The title slide in the project uses a large photograph of a salad bowl to gain the viewers' attention and to express the concept that they can make healthy food choices. The title and subtitle text reinforce the food concept by mentioning that the slide show will focus on taking vitamins and limiting salt to promote healthy eating. The following steps create the text for the title slide.

1 Click the title text placeholder.

2 Type foundations in the title text placeholder and then press the ENTER key.

③ Type for healthy eating in the second line of the title text placeholder.

④ Press CTRL+ENTER to move the insertion point to the subtitle text placeholder.

⑤ Type Take Your Vitamins; Watch Your Salt but do not press the ENTER key (Figure 4–2).

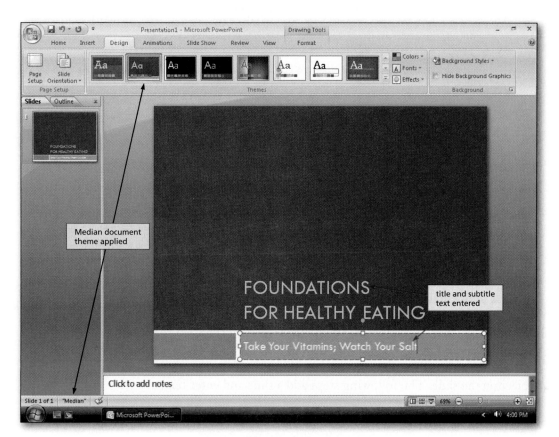

Figure 4–2

To Create Slide 2

An information graphic will be the primary content of Slide 2. The table on Slide 2 will give viewers details on which vitamins are necessary for healthy living. The title text of this slide will introduce this topic. The following steps create the title text for Slide 2.

① Click the New Slide button on the Home tab.

② Type Required Vitamins in the title text placeholder (Figure 4–3).

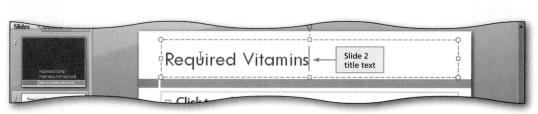

Figure 4–3

To Create Slide 3

Slide 3 will give information about sources of salt in the diet. The chart you will create will show where salt is found in the foods we ingest. The following steps create the title text for this slide.

1 Click the New Slide button on the Home tab.

2 Type `Limit Salt Intake` in the title text placeholder (Figure 4–4).

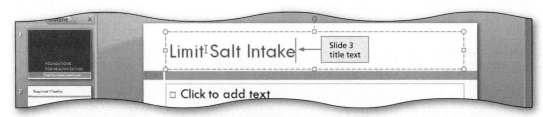

Figure 4–4

To Create Slide 4

Slide 4 in the presentation gives resources for additional information. Audience members can refer to these sources to learn more about the topics presented in the slide show or to obtain specific information that would benefit them personally.

Part of this slide will contain hyperlinks. A **hyperlink**, also called a **link**, is a connection from one slide to a Web page, another slide, a custom show consisting of specific slides in a presentation, or a file. Hyperlinks can be text or an object, such as a picture, graph, shape, or WordArt. The first step in creating hyperlinks is typing the text or inserting an object on the slide. The following steps add a slide and enter text.

1 Click the New Slide button on the Home tab.

2 Type `Nutrition Resources` in the title text placeholder.

3 Press CTRL+ENTER to move the insertion point to the body text placeholder.

4 Type `Consumer information` and then press the ENTER key.

5 Press the Tab key. Type `American Society for Nutrition` and then press the ENTER key.

6 Type `USDA Food and Nutrition Service` and then press the ENTER key.

7 Press SHIFT+TAB to demote the paragraph. Type `Meal planning` but do not press the ENTER key (Figure 4–5).

Figure 4–5

To Save the Presentation

You applied a design template and created four slides. The next step is to save the presentation.

Note: If you are using Windows XP, see Appendix F for alternate steps.

1 With a USB flash drive connected to one of the computer's USB ports, click the Save button on the Quick Access Toolbar to display the Save As dialog box.

2 Type `Nutrition` in the File name text box to change the file name.

3 Close the Folders list. If Computer is not displayed in the Favorite Links section, drag the top or bottom edge of the Save As dialog box until Computer is displayed.

4 Click Computer in the Favorite Links section, and then double-click your USB flash drive in the list of available drives.

5 Click the Save button in the Save As dialog box to save the document on the USB flash drive with the file name, Nutrition.

Customizing Entire Presentation Elements

With the basic elements of the slide show created, you can modify two default elements that display on all slides in the presentation. First, you will modify the template by changing the color scheme. Then, you will change the font.

BTW

Choosing Contrasting Colors
Researchers have determined that black or dark blue type on a white screen is an extremely effective color combination. The contrast increases readability. If you add a background color, be certain it has sufficient contrast with the font color. This contrast is especially important if your presentation will be delivered in a room with bright lighting that washes out the screen.

Presentation Template Color Scheme

Each presentation template has twelve complementary colors, which are called the **color scheme**. You can apply these colors to all slides, an individual slide, notes pages, or audience handouts. A color scheme consists of four colors for a background and text, six accent colors, and two hyperlink colors. The Theme Colors button on the Design tab contains a square with four colors; the top two colors indicate the primary text and background colors, and the bottom two colors indicate the accent colors. You also can customize the theme colors to create your own set and give them a unique name. Table 4–1 explains the components of a color scheme.

Table 4–1 Color Scheme Components

Component	Description
Background color	The background color is the fundamental color of a PowerPoint slide. For example, if the background color is black, you can place any other color on top of it, but the fundamental color remains black. The black background shows everywhere you do not add color or other objects.
Text color	The text color contrasts with the background color of the slide. As a default, the text border color is the same as the text color. Together with the background color, the text and border colors set the tone for a presentation. For example, a gray background with black text and border sets a dramatic tone. In contrast, a red background with yellow text and border sets a vibrant tone.
Accent colors	Accent colors are designed as colors for secondary features on a slide. They often are used as fill colors on graphs and as shadows.
Hyperlink colors	The default hyperlink color is set when you type the text. When you click the hyperlink text during a presentation, the color changes to the Followed Hyperlink color.

To Change the Presentation Theme Colors

The first modification to make is to change the color scheme throughout the presentation. The following steps change the color scheme for the template from a brown title slide background with orange and blue accent to a gray background with blue and gold accents.

1

- Click Design on the Ribbon to display the Design tab.

- Click the Theme Colors button in the Themes group to display the Theme Colors gallery.

- Point to the Module built-in theme to display a live preview of this color scheme (Figure 4–6).

Experiment

- Point to various themes in the Theme Colors gallery and watch the colors change on Slide 4.

Q&A Why does an orange circle surround the Median color scheme in the Themes Colors gallery?

It shows the Median document theme is applied, and those eight colors are associated with that theme.

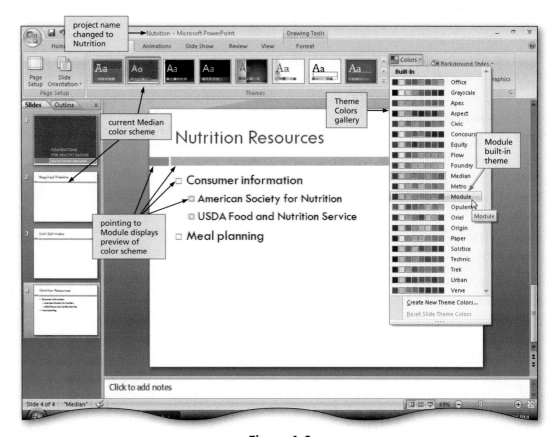

Figure 4–6

2

- Click Module in the Theme Colors gallery to change the presentation theme colors to Module (Figure 4–7).

Q&A What if I want to return to the original theme color?

You would click the Theme Colors button and then click Median in the Theme Colors gallery.

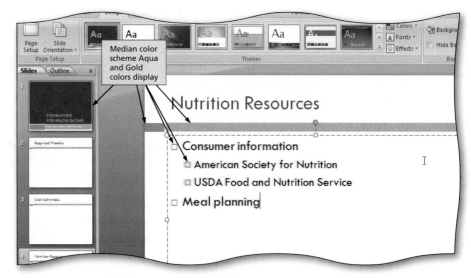

Figure 4–7

**Plan
Ahead**

Select an appropriate font.
Complex messages and formal settings call for simple fonts. If the topic of your presentation is to discuss corporate downsizing or elimination of a company pension, then a script or playful font, such as Comic Sans, sends a mixed message. This sentence uses the Comic Sans font. Some fonts are mono-spaced, which means the spacing for each letter is the same. Courier is a mono-spaced font. Most fonts are proportionally spaced, such as the font used in this sentence, so that different letters have varying spacing between them. Proportionally spaced fonts generally are easier to read than mono-spaced fonts.

PowerPoint designers often set their own guidelines on type usage. Some never use italic type or fancy fonts, such as Broadway Engraved or UMBRA. Some fonts, such as Blackadder, look good on a computer monitor but look distorted when they are projected on a screen, and others, such as Vivaldi, look better when they are projected. Use a maximum of four fonts in an entire presentation: one for title text, a second for body text, and one or two other fonts for emphasis.

To Change the Theme Fonts

The second modification to make is to change the theme fonts. Each document theme uses at least one font and several font sizes for the heading and body text. The Theme Fonts button displays a capital letter A with the current heading font associated with the document theme. When you click the Theme Fonts button, names and samples of the fonts are displayed for each document theme. As with the default document color scheme, you also can customize the theme fonts. The following steps change the theme heading and body fonts from Twentieth Century MT to Trebuchet MS and Georgia, which are associated with the Urban document theme.

- Click the Theme Fonts button in the Themes group to display the Theme Fonts gallery.

- Scroll through the Theme Fonts gallery until Urban is displayed and then point to Urban to display a live preview of the Urban font set (Figure 4–8).

Experiment

- Point to various font sets in the Theme Fonts gallery and watch the title text and body text fonts change in Slide 4.

Q&A

What elements are selected in the Urban theme font set?

The capital letter A in the square shows a sample of the heading font (Trebuchet MS); the lowercase letter a shows the body font (Georgia). The names of these fonts display to the right of the button.

Figure 4–8

2

• Click Urban in the Theme Fonts gallery to change the presentation theme fonts to Urban (Figure 4–9).

Q&A

What if I want to return to the original font set?

You would click the Theme Fonts button and then click Median in the Theme Fonts gallery.

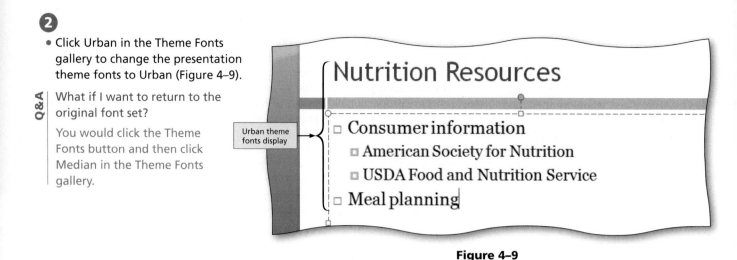

Urban theme fonts display

Figure 4–9

Inserting and Formatting a Picture and a Clip into Slides Without Content Placeholders

PowerPoint does not require you to use a content placeholder to add pictures and clips to a slide. You can insert these graphical elements on any slide regardless of its slide layout. The Slide 1 and Slide 4 layouts do not have a content placeholder for graphics, but you can insert files from the Microsoft Clip Organizer or from your Data Files for Students. Once these visuals are inserted, you can format them by applying a style, applying and coloring borders, recoloring, and changing the brightness or contrast.

To Insert a Picture into a Slide without a Content Placeholder

The next step in creating the presentation is to insert a picture of a salad bowl into Slide 1, which does not have a content placeholder. This picture is found in the Microsoft Clip Organizer and also on the Data Files for Students. See the inside back cover of this book for instructions on downloading the Data Files for Students, or contact your instructor for more information about accessing the required files. The following steps insert this picture.

1

• Click the Previous Slide button three times to display Slide 1.

• Click Insert on the Ribbon to display the Insert tab (Figure 4–10).

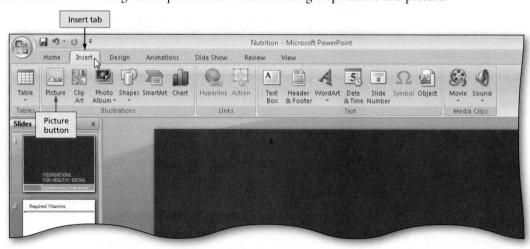

Insert tab

Picture button

Figure 4–10

2

- With your USB flash drive connected to one of the computer's USB ports, click the Picture button to display the Insert Picture dialog box.

- If the Folders list is displayed below the Folders button, click the Folders button to remove the Folders list.

- Click the Previous Locations arrow on the Address bar and then click Computer in the Favorite Links section. Double-click UDISK 2.0 (E:) to select the USB flash drive, Drive E in this case, as the device that contains the picture.

- Click Salad to select the file name (Figure 4–11).

 What if the picture is not on a USB flash drive?

Use the same process, but select the device containing the picture in the Favorite Links section. Another option is to locate the picture in the Microsoft Clip Organizer.

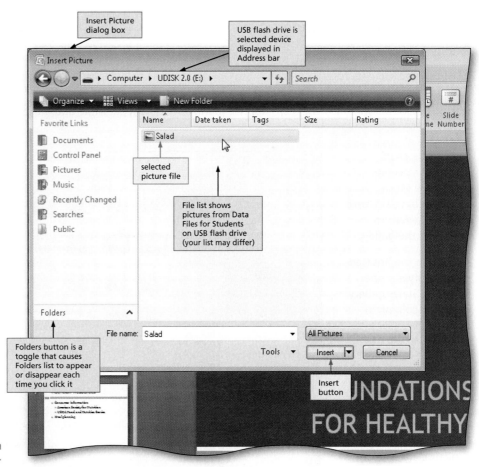

Figure 4–11

3

- Click the Insert button in the dialog box to insert the picture into Slide 1 (Figure 4–12).

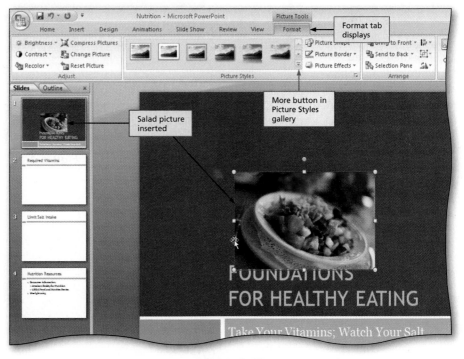

Figure 4–12

To Apply a Picture Style

A title slide should grasp the audience's attention, and one method of creating interest is by modifying graphical images. The salad picture is colorful, but you can increase its visual appeal by adding a style. PowerPoint has a wide variety of more than 25 styles to alter the rectangular shape. These styles include borders, shadows, reflections, and various shapes. The following steps apply a picture style with an angle and a reflection to the salad picture in Slide 1.

1

- With the salad picture selected, click the More button in the Picture Styles gallery to expand the gallery.

- Point to the Rotated, White style in the Picture Styles gallery (row 3, column 5) to display a live preview of that style applied to the picture in the slide (Figure 4–13).

🔎 **Experiment**

- Point to various picture styles in the Picture Styles gallery and watch the format of the picture change in the slide.

2

- Click the Rotated, White style to apply this selected style to the picture.

3

- Drag the picture to the location shown in Figure 4–1a on page PPT 227.

Figure 4–13

To Change a Picture Border Color

The Module presentation theme colors can be used to enhance the salad picture border. The area under the Picture Border button indicates the current border color, which is tan. To coordinate the colors on the slide, you can apply the Aqua color located in the lower-left corner of Slide 1 to the picture border. The theme colors associated with the Module document theme are displayed in the first row of the Picture Border color palette. The following steps change the border color.

1

- With the salad picture selected, click the Picture Border button on the Format tab to display the Picture Border color palette.

- In the Theme Colors area, point to the Aqua, Accent 2 color (row 1, column 6) to display a live preview of this color on the picture border (Figure 4–14).

Experiment

- Point to various colors in the Picture Border gallery and watch the border color on the picture change in Slide 1.

2

- Click the Aqua, Accent 2 color to apply this color to the salad picture border.

Q&A

If I had other pictures with borders, could I change their borders to Aqua easily?

Yes. Every picture border color will change to Aqua when you select the picture and then click the Picture Border icon.

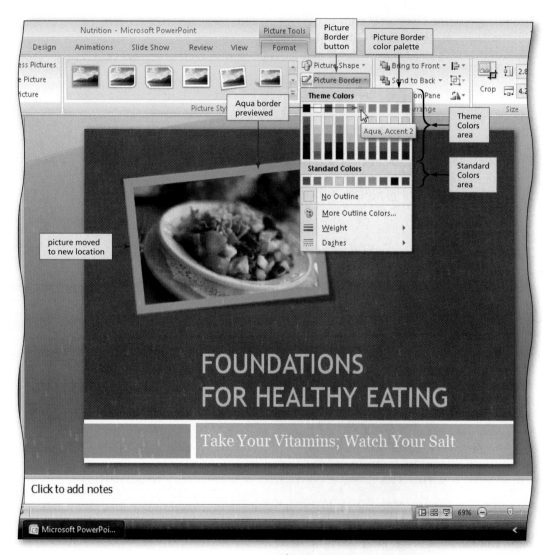

Figure 4–14

To Change a Picture Contrast

A photograph's color intensity can be modified by changing the brightness and contrast. **Brightness** determines the overall lightness or darkness of the entire image, whereas **contrast** is the difference between the darkest and lightest areas of the image. The brightness and contrast are changed in predefined percentage increments. The following steps increase the contrast to intensify the picture colors.

1

• With the salad picture still selected, click the Contrast button in the Adjust group to display the Contrast gallery.

• Point to +20 % to display a live preview of this contrast on the picture (Figure 4–15).

🔍 **Experiment**

• Point to various percentages in the Contrast gallery and watch the contrast change on the picture in Slide 1.

2

• Click +20 % to apply this contrast to the salad picture.

Q&A How can I remove all effects from the salad picture?
Click the Reset Picture button in the Adjust group.

Figure 4–15

Other Ways
1. In Format Picture dialog   enter number in box next
box, move Contrast slider or   to slider

To Insert a Clip into a Slide without a Content Placeholder

Slide 4 does not have a content placeholder, but you want to insert a clip of a placemat and utensils into this slide. This clip is found in the Microsoft Clip Organizer. Contact your instructor if you have difficulty locating this clip. The following steps insert this clip into Slide 4.

1

• Click the Next Slide button three times to display Slide 4.

• Click Insert on the Ribbon to display the Insert tab (Figure 4–16).

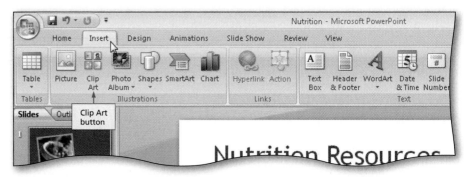

Figure 4–16

2

- Click the Clip Art button in the Illustrations group to display the Clip Art task pane.

- Type utensils in the Search for text box and then click the Go button.

- If necessary, scroll down the list to display the utensils clip shown in Figure 4–17.

- Click the clip shown in Figure 4–17 to insert it into Slide 4 (Figure 4–17).

What if the utensils image displayed in Figure 4–17 is not shown in my Clip Art task pane?

Select a similar clip. Your clips may be different depending on the clips installed on your computer and if you have an open connection to the Internet.

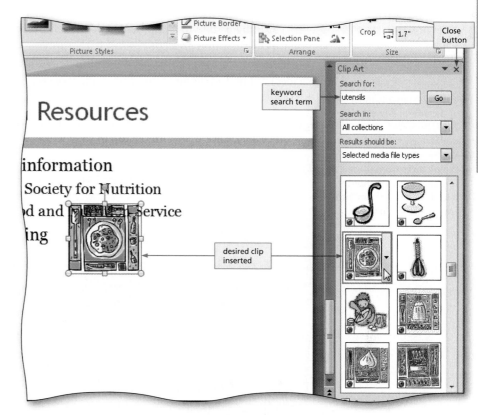

Figure 4–17

3

- Click the Close button on the Clip Art task pane title bar.

- Drag a corner sizing handle to increase the clip's size to approximately the size shown in Figure 4–18.

- Drag the clip to the location shown in Figure 4–18.

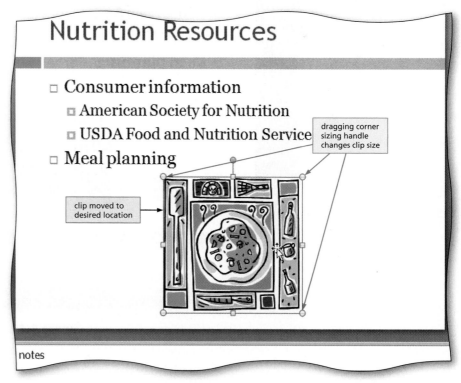

Figure 4–18

BTW

Importing Pictures from Scanners and Cameras
Previous PowerPoint versions allowed users to import pictures directly from a scanner or a camera. PowerPoint 2007, however, does not include this feature. You must download the pictures from these sources to your computer and then insert them into your presentation.

To Apply a Picture Style to a Clip

Adding a style to a clip helps add visual interest. To enhance the clip in this manner, you follow the same procedure used with applying a style to a picture. The same styles available for pictures can be used for clips, including shapes, borders, reflection, and shadows. The following steps apply a picture style with an angle and border to the clip in Slide 4.

1 With the utensils clip selected, click Format on the Ribbon to display the Format tab, if necessary. Click the More button in the Picture Styles gallery to expand the gallery.

2 Preview the various picture styles and then click the Relaxed Perspective, White style in the Picture Styles gallery (row 4, column 1) to apply this selected style to the clip (Figure 4–19).

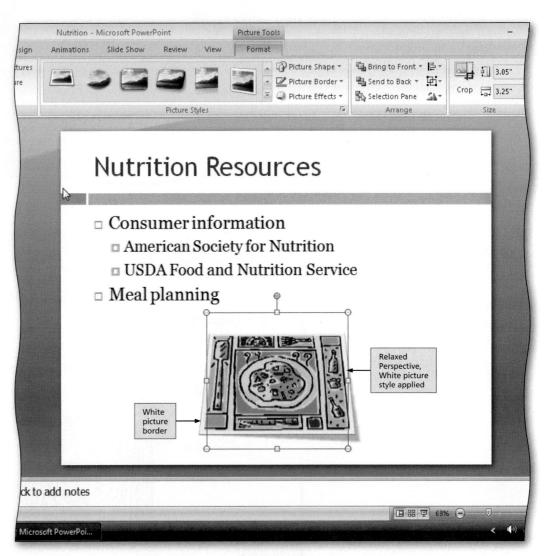

Figure 4–19

To Change the Border Color of a Clip

The Module presentation theme colors again can be used to enhance the utensils clip border color. For consistency, apply the Aqua color to this border. The Picture Border button is displaying with the Aqua color below the icon, so that color is the active color. If you select the clip and then click the Picture Border button, the active color will be added to the clip border. The following steps change the clip's border color.

1 With the utensils clip selected, click the Picture Border icon to apply the Aqua color to the clip border (Figure 4–20).

Q&A Can I select another color for the border?

Yes. Click the Picture Border button arrow and select one of the colors in the Theme Colors or Standard Colors areas.

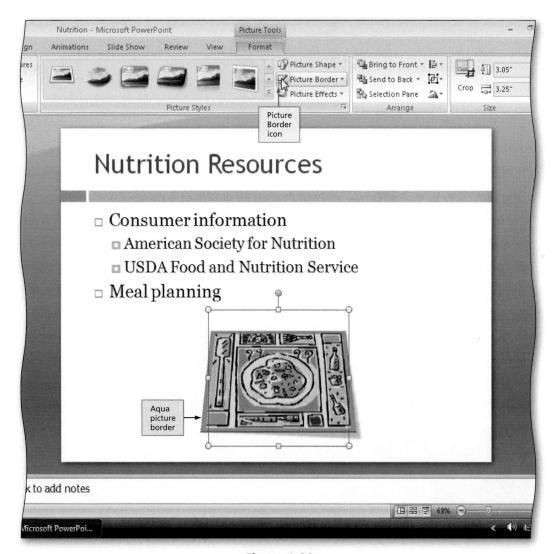

Figure 4–20

To Change the Brightness of a Clip

The final format change you will make is to increase the clip's brightness. The same steps used to modify a picture's contrast are used to modify a clip's brightness. The following steps increase the brightness.

1 With the utensils clip still selected, click the Brightness button in the Adjust group to display the Brightness gallery (Figure 4–21).

2 Preview the various percentages in the Brightness gallery and then click -10 % to apply this brightness to the utensils clip.

Q&A Do I remove all effects from a clip in the same manner as I would remove them from a picture?

Yes. Click the Reset Picture button in the Adjust group.

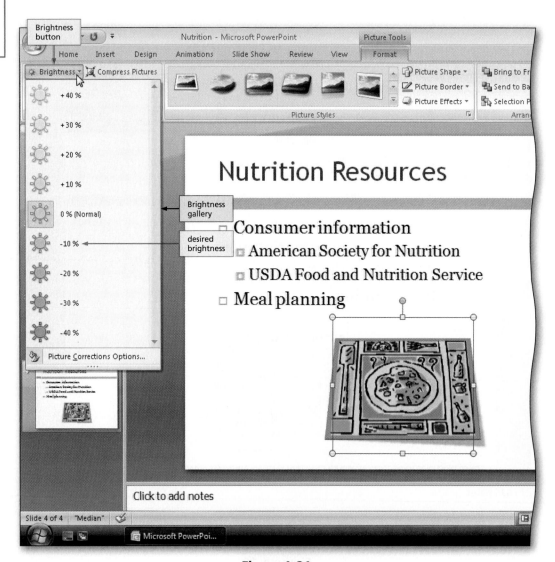

Figure 4–21

**Plan
Ahead**

Choose outstanding hyperlink text or images.
Outstanding speakers are aware of their audiences and know their speech material well. They have rehearsed their presentations and know where the hypertext is displayed on the slides. During a presentation, however, they sometimes need to divert from their planned material. Audience members may interrupt with questions, the room may not have optimal acoustics or lighting, or the timing may be short or long. It is helpful, therefore, to make the slide hyperlinks as large and noticeable to speakers as possible. The presenters can glance at the slide and receive a visual cue that it contains a hyperlink. They then can decide whether to click the hyperlink to display a Web page.

Adding Hyperlinks

Many speeches are presented in rooms with Internet access. Showing Web sites during a presentation can add much visual imagery, and this content can greatly enhance the overall message.

Hyperlinks

PowerPoint includes a hyperlink feature that allows you to access a specific Uniform Resource Locator (URL) from within your presentation if you are connected to the Internet. **Hyperlinks**, also called **links**, connect one slide to a Web page, another slide, a custom show consisting of specific slides in a presentation, or a file.

When you point to a hyperlink, the mouse pointer becomes the shape of a hand to indicate the text or object contains a hyperlink. A hyperlink can be any element of a slide. This includes a single letter, a word, a paragraph, or any graphical image. By default, hyperlinked text is displayed underlined and in a color that is part of the color scheme. When you click a hyperlink during a presentation, the Web browser will open a new window and display the Web address you specified when you created the presentation.

Slide 4 contains three hyperlinks to organizations' Web pages: two are text, and one is the utensils clip art. The following sections explain how to create the hyperlinks.

BTW

Customizing ScreenTips
You can create a custom screen tip that displays when you hover your mouse over a hyperlink. Click the ScreenTip button in the Insert Hyperlink dialog box, type the desired ScreenTip text in the Set Hyperlink ScreenTip dialog box, and then click the OK button.

To Add a Hyperlink to a Slide

On Slide 4, each second-level paragraph will be a hyperlink to a nutrition organization's Web page. If you are connected to the Internet when you run the presentation, you can click each of these paragraphs. Your browser will display the corresponding Web page for each paragraph. The following steps create the first hyperlink.

1

- Triple-click the first second-level paragraph, American Society for Nutrition, to select the text.

- Click Insert on the Ribbon to display the Insert tab (Figure 4–22).

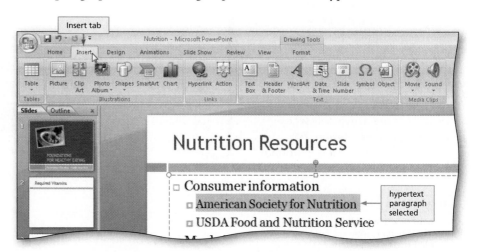

Figure 4–22

- Click the Insert Hyperlink button in the Links group to display the Insert Hyperlink dialog box.

- If necessary, click the Existing File or Web Page button in the Link to area.

- Type www.nutrition.org in the Address text box (Figure 4–23).

Q&A I did not type http://, but those letters displayed automatically in the Address text box. Why?

PowerPoint realizes you typed a URL and consequently inserted those letters automatically.

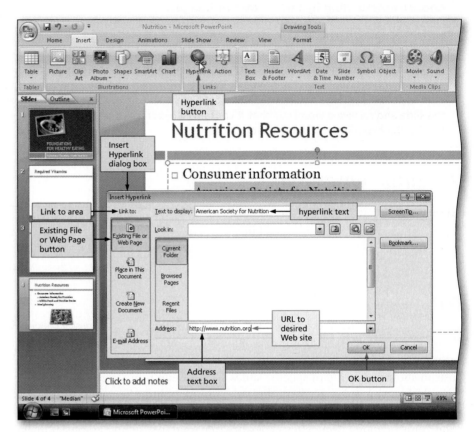

Figure 4–23

- Click the OK button to insert the hyperlink.

- Click Slide 4 anywhere except the text placeholder (Figure 4–24).

Q&A Why is this paragraph now displaying underlined and with a new font color?

The default style for hyperlinks is underlined text. The Module hyperlink color is Aqua, so PowerPoint formatted the paragraph to that color automatically.

Q&A I clicked the hyperlink, but the Web page did not display. Why?

Hyperlinks are active only when you run the presentation, not when you are creating it in Normal or Slide Sorter view.

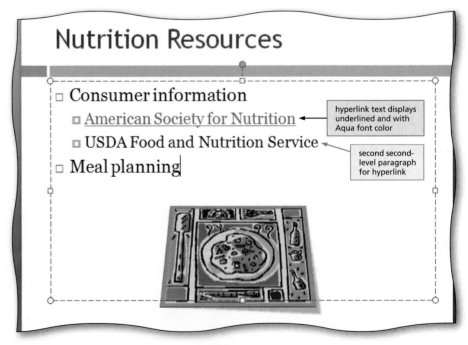

Figure 4–24

Other Ways
1. Right-click selected text, click Hyperlink, type address, click OK button   2. Press CTRL+K, type address, press ENTER

To Add a Hyperlink to the Second Paragraph

The hyperlink for the first second-level paragraph is complete. The next task is to create the hyperlink for the other second-level paragraph on Slide 4.

1 Triple-click the second second-level paragraph, USDA Food and Nutrition Service.

2 Click the Insert Hyperlink button and then type `www.fns.usda.gov/nutritionlink/` in the Address text box. Click the OK button.

3 Click Slide 4 anywhere except the text placeholder.

To Add a Hyperlink to a Clip

Pictures, shapes, and objects also can serve as hyperlinks. The next step is to create the hyperlink for the utensils clip on Slide 4.

1 Click the utensils clip to select it.

2 Click the Insert Hyperlink button and then type `www.mealsmatter.org/` in the Address text box. Click the OK button.

3 Click Slide 4 anywhere except the text placeholder (Figure 4–25).

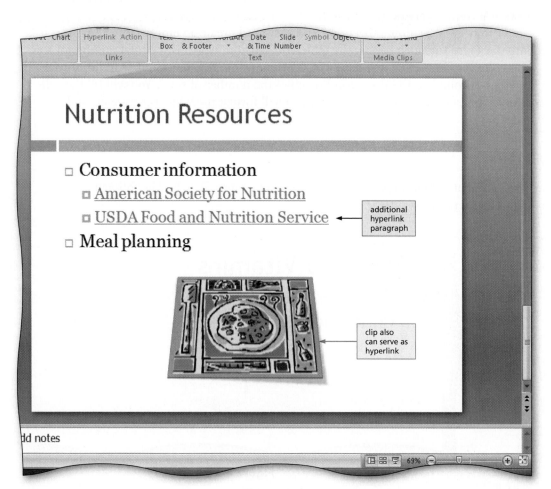

Figure 4–25

Plan
Ahead

Consider the graphic's function.
Determine why you are considering using an information graphic. The chart or graph should introduce meaningful information, support information in your speech, and help you convey details. If you are inserting the graphic simply for the sake of enlivening the presentation, then do not use it. Graphics should help your audience understand and retain information and should not merely repeat details they have seen or heard up to this point in the slide show. Take care in placing a manageable amount of information in your chart or table. Avoid overwhelming your audience with numerous slices or bars in your chart or lines in your table. If your audience is confused or struggling with comprehending the graphic, chances are they simply will abandon the task and wait for you to display the next slide.

Adding a Table to a Slide and Formatting

BTW

Copying Tables to and from Excel and Word
In this project you create a table, but you also can copy a table created in Microsoft Excel or Word to the Office Clipboard and then paste it into your slide. Similarly, you can copy a table you create in PowerPoint to an Excel worksheet or a Word document.

One effective method of organizing information on a slide is to use a **table**, which is a grid consisting of rows and columns. You can enhance a table with formatting, including adding colors, lines, fonts, and backgrounds. In this project you will create the table and then add borders and a shadow effect.

Tables

The table on Slide 2 (shown in Figure 4–1b on page PPT 227) contains information about specific vitamins, what food products contain them, and what part of the body they affect. This data is listed in three columns and seven rows. The intersections of these rows and columns are **cells**.

To begin developing this table, you first must create an empty table and insert it into the slide. You must specify the table's **dimension**, which is the total number of rows and columns. This table will have a 3 × 7 dimension; the first number indicates the number of columns, and the second specifies the number of rows. You will fill the cells with data pertaining to vitamins. Then you will format the table using a table style.

To Insert an Empty Table

The next step in developing the presentation is to insert an empty table into Slide 2. The following steps insert a table with three columns and seven rows into Slide 2.

1
- Click the Previous Slide button two times to display Slide 2 (Figure 4–26).

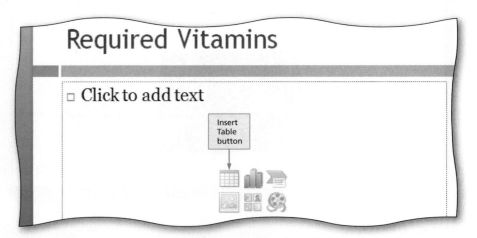

Figure 4–26

• Click the Insert Table button in the content placeholder to display the Insert Table dialog box.

• Click the down arrow to the right of the Number of columns text box two times so that the number 3 appears in the box.

• Click the up arrow to the right of the Number of rows text box five times so that the number 7 appears in box (Figure 4–27).

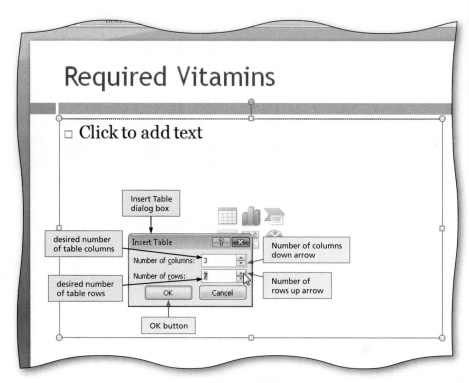

Figure 4–27

❸

• Click the OK button to insert the table into Slide 2 (Figure 4–28).

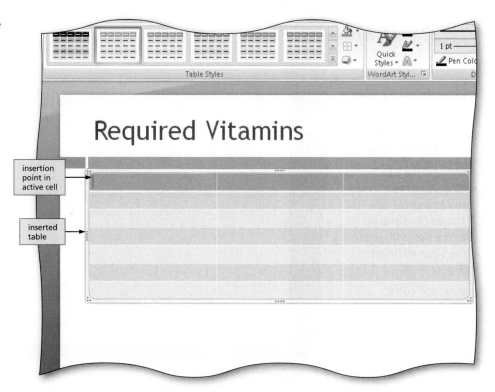

Figure 4–28

Other Ways

1. Click Table on Insert tab, drag to select columns and rows, press ENTER

To Enter Data in a Table

The Slide 2 table consists of three columns: one for the vitamin name, one for the vitamin source, and the third for how the body uses the vitamin. A **heading** identifies each column. The next step is to enter the data in the cells of the empty table. To place data in a cell, you click the cell and then type. Table 4–2 shows the three column headings and the corresponding data.

Table 4–2 Required Vitamins Data		
Vitamin	**Sources**	**Required for**
A	Milk, eggs, green vegetables	Eyes, skin
B	Whole wheat products, liver, soy beans	Energy production, nerves, skin
C	Oranges, tomatoes, fresh green vegetables	Blood vessels, preventing colds
D	Milk, eggs, fish oil, sunlight	Teeth, bones
E	Whole wheat products, eggs, butter	Heart, lungs, blood vessels
K	Fresh green vegetables	Blood clotting

The following steps enter the headings and data in the table.

1

- With the insertion point in the left cell of the table, type VITAMIN and then press the TAB key to advance the insertion point to the middle column heading cell.

- Type SOURCES and then press the TAB key to advance to the rightmost column heading cell.

- Type REQUIRED FOR and then press the TAB key to advance to the first cell under the Vitamin heading (Figure 4–29).

Q&A

How do I correct cell contents if I make a mistake?

Click the cell and then correct the text.

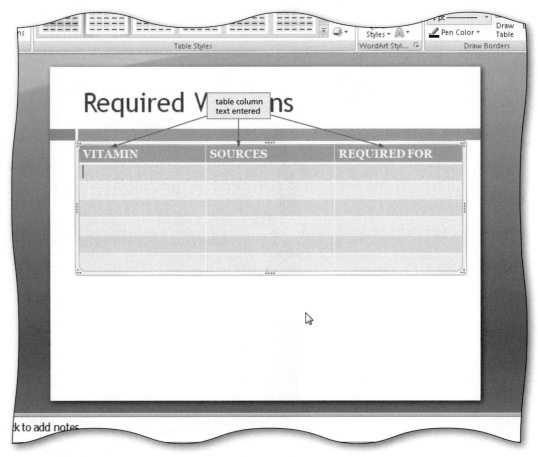

Figure 4–29

2

- Repeat Step 1 to enter the remaining table cells by using Table 4-2 as a guide (Figure 4–30).

Q&A

How can I add more rows to the table?

When the insertion point is positioned in the bottom-right cell, press the TAB key.

Q&A

What if I pressed TAB after filling in the last cell and added another row?

Right-click the unnecessary row and then click Delete Rows in the shortcut menu.

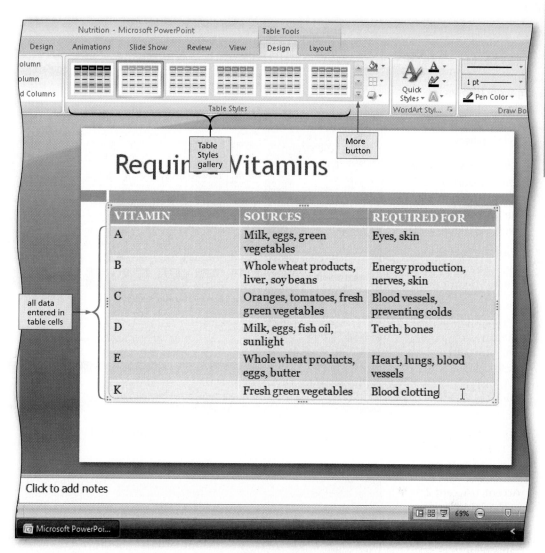

Figure 4–30

To Apply a Table Style

A table Quick Style is a combination of formatting options that use the theme colors applied to the presentation. When you inserted the table, PowerPoint automatically applied a style. Thumbnails of this style and others are displayed in the Table Styles gallery. These styles use a variety of colors and shading and are grouped in the categories of Best Match for Document, Light, Medium, and Dark. You want the Slide 2 table to coordinate with the Aqua border you applied to the photograph and clip in Slides 1 and 4, so you will select a table style that uses both the Aqua and Gold accent colors that are part of the Module color scheme. The steps on the following page apply a table style to the Slide 2 table.

1

- With the insertion point in the table, click the More button in the Table Styles gallery (shown in Figure 4–30) to expand the Table Styles gallery.

- Scroll down and then point to Dark Style 2 - Accent 1/Accent 2 in the Dark area (row 2, column 2) (Figure 4–31).

Q&A Does the Table Styles gallery have a live preview feature?

Yes, but the gallery is covering most the table, greatly limiting your ability to preview table styles.

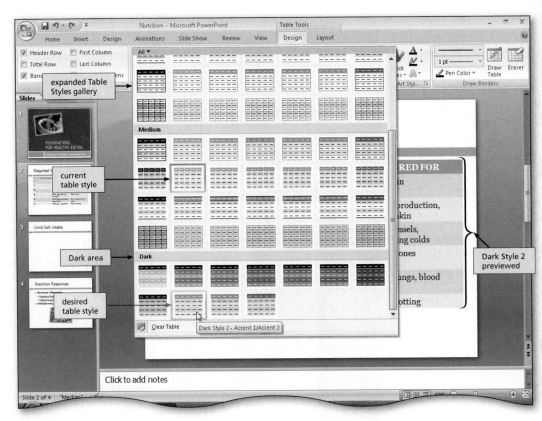

Figure 4–31

2

- Click Dark Style 2 - Accent 1/Accent 2 in the Table Styles gallery to apply the selected style to the table (Figure 4–32).

Q&A Can I resize the columns and rows or the entire table?

Yes. To resize columns or rows, drag a **column boundary** (the border to the right of a column) or the **row boundary** (the border at the bottom of a row) until the column or row is the desired width or height. To resize the entire table, drag a **table resize handle**.

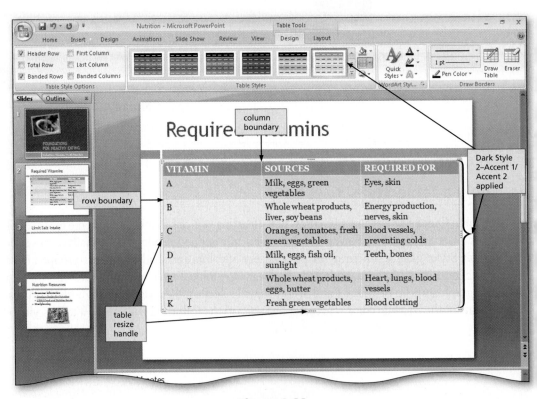

Figure 4–32

To Add Borders to a Table

The Slide 2 table does not have borders around the entire table or between the cells. The following steps add borders to the entire table.

1

- Click the edge of the table so that the insertion point does not appear in any cell.

- Click the No Border button arrow in the Table Styles group to display the Border gallery (Figure 4–33).

Q&A Why is the button called No Border?

The button name will change based on the type of border, if any, present in the table. Currently no borders are applied.

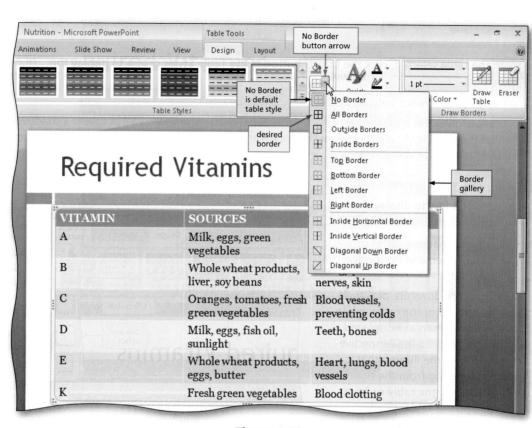

Figure 4–33

2

- Click All Borders in the Border gallery to add borders around the entire table and to each table cell (Figure 4–34).

Q&A Can I apply any of the border options in the Border gallery?

Yes. You can vary the look of your table by applying borders only to the cells, around the table, or in such combinations as the top, bottom, or left and right edges.

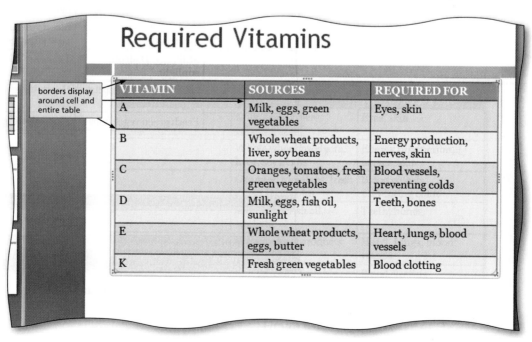

Figure 4–34

- Click the Insert Chart button in the content placeholder to display the Insert Chart dialog box.

- Scroll down and then click the Pie in 3-D chart button in the Pie area to select that chart style (Figure 4–40).

Q&A

Can I change the chart style after I have inserted a chart?

Yes. Click the Change Chart Type button in the Type group on the Design tab to display the Change Chart Type dialog box and then make another selection.

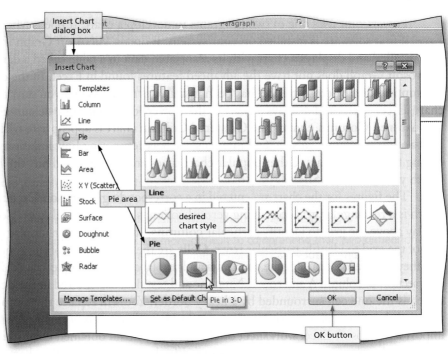

Figure 4–40

- Click the OK button to start the Microsoft Excel program and open a worksheet tiled on the right side of your Nutrition presentation (Figure 4–41).

Q&A

What do the numbers in the worksheet and the chart represent?

Microsoft Excel places sample data in the worksheet and charts the sample data in the default chart type.

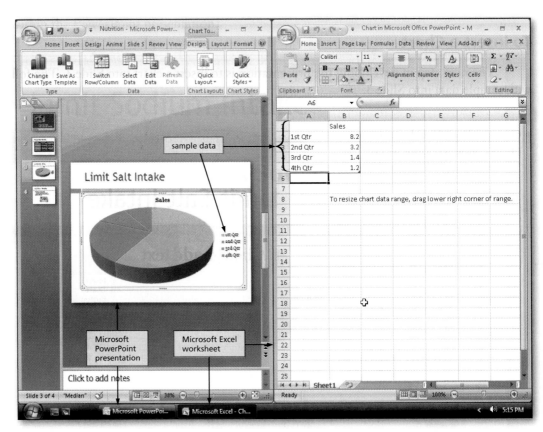

Figure 4–41

Other Ways

1. Click Chart button on Insert tab

Obtain information for the graphic from credible sources.
At times you are familiar with the data for your chart or graph because you have conducted in-the-field, or primary, research by interviewing experts or taking measurements. Other times, however, you have gathered the data from secondary sources, such as magazine or newspaper articles or from Web sites. General circulation magazines and newspapers, such as *Newsweek* and the *Wall Street Journal*, use experienced journalists and editors to verify their information. Also, online databases, such as EBSCO, OCLC FirstSearch, LexisNexis Academic, and NewsBank Info Web contain articles from credible sources.

On the other hand, some sources have particular biases and present information that supports their causes. Political, religious, and social publications and Web sites often are designed for specific audiences who share a common point of view. You should, therefore, recognize that data from these sources can be skewed and edited to support a cause.

If you did not conduct the research yourself, you should give credit to the source of your information. You are acknowledging that someone else provided the data and giving your audience the opportunity to obtain the same materials you used. Type the source at the bottom of your chart or graph, especially if you are distributing handouts of your slides. At the very least, state the source during the body of your speech.

Plan Ahead

To Replace the Sample Data

The next step in creating the chart is to replace the sample data, which will redraw the chart. The sample data is displayed in two columns and five rows. The first row and left column contain text labels and will be used to create the chart title and legend. A **legend** is a box that identifies each slice of the pie chart and coordinates with the colors assigned to the slice categories. The other cells contain numbers that are used to determine the size of the pie slices. The following steps replace the sample data in the worksheet.

1

- Click cell B1, which is the intersection of column B and row 1, to select it (Figure 4–42).

Why did my mouse pointer change shape?

The mouse pointer changes to a block plus sign to indicate a cell is selected.

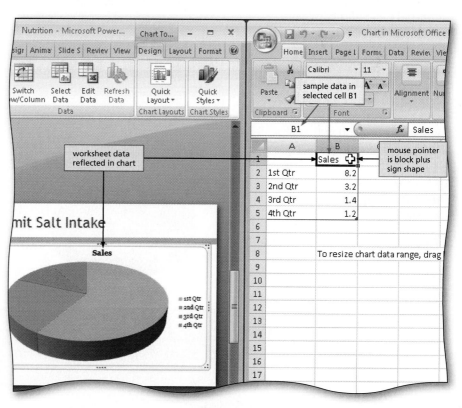

Figure 4–42

2

- Type Salt Sources in cell B1 to replace the sample chart title.

- Click cell A2 to select that cell (Figure 4–43).

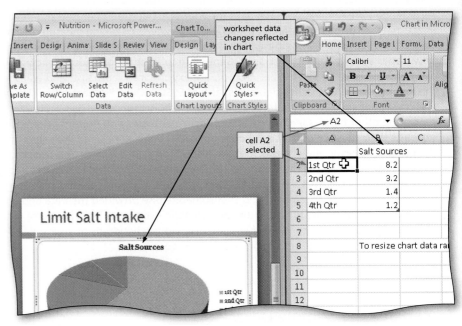

Figure 4–43

3

- Type Processed food in cell A2 and then press the DOWN ARROW key to move the mouse pointer to cell A3.

Q&A Why did some of the letters disappear in cell A2 when I moved the mouse pointer?

The default cell width is not wide enough to display the entire cell contents in the worksheet. The entire cell contents are displayed in the chart legend in the PowerPoint presentation.

- Type Occurs naturally in cell A3 and then press the DOWN ARROW key.

- Type Added at table in cell A4 and then press the DOWN ARROW key.

- Type Added during cooking in cell A5 (Figure 4–44).

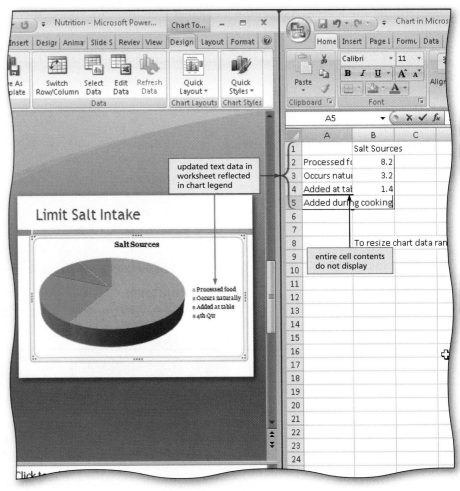

Figure 4–44

4

- Click cell B2, type 75% in that cell, and press the DOWN ARROW key to move the mouse pointer to cell B3.

- Type 10% in cell B3 and then press the DOWN ARROW key.

- Type 8% in cell B4 and then press the DOWN ARROW key.

- Type 7% in cell B5 and then press the DOWN ARROW key (Figure 4–45).

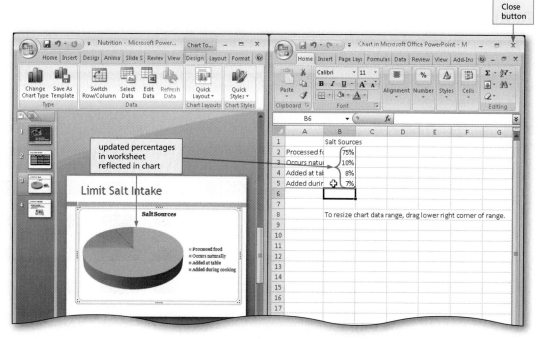

Figure 4–45

5

- Close Microsoft Excel by clicking its Close button (Figure 4–46).

Can I open the Excel spreadsheet once it has been closed?

Yes. Click the chart to select it and then click the Edit Data button in the Data group on the Design tab under Chart Tools.

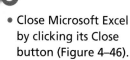

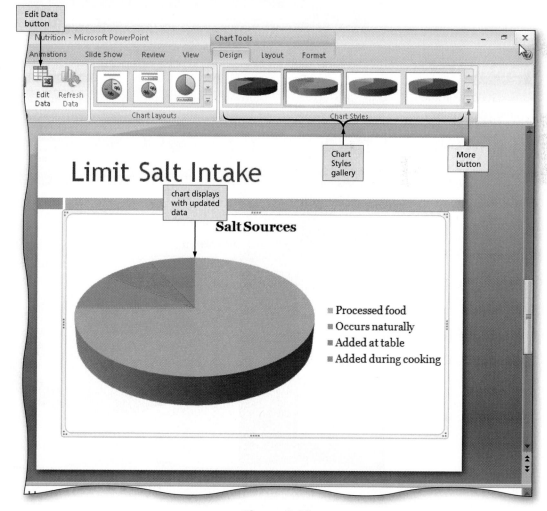

Figure 4–46

To Apply a Chart Style

Each chart type has a variety of styles that can change the look of the chart. If desired, you can change the chart from two dimensions to three dimensions, add borders, and vary the colors of the slices, lines, and bars. When you inserted the Pie in 3-D, a style was applied automatically. Thumbnails of this style and others are displayed in the Chart Styles gallery. The following steps apply a chart style to the Slide 3 pie chart.

1

- With the chart still selected, click the More button in the Chart Styles gallery (shown in Figure 4–46) to expand the Table Styles gallery.

- Point to Style 10 (row 2, column 2) (Figure 4–47).

 Q&A Does the Table Styles gallery have a live preview feature?

This feature is not available.

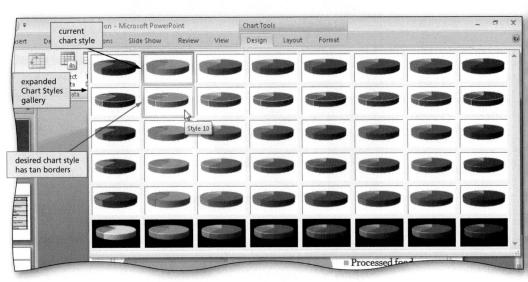

Figure 4–47

2

- Click Style 10 in the Table Styles gallery to apply the selected style to the table (Figure 4–48).

Q&A Can I change the chart type?

If you want to change the chart type, click the Change Chart Type button in the Type group on the Design tab and then select a different type.

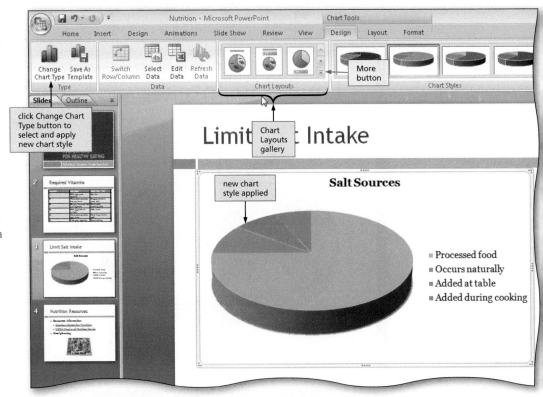

Figure 4–48

To Change the Chart Layout

Once you have selected a chart style, you can modify the look of the chart elements by changing its layout. The various layouts move the legend above or below the chart or move some or all of the legend data directly onto the individual chart pieces. For example, in the pie chart type, seven different layouts display only percentages on the pie slices, only the identifying information, such as the words Processed food, or combinations of this data. The following steps apply a chart layout with percentages to the Slide 3 pie chart.

1

- With the chart still selected, click the More button in the Chart Layouts gallery (shown in Figure 4–48) to expand the Chart Layouts gallery.

- Point to Layout 6 (row 2, column 3) (Figure 4–49).

Does the Chart Layouts gallery have a live preview feature?

This feature is not available.

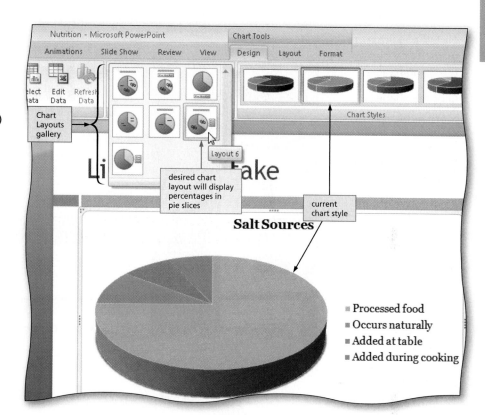

Figure 4–49

2

- Click Layout 6 in the Chart Layouts gallery to apply the selected layout to the chart (Figure 4–50).

Can I change the chart layout?

Because a live preview is not available, you may want to sample the various layouts to evaluate their effectiveness. To change these layouts, repeat Steps 1 and 2.

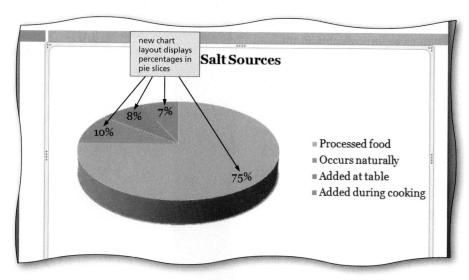

Figure 4–50

To Change the Shape Outline Weight

The new Style 10 has thin white outlines around each pie slice and around each color square in the legend. You can change the weight of these lines to accentuate each slice. The following steps change the outline weight.

- Click Format on the Ribbon to display the Format tab.

- Click the pie chart to select it and display the sizing handles.

- Click the Shape Outline button arrow in the Shape Styles group to display the Shape Outline color palette.

- Point to Weight in the Shape Outline menu to display the Weight submenu (Figure 4–51).

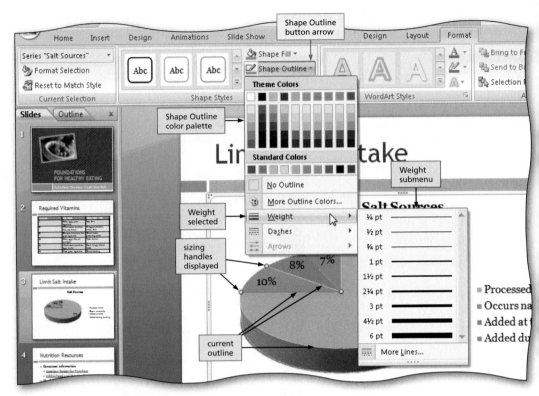

Figure 4–51

- Point to 3 pt to display a live preview of this outline line weight (Figure 4–52).

Experiment

- Point to various weights on the submenu and watch the border weights on the pie slices change.

Q&A What does pt mean after each number in the Weight submenu?

Pt is the abbreviation for point, which is the unit of measure used in the graphic arts industry.

- Click 3 pt to increase the border around each slice to that width.

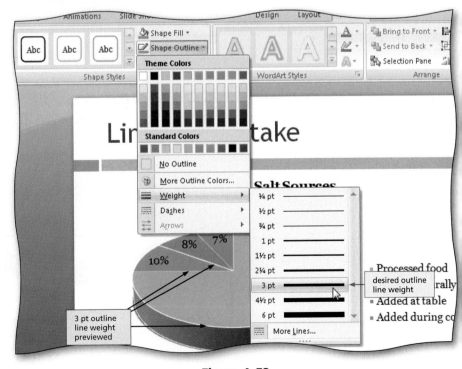

Figure 4–52

To Change the Shape Outline Color

The new Style 10 has white outlines around each pie slice and around each color square in the legend. You can change this color to add contrast to each slice and legend color square. The following steps change the border color.

1

- Click the Shape Outline button arrow in the Shape Styles group to display the Shape Outline color palette.

- In the Theme Colors area, point to the Black, Text 1 color (row 1, column 2) to display a live preview of this color on the pie shape borders (Figure 4–53).

Experiment

- Point to various colors in the Shape Outline gallery and watch the border color on the pie slices change.

What color is the active outline color?

Aqua. PowerPoint retains the setting of the previous border color selected.

2

- Click Black, Text 1 to add black borders around each slice and also around the color squares in the legend.

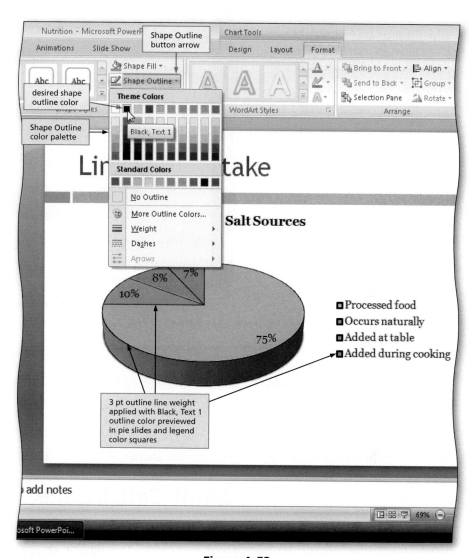

Figure 4–53

To Change the Title and Legend Font Size

Depending upon the complexity of the chart and the overall slide, you may want to increase the font size of the chart title and legend to increase readability. The steps on the following page change the font size of both of these chart elements.

- Click the chart title, Salt Sources, and then triple-click the paragraph to select the text and display the Mini toolbar.

- Click the Increase Font Size button three times to increase the font size of the selected text to 32 point (Figure 4–54).

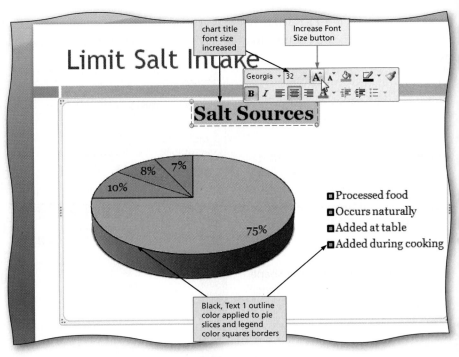

Figure 4–54

2

- Right-click the legend in the chart to display the Mini toolbar and a shortcut menu related to legends.

- Click the Increase Font Size button once on the Mini toolbar to increase the font size of the selected text to 20 point (Figure 4–55).

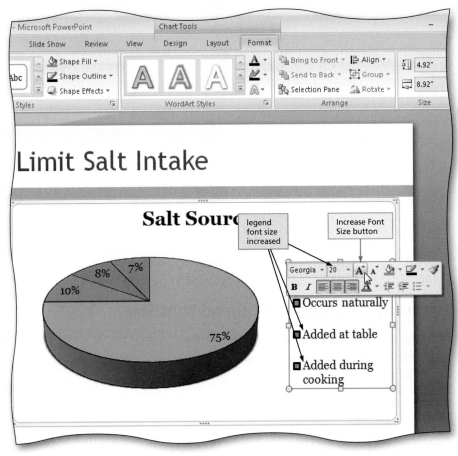

Figure 4–55

Plan Ahead

Test your visual elements.
Proofread your charts and tables carefully using these guidelines:

- Verify that your charts and tables contain the correct data. It is easy to make mistakes inputting large quantities of numbers or entering many lines of text. Check that numbers are not transposed and that pie chart percentages total 100.

- Be certain graphics are clearly labeled. The slide title text or the chart title should state the graphic's purpose. Table column headings must indicate the data below. Chart legends must accompany the graphic if the data are not displayed on the chart itself. Units of measurement, such as degrees, dollars, or inches, should appear for clarity.

- Show your graphic to people unfamiliar with your topic. Ask them to explain verbally what they gather from viewing the material. Determine how long it takes them to state their interpretations. If they pause or look confused, then your graphic either has too much or too little information and needs revision.

Revising and Customizing Individual Slides

The text and information graphics for all four slides in the Nutrition presentation have been entered. Once you complete a slide show, you might decide to change elements. PowerPoint provides several tools to assist you with making changes. The following pages discuss these tools.

Hiding a Slide

Slides 2, 3, and 4 present technical information in graphical form or with hyperlinks. Depending on the audience's needs and the time constraints, you may decide not to display one or more of these slides, particularly Slide 4 because it is a supporting slide. A **supporting slide** provides detailed information to supplement another slide in the presentation. For example, in a presentation to bank officers about the increase in student loans, one slide displays a graph representing the current year's loan amounts and the previous three years' loan figures. A supporting slide might display a table showing each branch office's loan application figures for every year in the graph.

When running a slide show, you may not always want to display the supporting slide. You would want to display it when time permits and when you want to show the audience more details about a topic. You should insert the supporting slide after the slide you anticipate may warrant more detail. Then, you use the **Hide Slide command** to hide the supporting slide. The Hide Slide command hides the supporting slide from the audience during the normal running of a slide show. When you want to display the supporting hidden slide, press the H key. No visible indicator displays to show that a hidden slide exists. You must be aware of the content of the presentation to know where the supporting slide is located.

When you run your presentation, the hidden slide does not display unless you press the H key when the slide preceding the hidden slide is displaying. For example, Slide 5 does not display unless you press the H key when Slide 4 display in Slide Show view. You continue your presentation by clicking the mouse or pressing any of the keys associated with running a slide show. You skip the hidden slide by clicking the mouse and advancing to the next slide.

BTW

Showing a Range of Slides
If your presentation consists of many slides, you may want to show only a portion of them in your slide show. For example, if your 40-slide presentation is designed to accompany a 30-minute speech and you are given only 10 minutes to present, you may elect to display only the first 10 slides. Rather than have the show end abruptly after Slide 10, you can elect to show a range of slides. To specify this range, click the Slide Show tab, click the Set Up Slide Show button to display the Set Up Show dialog box, and then specify the starting and ending slide numbers in the From and To boxes in the Show slides area.

To Hide a Slide

Slide 4 is a slide that supports information presented in the entire presentation. If time permits, or if the audience requires more information, you can display Slide 4. As the presenter, you decide whether to show Slide 4. You hide a slide in Slide Sorter view so you can see the slashed square surrounding the slide number, which indicates a slide is hidden. The following steps hide Slide 4.

• Right-click the Slide 4 thumbnail in the Slides tab to display the shortcut menu (Figure 4–56).

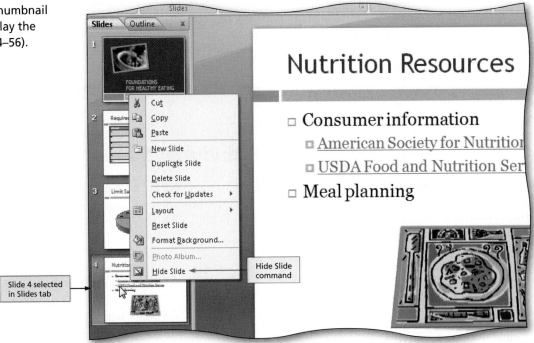

Figure 4–56

• Click the Hide Slide command on the shortcut menu to hide Slide 4 (Figure 4–57).

Q&A How do I know that Slide 4 is hidden?

The rectangle with a slash surrounds the slide number to indicate Slide 4 is a hidden slide.

Q&A What if I decide I no longer want to hide a slide?

Repeat Steps 1 and 2. The Hide Slide button is a toggle; it either hides or displays a slide.

Other Ways

1. Change view to Slide Sorter, right-click desired slide, click Hide Slide on shortcut menu
2. Click Hide Slide button on Slide Show tab

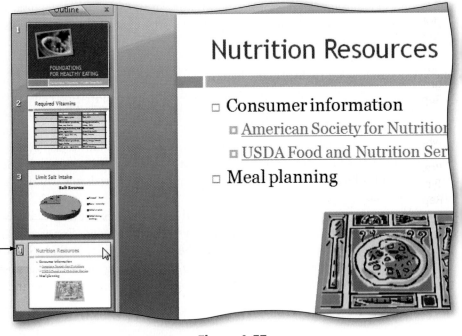

Figure 4–57

• Click
twice
the v
short

• Point
short
of sy

Find and Replace Dialog Box

At times you many want to change all occurrences of a word or phrase to another word or phrase. For example, a marketing representative may have one slide show to accompany a sales presentation given daily at a variety of offices, and he wants to update several sides with the name of the office where the presentation is occurring. He manually could change the words, but PowerPoint includes an efficient method of replacing one word with another. The Replace All button in the Find and Replace dialog box changes all occurrences of the Find what text with the Replace with text.

In some cases, you may want to replace only certain occurrences of a word or phrase, not all of them. To instruct PowerPoint to confirm each change, click the Find Next button in the Replace dialog box instead of the Replace All button. When PowerPoint locates an occurrence of the text, it pauses and waits for you to click either the Replace button or the Find Next button. Clicking the Replace button changes the text; clicking the Find Next button instructs PowerPoint to disregard the replacement and look for the next occurrence of the Find what text.

If you accidentally replace the wrong text, you can undo a replacement by clicking the Undo button on the Quick Access Toolbar. If you used the Replace All button to make the word changes, PowerPoint undoes all replacements. If you used the Replace button, PowerPoint undoes only the most recent replacement.

BTW

Finding Whole Words
The Replace dialog box contains an option to search for whole words. This feature is useful when your search term is embedded in unrelated words that are used frequently. For example, you may want to search for the word, use. PowerPoint will locate this combination of letters in other words, such as mouse and useful. To instruct PowerPoint to find only the word, use, click 'Find whole words only'.

To Find and Replace Text

While reading a nutrition label, you notice that food companies list sodium rather than salt content. You decide to use the term your audience members will see on their food packages and want to change all occurrences of salt to sodium. To perform this action, you can use PowerPoint's Find and Replace feature, which automatically locates each occurrence of a word or phrase and then replaces it with specified text. The following steps use Find and Replace to replace all occurrences of the word, salt, with the word, sodium.

• In th
the v
syno
word

What
displ

You
Rese
Thes
subm
with
Rese
anto
oppo

• Char
the v
lette

1

• If necessary, click Home on the Ribbon to display the Home tab. Click the Replace button in the Editing group to display the Replace dialog box.

• Type Salt in the Find what text box.

• Press the TAB key. Type Sodium in the Replace with text box (Figure 4–58).

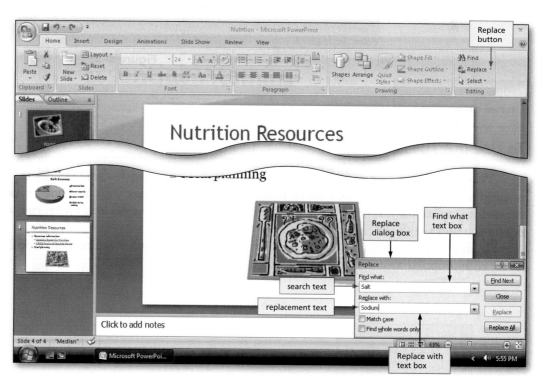

Figure 4–58

To Find a Second Synonym

Now that you have found a synonym for the word, Required, you want to find a synonym for the word, planning, on Slide 4. The following steps replace that word with a more appropriate one.

1 Click the Find button in the Editing group on the Home tab to display the Find dialog box.

2 Type planning in the Find what text box and then click the Find Next button.

3 With the word, planning, selected on Slide 4, click the Close button in the Find dialog box.

4 Right-click the word, planning, point to Synonyms on the shortcut menu, and then click the word, preparation, in the Synonyms submenu (Figure 4–62).

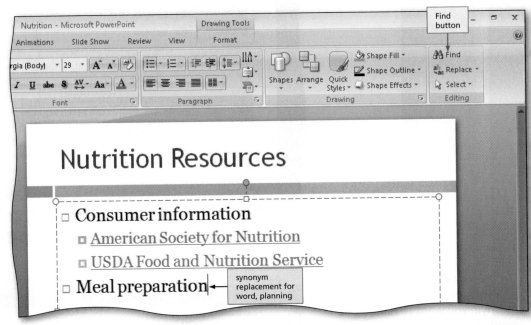

Figure 4–62

Adding and Formatting Action Buttons

When presenting the Nutrition slide show and discussing information on Slides 1, 2, or 3, a speaker might want to skip to the last slide in the presentation and then access a Web site for further information. Or the presenter may be discussing information on Slide 4 and want to display Slide 2 or 3 to re-emphasize information on the table or chart. One method of jumping non-sequentially to slides is by clicking an action button on a slide. An **action button** is a built-in 3-D button that can perform specific tasks such as display the next slide, provide help, give information, and play a sound. In addition, the action button can activate a hyperlink that allows users to jump to a specific slide in the presentation.

In the Nutrition slide show, you will insert and format the action button shape on Slides 2 and 3 and create a link to Slide 4 so that you will be able to display Slide 4 at any point in the presentation by clicking the action button. When you click the action button, a chime sound will play.

To Insert an Action Button

PowerPoint provides 12 built-in action buttons. You can customize one of them with a photograph, clip, logo, or any graphic you desire. The following steps insert an action button on Slide 2 and link it to Slide 4.

1

- Click the Previous Slide button two times to display Slide 2.

- Click Insert on the Ribbon to display the Insert tab. Click the Shapes button in the Illustrations group to display the Shapes gallery.

- Point to the Action Button: End shape in the Action Buttons area (column 4) (Figure 4–63).

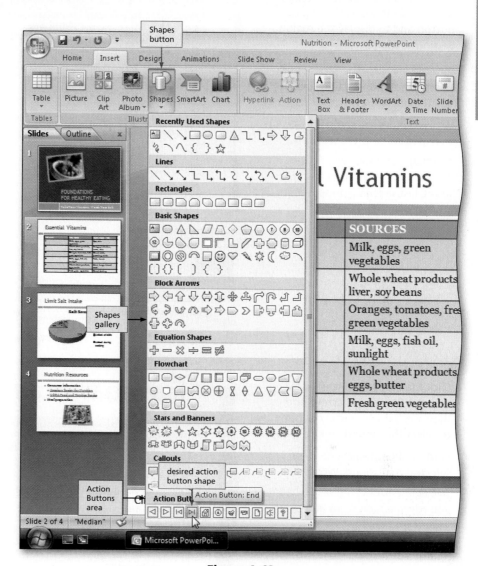

Figure 4–63

- Click the Action Button: End shape.

- Click the bottom-right corner of the slide to insert the action button and to display the Action Settings dialog box.

- If necessary, click the Mouse Click tab in the Action Settings dialog box (Figure 4–64).

Q&A Why is the default setting the action to hyperlink to the last slide?

The shape you selected, Action Button: End, establishes a hyperlink to the last slide in a presentation.

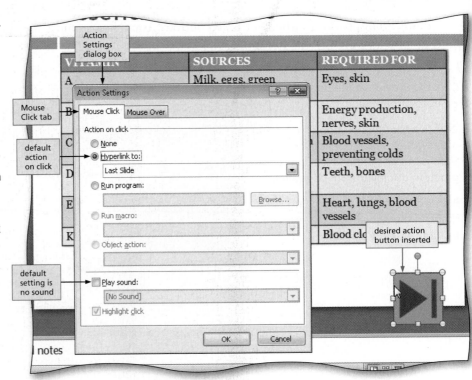

Figure 4–64

- Click the Play sound check box, click the Play sound arrow, and then scroll down and click Chime to select that sound (Figure 4–65).

Q&A I did not hear the chime when I selected that sound. Why not?

The chime sound will play when you run the slide show and click the action button.

4

- Click the OK button to apply the hyperlink setting and sound to the action button.

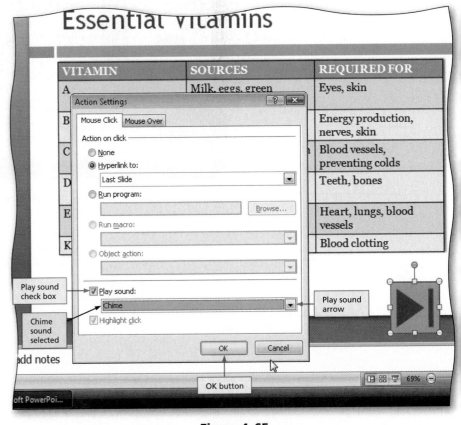

Figure 4–65

To Size an Action Button

The action button size can be decreased to make it less obvious on the slide. The following step resizes the selected action button.

1 With the action button still selected, point to the lower-right corner sizing handle on the button and then drag the sizing handle diagonally upward and inward until the button is the approximate size of the one shown in Figure 4–66.

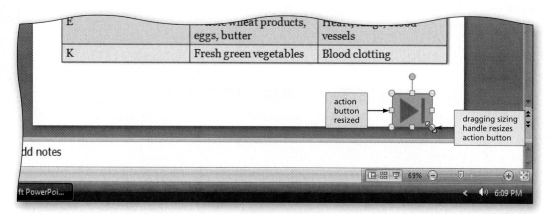

Figure 4–66

To Change the Action Button Fill Color

The action button's gold interior color is bright. To soften the hue, you can select a new fill color. The following steps change the fill to a lighter gold color.

1

- Right-click the action button to display the shortcut menu associated with the shape and the Mini toolbar (Figure 4–67).

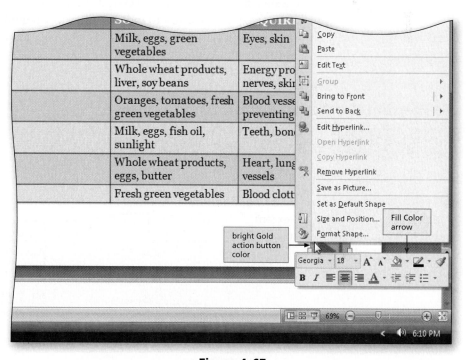

Figure 4–67

Click the Fill Color arrow on the Mini toolbar and then point to Gold, Accent 1, Lighter 80% in the Theme Colors palette (row 2, column 5) (Figure 4–68).

- Click Gold, Accent 1, Lighter 80% to apply this color to the action button.

- Click the slide to hide the Mini toolbar.

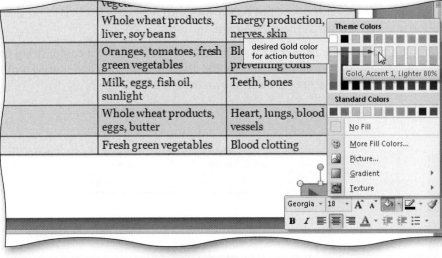

Figure 4–68

Guides

The PowerPoint guides help position shapes and objects on slides. **Guides** are two straight dotted lines, one horizontal and one vertical. When an object is close to a guide, its corner or its center (whichever is closer) **snaps**, or attaches itself, to the guide. You can drag a guide to a new location to meet your alignment requirements.

When you point to a guide and then press and hold the mouse button, PowerPoint displays a box containing the exact position of the guide on the slide in inches. The center of a slide is 0.00 on both the vertical and the horizontal guides. An arrow is displayed below the guide position to indicate the vertical guide either left or right of center. An arrow is displayed to the right of the guide position to indicate the horizontal guide either above or below center.

To Position the Action Button Using Guides

The action buttons should be displayed in precisely the same location on Slides 2, 3, and 4 so they appear static as you transition from one slide to the next during the slide show. Guides help you align objects on slides. The following steps display the guides and position the action button on Slide 2.

- Right-click Slide 2 anywhere except the chart and the title text to display the shortcut menu (Figure 4–69).

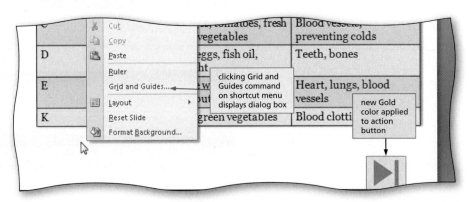

Figure 4–69

2

- Click Grid and Guides on the shortcut menu to display the Grid and Guides dialog box.

- Click the 'Display drawing guides on screen' check box in the Guide settings area (Figure 4–70).

Q&A Why does a check mark display in the Snap objects to grid check box?

The check mark indicates the action button and other shapes will snap to drawing guides that appear on the screen. This check mark is a default setting.

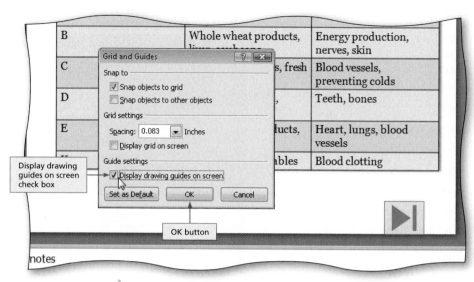

Figure 4–70

3

- Click the OK button to display the grids and the horizontal and vertical guides.

- Point to the horizontal guide anywhere except the table.

Q&A Why does 0.00 display when I hold down the mouse button?

The ScreenTip displays the horizontal guide's position. A 0.00 setting means that the guide is precisely in the middle of the slide and is not above or below the center.

- Click and then drag the horizontal guide to 2.75 inches below center. Do not release the mouse button (Figure 4–71).

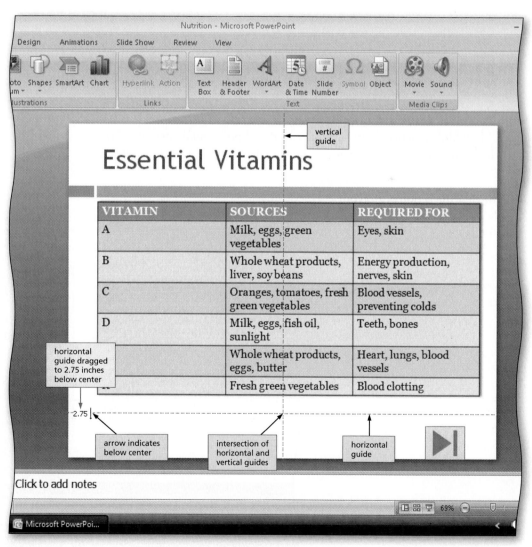

Figure 4–71

4

- Release the mouse button to position the horizontal guide at 2.75, which is the intended location of the action button's top border.

- Point to the vertical guide anywhere except the table.

- Click and then drag the vertical guide to 3.25 inches right of center.

- Drag the action button to the intersection of the vertical and horizontal guides to position the shape in the desired location (Figure 4–72).

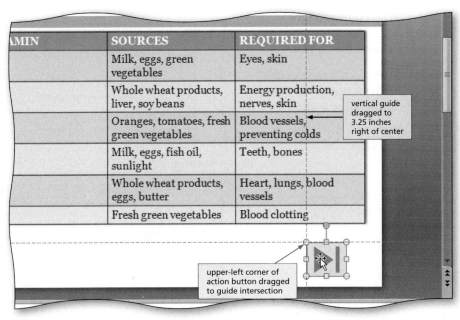

Figure 4–72

To Copy the Action Button

The Slide 2 action button is formatted and positioned correctly. You can copy this shape to Slides 3 and 4. The following steps copy the Slide 2 action button to the next two slides in the presentation.

1

- Right-click the action button on Slide 2 to display the shortcut menu (Figure 4–73).

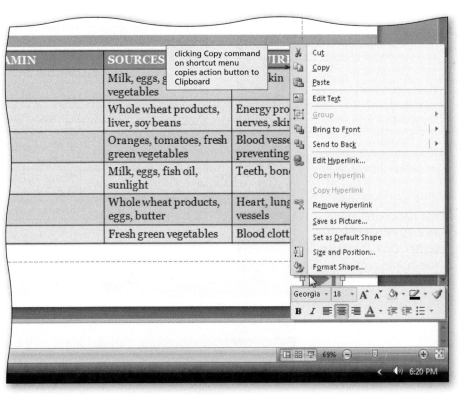

Figure 4–73

- Click Copy on the shortcut menu to copy the action button to the Clipboard.

- Click the Next Slide button to display Slide 3.

- Right-click Slide 3 anywhere except the chart and the title text to display the shortcut menu (Figure 4–74).

Why does my shortcut menu have different commands?

Depending upon where you right-clicked, you might see a different shortcut menu. As long as this menu displays the Paste command, you can use it. If the Paste command is not visible, click the slide again to display another shortcut menu.

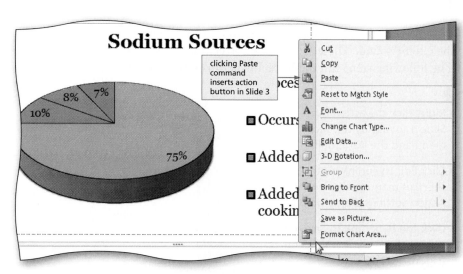

Figure 4–74

- Click Paste on the shortcut menu to paste the action button in the lower-right corner of Slide 3 (Figure 4–75).

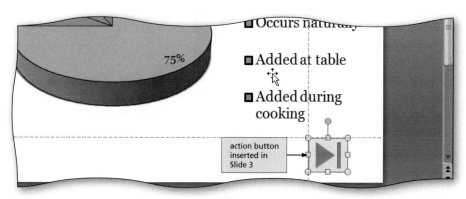

Figure 4–75

- Click the Next Slide button to display Slide 4.

- Right-click Slide 4 anywhere except the body text, title text, and clip to display the shortcut menu.

- Click Paste on the shortcut menu to paste the action button in the lower-right corner of Slide 4 (Figure 4–76).

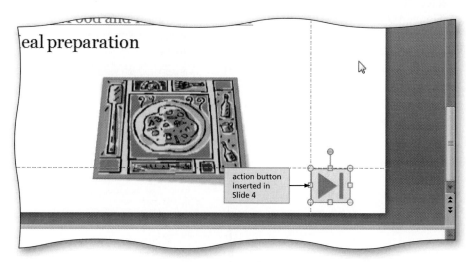

Figure 4–76

To Edit the Action Button Hyperlink Setting

When you copied the action button, PowerPoint retained the settings to hyperlink to the last slide and to play the Chime sound. These settings are correct for Slide 3, but you want the Slide 4 action button to hyperlink to Slide 2. The following steps edit the Slide 4 hyperlink setting to Slide 2.

- Right-click the action button on Slide 4 to display the shortcut menu and the Mini toolbar.

- Click Edit Hyperlink on the shortcut menu to display the Action Settings dialog box.

- Click the Hyperlink to arrow to display the Hyperlink to menu (Figure 4–77).

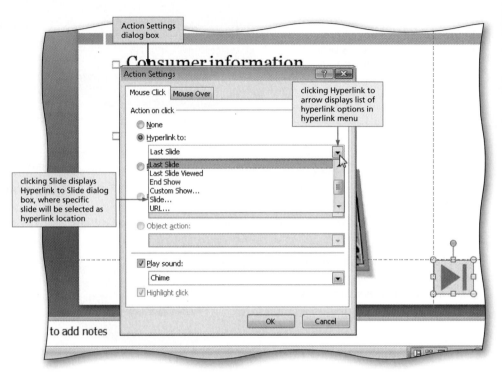

Figure 4–77

- Click Slide on the Hyperlink to menu and then click '2. Essential Vitamins' in the Slide title list to select Slide 2 as the hyperlink (Figure 4–78).

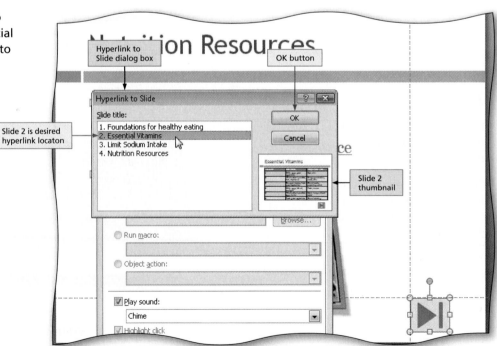

Figure 4–78

3

- Click the OK button in the Hyperlink to Slide dialog box to display the Action Settings dialog box (Figure 4–79).

4

- Click the OK button in the Action Settings dialog box to apply the new hyperlink settings to the Slide 4 action button.

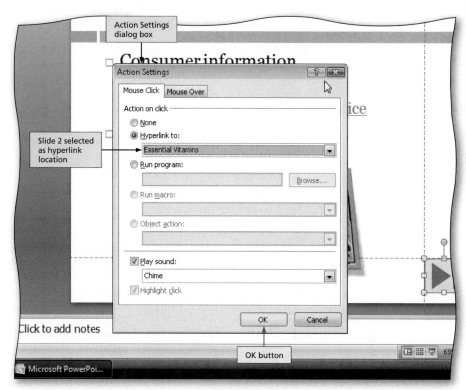

Figure 4–79

To Hide Guides

The three action buttons are copied and formatted, so the guides no longer are needed to display. The following steps hide the guides.

1 Right-click Slide 4 anywhere except the text, clip, or action button to display the shortcut menu.

2 Click Grid and Guides on the shortcut menu and then click the 'Display drawing guides on screen' check box in the Guide settings area so that the box is not selected.

3 Click the OK button to hide the guides.

To Add a Transition between Slides

A final enhancement you will make in this presentation is to apply the Split Vertical Out transition in the Wipes category to all slides and change the transition speed to Slow. The following steps apply this transition to the presentation.

1 Click Animations on the Ribbon to display the Animations tab and then click the More button in the Transition to This Slide group to expand the Transitions gallery.

2 Click the Split Vertical Out transition (row 4, column 6) in the Wipes category in the Transitions gallery to apply this transition to Slide 4.

3 Click the Transition Speed arrow in the Transition to This Slide group and then click Slow to change the transition speed for Slide 4.

4 Click the Apply To All button in the Transition to This Slide group to apply this transition and speed to all four slides in the presentation.

To Change Document Properties and Save the Presentation

Before saving the presentation again, you want to add your name, class name, and some keywords as document properties. The following steps use the Document Information Panel to change document properties and then save the project.

1 Click the Office Button to display the Office Button menu, point to Prepare on the Office Button menu, and then click Properties on the 'Prepare the document for distribution' submenu to display the Document Information Panel.

2 Click the Author text box, if necessary, and then type your name as the Author property. If a name already is displayed in the Author text box, delete it before typing your name.

3 Click the Subject text box, if necessary delete any existing text, and then type your course and section as the Subject property.

4 Click the Keywords text box, if necessary delete any existing text, and then type `nutrition, vitamins, sodium, Web links` as the Keywords property.

5 Click the Close the Document Information Panel button so that the Document Information Panel no longer is displayed.

6 Click the Save button on the Quick Access Toolbar to overwrite the previous Nutrition file on the USB flash drive.

BTW

Certification
The Microsoft Certified Application Specialist (MCAS) program provides an opportunity for you to obtain a valuable industry credential – proof that you have the PowerPoint 2007 skills required by employers. For more information see Appendix G or visit the PowerPoint 2007 Certification Web page (scsite.com/ppt2007/cert).

Running a Slide Show with Hyperlinks and Action Buttons

The Nutrition presentation contains a variety of useful features that provide value to an audience. The vitamin table and the sodium chart graphics should help viewers understand and recall the information being presented. The hyperlinks on Slide 4 show useful Web sites that give current nutritional information. In addition, the action button allows a presenter to jump to Slide 4 while Slides 2 or 3 are being displayed. If an audience member asks a question or if the presenter needs to answer specific questions regarding nutrition, the information on Slide 4 can be accessed immediately by clicking the action button.

To Run a Slide Show with a Hidden Slide and Hyperlinks

Running a slide show that contains hyperlinks is the same as running any other slide show. When a presentation contains hyperlinks and you are connected to the Internet, you can click the hyperlink text to command your default browser to locate the hyperlink file. The following steps run the Nutrition presentation.

1 Click Slide 1 on the Slides tab. Click the Slide Show button to run the slide show and display Slide 1.

2 Press the ENTER key to display Slide 2.

3 Press the ENTER key to display Slide 3.

4 Press the H key to display Slide 4.

5 Click the first hyperlink to start your browser and view The American Society for Nutrition Web page. If necessary, maximize the Web page window when the page is displayed. Click the Close button on the Web page title bar to close the browser.

6 Repeat Step 5 for the second hyperlink.

7 Click the ENTER key twice to display the black slide and then end the slide show.

To Run a Slide Show with Action Buttons

Once you have run the presentation and have seen all slides display, you should run the presentation again to use the action buttons. When you click the action buttons on Slides 2 and 3, PowerPoint will display Slide 4 because you hyperlinked the button to the last slide in the presentation. When Slide 4 is displayed and you view the information and Web sites, you want to return to Slide 2 in the presentation. The following steps run the slide show using the action buttons.

1 Click Slide 1 on the Slides tab, if necessary. Click the Slide Show button to run the slide show, and then display Slide 2.

2 Click the Slide 2 action button to display Slide 4.

3 When Slide 4 is displayed, click the action button to return to Slide 2.

4 Continue advancing through the slide show and using the action buttons until you have viewed all slides in the presentation and then ended the presentation.

BTW

Quick Reference
For a table that lists how to complete the tasks covered in this book using the mouse, Ribbon, shortcut menu, and keyboard, see the Quick Reference Summary at the back of this book, or visit the PowerPoint 2007 Quick Reference Web page (scsite.com/ppt2007/qr).

To Preview and Print Handouts

All changes are complete, and the presentation is saved. You now can create handouts to accompany the slide show. The following steps preview and then print the presentation.

1 Click the Office Button, point to Print, and then click Print Preview on the 'Preview and print the document' submenu.

2 Click the Print What arrow in the Page Setup group and then click Handouts (4 Slides Per Page) in the Print What list.

3 Click the Print button in the Print group.

4 Click the OK button in the Print dialog box to print the handout (Figure 4–80).

5 Click the Close Print Preview button in the Preview group on the Print Preview tab to return to Normal view.

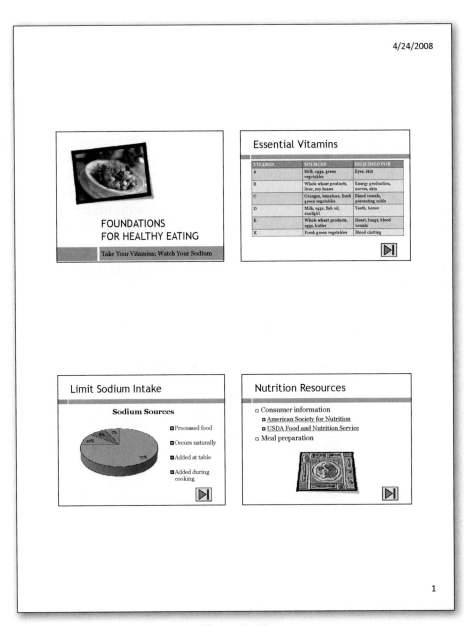

Figure 4–80

To Quit PowerPoint

This project is complete. The following steps quit PowerPoint.

1 Click the Close button on the right side of the title bar to quit PowerPoint.

2 If necessary, click the No button in the Microsoft Office PowerPoint dialog box so that any changes you have made are not saved.

Chapter Summary

In this chapter you have learned how to create and format a table, create a chart, develop a slide with hyperlinks to Web sites containing additional nutritional information, change the entire presentation color scheme and fonts, use the Thesaurus to change slide wording, and insert and format action buttons. The items listed below include all the new PowerPoint skills you have learned in this chapter.

1. Change the Presentation Theme Colors (PPT 232)
2. Change the Theme Fonts (PPT 233)
3. Insert a Picture into a Slide without a Content Placeholder (PPT 234)
4. Apply a Picture Style (PPT 236)
5. Change the Border Color of a Picture (PPT 237)
6. Change a Picture Contrast (PPT 238)
7. Insert a Clip into a Slide without a Content Placeholder (PPT 238)
8. Change the Border Color of a Clip (PPT 241)
9. Change the Brightness of a Clip (PPT 242)
10. Add a Hyperlink to a Slide (PPT 243)
11. Insert an Empty Table (PPT 246)
12. Enter Data in a Table (PPT 248)
13. Apply a Table Style (PPT 249)
14. Add Borders to a Table (PPT 251)
15. Add an Effect to a Table (PPT 252)
16. Insert a Chart (PPT 255)
17. Replace the Sample Data (PPT 257)
18. Apply a Chart Style (PPT 260)
19. Change the Chart Layout (PPT 261)
20. Change the Shape Outline Weight (PPT 262)
21. Change the Shape Outline Color (PPT 263)
22. Change the Title and Legend Font Size (PPT 263)
23. Hide a Slide (PPT 266)
24. Find and Replace Text (PPT 267)
25. Use the Thesaurus (PPT 268)
26. Find a Second Synonym (PPT 270)
27. Insert an Action Button (PPT 271)
28. Size an Action Button (PPT 273)
29. Change the Action Button Fill Color (PPT 273)
30. Position the Action Button Using Guides (PPT 274)
31. Copy the Action Button (PPT 276)
32. Edit the Action Button Hyperlink Settings (PPT 278)
33. Hide Guides (PPT 279)
34. Run a Slide Show with a Hidden Slide and Hyperlinks (PPT 281)
35. Run a Slide Show with Action Buttons (PPT 281)

 If you have a SAM user profile, you may have access to hands-on instruction, practice, and assessment. Log in to your SAM account (http://sam2007.course.com) to launch any assigned training activities or exams that relate to the skills covered in this chapter.

Learn It Online

Test your knowledge of chapter content and key terms.

Instructions: To complete the Learn It Online exercises, start your browser, click the Address bar, and then enter the Web address scsite.com/ppt2007/learn. When the Office 2007 Learn It Online page is displayed, click the link for the exercise you want to complete and then read the instructions.

Chapter Reinforcement TF, MC, and SA
A series of true/false, multiple choice, and short answer questions that test your knowledge of the chapter content.

Flash Cards
An interactive learning environment where you identify chapter key terms associated with displayed definitions.

Practice Test
A series of multiple choice questions that test your knowledge of chapter content and key terms.

Who Wants To Be a Computer Genius?
An interactive game that challenges your knowledge of chapter content in the style of a television quiz show.

Wheel of Terms
An interactive game that challenges your knowledge of chapter key terms in the style of the television show *Wheel of Fortune*.

Crossword Puzzle Challenge
A crossword puzzle that challenges your knowledge of key terms presented in the chapter.

Apply Your Knowledge

Reinforce the skills and apply the concepts you learned in this chapter.

Changing Theme Colors, Applying a Picture Style, Changing a Picture Border and Contrast, and Adding a Hyperlink
Instructions: Start PowerPoint. Open the presentation, Apply 4-1 Oral Hygiene, from the Data Files for Students. See the inside back cover of this book for instructions for downloading the Data Files for Students, or contact your instructor for more information about accessing required files.

The two slides in the presentation present general information about proper oral hygiene. The document you open is an unformatted presentation. You are to select a document theme and change the theme colors, add a style to the pictures on both slides, change the pictures' borders and contrast, and change the Slide 2 text to hyperlinks so the slides look like Figure 4–81.

Perform the following tasks:
1. Add the Solstice document theme and change the presentation theme colors to Flow. Move the subtitle text placeholder upward so that it is positioned under the title text placeholder, as shown in Figure 4–81a.
2. Apply the Reflected Bevel, Black picture style (row 5, column 1) to the Slide 1 picture and the Metal Oval picture style (row 5, column 4) to the Slide 2 picture. Change both picture borders to Bright Green, Accent 4, Lighter 60% (row 3, column 8 in the Theme Colors area). Change the contrast for both photographs to -30%.
3. Display the drawing guides. On Slide 1, set the horizontal guide to .50 above center and the vertical guide to 1.75 left of center. Move the picture so that its upper-left sizing handle aligns with the intersection of the guides. On Slide 2, set the horizontal guide to .08 below center and the vertical guide to 1.50 left of center, and then move the picture so that its upper-left sizing handle aligns with the intersection of the guides. Hide the guides.

4. On Slide 2, create hyperlinks for the two bullets. The American Dental Hygienists' Association bullet should be hyperlinked to adha.org/oralhealth, and the Amercian Dental Association's bullet should be hyperlinked to ada.org.

5. Apply the Wipe Down wipe transition (row 1, column 1) to both slides and change the transition speed to Slow.

6. Check the spelling, and then display the revised presentation in Slide Sorter view to check for consistency.

7. Use your name in place of Student Name in the footer. Change the document properties, as specified by your instructor. Save the presentation using the file name, Apply 4-1 Dental. Submit the revised document in the format specified by your instructor.

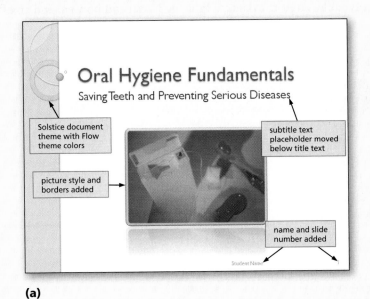

(a)

(b)

Figure 4–81

Extend Your Knowledge

Extend the skills you learned in this chapter and experiment with new skills. You may need to use Help to complete the assignment.

Inserting a Photograph and Creating a Table

Instructions: Start PowerPoint. Open the presentation, Extend 4-1 Animals, from the Data Files for Students. See the inside back cover of this book for instructions for downloading the Data Files for Students, or contact your instructor for more information about accessing required files.

You will add and format a picture on the title slide, add your name and slide number to the Slide 2 footer, insert an empty table, enter the data in Table 4–3, and add borders and an effect (Figure 4–82).

Table 4–3 Animal Longevity and Gestation

Animal	Longevity (Years)	Gestation (Days)
Hamster	2	14-17
Guinea Pig	3	58-75
Kangaroo	4-6	32-39
Rabbit	6-8	30-35
Parakeet	8	17-20
Horse	20-25	329-345
Hippopotamus	30	220-255

Perform the following tasks:

1. Add the Verve document theme and change the presentation theme colors to Origin. Change the theme font to Foundry.

2. Insert the Horses photograph from the Data Files for Students into Slide 1. Apply a picture style similar to the one shown in Figure 4–82a and a Glow picture effect. Change the border color and reduce the picture contrast.

3. In Slide 2, add the slide number and your name to the footer. Insert an empty table and enter the data shown in Table 4–2. Apply a table style and add borders around the outside of the table. Add a shadow effect from the Perspective category.

4. Center all text in the table by selecting all cells and then clicking the Center button in the Paragraph group on the Home tab.

5. Apply a transition to all slides.

6. Change the document properties, as specified by your instructor. Save the presentation using the file name, Extend 4-1 Revised Animals.

7. Submit the revised document in the format specified by your instructor.

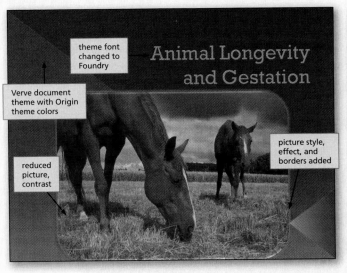

(a)

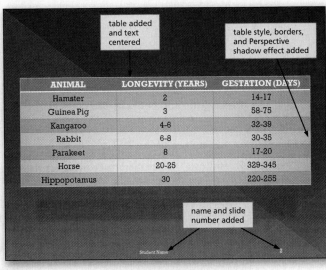

(b)

Figure 4–82

Make It Right

Analyze a presentation and correct all errors and/or improve the design.

Modifying a Table and Clips

Instructions: Start PowerPoint. Open the presentation, Make It Right 4-1 Birthstones, from the Data Files for Students. See the inside back cover of this book for instructions for downloading the Data Files for Students, or contact your instructor for more information about accessing required files.

Correct the formatting problems and errors in the presentation while keeping in mind the guidelines presented in this chapter.

Perform the following tasks:

1. Change the theme font to Origin. Increase the size of both gem clips at the top of the slide to 160% by right-clicking a clip, clicking Size and Position on the shortcut menu, changing the Height text box value in the Scale area to 160, and then clicking the Close button in the Size and Position dialog box. Rotate the right clip 90 degrees to the right. Apply the 25 Point Soft Edges picture effect to both gem photographs.

2. Display the drawing guides and set the horizontal guide to 4.75 above center and the vertical guide to 3.50 left of center. Move the left gem picture so that its upper-left corner aligns with the intersection of the guides. Set the vertical guide to 3.50 right of center and move the right gem picture so that its upper-right corner aligns with the intersection of the guides.

3. Replace the words, Student Name, in the text box with your name. Set the horizontal guide to 4.25 below center and the vertical guide to 3.50 left of center. Move the text box so that its upper-left corner aligns with the intersection of the guides.

4. Select the table and then apply the Medium Style 3 - Accent 1 table style (row 3, column 2 in the Medium area). Add borders to all table elements. Delete the empty rightmost column by right-clicking that column and then clicking Delete Columns on the shortcut menu. Set the horizontal guide to 3.00 above center and the vertical guide to 2.25 left of center. Move the table so that its upper-left corner aligns with the intersection of the guides. Hide the guides.

Continued >

Make It Right *continued*

5. Add a row for April by right-clicking either cell in the March row, pointing to Insert on the shortcut menu, and then clicking Insert Rows Below. Add the word, April, in the new left cell and the word, Diamond, in the new right cell. Add a row for September and add the gemstone Sapphire.

6. Use the spell checker to correct the misspellings.

7. Change the document properties, as specified by your instructor. Save the presentation using the file name, Make It Right 4-1 Gems.

8. Submit the revised document in the format specified by your instructor.

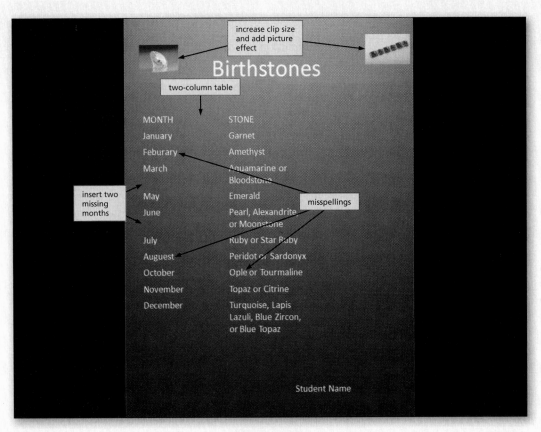

Figure 4–83

In the Lab

Design and/or create a presentation using the guidelines, concepts, and skills presented in this chapter. Labs 1, 2, and 3 are listed in order of increasing difficulty.

Lab 1: Inserting and Formatting a Clip and Chart

Problem: More than 50 million people travel throughout the United States each year to view natural land formations. Whether they trek to Niagara Falls, the rolling countrysides, the fertile plains, the lush forests, or the vast deserts, the country's physical features provide a variety of sights. You have been studying this country in your geography class and decide to begin a PowerPoint presentation with a clip of the United States and a chart of the land types. You insert this clip on Slide 1, create a chart on Slide 2 using the data in Table 4–4, and then modify these information graphics to enhance the visual message to create the slides shown in Figure 4–84 from a blank presentation.

Perform the following tasks.

1. Create a new presentation using the Technic document theme, and then change the presentation theme colors to Concourse. Delete the Slide 1 subtitle placeholder, type the slide title text shown in Figure 4–84a, and insert the United States clip from the Data Files for Students. Adjust the clip size and then add a text box with your name on the United States clip.

Table 4–4 U.S. Land Types	
Type	**Percent**
Forest	37.5
Farmland	29.5
Desert	12
Grassland	9.5
Tundra	5
Barren	3.5
Wetland	2.5
Built-up	.5

2. Apply the Bevel Perspective Left, White picture style (row 4, column 6) to the clip and change the border to Blue, Accent 4 (row 1, column 8 in the Theme Colors area). Apply the Accent color 2, 11 pt glow (row 3, column 2) glow variation picture effect, and change the brightness to -20%. Size and position the clip as shown in Figure 4–84a.

3. Insert a new slide and delete the title text placeholder. Create the chart shown in Figure 4–84b using the 'Exploded pie in 3-D' chart style. Use the data from Table 4–4. After you have replaced the sample data, you may need to drag the lower-right corner of the blue Excel box downward to select all the cells and consequently resize the chart data range.

4. Apply the Style 10 (row 2, column 2) chart style, increase the line weight to 2¼ pt, and change the line color to Blue. Change the chart layout to Layout 5. Increase the chart title font size to 24 and change the font color to Turquoise, Accent 1 (row 1, column 5 in the Theme Colors area).

5. Apply the Shape Circle wipe transition (row 5, column 5) and change the speed to Medium for both slides.

6. Change the document properties, as specified by your instructor. Save the presentation using the file name, Lab 4-1 United States Land.

7. Submit the revised document in the format specified by your instructor.

In the Lab *continued*

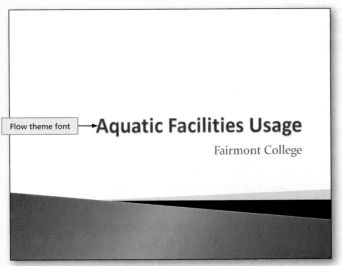

(a)

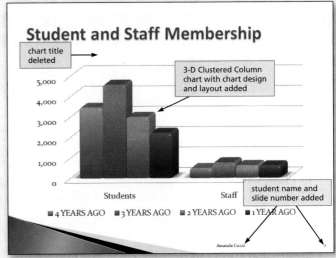

(b)

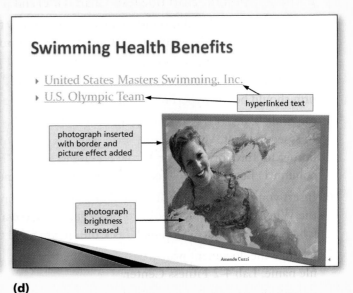

(c)

(d)

Figure 4–85

In the Lab

Lab 3: Creating a Presentation with Action Buttons and a Hidden Slide

Problem: Your public speaking instructor has assigned an informative speech, and you have decided to discuss orchestra instruments. You create the presentation in Figure 4–86 that consists of six slides and decide to hide one slide in case your speech runs longer than expected. The table on Slide 2 contains hyperlinks to Slides 3, 4, 5, and 6, and those slides contain hyperlinks to Slide 2.

Perform the following tasks.

1. Create a new presentation using the Civic document theme, and then change the theme font and the theme colors to Metro. Using Figure 4–86, create the six core presentation slides by typing the Slide 1 title and subtitle text, the Slide 2 title text, and the Slide 3, 4, 5, and 6 title and body text. Apply the Two Content layout to Slides 3 – 6

2. On Slide 2, create the table shown in Figure 4–86b. Apply the Dark Style 2 – Accent 1/Accent 2 table style (row 2, column 2 in the Dark area) and the Inside Diagonal Bottom Left Inner shadow (row 3, column 1 in the Inner area).

3. Insert the pictures from your Data Files for Students on all slides. Apply the 10 Point Soft Edges picture effect to each picture.

4. Insert a Sound action button to the right of each category on Slide 2. Hyperlink each button to the corresponding slide. For example, the Strings action button should hyperlink to Slide 3. Play the Push sound when the Strings button is clicked, the Wind sound for the Woodwind button, the Breeze sound for the Brass button, and the Drum Roll for the Percussion button. Size the buttons to fit in each table row and change the fill color to Turquoise, Accent 4 (row 1, column 8 in the Theme Colors area).

5. Insert a Back or Previous action button in the lower-left corner of Slides 3 – 6, and hyperlink the buttons to Slide 2. Change the action button fill color to Pink, Accent 2, Lighter 40% (row 4, column 6 in the Theme Colors area). Do not play a sound. Size and move the buttons as shown in Figures 4–86c through 4–86f.

6. Use the thesaurus to find a synonym for the word, Category, in the Slide 2 table. Hide Slide 2.

7. Insert the slide number in all slides except the title slide. Apply the Uncover Right-Up transition (row 3, column 1 in the Wipes category) to all slides. Change the speed to Medium. Check the spelling and correct any errors.

8. Click the Slide Sorter view button, view the slides for consistency, and then click the Normal view button.

9. Change the document properties, as specified by your instructor. Save the presentation using the file name, Lab 4-3 Orchestra Instruments.

10. Submit the revised document in the format specified by your instructor.

Continued >

STUDENT ASSIGNMENTS

In the Lab *continued*

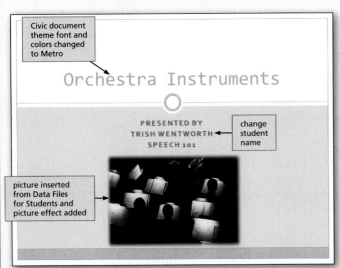

Civic document theme font and colors changed to Metro

change student name

picture inserted from Data Files for Students and picture effect added

(a)

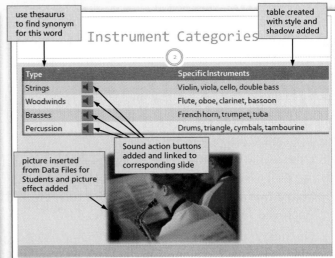

use thesaurus to find synonym for this word

table created with style and shadow added

Sound action buttons added and linked to corresponding slide

picture inserted from Data Files for Students and picture effect added

(b)

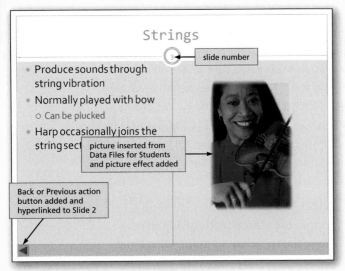

slide number

picture inserted from Data Files for Students and picture effect added

Back or Previous action button added and hyperlinked to Slide 2

(c)

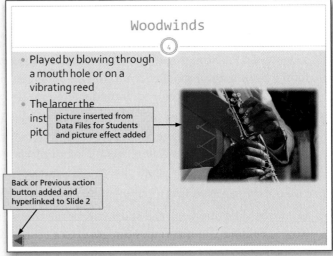

picture inserted from Data Files for Students and picture effect added

Back or Previous action button added and hyperlinked to Slide 2

(d)

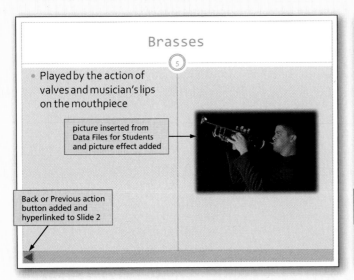

picture inserted from Data Files for Students and picture effect added

Back or Previous action button added and hyperlinked to Slide 2

(e)

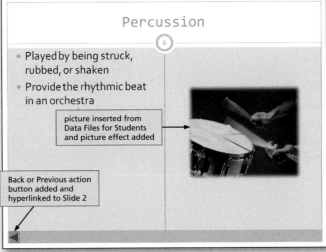

picture inserted from Data Files for Students and picture effect added

Back or Previous action button added and hyperlinked to Slide 2

(f)

Figure 4–86

Cases and Places

Apply your creative thinking and problem solving skills to design and implement a solution.

• EASIER   •• MORE DIFFICULT

Note: Remember to use the 7 × 7 rule as you design the presentations: a maximum of seven words on a line and a maximum of seven lines on one slide.

• 1: Design and Create an English Dialects Presentation

Much of the world speaks English as a primary language, but the grammar—vocabulary and pronunciation, or dialect—varies greatly. Linguists study the nature and structure of speech and focus on how language varies among countries and different regions within each country. Members of the American Dialect Society (www.americandialect.org) study English language use among people living in North America. They analyze how other languages influence English-speaking North Americans and how, in turn, North Americans influence speakers of other languages. Dialect numbers among native English speakers in America, Britain, Canada, and Australia are shown in Table 4–6.

Using the information in Table 4–6 create a chart and a hyperlink to the American Dialect Society as part of a presentation on dialects. Apply at least three objectives found at the beginning of this chapter to develop the presentation. Add a title slide with at least one clip to which you add an effect. Be sure to check spelling.

Table 4–6 English Dialects

Native Speakers	Number of Dialects
American	226,710
British	156,990
Canadian	19,700
Australian	15,316
Other	18,581

• 2: Design and Create a Gods and Goddesses Presentation

People have worshipped gods and goddesses since prehistoric times, thinking these spirits affect the destinies of humans and nature. These deities are believed to control forces beyond human power, and the rituals associated with worshipping them have held societies together. Some of these figures resemble humans, while others have part-human or part-animal forms. Many of the Roman gods are equivalent to earlier Greek versions, and their names and roles are listed in Table 4–7. Create a presentation about gods and goddesses, and include a table with the data in Table 4–7. Apply a table style and borders. Use clips from the Clip Organizer and add effects. Apply slide transitions and a footer with page numbers and your name on all slides. Be sure to check spelling.

Table 4–7 Gods and Goddesses

Role	Greek Name	Roman Name
Goddess of love	Aphrodite	Venus
God of the arts and medicine	Apollo	Apollo
God of war	Ares	Mars
God of travel, roads, and trade	Hermes	Mercury
God of the sea	Poseidon	Neptune
Ruler of the gods	Zeus	Jupiter

•• 3: Design and Create a Body Mass Index Presentation

The body mass index (BMI) is a tool used in assessing an individual's ideal weight. To calculate a person's BMI, multiply his height in inches by his height in inches and then divide that number into his weight. Multiply the result of that computation by 703. Compare the final number to the BMI Classification Table 4–8 to determine if he is healthy, overweight, obese, or very obese. Your campus fitness center director has asked you to prepare a presentation showing the formula, the data in Table 4–8, sample BMIs using a person with a height of 5' 7" and weights of 100, 125, 150, 175, and 200 pounds, and hyperlinks to the American Heart Organization and the National Institutes of Health Web sites. Create this slide show, and hide the BMI example slide. Use an action button to jump from the BMI formula slide to the slide containing the BMI classification table and a second action button to return to the formula slide from the table slide. Use at least one formatted clip from the Clip Organizer, apply a slide transition to all slides, and insert your name in a footer on all slides.

Table 4–8 Body Mass Index		
Range	**Condition**	**Risk Classification**
19 to 24.9	Healthy weight	Desirable
25 t0 29.9	Overweight	Borderline high
30 to 39.9	Obese	High
40 to 54	Very obese	Very high

•• 4 Design and Create an Energy Drinks Presentation

Make It Personal

Energy drinks are a popular alternative to coffee and caffeinated beverages. In this $4 billion industry, some energy drinks have up to four times the caffeine contained in popular colas. Visit your local grocery store and compare the ingredients in at least three different energy drinks, including the ones you or your friends drink regularly. Compare price, serving size, calories, sodium, carbohydrates, niacin, and B-group vitamins. Then read articles or search the Internet to find nutrition experts' reviews and opinions of these drinks' taste and effect. Then use the concepts and techniques presented in this chapter to develop and format a slide show reporting your findings. Include a formatted table comparing the energy drinks. Enhance the presentation with at least one formatted clip. Include hyperlinks to three of the drinks' Web sites. Be sure to check spelling. Print a handout with two slides on each page.

•• 5: Design and Create a Staging Presentation

Working Together

Homeowners attempting to sell their homes are turning to Staging, a trademarked term of Stagedhomes.com. Stagers prepare a home for sale by rearranging furniture, removing clutter, and accentuating the house's positive features. Have each member of your team call or visit a local Stager or conduct online research and gather information about how long the average staged home remains on the market compared to a non-staged home. Also find out the average increase in sale price between a staged and non-staged home. After coordinating the data, create a presentation with charts showing both these sets of statistics. As a group, critique each slide. Submit your assignment in the format specified by your instructor.

Collaboration Feature

Collaborating on and Delivering Presentations

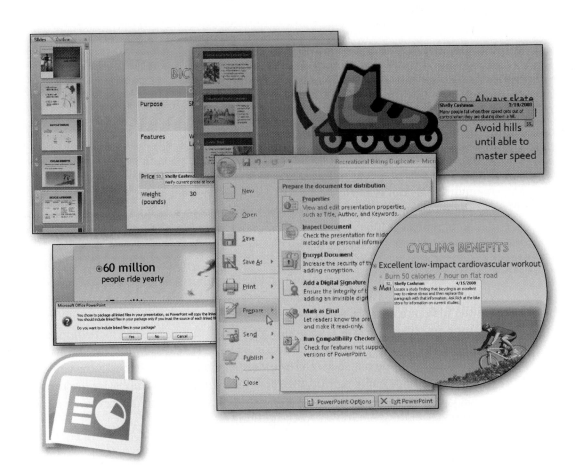

Objectives

You will have mastered the material in this Collaboration feature when you can:

- Insert, delete, and modify comments
- Inspect and protect files
- Compress files and mark them as final
- Create a digital signature
- Save files as a PowerPoint show
- Run shows with pens and highlighters
- Package presentations for a CD

Collaboration Feature Introduction

Often presentations are enhanced when individuals collaborate to fine-tune text, visuals, and design elements on the slides. A **review cycle** occurs when a slide show designer e-mails a file to multiple reviewers so they can make comments and changes to their copies of the slides and then return the file to the designer. The designer then can display the comments, modify their content and ask the reviewers to again review the presentation, and continue this process until the slides are satisfactory. Once the presentation is complete, the designer can protect the file so no one can open it without a password, remove comments and other information, and assure that it is authentic. The designer also can compress the overall file size and then save the presentation to a compact disc. In addition, a presenter can use PowerPoint's variety of tools to run the show effectively and emphasize various elements on the screen.

Project — Presentation with Comments, Protection, and Authentication

The six slides in the Recreational Biking presentation (Figure 1) give specific information about the sport, including statistics about who is riding, the history of the bicycles, and the benefits of participating in this activity. When you are developing a presentation, it often is advantageous to ask a variety of people to review your work in progress. These individuals can evaluate the wording, art, and design, and experts in the subject can check the slides for accuracy. They can add comments to the slides in specific areas, such as a paragraph, a graphic, or a table. You then can review their comments and use them to modify and enhance your work.

Once you develop the final set of slides, you can finalize the file by removing any comments and personal information, compressing the file size to aid in e-mailing and posting to a Web site, adding a password so that unauthorized people cannot see the file contents without your permission, saving the file as a PowerPoint show so it runs automatically when you open a file, and saving the file to a compact disc.

When running your presentation, you may decide to show the slides nonsequentially. For example, you may need to review a slide you discussed already, or you may want to skip some slide and jump forward. You also may want to emphasize, or **annotate**, material on the slides by highlighting text or writing on the slides. You can save your annotations to review during or after the presentation.

Overview

As you read through this chapter, you will learn how to use PowerPoint's commenting feature and presentation tools shown in Figure 1 by performing these general tasks:

- Review a presentation.
- Protect a presentation.
- Secure and share a presentation.
- Use presentation tools.
- Package presentations for a CD.

(a) Slide 1

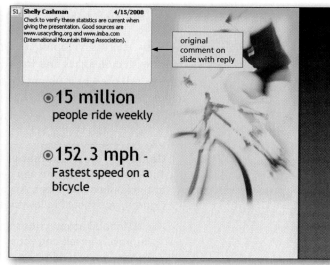

(b) Slide 2

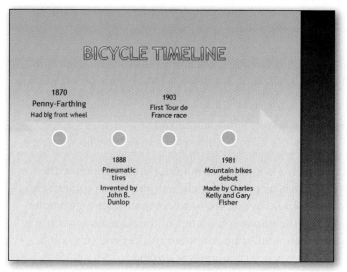

(c) Slide 3

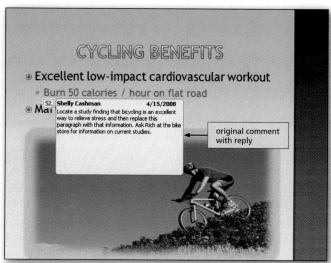

(d) Slide 4

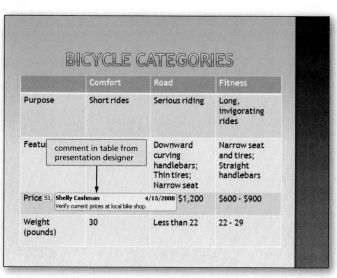

(e) Slide 5

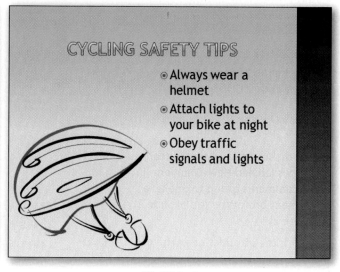

(f) Slide 6

Figure 1

Collaborating on a Presentation

When you are developing a presentation, it often is beneficial to share your ideas and work with colleagues and friends. These people can offer suggestions on how to enhance the overall presentation and specific slide elements. While adding this step to the development process increases the overall creation time, the end result most often is worth the effort. PowerPoint makes it easy to insert, review, modify, and delete comments.

Plan Ahead

General Project Guidelines

The actions you perform and decisions you make will affect the appearance and characteristics of the finished document. As you collaborate on a presentation, such as the project shown in Figure 1, you should follow these general guidelines:

1. **Ask for and accept criticism.** Feedback, both positive and negative, that enables you to improve yourself and your work, is called **criticism**. Written and oral comments from others can help reinforce the positive aspects and also identify the flaws. Seek comments from a variety of people who genuinely want to help you develop an effective slide show.

2. **Select an appropriate password.** A **password** is a private combination of characters that allows users to open a file. To prevent unauthorized people from viewing your slides, choose a good password and keep it confidential.

   When necessary, more specific details concerning the above guidelines are presented at appropriate points in the feature. The feature also will identify the actions you perform and decisions you made regarding these guidelines during the creation of the presentation shown in Figure 1.

To Insert a Comment

To prepare a presentation for review, you might want to insert a comment containing information for the reviewers. A **comment** is a description that normally does not display as part of the slide show. The comment can be used to clarify information that may be difficult to understand, to pose questions, or to communicate suggestions. PowerPoint adds a small rectangle, called a **comment marker**, to the upper-left corner of the slide along with a **comment box**, which is the area where you write or review the comment. The comment marker and box colors change depending upon your computer's settings. The following steps insert comments on Slides 2, 4, and 5.

- Start PowerPoint and then open the presentation, Recreational Biking, from the Data Files for Students.

- Click the Next Slide button to display Slide 2.

- Click Review on the Ribbon to display the Review tab.

- Click the Insert Comment button, which is labeled New Comment, in the Comments group to display a comment box at the top of Slide 2 (Figure 2).

Q&A

What is the information at the top at the comment box?

PowerPoint inserts the system date and the user's name that was entered when Microsoft Office 2007 was installed.

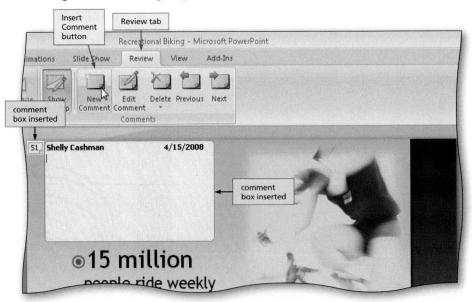

Figure 2

2

- **Type** Check to verify these statistics are current when giving the presentation. in the comment box (Figure 3).

Can I change the initials and name that display in the comment box and comment marker?

Yes. Click the Office Button, click PowerPoint Options, click Popular, and then change the information. When you are finished, click the OK button.

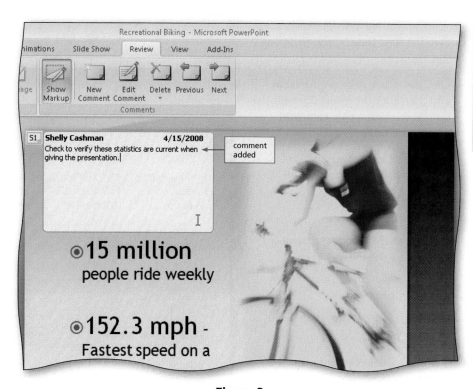

Figure 3

3

- Click anywhere outside the comment box to close the comment box.

- Click the Next Slide button twice to display Slide 4.

- Click after the second bullet and then click the Insert Comment button to display a comment box to the right of the bullet.

- **Type** Locate a study finding that bicycling is an excellent way to relieve stress and then replace this paragraph with that information. in the comment box (Figure 4).

Can I insert more than one comment on a slide?

Yes. Add the comments wherever they point out positive or negative slide elements.

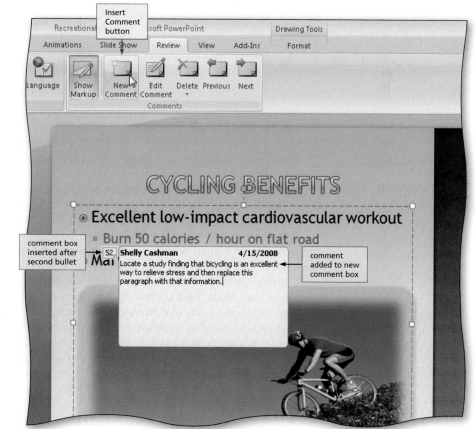

Figure 4

4

- Click anywhere outside the comment box to close the comment box.

- Click the Next Slide button to display Slide 5.

- Click the word, Price, in the table and then click the Insert Comment button to open a new comment box on the table.

- Type `Verify current prices at local bike shop.` in the comment box (Figure 5).

5

- Click anywhere outside the comment box to close the comment box.

Q&A Will the comments display if I run a presentation?

No. The comments are visible only in Normal view.

Q&A Will the comments display if I print a presentation?

Yes. If you do not want them to print, you can turn off this default setting by clearing the 'Print comments and ink markup' check box in the Print dialog box.

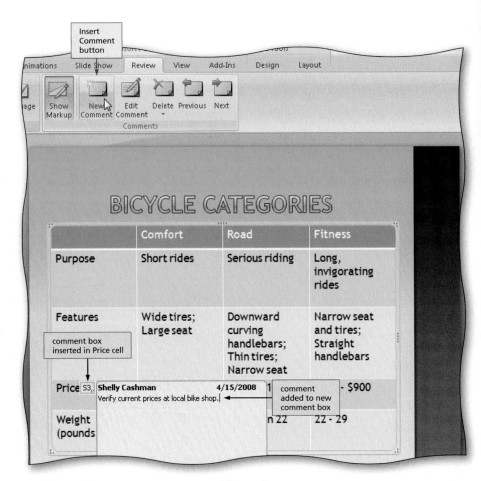

Figure 5

Plan Ahead

Ask for and accept criticism.

Receiving feedback from others ultimately should enhance your presentation. If several of your reviewers make similar comments, such as too much text appears on one slide or that a chart would help present your concept, then you should heed their criticism and modify your slides. Criticism from a variety of people, particularly if they are from different cultures or vary in age, gives a wide range of viewpoints. Some reviewers might focus on the font size, others on color and design choices, while others might single out the overall message. These individuals should make judgments on your work, such as saying that the overall presentation is good or that a particular paragraph is confusing, and then offer reasons of what elements are effective or how you can edit a paragraph.

When you receive these comments, do not get defensive. Ask yourself why your reviewers would have made these comments. Perhaps they lack a background in the subject matter. Or they may have a particular interest in this topic and can add their expertise.

If you are asked to critique a presentation, begin and end with positive comments. Give specific details about a few key areas that can be improved. Be honest, but be tactful. Avoid using the word, you. For example, instead of writing, "You need to give some statistics to support your viewpoint," write "I had difficulty understanding which departments' sales have declined in the past five months. Perhaps a chart with specific losses would help depict how dramatically revenues have fallen."

To Modify a Comment

Once a comment is added to a slide, you can review the wording and then edit the text or add more material. The following steps edit the comments on Slides 2 and 4.

1

- Display Slide 2 and then click the comment marker to display the comment on Slide 2.

- Click the Edit Comment button in the Comments group to open the comment box.

- At the end of the current text type Good sources are www.usacycling.org and www.imba.com (International Mountain Bicycling Association). in the comment box (Figure 6).

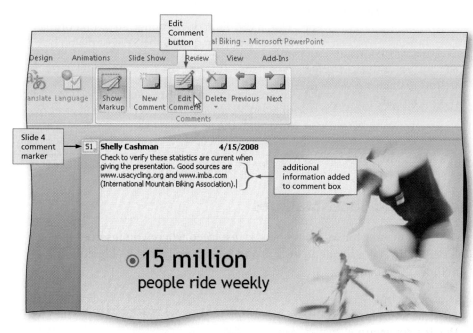

Figure 6

2

- Click the Next Comment button, which is labeled Next, in the Comments group to display the comment on Slide 4.

- Click the Edit Comment button and then type Ask Rich at the bike store for information on current studies. in the comment box (Figure 7).

Q&A

Can I move a comment on a slide?

Yes. Drag the comment marker to the desired location on the same slide.

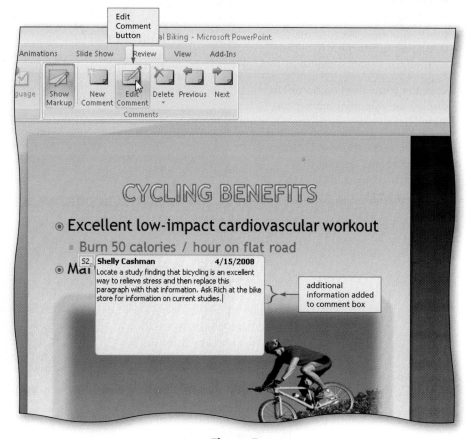

Figure 7

Other Ways

1. Right-click comment marker, click Edit Comment on shortcut menu

To Save the Presentation

You added comments to three slides. The next step is to save the presentation.

Note: If you are using Windows XP, see Appendix F for alternate steps.

1 With a USB flash drive connected to one of the computer's USB ports, click the Office Button and then display the Save As dialog box.

2 Type `Recreational Biking Revised` in the File name text box to change the file name.

3 Click Computer in the Favorite Links section, double-click your USB flash drive in the list of available drives, and then click the Save button to save the document on the USB flash drive with the new file name.

To Hide and Show Markups

The marker for each comment is displayed where you inserted it when you open the presentation. The Show Markup button is a toggle to display and hide these markers. The following steps hide and then show the markups on Slides 2, 4, and 5.

1
- Click the Show Markup button in the Comments group to hide the comment on Slide 4 (Figure 8).

2
- Display Slide 5 to view the slide with no comments showing.

- Click the Show Markup button to display the comment marker on Slide 5.

- Click the Next Comment button, which is labeled Next, in the Comments group to display the Slide 2 comment.

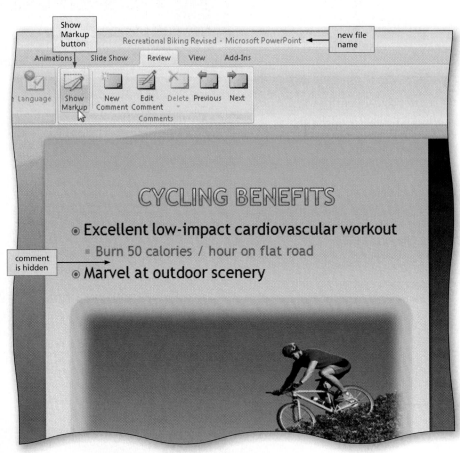

Figure 8

To Delete a Comment

If a particular comment no longer is useful, you should delete it from the slide. The following step deletes the comment from the Slide 2 table.

1

- With Slide 2 displayed, click the Delete Comment button in the Comments group to delete the comment (Figure 9).

Q&A

What options will I have if I click the Delete button arrow?

You can choose to delete just a selected comment, all comments on the current slide, or all comments in the presentation.

Figure 9

Protecting, Securing, and Sharing a Presentation

When your slides are complete, you can perform additional functions to finalize the file and prepare it for distributing to other users or running on a computer other than the one used to develop the file. For example, the Compatibility Checker reviews the file for any feature that will not work properly or display on computers running a previous PowerPoint version. In addition, the Document Inspector locates inappropriate information, such as comments, in a file and allows you to delete these slide elements. You also can reduce the overall file size to simplify sending the file as an e-mail attachment or posting to a Web page. With passwords and digital signatures, you add security levels to protect people from distributing, viewing, or modifying your slides. When the review process is complete, you can indicate this file is the final version. You also can save the file as a PowerPoint show so that it runs automatically when opened.

To Identify Presentation Features Not Supported by Previous Versions

PowerPoint 2007 has many new features not found in previous versions of PowerPoint. For example, WordArt formatted with Quick Styles is an enhancement found only in this current software. If you give your file to people who have a previous PowerPoint version installed on their computers, they will be able to open the file but may not be able to see or edit some special features and effects. You can use the **Compatibility Checker** to see which presentation elements will not function in earlier versions of PowerPoint. The following steps run the Compatibility Checker and display a summary of the elements in your Recreational Biking presentation that will be lost if your file is opened in an earlier PowerPoint version.

- Click the Office Button and then point to Prepare on the Office Button menu to display the Prepare submenu (Figure 10).

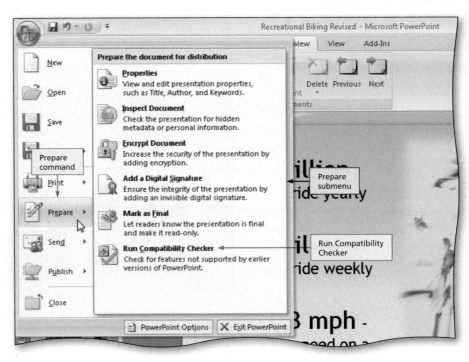

Figure 10

- Click Run Compatibility Checker to open the Microsoft Office PowerPoint Compatibility Checker dialog box.

- View the comments in the Summary area regarding the two features that are not supported by earlier versions of PowerPoint (Figure 11).

Q&A Why do the numbers 5 and 1 display in the right side of the Summary area?

The Compatibility Checker found five shapes in your presentation that cannot be edited in previous versions. These graphics will be converted to bitmap images in older versions, so they cannot be ungrouped and modified.

Q&A What happens if I click the Help links in the Summary area?

PowerPoint will provide additional information about the particular incompatible slide element.

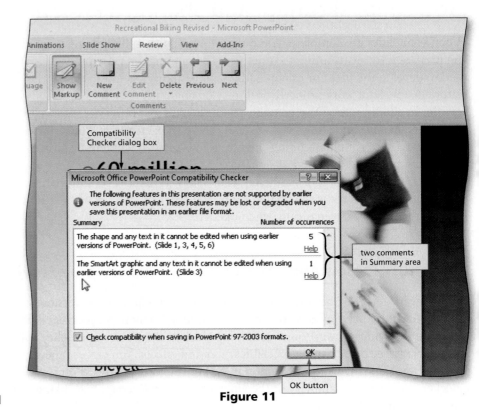

Figure 11

- Click the OK button to close the Microsoft Office PowerPoint Compatibility Checker dialog box.

To Remove Inappropriate Information

As you work on your presentation, you might add information meant only for you to see. For example, you might write comments to yourself or put confidential information in the Document Information Panel. You would not want other people to access this information if you give a copy of the presentation file to them. The Document Inspector provides a quick and efficient method of searching for and deleting inappropriate information.

If you tell the Document Inspector to delete content, such as personal information, comments, invisible slide content, or notes, and then decide you need to see those slide elements, quite possibly you will be unable to retrieve the information by using the Undo command. For that reason, it is a good idea to make a duplicate copy of your file and then inspect this new second copy. The following steps save a duplicate copy of your Recreational Biking presentation, run the Document Inspector on this new file, and then delete comments.

1

- Click the Office Button, point to Save As on the Office Button menu, and then click PowerPoint presentation.

- Type Recreational Biking Duplicate in the File name text box and then click the Save button to change the file name and save another copy of this presentation.

- Click the Office Button and then point to Prepare on the Office Button menu (Figure 12).

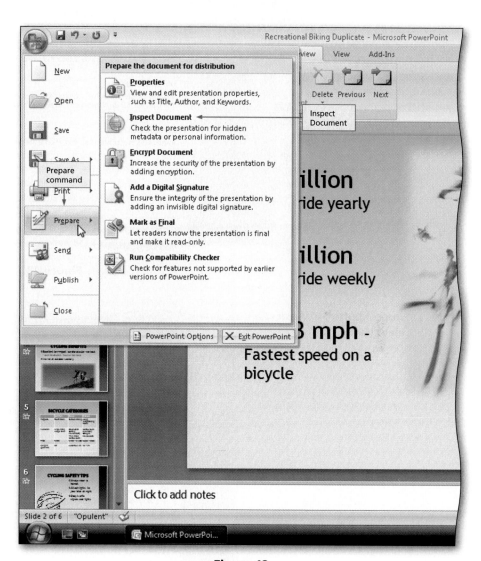

Figure 12

● Click Inspect
Document in the
Prepare submenu to
display the Document
Inspector dialog box
(Figure 13).

Q&A What information
does the Document
Inspector check?

This information
includes text in
the Document
Information Panel,
such as your name
and company. Other
information includes
details of when the
file was last saved,
objects formatted as
invisible, graphics and
text you dragged off
a slide, presentation
notes, and e-mail
headers.

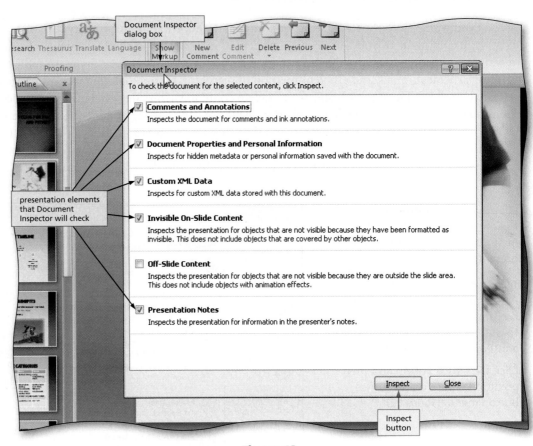

Figure 13

● Click the Inspect button to check
the document (Figure 14).

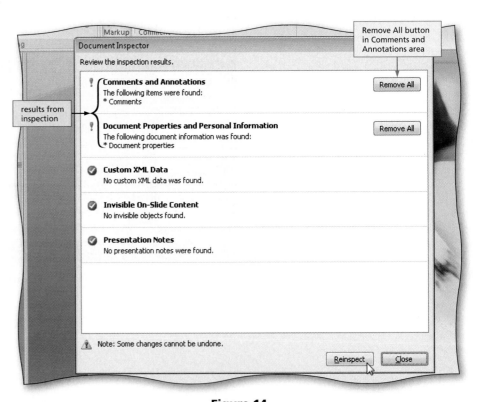

Figure 14

4

- When the inspection report is displayed, click the Remove All button in the Comments and Annotations area to remove the comments from the presentation (Figure 15).

Should I also remove the document properties and personal information?

You might want to delete this information so that no identifying information is saved. This information includes text that displays in the Document Information Panel, such as your name and company, and also comments and other hidden data.

5

- Click the Close button to close the Document Inspector dialog box.

Figure 15

Plan Ahead	**Select an appropriate password.**
	A password should be at least six characters and contain a combination of letters and numbers. Using both uppercase and lowercase letters is advised. Do not use a password that someone could guess, such as your first or last name, spouse's or child's name, telephone number, birth date, street address, license plate number, or Social Security number.
	Once you develop this password, write it down in a secure place. Underneath your keyboard is not a secure place, nor is your middle desk drawer.

To Set a Password

You can protect your slide content on CDs by using passwords on all packaged presentations. The passwords specify whether a user can look at or modify a file. The following steps set a password for the Recreational Biking Duplicate file.

1

• Click the Office Button and click Save As on the Office Button menu to display the Save As dialog box.

• Click the Tools button to display the Tools menu (Figure 16).

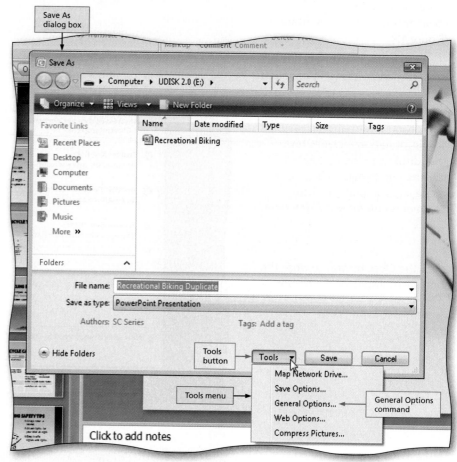

Figure 16

2

• Click General Options in the Tools menu to display the General Options dialog box.

• Type Biking4me in the 'Password to open' text box (Figure 17).

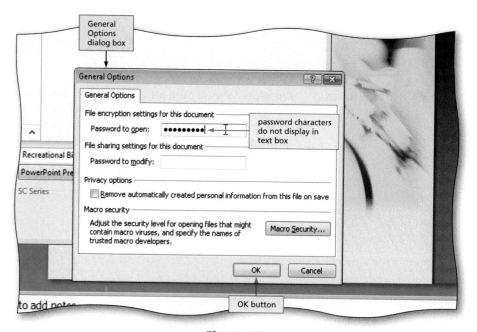

Figure 17

3

- Click the OK button to display the Confirm Password dialog box.

- Type `Biking4me` in the 'Reenter password to open' text box (Figure 18).

Q&A What if I forget my password?

You will not be able to open your file. For security reasons, Microsoft or other companies cannot retrieve a lost password.

4

- Click the OK button in the Confirm Password dialog box.

- Click the Save button in the Save As dialog box to add the password to the document.

- Click the Yes button in the Confirm Save As dialog box to replace the existing presentation.

Q&A When does the password take effect?

You will need to enter your password the next time you open your presentation.

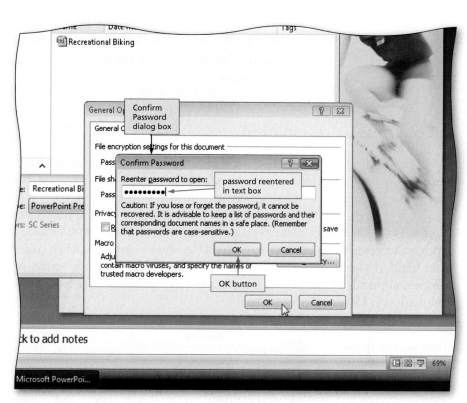

Figure 18

To Open a Presentation with a Password

To open a file that has been protected with a password, you would perform the following steps.

1. Click the Office Button and then click Open on the Office Button menu.

2. Locate the desired file and then click the Open button to display the Password dialog box.

3. When the Password dialog box appears, type the password in the Password text box and then click the OK button to display the presentation.

To Change the Password or Remove Password Protection

To change a password that you added to a file or to remove all password protection from the file, you would perform the following steps.

1. Click the Office Button and then click Open on the Office Button menu.

2. Locate the desired file and then click the Open button to display the Password dialog box.

3. When the Password dialog box appears, type the password in the Password text box and then click the OK button to display the presentation.

4. Click the Office Button and then click Save As to display the Save As dialog box. Click the Tools button and then click General Options in the Tools list.

5. Select the contents of the 'Password to modify' text box or the 'Password to open' text box. To change the password, type the new password and then click the OK button. When prompted, retype your password to reconfirm it, and then click the OK button.

6. Click the OK button, click the Save button, and then click the Yes button to resave the presentation.

To Compress a Presentation

PowerPoint file sizes can become quite large, especially if the slides contain many photographs and graphical elements. To reduce the file size, you can **compress** one or more pictures. When you compress a picture, however, some of the image's resolution or clarity may be lost. PowerPoint gives you options to decide on a particular amount of compression. The compression options are measured in **pixels per inch (ppi)**. A pixel, short for picture element, is the smallest element in an electronic image. A resolution's image quality improves when the number of pixels increases. If your presentation will be shown only on a Web page, the resolution can be low. On the other hand, if you are going to project your presentation on a large screen in a conference room, compression is not recommended because your images might appear blurry. The following steps compress all pictures in your presentation to 150 pixels per inch (ppi).

- Display Slide 4 and then click the bicycle picture to select it.

- Click Format on the Ribbon to display the Format tab under Picture Tools.

- Click the Compress Pictures button in the Adjust group to display the Compress Pictures dialog box (Figure 19).

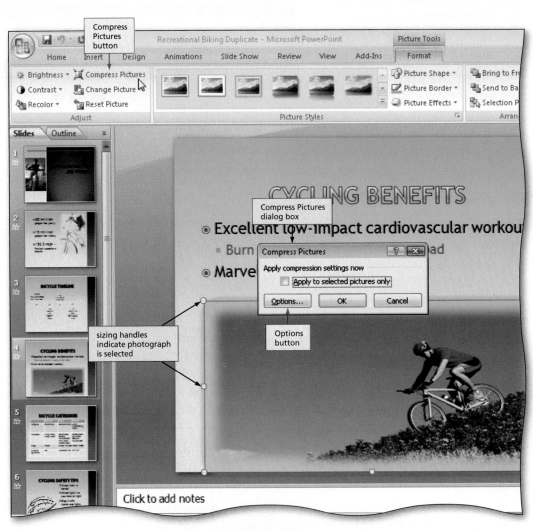

Figure 19

2

- Click the Options button in the Compress Pictures dialog box to display the Compression Settings dialog box.

- Click Screen to select the Screen (150 ppi) option (Figure 20).

Q&A

What is the option to delete cropped areas of pictures?

If you have cropped photographs and know you will not want to view the complete photographs, or if you have the original picture file stored in another location, you have the option to remove the cropped areas to save space.

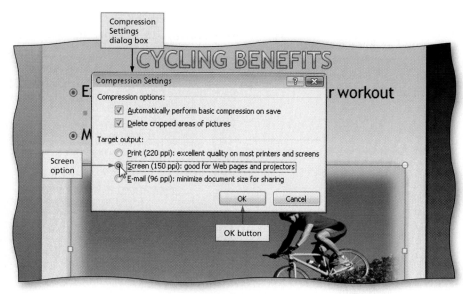

Figure 20

3

- Click the OK button to close the Compression Settings dialog box.

- Click the OK button to close the Compress Pictures dialog box and to compress all pictures in the presentation.

To Create a Digital Signature and Add It to a Document

Digital certificates, or digital IDs, verify that the file contents are authentic and valid. You can add a digital signature to files that require security, such as a presentation about a company's prototype or a patent application that will be submitted shortly. Only users with Office PowerPoint 2003 or later can view presentations protected by the digital signature. You can obtain an authentic digital certificate from a Microsoft partner, or you can create one yourself. Files protected with this certificate cannot be viewed in the PowerPoint viewer or sent as an e-mail attachment. The following steps create a digital signature and add it to the Recreational Biking Duplicate file.

1

- Click the Office Button and then point to Prepare on the Office Button menu to display the Prepare submenu (Figure 21).

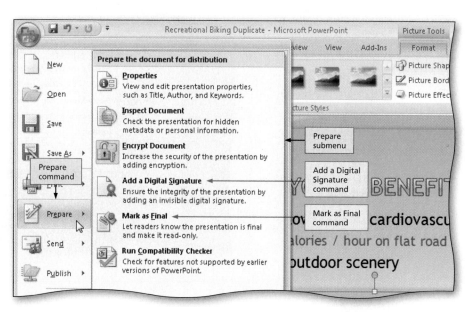

Figure 21

- Click Add a Digital Signature on the Prepare submenu to display the Microsoft Office PowerPoint dialog box (Figure 22).

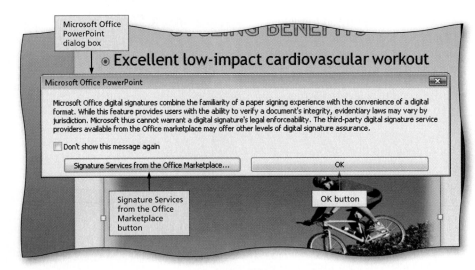

Figure 22

- Click the OK button to display the Get a Digital ID dialog box (Figure 23).

Q&A

What would have happened if I had clicked the Signature Services from the Office Marketplace button instead of the OK button?

You would have been connected to the Microsoft Office Marketplace, which is the same process that will occur if you click the 'Get a digital ID from a Microsoft partner' option button now.

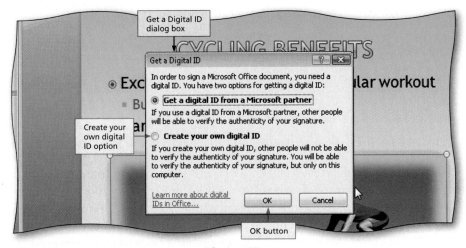

Figure 23

- Click 'Create your own digital ID' and then click the OK button to display the Create a Digital ID dialog box.

- Type `Mary Halen` in the Name text box.

- Type `mary_halen@hotmail.com` in the E-mail address text box.

- Type `Mary's Bike Shop` in the Organization text box.

- Type `Los Angeles, CA` in the Location text box (Figure 24).

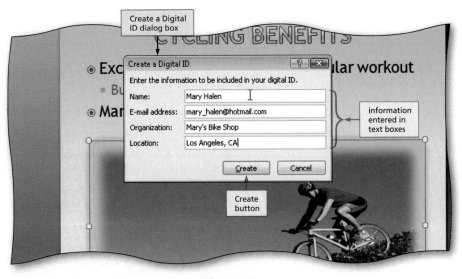

Figure 24

5

● Click the Create button to display the Sign dialog box (Figure 25).

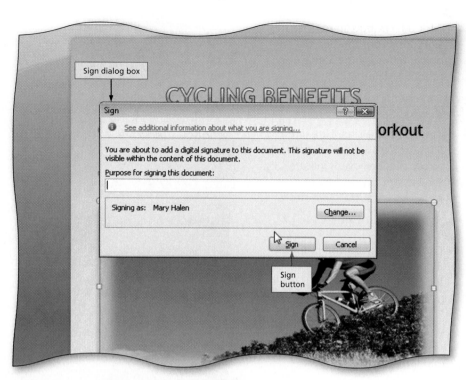

Figure 25

6

● Click the Sign button to display the Signature Confirmation dialog box (Figure 26).

Why would a company want to add a digital signature to a document?

The publisher, who is the signing person or organization, is trusted to assure the source and integrity of the digital information. A signature confirms that the file contents have not been altered since it was signed.

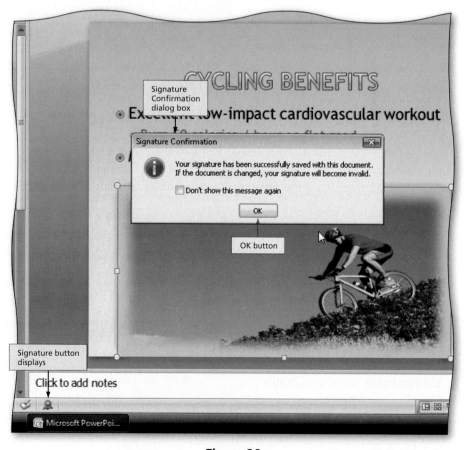

Figure 26

- Click the OK button to close the Signature Confirmation dialog box and display the Signatures task pane (Figure 27).

Q&A

Can I remove a digital signature that has been applied?

Yes. Point to a signature in the Signatures task pane, click the list arrow, click Remove Signature, click the Yes button, and then, if necessary, click the OK button.

- Click the Close button in the Signatures task pane so that it no longer is displayed.

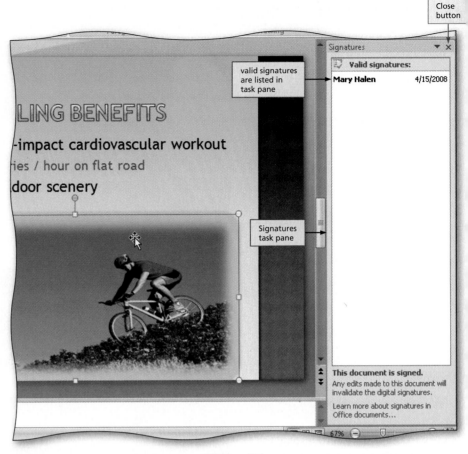

Figure 27

To Mark a Presentation as Final

When your slides are completed, you may want to prevent others or yourself from accidentally changing the slide content or features. If you use the **Mark as Final** command, the presentation becomes a read-only document. The following steps mark the presentation as a final (read-only) document.

- Click the Office Button and then point to Prepare on the Office Button.

- Click Mark as Final (shown in Figure 21 on PPT 313) to display the Microsoft Office PowerPoint dialog box (Figure 28).

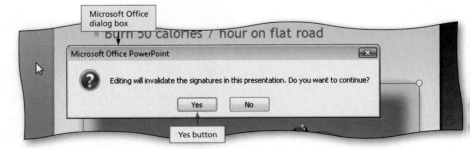

Figure 28

②

- Click the Yes button to invalidate the signatures in the presentation.

- If necessary, click the OK button to display a second Microsoft Office PowerPoint dialog box indicating that the presentation is final.

Q&A

Can I turn off this read-only status so that I can edit the file?

Yes. Repeat Step 1 above to toggle off the read-only status.

To Save a File in .PPS Format

To simplify giving a presentation in front of an audience, you may want your slide show to start running without having to start PowerPoint, open a file, and then click the Slide Show button. When you save a presentation as a **PowerPoint show (.pps)**, it automatically begins running when opened. The following steps save the Recreational Biking Duplicate file as a PowerPoint show.

- Click the Office Button, point to Save As on the Office Button menu, and then click PowerPoint Presentation.

- Type Recreational Biking Show in the File name text box.

- Click the Save as type arrow to display the Save as type list (Figure 29).

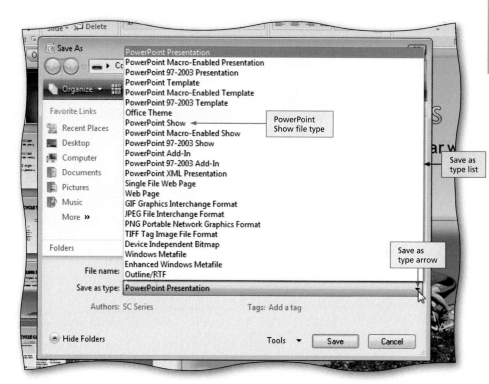

Figure 29

- Click PowerPoint Show in the Save as type list (Figure 30).

- Click the Save button to save the Recreational Biking presentation as a PowerPoint show.

- Click the Yes button in the Microsoft Office PowerPoint dialog box to remove all signatures in the presentation.

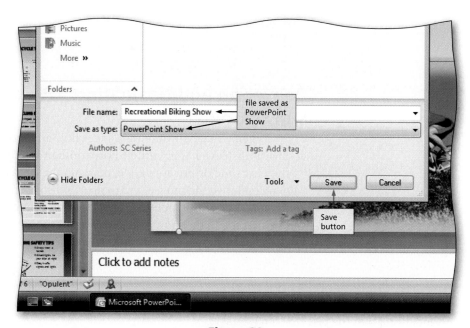

Figure 30

Using Presentation Tools to Navigate

When you click the slide show options button on the Slide Show toolbar, PowerPoint displays the Popup menu. This menu is described on page PPT 51.

When you display a particular slide and view the information, you may want to return to one of the other slides in the presentation. Jumping to particular slides in a presentation is called **navigating**. A set of keyboard shortcuts can help you navigate to various slides during the slide show. When running a slide show, you can press the F1 key to see a list of these keyboard controls. These navigational features are listed in Table 1.

Table 1 Navigation Shortcut Keys	
Keyboard Shortcut	**Purpose**
N Click SPACEBAR RIGHT ARROW DOWN ARROW ENTER PAGE DOWN	Advance to the next slide
P BACKSPACE LEFT ARROW UP ARROW PAGE UP	Return to the previous slide
Number followed by ENTER	Go to a specific slide
B PERIOD	Display a black screen Return to slide show from a black screen
W COMMA	Display a white screen Return to slide show from a white screen
ESC CTRL+BREAK HYPHEN	End a slide show

Delivering and Navigating a Presentation Using the Slide Show Toolbar

When you begin running a slide show and move the mouse pointer, the Slide Show toolbar is displayed. The **Slide Show toolbar** contains buttons that allow you to navigate to the next slide or previous slide, mark up the current slide, or change the current display. When you move the mouse, the toolbar is displayed in the lower-left corner of the slide; it disappears after the mouse has not been moved for three seconds. Table 2 describes the buttons on the Slide Show toolbar.

Table 2 Slide Show Toolbar Buttons

Description	Function
previous slide	Previous slide or previous animated element on the slide
pointer arrow	Shortcut menu for arrows, pens, and highlighters
slide show options	Shortcut menu for slide navigation and screen displays
next slide	Next slide or next animated element on the slide

To Highlight Items on a Slide

You click the arrow buttons on either end of the toolbar to navigate backward or forward through the slide show. The pointer arrow button has a variety of functions, most often to add **ink** notes or drawings to your presentation to emphasize aspects of slides or make handwritten notes. This feature is available in all views except Slide Sorter view. The following steps highlight items on a slide in Slide Show view.

- Click the Slide 1 thumbnail in the Slides tab and then run the slide show.

- If the Slide Show toolbar is not visible, move the mouse pointer on the slide.

- Click the pointer arrow on the Slide Show toolbar to display the shortcut menu (Figure 31).

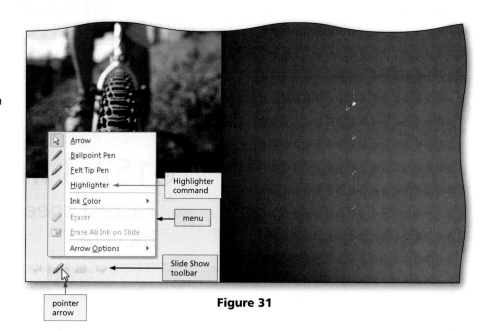

Figure 31

- Click Highlighter and then drag the mouse over the word, Fitness, until the entire word is highlighted (Figure 32).

- Move the mouse and then click to highlight any area of the slide.

Figure 32

In the Lab

Create a presentation using the guidelines, concepts, and skills presented in this feature. Labs 1, 2, and 3 are listed in order of increasing difficulty.

Lab 1: Adding Comments to and Protecting a Presentation

Problem: Registered dietitians provide a variety of nutrition services, including personal consultations on developing appropriate eating plans and preparing healthy meals. Jen Rowley, the registered dietitian at your community center, has created a presentation she would like to use during these consultations on the topic of choosing nutritious foods, and she asks you to review it. She sends you the slides and requests comments. You add several comments, check the slides for incompatibility with previous PowerPoint versions, and then protect the presentation with a password. When you run the presentation, you add annotations. The annotated slides are shown in Figure 38.

Instructions: Perform the following tasks.

1. Open the presentation, Lab SF-1 Healthy Meals, from the Data Files for Students.

2. On Slide 1, replace Jen Rowley's name with your name. Add a comment on the photograph with the following text: I suggest you enlarge this photo and add a border.

3. On Slide 2, add a comment in the Breakfast cell with the following text: Can you add a bullet on this slide to emphasize that breakfast is the most important meal of the day? Everyone should make the time to eat a healthy breakfast.

4. On Slide 3, add a comment on the apple graphic with the following text: I would change the color of the title text to red so that it blends with the clip.

5. Run the Compatibility Checker to identify the presentation features not supported in previous PowerPoint versions. Summarize these features in a comment placed on Slide 1.

6. Protect the presentation with the password, Food4Health.

7. Change the document properties, as specified by your instructor. Save the presentation using the file name, Lab SF-1 Healthy Meals Comments.

(a)

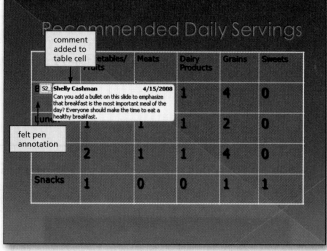

(b)

Figure 38

8. Run the presentation. On Slide 1, click the pointer arrow in the Slide Show toolbar and use the yellow highlighter to draw a circle around the word, Healthy, in the title text. Click the Next Slide button on the toolbar, click the pointer arrow, click Felt Tip Pen in the menu, and then draw two underlines under the word, Breakfast, in the table. Click the Next Slide button on the toolbar, click the pointer arrow, and then click Ballpoint Pen in the menu. Click the pointer arrow, point to Ink Color in the menu and then click Yellow in the Standard Colors row. Draw a check mark to the left of each of the three bullets on this slide. Save the annotations. Print the slides.

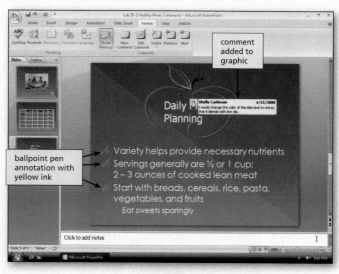

Figure 38 (c)

9. Submit the revised document in the format specified by your instructor.

In the Lab

Lab 2: Modifying and Deleting Comments in a Protected Presentation

Problem: Antibiotics are used to kill bacteria and can control infectious diseases. Some people, however, believe these drugs will help relieve the symptoms of viral infections, such as coughs and sore throats caused by colds and the flu. Many bacteria have become resistant to antibiotics because these drugs have been taken unnecessarily. You are working with a friend in your health class to develop a PowerPoint presentation on the topic of antibiotics. Your friend gives you a password-protected file that she created, and she asks you to review the slides, which are shown in Figure 39. She has inserted comments with questions, and you offer some suggestions. You modify her comments and remove inappropriate information.

Instructions: Perform the following tasks.

1. Open the presentation, Lab SF-2 Antibiotics, from the Data Files for Students. The password is Anti4Us.

2. Insert your name in the footer on all slides. On Slide 1, modify the comment on the photograph by adding the following text: `No. The photo's size is great. It introduces the topic and calls attention to the presentation.`

3. On Slide 2, modify the comment by adding the following text: `You can leave those words in past tense, or you can change them to the present tense words you recommend.  Either one is fine as long as you are consistent.`

4. On Slide 3, modify the comment by adding the following text: `Yes. I think it is better if you tell your audience why the drugs are prescribed rather than why they are not prescribed.`

5. On Slide 4, delete the comment.

6. Print the slides and comments.

7. Inspect the document and then remove all document properties and personal information.

Continued >

In the Lab *continued*

8. Save the presentation using the file name, Lab SF-2 Antibiotics Revised.

9. Submit the revised document in the format specified by your instructor.

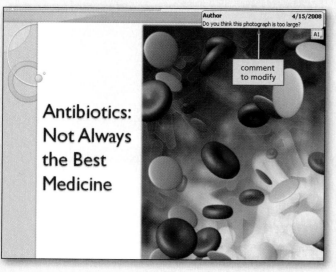

(a)

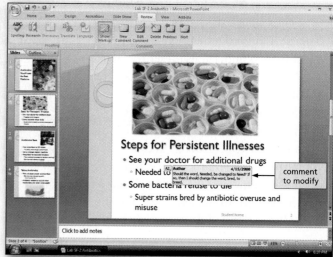

(b)

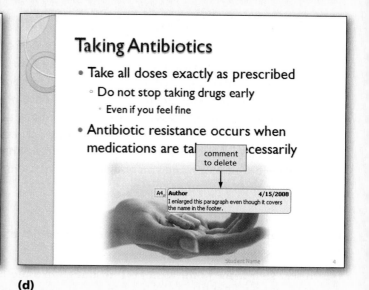

(c)

(d)

Figure 39

In the Lab

Lab 3: Compressing a Presentation, Saving in .PPS Format, and Packaging the Presentation for a CD

Problem: In-line skating is a popular method of exercising and having fun with friends and family. The owner of the sporting goods store in your town has created a presentation with skating safety tips and also with statistics about the number of people who participate in this sport. She sends you the slides shown in Figure 40. You delete her comments, compress the presentation, add a digital signature, save the file as a PowerPoint show, and then package the presentation on a CD.

Instructions: Perform the following tasks.

1. Open the presentation, Lab SF-3 Skating, from the Data Files for Students.
2. Show the markups, review the Slide 1 comment, and then click the Next Comment button in the Comments group to review the comment on Slide 2. Continue clicking the Next Comment button to review all the comments on the slides.
3. Inspect the document and then remove all comments and annotations.
4. Compress the presentation using the default settings.
5. Change the document properties, as specified by your instructor.
6. Save the presentation using the file name, Lab SF-3 Skating Revised. Protect the presentation with the password, 2Sk8.
7. Save the presentation as a PowerPoint show. Use the file name, Lab SF-3 Skating Show.
8. Mark the presentation as final.
9. Add a digital signature by creating your own digital ID. Enter your name in the Name text box, mary_halen@hotmail.com in the E-mail address text box, Sarah's Skate Shop in the Organization text box, and Los Angeles, CA in the Location text box.
10. Save the Skating Show presentation using the Package for CD feature.
11. Submit the revised document in the format specified by your instructor.

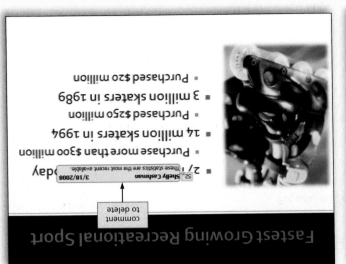

(b)

(a)

Figure 40

< *Continued*

In the Lab continued

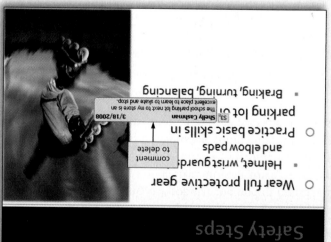

(d)

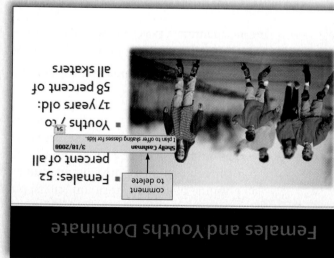

(c)

Figure 40 (continued)

(e)

2 Managing Calendars and Instant Messaging

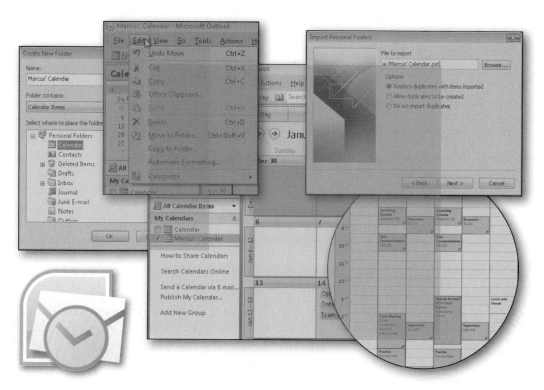

Objectives

You will have mastered the material in this project when you can:

- Start Outlook and open the Calendar folder

- Describe the components of the Calendar – Microsoft Outlook window and understand the elements of the Outlook Navigation Pane

- Enter, move, and edit one-time and recurring appointments

- Create an event

- Display the calendar in Day, Work Week, Week, and Month views

- Create and customize a task list and move it to a new folder

- Import, export, and delete personal subfolders

- Delegate tasks

- Schedule a meeting

- Customize the calendar

- Print the calendar in Daily Style, Weekly Style, and Monthly Style

- Enable and start instant messaging in Outlook

- Add an instant messaging address in the contact list

- Send an instant message and send a file with instant messaging

2 | Managing Calendars and Instant Messaging

Introduction

Whether you are CEO of a major company or president of an extracurricular activity group in school, you can take advantage of Outlook's features for scheduling and managing appointments, meetings, and tasks. You can view or print an Outlook calendar in Day, Week, or Month views (Figure 2–1). Using Outlook's Calendar component, you can schedule meetings and appointments, assign tasks for the other members of a group, and even keep track of meeting attendance and task progression. Outlook also allows you to store miscellaneous information using Notes.

Outlook is also helpful for scheduling personal time. Most individuals have multiple appointments to keep and tasks to accomplish in a day, week, or month. Outlook can organize activity-related information in a structured, readable manner.

Outlook has an instant messaging feature (bottom of Figure 2–1) that works in conjunction with Windows Messenger or MSN Messenger. This feature allows you to communicate instantaneously with people in your contact list who also use one of these instant messenger services.

Project — Calendar

Time management is a part of everyday life. Many people are constantly rearranging appointments, work schedules, or vacations in an attempt to efficiently utilize their time. The better you manage your professional or student life, the more time you will have for your personal life. Outlook is the perfect tool to maintain a personal schedule and help plan meetings. In this project, you use the basic features of Outlook to create a calendar of classes, work schedules, and extra-curricular activities for Marcus Cook, including scheduling meetings. In addition to creating the calendar, you learn how to print it in three views: Day, Week, and Month. The project also shows how to create a task list and delegate those tasks. Finally, you will learn how to use Windows Messenger with Outlook.

Overview

As you read through this chapter, you will learn how to create the calendar shown in Figure 2–1 by performing these general tasks:

- Enter appointments.
- Create recurring appointments.
- Move appointments to new dates.
- Schedule events.
- View and print the calendar.
- Create a task list.
- Assign tasks.

OUTLOOK CALENDAR

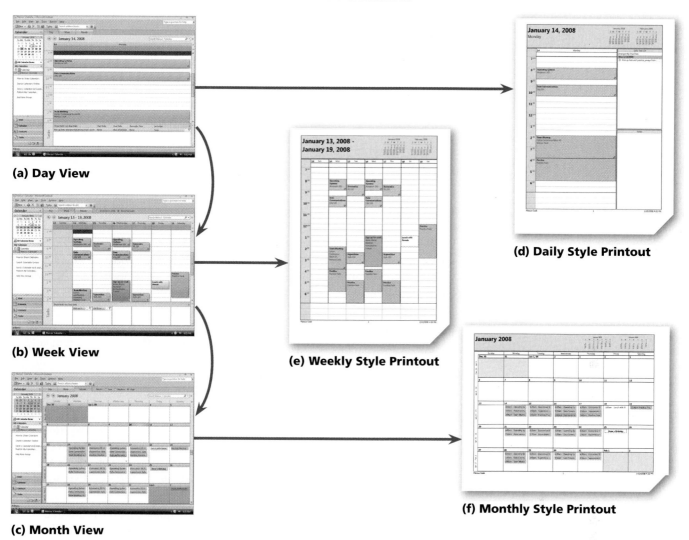

(a) Day View

(b) Week View

(c) Month View

(d) Daily Style Printout

(e) Weekly Style Printout

(f) Monthly Style Printout

INSTANT MESSAGING USING OUTLOOK

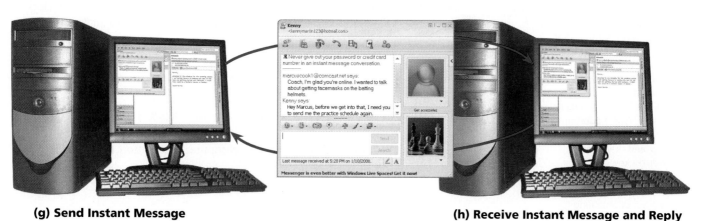

(g) Send Instant Message

(h) Receive Instant Message and Reply

Figure 2–1

- Accept a task assignment.
- Invite attendees to a meeting.
- Accept a meeting request.
- Propose and change the time of a meeting.
- Color code and label your calendar.
- Create and edit notes.
- Use AutoArchive.
- Use Windows Messaging with Outlook.

Plan Ahead

General Project Guidelines

When creating a schedule, the actions you perform and decisions you make will affect the appearance and characteristics of the finished schedule. As you create an appointment, task, or schedule a meeting as shown in Figure 2–1, you should follow these general guidelines:

1. **Determine what you need to schedule.** For students, a class list with room numbers and times would be a good start. For businesspeople, the schedule is a dynamic tool that will need frequent updating; however, you can schedule weekly staff meetings and other regular events or tasks.

2. **Determine if an activity is recurring.** Classes most likely recur through the semester. Work schedules can change week by week or month by month. If an activity happens regularly on the same day and time, it is recurring.

3. **Use good judgment when assigning a task.** If you are going to assign a task, you should be sure the person to whom you are assigning the task is capable of performing the task by the assigned due date.

4. **Be sure to have an agenda before scheduling a meeting.** A poorly organized meeting may be the least productive tool in the business world. Attendees become uninterested and sometimes angry knowing that their time could be better spent elsewhere. A carefully planned meeting with a defined agenda, however, can be a very productive tool if it is followed correctly.

When necessary, more specific details concerning the above guidelines are presented at appropriate points in the chapter. The chapter also will identify the actions you perform and decisions made regarding these guidelines during the creation of the schedule shown in Figure 2–1.

BTW

The Outlook 2007 Help System
Need Help? It is no further than the 'Type a question for help' box on the menu bar in the upper-right corner of the window. Click the box that contains the text, Type a question for help (Figure 2–2), type `help`, and then press the ENTER key. Outlook responds with a list of topics you can click to learn about obtaining help on an Outlook-related topic. To find out what is new in Outlook 2007, type `what is new in Outlook` in the 'Type a question for help' box.

Starting and Customizing Outlook

If you are using a computer to step through the project in this chapter and you want your screen to match the figures in this book, you should change your screen's resolution to 1024×768. For information about how to change a computer's resolution, read Appendix E.

To Start and Customize Outlook

The following steps, which assume Windows Vista is running, start Outlook based on a typical installation. You may need to ask your instructor how to start Outlook for your computer.

1
- Click the Start button on the Windows Vista taskbar to display the Start menu.

2
- Click All Programs at the bottom of the left pane on the Start menu to display the All Programs list, and then click Microsoft Office in the All Programs list to display the Microsoft Office list.

3
- Click Microsoft Office Outlook 2007 on the Microsoft Office list to start Outlook.

- If necessary, click the Calendar button in the Navigation Pane.

- If the Calendar – Microsoft Office Outlook window is not maximized, double-click its title bar to maximize the window (Figure 2–2).

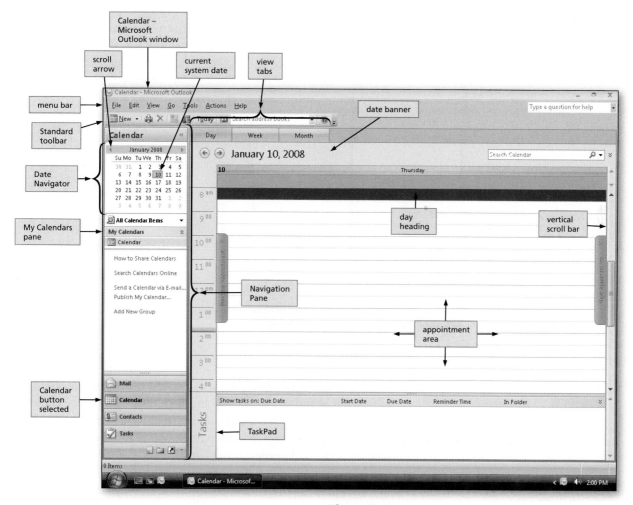

Figure 2–2

Calendars
Other users can give you access to their calendars. This allows you to make appointments, check free times, schedule meetings, check or copy contacts, or perform any other tasks that you can accomplish with your own calendar. This is useful when you need to schedule meetings or events that depend on other people's schedules.

The Calendar – Microsoft Outlook Window

The Calendar – Microsoft Outlook window shown in Figure 2–2 on the previous page includes a variety of features to help you work efficiently. It contains many elements similar to the windows in other Office applications, as well as some that are unique to Outlook. The main elements of the Calendar window are the Navigation Pane, the Standard toolbar, the appointment area, and the TaskPad. The following paragraphs explain some of the features of the Calendar window.

Navigation Pane The **Navigation Pane** (Figure 2–2 on the previous page) includes two sets of buttons and two panes: the Date Navigator pane and My Calendars pane. The **Date Navigator** shows a calendar for the current month with scroll arrows. When you click the scroll arrows to move to a new date, Calendar displays the name of the month, week, or day in the current view in the appointment area. The current system date has a square around it in the Date Navigator. Dates displayed in bold in the Date Navigator indicate days on which an item is scheduled.

Below the Date Navigator, the My Calendars pane includes a list of available calendars on your computer. In this pane, you can select a single calendar to view, or view other calendars side-by-side with your calendar.

On the lower part of the Navigation Pane are two groups of buttons (Figure 2–3). The first group of buttons are shortcuts representing the standard items that are part of Microsoft Outlook: Mail, Calendar, Contacts, and Tasks. The second group of buttons are shortcuts to other functions of Outlook: Notes, Folder List, Shortcuts, and Configure buttons. When you click a shortcut, Outlook opens the corresponding folder.

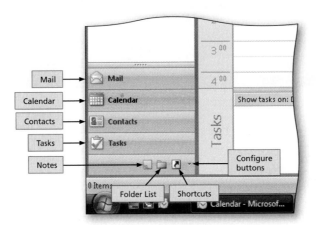

Figure 2–3

Appointment Area The **appointment area** (Figure 2–2 on the previous page) contains view tabs, a date banner, a day heading and, under the day heading, time slots for the current view. The date currently selected in the Date Navigator appears in the date banner. By default, workday time slots are set from 8:00 a.m. to 5:00 p.m. in one-hour increments. Time slots outside this period are shaded. A vertical scroll bar allows backward and forward movement through the time slots.

Scheduled items, such as appointments, meetings, or events, are displayed in the appointment area. An **appointment** is an activity that does not involve other resources or people. A **meeting**, by contrast, is an appointment to which other resources or people are invited. Outlook's Calendar can be used to schedule several people to attend a meeting or only one person to attend an appointment (such as when you attend a class). An **event** is an activity that lasts 24 hours or longer, such as a seminar, birthday, or vacation. Scheduled events do not occupy time slots in the appointment area; instead, they are displayed in a banner below the day heading.

Standard Toolbar Figure 2–4 shows the Standard toolbar in the Calendar window. The button names indicate their functions. Each button can be clicked to perform a frequently used task, such as creating a new appointment or printing a calendar.

Figure 2–4

To Create a Personal Folder

As in other features of Outlook, such as Contacts, you can create multiple folders within the Calendar component. If you were the only person using Outlook on a computer, you could enter appointments and events directly into the main Calendar folder. In many school situations, however, several people share one computer and therefore, each user needs to create a separate folder in which to store their appointments and events. The following steps create a personal folder for Marcus Cook. Marcus will store his class, work, and baseball practice scheduling information in his personal folder.

1

- With the Calendar – Microsoft Office window active, right-click Calendar in the My Calendars pane to display the Calendar shortcut menu (Figure 2–5).

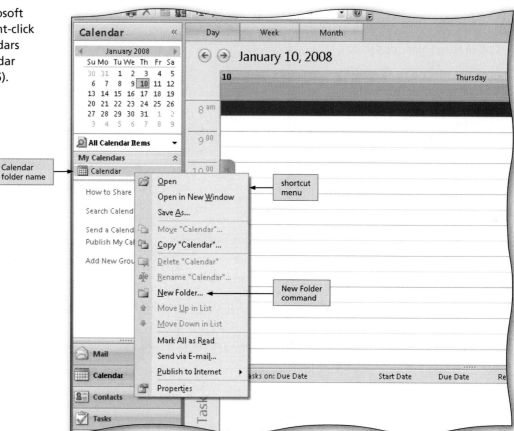

Figure 2–5

2

- Click New Folder on the Calendar shortcut menu to display the Create New Folder dialog box.

- Type `Marcus' Calendar` in the Name text box.

- If necessary, select Calendar Items in the Folder contains text box.

- Click Calendar in the 'Select where to place the folder' list box to specify where the folder will be stored (Figure 2–6).

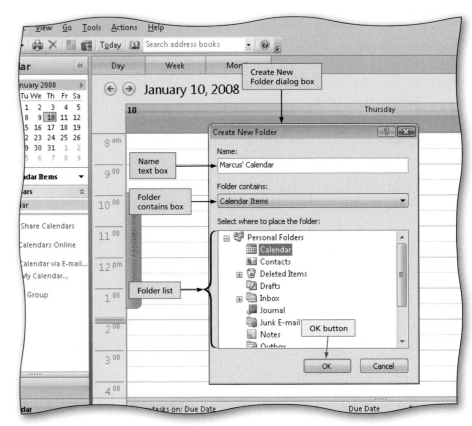

Figure 2–6

3

- Click the OK button to close the Create New Folder dialog box.

- Click the check box next to Marcus' Calendar in the My Calendars list to open Marcus' calendar.

- Click the check box next to Calendar to remove the existing check mark to remove the default calendar from view (Figure 2–7).

 Why does my view look different from what is shown?

Figure 2–7 shows the default view for Calendar. If this view does not appear on your computer, click View on the menu bar, point to Current View, and then make sure the Day/Week/Month option is selected.

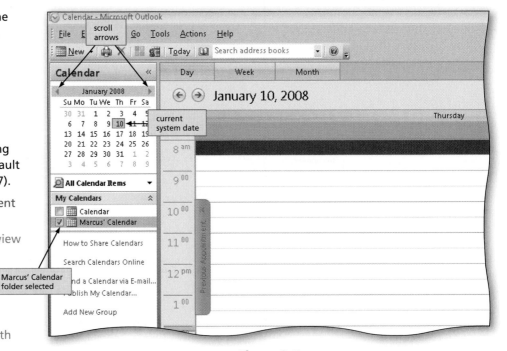

Figure 2–7

Other Ways

1. On the File menu point to Folder, click New Folder on Folder submenu

2. Press CTRL+SHIFT+E

Entering Appointments

Calendar allows you to schedule appointments, meetings, and events for yourself as well as for others who have given you permission to open their personal folders.

This section describes how to enter appointments, or in this case, classes, into Marcus Cook's personal folder, starting with classes for January 14, 2008. Work days and games are one-time appointments; classes and team meetings are recurring appointments.

When entering an appointment into a time slot that is not visible in the current view, use the scroll bar to bring the time slot into view. Once you enter an appointment, you can perform ordinary editing actions.

To Enter Appointments Using the Appointment Area

The following steps enter appointments using the appointment area.

1

- If necessary, click the scroll arrows in the Date Navigator to display January 2008.

- Click 14 in the January calendar in the Date Navigator to display it in the appointment area.

2

- Drag through the 8:00 a.m. – 9:00 a.m. time slot (Figure 2–8).

3

- Type Operating Systems as the first appointment.

4

- Drag through the 9:30 a.m. – 10:30 a.m. time slot.

- Type Data Communications as the second appointment.

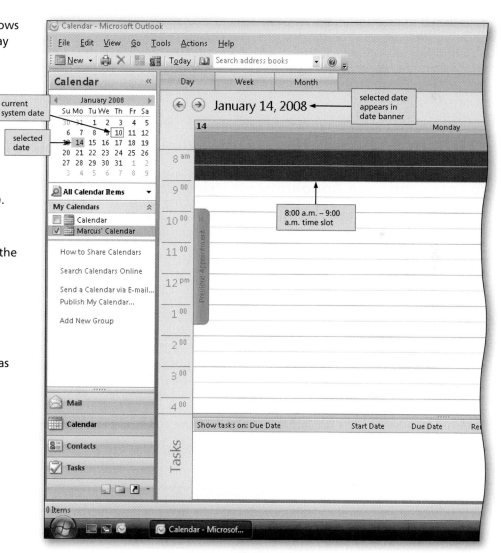

Figure 2–8

⑤

- Drag through the 11:30 a.m. – 12:30 p.m. time slot.

- Type Lunch with friends as the third appointment and then press the ENTER key (Figure 2–9).

Q&A What if I make a mistake while typing an appointment?

If you notice the error before clicking outside the appointment time slot or pressing the ENTER key, use the BACKSPACE key to erase the characters back to and including the error. To cancel the entire entry before clicking outside the appointment time slot or pressing the ENTER key, press the ESC key. If you discover the error after clicking outside the appointment time slot or pressing the ENTER key, click the appointment and retype the entry.

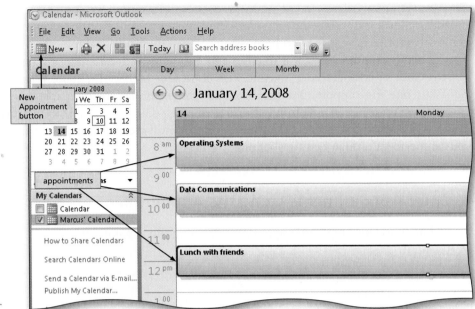

Figure 2–9

To Enter and Save Appointments Using the Appointment Window

Using the **Appointment window** is a slightly more involved process, but it allows the specification of more detail about the appointment. The following steps enter an appointment at 2:00 p.m. to 4:00 p.m. using the Appointment window.

❶

- Drag through the 2:00 p.m. – 4:00 p.m. time slot and then click the New Appointment button on the Standard toolbar to open the Untitled – Appointment window. If necessary, maximize the Untitled – Appointment window (Figure 2–10).

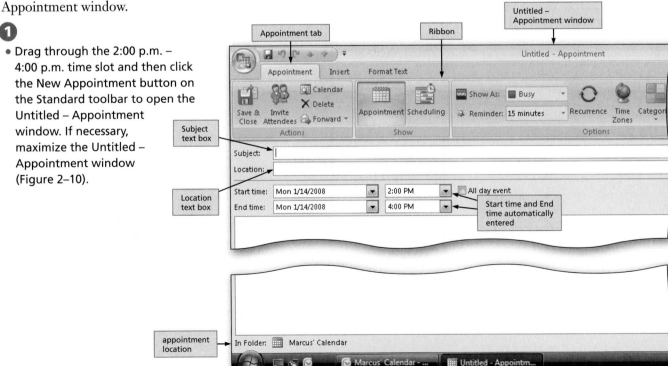

Figure 2–10

2

- Type `Team Meeting` in the Subject text box and then press the TAB key to move the insertion point to the Location text box.

- Type `Union Conference Room #1` in the Location text box (Figure 2–11).

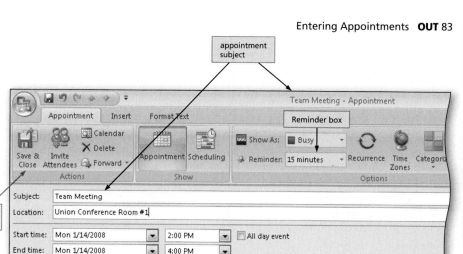

Figure 2–11

3

- Click the Save & Close button on the Ribbon to close the Team Meeting – Appointment window and return to the Calendar window (Figure 2–12).

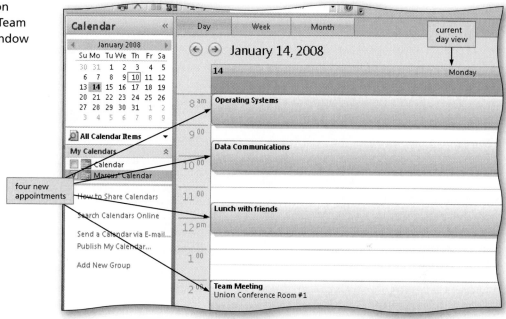

Figure 2–12

Other Ways

1. Double-click time slot, enter appointment
2. On Actions menu, click New Appointment
3. Right-click time slot, click New Appointment on shortcut menu
4. Press CTRL+N

Recurring Appointments

Many appointments are **recurring**, or occur at regular intervals. For example, a class held every Monday and Wednesday from 8:00 a.m. to 9:00 a.m. is a recurring appointment. In this project, Marcus' college classes and team meetings occur at regular weekly intervals. Typing these recurring appointments for each occurrence would be very time-consuming. Table 2–1 lists Marcus' recurring appointments.

BTW

Appointments
Appointments can be designated as busy, free, tentative, or out of office. The Private button in the Appointment window allows you to designate as private any appointments, tasks, meetings, or contacts. The private designation prevents viewing by other users with access to your calendar. Private calendar elements are identified with a lock symbol.

Table 2–1 Recurring Appointments

Time	Appointment	Occurrence
8:00 a.m. – 9:00 a.m.	Operating Systems (Anderson 203)	Every Monday and Wednesday (30 times)
9:30 a.m. – 10:30 a.m.	Data Communications (Lilly 105)	Every Monday and Wednesday (30 times)
2:00 p.m. – 4:00 p.m.	Team Meeting (Union Conference Room #1)	Every other Monday (15 times)

To Enter Recurring Appointments

By designating an appointment as recurring, the appointment needs to be added only once and then recurrence is specified for the days on which it occurs. The following steps enter recurring appointments.

- With Monday, January 14, 2008 displayed, double-click the words Operating Systems in the 8:00 a.m. – 9:00 a.m. time slot to open the Operating Systems – Appointment window.

- Click the Location text box and then type Anderson 203 to set the location of the class (Figure 2–13).

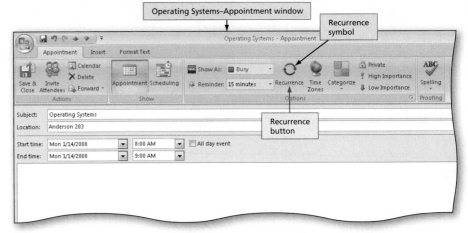

Figure 2–13

3

- Click the Recurrence button on the Ribbon to display the Appointment Recurrence dialog box.

- Click the Wednesday check box to select the days this appointment will recur.

- Click End after in the Range of recurrence area, double-click the End after text box, and then type 30 as the number of occurrences (Figure 2–14).

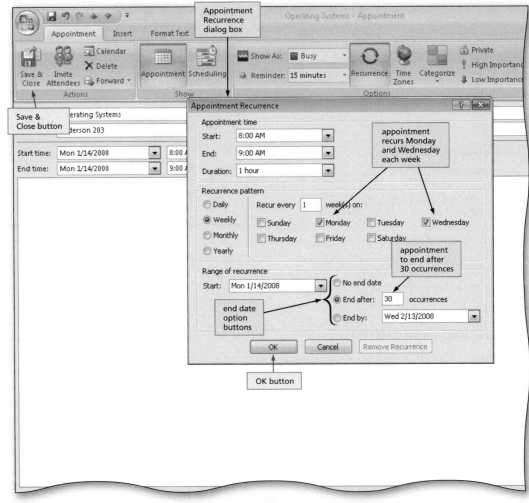

Figure 2–14

④

- Click the OK button to close the Appointment Recurrence dialog box.

- Click the Save & Close button on the Ribbon to close the Operating Systems – Recurring Appointment window and return to the Calendar window (Figure 2–15).

⑤

- Repeat Steps 1 through 4 to make the Data Communications and Team Meeting appointments recurring. Refer to Table 2–1 for the location, range, and ending dates.

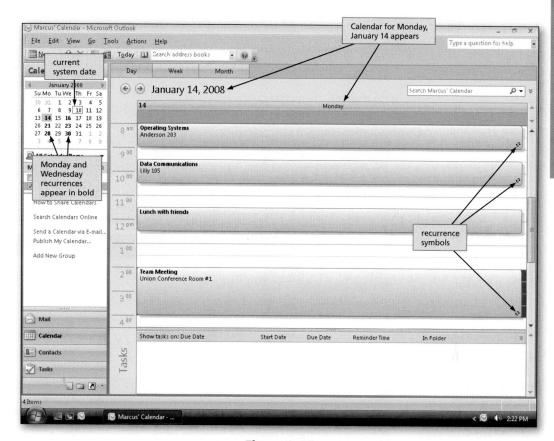

Figure 2–15

Completing Marcus' Calendar

With the Monday schedule entered, the next step is to move to the next day in the appointment area and complete the recurring appointments for every Tuesday and Thursday using the appointment information in Table 2–2.

Table 2–2 Additional Recurring Appointments

Time	Appointment	Occurrence
8:30 a.m. – 9:30 a.m.	Economics (EE 215)	Every Tuesday and Thursday (30 times)
2:30 p.m. – 3:30 p.m.	Supervision (Gyte 103)	Every Tuesday and Thursday (30 times)

To Move to the Next Day in the Appointment Area and Enter the Remaining Recurring Appointments

Because the recurring appointments start on Tuesday, Tuesday must be displayed in the appointment area. The following steps move to the next day using the Date Navigator and then enter the remaining recurring appointments.

- Click 15 in the January 2008 calendar in the Date Navigator to move to Tuesday, January 15, 2008.

- Drag through the 8:30 a.m. – 9:30 a.m. time slot (Figure 2–16).

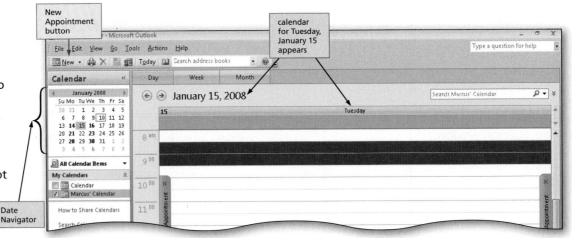

Figure 2–16

- Click the New Appointment button on the Standard toolbar to open the Untitled – Appointment window.

- Enter the recurring appointments listed in Table 2–2 on the previous page.

- Click the Save & Close button on the Ribbon to close the Appointment window and return to the Calendar window (Figure 2–17).

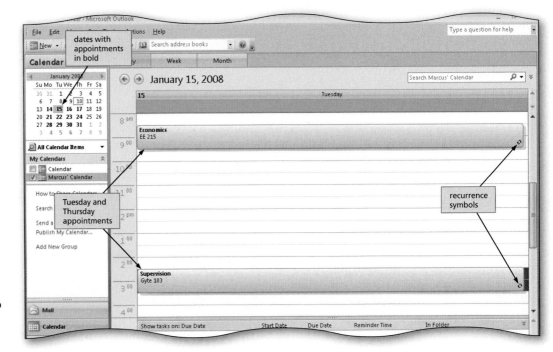

Figure 2–17

Q&A

What if I have appointments that recur other than weekly or semi-weekly?

Daily, weekly, monthly, or yearly recurrence patterns are possible in the Recurrence pattern options. An appointment can be set to occur a certain number of times or up to a certain day.

Other Ways

1. On Actions menu, click New Recurring Appointment

2. Press ALT+A, TYPE A

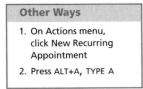

Natural Language Phrasing

BTW

Moving a Recurring Appointment
If a recurring appointment is moved, only the selected instance of the appointment is moved. If all instances of an appointment need to be moved, open the appointment, click the Recurrence button on the Ribbon, and then change the recurrence pattern.

In the steps just completed, dates and times were entered in the Appointment window using standard numeric entries. Outlook's **AutoDate function**, however, provides the capability of specifying appointment dates and times using **natural language phrases**. For example, you can type phrases, such as "next Tuesday," "two weeks from yesterday," or "midnight," and Outlook will calculate the correct date and/or time.

In addition to these natural language phrases, Outlook can convert abbreviations and ordinal numbers into complete words and dates. For example, you can type Feb instead of February or the first of September instead of 9/1. Outlook's Calendar application also can convert words such as "yesterday," and "tomorrow," and the names of holidays that occur on the same date each year, such as Valentine's Day. Table 2–3 lists various AutoDate options.

Table 2–3 AutoDate Options

Category	Examples
Dates Spelled Out	• July twenty-third, March 29th, first of December • this Fri, next Sat, two days from now • three weeks ago, next week • one month from today
Times Spelled Out	• noon, midnight • nine o'clock a.m., five twenty • 7 p.m.
Descriptions of Times and Dates	• now • yesterday, today, tomorrow • next, last • ago, before, after, ending, following • for, from, that, this, till, through, until
Holidays	• Cinco de Mayo • Christmas Day, Christmas Eve • Halloween • Independence Day • New Year's Day, New Year's Eve • St. Patrick's Day • Valentine's Day • Veteran's Day

To Enter Appointment Dates and Times Using Natural Language Phrases

Now that Marcus has entered his classes into his calendar, he will enter his work schedule. The following steps enter the date and time for the work schedule using natural language phrases.

- With Tuesday, January 15 displayed in the appointment area, click the New Appointment button on the Standard toolbar to open the Untitled – Appointment window.

- Type Sign up for work in the Subject text box and then press the TAB key to move to the location.

- Type Better Batter Baseball Instructional School in the Location text box and then press the TAB key once.

- Type next Wednesday in the Start time date box for the date (Figure 2–18).

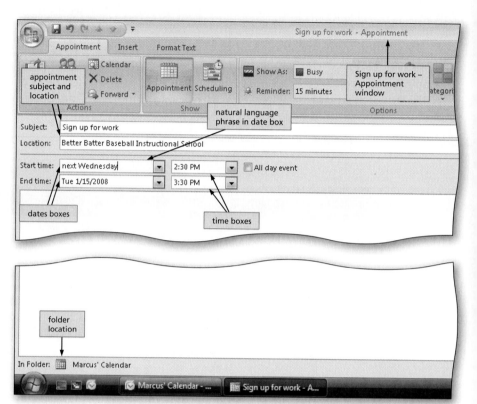

Figure 2–18

3

- Press the TAB key.

- Type one p.m. in the Start time time box.

- Press the TAB key twice to advance the cursor to the End time time box (Figure 2–19).

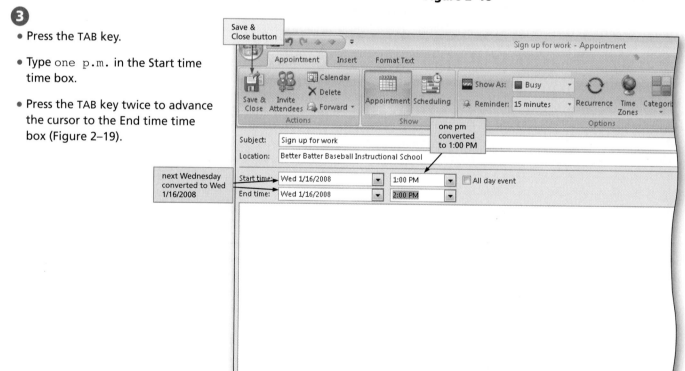

Figure 2–19

- Type three forty five in the End time time box and then press the ENTER key.

- Click the Save & Close button on the Ribbon to close the Sign up for work – Appointment window and return to the Marcus' Calendar window.

- Repeat Steps 1 through 4 to enter working at Better Batter Baseball Instructional School on January 26, 2008 from 9:00 a.m. to 1:00 p.m. Use work as the subject and Better Batter Baseball Instructional School as the location. Use natural language phrases to enter the dates and times. When you have completed entering the information, click the Save & Close button on the Ribbon to return to the Calendar window (Figure 2–20).

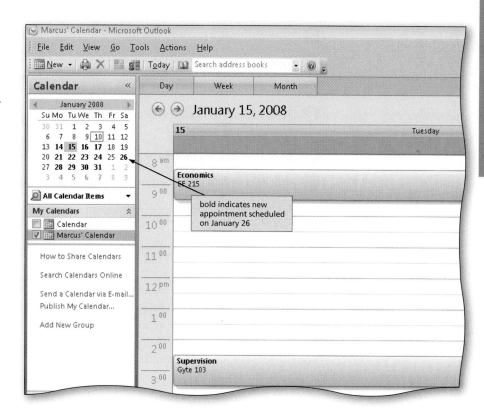

Figure 2–20

To Enter the Remaining One-Time Appointments

Table 2–4 contains the current week's practice schedule along with the schedule for the first seven games for the upcoming season. The following steps show how to enter the remaining one-time appointments.

Table 2–4 Additional One-Time Appointments			
Date	**Time**	**Appointment**	**Location**
1/14/2008	4:00 p.m. – 6:00 p.m.	Practice	Practice Field
1/15/2008	5:00 p.m. – 7:00 p.m.	Practice	Practice Field
1/16/2008	4:00 p.m. – 6:00 p.m.	Practice	Practice Field
1/17/2008	5:00 p.m. – 7:00 p.m.	Practice	Practice Field
1/19/2008	12:00 p.m. – 3:00 p.m.	Practice	Practice Field
2/16/2008	1:00 p.m. – 4:00 p.m.	Game	Beachcombe, FL
2/23/2008	11:00 a.m. – 2:00 p.m.	Game	Blackburg, TX
3/6/2008	7:00 p.m. – 10:00 p.m.	Game	Donner Field
3/8/2008	1:00 p.m. – 4:00 p.m.	Game	Donner Field
3/11/2008	7:00 p.m. – 10:00 p.m.	Game	Snow Hill, IL
3/15/2008	2:00 p.m. – 5:00 p.m.	Game	Donner Field
3/18/2008	7:00 p.m. – 10:00 p.m.	Game	Donner Field

1 With the Calendar window active, click January 14, 2008 in the Date Navigator.

2 Click the New Appointment button on the Standard toolbar.

3 Type `Practice` in the Subject text box, and then press the TAB key.

4 Type `Practice Field` in the Location text box, and then press the TAB key two times.

5 Type `4 p.m.` in the Start time time box, press the TAB key two times, and then type `six p.m.` in the End time time box.

6 Click the Save & Close button on the Ribbon.

7 Enter the remaining one-time appointments in Table 2–4.

Editing Appointments

Because schedules often need to be rearranged, Outlook provides several ways of editing appointments. Change the subject and location by clicking the appointment and editing the information directly in the appointment area, or double-click the appointment and make corrections using the Appointment window. You can specify whether all occurrences in a series of recurring appointments need to be changed, or a single occurrence can be altered.

To Delete an Appointment

Appointments sometimes are canceled and must be deleted from the schedule. For example, the schedule created thus far in this project contains appointments during the week of April 7, 2008. Because this week is Spring Break, no classes will meet and the scheduled appointments need to be deleted. The following steps delete an appointment from the calendar.

1
- Click the scroll arrow in the Date Navigator to display April 2008.
- Click 7 in the April 2008 calendar.
- Click the first appointment to be deleted, Operating Systems (Figure 2–21).

BTW

Editing Appointments
If you cannot remember the details about a specific appointment, you easily can check it. Click Tools on the menu bar, point to Instant Search, and then click Advanced Find to locate the appointment in question. In the Look for box, select Appointments and Meetings. You then may search for any word or subject.

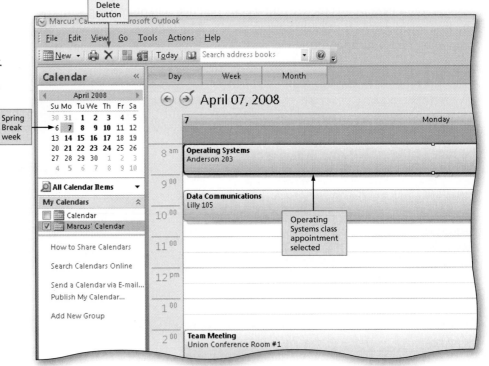

Figure 2–21

2

- Click the Delete button on the Standard toolbar to display the Confirm Delete dialog box (Figure 2–22).

- Click the OK button to delete the appointment and return to the Calendar window.

3

- Repeat Steps 1 and 2 to delete the remaining classes and meetings from the week of April 7, 2008.

Q&A Can I use the DELETE key to delete an appointment?

Yes. Select the appointment and then press the DELETE key. If only individual characters are being deleted when you press the DELETE key, you are just editing the appointment. Try clicking outside the appointment and then select it again.

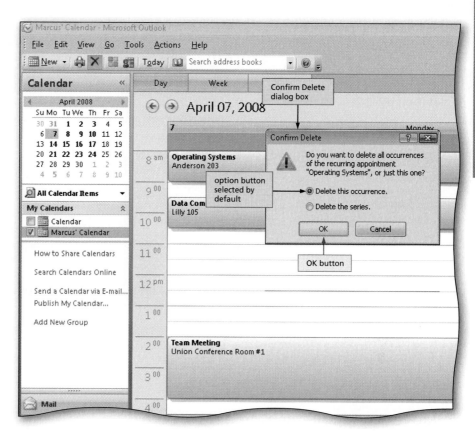

Figure 2–22

Other Ways

1. Right-click appointment to be deleted, click DELETE on the shortcut menu

To Move an Appointment to a New Time

Outlook provides several ways to move appointments. Suppose, for instance, that some of your friends cannot make it for lunch at 11:30 a.m. on Monday, January 14, 2008. The appointment needs to be rescheduled for 1:00 p.m. to 2:00 p.m. Instead of deleting and then retyping the appointment, simply drag it to the new time slot. The following steps move an appointment to a new time.

1

- Click the left scroll arrow in the Date Navigator to display January 2008.

- Click 14 in the January 2008 calendar in the Date Navigator.

- Position the mouse pointer over the Lunch with friends appointment (Figure 2–23).

Figure 2–23

2

- Drag the appointment down to the 1:00 p.m. – 2:00 p.m. time slot.

- Release the mouse button to drop the appointment in the new time slot (Figure 2–24).

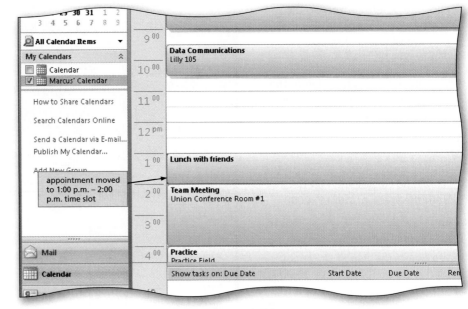

appointment moved to 1:00 p.m. – 2:00 p.m. time slot

Figure 2–24

Other Ways

1. Double-click appointment, edit Start time date box in Appointment window

---

To Move an Appointment to a New Date

If an appointment is being moved to a new date but remaining in the same time slot, simply drag the appointment to the new date in the Date Navigator. The following steps move an appointment to a new date.

1

- Position the mouse pointer over the Lunch with friends appointment.

- Click and drag the appointment from the appointment area to the 18 in the January 2008 calendar (Figure 2–25).

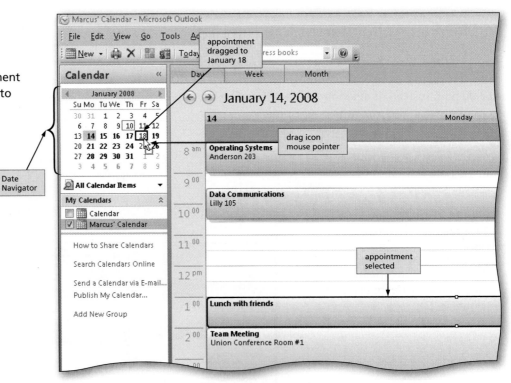

appointment dragged to January 18

Date Navigator

drag icon mouse pointer

appointment selected

Figure 2–25

- Release the mouse button to complete moving the appointment (Figure 2–26).

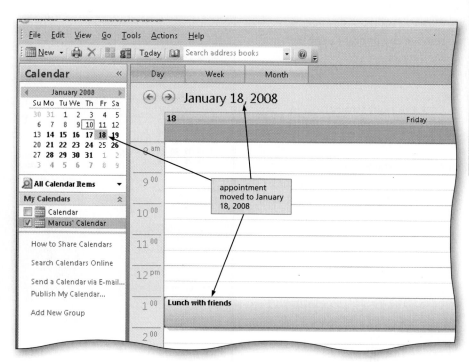

Figure 2–26

To Move an Appointment to a New Month

When moving an appointment to another month, you must cut and paste the appointment.

The baseball instructional school has decided to reschedule the Saturday time slot to a date in February. The new work date is moved from Saturday, January 26, 2008 to Saturday, February 2, 2008. The following steps show how to move an appointment to a new month using the cut and paste method.

1

- Click 26 in the January 2008 calendar in the Date Navigator.

- Click the Work appointment to select it.

- Click Edit on the menu bar to display the Edit menu (Figure 2–27).

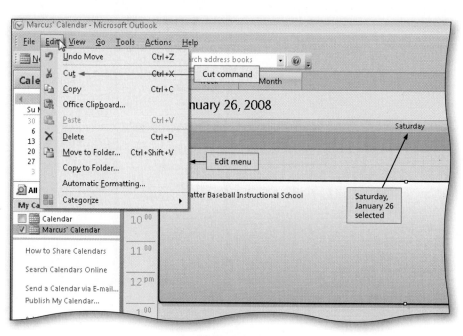

Figure 2–27

2

- Click Cut on the Edit menu to remove the appointment from January 26.

3

- Click the right scroll arrow in the Date Navigator to display February 2008.

- Click 2 in the February 2008 calendar in the Date Navigator to display it in the Appointment area (Figure 2–28).

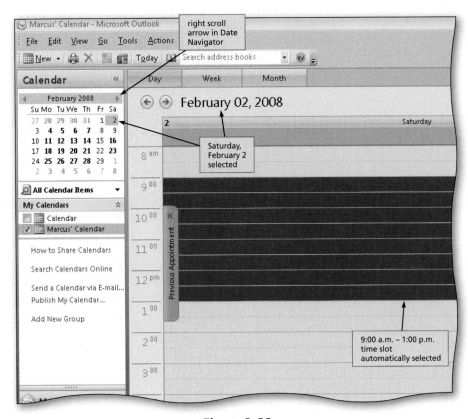

Figure 2–28

4

- Click Edit on the menu bar and then click Paste to complete moving the appointment to the new time slot (Figure 2–29).

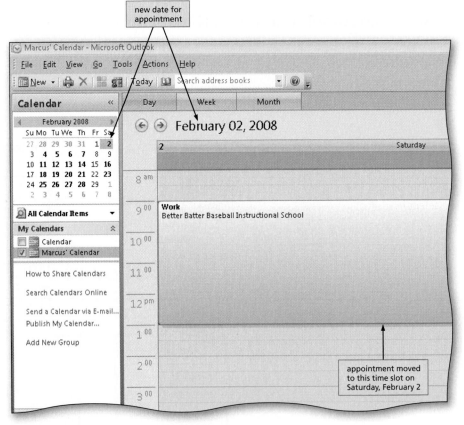

BTW

E-Mailing Appointments
To send an appointment to a coworker or classmate, right-click the appointment and click Forward on the shortcut menu.

Figure 2–29

Creating an Event

Outlook's Calendar folder allows you to keep track of important events. **Events** are activities that last 24 hours or longer. Examples of events include birthdays, conferences, weddings, vacations, holidays, and so on, and can be one-time or recurring. In Outlook, events differ from appointments in one primary way – they do not appear in individual time slots in the appointment area. When an event is scheduled, its description appears in a small **banner** below the day heading. The details of the event can be indicated as time that is free, busy, or out of the office during the event.

To Create an Event

The following steps enter a birthday as an event.

1

- If necessary, click the left scroll arrow to display January 2008 in the Date Navigator. Click 25 in the January 2008 calendar in the Date Navigator.

2

- Double-click the day heading at the top of the appointment area. When the Untitled - Event window opens, type Drew's Birthday in the Subject text box and then press the TAB key (Figure 2–30).

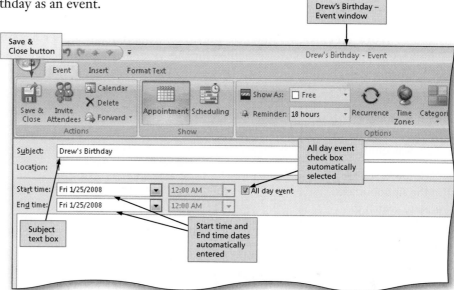

Figure 2–30

3

- Click the Save & Close button on the Ribbon to close the Event window and return to the Calendar window (Figure 2–31).

Do I have to enter every holiday into the calendar?

No. Outlook contains a folder of typical holidays for various countries that can be added to your calendar automatically. To do this, click Options on the Tools menu. Click Calendar Options, and then click Add Holidays in the Calendar Option sheet.

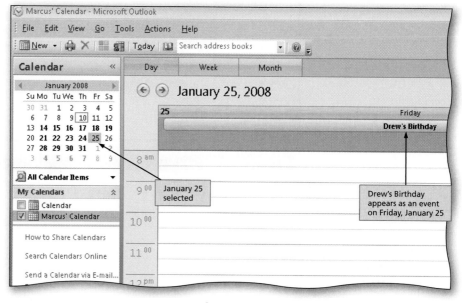

Figure 2–31

BTW

Locations
As appointments or events are entered with specific locations, the locations automatically are accumulated in a list. To access this list, open the appointment and click the Location box arrow. Frequently used locations can be selected from this list, thereby saving typing time.

Various Calendar Views

The default view type of the Calendar folder is the Day/Week/Month view. While in **Day/Week/Month view**, Outlook can display calendars in four different views: Day, Work Week, Week, and Month. So far in this project, you have used only the Day view, which is indicated by the Day tab selected in the Appointment area (Figure 2–31).

Some people may prefer a different view of their calendar, or you may need to use different views at various times. Now that the schedule is complete, it also can be displayed in Week or Month view. Although the screen looks quite different in Week and Month views, you can accomplish the same tasks as in Day view: you can add, edit, or delete appointments and events, and reminders can be set or removed.

To Change to Work Week View

The **Work Week view** shows five work days (Monday through Friday) in columnar style. This view lets you see how many appointments are scheduled for the Monday through Friday timeframe, eliminating the weekends. The following step changes the Calendar view to Work Week view.

1

- Click Tuesday, January 15 in the Date Navigator.

- Click the Week tab in the Appointment area to switch to Work Week view.

- If necessary, scroll up in the appointment area until the 8:00 a.m. time slot appears (Figure 2–32).

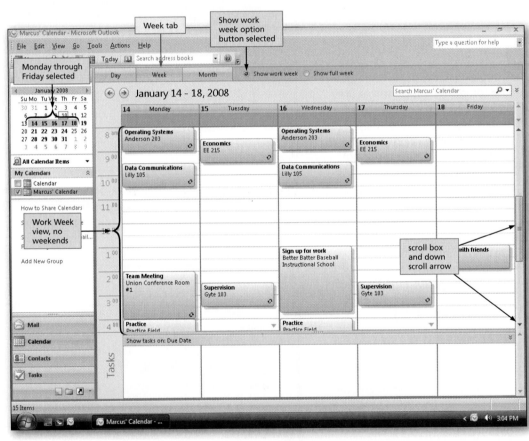

Figure 2–32

Other Ways

1. On the View menu click Work Week
2. Press ALT+V, type R
3. Press CTRL+ALT+2

To Change to Week View

The advantage of displaying a calendar in **Week view** is to see how many appointments are scheduled for any given week. In Week view, the seven days of the selected week appear in the appointment area. The following step displays the calendar in Week view.

1

• With the Week tab active, click the Show full week option button to switch to Week view (Figure 2–33).

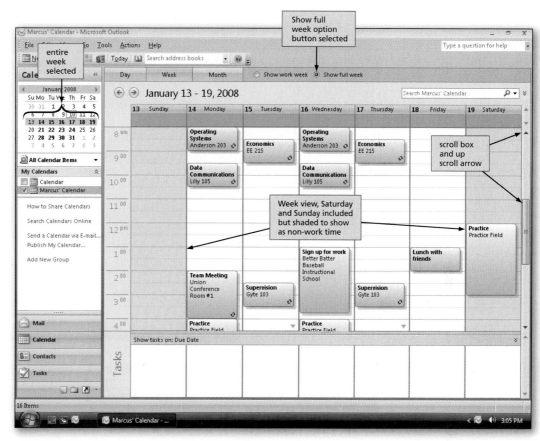

Figure 2–33

Other Ways
1. On the View menu click Week
2. Press ALT+V, type W
3. Press CTRL+ALT+3

To Change to Month View

The **Month view** resembles a standard monthly calendar page and displays a schedule for an entire month. Appointments are listed in each date frame in the calendar. The following step displays the calendar in Month view.

1

- Click the Month tab in the Appointment area to switch to Month view (Figure 2–34).

- Click the Day tab to return to Day view.

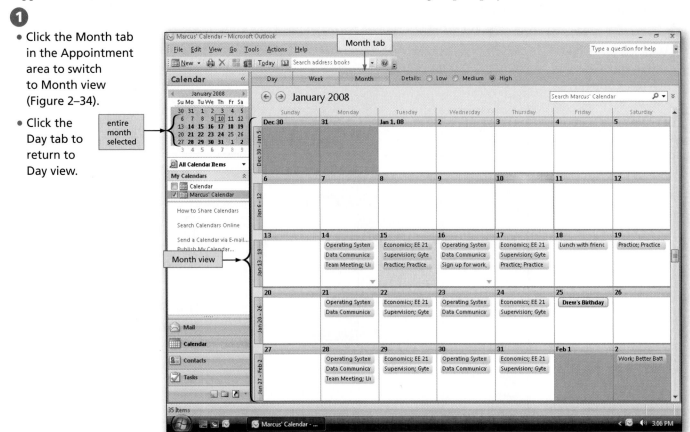

Figure 2–34

Organizing Tasks

With the daily appointments organized, you can use Tasks to organize the many duties and projects you need to complete each day. Tasks allow for the creation of a **task list** of items that need to be tracked through completion. **Tasks** can be simple to do items, daily reminders, assignments with due dates, or business responsibilities. Outlook can indicate whether a task is pending, in progress, complete, or has some other status.

When a task is complete, click the check box in the Sort by: Complete column to the left of the task's subject. A check mark called a **Completed icon** then appears in the Complete column and a line through the task indicates it is complete.

In this project, Table 2–5 contains tasks that occur once and will be later made into group tasks, assigned, or forwarded.

Table 2–5 Task List

Task	Due Date
Pick up hats and practice jerseys from coach	1/14/2008
Get Econ class book	1/15/2008
Set up meeting with advisor	1/11/2008
Make appointment with dentist	1/10/2008
Check on availability of parking lots for fund-raiser carwash	1/25/2008

To Create a Task List

The following steps create a task list.

1

• Click the Tasks button in the Navigation Pane to open the To-Do-List – Microsoft Outlook window.

2

• Click the Tasks folder in the My Tasks folder list to switch to the Tasks – Microsoft Outlook window.

• Click the Subject text box and then type `Pick up hats and practice jerseys from coach` as the first task.

• Press the TAB key and then type `1/14/2008` in the Due Date text box (Figure 2–35).

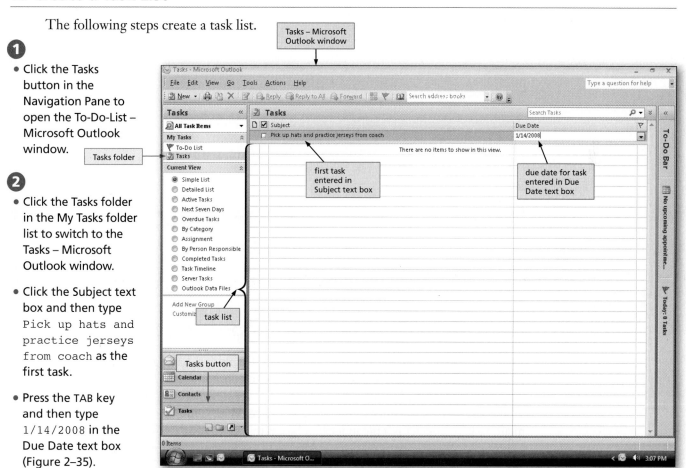

Figure 2–35

3

- Press the ENTER key.

- Repeat Steps 1 and 2 to enter the remaining tasks in Table 2–5.

- Click outside the task list to display the completed task list (Figure 2–36).

Q&A

Is there a way to add more detail to a task?

Yes. To add details to tasks, such as start dates, status, and priority, double-click a task in the task list to open a Task window.

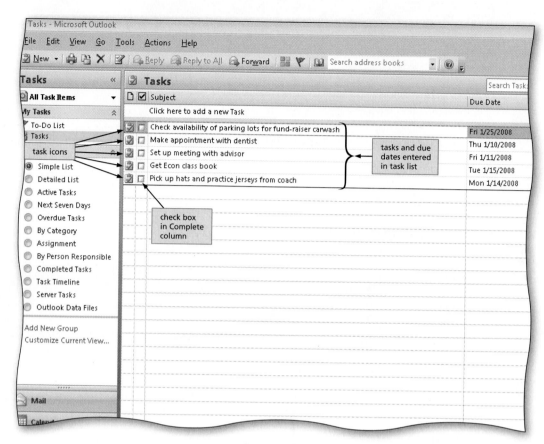

Figure 2–36

Other Ways

1. Click New Task button on Standard toolbar

2. On File menu point to New, click Task on New submenu

3. Press CTRL+N

Exporting, Deleting, and Importing Subfolders

The calendar is now ready to be saved to a USB flash drive. Saving your work to an external storage device allows you to take your schedule to another computer.

With many application software packages, a single file, such as a letter or spreadsheet, can be saved directly to an external storage device. With Outlook, however, each appointment, task, or contact is a file in itself. Thus, rather than saving numerous individual files, Outlook uses an **Import and Export Wizard** to guide you through the process of saving an entire subfolder. Transferring a subfolder to a USB flash drive is called **exporting**. Moving a subfolder back to a computer is called **importing**. Subfolders can be imported and exported from any Outlook application. Outlook then saves the subfolder to a USB flash drive, adding the extension **.pst**.

To Export a Subfolder to a USB Flash Drive

The following steps show how to export Marcus' Calendar subfolder to a USB flash drive.

• Connect the USB flash drive containing the Data Files for Students to one of the computer's USB ports.

• Click File on the menu bar and then click Import and Export to display the Import and Export Wizard dialog box.

• Click Export to a file in the Choose an action to perform list (Figure 2–37).

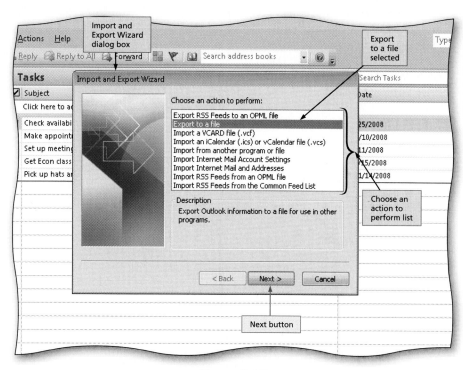

Figure 2–37

• Click the Next button.

• In the Export to a File dialog box, click Personal Folder File (.pst) and then click the Next button to display the Export Personal Folders dialog box.

• If necessary, scroll up until the Calendar folder is visible and then click the plus sign (+) to the left of the Calendar icon in the Select the folder to export from list to see Marcus' calendar in the list.

• Click Marcus' Calendar to select it as the folder to be exported (Figure 2–38).

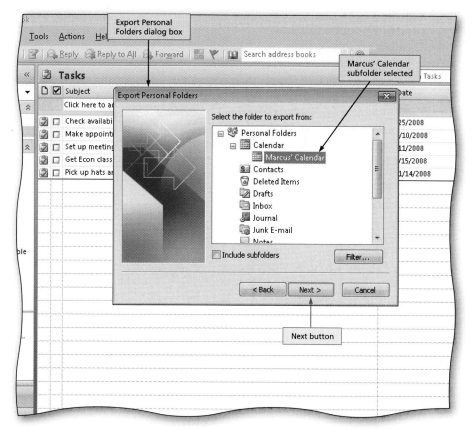

Figure 2–38

- Click the Next button.

- Type e:\Marcus' Calendar.pst in the Save exported file as text box and then click the 'Replace duplicates with items exported' option button (Figure 2–39). (If your USB flash drive is not labeled E, type the drive letter accordingly.)

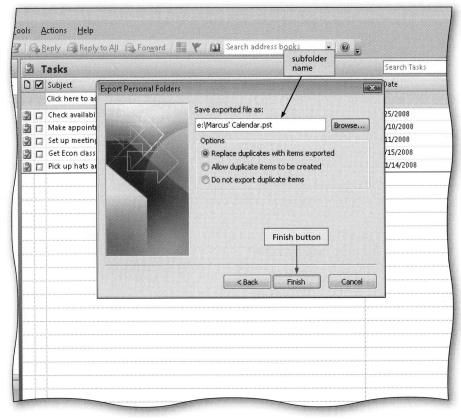

Figure 2–39

- Click the Finish button to display the Create Microsoft Personal Folders dialog box (Figure 2–40).

- Click the OK button to close the dialog box and return to the Tasks window.

Q&A

What programs can I use to view the exported subfolder?

Exported subfolders can be viewed only in Outlook. However, they can be saved as another file type, such as a text file, and then imported into other programs.

BTW

Saving
All appointments, events, meetings, and tasks are saved as separate files on your hard disk. As such, they can be edited, moved, copied, or deleted. These items can be saved as a group using the Import and Export Wizard on the File menu.

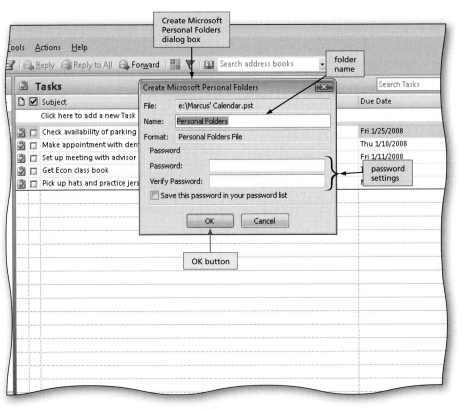

Figure 2–40

To Delete a Personal Subfolder

The Marcus' Calendar subfolder now has been exported to a USB flash drive. A copy of it is still present on the hard disk of your computer, however, and appears in Outlook's Folder List. To delete a subfolder from the computer entirely, use the Delete command. The following steps delete a personal subfolder. If you did not complete the previous set of steps, do not delete the Marcus' Calendar subfolder.

- Click the Calendar button in the Navigation Pane to display the Marcus' Calendar window.

- Right-click the date banner to display the shortcut menu (Figure 2–41).

- Click Delete "Marcus' Calendar" on the shortcut menu to delete the folder from Outlook's folder list.

- Click the Yes button in the dialog box that asks if you are sure you want to delete the folder.

Q&A

Is there a way to retrieve a deleted folder?

Yes. Outlook sends the deleted sub-folder to the **Deleted Items** folder in the Folder List. If you accidentally delete a subfolder without first exporting it to an external storage device, you can still open the subfolder by double-clicking it in the Deleted Items folder in the Folders List.

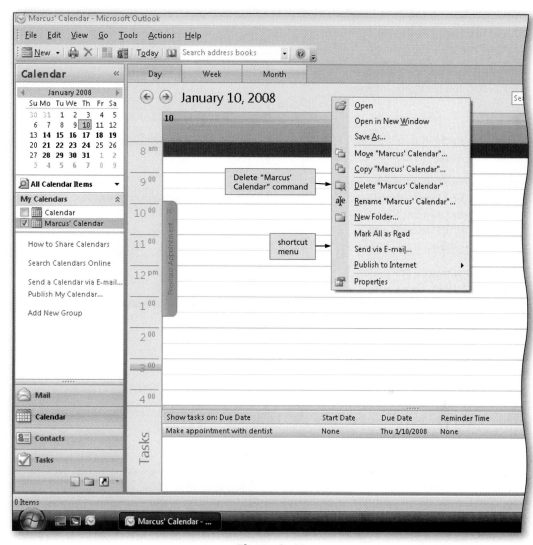

Figure 2–41

Other Ways

1. On File menu point to Folders, click Delete "Calendar" on Folders submenu

2. Press ALT+F, press F, press D

To Import a Subfolder

Earlier, the Calendar subfolder containing Marcus' appointment and event files was exported to a USB flash drive. The following steps import the same Calendar subfolder from the USB flash drive as well as other Data files to be used later in the chapter.

- If necessary, connect the USB flash drive containing the Data Files for Students to one of the computer's USB ports.

- If necessary, click the Calendar button in the Navigation Pane.

- Click File on the menu bar and then click Import and Export.

- When the Import and Export Wizard dialog box is displayed, click 'Import from another program or file' and then click the Next button.

- When the Import a File dialog box is displayed, click Personal Folder File (.pst) and then click the Next button.

3

- In the Import Personal Folders dialog box, type e:\Marcus' Calendar.pst in the File to Import text box or click the Browse button to access the USB flash drive and select the Marcus' Calendar subfolder (Figure 2–42). (If your USB flash drive is not labeled E, type the drive letter accordingly.)

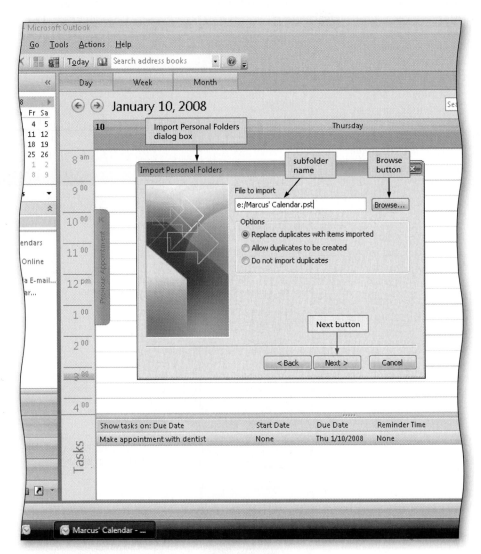

Figure 2–42

4

- Click the Next button to display the Import Personal Folders dialog box.

- Click Calendar in the 'Select the folder to import from' list (Figure 2–43).

5

- Click the Finish button to close the dialog box and return to the Calendar window.

6

- Repeat Steps 1 through 5 twice, once to import Marcus' Contacts subfolder (selecting the Contact folder in Step 4) and once to import Marcus' Inbox subfolder (selecting the Inbox folder in Step 4) from the Chapter 2 folder in the Data Files for Students.

Importing
Other contact information can be imported through the Import and Export Wizard on the File menu. This wizard allows you to copy to Outlook information that was created and saved in other applications.

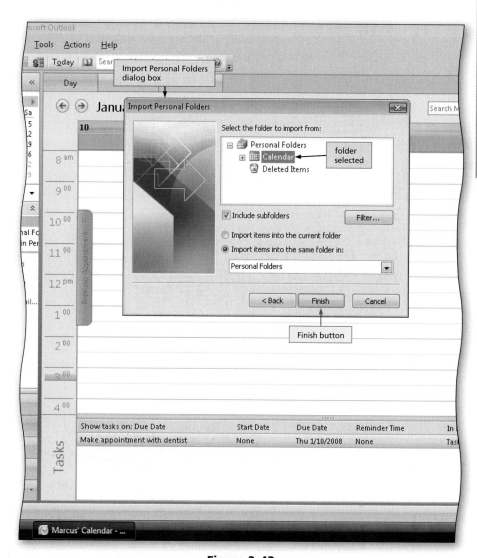

Figure 2–43

Meeting and Task Management

If you are in charge of an organization or group, you likely will have to schedule meetings and delegate tasks to other members of the group. Using your contact list, Outlook allows you to easily perform these functions. The following sections illustrate how to assign tasks and schedule meetings with individuals in the Marcus' Contact list.

To Assign a Task to Another Person

Using the task list previously created in this project and the imported Marcus' Contacts contact list, the following steps assign a task to an individual in the Marcus' Contacts contact list.

1

- Click the Contacts button in the Navigation Pane and then click Marcus' Contacts in the My Contacts list.

- Click the Tasks button in the Navigation Pane to display the Task window.

- Double-click the Pick up hats and practice jerseys from coach task to display the Pick up hats and practice jerseys from coach – Task window.

- Double-click the title bar to maximize the window (Figure 2–44).

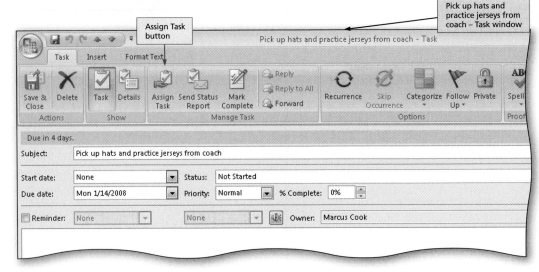

Figure 2–44

2

- Click the Assign Task button on the Ribbon.

- Type Jake Nunan in the To text box (Figure 2–45).

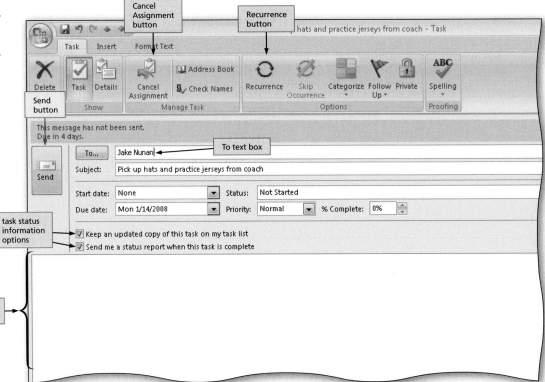

Figure 2–45

- Click the Send button to send the task to Jake Nunan and close the task window (Figure 2–46).

Q&A

Can I assign a task to more than one person at a time?

Yes. Outlook does allow you to assign a task to more than one person at a time; however, in order to have Outlook keep you up to date on the progress of a task, you must divide the work into separate tasks and then assign each task individually.

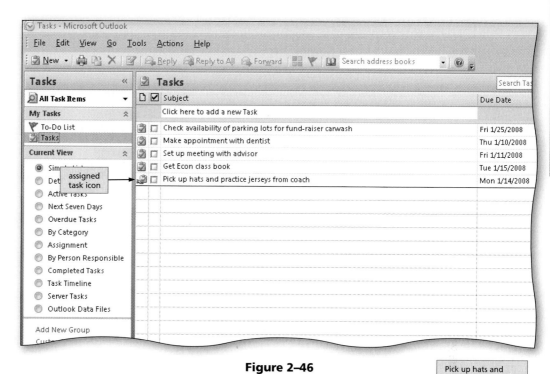

Figure 2–46

- Double-click the Pick up hats and practice jerseys from coach task to open the task window (Figure 2–47).

- Click the Close button on the Pick up hats and practice jerseys from coach task to close the task window.

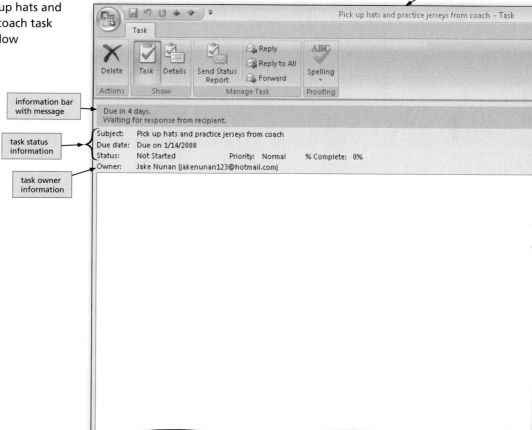

Figure 2–47

To Accept a Task Assignment

When a recipient receives a task assignment, it appears in his or her Inbox. Then, the recipient has the option to accept or decline the task. The following steps show how to accept a task assignment.

Note: The steps on pages OUT 108 through OUT 110 are for demonstration purposes only, thus, if you are stepping through this project on a computer, then you must have someone send you a task request so it appears in the Inbox as shown in Figure 2–48.

- If necessary, click the Mail button in the Navigation Pane.

- If necessary, click the plus sign (+) next to the Inbox folder in the All Mail Items list, and then select the Marcus' Inbox folder.

- Click the Mary Cook Task Request to display it in the Reading pane (Figure 2–48).

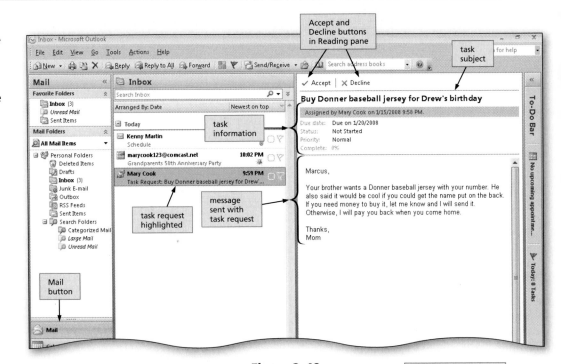

Figure 2–48

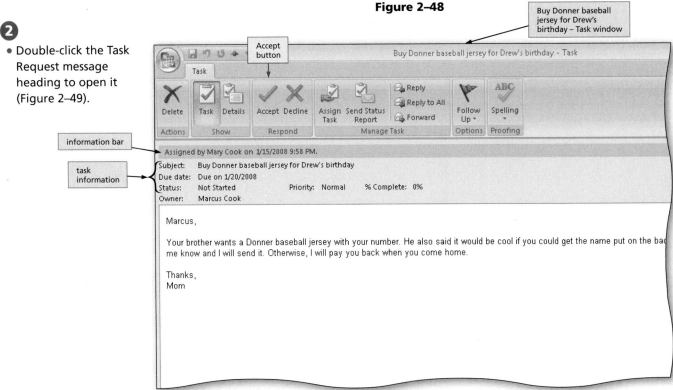

- Double-click the Task Request message heading to open it (Figure 2–49).

Figure 2–49

3

- Click the Accept button on the Ribbon to display the Accepting Task dialog box (Figure 2–50).

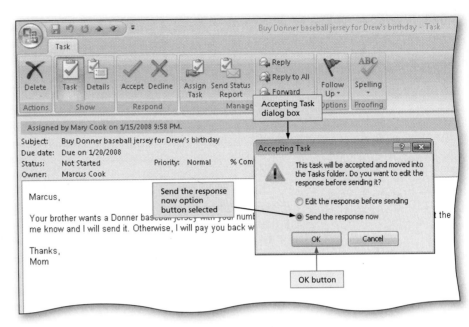

Figure 2–50

4

- Click the 'Send the response now' option button, and then click the OK button to send the response and close the Accepting Task dialog box.

5

- Click the Task button in the Navigation Pane to display the Task List. If necessary, click Tasks in the My Tasks list in the Navigation Pane (Figure 2–51).

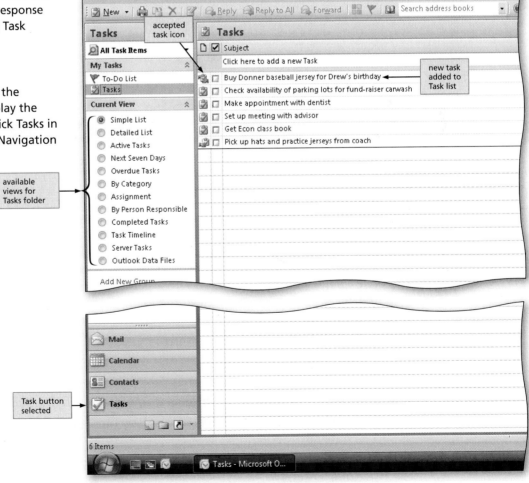

Figure 2–51

- When a recipient accepts a task request, the requestor receives a message indicating that the task has been accepted (Figure 2–52).

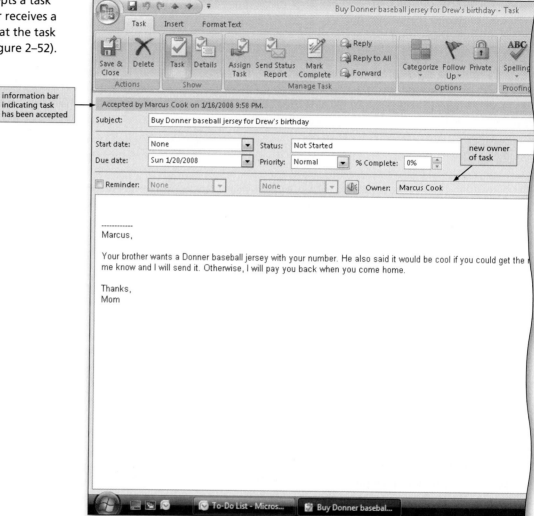

information bar indicating task has been accepted

new owner of task

Figure 2–52

To Customize the Tasks Window

The default view for the task list is shown in Figure 2–51 on the previous page. This view contains the Task icon, the completed task check box, the task description, and the due date. Outlook allows you to add or delete columns, or **fields**, so you can display only the information you want to view. To modify the current view of the task list, you would follow these steps.

1. On the View menu, point to Current View, and then click Customize Current View in the Current View submenu.

2. When the Customize View: Simple List dialog box is displayed, click the Fields button.

3. To add a new field, select a field in the Available fields list, and then click the Add button.

4. To delete a field, select a field in the Show these fields in this order list, and then click the Remove button.

5. When you are finished customizing the view, click the OK buttons in both open dialog boxes.

For the same reason you created a separate folder for calendar items, you may want to create a separate folder for tasks and move the current task list to that folder. The following steps describe how to create a personal tasks folder and move the current task list to that folder.

TO MOVE TASKS TO A NEW PERSONAL FOLDER

1. With the Tasks window active, right-click the Tasks title bar above the task list.

2. Click New Folder on the shortcut menu.

3. When the Create New Folder dialog box is displayed, type Marcus' Tasks in the Name text box and select Tasks in the select where to place the folder list. Click the OK button.

4. Click the first task in the task list, then, while holding the SHIFT key, click the last task in the task list to select all the tasks in the task list.

5. Right-click the task list. Click Move to Folder on the shortcut menu.

6. When the Move Items dialog box is displayed, select Marcus' Tasks in the Move the selected items to the folder list. Click the OK button.

BTW

Updating Tasks
To send a status report for a task on which you are working, open the task. Click Send Status Report on the Ribbon. If the task was assigned to you, the person who sent the task request will automatically be added to the update list.

To Schedule Meetings

Earlier in this chapter, you added an appointment for a team meeting. Outlook allows you to invite multiple attendees to a meeting by sending a single invitation. The following sections show how to invite attendees for that meeting.

1

- With the Calendar window active, click January 14 in the Date Navigator.

- Double-click the Team Meeting appointment to open the Team Meeting – Recurring Appointment window.

- When the Open Recurring Item dialog box is displayed, if necessary, click Open this occurrence, and then click the OK button.

- Double-click the title bar to maximize the window.

- Click the Scheduling button on the Ribbon to display the Scheduling sheet (Figure 2–53).

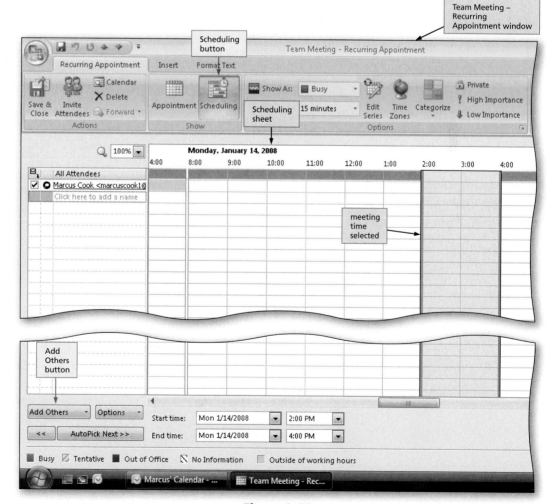

Figure 2–53

- Click the Add Others button, and then click Add From Address Book to display the Select Attendees and Resources dialog box (Figure 2–54).

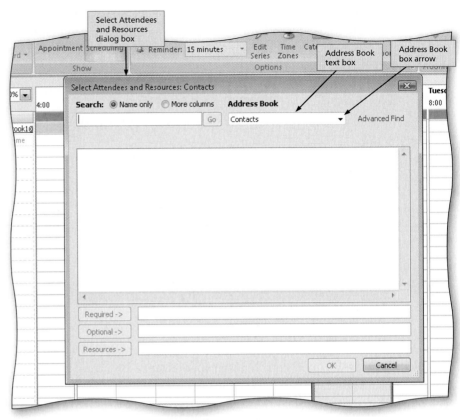

Figure 2–54

- Click the Address Book box arrow, and then click Marcus' Contacts.

- While holding the SHIFT key, click Trevor Walker to select the entire list.

- Click the Required button to add the selected names to the Required text box (Figure 2–55).

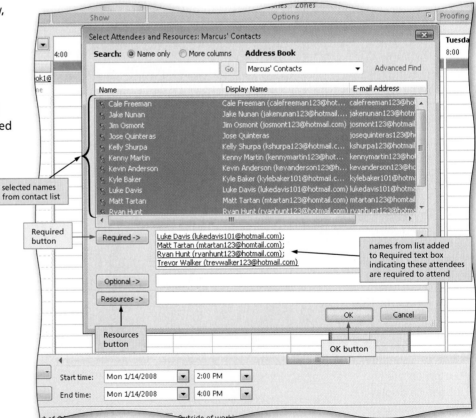

Figure 2–55

4

- Click the OK button to close the Select Attendees and Resources dialog box and display the Team Meeting – Recurring Appointment window (Figure 2–56).

- If the Microsoft Office Internet Free/Busy dialog box appears, click the Cancel button.

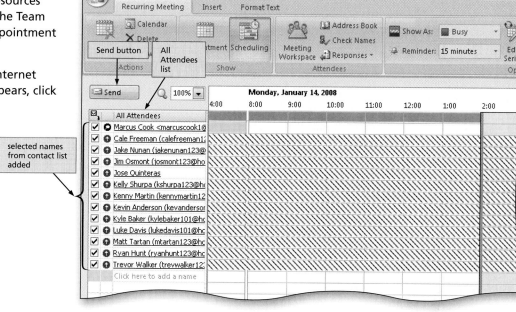

Figure 2–56

5

- Click the Send button to close the Meeting window and display the Calendar window (Figure 2–57).

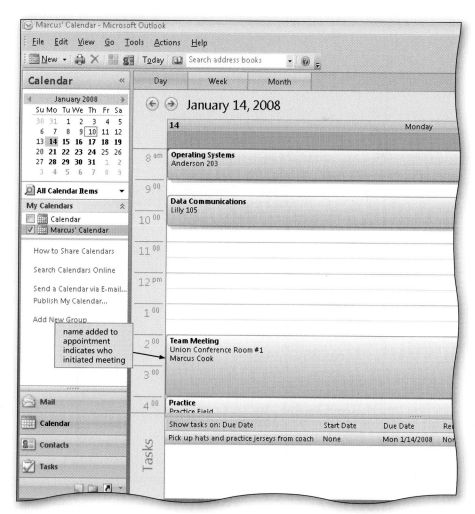

Figure 2–57

6

- Double-click the Team Meeting appointment and click OK in the Open Recurring Item dialog box to open the appointment to see the invitation recipients and whether any replies to the invitation have been received (Figure 2–58).

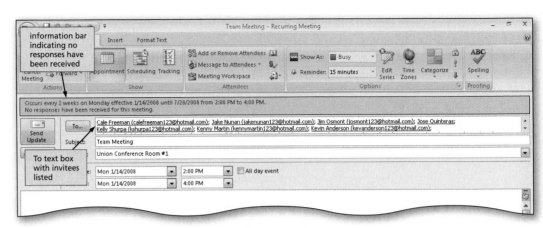

Figure 2–58

To Reply to Meeting Requests

Once you receive a meeting request, you will either accept it or decline it. A meeting request will appear in your Inbox similar to the one shown in Figure 2–59. Outlook allows you to choose from four responses: Accept, Tentative, Decline, or Propose New Time. The following steps accept a meeting request.

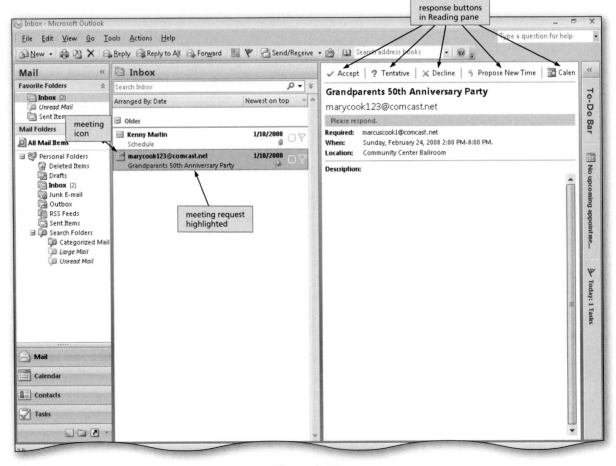

Figure 2–59

1

• If necessary, click the Mail button in the Navigation Pane to display the Inbox folder and then click the Grandparents 50th Anniversary Party message to select it (Figure 2–60).

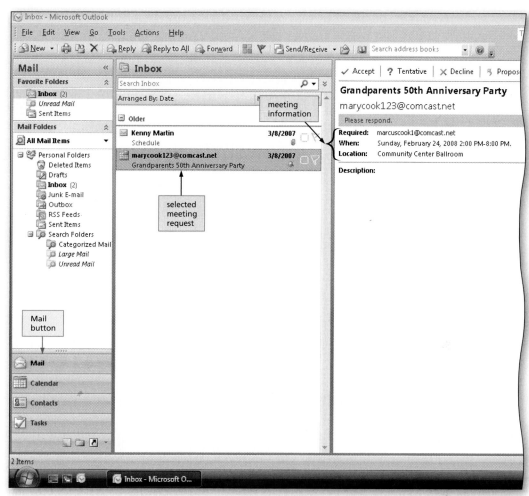

Figure 2–60

2

• Double-click the Grandparents 50th Anniversary Party message heading to open it (Figure 2–61).

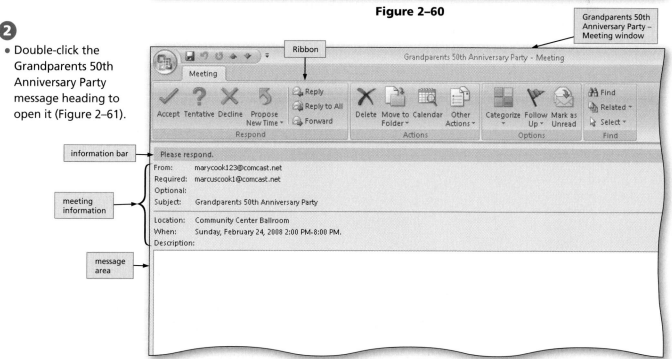

Figure 2–61

● Click the Accept button on the Ribbon to display the Microsoft Office Outlook dialog box (Figure 2–62).

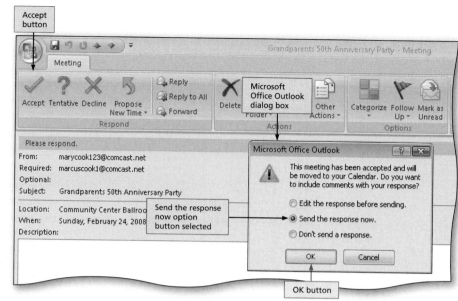

Figure 2–62

● Select the 'Send the response now' option button, and then click the OK button to close the dialog box and display the Inbox window.

● Click the Calendar button in the Navigation Pane.

● Click the right scroll arrow in the Date Navigator so the February 2008 calendar appears.

● Click 24 in the Date Navigator to display February 24 in the appointment area (Figure 2–63).

Q&A

How does the person organizing the meeting know whether I have accepted or declined a meeting request?

When a meeting is accepted, the meeting organizer receives a message indicating that the request has been accepted. If the meeting request is declined, the request is moved to the Deleted Items folder, and the meeting organizer receives a message indicating that the request was declined.

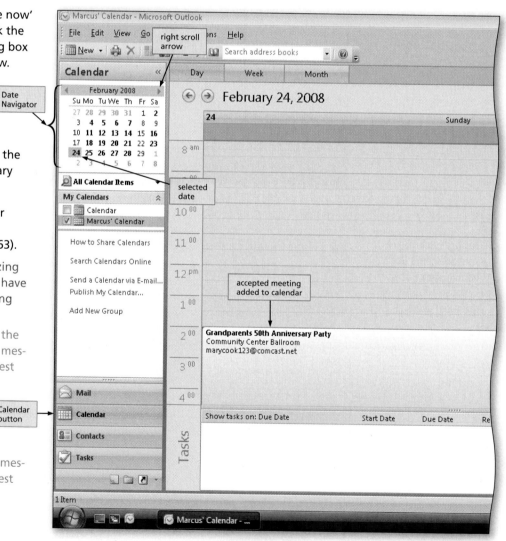

Figure 2–63

To Propose a New Meeting Time

One of the available responses to a meeting request is to propose a new time. When you click the Propose New Time button, Outlook allows you to send a response to the meeting organizer indicating that you tentatively accept the request, but propose the meeting be held at a different time. To propose a new time for a meeting, you would perform the following steps.

1. Double-click the appropriate meeting request to open the request.
2. Click the Propose New Time button on the Ribbon.
3. When the Propose New Time dialog box is displayed, drag through the time slot that you want to propose, or enter the appropriate information in the Meeting start time and Meeting end time time boxes.
4. Click the Propose Time button.
5. When the New Time Proposed – Meeting Response window opens, click the Send button.

To Change the Time of a Meeting and Send an Update

Once someone has proposed a new meeting time, it may be necessary to update the meeting request to the other potential attendees. Other reasons to update a meeting request may be that you have added or removed attendees, changed the meeting to a recurring series, or moved the meeting to a different date. To change the time of a meeting and send an update, you would perform the following steps.

1. With the Calendar window active, drag the meeting to its new time.
2. When the Microsoft Office Outlook dialog box is displayed, select the 'Save changes and send an update' option.
3. Click OK. If the appointment opens, click the Send button.

Q&A What if a meeting needs to be canceled?

If you need to cancel a meeting, open the meeting window, click Cancel Meeting on the Ribbon, and then click OK in the Confirm Delete dialog box. Click the Send Cancellation button to send the cancellation and remove the meeting from the calendar.

Creating and Editing Notes

Another organizational tool included with Outlook is Notes. **Notes** provides you with a medium on which to record thoughts, ideas, questions, or anything else that you might write down on a sticky note or note pad. Notes can remain open while you perform other work on your computer. You can add to your notes, and your changes are saved automatically. Notes can be categorized per your personal specifications.

BTW

Meeting Workspace
Microsoft Outlook and SharePoint Services offer Meeting Workspace to help you plan your meeting more efficiently. A Meeting Workspace is a Web site for centralizing all the information required for one or more meetings. To learn more about Meeting Workspace, type `Meeting Workspace` in the Type a question for help box and then press the ENTER key to display a list of topics related to Meeting Workspace.

BTW

Meeting Times
If you use Windows SharePoint Services and have access to other attendees' calendars, use the AutoPick Next button in the Scheduling sheet of the Meeting window to find the next available free time for all attendees.

To Create and Edit a Note

The following steps create and edit a note that serves as a reminder for Marcus.

- Click the Notes button in the Navigation Pane.

- Click the New Note button on the Standard toolbar to open the Untitled – Notes window (Figure 2–64).

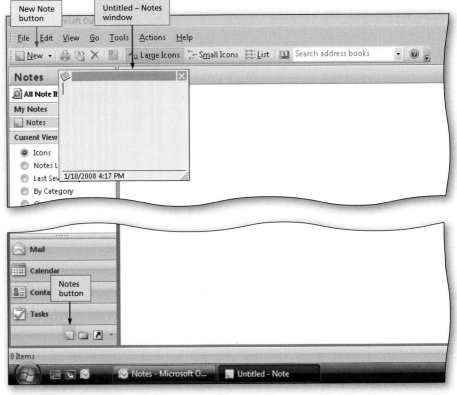

Figure 2–64

- Type `Talk to Coach about new equipment.` as the entry (Figure 2–65).

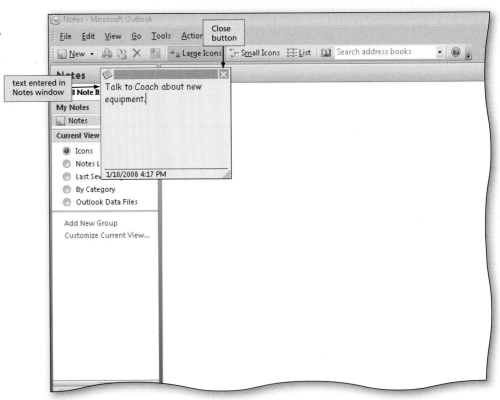

Figure 2–65

- Click the Close button to close the Notes window and place the note in the Notes folder (Figure 2–66).

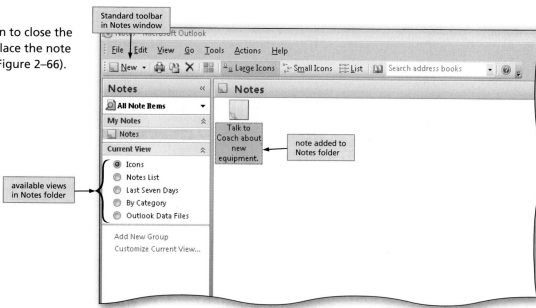

Figure 2–66

4

- Right-click the note and then point to Categorize on the shortcut menu (Figure 2–67).

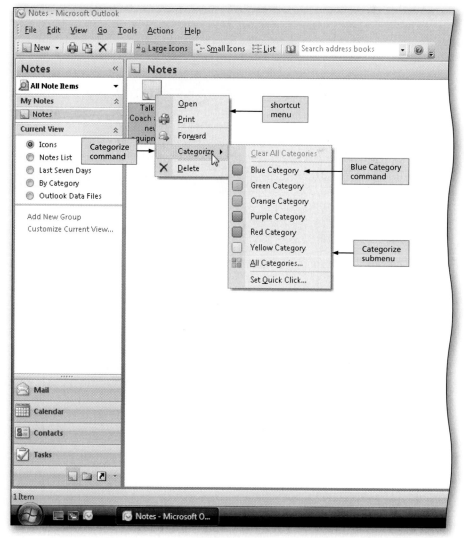

Figure 2–67

5

- Click Blue Category on the Categorize submenu to color the note blue (Figure 2–68). If the Rename Category dialog box is displayed, click the No button to close it.

Figure 2–68

Other Ways

1. Click Note icon in Notes window, click the Categorize button, click category on Categorize submenu

Customize Calendar Settings

Outlook provides you with several options to change the appearance of the Calendar window. You can customize your work week by selecting the days you work if they differ from the default Monday to Friday work week. You also can change the hours that appear as work hours in the appointment area. Additionally, you can categorize your appointments to make them easier to view.

To Set Work Week Options

Some people have schedules that differ from the standard Monday through Friday work week. Whether it is a six-days-per-week schedule, a four-days-per-week schedule, an alternating day schedule, or any other type of schedule, Outlook allows you to select the days that display in your calendar.

The following steps set work week options.

- Click Calendar in the Navigation Pane.

- With the Calendar window active, click Tools on the menu bar, and then click Options to open the Options dialog box (Figure 2–69).

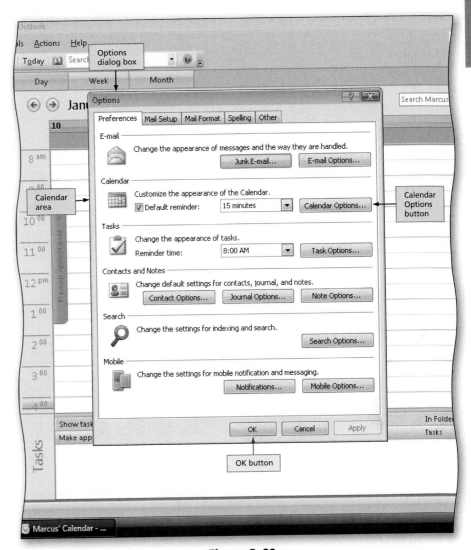

Figure 2–69

2

- Click the Calendar Options button to open the Calendar Options dialog box (Figure 2–70).

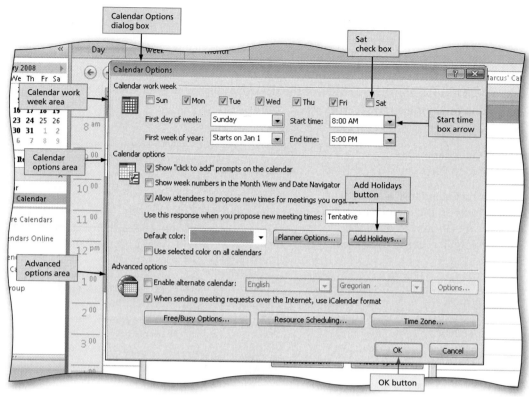

Figure 2–70

3

- In the Calendar work week area, click the Sat check box to add Saturday to your work week.

- Click the Start time box arrow and then select 7:00 a.m. as the new start time (Figure 2–71).

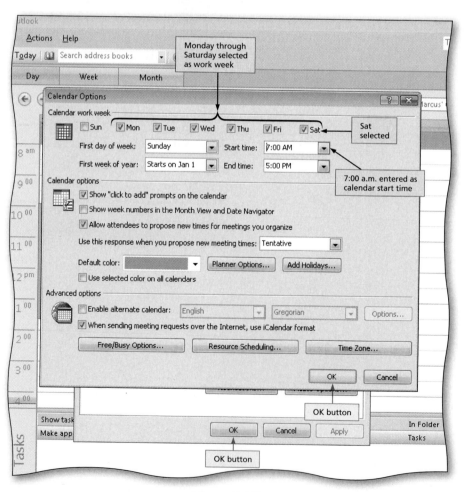

Figure 2–71

• Click the OK button in both open dialog boxes to close them.

• Scroll up in the Appointment area so that 6 a.m. shows as the first time slot (Figure 2–72).

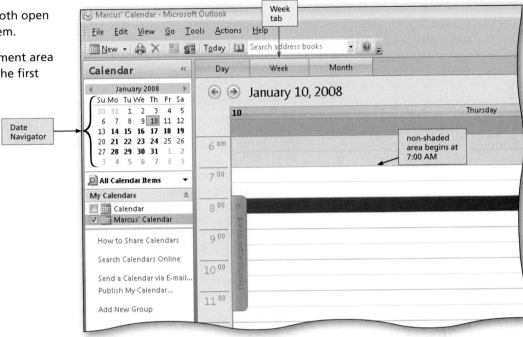

Figure 2–72

• Click January 14 in the Date Navigator.

• Click the Week tab in the Appointment area, and then, if necessary, click the Show work week option button to display the calendar in Work Week view (Figure 2–73).

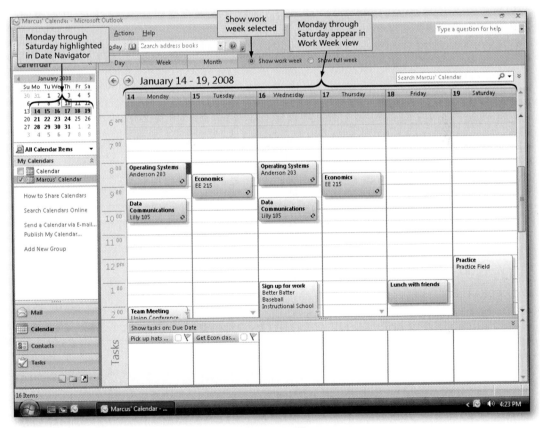

Figure 2–73

Other Ways

1. Press ALT+T, press O, press C

To Categorize the Calendar and Edit Category Labels

Outlook offers six default color categories from which to choose to categorize appointments and meetings. For example, you can categorize your class schedule, your work schedule, and your extracurricular activities. The categories can be renamed to fit your needs, or you can add your own categories.

The following steps categorize Marcus' calendar and edit the category labels.

1

- With the Calendar window active, click the Month tab in the Appointment area to display the calendar in Month view, and then click the Operating Systems appointment on January 14 to select it.

- Click the Categorize button on the Standard toolbar to display the Categorize menu (Figure 2–74).

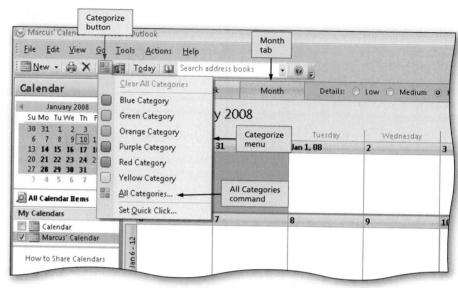

Figure 2–74

2

- Click All Categories on the Categorize menu to open the Color Categories dialog box.

- If necessary, click the Blue Category to select it, and then click the Rename button.

- Type Work as the new Category name.

- Rename the Green Category as Class, and the Orange Category as Practice (Figure 2–75)

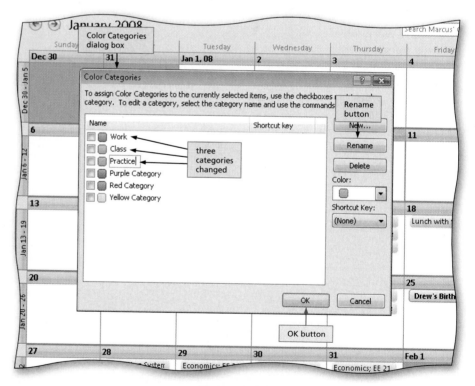

Figure 2–75

● Click the OK button to close the
Color Categories dialog box and
return to the Calendar window
and select the Operating Systems
appointment (Figure 2–76).

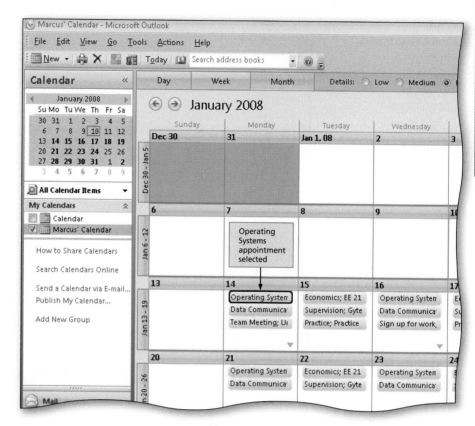

Figure 2–76

④

● Click the Categorize button on the
Standard toolbar to display the
Categorize menu (Figure 2–77).

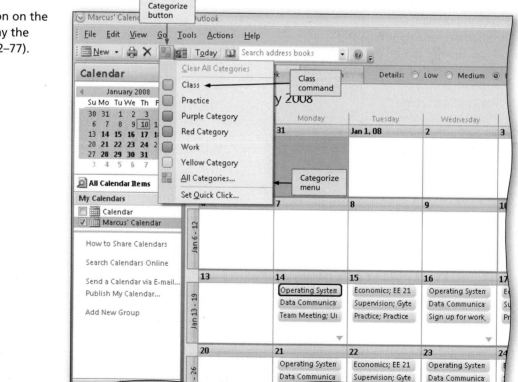

Figure 2–77

5

- Click Class on the Categorize menu to categorize the Operating Systems recurring appointment (Figure 2–78).

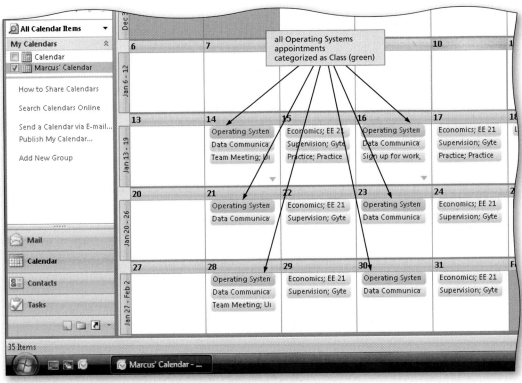

Figure 2–78

6

- Repeat Steps 3 through 5 to categorize the remaining recurring appointments and the work-related appointments in the calendar. Select Practice as the category for the Team Meeting recurring appointment (Figure 2–79).

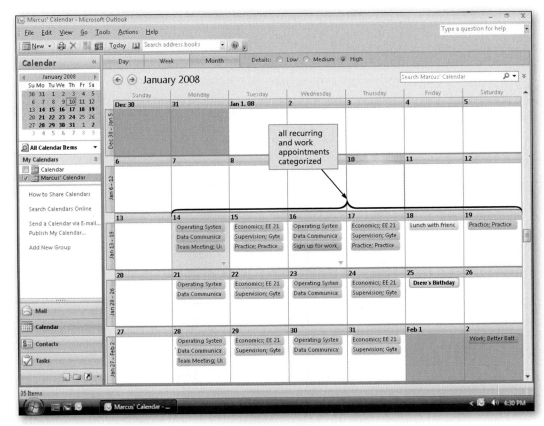

Figure 2–79

Printing a Calendar

All or part of a calendar can be printed in a number of different layouts, or **print styles**. The following section describes how to print the calendar in Daily, Weekly, and Monthly Styles.

To Print the Calendar in Daily Style

A printout of a single day of the calendar, called **Daily Style**, shows the day's appointments, tasks, and a two-month calendar. The following steps show how to print the calendar in Daily Style.

1

• Ready the printer.

• With the Calendar window active and January 14, 2008 selected in Day view, click the Print button on the Standard toolbar to display the Print dialog box (Figure 2–80).

2

• With the Daily Style selected in the Print Style list, click OK to close the dialog box and print the daily schedule of appointments for January 14, 2008 as shown in Figure 2–1d on page OUT 75.

Q&A

Is there a way to modify what is included on the printout?

Yes. The Page Setup button in the Print dialog box allows style modifications to include or omit various features, including the TaskPad and the Notes area. Specific time ranges also can be printed rather than the default 7:00 a.m. to 6:00 p.m.

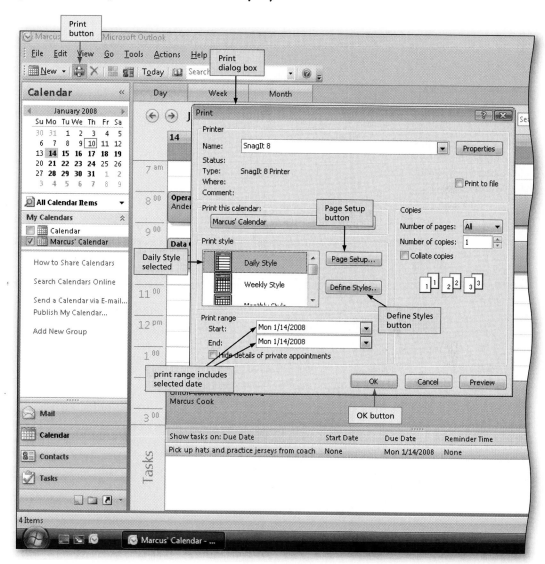

Figure 2–80

Other Ways

1. On File menu click Print
2. Press CTRL+P

To Print the Calendar in Weekly Style

Printing a calendar in Weekly Style can be accomplished through the Print button on the Standard toolbar while viewing the calendar in Week view, or by selecting the Weekly Style in the Print dialog box. The following step prints the calendar in Weekly Style.

1 Ready the printer. Click the Print button on the Standard toolbar. Click Weekly Style in the Print Style list and then click the OK button to print the document shown in Figure 2–1e on page OUT 75.

To Print the Calendar in Monthly Style

The following step prints the calendar in Monthly Style.

1 Ready the printer. Click the Print button on the Standard toolbar. Click Monthly Style in the Print Style list and then click the OK button to print the document shown in Figure 2–1f on page OUT 75.

To Print the Task List

To print only the task list, first open the Task folder. The following steps print the task list by itself.

1 Click the Tasks button in the Navigation Pane to display the task list.

2 Click the Print button on the Standard toolbar. When the Print dialog box is displayed, click the OK button to print the task list (Figure 2–81).

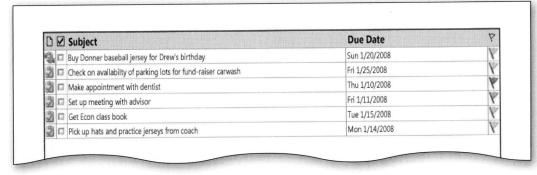

🗎 ☑ Subject	Due Date	▽
Buy Donner baseball jersey for Drew's birthday	Sun 1/20/2008	
Check on availabilty of parking lots for fund-raiser carwash	Fri 1/25/2008	
Make appointment with dentist	Thu 1/10/2008	
Set up meeting with advisor	Fri 1/11/2008	
Get Econ class book	Tue 1/15/2008	
Pick up hats and practice jerseys from coach	Mon 1/14/2008	

Figure 2–81

Archiving Items

Outlook has a built-in feature called **AutoArchive** that helps manage Outlook folders. AutoArchive is on by default and can be scheduled to run automatically. AutoArchive searches Outlook folders for items that are used infrequently, and items of which the content is no longer valid (a completed task, an old meeting, etc.). AutoArchive can be set up either to delete expired items permanently, and/or move old items to a special archive file. When AutoArchive is run for the first time, Outlook automatically creates this archive file. Outlook also creates an Archive Folders folder in the Folder List. AutoArchive does not delete any folders even if they are empty. If you decide that you want to move archived items back to their original folders, you can use the Import Export wizard to move the items back to the original folder or any folder you specify.

Customizing AutoArchive

Outlook allows you to change how AutoArchive works. The default settings, or global settings, of AutoArchive are set to archive all folders except the Contacts folder. You also can specify **per-folder settings** that override the global settings. With per-folder settings, you can have different archive settings for different folders.

To Change the Default Settings for AutoArchive

The following steps show how to change the default settings for AutoArchive.

- Click Tools on the menu bar, and then click Options to display the Options dialog box.

- Click the Other tab to display the Other sheet (Figure 2–82).

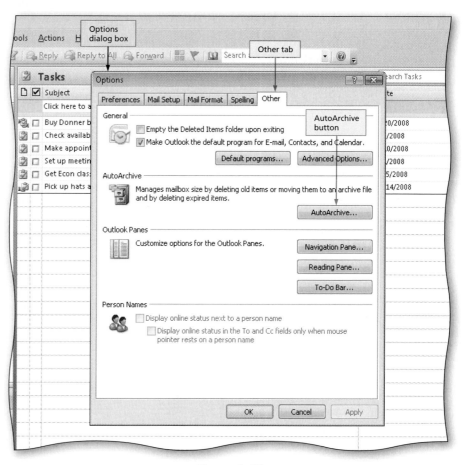

Figure 2–82

- Click the AutoArchive button to display the AutoArchive dialog box (Figure 2–83).

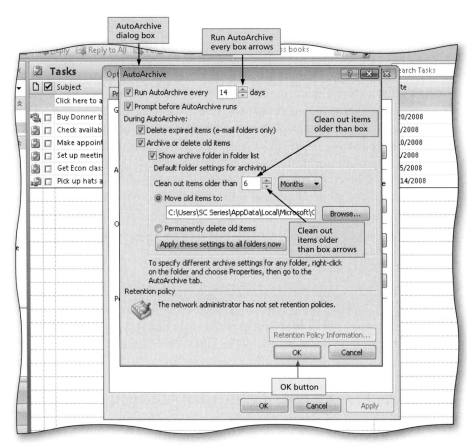

Figure 2–83

- If necessary, click the 'Run AutoArchive every' check box.

- Change the 'Run AutoArchive every' box to 10 by clicking the down arrow.

- Change the 'Clean out items older than' box to 8 by clicking the up arrow (Figure 2–84).

- Click the OK button on both open dialog boxes to close them and return to the Task window.

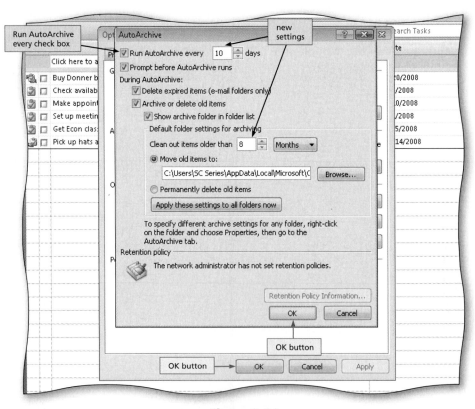

Figure 2–84

Other Ways

1. Press ALT+T, press O

Instant Messaging

One of the more useful communication tools available with Outlook is Windows Live Messenger. **Windows Live Messenger** allows you to communicate instantly with your online contacts using instant messaging. **Instant messaging (IM)** is real-time communication shown in a pop-up style application that occurs as a typed conversation between two or more participants. Windows Live Messenger is included with the Windows Vista operating system. The advantage of using Windows Live Messenger over e-mail is that the message you send appears immediately on the computer of the person with whom you are communicating, provided that person has signed in to Windows Live Messenger.

Before using Windows Live Messenger with Outlook, a contact first must have an MSN Hotmail account or a Windows Live ID and have Windows Live Messenger software installed and running on his or her computer. **MSN Hotmail** is a Microsoft service that provides free e-mail accounts to allow you to read your e-mail messages from any computer connected to the Internet. The **Windows Live ID** service is a secure way for you to sign in to multiple Web sites with a single user name and password. As an MSN Hotmail user, your MSN Hotmail sign-in name and password also are your Windows Live ID user name and password.

To Start and Sign In to Windows Live Messenger

Before using Windows Live Messenger with Outlook, you must enable instant messaging in Outlook, start Windows Messenger, and sign in to the .NET Messenger Service using your sign-in name and password. The following steps start Windows Live Messenger and sign in to the .NET Messenger Service using your sign-in name and password.

- Click the Minimize button on the Outlook window title bar to minimize the window to the Windows Vista taskbar.

- Click the Start button on the Windows Vista taskbar to display the Start menu.

- Click All Programs at the bottom of the left pane on the Start menu to display the All Programs list, and then click Windows Live Messenger in the All Programs list to open the Windows Live Messenger window (Figure 2–85)

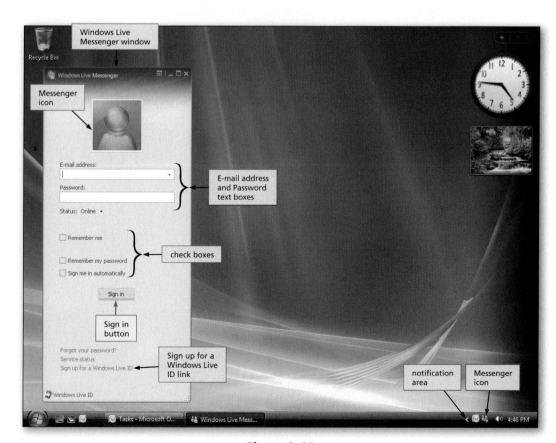

Figure 2–85

- Type your e-mail address and password in the appropriate text boxes in the Windows Live Messenger window (Figure 2–86).

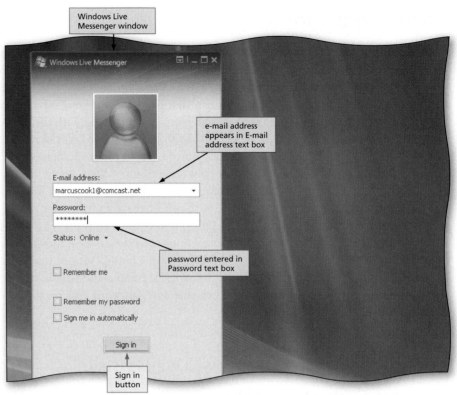

Figure 2–86

- Click the Sign in button to sign in to the Windows Live Messenger Service (Figure 2–87).

What happens if I click the Sign me in automatically check box?

Clicking the Sign me in automatically check box allows Windows Live Messenger to remember your e-mail address and password and sign-in automatically each time you start Windows Live Messenger.

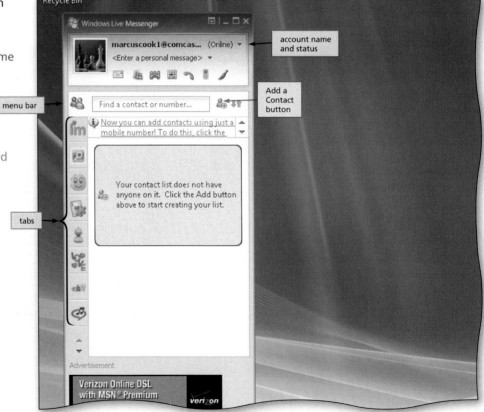

Figure 2–87

To Enable Instant Messaging in Outlook

After signing into Windows Live Messenger, the next step is to enable instant messaging in Outlook. The following steps enable instant messaging in Outlook.

- Click the Tasks – Microsoft Outlook button on the Windows taskbar to display the Outlook window.

- With the Contacts window active, click Tools on the menu bar and then click Options to display the Options dialog box (Figure 2–88).

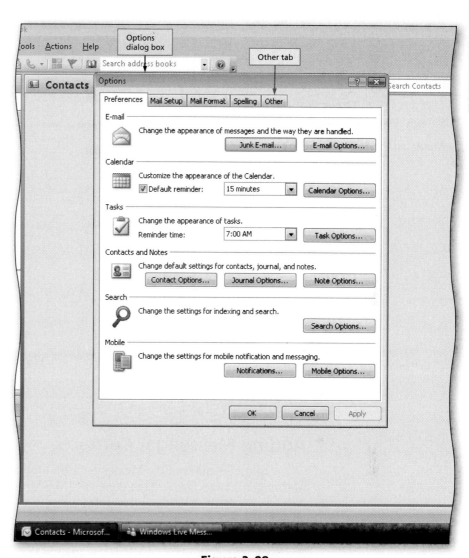

Figure 2–88

2

- Click the Other tab to display the Other sheet.

- In the Other sheet, confirm that the two boxes in the Person Names area have a check mark in each check box (Figure 2–89).

3

- Click the OK button to close the Options dialog box.

- Minimize the Outlook window.

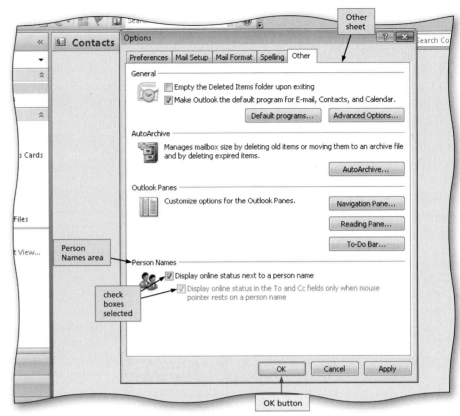

Figure 2–89

Adding Messenger Contacts

To use Windows Live Messenger with Outlook, contacts must be entered in the Messenger contact list, and the contact's IM address must be entered in the Outlook contacts list. Table 2–6 contains the IM addresses for the contacts in the Marcus' Contacts contact list.

Table 2–6 IM Addresses	
Contact Name	**IM Address**
Kevin Anderson	kevanderson123@hotmail.com
Kyle Baker	kylebaker101@hotmail.com
Luke Davis	lukedavis101@hotmail.com
Cale Freeman	calefreeman123@hotmail.com
Ryan Hunt	ryanhunt123@hotmail.com
Kenny Martin	kennymartin123@hotmail.com
Jake Nunan	jakenunan123@hotmail.com
Jim Osmont	josmont123@hotmail.com
Jose Quinteras	josequinteras123@hotmail.com
Kelly Shurpa	kshurpa123@hotmail.com
Matt Tartan	mtartan123@hotmail.com
Trevor Walker	trevwalker123@hotmail.com

After starting Windows Live Messenger, you can add a contact to the contact list if you know the e-mail address or Windows Live Messenger sign-in of the contact. A contact must have an MSN Hotmail account or a Windows Live ID and have the Windows Live Messenger or MSN Messenger software installed on their computer. If you try to add a contact that does not meet these requirements, you are given the chance to send the contact an e-mail invitation that explains how to get a passport and download the Windows Live Messenger or MSN Messenger software.

To Add a Contact to the Messenger Contact List

Windows Live Messenger allows you to add contacts to the contact list. The following steps add a contact to the Messenger contact list using the IM addresses listed in Table 2–6.

1
- Click the Add a Contact icon in the Windows Live Messenger window to display the Windows Live Contacts - Add a Contact dialog box (Figure 2–90).

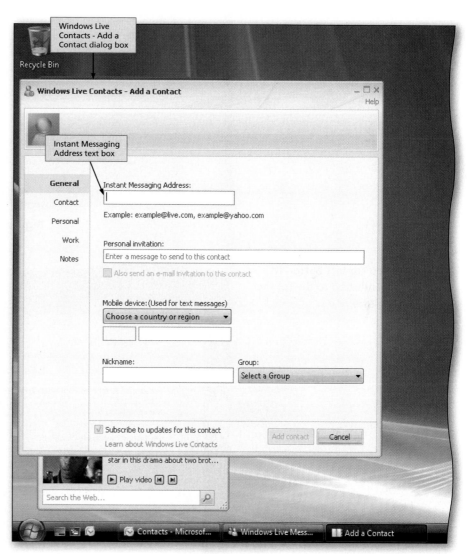

Figure 2–90

2

• Type kevanderson123@hotmail.
com in the Instant Messaging
Address text box (Figure 2–91).

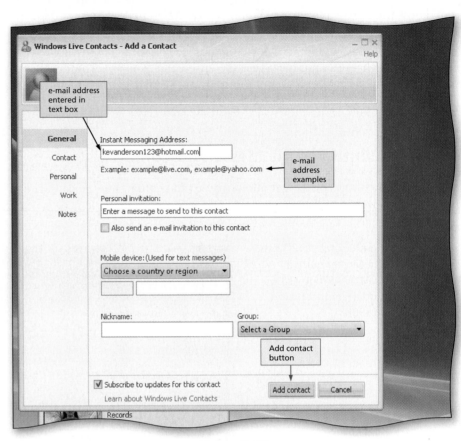

Figure 2–91

3

• Click the Add contact button to
add Kevin Anderson to the contact
list (Figure 2–92).

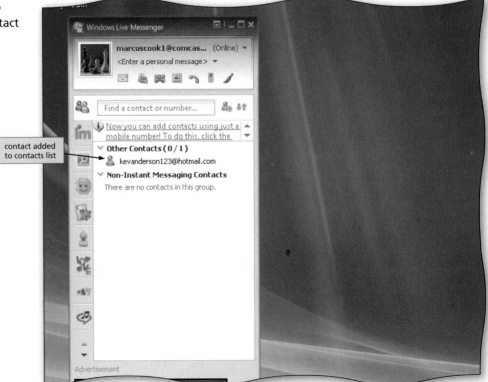

Figure 2–92

4

- Repeat Steps 1 through 3 to enter the remaining contacts in Table 2–6 and display the Windows Live Messenger window showing the added contacts (Figure 2–93).

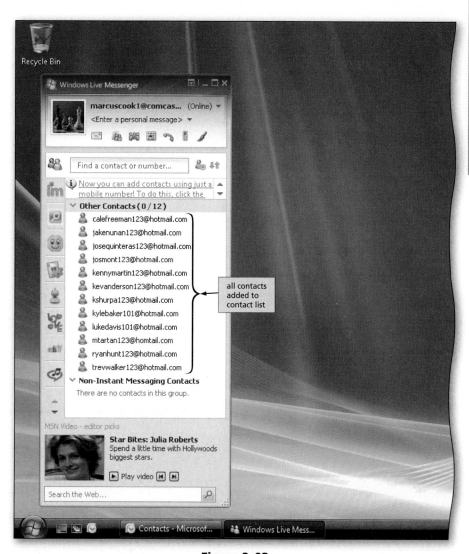

Figure 2–93

To Update the Outlook Contact List

To complete the process of setting up instant messaging with Outlook, the contact list must be updated with IM addresses of the contacts listed in Table 2–6.

The following steps show how to update the Marcus' Contacts contact list.

- If necessary, click the Contacts – Microsoft Outlook button on the Windows taskbar to display the Marcus' Contacts – Microsoft Outlook window.

- Double-click the Anderson, Kevin entry to open the Kevin Anderson – Contact window (Figure 2–94).

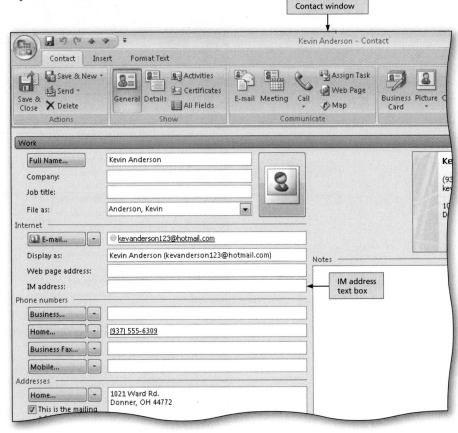

Figure 2–94

- Click the IM address text box.

- Type kevanderson123@hotmail.com as the IM address (Figure 2–95).

- Click the Save & Close button on the Ribbon to close the Contact window.

- Repeat Steps 1 through 3 to add the remaining IM addresses from Table 2–6 to the Marcus' Contacts contact list.

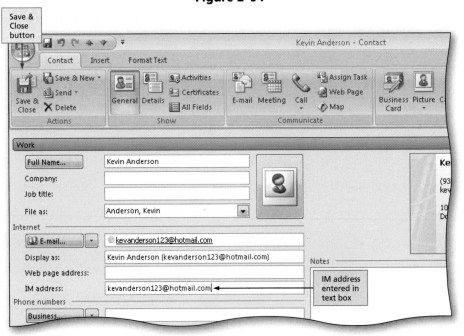

Figure 2–95

Communicating Using Instant Messaging

To use Windows Live Messenger with Outlook, the person with whom you want to communicate must be online, and, for this project, must have an e-mail message in an Outlook folder. Using Outlook, when you open an e-mail message from an individual or view the message in the Reading pane, the Person Names Smart Tag is shown next to the sender's name. Placing the mouse pointer over the Person Names Smart Tag will show a ScreenTip indicating the person's online status.

> **Note:** The following steps are for demonstration purposes only. Thus, if you are stepping through this project on a computer, you must have someone with an Instant Messenger address send you an e-mail so an ID appears in the Inbox, as shown in Figure 2–96.

BTW

The Person Names Smart Tag
The Person Names Smart Tag can indicate online status for any person whose instant messaging e-mail address you have added to your instant messaging contact list. The Person Names Smart Tag also shows online status for individuals using the Exchange Instant Messaging Service or SIP Communications Service, even if they are not in your contact list.

To Send an Instant Message

The following steps show how to send an instant message to someone you know is online.

1

- With the Inbox window active, click the Kenny Martin e-mail message.

- Click the Person Names Smart Tag in the Reading pane to display the Smart Tag menu (Figure 2–96).

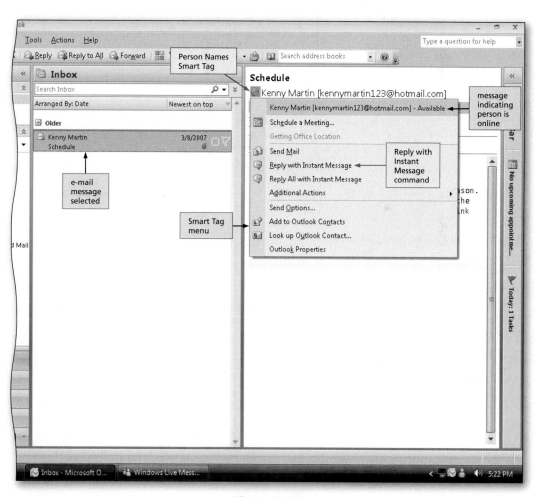

Figure 2–96

2

- Click Reply with Instant Message on the Smart Tag menu to open the Kenny window (Figure 2–97).

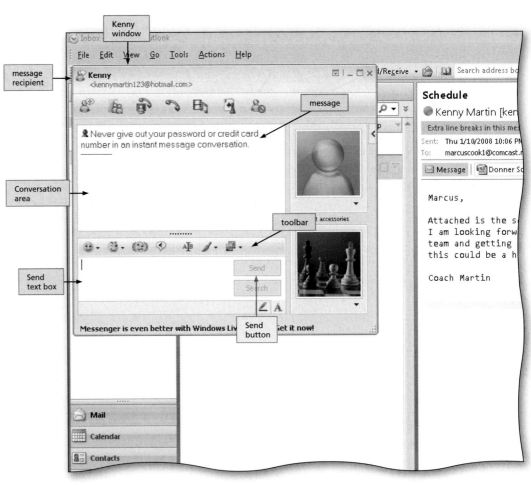

Figure 2–97

3

- Type Coach, I'm glad you're online. I wanted to talk about getting facemasks on the batting helmets. in the Send text box, and then click the Send button to send the message (Figure 2–98).

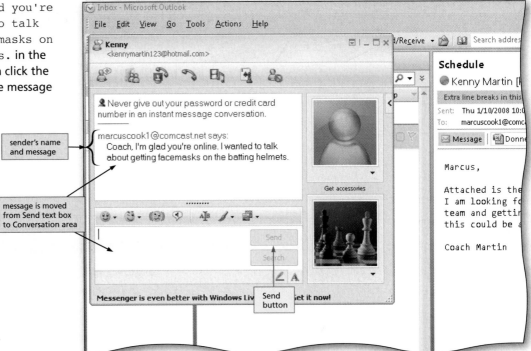

Figure 2–98

4

- The receiver of the message (Kenny Martin) types and sends a response (Figure 2–99).

Q&A

What can I do with the message toolbar above the Send text box?

The Emoticons, Wink, and Nudge buttons allow you to insert icons in a message that convey an emotion or a feeling. Icons are available that can convey happiness, surprise, confusion, and disappointment. The record a Voice Clip button allows you to insert a voice recording to your message. The Font button allows you to select a font, font style, font size, and apply special effects to the text in a message. The Change color scheme button allows you to change the appearance of the message window. The Background button allows you to select a background for your conversation window.

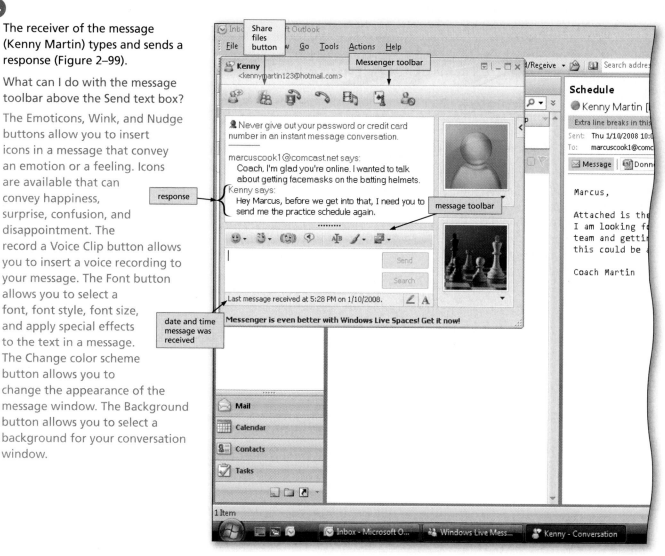

Figure 2–99

BTW

Certification
The Microsoft Certified Application Specialist (MCAS) program provides an opportunity for you to obtain a valuable industry credential – proof that you have the Outlook 2007 skills required by employers. For more information see Appendix G or visit the Outlook 2007 Certification Web page (scsite.com/out2007/cert).

To Attach and Send a File with Instant Messaging

The items in the Messenger toolbar in Figure 2–97 allow you to invite another person to the conversation, send a file or photo, start a Video Call, call a contact, see a list of activities, see a list of games, or block a contact from seeing or contacting you. The following steps show how to attach and send a file with instant messaging.

- Connect the USB flash drive containing the Data Files for Students to one of the computer's USB ports.

- Click the Share files button on the Messenger toolbar to display the Share files menu and then click the Send a file or photo command to display the Send a File to Kenny dialog box (Figure 2–100).

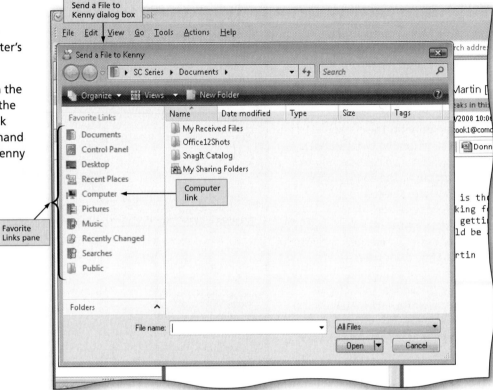

Figure 2–100

- Click Computer in the Favorite Links pane and then double-click UDISK 2.0 (E:) (Your drive name and letter may be different).

- Click Draft Practice Schedule in the Send a File to Kenny dialog box to select the file (Figure 2–101).

Figure 2–101

3

• Click the Open button to close the dialog box and display the Kenny window (Figure 2–102).

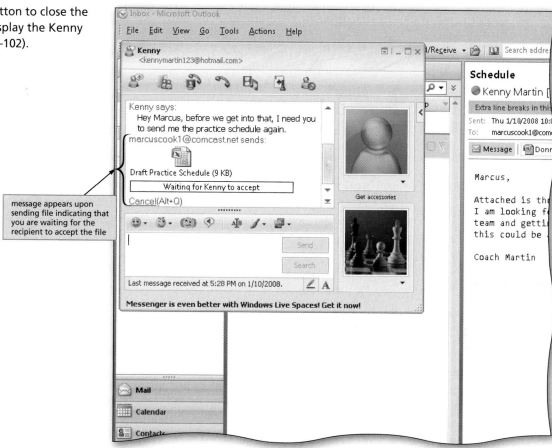

message appears upon sending file indicating that you are waiting for the recipient to accept the file

Figure 2–102

4

• The message in the window indicates the receiver (Kenny Martin) has accepted the file (Figure 2–103).

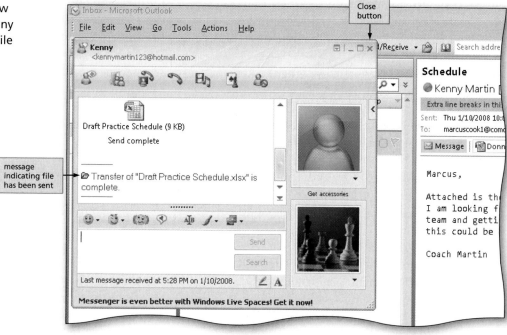

message indicating file has been sent

Quick Reference
For a table that lists how to complete the tasks covered in this book using the mouse, Ribbon, shortcut menu, and keyboard, see the Quick Reference Summary at the back of this book, or visit the Outlook 2007 Quick Reference Web page (scsite.com/out2007/qr).

Figure 2–103

To Close the Conversation Window

Participants can continue conversing in this manner, reading each other's messages and then typing their responses. When the conversation is complete, the Conversation window should be closed to end the conversation. The following step closes the Conversation window.

 Click the Close button in the Conversation window.

To Quit Outlook

With the project complete, the final step is to quit the Outlook program and return to the Windows desktop. The following step quits Outlook.

 Click the Close button on the right side of the title bar to quit Outlook.

Chapter Summary

In this chapter you have learned how to use Outlook to create a personal schedule, organize meetings, and create a task list, enter appointments, create recurring appointments, move appointments to new dates, schedule events, and view and print your calendar in different views and print styles, create a task list, assign tasks, and accept a task assignment; invite attendees to a meeting, accept a meeting request, and propose and change the time of a meeting; categorize your calendar to make it easier to view; create and edit notes; export your personal folder to an external storage device and import subfolders for further updating; use AutoArchive; enable and sign into Windows Live Messenger through Outlook; add contacts to the contact list, and send an instant message including sending a file through instant messaging. The following list includes all the new Outlook skills you have learned in this chapter.

1. Start and Customize Outlook (OUT 77)
2. Create a Personal Folder (OUT 79)
3. Enter Appointments Using the Appointment Area (OUT 81)
4. Enter and Save Appointments Using the Appointment Window (OUT 82)
5. Enter Recurring Appointments (OUT 84)
6. Move to the Next Day in the Appointment Area and Enter the Remaining Recurring Appointments (OUT 86)
7. Enter Appointment Dates and Times Using Natural Language Phrases (OUT 88)
8. Enter the Remaining One-Time Appointments (OUT 89)
9. Delete an Appointment (OUT 90)
10. Move an Appointment to a New Time (OUT 91)
11. Move an Appointment to a New Date (OUT 92)
12. Move an Appointment to a New Month (OUT 93)
13. Create an Event (OUT 95)
14. Change to Work Week View (OUT 96)
15. Change to Week View (OUT 97)
16. Change to Month View (OUT 98)
17. Create a Task List (OUT 99)
18. Export a Subfolder to a USB Flash Drive (OUT 101)
19. Delete a Personal Subfolder (OUT 103)
20. Import a Subfolder (OUT 104)
21. Assign a Task to Another Person (OUT 106)
22. Accept a Task Assignment (OUT 108)
23. Customize the Tasks Windows (OUT 110)
24. Move Tasks to a New Personal Folder (OUT 111)
25. Schedule Meetings (OUT 111)
26. Reply to Meeting Requests (OUT 114)
27. Propose a New Meeting Time (OUT 117)
28. Change the Time of a Meeting and Send an Update (OUT 117)
29. Create and Edit a Note (OUT 118)
30. Set Work Week Options (OUT 121)
31. Categorize the Calendar and Edit Category Labels (OUT 124)
32. Print the Calendar in Daily Style (OUT 127)
33. Print the Calendar in Weekly Style (OUT 128)
34. Print the Calendar in Monthly Style (OUT 128)
35. Print the Task List (OUT 128)
36. Change the Default Settings for AutoArchive (OUT 129)

37. Start and Sign In to Windows Live Messenger (OUT 131)
38. Enable Instant Messaging in Outlook (OUT 133)
39. Add a Contact to the Messenger Contact List (OUT 135)
40. Update the Outlook Contact List (OUT 138)
41. Send an Instant Message (OUT 139)
42. Attach and Send a File with Instant Messaging (OUT 142)
43. Close the Conversation Window (OUT 144)

If you have a SAM user profile, you may have access to hands-on instruction, practice, and assessment. Log in to your SAM account (http://sam2007.course.com) to launch any assigned training activities or exams that relate to the skills covered in this chapter.

Learn It Online

Test your knowledge of chapter content and key terms.

Instructions: To complete the Learn It Online exercises, start your browser, click the Address bar, and then enter the Web address scsite.com/out2007/learn. When the Outlook 2007 Learn It Online page is displayed, click the link for the exercise you want to complete and then read the instructions.

Chapter Reinforcement TF, MC, and SA
A series of true/false, multiple choice, and short answer questions that test your knowledge of the chapter content.

Flash Cards
An interactive learning environment where you identify chapter key terms associated with displayed definitions.

Practice Test
A series of multiple choice questions that test your knowledge of chapter content and key terms.

Who Wants To Be a Computer Genius?
An interactive game that challenges your knowledge of chapter content in the style of a television quiz show.

Wheel of Terms
An interactive game that challenges your knowledge of chapter key terms in the style of the television show *Wheel of Fortune*.

Crossword Puzzle Challenge
A crossword puzzle that challenges your knowledge of key terms presented in the chapter.

Apply Your Knowledge

Reinforce the skills and apply the concepts you learned in this chapter.

Creating a Schedule
Instructions: Start Outlook. Create a Calendar folder using your name as the name of the new folder.

Perform the following tasks: Create a schedule using the information in Table 2–7. Categorize the schedule using the following categories: School, Work, and Personal. This calendar is for the spring semester that begins Monday, January 14, 2008, and ends Friday, May 16, 2008. When the calendar is complete, print the calendar in Month view and submit to your instructor.

Table 2–7 Appointment Information

Appointment	Category	Days	Time	Occurrences
Chemistry	School	M, W	7:30 a.m. – 9:00 a.m.	30
Technical Report Writing	School	M, W	11:30 a.m. – 1:00 p.m.	30
Marketing	School	T, Th	7:00 p.m. – 8:30 p.m.	30
Work	Work	T, Th, Sa	7:00 a.m. – 3:30 p.m.	January 15 January 17 January 19
Doctor Appointment	Personal	W	4:00 p.m. – 5:00 p.m.	January 16
Work	Work	T, Th, Sat	9:00 a.m. – 6:00 p.m.	January 29 January 31 February 2
Volunteer for Park cleanup	Personal	Su	8:30 a.m. – 12:00 p.m.	February 3
Chemistry Study Lab	School	W	5:00 p.m. – 7:00 p.m.	Every other Wednesday for 15 occurrences

Extend Your Knowledge

Extend the skills you learned in this chapter and experiment with new skills. You may need to use Help to complete the assignment.

Customizing the Calendar

Instructions: Start Outlook. Using the calendar created in Apply Your Knowledge, use the Options command on the Tools menu to set up the calendar for a six-day work week with hours from 7:00 a.m. to 6:00 p.m..

Perform the following tasks: Export your personal folder to a USB flash drive and then delete the folder from the computer's hard disk. If possible, have your instructor verify that the folder is deleted.

Make It Right

Analyze a document and correct all errors and/or improve the design.

Editing a Calendar

Instructions: Start Outlook. Import the MIR 2-1 Calendar folder into Outlook. See the inside back cover of this book for instructions for downloading the Data Files for Students, or see your instructor for information on accessing the files required in this book.

Perform the following tasks:

1. Change the system date to February 4, 2008.
2. Change Kelly's Birthday Party from the 16th to the 23rd for the same time slot.
3. Reschedule the work on the 23rd for the 16th from 12:00 p.m. to 4:00 p.m.
4. The Chemistry Lab has been rescheduled for Wednesday evenings from 5:00 p.m. to 7:00 p.m. in CHM 225.
5. Intramural Basketball has been changed to Tuesdays and Thursdays for the same time slot.
6. Print the revised calendar in Month view and submit to your instructor.
7. Export the MIR 2-1 Calendar folder to a USB flash drive and then delete the folder from the hard disk.
8. Quit Outlook.

In the Lab

Design, create, modify, and/or use a document using the guidelines, concepts, and skills presented in this chapter. Labs are listed in order of increasing difficulty.

Lab 1: Planning a Meeting

Problem: You are the project manager for a large government project. The project involves working with individuals from county, state, and federal offices. With the project start date approaching, you need to organize a meeting to get all the required signatures on your contract.

Instructions:

1. Import the Lab 2-1 Contacts folder into Outlook (Figure 2–104).

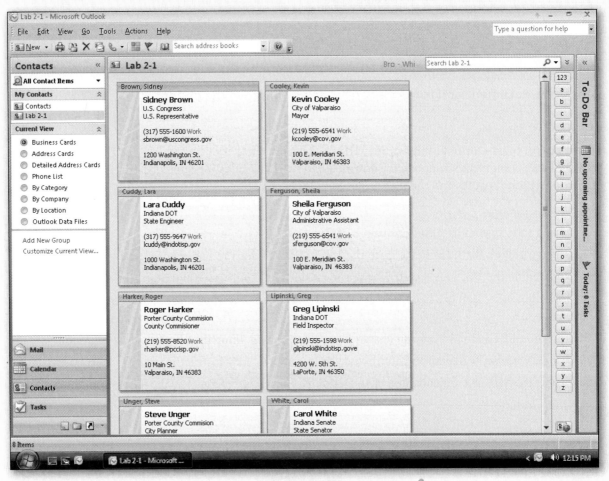

Figure 2–104

2. Organize a meeting for Wednesday, March 12, 2008 from 1:00 p.m. until 3:00 p.m., inviting only those contacts that hold a county, state, or federal office.

3. Submit a printout of the meeting to your instructor.

4. Change the date and time of the meeting from March 12, 2008 to March 14, 2008 from 9:00 a.m. to 11:00 a.m.

5. Send an updated meeting invitation.

6. Submit a printout of the updated meeting to your instructor.

7. You have just found out that your presence is required elsewhere on the meeting date. Cancel the meeting using the Cancel Meeting command on the Ribbon.

In the Lab

Lab 2: Using Windows Live Messenger with Outlook

Problem: You are preparing for an important meeting and need to have a file updated by a coworker in another department. You do not have that individual's information in your contact list, however. You leave a message on her voice mail about the file and she e-mails you a message requesting that you send the file to her. Because you have only a short time before the meeting begins, you decide to use Windows Live Messenger with Outlook to communicate and send the file to your coworker for her to revise. ***Note:*** To use instant messaging, you should complete this exercise with a classmate.

Instructions: Perform the following tasks:

1. Sign in to Windows Live Messenger using your own user name and password.
2. Send an e-mail message similar to the one shown in Figure 2–105 to your classmate.

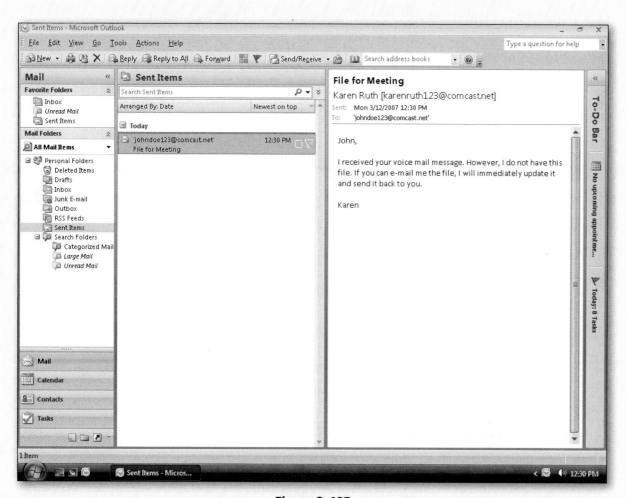

Figure 2–105

3. Add the sender to your Windows Live Messenger and Outlook contact list. Be sure to include his or her instant message address in Outlook.
4. Connect the USB flash drive containing the Data Files for Students to one of the computer's USB ports.
5. Send an instant message indicating that you will send the file using Windows Live Messenger.
6. Send the Quarterly Report file from the Data Files for Students to the sender.

Continued >

In the Lab *continued*

7. When you receive the file, open the file and submit a printout with your name and the name of the person you completed the exercise with to your instructor.

8. Sign out of Windows Live Messenger and close all the open windows.

In the Lab

Lab 3: Creating a Calendar and Task List

Problem: You are the owner of a small hardware store. Your company has experienced rapid growth during the last several months, and with spring approaching, you need to change to regular from seasonal stock. As the owner, you also have administrative duties to perform, such as staff meetings, payroll, advertising, and sales campaigns. To make your schedule even more hectic, you coach your child's spring soccer team on Wednesday nights from 5:30 p.m. to 7:00 p.m., and Saturdays from 1:00 p.m. to 3:00 p.m. at the Community Soccer Fields. You need to create a schedule of appointments as well as a task list to help you keep track of your various jobs and responsibilities each day.

Instructions Part 1: Perform the following tasks:

1. Create a personal Calendar subfolder named A-1 Hardware.

2. Change the start time of the calendar to 7:00 a.m.

3. Enter the appointments in the calendar, using the information listed in Table 2–8.

Table 2–8 Appointment Information

Desctiption	Date	Time
Staff meeting	Every Monday from March 10, 2008 – April 28, 2008	7:00 a.m. – 8:00 a.m.
Meeting to prepare Winter Closeout Sale	March 3, 2008	8:30 a.m. – 10:30 a.m.
Enter payroll	Every Thursday	4:00 p.m. – 5:00 p.m.
Eric's birthday	March 27, 2008	
Conference call with Liz & Greg	March 20, 2008	9:00 a.m. – 10:00 a.m.
Meet with lawn care supplier	March 21, 2008	1:00 p.m. – 2:00 p.m.
Lunch with Beth	March 31, 2008	12:00 p.m. – 1:00 p.m.

4. Create a task list containing the following tasks:

   a. Call Alex to confirm lawn care supplier's visit.

   b. Schedule meeting to discuss spring and summer sales goals.

   c. Call to check plumbing supplies delivery.

   d. Clear out snow blowers to make room for lawn mowers.

   e. Replace snow shovels with lawn and garden tools.

5. Print the calendar for the month of March and submit to your instructor.

Instructions Part 2: This part of the exercise requires that you work as a team with two classmates. With the growth of your hardware store, you have been able to hire a manager and assistant manager. Perform the following tasks:

1. Add the due dates in Table 2–9 to the tasks created in Part 1.

2. Using the tasks created in Part 1, assign the tasks per Table 2–9. Obtain and use the e-mail addresses of the two classmates for Manager and Assistant Manager.

3. Have the classmate representing the Manager accept one task and decline one task, and the classmate representing the Assistant Manager accept one task and decline one task.

4. Modify the current view of the task list to include the Owner field using the Customize Current View command accessed by pointing to Current View on the View menu.

5. Print the modified task list and submit to your instructor.

6. Create a personal Tasks subfolder called A-1 Tasks and move the task list you created to the new subfolder.

7. Export both the personal subfolders created in this exercise to a USB flash drive, archive the folders, and then delete them from the hard disk.

8. Close all open windows.

Table 2–9 Task Information

Tasks From Part 1	Assignment	Due Date
Call Alex to confirm lawn care supplier's visit	Manager	March 14, 2008
Call to check plumbing supplies delivery	Manager	March 10, 2008
Clear out snow blowers to make room for lawn mowers	Assistant Manager	March 28, 2008
Replace snow shovels with lawn and garden tools	Assistant Manager	March 17, 2008

Cases and Places

Apply your creative thinking and problem solving skills to design and implement a solution.

• EASIER   •• MORE DIFFICULT

• 1: Create a Personal Schedule

Create a personal schedule for the next month. Include any work and class time, together with study time. You also can include any extracurricular activities in which you participate. Use recurring appointments when possible. All day activities should be scheduled as events. Categorize the calendar as necessary. Print the calendar in Monthly Style and submit to your instructor.

•• 2: Create a Work Schedule for Employees

At work, you are in charge of scheduling for the month of May. Create a schedule of work times for four employees. Dan works Mondays, Wednesdays, and Fridays from 9:00 a.m. to 5:00 p.m. Sally works Tuesdays, Thursdays, and Saturdays from 9:00 a.m. to 5:00 p.m. Juan works from 12:00 p.m. until 9:00 p.m. on Mondays, Wednesdays, and Fridays. Bridgette completes the schedule working from 12:00 p.m. until 9:00 p.m. on Tuesdays, Thursdays, and Saturdays. Set the calendar to reflect a six-day work week with hours ranging from 9:00 a.m. to 9:00 p.m. Print the calendar in Monthly Style and submit to your instructor.

•• 3: Create a Journal

Create journal entries from your personal schedule for the past week. Comment on activities in which you participated and tasks that you accomplished. Write when the activity started and ended. Note the problems (if any) associated with the activity. When commenting on completed tasks, include notes about results of having completed it. Specify what would have happened had the task not been completed when it was. Write a brief summary of your journal and submit to your instructor.

•• 4: Create a Calendar of Events

Make It Personal

Use the natural language phrase option in the Start time date box to create a list of events for the year. Create a calendar that contains the following holidays: New Year's Day, Valentine's Day, St. Patrick's Day, Independence Day, Halloween, Veteran's Day, Thanksgiving Day, Christmas Eve, Christmas Day, and New Year's Eve. For the last four holidays, indicate that you will be out of the office all day. Also, add events for several family or friend birthdays or anniversaries, using the natural language phrase option. For instance, schedule these events by utilizing the phrase "two weeks from today" (or something similar) as a start date. Try at least three different phrase options to schedule these events. Categorize the events to separate birthdays from anniversaries, and so on. Select two months to print in Monthly Style and submit them to your instructor.

•• 5: Create Meeting Invitations

Working Together

Choose a member of your team to act as meeting organizer. The organizer will use Outlook to send out a meeting invitation to each group member. Each member either should accept the meeting time or decline the meeting time and propose a new meeting time based on their individual schedules using Outlook. Use a combination of e-mail and Windows Live Messenger with Outlook to discuss proposed meeting times with the organizer. Each team member should print out the appointment and hand it in to the instructor.

1 | Microsoft Office 2007 Integration Case Studies

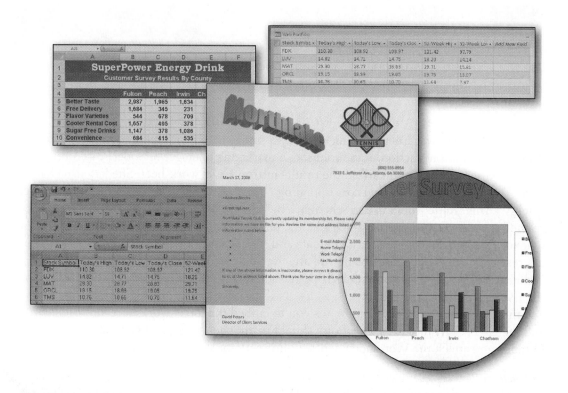

Objectives

You will have mastered the material in these case studies when you can:

- Create a memo with an embedded Excel spreadsheet
- Create a slide in PowerPoint with an embedded Excel chart
- Create a letterhead
- Create a form letter using an Access database table as the data source

- Set query conditions
- Convert an Access table to a Word document
- Convert an Access table to an Excel worksheet
- Convert among Word, Excel, and Access

Integration Case Studies Introduction

In these case studies, you will use the concepts and techniques presented in the chapters and special features in this book to integrate all of the Office 2007 programs. The first case study requires that you link an existing Excel worksheet into a Word document, embed an Excel chart into a PowerPoint presentation, and then insert (attach) the Word document and PowerPoint presentation to an e-mail message using Outlook. The second case study requires you to use an existing Access database table as the data source for a Word form letter; it also requires you to use WordArt to create the letterhead for the form letter. In the third case study, you will create an Access database table and then convert the table twice, first to a Word document and second to an Excel worksheet. You then will convert the Word document to an Excel worksheet and vice versa. The files for the first and second studies are provided on the Data Files for Students. See the inside back cover of this book for instructions on downloading the Data Files for Students, or contact your instructor for more information about accessing the required files.

Case Study

Use the concepts and techniques presented in the chapters and special features in this book to integrate all of the Office 2007 programs.

Case Study 1: Integrating Excel, Word, PowerPoint, and Outlook

Problem: SuperPower Energy Drink enclosed a survey along with its June invoices in order to collect data on customer satisfaction. Katie Johnson, a marketing manager at SuperPower, has received the completed surveys and summarized the results into an Excel worksheet. She has also charted the results using Excel. The worksheet and corresponding charts are saved in a workbook named SuperPower Energy Drink. Katie would like to schedule a meeting to discuss the survey results with the steering committee of SuperPower Energy Drink. She plans to send an e-mail message to the committee to schedule the meeting and ask for comments and suggestions. To ensure that the committee can review the results before the meeting, Katie will attach two documents to the e-mail message: (1) a memo that includes the Excel worksheet summarizing the survey results, and (2) a PowerPoint slide that includes the Excel chart depicting the survey results. As Katie's assistant, you are to create the memo in Word and the slide in PowerPoint. Katie wants you to embed the Excel worksheet into the Word document and the Excel chart into the PowerPoint slide. Finally, she wants you to create an e-mail message using Outlook and attach the Word document and PowerPoint slide.

Instructions Part 1:   To review the Excel Workbook, open the SuperPower Energy Drink workbook shown in Figures 1a and 1b from the Data Files for Students. Before you begin creating the memo and slide, familiarize yourself with their contents. Print each sheet of the workbook.

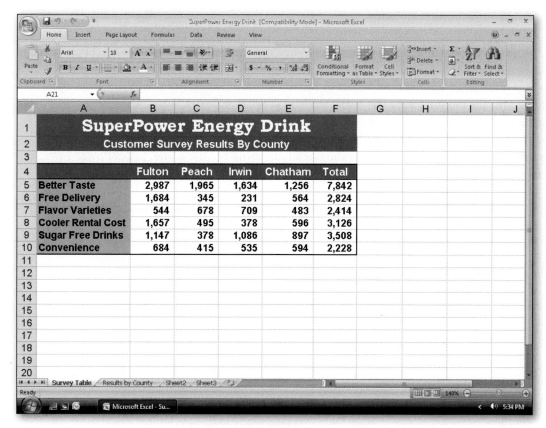

Figure 1a

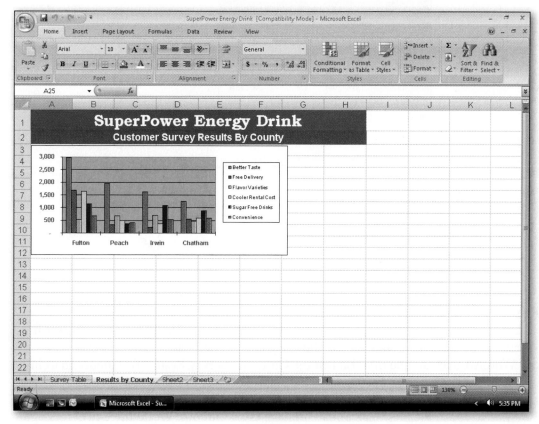

Figure 1b

Continued >

Case Study *continued*

Instructions Part 2:   Next, create a memorandum in Word with an embedded Excel worksheet. Create the memorandum to schedule the meeting with the steering committee, as shown in Figure 1c. After typing the text in the memo, embed the Customer Survey Results By County worksheet from the Excel workbook into the memo. Leave the Excel workbook open and start Word. Use the Professional Memo template to create the memo. Modify the template text so that the memo matches Figure 1c. Next, embed the Customer Survey Results By County worksheet into the memo. (Do not type the worksheet; rather, embed it from Excel.) Save the document using the file name, SuperPower Energy Drink. Submit the memorandum with the embedded worksheet to your instructor.

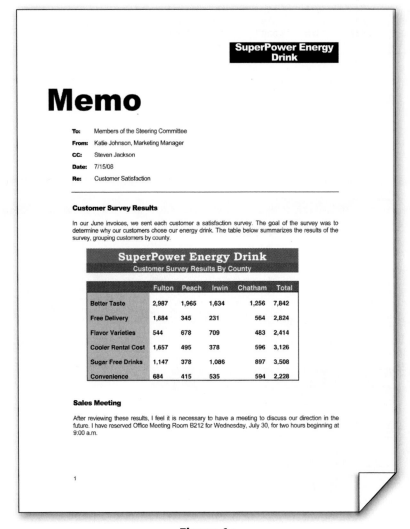

Figure 1c

Instructions Part 3:   To create a slide in PowerPoint with an embedded Excel chart, create a slide (Figure 1d) to be used in the presentation to the board of directors. Leave the Excel workbook open and start PowerPoint. Select a blank slide for the slide's layout and use a background color as shown in Figure 1d. Use WordArt to create the title. Embed the Customer Survey Results By County chart into the slide. Save the presentation using the file name, SuperPower Energy Drink.

Instructions Part 4:   To attach the files to an e-mail message using Outlook, create the e-mail message (Figure 1e) and attach the Word document and PowerPoint slide to the e-mail message. Print the e-mail message.

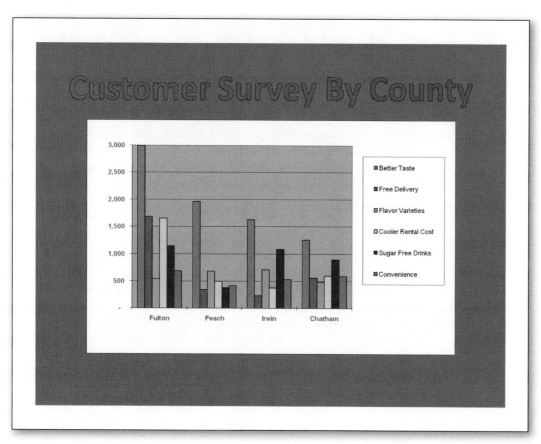

Figure 1d

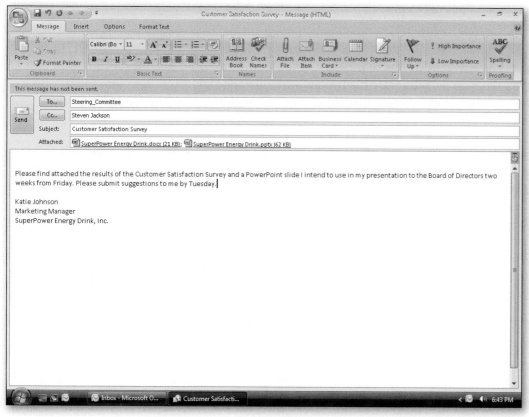

Figure 1e

Case Study

Case Study 2: Integrating Word, WordArt, and Access

Problem: Every spring, Northlake Tennis Club sends letters to its clients to verify the club's internal records. In the past, the club's director of client services, Greg O'Leary, has used Word to type these letters to each client individually. This year, he wants to automate the process even further. He has entered the list of clients into an Access table (Figure 2a), which is saved in a database named Northlake Tennis Club. He has asked you to prepare a form letter to be sent to all clients using the Access database table as a data source. He also would like you to develop a creative letterhead for Northlake Tennis Club that can be used on all its business correspondence. The completed form letter, with letterhead, is shown in Figure 2b.

Instructions Part 1:   The database table is in a file named Northlake Tennis Club, which is located in the Data Files for Students. To review and maintain the Access database table, open the database and then open the table named Client List. Familiarize yourself with the contents of the Client List table (Figure 2a). Add a record that contains information about yourself to the table — the table then should contain six records. Print the revised table and then close Access.

ID	Title	First Name	Last Name	Address1	Address2	City	State	ZIP code	Home Phone	Work Phone	Fax Number
1	Mr.	Troy	Jameson	798 Snead Ave		Atlanta	GA	30303-	(470) 555-4861	(470) 555-8856	(470) 555-3125
2	Dr.	Lindsey	Hawkins	6351 W. 73rd Ave		Atlanta	GA	30306-	(470) 555-8282	(470) 555-4523	(470) 555-1111
3	Ms.	Jo Anne	Brady	234 McArthure Blv	Apt. 3C	Atlanta	GA	30310-	(470) 555-3102	(470) 555-9087	
4	Mr.	Cameron	Osborne	4732 Brown St.		Atlanta	GA	30305-	(470) 555-5209	(470) 555-1523	(470) 555-6653
5	Mrs.	Julie	Hagar	5354 E. 101st St	Apt. 6	Atlanta	GA	30303-	(470) 555-2192	(470) 555-6666	(470) 555-8897

Figure 2a

Instructions Part 2:   Your first task is to develop the letterhead for the correspondence. Start Word and then display the Header area. Insert and format a WordArt object, using the text, Northlake, as shown in Figure 2b. Insert the tennis clip art to the right of the WordArt object. Reposition and resize the clip art as shown in Figure 2b. Finally, enter the telephone number and address of the club, add a bottom border, and color it dark blue. When you are finished with the header, save the file as Northlake Letterhead and submit to your instructor.

Instructions Part 3:   Create the form letter, shown in Figure 2b, using an Access database table as the data source, which is to be sent to each client in the Client List table. The form letter is to verify the accuracy of the following information for each client: name, address, home and work telephone numbers, fax number, and e-mail address. Using the Northlake Letterhead created in Part 2 above as the main document, create a form letter using the text shown in Figure 2b and the Access database table as the data source. Use the Mail Merge Wizard to set up your document. When you are finished with the main document, save the document using the file name, Northlake Membership Update, and print it. Finally, merge and submit the form letters for the six records.

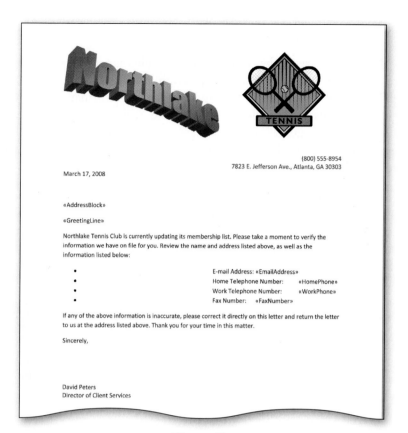

Figure 2b

Instructions Part 4:   Merge and submit form letters for only those clients with a zip code of 30303. On the resulting form letters, handwrite the condition you specified. Next, merge and submit form letters for only those clients that have fax numbers. On the resulting form letters, handwrite the condition you specified.

Case Study

Case Study 3: Integrating Access into Word and Excel

Problem: The owner of Money Making Investors, Inc., Nicole Wood, would like to work with the daily stock records. The problem is that the records are stored in an Access database table (Figure 3a) and Nicole is unfamiliar with Access. Instead, she wants to work with the records in both Word and Excel. Thus, she has asked you to convert the Access table to both a Word document and an Excel worksheet. She also has asked you to show her how to convert in any direction among the three applications, Word, Excel, and Access.

Stock Symbol	Today's High	Today's Low	Today's Close	52-Week High	52-Week Low	Add New Field
FDX	110.30	108.92	108.97	121.42	97.79	
LUV	14.82	14.71	14.75	18.20	14.14	
MAT	29.30	28.77	28.83	29.71	15.81	
ORCL	19.15	18.99	19.05	19.75	13.07	
TMS	10.76	10.65	10.70	11.64	7.97	

Figure 3a

Continued >

Case Study *continued*

Instructions Part 1:   Design and create the Access database table that contains the stock information. The field names are as follows: Stock Symbol, Today's High, Today's Low, Today's Close, 52-Week High, and 52-Week Low. Use the Internet to obtain stock market information for five different stocks. Enter the information as records in the table you create. The Access screen in Figure 3a shows sample data entered in the Web Portfolio table. The actual data you use will be different. When you finish creating the table, save the database using the file name, Money Making Investors. Submit the Access table along with the Web pages you used for stock quotes.

Instructions Part 2:   Convert the Web Portfolio table to a Word table. With the Access table selected in the Microsoft Access window, click the External Data tab on the Ribbon and then click the Word button in the Export group. When the Export – RTF File dialog box displays, click the OK button, and then click the Close button. Open the Word document to display the stock information as a Word table, as shown in Figure 3b. Submit the resulting Word table.

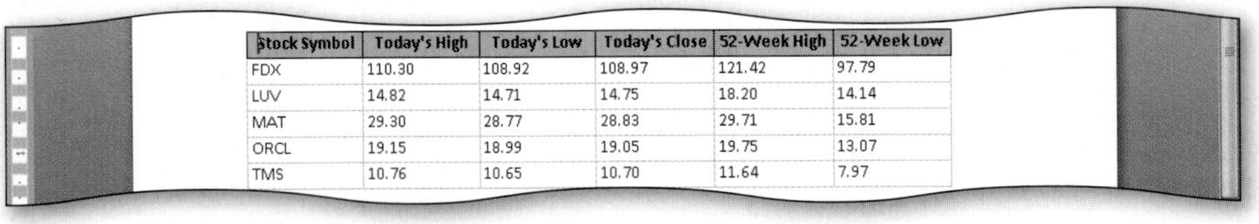

Stock Symbol	Today's High	Today's Low	Today's Close	52-Week High	52-Week Low
FDX	110.30	108.92	108.97	121.42	97.79
LUV	14.82	14.71	14.75	18.20	14.14
MAT	29.30	28.77	28.83	29.71	15.81
ORCL	19.15	18.99	19.05	19.75	13.07
TMS	10.76	10.65	10.70	11.64	7.97

Figure 3b

Instructions Part 3:   Convert the Web Portfolio table to an Excel worksheet. Return to the Access database table. With the Access table highlighted in the Money Making Investors: Database window, click the External Data tab on the Ribbon and then click the Excel button in the Export group. When the Export – Excel Spreadsheet dialog box displays, click the OK button, and then click the Close button. Open the Excel spreadsheet to display the stock information as a worksheet, and format it so that it is readable and professional, as shown in Figure 3c. Below the table, add two rows that use Excel's statistical functions to determine the highest and lowest values for each of the numeric columns in the table. (*Note:* you will need to format the stock quotes as numbers rather than text.) Submit the resulting Excel worksheet.

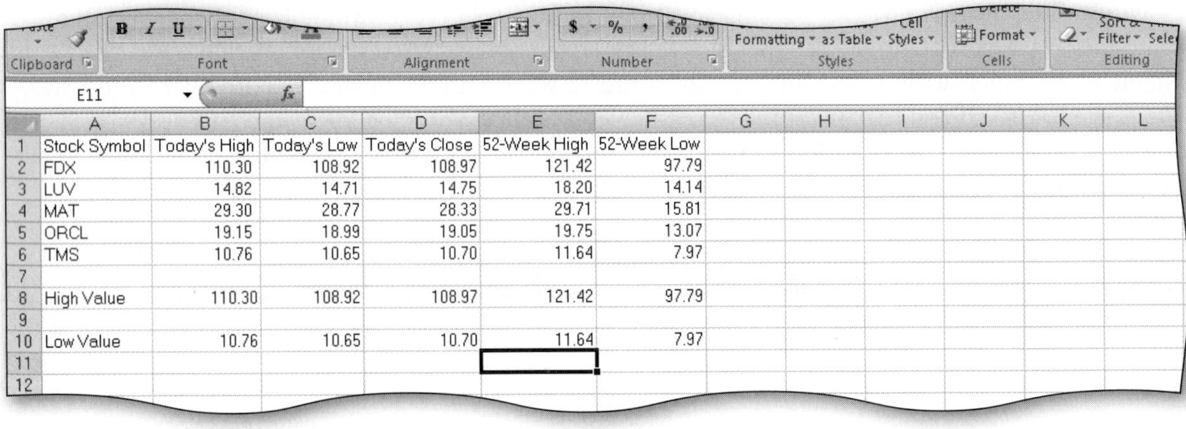

	A	B	C	D	E	F
1	Stock Symbol	Today's High	Today's Low	Today's Close	52-Week High	52-Week Low
2	FDX	110.30	108.92	108.97	121.42	97.79
3	LUV	14.82	14.71	14.75	18.20	14.14
4	MAT	29.30	28.77	28.33	29.71	15.81
5	ORCL	19.15	18.99	19.05	19.75	13.07
6	TMS	10.76	10.65	10.70	11.64	7.97
7						
8	High Value	110.30	108.92	108.97	121.42	97.79
9						
10	Low Value	10.76	10.65	10.70	11.64	7.97
11						
12						

Figure 3c

Instructions Part 4:   Use the following techniques described earlier in this book to convert in any direction among Word, Excel, and Access. For example, open the Excel workbook Web Portfolio and convert it to Word. Next convert the workbook to Access. Do the same for the Word document Web Portfolio. Submit each of the four files created.

Appendix A
Project Planning Guidelines

Using Project Planning Guidelines

The process of communicating specific information to others is a learned, rational skill. Computers and software, especially Microsoft Office 2007, can help you develop ideas and present detailed information to a particular audience.

Using Microsoft Office 2007, you can create projects such as Word documents, Excel spreadsheets, Access databases, and PowerPoint presentations. Computer hardware and productivity software such as Microsoft Office 2007 minimizes much of the laborious work of drafting and revising projects. Some communicators handwrite ideas in notebooks, others compose directly on the computer, and others have developed unique strategies that work for their own particular thinking and writing styles.

No matter what method you use to plan a project, follow specific guidelines to arrive at a final product that presents information correctly and effectively (Figure A–1). Use some aspects of these guidelines every time you undertake a project, and others as needed in specific instances. For example, in determining content for a project, you may decide that a bar chart communicates trends more effectively than a paragraph of text. If so, you would create this graphical element and insert it in an Excel spreadsheet, a Word document, or a PowerPoint slide.

Determine the Project's Purpose

Begin by clearly defining why you are undertaking this assignment. For example, you may want to track monetary donations collected for your club's fundraising drive. Alternatively, you may be urging students to vote for a particular candidate in the next election. Once you clearly understand the purpose of your task, begin to draft ideas of how best to communicate this information.

Analyze Your Audience

Learn about the people who will read, analyze, or view your work. Where are they employed? What are their educational backgrounds? What are their expectations? What questions do they have?

PROJECT PLANNING GUIDELINES

1. DETERMINE THE PROJECT'S PURPOSE
Why are you undertaking the project?

2. ANALYZE YOUR AUDIENCE
Who are the people who will use your work?

3. GATHER POSSIBLE CONTENT
What information exists, and in what forms?

4. DETERMINE WHAT CONTENT TO PRESENT TO YOUR AUDIENCE
What information will best communicate the project's purpose to your audience?

Figure A–1

Design experts suggest drawing a mental picture of these people or finding photographs of people who fit this profile so that you can develop a project with the audience in mind.

By knowing your audience members, you can tailor a project to meet their interests and needs. You will not present them with information they already possess, and you will not omit the information they need to know.

Example: Your assignment is to raise the profile of your college's nursing program in the community. How much do they know about your college and the nursing curriculum? What are the admission requirements? How many of the applicants admitted complete the program? What percent pass the state Boards?

Gather Possible Content

Rarely are you in a position to develop all the material for a project. Typically, you would begin by gathering existing information that may reside in spreadsheets or databases. Web sites, pamphlets, magazine and newspaper articles, and books could provide insights of how others have approached your topic. Personal interviews often provide perspectives not available by any other means. Consider video and audio clips as potential sources for material that might complement or support the factual data you uncover.

Determine What Content to Present to Your Audience

Experienced designers recommend writing three or four major ideas you want an audience member to remember after reading or viewing your project. It also is helpful to envision your project's endpoint, the key fact you wish to emphasize. All project elements should lead to this ending point.

As you make content decisions, you also need to think about other factors. Presentation of the project content is an important consideration. For example, will your brochure be printed on thick, colored paper or transparencies? Will your PowerPoint presentation be viewed in a classroom with excellent lighting and a bright projector, or will it be viewed on a notebook computer monitor? Determine relevant time factors, such as the length of time to develop the project, how long readers will spend reviewing your project, or the amount of time allocated for your speaking engagement. Your project will need to accommodate all of these constraints.

Decide whether a graph, photograph, or artistic element can express or emphasize a particular concept. The right hemisphere of the brain processes images by attaching an emotion to them, so audience members are more apt to recall these graphics long term rather than just reading text.

As you select content, be mindful of the order in which you plan to present information. Readers and audience members generally remember the first and last pieces of information they see and hear, so you should put the most important information at the top or bottom of the page.

Summary

When creating a project, it is beneficial to follow some basic guidelines from the outset. By taking some time at the beginning of the process to determine the project's purpose, analyze the audience, gather possible content, and determine what content to present to the audience, you can produce a project that is informative, relevant, and effective.

Appendix B
Introduction to Microsoft Office 2007

What Is Microsoft Office 2007?

Microsoft Office 2007 is a collection of the more popular Microsoft application software. It is available in Basic, Home and Student, Standard, Small Business, Professional, Ultimate, Professional Plus, and Enterprise editions. Each edition consists of a group of programs, collectively called a suite. Table B-1 lists the suites and their components. **Microsoft Office Professional Edition 2007** includes these six programs: Microsoft Office Word 2007, Microsoft Office Excel 2007, Microsoft Office Access 2007, Microsoft Office PowerPoint 2007, Microsoft Office Publisher 2007, and Microsoft Office Outlook 2007. The programs in the Office suite allow you to work efficiently, communicate effectively, and improve the appearance of the projects you create.

Table B–1

	Microsoft Office Basic 2007	Microsoft Office Home & Student 2007	Microsoft Office Standard 2007	Microsoft Office Small Business 2007	Microsoft Office Professional 2007	Microsoft Office Ultimate 2007	Microsoft Office Professional Plus 2007	Microsoft Office Enterprise 2007
Microsoft Office Word 2007	✓	✓	✓	✓	✓	✓	✓	✓
Microsoft Office Excel 2007	✓	✓	✓	✓	✓	✓	✓	✓
Microsoft Office Access 2007					✓	✓	✓	✓
Microsoft Office PowerPoint 2007		✓	✓	✓	✓	✓	✓	✓
Microsoft Office Publisher 2007				✓	✓	✓	✓	✓
Microsoft Office Outlook 2007	✓		✓				✓	✓
Microsoft Office OneNote 2007		✓				✓		
Microsoft Office Outlook 2007 with Business Contact Manager				✓	✓	✓		
Microsoft Office InfoPath 2007						✓	✓	✓
Integrated Enterprise Content Management						✓	✓	✓
Electronic Forms						✓	✓	✓
Advanced Information Rights Management and Policy Capabilities						✓	✓	✓
Microsoft Office Communicator 2007							✓	✓
Microsoft Office Groove 2007						✓		✓

Microsoft has bundled additional programs in some versions of Office 2007, in addition to the main group of Office programs. Table B–1 on the previous page lists the components of the various Office suites.

In addition to the Office 2007 programs noted previously, Office 2007 suites can contain other programs. Microsoft Office OneNote 2007 is a digital notebook program that allows you to gather and share various types of media, such as text, graphics, video, audio, and digital handwriting. Microsoft Office InfoPath 2007 is a program that allows you to create and use electronic forms to gather information. Microsoft Office Groove 2007 provides collaborative workspaces in real time. Additional services that are oriented toward the enterprise solution also are available.

Office 2007 and the Internet, World Wide Web, and Intranets

Office 2007 allows you to take advantage of the Internet, the World Wide Web, and intranets. The Microsoft Windows operating system includes a **browser**, which is a program that allows you to locate and view a Web page. The Windows browser is called Internet Explorer.

One method of viewing a Web page is to use the browser to enter the Web address for the Web page. Another method of viewing a Web page is clicking a hyperlink. A **hyperlink** is colored or underlined text or a graphic that, when clicked, connects to another Web page. Hyperlinks placed in Office 2007 documents allow for direct access to a Web site of interest.

An **intranet** is a private network, such as a network used within a company or organization for internal communication. Like the Internet, hyperlinks are used within an intranet to access documents, pages, and other destinations on the intranet. Unlike the Internet, the materials on the network are available only for those who are part of the private network.

Online Collaboration Using Office

Organizations that, in the past, were able to make important information available only to a select few, now can make their information accessible to a wider range of individuals who use programs such as Office 2007 and Internet Explorer. Office 2007 allows colleagues to use the Internet or an intranet as a central location to view documents, manage files, and work together.

Each of the Office 2007 programs makes publishing documents on a Web server as simple as saving a file on a hard disk. Once placed on the Web server, users can view and edit the documents and conduct Web discussions and live online meetings.

Using Microsoft Office 2007

The various Microsoft Office 2007 programs each specialize in a particular task. This section describes the general functions of the more widely used Office 2007 programs, along with how they are used to access the Internet or an intranet.

Microsoft Office Word 2007

Microsoft Office Word 2007 is a full-featured word processing program that allows you to create many types of personal and business documents, including flyers, letters, resumes, business documents, and academic reports.

Word's AutoCorrect, spelling, and grammar features help you proofread documents for errors in spelling and grammar by identifying the errors and offering suggestions for corrections as you type. The live word count feature provides you with a constantly updating word count as you enter and edit text. To assist with creating specific documents, such as a business letter or resume, Word provides templates, which provide a formatted document before you type the text of the document. Quick Styles provide a live preview of styles from the Style gallery, allowing you to preview styles in the document before actually applying them.

Word automates many often-used tasks and provides you with powerful desktop publishing tools to use as you create professional looking brochures, advertisements, and newsletters. SmartArt allows you to insert interpretive graphics based on document content.

Word makes it easier for you to share documents for collaboration. The Send feature opens an e-mail window with the active document attached. The Compare Documents feature allows you easily to identify changes when comparing different document versions.

Word 2007 and the Internet   Word makes it possible to design and publish Web pages on the Internet or an intranet, insert a hyperlink to a Web page in a word processing document, as well as access and search the content of other Web pages.

Microsoft Office Excel 2007

Microsoft Office Excel 2007 is a spreadsheet program that allows you to organize data, complete calculations, graph data, develop professional looking reports, publish organized data to the Web, and access real-time data from Web sites.

In addition to its mathematical functionality, Excel 2007 provides tools for visually comparing data. For instance, when comparing a group of values in cells, you can set cell backgrounds with bars proportional to the value of the data in the cell. You can also set cell backgrounds with full-color backgrounds, or use a color scale to facilitate interpretation of data values.

Excel 2007 provides strong formatting support for tables with the new Style Preview gallery.

Excel 2007 and the Internet   Using Excel 2007, you can create hyperlinks within a worksheet to access other Office documents on the network or on the Internet. Worksheets saved as static, or unchanging Web pages can be viewed using a browser. The person viewing static Web pages cannot change them.

In addition, you can create and run queries that retrieve information from a Web page and insert the information directly into a worksheet.

Microsoft Office Access 2007

Microsoft Office Access 2007 is a comprehensive database management system (DBMS). A **database** is a collection of data organized in a manner that allows access, retrieval, and use of that data. Access 2007 allows you to create a database; add, change, and delete data in the database; sort data in the database; retrieve data from the database; and create forms and reports using the data in the database.

Access 2007 and the Internet   Access 2007 lets you generate reports, which are summaries that show only certain data from the database, based on user requirements.

Microsoft Office PowerPoint 2007

Microsoft Office PowerPoint 2007 is a complete presentation graphics program that allows you to produce professional looking presentations. With PowerPoint 2007, you can create informal presentations using overhead transparencies, electronic presentations using a projection device attached to a personal computer, formal presentations using 35mm slides or a CD, or you can run virtual presentations on the Internet.

PowerPoint 2007 and the Internet　PowerPoint 2007 allows you to publish presentations on the Internet or other networks.

Microsoft Office Publisher 2007

Microsoft Office Publisher 2007 is a desktop publishing program (DTP) that allows you to design and produce professional quality documents (newsletters, flyers, brochures, business cards, Web sites, and so on) that combine text, graphics, and photographs. Desktop publishing software provides a variety of tools, including design templates, graphic manipulation tools, color schemes or libraries, and various page wizards and templates. For large jobs, businesses use desktop publishing software to design publications that are **camera ready**, which means the files are suitable for production by outside commercial printers. Publisher 2007 also allows you to locate commercial printers, service bureaus, and copy shops willing to accept customer files created in Publisher.

Publisher 2007 allows you to design a unique image, or logo, using one of more than 45 master design sets. This, in turn, permits you to use the same design for all your printed documents (letters, business cards, brochures, and advertisements) and Web pages. Publisher includes 70 coordinated color schemes; 30 font schemes; more than 10,000 high-quality clip art images; 1,500 photographs; 1,000 Web-art graphics; 340 animated graphics; and hundreds of unique Design Gallery elements (quotations, sidebars, and so on). If you wish, you also can download additional images from the Microsoft Office Online Web page on the Microsoft Web site.

Publisher 2007 and the Internet　Publisher 2007 allows you easily to create a multipage Web site with custom color schemes, photographic images, animated images, and sounds.

Microsoft Office Outlook 2007

Microsoft Office Outlook 2007 is a powerful communications and scheduling program that helps you communicate with others, keep track of your contacts, and organize your schedule. Outlook 2007 allows you to view a To-Do bar containing tasks and appointments from your Outlook calendar. Outlook 2007 allows you to send and receive electronic mail (e-mail) and permits you to engage in real-time communication with family, friends, or coworkers using instant messaging. Outlook 2007 also provides you with the means to organize your contacts, and you can track e-mail messages, meetings, and notes with a particular contact. Outlook's Calendar, Contacts, Tasks, and Notes components aid in this organization. Contact information is available from the Outlook Calendar, Mail, Contacts, and Task components by accessing the Find a Contact feature. **Personal information management (PIM)** programs such as Outlook provide a way for individuals and workgroups to organize, find, view, and share information easily.

Microsoft Office 2007 Help

At any time while you are using one of the Office programs, you can interact with **Microsoft Office 2007 Help** for that program and display information about any topic associated with the program. Several categories of help are available. In all programs, you can access Help by pressing the F1 key on the keyboard. In Publisher 2007 and Outlook 2007, the Help window can be opened by clicking the Help menu and then selecting Microsoft Office Publisher or Outlook Help command, or by entering search text in the 'Type a question for help' text box in the upper-right corner of the program window. In the other Office programs, clicking the Microsoft Office Help button near the upper-right corner of the program window opens the program Help window.

The Help window in all programs provides several methods for accessing help about a particular topic, and has tools for navigating around Help. Appendix C contains detailed instructions for using Help.

Collaboration and SharePoint

While not part of the Microsoft Office 2007 suites, SharePoint is a Microsoft tool that allows Office 2007 users to share data using collaborative tools that are integrated into the main Office programs. SharePoint consists of Windows SharePoint Services, Office SharePoint Server 2007, and, optionally, Office SharePoint Designer 2007.

Windows SharePoint Services provides the platform for collaboration programs and services. Office SharePoint Server 2007 is built on top of Windows SharePoint Services. The result of these two products is the ability to create SharePoint sites. A SharePoint site is a Web site that provides users with a virtual place for collaborating and communicating with their colleagues while working together on projects, documents, ideas, and information. Each member of a group with access to the SharePoint site has the ability to contribute to the material stored there. The basic building blocks of SharePoint sites are lists and libraries. Lists contain collections of information, such as calendar items, discussion points, contacts, and links. Lists can be edited to add or delete information. Libraries are similar to lists, but include both files and information about files. Types of libraries include document, picture, and forms libraries.

The most basic type of SharePoint site is called a Workspace, which is used primarily for collaboration. Different types of Workspaces can be created using SharePoint to suit different needs. SharePoint provides templates, or outlines of these Workspaces, that can be filled in to create the Workspace. Each of the different types of Workspace templates contain a different collection of lists and libraries, reflecting the purpose of the Workspace. You can create a Document Workspace to facilitate collaboration on documents. A Document Workspace contains a document library for documents and supporting files, a Links list that allows you to maintain relevant resource links for the document, a Tasks list for listing and assigning To-Do items to team members, and other links as needed. Meeting Workspaces allow users to plan and organize a meeting, with components such as Attendees, Agenda, and a Document Library. Social Meeting Workspaces provide a place to plan social events, with lists and libraries such as Attendees, Directions, Image/Logo, Things To Bring, Discussions, and Picture Library. A Decision Meeting Workspace is a Meeting Workspace with a focus on review and decision-making, with lists and libraries such as Objectives, Attendees, Agenda, Document Library, Tasks, and Decisions.

Users also can create a SharePoint site called a WebParts page, which is built from modules called WebParts. WebParts are modular units of information that contain a title bar and content that reflects the type of WebPart. For instance, an image WebPart would contain a title bar and an image. WebParts allow you quickly to create and modify a SharePoint site, and allow for the creation of a unique site that can allow users to access and make changes to information stored on the site.

Large SharePoint sites that include multiple pages can be created using templates as well. Groups needing more refined and targeted sharing options than those available with SharePoint Server 2007 and Windows SharePoint Services can add SharePoint Designer 2007 to create a site that meets their specific needs.

Depending on which components have been selected for inclusion on the site, users can view a team calendar, view links, read announcements, and view and edit group documents and projects. SharePoint sites can be set up so that documents are checked in and out, much like a library, to prevent multiple users from making changes simultaneously. Once a SharePoint site is set up, Office programs are used to perform maintenance of the site. For example, changes in the team calendar are updated using Outlook 2007, and changes that users make in Outlook 2007 are reflected on the SharePoint site. Office 2007 programs include a Publish feature that allows users easily to save file updates to a SharePoint site. Team members can be notified about changes made to material on the site either by e-mail or by a news feed, meaning that users do not have to go to the site to check to see if anything has been updated since they last viewed or worked on it. The search feature in SharePoint allows users quickly to find information on a large site.

Appendix C
Microsoft
Office 2007 Help

Using Microsoft Office Help

This appendix shows how to use Microsoft Office Help. At any time while you are using one of the Microsoft Office 2007 programs, you can use Office Help to display information about all topics associated with the program. To illustrate the use of Office Help, this appendix uses Microsoft Office Word 2007. Help in other Office 2007 programs responds in a similar fashion.

In Office 2007, Help is presented in a window that has Web browser-style navigation buttons. Each Office 2007 program has its own Help home page, which is the starting Help page that is displayed in the Help window. If your computer is connected to the Internet, the contents of the Help page reflect both the local help files installed on the computer and material from Microsoft's Web site. As shown in Figure C–1, two methods for accessing Word's Help are available:

1. Microsoft Office Word Help button near the upper-right corner of the Word window

2. Function key F1 on the keyboard

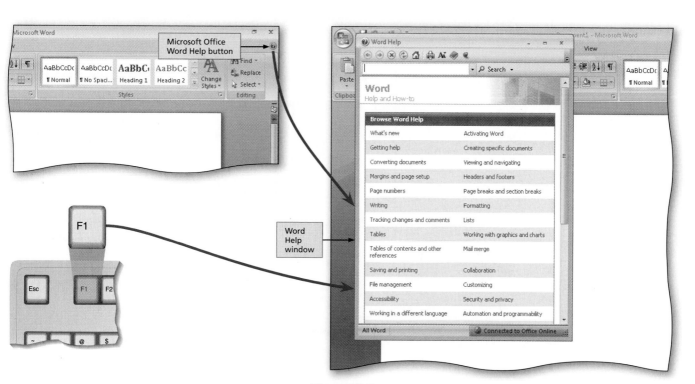

Figure C–1

To Open the Word Help Window

The following steps open the Word Help window and maximize the window.

- Start Microsoft Word, if necessary. Click the Microsoft Office Word Help button near the upper-right corner of the Word window to open the Word Help window (Figure C–2).

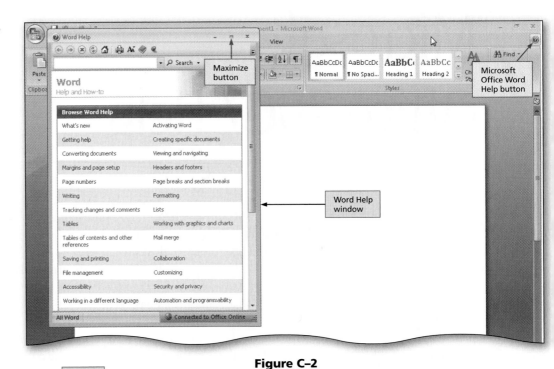

Figure C–2

2

- Click the Maximize button on the Help title bar to maximize the Help window (Figure C–3).

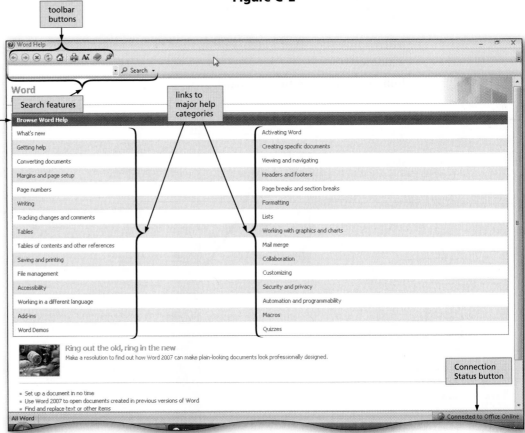

Figure C–3

The Word Help Window

The Word Help window provides several methods for accessing help about a particular topic, and also has tools for navigating around Help. Methods for accessing Help include searching the help content installed with Word, or searching the online Office content maintained by Microsoft.

Figure C–3 shows the main Word Help window. To navigate Help, the Word Help window includes search features that allow you to search on a word or phrase about which you want help; the Connection Status button, which allows you to control where Word Help searches for content; toolbar buttons; and links to major Help categories.

Search Features

You can perform Help searches on words or phrases to find information about any Word feature using the 'Type words to search for' text box and the Search button (Figure C–4a). Click the 'Type words to search for' text box and then click the Search button or press the ENTER key to initiate a search of Word Help.

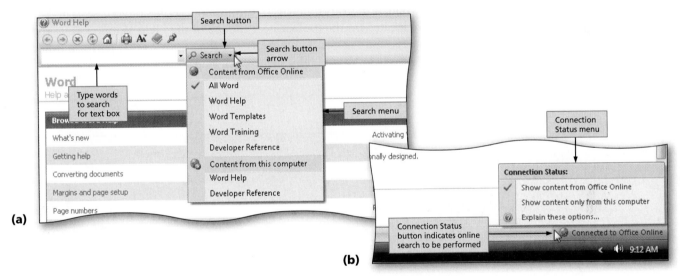

Figure C–4

Word Help offers the user the option of searching the online Help Web pages maintained by Microsoft or the offline Help files placed on your computer when you install Word. You can specify whether Word Help should search online or offline from two places: the Connection Status button on the status bar of the Word Help window, or the Search button arrow on the toolbar. The Connection Status button indicates whether Help currently is set up to work with online or offline information sources. Clicking the Connection Status button provides a menu with commands for selecting online or offline searches (Figure C–4b). The Connection Status menu allows the user to select whether Help searches will return content only from the computer (offline), or content from the computer and from Office Online (online).

Clicking the Search button arrow also provides a menu with commands for an online or offline search (Figure C–4a). These commands determine the source of information that Help searches for during the current Help session only. For example, assume that your preferred search is an offline search because you often do not have Internet access. You would set Connection Status to 'Show content only from this computer'. When you have Internet access, you can select an online search from the Search menu to search Office Online for information for your current search session only. Your search will use the Office Online resources until you quit Help. The next time you start Help, the Connection Status once again will be offline. In addition to setting the source of information that Help searches for during the current Help session, you can use the Search menu to further target the current search to one of four subcategories of online Help: Word Help, Word Templates, Word Training, and Developer Reference. The local search further can target one subcategory, Developer Reference.

In addition to searching for a word or string of text, you can use the links provided on the Browse Word Help area (Figure C–3 on page APP 10) to search for help on a topic. These links direct you to major help categories. From each major category, subcategories are available to further refine your search.

Finally, you can use the Table of Contents for Word Help to search for a topic the same way you would in a hard copy book. The Table of Contents is accessed via a toolbar button.

Toolbar Buttons

You can use toolbar buttons to navigate through the results of your search. The toolbar buttons are located on the toolbar near the top of the Help Window (Figure C–5). The toolbar buttons contain navigation buttons as well as buttons that perform other useful and common tasks in Word Help, such as printing.

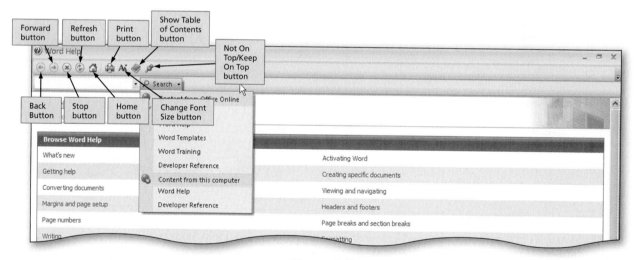

Figure C–5

The Word Help navigation buttons are the Back, Forward, Stop, Refresh, and Home buttons. These five buttons behave like the navigation buttons in a Web browser window. You can use the Back button to go back one window, the Forward button to go forward one window, the Stop button to stop loading the current page, and the Home button to redisplay the Help home page in the Help window. Use the Refresh button to reload the information requested into the Help window from its original source. When getting Help information online, this button provides the most current information from the Microsoft Help Web site.

The buttons located to the right of the navigation buttons — Print, Change Font Size, Show Table of Contents, and Not on Top — provide you with access to useful and common commands. The Print button prints the contents of the open Help window. The Change Font Size button customizes the Help window by increasing or decreasing the size of its text. The Show Table of Contents button opens a pane on the left side of the Help window that shows the Table of Contents for Word Help. You can use the Table of Contents for Word Help to navigate through the contents of Word Help much as you would use the Table of Contents in a book to search for a topic. The Not On Top button is an example of a toggle button, which is a button that can be switched back and forth between two states. It determines how the Word Help window behaves relative to other windows. When clicked, the Not On Top button changes to Keep On Top. In this state, it does not allow other windows from Word or other programs to cover the Word Help window when those windows are the active windows. When in the Not On Top state, the button allows other windows to be opened or moved on top of the Word Help window.

You can customize the size and placement of the Help window. Resize the window using the Maximize and Restore buttons, or by dragging the window to a desired size. Relocate the Help window by dragging the title bar to a new location on the screen.

Searching Word Help

Once the Word Help window is open, several methods exist for navigating Word Help. You can search for help by using any of the three following methods from the Help window:

1. Enter search text in the 'Type words to search for' text box
2. Click the links in the Help window
3. Use the Table of Contents

To Obtain Help Using the Type words to search for Text Box

Assume for the following example that you want to know more about watermarks. The following steps use the 'Type words to search for' text box to obtain useful information about watermarks by entering the word, watermark, as search text. The steps also navigate in the Word Help window.

1

- Type watermark in the 'Type words to search for' text box at the top of the Word Help window.

- Click the Search button arrow to display the Search menu (Figure C-6).

- If it is not selected already, click All Word on the Search menu to select the command. If All Word is already selected, click the Search button arrow again to close the Search menu.

Q&A Why select All Word on the Search menu?

Selecting All Word on the Search menu ensures that Word Help will search all possible sources for information on your search term. It will produce the most complete search results.

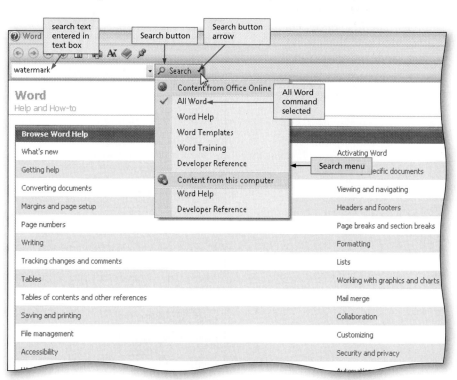

Figure C-6

2

- Click the Search button to display the search results (Figure C–7).

Q&A

Why do my results differ?

If you do not have an Internet connection, your results will reflect only the content of the Help files on your computer. When searching for help online, results also can change as material is added, deleted, and updated on the online Help Web pages maintained by Microsoft.

Q&A

Why were my search results not very helpful?

When initiating a search, keep in mind to check the spelling of the search text; and to keep your search very specific, with fewer than seven words, to return the most accurate results.

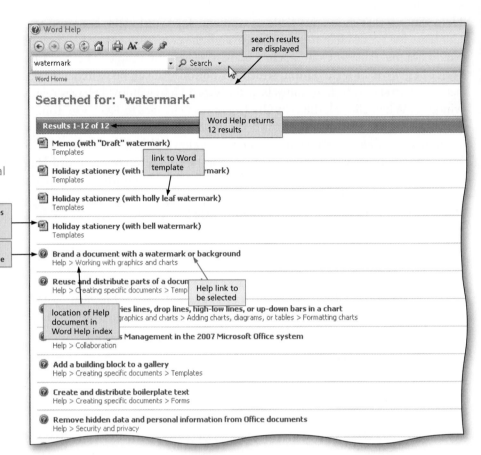

Figure C–7

3

- Click the 'Brand a document with a watermark or background' link to open the Help document associated with the link in the Help window (Figure C–8).

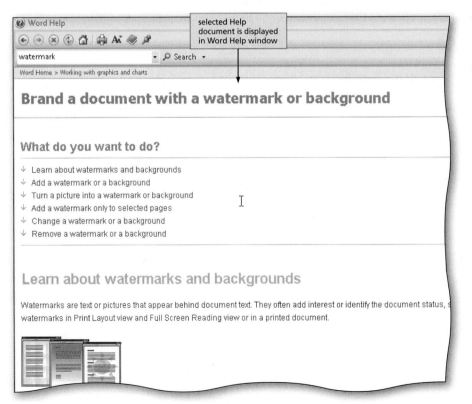

Figure C–8

4

- Click the Home button on the task-bar to clear the search results and redisplay the Word Help home page (Figure C–9).

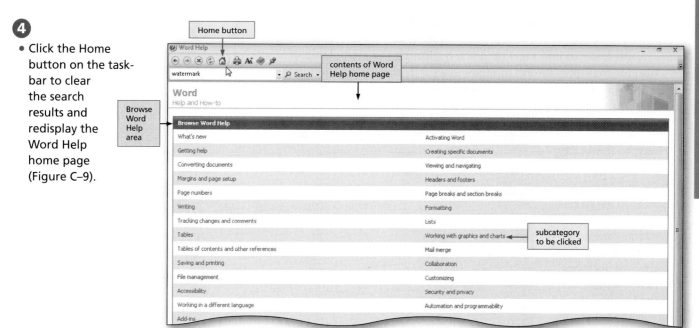

Home button

contents of Word Help home page

Browse Word Help area

subcategory to be clicked

Figure C–9

To Obtain Help Using the Help Links

If your topic of interest is listed in the Browse Word Help area, you can click the link to begin browsing Word Help categories instead of entering search text. You browse Word Help just like you would browse a Web site. If you know in which category to find your Help information, you may wish to use these links. The following steps find the watermark Help information using the category links from the Word Help home page.

1

- Click the 'Working with graphics and charts' link to open the 'Working with graphics and charts' page.

- Click the 'Brand a document with a watermark or background' link to open the Help document associated with the link (Figure C–10).

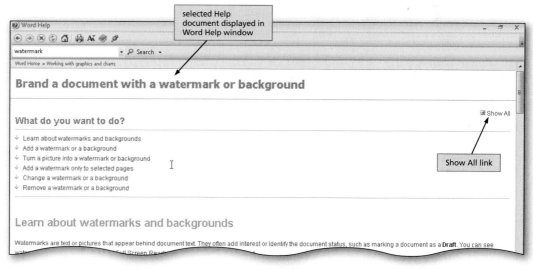

selected Help document displayed in Word Help window

Show All link

Figure C–10

Q&A

What does the Show All link do?

In many Help documents, additional information about terms and features is available by clicking a link in the document to display additional information in the Help document. Clicking the Show All link opens all the links in the Help document that expand to additional text.

To Obtain Help Using the Help Table of Contents

A third way to find Help in Word is through the Help Table of Contents. You can browse through the Table of Contents to display information about a particular topic or to familiarize yourself with Word. The following steps access the watermark Help information by browsing through the Table of Contents.

• Click the Home button on the toolbar.

• Click the Show Table of Contents button on the toolbar to open the Table of Contents pane on the left side of the Help window. If necessary, click the Maximize button on the Help title bar to maximize the window (Figure C–11).

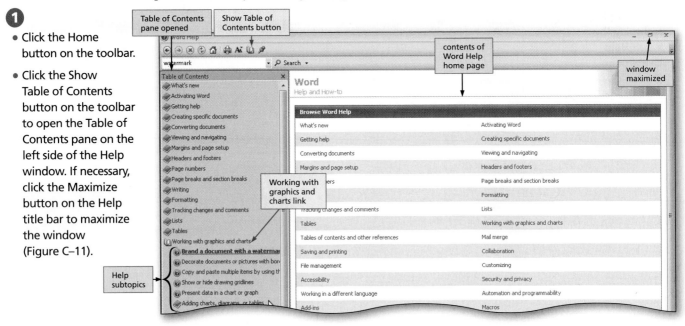

Figure C–11

❷
• Click the 'Working with graphics and charts' link in the Table of Contents pane to view a list of Help subtopics.

• Click the 'Brand a document with a watermark or background' link in the Table of Contents pane to view the selected Help document in the right pane (Figure C–12).

Q&A How do I remove the Table of Contents pane when I am finished with it?

The Show Table of Contents button acts as a toggle switch. When the Table of Contents pane is visible, the button changes to Hide Table of Contents. Clicking it hides the Table of Contents pane and changes the button to Show Table of Contents.

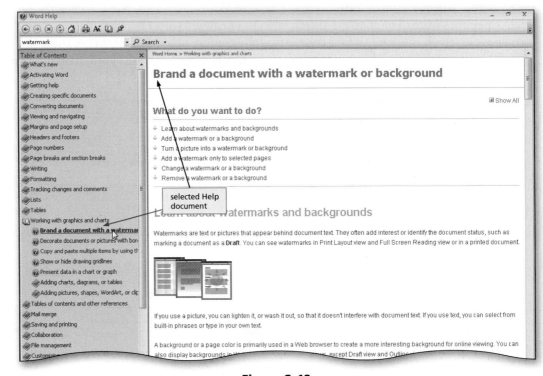

Figure C–12

Obtaining Help while Working in Word

Often you may need help while working on a document without already having the Help window open. For example, you may be unsure about how a particular command works, or you may be presented with a dialog box that you are not sure how to use. Rather than opening the Help window and initiating a search, Word Help provides you with the ability to search directly for help.

Figure C–13 shows one option for obtaining help while working in Word. If you want to learn more about a command, point to the command button and wait for the Enhanced ScreenTip to appear. If the Help icon appears in the Enhanced ScreenTip, press the F1 key while pointing to the command to open the Help window associated with that command.

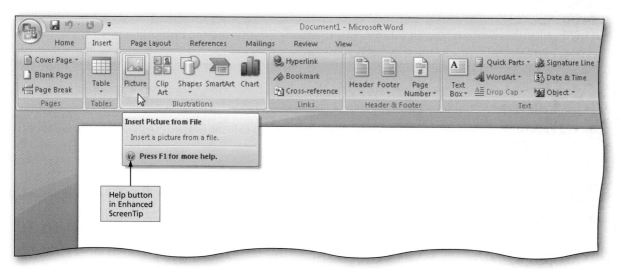

Figure C–13

Figure C–14 shows a dialog box with a Get help button in it. Pressing the F1 key while the dialog box is displayed opens a Help window. The Help window contains help about that dialog box, if available. If no help file is available for that particular dialog box, then the main Help window opens.

Figure C–14

Use Help

1 Obtaining Help Using Search Text

Instructions: Perform the following tasks using Word Help.

1. Use the 'Type words to search for' text box to obtain help about landscape printing. Use the Connection Status menu to search online help if you have an Internet connection.

2. Click Select page orientation in the list of links in the search results. Double-click the Microsoft Office Word Help window title bar to maximize it. Read and print the information. At the top of the printout, write down the number of links Word Help found.

3. Use the Search menu to search for help offline. Repeat the search from Step 1. At the top of the printout, write down the number of links that Word Help found searching offline. Submit the printouts as specified by your instructor.

4. Use the 'Type words to search for' text box to search for information online about adjusting line spacing. Click the 'Adjust the spacing between a list bullet or number and the text' link in the search results. If necessary, maximize the Microsoft Office 2007 Word Help window. Read and print the contents of the window. Close the Microsoft Office Word Help window. Submit the printouts as specified by your instructor.

5. For each of the following words and phrases, click one link in the search results, click the Show All link, and then print the page: page zoom; date; print preview; Ribbon; word count; and citation. Submit the printouts as specified by your instructor.

2 Expanding on Word Help Basics

Instructions: Use Word Help to better understand its features and answer the questions listed below. Answer the questions on your own paper, or submit the printed Help information as specified by your instructor.

1. Use Help to find out how to customize the Help window. Change the font size to the smallest option and then print the contents of the Microsoft Office Word Help window. Change the font size back to its original setting. Close the window.

2. Press the F1 key. Search for information about tables, restricting the search results to Word Templates. Print the first page of the Search results.

3. Search for information about tables, restricting the search results to Word Help files. Print the first page of the Search results.

4. Use Word Help to find out what happened to the Office Assistant, a feature in the previous version of Word. Print out the Help document that contains the answer.

Appendix D
Publishing Office 2007 Web Pages to a Web Server

With the Office 2007 programs, you use the Save As command on the Office Button menu to save a Web page to a Web server using one of two techniques: Web folders or File Transfer Protocol. A **Web folder** is an Office shortcut to a Web server. **File Transfer Protocol (FTP)** is an Internet standard that allows computers to exchange files with other computers on the Internet.

You should contact your network system administrator or technical support staff at your Internet access provider to determine if their Web server supports Web folders, FTP, or both, and to obtain necessary permissions to access the Web server. If you decide to publish Web pages using a Web folder, you must have the Office Server Extensions (OSE) installed on your computer.

Using Web Folders to Publish Office 2007 Web Pages

When publishing to a Web folder, someone first must create the Web folder before you can save to it. If you are granted permission to create a Web folder, you must obtain the Web address of the Web server, a user name, and possibly a password that allows you to access the Web server. You also must decide on a name for the Web folder. Table D–1 explains how to create a Web folder.

Office 2007 adds the name of the Web folder to the list of current Web folders. You can save to this folder, open files in the folder, rename the folder, or perform any operations you would to a folder on your hard disk. You can use your Office 2007 program or Windows Explorer to access this folder. Table D–2 explains how to save to a Web folder.

Table D–1 Creating a Web Folder

1. Click the Office Button and then click Save As or Open.

2. When the Save As dialog box (or Open dialog box) appears, click the Tools button arrow, and then click Map Network Drive... When the Map Network Drive dialog box is displayed, click the 'Connect to a Web site that you can use to store your documents and pictures' link.

3. When the Add Network Location Wizard dialog box appears, click the Next button. If necessary, click Choose a custom network location. Click the Next button. Click the View examples link, type the Internet or network address, and then click the Next button. Click 'Log on anonymously' to deselect the check box, type your user name in the User name text box, and then click the Next button. Enter the name you want to call this network place and then click the Next button. Click to deselect the 'Open this network location when I click Finish' check box, and then click the Finish button.

Table D–2 Saving to a Web Folder

1. Click the Office Button, click Save As.

2. When the Save As dialog box is displayed, type the Web page file name in the File name text box. Do not press the ENTER key.

3. Click the Save as type box arrow and then click Web Page to select the Web Page format.

4. Click Computer in the Navigation pane.

5. Double-click the Web folder name in the Network Location list.

6. If the Enter Network Password dialog box appears, type the user name and password in the respective text boxes and then click the OK button.

7. Click the Save button in the Save As dialog box.

Using FTP to Publish Office 2007 Web Pages

When publishing a Web page using FTP, you first must add the FTP location to your computer before you can save to it. An FTP location, also called an **FTP site**, is a collection of files that reside on an FTP server. In this case, the FTP server is the Web server.

To add an FTP location, you must obtain the name of the FTP site, which usually is the address (URL) of the FTP server, and a user name and a password that allows you to access the FTP server. You save and open the Web pages on the FTP server using the name of the FTP site. Table D–3 explains how to add an FTP site.

Office 2007 adds the name of the FTP site to the FTP locations list in the Save As and Open dialog boxes. You can open and save files using this list. Table D–4 explains how to save to an FTP location.

Table D–3 Adding an FTP Location
1. Click the Office Button and then click Save As or Open.
2. When the Save As dialog box (or Open dialog box) appears, click the Tools button arrow, and then click Map Network Drive... When the Map Network Drive dialog box is displayed, click the 'Connect to a Web site that you can use to store your documents and pictures' link.
3. When the Add Network Location Wizard dialog box appears, click the Next button. If necessary, click Choose a custom network location. Click the Next button. Click the View examples link, type the Internet or network address, and then click the Next button. If you have a user name for the site, click to deselect 'Log on anonymously' and type your user name in the User name text box, and then click Next. If the site allows anonymous logon, click Next. Type a name for the location, click Next, click to deselect the 'Open this network location when I click Finish' check box, and click Finish. Click the OK button.
4. Close the Save As or the Open dialog box.

Table D–4 Saving to an FTP Location
1. Click the Office Button and then click Save As.
2. When the Save As dialog box is displayed, type the Web page file name in the File name text box. Do not press the ENTER key.
3. Click the Save as type box arrow and then click Web Page to select the Web Page format.
4. Click Computer in the Navigation pane.
5. Double-click the name of the FTP site in the Network Location list.
6. When the FTP Log On dialog box appears, enter your user name and password and then click the OK button.
7. Click the Save button in the Save As dialog box.

Appendix E
Customizing Microsoft Office 2007

This appendix explains how to change the screen resolution in Windows Vista to the resolution used in this book. It also describes how to customize the Word window by changing the Ribbon, Quick Access Toolbar, and the color scheme.

Changing Screen Resolution

Screen resolution indicates the number of pixels (dots) that the computer uses to display the letters, numbers, graphics, and background you see on the screen. When you increase the screen resolution, Windows displays more information on the screen, but the information decreases in size. The reverse also is true: as you decrease the screen resolution, Windows displays less information on the screen, but the information increases in size.

The screen resolution usually is stated as the product of two numbers, such as 1024×768 (pronounced "ten twenty-four by seven sixty-eight"). A 1024×768 screen resolution results in a display of 1,024 distinct pixels on each of 768 lines, or about 786,432 pixels. The figures in this book were created using a screen resolution of 1024×768.

The screen resolutions most commonly used today are 800×600 and 1024×768, although some Office specialists set their computers at a much higher screen resolution, such as 2048×1536.

To Change the Screen Resolution

The following steps change the screen resolution from 1280×1024 to 1024×768. Your computer already may be set to 1024×768 or some other resolution.

1

- If necessary, minimize all programs so that the Windows Vista desktop appears.

- Right-click the Windows Vista desktop to display the Windows Vista desktop shortcut menu (Figure E–1).

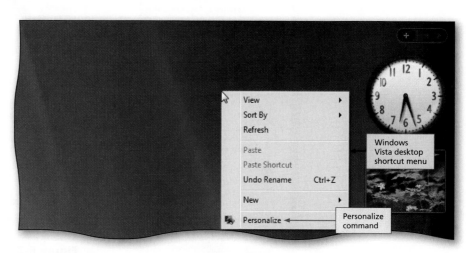

Figure E–1

- Click Personalize on the shortcut menu to open the Personalization window.

- Click Display Settings in the Personalization window to display the Display Settings dialog box (Figure E–2).

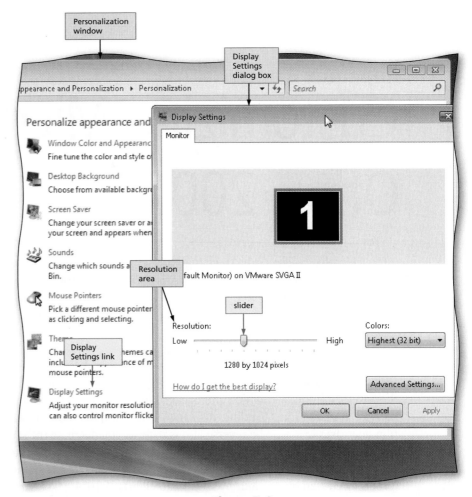

Figure E–2

- Drag the slider in the Resolution area so that the screen resolution changes to 1024 × 768 (Figure E–3).

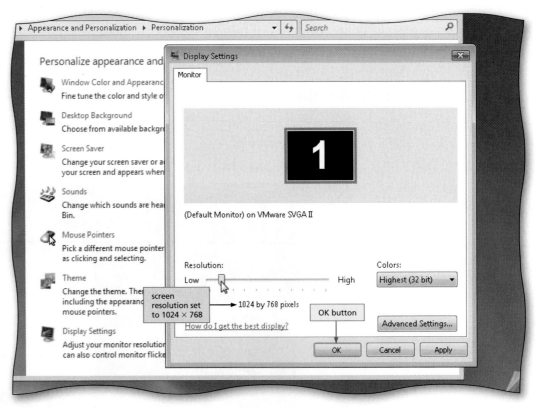

Figure E–3

4

- Click the OK button to change the screen resolution from 1280 × 1024 to 1024 × 768 (Figure E–4).

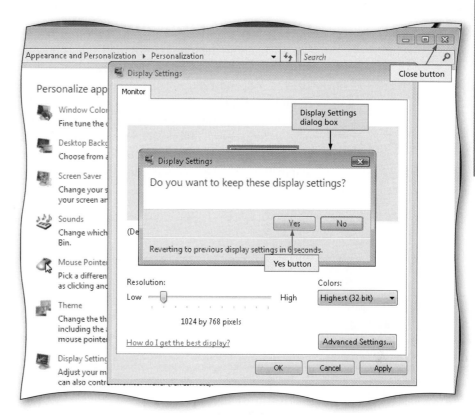

Figure E–4

5

- Click the Yes button in the Display Settings dialog box to accept the new screen resolution (Figure E–5).

 What if I do not want to change the screen resolution after seeing it applied after I click the OK button?

You either can click the No button in the inner Display Settings dialog box, or wait for the timer to run out, at which point Windows Vista will revert to the original screen resolution.

- Click the Close button to close the Personalization Window.

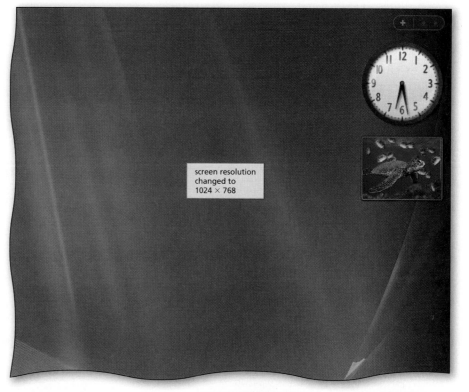

Figure E–5

Screen Resolution and the Appearance of the Ribbon in Office 2007 Programs

Changing the screen resolution affects how the Ribbon appears in Office 2007 programs. Figure E–6 shows the Word Ribbon at the screen resolutions of 800 × 600, 1024 × 768, and 1280 × 1024. All of the same commands are available regardless of screen resolution. Word, however, makes changes to the groups and the buttons within the groups to accommodate the various screen resolutions. The result is that certain commands may need to be accessed differently depending on the resolution chosen. A command that is visible on the Ribbon and available by clicking a button at one resolution may not be visible and may need to be accessed using its group button at a different resolution.

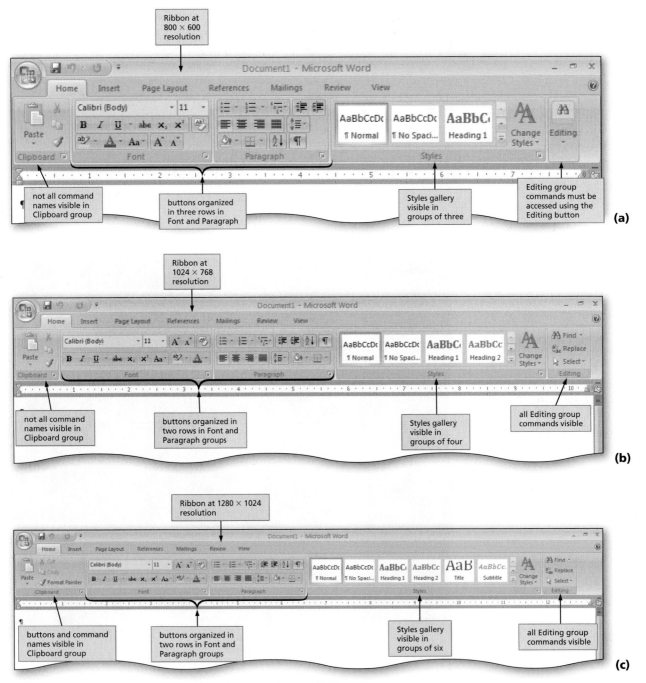

Figure E–6

Comparing the three Ribbons, notice changes in content and layout of the groups and galleries. In some cases, the content of a group is the same in each resolution, but the layout of the group differs. For example, the same buttons appear in the Font and Paragraph groups in the three resolutions, but the layouts differ. The buttons are displayed in three rows at the 800 × 600 resolution, and in two rows in the 1024 × 768 and 1280 × 1024 resolutions. In other cases, the content and layout are the same across the resolution, but the level of detail differs with the resolution. In the Clipboard group, when the resolution increases to 1280 × 1024, the names of all the buttons in the group appear in addition to the buttons themselves. At the lower resolution, only the buttons appear.

Changing resolutions also can result in fewer commands being visible in a group. Comparing the Editing groups, notice that the group at the 800 × 600 resolution consists of an Editing button, while at the higher resolutions, the group has three buttons visible. The commands that are available on the Ribbon at the higher resolutions must be accessed using the Editing button at the 800 × 600 resolution.

Changing resolutions results in different amounts of detail being available at one time in the galleries on the Ribbon. The Styles gallery in the three resolutions presented show different numbers of styles. At 800 × 600, you can scroll through the gallery three styles at a time, at 1024 × 768, you can scroll through the gallery four styles at a time, and at 1280 × 1024, you can scroll through the gallery six styles at a time.

Customizing the Word Window

When working in Word, you may want to make your working area as large as possible. One option is to minimize the Ribbon. You also can modify the characteristics of the Quick Access Toolbar, customizing the toolbar's commands and location to better suit your needs.

To Minimize the Ribbon in Word

The following steps minimize the Ribbon.

- Start Word.

- Maximize the Word window, if necessary.

- Click the Customize Quick Access Toolbar button on the Quick Access Toolbar to display the Customize Quick Access Toolbar menu (Figure E–7).

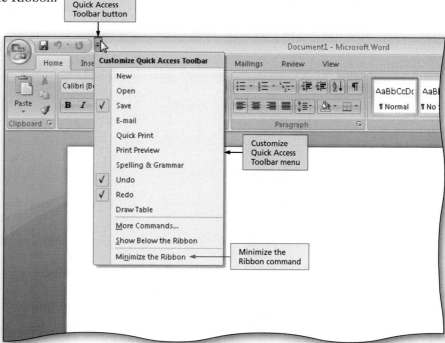

Figure E–7

2

- Click Minimize the Ribbon on the Quick Access Toolbar to reduce the Ribbon display to just the tabs (Figure E–8).

Figure E–8

Other Ways

1. Double-click the active Ribbon tab
2. Press CTRL+F1

Customizing and Resetting the Quick Access Toolbar

The Quick Access Toolbar, located to the right of the Microsoft Office Button by default, provides easy access to some of the more frequently used commands in Word (Figure E–7). By default, the Quick Access Toolbar contains buttons for the Save, Undo, and Redo commands. Customize the Quick Access Toolbar by changing its location in the window and by adding additional buttons to reflect which commands you would like to be able to access easily.

To Change the Location of the Quick Access Toolbar

The following steps move the Quick Access Toolbar to below the Ribbon.

1

- Double-click the Home tab to redisplay the Ribbon.

- Click the Customize Quick Access Toolbar button on the Quick Access Toolbar menu to display the Customize Quick Access Toolbar menu (Figure E–9).

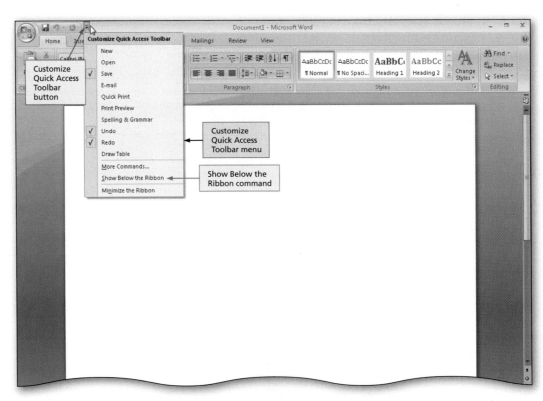

Figure E–9

- Click Show Below the Ribbon on the Quick Access Toolbar menu to move the Quick Access Toolbar below the Ribbon (Figure E–10).

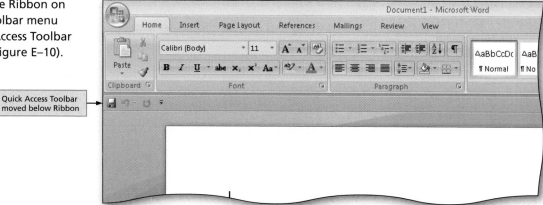

Quick Access Toolbar moved below Ribbon

Figure E–10

To Add Commands to the Quick Access Toolbar Using the Customize Quick Access Toolbar Menu

Some of the more commonly added commands are available for selection from the Customize Quick Access Toolbar menu. The following steps add the Quick Print button to the Quick Access Toolbar.

- Click the Customize Quick Access Toolbar button to display the Customize Quick Access Toolbar menu (Figure E–11).

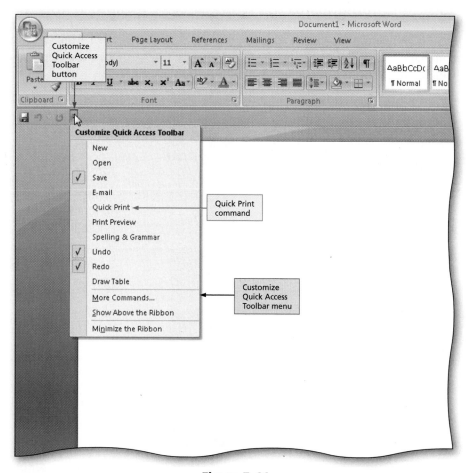

Customize Quick Access Toolbar button

Quick Print command

Customize Quick Access Toolbar menu

Figure E–11

- Click Quick Print on the Quick Access Toolbar menu to add the Quick Print button to the Quick Access Toolbar (Figure E–12).

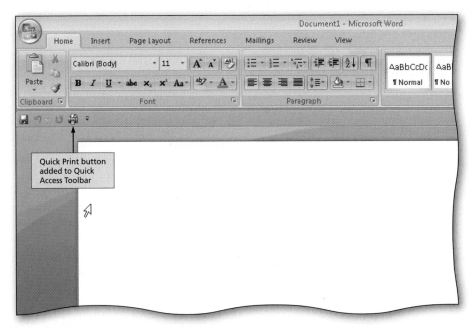

Figure E–12

To Add Commands to the Quick Access Toolbar Using the Shortcut Menu

Commands also can be added to the Quick Access Toolbar from the Ribbon. Adding an existing Ribbon command that you use often to the Quick Access Toolbar makes the command immediately available, regardless of which tab is active.

- Click the Review tab on the Ribbon to make it the active tab.

- Right-click the Spelling & Grammar button on the Review tab to display a shortcut menu (Figure E–13).

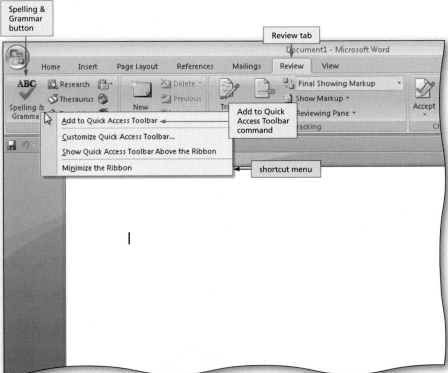

Figure E–13

2
- Click Add to Quick Access Toolbar on the shortcut menu to add the Spelling & Grammar button to the Quick Access Toolbar (Figure E–14).

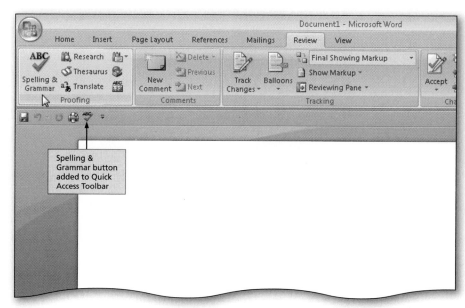

Figure E–14

To Add Commands to the Quick Access Toolbar Using Word Options

Some commands do not appear on the Ribbon. They can be added to the Quick Access Toolbar using the Word Options dialog box.

1
- Click the Office Button to display the Office Button menu (Figure E–15).

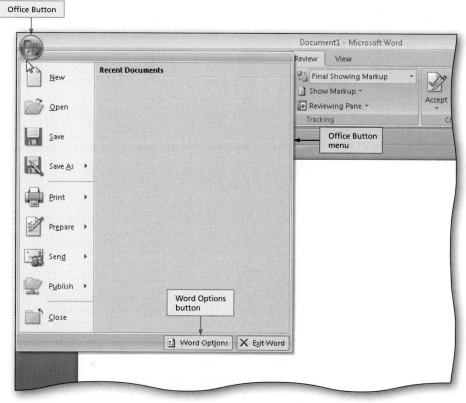

Figure E–15

- Click the Word
  Options button on
  the Office Button
  menu to display the
  Word Options dialog
  box (Figure E–16).

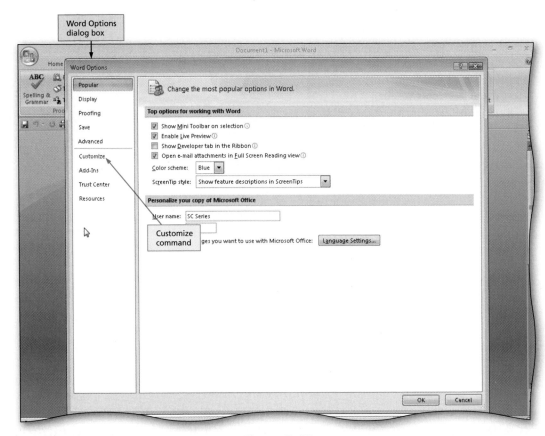

Figure E–16

- Click Customize in
  the left pane.

- Click 'Choose
  commands from'
  box arrow to
  display the 'Choose
  commands from' list.

- Click Commands Not
  in the Ribbon in the
  'Choose commands
  from' list.

- Scroll to display the
  Web Page Preview
  command.

- Click Web Page
  Preview to select it
  (Figure E–17).

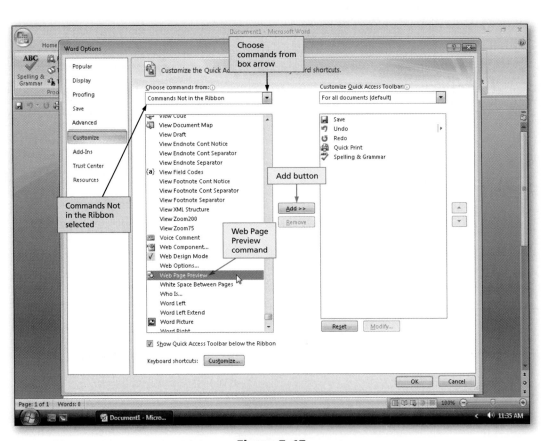

Figure E–17

4

- Click the Add button to add the Web Page Preview button to the list of buttons on the Quick Access Toolbar (Figure E–18).

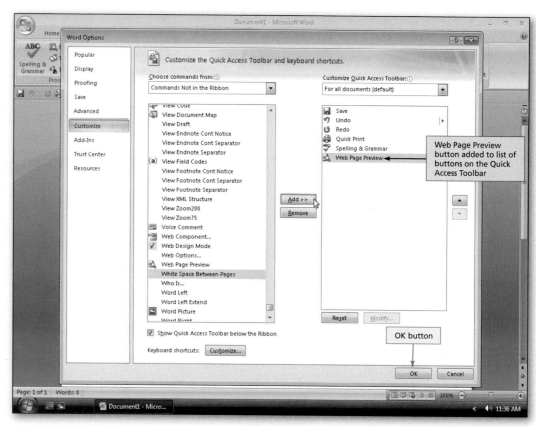

Figure E–18

5

- Click the OK button to add the Web Page Preview button to the Quick Access Toolbar (Figure E–19).

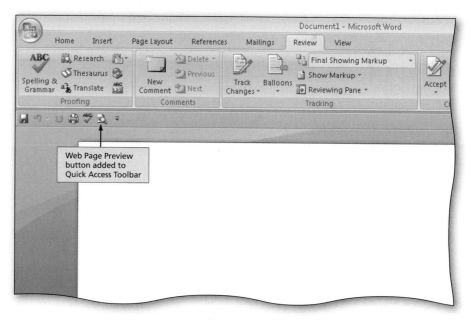

Figure E–19

Other Ways

1. Click Customize Quick Access Toolbar button, click More Commands, select commands to add, click Add button, click OK button

To Remove a Command from the Quick Access Toolbar

1

• Right-click the Web Page Preview button on the Quick Access Toolbar to display a shortcut menu (Figure E–20).

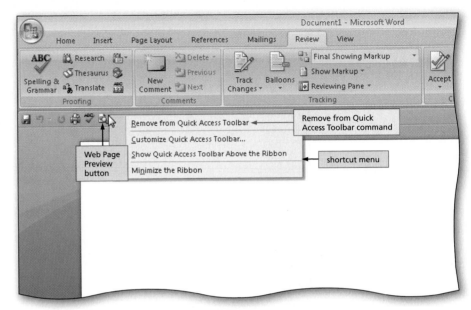

Figure E–20

2

• Click Remove from Quick Access Toolbar on the shortcut menu to remove the button from the Quick Access Toolbar (Figure E–21).

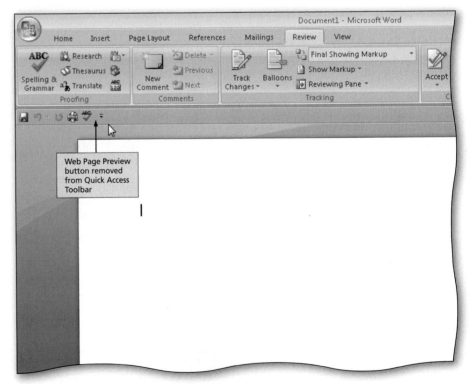

Figure E–21

Other Ways

1. Click Customize Quick Access Toolbar button, click More Commands, click the command you wish to remove in the Customize Quick Access Toolbar list, click Remove button, click OK button

2. If the command appears on the Customize Quick Access Toolbar menu, click the Customize Quick Access Toolbar button, click the command you wish to remove

To Reset the Quick Access Toolbar

1

- Click the Customize Quick Access Toolbar button on the Quick Access Toolbar.

- Click More Commands on the Quick Access Toolbar menu to display the Word Options Dialog box.

- Click the Show Quick Access Toolbar below the Ribbon check box to deselect it (Figure E–22).

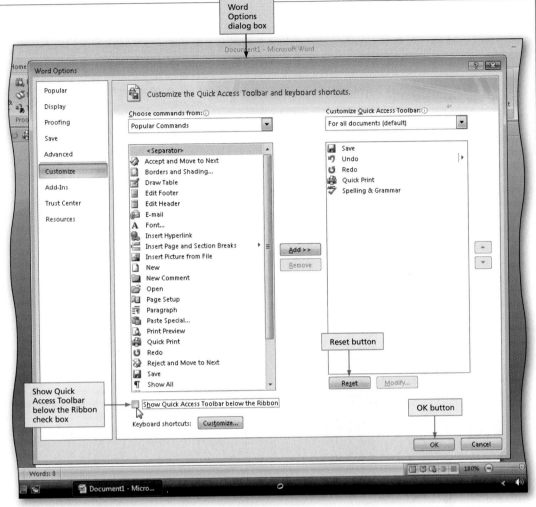

Figure E–22

- Click the Reset button, click the Yes button in the dialog box that appears, and then click the OK button in the Word Options dialog box, to reset the Quick Access Toolbar to its original position to the right of the Office Button, with the original three buttons (Figure E–23).

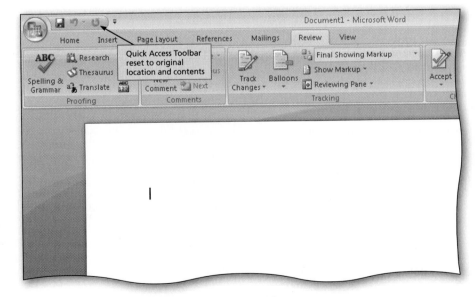

Figure E–23

Changing the Word Color Scheme

The Microsoft Word window can be customized by selecting a color scheme other than the default blue one. Three color schemes are available in Word.

To Change the Word Color Scheme

The following steps change the color scheme.

1
- Click the Office Button to display the Office Button menu.

- Click the Word Options button on the Office Button menu to display the Word Options dialog box.

- If necessary, click Popular in the left pane. Click the Color scheme box arrow to display a list of color schemes (Figure E–24).

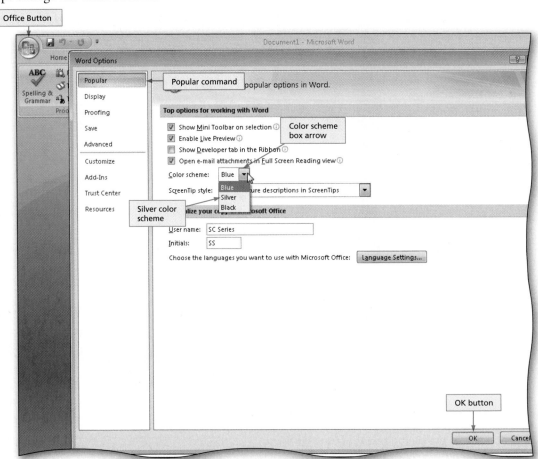

Figure E–24

2
- Click Silver in the list.

- Click the OK button to change the color scheme to silver (Figure E–25).

Q&A

How do I switch back to the default color scheme?

Follow the steps for changing the Word color scheme, and select Blue from the list of color schemes.

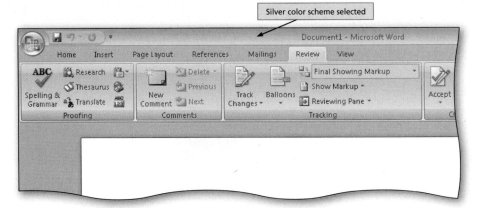

Figure E–25

Appendix F

Steps for the Windows XP User

For the XP User of this Book

For most tasks, no differences exist between using Office 2007 under the Windows Vista operating system and using an Office 2007 program under the Windows XP operating system. With some tasks, however, you will see some differences, or need to complete the tasks using different steps. This appendix shows how to Start an Application, Save a Document, Open a Document, Insert a Picture, and Insert Text from a File while using Microsoft Office under Windows XP. To illustrate these tasks, this appendix uses Microsoft Word. The tasks can be accomplished in other Office programs in a similar fashion.

To Start Word

The following steps, which assume Windows is running, start Word based on a typical installation. You may need to ask your instructor how to start Word for your computer.

1

- Click the Start button on the Windows taskbar to display the Start menu.

- Point to All Programs on the Start menu to display the All Programs submenu.

- Point to Microsoft Office on the All Programs submenu to display the Microsoft Office submenu (Figure F–1).

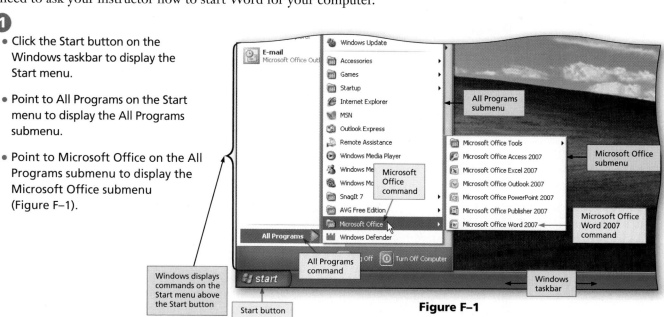

Figure F–1

- Click Microsoft Office Word 2007 to start Word and display a new blank document in the Word window (Figure F–2).

- If the Word window is not maximized, click the Maximize button next to the Close button on its title bar to maximize the window.

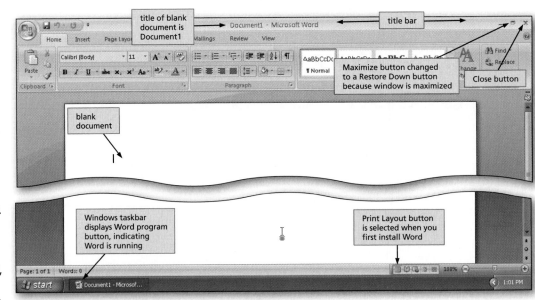

- If the Print Layout button is not selected, click it so that your screen layout matches Figure F–2.

Figure F–2

Other Ways
1. Double-click Word icon on desktop, if one is present   2. Click Microsoft Office Word 2007 on Start menu

To Save a Document

After editing, you should save the document. The following steps save a document on a USB flash drive using the file name, Horseback Riding Lessons Flyer.

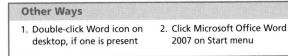

- With a USB flash drive connected to one of the computer's USB ports, click the Save button on the Quick Access Toolbar to display the Save As dialog box (Figure F–3).

Q&A

Do I have to save to a USB flash drive?

No. You can save to any device or folder. A **folder** is a specific location on a storage medium. You can save to the default folder or a different folder. You also can create your own folders, which is explained later in this book.

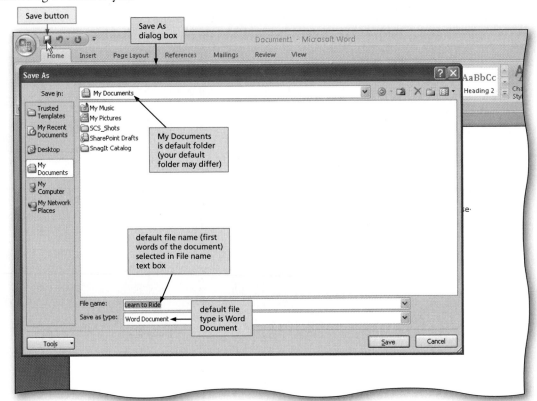

Figure F–3

2

- Type the name of your file (Horseback Riding Lessons Flyer in this example) in the File name text box to change the file name. Do not press the ENTER key after typing the file name (Figure F–4).

Q&A What characters can I use in a file name?

A file name can have a maximum of 255 characters, including spaces. The only invalid characters are the backslash (\), slash (/), colon (:), asterisk (*), question mark (?), quotation mark ("), less than symbol (<), greater than symbol (>), and vertical bar (|).

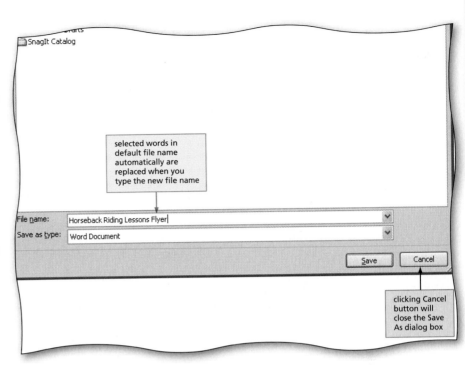

Figure F–4

3

- Click the Save in box arrow to display a list of available drives and folders (Figure F–5).

Q&A Why is my list of files, folders, and drives arranged and named differently from those shown in the figure?

Your computer's configuration determines how the list of files and folders is displayed and how drives are named. You can change the save location by clicking shortcuts on the **My Places bar**.

Q&A How do I save the file if I am not using a USB flash drive?

Use the same process, but be certain to select your device in the Save in list.

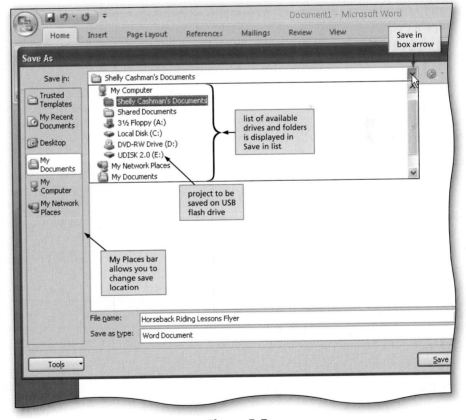

Figure F–5

4

- Click UDISK 2.0 (E:) in the Save in list to select the USB flash drive, Drive E in this case, as the new save location (Figure F–6).

- Click the Save button to save the document.

Q&A

What if my USB flash drive has a different name or letter?

It is very likely that your USB flash drive will have a different name and drive letter and be connected to a different port. Verify the device in your Save in list is correct.

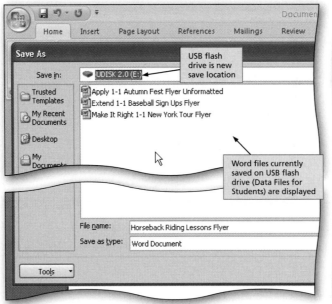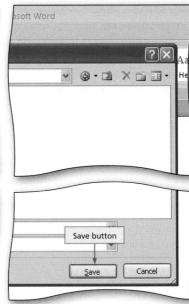

Figure F–6

Other Ways

1. Click Office Button, click Save, type file name, select drive or folder, click Save button

2. Press CTRL+S or press SHIFT+F12, type file name, select drive or folder, click Save button

To Open a Document

The following steps open the Horseback Riding Lessons Flyer file from the USB flash drive.

1

- With your USB flash drive connected to one of the computer's USB ports, click the Office Button to display the Office Button menu.

- Click Open on the Office Button menu to display the Open dialog box.

- If necessary, click the Look in box arrow and then click UDISK 2.0 (E:) to select the USB flash drive, Drive E in this case, in the Look in list as the new open location.

- Click Horseback Riding Lessons Flyer to select the file name (Figure F–7).

- Click the Open button to open the document.

Q&A

How do I open the file if I am not using a USB flash drive?

Use the same process, but be certain to select your device in the Look in list.

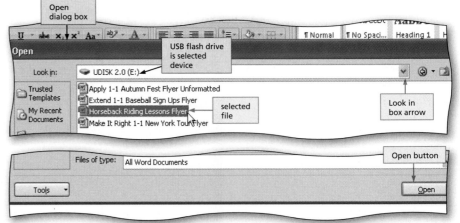

Figure F–7

Other Ways

1. Click Office Button, double-click file name in Recent Documents list

2. Press CTRL+O, select file name, press ENTER

To Insert a Picture

The following steps insert a centered picture, which, in this example, is located on a USB flash drive.

1 Position the insertion point where you want the picture to be located. Click Insert on the Ribbon to display the Insert tab. Click the Insert Picture from File button on the Insert tab to display the Insert Picture dialog box.

2 With your USB flash drive connected to one of the computer's USB ports, if necessary, click the Look in box arrow and then click UDISK 2.0 (E:) to select the USB flash drive, Drive E in this case, in the Look in list as the device that contains the picture. Select the file name of the picture file.

3 Click the Insert button in the dialog box to insert the picture at the location of the insertion point in the document.

To Insert Text from a File

The following steps insert text from a file located on the USB flash drive.

1 Click where you want to insert the text. Click Insert on the Ribbon to display the Insert tab. Click the Object button arrow in the Text group to display the Object menu. Click Text from File to display the Insert File dialog box.

2 With your USB flash drive connected to one of the computer's USB ports, if necessary, click the Look in box arrow and then click UDISK 2.0 (E:) to select the USB flash drive, Drive E in this case, in the Look in list as the device that contains the file. Click to select the file name.

3 Click the Insert button in the dialog box to insert the file at the location of the insertion point in the document.

To Create a New Database

The following steps create a database on a USB flash drive.

1 With a USB flash drive connected to one of the computer's USB ports, click Blank Database in the Getting Started with Microsoft Office Access screen to create a new blank database.

2 Type the name of your database in the File Name text box and then click the 'Browse for a location to put your database' button to display the File New Database dialog box.

3 Click the Save in box arrow to display a list of available drives and folders and then click UDISK 2.0 (E:) (your letter may be different) in the Save in list to select the USB flash drive as the new save location.

4 Click the OK button to select the USB flash drive as the location for the database and to return to the Getting Started with Microsoft Office Access screen.

5 Click the Create button to create the database on the USB flash drive with the file name you selected.

To Open a Database

The following steps use the More button to open a database from the USB flash drive.

1 With your USB flash drive connected to one of the computer's USB ports, click the More button to display the Open dialog box.

2 If necessary, click the Look in box arrow and then click UDISK 2.0 (E:) to select the USB flash drive in the Look in list as the new open location. (Your drive letter might be different.)

3 Select the file name. Click the Open button to open the database.

4 If a Security Warning appears, click the Options button to display the Microsoft Office Security Options dialog box. With the option button to enable this content selected, click the OK button to enable the content.

Appendix G
Microsoft Business
Certification Program

What Is the Microsoft Business Certification Program?

The Microsoft Business Certification Program enables candidates to show that they have something exceptional to offer – proved expertise in Microsoft Office 2007 programs. The two certification tracks allow candidates to choose how they want to exhibit their skills, either through validating skills within a specific Microsoft product or taking their knowledge to the next level and combining Microsoft programs to show that they can apply multiple skill sets to complete more complex office tasks. Recognized by businesses and schools around the world, more than 3 million certifications have been obtained in more than 100 different countries. The Microsoft Business Certification Program is the only Microsoft-approved certification program of its kind.

What Is the Microsoft Certified Application Specialist Certification?

The Microsoft Certified Application Specialist certification exams focus on validating specific skill sets within each of the Microsoft Office system programs. Candidates can choose which exam(s) they want to take according to which skills they want to validate. The available Application Specialist exams include:

- Using Windows Vista™
- Using Microsoft® Office Word 2007
- Using Microsoft® Office Excel® 2007
- Using Microsoft® Office PowerPoint® 2007
- Using Microsoft® Office Access™ 2007
- Using Microsoft® Office Outlook® 2007

> For more information and details on how Shelly Cashman Series textbooks map to Microsoft Certified Application Specialist certification, visit scsite.com/off2007/cert.

What Is the Microsoft Certified Application Professional Certification?

The Microsoft Certified Application Professional certification exams focus on a candidate's ability to use the 2007 Microsoft® Office system to accomplish industry-agnostic functions, for example Budget Analysis and Forecasting, or Content Management and Collaboration. The available Application Professional exams currently include:

- Organizational Support
- Creating and Managing Presentations
- Content Management and Collaboration
- Budget Analysis and Forecasting

Index

Quick Reference Summary

In the Microsoft Office 2007 programs, you can accomplish a task in a number of ways. The following five tables (one each for Microsoft Office Word 2007, Microsoft Office Excel 2007, Microsoft Office Access 2007, Microsoft Office PowerPoint 2007, and Microsoft Office Outlook 2007) provide a quick reference to each task presented in this textbook. The first column identifies the task. The second column indicates the page number on which the task is discussed in the book. The subsequent four columns list the different ways the task in column one can be carried out.

Table 1 Microsoft Office Word 2007 Quick Reference Summary

Task	Page Number	Mouse	Ribbon	Shortcut Menu	Keyboard Shortcut
1.5 Line Spacing	WD 86		Line spacing button on Home tab	Paragraph | Indents and Spacing tab	CTRL+5
Address, Validate	WD 348		Edit Recipient List button on Mailings tab | Validate addresses link		
AddressBlock Merge Field, Add	WD 357		Address Block button on Mailings tab		
Arrange All Open Documents	WD 435		Arrange All button on View tab		
AutoCorrect Entry, Create	WD 93	Office Button | Word Options button | Proofing | AutoCorrect Options button			
AutoCorrect Options Menu, Display	WD 92	Point to text automatically corrected, point to small blue box, click AutoCorrect Options button			
Background Color, Add	WD 221		Page Color button on Page Layout tab		
Bibliographical List, Create	WD 113		Bibliography button on References tab | Insert Bibliography		
Bibliographical List, Modify Source and Update List	WD 117		Manage Sources button on References tab | select source | Edit button		

Table 1 Microsoft Office Word 2007 Quick Reference Summary *(continued)*

Task	Page Number	Mouse	Ribbon	Shortcut Menu	Keyboard Shortcut
Bibliography Style, Change	WD 95		Bibliography Style box arrow on References tab		
Bold	WD 34	Bold button on Mini toolbar	Bold button on Home tab	Font | Font tab | Bold in Font style list	CTRL+B
Border, Paragraph	WD 161, WD 231, WD 396		Border button arrow on Home tab | Borders and Shading		
Building Block, Create	WD 170		Quick Parts button on Insert tab | Save Selection to Quick Part Gallery		ALT+F3
Building Block, Insert	WD 172		Quick Parts button on Insert tab | building block name		F3
Bullets, Apply	WD 32	Bullets button on Mini toolbar	Bullets button on Home tab	Bullets	ASTERISK KEY | SPACEBAR
Bullets, Customize	WD 278		Bullets button on the Home tab | Define New Bullet		
Capital Letters	WD 86		Change Case button on Home tab | UPPERCASE	Font	CTRL+SHIFT+A
Case of Letters, Change	WD 86		Change Case button on Home tab	Font | Font tab	SHIFT+F3
Center	WD 26	Center button on Mini toolbar	Center button on Home tab	Paragraph | Indents and Spacing tab	CTRL+E
Character Spacing, Modify	WD 240		Font Dialog Box Launcher on Home Tab | Character Spacing tab	Font | Character Spacing tab	
Character Style, Create	WD 276		More button in Styles gallery | Save Selection as New Quick Style	Styles | Save Selection	
Chart Table	WD 269		Object button arrow on Insert tab		
Chart Type, Change	WD 272			Chart Type | Standard Types tab	
Chart, Move Legend	WD 270			Format Legend | Placement tab	
Chart, Resize	WD 271	Drag sizing handle			
Citation Placeholder, Insert	WD 101		Insert Citation button on References tab | Add New Placeholder		
Citation, Insert and Create Source	WD 96		Insert Citation button on References tab | Add New Source		
Citation, Edit	WD 98	Click citation, Citation Options box arrow | Edit Citation			

Table 1 Microsoft Office Word 2007 Quick Reference Summary *(continued)*

Task	Page Number	Mouse	Ribbon	Shortcut Menu	Keyboard Shortcut
Close Document	WD 60	Office Button | Close			
Color Text	WD 152, WD 240	Font Color button arrow on Mini toolbar	Font Color button arrow on Home tab		
Column Break, Insert	WD 420		Insert Page and Section Breaks button on Page Layout tab | Column		
Column Break, Remove	WD 421		Cut button on Home tab		DELETE
Columns, Balance	WD 438		Insert Page and Section Breaks button on Page Layout tab		
Columns, Change Number	WD 410, 433		Columns button on Page Layout tab		
Columns, Increase Width	WD 414	Drag column boundaries	Columns button on Page Layout tab | More Columns		
Content Control, Change Text	WD 187	Triple-click content control, change text			
Copy	WD 189, WD 428		Copy button on Home tab	Copy	CTRL+C
Count Words	WD 107	Word Count indicator on status bar	Word Count button on Review tab		CTRL+SHIFT+G
Cut	WD 121, WD 257		Cut button on Home tab	Cut	CTRL+X
Data Source, Associate with Main Document	WD 340		Select Recipients button on Mailings tab | Use Existing List		
Data Source, Create	WD 323		Start Mail Merge button on Mailings tab		
Date, Insert	WD 168, WD 330		Insert Date and Time button on Insert tab		
Delete	WD 59				DELETE
Dictionary, Custom, View or Modify Entries	WD 127	Office Button | Word Options button | Proofing | Custom Dictionaries button			
Dictionary, Set Custom	WD 127	Office Button | Word Options button | Proofing | Custom Dictionaries button | select desired dictionary name | Change Default button			
Document Properties, Set or View	WD 51	Office Button | Prepare | Properties			
Documents, Switch Between	WD 189	Program button on Windows taskbar	Switch Windows button on View tab		ALT+TAB
Double-Space Text	WD 87		Line spacing button on Home tab	Paragraph | Indents and Spacing	CTRL+2

Table 1 Microsoft Office Word 2007 Quick Reference Summary *(continued)*

Task	Page Number	Mouse	Ribbon	Shortcut Menu	Keyboard Shortcut
Double-Underline	WD 35		Font Dialog Box Launcher on Home tab	Font | Font tab	CTRL+SHIFT+D
Drawing Canvas, Display Automatically	WD 314	Office Button | Word Options button | Advanced | Editing Options area			
Drawing Canvas, Format	WD 315		Drawing Tools Format tab		
Drawing Canvas, Insert	WD 314		Shapes button on Insert tab | New Drawing Canvas		
Drawing Canvas, Resize	WD 320	Drag a sizing handle	Shape Width and Shape Height text boxes on Format tab	Format Drawing Canvas | Size tab	
Drop Cap	WD 417		Drop Cap button on Insert tab		
Edit Linked Object	WD 476	Double-click linked object			
E-Mail Document, as Attachment	WD 478	Office Button | Send | E-mail			
E-Mail Document, as PDF Attachment	WD 449	Office Button | Send | E-mail as PDF Attachment			
Envelope, Address and Print	WD 203		Envelopes button on Mailings tab | Envelopes tab | Print button		
Field Codes, Display or Remove	WD 261, WD 331, WD 341			Toggle Field Codes	ALT+F9
Field Codes, Print	WD 342	Office Button | Word Options button | Advanced			
Field, Lock	WD 345				CTRL+F11
Field, Unlock	WD 345				CTRL+SHIFT+F11
File, Create from Existing File	WD 165	Office Button | New | New from existing			
Find Format	WD 274	Select Browse Object button on vertical scroll bar | Find icon	Find button on Home tab		CTRL+F
Find Text	WD 124	Select Browse Object button on vertical scroll bar | Find icon	Find button on Home tab		CTRL+F
Find and Replace Text	WD 123	Select Browse Object button on vertical scroll bar | Find icon | Replace tab	Replace button on Home tab		CTRL+H
First-Line Indent Paragraphs	WD 88	Drag First Line Indent marker on ruler	Paragraph Dialog Box Launcher on Home tab | Indents and Spacing tab	Paragraph | Indents and Spacing tab	TAB

Table 1 Microsoft Office Word 2007 Quick Reference Summary *(continued)*

Task	Page Number	Mouse	Ribbon	Shortcut Menu	Keyboard Shortcut
Folder, Create While Saving	WD 321	Save button on Quick Access Toolbar | Create a new, empty folder button			F12
Font, Change	WD 29	Font box arrow on Mini toolbar	Font box arrow on Home tab	Font | Font tab	CTRL+SHIFT+F
Font, Change Case	WD 243		Change Case button on Home tab		SHIFT+F3
Font Settings, Modify Default	WD 242		Font Dialog Box Launcher on Home Tab | Default button | Yes button		
Font Size, Change	WD 28	Font Size box arrow on Mini toolbar	Font Size box arrow on Home tab	Font | Font tab	CTRL+SHIFT+P
Font Size, Decrease	WD 152	Shrink Font button on Mini toolbar	Shrink Font button on Home tab	Font | Font tab	CTRL+SHIFT+<
Font Size, Decrease 1 Point	WD 86			Font | Font tab	CTRL+ [
Font Size, Increase	WD 151	Grow Font button on Mini toolbar	Grow Font button on Home tab		CTRL+SHIFT+>
Font Size, Increase 1 Point	WD 86			Font | Font tab	CTRL+]
Footer, Insert Formatted	WD 261		Footer button on Design tab		
Footnote Reference Mark, Insert	WD 100		Insert Footnote button on References tab		CTRL+ALT+F
Footnote, Delete	WD 106	Delete note reference mark in document window	Cut button Home tab		BACKSPACE | BACKSPACE
Footnote, Edit	WD 106	Double-click note reference mark in document window	Show Notes button on References tab		
Footnote, Move	WD 106	Drag note reference mark in document window	Cut button on Home tab | Paste button on Home tab		
Footnote Style, Modify	WD 102		Click footnote text | Styles Dialog Box Launcher | Manage Styles button | Modify button	Style | Footnote Text | Modify button	
Format Characters	WD 240		Font Dialog Box Launcher on Home Tab		
Formatting Marks	WD 14, WD 248		Show/Hide ¶ button on Home tab		CTRL+SHIFT+*
Formatting, Clear	WD 162		Clear Formatting button on Home tab		CTRL+ SPACEBAR
Go To, Section	WD 258	Page number in document button on status bar	Find button arrow on Home tab | Go To on Find menu		CTRL+G

Table 1 Microsoft Office Word 2007 Quick Reference Summary *(continued)*

Task	Page Number	Mouse	Ribbon	Shortcut Menu	Keyboard Shortcut
Graphic, Adjust Brightness	WD 404		Brightness button on Format tab	Format Picture | Picture	
Graphic, Flip	WD 403		Rotate button on Format tab		
Graphic, Format as Floating	WD 402		Text Wrapping button on Format tab	Text Wrapping	
Graphic, Insert	WD 153		Clip Art button on Insert tab		
Graphic, Recolor	WD 156		Recolor button on Format tab	Format Picture | Picture | Recolor button	
Graphic, Resize	WD 46	Drag sizing handle	Format tab in Picture Tools tab or Size Dialog Box Launcher on Format tab	Size | Size tab	
Graphic, Restore	WD 404		Reset Picture button on Format tab		
Graphic, Set Transparent Color	WD 157		Recolor button on Format tab | Set Transparent Color		
GreetingLine Merge Field, Edit	WD 332			Right-click field | Edit Greeting Line	
Hanging Indent, Create	WD 116	Drag Hanging Indent marker on ruler	Paragraph Dialog Box Launcher on Home tab | Indents and Spacing tab	Paragraph | Indents and Spacing tab	CTRL+T
Hanging Indent, Remove	WD 86		Paragraph Dialog Box Launcher on Home tab | Indents and Spacing tab	Paragraph | Indents and Spacing tab	CTRL+SHIFT+T
Header & Footer, Close	WD 83	Double-click dimmed document text	Close Header and Footer button on Design tab		
Header, Different for Section	WD 259		Header button on Insert Tab | Edit Header		
Header, Display	WD 80	Double-click dimmed header	Header button on Insert tab | Edit Header		
Header, Distance from Edge	WD 261		Page Setup Dialog Box Launcher on Page Layout tab | Layout tab		
Header, Insert Formatted	WD 260		Header button on Design tab		
Help	WD 60		Office Word Help button		F1
Hidden Text, Format Text as	WD 366		Font Dialog Box Launcher | Font tab	Font | Font tab	
Hidden Text, Hide/Show	WD 367		Show/Hide ¶ button on Home tab		CTRL+SHIFT+*
Hyperlink, Format Text as	WD 220		Insert Hyperlink button on Insert tab	Hyperlink	CTRL+K

Table 1 Microsoft Office Word 2007 Quick Reference Summary *(continued)*

Task	Page Number	Mouse	Ribbon	Shortcut Menu	Keyboard Shortcut
Hyperlink, Remove	WD 163		Hyperlink button on Insert tab | Remove Link button	Remove Hyperlink	
IF Field, Insert	WD 338		Rules button on Mailings tab		
Indent Paragraph	WD 196, WD 233	Drag Left Indent marker on ruler	Increase Indent button on Home tab	Paragraph | Indents and Spacing sheet	CTRL+M
Insert Document in Existing Document	WD 251		Object button arrow on Insert tab		
Insertion Point, Move to Beginning of Document	WD 24	Scroll to top of document, click			CTRL+HOME
Insertion Point, Move to End of Document	WD 25	Scroll to bottom of document, click			CTRL+END
Italicize	WD 36	Italic button on Mini toolbar	Italic button on Home tab	Font | Font tab	CTRL+I
Justify Paragraph	WD 86, WD 411		Justify button on Home tab	Paragraph | Indents and Spacing tab	CTRL+J
Left-Align	WD 86		Align Text Left button on Home tab	Paragraph | Indents and Spacing tab	CTRL+L
Line Break, Enter	WD 194				SHIFT+ENTER
Link Object	WD 469		Copy object; Paste button on Home tab | Paste Special		
Linked Object, Break Links	WD 476	Office Button | Prepare | Edit Links to Files | Break Link button		Linked Object | Links | Break Link button	CTRL+SHIFT+F9
Mail Merge Fields, Insert	WD 333		Insert Merge Field button arrow on Mailings tab		
Mail Merge to New Document Window	WD 363		Finish & Merge button on Mailings tab | Edit Individual Documents		
Mail Merge to Printer	WD 344		Finish & Merge button on Mailings tab | Print Documents		
Mail Merge, Directory	WD 358		Start Mail Merge button on Mailings tab		
Mail Merge, Envelopes	WD 356		Start Mail Merge button on Mailings tab		
Mail Merge, Identify Main Document	WD 309		Start Mail Merge button on Mailings tab		
Mail Merge, Mailing Labels	WD 350		Start Mail Merge button on Mailings tab		

Table 1 Microsoft Office Word 2007 Quick Reference Summary *(continued)*

Task	Page Number	Mouse	Ribbon	Shortcut Menu	Keyboard Shortcut
Mail Merge, Select Records	WD 345		Edit Recipient List button on Mailings tab		
Mail Merge, Sort Data Records	WD 348		Edit Recipient List button on Mailings tab		
Mail Merged Data, View	WD 349		View Merged Data button on Mailings tab		
Main Document File, Convert	WD 368		Start Mail Merge button on Mailings tab		
Margins, Change Settings	WD 313, WD 389	Drag margin boundary on ruler	Margins button on Page Layout tab		
Merge Condition, Remove	WD 348		Edit Recipient List button on Mailings tab | Filter link | Clear All button		
Move Selected Text	WD 121	Drag and drop selected text	Cut button on Home tab | Paste button on Home tab	Cut | Paste	CTRL+X; CTRL+V
Multilevel List, Change Levels	WD 336		Increase (Decrease) Indent button on Home tab	Increase Indent or Decrease Indent	TAB; SHIFT+TAB
Multilevel List, Create	WD 335		Multilevel List button on Home tab		
Nonbreaking Space, Insert	WD 171		Symbol button on Insert tab | More Symbols | Special Characters tab		CTRL+SHIFT+SPACEBAR
Open Document	WD 56	Office Button | Open			CTRL+O
Page Border, Add	WD 48		Page Borders button on Page Layout tab		
Page Break, Delete	WD 256		Cut button on Home tab	Cut	CTRL+X, BACKSPACE
Page Break, Manual	WD 112		Page Break button on Insert tab		CTRL+ENTER
Page Number, Insert	WD 82		Insert Page Number button on Design tab		
Page Numbers, Start at Different Number	WD 262		Insert Page Number button on Design tab | Format Page Numbers on Insert Page Number menu		
Page Orientation	WD 362		Page Orientation button on Page Layout tab		
Paragraph, Add Space Above	WD 79		Line spacing button on Home tab | Add Space Before (After) Paragraph	Paragraph | Indents and Spacing tab	CTRL+0 (zero)
Paragraph, Decrease Indent	WD 196	Decrease Indent button on Mini toolbar	Decrease Indent button on Home tab	Paragraph | Indents and Spacing tab	CTRL+SHIFT+M

Table 1 Microsoft Office Word 2007 Quick Reference Summary *(continued)*

Task	Page Number	Mouse	Ribbon	Shortcut Menu	Keyboard Shortcut
Paragraph, Remove Space After	WD 195		Line spacing button on Home tab | Remove Space After Paragraph	Paragraph | Indents and Spacing tab	
Paragraphs, Change Spacing Above and Below	WD 50		Spacing Before box arrow on Page Layout tab	Paragraph | Indents and Spacing tab	
Paste	WD 191, WD 430, WD 436		Paste button on Home tab	Paste	CTRL+V
Pattern Fill Effect for Background, Add	WD 222		Page Color button on Page Layout tab | Fill Effects | Pattern tab		
Picture Border, Change	WD 45		Picture Border button on Format tab		
Picture Style, Apply	WD 44		Picture Tools and Format tabs | More button in Picture Styles gallery		
Picture, Insert	WD 41		Picture button on Insert tab		
Print Document	WD 54	Office Button | Print | Print			CTRL+P
Print Document Properties	WD 130	Office Button | Print | Print | Print what box arrow			
Print Preview	WD 201	Office Button | Print | Print Preview			
Print Specific Pages	WD 253	Office Button | Print | Print			CTRL+P
Print, Draft	WD 347	Office Button | Word Options button | Advanced | Print area			
Quick Style, Create	WD 90		More button in Styles gallery | Save Selection as a New Quick Style	Styles | Save Selection as a New Quick Style	
Quit Word	WD 55	Close button on right side of Word title bar			ALT+F4
Remove Character Formatting (Plain Text)	WD 87		Font Dialog Box Launcher on Home tab | Font tab	Font | Font tab	CTRL+SPACEBAR
Remove Paragraph Formatting	WD 87		Font Dialog Box Launcher on Home tab	Font | Font tab	CTRL+Q
Research Task Pane, Use	WD 128	Hold down ALT key, click word to look up			
Reveal Formatting	WD 248				SHIFT+F1
Right-Align Paragraph	WD 81		Align Text Right button on Home tab	Paragraph | Indents and Spacing tab	CTRL+R
Rulers, Display	WD 87	View Ruler button on vertical scroll bar	View Ruler on View tab		

Table 1 Microsoft Office Word 2007 Quick Reference Summary *(continued)*

Task	Page Number	Mouse	Ribbon	Shortcut Menu	Keyboard Shortcut
Save Document as Web Page	WD 218	Office Button | Save As | Other Formats			F12
Save Document, Previous Word Format	WD 477	Office Button | Save As | Word 97-2003 Document			F12
Save Document, Same Name	WD 53	Save button on Quick Access Toolbar			CTRL+S
Save New Document	WD 19	Save button on Quick Access Toolbar			CTRL+S
Section Break, Continuous	WD 409		Insert Page and Section Breaks button on Page Layout tab | Continuous		
Section Break, Delete	WD 251			Cut	DELETE or BACKSPACE
Section Break, Next Page	WD 250, WD 418		Breaks button on Page Layout tab		
Section Number, Display on Status Bar	WD 249			Section	
Section, Formatting	WD 259	Double-click section break notation			
Select Block of Text	WD 33	Click at beginning of text, hold down SHIFT key and click at end of text to select; or drag through text			CTRL+SHIFT+RIGHT ARROW and/or DOWN ARROW
Select Browse Object Menu, Use	WD 118	Select Browse Object button on vertical scroll bar			ALT+CTRL+HOME
Select Character(s)	WD 120	Drag through character(s)			CTRL+SHIFT+RIGHT ARROW
Select Entire Document	WD 120	Point to left of text and triple-click			CTRL+A
Select Graphic	WD 46	Click graphic			
Select Line	WD 27	Point to left of line and click			SHIFT+DOWN ARROW
Select Lines	WD 30	Point to left of first line and drag up or down			CTRL+SHIFT+DOWN ARROW
Select Nonadjacent Text	WD 277	Drag through text | press and hold CTRL key | drag through more text			
Select Paragraph	WD 90	Triple-click paragraph			SHIFT+DOWN ARROW
Select Paragraphs	WD 30	Point to left of first paragraph, double-click, and drag up or down			
Select Sentence	WD 120	Press and hold down CTRL key and click sentence			CTRL+SHIFT+RIGHT ARROW
Select Word	WD 59	Double-click word			CTRL+SHIFT+RIGHT ARROW

Table 1 Microsoft Office Word 2007 Quick Reference Summary *(continued)*

Task	Page Number	Mouse	Ribbon	Shortcut Menu	Keyboard Shortcut
Select Words	WD 33	Drag through words			CTRL+SHIFT+RIGHT ARROW
Shade Paragraph	WD 232		Shading button arrow on Home tab		
Shape, Add Text	WD 319		Edit Text button on Drawing Tools Format tab	Add Text	
Shape, Apply Style	WD 318		Advanced Tools Dialog Box Launcher in Shape Styles group	Format AutoShape	
Shape, Insert	WD 316		Shapes button on Insert tab		
Single-Space Lines	WD 86		Line spacing button on the Home tab	Paragraph | Indents and Spacing tab	CTRL+1
Small Uppercase Letters	WD 86		Font Dialog Box Launcher on Home tab | Font tab	Font | Font tab	CTRL+SHIFT+K
SmartArt Graphic, Change Colors	WD 238		Change Colors button on SmartArt Tools Design tab		
SmartArt Graphic, Add Shape	WD 441		Add Shape button on Design tab		
SmartArt Graphic, Add Text	WD 237, WD 442	Click Text Pane control on SmartArt graphic	Text Pane button on SmartArt Tools Design tab		
SmartArt Graphic, Apply Style	WD 239		More button in SmartArt Styles gallery		
SmartArt Graphic, Change Layout	WD 440		Click selection in Layouts gallery on SmartArt Tools Design tab	Change Layout	
SmartArt Graphic, Insert	WD 235		Insert SmartArt Graphic button on Insert tab		
SmartArt Graphic, Outline	WD 446		Shape Outline button on Format tab		
SmartArt Graphic, Remove Formats	WD 240		Reset Graphic button on SmartArt Tools Design tab		
Sort Paragraphs	WD 200		Sort button on Home tab		
Source, Edit	WD 104	Click citation, Citation Options box arrow | Edit Source			
Spelling and Grammar	WD 125	Spelling and Grammar Check icon on status bar | Spelling	Spelling & Grammar button on Review tab	Right-click flagged text | Spelling	F7
Spelling and Grammar Check as You Type	WD 16	Spelling and Grammar Check icon on status bar		Correct word on shortcut menu	
Split Window	WD 434	Double-click split box	Split button on View tab		

Table 1 Microsoft Office Word 2007 Quick Reference Summary *(continued)*

Task	Page Number	Mouse	Ribbon	Shortcut Menu	Keyboard Shortcut
Split Window, Remove	WD 437	Double-click split bar	Remove Split button on View tab		
Status Bar, Customize	WD 249			Right-click status bar | click desired element	
Style Set, Change	WD 37		Change Styles button on Home tab | Style Set on Change Styles menu		
Styles Task Pane, Open	WD 25		Styles Dialog Box Launcher		ALT+CTRL+SHIFT+S
Styles, Apply	WD 24		Styles gallery		
Styles, Modify	WD 90, WD 405, WD 424		Styles Dialog Box Launcher	Update [*style name*] to Match Selection	
Subscript	WD 86		Font Dialog Box Launcher on Home tab	Font | Font tab	CTRL+EQUAL SIGN
Superscript	WD 86		Font Dialog Box Launcher on Home tab	Font | Font tab	CTRL+SHIFT+PLUS SIGN
Symbol, Insert	WD 398		Symbol button on Insert tab		ALT+0 | NUM LOCK key | type ANSI code
Synonym, Find	WD 124		Thesaurus on Review tab	Synonyms | desired word	SHIFT+F7
Tab Stops, Set	WD 158, WD 167	Click tab selector, click ruler on desired location	Paragraph Dialog Box Launcher | Tabs button	Paragraph | Tabs button	
Table Style, Apply	WD 176		More button in Table Styles gallery		
Table Wrapping	WD 284			Table Properties | Table tab	
Table, Add Column	WD 264		Insert Columns to the Left (or Right) button on Layout tab		
Table, Align Data in Cells	WD 268		Align [location] button on Layout tab		
Table, Border	WD 267		Line Weight box arrow on Design tab | Borders button arrow		
Table, Change Row Height	WD 290	Drag border	Table Properties button on Layout tab	Table Properties	
Table, Convert Text	WD 361		Table button on Insert tab | Convert Text to Table		
Table, Delete Column	WD 263		Delete button on Layout tab	Delete Columns	
Table, Delete Contents	WD 283				DELETE
Table, Delete Rows	WD 186, WD 264		Delete button on Layout tab | Delete Rows		
Table, Display Text Vertically in Cell	WD 284		Text Direction button on Layout tab		

Table 1 Microsoft Office Word 2007 Quick Reference Summary *(continued)*

Task	Page Number	Mouse	Ribbon	Shortcut Menu	Keyboard Shortcut
Table, Distribute Rows	WD 283		Select Table button on Layout tab | Select Table		
Table, Draw	WD 280		Table button on Insert tab | Draw Table		
Table, Erase Lines	WD 282		Eraser button on Design tab		
Table, Insert	WD 173		Table button on Insert tab		
Table, Merge Cells	WD 287		Merge Cells button on Layout tab	Merge Cells	
Table, Modify Properties	WD 364		Table Properties button on Layout tab		
Table, Move	WD 267	Drag move handle			
Table, Non-Breaking Across Pages	WD 279		Table Properties button on the Table Tools Layout tab | Row tab		
Table, Resize Columns	WD 177	Double-click column boundary	AutoFit button on Layout tab	AutoFit | AutoFit to Contents	
Table, Select	WD 179	Click table move handle	Select button on Layout tab | Select Table on Select menu		
Table, Select Cell	WD 178	Click left edge of cell			
Table, Select Column	WD 178	Click border at top of column			
Table, Select Multiple Adjacent Cells, Rows, or Columns	WD 178	Drag through cells, rows, or columns			
Table, Select Multiple Nonadjacent Cells, Rows, or Columns	WD 178	Select first cell, row, or column, hold down CTRL key while selecting next cell, row, or column			
Table, Select Next Cell	WD 178	Drag through cell			TAB
Table, Select Previous Cell	WD 178	Drag through cell			SHIFT+TAB
Table, Select Row	WD 178	Click to left of row			
Table, Shade Cells (Remove Shade)	WD 288		Shading button arrow on Design tab		
Table, Sort	WD 365		Sort button on Layout tab		
Table, Split Cells	WD 287		Split Cells button on Layout tab	Split Cells	
Table, Sum Columns	WD 265		Formula button on Layout tab		
Text Box, Insert	WD 427		Text Box button on Insert tab		

Table 1 Microsoft Office Word 2007 Quick Reference Summary (continued)

Task	Page Number	Mouse	Ribbon	Shortcut Menu	Keyboard Shortcut
Text Box, Position	WD 431	Drag text box			
Theme Colors, Change	WD 39		Change Styles button on Home tab | Colors on Change Styles menu		
Theme Fonts, Change	WD 40		Change Styles button on Home tab | Fonts on Change Styles menu		
Theme Fonts, Customize	WD 255		Change Styles button on Home tab | Fonts on Change Styles menu | Create new Theme Fonts		
Theme, Change	WD 467		Themes button on Page Layout tab		
Underline	WD 35		Underline button on Home tab	Font | Font tab	CTRL+U
Underline Words, Not Spaces	WD 86				CTRL+SHIFT+W
User Information, Change	WD 312	Office Button | Word Options button			
Watermark, Create	WD 245		Watermark button on Page Layout tab		
WordArt, Fill Color	WD 393		Shape Fill button arrow on WordArt Tools Format tab	Format WordArt | Fill Effects button	
WordArt, Insert	WD 391		WordArt button on Insert tab		
WordArt, Shape	WD 395		Change WordArt Shape button on Format tab		
Zoom	WD 46, WD 244	Zoom Out and Zoom In buttons on status bar	Zoom button on View tab		
Zoom, Two Pages	WD 447		Two Pages button on View tab		

Table 2 Microsoft Office Excel 2007 Quick Reference Summary

Task	Page Number	Mouse	Ribbon	Shortcut Menu	Keyboard Shortcut
Advanced Filter	EX 386		Advanced button on Data tab		ALT+A | Q
AutoCalculate	EX 62	Select range | right-click AutoCalculate area | click calculation			
AutoFilter	EX 380		Filter button on Data tab		ALT+A | T

Table 2 Microsoft Office Excel 2007 Quick Reference Summary (continued)

Task	Page Number	Mouse	Ribbon	Shortcut Menu	Keyboard Shortcut
Bold	EX 38	Bold button on Mini toolbar	Bold button on Home tab or Font Dialog Box Launcher on Home tab	Font tab	Format Cells	Font tab	Bold in Font style list	CTRL+B
Borders	EX 111	Borders button on Mini toolbar	Borders button on Home tab or Alignment Dialog Box Launcher on Home tab	Border tab	Format Cells	Border tab	CTRL+1	B
Cell Style, change	EX 35		Cell Styles button on Home tab		
Center	EX 113	Right-click cell	Center button on Mini toolbar	Center button on Home tab or Alignment Dialog Box Launcher on Home tab	Format Cells	Alignment tab	CTRL+1	A
Center Across Columns	EX 40	Right-click selection	Merge & Center button on Mini toolbar	Merge & Center button on Home tab or Alignment Dialog Box Launcher on Home tab	Format Cells	Alignment tab	CTRL+1	A
Chart, Add	EX 50, 205		Dialog Box Launcher in Charts group on Insert tab		F11
Clear Cell	EX 66	Drag fill handle back	Clear button on Home tab	Clear Contents	DELETE
Clear Worksheet	EX 66		Select All button on worksheet	Clear button on Home tab		
Close All Workbooks	EX 69	Office Button	Exit Excel			ALT+F	X
Close Workbook	EX 59		Close button on Ribbon or Office Button	Close		CTRL+W
Color Background	EX 110		Fill Color button on Home tab or Font Dialog Box Launcher on Home tab	Format Cells	Fill tab	CTRL+1	F
Color Tab	EX 216			Tab Color	
Column Width	EX 46, 122	Drag column heading boundary	Home tab	Format button	Column Width	Column Width	ALT+O	C	W
Comma Style Format	EX 44		Comma Style button on Home tab or Number Dialog Box Launcher on Home tab	Accounting	Format Cells	Number tab	Accounting	CTRL+1	N
Conditional Formatting	EX 119, 362		Conditional Formatting button on Home tab		ALT+H	L	ALT+O	D

Table 2 Microsoft Office Excel 2007 Quick Reference Summary *(continued)*

Task	Page Number	Mouse	Ribbon	Shortcut Menu	Keyboard Shortcut
Copy and Paste	EX 175		Copy button and Paste button on Home tab	Copy to copy; Paste to paste	CTRL+C; CTRL+V
Copy to adjacent cells	EX 27	Select source area | drag fill handle through destination cells	Select source area | click Copy button on Home tab | select destination area | click Paste button on Home tab	Right-click source area | click Copy | right-click destination area | click Paste	
Currency Style Format	EX 116		Currency Style button on Home tab or Format Cells | Number | Currency	Format Cells | Number | Currency	CTRL+1 | N
Custom Formats	EX XXX		Number Dialog Box Launcher on Home tab | Custom	Format Cells | Number | Custom	ALT+H | FM
Cut	EX 64		Cut button on Home tab	Cut	CTRL+X
Data Table	EX 2	What-If Analysis button on Data tab | Data Table			ALT+A | W | T
Data Validation, Cell	EX 348	Data Validation button on Data tab			ALT+A | V | V
Date	EX 184	Insert Function button in formula bar | Date & Time | NOW	Date & Time button on Formulas tab | NOW		CTRL+SEMICOLON
Date, Format	EX 113		Font Dialog Box Launcher on Home tab | Number tab | Date	Format Cells | Number tab | Date	
Decimal Place, Decrease	EX 115		Decrease Decimal button on Home tab or Number Dialog Box Launcher on Home tab | Number tab | Currency	Format Cells | Number tab | Currency	CTRL+1 | N
Decimal Place, Increase	EX 118		Increase Decimal button on Home tab or Number Dialog Box Launcher on Home tab | Number tab | Currency	Format Cells | Number tab | Currency	CTRL+1 | N
Delete Rows or Columns	EX 180		Home tab | Delete button arrow | Delete Sheet Rows or Home tab | Delete button arrow | Delete Sheet Columns	Delete | Entire row or Delete | Entire column	
Document Properties, Set or View	EX 55	Office Button | Prepare | Properties			ALT+F | E | P
Draft Quality	EX 309		Page Setup Dialog Box Launcher on Page Layout tab | Sheet tab		ALT+P | SP | S

Table 2 Microsoft Office Excel 2007 Quick Reference Summary *(continued)*

Task	Page Number	Mouse	Ribbon	Shortcut Menu	Keyboard Shortcut
E-Mail from Excel	EX 142	Office Button | Send | E-Mail			ALT+F | D | E
Embedded Chart, Delete	EX 67				Select chart, press DELETE
File Management	EX 259	Office Button | Save As | right-click file name			ALT+F | A | right-click file name
Find	EX 481		Find & Select button on Home tab | Find		CTRL+F
Fit to Print	EX 156		Page Setup Dialog Box Launcher on Page Layout tab		ALT+P | SP
Folder, New	EX 259	Office Button | Save As | Create New Folder button			ALT+F | A
Font Color	EX 39	Font Color box arrow on Mini toolbar	Font Color button arrow on Home tab or Font Dialog Box Launcher on Home tab	Format Cells | Font tab	CTRL+1 | F
Font Size, Change	EX 38	Font Size box arrow on Mini toolbar	Font Size box arrow on Home tab or Font Dialog Box Launcher on Home tab	Format Cells | Font tab	CTRL+1 | F
Font Size, Increase	EX 39	Increase Font Size button on Mini toolbar	Increase Font Size button on Home tab		
Font Type	EX 36	Font box arrow on Mini toolbar	Font box arrow on Home tab or Font Dialog Box Launcher on Home tab	Format Cells | Font tab	CTRL+1 | F
Formula Assistance	EX 101	Insert Function button in formula bar	Insert Function button on Formulas tab		CTRL+A after you type function name
Formulas Version	EX 136				CTRL+ACCENT MARK
Freeze Worksheet Titles	EX 182		Freeze Panes button on the View tab | Freeze Panes		ALT+W | F
Full Screen	EX 9		Full Screen button on View tab		ALT+V | U
Function	EX 101	Insert Function button in formula bar	Insert Function button on Formulas tab		SHIFT+F3
Go To	EX 48	Click cell	Find & Select button on Home tab		F5
Goal Seek	EX 225		What-If Analysis button on Data tab | Goal Seek		ALT+T | G
Gridlines	EX 309, 510		Gridlines check box on View tab or Page Setup Dialog Box Launcher on Layout tab | Sheet tab		ALT+W | V | G ALT+P | V | G

Table 2 Microsoft Office Excel 2007 Quick Reference Summary *(continued)*

Task	Page Number	Mouse	Ribbon	Shortcut Menu	Keyboard Shortcut
Header	EX 130, 472		Page Setup Dialog Box Launcher on Page Layout tab | Header/ Footer tab		
Help	EX 67 and Appendix C		Microsoft Office Excel Help button on Ribbon		F1
Hide Column	EX 122	Drag column heading boundary	Format button on Home tab | Hide & Unhide or Hide & Unhide button on View tab	Hide	CTRL+0 (zero) to hide CTRL+SHIFT+RIGHT PARENTHESIS to display
Hide Row	EX 126	Drag row heading boundary	Format button on Home tab | Hide & Unhide | Hide Rows	Hide	CTRL+9 to hide CTRL+SHIFT+LEFT PARENTHESIS to display
Hide Sheet	EX 316			Hide	
Hide Workbook	EX 317		Hide button on View tab		ALT+W | H
In-Cell Editing	EX 63	Double-click cell			F2
Insert Rows or Columns	EX 178		Home tab | Insert button arrow | Insert Sheet Rows or Home tab | Insert button arrow | Insert Sheet Columns	Insert	ALT+I | R or C
Insert Single Cell or Range of Cells	EX 179		Home | Insert button arrow | Insert Cells		
Italicize	EX 203		Italic button on Home tab or Font Dialog Box Launcher on Home tab | Font tab	Format Cells | Font tab	CTRL+I
Link Update	EX 138		Existing Connections button on Data tab		ALT+A | X
Margins, Change	EX 130, 472	In Page Layout view, drag margin in ruler	Margins button on Page Layout tab or Page Setup Dialog Box Launcher | Margins Tab		ALT+P | M
Merge Cells	EX 41		Merge & Center button on Home tab or Alignment Dialog Box Launcher on Home tab	Format Cells | Alignment tab	ALT+O | E | A
Move Cells	EX 177	Point to border and drag	Cut button on Home tab; Paste button on Home tab	Cut; Paste	CTRL+X; CTRL+V
Move Sheet	EX 217	Drag sheet tab to desired location		Move or Copy	

Table 2 Microsoft Office Excel 2007 Quick Reference Summary *(continued)*

Task	Page Number	Mouse	Ribbon	Shortcut Menu	Keyboard Shortcut
Name Cells	EX 270	Click Name box in formula bar and type name	Define Name button on Formulas tab or Create from Selection button on Formulas tab or Name Manager button on Formulas tab	Name a Range	ALT+M | M | D
New Workbook	EX 67	Office Button | New			CTRL+N
Open Workbook	EX 61	Office Button | Open			CTRL+O
Outline a Range	EX 273		Border button on Home tab	Format Cells | Border tab	CTRL+1 | B
Outline a Worksheet	EX 377		Group button on Data tab		ALT+A | G | G
Page Break, Insert	EX 478		Breaks button on Page Layout tab | Insert Page Break		ALT+P | B | I
Page Break, Move	EX 479	Click Page Break Preview button on status bar, drag page breaks	Page Break Preview button on View tab | drag page breaks		ALT+ W | I
Page Break, Remove	EX 478		Breaks button on Page Layout tab | Remove Page Break		ALT+P | B | R
Paste Options	EX 176		Paste button arrow on Home tab		
Percent Style Format	EX 118		Percent Style button on Home tab or Number Dialog Box Launcher on Home tab | Percentage	Format Cells | Number tab | Percentage	CTRL+1 | N or CTRL+SHIFT+%.
Picture, Insert	EX 522		Insert Picture from File button on Insert tab		ALT+N | P
Preview Worksheet	EX 132	Office Button | Print | Print Preview			ALT+F | W | V
Print Area, Clear	EX 310		Print Area button on Page Layout tab | Clear Print Area		ALT+P | R | C
Print Area, Set	EX 309		Print Area button on Page Layout tab | Set Print Area		ALT+F | T | S
Print Row and Column Headings	EX 309		Page Setup Dialog Box Launcher on Page Layout tab | Sheet tab		ALT+P | SP | S
Print Worksheet	EX 132	Office Button | Print			CTRL+P
Protect Worksheet	EX 313		Protect Sheet button on Review tab	Protect Sheet	ALT+R | PS
Quick Style, Add	EX 440		Cell Styles button on Home tab | New Cell Style		ALT+H | J | N
Quick Style, Apply	EX 443		Cell Styles button on Home tab		ALT+H | J

Table 2 Microsoft Office Excel 2007 Quick Reference Summary *(continued)*

Task	Page Number	Mouse	Ribbon	Shortcut Menu	Keyboard Shortcut
Quit Excel	EX 59	Close button on title bar Office Button | Exit Excel			ALT+F4
Range Finder	EX 106	Double-click cell			
Redo	EX 65	Redo button on Quick Access Toolbar			ALT+3 or CTRL+Y
Remove Splits	EX 223	Double-click split bar	Split button on View tab		ALT+W | S
Rename Sheet tab	EX 217	Double-click sheet tab | type sheet name		Rename	
Replace	EX 483		Find & Select button on Home tab | Replace		CTRL+H
Rotate Text	EX 169		Alignment Dialog Box Launcher on Home tab	Format Cells | Alignment tab	ALT+O | E | A
Row Height	EX 125	Drag row heading boundary	Format button on Home tab | Row Height	Row Height	ALT+O | R | E
Save Workbook, Different Format	EX 395	Office Button | Save As, choose from Save as type list			ALT+F | F | O
Save Workbook, New Name	EX 57	Office Button | Save As			ALT+F | A
Save Workbook, Same Name	EX 57	Save button on Quick Access Toolbar or Office Button | Save			CTRL+S
Select All of Worksheet	EX 67	Select All button on worksheet			CTRL+A
Select Cell	EX 15	Click cell or click Name box, type cell reference, press ENTER			Use arrow keys
Select Multiple Sheets	EX 218	CTRL+click tab or SHIFT+click tab		Select All Sheets	
Series	EX 169, 286	Drag fill handle	Fill button on Home tab	Fill Series	ALT+E | I | S ALT+H | F | I
Shortcut Menu	EX 12	Right-click object			SHIFT+F10
SmartArt	EX 510		SmartArt button on Insert tab		ALT+N | M
Spell Check	EX 127	Spelling button on Review tab			F7
Split Cell	EX 41		Merge & Center button on Home tab or Alignment Dialog Box Launcher on Home tab | click Merge cells to deselect	Format Cells | Alignment tab | click Merge cells to deselect	ALT+O | E | A
Split Window into Panes	EX 222	Drag vertical or horizontal split box	Split button on View tab		ALT+W | S
Stock Quotes	EX 138		Existing Connections button on Data tab		ALT+D | D | D ALT+A | X

Table 2 Microsoft Office Excel 2007 Quick Reference Summary *(continued)*

Task	Page Number	Mouse	Ribbon	Shortcut Menu	Keyboard Shortcut
Subtotals	EX 375		Subtotal button on Data tab		ALT+A │ B
Subtotals, Remove	EX 379		Subtotal button on Data tab │ Remove All button		ALT+A │ B │ R
Sum	EX 25	Function Wizard button in formula bar │ SUM	Sum button on Home tab	Insert Function button on Formulas tab	ALT+=
Table, Create	EX 346		Format as Table button on Home tab or Table button on Insert tab		ALT+H │ T
Table, Sort	EX 369		Sort & Filter button on Home tab or Sort A to Z button on Data tab	Sort	ALT+A │ A
Table Total Row, Add	EX 365		Total Row check box on Design tab of Table Tools contextual tab		ALT+J │ T │ T
Table Quick Style, Modify	EX 351		Format as Table button on Home tab │ right-click style │ Duplicate	Duplicate	ALT+H │ T
Underline	EX 203		Underline button on Home tab or Font Dialog Box Launcher on Home tab	Format Cells │ Font tab	CTRL+U
Undo	EX 65	Undo button on Quick Access Toolbar			ALT+2, CTRL+Z
Unfreeze Worksheet Titles	EX 194		Freeze Panes button on View tab │ Unfreeze Panes		ALT+W │ F
Unhide Column	EX 122	Drag hidden column heading boundary to right	Unhide button on View tab	Unhide	ALT+O │ C │ U
Unhide Row	EX 127	Drag hidden row heading boundary down	Unhide button on View tab	Unhide	ALT+O │ R │ U
Unhide Sheet	EX 316			Unhide	
Unhide Workbook	EX 317		Unhide button on View tab		ALT+W │ H
Unlock Cells	EX 313		Font Dialog Box Launcher on Home tab │ Protection tab	Format Cells │ Protection tab	CTRL+1 │ SHIFT+P
Unprotect Worksheet	EX 315		Unprotect Sheet button on Review tab	Unprotect Sheet	ALT+R │ PS
Web Page, Save Workbook As	EX 256	Office button │ Save As │ Save as type: arrow │ Single File Web Page or Office button │ Save As │ Save as type: arrow │ Web Page			

Table 2 Microsoft Office Excel 2007 Quick Reference Summary *(continued)*

Task	Page Number	Mouse	Ribbon	Shortcut Menu	Keyboard Shortcut
WordArt	EX 466		WordArt button on Insert tab		ALT+N | W
Workbook Theme, Change	EX 109		Themes button on Page Layout tab		
Worksheet Name, Change	EX 141	Double-click sheet tab, type new name		Rename	
Workspace, Save	EX 488		Save Workspace button on View tab		ALT+W | K
Zoom	EX 220	Zoom box on status bar or Zoom In and Zoom Out buttons on status bar	Zoom button on View tab		ALT+V | Z

Table 3 Microsoft Office Access 2007 Quick Reference Summary

Task	Page Number	Mouse	Ribbon	Shortcut Menu	Keyboard Shortcut
Add Additional Field Control	AC 316	Drag field name from field list to form			
Add Date to Form	AC 274		Date and Time button on Format tab		
Add Field to Form	AC 279		Add Existing Fields button on Format tab | select field in field list | drag field to form		
Add Field to Report	AC 265		Add Existing Fields button on Format tab | drag new field to report		
Add Fields to Table	AC 302			Right-click table in Navigation Pane | click Design View | click first open field	
Add Form Title	AC 323		Title button on Design tab		
Add Macro Actions	AC 368	In macro action column click box arrow | select action			
Add New Field	AC 24	Right-click Add New Field in Datasheet	Insert Rows button on Design Tab	Design View | INSERT	
Add Record	AC 30, 38	New (blank) record button	New button on Home tab	Open | Click in field	CTRL+PLUS SIGN (+)
Add Subform	AC 324		Subform/Subreport tool on Design tab | Control Wizards tool | click form		
Align Controls	AC 319		Select controls | click desired alignment button on Arrange tab		
AutoFormat Report or Form	AC 284		More button in AutoFormat group on Format tab		

Table 3 Microsoft Office Access 2007 Quick Reference Summary *(continued)*

Task	Page Number	Mouse	Ribbon	Shortcut Menu	Keyboard Shortcut
Calculate Statistics	AC 118		Totals button on Design tab		
Change a Control's Color	AC 275		Select control | click Font Color arrow on Format tab | click desired color		
Change Back Color on Form	AC 322			Right-click form | point to Fill/Back Color arrow | click desired color	
Change Chart Orientation	AC 407		Switch Row/Column button on Design tab		
Change Chart Type	AC 405		Change Chart Type button on Design tab | Type tab | select desired chart		
Change Colors and Font	AC 180		Alternate Fill/Back Color button arrow or Font Color button arrow or Font box arrow on Home tab		
Change Column Size	AC 309	Drag column boundary			
Change Database Properties	AC 60	Office button | Manage | Database Properties			
Change Form Label Color	AC 330		View button on Design tab | select label | click Font Color arrow | select color		
Change Form Tab Order	AC 336		Tab Order button on Arrange tab | Tab Order dialog box		
Change Form Title Format	AC 333		Design View on View Button menu on Design tab | select control | Property Sheet button		
Change Gridlines	AC 179		Gridlines button on Home tab		
Change PivotTable Properties	AC 398		Property Sheet button on Design tab		
Change Primary Key	AC 28	Delete field | Primary Key button	Design View button on Design tab | select field | Primary Key button		
Change Row Size	AC 309	Drag record selector boundary		Right-click field or record selector | click Column Width or Row Height	
Change Size Mode	AC 330		Click control | Property Sheet button on Design tab | Size Mode		

Table 3 Microsoft Office Access 2007 Quick Reference Summary *(continued)*

Task	Page Number	Mouse	Ribbon	Shortcut Menu	Keyboard Shortcut
Chart Axis Title	AC 408		Select axis title | Property Sheet button on Design tab | Format tab | Caption box | replace caption		
Chart Title	AC 409		Select chart | Property Sheet button on Design tab | General tab | Add title button | close property sheet | click title | Property Sheet button on design tab | Format tab | replace title (caption)		
Clear Form Filter	AC 282				
Clear Query	AC 98				Select all entries | DELETE
Clear Report Filter	AC 254			Right-click field | clear selected filter	
Close Object	AC 35	Close button for object		Right-click item | Close	
Close Switchboard	AC 388	Close button			
Composite Primary Key	AC 391	Click row selector for first field | press and hold SHIFT | click row selector for second field | Primary key button			
Conditionally Format Controls	AC 250		Select field | Conditional button on Format tab		
Create Calculated Field	AC 113			Zoom	SHIFT+F2
Create Crosstab Query	AC 123		Query Wizard button on Create tab | Crosstab Query Wizard		
Create Database	AC 14	Blank Database button or Office Button | Save			CTRL+S or SHIFT+F12 or ALT+I
Create Form	AC 142		Form button on Create tab		
Create Form in Design View	AC 315		Form Design button on Create tab		
Create Form with Datasheet	AC 343		Select "one" table in Navigation Pane | Form button on Create tab		
Create Form with Datasheet in Layout View	AC 345		Blank Form button on Create tab | Show All Tables | plus sign for "one" table | drag fields to form | plus sign for "many" table | drag first field to form | select datasheet | drag remaining fields		

Table 3 Microsoft Office Access 2007 Quick Reference Summary *(continued)*

Task	Page Number	Mouse	Ribbon	Shortcut Menu	Keyboard Shortcut
Create Form with Form Wizard	AC 269		More Forms button on Create tab | Form Wizard		
Create Macro	AC 366		Macro button arrow on Create tab | Macro		
Create PivotChart	AC 404	Open query | View button arrow | PivotChart View		PivotChart view on status bar	
Create PivotChart Legend	AC 404		Legend button on Design tab		
Create PivotTable	AC 396	Open query | View button arrow | PivotTable View | add fields to drop zones		PivotTable view on status bar	
Create Query	AC 78		Query Design button on Create tab		
Create Report	AC 51		Report Wizard button on Create tab		
Create Report using Report Wizard	AC 239		Report Wizard button on Create tab		
Create SQL Query	AC 430		Query Design button on Create tab | close Show Table dialog box | View button arrow | SQL View		
Create Switchboard	AC 380		Switchboard Manager button on Database Tools tab		
Create Table	AC 23	Office Button | Save button	Table button on Create tab		CTRL+S or SHIFT+F12
Customize Navigation Pane	AC 126	Navigation Pane arrow | Object Type			
Define Fields in a Table	AC 24		Right-click Add New Field on Datasheet tab | Rename Column	Right-click Add New Field | Rename Column	
Delete Record	AC 148	Click Record Selector | DELETE	DELETE button		
Enter Data in Attachment Field	AC 312			Right-click field | click Manage Attachments | click Add | navigate to file to add	
Enter Data in Date Field	AC 308	Type date in date field			Calendar button | select date
Enter Data in Hyperlink Field	AC 314			Right-click field | click Hyperlink | click Edit Hyperlink | enter desired Web address	
Enter Data in Memo Field	AC 308	Type data in memo field			
Enter Data in OLE Field	AC 310			Right-click field | click Insert Object	
Enter Data in Yes/No Field	AC 307	Click field's check box to indicate Yes			

Table 3   Microsoft Office Access 2007 Quick Reference Summary *(continued)*

Task	Page Number	Mouse	Ribbon	Shortcut Menu	Keyboard Shortcut
Exclude Field from Query Results	AC 112	Show check box			
Export Query	AC 221		Select query | desired application button in Export group on External Data tab		
Field Size	AC 46		Design View button on Design tab | select field | Field Size box		
Filter by Selection	AC 149		Selection button on Home tab | select criterion		
Filter Records in Report	AC 252			Right-click field | click selected filter	
Form Filter and Sort	AC 280		Advanced button on Home tab | Advanced Filter/Sort | select fields on which to sort | enter sort criteria | Toggle Filter button		
Format Calculated Field	AC 116		Property Sheet button on Design tab		
Format Field	AC 168	Select field | Format property box			
Gridlines in Form	AC 273		Gridlines button on Format tab		
Group in Query	AC 121	Total row or include multiple fields in query			
Group in Report	AC 244		Group & Sort button on Format tab | Add a group button		
Import Data	AC 212		Desired application in Import group on External Data tab		
Include All Fields in Query	AC 85	Double-click asterisk in field list	Query Design button on Create tab | Add All Fields button		
Include Field in Query	AC 85		Query Design button on Create tab | select field | Add Field button		
Input Mask	AC 304	In Design View | Input Mask property box | Build button			
Join Tables	AC 105		Query Design button on Create tab | bring field lists for tables into upper pane		
Link Tables	AC 217		Access button on External Data tab | select database | OK button		

Table 3 Microsoft Office Access 2007 Quick Reference Summary (continued)

Task	Page Number	Mouse	Ribbon	Shortcut Menu	Keyboard Shortcut
Lookup Field	AC 172	Data Type column for field | Lookup Wizard			
Macro Group	AC 377		Macro button arrow on Design tab | Macro | Macro Names button | enter macro names		
Modify Macro	AC 373			Right-click macro | Design view | insert new row | select new action	
Modify Switchboard Page	AC 383, 385		Switchboard Manager button on Database Tools tab | Edit | New | select item to add to switchboard		
Move Controls in Stacked or Tabular Control Layout	AC 277	Select controls | drag to new location			
Move Field List	AC 320	Drag field list title bar			
Move Form Control	AC 276	Point to control | drag to desired location			
Move to First Record	AC 39	First Record button			
Move to Last Record	AC 39	Last Record button			
Move to Next Record	AC 39	Next Record button			
Move to Previous Record	AC 39	Previous Record button			
Multi-Table Report	AC 257		Report Wizard button on Create tab | add fields for first table | click Tables/Queries arrow | select second table | add fields for second table		
New Item	various	Office button | Open			
Object Dependencies	AC 339		Select object in Navigation Pane | Object Dependencies button on the Database Tools tab | Objects that depend on me button		
Omit Duplicates	AC 100	Open Property Sheet, set Unique Values to Yes	Property Sheet button on Design tab | Unique Values	Properties | Unique Values	
Open Database	AC 37	More button | Open button or Office button | double-click file name			CTRL+O
Open Switchboard	AC 387			Right-click switchboard in Navigation Pane | Open	
Open Table	AC 26	Open button		Open	
Preview Table	AC 41	Office button | Print | Print Preview			ALT+F, W, V

Table 3 Microsoft Office Access 2007 Quick Reference Summary (continued)

Task	Page Number	Mouse	Ribbon	Shortcut Menu	Keyboard Shortcut
Print Form	AC 282	Office button | Print | Quick Print			
Print Report	AC 256	Office button | Print | Quick Print			
Print Object	AC 41, 56	Office button | Print | Quick Print or Print			CTRL+P
Quit Access	AC 36	Close button			
Referential Integrity	AC 186		Relationships button on Database Tools tab		
Remove Chart Drop Zones	AC 409		Drop Zones button on Design tab		
Remove Form Tab Stops	AC 335		Select controls | Property Sheet button on Design tab | select All tab | change Tab Stop property to No		
Resize Column	AC 175	In Datasheet view, double-click right boundary of the field selector		Right-click field name | Column Width	
Resize Column Headings	AC 263	Select column header | drag upper or lower boundary			
Resize Column in Report	AC 249	Select column | drag right column boundary			
Run Macro	AC 372			Select macro in Navigation Pane | right-click macro | click Run	
Save Form	AC 58	Office button | Save			CTRL+S
Save Query	AC 91	Save button or Office button | Save			CTRL+S
Save Report	AC 254	Save button			
Save Table	AC 27	Save button	Office button | Save	Save	CTRL+S
Search for Access Help	AC 62	Microsoft Office Access Help button			F1
Search for Record	AC 145		Find button on Home tab		CTRL+F
Search Memo Field in Query	AC 340	In Datasheet view, include wildcards in criterion			
Select Fields for Report	AC 51		Report Wizard button on Create tab | Add Field button		
Simple Query Wizard	AC 78		Query Wizard button on Create tab		
Single-Step Macro	AC 371		Single Step button on Design tab | Run button in Design view		
Sort Data in Query	AC 98		Select field in Design grid | Ascending		
Sort in Report	AC 244		Group & Sort button on Format tab | Add a sort button		

Table 3 Microsoft Office Access 2007 Quick Reference Summary *(continued)*

Task	Page Number	Mouse	Ribbon	Shortcut Menu	Keyboard Shortcut
Sort on Multiple Keys	AC 101	Assign two sort keys			
Special Effects for Form Labels	AC 330		Select label | Property Sheet button on Design tab | Special Effect property box arrow		
Split Form	AC 57		Split Form button on Create tab		
Start Access	AC 12	Start button | All Programs | Microsoft Office | Microsoft Office Access 2007			
Subtotals in Reports	AC 268		For each subtotal, select field to sum | Totals button on Format tab | Sum		
Summary Report	AC 256		Group report on desired field | include calculations | Hide Details button on Format tab		
Switch Between Form and Datasheet Views	AC 57	Form View or Datasheet View button			
Totals in Report	AC 248		Select field | Totals button on Format tab | Sum		
Update Query	AC 162		Update button on Design tab | select field, Update To row, enter new value	Query Type | Update Query	
Use Advanced Filter/Sort	AC 155		Advanced button on Home tab | Advanced/Filter Sort		
Use AND Criterion	AC 95				Place criteria on same line
Use Criterion	AC 81	Right-click query | Design View | Criteria row			
Use Date Field in Query	AC 340	In Datasheet view, type date with slashes as criterion			
Use Form	AC 337			Right-click form in Navigation Pane | Open | click navigation buttons	
Use OR Criterion	AC 96				Place criteria on separate lines
Use PivotChart	AC 411		Open query in PivotChart view | Drop Zones button on Design tab | click arrows and check boxes to experiment		
Use PivotTable	AC 400	View button arrow | PivotTable View | click plus or minus signs			
Use Yes/No Field in Query	AC 340	In Datasheet view, type Yes or No as criterion			

Table 4 Microsoft Office PowerPoint 2007 Quick Reference Summary

Task	Page Number	Mouse	Ribbon	Shortcut Menu	Keyboard Shortcut
Action Button, Change Fill Color	PPT 273		Shape Fill button on Format tab	Format Shape | Fill	
Action Button, Edit Hyperlink	PPT 278		Hyperlink button on Insert tab	Edit Hyperlink	
Action Button, Insert	PPT 271		Shapes button on Insert tab		
Add Shapes	PPT 119		Shapes button on Home tab | select shape		
Add Transition	PPT 122		Transition effect on Animations tab or More button in Transition to This Slide group on Animations tab | select transition		ALT+A | T
Background, Insert Picture	PPT 171		Background Styles button on Design tab | Format Background | Picture or texture fill | File button | select picture | Insert button	Format Background | Picture or texture fill | File button | select picture | Insert button	
Change Size, Clip Art, Photo, or Shape	PPT 101, 103, 117	Drag sizing handles	Dialog Box Launcher in Size group of Format tab | Size tab | enter height and width values or Size group of Format tab | enter height and width values		
Chart, Apply Style	PPT 260		More button in Chart Styles gallery		
Chart, Change Layout	PPT 261		More button in Chart Layouts gallery		
Chart, Insert	PPT 255	Insert Chart button in content placeholder | select chart | OK button	Chart button on Insert tab | select chart | OK button		
Chart Shape, Change Outline Color	PPT 263		Shape Outline button arrow on Format tab		
Chart Shape, Change Outline Weight	PPT 262		Shape Outline button arrow on Format tab | Weight		
Clip Art Border Color, Change	PPT 241		Picture Border button on Format tab		
Clip Art Brightness, Change	PPT 242	Drag Brightness slider or click increase or decrease Brightness arrow in Format Picture dialog box	Brightness button on Format tab		
Clip Art, Insert	PPT 96	Clip Art icon in slide	Clip Art button on Insert tab		
Clip Art, Insert into Slide without Content Placeholder	PPT 234		Clip Art button on Insert tab | type search term | Go button | click clip | Close button		

Table 4 Microsoft Office PowerPoint 2007 Quick Reference Summary *(continued)*

Task	Page Number	Mouse	Ribbon	Shortcut Menu	Keyboard Shortcut
Clip Art, Ungroup	PPT 198		Group button on Format tab | Ungroup | Yes	Group | Ungroup	
Color, Change Object	PPT 199	Shape Fill arrow | select color		Format Shape | Color	
Comment, Delete	PPT 305		Delete Comment button on Review tab		
Comment, Insert	PPT 300		Insert Comment button on Review tab		
Comment, Modify	PPT 303		Edit Comment button on Review tab		
Compatibility Checker, Start	PPT 306	Office Button | Prepare | Run Compatibility Checker			
Compress Presentation	PPT 312		Compress Pictures button on Format tab		
Copy	PPT 276		Copy button on Home tab	Copy	CTRL+C
Date and Time, Add	PPT 173		Date & Time button on Insert tab | Date and time | Update automatically arrow | select date and time format | Apply button or Apply to All button		
Demote a Paragraph	PPT 34	Increase List Level button on Mini toolbar	Increase List Level button on Home tab		TAB or ALT+SHIFT+ RIGHT ARROW
Digital Signature, Create	PPT 313	Office Button | Prepare | Add a Digital Signature			
Display a Presentation in Grayscale	PPT 59		Grayscale button on View tab		ALT+V | C | U
Document Inspector, Start	PPT 307	Office Button | Prepare | Inspect Document | Inspect			
Document Properties	PPT 44	Office Button | Prepare | Properties			
Document Theme, Choose	PPT 16		More button on Design tab | theme		
End Slide Show	PPT 54			End Show	ESC or HYPHEN
Fill, Insert Texture	PPT 168		Background Styles button on Design tab | Format Background | Picture or texture fill | Texture arrow | select background | Apply to All button	Format Background | Picture or texture fill | Texture arrow | select background | Apply to All button	
Final, Mark Presentation as	PPT 316	Office Button | Prepare | Mark as Final | Yes button			
Find and Replace Text	PPT 267		Replace button on Home tab		CTRL+H

Table 4 Microsoft Office PowerPoint 2007 Quick Reference Summary *(continued)*

Task	Page Number	Mouse	Ribbon	Shortcut Menu	Keyboard Shortcut
Font, Change	PPT 109	Font button or Font box arrow on Mini toolbar	Font button on Home tab or Font arrow on Home tab | select font or Font Dialog Box Launcher on Home tab | Latin text font arrow on Font tab	Font | Latin text font arrow on Font tab	CTRL+SHIFT+F | Font tab | Latin text font arrow
Font Color	PPT 23, 110	Font Color button or Font Color arrow on Mini toolbar	Font Color button on Home tab or Font Color arrow on Home tab | select color or Font Dialog Box Launcher on Home tab | Font color button on Font tab | select color	Font | Font color button on Font tab | select color	CTRL+SHIFT+F | Font tab | Font color button | select color
Font Size, Decrease	PPT 25	Decrease Font Size button or Font Size arrow on Mini toolbar	Decrease Font Size button on Home tab or Font Size arrow on Home tab | size	Font Size arrow | Size	CTRL+SHIFT+LEFT CARET (<)
Font Size, Increase	PPT 24	Increase Font Size button or Font Size arrow on Mini toolbar	Increase Font Size button on Home tab or Font Size arrow on Home tab | size	Font size arrow | Size	CTRL+SHIFT+RIGHT CARET (>)
Guides, Display	PPT 274			Grid and Guides | Display drawing guides on screen	
Guides, Hide	PPT 279			Grid and Guides | Display drawing guides on screen	
Help	PPT 63 and Appendix A		Office PowerPoint Help button		F1
Hide Slide	PPT 266		Hide Slide button on Slide Show tab	Right-click desired slide thumbnail in Slides tab or in Slide Sorter view | Hide Slide	
Highlight Item	PPT 319	Pointer arrow on Slide Show toolbar | Highlighter		Pointer Options | Highlighter	
Hyperlink, Add	PPT 243		Insert Hyperlink button on Insert tab | type hyperlink text | OK button	Hyperlink | type hyperlink text | OK button	CTRL+K
Ink Color, Change	PPT 320	Pointer arrow on Slide Show toolbar | Ink Color		Pointer Options | Ink Color	
Insert Photograph	PPT 98, 99	Insert Picture from File icon on slide	Picture button on Insert tab		
Move Clip Art or Photo	PPT 105	Drag			
Next Slide	PPT 47	Next Slide button on vertical scroll bar			PAGE DOWN
Normal View	PPT 91	Normal View button at lower-right PowerPoint window	Normal button on View tab		ALT+V | N
Object, Delete	PPT 202				DELETE

Table 4 Microsoft Office PowerPoint 2007 Quick Reference Summary *(continued)*

Task	Page Number	Mouse	Ribbon	Shortcut Menu	Keyboard Shortcut
Open Presentation	PPT 54	Office Button	Open	select file			CTRL+O
Open Word Outline as Presentation	PPT 165	Office Button	Open	All Outlines	select file	Open	New Slide button arrow on Home tab	Slides from Outline	select file	Insert		CTRL+O
Package for CD	PPT 321	Office Button	Publish	Package for CD			
Password, Set	PPT 310	Office Button	Save As	Tools	General Options			
Paste	PPT 277		Paste button on Home tab	Paste	CTRL+V
Picture, Insert into Slide without Content Placeholder	PPT 234		Picture button on Insert tab	select file	Insert button		
Picture Border Color, Change	PPT 237		Picture Border button on Format tab		
Picture Contrast, Change	PPT 238	Drag Contrast slider or click increase or decrease Contrast arrow in Format Picture dialog box	Contrast button on Format tab		
Picture Style, Apply to Clip	PPT 240		More button in Picture Styles gallery on Format tab		
Picture Style, Insert in Picture	PPT 236		More button in Picture Styles gallery on Format tab		
Preview Presentation as Web Page	PPT 151	[Assumes Web Page Preview button has been added to Quick Access toolbar] Web Page Preview button			
Previous Slide	PPT 50, 51	Previous Slide button on vertical scroll bar			PAGE UP
Print a Presentation	PPT 61	Office Button	Print			CTRL+P
Print an Outline	PPT 122	Office Button	point to Print	Print Preview	Print What arrow	Outline View			
Promote a Paragraph	PPT 34	Decrease List Level button on Mini toolbar	Decrease List Level button on Home tab		SHIFT+TAB or ALT+SHIFT+ LEFT ARROW
Quick Access Toolbar, Add Buttons	PPT 148	Customize Quick Access Toolbar button	select from command options			
Quick Access Toolbar, Reset	PPT 154	Customize Quick Access Toolbar button	More Commands	Reset button			

Table 4 Microsoft Office PowerPoint 2007 Quick Reference Summary *(continued)*

Task	Page Number	Mouse	Ribbon	Shortcut Menu	Keyboard Shortcut
Quit PowerPoint	PPT 53	Double-click Office Button or Close button on title bar or Office Button | Exit PowerPoint		Right-click Microsoft PowerPoint button on taskbar | Close	ALT+F4 or CTRL+Q
Save a Presentation	PPT 27	Save button on Quick Access toolbar or Office Button | Save			CTRL+S or SHIFT+F12
Save as Web Page	PPT 152	Office Button | Save As | add File name | change Save as type to Single File Web Page | Save button			ALT+F | G or F12
Save in .PPS Format	PPT 317	Office Button | Save As | PowerPoint Presentation | type file name | Save as type arrow | PowerPoint Show | Save			
Slide, Add	PPT 29		New Slide button on Home tab or New Slide arrow on Home tab | choose slide type		CTRL+M
Slide, Arrange	PPT 41	Drag slide in Slides tab to new position or in Slide Sorter View drag slide to new position			
Slide, Background	PPT 89		Background Styles button on Design tab | select style	Format Background	
Slide, Duplicate	PPT 40		New Slide arrow on Home tab | Duplicate Selected Slides		
Slide Layout	PPT 92, 94		Layout button on Home tab		
Slide Show View	PPT 49	Slide Show button at lower-right PowerPoint window	Slide Show button on View tab or From Beginning button on Slide Show tab		F5 or ALT+V | W
Slide Sorter View	PPT 91	Slide Sorter View button at lower-right in PowerPoint window	Slide Sorter button on View tab		ALT+V | D
SmartArt Graphic, Add SmartArt Style	PPT 184		More button in SmartArt Styles group on Design tab		
SmartArt Graphic, Adjust Size	PPT 210	Drag sizing handle to desired location			
SmartArt Graphic, Change Color	PPT 186		Change Colors button on Design tab		
SmartArt Graphic, Insert	PPT 205		SmartArt button on Insert tab | select category | select graphic		

Table 4 Microsoft Office PowerPoint 2007 Quick Reference Summary *(continued)*

Task	Page Number	Mouse	Ribbon	Shortcut Menu	Keyboard Shortcut
SmartArt Graphic, Insert Image	PPT 183	Double-click icon in shape | select picture | Insert button			
Spelling Check	PPT 55		Spelling button on Review tab		F7
Table, Add Borders	PPT 251		No Border button arrow on Design tab | All Borders		
Table, Add Effect	PPT 252		Effects button on Design Tab		
Table, Apply Style,	PPT 250		More button in Table Styles gallery on Design tab		
Table, Insert	PPT 246	Insert Table button in content placeholder | click Number of columns and Number of rows up or down arrows | OK button	Table button on Insert tab | drag to select columns and rows		
Text, Add Shadow	PPT 110		Text Shadow button on Home tab		
Text, Bold	PPT 25	Bold button on Mini toolbar	Bold button on Home tab		CTRL+B
Text, Change Color	PPT 23	Font Color button or Font Color arrow on Mini toolbar	Font color arrow on Home tab | choose color	Font | Font color button | choose color	
Text, Convert to SmartArt Graphic	PPT 181		SmartArt button on Insert tab	Convert to SmartArt	
Text, Delete	PPT 42		Cut button on Home tab	Cut	DELETE or CTRL+X or BACKSPACE
Text, Formatting with Quick Styles	PPT 119		Quick Styles button on Home tab | select style		
Text, Italicize	PPT 22	Italic button on Mini toolbar	Italic button on Home tab	Font | Font style arrow | Italics	CTRL+I
Text, Select	PPT 21	Drag to select | double-click to select word | triple-click to select paragraph			SHIFT+DOWN ARROW or SHIFT+RIGHT ARROW
Text Box, Format	PPT 191		Shape Fill button or Shape Outline button or Shape Effects button on Format tab		
Text Box, Insert	PPT 188		Text Box button on Insert tab | click in desired location		
Text Box, Rotate	PPT 189	Drag Free Rotate pointer	Rotate button on Format Tab		
Texture Fill, Insert	PPT 168		Background Styles on Design tab | Format Background		
Theme Colors, Change	PPT 233		Theme Colors button on Design tab		

Table 4 Microsoft Office PowerPoint 2007 Quick Reference Summary *(continued)*

Task	Page Number	Mouse	Ribbon	Shortcut Menu	Keyboard Shortcut
Thesaurus	PPT 269		Thesaurus button on Review tab	Synonyms	SHIFT+F7
Transparency, Change	PPT 172	Drag Transparency slider in Transparency text box or click increase or decrease Transparency arrow in Format Background dialog box			
Use Format Painter	PPT 112	Format Painter button on Mini toolbar	Double-click Format Painter button on Home tab	select text with a format you want to copy	select other text to apply previously selected format	press ESC to turn off Format Painter		
WordArt, Apply Style	PPT 175		More button on Format tab		
WordArt Outline Weight, Change	PPT 178		Text Outline arrow on Format tab	Weight		
WordArt Text Effect, Add	PPT 179		Text Effects button on Format tab		
WordArt Text Fill, Format	PPT 176		Text Fill arrow on Format tab		
Zoom for Printing	PPT 128	Drag Zoom slider on status bar or Office Button	point to Print	Print Preview		Zoom button on View tab	select zoom		
Zoom for Viewing Slides	PPT 127	Drag Zoom slider on status bar	Zoom button on View tab	select zoom		

Table 5 Microsoft Office Outlook 2007 Quick Reference Summary

Task	Page Number	Mouse	Ribbon	Shortcut Menu	Keyboard Shortcut
Accept Meeting	OUT 114		Open message	Accept button	send response	OK button		
Accept Task	OUT 108		Double-click Task Request	Accept		
Address E-Mail Message	OUT 27	Mail button in Inbox window	New Mail Message button on Message tab	To button		
Assign Task	OUT 106, 110		Assign Task button in Task window	Assign Task	
Attach File to E-Mail Message	OUT 31	Attach File button on Standard toolbar in Message window	Attach File button on Insert tab		

Table 5 Microsoft Office Outlook 2007 Quick Reference Summary (continued)

Task	Page Number	Mouse	Ribbon	Shortcut Menu	Keyboard Shortcut
Categorize Calendar	OUT 124		Categorize button | All Categories *		
Change Appointment Date	OUT 92	Drag appointment to new date			
Change Appointment Month	OUT 93			Select appointment | Edit | Cut |scroll | click selected date | Paste	
Change Appointment Time	OUT 91	Drag appointment to new time or double-click appointment | edit Start time			
Change Meeting Time	OUT 117	Drag meeting to new time | Yes button | Send Update button			
Change Work Week	OUT 121	Open Calendar | Tools | Options | Calendar Options button | change dates in work week area			ALT+T, O, C
Close an E-Mail Message	OUT 15	Click Close button on title bar in Message window			ALT+F, C
Compose E-Mail Message	OUT 27	New button on Standard toolbar	New | Mail Message*		CTRL+N
Create Contact List	OUT 47	New button on Standard toolbar	Actions | New Contact*	New Contact	CTRL+SHIFT+C
Create Distribution List	OUT 58	New Contact button on Standard toolbar	New Contact button | Distribution List*		CTRL+SHIFT+L
Create E-Mail Signature	OUT 24		Tools | Options | Mail Format tab | Signatures button*		ALT+T, O
Create Event	OUT 95	Double-click appointment area day heading			
Create Personal Folder	OUT 44	Contacts button in Navigation pane	File | New | Folder*	New Contacts | New Folder	CTRL+SHIFT+E
Create Note	OUT 118		New Note button*		
Create View Filter	OUT 36		View | Arrange By*	Custom	
Delete Appointment	OUT 90		Select appointment | Delete button | OK*		
Delete E-Mail Message	OUT 21	Delete button on Standard toolbar	Select message | Delete*		CTRL+D or DELETE
Delete Subfolder	OUT 103			Right-click date banner | Delete | Yes	ALT+F, F, D
Display Contacts	OUT 52	Find a Contact box on Standard toolbar	Tools | Instant Search*		CTRL+E or ALT+T, I
Enter Appointment in Appointment Area	OUT 81	Select date in Date Navigator | select time | type appointment		File | Import and Export | Export to a file	
Enter Appointment in Appointment Window	OUT 82		Select date in Date Navigator | select time | click New Appointment button*	Actions menu | New Appointment	CTRL+N

Table 5 Microsoft Office Outlook 2007 Quick Reference Summary *(continued)*

Task	Page Number	Mouse	Ribbon	Shortcut Menu	Keyboard Shortcut
Export Subfolder	OUT 101				
Find a Contact	OUT 50	Find a Contact box on Standard toolbar	Tools | Instant Search | Advanced Find*		CTRL+SHIFT+F
Flag E-Mail Messages	OUT 34	Follow Up button on Standard toolbar	Actions | Follow Up*	Follow Up	ALT+A, U
Forward E-Mail Message	OUT 20	Forward button on Standard toolbar		Forward	CTRL+F
Import Subfolder	OUT 104			File | Import and Export | Import from another program or file	
Month View	OUT 98	Month tab			
Move to Next Day	OUT 86		Go | Go to Date*	Go to Date	CTRL+G
Natural Language Phrasing	OUT 88			New Appointment button | enter time as natural language	
Open E-Mail Message	OUT 10	Double-click message	File | Open*	Open	CTRL+O
Print Calendar	OUT 127		Select calendar view | Print button | select style | OK*	File | Print	CTRL+P
Print Contact List	OUT 53	Print button on Standard toolbar	File | Print* or File | Print Preview | Print*		CTRL+P
Print E-Mail Message	OUT 15	Print button on Standard toolbar	File | Print | OK button*		CTRL+P, ENTER
Print Task List	OUT 127		Display task list | Print button | OK*		
Propose New Meeting Time	OUT 117		Propose New Time button in Meeting window	Propose New Time	ALT+A, S
Recurring Appointment	OUT 84		Recurrence button | Appointment Recurrence dialog box		
Reply to E-Mail Message	OUT 16	Reply button on Standard toolbar	Reply button on Message tab		CTRL+R
Save Contact List as Text File	OUT 60	Select name bar of contact | CTRL+A | File | Save As	File | Save As*		
Schedule Meeting	OUT 111		Open appointment | Scheduling button | Add Others button		
Send E-Mail Message	OUT 31	Send button in Message window	Send button on Insert tab		
Send Instant Message	OUT 139			Reply with Instant Message	
Send Meeting Update	OUT 117	Send Update button in Meeting window			
Set Message Importance, Sensitivity, and Delivery Options	OUT 38	New Mail Message button on Standard toolbar in Message window	Options dialog box launcher in the Options group on the Message tab		

Table 5 Microsoft Office Outlook 2007 Quick Reference Summary *(continued)*

Task	Page Number	Mouse	Ribbon	Shortcut Menu	Keyboard Shortcut
Sort E-Mail Messages	OUT 35	Arrange By Command on View menu			ALT+V, A, E
Task List	OUT 99	Tasks button	New Task	New Task*	New	Task	CTRL+N
Work Week View	OUT 96	Week tab	Work Week on View menu*		ALT+V, R or CTRL+ALT+2